Economic Principles and Problems

Economic Principles and Problems: A Pluralist Introduction offers a comprehensive introduction to the major perspectives in modern economics, including mainstream and heterodox approaches. Through providing multiple views of markets and how they work, it leaves readers better able to understand and analyze the complex behaviors of consumers, firms, and government officials, as well as the likely impact of a variety of economic events and policies.

Most principles of economics textbooks cover only mainstream economics, ignoring rich heterodox ideas. They also lack material on the great economists, including the important ideas of Adam Smith, Karl Marx, Thorstein Veblen, John Maynard Keynes, and Friedrich Hayek. Mainstream books tend to neglect the kind of historical analysis that is crucial to understanding trends that help us predict the future. Moreover, they focus primarily on abstract models more than existing economic realities. This engaging book addresses these inadequacies. Including explicit coverage of mainstream economics and the major heterodox schools of economic thought—institutionalists, feminists, radical political economists, post-Keynesians, Austrians, and social economists—it allows the reader to choose which ideas they find most compelling in explaining modern economic realities.

Written in an engaging style and focused on real-world examples, this textbook brings economics to life. Multiple examples of how each economic model works, coupled with critical analysis of the assumptions behind them, enable students to develop a sophisticated understanding of the material. Digital supplements are also available for students and instructors. *Economic Principles and Problems* offers the most contemporary and complete package for any pluralist economics class.

Geoffrey Schneider is Presidential Professor of Economics at Bucknell University, Pennsylvania, U.S.A. He is an award-winning teacher, author or co-author of six books and numerous scholarly articles, and executive director of the International Confederation of Associations for Pluralism in Economics.

Economic Principles and Problems

A Pluralist Introduction

Geoffrey Schneider

Routledge
Taylor & Francis Group

LONDON AND NEW YORK

First published 2022
by Routledge
2 Park Square, Milton Park, Abingdon, Oxon OX14 4RN

and by Routledge
605 Third Avenue, New York, NY 10158

Routledge is an imprint of the Taylor & Francis Group, an informa business

British Library Cataloguing-in-Publication Data
A catalogue record for this book is available from the British Library

Library of Congress Cataloging-in-Publication Data
A catalog record has been requested for this book

ISBN: 978-1-138-63994-2 (hbk)
ISBN: 978-1-138-64000-9 (pbk)
ISBN: 978-1-315-63692-4 (ebk)

DOI: 10.4324/9781315636924

Typeset in Bembo
by Deanta Global Publishing Services, Chennai, India

I dedicate this book to my spouse and partner for more than 35 years, Lori Schneider. Lori has been at my side throughout all of the ups and downs. She put up with the many hours I spent writing this book. And she tolerated all of the evenings she had to spend surrounded by economists (!) talking endlessly about the economic system, despite the fact that economics was her least favorite subject as an undergraduate. Without her love and support, none of this would have been possible.

Contents

Detailed table
of contents

Preface

In 2008, the housing bubble and financial crisis confounded mainstream economists. Only a few of them predicted that the meltdown was coming, and most were caught completely surprised.

Interestingly, large numbers of political economists who were not part of the mainstream, including this author, spotted the real estate bubble, anticipated the financial crisis, and advised their friends and colleagues to pull their money out of financial markets prior to the collapse. What did political economists know that mainstream economists did not?

First, political economists drew on the lessons of economic history. There are numerous examples demonstrating that the deregulation of financial markets encourages speculative behavior, which can lead to spectacular booms and equally spectacular busts. The Great Depression of the 1930s, the savings and loan crisis of the 1980s, and the Asian financial crisis of the 1990s all featured deregulated lenders taking incredible risks with other people's money. Similarly, the deregulation of financial markets in the 1980s and 1990s paved the way for the great financial crises of 2008–2010, which sparked the Great Recession. Studying the evolution of economic systems is particularly helpful in predicting when conditions are ripe for the next crisis.

Second, political economists drew on the economic ideas of Keynes, Marx, and Veblen, among others—economists who studied the roots of economic crises carefully and had much to say on the topic. Meanwhile, mainstream economists were utilizing mathematical models in which it was assumed that markets would always be rational and efficient and could never experience a crisis.

Thus, the analysis of the evolution of economic systems and a broader knowledge of economic ideas could have saved the profession from the embarrassment it suffered in 2008. Even more surprising, perhaps, is the fact that most mainstream principles of economics texts still ignore economic history and some of the major economists whose ideas were most useful in predicting the housing bubble and the financial crisis. This book seeks to remedy those omissions.

More specifically, most current principles of economics textbooks cover only mainstream economics, ignoring the rich ideas of the heterodox schools of thought. They also tend to lack material on the great economists, so readers usually leave the introductory course without learning in depth about who Adam Smith, Karl Marx, Thorstein Veblen, Joseph Schumpeter, John Maynard Keynes, and Friedrich Hayek were and why their ideas are important.

Mainstream books are also missing the kind of historical analysis that is crucial to understanding trends and patterns that can help us predict the future. In addition, they tend to focus more on abstract models rather than existing economic realities.

This book attempts to addresses these inadequacies. The book includes explicit coverage of mainstream economics and the major heterodox schools of thought. This allows the reader to choose which ideas they find most compelling in explaining modern economic realities.

This book is intended to give you a broader background that will help save you from the tunnel vision that infected mainstream economics in recent decades. By understanding the evolution of economic systems and the ideas of the great economists, you will be better prepared to confront the complex realities of the modern world. By understanding multiple views of markets and how they work, you will gain a more sophisticated understanding of the functioning of a market economy. This will help you better understand the behavior of firms, consumers, and government officials.

As you approach this material, it is important to keep an open mind. All of the major economists you will read about in this book were brilliant, and their ideas are worth studying. Each of them has devoted followers among modern economists. Your task is to consider all of these ideas and then, observing the world around you, decide which ideas make the most sense in understanding our modern economic system.

Acknowledgments

I would like to thank all of the research assistants who helped with the writing of this book. Those research assistants include Spandan Marasini, James Weissenborn, Marissa DiPalo, Kailyn Angelo, Nghia (TN) Doan, James Elmendorf, Colin Randles, Kathryn Tomasi, Katelyn Schneider, and many others.

I would also like to thank my mentors who stimulated my interest in a broad-based, pluralist approach to economics. In graduate school, William (Sandy) Darity and Vincent Tarascio taught pluralistically, embodying the values that I came to embrace. My colleagues at Bucknell University also provided a rich, engaging environment where our regular discussions of how to develop a pluralist course and curriculum were invigorating. My regular collaborators on writing projects were particularly instrumental in developing a pluralist approach, including Charles Sackrey, Janet Knoedler, Jean Shackelford, Berhanu Nega, Erdogan Bakir, and Steve Stamos. I am also deeply indebted to a number of economists whose ideas I draw on heavily in this book. In particular, Karl Polanyi's masterwork *The Great Transformation* looms large.

A thanks is also due to the staff at Routledge and to editor Andy Humphries, who made this project possible. And thanks to the many colleagues who offered feedback on the book at various stages, including Nathan Sivers Boyce, Barbara Hopkins, Paula Cole, Zdrvaka Todorova, Xiao Jiang, and my department colleagues.

Chapters 1–8 of this book were previously published as Schneider, G. (2018) *The Evolution of Economic Ideas and Systems: A Pluralist Introduction*. London: Routledge. Chapters 9–23, parts of Chapter 34, in particular sections 34.1–34.3, and parts of Chapter 35, including sections 35.1–35.3, were previously published in Schneider, G. (2019) *Microeconomic Principles and Problems: A Pluralist Introduction*. London: Routledge. All materials have been revised and updated since the previous versions.

Economics
A pluralist definition

Part I explores several different definitions of what economics is and the different ways in which economists practice the social science of economics (economic methodology).

The first chapter, What Is Economics?, begins by describing why economic policy matters to the country and to every person. It describes the debate over whether or not politicians should balance their budgets every year given the regular occurrence of recessions in the economy (downturns in which unemployment increases and business activity decreases). The chapter then offers four different definitions of economics: One offered by mainstream economists (who tend to advocate a capitalist market system with limited government intervention), one preferred by economists practicing progressive political economics (PPE, which includes institutionalist, social, post-Keynesian, and feminist economists who believe that capitalism can and should be reformed), another from economists who engage in radical political economics (RPE—Marxists and others who believe that capitalism is fatally flawed and should be replaced), and a broad definition of pluralist economics that synthesizes the other definitions.

Chapter 1 then takes up methodology, or how economists attempt to "do" economics. This will give you an idea of what it means to be an economist from the various perspectives—the kind of things you study, what you look for, and how you construct knowledge about the economy. The chapter then goes through a series of short examples so you can see different types of economic analysis in action when economists study consumer behavior, labor markets, and the business cycle. The chapter concludes by briefly laying out the ten different schools of economics that will be discussed in the book.

DOI: 10.4324/9781315636924-1

Chapter 2 takes up a simple mainstream economics concept, opportunity costs, and a simple economic model, the production possibilities curve (PPC). The PPC model is applied to several economic issues, including a treatment of defense spending and its impact on economic growth. The chapter concludes with a section on the potential limitations of economic models in capturing economic reality, building on the work of PPE and RPE economists.

What is economics?

The answer depends on who you ask

In his famous book, *The General Theory of Employment, Interest and Money*, John Maynard Keynes said, "The ideas of economists and political philosophers, both when they are right and when they are wrong, are more powerful than is commonly understood. Indeed the world is ruled by little else." This quote highlights the extent to which economic policy is a major determinant of what our lives are like. Economic ideas led the followers of Adam Smith to demand an end to mercantilism and ushered in the beginnings of capitalism in the late 1700s. Karl Marx provoked the masses to strike and revolt against the oppressions of unregulated capitalism in the 1800s. Thorstein Veblen and Keynes provided a vision of regulated, mixed market capitalism that proved compelling in the Great Depression of the 1930s, and Friedrich Hayek's critique of bloated bureaucracy helped persuade Ronald Reagan and Margaret Thatcher to reduce the size of government in the 1980s. Economic ideas play a significant role in shaping the type of economic system you live in, which has a major impact on the opportunities you have and the challenges you face.

This is why everyone needs to have a solid understanding of economics. To help you grasp the material, each chapter in this book will begin with a list of learning goals. These goals will help you to focus on the key themes.

1.0 CHAPTER 1 LEARNING GOALS

After reading this chapter you should be able to:

- Explain in your own words the importance of economics for you and for society as a whole.

- Briefly contrast unregulated market capitalism with mixed market capitalism.

DOI: 10.4324/9781315636924-2

- Describe the difference between mainstream economics, progressive political economics (PPE) and radical political economics (RPE), using their different definitions of economics and their different methods.

- Explain and begin to apply the methods of mainstream, PPE, and RPE economists to economic issues.

- Understand how the ten different schools of economics match up with conservative, moderate, liberal, and radical political approaches to the economy.

Note that there are a lot of new ideas in this chapter. However, the topics in this chapter will become clearer as the book progresses, so do not feel like you need to get all the details down now. Instead, work to grasp the basic ideas and gain a general understanding of the material.

1.1 WHY ECONOMICS MATTERS: ECONOMIC POLICY

Economics is a crucial subject that every educated voter and politician should understand. To show this, we begin with a brief example of how economic debates and a government's economic policy can matter to us all. As we go through this book, it is especially important for you to try to understand all of the different views of the various schools of economic thought that we will be studying. Understanding their differences teaches us more about this subject than any other way we might study it. As you read through this first example, and as a general rule while going through this book, take the time to try to figure out the meaning of each part of each section, including the key terms that are used, what they mean, and how they work.

Let's begin by taking a look at a government policy called austerity, **where governments reduce or eliminate social programs like food stamps, unemployment insurance, and education in order to balance the government budget** (they try to balance the incoming tax revenues with the spending amounts going out). Political leaders around the world regularly make the argument that the government should balance its budget each year, spending no more than it takes in via tax revenue. Such a policy is frequently justified by folksy expressions such as, "if households balance their checkbooks, then the government should balance its budget." And this policy is sometimes supported by a few "crank" economists who are, in general, opposed to any type of government inter-vention. (These economists can be labeled "cranks" because their views have been dismissed by the vast majority of the economics profession.) The problem is that an obsession with balancing the government budget each and every year could cause an economic disaster. Here is a brief explanation for why it is a bad idea to try and balance the government budget when a recession hits.

In the modern United States, the economy tends to hit a major crisis, called a recession, every eight to twelve years. As you can see in Figure 1.1, the United States experienced recessions beginning in 1980, 1990, 2000, 2008, and 2020, when the U.S. real gross domestic product, which is the total output of goods and services, declined. A recession is usually sparked by a major panic of some sort, such as the financial crisis of 2007–2008 when stock markets plunged, banks failed, and the global economy shrank considerably. After a financial market collapse, busi-nesses and consumers become pessimistic. Businesses lay off workers and consum-ers stop spending. This reduces overall spending in the economy, which reduces the incomes of both workers and business owners.

Reduced incomes in the economy mean that governments take in less tax revenue from income and sales taxes and that the government will start running a large budget deficit because tax revenues will have fallen below the level of govern-ment spending. How should the government respond to the fact that a recession caused a decline in incomes, which caused a decline in tax revenues and an increase in the government deficit? If the government decides to balance the government budget right away, then it must either raise taxes or cut spending, an economic

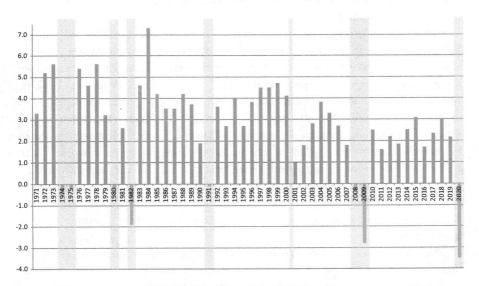

FIGURE 1.1 U.S. real gross domestic product (GDP) growth in the modern era (1971–2020).

policy called **austerity**. But—and here is where the crucial knowledge of economics comes in—*austerity will not succeed in balancing the budget in a recession!*

Here is why: If a nation's economy is in a recession, and if its government responds by raising taxes and cutting government spending, then the result will be that consumers and businesses have even *less* money to spend than before. Raising taxes directly reduces the money consumers and businesses have to spend. Reducing government spending directly reduces incomes: Teachers and other government personnel are laid off, construction firms see less revenue from building fewer roads and bridges, and so on. So cutting government spending and raising taxes directly reduce income and spending. Also, the decline in incomes and spending means additional reductions in tax revenues from income and sales taxes, making the government deficit *worse*! Thus, as any student of economics should know, trying to balance a government budget in a recession via austerity makes the recession worse, which makes the government deficit worse, not better.

Furthermore, even though it seems counterintuitive, governments can actually improve the deficit situation over the long term by spending more in a recession and running larger deficits! If the government cuts taxes and increases spending when a recession hits, which means running a larger budget deficit, it directly increases the incomes of consumers and the revenues of businesses. This leads consumers to spend more money and businesses to hire more people, raising incomes further and increasing tax revenues in the process. By stimulating economic growth, government spending and tax cuts can help to pay for themselves. (Before you go on, try reading back through the last two paragraphs until you understand the material. They contain a number of terms that we will deal with throughout the book.)

There are some major lessons to be learned from this example. First, what seems to be logical to most people (balancing one's budget every year) can fly in the face of what economists have learned. For example, the best way to combat a recession is for the government to increase spending, cut taxes, and inject money into the banking system to promote lending. Even though this will increase government deficits in the short term, it will likely stimulate economic growth, which will actually reduce deficits over the long term once economic growth is restored. However, efforts to balance the government budget in a recession via austerity will not work. When a recession hits, incomes and spending fall, and that reduces tax revenues, leading to substantial government deficits. If the government responds by raising taxes and cutting spending (austerity), this makes a fragile economy even worse, slowing economic growth and reducing incomes and tax revenues further, resulting in even more deficits.

Second, our example demonstrates that economics is an uncertain field, and there is much disagreement between economists from the different economic schools of thought. This means that it is usually possible for politicians to find support for their ideas, no matter how bad those ideas are. Politicians frequently seize on bad ideas from crank economists because those ideas support their political perspective, even though most of the economics profession would consider those ideas to be ridiculous. This was certainly true of austerity policies, which have been promoted recently by a few crank economists but opposed by most economists.

Your job, as you read through this book, is to understand and evaluate the best ideas that economists have about how the economy works and what economic policies should be used in certain situations. However, we need to avoid making the mistake that some politicians do when they listen only to the economists who say what they want to hear. Instead, critically evaluate the ideas of all the economists you study, assess the available evidence, and develop your own perspective regarding which economic ideas best explain the world you see around you. The world is desperately in need of economically literate people who will call politicians on their craziest economic ideas. You will find that a solid understanding of the economy will help you in your personal life as well.

Key objective

1.2 HOW DOES THE ECONOMY AFFECT YOUR LIFE?

The economy is vitally important to each of us. Consider for a minute the following factors that affect what your life and your community are like:

- An austerity program could slash government funding for financial aid and other programs at your college, resulting in huge increases in tuition and lay-offs (possibly of a family member). *No school activities. Free school meals*
- The economic system largely determines whether you get enough food to eat, the various kinds of opportunities for work that are available to you, what your workday is like, and whether or not our society is equal or unequal.
- Major economic events, such as financial crises, economic booms, and shifts in major industries, can have a huge influence on your life and your community.
- The functioning of the global economy determines what the planet is like, including how much pollution there is and whether beautiful coastlines are owned by particular people or whether they are public parks. *No spending on climate*
- In the modern economy, businesses produce an ever-changing, ever-expanding quantity of goods and services for sale to people, often using extensive advertising to increase sales.
- Large corporations play a particularly important role in today's global economy, determining what goods are sold, where they are produced, and what future endeavors they think are worth investing in.

- Governments play a major role in establishing the rules of the economic system, shaping what types of economic activities are undertaken—often regulating the behaviors of companies and individuals—and sometimes developing or promoting key industrial sectors.
- Global trade has a significant impact on jobs and communities, promoting growth in some places while undermining it in others.

To study such important topics, the social science of economics developed. Economists seek to understand the above factors and many more. If they can successfully determine how the economy works, economists can then make useful recommendations regarding how the economy can be improved.

The study of the economy can be quite difficult, however. The world economy is extremely complex, involving almost 200 countries, more than 7 billion people from culturally diverse backgrounds, and millions of organizations interacting in a variety of situations. Economists are often able to recognize trends and patterns, which can allow us to make accurate predictions. Yet, as is commonly known, economists are frequently wrong in their predictions due to the complex nature of the economy. In other words, economics is an inexact social science. Furthermore, the fact that the study of the economy is uncertain and inexact means that at any given time economists will often disagree with each other over what is happening in the economy and what should be done in order to improve its outcomes.

Economists also disagree over what type of economy we should have. As we will see below, some advocate an economy based on unregulated markets in which private individuals and corporations make most of the economic decisions without the interference of government (unregulated market capitalism). Others tend to see markets as bad for people and the environment, preferring to have workers and a democratically elected government in control of the major economic decisions (democratic socialism). Most economists advocate a middle path between these two perspectives: Mixed market capitalism.

1.3 WHY TAKE A PLURALIST APPROACH TO THE STUDY OF ECONOMICS?

Because there are debates and divisions among economists regarding the nature of the economy and the role of public policy in it, this book takes a *pluralist* approach. Pluralist economics seeks to include the best ideas from *all* major economic perspectives, while also highlighting the important areas of agreement and disagreement. This book will share the best ideas from a wide variety of economists, and you are tasked with the job of deciding which ideas are most relevant to the world you see around you. For instance, do you think markets are usually efficient and effective, as Adam Smith believed, or do they tend to be ruthless and exploitative as Karl Marx argued? Is government intervention in markets inherently inefficient, as Friedrich Hayek believed, or is government intervention essential to the healthy functioning of markets, as John Maynard Keynes maintained?

One clear way to differentiate between some of the different schools of thought is to consider their definitions of the study of economics.

Mainstream economics (ME) is **the study of how society manages its scarce resources to satisfy individuals' unlimited wants**. To mainstream economists, economics involves studying the costs and benefits of the decisions facing consumers, producers, and governments and making rational choices between alternatives using society's limited resources. Mainstream economists are particularly good at establishing the consistent statistical relationships between economic variables. These ideas can be used to predict, for example, how an increase in the price of gasoline is likely to affect the demand for gasoline or how an increase in consumer spending will affect a country's total income and its unemployment rate and inflation rate. Mainstream economics includes both conservative economists who prefer little government intervention in markets and liberal economists who see government intervention in markets as essential.

Important Today

Progressive political economics (PPE) is **the study of social provisioning—the economic processes that provide the goods and services required by society to meet the needs of its members**. These economists study culture, history, and technology to understand how the economy is evolving over time and how different societies function in distinct ways. Progressive political economists are particularly good at analyzing matters such as how consumers in Germany behave differently than consumers in the United States or how the legal and political systems in a particular country affect their economic system.

+ International

Radical political economics (RPE) is **the study of power relations in society, especially conflicts over the allocation of a society's resources by various social classes and how those conflicts cause society to evolve**. Radical political economists see power, conflict, and technology as the major drivers of changes in economic systems. They are particularly good at analyzing how class relations affect the economic system and the dynamics of how economic crises form.

Diversity econ

If we combine definitions, a pluralist definition of economics would be as follows: Pluralist economics is **a social science whose practitioners, from a variety of distinct schools of thought, study economies, how they grow and change, and how they produce and distribute the goods that societies need and want**.

Another important topic is the different ways to study the economy. Next, we turn to the different *methods* that economists use in economics.

1.4 ECONOMIC METHODOLOGY: HOW TO "DO" ECONOMICS

Given the vast complexity of the global economy, it is impossible for economists to study everything. Thus, they choose to narrow their focus on the variables that they see as most important.

Mainstream economists attempt to be as scientific as possible. The mainstream economics methodology can be summarized as follows:

1. **Mainstream economists make simplifying assumptions about the economy so that they can focus on what they determine to be the most important economic variables**

    For example, mainstream economists typically believe that consumers are rational, calculating, fully informed, and self-interested most of the time. In theory, this allows mainstream economists to assume that all consumers behave in a consistent manner, which should allow mainstream economists to make reasonable predictions about consumers' economic behaviors. Thus, mainstream economic models are based on a hypothetical "**economic man**" who behaves quite predictably.

2. **Mainstream economists construct mathematical models of the economy so that they can make predictions about how it will behave**

    Mainstream economists make logical deductions based on their assumptions and construct hypotheses about how the economy should work if their assumptions hold. For example, if we assume that consumers are rational, well-informed, and self-interested, then we can construct a model of consumer demand demonstrating that when the price of a product increases, consumers will buy less of that good for themselves. This is known as the law of demand, and it can be expressed as a mathematical equation or as a graph, such as Figure 1.2.

3. **Mainstream economists test their models using statistical analysis and observations of whether or not the real world conforms to their predictions**

    If the assumptions are reasonably accurate and the models are good, then the predictions of mainstream economic models should match what we see in the real world. For example, historically, a 10% increase in the price of gasoline caused a 2% decrease in the quantity of gasoline purchased by consumers. Thus, assuming no changes in the assumptions behind the model, and holding all other economic variables constant, we could predict that a gasoline tax that raised the price of gasoline by 100% would cause consumers to purchase 20% less gasoline than usual.

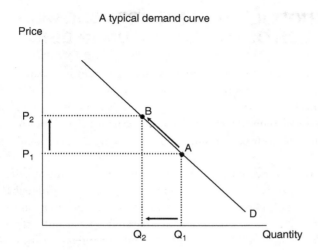

FIGURE 1.2 A typical demand curve.

Political economists—those from the PPE and RPE groups—believe that the methods adopted by mainstream economists are fundamentally flawed and thus approach the study of economics quite differently. Indeed, they see each of the assumptions behind "economic man" as flawed in key ways. From the political economy perspective, consumers can be irrational and ill-informed much of the time. And whereas a fully informed, calculating and rational individual would never be convinced to buy something he or she doesn't need, we know that most of us are affected by advertising in key ways, such as making impulsive purchases or buying products we do not really need at prices that we know are too high for our budgets.

More interesting and more important, from the political economy perspective, are the social factors that shape consumers and their decisions. How does culture (peer pressure, social groups, etc.) shape consumers' tastes and purchases? How do companies manipulate consumers via advertising and attempting to control the market? How does one's gender, race, and social class affect one's purchases? Is it truly rational to buy consumer goods that are not necessary for survival when those goods use resources that contribute to global warming? Or is such consumerist behavior the unique product of a particular culture in a particular place at a specific time?

In order to differentiate between the two approaches to economics highlighted above, the next section uses the ideas of both mainstream and political economists to analyze consumer shopping behavior on Amazon.com. Notice that *both* perspectives contribute something valuable to our understanding of consumer behavior, which is why a pluralist approach to economics is likely to leave you with a better understanding of the economy!

1.5 METHODOLOGY IN MICROECONOMICS: AMAZON.COM AND CONSUMER BEHAVIOR

Economics is traditionally broken up into the study of microeconomics and macroeconomics. Microeconomics is the study of how individual markets work, such as the market for labor, cell phones, or other specific goods and services. Macroeconomics is the study of the dynamics of national and international economies, including the factors affecting recessions and booms, economic growth, and financial markets.

To explore microeconomic analysis from a mainstream and a political economy (PPE/RPE) perspective, we turn to an analysis of the shopping behavior of consumers with the online retailing giant Amazon.com. Amazon.com is the world's largest online retailer, and it analyzes consumer behavior relentlessly in the pursuit of higher sales. Thus, we learn a lot about consumers from the various strategies that Amazon.com uses successfully.

To improve sales, mainstream economists would emphasize the importance of providing rational, calculating, fully informed, and self-interested consumers with the best product at the best price. This is, indeed, one of Amazon.com's signature strengths. For books, music, and electronics, Amazon.com is consistently cheaper than its competitors. For other goods, such as groceries or household appliances, Amazon.com tends to be slightly more expensive than Walmart or local grocery stores. However, many consumers continue to shop for these goods at Amazon.com for the convenience (consumers' time is also a "cost"). Amazon.com provides a lot of information for consumers about their products, including customer reviews, so that consumers can make an informed decision. Thus, much consumer behavior on Amazon.com confirms the mainstream view.

However, PPE and RPE economists look at additional factors. First, consumers on Amazon.com are often impulsive. This is why Amazon.com often gives you suggestions when you shop, telling you what other consumers bought who purchased the same items you did and giving you personalized recommendations. As we know, for many consumers, the suggestions have a significant impact on their buying behavior. Thus, from a PPE or RPE perspective, we must also study consumers' impulsive side, especially the ways in which sellers work on us, even to the point of hiring psychologists to study how we can be tricked and fooled.

Second, consumers are affected by culture, and especially the behavior of their peers. This is one of the reasons why customer reviews are so successful. People feel much more secure in making a purchase if their peers approve of the item. For this and many other reasons, PPE and RPE economists view culture as an essential subject of study.

Third, Amazon.com exercises its market power to compete unfairly. The company demands that publishers discount books and other sellers discount items that are provided to Amazon.com or it will refuse to offer those entities' items for sale. This is a strategy also pursued by Walmart. By demanding and getting lower prices from their suppliers, the big retailers get a cost advantage over smaller competitors, allowing them to sell goods for lower prices and to reap higher profits because they are bigger and more powerful, not because they provide better goods or services. Analyzing the main institutions in a society, and the power and control exercised by those institutions, is another important topic to PPE and RPE economists and surely among the most important differences between the methodology of political economists and that of mainstream economists.

Fourth, some retailers whose products are sold on Amazon.com try to cheat the system by paying people to review their products favorably. Consumers who are taken in by these reviews will not be purchasing an item based on valid information. Understanding a country's legal system and how the profit motive can lead to unsavory behavior is another topic of focus for PPE and RPE economists.

What we can see is that mainstream economics focuses on certain aspects of consumer behavior and PPE and RPE economists broaden that focus considerably. We see similar divisions in the area of macroeconomics, as will be found below. But first, it is worth considering the scientific approach to economics more carefully.

1.6 THE SCIENTIFIC METHOD IN ECONOMICS: HOW SCIENTIFIC CAN ECONOMICS BE?

The scientific approach to economics, in which economists make simplifying assumptions to construct models and then test those models against the real world, is often called positive economics. This is named after the economic philosophy of positivism, which seeks to determine definitive, "positive" facts about how the economy works, without the influence of political biases. This approach has yielded some very useful information about the economy, but there are limits to how scientific economics can be.

For example, for many years economists using a model of the labor market believed that there was an inverse relationship between wages and employment: It seemed logical that if wages were increased, businesses would hire fewer workers due to the increase in costs (assuming there were no other major changes in the economy happening at the time that might alter that basic relationship). However, in a groundbreaking study in the 1990s, economists David Card and Alan Krueger proved that a higher minimum wage had no effect on employment; businesses needed a certain minimum number of employees to serve their customers and did not lay off workers after the minimum wage went up. Following the work of Card and Krueger, many other studies of the minimum wage were undertaken, with most supporting their work (some contradicted the findings, though). Overall, the studies seem to indicate that raising the minimum wage by a modest amount usually has little or no effect on employment, although sometimes a higher minimum wage may reduce employment very slightly.

We learn several important things from this example. First, scientific economics can be extremely useful if it can successfully determine how the economy works, which can then inform governments of the best economic policies to use. Second, it is very difficult to establish "positive" and conclusive economic facts. Due to the conflicting findings of numerous studies, economists still disagree on whether or not we should raise the minimum wage. Third, the uncertain nature of the "science" of economics means that economists usually disagree about the way the world works and what policies should be adopted. There are limits to how scientific the study of economics can be. Fourth, logical analysis, though useful, can have serious pitfalls. The logic of the model of the labor market implies that any increase in the wage rate will lead to a decrease in employment, but real-world data indicate that this logic seems to be flawed much of the time.

We see similar disagreements in macroeconomics, especially in the study of economic crises.

1.7 MACROECONOMIC ANALYSIS OF ECONOMIC CRISES

One of the most striking differences between mainstream economics and political economics became apparent in the lead-up to the financial crisis of 2007–2008. Prior to the crisis, most mainstream economists held the view that the macroeconomy tended to be stable. They believed the macroeconomy tended to reach a stable equilibrium from which there would only be small, unimportant deviations. Mainstream economists, using sophisticated mathematical and statistical techniques, were able to develop elaborate general equilibrium models to analyze the interaction between key macroeconomic variables. These models helped the Federal Reserve Bank of the United States and other national banks tweak interest rates in order to keep economies growing and relatively stable. These models, however, did not account for the possibility of an economic crisis occurring.

Meanwhile, political economists, especially those who study economic crises and how they form, began to be concerned with the housing bubble forming in the United States, which was causing an the exceptionally rapid increase in the value of financial assets associated with housing markets. To political economists, economic crises are frequent occurrences, due to the fundamental instability in businesses' investment decisions and the potential for a shortfall in consumer and investor spending once confidence is eroded by some sort of economic shock.

From the political economy perspective, economies typically follow a business cycle of about ten years in length. After a recession starts, businesses are very pessimistic and investment spending on factories and equipment declines. Households are pessimistic and millions of people have lost jobs, so consumer spending also declines. After a few years of sluggish growth, the economy usually starts to pick up. Businesses need to replace outdated and worn-out equipment, and new, profitable opportunities emerge, so business investment rises. This puts more people to work, improving consumer confidence, and consumer spending also increases, raising businesses' profits. This, in turn, stimulates more business investment and hiring. The economy begins to boom and businesses' profits grow rapidly. Businesses have substantial profits, and they invest heavily to take advantage of new opportunities. But eventually, after the economy has boomed for several years, the most secure business opportunities are already taken, and businesses invest their profits in increasingly risky ventures. Eventually, these risky ventures crash and the economy falls into another recession.

For example, in the early 2000s, businesses in the United States invested in extremely risky financial securities tied to real estate markets, which tend to be quite volatile. The value of these risky securities increased incredibly rapidly as more and more money poured in. But eventually investors realized that the real estate market was overvalued, and they sold the risky securities in a panic. The result was a crash in the financial markets, which eliminated billions of dollars in investor wealth, undermined consumer confidence, and threw the economy into the Great Recession of 2008. Prior to the Great Recession, a number of political economists (and one mainstream economist!) published material predicting the financial crisis, and a number of political economists (including the author of this book) quietly began advising their friends that a crisis was coming.

In the wake of the Great Recession, most mainstream economists returned to the work of the great economist John Maynard Keynes, whose analysis of recessions formed the basis of the ideas political economists used to anticipate the recession. During the coronavirus recession of 2020, both mainstream and political economists called for a dramatic increase in government spending, a cornerstone of Keynesian ideas. There is now more similarity between mainstream economics and political economics in macroeconomics, although mainstream economists still see the macroeconomy as fundamentally stable, whereas political economists see it as volatile and unstable. It would be wise for an economics student to understand both views! This is a topic we will take up at length in later chapters.

1.8 THE RICH SOCIAL SCIENCE OF ECONOMICS

Previous sections of this chapter explored microeconomic and macroeconomic examples of how different economists view important economic issues. You should now have some idea of the richness of the field of economics and the insights you can gain from some of the schools of thought. Each school of thought has crucial ideas that you will find useful in understanding certain aspects of the economy you see around you.

Note that, at times, we will broaden our definition of economics to cover ten different schools of economic thought. Each of these schools of thought uses a particular method of analysis and has areas in which their analysis is particularly insightful. Those schools of thought are listed in Figure 1.3.

There is often much overlap between various groups, so do not view the schools of thought as rigid. Conservative mainstream economists, including monetarist, new classical, and supply-side economists, share much with Austrian

Economic school of thought	Methodology	Key areas of strength	Some major thinker(s)
Austrian	Focus on individual choices and their impact on the economy; avoid the use of models and statistics and the analysis of group behavior	Efficiency of markets and how public policy can be stifling, corrupted, and inefficient	Friedrich Hayek, Ludwig von Mises
Monetarist	Mainstream economics: Make simplifying assumptions about economic actors, construct economic models to make predictions, and (to the extent possible) test those predictions using statistical analysis	Importance of the money supply in affecting inflation, gross domestic product	Milton Friedman
New classical (rational expectations)		How individuals' rational decisions can anticipate market changes and affect the economy	Robert Lucas, Eugene Fama
Supply side		How tax rates and regulations affect individuals and businesses and economic activity in general	Martin Feldstein
Moderate (New Keynesian)		Where markets are effective but where they need appropriate regulation to fix market failures and operate more efficiently.	Paul Krugman, Joseph Stiglitz, Gregory Mankiw
Institutional	Focus on the evolution of key human institutions and group behaviors, including technology and culture	How an economy is fundamentally shaped by its institutions, including culture, social norms, companies, the legal system, and government	Thorstein Veblen, John Kenneth Galbraith
Social	Focus on the ethics and social impact of economic activities and policies, along with social (as well as self-interested) behavior	The ethical and social causes and consequences of economic behavior, institutions, organizations, theory, and policy	E. K. Hunt, John B. Davis
Feminist	Attempt to overcome male, patriarchal biases by analyzing social constructs, discrimination, and inequities	Economics of households and the impact of gender on economic outcomes	Marilyn Waring, Nancy Folbre
Post-Keynesian	Focus on effective demand (spending), investment instability, and money creation of banks as major economic factors	How demand affects the macroeconomy and how instability and uncertainty affect investment	Hyman Minksy, Paul Davidson
Marxist	Focus on class conflict over the wealth (surplus product) produced by workers and the dynamics produced by this conflict	Exploitative and unstable nature of markets and the effect of capitalism on workers and communities	Karl Marx, Friedrich Engels

FIGURE 1.3 Table displaying methodology and strengths of ten major economic schools of thought.

economists, preferring a mostly unregulated capitalist market system in which private firms own and control the major economic resources of society and allocate those resources based on the activities that earn the most profit. This approach is known as *laissez-faire* economics, after the French phrase meaning "let it be." Moderate mainstream economists, also known as New Keynesians, believe that markets must be carefully regulated by the government in order to reduce the negative side of markets, such as economic crises, pollution, and inequality. Progressive political economists, including institutional, social, feminist, and post-Keynesian economists, along with the most liberal mainstream economists, want the government to play a larger role in society, managing and guiding markets rather than letting markets dictate the direction of the economy. Finally, radical political economists, drawing on the ideas of Karl Marx, see markets as ruthless and exploitative, and they would rather replace capitalist markets with some variety of socialism or communism.

The ten schools of economic thought are laid out in Figure 1.4, based on how much or how little government the economists from each school tend to prefer, which is perhaps the central issue that creates the different approaches to each school of thought.

Fortunately, there is enough overlap between various schools of thought that we will often simplify our discussion to a few major perspectives on key topics. With respect to policy issues, it is often possible to break economists down into conservative (laissez-faire), moderate (New Keynesian), liberal (progressive political economy), and radical (radical political economy) groups.

Conservative economists generally favor unregulated market capitalism with less government intervention. Unregulated market capitalism is **an economic system in which the main productive resources of society—the labor, land, machinery, equipment, and natural resources—are owned by private individuals who use those resources to produce goods and services that are bought and sold in markets for profit**.

Moderate economists believe in regulated or "mixed" market capitalism. Mixed market capitalism is **an economic system in which private sector firms and individuals produce goods and services for markets for profit and a public sector established by the government regulates those markets and provides public goods such as schools, roads, airports, health care, and other goods and services that are usually provided inadequately by private markets**. Most of the economies in the world have chosen this type of economic system because it has the benefits of a market system, including innovations, competition, and economic growth, without the worst problems you tend to see in unregulated market capitalism, such as exploitation of workers or the environment.

Liberal economists are highly suspicious of markets, seeing them as dominated by a handful of wealthy corporations and rich individuals. They prefer

More Markets, Less Government				PPE	RPE	Less Markets, More Government
		Mainstream				
Economic school of thought	Austrian	Monetarist, New Classical	Supply Side	Moderate (New Keynesian)	Institutional, Social, Feminist, Post-Keynesian	Marxist	Economic school of thought
Preferred economic system	Unregulated Market Capitalism	Unregulated Market Capitalism	Pro-Business Capitalism	Regulated Market Capitalism	Managed Market Capitalism	Socialism, Communism	Preferred economic system
Political views	Conservative			Moderate	Liberal	Socialist	Political views

FIGURE 1.4 Table showing different kinds of economics.

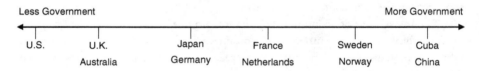

FIGURE 1.5 The size of government in select economies.

strictly regulated capitalism. Radical economists go even further, preferring democratic socialism, **an economic system in which the most important resources of society are controlled democratically by all citizens, including workers, who usually have little say in how market capitalist economies are run**. From this perspective, markets are not particularly efficient, because they produce wasteful and unnecessary goods while neglecting other, more important things such as public health, leisure time with one's family, workers' quality of life, and the environment.

Depending on which economists have the most influence and the economic views of politicians, the economic systems of countries around the globe exhibit substantial variations. Almost all modern economies can be classified as mixed market capitalist, in that they depend on markets for the production and distribution of most goods and services but they also utilize a substantial degree of government intervention.

As you can see from Figure 1.5, which depicts the size of the government sector in selected economies around the world, the United States has the smallest government of any developed economy, coming the closest to unregulated market capitalism. One of the reasons for this is that the United States is the only developed economy without a national health care system. Even very market-oriented countries like the United Kingdom and Australia provide national health care to all citizens. Economies such as Sweden's and Norway's, though still predominantly market based, come closer to democratic socialism in that they have very large state sectors that provide important goods and services such as college education, childcare, dental care, and housing for any citizen who needs them.

As communist countries, Cuba and China have the most government intervention. Communism **is an economic system in which the government controls society's productive resources and makes the major economic decisions.** However, both Cuba and China utilize markets to some degree, so even their economies are "mixed."

1.9 CONCLUSION

This chapter described why economics is an important subject to study. It also detailed various definitions of what economics is. The differences between mainstream economics and political economics (PPE and RPE) were covered, along with how the conservative, moderate, liberal, and radical political approaches to economics affect the size of government in various economies. Remember that each school of economic thought has something useful to add to our understanding of the economy, so it is important to study each approach. In the areas where economic approaches disagree, your job is to critically analyze the different perspectives and to decide for yourself which ideas best capture the world you see around you. This should leave you with a sophisticated and useful understanding of the world.

Also, the economic views that a society chooses to adopt determine the type of economic system that a society develops. Conservative economic views result in an economy closer to unregulated market capitalism. Moderate economic views result in a mixed market capitalist economic system that is mostly market oriented but that includes government intervention to fix the worst problems in markets. If liberal economic views are adopted, the result is a mixed market capitalist economic system with a larger role for government in directing and guiding markets. Finally, a radical economic view would result in a democratic socialist or communist economic system, in which the role of markets is very small and where most economic decisions are made by citizens or by the government.

To clarify the different types of economics, Chapter 2 goes through a mainstream economic model, the production possibilities curve, and contrasts this approach with the views of political economists.

QUESTIONS FOR REVIEW

1. What is **austerity**? Why do most economists think it is a bad economic policy to pursue in a recession?

2. Read about what is happening in the nation or around the globe in a reputable magazine or newspaper, such as *The New York Times, Wall Street Journal, The Economist, The Financial Times,* or *The Guardian.* Which events would be considered relevant to the study of *economics,* given the definitions of economics in this chapter? How are these events important to people and their communities? Explain briefly.

3. What are the primary differences between mainstream economics and political economics (PPE and RPE)? Explain briefly in your own words.

4. Consider the description of "economic man" above and the description of positive, scientific economics. Also consider how political economists (PPE and RPE) study human behavior. Then reflect carefully on your own shopping habits. Do you usually make rational, calculated, fully informed purchases (like "economic man"), or do you tend to buy on impulse for a variety of reasons, or do you do both? Analyze how much of your purchasing behavior can be captured by "positive economics" and when the methods used by political economists would better reflect your behavior. How much of your shopping behavior could be predicted scientifically? How much of it would be hard to predict?

5. Briefly explain the main differences between the economic systems of unregulated market capitalism, mixed market capitalism, and democratic socialism. Using a recent issue of *The Economist* or another reputable publication that features significant international economic news, find examples that show how two countries exhibit characteristics of one or more of these types of economic systems.

6. One of the main economic problems in the modern world is climate change. Scientists have concluded that the world is likely to experience a major ecological crisis unless we reduce the amount of greenhouse gases (especially carbon) that we produce. Greenhouse gases are generated by economic activity. Almost all economists acknowledge the problem but disagree vehemently on how to solve it. Given the definitions of radical, moderate, and conservative economists in the reading, identify which group would be most likely to support each set of policies listed below. Explain your answer briefly.

   a. Establish a carbon tax (on fossil fuels) to give businesses and consumers incentives to change their behavior.

   b. Subsidize the development of solar and wind power industries while taxing carbon to push the economy toward more sustainable practices.

    c.   Close down the most harmful industries (coal, shale gas); tax carbon and mandate the comprehensive use of renewable energies in the very near future; create jobs for any displaced workers.

7.   Which of the ten schools of economic thought listed in Figure 1.3 do you find most interesting? Which do you find least interesting? What does this indicate about your own background and approach to economics at this point?

Scarcity, choice, and opportunity cost

The mainstream approach, the PPC model, the limits of this approach, and the importance of institutions

In this chapter we will examine some mainstream economic concepts, including scarcity, opportunity cost, efficiency, cost–benefit analysis, and how those concepts frame the choices faced by a society. We will also use a simple mainstream economic model, the production possibilities curve (PPC), to capture some of these concepts and to display a variety of choices that a society might face. We will apply these concepts and the PPC model to several economic issues, including an analysis of defense spending and its impact on economic growth. The chapter concludes by drawing on the work of political economists to show the limitations of these mainstream economic concepts and the PPC model in capturing economic reality. Rather than focusing on scarcity and choice, political economists tend to focus on the institutions that shape a society and its choices.

2.0 CHAPTER 2 LEARNING GOALS

After reading this chapter you should be able to:

- Define and apply the concepts of scarcity, opportunity cost, efficiency, and cost–benefit analysis.

- Use a production possibilities curve to analyze the opportunity cost of allocating resources in a particular way.

DOI: 10.4324/9781315636924-3

■ Identify and explain the difference between capital goods and consumer goods and analyze their impact on economic growth using a PPC.

■ Explain why political economists find the mainstream approach to scarcity and cost–benefit analysis limited and how political economists would approach these topics differently using an analysis of the institutional factors that shape a society's choices.

■ Critically analyze the strengths and limitations of the production possibilities curve model and the political economy approach to choices regarding the allocation of resources.

Work on understanding each new concept in this chapter carefully. Also, spend some time working with the production possibilities curve to make sure you understand how it works and what it can be used for. Finally, the chapter is primarily concerned with how mainstream economists and political economists study the choices a society makes to allocate its resources. As always, critically analyze the different approaches and develop your own ideas on the topic.

2.1 SCARCITY, CHOICE, AND OPPORTUNITY COST

The problem of scarcity is absolutely central to mainstream and Austrian economics (this is one of several areas in which mainstream economics and Austrian economics overlap). Scarcity exists **when a society's seemingly unlimited desire for goods and services exceeds the resources available to produce and provide those goods and services**. From this perspective, scarcity exists everywhere because there are never enough resources to produce everything society wants, and much of human life is a struggle to overcome scarcity. Consumers always want more than they have—bigger houses, better cars, faster smart phones, trendier clothes, more new stuff of all kinds—but they have limited budgets. Companies want to produce more goods so they can generate higher profits, but they have limited inputs (labor, machinery, technology, buildings, raw materials). Governments would like to build more roads, improve the environment, spend more on social programs, and expand their militaries, but they have limited tax revenues to spend. Thus, society as a whole wants more of everything it values. However, because of limited resources, people cannot have everything they want, which necessitates making difficult choices. Choice involves **consumers, producers, and governments selecting from among the limited options that are available to them due to scarcity**.

Mainstream economists like to frame making choices in terms of cost–benefit analysis: Good decisions depend on carefully weighing the costs and benefits involved in a decision. In order to undertake such analysis, economists use the concept of opportunity cost: **What is given up when a choice is made to allocate resources in a particular way**. When a consumer is considering the purchase of a $40,000 car, what is the **next best alternative** for which they could use that money? They could put an addition on their home, work 2000 fewer hours at their job, or buy 4000 cases of cheap beer, among many other things. A rational decision would weigh the benefits of the new car against the value of what is perceived as the next best alternative to that car, which would be considered the car's opportunity cost.

The concept of opportunity cost can be a powerful tool in improving decision making because it forces us to consider not just the benefit of what we are choosing to devote resources to but all alternative uses of those resources as well. Consider the following examples.

2.1.1 The opportunity cost of attending college

The average cost of four years of tuition and room and board in 2020–2021 was $103,000 at a public university and $216,000 at a private university in the United States. But one must consider more than just the financial cost. Instead of going to college, a person with a high school degree could go to work full-time and earn, on average, $30,000 per year. So the financial opportunity cost of attending college for four years is about $223,000 at a public university, including $120,000 in foregone salary and $103,000 in tuition and room and board. Similarly, the opportunity cost of attending a private college would be $336,000, on average. Is this a good investment? Fortunately for college students, the lifetime earnings of a typical U.S. college graduate—about $1,200,000—are more than double the $580,000 that a typical high school graduate would earn in their lifetime, so a college education clearly has a substantial financial benefit. Also, college education provides opportunities to cultivate one's passions, become an informed voter, learn to work with diverse people, and much, much more.

2.1.2 The opportunity cost of Sony devoting resources to its computer division

The Japanese company Sony once had a very large computer division. However, personal computer sales began to drop whereas mobile device (smart phones and tablets) sales surged after 2010, so Sony decided to sell off its computer division. Given the poor prospects for personal computers, it made little sense to continue to devote so many resources to that area. For Sony, the opportunity cost of running its computer division was the resources and staff that it could instead devote to the rapidly growing market for mobile devices.

2.1.3 The opportunity cost of the U.S. government spending $55 billion on B-2 Stealth Bombers

The stealth bomber was designed during the Cold War to evade Soviet radar systems and empower the United States to drop nuclear bombs on them. The Soviet Union collapsed in 1990, and most modern conflicts utilize drones much more than old-fashioned bombers. Nonetheless, the U.S. Air Force recently asked for $55 billion for a fleet of new B-2 bombers. What is the opportunity cost of this purchase? In other words, what else could the government do with $55 billion? They could provide 533,980 people with a free education at a public university. They could give every taxpayer a $450 tax cut. These are just two of many worthwhile options.

As you can see from the above examples, the concept of opportunity cost can be applied to almost any decision facing consumers, companies, or governments. An analysis of opportunity cost can help people make a carefully considered choice between two viable alternatives.

Note that the idea of opportunity cost only makes sense if resources are being used efficiently. Efficiency in mainstream economics refers to a situation in which **all resources are employed as productively as possible**. No resources are being wasted or used inefficiently. Efficiency matters because if there are unused resources or if resources are being used inefficiently, then more goods can be produced by putting all resources into use or by using resources more efficiently. There is *no opportunity cost* when production is increased by employing unused or inefficiently used resources. Nothing has to be given up.

For example, if everyone in a country is employed, then producing more of one good necessarily means producing less of other goods. Producing more bombers for national defense means producing fewer cars for consumers. However, the average U.S. unemployment rate from 2005 to 2015 was 6.8%. If all the unemployed were put to work, a huge amount of additional goods and services could be provided for no opportunity cost (without sacrificing the production of any other good or service).

Mainstream economists have developed a simple economic model to display the choices that societies, especially individuals, companies, and governments, face when allocating scarce resources: The production possibilities curve.

2.2 THE PRODUCTION POSSIBILITIES CURVE: A SIMPLE, MAINSTREAM MODEL

An economic model is **a theoretical, simplified construct designed to focus on a key set of economic relationships**. Economists use models because they cannot conduct real-world experiments that isolate key factors, like scientists do, to determine how the real world functions. The best they can do is to construct a theoretical picture of how they think the economy works—a model—and then see whether their model fits with what they observe happening around them. For example, as we saw in Chapter 1, economists have created a model of the demand curve that suggests that when the price of a good goes up, consumers buy less of it. This model is reasonably accurate much of the time, as we will see later.

However, models are only as good as the simplifying assumptions upon which they are based. Any failing in the underlying assumptions will render the model inaccurate. Additionally, all models are based on a major, additional ceteris paribus assumption that **all other relevant factors do not change**. When economists draw a demand curve showing that higher prices cause people to purchase less of a good, they have to assume, ceteris paribus, that consumer confidence remains unchanged (improved consumer confidence would likely mean additional consumer spending on all goods even if prices were higher) and that the product did not become a hot item (which would also increase consumer demand even if prices were higher).

To demonstrate the usefulness and limitations of economic models, we will use a production possibilities curve (PPC), which is **a model that shows all combinations of two goods that can be produced, holding the amount of resources and the level of technology fixed**. The PPC model is designed to show the trade-offs (opportunity costs) that occur when more of a single good is produced.

Consider the production possibilities curve in Figure 2.1, which shows all possible combinations of two services, defense and education, that the U.S. government can provide using all of its available resources and current technology. If the U.S. government decides to devote all of its available resources to defense, it would select option A, with 40 units of defense and 0 units of education. Or, the U.S. government could produce 100 units of education, but this would leave no resources

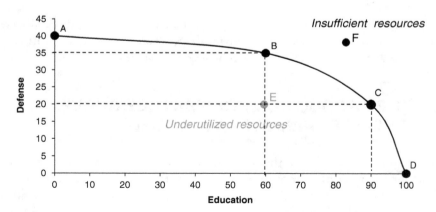

FIGURE 2.1 Production possibilities curve for U.S. government spending on defense, education.

left to use for defense, reducing defense production to 0. Thus, the opportunity cost of increasing the production of education from 0 units to 100 units, moving from point A to point D, is 40 units of defense (what is sacrificed when the government chooses to switch all of its available resources from defense to education). The government can also choose to produce at any point between point A and point D on the production possibilities curve. Figure 2.2 displays the combinations of defense and education that the U.S. government can choose in table form, matching the options that are graphed in Figure 2.1.

Suppose that the government is currently at point B, producing 35 units of defense and 60 units of education. Now suppose the government decides to increase the production of education to 90 units, moving from point B to point C. The only way they can increase the production of education, given that they are stuck with existing resources and technology, is by reducing the production of defense from 35 units to 20 units. The opportunity cost of moving from point B to point C would be 15 units of defense, which is what is given up in exchange for 30 additional units of education.

The assumptions behind the PPC model include the following: (1) There are only two relevant goods, (2) any point on the PPC curve involves the full employment of available resources, (3) resources are fixed, (4) technology is fixed, and (5) any other factors that might affect the production of the two goods in question will remain unchanged (the ceteris paribus assumption).

Note that any point on the PPC, including points A, B, C, and D, involves utilizing *all* of the government's available resources efficiently. If some resources were not being used, or if resources were being used inefficiently, then the U.S. government would be at a point *inside* the production possibilities curve, such as point E.

Also note that though the U.S. government would like to be able to provide more defense and more education for its citizens, it cannot choose a point outside the PPC because it does not have sufficient resources or effective enough technology (scarcity). The only way for the U.S. government to reach point F, which is beyond the PPC, would be if it had additional resources or if there were an improvement in technology that allowed more production of both education and defense than is currently possible. Any change in the availability of resources or technology, however, would be a change in the assumptions behind the model, and we would have to draw a new PPC reflecting the new assumptions.

Choice	Education	Defense
A	0	40
B	60	35
C	90	20
D	100	0

FIGURE 2.2 Table showing the production possibilities combinations in Figure 2.1.

2.3 THE SPECIALIZATION OF RESOURCES

The shape of the production possibilities curve is also important. The PPC above has a downward (negative) slope that becomes steeper and steeper (it is concave to the origin). This occurs whenever a PPC reflects the specialization of resources: **When some resources cannot be easily adapted from one use to another**. For example, some resources that are used to produce defense, such as tanks and bombers, are not well suited for producing education. Similarly, some resources that are used to produce education, such as schools and school buses, are poorly suited for producing defense.

We can see the specialization of resources in the PPC in Figure 2.1 and in the table in Figure 2.2 when the amounts of education exchanged for defense vary. If we begin at point A, the government is producing all defense and no education. Even schools, buses, and teachers are being used for national defense! Now suppose that the government decides to shift some resources out of defense and into education, moving from point A to point B. They will, of course, shift the resources most specialized for education first. By shifting the schools, buses, and teachers from producing defense to producing education, the result is very little loss in defense (5 units) for a very large gain in education (60 units). Between point A and point B, 5 units of defense (D) use the same resources that could produce 60 units of education (E). To put this in mathematical terms:

$$\text{From A to B}, 5D = 60E.$$

Dividing both sides by 5 to find the opportunity cost of 1 unit of defense, we get

$$\text{From A to B,} \left(\frac{5}{5}\right)D = \left(\frac{60}{5}\right)E; \text{ and } 1D = 12E.$$

From A to B, each unit of defense sacrificed results in 12 units of education being produced.

Now suppose that the government wants to devote even more resources to education. Moving from B to C involves producing 30 additional units of education while giving up 15 units of defense. The resources that were best suited for education were already shifted into education when the government moved from A to B. Now the government is shifting resources that are well suited for either defense or for education. This would include soldiers, who could also be teachers; computers; equipment that could be used for education or for defense; and so on. Now the opportunity cost of each unit is different. From point B to point C, 15 units of defense (D) are given up for 30 units of education (E). In mathematical terms,

From B to C, $15D = 30E$; and if we divide both sides by 15, $1D = 2E$.

Similarly, if the government moves from point C to point D, 20 units of defense are given up in exchange for only 10 units of education. Now the government is shifting all of their resources into education, even those that are well suited for defense but very poorly suited for education, such as bombs, bombers, tanks, and guns.

$$\text{From } C \text{ to } D, 10E = 20D; \text{ and } 1D = \frac{1}{2}E.$$

From C to D, each unit of defense that is given up only results in half of a unit of education (½E) being produced.

The last column in Figure 2.3 shows how the opportunity cost of 1 unit of defense changes as the government moves from point A to point D.

Similarly, we can compute the opportunity cost of one unit of education in each region of the PPC, which you can see in the fifth column of the table in Figure 2.3.

The change in the opportunity cost of one unit of each good on a curved production possibilities curve displays something mainstream economists refer to as the law of increasing opportunity cost: **If resources are specialized and if all resources are being used efficiently, then, as more and more of a particular good is produced, the opportunity cost of producing each additional unit of that good will increase**. In other words, as we produce more and more units of education, moving from point A to point D on the PPC in Figure 2.1, each unit of education will have a higher opportunity cost. This occurs because we have to give up more and more units of defense to get one unit of education as we shift resources that are better suited to defense into the production of education. This situation also works in reverse: As we produce more and more units of defense, moving from point D to point A on the PPC in Figure 2.1, each unit of defense has a higher opportunity cost because we are shifting resources into defense that are better suited to education as we get closer to point A.

Choice	Education	Defense	Opportunity cost	Opportunity cost of one unit of education	Opportunity cost of one unit of defense
A	0	40			
A-B			$60E = 5D$	$1E = (1/12)D$	$1D = 12E$
B	60	35			
B-C			$30E = 15D$	$1E = (1/2)D$	$1D = 2E$
C	90	20			
C-D			$10E = 20D$	$1E = 2D$	$1D = (1/2)E$
D	100	0			

FIGURE 2.3 Table showing changes in opportunity cost due to the specialization of resources.

There are some important real-world examples of the law of increasing opportunity cost at work. For instance, in the 1980s, the Soviet Union devoted about 17% of its economy to national defense. The Soviet Union collapsed in 1990, ending the Cold War in which the United States and the Soviet Union built up huge military arsenals. The Soviet Union became Russia and a group of independent countries. Russian officials decided to reduce the size of their military to 3% of the economy and shift from the production of defense into the production of consumer goods, energy, health care, and other non-defense items that Russia needed. They hoped to see a huge boom in other sectors as they shifted resources out of defense. But the boom was much smaller than they anticipated. Why? One of the biggest reasons was the specialization of resources: All of the huge defense factories and specialized defense workers who built tanks and served as soldiers were not very productive when it came to producing non-defense goods. After 1990, Russia sacrificed a vast amount of defense in exchange for a much smaller increase in the production of non-defense goods.

Investor T. Boone Pickens once proposed that the United States stop using so much imported oil by converting automobiles to use U.S.-produced compressed natural gas. It is an interesting proposal, but due to the specialization of resources, we must carefully consider the opportunity cost of doing so. The transportation infrastructure in the United States is built around using gasoline made from oil; converting all of the cars, gas stations, and refineries to produce compressed natural gas would be difficult and expensive—and would come with a significant opportunity cost.

The above examples all refer to cases in which resources are specialized. However, if resources are not specialized, then opportunity costs would be constant along a PPC rather than increasing, and the PPC would be a straight line. For example, Figure 2.4 shows a production possibilities curve for a company

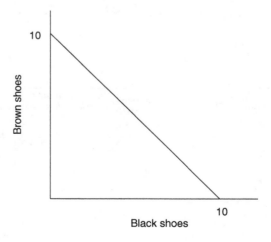

FIGURE 2.4 A PPC without specialized resources.

producing black shoes and brown shoes. Because the only difference between the shoes is the color of the dye used, resources (labor, machinery, etc.) can be shifted easily from the production of black shoes to the production of brown shoes.

2.4 SHIFTS IN THE PRODUCTION POSSIBILITIES CURVE

A production possibilities curve is drawn based on the assumption that resources and technology are fixed. But what would happen if more resources or better technology were made available? We would need to draw a new PPC that is shifted outward. The type of shift would depend on whether or not the resources or technology were better suited for the production of one good or both goods.

For example, consider an economy producing cars and food. If better robots were invented that can produce either item, then the PPC would shift out, showing that society can now have more of both goods. This is shown in example (a) in Figure 2.5. What if the newly invented robots can only be used to produce cars? Then the PPC shifts out on the "cars" axis, but not on the "food" axis, as shown

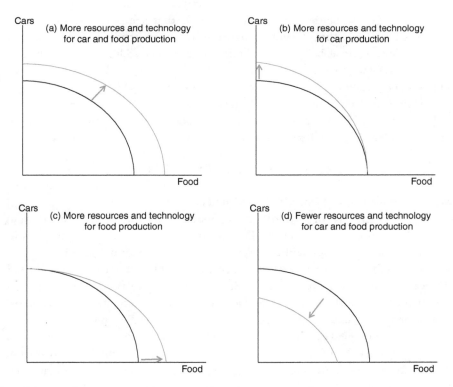

FIGURE 2.5 Shifts in the PPC from changes in resources or technology.

in Figure 2.5, example (b). If the robots could only be used for producing food, the PPC would shift out only on the "food" axis, as shown in Figure 2.5, example (c). Finally, suppose that a natural disaster reduced the resources available for food and car production. The result would be a PPC that has shifted in on both axes, as shown in Figure 2.5, example (d).

2.5 CAPITAL GOODS, CONSUMER GOODS, AND ECONOMIC GROWTH

One of the key issues in determining whether or not an economy (and its PPC) grows is the priority that the people in an economy give to generating productive resources. Capital goods are **the machinery, equipment, buildings, and productive resources (other than labor) used to produce goods and services**. When an economy produces capital goods, it becomes more productive, shifting out its PPC. A PPC could also shift out from an improvement in **technology**, which would make capital goods more productive. **Labor** is another productive resource. When an economy has more laborers, it can produce more goods and services, shifting out its PPC. Economists also consider **human capital** to be a capital good: Education and training make our labor force more productive, which also shifts out the PPC. Consumer goods, on the other hand, are **goods that are purchased and used by consumers but that do not contribute to future productivity**. Consumer goods include items such as beer, clothing, and food. The addition of labor, human capital, or capital goods increases an economy's productivity and shifts out its PPC, but producing additional consumer goods does not shift the PPC.

Mainstream economic theory suggests that, in general, economic growth (growth in the PPC) is a result of increases in labor, increases in capital goods, and increases in productivity (from better technology or greater human capital):

$$\text{Economic Growth} = \Delta L + \Delta K + \Delta \text{Productivity},$$

where Δ = change, L = labor, and K = capital.

An economy that draws more of its population into the labor force, devotes more of its resources to capital goods than to consumer goods, and improves its education and technology will experience more rapid economic growth.

Much of China's recent growth can be explained by these factors: For the last 35 years, China drew millions of relatively unproductive rural workers into its highly productive urban factories, and it invested heavily in capital goods, technology development, education, and infrastructure (roads, bridges, ports, and airports, also considered capital goods), which in turn increased productivity. The result was an astounding economic boom and economic growth averaging 9.8% a year from 1979 to 2013. For comparison, the average annual U.S. economic growth rate during the same period was 2.7%.

2.5.1 Defense spending and growth

Interestingly, government spending on national defense is considered to be a consumer good. Defense spending protects people within a country, but it does not
increase the economy's productive capacity. Thus, we "consume" defense much
like we do other services that we value but that do not contribute to economic
growth.

Consider Figure 2.6, which shows a PPC for capital goods and consumer
goods. If the society depicted in Figure 2.6 chooses point A, with more capital
goods and fewer consumer goods like national defense, it will experience greater
economic growth, its PPC will shift out further, and it will have a higher standard
of living in the future (a larger PPC, which allows it to consume more of both
goods). If the society chooses point B, with fewer capital goods and more consumer
goods, the PPC will shift out less in the future.

The facts that economic growth is generated in part by capital goods and that
defense spending is a consumer good make the choice of whether or not to devote
significant resources to national defense a very important one for a society. As you
can see in Figure 2.7, the United States devotes more of its resources to military
spending than any other country in the world. In fact, the United States devotes
more money to defense than the next nine countries combined! The United States
spends more than twice as much on defense as the countries the United States sees
as major security risks: China, Russia, Iran, and North Korea. The opportunity

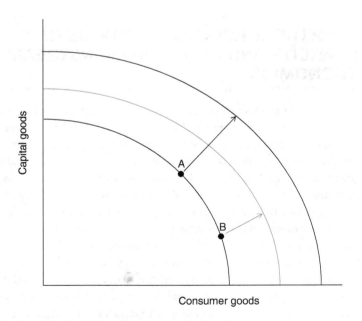

FIGURE 2.6 Growth in the PPC from more capital goods.

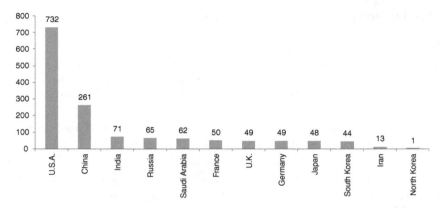

FIGURE 2.7 Ten largest military spenders in 2018, plus Iran and North Korea (billions of dollars). Source: Stockholm International Peace Research Institute (SIPRI).

cost of spending so much on defense is both the current goods that are given up *and* the future goods that are sacrificed due to lower economic growth.

Thus, the mainstream PPC model focuses on how society chooses to allocate its scarce resources. In doing so, the model encourages society to carefully consider the opportunity costs of making choices. However, as we will see in the next section, political economists extend their analysis of scarcity and choice into additional areas.

2.6 A POLITICAL ECONOMY CRITIQUE OF SCARCITY AND CHOICE IN MAINSTREAM ECONOMICS

The economies of the modern developed world produce enough goods and services for everyone to have a standard of living that would have been unthinkable a century ago. Thus, to characterize economics as the study of scarcity rather than abundance is a reflection of a particular set of assumptions and value choices. To mainstream economists, an efficient allocation of resources occurs when no one can be made better off without making someone else worse off. The idea of redistributing goods and services from one person to another is considered outside of the realm of analysis. This is a reflection of the mainstream's attempt to practice value-free, "positive" analysis rather than taking into consideration values and other normative elements of economic issues. Political economists of various types find the mainstream analysis of scarcity and choice overly limiting, and they extend their analysis into a number of areas, including ethics, culture, underemployment of resources, inequality, and gender empowerment. A brief analysis of each of these areas will provide an excellent introduction to the crucial differences between mainstream analysis and that of different schools of political economy.

2.6.1 Ethical considerations

Social economists urge us to consider the ethical considerations of our decisions regarding resource allocation. Is it ethical to devote additional resources to B-2 bombers and other defense goods when many children do not have enough food to eat? One of the most important economic decisions a society can make is how it chooses to allocate its resources, and such ethical considerations play a crucial part in that choice.

2.6.2 Culture and conspicuous consumption

The fact that rich consumers in wealthy countries want to buy more and more lavish goods can be seen as an indication not of scarcity but of what the **institutionalist** economist Thorstein Veblen called conspicuous consumption: **Purchasing goods in order to display social status**. To Veblen and other institutionalists, a crucial aspect of an economic system is the cultural forces that encourage conspicuous consumption at the expense of other worthwhile societal goals. Why do human beings seem bent on showing off their wealth to achieve social status? From this perspective, understanding consumer choices is less about scarcity than the fact that consumers with an unprecedented level of material well-being, drowning in high-tech gadgets and luxury goods, think that they need to buy even more goods than they already have. Determining the cultural processes that drive consumerist attitudes is therefore important to our understanding of resource allocation in the economy.

2.6.3 Underemployed resources

Another issue concerns whether or not resources are ever fully employed and how easily they can be switched to new uses. The production possibilities curve model implies that resources are usually fully employed and that resources can always be shifted to another use, although there may be increasing opportunity costs when that is done. Does this match the real-world experiences we see around us? As U.S. manufacturers have increasingly moved their factories to foreign sites in China, Mexico, and elsewhere, there has been a significant increase in availability of resources. Buildings, factories, machines, and manufacturing workers in the United States are now available to produce different goods instead of the steel, cars, and other manufactured goods that they used to produce. However, instead of shifting easily and quickly into other productive activities, most of the old factories sit unused, and many manufacturing workers remain unemployed. The "rust belt" of the United States, with depressed cities like Detroit, Youngstown, and Allentown, shows us that the shift of resources to new uses has not happened effectively. In reality, given chronic unemployment and underutilized resources, the United States may never have been on its PPC. From a **post–Keynesian** perspective, the key economic problem is not scarcity but how society can put all of its productive resources to their best possible use. In every society, there are people who need work and work that needs to be done. The key economic issue is not so much scarcity as the underemployment of resources, something that can be addressed by good government policies.

2.6.4 Inequality

It is also worth pointing out that abundance for the few is accompanied in wealthy countries by vast poverty. At the same time that the rich are consuming ever more luxury goods, more than 1.5 million people experience homelessness in a single year in the United States. To a **Marxist** (radical political) economist, the key issue is not scarcity but the structure of the class system and power structures of society that result in abundance for a few, and poverty and homelessness for millions. Why are the lower classes in the United States, and especially citizens from Black and Latino backgrounds, so poor while others are so rich? Scarcity, from a Marxist perspective, is a condition imposed on the working class by greedy capitalists who want more for themselves while denying workers a decent standard of living. Only in countries where strong labor movements have reduced the power of corporate interests do we see workers earning a decent share of what is produced. Marxists focus on the analysis of social classes to understand resource allocation in societies, a topic that is omitted from mainstream analysis.

2.6.5 Gender empowerment

Another key issue, from the perspective of **feminist** economists, involves who is making the decisions and what priorities their decisions reflect. If women had greater political and economic power, would the decisions of society reflect different priorities? The Northern European countries that lead the world in gender empowerment tend to have much more generous family leave policies and welfare states. They provide new parents with up to a year of paid leave to care for a child (compared with six weeks of unpaid leave in the United States), and they provide all citizens with high-quality health care and education (including college), paid for by taxes on income and consumption. These countries have decided to devote more resources to family time, health, and education, while devoting fewer resources to consumer goods. There is a gendered component to decision making that reflects crucial aspects of an economic system, so any analysis of resource allocation must include an analysis of gender.

The above examples of how various groups of political economists view scarcity and choice illustrate the fundamental difference between mainstream economics and political economy: Mainstream economists prefer focusing on specific decisions using the concepts of scarcity and opportunity cost, whereas political economists prefer a **much broader approach** that emphasizes various crucial **institutions** in the economy. That approach is described in more detail in the next section.

2.7 INSTITUTIONAL ANALYSIS: A POLITICAL ECONOMY APPROACH TO THE STUDY OF RESOURCE ALLOCATION

When political economists study resource allocation they focus on institutions. Institutions are **the organizations, social structures, rules, and habits that structure human interactions and the economy**. Formal institutions include the laws, regulations, firms, government bodies, and the political system. Informal institutions include culture, social classes, habits, and other patterns of behavior that shape how people act and interact. Institutions are specific to a particular time and place. From this perspective, the opportunity cost of producing bombers is less informative than the factors that shape the actual choice of bombers and national defense over education in the modern United States.

In analyzing why the United States has chosen to devote vast resources to B-2 bombers and other defense goods over education, political economists focus on power structures, class, politics, culture, and other key institutions. The economic system in the modern United States is dominated by huge corporations. Similarly, the political system is dominated to a large degree by those corporations and the wealthy individuals who own them and who give vast sums of money to politicians. Some of the most powerful corporations and wealthy individuals have financial interests in the defense industry, and via political donations they encourage politicians to keep building B-2 bombers. U.S. corporate interests in foreign countries sometimes need the U.S. military to intervene on their behalf, which requires a U.S. military presence around the globe. In general, political economists see the U.S. military as supporting the dominant class of corporate leaders, wealthy owners, and politicians.

The U.S. military is itself a powerful institution that has been very successful in persuading Congress to continue funding defense expenditures at an extremely high level, even in times of peace. Furthermore, Congress can safely spend huge sums of money on defense due in part to U.S. cultural attitudes. The United States is known to be much more patriotic than other countries, as measured in the World Values Surveys. This contributes to a willingness of citizens to devote more resources to the military than other countries do and the ability of politicians to appeal to patriotism when they increase funding for national defense.

These factors led President Dwight D. Eisenhower, a five-star general during World War II, to warn against the powerful alliance of the corporate defense industry and the military. In a famous speech in 1961, he warned, "In the councils of government, we must guard against the acquisition of unwarranted influence, whether sought or unsought, by the military–industrial complex. The potential for the disastrous rise of misplaced power exists and will persist." The fact that defense spending in the United States continues to be at a level much higher than that of other countries indicates the ongoing vitality of the military–industrial complex.

From a political economy perspective, the decision of the United States to place a very high priority on national defense and a lower priority on education in comparison to most developed countries is a product of a variety of institutional factors. Scarcity is one of the important issues that affects how many resources can be devoted to defense and education. Nonetheless, political economists prefer a much broader focus for economics than scarcity. Economic models can be useful in helping us to focus on a few key economic relationships, but they can ignore many other important factors that come into play. The question of which relationships to focus on deeply divides mainstream and political economists.

2.8 CONCLUSION

To mainstream economists, economics is about the difficult choices an individual, firm, or society must make when resources are scarce. By carefully considering the opportunity cost as well as the benefits of choosing to devote resources in a particular way, decision making can be improved. A simple mainstream model, the production possibilities curve, can be used to analyze the opportunity cost of a particular allocation of resources, including the relationship between capital goods, consumer goods, and economic growth. This is a flexible approach that can be applied to numerous situations.

Political economists acknowledge the usefulness of cost–benefit analysis, while also stressing the need to broaden this approach. From a political economy perspective, economists must go beyond scarcity to study the institutions that shape choices in a society. By combining the focused cost–benefit analysis of mainstream economics with the breadth of political economy, you are likely to get a very clear picture of the trade-offs facing society and how those trade-offs are shaped by key institutional factors.

To be sure, the analysis above is but a quick glance at a set of different approaches taken by mainstream and political economists. As we continue, these differences will become more apparent. Also, it is important to recognize that the example of the mainstream PPC model suggests a fundamental focus by the mainstream on mathematical approaches and an attempt to make their analysis as scientific as possible. Political economists, on the other hand, prefer to bring in additional factors that cannot always be measured precisely but that nevertheless can have an important influence on the economy.

Now that you are familiar with some of the fundamental premises and applications of mainstream economics and political economy, the next crucial topic to explore is the evolution of the global economy over time. The institutions of society were developed in the past and shape the future in key ways. The best way to understand where the economic system is going is to understand where it has been. Analyzing economic history can help you anticipate the likely trends in the future, and such economic forecasting is an invaluable economic skill.

QUESTIONS FOR REVIEW

1. Explain how each of the following events would affect scarcity:
   a. Consumers' desire for goods and services decreases.
   b. Resources become less plentiful.
   c. The government discovers a large amount of unused resources.
2. Use the concept of opportunity cost to analyze the decision of whether or not you should study economics tonight.
3. The graph in Figure 2.8 displays a production possibilities curve for the world in choosing between allocating resources to food or machinery.
   a. What is the opportunity cost of moving from point B to point D?
   b. What is the opportunity cost of 1 unit of machinery between point D and point C?
   c. Which points on the graph are considered to be efficient and feasible? Explain briefly.

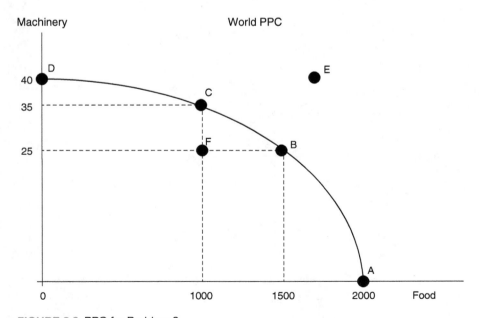

FIGURE 2.8 PPC for Problem 3.

    d.   The reason for the curved shape of the PPC above is that (choose the best answer):
- (i) Resources are scarce.
- (ii) Increasing food production causes a decrease in machinery production.
- (iii) There are opportunity costs for producing more of either good.
- (iv) Some inputs are better at producing food than machinery.
- (v) None of the above.

    e.   Scientists estimate that global climate change will destroy 10% of land that is current used to produce food. Show on a graph how this will affect the PPC.

    f.   Assuming that the world is at point B on the PPC, producing and consuming 1500 units of food, and that the world will need to continue consuming the same amount after global climate change destroys 10% of land, how will the destruction of land affect the production of machinery? Will economic growth in the future be affected by these changes? Why or why not?

    g.   How would political economists broaden the analysis in parts e and f of this question? What institutions would they think are most relevant to the issues being raised?

4.   The graph in Figure 2.9 displays a production possibilities curve for the United States in choosing between allocating resources to transportation or beer.

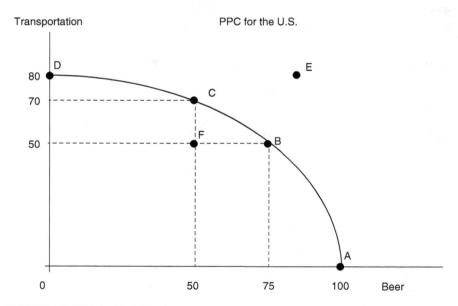

FIGURE 2.9 PPC for Problem 4.

a. What is the opportunity cost of 1 unit of beer between point A and point B?

b. What is the opportunity cost of moving from point A to point C?

c. Show what would happen to the graph if the government fails to maintain their transportation infrastructure.

d. The President of the United States recently proposed that the United States should dramatically increase its transportation spending. Assume that the economy is currently at point B in Figure 2.9. If we follow the President's plan and increase transportation spending dramatically, what would be the immediate, short-term effect?

e. Economic data indicate that transportation spending by the government improves businesses' productivity. Using the PPC model, analyze what the President's proposal to increase transportation spending will do in the long run to the U.S. economy.

f. How would political economists respond to the analysis in parts d and e?

5. Given the factors that mainstream economists believe contribute to economic growth, what would happen to economic growth and to the production possibilities curve for the United States if it halts all immigration into the country and the United States population actually declines?

6. Scientists are convinced that the burning of fossil fuels is contributing to global climate change, which will harm future economic growth.

a. Construct a PPC showing the trade-off between fossil fuels and renewable energy. Explain how different points on the PPC will affect future growth in the PPC.

b. Undertake an analysis from a political economy perspective about the choice of whether or not to devote resources to renewable energy. Why do you think the United States devotes fewer resources to renewable energy than many other developed countries?

PART II

The evolution of economic ideas and systems

The economic systems of the world have changed dramatically over the course of human history. The only certainty about economic systems appears to be that they will continue to change as they are forced to confront inherent contradictions and new problems. Human economic systems evolved from cooperative hunting and gathering communities to kingdoms that exploited slaves to variations of market capitalism in which privately owned firms controlled the bulk of society's resources. The fact that no economic system has lasted forever leads to an interesting question: *What type of economic system might replace contemporary market capitalism?*

As economic systems evolved, so did economic thought. All economic thinkers reflect the society and the economic problems of their era. Some of the earliest authors who took up economic topics, including Plato and Aristotle, justified slavery on the grounds that some people were naturally inferior. Adam Smith lived toward the end of the mercantilist era, when giant monopolies working with autocratic governments dominated global trade and extracted resources from the rest of society. He believed that unregulated market capitalism would be preferable to mercantilism because competition would limit the power of monopolistic firms and enhance the well-being of workers. Karl Marx wrote during the dark ages of capitalism, when it was not uncommon for children to be shackled to machines for up to 78 hours a week. Marx hoped that a socialist or communist system would solve the worst excesses of capitalism. In the early 1900s, Thorstein Veblen saw that small U.S. firms were being displaced by vast corporations run by the robber barons, who ruthlessly extracted profits from their workers and from society. Like Smith, Veblen believed that only by reining in large corporations would market capitalism be able to function for the well-being of all people. John Maynard Keynes wrote his masterwork, *The General Theory of Employment, Interest and Money*, during the Great Depression, a crisis that convinced him and many others that unregulated market capitalism could not work. Keynes advocated a regulated form of capitalism, which is the economic system that came to dominate the modern world.

DOI: 10.4324/9781315636924-4

But, as Keynes was advocating the development of a government-regulated market capitalist economy, the rise of Hitler in Germany and Stalin in the Soviet Union caused Friedrich Hayek to question whether or not we should put our trust in government.

Part II describes the evolution of economic systems from ancient times to the present. In the process, we will take up the best ideas of the most influential economists in the context in which they wrote their ideas. As we study the different forms that economic systems have taken, think carefully about what lessons emerge regarding human nature from the many ways in which human beings have organized themselves to produce the goods and services necessary for survival. And, as we study the theories of the great economists, critically evaluate their ideas against the economy you see around you to decide for yourself which theories are still relevant to the modern world.

Chapter 3 takes up the evolution of economic systems from communal, tribal societies to slave-based empires, followed by feudalism and mercantilism. Chapter 4 describes the establishment of capitalism and the ideas of Adam Smith. Chapter 5 goes through the labor unrest and economic crises that were a product of the dark ages of capitalism in the mid-1800s and the ideas that Karl Marx developed during this period. Chapter 6 lays out the principal ideas of Thorstein Veblen, along with the rise of monopoly capitalism that culminated in the Great Depression and the fall of laissez-faire. Chapter 7 describes the rise of mixed market capitalism based on the ideas of John Maynard Keynes. Part II concludes with Chapter 8, which examines the market-dominated, social market, and state-dominated economies we see in the modern world.

The evolution of pre-capitalist economic systems

From communal societies to empires, feudalism, and mercantilism

Every society needs an economic system of some sort to provide the goods and services its people need to survive and thrive. But only in modern times, under capitalism, has that economy been controlled by markets and the pursuit of private profit. Early human societies did make use of markets, but their use was extremely limited and markets were almost never entrusted with the provision of the main goods that a society needed for its survival.

The harsh conditions of the ancient world required people to band together for survival. The survival of individuals required doing everything necessary for the group to ensure its survival. The largest, most closely knit groups were the ones that triumphed over smaller, less cohesive ones. Thus, due to our evolutionary history, individual motivations seem to be group oriented rather than completely self-interested. This is one of the biggest reasons why political economists dispute the mainstream economics portrayal of economic man as primarily individualistic and self-interested: Throughout human history people have cared deeply about their place in their social group. In fact, their survival depended on it.

Human beings have lived and worked in a wide variety of economic systems, which they have designed over the centuries. As we will see below, early human societies were usually characterized by reciprocity, redistribution, sharing, and trust. They also engaged in some specialization of tasks and a simple division of labor to facilitate their survival.

Once societies began to produce enough surplus food that everyone did not have to work, hierarchical class systems began to develop. These grew in size and complexity as the surplus expanded, accompanied by a gradual increase in the

DOI: 10.4324/9781315636924-5

use of trade and markets to provide goods for the elites. In slave societies, a small minority controlled the resources and most of the population barely earned enough to survive. However, slave societies proved to be unstable, and they were followed by the static, hierarchical system of feudalism, where lords controlled the labor of serfs. Feudalism lasted for 1000 years, but it too eventually became untenable, and it was replaced by mercantilism in the 1500s. Markets began to take on an important role when kings and merchants constructed and expanded markets for their own benefit. But even under mercantilism, markets did not control the allocation of a majority of society's resources. It was only with the advent of full-fledged capitalism in the 1800s that market capitalism became the dominant economic system and society's productive resources, land, labor, and capital came to be allocated by markets.

This chapter will describe the evolution of human economic systems from communal, tribal societies to the more hierarchical systems of slave-based empires, feudalism, and mercantilism. It draws on the classic work by Karl Polanyi, *The Great Transformation*, along with recent discoveries in economic anthropology, psychology, and evolutionary biology that address the evolution of human societies over time.

3.0 CHAPTER 3 LEARNING GOALS

After reading this chapter you should be able to:

- Outline the main characteristics of (1) traditional, hunter-gatherer societies; (2) slave-based empires (Rome); (3) feudalism; and (4) mercantilism, and describe the common threads and major differences of these human societies.

- Analyze the role of tradition, authority, and markets, along with the specialization of labor and the use of the surplus product, in each of these four economic systems.

- Explain how cooperation, specialization, redistribution, and reciprocity were important to the survival of people living in hunter-gatherer societies and in other economic systems.

- Describe the types of social classes and role of private property in the different economic systems.

- List and analyze the major forces that eroded each economic system and paved the way for the next economic system.

We begin by considering what we know about the earliest human societies that existed.

3.1 TRADITIONAL ECONOMIES: ANCIENT HUNTER-GATHERER SOCIETIES

So, what were the earliest economic systems like?

Human beings are inherently group-oriented, social creatures. Archaeological evidence indicates that the earliest tool-using human ancestors of 2 million years ago were nomadic hunter-gatherers living in groups of around 70 members, usually formed by large kinship groups (extended families). It is worth analyzing why working in groups was essential to survival because this helps us to understand how we evolved as a group-oriented species.

The earliest human societies lived on the edge of survival. They did not have the ability to store food for long periods, so obtaining a steady supply of food every day was the primary human activity. Any shortfall for a sustained period of time meant starvation. In this environment, cooperative communities had an advantage, and individuals or very small groups usually did not last long.

Cooperation was useful in protecting the community from predators, including animals as well as other human groups. A larger community could also engage in larger scale, risky activities. While some community members were devoted to the regular hunting and gathering activities, some high-risk endeavors with potentially large payoffs, such as hunting large game, would be undertaken by a small portion of the community. This allowed for a degree of **specialization** and innovation in performing tasks and resulted in a more secure food supply.

Redistribution (sharing) and **reciprocity** within the group were defining characteristics of these early societies. As Karl Polanyi observes in *The Great Transformation*, "The Bergdama returning from his hunting excursion, the woman coming back from her search for roots, fruit, or leaves are expected to offer the greater part of their spoil for the benefit of the community." Producers share with their community because they can expect reciprocity: When another member of the community finds food, they too will share it.

Redistribution was crucial to survival in that a family without the support of a larger group was at high risk of starvation. One bout of serious illness or a run of bad luck in hunting and gathering and the family could starve. However, with the support of the community, they could survive the lean times. Thus, though independent families did sometimes live on their own (householding), it was the larger groups that were more successful.

Sometimes chiefs controlled the method of redistribution in larger groups, and sometimes redistribution was done based on traditional social roles. This type of system has sometimes been labeled **primitive communism** because of the emphasis on common production and the relatively egalitarian sharing of the collectively produced goods.

To effectively allocate tasks and goods, our human ancestors developed customs or traditions. A traditional economy is one in which **resources are allocated based on communal patterns of reciprocity and redistribution, and**

in which tasks are allocated and knowledge and skills preserved through established social relationships. In this sense, a traditional economy is dominated by the cultural forces that shape the allocation of resources, goods, and tasks. In such societies, culture and tradition were crucial in making sure that society's knowledge was passed down to the next generation, guaranteeing that a community had enough people with the appropriate skill set allocated to each task (hunting, tracking, gathering, tool making, etc.), and in uniting society in the face of external threats.

Anthropologists have been able to observe hunter-gatherer societies that have survived until the modern era, and they have seen redistributive and reciprocal behaviors firsthand. For example, Pierre Robbe describes the Inuit dividing up the meat from a bear that had been killed:

> Virtually all the inhabitants of the village were there, standing around the animal in three roughly concentric circles: Harald [the first person to see the bear] and the five participants (those who had been members of the hunt), then the other men of the village who were going to take part in the cutting up of the bear … and finally the women and the children.

Although more of the bear meat goes to the person who spotted the bear and to those who killed the bear, some must be shared with the entire community. We see similar methods of redistribution in other societies, with all hunters and gatherers sharing what they find or kill with the community according to established social rules.

In the harsh hunter-gatherer environment, the highest social status was given to those who were the most productive members of society. One of the characteristics of people in all human societies seems to be the desire to achieve social status. The desire for status is probably hard-wired into us by the evolutionary process: Those who achieved a higher social status were more likely to survive and procreate. Historical evidence indicates that human beings are inherently status-seeking, which is **the human propensity to strive to achieve the highest social status possible, given the values of the community in which they live**.

The criteria for achieving a high social status vary substantially based on the society and its priorities. Traditional economies valued the production of food and held the most productive hunters and gatherers in high esteem. Some traditional societies also developed elaborate systems of gift-giving as displays of status. As ethnologist Marcel Mauss observed in his classic work, *The Gift*, these communities engaged in a competitive exchanging of gifts in which gift-givers tried to outdo others in order to achieve social status. A modern parallel would be some countries in Europe, Asia, and the Middle East in which generous gestures to others, such as paying for the entire group's dinner and drinks when dining out, are considered acts worthy of esteem and praise. In contrast, capitalist economies tend to celebrate the accumulation of personal wealth. To political economists, one of the keys to analyzing the economy of a particular place is understanding how its culture shapes the status-seeking of its members. Human beings work to succeed in their particular community, which means they try to **act rationally within a cultural context** to achieve social status.

In addition to valuing productivity above other activities, most traditional communities tended to practice a form of direct democracy. Each adult had a say in major decisions, so the power of the chief was quite limited.

In such communities, there was limited specialization of tasks. Everyone needed to perform a large number of tasks every day just to stay alive. The most significant division of tasks was along gender lines, with men performing the hunting and women focused on gathering, child-rearing, and cooking. Mothers would teach their daughters the knowledge and skills associated with their specialized tasks, and their daughters would follow in their footsteps. Fathers and sons followed the same pattern.

The development of technology was severely limited because traditional economies produced barely enough food to survive and because of the limited amount of specialization. Technology refers to **the tools, skills, and scientific knowledge that society develops in the use of resources to produce goods and services**. Technology, along with cultural factors, plays a crucial role in structuring what an economic system is like. Societies that face a constant threat of starvation tend to be deeply risk averse, and they are rarely willing to expend the labor and resources necessary to develop new technologies. Nor do they have enough surplus labor or resources to undertake substantial investments in new technologies due to their low level of productivity.

Despite these limitations, archaeological evidence has proven that human groups steadily increased in size over time, indicating that larger groups had an evolutionary advantage over smaller groups. As noted above, larger groups can have a greater degree of specialization of labor. Specialization of labor is a fundamental characteristic of all human societies in which **particular tasks are performed by specific individuals, rather than everyone performing all tasks**. Specialization tends to improve productivity because people develop **skills**, becoming very good at the tasks they specialize in (tracking game, finding roots and berries, etc.). Via their expertise, they can develop simple **tools** (technology) for their work. The larger the group, the more specialized the tasks that can exist and the more productive that society is likely to be. Furthermore, larger groups have greater **military power** and are better able to dominate smaller groups. Correspondingly, those humans who could successfully function in large groups were more likely to survive. Our evolutionary past indicates that we evolved to function effectively in a large group setting.

For many thousands of years, human economies continued to be dominated by traditions that specified who would undertake which tasks; how food, tools, and other resources would be used and shared; and who would achieve the highest status in the community based on his or her productivity. Human groups faced increasing pressures to grow larger in size in order to increase their military power, which necessitated improvements in productivity (via specialization and risk-taking) to produce more food to support a larger population.

The invention of agriculture and food storage ushered in a new era of human development, involving settled life and the establishment of villages, towns, and even cities. The importance of being successful in a large group became even more crucial as societies grew larger and more complex.

3.2 AGRICULTURE AND THE ESTABLISHMENT OF CITIES, SOCIAL CLASSES, AND SLAVE-BASED EMPIRES

About 12,000 years ago, the invention of agriculture (farming and herding), sharper tools, and new materials—especially pottery for food storage—caused a dramatic increase in the ability of communities to support a larger population due to the larger supply of food.

Instead of providing subsistence just for themselves and their family, farmers were now able to produce enough food to provide for more people. In the harsh climates of sub-Saharan Africa, it took about six farmers to produce enough food to provide for themselves and one additional adult, who no longer needed to grow food and could concentrate on other things. In the more fertile regions of the Middle East, two farm families could support one non-farm family. In all agricultural regions, farming could support a larger population than had been previously possible due to the increase in productivity.

As groups grew larger, it became important to develop institutions, including codes of behavior and other rules, to develop the high degree of trust that is crucial to the functioning of a larger society. The development of a strong group identity, with cultural or religious bonds and a prevailing ideology, took on increased significance.

The importance of group identification was now even more crucial because the production and storage of surplus food made warfare increasingly important. In earlier hunter-gatherer societies, taking over another group had little benefit because they possessed little of value. In agricultural societies, however, the rewards of military aggression were substantial. A powerful army could seize the stored food and the most productive land of other groups. Then the army could force the conquered people to work as slaves and seize any surplus that was produced. This highlights a key aspect of all economic systems, the production and allocation of **surplus product**.

The surplus product is **the amount that is produced over and above what is needed for the community's survival**. The necessary product, **what is necessary for a community's survival, includes food and shelter**

for everyone, plus the replacement of tools and materials used up in production.

The generation of surplus product caused dramatic changes in society. In addition to causing warfare, surpluses were as a source economic growth when they were used to augment the productive resources of society (investment). For example, excess grain that was used to feed horses or oxen, which could be used as draft animals, made farms more productive. Labor could be used to build irrigation canals and aqueducts to increase crop yields. In these cases, sacrificing current resources (grain and labor) in the short term to invest in the development of capital goods caused increased output in the future.

Surplus product was also necessary for cities to develop, because larger population centers relied on the surplus food produced by the agricultural areas for their sustenance. In those cities, artisans specialized in the development of more sophisticated tools, which increased productivity further. Human civilization as we know it grew out of the production of surplus food.

In all economic systems, **how much surplus product is generated and how it is allocated has a large impact on economic growth**. Hunter-gatherer societies had little or no surplus, so they could not invest time and resources into more elaborate endeavors; they had to concentrate on finding food. Agricultural societies could devote their surplus to raising draft animals, building irrigation systems, or developing tools (capital goods), which would increase their productivity and economic growth. Or they could devote their surplus to amassing vast conquering armies, building temples and monuments like the pyramids of ancient Egypt or the Coliseum in Rome, and supporting an idle religious or noble class.

Control of surpluses proved to be a major source of power. The surplus of food allowed a more elaborate social hierarchy to develop in which some members of society no longer had to work to produce food. Kings, emperors, chiefs, and priests seized and controlled the land and resources, sitting atop the hierarchy and avoiding manual labor while slaves or peasants did the most productive tasks of society. With the advent of agriculture in 10,000 BCE, property rights came into existence for the first time in human history. Property rights exist when **a productive resource such as land or slave labor belongs to a particular person or group instead of to society as a whole**. The production of surplus is therefore also associated with the rise of private property and the establishment of social classes in human society. In economics, class refers to **a group of people that has a specific relationship with the production process**.

In order to protect property rights, stave off slave revolts, fend off invaders, provide public goods (irrigation, flood control, roads, etc.), and organize larger and more complex societies, it was necessary to develop a system of government for the first time. The role of a government is to **provide the institutions that develop and implement policies for the state**. The state can be a kingdom, a democratic republic, or something in between, but every state needs a government to undertake key tasks and to maintain the functioning of the economic system.

Closely related to the system of government was the **ideological system that justified the existing class structure**. Religions developed that supported the status quo, preaching, for example, the divinity of the Pharaohs and erecting the great pyramids to cement those views. Along with the rise of class interests, we also see the values of the community change. Instead of the solidarity and equality of hunter-gatherer communities, societies divided by classes tended to be much **more individualistic**, with people working more for themselves.

Despite the rise of an unproductive, elite class along with the creation of occupations in government, the army, and the priesthood, the major work of society was still agricultural and done by peasants or slaves. The **peasants** of antiquity did not own their land, which was now owned or controlled by a great lord. But peasants did tend to have rights to farm certain land, and that right was usually passed down to their children. Peasants produced for their own family and handed over a portion of their output (the surplus) to their lord. Peasants produced barely enough food to survive, so they tended to stick with well-known methods and avoid any risky undertaking that could result in starvation. Thus, peasants represented a particular class of people in agricultural systems, with some rights of access to land but with obligations to their lord. Their behavior was governed by **tradition**, including the established social relations; the basic, almost unchanging level of technology; and the **authority** of the lord.

In addition to peasants, the largest ancient human societies relied extensively on slave labor. A **slave** had no control over the resources used to produce goods and services, received only enough food to survive on, and was completely subject to the **authority** of the merchant or lord who owned them. In the city state of ancient Athens in Greece as well as in the Roman Empire, between 30% and 80% of the people were slaves at various times. Slave economies required large governments and military operations to maintain power and control in the face of regular slave rebellions.

While the peasants and slaves toiled in the rural areas to provide food for society, dynamic but mostly parasitic cities began to develop and grow. In the great cities of ancient Egypt, Greece, or Italy, one could find goods in markets from all over the known world. However, most of these goods were luxuries intended for the upper classes and food for the elites and their slaves and servants. The markets of this era fulfilled a limited role compared to their function in modern capitalism. Most of the important resources of society were allocated by tradition or authority (the peasant–lord or slave–owner relationship), whereas markets supplied only a tiny proportion of goods. Furthermore, status (and wealth) was now a product of political, military, or religious power more than one's productivity for the community. With the rise of slavery, productive work came to be denigrated by the elites. Hence, we have the development of the first "leisure class," as Veblen labeled the idle rich of this era, who looked down upon hard agricultural labor and aspired to a life of leisure or nonproductive work in warfare, priesthood, or government.

Societies of this era did not develop at an equal rate, as Jared Diamond lays out in his book, *Guns, Germs, and Steel*. The groups living in the Middle East, Europe, and Asia had the great luck to have access to the most nutritious grains and the most easily domesticated animals (beasts of burden and animals for food). Greater food production led to higher population densities, and in those densely populated cities people developed resistance to germs. Larger populations also meant more specialization and development of better technology, especially weapons and ships, and more elaborate political and military organizations.

Because of these advantages, the peoples living in the Fertile Crescent area of the Middle East were the first to develop large states, making this region the "cradle of civilization." A series of large empires developed in and around the Fertile Crescent (see Figure 3.1), beginning with Mesopotamia around 2300 BCE, Egypt around 1500 BCE, the Hittites around 1300 BCE, the Assyrians around 715 BCE, the Persians in 539 BCE, Alexander in 334 BCE, and eventually Rome from 50 BCE to 456 CE. It is worth briefly examining the Roman Empire as an important example of this type of economic system.

3.3 THE ECONOMIC SYSTEM OF THE ROMAN EMPIRE

At the height of the Roman Empire (see Figure 3.2), 1 million residents of the city of Rome were supported by 80–100 million subjects. Impressive military power, effective communication, and efficient transportation networks (roads and ships) allowed Rome to control a huge land area and to generate a steady inflow of goods and wealth. Rome was able to demand rents, taxes, tributes, and gifts from citizens and conquered provinces because of its military control of the region. Imported products included food (fruits, grains, honey, wine, olive oil, meats), metals (gold and silver to make coins, copper, tin, iron, and lead), materials (marble, ivory, pottery, and cloth), and slaves. These resources were used to maintain the army, administer the government, support the city, and allow the elite to live in luxury.

The class system was complex. The emperor and Roman elite who controlled the Senate, the *patricians*, sat atop the empire and received most of the wealth. They were expected, however, to redistribute some of their wealth to the poor during food shortages and to support public buildings and temples and the army when needed, so some measure of reciprocity still existed. Most professions, including crafts and trading, were considered dishonorable by the elite. Positions were hereditary, with titles and wealth being passed down from fathers to sons. Later, Romans of lower status could become a member of the elite if they amassed enough property.

Underneath the upper class were the freeborn Roman *plebeians*, who varied in rank by wealth and position. Depending on their position, they could be free

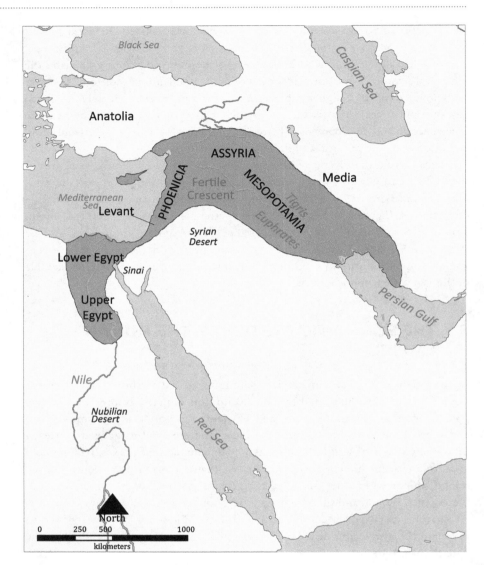

FIGURE 3.1 The Fertile Crescent.

farmers, merchants, priests, government officials, and craftsmen, or they could be poor peasants and soldiers. They often worked in a variety of occupations alongside freed slaves, who had fewer rights than plebeians, and non-Roman free people.

Slaves were the largest class of people, and they had no rights. Some of the luckier slaves served the emperor and the elite or worked as craftsmen or teachers, whereas others toiled in the mines or on farms under brutal conditions. In general, slaves only received subsistence—just enough food, clothing, and shelter to survive—and their surplus production went to their owner.

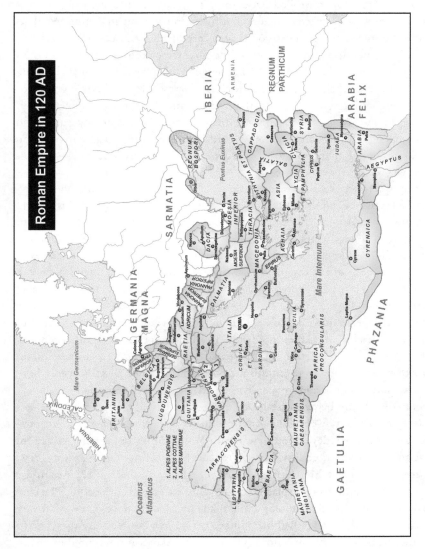

FIGURE 3.2 The Roman Empire.

Although there was growth in many nonagricultural professions, including soldiers, traders, priests, entertainers, and government, 90%–95% of the population of the Roman Empire was involved in agriculture. In fact, agriculture would continue to dominate the economies of the world until the industrial revolution.

In general, the aristocracy owned and controlled the land and labor of the economy. The emperor controlled trade, shipping, crafts, mines, coinage, tax collection, and markets via a centralized administration housed in Rome. Markets were quite limited, because most goods were produced by peasants or slaves for their master and because transport costs of the time were prohibitive. Also, most of the population consisted of slaves and other people with very little money, limiting the extent of the market. Hence, trade was mostly restricted to luxury goods for the elite, along with goods needed by the military and the state. The government, funded by taxes as well as funds from the emperor and the aristocracy, subsidized grain to reduce civil strife and economic hardship. So Rome had an early version of a welfare state—state support for the least well-off members of society—to limit the negative consequences of poverty.

Not only were class relations vastly different in the Roman Empire when compared to traditional economies, but there were substantial gender differences as well. By the time of the Roman Empire, women had gone from being roughly equal to men in hunter-gatherer societies to being in a subordinate position. This accompanied the rise in the importance of warriors and the allocation of captured slaves to those warriors. Men came to dominate farming, using their slaves to do the farmwork for them. Cultural attitudes shifted along with these changing roles, until the belief that women were inferior to men became widespread. Women did not have the same rights and privileges as men in Rome, although they were generally considered to have the same social status as their husbands. The importance of male inheritance of property led to greater restrictions on the sexual behavior of women, as men sought to ensure that their spouses were faithful and bore their children. Men, however, bore no such sexual restrictions and frequently took advantage of their slaves.

Eventually Rome began to stagnate as its slave-based economy became less productive and as the power of the army declined. Slavery was initially very productive as free farmers developed new farming techniques (especially irrigation) and brought new land into cultivation using slave labor. However, over time, economic growth stagnated. Free farmers, who were driven to increase their status by increasing their wealth, were displaced by the vast slave estates of the elite. The elite looked down on work and technology, and made no effort to develop new farming techniques. Slaves themselves had little interest in innovation because they had to work endlessly, no matter how innovative they were. Slaves also required intensive supervision and could not be trusted with complex independent tasks or tools that could be used as weapons. Also, the Roman Empire began to run short of slaves because so many died young or were killed (in revolts or in sport), and because of a reduction in conquests as the army's power decreased. The army shrank as the supply of free farmers and peasants dwindled due to war and economic stagnation.

After many years of decline, Rome fell in 456 CE to Germanic invaders and the era of empires in the Fertile Crescent came to an end. What followed in Europe was the era of feudalism, which lasted for the next 1000 years.

3.4 FEUDALISM AND THE MANOR ECONOMY IN WESTERN EUROPE

Once the Roman Empire collapsed, chaos spread across Europe and the Middle East. Trade routes became dangerous and lawless, and the great cities of the empire could no longer gain access to the goods they needed to survive. Cities shrank, knowledge and expertise were lost, and societies turned inwards.

Amidst the chaos, security and survival became the highest priority. In response, the Roman elite, and later the chiefs of Germanic tribes and other European leaders, turned to a new economic system: Feudalism. Feudalism was organized around independent **manors**, which consisted of large tracts of land (often thousands of acres) controlled by a lord. Slaves were granted greater freedom and became serfs. **Serfs** were obligated to work for their lord on his land a certain number of days each year, in exchange for protection and the right to farm a small amount of land for themselves using the lord's tools (ploughs) and draft animals (oxen and horses). Serfs also had access to common lands where they could farm, graze animals, and collect wood. Thus, there was a degree of reciprocity to the relationship between serfs and lords, even though the relations were highly slanted in favor of the lord.

The serf system was more productive and sustainable than slavery. Serfs had more of an incentive than slaves to work hard for the lord thanks to the protection, stability, and small quantity of property and independence they were granted. Serfs did not need to be supervised the way slaves did, they had little interest in revolting, and they even had an interest in fighting for their lord to protect their own land and house from invaders.

Eventually, all of Western Europe came to be divided into independent, self-sufficient, isolated manors. On the manor, the lord was the master of all who lived there, serving as judge, general, and governor. Serfs were tied to the land and to the lord, but they had a measure of security because they could not be removed from their land or their family. The most powerful lords gained control over the most land, becoming kings and demanding loyalty and military support from lesser lords. However, the kings of the feudal era were not very powerful, and most of the wealth and control of the economy rested with the lords.

Like the agriculture-based empires of the Fertile Crescent, feudalism was a system in which resources were allocated by **authority** and **tradition**. The authority of the feudal lord was paramount, and one's station in life was determined traditionally by one's birth. The eldest son of the lord became the next lord. The son of a serf was also a serf. The son of a blacksmith would also become a blacksmith. Serf women worked for lords as servants or makers of clothing, and at home they prepared food, raised the children, and maintained the household. Many serf women were sexually exploited by their lords, however, and women could not own property, so women still occupied an inferior position in society.

Because most feudal manors were self-sufficient, there was very little trade other than a few luxury goods for the lords. However, there were small cities that depended on trade and that hosted traveling fairs of merchants and entertainers, so a small amount commerce did occur in exchange for money.

The towns did have some tradespeople, such as armorers, blacksmiths, shipwrights, potters, weavers, and dyers, indicating that some specialization of labor did exist. But anyone who wanted to produce and sell such goods and services had to join a guild. Guilds were a type of union governing a particular trade or profession. Independent manufacturers, known as guild masters, banded together to set quality standards and wages, limit competition by dividing up territory, and establish rules and codes of conduct. Working for the guild masters were apprentices (usually children of ages 10–12) and adult journeymen who someday hoped to be guild masters.

The guilds were incredibly detailed in the prescriptions governing their members. Rules could include prohibitions on indecent language, the number of threads in a fabric, the type of equipment to be used in construction, how a particular task was to be completed, etc. Traditional methods of production were passed down through the guilds, and innovation was strongly discouraged. A new product or new process for making a product had to be approved by the guild, but such innovations were usually rejected as a threat to other producers. If one craftsman developed a superior technique, it might displace other craftsmen and upset the accepted order of things. In a society that prized safety and stability above all else, this was unacceptable, so any deviation from approved procedures often resulted in imprisonment, torture, or even death! The emphasis was clearly on maintaining the status quo and resisting change. Unsurprisingly, given that the utilization of new techniques could lead to dire outcomes, very little innovation occurred during the feudalist era. Over these 1000 years, there were only a handful of major innovations, with clocks, the blast furnace, eyeglasses, the spinning wheel, and the printing press being among the most important.

In this system of decentralized manors, the Catholic Church was the largest owner of land. As a result, the Catholic religion played a huge role in shaping society and its values. A tour of the cathedrals of Europe built during the feudal era demonstrates that of the little surplus that was produced, the majority went to the church. In addition, religious prescriptions played a prominent role in the economy. For example, merchants were expected to charge a "just price," selling items for what they were worth and no more. Greed was considered to be a sin, a corrupting influence to be scorned and even punished. The notion of profit or personal gain was largely condemned until very recently in human history.

In fact, moneylending was considered to be so sinful under Catholicism that moneylenders were to be excommunicated from the church. The prohibition against moneylending was grounded in the New Testament of the Bible, which condemned usury. However, the Old Testament of the Bible allowed Jews to lend to non-Jews. As a result, many European Jews, barred from most professions by guilds and prohibited from owning land, turned to moneylending to Christians in order to make a living. The Jewish monopoly on moneylending meant that they could make a lot of money, but Christians resented the success of Jewish moneylenders based on biblical condemnations of usury. There was much Christian hostility toward Jews stemming from this strained relationship. As an example, the entire community of 150 Jews of York, England, was killed in 1190 due to religious intolerance and the anger of those who were indebted to them. The roots of much anti-Semitism in Europe can be traced to the feudal era and the differing views of Christians and Jews on the acceptability of moneylending.

The characteristics of feudal society help us to understand why life in Europe went largely unchanged for 1000 years. The small amount of surplus that was produced went to provide military protection or was squandered on luxuries for the lords and the church. Without any substantial investment, and with substantial resistance to technological change, there was very little economic growth. However, over time, a series of changes undermined feudalism, stimulated the rise of markets, and reshaped European societies.

3.5 THE FORCES BEHIND THE DECLINE OF FEUDALISM AND THE RISE OF MARKETS

The major changes that eroded the institutions of feudalism and created the conditions for the development of markets were changes in technology, urbanization and specialization, increased long-distance trade, the Crusades, the establishment of the nation-state, exploration and colonization, the rise of Protestantism, the development of early manufacturing and factories, the monetization of the economy, and the establishment of private property rights. The section below describes these changes and how they moved the feudal economies of Europe toward the market capitalist system of mercantilism. One crucial change that prompted many of the other changes was the increase in the surplus of food that occurred when better agricultural technology was developed.

3.5.1 An increase in the surplus from improvements in agricultural technology

In an agriculturally based economy, agricultural technology is the primary determinant of the amount of surplus a community has. Yearly planting of the same crops in the same soil eventually depletes the land and can even render the land unusable. To avoid this problem, farmers had developed a system where land would be used to grow crops one year but then it would lie fallow (unused) the next year to allow the soil to recover. Eventually, around the year 1000, a three-field crop rotation system was developed. A grain (rye or winter wheat) would be planted in one field in the fall, a second crop (peas, oats, or beans) would be planted in a second field in the spring, and a third field would lie fallow. Rotating crops between these three uses improved the health of the soil, and the land only had to lie fallow one-third of the time instead of half of the time. Productivity increased significantly, generating additional food that could support more people and surplus grains that could support more horses and other farm animals. Horses not only made farming more productive, but they could be used to transport goods for trade. With the rise in food production, Europe's population doubled between 1000 and 1300 and, as a consequence, there was a significant increase in urbanization.

3.5.2 Urbanization and specialization

The towns of Europe began to grow steadily as food supplies increased. Because they existed outside of the influence of the feudal lords, who controlled rural areas but not the towns, the urban areas were forced to develop their own codes of law, monetary system, and governing institutions. For their survival they depended on local trade, which meant that they needed to produce specialized goods that the rural areas needed and would buy in exchange for food. Greater surpluses and better transportation made trade easier, encouraging still more specialization and exchange. Local trade grew steadily, but it was carefully regulated by town officials to preserve stability, especially jobs, incomes, and food supplies. Long-distance trade, on the other hand, was the province of international traveling merchants and was not subject to the same regulation.

3.5.3 Long-distance trade and traveling merchants

Traveling merchants became more prominent from 700 to 1300. Originally, they traded spices, salted fish, wine, and goods that were only produced in certain places (dyes, special cloth, fine metalwork, etc.). As trade routes became more established (around the 1400s), permanent markets featuring goods from distant lands became a feature of towns. Regions of Europe began to specialize increasingly in the production of specific types of goods, which led to improvements in skill and productivity, resulting in even more surplus to trade. Great trading cities developed to facilitate long-distance trade, and they created legal and banking systems for businesses that formed the basis for modern market capitalist systems. Further facilitating this trade was the Crusades.

3.5.4 The Crusades and the opening of Europe

From 1095 to 1291, hundreds of thousands of European knights and peasants traveled to the Middle East at the behest of the Catholic Church to protect Catholic interests and free the holy lands from non-Catholics. The Crusades were only somewhat successful militarily, and the crusading soldiers were often manipulated by the commercial interests of Venice into attacking Venetian rivals instead of their intended targets. But the major long-term effect of the Crusades was economic: Sheltered Europeans came in contact with the thriving, dynamic commercial societies of Venice and Byzantium. They were impressed by the opulent lifestyle, and they returned to Europe with spices, exotic trinkets, and tales of luxury that could be obtained by trade. Europe began to look increasingly outward. But this outward orientation required different political arrangements.

3.5.5 The rise of the nation-state and commercial interests

Trade under feudalism was a complicated affair. Every time a merchant set foot on the land of an estate or a town, they would have to pay a tax or duty of some sort. Along the German section of the Rhine in 1400, there were more than 60 toll stations! It was not uncommon for tolls to double the prices of goods as they were hauled by merchants from where they were produced to where they were sold. As trade increased in importance, merchants chafed under the stifling commercial system of feudalism. They found an ally in the kings, who were looking to expand their influence over the largely independent feudal lords. Kings, with the financial support of merchants, began to expand their power and influence and develop larger and larger kingdoms. They amassed armies and built navies using the revenues from trade, stimulating manufacturing in the process. By the 1500s, Europe was a collection of nation-states with growing economic and military power under the control of kings and merchants. Kings and merchants relied on trade to generate gold and silver, which were needed for hiring mercenaries and maintaining an army and navy. Because money meant the ability to purchase military power (gold meant power), they worked incessantly to increase trade and the supply of gold as much as possible. One of the ways that they could do this was by finding new places to trade with and new sources of raw materials and gold.

3.5.6 Exploration and colonization by nation-states

Though some exploration did occur during feudalism, it took the concentrated power and wealth of the new kings of Europe to undertake large scale exploration. Kings outfitted fleets for exploration under the direction of the likes of Vasco Da Gama (Portugal), Christopher Columbus (Spain), John Cabot (England), Jacques Cartier (France), and Olivier van Noort (the Netherlands). In addition to exotic goods and trade routes, explorers sought gold, silver, and slaves to pay off the high costs of these ventures and to support the kings who financed them.

Christopher Columbus's log describing his landing in the Bahamas, quoted in Howard Zinn's book, *A People's History of the United States*, illustrates the attitudes of the merchants and explorers of the newfound nation-states of Europe:

> [The Arawaks] brought us parrots and balls of cotton and spears and many other things, which they exchanged for the glass beads and hawks' bells. They willingly traded everything they owned. ... They were well-built, with good bodies and handsome features. ... They do not bear arms, and do not know them, for I showed them a sword, they took it by the edge and cut themselves out of ignorance. They have no iron. Their spears are made of cane. ... They would make fine servants. ... With fifty men we could subjugate them all and make them do whatever we want.

Europe's advanced weaponry and resistance to disease, a product of a longer history of close-quarters living, allowed them to dominate and decimate large areas of the earth as they roamed the planet in search of riches. Eventually, the European countries established colonial empires in the Americas, Africa, and Asia designed to funnel resources and gold to Europe, often using slave labor. This was trade of a particularly exploitative sort, but it served to stimulate Europe tremendously and transform it into a vibrant commercial center. In the process, greed had displaced the feudal prohibitions on such behavior, marking a major shift in ideology and religion.

3.5.7 The rise of Protestantism, individualism, and greed

Following close on the heels of the first wave of exploration was the development of Calvinism, the first Protestant religion, in the 1500s. The Catholic Church of the feudal era was primarily concerned with the afterlife, and it explicitly condemned any obsession with the accumulation of worldly possessions and any form of greed. Also, the church was supposed to be the primary focus of the community, not the individual. Individuals were supposed to know their place in society and work to maintain their station in life, not to change it.

Calvinists, in contrast, saw hard work and professional activity as one's calling and a sign of godliness. Individual wealth accumulation from hard work was actually considered to be evidence of doing God's work. Additionally, wealth was to be invested in further productive endeavors rather than wasted on luxuries. Even earning income from interest on loans was acceptable as a sign of engaging in a productive, profitable venture.

In many ways, Calvinism and later variations of Protestantism provided the ideal ideological support for a market capitalist economic system based on self-interest, greed, hard work, and reinvestment. The idea of improving one's standing in society and celebrating the riches earned through hard work helped foster economic growth. Unsurprisingly, it was the nations in which Protestantism took the greatest hold that developed the earliest and most robust market systems. England, in particular, had the strongest departure from Catholicism and embracing of Protestantism when King Henry VIII and the Church of England broke with the papacy in the 1530s. Meanwhile, the earliest forms of capitalist manufacturing were also getting started.

3.5.8 The putting-out system and the beginnings of capitalist factories

As markets expanded rapidly in the 1500s, merchants operating in export industries needed a larger and more reliable supply of goods to sell. Instead of relying on small, independent craftsmen to produce goods for them, they started the **putting-out system**. The merchant provided the craftsman with the materials, the craftsman worked the materials into finished products using their tools and skills, and the merchant collected and sold the finished products. Merchants eventually began to set up entire buildings with tools and equipment and hired journeymen and apprentices with the requisite skills, bypassing independent craftsmen entirely. These were the first capitalist factories. Independent craftsmen were gradually replaced by larger-scale factories and workers, breaking down the guilds that had governed production and turning independent craftsmen into laborers who worked for a merchant-capitalist. Merchant-capitalists began developing markets for buying and selling inputs, including labor, to use in their new factories. Consider, for a moment, how revolutionary this was. In prior human history, labor had always been allocated based on a social relationship governed by tradition or authority. Now, labor was starting to be allocated to the highest bidder. For the first time in human history, labor and significant amounts of resources were allocated based on money in markets and not by tradition or authority.

3.5.9 The monetization of the economy and the decline of the manor

The growing urban populations of Europe needed increasing amounts of food, which they paid for with money earned from manufacturing and trading. Meanwhile, the rural lords wanted additional money to buy all of the new goods that were becoming available. As a result, lords began switching from demanding payments from serfs in fixed amounts of goods (in-kind payments) to demanding payments in fixed amounts of money. Ironically, this set the stage for the economic decline of the manor. As gold from the new world flooded Europe, prices began to rise dramatically. From 1520 to 1650, prices in Europe increased by between 150% and 400%. Lords found that their fixed payments from serfs bought fewer and fewer goods, and many became impoverished.

These trends were exacerbated by a significant decline in the population from the Black Death of the 1300s and the Hundred Years' War between England and France (1337–1453). These events wiped out almost 40% of England's population and led to a labor shortage there and elsewhere in Europe. Without enough labor, lords attempted to squeeze the remaining serfs to generate enough money to support the manor. The serfs responded with a series of revolts. The serf resistance—combined with the competition between lords for the labor services of the serfs—led many serfs to gain the status of independent, free peasants with the right to farm their traditional plot as well as the common lands. This put the rural lords in a desperate situation. Their only recourse was to seize as much land as possible to generate cash to support the manor.

3.5.10 The enclosure movement and the establishment of private property rights

To generate cash income, lords began seizing the common lands for their own use. In England, lords fenced off (enclosed) common lands in order to raise sheep for the booming textile industry. Similar patterns followed in continental Europe as lords seized common lands to raise animals or crops that could be sold for cash. By the 1700s, 75%–90% of peasants had been forced off of farms all over Europe and into urban slums. This, coupled with a rising population and rising rural rents, meant that cities had huge, desperate populations of former peasants with no means of subsistence. They had no land or tools and only their labor power to sell.

At the same time, the enclosure movement established the legal right of lords to the land they seized. The lords began to use the land as productively as possible to generate the income they needed, and the use of land came to be associated with the amount or revenue or rent that it could bring. Lands were sometimes rented out to others in exchange for money because money was of higher value to lords than produced goods.

Thus, the enclosure movement had the doubly important impact of creating a market for labor power (former serfs and peasants who had to sell their labor in order to survive) and a market for land (which now could be sold or rented). Labor and land had become commodities to be bought and sold. This is a far cry from traditional feudal relationships in which labor was a social obligation and land was a family's estate or plot, both established by birth.

We also see how private property can be both constructive and destructive. If a property owner is secure in their ownership of the land for the foreseeable future, they are willing to invest in the productivity of the land by adding irrigation, breeding draft animals, fertilizing, and so on. On the other hand, privatizing the common lands cast millions of peasants into desperate, landless poverty.

The culmination of all of these changes in the feudal era was the establishment of the first market-based economic system, mercantilism. By the late 1500s and early 1600s, most of the major cities of England, France, Spain, Belgium, and Holland were incorporated into countries that were dominated by huge merchant-capitalists and the monarchs who were allied with them. These merchant-capitalists controlled almost all trade and manufacturing.

3.6 MERCANTILISM AND THE UNEASY BEGINNINGS OF CAPITALISM

National, market-based economic systems did not evolve naturally during mercantilism. They were created by the merchant-capitalists and monarchs of Europe for their benefit. A national market system was resisted vigorously by the smaller towns and rural areas, which fought to maintain their tight regulation of local trade and preserve existing jobs. As Polanyi noted in *The Great Transformation*, "The towns raised every possible obstacle to the formation of a national or internal market for which the capitalist wholesaler was pressing." It took deliberate actions by the state in the 1400s and 1500s to break down the fiercely protectionist policies of the towns. Once local resistance was broken, the state replaced local rules on trading and manufacturing with national rules, so mercantilism was not freewheeling, competitive market capitalism. It was tightly controlled national capitalism run by and for the merchant-capitalists and monarchs, grounded in the social hierarchies of the period.

The early mercantilist countries tried to maximize the inflow of gold, an approach known as **bullionism**, to cement their power and wealth. To do this, they tried to maintain a trade surplus by subsidizing and encouraging exports while taxing and discouraging imports. One of the best ways to do this was to grant companies trading monopolies in specific areas of the market. If only one British merchant was allowed to purchase red dye from France, he could buy it more cheaply than if multiple British merchants were bidding for the same dye. If only one British merchant was allowed to sell red cloth in England, that merchant could sell it for the highest possible price. Trading was carefully regulated so that the system maximized the profits of the monopoly merchant-capitalists and insured an inflow of gold.

Colonial empires also improved profits from trading. Resources, especially raw materials and slave labor, could be had cheaply from the colonies. The British dismantled the thriving textile industry in India and forced the colony to export raw cotton to England, where it could be used by British industries to manufacture textiles. Similar practices occurred in Africa, Asia, and the Americas, as industries in the colonies were displaced in favor of the production of raw materials for export to the colonial power.

The Transatlantic Slave Trade was a particularly horrific example of mercantilist trading patterns. Slave ships left England for West Africa carrying cloth, guns, alcohol, iron wares, and other manufactured goods. These were traded in West Africa for slaves who were captured by African chiefs collaborating with the English traders. The ships then traveled to the West Indies in the Caribbean (and later the United States) where the slaves were sold at auctions to plantation owners. The ships were then loaded with the produce from the plantations, especially commodities like sugar, coffee, tobacco, and cotton, which were brought back to England. Merchants profited from each stage of the trade, while extracting resources from Africa and the Americas.

In some cases, private companies such as the Dutch East India Company were put in charge of vast colonial territories and granted the power to wage war, mete out justice, execute convicts, establish new colonies, mint coins, and so on. They exploited colonial territories ruthlessly for their own profit. Imagine how the most racist and rapacious company without any check on its behavior might exploit a country in Africa, Asia, or the Americas for its own benefit and you will get some idea of the horrors of mercantilism.

Initially, countries experienced economic growth under tightly controlled mercantilism. The expansion of markets internally within the countries and externally to their colonies enhanced profits and stimulated the development of new industries. But the control of the economy by the monarch and a handful of huge firms began to stifle the development of new firms and industries. Stimulated by the growth of trade, an emerging group of capitalists working in mining, manufacturing, and other industries chafed at the restricted, monopolized markets. They wanted more trade, greater access to domestic and foreign markets, and fewer government restrictions on their behavior. At the same time, mercantilism experienced some major economic problems: The enclosure of the common lands had created large pools of desperately poor workers without sufficient jobs or opportunities, and fluctuations in the supply of gold caused large swings in prices. Such a system, which worked well only for a small part of the population, ultimately proved to be unstable.

Just as the mercantilist economy was becoming more and more untenable, Adam Smith offered a vision of how capitalism could solve the problems created under mercantilism. His vision of a lightly regulated market capitalist economy proved to be very attractive to the increasingly powerful capitalists of England in the late 1700s and early 1800s. By 1834, England had abandoned mercantilism and embarked on an experiment in market capitalism that would reshape the entire world. This is the subject of the next chapter.

3.7 CONCLUSION

As we have seen, the economic systems of human societies have taken a wide variety of forms. The traditional economies of hunter-gatherer societies were small, egalitarian, self-sufficient, redistributive, and cooperative. The slave empires of Rome and the Fertile Crescent were large, hierarchical, and exploitative, with a small volume of trade primarily for the elites. The feudal manors of Europe were small, self-sufficient, and hierarchical, with less trade than the Roman Empire. Finally, the mercantilist countries of Europe were large, profit and trade oriented, and monopolistic. Tradition and authority were the main methods by which resources were allocated under all human societies until mercantilism in Europe, when markets came to dominate the economic system for the first time. But even under mercantilism, the social structure of society, especially which class a person was born into, was crucial in determining who had access to resources and who did not. The specialization of labor and the generation and use of the surplus product were important features of all human societies, determining whether an economy experienced growth or stagnation. Stagnation, and other intractable contradictions, tended to result in the elimination of one type of economic system and the gradual development of another.

Stagnation and the pressures from the new capitalist class provoked changes in the mercantilist economic system. First in England and then around Europe, one country after another switched from mercantilism to lightly regulated market capitalism. The next chapter turns to the fall of mercantilism, the rise of capitalism, and the ideas of Adam Smith, who provided a powerful intellectual argument in favor of a capitalist economic system.

QUESTIONS FOR REVIEW

1. What factors determined who did what job (how labor was allocated) in (a) traditional, hunter-gatherer societies, (b) slave-based empires such as Rome, (c) feudalism, and (d) mercantilism?
2. Why do political economists think that human beings are inherently social beings with strong levels of group identity? Is there evidence from economic history to support this view? Why or why not?
3. Describe the role played by (a) tradition, (b) authority, and (c) markets in traditional, slave, feudal, and mercantilist economic systems.
4. How did the role and status of women change as economic systems evolved from traditional economies to mercantilism?
5. Why is the specialization of labor important to understanding historical economic development?
6. How is the generation and utilization of the surplus product important to understanding economic development?
7. Construct an argument agreeing or disagreeing with the following statement: *All human societies involve a large degree of cooperation, redistribution, and reciprocity.* Use specific examples to support your argument.
8. List the main social classes in each of the following economic systems: (a) traditional (hunter-gatherer), (b) the Roman Empire, (c) feudalism, and (d) mercantilism.
9. Describe how social classes evolved from traditional economies through mercantilism. How did the determination of status (which people were held in highest esteem) change?
10. How has the role of private property changed as economic systems evolved?
11. How did attitudes toward greed change as economic systems evolved?
12. List and analyze the major forces that eroded each economic system and paved the way for the next economic system.
13. Construct an argument for which two factors were most important in eroding feudalism and paving the way for mercantilism. Use specific examples to support your argument.

Adam Smith and the rise of capitalism

The era of laissez-faire

As the problems of mercantilism began to mount, a dynamic new economic system began to develop in England. A group of early entrepreneurs was able to make large sums of money manufacturing textiles and a few other goods using new technologies they developed. They reinvested their profits in new ventures, spurring rapid economic growth.

Adam Smith saw the earliest stages of capitalism occurring around him and realized the tremendous potential of the system. Smith believed that lightly regulated capitalism would be preferable to mercantilism, a system where the king and a select group of monopolistic merchants dominated the economy for their own benefit. Smith hoped that a capitalist system, with sufficient competition to keep businesses innovative and efficient, would result in greater productivity and lower prices for goods. This would, in theory, result in a higher standard of living for all people as the number of jobs increased and the prices of necessities decreased. Thus, Smith hoped that capitalism would solve the major problem that mercantilism had been unable to fix: The vast amount of poverty created by the enclosure movement. Smith and some other pro-market economists, along with their allies among the capitalist class, were able to push England to adopt the world's first capitalist economic system.

This chapter describes the roots of capitalism in England. We then take up Adam Smith's ideas regarding how he thought capitalism would work and why he thought it was preferable to mercantilism. Next, the chapter describes the triumph of laissez-faire ideas in the debates over the Poor Laws, macroeconomic crises, and restrictions on trade. By the mid-1800s, England had eliminated most of its mercantilist regulations and embarked on a radical experiment in laissez-faire capitalism.

DOI: 10.4324/9781315636924-6

4.0 CHAPTER 4 LEARNING GOALS

After reading this chapter you should be able to:

- List and analyze the key institutions that supported the establishment of capitalism in England.

- Describe the major economic concepts in Smith's critique of mercantilism.

- Identify the major components of Smith's analysis of capitalism and critically evaluate which of his ideas still hold true when applied to modern capitalism.

- Explain and critically assess the arguments of laissez-faire economists against English Poor Laws, macroeconomic intervention, and trade protectionism.

- Define Karl Polanyi's concept of the double movement and apply this concept to the modern world.

We begin by considering what differentiates capitalism from other economic systems and the institutional factors that provided the foundation for capitalism in England in the 1700s.

4.1 THE INDUSTRIAL REVOLUTION AND CAPITALISM IN ENGLAND

Hunter-gatherer societies revolved around using labor to generate enough food to survive. The invention of agriculture spawned the empires and later the feudal system. These economies relied on agricultural production and the exploitation of slave and peasant labor by the elites, who seized any available surpluses for themselves. During the era of mercantilism, the importance of trade and commerce came to the fore—although the wealth of mercantilist economies was still primarily based on agricultural output from slave and peasant labor. Thus, human economies from the beginning of time revolved around labor and agriculture.

The industrial revolution changed everything. The creation of the industrial factory signaled the rise in importance of **capital**, machinery, equipment, buildings, and other technological resources used to produce factory goods. First in

England, then across Europe and around the globe, the Industrial Revolution made ownership of capital the major source of economic power and the foremost driver of change in the economy. Capitalism is **an economic system in which the capital goods and other productive resources (land, natural resources) are privately owned and are bought and sold in markets based on the pursuit of profits**. Under a capitalist economic system, workers, instead of laboring for themselves and keeping the proceeds, sell their labor power to the capitalist in exchange for wages. The capitalist, as the owner, gets to keep any surplus that is produced.

Under capitalism, the primary focus of all economic activity is profit. An owner takes a large sum of money and invests it in setting up a factory and hiring workers. Those workers produce a commodity of some kind. That commodity is (hopefully) sold for a greater value than the initial investment.

$$\text{Money}(M) \rightarrow \text{Commodities}(C) \rightarrow \text{More Money}(M').$$

Early entrepreneurs had to advance a considerable sum of money ahead of time to cover costs, with no assurance that they would get a substantial return once a commodity was produced. This uncertain situation made them, as described by economic historian Paul Mantoux, "tyrannical, hard, sometimes cruel."

The Industrial Revolution began around 1760 in England with just such a group of "hard" entrepreneurs. The reasons for the Industrial Revolution's conception in England, as opposed to elsewhere, are important because they help us understand the key institutions that provide the basis for a capitalist economic system.

First, England was **ideologically** better suited toward a money-oriented, invention-driven capitalist economy. As the heart of the Protestant reformation, English society was less opposed to the notion of making money. As a result, members of the English aristocracy were early supporters of commerce and manufacturing, and businessmen who made a lot of money were accepted into high society much more readily than elsewhere in Europe. This "worldly" attitude also carried over into an interest in science and engineering. The Royal Society was founded in London in 1660 to promote "natural knowledge" and establish principles of scientific inquiry and experimentation. England became the international scientific leader, which led to a host of discoveries and inventions. The establishment of a national patent system to protect the rights of inventors to the profits from their discoveries further spurred technological change.

Second, England was the site of the most comprehensive enclosure movement and, consequently, the most complete elimination of feudal society, which resulted in the most secure system of **property rights**. The interest of the English aristocracy in exporting wool to obtain gold and foreign luxuries made it particularly aggressive in seizing the common lands from the peasants. Thus, the privatization of land and the creation of a vast quantity of **landless laborers** were more prevalent in England than elsewhere. A factory owner could only start an industrial operation if the inputs he needed were available: He needed laborers who were willing and able to work for reasonable wages and land that could be rented or purchased for the site of his factory. Both of these conditions were present in England.

Third, England was wealthy, and this created a **large market** for manufactured products. Manufacturing large quantities of goods in a factory is only profitable if there is a sizable market for those goods. There must be enough people with ample income to create sufficient demand for large quantities of products. England's vast colonial empire, rigged to generate profits from slave trading, piracy, colonial commerce, and more, created a relatively large (for that time) upper-middle class and a very rich upper class. These groups were only too happy to consume the latest manufactured goods. The colonies also served as suppliers of cheap raw materials and as market outlets for English manufactured goods. The extensive colonial trade of England also included a well-developed transportation system that made trade in manufactured goods relatively easy and low-cost. Also, England was lucky to have large deposits of coal and iron ore, which were crucial in early manufacturing. Luck, alongside the vast colonial empire, meant plenty of **cheap inputs** and **captive markets** for English manufacturers. The result was a system in which immense profits could be earned if entrepreneurs were willing to invest sufficient sums of money. Many were willing to do so, and their successes encouraged other entrepreneurs to follow.

With cheap labor and inputs available to purchase, land available to rent, profits to invest, and an ideological approach favoring the acquisition of money, the way was paved for the rise of capitalism. In the process, there was a fundamental shift from labor and land as a part of social and cultural relations to labor and land as commodities to be bought and sold.

In such a system, the owners of capital had the greatest amount of power in society. Landowners needed rent from their land in order to generate income. The best way to generate income from the land was to rent to a capitalist, who would use the land to its greatest capacity. The best way for a laborer to earn a living was to work for a capitalist. Given that there were many more people looking for work than there were jobs, the capitalist employer had a huge advantage in the relationship with workers. Most workers of the time had to take whatever wage rate the employer offered and accept work even in oppressive conditions because the alternative was starvation. As British economist Joan Robinson observed in her book, *Economic Philosophy*, "The misery of being exploited by capitalists is nothing compared to the misery of not being exploited at all." Meanwhile, the capitalists, who had to advance a considerable amount of money without the guarantee of a return on their investment, worked to drive very hard bargains with workers and landowners. Thus, with the rise of capitalism in the mid-1700s, we see for the first time in human history the notion of individual gain—the profit motive—becoming an all-pervasive force in society, driving the behavior of workers, landowners, and capitalists.

There was deep unease in England as capitalism was stirring. The mercantilist system was not able to solve the major problems of society, especially the massive amount of poverty. The early capitalist enterprises were very promising, but their expansion was limited by the strict regulations on trade put into place to benefit the monopolistic merchants. Into this environment stepped Adam Smith, who is usually credited with inventing the field of economics and who argued that a lightly regulated market capitalist economic system would solve the problems of mercantilism.

4.2 ADAM SMITH, LAISSEZ-FAIRE CAPITALISM, AND SMITH'S CRITIQUE OF MERCANTILISM

In the budding capitalism occurring around him, Smith saw the possibilities for an economic system that he hoped could solve the major problems of mercantilism. That system was limited laissez-faire (lightly regulated) capitalism. Laissez-faire is French for "let it be." When applied to the economy, a laissez-faire approach means letting the market run without significant interference from the government.

Adam Smith, pictured in Figure 4.1, lived most of his life in Scotland, where he was surrounded by dynamic entrepreneurs such as his friend James Watt. Watt

FIGURE 4.1 Adam Smith (1723–1790).

invented a revolutionary steam engine that was an essential part of the Industrial Revolution.

These entrepreneurs needed access to new markets for inputs and goods so that they could produce on a larger scale. The only way to recoup the large investment needed to set up a factory was to get inputs at low prices and to sell large quantities of the product that the factory was producing. But mercantilist monopolies dominated trade, charging high prices for the commodities that entrepreneurs needed as inputs and limiting entrepreneurs' access to foreign markets. Smith argued that mercantilist policies were limiting economic growth and preventing the alleviation of poverty for three main reasons.

First, with every European country strictly regulating trade and preventing imports of manufactured goods, manufacturing firms could only produce for the domestic market. With free trade, firms would be able to sell their products to multiple countries, and that would allow them to produce more goods on a larger scale, which would be more efficient. Factories could be larger, which would promote the development of additional machinery and workers with more specialized skills. Below, we will go into more detail about the importance of specialization.

Second, mercantilist policies reduced competition, allowing monopolies to form in key sectors. Without competition, monopolistic firms did not have to be efficient or innovative to make a profit. Thus, the creation of monopolistic markets was a major barrier to development, keeping prices high and growth low.

Third, Smith objected to mercantilist policies to suppress wages. These policies encouraged employers in a particular trade or geographical area to form a trade association, which could then meet to set wages at the lowest possible level. If employers were instead forced to compete with each other for workers, they would tend to bid up wages in seeking to lure the best people from other firms. Agreeing to a fixed wage rate for the area eliminated such competition and kept wages low.

In Smith's view, the two great evils of his era were the **government** and the **monopolies** that set up the mercantilist system for their own benefit. The way to solve the poverty problem was, he thought, to stop the government from interfering with markets and to let competition force firms to be efficient and innovative. This, he hoped, would raise the standard of living of all citizens, especially the poor.

4.3 SMITH'S IDEALIZED PICTURE OF A CAPITALIST SYSTEM

Smith believed that lightly regulated capitalism was preferable to mercantilism based on how he envisioned a competitive market capitalist system working. The key difference between this system and mercantilism would be its effect on economic growth. Smith's economics book was titled *The Wealth of Nations* in large part because he sought to analyze the determinants of wealth.

Smith's first important insight was that **wealth comes from productivity**, not from money (gold). Money is only useful if it can lead to a high standard of living, but a country's standard of living is determined by how productive it is—how many goods and services it can produce and consume—not how much money it has. A country that has lots of gold but produces very few goods will quickly find that the prices of those few goods are very high. But a country that is very productive will be able to consume lots of goods and services, no matter how much money it has. The fact that countries today use gross domestic product, which is the total production of goods and services in an economy, to measure the standard of living of people in an economy is a testament to Smith's enduring insight.

Second, Smith identified **the importance of the specialization of labor in enhancing productivity** (and wealth). As noted before, the specialization of labor occurs when particular tasks are performed by specific individuals, rather than everyone performing all tasks. This enhances productivity for three reasons, according to Smith. First, workers get better at their job, improving their skill and dexterity, when they specialize in one task instead of many tasks. Second, less time is spent moving from one job to another. Third, specialization leads to the invention of machines that facilitate and replace labor. The last of these tends to be the most important driver of increases in productivity.

A good example of the importance of specialization comes from the car industry. The first cars were produced by teams of skilled craftsmen and entrepreneurs. But once entrepreneurs divided the manufacturing process into discrete tasks and developed specialized machinery, the manufacturing process became much more productive. Each car part could be manufactured using a specialized process, which was subdivided into a series of even more specialized tasks. In Figure 4.2, we see workers on the first moving assembly line in 1913 assembling magnetos and flywheels, which were parts of a Ford car.

Another crucial insight in Smith's analysis was the importance of **competition** in making markets work efficiently and fostering growth. In the absence of competition, monopolistic companies could produce shoddy products and charge high prices because consumers had no other options. These companies also had no incentive to invest in new technology or products because they could continue to make profits indefinitely without fear of new competition. Additionally, they could pay workers very little because other companies were not competing to hire workers. Competition changes all of this. Competitive markets tend to generate better quality, lower prices, more innovations, and higher wages.

Ideally, Smith hoped, **competition would** even **regulate incomes and benefit the poor**, solving the huge poverty problem of the day. Smith envisioned the pattern unfolding as follows:

1. Bold entrepreneurs, trying to get ahead of their competition, engage in risky innovations, such as creating a new product or designing a more cost-effective method of production (technology).

FIGURE 4.2 The first moving assembly line for 1913 Ford cars.

2. If effective, the new product or technology yields substantial economic (above-normal) profits and the business expands.
3. Timid entrepreneurs, once they see that the innovation is effective, copy the new product or imitate the new technology, causing new firms to enter the market to compete with the bold entrepreneur.
4. The entrance of more competition increases the supply of the product, lowering the price and eliminating the excess profits earned by the bold entrepreneur.
5. The industry as a whole experiences economic growth as multiple businesses expand operations as a result of building the new product or utilizing the new technology.
6. This process tends to limit the incomes of the rich via competition and raise the standard of living of the poor because goods' prices are kept low and demand for workers increases as industries expand.

The result, according to Smith, is that a much more equal distribution of income would result in this capitalist economic system than was the case under mercantilism!

In highlighting the importance of competition, Smith also identified **self-interest** as a useful component of a market capitalist economy. The dynamic entrepreneurs of his era were providing essential goods and services to society, but they were doing so for selfish reasons—to make a profit:

> It is not from the benevolence of the butcher, the brewer, or the baker, that we expect our dinner, but from their regard to their own interest. We address ourselves, not to their humanity but to their self-love, and never talk to them of our own necessities but of their advantages.

To Smith, the profit motive, in the presence of sufficient competition, was a positive force providing the essential goods that society wanted and leading to economic growth in the process.

Along with competition, Smith believed that **moral sentiments** and a **system of justice** were key regulators of the competitive process. In his first important book, *The Theory of Moral Sentiments*, Smith states, "How selfish soever man may be supposed, there are evidently some principles in his nature, which interest him in the fortune of others, and render their happiness necessary to him." Smith evidently saw people as both self-interested *and* interested in the welfare of others. Along with moral sentiments, Smith envisioned a government that had "the duty of protecting, as far as possible, every member of the society from the injustice and oppression of every other member of it, or the duty of establishing an exact administration of justice."

Combining these crucial ideas, to Smith, *a self-interested entrepreneur who (a) operates in a competitive market, (b) cares about the welfare of others, and (c) is prevented by law from exploiting others would tend to serve the public interest by producing good products at low prices, innovating regularly, fostering economic growth, and benefiting the poor.* This led Smith to his famous analogy of the **invisible hand** of the market:

> As every individual … endeavours as much as he can both to employ his capital in the support of domestic industry, and so to direct that industry that its produce may be of the greatest value; every individual necessarily labours to render the annual revenue of the society as great as he can. He generally, indeed, neither intends to promote the public interest, nor knows how much he is promoting it. By preferring the support of domestic to that of foreign industry, he intends only his own security; and by directing that industry in such a manner as its produce may be of the greatest value, he intends only his own gain, and he is in this, as in many other cases, led by an invisible hand to promote an end which was no part of his intention. Nor is it always the worse for the society that it was no part of it. By pursuing his own interest he frequently promotes that of the society more effectually than when he really intends to promote it.

This was a powerful and counterintuitive claim. Self-interest, via the competitive market system, can end up benefiting society more effectively than intentionally benevolent acts! Consider this idea carefully and evaluate whether or not you think it holds true in our world.

Given what Smith actually said about capitalism, as described above, it is interesting how many commentators cite the portion of Smith's work on self-interest without acknowledging the other crucial components of the system that Smith discussed. Smith only mentioned the invisible hand once in *The Wealth of Nations*, so selecting this metaphor as the key to understanding Smith's work is questionable.

Smith was also a strong advocate of reducing regulations on imports and exports. He thought that with less regulated trade companies could sell goods to a larger market (foreign as well as domestic consumers). This in turn would allow companies to increase the size of their factories, leading to greater specialization, the development of new machines, and ultimately greater productivity and economic growth. Smith thought that the result would be an improvement in everyone's standard of living as productivity increases resulted in lower prices and greater quantities of goods.

Despite Smith's distrust of government, which in his day acted on behalf of monopolistic interests rather than promoting the public welfare, Smith still saw a limited role for government policy. Smith's approach to government regulation is termed "limited laissez-faire" because he did envision a few limits being placed on market capitalism. First, as noted earlier, Smith wanted the government to establish a strong system of justice to protect every member of society from injustice and oppression. Second, the government needed to maintain order and provide for national defense. Third, the government needed to provide public goods, including roads, harbors, and education, all of which contribute to commerce and the functioning of the market.

Smith wanted greater investment in human capital via education. Without such efforts, Smith feared that most people would be poor and would have mindless jobs. Also, he hoped that education would lead to more innovations, possibly generated by workers themselves, and increase productivity.

Smith believed firmly that limited laissez-faire capitalism would be a better, more egalitarian system than mercantilism. Smith's goal was to create a society that was so productive that there would be enough for the "slothful and oppressive profusion of the great, and at the same time abundantly to supply the wants of the artisan, the laborer, and the peasant." In these words we see Smith's disdain for the rich and powerful of his era and his hope that capitalism would lead to a better world.

Such an idealistic vision was very powerful, especially in the face of ongoing problems of the mercantilist economies. The mercantilist governments in England had attempted to alleviate the plight of the poor with a series of welfare programs and wage subsidies beginning around 1600, but these programs came under attack in the early 1800s with the rise of the philosophy of laissez-faire.

4.4 FROM SUPPORTING THE POOR TO LAISSEZ-FAIRE CAPITALISM

4.4.1 Poor Laws

The expansion of markets under mercantilism was accompanied by major economic problems. Most important was the vast amount of poverty created when the peasants were thrown off their land by the enclosure movement. The poverty often provoked crime, food riots, and other desperate acts by the poor. To reduce some of the negative consequences, England established the Poor Laws beginning around 1600 to ensure that the poor had enough food to survive. These laws were continued in various forms until 1834.

The Speenhamland system, for example, was established in 1795 to reduce rural poverty at a time when high grain prices were making the situation of the poor even more tenuous. Speenhamland subsidized wages based on the price of bread in order to guarantee a minimum income, a "living wage," to the poor irrespective of their earnings. In essence, any worker who received less than a living wage would receive a subsidy from the government up to a minimum level necessary to support a family. The problem with the Speenhamland system was that it eroded incentives. Workers had no reason to work hard. If their pay was slashed because they slacked off on the job, they would then receive a higher subsidy from the government to compensate for their lower wages. Employers had an incentive to pay workers less than a living wage because the government would subsidize low wages until they reached a living wage. The result was that productivity declined and the cost to taxpayers of the Speenhamland system became higher and higher.

In addition to the lower productivity and increasing cost of the Speenhamland system, Thomas Malthus, a minister and influential writer on economics, helped erode support for aiding the poor with his theory of population. Malthus argued that the population would expand as long as there was sufficient food available. Furthermore, he argued that the limited amount of land available could only produce enough food for a certain number of people. With a limited supply of food and an ever-increasing population, Malthus thought famine was inevitable.

Many members of the British Parliament used the population theory of Malthus to argue that giving money to the poor would only lead them to have more children and cause a famine. To eliminate this possibility, Parliament passed the Poor Law Reform Act of 1834, which eliminated relief for the poor except for those who were disabled and created an unregulated market for labor. Subsidies for the poor were replaced by a competitive labor market, and anyone who could not find a job was thrown into a harsh workhouse. No longer was there a commitment to help those who fell upon hard times. Instead, the poor and the unemployed, and often their children, were subject to the brutal treatment of the workhouse. These were the conditions described by Charles Dickens in *Oliver Twist* after visiting a series of workhouses (see Figure 4.3). Even those who worked in factories faced a harsh environment, as we will see in the next chapter.

It is unfortunate that the hardships of the poor after 1834 in England were a product of bad economic theory. Modern economic research has proven that when the poor have higher incomes and more opportunities, they tend to have fewer (not more) children. Families that have lower incomes and are less secure tend to have more children because the extra labor is helpful and the children might earn enough money to support their parents once they reach old age. For poor families in countries

FIGURE 4.3 *Oliver Asks for More*, by George Cruikshank.

without secure retirement benefits, children are the primary provider of security for the elderly. Thus, the removal of support for the poor was based on faulty perceptions of the relationship between incomes for the poor and population growth.

4.4.2 Say's law and macroeconomic intervention

Laissez-faire policies were also promoted in England in another key area in the early 1800s: Macroeconomic policy. Malthus and a few other economists were worried about the instability of the macroeconomy, which was experiencing frequent recessions; when spending and investment fell, products piled up on store shelves (gluts of goods) and unemployment increased as businesses laid off workers due to slack demand for their products. Despite the problem of frequent recessions, most politicians and economists were convinced by the arguments of Jean-Baptiste Say, who popularized and extended Smith's argument that a capitalist economy was fundamentally stable over the long term.

The key theory in Say's "law of markets" was that **supply creates its own demand**. When entrepreneurs make a product, they hire workers, rent land, and buy raw materials, putting money into the hands of workers, landowners, and input suppliers. The money they pay for raw materials becomes income for those businesses, which goes to pay their wages, rent, and materials costs. Businesses also generate profits, which becomes the owners' income. Thus, the act of producing and supplying goods and services generates wages for laborers, rent for landowners, and profits for owners. What do people do with this income? They buy the goods and services that are produced. This is the famous circular flow of economic activity depicted in Figure 4.4.

According to Say's law, the income from producing goods and services generates exactly enough money to buy those goods and services.

Say's law is based on a number of crucial assumptions about how the economy works. Recall from Chapter 2 that a model is only as good as its underlying assumptions, and when the assumptions fail the model is usually inaccurate. The **assumptions behind Say's law** are the following:

1. Consumers' demand for goods and services is unlimited because they get satisfaction from consumption, so they always tend to spend most of their incomes.
2. An unregulated capitalist system will generate enough income for consumers to buy everything that is produced.
3. All money that is saved or earned as profits will be invested by entrepreneurs due to the (almost unlimited) profitable opportunities provided by capitalism.
4. Wages, prices, and interest rates will adjust very rapidly so that supply will equal demand.
5. The (standard) ceteris paribus assumption holds; all other relevant factors do not change.

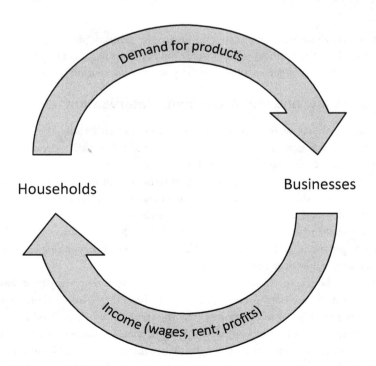

FIGURE 4.4 The simple circular flow model of the economy.

If all of these assumptions hold, then it is likely that enough income is generated to produce enough demand to buy all of the goods that are supplied. There may be temporary downturns in the economy, but these should be short-lived. Therefore, economists following Say's law believed that no government intervention was necessary in recessions because they thought that the market would fix itself quickly.

As we will see in more detail later, there are several fundamental flaws with Say's law. For now, we will focus on one crucial problem: The view that there will always be enough demand for products. This flaw was pointed out by Malthus, Marx, and Keynes but ignored by most economists until the Great Depression of the 1930s. What economists now know is that in recessions, consumers are reluctant to spend because they are worried about keeping their jobs, and businesses are reluctant to invest when they are pessimistic about future sales. Consumer demand and businesses investment purchases both fall, tending to stay low until confidence returns. Pessimistic consumers reduce spending and save more. If the extra money that consumers saved in banks were then spent by businesses on investment goods, the economy would not experience a prolonged recession. However, economic research indicates that *the most important determinant of business investment is expected sales*: Businesses are only willing to buy new machinery and equipment to expand the size of their operations if they think that they will be able to sell more goods in the future. Certainly this is not the case if consumers are buying fewer goods than normal. Say and most economists of his era assumed that there would always be enough opportunities that businesses would want to invest all of the money available in the banking system. In reality, when the business environment is poor and expected sales are low, businesses tend to reduce their investment spending. Money piles up in banks, which are then unable to loan out all the money in their vaults. Even if banks lower their interest rates on loans, businesses are reluctant to borrow money to invest as long as they believe they will not be able to sell all of the products that they produce. One of the key implications is that if businesses expect a bad economy in the future, they reduce investment right away, which then helps to create the bad economy that they expected! Hence, we see that recessions occur regularly due to shortages in demand.

Despite the major flaw in Say's law, most economists subscribed to this theory and believed that the market would always fix itself very rapidly. They believed that no government intervention was necessary to alleviate unemployment and stimulate a stagnant economy because those problems would always be promptly righted by the market system. Another economic dogma of the economists of this era was the belief in unregulated ("free") trade, based on the theory of comparative advantage developed by David Ricardo.

4.4.3 Free trade and comparative advantage

Under the mercantilist system, trade was heavily protected and imported goods faced stiff tariffs. Given the importance of agriculture to mercantilist economies, agriculture was one of the most protected sectors. In England, the Corn Laws established a high domestic price of grains (corn, wheat) to generate wealth for landlords. However, entrepreneurs and workers objected to the high cost of food, which had the effect of raising wages because workers had to be paid more in order to survive.

David Ricardo argued that England should deregulate trade. That would allow entrepreneurs to earn greater profits, which would be reinvested as purchases of capital goods, which would stimulate economic growth and make everyone better off. According to Ricardo's (1817) theory of comparative advantage, which we will study in more detail later, if all countries engaged in unregulated trade, each country would end up producing the goods that it was relatively best at producing. The competition of the market once tariff protections were eliminated would lead to the most efficient firms surviving, and it would decrease the costs of all goods, which would raise everyone's standard of living. Also, if firms could sell to a larger market, including domestic and foreign consumers, they could increase their level of specialization, which would then increase productivity, as Smith had argued. The result would (in theory) be an economy with more rapid economic growth and a higher standard of living than under regulated (mercantilist) trade.

The Corn Laws were repealed in 1846 based on Ricardo's arguments, marking the completion of England's transition to a grand experiment: Laissez-faire capitalism. Under this economic system, the economic power no longer resided with the merchants and the king. Instead, the most powerful individuals were the entrepreneurial factory owners, and the factory became the center of economic life.

4.5 THE RISE OF THE FACTORY AND THE "DOUBLE MOVEMENT"

Once the Industrial Revolution was underway, it quickly became self-sustaining. The earliest entrepreneurs made huge sums of money, which they invested in new ventures. Many of these new ventures were successful, generating additional profits to be reinvested. As this process continued, the factory came to be the center of the economy, transforming the commercial, agricultural, mercantilist system into a more urban, industrial capitalist system. The pace of change was breathtaking. In 40 years, Glasgow was transformed from a sleepy farming center to an industrial powerhouse with 100 mills producing manufactured goods, iron, leather, chemicals, and more.

By the mid-1800s, many factory owners were wealthy and politically powerful. The factory was the most important institution in the community, determining what life was like for much of the population. Unfortunately for many workers, the transition to factory life was a difficult one. Agrarian peasants did not have an easy life, but they worked at their own pace, and there were times of the year when they did not have to work much, especially in the winter. In the unregulated factories of early capitalism, the pace of work was dictated by the machine, and the work hours pushed people to the brink of human endurance.

So horrific were the conditions that in the late 1700s and early 1800s workers regularly smashed machines and burned factories as part of the Luddite movement. However, the Luddites were arrested and many were hanged in 1813. In essence, the factory system was imposed on a resisting population by force and by the lack of viable alternatives for poor and desperate people.

If we reflect on the major trends in the development of the market system, we see that national markets were initially created by mercantilist firms and monarchs in pursuit of gold and power. However, the expansion of markets was actively resisted by guilds and workers who sought to maintain their standard of living in any way they could, often using violence. Similarly, as England moved to manufacturing factories and laissez-faire capitalism in the 1800s, workers resisted the horrific conditions, as we will see in the next chapter. Along with the workers' movements, laws regulating factories and various forms of social legislation began to be introduced to mitigate the worst effects of industrial capitalism.

This process of the relentless expansion of markets into new areas at the behest of the most powerful economic interests, coupled with the resistance of workers and communities to market expansion that threatened their livelihood, has been termed "the double movement" by Karl Polanyi. More specifically, the double movement describes how **the push for the development of markets by businesses** (first mercantilists and then capitalists) **was met by a counter movement by workers and communities to regulate markets** to prevent them from doing too much destruction to society.

In many ways, early capitalism was, indeed, an ugly thing, and it provoked strong reactions from those it victimized. This is the form of capitalism that Karl Marx described when he wrote, "Capital comes [into the world] dripping from head to foot, from every pore, with blood and dirt." We turn to Marx and workers' resistance to the dark ages of capitalism in the next chapter.

4.6 CONCLUSION

Capitalism began in England based on set of unique institutions that help us to understand the crucial ingredients in a capitalist economic system. The key institutions include a money-driven, scientifically oriented culture; secure property rights; and a large domestic and colonial market. The successes of the early capitalists prompted Adam Smith to write *The Wealth of Nations*, in which he proposed that lightly regulated market capitalism would improve the well-being of all people. To Smith, the great evils of mercantilism—monopolies and government manipulation of markets for the elites—would be eliminated via the installation of a competitive capitalist system. Competition, moral sentiments, and a sound legal system would, he thought, harness the power of self-interest to generate rapid economic growth that would raise the standard of living for all.

Smith was followed by Say, who argued against the need for government to intervene in recessions, and Ricardo, who argued in favor of unregulated trade with other countries. These powerful ideas, coupled with the elimination of the Poor Laws, resulted in the installation of the world's first laissez-faire capitalist economic system in England between 1834 and 1846. Yet, as England was moving toward laissez-faire capitalism, a countermovement grew in opposition to capitalism, a phenomenon that Karl Polanyi described as the "double movement."

QUESTIONS FOR REVIEW

1. What were the major institutional factors that spurred the development of capitalism in England? Which of these factors do you think was most important? Why?

2. Given the institutional factors that provided the foundation for capitalism in England, do you think capitalism would work as effectively in other countries with different institutions? Why or why not?

3. Why was Adam Smith critical of mercantilism? Why did he think capitalism was preferable to mercantilism?

4. Smith argued that unregulated (laissez-faire) capitalism would lead to substantial increases in income for all, and especially for workers. Carefully explain how Smith thought this would come about. Critically evaluate his analysis.

5. Smith believed that laissez-faire capitalism would be almost completely self-regulating via the invisible hand, as long as moral sentiments and an effective legal system were in place. Evaluate his argument and use examples of current events to support your analysis.

6. Smith was an opponent of mercantilist governments. What role (if any) does Adam Smith envision for government in a capitalist economy?

7. Why did Malthus (and others) oppose the Poor Laws such as the Speenhamland system? What parts of their arguments were valid and what parts would modern economists consider invalid?

8. Describe Say's law and why it is important. Also explain the major criticism of Say's law.

9. Apply Say's law to the modern economy. Has the economy recently experienced a shortfall in demand, or has the economy operated smoothly without such a problem in recent decades?

10. Why did Smith and Ricardo advocate unregulated trade? What problems might occur when a country moves to unregulated trade? Do we see any such problems in the modern world?

11. Define Karl Polanyi's concept of the double movement and apply this concept to the modern world. Do we see businesses pushing for fewer regulations and access to more markets today? Is there opposition to these business initiatives from people and communities? Give specific examples.

Karl Marx and the dark ages of capitalism

Historical materialism, surplus value, and the exploitation of labor

By the mid–1800s, unregulated capitalism dominated economic systems of Europe and the United States. Adam Smith had hoped that unregulated capitalism would benefit workers, but this was not the case. Instead, this was the dark ages of capitalism: Children were sometimes shackled to machines to keep them at their jobs; workers regularly lost limbs on the job, at which point they were fired because they were no longer productive; work hours were pushed to the brink of human endurance so that laborers spent almost every waking minute working; and work was mind-numbingly dull and repetitive for most industrial laborers.

In this context, Karl Marx wrote his famous critique of capitalism, advocating socialism and communism as alternatives. Although Marx is often thought of as the father of communism, he had very little to say about communism and how it might work. Instead, he concentrated on analyzing the functioning of capitalism.

As we will see, even though he wrote in the mid-1800s, Marx was able to anticipate many of the characteristics of modern capitalism. His analysis predicted, among other things, globalization, the rise of huge corporations, the influence of money in democratic political systems, the abiding alienation of wage workers, and much more. The power of the analytical framework he developed accounts for why many of his ideas still remain relevant today.

This chapter begins by describing the spread of capitalism from England to the United States and Europe and the horrible conditions that characterized capitalism of the mid-1800s. We then turn to Marx's ideas regarding the evolution of economic systems and his analysis of capitalism.

DOI: 10.4324/9781315636924-7

5.0 CHAPTER 5 LEARNING GOALS

After reading this chapter you should be able to:

■ Define and give an example of an infant industry promotion strategy.

■ Describe the conditions of workers in the 1800s, assess the implications of these conditions for the functioning of laissez-faire capitalism, and determine whether or not you think laissez-faire capitalism inevitably results in exploitation.

■ Explain the components of historical materialism and Marx's method of analysis and apply this method to the evolution of economic systems.

■ Use the concept of surplus value to analyze the functioning of a capitalist economic system.

■ Evaluate Marx's views on competition and commodification using specific examples from history and from modern capitalism.

■ Explain the forces in capitalism that Marx thought would result in a workers' revolution and the factors that mitigated those pressures.

5.1 INFANT INDUSTRY PROTECTION AND THE SPREAD OF CAPITALISM IN EUROPE AND THE UNITED STATES

Beginning in the 1300s, England enacted policies to develop the wool industry. They used measures such as protective tariffs, subsidies, and the poaching of skilled workers from foreign manufacturers to give their industry an advantage. This classic approach to economic development is known as an infant industry promotion strategy, in which **a country protects and subsidizes a new industry until it can be globally competitive**. In the 1700s, England used similar policies to promote additional industries. By the 1800s, England was the world's technological and industrial leader, and its shift to free trade policies in 1846 was designed to cement the advantages of British industries and undermine the development of competing industries among its European rivals. When you are the global leader with the most efficient industries, free trade benefits your economy while undercutting the industries of other countries.

Most other countries followed England's example, protecting new industries until they could compete with the established industries of other countries. The United States used infant industry promotion strategies once it was independent from England in 1780. Alexander Hamilton, a founding father and the country's first secretary of the treasury, successfully persuaded the U.S. Congress to install protective tariffs to allow U.S. industries to develop and compete with British industries. In Germany, the state provided subsidies and established a number of factories itself. The French hired skilled British workers and engaged in industrial espionage to close the technological gap with Britain. In country after country, governments protected and encouraged industrial development to stimulate the economy and to catch up with the technological leaders. Only small countries such as Switzerland that were already technologically developed and that needed to sell to larger markets in other countries pursued free trade policies as they were industrializing.

But as capitalist industries spread to Europe and across the globe, they were accompanied by horrific working conditions. The rosy scenario that Adam Smith anticipated, where the growth of competitive capitalism would dramatically improve the welfare of workers and the poor, did not play out as he had hoped.

5.2 THE CONDITIONS OF WORKERS UNDER CAPITALISM IN THE 1800S

The scores of impoverished people created by England's enclosure movement meant that many people were desperate for work. As a result of the large surplus of laborers, workers had no bargaining power with employers because they could be easily replaced. Consequently, workers had to accept whatever wages and working conditions were offered. And, as noted previously, the earliest entrepreneurs were hard men, uncertain in their ability to make a profit and driven to squeeze every drop of profit out of their operations. The result was that working and living conditions for the average person were incredibly horrific.

Consider some of the following characteristics of work in England, the wealthiest country in the world in the mid-1800s.

*   Employers often preferred women and children for manufacturing work because they were more submissive. Children of the working class began to work as young as four years old. They worked for 14–18 hours every day, or until they dropped from exhaustion. Sometimes they were chained to machines and beaten to keep them working. Figure 5.1 depicts Addie Card, a 12-year-old cotton mill worker in 1910.[1]
*   There were very few safety precautions, and workers regularly lost fingers, hands, arms, and legs in industrial accidents. Upon experiencing a debilitating

FIGURE 5.1 Addie Card in 1910.

injury, workers were usually fired and received no compensation or medical care from their employer.
- Once at the factory, workers had no control over their lives. Breaks were limited to a few minutes each day, despite the incredibly long workdays. Factory owners and managers regularly took sexual advantage of female employees.

As businesses sought to expand markets and gain access to additional resources, there was a countermovement to regulate the worst excesses of markets (Polanyi's double movement, for example, as discussed in Chapter 4). But the reforms themselves were modest, and they confirm the overall ugly state of affairs. As a brief example, consider some of the following child labor "reforms" in England:

- 1819: The employment of children under the age of 9 was prohibited in cotton mills.
- 1833: The work week for children under the age of 18 was limited to 69 hours.
- 1842: Children under the age of 10 were prohibited from working in coal mines.
- 1847: The workday for women and children was limited to 10.5 hours.

The low wages paid by the factories also resulted in squalid living conditions for working-class families. Most families lived in single-room apartments. They often could not afford clothes, furniture, or even food. Many people died from disease or malnutrition. To give but a few examples of the human toll of this system, the life expectancy in the manufacturing city of Manchester, England, in the mid-1800s was only 17 years. J. C. Symons, a government commissioner, described a working-class neighborhood in Glasgow in 1839 in this way:

> The wynds of Glasgow house a fluctuating population of between 15,000 and 30,000 persons. This district is composed of many narrow streets and square courts and in the middle of each court there is a dung-hill. Although the outward appearance of these places was revolting, I was nevertheless quite unprepared for the filth and misery that were to be found inside. In some of these bedrooms we visited at night we found a whole mass of humanity stretched out on the floor. There were often 15 to 20 men and women huddled together, some being clothed and others naked. Their bed was a heap of musty straw mixed with rags. There was hardly any furniture there and the only thing which gave these holes the appearance of a dwelling was fire burning on the hearth. Thieving and prostitution are the main sources of income of these people ... In this part of Glasgow most of the houses have been condemned by the Court of Guild as dilapidated and uninhabitable—but it is just these dwellings which are filled to overflowing, because, by law no rent can be charged on them.[2]

The squalid conditions led to regular outbreaks of cholera, typhoid, and other diseases. Unsurprisingly, the dreadful working and living conditions prompted regular uprisings. Various types of riots and rebellions occurred in England in most years between 1811 and 1850. And yet, employers saw no need to address the desperate conditions of their workers. Their belief was that once an employer had paid employees their wages, he had no further obligation to them. This was the embodiment of the laissez-faire, every-man-for-himself philosophy that dominated the business community in the early stages of capitalism.

It was in response to this world that Karl Marx wrote his critique of capitalism.

5.3 KARL MARX, HISTORICAL MATERIALISM, AND CLASS CONFLICT

Karl Marx, pictured in Figure 5.2, was born in 1818 into a German economy that was structured to funnel almost all of the resources to the rich. As in England, German factories were organized in a brutal, militaristic structure designed to discipline and exploit desperate workers. They could do so with impunity due to the support of the government and the elites. Outraged by this society, Marx gravitated toward radical politics during his university years, where he studied philosophy and earned a Ph.D. at age 23. Due to his radical politics, Marx was unable to secure a teaching position, and he was thrown out of Germany, France, and Brussels for his

FIGURE 5.2 Karl Marx (1818–1883).

activism on behalf of workers. He eventually settled in England, where he collaborated with Friedrich Engels (1820–1895). Note that Engels acknowledged Marx as the major thinker behind their writings, so most economists attribute the ideas of their co-authored works to Marx.

In 1848, Marx and Engels wrote one of their most powerful documents, *The Communist Manifesto*. In it, they encouraged workers to rise up against their exploitative employers. They also developed a powerful theory of historical change featuring class conflict and technology as the driving factors behind the major shifts in society.

Marx was interested in understanding and analyzing historical change. Adam Smith wrote about capitalism as if it would always operate in a particular way, with small, competitive firms acting to enhance the well-being of society. Marx, however, observed that no economic system was permanent. Within each economic system were forces that threatened to break it apart, sometimes resulting in a new economic system. Marx cited historical evidence indicating that the driving force of the major changes in economic systems was class conflict. Marx and Engels began *The Communist Manifesto* with a famous statement regarding the importance of class conflict to historical change:

The history of all hitherto existing society is the history of class struggles. Freeman and slave, patrician and plebeian, lord and serf, guild-master and journeyman, in a word, oppressor and oppressed, stood in constant opposition to one another, carried on an uninterrupted, now hidden, now open fight, a fight that each time ended, either in a revolutionary reconstitution of society at large, or in the common ruin of the contending classes. … Our epoch, the epoch of the bourgeoisie [capitalists], … has simplified class antagonisms. Society as a whole is more and more splitting up into two great hostile camps, into two great classes directly facing each other—Bourgeoisie and Proletariat [workers].

Marx focused on the contradictions within each economic system that would eventually force the system to change. This **method of analysis, focusing on contradictions and the struggle of opposing forces**, is known as dialectics.

Consider for a moment how powerful Marx's observation on class conflict is in helping us to understand the major shifts in economic systems. In each major shift in economic systems—Roman Empire to feudalism, feudalism to mercantilism, and mercantilism to capitalism—class antagonisms featured prominently. For example, the clash of the feudal elites (lords and church officials) with kings and merchants destroyed feudalism and ushered in mercantilism, as kings and merchants reshaped society based on their interests in extending markets. With their rise in power and importance, capitalists were able to prevail against the interests of merchants and kings and replace mercantilism with laissez-faire capitalism. And, as we shall see later, the conflict between capitalists and workers under laissez-faire capitalism produced the mixed market capitalist economies of the modern world. In each case, an economic system was unable to resolve major conflicts over resources in society, resulting in conflicts between key classes and leading to a new type of economic system.

Technology also plays an important role in reshaping economic systems. The development of agriculture prompted the change from hunter-gatherer societies to agriculture-based empires. The rise in agricultural productivity during feudalism promoted urbanization and trade and established conditions that were ripe for mercantilism. The development of shipping, guns, and steel in Europe made mercantilism and colonial empires possible. The steam engine stimulated the development of factories in early capitalism. In all of these examples, technological changes prompted changes in class structures, which helped to undermine existing class relations.

Given that no economic system has lasted forever and that there are many conflicts and technological changes occurring in contemporary society, think for a moment about how the next economic system might arise and what it might look like:

- What do you see as the major contradictions in our current society?
- What technological changes are fundamentally reshaping society?
- What are the key social classes engaged in conflicts over resources?
- What type of economic system might emerge from these contradictions, changes, and conflicts?

Identifying the major contradictions, technological changes, and conflicts helps us to identify the major sources of change in an economic system. Conflicts, which arise from contradictions and technological changes that advantage some groups over others, often drive major changes. Marx focused on the fight over economic resources as the primary source of conflict because, historically, this battle has been the most important factor behind changes in economic systems. Also, the **material conditions** of society are the primary influence on what our lives are like, determining whom we interact with during most of the day, how hard we have to work, our status in society, who we are likely to marry, and so on.

For example, what social class you are born into has a huge influence on what your life will be like, affecting whether or not you are likely to go to an elite college, whether you are more likely to end up working on Wall Street or at Walmart, and whether you are likely to be a manager or a laborer. The **relations of production** are the relationships between people in the workplace, and they are primarily determined by your social class.

Also important in shaping the conditions of society are technological factors, including tools, machinery, infrastructure, resources, labor power, and knowledge. These Marx called the **forces of production**. The physical, non-human parts of the forces of production, including machinery, tools, buildings, infrastructure, and natural resources, are called the **means of production**. In a capitalist economic system, capitalists own and control the means of production whereas workers have to sell their labor to capitalists in order to survive. Together, the forces of production (technology, knowledge) and the (class) relations of production are the driving forces behind the changes in society. **Marx's approach to the study of economics, focusing on the class conflicts and technological changes that provoke changes in the material conditions of society over time**, is called historical materialism.

Marx turned his sophisticated analytical method to the study of the laissez-faire capitalist system of the mid-1800s. Where Smith saw profit-seeking as a positive force, Marx saw a system that brutalized workers and turned everything—people, love, religion, democracy, justice—into a commodity to be bought and sold. The key to understanding how exploitation and commodification come about is Marx's concept of surplus value.

5.4 SURPLUS VALUE AND THE EXPLOITATION OF LABOR

In the capitalist system of the mid-1800s there were two main social classes, the capitalists who owned the means of production and the workers who were forced to sell their labor. During Marx's era, the small middle class that existed, consisting of skilled craftspeople and owners of small shops, was being rapidly displaced by the ever-growing capitalist firms. Thus, Marx concentrated on the two main social classes of his day, capitalists and workers.

The main dynamic between capitalists and workers is shaped by the pursuit of profit by the capitalist. In a competitive capitalist system, owners are forced to be "hard men" who extract the most they can from their business. In the cutthroat capitalist world, if you can't produce the best product for the lowest possible price, then you will likely get displaced by a competitor who is better or more efficient. And you must constantly reinvest your profits in new ventures and new technology to stay one step ahead of your competitors. Indeed, the reinvestment of profits into new production techniques and products is usually the key to long-term survival. Thus, in order to survive, firms must keep costs as low as possible and accumulate sufficient profits for reinvestment. These profits are invested in capital goods (machinery, equipment, research and development, etc.), resulting in capital accumulation (a larger and larger capital stock). Marx saw capital accumulation as one of the key forces in capitalism, driving the development of new products, the search for new markets, and the exploitation of labor.

In their relentless pursuit of profit (and capital accumulation), firms have to extract as much effort as possible at as low a wage as possible from their workers. In other words, firms seek the maximum production from workers for the lowest cost.

To demonstrate this fundamental aspect of capitalism, Marx developed a simple model of the workday based on the concept of **surplus value**. During the first part of the workday, the worker produces goods or services to generate enough profits to pay for their wages (and benefits) for the day. Once a worker has paid for his or her wages, the rest of the work for the day generates profits for the owner. Thus, the workday can be broken down into the following:

$$A - - - - - - - - - - - - - B - - - - - - - - - - - - -C,$$

where A–B pays for the wage and B–C is profit (surplus value).

Surplus value is defined as **the amount of value produced by workers over and above the cost of their wages (including benefits)**.

In this relationship, a firm that is pursuing maximum profits must increase the B–C part of the workday as much as possible. That can be done in two different ways:

1. Increasing the length of the workday (moving C to the right from C to C_2, as shown in Figure 5.3).
2. Reducing the amount of time necessary to pay for a laborer's wage (moving B to the left from B to B_2, as shown in Figure 5.3). This can be done by (a) reducing wages, (b) replacing workers with more cost-effective machinery, or (c) increasing the productivity of workers by speeding up the pace of work or other measures that target productivity.

This is where the fight over the workday in capitalism arises. Clearly, employers want to maximize profits, and that means getting the most surplus value possible

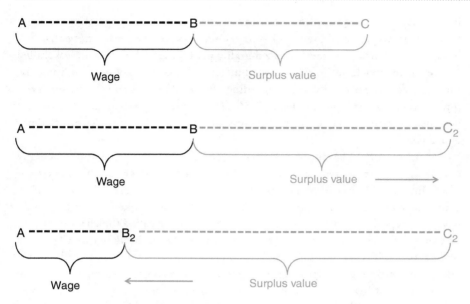

FIGURE 5.3 The fight over the workday.

from their workers. Once employers have paid their workers' daily salaries, the incentive is to work them as many hours as possible. And employers always want to pay the lowest wages possible. But what do workers want? Mostly, they prefer just the opposite: Workers want higher pay and shorter hours.

During the years of unregulated capitalism, factory owners went to great lengths to increase their profits and undercut their competitors. With daily wages fixed, employers engaged in relentless efforts to expand work hours, as documented in Juliet Schor's (1991) book, *The Overworked American*:

- The invention of artificial lighting was used to increase work from daylight hours (about 12 hours a day) to as many as 16 hours a day.
- Mealtimes and breaks were shortened to only a few minutes each day.
- Holidays and days off were eliminated.
- Clocks at factories were set ahead in the morning and turned back at night to manipulate laborers into working more hours. Workers, who usually did not own watches and who lived in fear of beatings or being fired, could only accept these manipulations.

In the mid-1800s, factory work hours reached between 75 and 90 a week in England and the United States. As a show of how much power employers had, they challenged human endurance by pushing work hours to extremes.

In addition to extending work hours, employers sought to increase surplus value in other ways. They tried to reduce wages by employing children and women instead of men, using slave labor if it was allowed, and moving operations to locations where wages were lower. They replaced workers with machinery that was less costly. In particular, they replaced highly paid skilled laborers with less skilled workers using machines, which resulted in considerable cost savings. Additionally, they increased the pace of work by speeding up assembly lines and closely supervising workers. For example, Frederick Taylor (1856–1915) developed factory systems in which every motion of every worker was monitored and controlled for optimum efficiency.

Marx saw the relationship between capitalists and workers as fundamentally exploitative. First, employers have more power than workers in the market for labor. Employers control the number of jobs, and they are able to select from an abundant supply of workers. As long as there are surplus workers around, workers have to accept the conditions set by the employer. Marx called the chronic surplus of workers the **reserve army of the unemployed**, and he noted that having a ready supply of disciplined, desperate, unemployed laborers was very useful to capitalists. Unemployment helps to push wages down and to keep workers in line due to their fears of being replaced by an unemployed person. Also, the unemployed provide a ready pool of labor if a firm needs to expand the size of its operations.

Second, surplus value is exploitative because if a worker owned the business herself, she would get to keep the surplus value instead of having it seized by the capitalist. Surplus value goes to whoever owns the business (the means of production). But why do capitalists own the factory instead of workers? In the 1800s, most wealth could be traced back to the era when resources (especially land) were seized in the enclosure movement, establishing a wealthy class that in turn became factory owners. To Marx, ownership of factories and businesses was usually a product of the theft of public resources or luck of birth, so he saw the seizure of surplus value as an exploitative and unjustified act. It was this idea—that private property was born out of theft and exploitation—that led Marx to advocate a socialist or communist system in which workers would own and control the factories.

Workers, of course, resisted the extension of work hours, intensification of work, and efforts to reduce wages in any way they could. When workers functioned as individuals, they were expendable and had little power. But when they joined together to form labor unions, they were able to demand changes. Their major weapon was the strike: When all workers refused to work at the same time, they could bring production to a halt. When workers were united and when employment conditions were favorable (a high demand for labor to produce goods during an economic boom), workers were able to demand shorter hours, better conditions, and higher pay. This is exactly what Marx and Engels were arguing when they ended *The Communist Manifesto* with their famous call-to-arms: "Workers of the world, unite! You have nothing to lose but your chains!"

Marx was describing capitalism of the mid-1800s, but it is worth noting the extent to which the processes he described are still visible in modern capitalism. Every year, firms such as Walmart are convicted of forcing laborers to work off the clock (work for no pay). Employers increasingly demand that workers be available evenings and weekends for work. Firms still shift their operations around the globe in search of cheaper, more vulnerable workers. They continue to replace skilled labor with mechanization and less skilled workers. They also monitor workers to keep them on task and working efficiently.

Nothing indicates the enduring importance of the idea of surplus value more strongly than the modern employment relationship. Ask yourself, "When I graduate from college, why will a company want to hire me?" The answer, as Marx noted so many years ago, is "because you will make the company more money than you will cost them." In other words, you will produce profit (surplus value), which your employer gets to keep. If you ever find yourself in a situation where you cost your employer more money than you make them, you can expect to be cast into the reserve army of the unemployed.

The power of Marx's concept of surplus value can also be seen in the major trends that Marx predicted in modern capitalism. These include Marx's view of competition as a race to the bottom and his predictions of globalization, the concentration of capital, and the commodification of most aspects of life.

5.5 MARX ON COMPETITION, GLOBALIZATION, ECONOMIC CONCENTRATION, AND COMMODIFICATION

As noted above, Adam Smith saw competition as a positive force in the economy, keeping firms innovative, prices low, and demand for workers high. Marx, however, saw a darker side to capitalist competition. Marx acknowledged that the Industrial Revolution and the capitalist economic system that sparked it had generated impressive amounts of new products and worthwhile inventions. But the effect on workers had not been the rosy scenario Smith had laid out, with upstanding, moral employers creating better and better conditions for workers. Instead, many workers were worse off under capitalism than they had been under feudalism.

The problem was that competition also put pressures on firms to engage in the most ruthless, merciless practices possible. If one employer found it cheaper to use child laborers rather than adults, other firms would follow suit or be outcompeted and out of business. If one employer spent less money on worker safety and extracted more work out of each worker, that employer could undercut the competition. In essence, competition served as a race in which each firm was forced to sink to the level of the least scrupulous firm in the market.

In a competitive, laissez-faire, market economy, employers could not adhere to their moral beliefs as Smith hoped. Instead, they were forced to adopt the morals of their least ethical, most merciless competitor in order to survive. In other words, Marx saw competition as a **race to the bottom**.

This is another of Marx's insights that still has relevance. To give a modern example, for most of its history, Levi Strauss prided itself on being a socially responsible company that manufactured jeans in the United States and paid its workers well. But in 1999, it began closing its U.S. factories and using sweatshop labor overseas to manufacture its products. As Levi's CEO Robert Haas stated, despite investing tens of millions of dollars to keep U.S. plants competitive, "We can't swim against the tide." In a throwback to the dark ages of capitalism, Levi's factories abroad were accused of exploiting Chinese prison labor, firing workers who tried to unionize, and forcing laborers to work more than 12 hours per day while withholding overtime pay. Levi's factories in Saipan paid workers $3 an hour, much less than the $18 an hour that U.S. workers earned. Although Levi's was one of the last holdouts against using sweatshop labor abroad, they eventually succumbed to the race to the bottom provoked by competitive pressures. They joined the company of firms like Nike, who boasted in the late 1990s that workers in their factories were required to be at least 16 years old and to work no more than 60 hours a week. Evidently Nike considered these employment rules to be a form of progress!

We see many other examples of the race to the bottom in contemporary capitalism. Firms sometimes move operations overseas to escape taxes, labor laws, or environmental regulations. There have been numerous attempts by companies around the globe to bribe government officials so that they do not enforce laws and regulations. The fact that we have had to outlaw child labor, deceptive advertising, unsafe working conditions, hazardous waste dumping, and other unsavory business activities indicates the powerful drive toward the bottom produced by competitive capitalism.

The drive to increase profits is at the root of **globalization**. As Marx and Engels observed in *The Communist Manifesto*, "The need of a constantly expanding market for its products chases the bourgeoisie over the whole surface of the globe. It must nestle everywhere, settle everywhere, establish connections everywhere." The efforts of large multinational firms to establish operations to open markets in China and to gain access to raw materials and labor in Africa, South Asia, and South America demonstrate the ongoing relevance of this part of Marx's analysis.

Another characteristic of capitalist markets that Marx anticipated was the **increasing concentration of capital** into fewer and fewer hands. In other words, Marx predicted the domination of markets by huge companies that would, if allowed, monopolize markets. Whereas Smith hoped that there would always be a sufficient amount of competition, Marx noted that in competition there were winners and losers, and the winning firms would get larger and larger as they swallowed up competitors and used their size as an advantage. One glance at the landscape of modern capitalism reveals the accuracy of Marx's prediction. In each major industry, we see a handful of huge companies dominating: Internet searches and ads (Google), smart phones (Apple, Samsung), breakfast cereals (General Mills, Kellogg, Post), soft drinks (Coke, Pepsi), fast food (McDonald's, Subway, Burger King, Wendy's), pizza (Pizza Hut, Domino's), beer (Budweiser/InBev, SABMiller–Molson Coors), and so on. Some industries are moderately competitive, such as cars (Toyota, General Motors, VW, Hyundai, Ford, Nissan, Fiat Chrysler, Honda) and small retail businesses, but most manufacturing industries are dominated by a few huge firms. If not for antitrust laws that limit the ability of huge firms to get even larger, it appears that most markets would end up being monopolized because of the advantages that huge firms have. Not only can large firms achieve greater efficiency (greater size leads to greater degrees of specialization and lower costs) but they can use their financial resources to buy up competitors or to snap up the latest innovations, staying atop the heap for long stretches of time.

Marx also observed how economic systems tended to shape the values of society. In capitalism, the emphasis on making money affects everything; or, as Marx put it in 1846, "Money abases all the gods of mankind and changes them into commodities." This is the process of **commodification**. Christianity had been transformed from a religion in which greed was considered to be a sin during feudalism to a religion that celebrated greed and wealth during mercantilism and even more so during capitalism.

Even more destructive was the commodification of labor under capitalism. Instead of seeing workers as human beings, capitalists were forced by competitive pressures to view workers as tools to be used up and then cast aside. The brutal conditions of laissez-faire capitalism, some of which were described above, were evidence of the dehumanizing effect capitalism had on the relationship between workers and owners.

Marx developed the term **alienation** to describe how work under capitalism tended to be unnatural and isolating. In previous human societies, people were usually connected to their work as a farmer or skilled craftsperson. They were connected to nature and to work that was usually social, involved a variety of tasks, and could even be interesting and creative at times. Under capitalism, however, work became isolated, repetitive drudgery. **Deskilling** took place, where skilled craftspeople were replaced by unskilled workers using a machine. These unskilled workers toiled by themselves at a machine for 16 hours a day in a dreary, unsafe factory. It is difficult to imagine a more mind-numbing experience.

Even in modern, regulated capitalism, most workers find their jobs to be alienating. A 2014 Gallup survey asked more than 5 million workers whether they found their jobs to be "engaging," by which it meant "involved in, enthusiastic about and committed to their work and workplace." Only 31.5% of employees in the survey reported being engaged at work; 51% were not engaged and 17.5% were actively discouraged. Drudgery, it seems, is a defining characteristic of work in a capitalist system for most people.

In addition to the commodification of labor, another particularly glaring example is the commodification of holidays and major societal events. If you are the CEO of a company that must generate the maximum amount of profits possible to survive, you have to push for new sales in every way possible. One of the best ways to do this is to connect your product to deep human emotions, such as those associated with love or a religious holiday.

The diamond engagement ring exemplifies the commodification of love under modern capitalism. Human beings have used rings as a symbol of unity for thousands of years. But the widespread use of the diamond engagement ring was a product of a particularly effective marketing campaign by the De Beers Corporation, a South African mining company that controls most of the world's supply of diamonds. In the 1930s, only 10% of engagement rings contained diamonds. De Beers began featuring glamourous movie stars adorned in diamonds in movies and magazines. The company emphasized the purity, sparkle, and durability of the diamond as a symbol of a man's love for a woman, and it suggested that men spend one month's salary on an engagement ring, putting a very specific price on love! De Beers later raised their definition of the appropriate amount of salary to spend to two months in the 1980s. The idea that love and engagement to be married have come to be associated with a specific value and a specific commodity is a classic example of commodification.

Another classic example is the commodification of Christmas. Visitors to the United States from different cultures are often astounded by the various manifestations of Christmas under capitalism. Rather than a religious holiday, it appears to an external observer as an orgy of consumerism in which people are told via a massive advertising effort that if they love someone they should express that love by buying them expensive commodities. The modern messages are very explicit about what you should do for your loved ones at Christmas:

- De Beers says, "This Christmas go straight for the heart: A diamond is forever."
- A flower company encourages people to "show your loved ones how much you care with a gift from 1-800-Flowers."
- Godiva chocolates tells us, "This holiday season give the finest to those you love."
- Hallmark invites us to buy their cards when we "care enough to send the very best."

And there are a thousand more examples, all equating love, caring, and Christmas sentiment with purchasing commodities.

It is also worth noting the extent to which capitalism commodifies public services such as the administration of justice. In the United States, those who can afford better lawyers are much more likely to get better legal outcomes than those who cannot. Even democracy has been commodified to a significant degree in the United States, where it takes millions of dollars to mount a political campaign for Congress and a trillion dollars to compete in a Presidential election. More than half of the members of Congress are millionaires. In another perceptive prediction, Marx argued that politicians in a capitalist system would become beholden to the capitalists and that this would limit the ability of democracy to work on behalf of workers.

The commodification and exploitation of labor led Marx to believe that capitalism was irredeemable. Ultimately, given the corrupt nature of political systems and the brutal conditions of workers, Marx predicted that a workers' revolution was inevitable. He thought that a revolution would likely occur during one of the prolonged economic crises that plagued laissez-faire capitalism.

5.6 CRISIS AND REVOLUTION

Not only was capitalism of the mid-1800s incredibly unequal and exploitative but it was also prone to regular economic crises. To Marx, this was a product of the inherent contradictions in capitalism. On the one hand, capitalists are driven to invest in new machinery and new markets, relentlessly increasing the amount of goods they produce. At the same time, they work as hard as possible to suppress wages and minimize costs. But if output is constantly growing while wages are stagnant or falling, the economy will eventually reach a point where a large supply of goods exists but workers have limited incomes to buy those goods. The result of too much supply and too little demand is a crisis of underconsumption. As goods sit unsold on store shelves, businesses are forced to cut back on production, resulting in layoffs of workers and increasing poverty, which further undermines spending and ultimately results in a crisis (recession).

Along with experiencing regular crises, capitalism was becoming more unequal during Marx's day; firms were growing larger and a rising number of independent craftspeople were being displaced by capitalist firms. The combination of regular crises and increasing inequality led Marx to believe that some sort of major change was inevitable. He hoped that a revolt of the working class would replace capitalism with socialism, a system in which the means of production would be used for the benefit of all instead of to generate profits for the elite. Moreover, he hoped that once people became more communally minded and less selfish, they might be willing to replace socialism with an even more egalitarian system, communism, in which all of society's resources are shared equally. In a communist system, people would work "each according to their ability" and they would be provided for "each according to their needs."

This is, without question, an idealistic vision. Like Smith, Marx truly wished for an economic system that would create a better life for all, and especially for those who were most exploited under capitalism.

As workers increasingly joined unions and became more powerful, there was talk of revolution, especially in the most unequal societies. However, as we will see in the next chapter, pressure from labor unions and reformers and the severity of the worst crisis in capitalist history, the Great Depression, undermined the credibility of laissez-faire capitalism and ushered in the era of regulated capitalism. As Marx predicted, the combination of a major economic crisis (the Great Depression) and great inequality did result in a change in economic systems. But the new system in Europe and the United States was a more humanized form of capitalism rather than social-ism. Under pressure, democratic leaders passed laws limiting work hours, promoting worker safety, regulating child labor, and providing a safety net for the poor, the elderly, and the unemployed. Also, encouraged by the ideas of John Maynard Keynes, capitalist countries began successfully engaging in stabilization policies to reduce the length and severity of crises. Additional government spending in recessions helped to put money in peoples' pockets and to put people back to work.

Whereas laissez-faire capitalism was quite unstable, regulated capitalism proved to be more stable, and the gains of regulated capitalism were distributed more widely. The improvement in the conditions of the working class eased the pressures for revolution in the United States and Europe. However, the most une-qual societies that were not able to spread the wealth more widely, such as Russia, Cuba, and China, proved to be ripe for communist revolutions.

It is important to note that Marx said very little about communism and how it might work. Given that he was throughout his life a tireless advocate of workers' power and well-being, it is unlikely that he would have approved of dictatorial com-munism such as the kind that developed during later periods in the Soviet Union. In Soviet Russia, workers were exploited and had very little power and control over their work and lives, much as was the case under unregulated capitalism. In the ultimate irony, the fall of the Soviet Union and the Eastern Bloc was sparked by a workers' revolt in Poland led by the Solidarity movement, an independent, self-governing trade union! Thus, it is more correct to consider Marx an astute analyst of laissez-faire capitalism than the architect of totalitarian communism.

5.7 CONCLUSION

Capitalism spread across Europe and the United States in the mid-1800s as countries used infant industry promotion strategies to develop their economies. However, the conditions for workers under laissez-faire capitalism were abhorrent, sparking strikes and other forms of resistance. It was in this world that Karl Marx developed his sophisticated analysis of capitalism, exposing the contradictory forces within the system that led to rapid growth and development on the one hand and utter desperation and poverty for most workers on the other. His method of analysis, historical materialism, and key analytical concept, surplus value, help us to under-stand how unregulated capitalism tends to work. In particular, Marx emphasized how competitive pressures all too often produced a race to the bottom and how the commodification of labor and other key aspects of society would demean and distort labor, culture, justice, and democracy.

Despite the accuracy of many of his predictions, Marx and his ideas were ignored by mainstream economists, who continued to see the market as efficient and effective.

However, changes in the structure of capitalism made such views increasingly difficult to maintain. With the rise of the robber barons and huge corporations in the United States, the era of competitive capitalism was replaced by a new era of monopoly capitalism in the late 1800s and early 1900s. It was in that period that Thorstein Veblen wrote his famous critique of the leisure class and the monopolistic forces that had come to dominate laissez-faire capitalism. In the process, Veblen developed a very sophisticated and useful economic methodology known as institutionalism. Veblen was followed by John Maynard Keynes, probably the most important economist of the 1900s. Keynes founded the study of macroeconomics, which focuses on the large, aggregate forces that shape an economic system. Keynes argued that the worst excesses of capitalism, including the problem of recurring economic crises, could be eliminated with appropriate government intervention. Keynes was opposed by Friedrich Hayek, who feared that any increase in government power would lead to totalitarianism. We turn next to the rise of monopoly capitalism, the ideas of Thorstein Veblen and the Great Depression.

QUESTIONS FOR REVIEW

1. Explain in your own words the concept of an infant industry promotion strategy. Do you think such strategies could work in the modern world? Why or why not?

2. Given the experiences of workers under laissez-faire capitalism, analyze Smith's argument that laissez-faire capitalism would benefit workers. Which of Smith's ideas hold up and which do not?

3. What are the key components of Marx's method, historical materialism? Explain briefly. Use historical materialism to explain the transition from one specific economic system to another.

4. Describe what you see as the major contradictions, technological changes, and class conflicts in our current society. What factors do you think are most likely to provoke a crisis? What type of economic system might evolve out of the crisis to resolve the existing contradictions?

5. List all of the factors that would increase the surplus value going to an employer.

6. Find three examples from a reputable news source that illustrate the drive by modern employers for greater surplus value.

7. Would it be possible for an employer to pay and treat workers well and still increase the amount of surplus value it takes in? Why or why not?

8. Do you or most people you know find work to be alienating? Explain and give specific examples.

9. Find three examples of commodification that you see around you. Choose different examples than those given in this chapter.

10. Contrast Marx's view of competition with Adam Smith's. Analyze which aspects of their views of competition you think are most accurate and support your answer with specific examples.

11. Explain why Marx thought capitalism would eventually lead to a workers' revolt. Assess the strengths and weaknesses of Marx's argument regarding the inevitable fall of laissez-faire capitalism.

NOTES

1 Source: https://commons.wikimedia.org/wiki/File%3AAddieCard05282vLewisHine .jpg.

2 Quoted in Friedrich Engels, *The Condition of the Working Class in England*, 1845.

6

Thorstein Veblen and monopoly capitalism

The rise of manufacturing and the fall of laissez-faire

By the end of the 1800s, capitalist firms had evolved from small, local factories to huge, national corporations. The development of the limited liability corporation in the United States facilitated that change and led to the era of the robber barons. This era is sometimes termed "monopoly capitalism" because industries came to be dominated by huge firms with significant monopoly power. But monopoly capitalism contained within it numerous contradictions. In particular, it was prone to frequent booms and busts and marked by inequality, with fabulous wealth generated for the few, poverty and desperation for the many, and only a small middle class.

Economic divisions were particularly dramatic with respect to race, ethnicity, class, and gender. Despite the abolition of slavery at the end of the U.S. Civil War, African Americans faced racial discrimination on a massive scale. Women continued to be barred from most professions. And workers in the new manufacturing firms faced harsh conditions and an unsympathetic government. Meanwhile, workers in less developed countries endured even worse experiences under imperial rule by European countries, the United States, and Japan.

During the unrest and unevenness of the economic system of the time, a new approach to studying the economy, neoclassical economics, developed. This approach attempted to be scientific, emulating the approaches of physics and other sciences, in developing simplified mathematical models of economic behavior. Meanwhile, Thorstein Veblen developed a completely different approach.

Veblen focused on the forces in the economy that cause it to evolve and change, as well as the institutions—the culture, legal system, corporations, government, and other patterns of human interaction—that shape human actions in the economy. Veblen incorporated psychology, anthropology, and history to arrive at a detailed and complex analysis of the economy. As the economy experienced fitful booms and busts and as the elites of the era grew richer and richer, Veblen criticized a system he saw as wasteful, destructive, and fundamentally unfair.

DOI: 10.4324/9781315636924-8

This pinnacle of monopoly capitalism came in the boom of the Roaring Twenties (1920s), but this was followed by the worst crisis capitalism had ever experienced, the Great Depression. The Depression was so devastating that it caused a fundamental shift in economic systems and in the field of economics.

This chapter starts by describing the evolution of laissez-faire capitalism from small firms to large limited liability corporations in the United States and the ideas of Thorstein Veblen regarding this society. Subsequently, we examine race, ethnicity, gender, and imperialism in the United States and less developed countries. We then turn to a brief sketch of the ideas of neoclassical economists (who we will study in more depth later), before taking up the ideas of Thorstein Veblen. The chapter concludes with a section on the Great Depression.

6.0 CHAPTER 6 LEARNING GOALS

After reading this chapter you should be able to:

- Describe the rise of U.S. monopoly capitalism and how this system was structured relative to owners, workers, the government, as well as race, gender, ethnicity, and imperialism.

- Explain the approach taken by neoclassical economists and what they were trying to achieve with their approach.

- Define and apply the major concepts developed by Thorstein Veblen: Evolution, institutions, culture, pecuniary emulation, conspicuous consumption, making money vs. making goods, and the vested interests.

- Describe how the Roaring Twenties in the United States created the conditions for the Great Depression, and how the Great Depression created the conditions for a new approach to economics.

6.1 THE DEVELOPMENT OF MONOPOLY CAPITALISM IN THE UNITED STATES

When Adam Smith first wrote about capitalism, firms were small and markets primarily local. High transportation costs and the limited size of local markets created conditions favorable for small firms manufacturing and selling goods locally. A series of factors changed the structure of capitalism in the late 1800s.

1. Changes in transportation technology (canals and trains, followed by automobiles) and communication (the telegraph, then the telephone) made it possible to travel and communicate across large distances, creating a national, interconnected market.

2. New manufacturing technologies (steel, chemicals, engines, electricity) allowed large firms who made substantial investments to dominate smaller firms.

3. Laws establishing limited liability corporations promoted investment by ensuring that stockholders would receive a share of profits, but the most they could lose would be the amount of their investment and they would not be liable for any debts incurred by the company.

4. The development of the banking sector provided financing for large firms to expand, and larger firms were able to borrow at lower interest rates than smaller firms.

5. Large firms had more influence over the government and were able to obtain government contracts, subsidies, and protection from foreign competition more easily than small firms.

6. Once a large firm came to dominate an industry, it could raise prices and increase profits, which gave the owners even more money with which to make investments and buy out competition.

The **ability to control prices** is defined as monopoly power, and the amount of monopoly power a firm has is directly proportional to its market share.

Industry after industry came to be dominated by a few huge firms. In the early 1800s, no company controlled more than 10% of the output in a manufacturing industry. By the early 1900s most industries were dominated by a few large firms, and in more than 160 industries a single firm produced more than half of the output. U.S. Steel controlled 85% of steel production, and Standard Oil owned 95% of the oil industry. Companies used size, collusion (forming secret trusts), mergers (buying out competitors), bribes (to get favorable treatment from the government or shipping companies), and even illegal means to dominate their industry.

The story of how Standard Oil came to dominate the oil industry is emblematic of the robber baron era. John D. Rockefeller purchased an oil refinery in Cleveland in 1862. He then merged with and purchased other competitors, forming Standard Oil as a limited liability corporation in 1870. Now that Standard Oil had a degree of monopoly power, Rockefeller began to collude and combine secretly with other large refineries to raise prices and profits, forming the Standard Oil Trust in 1882. Standard Oil used its large size to demand lower shipping costs from the railroads, and the lower costs allowed it to double the size of the company by undercutting competitors. Once it was the dominant company, Rockefeller then demanded that railroads pay Standard Oil rebates whenever they shipped the oil of competitors, and he required that the railroads share all data from shipments of their competitors, including the buyer and price of the shipment. This gave Rockefeller immense advantages. Rockefeller was also known for bribing and threatening competitors, and Standard Oil officials even arranged for an explosion to occur at a rival refinery.

Other robber barons engaged in similar manipulations. Andrew Carnegie copied the Bessemer method of producing steel from England, built his own huge plant in the United States, and persuaded Congress to protect the steel industry from foreign competition, making him hundreds of millions of dollars. J. P. Morgan bought up half of the country's railroads along with a series of banks and insurance companies. He eventually bought out Carnegie and formed U.S. Steel. As Howard Zinn described it in *A People's History of the United States*, "And so it went, in industry after industry—shrewd, efficient businessmen building empires, choking out competition, maintaining high prices, keeping wages low, using government subsidies."[1]

The robber barons made a special point of crushing any attempt by workers to form unions and to get higher pay and better conditions. As in England, work hours were long and working conditions harsh. Workers responded the only way they could, by forming labor unions and going on strike. However, the police, at the urging of employers, responded brutally; striking men, women, and children were shot with disturbing frequency.

The ruthless behavior of the robber barons did provoke resistance from farmers and workers, who increasingly demanded laws to rein in the power of corporations. Also, government officials became worried about the increasing power of corporations as the size of the biggest firms became larger than entire states. The Sherman Antitrust Act, passed in 1889, outlawed trusts and conspiracies that would lead to monopolies or otherwise restrain trade. However, the law was twisted by pro-corporation courts from an antitrust law to a measure to prevent labor unions from striking, and numerous labor leaders were arrested based on the new law. In a similar fashion, many federal regulatory agencies, such as the Interstate Commerce Commission, that were originally charged with regulating industries eventually were manipulated into helping industries make excess profits at the expense of the public. At this point in U.S. history, the duly elected government was operating almost entirely on the side of business, just as Marx predicted it would.

Despite these problems, the U.S. economy became the largest and most advanced in the world under monopoly capitalism. Meanwhile, the working class was not able to effectively counter the power of the robber barons. Divisions that existed with respect to race, ethnicity, and gender made it difficult for the working class in the United States to unite.

6.2 RACE, ETHNICITY, CLASS, AND GENDER IN THE UNITED STATES

Slaves were introduced into the American colonies in 1619, establishing racist exploitation as one of the foundations of the early economic system. Slavery was immensely profitable for plantation owners until the end of the Civil War. James Madison, instrumental in writing the U.S. Constitution, once boasted to "a British visitor shortly after the American Revolution that he could make $257 on every Negro in a year, and spend only $12 or $13 on his keep."[2] However, wealthy land-owners feared a revolt by black slaves allied with poor white indentured servants. They began giving whites who completed their period of indentured servitude land, money, and greater status in order to separate their interests from those of black slaves.

In the United States, wealthy white landowners sat atop the class structure. Underneath them were a small number of free white merchants and small farmers. Next were white sharecroppers and indentured servants. At the bottom were black slaves. Native Americans were primarily excluded from white society and were thus outside the class system.

Even after the end of slavery after the Civil War, the black population of the United States remained at the bottom rung of society. Although African Americans were no longer slaves, they had no land and no money, so they had little choice other than to work for landowners as sharecroppers: They farmed the owner's land and gave the owner half of what was produced, similar to the system that existed during feudalism in Europe. But the value of the crops they produced was not enough to live on most years, so sharecroppers fell increasingly into debt. In addition to their desperate economic situation, African Americans faced the ter-roristic violence of the Ku Klux Klan, who tortured, raped, and murdered blacks in the southern United States. Furthermore, legal racial segregation established by the "Jim Crow laws" made it difficult for blacks to vote and established segre-gated schools, transportation, bathrooms, restaurants, drinking fountains, and so on. With such a deep history of racial discrimination, most labor unions actively discriminated against black workers, refusing to let them join white unions.

Ethnic differences also splintered the white working class. In U.S. cities, white immigrants from Ireland, Italy, and other countries faced discrimination and ste-reotyping, making it difficult for workers to unite. Gender divisions were even more intractable.

Many women worked in factories, but they were paid lower salaries than men. Almost all labor unions excluded women. Women were barred from many profes-sions, especially the highest paid jobs in law and medicine. Additionally, women were still not allowed to vote. As a consequence, an increasingly powerful women's movement lobbied for greater rights and especially the right to vote, which was finally achieved in 1920.

If we fast forward to today, although there is greater class mobility now, the descendants of slaves and indentured servants are more likely to be members of the lower classes than the descendants of the wealthy landowners. Many Native Americans are still separated from white society. Women today are, on average, paid significantly less than men and are less likely to be selected for top positions in corporations and government. The social classes and race and gender structures at the beginning of U.S. history evidently have had a significant impact on its current class structure. This is partly because the social classes on top have numerous advantages, including better education, health, wealth, and connections, which they use to stay on top. Also, as we will study later, discrimination with respect to race and gender has proven very difficult to root out.

As U.S. workers struggled with their lot under monopoly capitalism, a new type of exploitation was underway in less developed countries. More developed and militarily powerful countries in Europe along with the United States and Japan engaged in imperialism.

6.3 THE AGE OF IMPERIALISM

Imperialism, when **one country gains control of another country or territory**, has happened throughout much of human history. From 1415 to the mid-1800s, European powers gained control of the Americas, India, and the coastal areas of Southeast Asia. A second, more rapid wave of imperialism occurred from 1870 to 1914. Britain, France, Germany, Belgium, and Portugal seized more than 10 million square miles of territory inhabited by more than 180 million people. Almost the entire continent of Africa was part of this seizure. Japan pushed into China and Korea. Meanwhile, the United States seized the Philippines and Cuba and began extending its influence into much of Latin America, dispatching troops to Mexico and countries in the Caribbean 12 times between 1906 and 1929 to shape political and economic structures in a way favorable to the United States.

This era had important long-term impacts on economic development. Most imperial countries structured their colonies or territories to serve their national interests. Their goals were to obtain cheap raw materials for their industries and to find additional outlets for their manufactured goods. For example, Britain destroyed India's textile industry, forcing India to produce raw cotton instead, which was then exported to Britain at low prices. Britain manufactured the cotton into textiles, which it sold back to India at a substantial profit. In South Africa, Britain seized land from Africans and forced them to work in gold and diamond mines. The result in colony after colony was an underdeveloped economy that produced natural resources but little else. This was extremely deleterious to the development of the colonial economies.

Like Marx, British economist J. A. Hobson saw imperialism as an inevitable product of a capitalist economic system. As technology continued to improve, the industrial economies of the world were producing ever larger quantities of goods. But with workers' wages limited, there often was insufficient demand for all of the products produced: The rich owners could only buy so many things, and low-paid workers could not afford to buy very much. In order to increase profits, companies needed to find lower costs of production, cheaper labor, or new markets in which to sell goods. Colonies offered a potential solution to the problem. Hobson's ideas were later developed and expanded by Vladimir Lenin, the leader of the communist revolution in Russia. By the end of the Age of Imperialism, most of the world had been incorporated into the capitalist economic system, though the colonial economies were structured very differently from those of the industrial powers.

In this world of powerful robber barons; rapidly advancing technology; exploited colonies; a working class in developed economies splintered along racial, ethnic, and gender lines; and ongoing poverty and inequality, mainstream economists attempted to develop a scientific approach to the study of economics building on the ideas of Adam Smith. Their approach was based on a view of markets as competitive, stable, and efficient, and of economic actors as rational and calculating (the rational economic man that we studied in Chapter 1).

6.4 THE RISE OF NEOCLASSICAL ECONOMICS

Impressed by the advances in the natural sciences, mainstream economists of the late 1800s attempted to develop a scientific approach to the study of economics. Stanley Jevons, Carl Menger, and Leon Walras developed elegant mathematical models of the economy based on a series of assumptions. They used as the core of their theories some selected ideas of the classical economists (Smith, Say, Ricardo, Malthus) but they incorporated new mathematical approaches, so this approach was labeled "neoclassical" economics. The neoclassical approach forms the basis for modern mainstream economics, and we will study it in much greater detail later in the book. For now, it is worthwhile to sketch out a few key neoclassical ideas to illustrate the differences between this approach and those of Smith, Marx, Veblen, and Keynes.

The possibility of developing a scientific approach to economics is captured by the famous neoclassical economist Alfred Marshall, whose 1890 book, *Principles of Economics*, established the approach still used by many mainstream economists today:

> The raison d'être of economics as a separate science is that it deals chiefly with that part of man's action which is most under the control of measurable motives; and which therefore lends itself better than any other to systematic reasoning and analysis. ... [W]ith careful precautions money affords a fairly good measure of the moving force of a great part of the motives by which men's lives are fashioned.

If we assume that people behave in a rational and systematic fashion, then we can measure human activity using the dollars that they spend as our guide to understanding their behavior. This, in turn, allows us to construct economic theories and models based on that behavior and to test our models against actual economic behavior in true scientific fashion.

In the area of consumer theory, neoclassical economists focused on the idea that consumers maximized pleasure or "utility" by selecting rationally from all of the goods available to them, given their tastes, preferences, and income. Similarly, producers maximized profits by using all inputs as efficiently as possible and by selling goods as long as the revenue from selling a good exceeded its cost. Competitive markets also were seen as behaving in a predictable manner according to the neoclassical perspective, with small firms producing goods efficiently at the lowest possible cost and with any excess profits being competed away by the entry of new firms. Thus, the picture of the economy was of a smoothly functioning, stable machine, with everyone making rational, calculated decisions and with free markets providing the best possible outcomes for society, allocating income to the most productive people and producing exactly the amount of goods that people want at the lowest possible price. (To see more examples of the neoclassical approach to economics, look at the model of the production possibilities curve, the supply and demand model, and the model of firm behavior.) Putting this together, neoclassical economics focuses on **how rational actors in competitive markets determine incomes and the prices and quantities of goods and services through the interaction of supply and demand**.

At its best, when all of the assumptions of the models hold, neoclassical economics can be extremely useful. When markets are sufficiently competitive we

FIGURE 6.1 Thorstein Veblen (1857–1929).

can use the supply and demand model to predict how prices and quantities will change in response to variations in consumer demand, producer costs, or government policies. This gives us powerful tools to predict how various factors will affect particular markets.

However, some economists found the neoclassical view of the economy to be a far cry from the robber baron capitalism of the late 1800s. Thorstein Veblen, pictured in Figure 6.1, developed an approach to economics that emphasized power structures, culture, and change. Veblen saw little chance of a workers' movement overthrowing capitalism, as Marx had envisioned. Nonetheless, like Smith and Marx before him, Veblen sought to understand the underlying workings of capitalism and, in the process, to develop an economic system that would lead to a fuller unfolding of human life.

6.5 VEBLEN ON EVOLUTION AND INSTITUTIONS

One of the most important aspects of Veblen's analysis was his methodology—his approach to the study of economics. When Veblen looked around him, he saw an economic system that was dynamic and constantly changing. Whereas Smith and Marx saw certain "laws" governing how a capitalist economy worked, Veblen saw a world in which the patterns were constantly shifting. To Veblen, anyone who adopted a rigid view of the economy and assumed the future would always work the same as the past was doomed to failure. Instead, Veblen adopted an **evolutionary** approach, studying the forces causing the economy to change (or resist change) over time. Veblen believed that economists should analyze the key processes that shape the economy and economic behavior. For example, consumers' behaviors are shaped by biological needs (for food and shelter, procreation, etc.), cultural factors (the need to fit in and succeed in a particular society), industrial factors (competition or the lack of it in various industries, advertising and other media, etc.), government structures (the system of law, regulation, and taxation), and more.

But if the economy is constantly changing and if consumers and firms are constantly buffeted by a variety of factors that affect their behavior, what should economists focus on? To Veblen, the answer was to study institutions, which, as noted in Chapter 2, are **the organizations, social structures, rules, and habits that structure human interactions and the economy**. Once we understand the major institutions in a society, we should have a good grasp of the forces that are promoting and resisting change, which will allow us to analyze the evolution of the economy. The result of Veblen's unique approach was the founding of institutional economics, based on the following core ideas:

1. Institutions are the key factors shaping an economy and should be the primary focus of economists.

2. The economy is constantly changing, and studying how those changes are shaped by technology and key institutions (culture, power structures, and so on) gives us the best possible understanding of the structure of the economic system, how it is evolving, and how it might be improved with effective government policy.

3. Humans are social beings whose behavior is shaped fundamentally by the institutions of society and who seek status and power based on their cultural values.

Implicit in this approach is a critique of neoclassical economics. To Veblen, individual behavior is much less important than studying culture and other institutions that shape human behavior.[3] Utilizing this approach, Veblen made a series of penetrating observations about capitalism, culture, and the "leisure class" that still are relevant today.

6.6 VEBLEN ON CULTURE, PECUNIARY EMULATION, AND CONSPICUOUS CONSUMPTION

In his studies of human societies throughout history, Veblen saw a pattern. In each human society, the members strove to fit in and succeed within the existing cultural norms of that society. As we discussed in Chapter 3, human beings tend to be status-seeking and to act rationally within a cultural context. If, due to a harsh climate or difficult conditions, a society prioritized the sharing of food and resources, people would tend to work cooperatively within that society, seeking status by becoming the most prolific producers of food to share. In a cooperative society, those who were selfish were a threat to the community's survival, and they would be ostracized and shunned, making it less likely that they would survive and reproduce. Survival meant succeeding within the cultural norms of that particular society.

Meanwhile, if a society was more hierarchical, with those on top living ostentatiously and eschewing work while the masses did all of the productive tasks, a different set of cultural values would develop. Overt displays of wealth and leisure came to be valued because they demonstrated that a person was important and of high status in that society. Veblen observed that over time societies with emperors, kings, and nobility came to value outward displays of wealth, such as jewelry, fine clothes, fancy vehicles, and vast estates. They also tended to avoid the type of productive work associated with the common laborers. The elites formed a "leisure class" that sought to develop knowledge of fine wines, food, music, sports, and other cultural markers that showed they had the leisure time to spend on developing these skills instead of work skills. Thus, the leisure class worked very hard at displaying that they did not need to engage in productive work by cultivating useless skills and hobbies!

Veblen saw in all people an **instinct of workmanship**—a desire to work at productive tasks and to achieve something in the process. This too was probably a product of our evolutionary history: Lazy, unmotivated people most likely did not survive. However, in hierarchical societies the fundamentally productive instinct of workmanship in all people became perverted into a vehicle for conspicuous leisure and conspicuous consumption. People worked very hard at acquiring useless goods or skills.

These values of the leisure class were then imitated by the classes below who sought to move up in society, and as a result they became the values of society as a whole. This is the Veblenian concept of pecuniary emulation, where **people from the lower classes imitate the culture, habits, and spending of the upper classes to achieve status for themselves**. This helps us a great deal in understanding how consumption habits in particular societies get established.

Let us consider some specific examples of how human behavior is shaped directly by the culture of the leisure class and how culture evolves over time. Europeans wore cloth around their necks for centuries to use as napkins or to keep their shirts closed in cold weather. However, when King Louis XIV of France began wearing a fancy lace necktie, or cravat, the necktie became a hot fashion accessory and, eventually, a symbol of status and respect among European nobility. Once the necktie became a symbol of status, it was adopted by businessmen who wanted to improve their social standing. Eventually, wearing a necktie came to symbolize one's seriousness in business and it became a required article of clothing for men at formal occasions in Western societies, even when it no longer fulfilled its once practical purpose as a napkin or neck warmer. This convention spread to other societies around the globe as European countries dominated the global economy during the colonial era. One can find businessmen and government officials wearing neckties in the summer in tropical Africa! Thus, the only way to understand why men in modern societies still purchase and wear neckties is to grasp how the necktie came to symbolize status and respect in the European leisure class in a particular era.

We can see another example in the origins of certain fashion trends for women which developed in the late 1800s when women of status wanted to differentiate themselves from women who worked in factories. Veblen discusses this in his famous book, *The Theory of the Leisure Class*:

> The woman's shoe adds the so-called French heel to the evidence of enforced leisure afforded by its polish; because this high heel obviously makes any, even the simplest and most necessary manual work extremely difficult. The like is true even in a higher degree of the skirt and the rest of the drapery which characterizes woman's dress. The substantial reason for our tenacious attachment to the skirt is just this; it is expensive and it hampers the wearer at every turn and incapacitates her for all useful exertion.[4]

High heels, polished shoes, long hair, long nails, and skirts became signs of status in distinguishing upper-class women from working-class women in the United States and other industrial societies in the late 1800s. No one could possibly engage in productive work in a factory or on a farm when dressed in this way. Ironically, women's fashions still reflect these trends to a certain degree: Business environments and formal occasions usually are associated with women wearing a skirt and polished shoes with high heels.

Thus, in Veblen's era, those at the top of the pecking order, the "leisure class," displayed that they were too important to work via their "conspicuous consumption" and "conspicuous leisure" patterns. Others then emulated the leisure class, wearing skirts and high heels to work and to important events. This tradition became institutionalized, and it persists to some extent even today, more than a century after it became a cultural norm.

The concept of conspicuous consumption is emblematic of Veblen's sophisticated analysis of how culture and human institutions shape purchasing patterns. Conspicuous consumption refers to **the practice of consumers purchasing and using goods for the purposes of displaying their status and importance to others**. All goods have a "use value" or "utility," meaning that they are useful to us and improve our well-being. But conspicuous consumption goods also have a "display" or "honorific" value. A good example can be found in the difference between a normal watch such as a Timex and a luxury watch such as a Rolex. Both watches have "use value": They tell us what time it is. But luxury watches also have "display" value. Wearing a Rolex sends a signal to others from our culture that the wearer is a wealthy, important individual. Another obvious example would be the difference between an economy car and a luxury car. Both cars will get the riders to their destination. But only the luxury car will get the rider to their destination in style, impressing others on the way. In both cases, the luxury items send a signal to others from that particular culture that the person who possesses them is important and of high status.

As noted above, the definition of what signifies status varies widely by culture. In ancient tribal societies, everyone knew who the chief was, so it was not as important for the chief to consume conspicuously. In modern, large-scale societies, however, people tend to try to impress others by wearing expensive clothes, jewelry, and watches and driving expensive cars. A fashionably dressed person driving up in a limousine or an expensive car signals that someone important has arrived. Social media today involves substantial conspicuous displays. People attend a concert, for example, to listen to the music. But now that social media is a powerful cultural force, some people spend large amounts of time at concerts taking and posting pictures and videos to their social media accounts. The use value of the event, listening to beautiful music, is only part of the experience. The conspicuous display value of proving that you were at a particularly coveted concert or show is just as important for many people.

Cultural values and consumption patterns do shift over time. In Veblen's era, the elites demonstrated their status via displays of leisure, proving to the world that they were not engaged in productive work via their impractical and impeccable clothing and their knowledge of fine wine and high culture. In the modern United States, a different value set seems to be emerging. New studies by Neeru Paharia, Silvia Bellezza, and Anat Keinan indicate that in the modern knowledge economy of the United States, where hard work is prized, people associate busyness with high status.[5] People go out of their way to show and discuss their busy schedules, and this is taken as a sign of how important they are, which indicates a high status in the knowledge sector. Ironically, when the same studies were conducted in Italy the researchers got the opposite results: Participants tended to think those with leisure time were of higher status and those who were busy were of lower status. Thus, the aspiration to be part of the leisure class is still alive and well in Italy!

In these examples, we see that human institutions such as culture have a past-binding, ceremonial aspect that holds onto traditions. However, institutions also have an industrial, technological aspect that promotes change. This dualistic character is readily apparent in the fundamental contrast that often manifests in capitalism between making money and making a useful product that enhances human well-being.

6.7 MAKING MONEY VS. MAKING GOODS

Veblen observed a conflict that often existed in capitalist businesses between making money and money goods. The productive aspect of capitalist businesses occurred when they sought to provide a high-quality product that consumers needed at the best possible price. The pursuit of newer technologies to reduce costs and the invention of new, useful products also stemmed from this productive impulse. This side of capitalism was beneficial. Businesses' investments in new technologies after the Civil War ushered in the U.S. Industrial Revolution, developing entirely new industries such as automobiles, telephones, photography, and electricity. These products were often invented by individuals, but it was large-scale businesses engaging in mass production that made these products affordable to the common people.

However, the useful, industrial side of capitalism is often countered by the focus on making money. Businesses could increase profits by eliminating competition or by manipulating consumers via questionable marketing and advertising practices. In the robber baron era, Veblen thought that too much business activity was devoted to wasteful and destructive activities, which he called **industrial sabotage**, and too little was spent on productive efforts. Businesses during the monopoly capitalism era were relentless in colluding (forming "trusts" to fix prices and reduce competition), merging, or using other means to stomp out competition.

They bribed or manipulated politicians to get subsidies, prevented foreign competition from entering the market, and kept wages low. In addition to the focus on keeping prices high by reducing competition and wages low by clamping down on workers, companies engaged in deceptive advertising.

Prior to government regulations, advertising was often misleading or dishonest. Post Foods Company advertised that Grape-Nuts cereal would cure malaria, heart disease, appendicitis, and other maladies and that it would straighten teeth. Early pharmaceutical companies sold cocaine and opium as elixirs that could cure cancer or as cough remedies, fostering drug addiction in the process. Coca-Cola was developed originally as a "medicine" containing cocaine and caffeine (from kola nuts) that, according to its creator, would cure indigestion, headaches, impotence, and other health problems. These efforts highlight a potentially significant flaw with capitalism: Firms may be able to increase their profits more via manipulative advertising than they can by producing a good product at a low price. This encourages firms to focus more on advertising and marketing than on the product they are producing.

A quick look around the U.S. economy indicates that these opposing forces—making a good product vs. making money—are still a feature of modern capitalism. Each year firms improve old products and invent useful products or new methods for producing existing products for a lower cost. From 2000 to 2019, firms invented or refined numerous products, including the smart phone and mobile broadband, social media websites, tablets (iPads, Kindles), electric and hybrid cars, GPS navigation systems, robots for surgery and manufacturing, smart devices of all types controlled via voice commands, artificial limbs and medical devices, lifesaving drugs, and many more. The ability of capitalist firms to innovate continues unabated.

Unfortunately, there are also many examples of firms prioritizing making money over making a good product. Firms change the styles, colors, packaging, or outward design of their products to manipulate consumers into thinking they should purchase the latest versions instead of living with the ones they have. For example, some clothing firms, including Zara and Forever 21, are now churning out new styles every week ("fast fashion") so that consumers keep purchasing new clothes that they do not need in order to stay up with the latest trends. Car companies change models almost every year, so consumers keep buying new models instead of keeping their cars for the normal life span of more than ten years.

Companies still engage in deceptive or manipulative advertising. Kellogg advertised that Rice Krispies could boost your immune system and Mini-Wheats could make you smarter, making unsubstantiated claims that harken back to the snake oil salesmen of old. Fortunately, we now have laws, enforced by the Federal Trade Commission, that prevent such distortions, and Kellogg was forced to pay fines and compensate consumers for making unsubstantiated health claims.

As a result, most modern advertising is much subtler now, and companies concentrate on manipulating cultural norms and pecuniary emulation to increase sales. Companies sell an image of their product that connects with our cultural values rather than emphasizing the product's practical and useful characteristics. SUV companies show their cars driving up mountains and across rugged terrain, cultivating an image of freedom and adventure even though the vast majority of SUV owners will never drive their vehicle off-road. Marketing to teenagers shows people having fun, fitting in, and being "cool" when they buy certain products.

Companies even work hard to reshape cultural norms to sell more stuff. When Miller Lite was developed in the 1970s, the company could not persuade men to buy a "diet" beer, which was seen as a product for women. To break through this cultural barrier and reach men, who are the main consumers of beer, Miller started featuring macho men (often professional athletes), usually surrounded by beautiful women, in their commercials. Their advertising investment worked, doubling sales and making it socially acceptable for men to drink light beer. This has been so successful that the main beer consumed on many college campuses today is a lite beer such as Natural "Natty" Light, which is the favorite on the campus of Bucknell University where I teach.

In all of these cases, advertisers are playing on the basic human tendency to engage in pecuniary emulation of those who are successful. It is no accident that celebrities are featured prominently in most ads or that the message of many commercials is that you will appear to be more successful if you buy a particular item.

Similar to the monopoly capitalism era, we also see regular mergers and acquisitions as large firms preserve their dominance of industries by reducing competitive pressures. Apple, Facebook, Amazon, and Google are famous for buying up patents and small companies with new ideas who operate in their markets, in the process ensuring their continued market dominance.

Additionally, firms continue to curry favor with the government. In the United States, firms and their executives donate vast sums of money to the campaigns of candidates *from both political parties* to ensure that they will receive favorable treatment no matter who wins. If any candidate seems likely to question the status quo, businesses donate huge amounts of money to the competitor. In this way, firms can continue to dominate the economy even if they are not efficiently producing good products. The ability of the dominant powers in a society to resist productive change was one of the worst characteristics of a society to Veblen.

Veblen objected to the domination of the economy by a small group of political and economic elites. Veblen called this group the vested interests, because **their goal as the group dominating society is to preserve the status quo that they benefit from**. Their focus is to resist any changes that would displace them from their privileged position atop the social structure. This means preventing new competition in the markets that they dominate via mergers, collusion, and threats, and using their power and influence to manipulate the government to do what they want. In Veblen's view, the vested interests tend to impede progress and distort the allocation of resources, preventing the economy from functioning as efficiently as it might otherwise.

Veblen's core ideas—that the economy is structured primarily for the benefit of the few rather than the many and that it was deeply inefficient due to industrial sabotage, conspicuous consumption, and other wasteful activities—had little influence on the economics profession of his era. Veblen's call to rein in the powers of the vested interests on behalf of the common people went unheeded. As the monopoly capitalist era proceeded, it was subject to vast economic fluctuations, and inequality exploded to levels never before seen in the United States.

6.8 THE MANUFACTURING BOOM AND THE ROARING TWENTIES

From 1900 to 1929, the U.S. economy grew rapidly alongside the rising power and influence of large corporations. The development of electric power drove a huge expansion in manufacturing, which also fed on the large influx of immigrants from Europe and resulted in a significant increase in urbanization. Figure 6.2 shows the dramatic increase in production that occurred in various manufacturing industries. Manufacturing output nearly tripled during this period.

Some of these increases in production were driven by new inventions in manufacturing, in particular, the assembly line. Henry Ford pioneered the assembly line and began making large numbers of the Model T car in 1908. Despite the difficult working conditions, Ford was able to keep his workers by paying them $5 a day, more than twice the going wage rate of $2.25. Also, with the higher wages his workers were better able to afford the cars that they were producing.

The advent of World War I further stimulated production in the United States and cemented the role of the United States as the dominant manufacturing power. Following a short recession after the war, the economy boomed with an explosion in mass-produced consumer goods such as cars and appliances. But the economic growth was extremely uneven and unequal. From 1900 to 1929, the United States experienced eight recessions, though they were usually short in duration. (The modern U.S. economy typically experiences one recession every ten years.) During

Textiles and apparel	158%
Metals	364%
Steel products	365%
Paper	420%
Chemicals	483%
Printing and publishing	500%
Petroleum and coal	980%
Transportation equipment	1220%
All manufacturing	273%

FIGURE 6.2 Table showing increases in manufacturing production, 1899–1929.

the rapid growth of the Roaring Twenties, inequality rose to unprecedented levels. One useful way to measure inequality is to look at the share of national income that goes to the richest 1% of the population. Figure 6.3 shows that, in 1920, the richest 1% of the U.S. population made 14.8% of the country's income. By 1928, that amount had grown to 23.9%.

Inequality can be a major problem for an economy in that it can result in macroeconomic instability. On average, rich people save much more than poor people. When more income goes to those at the top rather than those at the bottom, the result is more savings and less spending on goods. Unless the increase in savings is invested (spent on investment goods such as machines and factories), there will be a shortage of demand (purchases of goods) and the economy will spiral into a recession. Businesses that aren't selling all of their goods lay off workers, which reduces incomes further, causing spending to decline even more. What we know from economic history is that the savings of the richest 1% is usually invested in sufficient quantities when investors are confident about that future of the economy, but when investors get spooked for some reason, investment falls below the amount of savings and the economy enters a recession.

In general, the government of the day took a pro-business, laissez-faire approach. In many locations, the Progressive Movement during this era succeeded in making small changes to the economy for the benefit of workers, such as factory inspections to improve worker treatment and safety; public utilities commissions

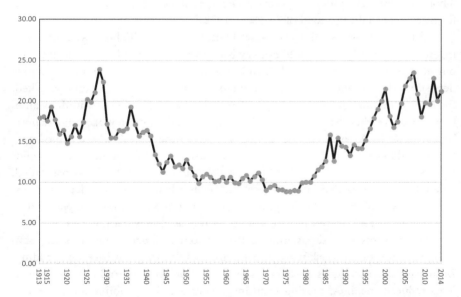

FIGURE 6.3 Income share of the top 1% in the United States, 1913–2014. Source: Saez, "Striking It Richer: The Evolution of Top Incomes in the United States," June 25, 2015. https://eml.berkeley.edu/~saez/saez-UStopinco mes-2014.pdf, accessed July 26, 2021.

to limit the pricing of train travel, streetcars, water, and gas; and public health bureaus to address issues of housing, food safety, and disease. At the national level, repeated crises, and especially the Panic of 1907, led to the creation of the Federal Reserve, the U.S. national bank, to control the money and banking system. But the economy remained mostly unregulated until the Great Depression.

6.9 THE GREAT DEPRESSION AND THE FALL OF LAISSEZ-FAIRE

As the economy boomed during the 1920s, very few people recognized the increasingly fragile nature of the economic system. The 1920s saw a doubling of consumer debt, including mortgages for houses as well as installment debt for purchases of cars and appliances. At the same time, investors increasingly bought stocks with borrowed money, called "buying on the margin." Investors were only required to put a 10% down payment on their stock purchases. The increased demand for stocks and the boom of the 1920s caused stock markets to soar. The stock market doubled in 1928 alone! But a bubble based on debt can pop at any time when investors realize that their investments are not safe.

On October 23, 1929, the stock market started to fall toward the day's end, especially in automobile stocks. As one investor after another panicked, it fell faster and faster, dropping 13% on October 28th and 12% more on October 29th. Though there were some temporary recoveries, stock prices continued declining for three years, falling a total of 73.4% by 1932.

As the stock prices fell, banks started failing. People who borrowed money to invest in the stock market could not pay back their loans, and banks started to run out of money. When a few banks had lost so much that they were unable to give depositors their money when they wanted to withdraw it, depositors panicked. Even those depositors whose money was in stable banks decided to withdraw all of their deposits rather than worry that they might lose their money like other depositors at other banks had. The result was a "run on the bank," where banks, who had loaned out most of the money of their depositors, could not meet the demands for cash withdrawals. By 1933, 11,000 of the country's 25,000 banks had failed. There was no federal deposit insurance yet, so when banks failed the depositors lost their money. This resulted in a significant decline in the U.S. money supply and an increase in the real interest rate of more than 10% as money became scarce.

These events were devastating to the economy. As people saw their life savings evaporate in the stock market or in failed banks, they cut back on spending. Businesses saw their sales plummet, so they laid off workers and cut investment. This reduced incomes, causing even more decreases in spending and more layoffs and declines in investment. The decline in consumer demand caused prices for farmers to plunge, driving thousands bankrupt. More than 85,000 businesses closed, and unemployment reached an astounding 25%. Unemployment insurance and welfare programs did not exist at the time, so people became desperate. Some starved, and others depended on charities, begging, or picking through garbage dumps for food. U.S. National Income fell from $87 billion in 1929 to $42 billion in 1932 and kept falling. The U.S. economy was the largest in the world, and it was closely tied with Europe, so the contagion quickly spread to Europe and then the rest of the world. Soon the entire world was in a depression.

U.S. President Herbert Hoover, and most economists of the day, thought that the depression would pass as quickly as others had. Hoover refused to take dramatic action, arguing that involving the government in the economy would be akin to socialism. Meanwhile, the neoclassical economists of the day kept arguing that the economy would return to equilibrium in the "long run," which would happen very soon. Hoover and his economic advisors also pushed austerity (see Chapter 1). Believing that a balanced government budget was necessary, they slashed spending and enacted the largest tax increase in history (for that time) in 1932, throwing even more people out of work, all in the belief that the depression would soon disappear. The response of the great macroeconomist John Maynard Keynes to this type of argument was a devastating critique of this approach. Keynes said, "The long run is a misleading guide to current affairs. **'In the long run we are all dead'**. Economists set themselves too easy, too useless a task if in tempestuous seasons they can only tell us that when the storm is past the ocean is flat again."[6] To Keynes it was ridiculous to wait for the long run equilibrium, which might take years to come, when we have the tools to end the depression much sooner.

Franklin Delano Roosevelt was elected President in 1932 by promising a "New Deal" for Americans in which the government would get much more directly involved in the economy, regulating huge firms, creating jobs, and providing a safety net for workers. Drawing on the ideas of Thorstein Veblen's students and, especially John Maynard Keynes, Roosevelt ushered in the modern era of the mixed economy in which the core economic system is still capitalist, but the government takes on a significant role in regulating and stabilizing the economy. The era of laissez-faire capitalism had come to an end, destroyed by the Great Depression and the Keynesian Revolution.

6.10 CONCLUSION

The period from the mid-1800s to 1932 was a tumultuous one for the United States. After the Civil War, the manufacturing sector in the United States exploded, driven first by government-led investment in railroads and later by huge, monopolistic corporations and trusts. The first attempts to regulate corporations were undertaken as the Progressive Movement grew but, in general, the government took a pro-business, laissez-faire approach to regulation. Despite the rapid rate of growth, there were warning signs in the frequent crises and rising inequality of the period.

Neoclassical economists of this era devoted their energies to developing a mathematical approach to the discipline that would be rigorous, logical, and scientific. They constructed elaborate models of consumer and producer behavior based on assumptions that all markets were efficient and competitive and all consumers and firms were rational actors motivated by money. This allowed neoclassical economists to make predictions regarding economic behavior. However, the assumption that all markets would reach equilibrium in the long run became increasingly untenable as the Great Depression grew longer and longer, with markets staying in disequilibrium for years at a time.

Meanwhile, Thorstein Veblen was developing the evolutionary, institutionalist approach to economics, bringing anthropology and psychology into his analysis to understand human behavior. He observed the status-seeking behavior common to human societies and noted how conspicuous consumption and conspicuous leisure had become the markers of respectability in the United States, demonstrating to the outside world the status and importance of a person.

Recent trends in economics demonstrate the ongoing importance of Veblen's methodology. Mainstream economists have increasingly been incorporating institutions into their analysis. Marxian economists have moved away from deterministic attitudes toward capitalism to a more evolutionary perspective. Thus, Veblen's contributions to the field are significant and enduring, as are those of John Maynard Keynes, whose ideas we take up next.

- -

QUESTIONS FOR REVIEW

1. How was the era of monopoly capitalism different from the competitive capitalism of Adam Smith's era? Does Smith's argument that unregulated capitalism will tend to benefit the workers hold up under monopoly capitalism?

2. How do race and gender interact with social class to affect opportunities?

3. How did the Age of Imperialism restructure the global economic system?

4. Describe how Veblen's "evolutionary" approach to economics differs from the approaches of Smith, Marx, and neoclassical economics.

5. Describe the role of the leisure class, conspicuous consumption, and pecuniary emulation in the economy. Apply the concepts of conspicuous consumption and pecuniary emulation to the modern world, including examples from your community or university.

6. Define what Veblen means by conspicuous consumption. Make a list of at least three items that people in your community or university seem to purchase more for the purposes of conspicuous consumption than for the usefulness of the item. Briefly explain why you chose these particular items. Do not use examples already given in this book.

7. Why does Veblen distinguish between making money (via industrial sabotage) vs. making goods? Explain briefly.

8. Why does Veblen think that culture is important in understanding human behavior? Explain.

9. How did the "Roaring Twenties" set the stage for the Great Depression? How did the Great Depression create the conditions for the Keynesian Revolution in economics?

10. Veblen focused on institutions and how those institutions tend to persist over time, largely due to the forces of culture and the power of the vested interests to resist change. But these institutions also evolve. Using Veblen's approach, analyze the persistence and evolution of one of the following factors over time: (a) Racial inequality, (b) gender inequality, (c) class inequality, (d) domination of the economy by large corporations, or (e) domination of the global economy by the former imperial powers.

NOTES

1 Howard Zinn, *A People's History of the United States*, Abridged Teaching Edition (The New Press, New York, 2003), p. 190.

2 Ibid., p. 33.

3 See Geoffrey M. Hodgson, "What Is the Essence of Institutional Economics," *Journal of Economic Issues* 34, no. 2 (June 2000), pp. 317–329, for a broader description of institutional economics.

4 Thorstein Veblen, *The Theory of the Leisure Class* (Dover, New York, 1994), p. 105. Originally published in New York by Macmillan, 1899.

5 Silvia Bellezza, Neeru Paharia, and Anat Keinan, "Research: Why Americans Are So Impressed by Busyness," *Harvard Business Review*, December 15, 2016. https://hbr.org/2016/12/research-why-americans-are-so-impressed-by-busyness, accessed July 29, 2017.

6 John Maynard Keynes, *A Tract on Monetary Reform* (MacMillan, New York, 1923), p. 80.

Keynes and mixed market capitalism

How to save capitalism from itself

In the United States and Europe, a new role for government inspired by the ideas of Thorstein Veblen and John Maynard Keynes emerged, aiming to reduce the worst excesses of markets while still preserving the best aspects of market capitalism—competition, innovation, and economic growth. Followers of Veblen and Keynes worked in the U.S. government to establish stabilization policies, unemployment insurance, Social Security, and other programs to create a safety net for all citizens and to legalize labor unions.

Keynes revolutionized economic thinking by establishing the field of macro-economics, which is **the study of the aggregate forces that shape national economies**. Macroeconomics studies large-scale, aggregate patterns in spending, saving, and investment and how these patterns create the business cycle—**the pattern of booms and busts created by economic fluctuations in market capitalist economies**. Keynes demonstrated that aggregate forces at the national and international levels have fundamentally different dynamics than microeconomic markets. National economies, and especially financial markets, are subject to "animal spirits" that spark booms and busts, rendering the economy unstable at times. Keynes advocated stabilization policy to smooth out the business cycle, reduce the severity of recessions, and create a more sound economic system. In this way, Keynes sought to save capitalism from the destructive forces within it.

As governments began implementing Keynesian policies and regulating markets, the result was the modern, mixed economy consisting of some government and some market influence. Mixed market capitalism proved to be a relatively stable and robust system, generating rapid economic growth and a much less unequal distribution of the gains from capitalism.

Friedrich Hayek criticized this growth of government's role, worrying that it would lead to totalitarianism of the kind seen in Nazi Germany and the Soviet

DOI: 10.4324/9781315636924-9

Union. Despite Hayek's cautions, most Western democracies adopted mixed market capitalism, though with varying degrees of government intervention and varying degrees of success. However, the oil shocks of the 1970s, and the era of globalization and environmental crisis that followed, exposed some of the main contradictions in mixed market capitalism.

This chapter begins by describing the economic theories that led neoclassical economists to advocate a laissez-faire, hands-off approach to the economy even in the depths of the Great Depression. Next, we take up the ideas of John Maynard Keynes in more detail, describing his critique of neoclassical economics of his day and his major ideas regarding the circular flow of the economy, leakages and injections, the multiplier, sticky wages, and other market rigidities. Subsequently, we discuss the New Deal and the government policies that were established in the United States and elsewhere to stabilize economies and end the Great Depression. We then turn briefly to the ideas of Friedrich Hayek and his critique of Keynesian policies and central planning. The chapter concludes by looking at the mixed market economy that developed in the United States after the New Deal and that still exists today.

7.0 CHAPTER 7 LEARNING GOALS

After reading this chapter you should be able to:

■   List, explain, and evaluate the three core theoretical ideas that drove neoclassical economists of the early 1900s to advocate a hands-off, laissez-faire approach to the economy: The marginal productivity theory of distribution, markets always clear, and Say's law.

■   Reproduce the circular flow model of the economy and use it to explain how neoclassical economists and Keynes differ in their analysis of savings and investment (leakages and injections).

■   List, explain, and evaluate the major ideas of John Maynard Keynes, including the volatility of investment, sticky wages and prices, the macroeconomic problems created by wage and price deflation, the multiplier process, and stabilization policy.

■   Compare and contrast the ideas of Hayek and Austrian economists with those of Keynes.

■   Describe and analyze the economic interventions made by the U.S. government from the New Deal to the present.

■   Define and evaluate the effectiveness of an economic system of "regulated" or "mixed" market capitalism.

7.1 NEOCLASSICAL ECONOMICS AND THE IDEOLOGY OF LAISSEZ-FAIRE

The neoclassical economists of the early 1900s held three theoretical beliefs that led most of them to conclude that a laissez-faire approach to economic regulation was always preferable to government intervention. These theories were the marginal productivity theory of distribution, markets always clear (supply equals demand, along with the "invisible hand"), and Say's law. We take each of these up below.

1. **The** marginal productivity theory of distribution: **The neoclassical theory that people are paid exactly what they are worth based on their marginal productivity under a competitive, capitalist economic system**

   This theory assumes that there are no power imbalances, so no exploitative relationships exist. The implications of this theory are important to understand. Because all markets are assumed to be fully competitive, workers should always have multiple employers trying to hire them, and employers should always have multiple workers to choose from. In essence, workers are assumed to have as much bargaining power as their bosses. Under such conditions, a worker will end up getting paid exactly what they are worth based on how productive they are. If a worker is particularly productive (a high marginal productivity), many employers will bid for their services and their wages will be high. If a worker is less productive (a low marginal productivity), they will be paid a lower wage in a competitive marketplace. Also, another assumption behind this theory was that everyone had equal access to education and opportunities, so it did not matter if someone was well connected. If this theory holds true, then the government should never take steps to reduce inequality, because that would mean taking money from highly productive people and giving it to less productive people, reducing the efficiency of the economy. Thus, despite the exploding inequality of the 1920s, no efforts were made to equalize incomes.

2. Markets always clear: **The neoclassical theory that supply always equals demand in all markets, so the invisible hand of the market always allocates resources efficiently**

   If all markets are competitive and there is easy entry and exit of firms, then prices will always adjust to eliminate any surplus or shortage. If there is a glut of goods produced, then the prices of those goods will fall, causing consumers to buy more and eliminating the glut. So, the surplus of goods in a depression will be eliminated once prices of goods fall, which causes consumers to buy more of them. If there is unemployment, otherwise known as a surplus of laborers, unemployment will disappear as soon as wages fall because then firms will hire more workers and the surplus will be eliminated. According to this theory, the only possible reason for unemployment was if workers demanded higher wages than they were entitled to. Edwin Cannan, President of the Royal Economic Society in England, put it this way in 1932: "General unemployment appears when asking too much is a general phenomenon. ... [T]he world ... should learn to submit to declines of money-incomes without squealing."[1] Neoclassical economists saw no need to intervene in the economy to help the unemployed or producers. Any government intervention was seen as reducing the efficiency of the market mechanism: Capitalist markets were seen as the ideal, rational, and efficient way to allocate society's resources.

3. **Say's law**: **Supply creates its own demand, and savings is always equal to investment**

    As we saw in Chapter 4, Say's law posits that in the act of supplying products firms generate income. Because every penny a firm earns in revenue is income for someone—either the workers, suppliers, or owners—there is always enough income generated to purchase all of the goods produced. Also, any amount of income that people save will automatically be invested. When people save money, they put it in banks. The banks need to loan that money out to make a profit, so they offer loans at favorable interest rates. Businesses looking to expand their operations and consumers desiring more goods borrow from banks, and when they spend the money they borrowed, the money in banks has been returned to the economy and the circular flow is complete. Any time there is a decline in spending and an increase in savings, perhaps because consumers are pessimistic after a stock market crash, there will be a larger amount of money in banks, which in turn causes the banks to reduce interest rates, which then stimulates investment and consumption spending, eliminating any problems created by the original decline in spending. There is always exactly enough demand to buy all the goods that are supplied. This is the famous "Circular Flow Model of the Economy," depicted in Figure 7.1.

Recall that in the circular flow model, firms produce goods and services, which they sell to consumers and to other businesses (businesses purchase capital goods, such as machinery and equipment). Every dollar of income that the producers generate when they sell goods and services becomes income for somebody: Firms pay wages to workers hired in labor markets, they pay rent on land to landowners in real estate markets, and they pay interest to banks, dividends to shareholders, and profits to owners in capital (financial) markets. What do households do with the income they earn? They either spend it, in the form of consumer spending on goods and services, or they save it, putting their money in banks. The money placed in banks is then loaned out to businesses for purchases of capital goods or to consumers for the purchase of consumer durables (houses, cars, and appliances), putting the money back into the economy. Note that businesses' purchases of capital goods and consumer purchases of durable goods are considered to by physical investment.

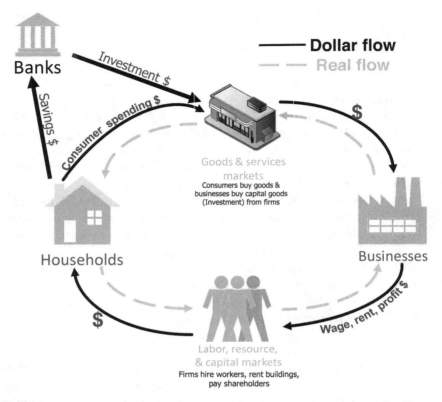

Dollar flow

Real flow

Banks

Investment $

Savings $

Consumer spending $

Goods & services
markets
Consumers buy goods &
businesses buy capital goods
(Investment) from firms

$

Households

Businesses

$

Wage, rent, profit $

Labor, resource,
& capital markets
Firms hire workers, rent buildings,
pay shareholders

FIGURE 7.1 The circular flow model of the economy, with savings and investment.

According to Say's law, all of the money that is taken out of the economy in the form of savings is put back into the economy in the form of investment.

7.2 THE MACROECONOMIC REVOLUTION OF JOHN MAYNARD KEYNES

John Maynard Keynes (1883–1946), pictured in Figure 7.2,[2] was born in Cambridge, England. His father was a well-known economist, and he studied with the famous neoclassical economist Alfred Marshall at Cambridge. Even early in his career, he demonstrated extraordinary sophistication and foresight in his analysis. In his famous book, *The Economic Consequences of the Peace* (1919), he predicted that the harsh financial conditions imposed on Germany after World War I, requiring it to pay more than 80% of gross domestic product (GDP) in reparations, would cause impoverishment and starvation and would eventually lead to another war even worse than World War I. The German hyperinflation and crisis of the 1920s, followed by the rise of Adolf Hitler and Nazi Germany, and the advent of World War

FIGURE 7.2 J. M. Keynes (1883–1946).

II in 1939, showed just how accurate Keynes' predictions were. He was also able to use his knowledge of the economy to make a fortune for himself and for King's College in financial markets.

Rather than depending on abstract, deductive theory based on questionable assumptions, Keynes based his ideas on observations of actual investor and worker behavior. What he saw was a picture very different from the one described in the neoclassical theories of the day.

The first major flaw in neoclassical analysis, according to Keynes, was with Say's law. As you can see with the circular flow model above, Say's law only holds if savings and other leakages out of the economy are equal to investment and other injections into the economy. (Later, we will include additional leakages such as export spending and taxes, and additional injections such as import spending and government spending.) However, Keynes observed that when a crisis hits, savings increases but investment falls as businesses lose confidence, leakages then exceed injections, and the economy spirals into a recession. Thus, the first pillar of Keynesian analysis is the inherent volatility of investment.

1. Volatility of investment: **The Keynesian theory that business purchases of capital goods (investment) depend primarily on expected future profits, which are driven largely by expected sales, and expectations can vary dramatically.** When businesses' expectations change, we

can anticipate large changes in investment, resulting in the booms and busts of the business cycle.

Say's law fails precisely because it does not incorporate this fundamental driver of investor behavior. The stock market crash of 1929 and failures of banks undermined business confidence and reduced consumer spending as people saw their wealth decline. According to Say's law, the decrease in spending meant that people were saving more, and more money in banks should have led to lower interest rates, which should have prompted more investment. But few businesses were investing despite lower interest rates. Why? Because expected sales were very low. With consumer spending down and unemployment spiraling out of control, no sane businessperson would see 1932 as a good time to increase investment.

Recall that investment, the purchase of capital goods, usually increases the size and scale of business operations. Businesses will not invest unless they expect to sell more goods in the future. The main reason for this is that it can take a long time, often more than a year, for a business investment to start earning profits. A business that builds a new factory must lay out large sums of money now for a plant that could take two years before it has been built, staffed, and become operational. When it invests, the business is making a bet that it can sell more goods in two years than it does now. The only conditions under which the business will make the investment in the new factory is if it expects sales to be very good in two years. A pessimistic sales forecast would likely mean that the business will not undertake the investment. This is why business expectations are such an important driver of investment, which is an important driver of the business cycle.

In the Great Depression, as unemployment increased and consumer spending fell, businesses cut their investment even though interest rates were low. Thus, there was no increase in investment forthcoming, as Say's law had predicted, and the economy languished in the Great Depression for years. Savings continued to exceed investment. This problem was exacerbated when banks failed, reducing the money supply and causing interest rates to increase. Furthermore, the unemployment rate failed to decrease, as the neoclassical economists had predicted. One of the main causes of this was sticky wages.

2. Sticky wages and prices: **Keynes' observed that, in a recession, wages and prices do not fall fast enough to encourage businesses to hire more workers and consumers to buy more goods**

What Keynes found was that it took a very long time after the start of a recession for wages to fall. Workers and their unions fought any wage cuts vigorously and angrily, so slashing wages often meant strikes and lower productivity, which were bad for profits. However, employers have found that if they keep wages the same and lay off some of their workforce, the results are different. Workers who keep their jobs in the face of layoffs are very happy to have them. They will work harder and more productively to keep their jobs so that they do not get laid off in the future. In this sense, wages are "sticky downward": They tend to increase in booms when the unemployment rate falls and workers are in demand, but wages tend to stay the same for a long time in recessions before falling eventually if the recession persists for several years.

For example, Leo Wolman of the National Bureau of Economic Research reported that after the stock market crash in 1929, real wages fell very little in 1930 and 1931 and only fell in 1932 in non-union and non-utilities industries.[3] Meanwhile, unemployment surged. So three years after the crash, the Great Depression persisted with large increases in layoffs but only small declines in wages in some sectors. Wages did not fall far enough and fast enough to spark a rise in employment that would have helped to end the Great Depression, as neoclassical economic theory implied. But even where wages did fall, there was not the desired increase in employment that neoclassical economic theory had predicted, as we will see below.

The story with prices is a bit different. Prices of goods did not fall significantly for the first six months after the stock market crash, but then they began to fall quickly. As the economy crashed, surpluses of goods began to pile up because no one was buying them, and that caused prices to fall in one market after another. Prices fell by more than 20% from 1930 to 1933. According to the neoclassical theory of the day, that decline in prices should have sparked an increase in consumer purchases, helping to solve the Depression. Instead, deflation and declines in wages proved to be ruinous.

3. Macroeconomic problems created by wage and price deflation: **Declines in wages undermine aggregate demand and declines in goods' prices undermine business profitability, both of which harm the economy in particular ways**

One of the important economic facts that Keynes established was that, in general, wage declines are bad for economic growth. Neoclassical economic theory of the time predicted that a decline in wages, by reducing the cost of hiring, would cause employers to hire more workers and boost the economy. However, neoclassical economists were only focusing on the cost, or supply, side of the wage issue, ignoring the demand side. When wages fall, workers have less money to spend. When workers spend less, sales fall at businesses, which then lay off workers due to poor sales. Thus, when wages decline, the total demand for goods and services (aggregate demand) falls, which prevents employment from increasing (despite the decrease in wage costs) and harms real GDP growth.

Declines in prices are also destructive to economic growth. In fact, deflation is one of the worst things that can happen to a business. Imagine Henry Ford producing 1 million basic Model A cars for an average cost of $450 in 1930 and being able to sell them for $500 to make a reasonable profit. But with deflation, if the price at which he can sell the Model A car falls 11%, to $445, then he takes a loss on every car he sells. Losses, if they continue, will result eventually in bankruptcy. By reducing the prices that businesses can sell their goods to below what it costs to produce, deflation can be ruinous to producers.

As a classic example from the Depression, the price of milk fell so low that farmers lost money on each gallon they sold. In desperation, the farmers went on strike, dumping their milk and blocking milk shipments of nonstriking farmers to try to boost prices and call attention to their plight. Similar dumping and destruction of food happened with oranges, potatoes, pigs, and other farm products. It is remarkable to think of children dying of malnutrition at the same time that food was being destroyed due to low prices, something John Steinbeck called "a crime ... that goes beyond denunciation" in his famous novel about the Depression, *The Grapes of Wrath*. Deflation was one of the most devastating aspects of the Depression, and it remains a significant problem for economies in recessions. It also is important to understand how the contagion of a downturn spreads from one sector to another via the multiplier process.

4.   Multiplier process: **A respending process whereby a dollar in spending becomes income for someone else, which they then spend, which becomes additional income, and so on, so that a dollar of spending is respent multiple times.** Similarly, when a firm lays off workers and incomes decline, those workers spend less, which reduces incomes at the businesses they usually patronize, which lowers revenues of those businesses, which causes them to lay off workers, who then spend less, which lowers incomes more, which lowers spending more, and so on.

The stock market crash of 1929 caused businesses to cancel investment projects such as the building of new factories, and it caused consumers to cut their spending on expensive, durable goods such as houses, cars, and appliances. These declines in spending reduced the incomes of firms in the construction and durable goods sectors. Those firms, in turn, laid off workers and cut their investment spending. When the workers in construction and durable goods lost their jobs, they too cut their spending, buying fewer goods of all types, which hurt those businesses that they usually patronized. And on and on it went. Thus, one major macroeconomic event, like a stock market crash, can spread like a contagion to other parts of the economy. Fortunately, Keynes observed, crashes can be reversed if the government will engage in appropriate stabilization policy.

Taken together, these key Keynesian insights tell us that there is no reason to expect recessions to fix themselves. Given that the economy can linger in a recession for long periods of time, as it did in the Great Depression, Keynes argued that in recessions, the government should use all of the tools at their disposal to stimulate the economy. This "stabilization policy" meant abandoning the laissez-faire approach and actively using government policy to improve the economy.

7.3 MACROECONOMIC STABILIZATION POLICY

As we noted in the previous chapter, Keynes thought it was ridiculous to wait for the economy to eventually improve, stating sarcastically, "In the long run we are all dead." Instead, he advocated taking concrete, immediate government action to stimulate the economy. He thought the government should engage in macroeconomic stabilization policy: **(1) Increase government spending, (2) reduce taxes, and (3) reduce interest rates in recessions, while doing the opposite when the economy is growing too quickly**.

Increasing government spending was the surest way to improve economic conditions in a recession. The biggest problem in a recession was that there was too little spending (a shortage of aggregate demand): Investors and consumers weren't buying enough goods to keep the economy going at its normal rate. Therefore, the best way to correct the economy was for the government to increase spending because this would directly increase incomes and then, via the multiplier, spark additional rounds of spending. If the government were to spend billions of dollars building roads, bridges, parks, and schools, it would create jobs and income for millions of workers necessary to build those things. Those workers would then spend the income they received, further stimulating the economy.

The government could also cut taxes, giving consumers and businesses more money to spend. As they spend more, this will stimulate income and job growth. Tax cuts should be targeted at poor and middle-class families, who will spend the largest percentage of their tax cut and therefore stimulate spending the most. However, tax cuts tend to be less effective than government spending in recessions because of poor consumer and business confidence. If consumers are pessimistic about the future, worrying that they might lose their job or fall on hard times, then they will likely save the tax cut instead of spending it. Similarly, businesses that get a tax cut in a recession might use that money to invest in new plants and equipment, but if they expect slow sales to continue, they too might save the money from the tax cut instead of spending it. Tax cuts tend to be less effective than government spending in a recession because some (and possibly a lot) of the tax cut will be saved, whereas all of the government project money is spent.

The government should also increase the money supply in order to reduce interest rates in a recession. As the government floods the banking system with money, banks will seek to loan out the new money to new borrowers, which will require them to lower interest rates to entice new borrowers. One of the major problems in the Great Depression was that when banks failed, this significantly reduced the money supply and increased real interest rates, which made businesses and consumers reluctant to borrow for spending on investment and consumer durable goods. Increasing the money supply would help to reverse that problem.

Unfortunately, like tax cuts, declines in interest rates can have limited effectiveness in a recession due to pessimism. Consumers might not be willing to borrow more money for new houses and cars if they are worried about keeping their job in the future. And employers might not be willing to borrow money to finance new investment purchases of plants and equipment if they expected slow sales to continue in the future. There is no guarantee that lowering interest rates will spark significant increases in investment and consumer spending.

The best possible way to combat a recession would be to enact all three policies, increasing spending, reducing taxes, and reducing interest rates so that every possible lever is used to stimulate the economy. In fact, the government did all of these things to combat the recessions of 2008–2009 and 2020. Note that enacting stabilization policy not only requires the government to intervene in the economy, but it also requires that the government run a deficit and borrow money in a recession. Running deficits, however, was the opposite of the policy of austerity recommended by most neoclassical economists of the day.

As we noted in Chapter 1, government deficits tend to increase automatically in recessions, and this was particularly true during the Great Depression. As incomes and spending fell after the stock market crash, tax revenues fell as well, creating budget deficits for the government now that tax revenues were below spending. Neoclassical economists argued that the government should increase taxes and cut government spending to balance the budget. But in cases where the government did this, the recession worsened. Increases in taxes reduced spending, as did cuts in government programs. Keynes suggested the opposite. Even though the budget deficit has increased in a recession, the government should run even larger deficits by cutting taxes and increasing spending. Those policies will increase income and stimulate economic growth, which will then increase tax revenues in the future. In essence, running government deficits during recessions pays for itself once economic growth returns.

Here, Keynes argued for a revolution in thinking about government intervention and government budgets. Instead of running a balanced budget each and every year, governments should run deficits in recessions, which could then be paid off by surpluses that are run during expansions when economic growth is more rapid and incomes (and tax revenues) are higher. The government budget should be balanced over the entire business cycle, not each year. Governments must have the flexibility to run deficits when conditions are bad and to slow down the economy by running a surplus when they see the economy growing too quickly—an overheated economy—which can lead to a bubble and a crash.

7.4 THE NEW DEAL AND THE RISE OF THE MIXED ECONOMY

In the 1932 U.S. campaign for President, Franklin Delano Roosevelt promised to stop following a laissez-faire approach and to take direct government action to end the Great Depression, adopting a philosophy similar to Keynes' called the "New

Deal." He won the election in a landslide over Herbert Hoover, winning by 18 percentage points and bringing a Democratic Congress into office with him. After inauguration in 1933, Roosevelt and Congress enacted 15 major bills in the first 100 days to begin to transform the United States into a mixed market economy. Over the next two years, even more changes were made. The major areas of reform were (1) regulation of banking, financial markets, and the money supply; (2) the creation of a safety net for people who had fallen on hard times; (3) the direct provision of jobs for the unemployed; (4) the establishment of the Social Security retirement program for the elderly; and (5) the creation of an agricultural price support system.

7.4.1 Regulation of banking, money, and financial markets

One of the major problems after the stock market crash had been bank failures. Consumers and businesses lost their savings when the banks failed, which made everyone reluctant to put their money into banks once they had some. Many people hid cash under their mattresses rather than entrust their money to a bank! But the lack of savings in banks was very bad for the economy. There was little money for businesses and consumers to borrow, which stifled business investment and consumer purchases of houses, cars, and appliances.

To solve this problem, the Roosevelt administration created Federal Deposit Insurance, where the government would guarantee deposits of up to $5000 per individual in banks (that amount has grown to $250,000 per individual today). This means that if the bank fails, the government would reimburse depositors for any money the bank lost. In exchange for providing this insurance, the government imposed strict regulations on banks. Insured banks were prohibited from engaging in speculative investments in the stock market, they had to agree to keep a certain amount of cash on hand (reserves) to prevent runs on the bank, and they were required to submit to regular inspections from bank regulators. The government split the banking sector into safe, insured mortgage banks and riskier, noninsured investment banks. The government also established itself as the "lender of last resort," meaning that if a bank ran short of cash, it could borrow from the Fed. And it established the possibility of the federal government seizing insolvent banks and bailing out banks experiencing financial difficulty.

Investment banks and stock markets were now to be regulated by the newly created Securities and Exchange Commission. The SEC established rules and guidelines for financial markets, mandated transparency, and outlawed insider trading and other unethical market manipulations.

The government also took greater control of the money supply—which at the time meant controlling the supply of gold and the issuance of Federal Bank notes backed by gold. By devaluing the dollar relative to gold (and also relative to other currencies backed by gold), the money supply increased. By flooding banks with money, real interest rates dropped as banks sought to find new borrowers, stimulating investment and consumer spending. Devaluing the dollar relative to other currencies also increased U.S. exports because it made U.S. goods cheaper to foreign consumers.

Together, the banking, financial market, and money supply reforms restored faith in the financial system. People began putting their savings in banks and stock markets once again, the money supply expanded significantly, real interest rates fell, and consumer spending and business investment started to increase. Ironically, although many of these reforms were looked at as "socialism" by those opposing government intervention, they were proposed and enacted by conservative bankers who saw these changes as the only way to save capitalism.

7.4.2 The safety net: Social Security, unemployment insurance, and welfare

In addition to its pathbreaking regulation of banks, financial markets, and the money supply, the New Deal established a "safety net" for those who fell on hard times with the Social Security Act. This too was a revolutionary change in philosophy, with the government for the first time taking on the role of insuring that its citizens "fared well," in what came to be termed the "welfare state." The first key component of the new welfare state was the Social Security program.

In the 1930s, the elderly were among the poorest segments of the population. Most workers in that era did not receive pensions, there was no government-provided old age insurance, the jobs that did exist in the Depression went to younger workers, and many of the elderly had lost their life savings in the bank failures of the early 1930s. To rectify this situation, the Roosevelt administration established the Social Security program as a national system of old age insurance. Once workers reached age 65, they would receive a payment from the government based on the amount they had earned during their lifetime, up to a limit. In order to start the program immediately to address the poverty of the elderly, the Social Security program was established as a pay-as-you-go system: Workers and employers in the 1930s would pay a Social Security tax that would go directly to existing retirees. When those workers and employers retired, say, in the 1950s, their Social Security benefits would be paid out of taxes from new workers and employers. There are no retirement accounts within the U.S. Social Security system. Rather, by working in the United States, you acquire the right to a certain amount of Social Security retirement benefits, which will be paid as long as there are enough workers and employers paying Social Security taxes to support you and other retirees.

Another major innovation of the Social Security Act was the establishment of unemployment insurance. This program provides temporary assistance, usually for up to six months, to a worker after she or he loses their job. (In recent recessions, the government has regularly extended unemployment benefits beyond six months when conditions are such that unemployed workers have little chance of finding a job.)

Workers who were unable to find jobs or generate income for prolonged periods of time and who became destitute would qualify for welfare programs, designed to help the poorest, most desperate people in society. These programs also helped to support single mothers and their children and the disabled. During the Depression, because many families were no longer able to support their relatives who had fallen on hard times, the government increasingly took on this role.

7.4.3 Intervention in the labor market: Job creation and labor laws

Due to the massive nature of the unemployment problem, Roosevelt also created new programs to put people back to work directly. The Civilian Conservation Corps employed hundreds of thousands of unemployed, unmarried men between the ages of 17 and 27. These men planted more than 3 billion trees to stop land erosion and beautify towns. The Civil Works Administration, the National Industrial Recovery Act, and the Works Progress Administration employed people to build roads, schools, national parks, and airports or to serve as teachers. Until the United States entered World War II, these programs employed more than 15 million people at various times on a variety of public works projects. The efforts were so successful at job creation and achieved so many useful things in communities that some reformers began to consider the idea that the government should be the "employer of last resort" in recessions, employing people who wanted to work but could not find a job.

Other dramatic actions were taken in labor markets as well. The government legalized the right of workers to unionize and the right of unions to collectively bargain with employers. Collective bargaining occurs **when workers bargain as a group (union) with employers instead of each worker bargaining separately with an employer**. This significantly strengthens the bargaining power of employees, allowing them to get better wages and benefits and greater job security. When employees bargain on their own with their employer, they have little power in negotiations. When the workers bargain as a group, they can threaten to go on strike and shut down the entire company if their demands are not met, giving them much more say in pay and working conditions. The government also established minimum wages in many industries, reduced the standard work week to 40 hours, and abolished child labor. In addition to these interventions in labor markets, the government began regulating agricultural markets.

7.4.4 Agricultural price supports

Farmers were among the groups hardest hit by the Depression, when agricultural prices plummeted in the early 1930s. To alleviate the farmers' plight, Roosevelt paid them to produce less, reducing the supply of agricultural products so that prices would increase and farmers would make more money. Although this policy was condemned by many given that there were a lot of hungry people in the United States at the time, it succeeded in stabilizing agricultural markets.

7.4.5 The success of the New Deal

The New Deal reforms had a very positive effect on the economy, finally ending the freefall that began in 1929. Financial markets and banks were stabilized by the reforms. Unemployment insurance, welfare, job creation, and Social Security programs directly put money into the hands of poor households, and they spent it, stimulating aggregate demand, increasing businesses' sales, and sparking even more hiring. From 1933 to 1937, business investment increased by more than 1200%, consumer spending increased by more than 46%, and real GDP had returned to its 1929 level.

In general, the New Deal was pragmatic and modest in scope, intending to stabilize markets and to correct market failures where they were most glaring—especially in labor, finance, banking, and agriculture. Despite these modest goals, it ushered in a new era of government intervention in the economy, with the state assuming the role of stabilizer of markets and insurer of the welfare of its citizens. Nonetheless, many people were worried about this unprecedented increase in the government's role and especially the 83% increase in government spending.

7.4.6 The Recession of 1937–1938

Despite all the successes of the New Deal and the positive growth that had been achieved, the Roosevelt administration still had not completely embraced Keynesian economics and the need to run substantial deficits and engage in expansionary monetary policy until the economy had fully recovered. Business investment was still 27% lower in 1937 than it had been in 1929, despite Roosevelt's efforts. Even with the fragility of the recovery, the Roosevelt administration decided to raise taxes, slash spending by $1 billion, and reduce the money supply. This produced another devastating recession, with real GDP falling by $5 billion (another example of the multiplier in action). This experience produced an important lesson for economists: When the economy is still in fragile condition from a major recession, it is a mistake to cut spending, raise taxes, or raise interest rates because these can derail the expansion by undermining business and consumer confidence just as they are beginning to rebound. Fortunately, after the financial crisis of 2008–2009, the government heeded that lesson and continued to stimulate the economy until 2017, when the economy had returned to full strength.

7.4.7 World War II proves Keynes right

After 1938, the economy made a sluggish recovery, and it was not until the United States entered World War II and engaged in a massive increase in military spending that the Great Depression finally ended. But World War II did demonstrate conclusively that the government can end any recession, no matter how severe, if it is willing to spend enough money. The wartime spending also proved another of Keynes' ideas true: Running budget deficits for short periods of time does not necessarily create macroeconomic problems. The U.S. government ran huge deficits to finance war spending, but rather than constrain economic development, business investment surged along with government spending. The U.S. public national debt reached 106% of GDP in 1946—the government owed more money than the value of all goods and services produced in a year! Yet, not only did the economy remain strong but this set the stage for one of the most rapid periods of economic growth that the United States has ever seen.

7.5 HAYEK'S CRITIQUE OF GOVERNMENT INTERVENTION

Following the success of Keynesian policy in the United States and other countries where it was used, economists became more and more comfortable with the idea of government intervention in the economy to fix market failures. However, one group of economists, the **Austrian** school, led by Ludwig von Mises and Friedrich Hayek, found this approach to be deeply problematic.[4]

The Austrian economists had much in common with neoclassical economic theory, believing that the individual (not groups or institutions) should be the focus of economic analysis. However, they tended to avoid the use of the mathematical models that neoclassical economists favored. Austrian economists also harbored a deep suspicion of government intervention. With the rise of authoritarian regimes on either side of Austria—Nazi Germany and the Soviet Union—this revulsion of government grew even stronger with time.

Hayek was an insightful economist in several key areas, and his ideas had substantial influence on conservative politicians in the United States and England. Both Ronald Reagan and Margaret Thatcher cited him as a major influence and inspiration. His often-controversial ideas on the business cycle, central planning, freedom, and the efficiency and effectiveness of markets provide an important potential counterargument to Keynesian approaches.

7.5.1 The business cycle

One of Hayek's major disagreements with Keynes was on the business cycle. Hayek believed that periods of overinvestment create a boom and an imbalance between savings and investment. A shortage of savings causes interest rates to rise, which halts investment and leads to a crash. He thought that after a crash, financial markets would return to equilibrium, and he believed that there were no major consequences to recessions. In fact, recessions could be useful in his view by weeding out inefficient firms, so recessions should not necessarily be avoided. However, most economists today reject the idea that the government should do nothing to alleviate extraordinarily high levels of bank and business failures and unemployment, believing that the costs of recessions are too high.

7.5.2 Central planning and freedom

Hayek also disagreed with the idea that government should become a welfare state or intervene extensively in industrial development. He saw the New Deal moving the United States closer to command communism, and he believed this increased level of government intervention was a threat to freedom, which he defined as freedom from government interference. He argued in *The Road to Serfdom* that "planning leads to dictatorship because dictatorship is the most effective instrument of coercion and the enforcement of ideals and, as such, essential if central planning on a large scale is to be possible." He worried that any government venture into planning would ultimately lead to dictatorships, so he resisted public health care, public education, and government economic development programs.

In contrast, Karl Polanyi, who wrote *The Great Transformation* during the same time when Hayek was active, thought that Hayek's definition of freedom would result in freedom being available only for the rich and powerful. Polanyi believed that workers and the nonelites needed government intervention to protect them from market outcomes, arguing that unemployment and destitution are "brutal restrictions of freedom." To Polanyi, true freedom, the freedom to live a good life and make choices, comes from having security, a decent income, and job opportunities. He saw government intervention as a crucial part of creating an economy in which everyone, including working people, has significant freedoms.

In Hayek and Polanyi, we see two sides to economic freedom. In philosophy, negative freedom is the absence of barriers or constraints, whereas positive freedom is the ability to have opportunities and to control one's life. Hayek's (negative) definition of freedom emphasizes the right of individuals to do as they will with their person and their property, free from government interference. This view supports a laissez-faire approach in which government plays as little a role as possible. Polanyi's (positive) definition of freedom focuses on the factors that enable most people to live a good life free from the threat of starvation, poverty, and exploitation. This view supports the use of government intervention to regulate the functioning of the economy so that all citizens can live a good life. When we study modern economic systems, we will see this ongoing tension between "freedom from" government, which is the hallmark of most market-dominated (laissez-faire) economies, and "freedom to" have a good life, which is the hallmark of most government-centered economies.

7.5.3 Markets and information

One of Hayek's most important insights was his understanding of markets as superb gatherers and disseminators of information. Hayek pointed out that markets and prices are perfect vehicles for transmitting massive amounts of information to coordinate an economic system. Consumers transmit exactly how much they value goods and how many they want via their purchases. Manufacturers respond to consumer demand by making goods that consumers want in the right quantities.

In the process, manufacturers send signals to input markets about what materials they need—how much machinery, raw materials, and labor are required to build their goods. The suppliers of inputs then know how many people they need to hire and they can figure out what materials they need to obtain for their production. And so on.

One of Hayek's most astute insights was the prediction that the central planning of the Soviet Union could never compete with the efficiency of markets. Planners, he thought, could never duplicate the sophisticated signaling inherent to markets in order to coordinate an entire economy and were doomed to produce inefficiently. Certainly the Soviet Union did run into numerous problems deriving from central planning. Despite developing sophisticated measures of the input requirements for each industry, it regularly experienced gluts or shortages of a huge magnitude that resulted in delays and inefficiencies.

7.5.4 Joseph Schumpeter and creative destruction

In addition to production inefficiencies, the Soviet Union lagged behind the United States in innovation. A key reason was what another Austrian economist, Joseph Schumpeter, called the "creative destruction" of capitalism. Building on Marx's ideas but coming from a very different perspective, Schumpeter noted that one of the keys to understanding capitalism was the constant innovation and remaking of industries. As he put it in his 1942 book, *Capitalism, Socialism and Democracy*,

> The opening up of new markets, foreign or domestic, and the organizational development from the craft shop and factory to such concerns as U.S. Steel illustrate the same process of industrial mutation … that incessantly revolutionizes the economic structure from within, incessantly destroying the old one, incessantly creating a new one. This process of Creative Destruction is the essential fact about capitalism.

Creative destruction is **the process by which businesses are forced to invent constantly to stay one step ahead of the competition and where creative new industries inevitably destroy and replace older ones**. Certainly capitalism in the United States was much more innovative than the command economy of the Soviet Union. Whereas Russia faced a stifling bureaucracy, firms in competitive U.S. capitalist markets were constantly investing and innovating, although this was less true during the Great Depression than it had been previously.

Schumpeter thought that the process of creative destruction would be too destabilizing for markets, as was the case when entire communities were devastated by the loss of an outmoded industry. Ironically, an adequate safety net can help communities recover from creative destruction and prevent the destabilizing properties of markets from manifesting. So, although Hayek and Schumpeter might not approve given their preference for laissez-faire approaches, modern economies have found a certain amount of government intervention crucial to stabilizing markets, thereby reducing the pressures to rein in markets when communities are suffering from creative destruction, which in turn allows the process of creative destruction to continue.

7.5.5 Market institutions

Hayek also understood that capitalism depends on an important set of supporting institutions in order to function properly. These include the sanctity of private property so that businesses will invest in their enterprises. There also need to be social norms of trust facilitated by systematic and fair laws so that people freely and willingly enter into exchanges and bargains. No one will invest and start a business if they think it will be seized by others once it is successful. Markets also must be contestable—open to the entry of new firms. The government's role, according to Hayek, was to enforce contracts and laws fairly rather than discriminating arbitrarily among individuals. Where market-supporting institutions are absent, markets will not perform effectively, as we see in many cases in less developed countries.

Hayek has had an important influence on economic systems, especially in the United States and the United Kingdom, where conservative politicians regularly cite him as a major influence. Even though most economies today utilize more government intervention than Hayek preferred, his cautions about the need to avoid authoritarianism and the inefficiencies of central planning have played a major role in spurring most democracies to impose checks on government behavior.

Next, we turn to the U.S. economy in the post-World War II era. We will only cover this period briefly to give you a flavor of the broad sweep of U.S. history and the most important trends.

7.6 THE MIXED ECONOMY AND THE GOLDEN AGE OF U.S. CAPITALISM, 1945–1973

The establishment of a mixed economy in the United States after the Great Depression and the global dominance of U.S. manufacturing created the perfect combination for a period of unprecedented growth and stability. By the early 1950s, the United States was producing 80% of the world's manufacturing output due to its advanced technology and the devastation that other manufacturing industries in Europe and Japan had experienced during World War II.

This era is sometimes termed the "capital–labor accord" in that workers and management got along very well for the most part. Manufacturers could afford to pay their workers well due to their domination of industries, and they had to pay their workers well because unions had become quite powerful now that they were legal. The unionization rate peaked in 1954 with 35% of the workforce being represented by a union, and unions were heavily concentrated in manufacturing. Workers experienced rising wages and were able to afford a middle-class lifestyle with a car, a house, and all the appliances and accoutrements that go with a house purchase. The creation of a large middle class in the United States stems from this era, and the spending by the middle class proved to be very good for businesses, sparking growth in one consumer industry after another.

The economy grew rapidly and experienced only short recessions in this era, with per capita real GDP growth averaging 2.49% per year from 1948 to 1973. This was much faster than the per capita real GDP growth rate during the monopoly capitalism era of 1890–1929, when growth averaged 1.92%. It was also faster than growth during the global capitalism era of 1974–2015, which averaged 1.65%. The increase in incomes during the "golden age" was also very equally distributed. Rich, middle-class, and poor citizens all experienced significant increases in income. Rapid economic growth and strong unions meant that workers received a substantial share of the wealth that was being generated. But firms still benefited significantly as record consumer spending expanded sales and profits. The wealth injected at the bottom to workers trickled up to the owners of businesses.

Despite the rapid growth of the era, African Americans and women were still excluded from the best positions. Overt racial discrimination, separate but unequal education and facilities, and lynchings combined to provoke the Civil Rights Movement, led by Rev. Martin Luther King, Jr.. It achieved some major victories, with new laws enacted in the 1960s prohibiting discrimination in employment and preserving voting rights.

Women and minorities were assisted by affirmative action laws, which mandated that, in cases where two applicants for a position had equal qualifications but differed by race or gender, the job should go to the person from the underrepresented group (women or minorities). This helped pry open jobs in law and business that had previously been the purview of white males.

The government also began intervening more directly in helping the poor. As part of the "War on Poverty," President Lyndon Johnson and Congress established Medicare and Medicaid to provide health care for the elderly and the poor, respectively. The Food Stamps program was established, as well as the Head Start program to provide subsidized preschool for poor children. The government also made its first major attempts to regulate environmental damage. By the end of the 1960s, the government was firmly established in the United States as a major factor in markets. However, the stagflation of the 1970s and the deindustrialization associated with globalization that began at the same time would set the stage for a new effort to bring back rapid growth by deregulating the economy.

7.7 THE ERA OF NEOLIBERALISM AND GLOBALIZATION, 1974–2021

In 1973, the Organization of the Petroleum Exporting Countries (OPEC) cut production and imposed an embargo on selling oil to the United States due to U.S.

support for Israel. Oil prices surged from $3 per barrel to $12 a barrel internationally (a 300% increase!), and prices were even higher in the United States because of the embargo. This devastated the U.S. economy, which had become completely dependent on oil to run its cars and factories. The explosion in the price of energy caused businesses' costs to rise and profits to fall, so they laid off workers. The result was stagflation—**stagnation and inflation at the same time**—as businesses laid off workers to cut costs and raised prices to try to recoup the higher cost of energy. A major recession resulted. A second oil crisis occurred in 1979, when oil supplies were disrupted by the Iranian Revolution. This time oil prices doubled, once again spurring a major recession in the United States and other oil-dependent economies.

Meanwhile, in a decade that saw two major recessions, there was also a steady erosion of manufacturing jobs due to mechanization and overseas competition from Japan and Europe. Wages for workers stagnated while unemployment and inflation stayed disturbingly high.

Ronald Reagan was elected President in 1980, running on a platform of reducing government and its scope of intervention in the economy—a return to laissez-faire principles. This was known as the era of **neoliberalism**, in that it sought a return to the liberalism of Adam Smith. Many countries followed the lead of Reagan in the United States and Thatcher in England and began moving toward a more laissez-faire economic system.

Reagan was able to enact large tax cuts for businesses and the wealthy, known as supply-side tax cuts because the money went to suppliers (firms and entrepreneurs) rather than demanders (consumers). The Reagan administration also reduced spending on social programs while increasing spending on the military. The U.S. economy did recover by 1984; however, growth in the 1980s was less robust than in previous decades, and the federal deficit quadrupled in size from 1980 to 1990. The tax cuts did not generate sufficient growth to pay for themselves, as supply-side supporters had hoped. Similar policies emphasizing deregulation and scaling back of government programs were pursued by subsequent Presidents George Bush, Bill Clinton, and George W. Bush. Nonetheless, these administrations did follow basic Keynesian stabilization policy, stimulating the economy whenever it hit a recession, so these actions were not a complete reversal of Keynesian policy.

A recession in 1991 was followed by the tech boom of the 1990s under President Clinton. However, a stock market bubble formed toward the end of the 1990s as investors clamored for the latest internet stock offerings, even from companies that had never made a profit. That bubble burst in 2000, with tech stocks plummeting by 78% and the economy falling into a recession. After a period of modest growth, another bubble formed in the mid-2000s, this time in real estate.

From 2004 to 2007 a huge speculative bubble, fueled by massive debt and unsound loans in the sub-prime housing market, formed. Deregulation of financial markets pursued by Reagan, Bush, Clinton, and W. Bush allowed banks to invest in very risky and volatile financial instruments. When these investments crashed, they brought the stock market and the entire banking system with them, sparking the worst recession since the Great Depression. Fortunately, the George W. Bush administration and, after 2008, the Obama administration, engaged in a massive bailout of the banking system and a significant increase in government spending. Rather than repeat the errors of 1937 and the Great Depression, the Fed kept stimulating the economy by injecting money into financial markets for years after the worst part of the recession was over. Obama also signed the Affordable Care Act, making the United States the last developed country to install a national health care system of some kind. Keynesian policy had returned to the United States, and it reduced the length of the recession significantly. As conclusive evidence of how useful Keynesian policy is, the European Union, which imposed austerity programs on the economies of Greece, Spain, and other poorly performing economies, fared very poorly compared to the United States, which instead injected large amounts of money into the economy.

The recovery from the Great Recession was slow, as is often the case after a major financial crisis. Hoping for a change in policies that would reinvigorate economic growth, U.S. voters elected Donald Trump President in 2016. Trump promised to bring back jobs to the United States from abroad by renegotiating trade deals and by cutting taxes and regulations on businesses. In essence, Trump was promising more government intervention in some areas (trade) and less in others (deregulation). The unrest that propelled Trump to the presidency was also present in other developed economies where workers' wages stagnated and communities experienced deindustrialization as jobs shifted to China and other inexpensive manufacturing locations.

Trump's tax cuts and deregulation efforts had no measurable impact on economic growth. With the advent of the devastating coronavirus recession of 2020, the U.S. adopted Keynesian policy, spending trillions of dollars on stimulus programs to reduce the severity of the downturn. Joseph Biden was elected to replace Trump in 2020, promising to restore the government programs Trump cut and invest more significantly in health care and environmental programs. Around the world, the pandemic and the accompanying recession prompted a return to Keynesian policy to deal with the crisis. Whether this will lead to a significant move away from neoliberalism remains to be seen.

7.8 CONCLUSION: THE MIXED ECONOMY OF THE UNITED STATES

In general, there has been a trend toward greater deregulation in the United States since 1980, but the country continues to use government policy and programs to fix market failures. The United States is a laissez-faire-leaning mixed economy, with less government intervention than most other developed countries but much more government intervention than was the case in the United States prior to the Great

Depression. Keynesian economic policy has been very good for the U.S. economy in general. As you can see from Figure 7.3, prior to 1950, the U.S. economy experienced dramatic fluctuations in economic growth. After 1950, the United States experienced more rapid and steady growth, which was achieved with the help of government efforts to stabilize the economy. A stable business environment makes firms more likely to invest, which drives growth and prosperity.

This type of economic system is called "regulated capitalism" or a mixed economy: **Where markets are seen as worth preserving due to the efficiency and innovation they promote, but sound government policy can improve the functioning of the capitalist market system by reducing or eliminating market failures such as recessions**. A mixed economy relying on markets and government is seen by most economists as preferable to a laissez-faire or a state-dominated economy.

Keynes can be thought of as wanting to save capitalism from itself. In its unregulated state, capitalism can result in lengthy recessions, as well as bad outcomes for workers and the environment. Appropriate government policy can solve those problems. In a recession, the government can spend money, cut taxes, and increase the money supply to pump money back into the economy and, via the multiplier, increase spending significantly to end the recession. If banks are prone to speculative bubbles and risky behavior, the government can regulate them to make sure they behave in a financially sound manner. Where markets fail to safeguard workers or the environment, the government can impose laws or regulations to force markets to address these shortcomings.

As we will see in the next chapter, which looks at modern economic systems, other economies strive for a different balance of state and markets than the United

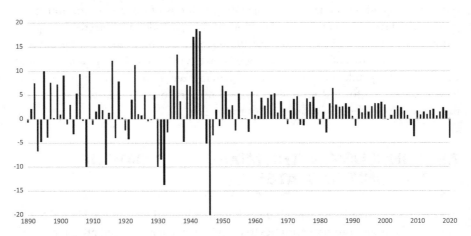

FIGURE 7.3 Economic instability in the U.S. economy: Real GDP growth per capita, 1890–2020. Sources: Our World in Data, https://ourworldindata.org/grapher/gdp-per-capita-over-the-long-run-Maddison, World Bank, and Federal Reserve Economic Data (FRED).

States. The United States is a **market-dominated economy**, striving for the least amount of government intervention possible to keep markets functioning effectively. Even though our government is large, it controls only about 30% of the economy while the rest of the economy is controlled by private sector firms. In other countries, such as most of Europe and Japan, we find **social market economies** where the government controls a much larger share (sometimes over 50%) and strives to manage the economy in accordance with domestic social values. Meanwhile, in **state-dominated economies** like China, the government plays an even larger role in controlling the economic system. All of these economic systems use some degree of markets and some amount of government intervention, so they are all considered mixed market economies, but the mix of market and government can be quite different.

QUESTIONS FOR REVIEW

1. Explain how the neoclassical concepts (a) marginal productivity theory of distribution, (b) markets always clear, and (c) Say's law combine to result in a conclusion that no government intervention is necessary in a capitalist market system.
2. Describe the nature of the Keynesian "revolution" in economics. How did Keynes reshape the way economists thought about the economy? How did he address the major flaws in the neoclassical economics of his time?
3. Why do many economists see the volatility of investment along with the multiplier as the key to understanding the business cycle (the cycle of booms and busts that characterize our economic system)?
4. How do sticky wages and prices prevent the economy from adjusting in a recession?
5. In what areas of the economy do we tend to see the market fail to work well? What government programs have been designed to address those market failures?
6. How would you explain to someone with no economics background why deflation can be a major macroeconomic problem?
7. How do Keynes' ideas relate to those of Smith and Marx?
8. Which of Keynes' ideas do you find most compelling in capturing the realities of the modern world? Explain and give examples.
9. Which of Hayek's ideas do you find most compelling? Which are least compelling? Support your answer with examples and analysis.
10. Compare and contrast Keynes' ideas with those of Hayek.
11. Explain the concept of creative destruction and give examples from the world around us.
12. Describe the evolution of the U.S. economic system from 1920 to the present. How has our approach to regulating the economy shifted over time?

NOTES

1 Edwin Cannan, "The Demand for Labour," *The Economic Journal*, September 1932, pp. 357–370.

2 Source: https://commons.wikimedia.org/wiki/File:Lord_Keynes.jpg.

3 Leo Wolman, "Wages During the Depression," *National Bureau of Economic Research Bulletin* No. 46, May 1, 1933, pp. 1–5. www.nber.org/chapters/c2256.pdf.

4 The founder of the Austrian school is considered to be Carl Menger, who taught at the University of Vienna in Austria in the late 1800s. Although later scholars from this tradition worked and lived outside of Austria, the original label stuck.

Modern economic systems

Market-dominated, social market, and state-dominated economies

The economic systems of the modern world draw extensively on the ideas and philosophies of the great economists. From Smith, we see the widespread use of markets and the tendency to allow firms to compete and to make major economic decisions for society based on the profit motive. From Marx and Veblen, we see the need to check the unfettered power of large firms and to safeguard workers and communities from exploitation. From Hayek and Smith, we see the need to check the coercive power of the state to prevent it from becoming too powerful and bureaucratic. From Keynes, we see the approach that dominates modern economic systems: The construction of a mixed economy that builds on the best aspects of market capitalism while regulating market failures is likely to deliver the best outcomes.

All modern economies combine a mix of markets and government to some degree. Even market-dominated economies, such as the U.S. economy, have a substantial amount of government (state) intervention. And even state-dominated economies, such as China, Cuba, and North Korea, use markets, often extensively. The key to understanding modern economic systems is therefore to grasp the mix of state and market in a particular economy.

In general, we can group economies into three broad categories.

1. Market-dominated economies (MDEs), also called liberal market economies, are **economic systems in which the primary economic decisions are made by private actors (businesses, individuals) in the market. Government and social values play a secondary role**.
2. Social market economies (SMEs), also called coordinated market economies, are **economic systems in which social values take a leading role in directing the economy, usually through the actions of a government that manages the economy in accordance with social values**.

DOI: 10.4324/9781315636924-10

3.   State-dominated economies (SDEs) are **economic systems in which the government is the main economic actor in most major industries or economic decisions, owning or controlling most of the economy**.

This chapter will briefly survey the different types of successfully developed economic systems in the world and offer some case studies of each type. (We consider developing countries later.) We begin by contrasting MDEs and SMEs, followed by a case study of the U.S. MDE and the Nordic SME. Next, we take up socialism and communism, which culminates in a case study of China's SDE.

8.0 CHAPTER 8 LEARNING GOALS

After reading this chapter you should be able to:

■   Define and describe the characteristics of market-dominated economies, social market economies, and state-dominated economies.

■   Analyze, compare, and contrast the characteristics and functioning of an MDE such as the United States, an SME such as the Nordic countries, and an SDE such as China.

■   Explain the difference between socialism, communism, and capitalism.

■   Evaluate the strengths and weaknesses of a market capitalist approach (United States), a guided market approach (Nordic model), and a central planning approach (U.S.S.R.) to economic development.

8.1 COMPARING MARKET-DOMINATED ECONOMIES AND SOCIAL MARKET ECONOMIES

Most of the world's developed economies are either market-dominated economics or social market economies. We begin by describing and comparing those economies and looking at their effectiveness as economic systems in delivering economic growth and human well-being.

In market-dominated economies, most major economic decisions are made by corporations and other private sector businesses. These businesses determine what society produces and how it is produced. The private sector dictates how a society's scarce resources are allocated based on the profit motive and businesses' desire to persuade consumers to buy more of their products.

The government's major role in MDEs is to support the market system by building and maintaining infrastructure (roads, airports, ports, a postal system), providing a fair and effective judicial system that enforces contracts, and fixing market failures when they threaten the functioning of the market system. The major market failures that are usually addressed by government include macroeconomic instability (especially major recessions), poverty and inequality, the exploitation of laborers and the environment, and the lack of sufficient private health or education.

Interestingly, when we look at wealthy countries in the world that have adopted a market-dominated economic system (the United States, Canada, Ireland, Australia, New Zealand, and the United Kingdom), we see that they were all part of the British Empire at one point. The culture and values of that empire, emphasizing Protestantism, self-interest, hard work, and material rewards, fits well with a market economy. In this sense, MDEs reflect a particular set of cultural values.

In SMEs the role of social interests is more balanced compared to the role of the market. Social values often take precedence over market outcomes in SMEs. Some economic decisions are made by markets, especially those related to consumer goods. Many, and sometimes most, decisions are made by society, acting through government. Many services are considered to be human rights, including health care, childcare, dental care, housing, education (including college), and even a job. The government is charged with providing all citizens with these services, sometimes through government agencies and sometimes by working with and through the private sector. In SMEs, the state can also play a role in preserving domestic culture, such as the French government's efforts to protect traditional agriculture, food, and wine.

Although the SMEs represent a variety of very different cultures, they do have some commonalities. Though England was the first country to industrialize, countries that industrialized later usually utilized government intervention to spur industrialization and to catch up with England. SMEs therefore are accustomed to a larger degree of government intervention in determining the direction of the economy. Most SMEs have industrial policies that they use to stimulate economic development in key sectors in order to gain advantages in these industries relative to other countries.

Lest you be tempted to think that one of these models is superior to the other, consider carefully the data in Figure 8.1, which compares key economic indicators of the largest and wealthiest MDEs and SMEs in the world. First, a good indicator of whether or not a country is an MDE or an SME is the amount of its gross domestic product (GDP) devoted by the public sector to social expenditures, such as health, welfare, unemployment, job assistance, and childcare. Social expenditures also go along with a high tax rate: If you spend a lot on social services for your citizens, then you have to raise a lot of tax revenue. As you can see from the first two columns of Figure 8.1, MDEs tend to spend less on social expenditures and have lower taxes than SMEs.

Market Dominated Economies	GDP Devoted to Social Expenditures, 2019 (%)	Tax Revenue % of GDP, 2019	Real GDP per capita, 2019	Growth in Real GDP per capita, 1971–2019 (%)	Poverty Rate, 2017 (%)
Australia	16.7	28.7	$ 57,071	112	12.4
Canada	18.0	33.5	$ 51,589	113	12.1
United States	18.7	24.5	$ 55,670	141	17.8
New Zealand	19.4	32.3	$ 38,993	93	10.9
United Kingdom	20.6	33.0	$ 43,688	144	11.7
MDE Average	**18.7**	**30.4**	**$ 49,402**	**120**	**13.0**
Social Market Economies					
Japan	22.3	32.0	$ 49,188	162	15.7
Norway	25.3	39.9	$ 92,556	186	8.4
Sweden	25.5	42.9	$ 57,975	118	8.9
Germany	25.9	38.8	$ 47,628	140	10.4
Denmark	28.3	46.3	$ 65,147	116	5.8
Belgium	28.9	42.9	$ 47,541	139	10.1
France	31.0	45.4	$ 44,317	120	8.1
SME Average	**26.7**	**41.2**	**$ 57,765**	**140**	**9.6**

FIGURE 8.1 Table showing key data on select MDEs and SMEs. Source: OECD. http://stats.oecd.org, accessed January 30, 2021.

One of the key issues for economists when evaluating an economic system is how well it performs. Column 3 displays real GDP per capita in MDEs and SMEs, and column 4 looks at the rate of growth in GDP per capita over the last 48 years. Interestingly, there is no clear pattern. Both MDEs and SMEs are rich, and both have experienced substantial economic growth (1.69% per year in MDEs, 1.86% per year in SMEs). There is no reason to prefer one system over another based on growth performance: An effective MDE can perform just as well as an effective SME. Where we do see significant differences are in terms of inequality. Because of the substantial amount of money devoted to social expenditures, SMEs tend to have very low levels of poverty and inequality. MDEs that spend less on these programs have much higher levels of poverty and inequality.

Another way to look at the success of economic systems is to consider a broad range of indicators. For example, the Organisation for Economic Cooperation and Development (OECD) Better Life Index ranks OECD countries according to the following factors: Housing, income, jobs, community, education, environment, civic engagement, health, life satisfaction, safety, and work–life balance (Figure 8.2). The United Nations (U.N.) Human Development Index focuses on a subset of the OECD measures: Life expectancy, education, and income per capita indicators. Notice that the Scandinavian countries (Norway, Iceland, Denmark, Sweden, and Finland) do particularly well on these broader measures of welfare, something we will discuss below when we take up the Nordic model. Nonetheless,

Country (MDE or SME)	OEC Better Life Index	UN Human Development Index
Norway (SME)	1	1
Australia (MDE)	2	6
Iceland (SME)	3	6-T
Canada (MDE)	4	13
Denmark (SME)	5	11
Switzerland (SME)	6	2
Netherlands (SME)	7	10
Sweden (SME)	8	8
Finland (SME)	9	12
United States (MDE)	10	15
New Zealand (MDE)	12	14
Belgium (SME)	13	17
United Kingdom (MDE)	14	15
Germany (SME)	15	4
Ireland (MDE)	16	3
Austria (SME)	17	20
France (SME)	18	26
Spain (SME)	19	25
Japan (SME)	25	19

FIGURE 8.2 Table depicting OECD Better Life and U.N. Human Development rankings, 2019.

both MDEs and SMEs perform well for the most part, providing another indication that there are different paths to wealth and well-being.

Next, we take up case studies of each type of economic system. We begin by describing the unique characteristics of the modern U.S. MDE relative to other economics systems. We follow that with a case study of the Nordic model of SMEs. Then we take up state-dominated economies, focusing primarily on China.

8.2 THE U.S. MODEL OF A MARKET-DOMINATED ECONOMY

Having traced the evolution of the U.S. economy in previous chapters, here we only describe the key aspects of the U.S. system as they compare to other economies. The major characteristics of the U.S. economic system include ready access to productive resources, a Protestant work ethic and melting pot of immigrants, early protectionism followed by later globalization, a business-friendly legal system, massive multinational corporations, an innovation system promoting revolutionary innovations, a small welfare state and few regulations, and macroeconomic stabilization policies.

8.2.1 Ready access to productive resources

One of the important reasons for U.S. economic success was its access to human and natural resources. The United States has historically had a large pool of mobile and highly motivated immigrant labor. Immigrant groups included religious dissidents, people pursuing commercial enterprises, convicts, indentured servants, slaves, and waves of migrants from Europe. The United States also had rich land and abundant natural resources, acquired via war, negotiation, or purchase, which were crucial in agricultural and industrial development. This ready supply of labor and resources provided fuel for economic growth.

8.2.2 Protestant work ethic and the melting pot

The United States has a culture that is very hardworking and individualistic. This is often attributed to that fact that many of the early settlers were Protestants who valued personal independence and material success. Later immigrants from Europe, Mexico, India, China, and many other countries also tended to be extremely hardworking and willing to take the least desirable jobs just so that they or their children would have a chance to move up in the future. Hard work is so ingrained into the U.S. culture that American workers put in more hours than most other developed countries, and surveys indicate that social status is strongly associated with hard work. Highly motivated labor facilitates production and growth.

8.2.3 Early protectionism, later globalization

The split with Great Britain in the Revolutionary War prompted the United States to protect its market from British competitors, which allowed domestic industries to develop and sell to the large internal U.S. market. This allowed infant industries that would not have been able to survive otherwise to grow and develop. However, after World War II, the United States increasingly embraced globalization and free trade now that its industries dominated international manufacturing. U.S. corporations moved their operations all over the globe in search of new markets and cheap labor and resources.

8.2.4 Business-friendly legal system

The stable U.S. Constitution and a pro-business legal system provided solid grounding for market exchange. Checks and balances with an independent judiciary tended to keep corruption to an acceptable level and to safeguard contracts and property rights. Civil liberties and democratic rule meant that many citizens had opportunities to succeed and to change the system, although this was mitigated by systemic racism and sexism. Corporations were given substantial power in the U.S. system, including legal standing as a person with all the rights that citizens have, along with low taxes and other forms of government support. As we saw earlier, the U.S. government sided with corporations and against workers throughout much of its history.

8.2.5 Massive multinational corporations

U.S. corporations were allowed to grow into vast, market-dominating enterprises that controlled entire global industries. The typical U.S. multinational corporation (MNC) is huge and very hierarchical, with power and decision-making resting in the hands of the chief executive officer (CEO) and upper administration. Workers tend to have very little power and control, given the low unionization rates in the modern United States and in the countries in which MNCs operate. These huge companies are almost all owned by shareholders, and their shares are traded publicly in stock markets, so their primary goal is to maximize short-term profits to please shareholders. Massive MNCs dominate the United States and much of the world economy.

8.2.6 Innovation system promoting revolutionary innovation

The U.S. government has always invested substantially in public goods, especially infrastructure, building canals, railroads, roads, ports, and airports to stimulate economic development. Free public education and the vast public university system helped to develop a skilled workforce and to stimulate scientific research, which fostered numerous inventions. A 2017 study published in *Science* found that 80%

of high-impact scientific papers (those cited frequently by other scientists) can be traced forward to some future marketplace invention, demonstrating how crucial basic scientific research is for innovation.[1] The strong patent system in the United States, which gives inventors a monopoly over their new product for 20 years, also provides a strong incentive for investment and innovation. The combination of low taxes on corporations and wealthy individuals, along with strong higher education and patent systems, and a hardworking, individualistic culture provides excellent conditions to prompt people to come up with the next big product. The United States is one of the world leaders in revolutionary innovation (inventing brand-new products and industries) due to these conditions.

8.2.7 Small welfare state and few regulations

In general, the United States has the least generous welfare state of any developed country. The most glaring difference is in the area of health care: The United States is the only developed country without a national health care system. Even other MDEs consider basic health care a human right that should not be left up to the market to provide, meaning that millions who cannot afford health care will have to do without it or to depend on charity. The Affordable Care Act (ACA) enacted by President Obama caused the number of uninsured in the United States to decline from a high of 18% in 2013, just before the ACA went into effect, to 11% in 2017. However, there remain political pressures to repeal or replace the ACA from conservative politicians who prefer to leave health care in the hands of individuals and markets.

The United States also does less to address inequality and poverty than any other developed country. Taxes on the wealthy are relatively low, and financial assistance for the poor for housing, food, childcare, dental care, and higher education is also low. Welfare and unemployment benefits are also less generous, and the United States provides very little in the way of job training. This explains why the United States has the highest poverty rate of any developed country.

The United States tends to have fewer regulations on business behavior than other countries, with relatively lax approaches to regulating the environment, labor markets, and food and product safety. The United States has the highest per person carbon emissions in the world, but it has yet to take significant steps to address climate change, unlike most other developed countries.

Note that we are discussing the United States in comparison to other countries. Despite the tendency to have fewer regulations than other countries, the United States still regulates food and drug safety, water and air quality, traffic safety, agricultural safety, workplace safety, and consumer product safety.

8.2.8 Macroeconomic stabilization policy

Though the United States does not intervene much in specific (microeconomic) markets, it does take an activist role in stabilizing the macroeconomy to reduce the severity of recessions and to stave off inflation. The U.S. government spends more, taxes less, and injects more money into financial markets in most recessions. This is very distinct from the European Union (E.U.), which adopted austerity policies that slashed spending and raised taxes while keeping interest rates stable after the 2008 financial crisis. Ironically, though the E.U. intervenes less in the macroeconomy, most corporations and markets in the E.U. are tightly regulated, with strict laws regarding environment, workers, and product safety.

In general, the United States is the quintessential model of a market-dominated, mixed economy. Most decisions are made by private sector firms and individuals. The government corrects the most egregious forms of market failure but does not take more proactive steps. The model has worked well in terms of generating economic growth and a steady stream of innovations. Those successes are marred somewhat by the inequality, poverty, and environmental degradation that are generated in the process. Interestingly, the Nordic countries are also wealthy and innovative, but their success is achieved in a more government-centered economic system.

8.3 THE NORDIC MODEL OF A SOCIAL MARKET ECONOMY

The Nordic model is often referred to as the "middle way" between the two extremes of an MDE and an SDE. The Nordic countries—Sweden, Norway, Denmark, Iceland, and Finland—are considered SMEs because of the manner in which their egalitarian social values inform government intervention in their economies. They are ultimately still capitalist economies utilizing markets for many economic decisions, but their governments play a much larger role than is the case in MDEs. One of the interesting questions for economists is why this region of the world evolved more cooperative, egalitarian systems than most other regions.

8.3.1 Cooperative culture and homogeneous population

Driven by the harsh climate of northern Europe, Scandinavians were forced to work hard and to cooperate in order to survive. The cooperative culture has persisted into the modern era in part due to its success—all of the Nordic countries are wealthy. In addition, the homogeneity and small size of the population tend to foster empathy. When someone in a Nordic country is destitute, it is easy for their neighbors to imagine that they too might experience the same fate. Note, however, that the Nordic countries were not particularly equal 100 years ago. It took powerful, well-organized labor movements to create the Nordic model over the last century. This, of course, implies that any country in which workers have strong solidarity and organization might be able to emulate the Nordic model.

8.3.2 Gender equity

Another area in which we see the Nordic culture at work in affecting market outcomes is gender equity. A Norwegian law requires 40% of corporate boards of directors to be women so that it is more likely that larger numbers of women will be selected for upper management. Norway's parental leave policies are quite generous, as are those of other Nordic countries. Together, Norwegian parents are allowed to take 46 weeks off at 100% of pay or 56 weeks off at 80% of pay. Employers are required to allow workers to return to their old jobs at the end of parental leave, which means that there is little or no detriment to your career if you choose to have children. The employment guarantee, along with free childcare, results in 75% of Norwegian women working outside the home, as opposed to 68% in the United States. There are also payments for parents who choose to be stay-at-home parents.

With similarly generous policies, in 2015, the five Nordic countries ranked at the very top of the world in terms of best places to be a mother, whereas the United States ranked 33rd. The United States only requires employers to grant new mothers 12 weeks of *unpaid* maternity leave. The intentional efforts by Nordic countries to create greater gender equity have spilled over into the political realm: 40% of representatives in Parliament in Nordic countries are women, compared with 19.4% in the United States.

8.3.3 Dramatic expansion of human rights

The egalitarian culture led Nordic countries to expand the definition of human rights well beyond what we find in MDEs. All Nordic citizens have the right to childcare, health care, dental care, free education (through college), housing, and food. These essentials are either provided by government agencies or the government subsidizes the private sector to provide them. The government invests substantially in all of these services so that they are of very high quality. As one might expect, the provision of such extensive services comes with a hefty price tag, which requires high tax rates in order to pay for them.

8.3.4 Government-guided development

Rather than letting market forces determine the direction of the economy, the state in Nordic countries guides and facilitates economic development with a sophisticated set of policies. Sweden, for example, is famous for its "triple helix" economic development approach utilizing government, universities, and the private sector. In the 1970s and 1980s, Sweden began experiencing deindustrialization in the face of increased global competition, just as the United States did. Rather than trying to save dying industries, Sweden implemented an initiative to attract new high-wage industries based on government, university, and private sector partnerships. The government would identify new key industries that were likely to generate high-wage jobs and that were suitable for the local economy. These industries included biotechnology, research and development, computer programming, and information technology. After consulting with private sector firms, the government would provide state-of-the-art infrastructure, and universities would provide training and education to make sure that the workforce had exactly the right set of skills. This made Sweden an ideal location for industries in the targeted sectors, attracting a huge influx of foreign investment and leading to the creation of new jobs in each of the above industries. This focus on cutting-edge industries, education, and research and development has resulted in Sweden generating more patent filings per resident than the United States.

Note that other countries, including Japan and South Korea, have also been very successful in targeting cutting-edge industries and developing them via substantial state support. Many economists see such industrial policies as a key step in developing an industrial sector in an underdeveloped region. However, such policies require an efficient, noncorrupt government sector. In countries with poor quality state institutions, industrial policies have not worked well.

Another interesting example of state-guided development is Norway's state oil company, Statoil. This public company was created to manage North Sea oil drilling to ensure that all Norwegian citizens benefitted from the oil discoveries. The government places all profits from Statoil into an oil fund, which is used to pay for much of the Norwegian welfare state and to provide Norway with economic security in the future, even after the oil runs out. The government treats the oil fund like an endowment, spending only the interest and 4% of the principal in any year. In 2020, the oil fund was valued at $1.2 trillion, which was almost 1% of global equity markets!

We also see substantial government intervention in Sweden's ultra-Keynesian macroeconomic policies. Sweden was the first country to use Keynesian stabilization policies extensively, beginning in the early years of the Great Depression. In addition to generous unemployment and welfare benefits, Sweden provides public employment for many of those who cannot find jobs otherwise. The idea is that in each community there are plenty of tasks that need to be done. The government should hire those willing and able to work but unable to find a private sector job to complete useful tasks, in the process pumping money into the economy. Businesses are also allowed to make tax-free investments if they do so in a recession, which stimulates investment when it is needed most. Sweden recovered very rapidly from the 2008 financial crisis thanks to these stabilization policies.

8.3.5 Active labor market policies (flexicurity)

When workers in Sweden lose their job, they are given generous benefits with a time limit and provided with free education, training, and money for relocation costs so that they can find a new job. If they are still unable to find a job at that point, they can get a job on a public works project. This makes Sweden's labor market flexible in that workers are regularly moving from one job to another, but it also offers workers significant job security because they will almost always have a job or state support. Note that this is not a "soft" system—everyone is expected to work. These flexicurity programs resulted in Sweden having the highest rate of labor market participation in the world (the highest percentage of the population working).

It is also interesting that, like the United States, Nordic countries are hotbeds for entrepreneurship and innovation. Startup rates in Norway are among the highest in the developed world, and Norway has more entrepreneurs per capita than the United States. This can be traced to state support for entrepreneurs in Norway. First, the security of the welfare state means that you have little to lose if your business fails. If it does fail, you will still get guaranteed retirement and health benefits, along with education and training for a new job. Free college education means that you have no student loan debt that has to be paid off if your business fails, so you can start a business right out of college. There are free courses on starting a business, you can get a state-sponsored three-month internship in a startup company, and it is easy to start a company, taking only seven days.

8.3.6 Inequality and poverty

As Figure 8.1 shows, the poverty rate in the Nordic countries is half that of the United States. This reflects the disparate levels of government spending to fight poverty and create opportunities for the poor. Similarly, the United States is the most unequal developed country, whereas the Nordic countries are the most equal in terms of income and wealth, which is reflected in the differences in tax policies. Sweden imposes a 1.5% annual wealth tax on rich individuals, whereas the United States has no wealth tax, and the richest people in Sweden pay 60% of their income in taxes, whereas the tax rate for the richest Americans is 39.6%. The 400 richest families in the United States only paid 20% of their income in taxes thanks to a plethora of tax deductions and low taxes on investment income.

Greater equality is also associated with a greater likelihood of moving up in the world. There is significantly greater class mobility in Nordic countries than in the United States. Statistically, a poor child in Denmark has a 22% chance of becoming rich, whereas a poor child in the United States has only a 1% chance. This disparity is a product of the greater resources available to poor children in Denmark, especially high-quality education and health care, which give them a better chance to succeed.

In general, we see in the Nordic model a set of countries that is globally competitive because of their effective use of the state to facilitate economic development. They also have exceptionally high measures of human development because of their use of heavily progressive taxes to provide high-quality services and support for all citizens.

8.4 OTHER VARIETIES OF SOCIAL MARKET ECONOMIES

Because there is so much variety in social market economies, it is worthwhile documenting some of the ways in which other SMEs differ from the Nordic model and reflect unique sets of cultural and institutional factors. Below, we briefly describe some of the unique characteristics of the largest SMEs, Germany, France, and Japan.

8.4.1 Germany, co-determination, and precision manufacturing

Germany is a world leader in producing high-value manufactured goods such as robotics, cars, and electronics. The German emphasis on technology is reflected in the fact that most CEOs of manufacturing firms are engineers, whereas in the United States it is more common to find CEOs with finance or marketing backgrounds. German education has two tracks, one targeting college and the other the development of sophisticated vocational skills that will culminate in an internship and a skilled job. Workers in Germany are extremely well paid, as you can see in Figure 8.3, whereas U.S. workers make $6 less per hour. German workers also have substantial input into how work is done, and at large firms workers elect members to the supervisory boards of corporations that appoint the members of

Country	Hourly Compensation (wages and benefits)
Belgium	$45.62
Norway	$43.32
Switzerland (2016)	$43.08
Germany	$42.00
France	$41.34
Netherlands	$40.37
Denmark	$39.85
Sweden	$39.21
Austria	$39.17
United States	$35.87
Italy	$35.62
Finland	$35.06
Iceland	$33.09
Ireland	$31.72
United Kingdom	$29.78
Spain	$29.64
Canada	$26.27
Australia (2011)	$20.12
New Zealand	$19.15

FIGURE 8.3 Table showing hourly compensation costs in manufacturing, 2012. Source: ILOStat, https://ilostat.ilo.org/, accessed January 31, 2021.

the board of directors. This system is called co-determination because both workers and firms together make major decisions regarding the future of the company.[2] Thus, German workers have much more input into how corporations are run than American workers do. This has translated into an empowered workforce that displays some of the highest productivity and greatest skill levels in the world. Interestingly, though Germany is a highly regulated economy, it tends to avoid substantial macroeconomic intervention, a philosophy which it has carried over into the E.U.

8.4.2 France, fashion, and leisure

France is another large, wealthy country in which cultural considerations play a large role in structuring the economy. The French work very hard to preserve their culture and way of life. This includes strict rules designed to preserve local food sources and cuisine. Correspondingly, France has very strong culturally based industries, including tourism (France is the most visited destination in the world) and fashion. France is home to the world's two largest luxury products companies, LVMH (Moët Hennessy Louis Vuitton) and Kering (Gucci, Yves San Laurent, etc.).

The French government also works as a member of the European Union to guide and protect established industries such as clothing and steel. It is well known for utilizing expert government planners to work with industry to construct economic development programs. In addition to guiding the economy, the government imposes strict regulations on businesses, including laws that make it difficult for firms to fire workers or to close an unprofitable manufacturing plant.

After it experienced the same forces of deindustrialization that hit other developed countries, France decided to deal with its high unemployment rate by reducing work hours for existing laborers and increasing leisure time. The maximum work week was reduced to 35 hours, or 39 hours for CEOs and upper management. (This did reduce the unemployment rate, although France still has chronically high unemployment.) To enforce the law, the government hired inspectors to count cars in parking lots after business hours, scrutinize office entry and computer records, grill employees about their schedules, and make sure no one was bringing work home with them! (Isn't there something appealing about a government inspector telling you to go home because you are working too hard?)

With the short work week, five weeks of paid vacation, and 11 paid holidays, the French work fewer hours than most other countries. France and the United States both generate about $60 in GDP per hour worked, so the main reason GDP per capita in the United States is higher than France is because people in the United States work 19% more hours than the French do. Essentially, the French work four days a week and Americans work five days a week, on average. This brings up an interesting question: Would you rather have more money or more leisure time? The French have chosen the latter.

8.4.3 Japan, keiretsu, and lifetime employment

Japan has the third-largest economy in the world, behind the United States and China and just ahead of Germany, the United Kingdom, and France. As with other SMEs, Japan's unique culture shapes its economy in significant ways. Like France, Japan's government uses highly skilled planners to work with industry to determine the direction of the economy. Top university graduates often go into government work and then move from government to industry leadership positions, which is a sign of how highly valued public service is.

As a deeply Confucian society featuring an emphasis on respect for elders, loyalty, and harmony, Japan has evolved unique organizational structures. The Japanese economy is dominated by six huge conglomerates, known as keiretsu. Each keiretsu is owned primarily by a bank, and these banks tend to prefer long-term growth and steady returns over short-term profits. This gives Japanese corporations a much longer focus than we tend to see in U.S. corporations. Within each keiretsu one finds networks of companies working together for a common goal. For example, Toyota works closely with all of its suppliers so that production changes can be made swiftly and seamlessly with minimal disruptions. This close integration of Toyota with all of its suppliers within the same keiretsu reduces costs, fosters innovation, and allows Toyota to respond more rapidly to changes in consumer preferences.

Within each large corporation, employees tend to act like an extended family. It is common for employees at the top Japanese firms to stay at the same firm for their entire career—lifetime employment! Workers socialize together, and promotions often come from within the company. This family-like atmosphere fosters cooperation and loyalty, leading to high levels of productivity and trust and a flat organizational structure in which workers need little supervision.

In all of the SMEs we see much larger government involvement in the strategic direction of the economy, with government planners working with industry officials to determine what industries to focus on and where to invest. Government regulation of the economy is more in line with local social values than it is with the market. Some commentators call such economies "socialist," but private sector firms still dominate most industries, so SMEs are actually still mixed market capitalist systems. True socialism or communism is a very different system, as we will discuss in the next section.

8.5 SOCIALISM AND COMMUNISM

Anyone who has experienced the dark side of capitalism—especially poorly paid workers abused by powerful, uncaring bosses—has likely longed for an alternative economic system. Since the very beginnings of capitalism more than 200 years ago, the downtrodden have turned to socialism and communism as a possible solution to the problems with capitalism.

A socialist economic system is one in which the means of production and distribution are either owned or regulated by society. Note that in most SMEs, only 40%–60% of the economy is controlled or regulated by the state, whereas a fully socialist system would mean control or regulation of almost all industries. A communist economic system is one in which the means of production and distribution are publicly owned and each person works according to their abilities and is paid according to their needs. Socialism can be considered the first step of an economy on the way toward communism. In general, communist systems involve central planning, with the government determining what is produced, how it is produced, who does what job, and how goods and services are distributed. State ownership and control of the economy is nearly absolute.

Beginning with the Russian Revolution of 1917, numerous countries experienced communist uprisings in the 20th century. Just before the fall of the Union of Soviet Socialist Republics (U.S.S.R.) in Russia in 1989, a third of the world's population lived in a communist country. However, although Marx proposed communism as a solution to the problems of capitalism, he never laid out how a communist system would work in practice. Countries attempting to implement communism had no blueprint to follow, so they had no choice but to try various methods and hope that they worked.

The U.S.S.R. developed a system of central planning where the state made all major economic decisions. Fearing invasion by the United States and other hostile capitalist countries, the U.S.S.R. undertook an effort to industrialize a previously rural and backward economic system. Planners instructed every industry on what to produce, along with when and how to produce it. They set up elaborate input–output tables for the entire economy detailing every input needed for every product so that they could allocate the correct resources in the right quantities to each manufacturer. They focused on manufacturing and especially on defense, given the external threats they faced.

Initially, this system was remarkably successful. While most of the world was experiencing the Great Depression, the economy of the U.S.S.R. grew rapidly, between 4% and 13% per year. The Soviet Union succeeded in industrializing a previously rural, agrarian economy with remarkable speed. This success prompted worries in Western capitalist countries, where it appeared that the communist system was more successful than capitalism.

But it was not to last. The centralization of control allowed ruthless dictators like Joseph Stalin to seize power in the U.S.S.R. Stalin killed more than a million people during his time as Soviet general secretary and premier. As the bureaucracy became more entrenched, efficiency declined, and the U.S.S.R. began to experience regular shortages of inputs and even basic consumer goods.

Most other communist countries that imitated the Soviet central planning model experienced similar problems. In places where control was more decentralized, however, more positive results were achieved. And in places in which local culture was already communal in nature, the system worked reasonably well.

In Cuba, though political power was controlled by the communist party under Fidel Castro and subsequent leaders, workers had substantial power and control over the workplace. This is an ironic reversal of the United States, where workers have the political power that comes with voting but lack power in the workplace. Cuba was able to achieve impressive results in education, literacy, and health, reaching levels of developed countries. Cuba's economic growth averaged 2% from 1990 to 2016, which is impressive given that it faced a huge cut in subsidies when the U.S.S.R. collapsed in 1990 and that it has continually faced U.S. economic sanctions during that period.

Yugoslavia, like Cuba, gave workers substantial control over workplaces, developing a series of worker-owned cooperatives as the basic organizational unit. They experienced some substantial successes before being derailed by regional and ethnic differences.

After a century of efforts by various countries to construct communist economic systems, the following lessons have emerged:

- Central planning can be a good way to organize and mobilize resources to industrialize in societies that were previously underdeveloped.
- Central planning does not tend to be as dynamic, efficient, or inventive as capitalism over the long term.
- Communist systems can result in better economic outcomes than exploitative capitalist systems—most Cuban citizens were better off after their communist revolution than they were under colonial capitalism; most Russian citizens were better off economically under the U.S.S.R. than they are now under oligarchic capitalism.
- When it builds on a culture of communal values and production and when it empowers workers, communism can work reasonably well.
- External pressures can derail any inclination toward democracy in state-dominated systems.
- Central control can and frequently does devolve into bureaucracy, inefficiency and dictatorship, which tends to undermine the effectiveness of communist systems and result in human rights abuses.

When the U.S.S.R. collapsed in 1990, most communist countries began a transition from communism to capitalism. The transition went very poorly in most cases. It proved much more difficult for communist countries that had little experience with markets to develop market-based economies than economists thought. Too little attention was paid to the need to develop all of the detailed legal and institutional structures and even the cultural characteristics that drive markets. Economists had evidently forgotten the lessons of history highlighted by Polanyi that the market system is complex and needs to be constructed carefully by the state. The biggest success story in the transition from a centrally planned economy to a market-based one was the case of China, which we turn to next.

8.6 THE CHINESE STATE-DOMINATED ECONOMY

Under Mao Zedong, China's centrally planned economy emphasized rural indus-trialization, regional self-reliance, and decentralization. This differed dramatically from the centralized approach of the U.S.S.R. The Chinese government confis-cated the lands of feudal lords and developed rural markets, giving farmers and workers more freedom and control over their work. This worked well initially, boosting productivity and rural incomes.

However, when the state tried to force farmers and workers into collectives, a more Soviet-style approach, the results were disastrous, with production declines, shortages, and extremely unhappy workers. In response, Mao implemented the "Hundred Flowers Campaign" and the "Great Leap Forward" to prompt creative thinking and solutions to the problems that China was experiencing. Efforts to develop the countryside utilizing traditional technology rather than cutting-edge methods did prompt the creation of numerous collective firms in rural China, which would later prove useful. However, the strategy was not effective in produc-ing goods efficiently, and China again faced repeated shortages and crises. These crises led to the re-imposition of central planning, as China returned to a more traditional communist economy.

With Mao's death in 1976, the way was opened for a new approach led by Deng Xiaoping. Deng gradually incorporated market reforms into the centrally planned system. Communes were eliminated and rural farmers were granted prop-erty rights and the right to farm small private plots for their own benefit. The household once again became the main agricultural unit, and rural markets were created so farmers could sell their goods.

In a particularly adept policy, farmers and privatized small firms were required to sell a certain amount of produce to the state at a low price so that the state could preserve the central planning system. Any goods produced over the state quota could be sold in the newly created markets. This allowed enterprises to adapt to markets and market prices over time while preserving the stability of the eco-nomic system. Rather than experiencing a collapse as most communist countries did when markets were introduced, the gradual introduction of markets to China resulted in a huge economic boom.

Locally owned town and village enterprises (TVEs), started under Mao's ear-lier efforts at rural industrialization, began to serve as a dynamic component of new markets. TVEs were owned by a village or town, and the manager was selected by local government officials, freeing them from centralized control. Profits from a TVE went to the community that owned it to pay wages, provide local public ser-vices, and generate funds for reinvestment. This gave TVEs an incentive to be suc-cessful, proving to be a source of entrepreneurship as the TVEs sought out niches in the newly created markets. By this point, China had moved away from a centrally planned, communist economy toward a market socialist economy.

The creation of markets also involved the use of special economic zones (SEZs) in China. SEZs were free trade zones within which firms could function in a market-based, capitalist manner while the rest of the economy was separate and protected. China attracted foreign investors to SEZs by offering low wages and taxes, few rules or regulations governing treatment of workers or the environment, a highly disciplined and skilled workforce, and a devalued currency that made exporting from China extraordinarily profitable. In exchange for such attractive conditions, China mandated that foreign investors work with local partner firms and share their technology so that Chinese firms would gain experience with international manufacturing. Foreign firms were only too happy to comply with these conditions in order to gain access to the vast Chinese market.

Foreign investment poured in beginning in the 1980s. The SEZs coupled with the rural market reforms caused an astounding economic boom in China. From 1978 to 2016, China's annual per capita economic growth averaged 8.6% while most other countries were experiencing average growth rates of less than 2%! With this rate of growth, the Chinese economy has been doubling in size every 8.4 years. China is now the world's second largest economy and will likely pass the United States as the largest economy in 2029. China is now the world's largest exporting country, the largest manufacturer of automobiles, and the largest manufacturing country in general.

Although there is much economic independence of firms in China, the government still maintains a significant degree of control. The communist party preserves close ties to all large firms, and the Red Army even runs a lot of firms. The government determines the main direction of investment, and new ventures cannot take place without government approval. Some economists have actually referred to modern China as a form of state capitalism, given that the state is so closely involved in profit-making activities.

China is frequently criticized by other countries for its human rights violations and poor environmental record. Media and internet searches are still censored, and dissidents are regularly arrested and imprisoned. The student-led Tiananmen Square protests of 1989 were met with brutal repression, and between 200 and 1000 people were killed.[3] Since that crackdown, protests have been more muted. China is facing numerous ecological disasters thanks to its rapid growth without substantial environmental regulation. Its largest cities are choked with smog, and it also faces water and soil problems as well as habitat destruction and biodiversity loss.

It is not clear at this point whether China will move in a more democratic direction or whether it will continue to be led by a one-party, communist state. A 2014 Pew Research Global Attitudes survey indicated that Chinese citizens are more satisfied with the direction their country is heading than any other country in the world, with 87% of citizens satisfied (compared with 33% in the United States). There appear to be no major pressures for change coming from within China.

China's success as a state-dominated economy (SDE) has been matched to some degree by recent growth spurts in Russia and Brazil, who have also taken a state-directed approach to economic development. It is interesting that so many emerging markets are successfully adopting this approach. This seems to support the idea that utilizing an SDE approach in an underdeveloped country can be effective.

However, many other SDEs have been dismal failures when it comes to economic development. In countries where the state is kleptocratic—stealing resources for itself at the expense of the rest of society—or where the state bureaucracy is overly controlling and inefficient, SDEs tend to work very poorly. Dozens of countries have failed at utilizing a state-centered approach to development. There are actually more failures than success stories at this point, which you will study if you take a course on developing countries. Interestingly, it does not seem to matter if an abusive government adopts a capitalistic or a socialistic approach: Its stranglehold over the economy will stifle development either way. However, where SDEs work in the public interest and offer a more flexible, pragmatic approach, as is the case in China, the results can be quite positive.

8.7 CONCLUSION

This chapter has briefly sketched out the types of economic systems that we see in the modern world. Modern economic systems can be grouped into three broad categories: Market-dominated economies, social market economies, and state-dominated economies. We have focused on successful developed economies in this chapter as a guide to the possible recipes for economic prosperity.

The United States is the dominant MDE, generating high levels of income and wealth and spawning a noteworthy amount of innovation and entrepreneurship while struggling with inequality and poverty. The Nordic model of an SME combines substantial government intervention with private sector development to achieve a similar level of income and innovation to the United States with fewer social problems. China's SDE has produced the most rapid rate of growth in the world for 40 years, a remarkable, sustained success story marred by human rights abuses and significant environmental problems.

In the modern economic systems, we see reflections of the ideas of the great economists that we studied earlier. In a nod to Adam Smith, all modern economies use market capitalism substantially. Fueled by competition, markets produce the products that consumers want while keeping prices low and fostering innovations. In a nod to Karl Marx, all economic systems work to safeguard the rights and safety of laborers and use the state to make peoples' lives better than the market would on its own. Two countries, Cuba and North Korea, still reject capitalism and espouse a communist philosophy. Reflecting Veblen's ideas, modern economies work to promote the productive side of markets, striving to develop new, productive industries via public-private partnerships. But, responding to Hayek's cautions, most economic systems are wary of having too much state interference in the economy. Ultimately, all modern economic systems reflect the ideas of John Maynard

Keynes, having developed mixed economic systems that rely on market capitalism for some economic decisions while using the state for others. What is interesting is the variation one finds in modern economic systems, with MDEs leaning more toward Smith, SDEs leaning more toward Marx, and SMEs in the middle.

QUESTIONS FOR REVIEW

1. Explain the key differences between market-dominated economies, social market economies, and state-dominated economies. Use specific examples to support your answer.
2. What are the key elements of the U.S. MDE? What factors do you think are essential contributors to U.S. economic success? What are the major problems with the U.S. MDE?
3. What are the key elements of the Nordic SME? What factors do you think are essential contributors to its economic success? What problems do you see with the SME approach?
4. How do socialism and communism differ from capitalism?
5. What are the strengths and weaknesses of a market capitalist approach (United States), a guided market approach (Nordic model), and a central planning approach (U.S.S.R.) to economic development?
6. The most successful countries in the last 50 years have used the government extensively in economic development efforts. However, many developing countries in sub-Saharan Africa, Latin America, and Southeast Asia have adopted similar approaches with little success. Why might a government-centered approach to development have such an uneven track record?
7. What are the key ingredients in China's economic success? Why was China's transition from a centrally planned system to a market-oriented system more successful than the transition in Russia?
8. Innovation is a key ingredient in economic success over time. What are the lessons regarding innovation that emerge from the experiences of the countries described in this chapter?
9. Write an essay in which you compare and contrast the U.S. economic system with the Nordic model. In your essay, take up the following issues: (a) What role does government play in each economy? (b) How does each economy reflect the ideas of Adam Smith, Karl Marx, Thorstein Veblen, John Maynard Keynes, and Friedrich Hayek? (c) What are the strengths and weaknesses of each economic system?
10. What role does culture seem to play in structuring economic systems? Explain using specific examples.
11. Would it be possible to implement a social market economy in the United States? Why or why not?

NOTES

1 Satyam Mukherjee, Daniel Romero, Benjamin F. Jones, and Brian Uzzi, "The Nearly Universal Link Between the Age of Past Knowledge and Tomorrow's Breakthroughs in Science and Technology," *Science Advances* 3, No. 4 (April 19, 2017).

2 Note that the co-determination system has been weakened in recent years in the face of global competition. It will be interesting to see how much of this system is maintained in the future. Given that it is credited with Germany's much-vaunted labor skill and productivity, it is difficult to imagine the system going away altogether.

3 Official Chinese government estimates range from 200 to 300, whereas journalists put the number of deaths between 300 and 1000.

PART III

Markets, supply and demand

This section of the book takes up markets and how they work in modern capitalism. Understanding markets is important for all economic actors—consumers, businesses, governments, nonprofits, and all those who depend on markets to provide the goods that are essential to their survival. Markets are the central organizing principle for most capitalist economies. Knowing how markets work, when they work well and when they work poorly, and what supporting state institutions are necessary to make them work effectively are keys to economic analysis. Once you understand the forces that make markets work, you will be better able to predict market outcomes, such as changes in prices, and anticipate changes in markets utilizing the supply and demand model and other tools.

To help you understand markets, in Chapter 9 we describe their characteristics and the institutions that make markets tick. Then we explain in detail the supply and demand model and how you can use it to analyze how changes in key variables will affect the prices and quantities of goods sold in markets. Supply and demand is the cornerstone of modern mainstream economics, so you should spend a significant amount of time mastering this material.

Chapter 10 contains a series of applications of the supply and demand model that demonstrate the insights this model can give us into market behavior and the impact of economic policies on markets. In addition to giving examples of how to use the supply and demand model to analyze specific markets, the chapter takes up government regulations of markets via price floors, price ceilings, excise taxes and subsidies, and the effect of these policies on consumer and producer surplus. We also discuss the concept of elasticity and how it helps us anticipate the magnitude of changes in quantities in response to changes in price and income.

DOI: 10.4324/9781315636924-11

In addition to the supply and demand model, we will develop some analysis of aspects of markets that are difficult to model but still important to understanding how markets work. Chapter 11 explores alternative ways of analyzing markets from political economics and behavioral economics perspectives. It takes up consumer and producer behavior in more detail, drawing on ideas from political, behavioral, and mainstream economics.

Markets and how they work

The institutional foundations of markets and the supply and demand model

Markets have existed in one form or another for much of human history, but their forms have often been very different, and it is only since the advent of capitalism that we have depended on markets to provide the goods and services we need for our survival. Even in the modern world in which markets are dominant, markets vary widely in how they work.

As a brief case study of markets, let's consider what has happened to the price of oil over the last 20 years. As Figure 9.1 shows, there has been a huge variation in the price of oil. Understanding the oil market involves knowledge of the factors that affect the supply and demand for oil, as well as geopolitical affairs and other political and industrial factors. The dramatic increase in the price of oil from a low of $17.50 per barrel in 2001 to a high of $145.16 in 2008 was a product of several factors. Rapid economic growth in China and other emerging market economies led to a huge increase in the demand for oil. There were also changes on the supply side of the market. About 40% of crude oil is produced by a group of countries that form a cartel, the Organization of the Petroleum Exporting Countries (OPEC). As such a large player in the oil market, OPEC plays a major role in oil supply. OPEC countries agreed to reduce their production in the early 2000s in order to increase the price of oil. The combination of an increase in demand and a decrease in supply sent crude oil prices soaring.

Then the Great Recession hit in late 2008. The demand for crude oil decreased dramatically as economic growth slowed and companies cut back significantly on their production, using less energy in the process. As the economy recovered from the Great Recession, demand increased again, and crude oil prices rose until 2014. But in 2014, economic growth in China and emerging markets fell, once

DOI: 10.4324/9781315636924-12

FIGURE 9.1 The price of a barrel of crude oil, September 1997–November 2020. Source: FRED.

again reducing the demand for oil. Alternative energies such as solar and wind power also led to some decreases in the demand for oil. At the same time, new hydraulic fracturing (fracking) techniques increased the supply of oil, especially in the United States and Canada. This combination of a decrease in demand and an increase in supply caused oil prices to drop dramatically in 2014 and then to stay low for the next several years. The COVID-19 pandemic recession of 2020 caused another crash in oil prices as factories closed and people stopped traveling, decreasing demand for oil sharply. The price of oil briefly fell into negative territory on April 20, 2020! There was such a large surplus that oil suppliers were willing to pay people to take it off their hands rather than make costly storage arrangements for surplus oil.

What we learn from this example is that most of the price of oil can be explained by straightforward supply and demand factors. But we also need to be aware of OPEC's strategies to manipulate the price of oil and the likely impact of new technologies in renewable energies and oil extraction. Governments around the world are pushing for more sustainable sources of power that contribute less to global warming than the burning of fossil fuels, which will probably have an increasing impact on the oil market in coming years. In short, market analysis involves understanding supply and demand along with the major institutional and technological structures that affect market behavior. That is the topic of this chapter.

9.0 CHAPTER 9 LEARNING GOALS

After reading this chapter you should be able to:

- Define and give examples of a market and a market transaction.

- Describe the key institutions that make markets work and analyze how those institutions support markets.

- List and critically evaluate the assumptions upon which the supply and demand model rests.

- Using supply and demand curves, explain the concept of equilibrium and why markets tend toward an equilibrium price and quantity.

- Explain the theory of demand and the theory of supply.

- Analyze how changes in the determinants of demand and the determinants of supply shift demand and supply curves and affect equilibrium price and equilibrium quantity.

9.1 MARKETS AND MARKET TRANSACTIONS

Markets are a central part of our lives, but they can be difficult to understand fully because so much of what makes markets work is hidden from plain sight. In simple terms, a market is **an institution that organizes and facilitates transactions between buyers and sellers**. A transaction is **an agreement between economic agents—buyers and sellers—to exchange goods, services, or assets**. Each market has a set of formal and informal **rules** that govern the behavior of economic agents. Economic agents can be individuals or groups such as corporations or government agencies.

There are many different types of markets in a capitalist economic system, each with its own characteristics. The market for food or clothing includes all of the stores and venders in your area and online that you could patronize to buy the food or clothes that you need or want. We can analyze the market for food at a local, national, or even a global level. Each level would have its own characteristics and dynamics. The market for stocks includes all the companies with publicly issued stocks and the investors and brokers who are interested in buying those stocks. The local market for labor includes all of the businesses in your area that are looking for employees and all of the people who want to find jobs. We usually subdivide the labor market into the market for particular skills because not everyone is qualified for every job. As you can see from the examples above, when analyzing a market, it is very important to specify the scope of the market you are describing so you can determine which factors are most important to incorporate into your analysis.

The most common markets in capitalist economies are structured as follows.

- Retail markets are **firms such as Walmart and Amazon (suppliers) that sell directly to consumers (demanders)**.
- Wholesale markets are **retailers like Walmart and Amazon (demanders) that purchase the goods they sell from the companies that produce them (suppliers)**. For example, Walmart buys food containers from Rubbermaid, which it then resells directly to consumers.
- Resource markets are **the markets for labor, land, capital, and natural resources where producers purchase the inputs they need (producers are the demanders) from the owners of those resources (suppliers)**.
- Financial markets are where **those wishing to borrow money (demanders) are matched with those with money to lend (suppliers)**.

We also see informal markets and markets for illegal drugs and other illicit products in all economies. Informal markets have a different dynamic because most transactions take place in cash and are based on trust rather than established rules and laws.

In each of these markets, the interaction of suppliers (sellers) and demanders (purchasers) will determine the market price, as we will study in some detail. In competitive markets the conditions affecting supply and demand are the primary determinant of prices. In less competitive markets, issues of monopoly power and bargaining power come into play. And government intervention can always play a role in determining prices.

Markets are actually quite complicated in that they require a host of formal and informal institutions to make them work. The key institutions that make markets and market transactions work effectively are described in the next section.

9.2 THE INSTITUTIONS THAT MAKE MARKETS WORK

Economists have identified a **set of market-supporting institutions that must exist in order for markets to function effectively**. Understanding these institutions and how they work will give you a deeper understanding of markets. If you go to work for a private sector business, you will need to gain an intimate understanding of the institutions that affect the market in which your business operates. The key market-supporting institutions include **property rights, laws to facilitate the aggregation of capital, trust, contract laws, competition, a lack of coercion, and infrastructure to lower transactions costs**. The most important market institution, according to mainstream economists, is that of property rights.

9.2.1 Property rights

In order to sell something to someone else, you must own it. Technically, this means you have been granted a property right to that thing by society. Property rights in a capitalist economic system stem from ownership of productive resources, and property can be owned by individuals, businesses, or governments. Most mainstream economists see property rights as the essential characteristic of capitalist markets. Property rights give the owners of resources the incentive to be as productive as possible with their property so they can make as much money as possible.

Where property rights are unstable, such as places where property can be seized at any time, people are reluctant to make investments. In his classic book *Tropical Gangsters*, Robert Klitgaard describes how businesses owners in Equatorial Guinea would not invest in their businesses because as soon as their business became profitable, it would be seized by corrupt government officials. When cocoa was profitable, the government nationalized cocoa farms. Government food inspectors stole chickens from the farms they inspected. And so on. These efforts completely undermined investment in the country. But where property rights are stable, owners are willing to build factories and invest in productivity enhancements because they are confident that they will reap the benefits of their investments.

One fact noted particularly by progressive and radical political economists is that property rights confer power upon property owners. Owners of the means of production have the right to hire and fire workers, which gives them power and control over the lives of laborers, and their wealth gives them immense power over governments.

Most property rights are inherited in capitalist countries (children inherit the businesses and properties owned by their parents), but there is no particular reason that property rights need to be associated so strongly with inheritance. Norway, France, Switzerland, and Spain have a wealth tax in order to reduce the amount of inequality that is caused by unequal property rights. Socialists argue that if property rights to society's productive resources were granted to workers, the result would be a much more equitable economic system. In a typical capitalist firm, workers do not own what they produce, so they cannot sell it—that right goes to the owner of the firm, and the owner gets to keep all of the profits from sales. But in a worker-owned firm, the people who do the work also get to sell the product because they collectively own the resources. As the worker-owned Mondragon Cooperative Corporation in Spain has demonstrated, workers running firms can make them efficient, productive, and profitable.

Feminist economists note that property rights in most societies are distributed unequally by gender. Around the world, men are more likely to own property and assets, which means that governments that strictly protect property rights and refuse to redistribute property cement existing gender inequality. The same is also true of the racial distribution of property. African Americans and Latino Americans are much less likely to own property and businesses than whites.

Given that property rights are the cornerstone of markets, the World Bank has made the establishment of clear property rights a key component of many of its development programs in poor countries. However, due to gender inequities, this has had some significantly negative consequences. In several countries in Africa, efforts to establish secure property rights led to landownership being granted almost exclusively to men, taking the land away from women who had farmed it for decades under traditional land rights allocated by tribal elders. Sadly, taking access to the land from productive women and giving it to men with no farming experience led to declines in agricultural production.

Property rights are therefore both the cornerstone of economic markets and a source of much dissatisfaction with markets on the part of those who have been historically excluded from having property rights. Laws facilitating the aggregation of capital are similarly divisive.

9.2.2 Laws to facilitate the aggregation of capital

In the modern world, firms in many industries need to be large in order to achieve economies of scale to compete with other huge firms. Correspondingly, every country has laws that allow individuals or groups to pool their resources in order to form large businesses. Many economists see the law that established the limited liability corporation as an essential component of U.S. economic success because it facilitated the pooling of capital into huge trusts that became the first large manufacturing companies. Other countries such as Japan and Germany allow banks to own a controlling interest in companies so that banks can directly use their vast financial resources for producing goods and services.

As with property rights, laws that foster huge corporations are controversial. By facilitating the pooling of financial resources, corporations grow larger and more powerful than they might otherwise, augmenting and centralizing the power of property rights significantly. Economist E. F. Schumacher argued in his book *Small Is Beautiful* that once corporations became huge and impersonal, it was easier for them to exploit workers they did not know and ruin the environment in locations the owners did not live in. The solution to problems of exploitation and environmental degradation was, to him, a return to local, small-scale production. The power of huge multinational corporations over workers, resources, and governments is an issue we return to throughout the book as one of the defining issues in modern capitalism.

9.2.3 Trust and contract laws that foster trust

Most transactions in markets are based on trust. Buyers have to trust that the seller will deliver a product of the expected quality at the expected time. Sellers have to trust that the buyer's payment will be made in the appropriate amount in the correct currency at the required time. Both agents have to trust that the other party will not try to steal or cheat during the transaction. Because trust is so essential to transactions, personal relationships are a major facilitator of exchange.

Another way to get people to trust you is to establish a solid reputation. Indeed, one of the reasons why marketers work so hard to establish a brand's reputation is because when people trust a particular brand, they are often willing to pay more for it and to purchase that brand over similar products that do not have as solid a reputation. It is hard to overstate how valuable reputation is. A survey by the World Economic Forum and Fleishman-Hillard, a public relations firm, found that "corporate reputation is a more important measure of success than stock market performance, profitability and return on investment, according to a survey of some the world's leading CEOs and organization leaders. Only the quality of products and services edged out reputation as the leading measure of corporate success."[1] Most CEOs think that a corporation's brand and reputation are worth *more than 40%* of their company's value.

Cultural norms can also facilitate or inhibit trust and particular types of transactions. For example, in countries adhering to strict Islamic law, religious beliefs prohibit charging interest. This makes banking very complex and inhibits numerous types of banking transactions. Instead of making traditional loans, Islamic banks have to engage in joint ventures and share in the profits of the ventures rather than charging interest. This requires a higher degree of trust on the part of the bank, and that makes it quite difficult for businesses to obtain funding. In countries that value honesty and transparency, such as Denmark and New Zealand, which rank as the least corrupt countries in Transparency International's Corruption Perceptions Index, market transactions are safer to engage in because it is less likely that someone will try to cheat or steal.

One of the ways in which large, impersonal, capitalistic markets achieve trust is via a system of contract laws. Contract laws specify the terms of a transaction. They are legally binding, so if one party violates the conditions of the contract, the other party has a legal right to seek compensation. Similarly, the Universal Commercial Code in the United States specifies the general rules governing transactions. With these laws in place, it is safe to assume that most transactions can be trusted. This makes people much more confident when engaging in market transactions.

There are other government functions that also facilitate trust. One of the main reasons that people are willing to entrust their food supply and health to private firms operating in a market is because of laws, regulations, and regular inspections by government regulators. Regulations protecting worker safety and the right to unionize ensure that workers participate in fair transactions with employers.

Interestingly, macroeconomic stability also encourages market transactions. If consumers are secure in their jobs, they tend to spend more, and if businesses are secure in their sales expectations, they tend to invest more. Therefore, successful government stabilization policies also facilitate transactions by instilling trust in the future of markets. Laws and regulations to reduce monopoly power and ensure competition also make markets work more effectively.

9.2.4 Competition and a lack of coercion

Markets tend to work well when all of their components are competitive. In product markets, prices stay low and firms remain innovative when they face the threat of significant competition. In labor markets, workers get paid and treated well when they have many employers bidding for their services. In market systems dominated by huge firms with monopoly power, the result is usually extreme inequality, which causes people to lose faith in the market system and demand an alternative. Similarly, in markets with rampant discrimination with respect to gender, race, and ethnicity, excluded groups will see the market as illegitimate and seek changes, potentially destabilizing markets.

9.2.5 Infrastructure to lower transactions costs

One of the biggest impediments to markets is the cost of engaging in a transaction. If transaction costs are too high, then no seller will participate in a market. For example, this might happen if it costs a seller too much to transport goods to where consumers are. There are many different types of transactions costs. These include **transportation costs, information costs incurred when actors identify and evaluate different opportunities, bargaining, monitoring and enforcement costs, and other costs associated with engaging in a transaction**.

The government plays a primary role in reducing transactions costs. An effective transportation infrastructure of roads, rails, ports, and airports is crucial, as is a fast, efficient, and safe internet service. Establishing the market infrastructure itself is another key role of government. The government can create a local farmer's market by providing a place, parking, and information to buyers and sellers. It can create a stock market by creating rules, laws, and regulations governing transactions. By providing a stable currency, economic actors are more willing to engage in all types of transactions. An efficient postal service that can deliver bills and goods to any address is also essential. The government needs to provide physical infrastructure **(roads, buildings, ports, airports, etc.),** market infrastructure **(information, rules, regulations, laws, and internet services),** and financial infrastructure **(a stable currency and banking system) to make markets work effectively**.

An understanding of market institutions is crucial for a business owner. It is very difficult to operate a business successfully unless you fully understand all of the key aspects of the markets in which you operate. You need to know the laws and regulations that affect all aspects of your operations, the competitive landscape, financial options for raising capital, the characteristics of consumers and consumer financing, and so much more.

If we assume that the government has put all of the necessary characteristics of markets in place, then we can use the supply and demand model to analyze how prices and quantities of various goods are likely to change in response to shifts in consumer, producer, and government regulatory behavior. The supply and demand model is the cornerstone of mainstream economics.

9.3 THE ASSUMPTIONS OF THE SUPPLY AND DEMAND MODEL OF MAINSTREAM ECONOMICS

Analysis of changes in prices and quantities is at the center of much mainstream economic analysis. Together, prices and quantities are the main mechanism by which resources are allocated in market capitalist economies. In markets that pursue maximum profits, prices provide crucial information, signaling whether companies should allocate more or less resources to the production of a particular product and causing firms to change the quantity of the product they supply. Similarly, prices signal to consumers that an item is more or less expensive relative to other commodities, which affects their purchasing decisions. Quantity is another crucial variable, indicating how many goods or services that businesses produce, something that affects how many resources they need to purchase and how many workers they need to hire in order to produce those goods and services. Their demand for workers in turn affects workers, households, and communities.

To analyze the forces that cause prices and quantities to change, economists developed the model of supply and demand. Like all economic models, the supply and demand model rests on a series of assumptions. Understanding these assumptions helps you determine when the model is useful in understanding economic phenomena and when it is less likely to apply.

The supply and demand model makes assumptions about what markets are like as well as assumptions about suppliers and demanders. Making these assumptions is what allows us to make systematic predictions about how supply and demand will change in response to a variety of factors and how these changes will likely affect prices and quantities. The supply and demand model is a simplified approximation of how markets work that focuses on a key set of characteristics present in most markets.

This chapter focuses on markets for commodities like pizza, beer, gas, wheat, and clothing operating in the short run. Markets for inputs such as labor and markets for financial assets work on slightly different principles. We will examine these markets later in the book. Also, different dynamics play out in the long run that cannot be captured by the supply and demand model alone.

The supply and demand model of commodities markets is based on ten major assumptions.

1. **Transactions take place in a capitalist market system with privately owned firms and individual consumers.**
2. **Markets are perfectly competitive or at least competitive enough to mirror the behavior of perfectly competitive markets.** In perfectly competitive markets, (a) suppliers sell an identical good or service and (b) no individual buyer or seller can influence the market price by themselves.
3. **Suppliers and demanders engage in optimizing behavior, with suppliers maximizing profits and demanders maximizing the satisfaction, or "utility," that they get from purchases.**
4. **Markets tend toward a stable equilibrium, settling on an equilibrium price and quantity.**

The specific assumptions about demanders (consumers) are as follows:

5. **Consumers are rational, calculating, fully informed, and self-interested about their purchasing options.** They engage in optimizing behavior, carefully weighing their options. Note that this assumption eliminates purchases driven by impulse buying and by emulating one's peers.
6. **Consumers prefer having more to having less, but they have a limited budget so they cannot buy all that they want, and they get less and less satisfaction from having more and more of the same good.** This assumption implies that consumers have an insatiable demand for goods and services in general but they don't want too much of any one item.
7. **There are substitutes for each good, and consumers can rank goods according to how much of each good they want at various prices. This leads them to want more of a good at lower prices and less of a good at higher prices.** Consumers have a good idea about the quality of substitute goods and how much satisfaction they will get from each type of good. Consumers behave like mini-computers, tabulating how much satisfaction they will get from each dollar of spending on each good, choosing to purchase the items that give them the most satisfaction per dollar until they exhaust their budget. The result is that rational, fully informed consumers desire to purchase smaller quantities of a good at high prices and larger quantities of a good at low prices.

The specific assumptions about suppliers are the following:

8. **Firms pursue as much short-term profit as possible and, in doing so decide what to produce, how much to produce, and how to produce it.**
9. **Capital and technology are fixed in the short run.** The short run is a period in which firms are stuck with the existing size of operations, usually a period of 1–12 months during which firms do not have time to dramatically expand the size of their business or develop new technologies. This means they cannot produce beyond their maximum capacity in the short run.

10. **Firms are encouraged to increase the quantity of a good supplied when the price increases.** With a fixed size of operations in the short run, it usually costs firms more to supply more. Thus, the only way to encourage firms to supply more is to offer them a higher price.

If these assumptions hold reasonably well, then the supply and demand model can be a powerful tool to analyze markets.

Let's consider the local market for pizza in the United States as it compares to the assumptions above. Most of the assumptions hold reasonably well: The pizza market in the United States is operated by private firms in a market capitalist system. Consumers are generally well informed about the quality of pizzas from different pizzerias in their town, along with other options for quick food (substitutes) such as sandwich shops and Chinese restaurants. However, pizza is not a completely homogeneous product: There are quality and location differences. Nonetheless, most economists think that pizzas are close enough substitutes for each other that we can still talk about a local market for pizza. Pizza firms are not all small operations, either. As Figure 9.2 shows, Domino's and Pizza Hut both have very large shares of the market. On the other hand, even small towns have lots of local competitors in addition to the national chains, so the pizza market is reasonably close to being a competitive market.

The prices that different restaurants charge for a similar size and type of pizza in a particular location cluster together, varying only slightly. This makes sense, because no restaurant wants to charge significantly more than its competitors for fear of losing business. The price of a large cheese pizza in the Theater District in Manhattan was $13.50 in 2014, and there was remarkably little variation among various restaurants. In Lewisburg, Pennsylvania, a 14-inch cheese pizza went for $10 in 2018. Gourmet pizzerias can charge more, and some discount pizzerias charge less, but most pizzerias charge a price within $1 of each other. To mainstream economists, this means that the market for pizza has settled on an equilibrium

Restaurant Name	Market Share
Domino's	30.10%
Pizza Hut	27.14%
Little Caesars Pizza	10.60%
Papa John's	7.78%
Papa Murphy's	1.80%
California Pizza Kitchen	1.74%
Marco's Pizza	1.42%
Chuck E. Cheese/Peter Piper Pizza	1.11%
Sbarro	1.07%
Round Table Pizza	1.04%

FIGURE 9.2 Table showing the ten largest pizza companies in 2019. Source: Pizza Today.

price, and we can safely analyze a market for a commodity like pizza using the supply and demand model, even though there are some slight variations in the product and the price.

9.4 OVERVIEW OF THE SUPPLY AND DEMAND MODEL AND EQUILIBRIUM

According to the supply and demand model, in competitive markets supply and demand interact to determine the equilibrium price and equilibrium quantity in the market. In this section we will briefly describe the model and how it works at a general level. In subsequent sections we go through each part of the model in detail.

In studying the relationship between price and quantity, economists have identified two major tendencies that dominate markets: (1) Firms tend to increase the amount of a good they want to sell as the price rises because it gets more and more profitable for the firm to supply a good as the price increases and (2) consumers tend to decrease the amount of a good that they want to purchase as the price increases, switching instead to lower priced goods or doing without the good altogether.

If we plot out the positive relationship between price and the quantity firms want to supply, we get the positively sloped supply curve in Figure 9.3. The supply curve has a positive slope because the higher the price, the larger the amount of the good that firms want to supply. Similarly, if we plot out the inverse relationship between price and quantity demanded, we get the negatively sloped demand curve in Figure 9.3. The demand curve has a negative slope because the higher the price

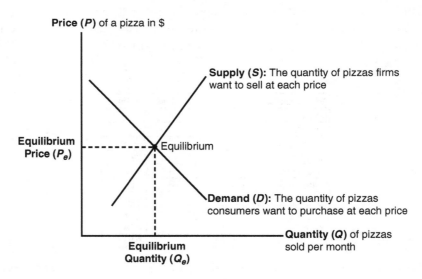

FIGURE 9.3 A graph of the supply and demand model for pizzas.

of the good, the smaller the quantity of the good consumers want to purchase. Where the supply and demand curves intersect we find the equilibrium point, where the quantity supplied is exactly equal to the quantity demanded, which determines the equilibrium price and equilibrium quantity.

Competitive markets always tend to move toward an equilibrium price and quantity due to the innate characteristics of markets—the invisible hand of the market that Adam Smith identified. In fact, markets abhor surpluses and shortages, and unless prevented by law, prices in markets will adjust to eliminate any surplus or shortage and move the market into equilibrium.

Consider graph (a) in Figure 9.4. We know that the equilibrium price (P_e) of a large cheese pizza in Lewisburg, Pennsylvania, is \$10. Now suppose that pizza restaurants in town try to charge a higher price than that, (P_H), of \$14. What will happen? Pizza restaurants want to sell more pizzas at a price of \$14 than they do at \$10. Making pizzas would be so profitable at that price that they could afford to hire more workers, buy more pizza delivery vehicles, and increase the quantity of pizzas they supply. The quantity they want to produce increases substantially. However, consumers have the opposite reaction. At \$14 pizzas are too expensive for many people, who will cook for themselves or buy other types of fast food instead of buying a pizza. When the price increases from \$10 (P_e) to \$14 (P_H), the quantity demanded decreases.

The result in Figure 9.4(a) is that at the high price, (P_H), the quantity of pizzas supplied is much greater than the quantity of pizzas demanded ($Q_S > Q_D$). This results in a surplus of pizzas: More pizzas are produced than are purchased. But for pizza producers, this is an unsustainable situation. As pizzas pile up, businesses cut back on production and lower prices to get rid of the surplus. As prices fall, consumers buy more pizzas. This process continues until we return back to

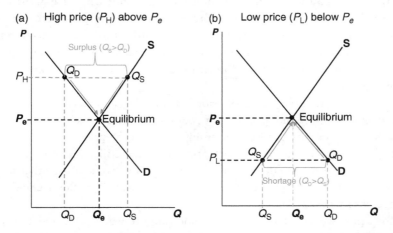

FIGURE 9.4 Prices adjusted to eliminate surpluses or shortages.

equilibrium at P_e where there is no longer any pressure for restaurants to cut prices and production.

Similarly, suppose pizza restaurants were to cut their prices below the equilibrium price of P_e = \$10 to a price of P_L = \$6 per pizza, which is depicted in Figure 9.4(b). That price is so low that many pizza restaurants would go out of business, and all firms would produce fewer pizzas because it is less profitable to do so. (They would probably start selling other types of food such as pasta and wings that are more profitable.) The quantity of pizzas supplied, (Q_S), declines as the price falls. Consumers, on the other hand, want to purchase a lot more pizzas at the new, lower price P_L. Quantity demanded, (Q_D), increases as the price falls. The result is a large shortage: consumers want a lot more pizzas than restaurants are willing to supply: $Q_D > Q_S$. How will the market respond to this shortage? Once businesses realize there is a shortage, they know they can increase prices and sell more pizzas. As they increase the price of pizza more and more in response to the shortage, the quantity of pizzas demanded falls steadily. Eventually we once again reach equilibrium at P_e and Q_e.

Next, we turn to how the supply and demand model works in more detail, analyzing the key factors that affect each curve. We can use this model to analyze how supply and demand interact to determine the price and quantity of goods and services and how price and quantity change in response to variations in key determinants of supply and demand.

9.5 THE THEORY OF DEMAND

To use the supply and demand model you need to understand each of its components and the major factors that affect them. We will start with the **theory of demand** and the **demand curve**.

According to the theory of demand in mainstream economics, **consumers' willingness to pay for a product (demand) depends on the benefit (marginal utility) they expect to get from consuming the product, the price of the product, disposable income and wealth, tastes and preferences, the prices of substitute and complementary goods, the number and size of buyers, expectations about the future, and the availability and cost of consumer credit.**

In order to determine the relationship between the factors that affect consumer demand and the prices and quantities of goods, economists developed the demand curve, which shows the precise relationship between the price of a good and the quantity of the good demanded at each price. Marginal utility and price determine the slope of the demand curve (whether it is steep or flat), and the other factors, known as the determinants of demand, affect the location of the demand curve (whether it shifts to the left or to the right).

To begin, we will focus on the relationship between price and the quantity demand. Quantity demanded is **the amount of a good or service that**

buyers are willing to purchase at each price in a particular time period.
Neoclassical economist Alfred Marshall's law of demand states that, **other
things being equal, the quantity of a good demanded is inversely related
to its price. When price increases, quantity demand decreases. When
price decreases, quantity demanded increases.** The law of demand focuses
exclusively on the relationship between price and quantity demanded, whereas the
theory of demand includes the effect of price and other factors on demand.

Consider your own purchases of a product like a pizza. If pizza is extremely
expensive—perhaps if it sells for a price of $30 per pizza—you would probably only
purchase it on rare occasions as a treat. If pizza is really cheap—if the price is only
$4 a pizza—you might buy it much more regularly. Note, however, that consumers
tend to be less and less willing to purchase an item the more they have of it. If you
have had pizza three nights in a row, on the fourth night you are much less likely to
want pizza again. This means, in economic terms, that you are less willing to pay
as much for pizza that night.

Economists use the concept of utility to explain this phenomenon. Utility
is **the amount of satisfaction a person gains from consuming a product.**
The law of diminishing marginal utility reflects the fact that **as a person
consumes more and more of one product, while holding consumption of
other products constant, that person experiences a decline in the additional (marginal) utility from each additional unit of that product consumed.** The law of diminishing marginal utility is the source of the negative
relationship between price and willingness to pay (quantity demanded). Consumers
are willing to pay a lot for something that is scarce and that they want very badly.
They are much less willing to pay for something that they have had a lot of and are
sick of having.

Economists construct a model of the demand curve based on such behavior.
Figure 9.5 shows the quantity of large cheese pizzas demanded at each price every
month by three consumers, Kate, Juan, and Bo. At a price of $14 per pizza, none
of them want to buy any. At that price, they prefer to buy less expensive alternative
forms of fast food. If the price falls to $12 per pizza, Kate will buy one pizza per

Price	Kate's quantity demanded	Juan's quantity demanded	Bo's quantity demanded	Market quantity demanded (sum of all 3)
$ 14.00	0	0	0	0
$ 12.00	1	2	3	6
$ 10.00	2	4	6	12
$ 8.00	3	6	9	18
$ 6.00	4	8	12	24
$ 4.00	5	10	15	30
$ 2.00	6	12	18	36
$ 0	7	14	21	42

FIGURE 9.5 Table showing the quantity of pizza demanded per month at each price.

month, Juan will buy two, and Bo will buy three. At a prize of $10 per pizza, Kate will buy two pizzas per month, Juan will buy four, and Bo will buy six. And so on.

To construct a market quantity demanded, we simply add up the quantity demanded for all economic actors in the market. If we assume that Kate, Juan, and Bo are the only consumers, the market quantity demanded is found by adding up all of the individual quantities demanded at each price. The result is the market quantity demanded in Figure 9.5.

We can use the information in Figure 9.5 to construct a graph of the demand curves for Kate, Juan, Bo, and the market. A demand curve **shows the quantity of a good buyers would like to purchase at each price within a particular period of time**. Figure 9.6 plots out the demand curves for Kate, Juan, Bo, and the market (if Kate, Juan, and Bo make up the entire market) using the data from Figure 9.5. As you can see, all of the demand curves have a negative slope, in keeping with the law of demand.

We can also use an equation to express a demand curve. In general, quantity demanded depends on price. In mathematical terms, $Q_d = f(P)$. Linear demand curves take the form

$$Q_d = a + bP,$$

where a is the quantity demanded when $P = 0$ and b is the inverse of the slope. The slope of the demand curve is the rise over the run. Slope = $(\Delta P / \Delta Q_d) = (1 / b)$.

b is always a negative number because when price increases, quantity demanded decreases and vice versa.

In Figure 9.6, the equation for Kate's demand curve is $Q_d = 7 - (0.5)P$. The equation for the market demand curve is $Q_d = 42 - 3P$.

The slope of the demand curve shows how quantity demanded changes whenever price changes. The location of the demand curve, whether it shifts to the left or to the right, depends on the **determinants of demand**.

9.6 THE DETERMINANTS OF DEMAND THAT CAUSE SHIFTS IN THE DEMAND CURVE

The demand curve is designed to show the direct relationship between price and the quantity demanded for a particular product (the law of demand). A change in price produces a change in the quantity demanded and causes a movement along the demand curve. For example, in Figure 9.6, if the price of a pizza falls from $12 to $10, the quantity of pizzas demanded in the market will increase from 6 to 12 (the second and third points on the market demand curve).

There are six factors that cause a shift in the entire demand curve. These are known as the determinants of demand: **The six factors that determine the location of the demand curve and whether or not it shifts to the left or**

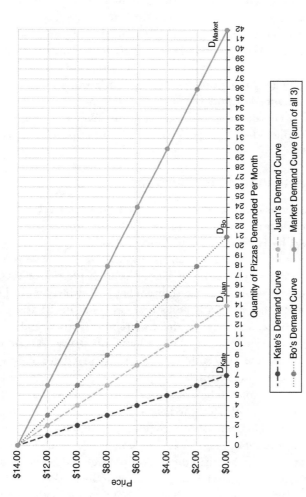

Quantity of Pizzas Demanded Per Month

Price

Kate's Demand Curve   Juan's Demand Curve
Bo's Demand Curve   Market Demand Curve (sum of all 3)

FIGURE 9.6 Demand curves for Kate, Juan, Bo, and the market.

to the right. **The determinants of demand are (1) disposable income and wealth, (2) tastes and preferences, (3) the prices of substitute and complementary goods, (4) the number and size (buying power) of buyers, (5) buyers' expectations about the future, and (6) the availability and cost of consumer credit**. The determinants of demand are held constant (the ceteris paribus conditions) when we draw a particular demand curve. This also means that when the determinants of demand change, we have to draw an entirely new demand curve reflecting the new information—the demand curve will have shifted.

Before we proceed, we need to highlight some very specific and precise language economists use when they talk about changes in demand. A change in the quantity demanded is **a movement along the demand curve caused by a change in the price of the good being demanded**. A change in demand refers to **a shift in the demand curve to the left or to the right due to a change in one of the determinants of demand**. We go through each of the determinants of demand below, starting with the most important one, disposable income and wealth.

9.6.1 Disposable income and wealth

Disposable income is **the income people have to spend after the government has taken out taxes (after tax income)**. Household wealth is **the value of the assets held by individuals and households**.

In general, for all normal goods an increase in income or wealth will lead to consumers wanting to buy more of a good at each price than they used to. The entire demand curve shifts to the right. Suppose that incomes in Lewisburg, Pennsylvania, double because of a huge natural gas boom in the area that creates a lot of jobs and income. When people have more money, they tend to buy more goods in general, and they definitely tend to buy more pizzas. As you can see in Figure 9.7(a), when income or wealth increases, the demand curve moves further to the right at each price. For example, at a price of $10, consumers in Lewisburg wanted 30,000 pizzas per month before the increase in income (point A), but they want 50,000 pizzas per month after the increase in income. The entire curve has shifted to the right by 20,000 pizzas: At each price, people want 20,000 more pizzas than they used to as a result of the increase in income. (Note that we are depicting the full market for pizzas, rather than the market of three people we used earlier as an example. Now we have thousands of consumers in the market.)

If we put the demand curve from Figure 9.7(a) together with a supply curve, we can see how a rightward shift in demand affects the equilibrium price and quantity of pizzas. The rightward increase in demand creates a shortage of pizzas at a price of $10: 50,000 people want pizzas (point B in Figure 9.7(b)), but suppliers only want to supply 30,000 pizzas (point A) at that price. Once pizza producers see that more people want their pizzas than pizzerias can provide, they will take advantage of the increase in demand to raise their prices and hire more workers so they can

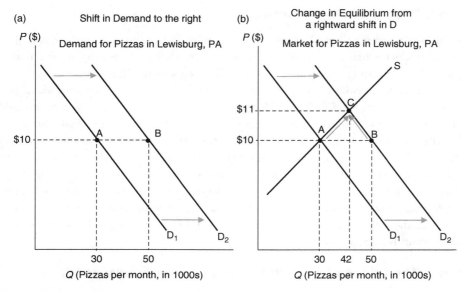

FIGURE 9.7 A shift in demand to the right (increase in demand).

increase pizza production, moving from point A to point C along the supply curve. As the price of pizzas increases, consumers purchase fewer of them, reducing their quantity demanded from 50 to 42 and moving from point B to point C, which is the new equilibrium.

A decrease in income or wealth would do the opposite. When the stock market crashed in 2008 and people saw the value of their assets decline by 60%, they purchased fewer goods of all types and the demand curves for most goods, including pizza, shifted to the left (decreased).

The examples given above describe normal goods, which are defined as **goods that consumers want to buy more of when their income or wealth increases and that they want to buy less of when their income or wealth decreases**. But we do sometimes find inferior goods, which are **goods that consumers want to buy less of as their income or wealth increases or more of as their income or wealth decreases**. Examples of inferior goods include used clothing, used cars, inexpensive brands of all types, less desirable types of foods, and other goods that people would choose not to buy if they had more money. If people have more money, they tend to increase their demand for higher quality items and decrease their demand for lower quality items. For example, during economic booms when incomes and wealth increase, people buy more expensive brands of beer, including imported brands (Heineken, Stella Artois) and microbrews (Samuel Adams, Victory, Dogfish Head), while buying less bargain brands (Pabst Blue Ribbon, Natural Light, Old Milwaukee). The demand for premium beers *increases* when income increases, but the demand for bargain beers (inferior goods) *decreases*.

9.6.2 Tastes and preferences

Consumers' tastes and preferences can have a significant influence on the demand for a product when large numbers of consumers shift their buying habits. For example, as health concerns about obesity, diabetes, and artificial sweeteners grew and as anti-carbohydrate diets became prominent, demand for sodas (soft drinks) plummeted. From 2004 to 2017, U.S. consumers decreased their purchases of sodas from 10.2 billion cases to 8.6 billion cases, a drop of 15%. In Figure 9.8(a) you can see that the demand curve for sodas shifts to the left by 3.2 billion cases due to the decrease in consumers' interest in soda. Figure 9.8(b) shows how the leftward shift in demand creates a surplus of soda (the line between point A and point B). As surplus soda builds up in inventories, soda companies like Coca-Cola and Pepsi cut back production and lower prices, moving the quantity supplied from point A to point C, the new equilibrium. As firms drop their prices, consumer demand moves from point B to point C.

9.6.3 The prices of substitute and complementary goods

Demand curves also shift when the prices of closely related goods change. A sub–stitute good is **a product that consumers are willing to purchase instead of another good; when the price of one good increases, many consumers will switch to buying the substitute good, increasing the demand for the substitute**. A substitute for Coca-Cola is Pepsi. A substitute for beef is chicken. A complementary good is **a product that consumers tend to purchase along**

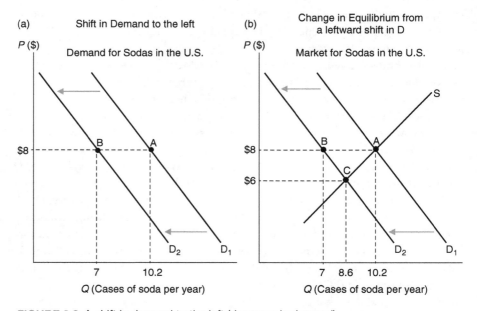

FIGURE 9.8 A shift in demand to the left (decrease in demand).

with another good; when the price of one good increases and consumers buy less of it, there will also be a decrease in the demand for any complementary goods. Complements for peanut butter are bread and jelly. A complement for a cell phone is a case for the phone.

As an example of substitute goods, when deciding how to heat their homes, households choose between electric, coal, wood, oil, and natural gas—these goods are substitutes for each other. As you can see in Figure 9.9, the increase in the supply of natural gas from fracking has led to a dramatic drop in natural gas prices during the last decade, which has caused households to increase the quantity of natural gas demanded (moving along the natural gas demand curve down and to the right from point A to point B). There is a movement along the demand curve for natural gas because of the decrease in the price of natural gas. In the heating oil market, however, there is a shift in the demand curve for heating oil to the left as households buy more gas and less heating oil. Equilibrium in the heating oil market moves from point C to point D, with a lower equilibrium price and quantity. Note that in these graphs we use P_1, P_2, Q_1, and Q_2 instead of putting in specific numbers. Economists are often interested in general trends in markets. In this case, economists were able to predict that the decrease in the price of natural gas and the increase in the quantity of natural gas demanded in Figure 9.9(a) would be matched by a decrease in demand (leftward shift) for heating oil that we see in Figure 9.9(b).

There are also numerous examples of complementary goods. When someone buys a laptop computer, they also tend to buy a laptop bag, an external mouse, a monitor, and a printer. When you buy a printer, you will eventually need more ink for it. When you buy a car, you will also need to buy gas, tires, and car insurance.

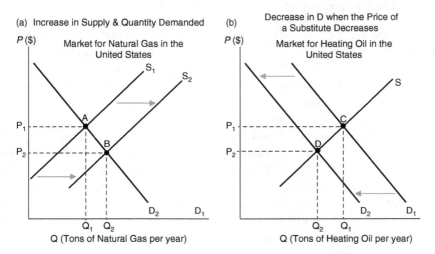

FIGURE 9.9 A decrease in the price of a substitute good (gas) causes a decrease in demand (oil).

For another concrete example, there was a large increase in the market supply of gasoline from 2014 to 2015, which caused gas prices to fall by more than 50%. Gasoline is a strong complement for large trucks and sport utility vehicles (SUVs). SUV sales increased by 16% as gas prices fell, a significant increase in demand (rightward shift). However, sales of passenger cars fell by 2%—passenger cars are substitutes for SUVs. When consumers shift their tastes toward SUVs because of low gas prices, this causes a decrease (leftward shift) in the demand for passenger cars. (See if you can draw this situation on a set of three graphs of the gasoline market, the SUV market, and the passenger car market.)

9.6.4 The number or size of buyers

The number of buyers, and especially the number of larger buyers, has a big influence over the demand for a product. If there is an increase in the number or size of buyers, the demand for a product will increase (shift to the right). If there is a decrease in the number or size of buyers, the demand for a product will decrease (shift to the left). For example, when the government raised the national drinking age to 21 in 1984, this meant that fewer consumers could legally drink in bars. Many bars started losing money due to the *decrease in demand* for drinks at bars, causing some bars to close. Interestingly, most data indicate that the increase in the drinking age had no significant impact on alcohol consumption; there was just less alcohol consumption in public settings such as bars.

The size of buyers also impacts demand significantly. If you manufacture a product and Walmart, the largest retailer in the United States, decides to stock your product to sell to consumers, you will experience a significant *increase in demand* because you have attracted a huge buyer.

9.6.5 Buyers' expectations about the future

Expectations can affect the demand for a product in several ways. If consumers expect their incomes or wealth to increase, or if they are confident about the future, they tend to *increase their demand* for goods. If consumers worry that they might lose their job or that the value of their stock market portfolio might drop significantly, they will *decrease their demand* for goods. Ironically, if consumers expect a recession, they can help to cause one by reducing their purchases due to pessimism! Consumers might also change their demand for a particular good if they expect its price to change: If people expect home prices to drop, they often wait to purchase a home. People also shift their demand for a product if they think they might lose access to it. A mass shooting in San Bernardino in 2015 led President Obama to call for stricter background checks and gun regulations. This caused a significant *increase in demand* for guns by consumers who were worried they might not be able to buy guns in the future. Thus, consumer expectations of all types affect the demand for products.

9.6.7 The availability and cost of consumer credit

The more access that consumers have to borrowing and the lower the interest payments they have to make on their debt, the more purchases they can make. In 2017 consumer credit card debt reached $784 billion—that means consumers were able to buy over $700 billion more goods than they could have if they just relied on their income and wealth to make purchases. That amounts to a huge *increase in demand* for many products. Low interest rates on car loans and easier access to those loans increased the demand for cars in the 2010s.

Now that we have discussed the factors that drive the behavior of the demand curve, it is time to turn to the supply curve and the behavior of sellers in more detail.

9.7 THE THEORY OF SUPPLY

According to the theory of supply in mainstream economics, **sellers' willingness to offer a product for sale (supply) in a perfectly competitive market depends on the price they expect to get from selling the product, the cost, productivity and availability of inputs, the technology available to make the product, sellers' expectations about the future, changes in the profitability of other markets the seller can supply, and the number and size of suppliers**.

In order to determine the relationship between the factors that affect suppliers and the prices and quantities of goods, economists developed the supply curve that shows the precise relationship between the price of a good and the quantity of the good supplied at each price. The marginal cost of producing a product, which is driven by the cost and marginal productivity of inputs, determines the slope of the supply curve (whether it is steep or flat), and the other factors affect the location of the supply curve (whether it is shifted to the left or to the right).

First, we will focus on the relationship between price and the quantity supplied. Quantity supplied is **the amount of a good or service that sellers are willing to offer for sale in a particular time period at each price**. The law of supply states that, **other things being equal, the quantity of a good supplied is directly related to its price. When price increases, quantity supplied increases. When price decreases, quantity supplied decreases**. This means that the supply curve is upward sloping in the short run.

The short run is **the period of time in which one or more inputs are fixed and cannot be changed, so only variable inputs can be adjusted**. For a pizzeria, in the short run they are stuck with the size of their restaurant and kitchen—their capital stock is fixed. If they experience an increase in demand for pizzas, they can supply pizzas quickly and easily until all of the specialized jobs in the pizzeria are taken. But once all of the ovens are baking and all of the waiters, cooks, delivery persons, and cashiers are working at capacity, it is extremely difficult to increase pizza production any further. And it would be less efficient to do so, involving people crowding in each other's way to do their work, waiting for a pizza oven to become free, and so on. The cost of each additional pizza would rise as more are produced under these conditions. Thus, the only way the pizzeria will continue to increase production when the restaurant is running out of capacity and costs per pizza are increasing is if the price of pizza is high enough to offset the increasing costs. In other words, the only way to entice a pizzeria to produce more pizza is for consumers to offer a higher price: An upward sloping supply curve.

Economists construct a model of the supply curve based on these characteristics of small firms in competitive markets. Figure 9.10 shows the quantity of large cheese pizzas supplied every month at each price by two firms, Pizza Hut and Domino's. At a price of $4 per pizza, neither pizzeria wants to sell any pizzas: That price isn't high enough to cover their costs and they would have to close down. If the price increases to $6, Pizza Hut will offer 1000 pizzas for sale and Domino's will offer 2000 pizzas for sale. If the price increases to $8, Pizza Hut will offer 2000 pizzas for sale and Domino's will offer 4000. And so on. Notice that as the prize of a pizza rises and selling pizzas becomes more profitable, the quantity of pizzas supplied per month increases.

To construct a market quantity supplied, we add up the quantity supplied for all sellers in the market. If we assume that Pizza Hut and Domino's are the only sellers, the market quantity supplied is found by adding up all of the individual quantities supplied at each price. The result is the "quantity supplied" column in Figure 9.10.

We can use the information in Figure 9.10 to construct a graph of the supply curves for Pizza Hut, Domino's, and the pizza market. A supply curve **shows the quantity of a good that a seller will offer for sale at each price within a particular period of time**. Figure 9.11 plots out the supply curves for Pizza Hut, Domino's, and the pizza market (if Pizza Hut and Domino's make up the entire sellers' side of the market). All of the supply curves have a positive slope, in keeping with the law of supply.

Price	Pizza Hut's quantity supplied	Domino's quantity supplied	Market supply (sum of both)
$14.00	5000	10,000	15,000
$12.00	4000	8000	12,000
$10.00	3000	6000	9000
$ 8.00	2000	4000	6000
$ 6.00	1000	2000	3000
$ 4.00	0	0	0

FIGURE 9.10 Table showing the quantity of pizza supplied per month at each price.

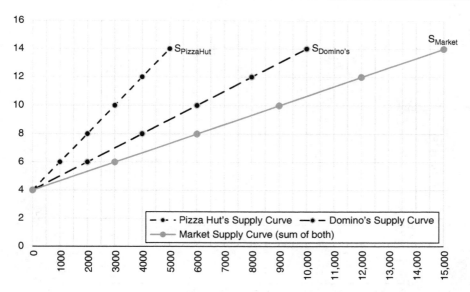

FIGURE 9.11 Supply curves for Pizza Hut, Domino's, and the market for pizzas.

We can also use an equation to express a supply curve. Quantity supplied depends on price. In mathematical terms, $Q_s = f(P)$. Linear demand curves take the form

$$Q_s = a + bP.$$

$-\dfrac{a}{b}$ is the intercept on the price axis when $Q = 0$ and b is the inverse of the slope. The slope of the supply curve is the rise over the run. Slope = $(\Delta P / \Delta Q_s) = (1 / b)a$.

b is always a positive number in the equation for a supply curve because when price increases, quantity supplied increases and when price decreases, quantity supplied decreases.

In Figure 9.11, the equation for Pizza Hut's supply curve is $Q_s = -2000 + (500)P$. The equation for the market supply curve is $Q_s = -6000 + 1500P$.

We can use equations for supply and demand to solve for equilibrium price and quantity. Suppose that the equation for the market demand curve is $Q_d = 12,000 - 300P$.

In equilibrium we know that $Q_S = Q_D$. Setting the equations for Q_S and Q_D equal to each other, we get the following:

$$Q_S = -6000 + 1500P; Q_d = 12,000 - 300P;$$
$$Q_S = Q_D; (-6000 + 1500P) = (12,000 - 300P)$$

Solving for P we get $1800P = 18,000$. The equilibrium price $P_e = 10$. If we plug $P = 10$ into the equations for Q_S and Q_D, we find that the equilibrium quantity $Q_e = 9000$.

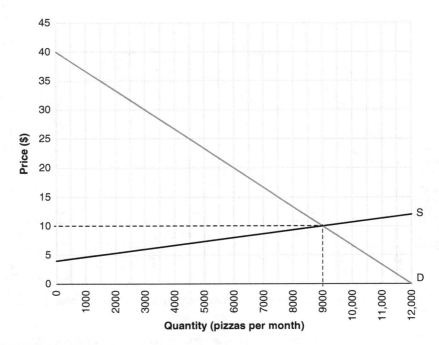

FIGURE 9.12 Equilibrium where $Q_S = Q_D$.

If we plot out the equations for the demand curve and the supply curve, we get Figure 9.12. The supply (S) and demand (D) curves intersect at the equilibrium price of $10 and the equilibrium quantity of 9000 pizzas per month. Therefore, we can use either an equation or a graph to show the relationship between supply and demand and to find equilibrium price and quantity.

The slope of the supply curve shows how the quantity supplied changes whenever price changes. The location of the supply curve, and whether it shifts to the left or to the right, depends on the **determinants of supply**.

9.8 THE DETERMINANTS OF SUPPLY

The determinants of supply are **the five factors that determine the location of the supply curve and whether or not it shifts to the left or to the right. The determinants of supply are (1) the cost, productivity, and availability of inputs; (2) the technology available to make the product; (3) sellers' expectations about the future; (4) changes in the profitability of other markets the seller can supply; and (5) the number and size of sellers.** The determinants of supply are held constant (the ceteris paribus conditions) when we draw a particular supply curve. When the determinants of supply change, we draw an entirely new supply curve reflecting the new information that caused the supply curve to shift.

9.8.1 The cost, productivity, and availability of inputs

Inputs are **the factors of production—labor, capital, land, and natural resources—used to produce goods and services**. Let's focus on labor for now because it is the most important input for most firms, making up about 61% of the costs of production on average. Suppose that the President of the United States suggests a complete ban on the use of illegal immigrant labor and threatens to impose huge fines on any companies that are caught employing illegal immigrants. Businesses that slaughter and process chickens depend on illegal immigrant labor to do much of the work in their industry—they find that legal U.S. citizens do not want to do this kind of work at the wages that businesses want to pay. The result of a crackdown on illegal immigration would be a reduction in the availability of laborers for chicken processing firms. Suppliers of chicken would not be able to supply as much chicken at each price as they used to, so the entire supply curve for chicken shifts to the left, as we see in Figure 9.13(a).

When we put the shift in supply on a graph with the demand curve for chicken, we see that when the supply curve shifts to the left, this creates a shortage (the distance from point A to point B). This causes the equilibrium price to rise from $1.50 per pound of chicken to $1.75 per pound, and the equilibrium quantity falls from 39 billion pounds per year to 32 billion.

Anything that raises the cost, reduces the productivity, or reduces the availability of inputs will cause the supply curve to decrease (shift to the left). Anything that lowers the cost, increases the productivity, or increases the availability of inputs will cause the supply curve to increase (shift to the right).

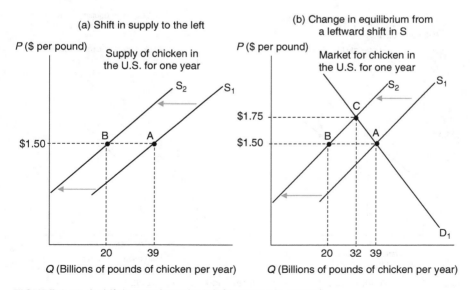

FIGURE 9.13 A shift in supply to the left (decrease in supply).

9.8.2 The technology available to make the product

Technology can be a major driver of the costs of production and therefore a major determinant of the location of the supply curve. Improvements in technology increase productivity and reduce the cost of producing each unit of output, reducing a supplier's costs of production.

The invention of robots to produce cars and trucks dramatically increased productivity and reduced the cost of producing cars. This caused the supply curve for cars to shift to the right: At each price, car suppliers were willing to offer more cars and trucks for sale than before. This is shown in Figure 9.14(a) with the shift in the supply curve for cars and trucks to the right. In Figure 9.14(b) we see that when we include the demand curve in the market for U.S. cars and trucks, the increase in supply from point A to point B creates a surplus of cars and trucks: At a price of $35,000 suppliers offer 20 million new cars and trucks for sale (point B) but consumers only want to purchase 16 million cars and trucks. The surplus causes suppliers to drop prices and reduce the number of cars and trucks they offer for sale (the quantity supplied) and they move from point B to point C. As producers of cars and trucks drop prices, the quantity demanded increases, moving from point A to point C. Notice that, compared with the original equilibrium at point A, the increase in supply causes the equilibrium to move to point C. The equilibrium price falls from $35,000 to $34,000, and the equilibrium quantity increases from 16 million to 18 million cars and trucks sold per year.

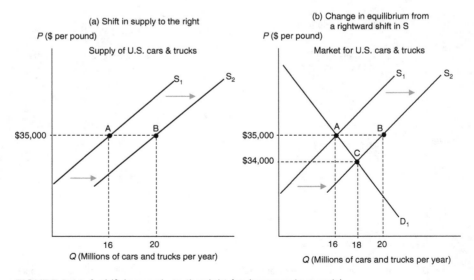

FIGURE 9.14 A shift in supply to the right (an increase in supply).

9.8.3 Sellers' expectations about the future

Sellers change the amount of goods and services they offer for sale based on **expected profitability**. If firms expect an increase in price or profitability in their market in the future, they will often decide to increase production and offer more goods for sale (an increase in supply) immediately to take advantage of the expected opportunity. This is partly because it can take a significant amount of time between the decision to increase production and the actual sale of a product to consumers. For complex manufactured goods it can take more than six months. Correspondingly, if firms expect a recession in the near future, they may well curtail production right away, reducing their supply of goods and laying off workers. This can, of course, help to bring about the recession that firms anticipated.

9.8.4 Changes in the profitability of other markets the seller can supply

Changes in profitability in other markets a firm operates in can also cause a shift in the supply curve. For example, IBM was once a big player in the personal computer and laptop market. But in the early 2000s it was losing money on personal computers, while its business consulting division was highly profitable. The logical decision was for them to reduce their supply of computers, which they did by selling off their computer division to Lenovo, which now produces the (originally IBM-designed) ThinkPad. IBM poured the resources they garnered from selling their personal computer division into business consulting and other ventures, increasing their supply of services in these markets.

As another example, milk prices fell by 34% from 2014 to 2015, due to a decline in demand from foreign buyers. Faced with low prices and poor profitability in milk markets, farmers reduced their supply and turned to other products, increasing their supply of beef and soybeans. Because farmers can use their land to produce a variety of products, when one good is less profitable, they will reduce their production of that good and increase their supply of the other goods they can produce. In terms of supply and demand, with the recent milk example we saw the following: In the milk market, the demand curve shifted to the left as foreign buyers purchased less U.S. milk. This caused the price of milk to fall, which in turn resulted in a decrease in the quantity of milk supplied (a movement along the supply curve). In the soybean market, farmers decided to raise fewer cattle on their land and to grow soybeans instead, increasing the supply (rightward shift) of soybeans. This caused the equilibrium price of soybeans to fall while the equilibrium price declined as well. (Exercise: See if you can draw this chain of events on your own.)

9.8.5 The number and size of suppliers

If more suppliers enter a market, and especially if more large suppliers enter a market, the market supply curve will increase (shift to the right). The early smartphone market was dominated by Ericsson, Palm, and Blackberry. In 2007 Apple changed the market significantly with the iPhone, which was the first commercial smartphone to use touchscreen input instead of relying primarily on a stylus or keyboard. Apple completely dominated the smartphone market and charged very high prices until 2010 when Samsung released the Galaxy and began making larger, slimmer, and cheaper touchscreen smartphones. With the increase in the supply of smartphones in 2010 as the huge firm, Samsung, entered the market, the market supply of smartphones shifted to the right and the market price of smartphones fell. Even Apple was compelled to lower its prices to compete.

Now that you understand the basics of how the supply and demand model works, you are ready for more complex supply and demand problems. Take some time to practice using the supply and demand model and then go on to the new applications of supply and demand in the next chapter.

9.9 CONCLUSION

In this chapter we began by defining what a market is and giving examples of the different kinds of market transactions we see in modern capitalism. We also described the major institutions that make markets work and how those institutions support markets. In a market capitalist economy, creating and safeguarding the institutions that make markets work is a major role for government.

We then turned to the supply and demand model and the assumptions upon which that model rests. When these assumptions are violated, the supply and demand model may not apply accurately to the real world, something that is very important to understand.

Subsequently, we used supply and demand curves to explain why markets tend toward an equilibrium price and quantity and why markets inevitably work to eliminate surpluses and shortages via changes in prices. Then we went through the supply and demand model in greater detail, working through what moves the market along a curve and what shifts a curve. The basics of the supply and demand model are as follows:

- A **movement along the demand curve** (an increase or decrease in the quantity demanded) is caused by a shift in the supply curve or, as we will see in the next chapter, a government law mandating a legally set minimum or maximum price.
- A **shift in the demand curve** (increase or decrease in demand) is caused by a change in one of the six determinants of demand.
- A **movement along the supply curve** (an increase or decrease in the quantity supplied) is caused by a shift in the demand curve or, as we will see, a government law mandating a legally set minimum or maximum price.
- A **shift in the supply curve** is caused by a change in one of the five determinants of supply.

In almost all cases, a change in a determinant will cause a shift in either the demand curve or the supply curve. Only one curve will shift. However, as we will see in more detail in the next chapter, there are two exceptions to this rule: wages and advertising. **Wages affect consumers' incomes, which shifts the demand curve, but wages also affect suppliers' costs of production, which shifts the supply curve.** Similarly, **advertising affects consumers' tastes and preferences, which shifts the demand curve, but advertising is very costly and any change in costs shifts the supply curve**. We go through these and other more complicated aspects of the supply and demand model in the next chapter.

· ·

QUESTIONS FOR REVIEW

1. Carefully explain what a market is and give *specific* examples of two different kinds of markets.
2. Which of the institutions that make markets work do you think is most important? Why? Explain carefully.
3. Cuba has little history of using markets over the last half century. Suppose that the Cuban government wants to develop a robust market system while still preserving the equality and high level of human development they have achieved via a communist approach. What should they do? Explain in terms of the institutions necessary to support markets.
4. Suppose that the cost of engaging in internet transactions increases substantially due to cybercrime. What are the likely consequences? What markets would be affected, and what types of impacts would you expect to see?
5. Which of the assumptions of the supply and demand model are most likely to cause the model to lead to inaccurate results. Explain carefully. Give specific examples to support your argument.
6. Using the graph of the U.S. market for wheat in Figure 9.15 as your starting point, show how the supply and demand curves for **wheat** will be affected

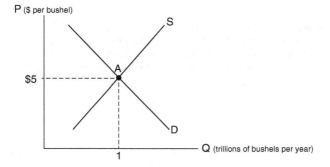

FIGURE 9.15 The U.S. market for wheat.

by specific events and show what happens to equilibrium price and quantity. (Note: Make sure to identify whether or not the demand and supply curves shift or whether you are moving along the demand and supply curves.) Draw a new graph for each part (a to d), and begin each graph at point A.

a. Wealth increases due to a boom in the stock market.

b. Lower oil prices cause the price of fertilizer used in growing wheat to decrease.

c. Consumers' preferences change toward buying more gluten-free products, so they reduce the amount of products they buy that contain wheat (which contains gluten).

d. Corn prices increase. (Note: Most farmers grow both corn and wheat on their farms. Consumers do not consider wheat and corn to be substitutes or complements.)

7. Using a graph of the U.S. market for Uber rides, show how the supply and demand curves for Uber rides will be affected by specific events, and show what happens to equilibrium price and quantity. (Note: Make sure to identify whether or not the demand and supply curves shift or whether you are moving along the demand and supply curves.) Draw a new graph for each part (a to d).

a. New, inexpensive technology allows all Uber vehicles to become driverless, replacing existing drivers without compromising service.

b. The price of Lyft, another type of taxi/ride-sharing service, increases significantly.

c. An Uber self-driving vehicle has a major accident in which several people die due to a software glitch. Consumers start to prefer rides with non-Uber companies.

d. Wages increase for workers around the country (including Uber drivers and others) due to an economic boom.

8. Find an article in a major newspaper that describes a change in the price of some type of good or service. Use a graph of supply and demand to explain the forces that caused the price of the good or service to change.

NOTE

1 World Economic Forum, "Corporate Brand Reputation Outranks Financial Performance as Most Important Measure of Success," January 22, 2004. https://www.csrwire.com/press_releases/21696-corporate-brand-reputation-outranks-financial-preformance-as-most-important-measure-of-success, accessed July 26, 2021.

Applications of supply and demand

Wages, advertising, price floors and ceilings, excise taxes and subsidies, consumer and producer surplus, and elasticity

This chapter contains a series of applications of the supply and demand model that was introduced in the previous chapter. We begin by analyzing the impact of changes in wages and advertising on markets. These are the only two factors that shift *both* the supply and demand curves. Other determinants shift only one curve at a time.

Subsequently, the chapter takes up government regulations of markets. Governments intervene directly in markets in many ways. They install price floors, also known as price supports, to help out suppliers such as farmers. They impose price ceilings to reduce prices for consumers on products like apartments and food staples. They impose excise taxes on suppliers of products like cigarettes and alcohol to raise tax revenue and to discourage consumers from buying these products. They subsidize producers of goods like electric cars or vaccinations to encourage the production of these goods. These government policies have an impact on the welfare of producers and consumers that we can analyze using the concepts of consumer surplus, producer surplus, and deadweight loss, which we will explain below.

This chapter also takes up the topic of elasticity, which shows the precise responsiveness of the quantity demanded and the quantity supplied to changes in prices and income. Using elasticity we can anticipate the likely magnitude of changes in quantities in response to changes in price and income.

Note that to obtain a comprehensive understanding of how to use the supply and demand model, you will need to practice with this material extensively. After reading each section, try some of the relevant problems at the end of this chapter. This will help to cement your understanding of the material.

DOI: 10.4324/9781315636924-13

10.0 CHAPTER 10 LEARNING GOALS

After reading this chapter you should be able to:

- ▪ Use the supply and demand model to analyze the impact of changes in wages or advertising.

- ▪ Use the supply and demand model to analyze the impact of price floors, price ceilings, excise taxes, and subsidies on consumers, producers, and the government.

- ▪ Explain the concepts of consumer surplus, producer surplus, and deadweight loss and how these concepts can be used to evaluate the impact of government policies.

- ▪ Compute the price elasticity of demand or supply and apply the concept of price elasticity to analyze supply and demand problems.

- ▪ Utilize income elasticity of demand and cross-price elasticity of demand to analyze how the demand for a particular product is affected by changes in incomes and changes in the prices of substitute and complementary goods.

10.1 DOUBLE SHIFTS: THE IMPACT OF CHANGES IN WAGES AND ADVERTISING

Figure 10.1 lays out the key elements of the supply and demand model that were explained in the previous chapter. In almost all cases, a change in a determinant of demand or supply will cause a single shift in either the demand or the supply curve.

For example, the following changes in the determinants of demand would cause an **increase in the demand curve** for a normal good and a movement along the supply curve up and to the right, as we saw in Figure 9.7(b):

- An increase in wealth
- An increase in the price of a substitute good
- An increase in the number of buyers
- More positive expectations about future income and wealth
- Easier access to credit cards.

The following changes in the determinants of supply would cause an increase in the **supply curve** for a typical good and a movement along the demand curve down and to the right, as we saw in Figure 9.14(b):

Factors that cause a **movement along a demand curve** (change in quantity demanded) for a particular good: A change in the price of the good, caused by:

1. a shift in the supply curve, or
2. the installation of a government price ceiling or price floor.

Factors that cause a **shift in the demand curve** (change in demand) to the right or left: A change in:

1. disposable income (including *wages*) and wealth,
2. tastes and preferences (shaped in part by *advertising*),
3. the prices of substitute and complementary goods,
4. the number and size of buyers,
5. buyers' expectations about the future, and
6. the availability and cost of consumer credit.

Factors that cause a **movement along the supply curve** (change in quantity supplied) for a particular good: A change in the price of the good caused by:

1. a shift in the demand curve, or
2. the installation of a government price ceiling or price floor.

Factors that cause a **shift in the supply curve** (change in supply) to the right or left: A change in:

1. the cost, productivity, and availability of inputs(including *wages, advertising costs*),
2. the technology available to make the product,
3. sellers' expectations about the future,
4. changes in the profitability of other markets the seller can supply, and
5. the number and size of sellers.

FIGURE 10.1 Movements along and shifts in supply and demand curves.

- The cost of energy declines.
- A new technology that reduces costs is invented.
- Sellers expect profits to increase in the future.
- Profits from selling other goods sold by sellers in this market decline.
- The number of sellers in the market increases.

In these cases, one curve shifts and then you move along the other curve to a new equilibrium price and quantity. If you can successfully identify which curve shifts in what direction, you should be able to solve any basic supply and demand problem.

There are two cases in which both supply and demand curves shift. Notice that in Figure 10.1 wages and advertising appear in the list of factors that shift the demand curve *and* the list of factors that shift the supply curve. These are the only factors that consistently shift both supply and demand curves.

Suppose that the U.S. government increases the federal minimum wage to $15 per hour from its 2021 level of $7.25 per hour. This would be a significant increase in wages for many workers, giving them more money to spend and increasing their demand (shifting demand to the right) for all normal goods and services. However, that increase in wages is also a cost paid by sellers. Their costs have increased, which causes the supply curve to decrease (shift to the left) for those businesses affected by the higher minimum wage. (Businesses that already pay their workers more than $15 per hour would not experience an increase in costs.)

McDonald's Corporation is one of the nation's largest employers of low-wage labor. Let's consider how raising the minimum wage would affect the market for McDonald's Big Mac hamburgers. First, given that most of McDonald's employees make less than $15 an hour, McDonald's would experience higher costs of production. Although some of that increase in costs would be offset by the fact that higher paid workers tend to be more productive, their costs would increase somewhat. Therefore, the supply curve decreases, shifting to the left from S_1 to S_2 in Figure 10.2.

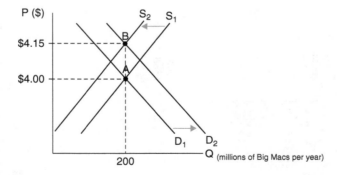

FIGURE 10.2 The effect of an increase in wages on the U.S. market for McDonald's Big Macs.

But workers at McDonald's and other low-wage employers now have a lot more money than they used to, and they use it to buy a lot more goods, including Bic Mac hamburgers (Big Macs are a normal good). The demand for Big Mac hamburgers increases, shifting to the right from D_1 to D_2 in Figure 10.2. What is the end result? The double shift caused by a change in wages—the increase in demand and the decrease in supply—results in little or no change in the equilibrium quantity but a small increase in the equilibrium price, as the market moves from point A (where D_1 and S_1 intersect) to point B (where D_2 and S_2 intersect) in Figure 10.2.

Advertising also shifts both supply and demand curves. Advertising is very expensive, so implementing an advertising campaign causes an increase in costs, which causes a decrease in the supply curve (a shift to the left). But effective advertising increases demand and, if it increases brand name recognition, makes the demand curve steeper because consumers are willing to pay a higher price for each unit of a good. A recent study by Rob Nelissen and Marijn Meijers of Tilburg University in the Netherlands showed that wearing clothes with designer labels leads other people to regard you as wealthier and of higher status, whereas wearing the same clothes with no label does not have the same impact.[1] The logo of the brand is what makes the product more valuable, conveying status and importance. But brand name recognition has to be created over time, often with large expenditures of advertising.

Consider the case of Apple laptops. By the 2010s Apple laptops dominated the market on college campuses, with over 70% of students purchasing an Apple laptop. But in the 2000s, Apple had only a tiny share of the market, even though they were making superb laptops. Apple changed this with one of history's most successful advertising campaigns, "Mac vs. PC," launched in 2006. The ads first labeled PCs as good for business and boring while displaying Apple Macs as better for photos, music, videos, and fun. Then the ads ridiculed the tendency of PCs to freeze and catch viruses whereas Macs were largely immune from such things. After more than 60 different commercials over four years, Apple had successfully persuaded college students that Apple Mac laptops were fast, fun, and hip whereas PCs were slow, boring, and only good for business.

In terms of supply and demand, the huge Mac vs. PC ad campaign cost Apple a lot of money. Apple spent $264 million on television advertising in 2008 alone, over $100 million more than Microsoft spent on PC advertising. This large increase in costs shifted the supply curve to the left, a decrease in supply depicted in Figure 10.3 as the shift from S_1 to S_2. The decrease in supply was more than matched by the huge increase in demand. The campaign was so successful that sales of Apple Mac laptops quadrupled. College students became more and more convinced that the Apple Mac was the only laptop they should consider purchasing. This brand name recognition meant that students were willing to buy a Mac laptop even if the price increased. This is evidence of a steeper demand curve, which we see in the movement from D_1 to D_2 in Figure 10.3. The equilibrium has moved from point A, where D_1 and S_1 intersect, to point B where D_2 and S_2 intersect.

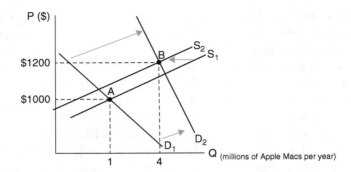

FIGURE 10.3 The effect of an increase in advertising on the U.S. market for Apple Macintosh (Mac) computers.

The Apple ad campaign was extremely successful because the increase in demand more than offset the decrease in supply from the costs of the campaign, making Apple a lot more money in the process. An unsuccessful ad campaign would be one in which the ads fail to increase and steepen the demand curve enough to offset the higher costs that decrease the supply curve. If demand increases less than supply decreases from an unsuccessful ad campaign, the equilibrium quantity will actually decline.

As the Apple example shows, the steepness of the demand curve is important in affecting outcomes. The slope of the demand curve is related to a concept called price elasticity, which measures the responsiveness of quantity demanded to changes in price. Demand curves can be flat (elastic), steep (inelastic), or somewhere in between.

A flat, or elastic, demand curve means that even a small increase in price will result in a large decrease in the quantity demanded, such as the demand curve in Figure 10.4(a) for Natty Light Beer. Goods that have lots of substitutes and are not necessities tend to have elastic demand curves. There are many, many substitutes for Natty Light, so consumers will buy a lot less of it if Natty Light becomes more expensive than similar products.

A steep, or inelastic, demand curve means that even with a large increase in price, most consumers will continue to buy a product, such as the demand curve for gasoline in Figure 10.4(b). Even if the price of gasoline increases a lot from P_1 to P_2, the quantity demanded in Figure 10.4(b) only falls slightly from Q_1 to Q_2. Necessities, goods that have few substitutes, or products with strong brand name recognition (like Apple MacBooks) tend to have inelastic demand curves. Most people need to drive a car that uses gasoline in order to get to work or to buy necessities, so they are not able to drive much less when gasoline prices increase. In the short term, the demand for gasoline is extremely inelastic.

We tend to see elastic (flat) **supply** curves when it is easy for firms to increase the quantity supplied when the price increases. Pizza firms that can easily increase

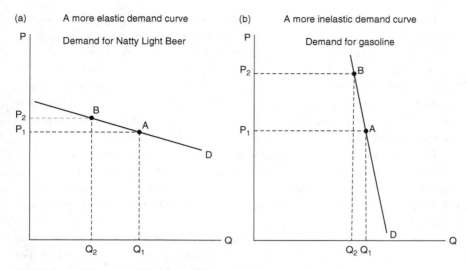

FIGURE 10.4 Elastic and inelastic demand curves.

their production of pizzas by hiring more workers and buying more pizza ingredients have elastic supply curves. However, supply curves tend to be inelastic (steep) when it is difficult to increase the quantity supplied as price increases. It is extremely difficult for suppliers of apartments in a city to increase the number of apartments they offer for rent when the price of renting an apartment increases. Building sizes are fixed, and it can take several years to build another apartment building. We will study price elasticity in more detail later in this chapter.

Another major player impacting markets is the government. One of the main ways in which governments intervene in specific markets is by installing price floors to raise prices and support sellers or price ceilings to lower prices and help purchasers.

10.2 PRICE CEILINGS AND PRICE FLOORS

10.2.1 Price ceiling

A price ceiling is **a legally set maximum price. Suppliers cannot raise their price above the price ceiling. A price ceiling must be set BELOW the equilibrium price to be effective**. If a price ceiling were set equal to or above equilibrium price, businesses would just charge the equilibrium market price where supply equals demand. However, if the price ceiling is set below the equilibrium price, the price falls and a shortage ensues. Price ceilings have been used in poor countries to reduce the price of food and in expensive cities to reduce the price of rent.

It is extremely expensive to live in many cities. To make living in cities more affordable, many city governments have turned to rent control, which is a price ceiling on the price of renting an apartment. The government of New York City tried to make it more affordable to live in the city, which is very important to the health of the city economy, by installing a maximum rent. The average rent of a two-bedroom apartment in Manhattan in 2020 was $5400. What would happen if the New York City government installed a price ceiling of $4000 on two-bedroom apartments? Figure 10.5 shows that the result would be a shortage.

First, the supply curve for apartments tends to be very steep (inelastic). It is very difficult to increase or decrease the quantity of apartments supplied in the short run. And the demand curve for apartments also tends to be very steep (inelastic). People who work in New York need and want to live there, and they have few other options.

The result of imposing rent control of $4000 on two-bedroom apartments is a shortage. When the price of renting an apartment falls from $5400 to $4000 per month, the quantity of apartments supplied is reduced from 75,000 to 70,000, the movement from point A to point B in Figure 10.5. As the rent falls, some apartment owners convert their buildings to condominiums or offices, which are more profitable. But the decrease in the price of renting an apartment from $5400 to $4000 causes more people to want city apartments: The quantity of apartments demanded increases from 75,000 to 80,000, which is the movement from point A to point C

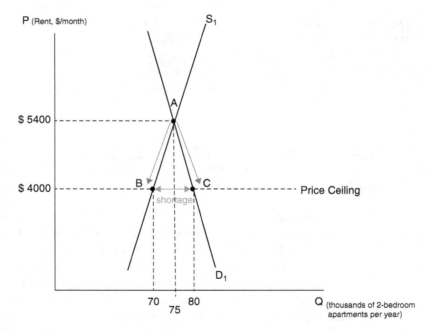

FIGURE 10.5 The effect of rent control on the market for two-bedroom apartments in NYC.

on the graph. This creates a shortage of 10,000 apartments, which is the distance between point B and point C in Figure 10.5.

The result of the installation of rent control is that 70,000 people now pay a lot less rent than they used to, making living in the city more affordable. However, *fewer* people are able to find apartments than was the case before rent control, which is not what rent control was designed to achieve. In addition, the chronic shortage of apartments created by rent control results in non-price rationing, which is **the development of methods of rationing goods and services other than by price, such as queues and black markets**. For example, there are long waits for people to find rent-controlled apartments. A black market develops where people can rent apartments illegally, or they can pay a bribe to the apartment owner to get access to a rent-controlled apartment. Some landlords would ask for a nonrefundable "key deposit" of thousands of dollars!

The chronic shortage of apartments created by rent control also results in poor maintenance and services. Landlords can tell renters that if they don't like the conditions in the apartment building, they should leave, because there are dozens of others who want the apartment. All of these methods of non-price rationing are, in essence, market forces trying to find a way around the rent control policy. The invisible hand of the market circumvents the best intentions of the city council.

After bad experiences with rent control, most cities today trying to reduce the cost of housing use soft rent controls, also known as rent stabilization. These policies guarantee landlords a "fair return" on their properties while limiting the amount of annual rent increases. Owners are required to maintain the building, but they are also allowed to pass along maintenance and improvement costs to tenants, making building upkeep more lucrative. New buildings are usually exempt from rent controls so that there is no disincentive to the construction of new apartment buildings.

Note that the government could also reduce rents by increasing the supply of apartments via subsidies or by building apartment buildings themselves. However, this would be very expensive, whereas price ceilings are free to implement.

They key takeaways regarding price ceilings are the following: Price ceilings are always set below the equilibrium price. Price ceilings do not shift demand or supply: The lower price set by the government causes a movement along both the supply and the demand curve. A price ceiling creates a shortage that results in non-price rationing. The opposite of a price ceiling is a price floor.

10.2.2 Price floor

A price floor is **a legally set minimum price. Sellers cannot lower their price below the price floor. A price floor is set above the equilibrium price in order to support sellers of a particular good**. Price floors are used to support farmers and unskilled laborers (the minimum wage is a price floor). However, price floors create a chronic surplus, which has important consequences.

To see how a price floor works, let's consider a government-installed price floor on corn. Suppose that the equilibrium price of corn is $3 per bushel but corn farmers are losing money at that price. In order to keep corn farmers in business and ensure a stable supply of corn, suppose that the government sets a price floor on corn at $4 per bushel. As you can see from Figure 10.6, when the government increases the price of corn from the equilibrium price of $3 per bushel to the price floor of $4 per bushel, the result is a surplus. Increasing the price of a bushel of corn to $4 causes corn sellers to grow more corn, which increases the quantity supplied from 13 billion bushels per year at point A to 14 billion bushels at point C. Meanwhile, when the price increases from $3 to $4 per bushel, corn buyers reduce their purchases of corn from 13 billion bushels per year at point A to 12 billion bushels per year at point B. The result is a surplus of 2 billion bushels of corn per year, which is the distance from point B to point C on the graph.

As with a chronic shortage, a chronic surplus will also lead to non-price rationing. With a surplus of corn piling up, corn farmers would be tempted to sell it illegally at a price below the price floor, and this will tend to undermine the price floor over time. The only way the government can stop non-price rationing from happening is to buy up the surplus. Thus, in many agricultural markets the government buys up the surplus created by their price floor. In Figure 10.6, this would mean purchasing 2 billion bushels of corn per year (the amount of the surplus) at $4 per bushel (the legally set price), for a cost of $8 billion per year.

If the government does purchase the surplus, suppliers will end up at point C, selling 12 billion bushels of corn to private buyers and 2 billion bushels to the government for a total of 14 billion bushels. The total revenue that a supplier takes

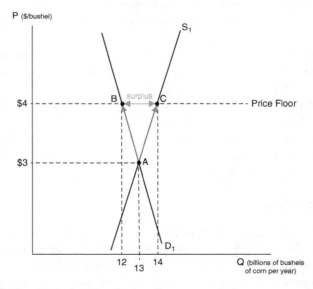

FIGURE 10.6 The effect of a price floor on the corn market.

in is found by taking the price of the product and multiplying by the quantity of the product sold,

$$\text{Total revenue} = \text{TR} = \text{Price} \times \text{Quantity sold} = P \times Q.$$

At point C the total revenue taken in by suppliers is $(14\,\text{billion} \times \$4) = \$56\,\text{billion}$. This is substantially more than the $39 billion of total revenue they took in when the equilibrium was at point A.

Often the government likes having surplus stores of agricultural crops in case of droughts or famines, or they can use the surplus to supply the military or school lunch programs. However, because storing surplus crops is expensive, sometimes the government actually pays farmers not to produce. For example, in Figure 10.6, the government could have paid farmers not to produce 2 billion bushels of corn. Shifting the supply curve to the left by 2 billion would have moved the market equilibrium from point A to point B, and farmers would still be making more money than before.

The key takeaways regarding price floors are the following: Price floors are always set above the equilibrium price. Price floors do not shift demand or supply: The higher price causes a movement along both the supply and demand curves. A price floor creates a surplus that results in non-price rationing, the government purchasing the surplus, or the government paying to eliminate the surplus. Another type of government intervention in markets occurs when they use excise taxes or per unit subsidies to discourage or encourage production of particular goods.

10.3 PER UNIT SUBSIDIES AND EXCISE TAXES

10.3.1 Per unit subsidy

With a per unit subsidy, **the government pays suppliers a fixed amount for each unit they sell**. Per unit subsidies increase the supply curve because they lower the costs for suppliers. More specifically, per unit subsidies shift the supply curve down (vertically) by exactly the amount of the per unit subsidy.

For example, suppose the federal government decides to help corn farmers with a $1 per bushel subsidy instead of a $4 per bushel price floor (see Figure 10.6). In Figure 10.7, the corn market starts out in equilibrium at point A with a price of $3 and a quantity of 13 billion bushels of corn. A per unit subsidy of $1 per bushel of corn shifts the supply curve down by exactly $1 to S_2. Suppliers are now able to sell each bushel of corn for $1 less than before and still make the same amount of money. Notice that point B on the new supply curve S_2 is exactly $1 below point A on S_1.

But at a price of $2, more corn is demanded than can be supplied, resulting in a shortage and causing the new equilibrium price is rise to $2.30 and the new equilibrium quantity to reach 13.7 billion bushels of corn. The new equilibrium

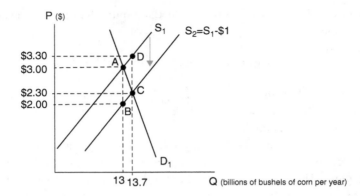

FIGURE 10.7 Effect of a $1 subsidy on the U.S. market for corn.

can be found at point C on the graph in Figure 10.7, where the new supply curve S$_2$ intersects the demand curve D$_1$. Notice that the equilibrium price fell as a result of the subsidy, but not by $1.

Next it is important to determine who benefits from the subsidy and how much this subsidy costs the government. Farmers used to receive $3.00 for each bushel of corn. Now they get $2.30 (the new equilibrium price), plus the $1 subsidy they receive from the government for each bushel they sell. Thus, farmers now receive $2.30 + $1.00 = $3.30 per bushel (point D on the graph in Figure 10.7), which is $0.30 more than they used to get before the subsidy. But why did a subsidy of $1 only make farmers $0.30 more? The rest of the subsidy goes to consumers in the form of lower prices. Consumers used to pay $3.00 per bushel for corn, and now they pay only $2.30. So in this example, consumers receive $0.70 of the $1.00 subsidy (70%), whereas farmers get only $0.30 (30%).

After the subsidy, the total revenue of corn producers at point D is $3.30 multiplied by 13.7 billion, which equals $45.21 billion. The cost to the government is the amount of the per unit subsidy multiplied by the new equilibrium quantity. 1×13.7 billion $= 13.7 billion.

Now let's compare the results of the price floor in Figure 10.6 and the per unit subsidy in Figure 10.7. With the price floor in Figure 10.6, corn farmers take in $56 billion, and it costs the government $8 billion to buy the surplus. Thus, farmers make more total revenue at less cost to the government with the price floor. In general, when supply and demand curves are inelastic, as they are with corn, price floors generate only a small surplus for the government to buy, making a price floor less expensive than a per unit subsidy. Of course, consumers always prefer a per unit subsidy to a price floor because a per unit subsidy lowers prices, whereas a price floor raises prices.

To recap, per unit subsidies shift the supply curve down by exactly the amount of the subsidy, and that causes the equilibrium price to decrease by some amount less than the subsidy. Part of the subsidy goes to consumers in the form of lower prices, and some of the subsidy goes to producers in the form of higher revenues. The opposite of a per unit subsidy is an excise tax.

10.3.2 Excise tax

An excise tax is a **per unit tax paid by sellers to the government**. Excise taxes affect the supply curve because they raise costs for suppliers. In general, when an excise tax is imposed on a good, this causes a decrease in supply, with the supply curve shifting by exactly the amount of the tax.

For example, in the graph in Figure 10.8, the initial equilibrium is at point A, with a price of $4 and a quantity of 13 billion packs of cigarettes per year. A $3 excise tax on each pack of cigarettes shifts the supply curve of cigarettes up by exactly $3 (notice that point B is exactly $3 above point A). Producers used to be willing to supply 13 billion packs at a price of $4. Now that they must pay the government $3 for each pack they sell, producers would like to sell 13 billion packs of cigarettes for $7 per pack to make the same amount of money (point B on the graph). (Note: We usually say that higher costs shift the supply curve to the left. In the case of an excise tax, it is more useful to shift the supply curve up by exactly the amount of the tax. This allows us to determine more precisely the impact on price and quantity.)

Producers will try to pass on some or all of the excise tax to consumers in the form of higher prices. However, cigarette companies can't pass all of the tax on to consumers. At a price of $7 there is a small surplus of cigarettes—some consumers stop buying cigarettes at $7 per pack—which forces cigarette producers to lower their prices. The cigarette market finally reaches a new equilibrium at point C in Figure 10.8, at a new equilibrium price of $6.50 and a new equilibrium quantity of 12 billion packs.

Cigarette companies were able to raise their prices by $2.50, passing on most of the $3 tax to consumers. After the tax, cigarette companies receive $6.50 from

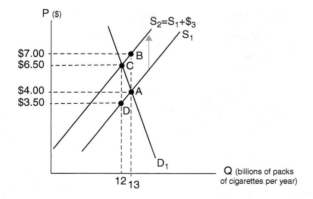

FIGURE 10.8 The effect of a $3 excise tax on the U.S. market for cigarettes.

consumers, but then they must pay $3 to the government, so cigarette producers receive $6.50 − $3.00 = $3.50 after the tax (point D in Figure 10.8). This is $0.50 less than they received before the tax, so cigarette sellers end up paying $0.50 of the tax and cigarette buyers pay $2.50 per pack more than before (point C). Meanwhile, the government takes in quite a bit of tax revenue from the cigarette excise tax. The **government revenue from an excise tax is found by multiplying the amount of the tax times the new equilibrium quantity after the tax**. Here, the government takes in $3 per pack multiplied by 12 billion packs for a total of $36 billion.

In general, excise taxes shift the supply curve up by exactly the amount of the tax, and this shift causes the equilibrium price to increase by some amount less than the tax. Part of the excise tax is paid by consumers in the form of higher prices, and part of the tax is paid by producers in the form of lower revenues.

Another interesting application of the supply and demand model is the notion of consumer and producer surplus. This helps economists evaluate when government interventions in the marketplace are effective and when they do more harm than good.

10.4 CONSUMER AND PRODUCER SURPLUS AND DEAD WEIGHT LOSS

Consumer surplus is **the difference between the amount consumers are willing to pay for a good and the price of that good. On a graph, consumer surplus is the area below the demand curve and above the equilibrium price**, as seen in Figure 10.9(a). Producer surplus is **the difference between the amount for which sellers are willing to sell each unit of a good and the price at which they actually sell the good. On a graph, producer surplus is the area above the supply curve and below the equilibrium price**, which is

(a)   Consumer and producer surplus in the market for sugar

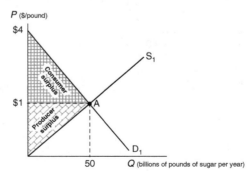

FIGURE 10.9 (a) Consumer and producer surplus in the market for sugar.

also depicted in Figure 10.9(a). To mainstream economists, consumer and producer surplus are important concepts because they demonstrate the benefits that consumers and producers gain from market exchanges. Both parties benefit significantly from trade, especially consumers who would have been willing to pay a lot more for a good and sellers who would have been willing to sell the good for much less.

Consumer and producer surplus can also be used to show deadweight loss, which is **the decrease in consumer and producer surplus that results from a market regulation, such as an excise tax, subsidy, price floor, or price ceiling**. For example, Figure 10.9(a) depicts the market for sugar without any regulation. Now suppose that the government decides that sugar is harmful to people's health because it contributes to major health problems such as obesity and diabetes. To discourage sugar consumption, the government installs a $1 per pound excise tax on sugar. As depicted in Figure 10.9(b), this shifts the supply curve up by exactly $1, causing the equilibrium price to rise from $1 to $1.60 and the equilibrium quantity to fall from 50 to 40. This results in a significant loss in consumer and producer surplus. Not only does the government take some of the consumer and producer surplus in the form of excise tax revenue but there is a deadweight loss that everyone loses that is equal to the area of the triangle labeled DL. Both consumers and producers lose out because fewer goods are exchanged.

Does this mean that government intervention of this sort is a bad thing? Not necessarily. Governments must carefully weigh the costs and the benefits of regulation. All forms of regulation will interfere with the market mechanism and cause some form of deadweight loss. But often the benefits of government regulation exceed the amount of deadweight loss. If the health benefits from the reduction in sugar consumption outweigh the loss in consumer and producer surplus, then the excise tax would be a sound policy to implement.

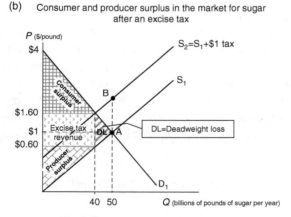

(b)   Consumer and producer surplus in the market for sugar after an excise tax

FIGURE 10.9 (b) Consumer and producer surplus in the market for sugar after an excise tax.

Now that we have described how price floors, price ceilings, excise taxes, and per unit subsidies affect the supply and demand model, we need to explore the topic of elasticity in more detail. Elasticity is an extremely useful concept for both consumers and producers to understand. It is particularly important for business owners trying to understand their consumer base and how they will respond to different pricing strategies.

10.5 THE PRICE ELASTICITY OF DEMAND

Price elasticity of demand refers to **the responsiveness of quantity demanded to changes in price. In mathematical terms, the price elasticity of demand, e_d, is equal to the percentage change in the quantity demanded divided by the percentage change in price**. The price elasticity of demand is less than or equal to zero, $e_d \leq 0$, because of the negative slope of the demand curve. In mathematical terms, the price elasticity of demand[2] (e_d) can be written as follows:

$$e_d = \frac{\%\Delta Q_d}{\%\Delta P} = \frac{\dfrac{\Delta Q}{Q_1}}{\dfrac{\Delta P}{P_1}} = \frac{\dfrac{(Q_2 - Q_1)}{Q_1}}{\dfrac{(P_2 - P_1)}{P_1}}.$$

10.5.1 Inelastic demand

In general, a demand curve is said to be price inelastic if **a change in price causes very little change in the quantity demanded**. Inelastic demand curves tend to be steep. Notice that in the equation for the price elasticity of demand, if the percentage change in quantity is very small compared to the percentage change in price, we will get a fraction for e_d because the numerator will be smaller than the denominator in absolute value. We use the absolute value to compare the magnitude of the change in price and the change in quantity demanded because one of the numbers will be negative given the negative slope of the demand curve. So when the demand curve is price inelastic, the absolute value of the price elasticity of demand is between 0 and 1: $0 < |e_d| < 1$. For this to happen, the absolute value of the change in quantity demanded has to be less than the absolute value of the change in price—the change in price must be larger than the change in quantity demanded.

Price inelastic demand: $\left|(\%\Delta Q_d)\right| < \left|(\%\Delta P)\right|$.

To compute the price elasticity of demand and determine whether a demand curve is price inelastic or price elastic, you need two points along a demand curve. For example, in Figure 10.10, suppose that OPEC (Organization of the Petroleum Exporting Companies) dramatically reduces the supply of oil such that the equilibrium quantity of gasoline, which is made from oil, declines by 10% from 150 billion gallons per year to 135 billion gallons per year. The result is a doubling in the price of gas from $2.00 to $4.00 per gallon. We can use this information to compute the price elasticity of demand between point A and point B. We start at point A, where P_1 = $2 and Q_1 = 150. We move to point B where P_2 = $4 and Q_2 = 135. Using the formula above,

$$e_d = \frac{\dfrac{\left(Q_2 - Q_1\right)}{Q_1}}{\dfrac{\left(P_2 - P_1\right)}{P_1}} = \frac{\dfrac{\left(135 - 150\right)}{150}}{\dfrac{\left(4 - 2\right)}{2}} = \frac{\dfrac{-15}{150}}{\dfrac{2}{2}} = -0.1.$$

The demand for gasoline is extremely inelastic in the short run, so a 10% decline in the equilibrium quantity of gasoline causes a 100% increase in the price of gasoline. The change in quantity demanded was much smaller (in absolute value) than the change in price.

Notice what happens to total revenue in this example. Recall that Total revenue = $TR = P \times Q$. Total revenue at point A in Figure 10.10 is 2×150 billion = $300 billion. After OPEC reduces the supply of gasoline, total revenue at point B is 4×135 billion = $540 billion. Because of the extremely inelastic demand curve for gasoline, OPEC makes a lot more revenue because prices increase much more than quantity decreases. This is why OPEC regularly engages in production cuts. Results are very different if a producer faces an elastic demand curve.

10.5.2 Elastic demand

If a demand curve is price elastic, a **change in price causes a large change in the quantity demanded**. Using the equation for e_d above, if the magnitude of the

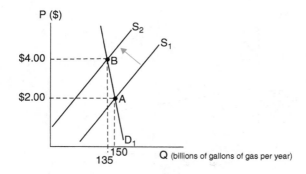

FIGURE 10.10 An inelastic demand curve for gasoline.

percentage change in quantity demanded is much larger in absolute value than the percentage change in price, then the numerator is larger than the denominator, and e_d will be greater than one in absolute value: $|e_d| > 1$. With a price elastic demand curve, the percentage change in the quantity demanded is greater in absolute value than the percentage change in price.

$$\text{Price elastic demand: } |(\%\Delta Q_d)| > |\%\Delta P|.$$

With flatter, price elastic demand curves, small changes in price cause very large changes in the quantity demanded. For example, in Figure 10.11 the price elasticity of demand for Coca-Cola is −3 ($e_d = -3$), which is very elastic. Suppose that Coca-Cola reduces the supply of soda and raises the price of a soda from $0.50 to $0.55, a 10% increase. What will happen to the quantity demanded? We can use the formula for the price elasticity of demand and the information in the graph to solve for the change in quantity demanded. At point A, $P_1 = \$0.50$ and $Q_1 = 2$. At point B, $P_2 = \$0.55$. We can solve for Q_2:

$$e_d = \dfrac{\dfrac{(Q_2 - Q_1)}{Q_1}}{\dfrac{(P_2 - P_1)}{P_1}} = \dfrac{\dfrac{(Q_2 - 2)}{2}}{\dfrac{(.55 - 50)}{.50}} = \dfrac{\dfrac{(Q_2 - 2)}{2}}{.1} = \dfrac{10(Q_2 - 2)}{2} = 5(Q_2 - 2) = 5Q_2 - 10.$$

Because we know $e_d = -3$, we can substitute that in for e_d, giving us the equation:

$5Q_2 - 10 = -3.$

Solving for Q_2, we get $5Q_2 = 7$ and $Q_2 = \dfrac{7}{5} = 1.4$. Thus, a 10% increase in price would cause a 30% decrease in the quantity demanded (from 2 to 1.4). The demand curve is extremely elastic because when Coca-Cola raises their prices, consumers switch to other drinks such as Pepsi. In fact, the primary determinant of the price

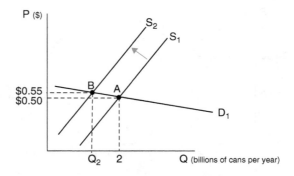

FIGURE 10.11 An elastic demand curve for Coca-Cola.

elasticity of a demand curve is the number and closeness of substitutes. The more substitutes there are and the more that consumers consider the substitutes to be almost identical, the more elastic the demand curve.

Note what happens to Coca-Cola's total revenue when they raise their prices while facing an elastic demand curve. At point A, total revenue is $P_1 \times Q_1 = \$0.50 \times 2\,\text{billion} = \$1\,\text{billion}$. After raising the price to $0.55, their total revenue at point B is $P_2 \times Q_2 = (\$.55 \times 1.4\,\text{billion}) = \$0.77\,\text{billion}$. They lose a lot of money when they raise their prices because, with an elastic demand curve, they lose too many customers to their rival, Pepsi. Most consumers, when choosing between a Coke and a Pepsi, will buy whichever one is cheaper. In addition to inelastic and elastic demand curves, a demand curve can be perfectly inelastic, perfectly elastic, or unit elastic.

10.5.3 Perfectly inelastic demand

A perfectly inelastic demand curve is "perfectly" steep and has a price elasticity of demand of zero: $|e_d| = 0$. This means that quantity demanded *does not change* as price changes. As an example, if you needed a certain amount of kidney dialysis to live, you would have a perfectly inelastic demand curve. You would pay any price for the amount you needed.

With a perfectly inelastic demand curve, quantity demanded does not change at all as price increases. The change in quantity demanded is zero when price changes. This gives us a vertical (perfectly steep) demand curve like the one depicted in Figure 10.12(a). No matter how high the price goes, consumers would still buy the same amount. Such demand curves are rare, but we see them in cases where people need a life-saving treatment and have no other options.

10.5.4 Perfectly elastic demand

A perfectly elastic demand curve is perfectly flat (horizontal). In this case, the price of the good never changes, no matter how much the supply changes. $|e_d|$

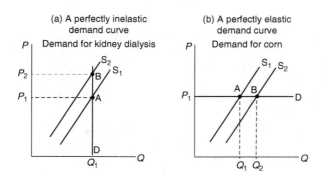

FIGURE 10.12 Perfectly elastic and perfectly inelastic demand curves.

approaches infinity because the change in price is 0. This too is extremely rare. But in some agricultural markets, such as the market for corn in which tens of thousands of farmers are growing an identical product, we find flat demand curves such as the one in Figure 10.12(b). If one corn farmer raises her price even a tiny amount over the market price that other corn farmers are charging, she will lose all of her business and the quantity demanded would fall to zero. No purchaser will pay a higher price when they can buy all they want at the market price. Also, one corn farmer is such a small part of the market that she could double or triple her output and have no effect on corn prices. With a perfectly elastic demand curve, if the corn farmer increases her supply of corn from S_1 to S_2, there is no change in price but only a change in the equilibrium quantity as we move from point A to point B in Figure 10.12(b).

10.5.5 Unit elastic demand

A unit elastic demand curve is in between inelastic and elastic: The percentage change in quantity demanded is exactly equal in absolute value to the percentage change in price:

$$\left|\%\Delta Q_d\right| = \left|\%\Delta P\right|.$$

When the price elasticity of demand is unit elastic, $\left|e_d\right| = \left|\dfrac{\%\Delta Q_d}{\%\Delta P}\right| = 1.$

A demand curve that is always unit elastic looks like the one in Figure 10.13. From point A to point B the price falls by 50% from $90 to $45 and the quantity demanded increases by 50% from two to three. From point B to point C the price decreases by 33.3% from $45 to $30 and the quantity demanded increases by 33.3% from three to four.

It is also important to note that the price elasticity of demand changes along a linear (straight line) demand curve. This is because at small quantities, the percentage changes in quantity are very large and at large quantities the percentage changes in quantity are very small. This means that linear demand curves are elastic at low

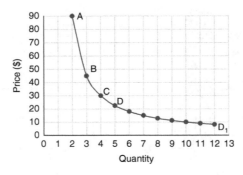

FIGURE 10.13 A unit elastic demand curve.

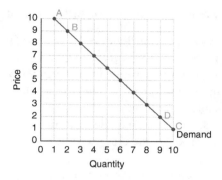

FIGURE 10.14 A linear demand curve.

quantities and inelastic at high quantities. For example, in Figure 10.14, when we move from point A to point B, the percentage change in quantity demanded is $(2 - 1)/1 = 100\%$ and the percentage change in price is $(9 - 10)/10$ or -10%. This makes the price elasticity of demand in the A–B region of the demand curve $100\%/(-10\%) = -10$, which is very elastic.

But if we compute the price elasticity of demand when we move from point C to point D, the percentage change in quantity demanded is $(9 - 10)/10 = -10\%$ and the percentage change in price is $(2 - 1)/1 = 100\%$. The price elasticity of demand in the C–D region of the demand curve is $-10\%/100\% = -0.1$, which is very inelastic.

Note that most real-world demand curves do not tend to have that much variation in elasticity. A study by Peter Cohen, Robert Hahn, Jonathan Hall, Steven Levitt, and Robert Metcalfe found that the price elasticity of the demand for Uber rides varied only slightly, from -0.4 to -0.6. Nonetheless, it is important to recognize that *the price elasticity of demand measures elasticity in a particular place on the demand curve*, and elasticity can be different elsewhere on the same demand curve.[3]

Next, it is important to understand what factors make a demand curve elastic or inelastic. These factors are called the determinants of the price elasticity of demand.

10.6 THE DETERMINANTS OF THE PRICE ELASTICITY OF DEMAND

The main factors that determine how sensitive the quantity demanded is to changes in price are related to how many options people have when buying an item and how important the item is to them. More specifically, the main determinants of the price elasticity of demand for a particular good or service are the availability and closeness of substitutes, the time frame, the nature of the product, and the fraction of the budget the purchase would take up.

10.6.1 Availability and closeness of substitutes

For most goods and services, the availability and closeness of substitutes is the major determinant of the price elasticity of demand. Figure 10.15 lists some estimates of price elasticities that economists have identified over the years. Notice that the goods that have the most substitutes and the closest substitutes have the largest price elasticities in absolute value. There are many different kinds of cars other than Chevrolets. Coca-Cola and Pepsi are such close substitutes that if one of them raises prices consumers will flock to buy the other. There are many other vegetables than just peas. And so on.

But if there are few substitutes, the price elasticity of demand will be very low in absolute value. Most people do not consider other types of meat to be good substitutes for beef, so the demand for beef is quite inelastic: Price increases for beef cause only small decreases in the quantity of beef demanded. Even though the demand for Chevrolet automobiles is quite elastic, the demand for automobiles in general in the United States over the long run is very inelastic because most people must have a car to get to work and to get food and run essential errands. There are few good substitutes in the United States for cars given the limited availability of public transportation options in most places. In general, we see the same pattern in many industries where the demand for one brand of the product is very elastic but the demand for the product in general is quite inelastic. The demand for one brand of beer will tend to be much more elastic than the overall demand for beer, for example.

10.6.2 Nature of the product (necessities and vices)

Goods or services that are necessities and are essential to survival have more inelastic demand curves. Notice that in Figure 10.15 physicians' services, medical insurance, and electricity all have very inelastic demand curves. Food in general has a very inelastic demand curve, although particular types of food such as peas face a very elastic demand curve because there are so many substitutes. Correspondingly,

Good or service	Price elasticity of demand	Good or service	Price elasticity of demand
Chevrolet automobiles	−4.0	Soda	−0.8
Coca-Cola, Pepsi	−3.3	Beef, physicians' services	−0.6
Peas	−2.8	Uber rides	−0.5
Restaurant meals	−2.3	Alcoholic drinks	−0.4
Olive oil	−1.9	Medical insurance	−0.3
Peanut butter	−1.7	Beer, coffee	−0.3
Ketchup	−1.4	Automobiles, long run	−0.2
Wine, furniture	−1.0	Cigarettes	−0.2
Movies, housing	−0.9	Electricity, salt, toothpicks	−0.1

FIGURE 10.15 Table showing elasticity estimates for a variety of goods.

goods that are luxuries or considered nonessential, such as restaurant meals, face elastic demand curves.

Goods that are considered vices also seem to have inelastic demand curves, including alcohol and cigarettes. Cigarettes are also addictive, and that contributes to the inelastic nature of their demand curve. The same is true of coffee—there are many people, including the author of this textbook—who can't get through the morning without several cups of coffee and are willing to pay a high price for it.

10.6.3 Fraction of budget

In general, people do not care much about price increases for inexpensive items. When the price of salt or toothpicks increases, consumers don't seem to notice the difference and keep buying about the same quantity, making the demand curve for these items extremely inelastic. But with more expensive items, the demand curve is much more elastic. Even though housing is a necessity, the price elasticity of the demand for housing in the United States is estimated at −0.9 (almost unit elastic). Housing is so expensive that a large percentage increase in the price of housing can cause a similarly large percentage decrease in the quantity of housing demanded.

10.6.4 Time frame (short term or long term)

The more time buyers have to adjust to changes in prices, the more elastic their demand curves will tend to be. In Figure 10.16 we see that the price elasticity of demand for gasoline is very inelastic in the short run (−0.1) but more elastic in the long run (−0.8). In the short run, when the price of gas increases, people can reduce their purchases of gas only slightly because they still have to get to work and they do not have other good transportation options. However, their quantity of gas demanded can change significantly over a period of several years. When gas prices stayed high from 2010 to 2014, people changed their buying behavior over time. The next time they purchased an automobile, they tended to buy smaller cars and more fuel-efficient hybrids rather than large SUVs. So the increase in the price of gasoline caused a small decrease in the quantity of gasoline demanded in the short term but a larger decrease in the quantity demand in the longer term.

We see something similar with airline travel. People booking airline tickets at the last minute tend to have extremely inelastic demand curves: They are traveling for an important business meeting or family emergency and they are willing to pay a high price. But people booking air travel far in advance, for their next vacation in

Good or service	Price elasticity of demand
Gasoline, short run	−0.1
Gasoline, long run	−0.8
Air travel, short run (last minute)	−0.1
Air travel, long run	−2.4

FIGURE 10.16 Table showing short-run and long-run price elasticities.

six months, will shop around and will consider alternative modes of transportation if the price of an airplane ticket is too high, making their demand more elastic. Airlines, of course, take advantage of this as much as they can. They sell advance tickets for lower prices to lure long-run purchasers with elastic demand curves, but as seats become more scarce and as the departure date nears, airline tickets jump in price because airlines know that last-minute travelers have few options and hence a very inelastic demand curve.

Price elasticity of demand is the most important and useful type of elasticity. But there are other types of elasticity that can be helpful in analyzing the demand for particular products. These include income elasticity of demand and cross-price elasticity of demand.

10.7 INCOME ELASTICITY AND CROSS-PRICE ELASTICITY OF DEMAND

10.7.1 Income elasticity of demand

Income elasticity of demand is important in telling us how particular markets will respond to changes in income due to the business cycle. In recessions, when incomes fall dramatically, those goods that are highly sensitive to changes in income—and have large income elasticities of demand such as automobiles, vacations, and housing—will take a big hit. But inferior goods, with negative income elasticities of demand, will actually see sales increase when incomes fall.

Income elasticity of demand (e_{GDP}) **measures the responsiveness of the quantity demanded to changes in income (GDP).**

$$e_{\text{GDP}} = \frac{\%\,\text{Change in quantity demanded}}{\%\,\text{Change in income}} = \frac{\%\Delta Q_d}{\%\Delta \text{GDP}}.$$

Economists determine how much the demand curve *shifts* in response to a change in income via the income elasticity of demand. Normal goods **have an income elasticity of greater than 0: $e_{\text{GDP}} > 0$.** When incomes increase, the demand for normal goods also increases, shifting to the right. Examples of normal goods from Figure 10.17 include food, housing, gas, electricity, and tobacco.

Economists have also identified superior goods that are **normal goods whose income elasticity is greater than 1: $e_{\text{GDP}} > 1$.** Examples of superior goods include automobiles, vacations, health care, books, restaurant meals, and meats. Superior goods tend to be luxuries or expensive items such as health care and housing that people are willing spend more on when their incomes increase. Notice, for example, that automobiles have an income elasticity of 3.0. Using the formula for the income elasticity of demand, this means that that a decrease in

Good or service	Income elasticity
Automobiles	3.0
Vacations	1.9
Books, restaurant meals	1.4
Health care, meat	1.2
Housing, physicians' services	0.7
Tobacco, fruits, vegetables	0.6
Gas	0.5
Electricity, food	0.2
Margarine	−0.2
Public transportation, rice, flour	−0.4

FIGURE 10.17 Table with examples of income elasticities.

income of 10% would result in a decrease in the demand for automobiles of 30%! This is one of the main reasons why the car industry fares so poorly in recessions.

On the opposite end are inferior goods that **have an income elasticity of less than 0:** $e_{GDP} < 0$. People buy less of these goods when their incomes increase. Examples of inferior goods include margarine, rice, flour, and public transportation. Think about what goods you would stop buying if you had a lot more money than you do now. These are inferior goods to you.

10.7.2 Cross-price elasticity of demand

Cross-price elasticity of demand measures the **responsiveness of the quantity demanded of one good to the price of a different good**. Specifically, **the formula for cross-price elasticity, e_{xy}, is:**

$$e_{xy} = \frac{\text{Percentage change in quantity demanded of good } x}{\text{Percentage change in the price of good } y} = \frac{\%\Delta Q_{dx}}{\%\Delta P_y}.$$

Economists use cross-price elasticity of demand to measure the closeness of substitutes and complements. **A** substitute good **has a cross-price elasticity that is greater than 0:** $e_{xy} > 0$. When the price of Coca-Cola increases, the quantity of Pepsi, a close substitute, demanded increases. A higher price for Coca-Cola causes consumers to buy less Coke and more Pepsi. For example, a 10% increase in the price of Coca-Cola typically causes a 6% increase in the quantity of Pepsi demanded. From this information, we can compute a cross-price elasticity of Pepsi relative to the price of Coca-Cola of

$$e_{\text{Pepsi-Coke}} = \frac{6\%}{10\%} = 0.6.$$

Similarly, whole-fat and low-fat milk have a cross-price elasticity of 0.5. The larger the cross-price elasticity, the closer the substitute.

A complementary good has a **cross-price elasticity of less than 0:** $e_{xy} < 0$. When the price of a good increases, consumers buy less of that good and less of any complementary goods. For example, when the price of gasoline goes up, consumers reduce their purchases of gasoline *and* very large SUVs. A 10% increase in the price of gasoline (P_{Gas}) causes a 3% decrease in the quantity of large SUVs demanded (Q_{dSUVs}), giving SUVs a cross-price elasticity $e_{SUVs\text{-}Gas} = -0.3$. Similarly, meat and potatoes are complements for many consumers, with a cross-price elasticity of -0.2.

We also find goods that are neither substitutes nor complements for each other, in which case the cross-price elasticity is zero. The price of Coca-Cola has no impact on the demand for iPhones, so $e_{Coke\text{-}iPhones} = 0$.

Now that we have studied how elasticities affect the demand curve, we can move on to the price elasticity of supply, which helps us determine when supply curves are elastic or inelastic.

10.8 PRICE ELASTICITY OF SUPPLY

The price elasticity of supply measures **the responsiveness of quantity supplied to changes in price**. In mathematical terms, **the price elasticity of supply, e_s, is equal to the percentage change in the quantity supplied divided by the percentage change in price**. The price elasticity of supply is greater than or equal to 0, $e_s \geq 0$, because of the positive slope of the supply curve. The formula for the price elasticity of supply, e_s, is

$$e_s = \frac{\dfrac{\Delta Q}{Q_1}}{\dfrac{\Delta P}{P_1}} = \frac{\dfrac{(Q_2 - Q_1)}{Q_1}}{\dfrac{(P_2 - P_1)}{P_1}}.$$

The formula for the price elasticity of supply is the same as the formula for the price elasticity of demand, but *we use two points along the supply curve to compute it*. For example, in Figure 10.18(a) we see an elastic supply curve for hamburgers. The supply of hamburgers is elastic because there is a large amount of frozen hamburgers available in storage, so suppliers can get more hamburgers very easily in the short run if demand increases. In Figure 10.18(a), the demand for hamburgers increases, shifting to the right from D_1 to D_2 and causing an increase in the equilibrium price from $1.00 to $1.05. This causes a large increase in the quantity of hamburgers supplied from 80 to 100 million hamburgers per day.

Using this information, we can compute the price elasticity of supply in this example:

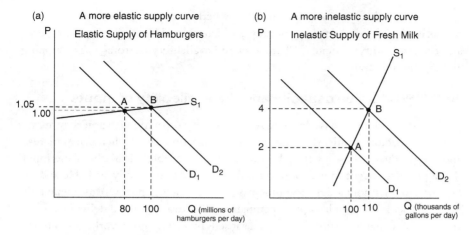

FIGURE 10.18 Elastic and inelastic supply curves.

$$e_s = \frac{\dfrac{\Delta Q}{Q_1}}{\dfrac{\Delta P}{P_1}} = \frac{\dfrac{(20)}{80}}{\dfrac{(0.05)}{1}} = 5.$$

When $e_s = 5$, a 1% increase in price causes a 5% increase in the quantity of hamburgers supplied and a 5% increase in price (like the example in Figure 10.18(a)) causes a 25% increase in the quantity supplied.

Figure 10.18(b) features an inelastic supply curve for fresh milk. Dairy farmers only have a certain number of milk-producing cows available. It will take farmers more than a year to generate more cows to produce fresh milk, so other than doing some small things to increase the yield of their existing cows (better feed, for example), they can do little to increase their milk production in the short run. In Figure 10.18(b) an increase in demand causes the price to double (increase by 100%) from $2 to $4, but this causes only a small increase of 10% in the quantity of milk supplied (quantity supplied increases from 100 units at point A to 110 units at point B). In this case, the price elasticity of supply can be computed as follows:

$$e_s = \frac{\dfrac{\Delta Q}{Q_1}}{\dfrac{\Delta P}{P_1}} = \frac{10\%}{100\%} = 0.1.$$

The supply curve for milk in Figure 10.18(b) is very inelastic.

There are three main determinants of whether or not a supply curve is elastic or inelastic. The price elasticity of supply is determined by (1) productive capacity and the availability of inputs, (2) the cost and availability of storage and shipping, and (3) the time frame.

10.8.1 Productive capacity and the availability of inputs

If a firm or an industry has a lot of excess productive capacity, such as if they are not using their factories fully, they can increase production easily when prices increase and the product they are selling becomes more profitable. Similarly, if the inputs that a producer needs to use to produce their product are readily available and can be purchased without a significant increase in costs, then supply will also tend to be more elastic. For example, a pizza company with extra ovens and delivery vehicles could easily expand the number of pizzas it sells by hiring more workers and ordering more dough, cheese, sauce, and toppings from distributors.

10.8.2 Cost and availability of storage and shipping

If a firm can maintain a large inventory and if it has access to rapid and inexpensive shipping, it will tend to have an elastic supply curve. Such a firm would be able to increase the quantity of goods offered for sale quickly and easily in response to changes in prices. This has been one of the keys to Amazon's success. When the demand for a product they are selling increases, they can quickly increase the quantity of the good they offer for sale out of their vast system of warehouses and their inexpensive shipping network. However, a producer with no significant inventory will not be able to increase the quantity supplied quickly when the price increases.

10.8.3 Time

As producers have more time to adjust, their supply curve becomes more elastic. A dairy farmer producing milk cannot increase the supply of milk much this year if the price of milk increases. But if milk prices stay high, they can buy or breed more cows, build new barns, grow more cattle feed, and increase their quantity of milk supplied substantially within two years. In general, supply curves tend to be more inelastic in the short run than they are in the long run.

Overall, the price elasticity of supply depends on how easy it is for a producer to expand operations. If their size of operations is relatively fixed, they will have an inelastic supply curve. If they can easily and inexpensively increase the amount they supply, they will have a more elastic supply curve.

10.9 CONCLUSION

In this chapter we have refined and extended our understanding of the supply and demand model. We began by analyzing the two factors that cause *both* the supply curve and the demand curve to shift: Wages and advertising. An increase in wages or advertising causes an increase in demand and a decrease in supply.

We then explored government interventions in the marketplace. The installation of price ceilings or price floors does not shift either the supply or the demand curve. Instead, you move along both curves to determine the shortage or surplus that the policy creates. Excise taxes shift the supply curve up by the amount of the tax, and per unit subsidies shift the supply curve down by the amount of the subsidy. All of these government interventions tend to cause reductions in consumer and producer surplus and create deadweight loss that must be weighed against the benefits of the government policy.

We also explored elasticity in some detail. There are five different possibilities for the price elasticity of demand $\left(e_d = \dfrac{\%\Delta Q_d}{\%\Delta P} \right)$:

1. Perfectly inelastic (vertical demand curve): $|e_d| = 0$.
2. Inelastic (steep demand curve): $0 < |e_d| < 1$.
3. Unit elastic (neither steep nor flat): $|e_d| = 1$.
4. Elastic (fairly flat demand curve): $|e_d| > 1$.
5. Perfectly elastic (horizontal demand curve): $|e_d|$ approaches ∞.

The same possibilities apply to the price elasticity of supply, except that the price elasticity of supply is always greater than zero.

This chapter also explained how income elasticity of demand helps us to understand the demand for superior, normal, and inferior goods. And we worked through how cross-price elasticity of demand can be used to analyze markets for substitute and complementary goods.

This is a lot of material that can only be mastered with practice. Work as many problems as possible until you are comfortable using the supply and demand model with all of its applications. Fortunately, supply and demand analysis follows a consistent, logical pattern that can be mastered with time.

QUESTIONS FOR REVIEW

1. Using a graph, show how the supply and demand curves for U.S.-made SUVs will be affected by each of the events listed below. Also show what happens to equilibrium price and quantity. Assume that the equilibrium price of a U.S.-made SUV is $35,000 and the equilibrium quantity is 500,000 U.S.-made SUVs sold per year.
   a. Wages for all U.S. workers increase due to an economic boom.
   b. SUV companies institute a very successful "Buy American SUVs" advertising campaign.
   c. Lower oil prices cause energy *and* gas prices to decrease.

    d.   The Environmental Protection Agency convinces Congress that SUV pollution is contributing to global warming, so Congress institutes a $30,000 per SUV excise tax (with the revenues to be used to clean up pollution).

    e.   Consumers find out that the markup on SUVs is higher than that on all other cars and demand that prices come down. In response, politicians install a price ceiling of $20,000 on SUVs. In addition to showing what happens on a graph, explain the likely consequences of the price ceiling.

2.   The equilibrium price of eggs is $2 per unit (a dozen eggs is one unit) and the equilibrium quantity of eggs is 300 million units per day. The demand and supply of eggs are both inelastic (very, very steep). In order to help egg producers, the government is considering a $4 price floor or a $2 per unit subsidy.

    a.   Draw a graph of the egg market in equilibrium based on the information above. Now show how the graph will be affected by a $4 price floor on a unit of eggs. How will the price floor affect the total revenue (Total revenue = Price × Quantity) of egg producers? How much will the price floor cost the government if the government buys up the surplus?

    b.   Draw a new graph of the egg market in equilibrium at a price of $2 and a quantity of 300. Now suppose that the government institutes a $2 per unit subsidy on eggs. How will the subsidy affect the equilibrium price and quantity and the total revenue of egg producers? How much will the subsidy cost the government?

    c.   Given your answers in parts a and b above, which policy should the government choose? Explain briefly.

3.   Suppose that the government imposed a $3 per pack excise tax on cigarettes. Using the graph in Figure 10.19, show how the cigarette market is affected by the $3 per pack excise tax. Discuss how the cigarette excise tax will affect consumers and producers and how much revenue it will generate for the government. Also discuss how the excise tax will affect consumer surplus, producer surplus, and deadweight loss, and evaluate if this policy is likely to be a good one given these impacts.

4.   The city council of San Francisco wants to lower the price of housing to increase their tax base and revitalize the city economy. The supply of apartments is very inelastic, and the demand for apartments is very elastic. The average price (monthly rent) of a typical apartment is $1600 per person, and 500,000 people rent apartments in San Francisco at this price. Using a graph, determine whether the city council should use a price ceiling of $1200 or a $400 per apartment subsidy to lower rents and increase the number of city residents. Explain carefully which policy will most effectively lower rents and increase the number of city residents, how much each policy will cost the government, and how both policies affect the graph. Draw your graph as precisely as possible.

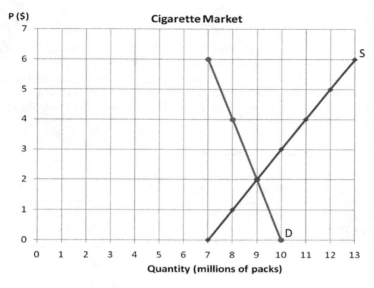

FIGURE 10.19 The cigarette market.

5. Suppose that the price elasticity of demand for gasoline is −0.2 and the equilibrium price of gasoline is $4 per gallon. Now suppose that OPEC reduces the supply of gasoline such that the equilibrium quantity falls by 20% from 100 million gallons per day to 80 million gallons per day. What will happen to the price of a gallon of gasoline?

6. Large Colorado ski areas discover that the price elasticity of demand, e_d, is very elastic ($e_d = -1.9$) for in-state skiers and very inelastic ($e_d = -0.6$) for out-of-state skiers. How can we explain the difference in price elasticities? What pricing policy should the ski areas pursue?

7. Suppose that the cross-price elasticity of demand for ski area lift tickets with respect to the price of ski lodging is −1. What should happen to the quantity of ski lift tickets demanded if the price of ski lodging increases by 20%? Explain your answer briefly and show your work.

8. The income elasticity of the demand for designer clothes is 2.5. What will happen to the quantity of designer clothes demanded if the economy hits a recession and income (GDP) falls by 5%? Explain and show your work.

9. If the price of energy increases dramatically as we run out of fossil fuels and this increases the price of storing and shipping goods significantly, what effect is likely to happen to the price elasticity of supply curves? What impact will this have on the equilibrium prices and quantities of goods whose supply curves are impacted?

NOTES

1 See *The Economist*, "Status Displays: I've Got You Labelled; Clothes May Make the Man, but It Is the Label That Really Counts," March 31, 2011.

2 Note that you can use several different formulas for the price elasticity of demand, each of which measures the price elasticity at a different point. The formula above measures the price elasticity at the starting point, (P_1, Q_1). You could substitute (P_2, Q_2) in the denominators of the price elasticity equation to measure the price elasticity at point (P_2, Q_2). Or you could use the midpoint formula: $e_d = \dfrac{\dfrac{(Q_2 - Q_1)}{(Q_1 + Q_2)}}{\dfrac{(P_2 - P_1)}{(P_1 + P_2)}}$.

3 Most research indicates that real-world demand curves are curved slightly, like the unit elastic demand curve, and they can be either steeper or flatter than the unit elastic demand curve. However, in terms of making general predictions regarding how changes in supply and demand are likely to affect equilibrium price and equilibrium quantity, using linear supply and demand curves will suffice.

Consumer and supplier behavior

The complexities of market analysis

In the previous two chapters, we worked through the supply and demand model in detail, showing how the model can be used to analyze markets and to predict how a variety of determinants will affect equilibrium prices and quantities in various markets. In this chapter we turn to some of the aspects of markets that are harder to quantify and model—the often less rational and more impulsive and culturally determined behavior of consumers and the complex decisions made by sellers in complex firms facing issues related to creative destruction and market power.

The first section of this chapter focuses on consumers and how they think in complex situations. Recall that in mainstream economic analysis, consumers are viewed as rational, self-interested, calculating, and fully informed decision makers. However, there are circumstances in which we need to refine that model of human behavior. Utilizing Veblen's institutionalist approach to economic behavior, along with modern behavioral economics that builds on many of Veblen's ideas, we will explore some of the complexities of consumer behavior.

Veblen emphasized the cultural factors that shape economic decisions. To Veblen, human beings are a product of a specific culture and the value system contained within it. This culture can have a dominant impact on our decisions. Similarly, behavioral economics studies the social and psychological influences on economic behavior and compares these aspects of behavior with the mainstream model of economic man. The results are fascinating, as we explore below.

The second section of the chapter focuses on the behavior of the actors in the supply side of the market. We describe the mainstream model of producer profit maximization and contrast this with views of producer behavior coming from behavioral economists and political economists. Rather than seeing producers as being engaged in optimizing behavior, behavioral economists see producers engaged in satisficing—making decisions that are good enough given limited information and complex workplace relationships. Political economists stress the role of innovation and corporate power in driving market changes, focusing on

DOI: 10.4324/9781315636924-14

the evolution and power dynamics of markets rather than equilibrium prices and quantities.

In short, the previous two chapters studied the consistent, predictable side of how competitive markets operate in the short run. This chapter focuses on the less predictable, less competitive side of markets and some of the complexities related to consumer and producer behavior.

11.0 CHAPTER 11 LEARNING GOALS

After reading this chapter you should be able to:

- Explain and give examples of a Veblen good.

- Analyze how pecuniary emulation and herd behavior affect consumer decisions.

- Evaluate how households, communities, and cultures shape consumer decisions.

- Describe the factors that lead consumers to make nonrational choices and apply these factors to real-world examples.

- Define and illustrate the short-run production function and the laws of specialization and diminishing returns.

- Use a table containing information on labor and output to compute the marginal product of labor, total variable cost, marginal cost, and average variable cost.

- Explain the derivation of a firm's supply curve in words and using a graph.

- Describe how behavioral economists and political economists analyze supply decisions and apply the ideas of satisficing, competition for innovation and monopoly power, and countervailing power to supply decisions.

11.1 VEBLEN GOODS AND PECUNIARY EMULATION

The mainstream model of economic behavior describes consumers as rational, calculating, and fully informed optimizers. They are subject to the law of diminishing marginal utility, which means the more they consume of a particular good, the less they want additional units of that good. This gives the demand curve its downward slope. However, we do not always see downward-sloping demand curves.

11.1.1 Veblen goods

As we saw earlier when we studied Veblen's ideas, most goods have a "use value" or "utility," as well as a "display value" or "honorific" character. When people think that purchasing a good will give them higher status, they are willing to pay more for it—as in the case of buying a Rolex watch instead of a Timex. This can result in a different outcome than we normally see with a downward-sloping demand curve: With a Veblen good, **the quantity of the good demanded increases as the price increases because the scarcity and exclusivity associated with the good increase the display value and honorific character of the good**. Most luxury goods are Veblen goods. Luxury goods depend on scarcity and exclusivity to drive the demand for their products. If the companies that produced luxury goods were to lower their prices, this could erode the aura of exclusivity associated with the product and reduce the demand for it.

Elite universities have found that raising the price of tuition signals a degree of exclusivity and actually *increases* the number of applications, which is a sign of the demand for a college education at that university. On the other hand, lowering the price of tuition can signal to applicants that a university is of lower quality.

Interestingly, recent research indicates that the act of paying more for a status good even increases consumers' satisfaction with that good! Researchers at the Stanford Graduate School of Business and the California Institute of Technology found that a person who thought they were tasting a $45 bottle of wine would experience more pleasure than a person who thought they were tasting a $5 bottle of wine, even though the wines were identical.[1] Believing that you are consuming something that is expensive makes it more likely you will actually enjoy consuming it! This shows how hard-wired we are to think in terms of expensive and exclusive items being better than others. This is sometimes called the snob effect, where **a higher price is assumed to represent better quality**. Similarly, low prices are assumed to represent low quality.

11.1.2 Pecuniary emulation and herd behavior

Another area in which we see Veblen's analysis come to life is with the band-wagon effect, where **the more people who have a good, the more other people also want that good**. In this case, we see Veblen's notion of pecuniary emulation in action: People desperately want to have the same goods that everyone else has—they want to jump on the bandwagon and fit in with their social group. College campuses are often prime examples of the bandwagon effect. One year Ugg Boots are the hot item that everyone has to have. The next year the hot product might be Vineyard Vines shirts. Yoga pants were only worn to exercise in until the mid-2010s, when they became normal dress for college women. In cases of the bandwagon effect, demand keeps increasing the hotter the item becomes, even if prices increase. This contradicts the normal "law of demand."

We see similar behavior when consumers buy products based on online reviews and recommendations. By trusting the opinions of online reviewers, we jump on the bandwagon and buy the same goods that others like. And we see this when consumers bypass an empty restaurant to wait in line at a busy restaurant that they are unfamiliar with, assuming that there is a reason why other consumers want to eat at the busy restaurant. We even see such behavior in financial markets. Investment banks followed each other into the sub-prime mortgage market on the assumption that others already in that market knew about a good business opportunity. Similarly, in the early 1980s banks followed each other in loaning large sums of money to governments of impoverished developing countries, despite the high risks. In both cases, this herd behavior resulted in financial crises!

We also sometimes see herd behavior due to network efficiencies, when consumers benefit by purchasing the same products used by others so that collaboration is easier. For example, it is easier to work collaboratively if everyone uses Google Docs or Skype.

It is hard to overstate how important pecuniary emulation and herd behavior are in shaping human decisions. However, it is difficult to analyze such behavior systematically. It is hard to predict when a particular item will become hot or when a particular bandwagon will prove irresistible to jump on. Such analysis requires deep knowledge of actors and close observation of their behavior.

11.2 HOUSEHOLD, COMMUNITY, AND CULTURE

Mainstream economic theory tends to ignore the role of households, communities, and cultures in shaping economic decisions. As we will see below, a variety of factors shape our value systems, and value systems shape the economic decisions we make.

11.2.1 Household decision making

As feminist economists note, the household is at the center of many economic decisions. The idea that purchases are made by individuals acting purely out of self-interest ignores key aspects of economic decision making. Most decisions within a household are negotiated. Major purchases of large ticket items are usually made jointly by both partners in a relationship.

There is, however, a gendered aspect to who makes which decisions that involves power and existing gender roles. In a heterosexual U.S. household, women usually make most of the decisions regarding furniture, home accessories, small appliances, and cell phones, whereas men make most of the decisions regarding power tools, lawn and garden care, and consumer electronics. Even though women tend to do more work than men in most households, averaging 50 more minutes of work per day according to the World Economic Forum, much of this is unpaid work that comes with less earning power and status. Therefore, household dynamics, including gender roles and power relations in each culture, are important in understanding household behavior regarding purchases, labor decisions, and other key aspects of the provisioning process by which households get the goods and services they need.

11.2.2 Fairness and cultural bonds

Most transactions also involve a concern with fairness and the welfare of others. In the United States most people leave a tip of 15% at restaurants even though there is no law requiring them to do so. This is a display of a cultural norm that trumps selfish economic gain. People give each other gifts and volunteer in their communities with no expectation of economic gain. We also see clear evidence of the importance of cultural norms and the value of fairness in the results from the ultimatum game from behavioral economics.

In the ultimatum game, there are two players and a possible monetary payout. One player, known as the proposer, **proposes a split of the payout**. The second player, known as the responder, **decides to accept or reject the split offered by the proposer**. The two players each get to keep their share of the payout *if* the responder agrees to the split offered by the proposer. If the responder rejects the split, then neither player gets any money.

According to economic theory, rational economic man, who is utterly self-interested and perfectly informed and has no notion of fairness and no cultural norms to abide, would always propose a very inequitable split as the proposer. As the responder, rational economic man would also accept any proposal no matter how unequal, because even an offer of $1 out of a $100 split would make the responder $1 better off. Knowing this, if the possible monetary payout is $100, the proposer should propose a split of $99 for himself and $1 for the responder, knowing that a rational responder would accept $1 even though it is highly inequitable.

But how do people really behave? In repeated experiments in a variety of settings, most proposers offer 50%—a fair split of the money. Also, offers of a split of 25% or less are frequently rejected by responders—they reject unfair proposals even though they would benefit financially from accepting the proposals. In these cases, it is more important to the responder that the proposer be punished by losing the payout than it is for the responder to benefit financially. What we see is that human beings have a preference for **fairness** and **reciprocity**, and they are willing to make a sacrifice in order to punish someone whose actions are viewed as unfair.

Bowles et al. also report that proposers in societies in which gift-giving garners status often offered more than a 50% split, and societies that depended on cooperation for survival tended to offer more than other societies. Interestingly, people with exposure to markets, which require people to cooperate, bargain, and trade with others, also tended to make higher offers and were more likely to reject lower offers.[2] Markets themselves evidently cultivate norms of fairness and reciprocity that are an important element in exchanges. This, of course, has important implications for how someone should conduct business dealings. Taking advantage of people is unlikely to be a sound business practice!

We also see cultural norms at play in the Haifa childcare experiment conducted by behavioral economists Uri Gneezy and Aldo Rustichini. Parents picking up children late from childcare is a chronic problem at almost all childcare centers. Gneezy was interested in how parents' behavior might change if they faced fines when they picked up their children late. According to economic theory based on rational economic man, levying a fine would discourage people from picking up their children late, and that would then reduce the number of late pickups.

In six of ten childcare centers in the town of Haifa, a small fine was levied on any parents who showed up more than ten minutes late to pick up their child. In the other four childcare centers no fine was imposed. The results were fascinating: *In the childcare centers where fines were levied for late pickups, parents were twice as likely to show up late as they were in childcare centers without fines*! Ironically, the guilt parents felt from inconveniencing a day care worker was a much more powerful motivator than the fine. Breaking a social contract is seen as unacceptable behavior by many people. But once arriving late became a monetary transaction, many parents simply chose to pay a little more money to arrive late at the day care center, absolved of guilt now that the relationship had changed from a personal one to a financial one.

Similarly, researchers have found that blood donations decline when people are paid to donate blood. People are more likely to donate blood when it is seen as a good deed for one's community than they are when a blood donation is seen as a monetary transaction.

These examples show us that a series of complex factors influence how consumers make decisions. First, their decisions depend on their household dynamics. Second, decisions are shaped fundamentally by a community's cultural values, including norms of fairness and equity. Consumers also sometimes behave in ways that seem nonrational from the perspective of mainstream economics.

11.3 NONRATIONAL CHOICES

Rational economic man is supposed to be fully informed and to make rational decisions taking into account all variables. This often fails to capture all aspects of economic decisions. For example, often we are overwhelmed with too many choices and too much information, so we tend to make quick, impulsive, emotional decisions that are not fully rational or well informed. Slower, deliberative thinking is much more likely to be rational and well informed. There are a number of categories in which people make decisions that, though not necessarily being irrational (not reasonable or logical), are nonrational at least when compared to how rational economic man is supposed to act. Nonrational decisions are made by relying on intuition rather than on logic or close observation.

11.3.1 Anchoring

One example of nonrational judgment occurs with anchoring, a phenomenon that occurs **when people rely too heavily on the first piece of information shared with them when making a decision**. This is a tactic used very effectively by retailers. There is a reason that Amazon and other retailers create a "list" price and then show you an "actual" or "deal" price that is lower: By establishing a high anchor point, it makes consumers think they are getting a good deal even when they are not. This is an example of what psychologists call cognitive bias, where **people experience systematic deviations from logical, rational behavior due to characteristics of our cognitive abilities**.

Another example of cognitive bias occurs when stores list the price of a product as $49.99 instead of $50. Our brains tend to latch onto the first digit, which makes us feel like a product whose price is $49.99 has a much lower price than a product selling for $50. In his book *Priceless*, William Poundstone reports on eight studies that demonstrated that items priced just below the "rounded" prices (99 cents vs. $1.00) sell on average 24% more often. Apple iTunes is famous for getting people who previously downloaded music for free illegally to pay 99 cents for each song. Evidently consumers see 99 cents as almost free. In many cases, human beings make choices based on some anchor or reference point, which often pushes our decision making into the realm of nonrational behavior.

11.3.2 Overoptimism

People also tend to be overly optimistic about many things. Homeowners tend to assume that home renovations will cost half as much as they actually will. Students tend to assume that it will take much less time to write a paper than it actually does. The author of this textbook assumed that he would be able to write this book more quickly than was actually the case. Investors are often wildly optimistic about the potential returns from an investment, especially during boom periods (which eventually turn into busts). Lottery winners assume that they will be responsible with their money, so they take it all as an immediate, lump sum. When we are overly optimistic, we are also being nonrational with our decision making.

11.3.3 Loss aversion

Ironically, at the same time we are overly optimistic about some things, we are also extremely reluctant to accept losses. Daniel Kahneman and Amos Tversky conducted a series of experiments to demonstrate that people feel a loss much more acutely than they feel a gain. For example, once investors have lost money on a stock they purchased, they become reluctant to sell the stock and "realize" the loss even if the stock's future prospects are not good. Similarly, homeowners are extremely unwilling to sell their house for less money than they paid for it, even if the real estate market has changed fundamentally. This causes many homeowners to reject sound offers and to continue to pay out money for taxes and maintenance rather than to accept a loss on their house's value. This, too, is nonrational, allowing one's feelings to trump sound decision making.

11.3.4 Status quo bias

Loss aversion is related to status quo bias, where we oppose changing our minds unless we have a very strong reason to do so. For example, many people tend to stick with their cell phone company, cable television provider, and electricity supplier, even if better options exist. The risk of making a change does not outweigh the potential benefits for most people. In these instances, we do not behave as fully rational, calculating individuals. We stick with what we know.

11.3.5 Nudge

People also tend to choose the default option that is given to them unless they have a strong reason to do otherwise. Economist Richard Thaler calls this a *nudge*— when consumers are gently encouraged to make a particular choice. Workers are more likely to save for retirement if enrollment in a retirement plan is automatic instead of optional. More people choose to be an organ donor if that is the default option than if the default option is not to be an organ donor. People tend to view the default option as the safe, authoritative choice, and if they trust the person giving them the options they are more likely to choose the default option than to make other choices. Retailers also give consumers nudges when they put up big displays to draw attention to particular products and when they put up a big sign advertising an "everyday low price" that is not a sale price. By drawing attention via displays and signs, retailers are nudging consumers in a particular direction, often in a somewhat manipulative fashion.

In all of these cases, we see that people do not always behave like rational economic man. Rather, they often behave like imperfect human beings with limited information and a host of cognitive biases that influence their behavior.

One of your tasks as a student of economics is to develop your own sophisticated analysis of which factors you find most important in human decision making based on the ideas of mainstream economists, behavioral economists, and political economists such as Veblen. We also find similar differences between how mainstream economists and political and behavioral economists analyze the profit-maximizing behavior of suppliers. The mainstream model focuses on short-term optimizing behavior, whereas political economists and behavioral economists look at longer-term decision making and a decision-making process that is more complex.

11.4 THE MAINSTREAM MODEL OF SUPPLY DECISIONS: DERIVING THE SUPPLY CURVE

As with the consumer model, mainstream economists view suppliers as rational maximizers who make optimal, informed decisions. Specifically, suppliers maximize profits by producing every unit that allows the firm to generate more in revenue than it generates in costs.

The mainstream model of supply decisions rests on several key assumptions:

1. Markets are competitive.
2. Firms are small and experience an upward-sloping marginal cost (supply) curve in the short run.
3. Firms engage in optimizing behavior, maximizing short-run profits by comparing marginal revenue and marginal cost based on complete information.
4. Markets tend toward an equilibrium price in the short term.
5. Long-term considerations such as innovation and achieving monopoly power are beyond the scope of the model.

As we will see later, political economists and behavioral economists have somewhat different views on how suppliers make decisions and what types of decisions are important.

In the mainstream model of supply and demand, supply curves are derived from the firm's short-run costs of production. The short run is **the period of time in which the supplier cannot adjust the size of operations (their capacity). The supplier's capital stock (buildings, machinery, and equipment) is fixed. Suppliers are only able to adjust their variable inputs in the short run, especially the amount of labor they hire**. The long run is **the period of time in which all inputs are variable and can be adjusted. Suppliers can build entirely new plants, install new technology and equipment, and increase their productive capacity in the long run**.

For example, consider the costs in the short run and long run of a small restaurant that specializes in selling burritos. In the short run, the restaurant has a fixed size of kitchen, with a fixed number of stoves, a fixed amount of equipment, and a fixed seating area with a certain number of tables and chairs for patrons. Suppose that the restaurant expects a large increase in the demand for burritos next weekend due to a big festival in town. What can they do? They don't have enough time to build an addition onto their building, install new equipment, or find and set up a larger space. Their capital goods—buildings, machinery, and equipment—are fixed in the short term. All the burrito restaurant can do in the short term is adjust their variable inputs, such as hiring more labor and increasing the amount of ingredients they purchase.

It would take the burrito restaurant several months to increase the size of their operation significantly by building an addition onto their restaurant or finding a new, larger location that can accommodate and serve more people. Thus, the long term for the burrito restaurant is a period of more than three months, a time period during which they have the ability to adjust *all* of their inputs to increase their capacity.

In the mainstream economics theory of the firm, short-run costs of production are derived from a short-run production function that **shows the relationship between the quantities of variable inputs (such as labor) and the amount of output produced, holding fixed inputs (such as capital) constant.** The most important variable input is labor—without labor, nothing would be produced—so we will focus on labor as we explain how a short-run production function works.

The short-run production function is governed by two economic laws: The law of specialization and the law of diminishing returns. According to the law of specialization, **when laborers specialize in a specific task, their productivity increases because (a) their skill and dexterity in completing that task improves, (b) they spend less time switching between jobs, and (c) specialized machinery and equipment can be developed to increase productivity related to the specialized task.** Workers in a burrito restaurant get particularly good at preparing the ingredients, wrapping burritos, waiting tables, and taking orders and payments. Specialized equipment including kitchen appliances, automated burrito wrapping machines, and cash registers improve the efficiency and productivity of these jobs.

But in a small restaurant with a fixed size of operations, eventually all of the specialized jobs are filled. Once the restaurant has one person specialized in cooking the ingredients, one person assembling and wrapping burritos, one person running the cash register, and one person waiting tables, there are no additional specialized tasks that exist to fill. Continuing to add workers once all of the specialized tasks are filled will increase the output of burritos, but output will start to increase by smaller and smaller increments because there is no longer a productivity bump from specialization. We have now entered the realm of diminishing returns.

According to the law of diminishing returns, **as more units of a variable input (such as labor) are added to a fixed amount of other inputs (such as capital), the marginal productivity of the variable input will eventually decrease (after all specialized tasks are filled).** In other words, as you have more and more workers utilizing a limited amount of machinery and equipment in a limited size operation, eventually adding additional workers will add smaller and smaller amounts to output. Once the restaurant is fully staffed, adding an additional worker may result in a small increase in output, but the increase in output will be much smaller than when previous workers were added.

As a real-world example of the law of diminishing returns, in the mid-1970s IBM found that increasing the number of programmers on a project definitely resulted in lower productivity of each additional programmer as more were hired. More programmers meant more time wasted in meetings, drafting plans, exchanging emails, reaching consensus, conducting staff evaluations, and so on. We see similar phenomena in most small businesses and in some large businesses.

Figure 11.1 shows a hypothetical short-run production function for Mercado Burrito that displays the law of specialization and the law of diminishing returns. The first two columns, showing the number of laborers hired (L) and the quantity of burritos produced by those laborers per hour worked (Q) constitute the short-run production function. In this example, there is only one variable input, labor. All other inputs are fixed. The production function focuses on the output of burritos from hiring a certain number of laborers for one hour.

The third column in Figure 11.1 shows the marginal product of labor (MPL), which is **the additional output that results from hiring an additional unit of a variable input (labor)**: $MP_L = (\Delta Q / \Delta L)$.

In this case, the marginal product of labor is the additional output of burritos that occurs when one more worker is hired for one hour. Notice that the marginal product of labor increases at first, when the first four laborers are being hired to fill specialized tasks, indicating the law of specialization. After hiring four laborers, the marginal product of labor declines. Hiring additional laborers increases the output of burritos by smaller and smaller amounts. Eventually, hiring the 11th laborer doesn't increase output at all. By this point, there are so many laborers working in a small space that they are actually getting in each other's way. Eighty-three burritos an hour is the maximum capacity for this small restaurant. When a 12th laborer is hired, output actually declines.

Figure 11.2 plots out the production function, also called the total product of labor, TP_L, and the marginal product of labor, MP_L. Notice that while specialization is occurring, MP_L is increasing and the slope of the TP_L curve is also increasing (the slope of the TP_L curve is the MP_L). When the law of diminishing returns sets

Number of laborers L	Quantity produced Q	Marginal product of labor $MP_L = \Delta Q/\Delta L$	Total variable cost TVC=$w \times L$	Marginal cost MC=$\Delta TVC/\Delta Q$	Average variable cost AVC=TVC/Q
0	0	-----	$ 0	-----	-----
1	5	5	$ 15	$ 3.00	$ 3.00
2	15	10	$ 30	$ 1.50	$ 2.00
3	27	12	$ 45	$ 1.25	$ 1.67
4	41	14	$ 60	$ 1.07	$ 1.46
5	53	12	$ 75	$ 1.25	$ 1.42
6	63	10	$ 90	$ 1.50	$ 1.43
7	71	8	$ 105	$ 1.88	$ 1.48
8	77	6	$ 120	$ 2.50	$ 1.56
9	81	4	$ 135	$ 3.75	$ 1.67
10	83	2	$ 150	$ 7.50	$ 1.81
11	83	0	$ 165	-----	$ 1.99
12	81	-2	$ 180	-----	$ 2.22

FIGURE 11.1 Table showing specialization, diminishing returns, and firm costs for Mercado Burrito.

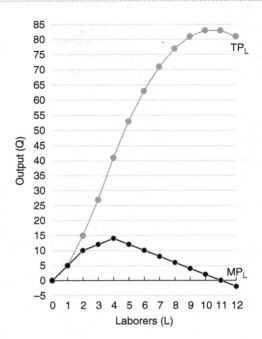

FIGURE 11.2 Production function (TP$_L$) and the marginal product of labor (MP$_L$).

in, MP$_L$ falls and the slope of the TP$_L$ curve declines. Eventually the TP$_L$ curve hits its maximum when MP$_L$ hits 0.

The next important step is to use the marginal product of labor to calculate the marginal cost of each burrito. First, we need to compute the total variable cost, which is **the total cost of hiring variable inputs, such as labor**. When labor is the only variable input, as it is in this case, total variable cost per hour is equal to the wage per hour multiplied by the number of laborers hired:

$$TVC = w \times L.$$

In general, the wage rate is fixed at the equilibrium local wage rate, which in this example is $15 per hour. TVC can be seen in column 4 of Figure 11.1. We can then use the changes in TVC and Q to compute the marginal cost of each unit. Marginal cost is an extremely important concept in mainstream economics. Marginal cost (MC) is **the increase in cost from producing another unit of a good**. In mathematical terms,

$$MC = \frac{\Delta TVC}{\Delta Q}.$$

Marginal cost is computed in column 5 of Figure 11.2. Notice that in this case, because the wage rate is considered to be fixed, we can rewrite the formula for MC:

$$MC = \frac{\Delta TVC}{\Delta Q} = \frac{w \times \Delta L}{\Delta Q} = \frac{w}{MP_L}.$$

Marginal cost in inversely related to the marginal product of labor. When workers become more productive due to the law of specialization, productivity increases and the cost of producing each additional unit decreases. Or, in economic lingo, when the marginal product of labor (MP_L) increases, the marginal cost of producing each unit of output (MC) decreases. Similarly, when workers become less productive due to the law of diminishing returns, productivity decreases and the cost of producing an additional unit of output increases. When MP_L decreases, MC increases.

We can also use the data in Figure 11.1 to compute average variable cost, which is **the variable cost per unit of output:** AVC = (TVC / Q). This can be found in the sixth column of Figure 11.1.

We can use the information on MC and AVC to construct the firm's supply curve. The supply curve for a firm is **the marginal cost curve above where MC intersects AVC**. Let's explore why this is the case.

First, in general, when firms engage in optimizing behavior, they use marginal cost to determine how many units to produce. Optimizing firms always build a small profit into their costs of production in order to accurately reflect the opportunity cost of spending money on inputs. This usually means adding a profit of about 10% into all costs of production. If a firm has to pay $13.64 for an hour of labor, they will want to recoup 110% of that amount, $15, to cover the opportunity cost of using their money to hire labor (instead of investing it in the stock market or some other profitable activity). *All costs in economics include a built-in normal profit* to capture the opportunity cost of engaging in production. A normal profit is the rate of profit that is typical in competitive industries. (We will explore the idea of normal profit more in subsequent chapters.) A 10% profit is built into the cost of each item produced in such markets.

In Figure 11.1, when six laborers are hired and the marginal cost of a burrito is $1.50, the firm is willing to sell those burritos for $1.50 each because the firm will make a small profit on each burrito at a price of $1.50. A 10% profit is included in the marginal cost figures. Thus, the marginal cost column tells us the lowest price for which a firm is willing to supply a certain quantity of goods, and that is the definition of a supply curve.

The only exception to this rule is that the firm will not want to supply any burritos if the price falls below the minimum number in the average variable cost column. The minimum AVC tells us the lowest price at which the firm can cover its labor costs. At any price below that, the firm would lose too much money by staying open and should shut down its operations. Thus, **the firm's supply curve is the marginal cost curve above the minimum average variable cost**, as depicted in Figure 11.3.

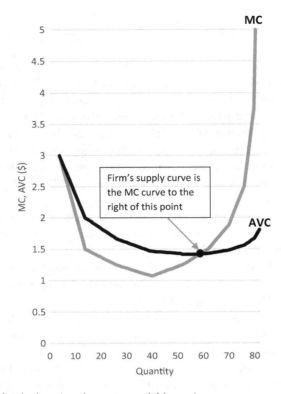

FIGURE 11.3 Marginal cost and average variable cost curves.

Using the table in Figure 11.1 or the graph in Figure 11.3, we can determine that at a price of $1.50, Mercado will supply a quantity of 63 burritos. If the price increases to $2.50, Mercado will supply 77 burritos. At a price of $7.50, Mercado will offer 83 burritos for sale, the maximum amount they can produce in an hour. Our restaurant maximizes profits by selling every unit for which the price is greater than or equal to the marginal cost.

We will explore firms and their supply curves extensively in the next section of the book. Now that we have gone in depth into the mainstream economics model of the supply curve, it's time to consider additional perspectives on how suppliers make decisions.

11.5 POLITICAL ECONOMISTS AND BEHAVIORAL ECONOMISTS ON SUPPLY DECISIONS

The mainstream supply and demand model focuses on short-term optimizing behavior. This captures some essential characteristics of markets and how they work much of the time. Political economists and behavioral economists focus on different aspects of markets. Regarding supply decisions, they are much more concerned with the complex realities of specific supply decisions. This includes understanding how groups within firms negotiate decisions and the key issues involved in longer-term strategic decision making, including the cultivation of innovations and monopoly power.

11.5.1 Satisficing

The mainstream model of supply decisions assumes that suppliers engage in optimizing behavior, comparing marginal revenue and marginal cost to determine the optimal level of output. This results in an elegant model in which supplier behavior is nicely predictable. But how often do real suppliers actually behave this way? According to both political economists and behavioral economists, rather than making fully informed, optimal decisions, most suppliers engage in satisficing—**making prudent decisions using rules of thumb given limited information**.

Firms rarely know what their marginal cost curve actually looks like. But they can easily determine the average cost of each unit they produce by adding up all of their costs and dividing by the quantity they are producing. Many firms simply take the average cost of a unit they are producing (including any opportunity costs) and then add a markup to average cost in order to figure out what price to charge. The amount of the markup they add on will depend on their best assessment of market conditions, including the interest of consumers in their product and the pricing and marketing campaigns of competitors.

In addition, decision making within a firm is often complex. Behavioral and political economists see firms as coalitions of groups including managers, stockholders, workers, and suppliers. Decisions within firms are usually made via compromises between the groups. Managing a firm is incredibly complex. For example, a firm can choose to pay the lowest wages possible to employees in order to minimize costs. Or a firm can pay workers more than the lowest possible wage rate to improve morale and productivity and thereby reduce the need to monitor workers closely. Well-paid workers who are given autonomy and responsibility are highly motivated and need little supervision, which boosts productivity and can actually reduce costs.

And as we saw earlier in the case of Veblen goods, simply setting prices as low as possible does not make sense in some markets. A firm that produces luxury goods needs to work more to establish brand name recognition and to cultivate exclusivity rather than to sell products as cheaply as possible.

From this perspective, the act of managing a firm is an artistic balancing act, rather than a mechanical decision to produce as long as marginal revenue is greater than or equal to marginal cost. This is the reason why the great "value investor" Warren Buffet puts so much weight on the management team of a firm when he is deciding where to invest. Management and the organizational structure of a firm are especially crucial in the long-term strategic success of a business.

11.5.2 Long-term strategic decisions

Firms certainly need to pay attention to prices, revenues, and costs, which are the focus of the supply and demand model. But they also need to attend to much broader, long-term considerations, especially the strategic direction of the firm and the best way to insure a steady flow of profits. From a political economy perspective, business competition is **competition for profits**. The goal and focus is making profits in whatever way possible. This includes price competition and efforts to optimize revenues and minimize costs. But it also includes competition for **breakthroughs** and to establish **monopoly power**. Indeed, the primary determinants of the long-term success of a company include the ability to cultivate innovation and to dominate and control markets.

As we discussed earlier in the book, one of the major dynamics in capitalism is creative destruction. Businesses are forced to invent constantly to stay one step ahead of the competition, and creative, new industries inevitably destroy and replace older ones. A major determinant of the long-term survival of a business is its ability to anticipate and manage the forces of creative destruction. A business must be constantly on the watch for new opportunities and threats.

Figure 11.4 lists some of the major U.S. industries that are in the midst of suffering steep declines, and Figure 11.5 lists the industries expected to grow the most rapidly in the near future. Currently the major sources of creative destruction are competition from online and foreign competition.

The major industries with highest expected growth in employment often surprise people, but some analysis of the trends makes it possible to anticipate such changes. Given the aging population of the United States, it makes sense that health care is among the list of growth industries. The increasing emphasis on sustainability, especially in energy production, has increased the demand for installers of wind turbines and solar panels. In addition, the increasing importance of online sales and social media, along with the massive amount of data being accumulated in this arena, is increasing the need for statisticians and data scientists, as well as cybersecurity.

Consider the implications of the constant destruction of old industries and development of new ones for existing businesses. Any firm that is content to maximize its current profits without taking steps to plan for the future is likely to end up in the dustbin of history. A key part of business activity is investing substantial

Industry	What's killing it
Printing and film development	Digital photography and screen viewing
Appliance repair	Cheap cost of new appliances
DVD, game, and video rental	Streaming and pirating
Newspaper publishing	Free online media
Recorded media manufacturing (DVDs, CDs)	Streaming, pirating
Tools and hardware, clothes, shoes	Cheap foreign competition
Retail sales (Sears, Macy's, malls)	Online sales (Amazon)

FIGURE 11.4 Table showing U.S. industries in decline.

Occupation	Growth rate	2019 Median pay
Wind turbine service technicians	61%	$52,910
Nurse practitioners	52%	$109,820
Solar photovoltaic installers	51%	$44,890
Occupational therapy assistants	35%	$61,510
Statisticians	35%	$91,160
Home health & personal care aides	34%	$25,280
Physical therapist assistants	33%	$58,790
Medical & health services managers	32%	$100,980
Physician assistants	31%	$112,260
Information security analysts	31%	$99,730
Data & mathematical scientists	31%	$94,280

FIGURE 11.5 Table showing industries with highest projected growth in employment. Source: Bureau of Labor Statistics.

funds to generate innovations that will keep the firm ahead of the competition or that will move the firm out of a dying industry and into a growing one. Amazon is famous for making very little in the way of annual profits because Amazon invests relentlessly in new initiatives for the long term. These investments have clearly paid off: Amazon's value as a company increased from $438 million in 1997 to $1,672,000 million in 2021, and their sales increased from $90 million per quarter in 1998 to $125,600 million in the last quarter of 2020. Innovation may be the single most important ingredient in a company's long-term economic success, followed closely by the firm's ability to cultivate a degree of monopoly power.

11.5.3 Cultivation of monopoly power

In extremely competitive markets, it is impossible to make much profit. So in an economic system focused on profit, one of the essential business tactics is to make an industry less competitive. This can be done in a number of ways. You can drive competitors out of business with fair or unfair practices. You can create brand name identity so consumers buy your products instead of those of your competitors. Once you grow bigger than your competitors, you can use your financial power to buy out or merge with competitors. You can buy up patents and innovations and either use them or shelve them so competitors cannot use them.

The most profitable industries in the United States are those with significant degrees of monopoly power when firms have the power to raise prices without losing too many consumers. As Warren Buffett, the most successful investor in modern history, once said,

> The single most important decision in evaluating a business is pricing power. If you've got the power to raise prices without losing business to a competitor, you've got a very good business. And if you have to have a prayer session before raising the price by 10%, then you've got a terrible business.

There is a direct correlation between market share and profitability: The more a firm dominates its market, the higher its profits are likely to be. As you can see in Figure 11.6, Apple was the most profitable U.S. company in 2019 thanks to its dominance (monopoly power) in the smart phone, tablet, and laptop markets. The financial industry has seen many mergers and acquisitions over the last two decades, leaving the industry heavily concentrated. By the late 2010s three huge banks, JPMorgan Chase, Bank of America, and Wells Fargo, controlled about one-third of U.S. banking, with Citigroup not far behind. With this degree of monopoly power, four of the ten most profitable U.S. companies in 2019 were financial institutions. Meanwhile, Google (Alphabet) with its dominance of search engines finished third, and Facebook with its control over social media was the sixth most-profitable company. These companies can use their market dominance to stay on top, buying up competitors and new technologies. It will likely take significant antitrust action by the government to break up the control that these huge companies have over the industries in which they operate.

Another key point here is that in many industries there are significant economies of scale: It is more efficient to be large than it is to be small. Large companies do not experience the law of diminishing returns in the same way as small firms. In fact, for huge firms in manufacturing and software, the larger they get, the lower their average cost of supplying each unit becomes as they create new specialized jobs and technologies.

Market power also allows firms to negotiate better deals that reduce costs. Large firms like Apple and Walmart can demand lower prices from their suppliers as a result of their market dominance. Similarly, in financial services, more financial clout means more opportunities to make profits. Huge banks can pursue opportunities around the globe and they can secure favorable rates for their services.

Supply curves for such industries may be downward sloping rather than upward sloping because the firm's costs may decline as they get bigger, and the biggest firms

Company	Profits (millions of $)
Apple	$59,531.0
JPMorgan Chase	$32,474.0
Alphabet	$30,736.0
Bank of America	$28,147.0
Wells Fargo	$22,393.0
Facebook	$22,112.0
Intel	$21,053.0
Exxon Mobil	$20,840.0
AT&T	$19,370.0
Citigroup	$18,045.0

FIGURE 11.6 Table showing the most profitable U.S. companies in 2019. Source: Fortune, https://fortune.com/fortune500/.

will tend to have the lowest costs and the most options. A market with vast economies of scale like this would not work in the same way the supply and demand model predicts.

11.5.4 Power and countervailing power

The issue of monopoly power highlights a more general issue with markets: The power of large corporations and the countervailing power of consumers, unions, communities, and governments. The famous institutionalist economist John Kenneth Galbraith observed that there were three main power centers in market economies: Businesses, governments (and the communities they represent), and workers (and the unions that represent workers). Galbraith believed that capitalism worked well when power was distributed relatively equally between those three power blocks. When businesses were too powerful, they exploited workers and gouged consumers. When governments were too powerful, they became authoritarian and bureaucratic. If unions became too powerful, they could harm economic productivity. The ideal system, to Galbraith, was one in which the countervailing power of each block could counteract the worst impulses of the other blocks: Businesses' bad behavior could be checked by unions and government regulations; government could be kept in line by businesses and workers; and workers' power would be checked by businesses and government regulations. But that perfect balancing act is hard to maintain.

Even in competitive markets there are power imbalances. We noted above that the pizza market is quite competitive, with dozens of restaurants in each town. In theory, the competitive nature of the pizza market limits the power of any one company and provides options and opportunities for consumers and workers. And yet we find that the big players in the pizza market, especially Domino's and Pizza Hut, have substantial monopoly power. Workers at Domino's and Pizza Hut are paid low wages, usually near or at the local minimum wage. Both restaurant chains make large political donations to make sure that politicians enact laws that are good for their business. This includes lobbying efforts to oppose increases in the minimum wage and to fight labeling laws that require health information to be put on menus and product labels. If the pizza industry lobbyists have their way, pizza will be classified as a "vegetable" for school lunch programs, so it can be served instead of dishes made up entirely of vegetables!

Even the most competitive markets involve power relations of some sort, so understanding markets means grasping how those power relations are structured. The locus of power in a market starts with the firm and the power it has by controlling resources (the means of production). Firms have direct control over their workers, what they are paid, and the conditions of work. If workers are skilled and/or unionized, they will have some countervailing power to ensure that they are paid and treated well. If they are unskilled and non-union, workers will have very little power and will have to accept what they are offered by the firm.

Company	Subsidy (millions of $)
Amazon	$750.0
Cree, Inc. (semiconductors)	$617.1
General Atomics	$533.6
Fiat Chrysler	$405.0

FIGURE 11.7 Table displaying the largest corporate subsidies of 2019. Source: Good Jobs First, "Subsidy Tracker," https://www.goodjobsfirst.org/subsidy-tracker, accessed January 29, 2021.

Firms have substantial control over communities. When a large firm is deciding where to locate its operations, communities will engage in bidding wars to attract the firm. This will often include decades of tax holidays and the provision of free infrastructure and government services. The biggest corporate subsidies of 2019 are listed in Figure 11.7, showing four companies that received hundreds of millions of dollars in tax breaks or direct subsidies to locate operations in a particular place. The largest corporate subsidy in history was an $8.7 billion tax break given to Boeing by Washington State. By 2021, Amazon amassed $3.7 billion in subsidies from state and local governments, including the $750 million they received in 2019. The larger the size of the corporation, the more power they have to demand subsidies and tax breaks. Communities, along with the local, state, and federal governments that represent them, do have some countervailing power. They can pass laws that restrict corporate power and enact taxes that make corporations pay for their fair share of infrastructure and education costs. But judging by the huge expansion in corporate subsidies and the decline in corporate regulations and oversight over the last few decades, corporations have the upper hand.

11.5.5 Evolution and change vs. stability and equilibrium

In general, the supply and demand model focuses on how short-term prices tend to stabilize around an equilibrium price and quantity. The supply and demand model is particularly useful for analyzing how a variety of key determinants affect equilibrium prices and quantities in the short term. The political economy approach is useful in studying the factors that cause industries to evolve and change, such as the forces of creative destruction and monopolization and the power relations within particular industries. One can find both of these tendencies in most markets. The key is to determine which tendency is most useful for particular types of analysis.

11.6 CONCLUSION

This chapter has expanded our analysis of markets to go beyond the supply and demand model in some key areas. The chapter began by analyzing consumer behavior that cannot be captured by a typical demand curve. This included the idea of

Veblen goods, where demand increases as an item becomes more exclusive and honorific. We also studied how pecuniary emulation, herd behavior, and culture impact purchasing decisions. And we discussed instances where consumers make decisions that do not conform to the standard model of a rational, fully informed consumer. Consumers are subject to a number of cognitive biases that can shift their decisions in a direction that mainstream economists would describe as irrational.

Next we turned to the model behind the supply curve in mainstream economics. The supply curve is derived from a short-run production function subject to the laws of specialization and diminishing returns. The information from the production function can be used to determine the marginal cost of each unit. Marginal cost becomes the firm's supply curve after it crosses the average variable cost curve.

Behavioral economists and political economists analyze supply decisions somewhat differently, going beyond optimizing behavior to analyze how businesses often engage in satisficing, where they make decisions based on competing interests using rules of thumb. Firms also compete on more than prices. They engage in competition for innovation and to develop monopoly power, which is likely to generate the highest rates of profits. Corporate power, and the idea of countervailing power of governments and workers, is also an important aspect of markets.

Now that we have explored market analysis in some detail, it is time to study the different market structures that exist in capitalist economic systems. On the supply side of the market, one of the most fascinating things to study is the dynamics of particular industries. You will find vast differences in markets: Local farm markets are very different from the market for local restaurants. More different still is the market for technological goods like smartphones and the market for processed foods, both of which are dominated by huge, global conglomerates. Local utilities markets such as the market for electricity operate on still different principles. Understanding these differences is crucial to any sophisticated analysis of markets. These differences are taken up in the next section of the book.

* *

QUESTIONS FOR REVIEW

1. Give an example of a Veblen good that is different from the examples given in the book. Explain why this is considered to be a Veblen good.

2. How do the consumption habits on your campus or in your community relate to Veblen's concept of pecuniary emulation and the concept of the bandwagon effect? Explain and give specific examples.

3. In your household and other households that you have observed, how does gender affect major decisions on purchases of goods and services? Explain and give examples.

4. The results of the ultimatum game and the Haifa childcare experiment demonstrate that most people value fairness and reciprocity in their dealings with

each other. Looking at the transactions that you have been involved in or observed, do you see similar examples of fairness and reciprocity on display? Explain and give examples.

5. Using your own behavior and the behavior of people close to you, find examples of anchoring, overoptimism, loss aversion, and status quo bias that are different from those given in the book. How widespread do these issues seem to be? Do they affect most human behavior most of the time, or are these rare examples? Explain and support your answer.

6. The table below shows information on labor and output for one week for a firm that manufactures the Slinky toy. The wage rate is $800 per week.
   a. Complete the table in Figure 11.8.
   b. Does this table display the law of specialization and the law of diminishing returns? Explain briefly.
   c. If the equilibrium price of a Slinky is $5, how many laborers should the firm hire, and how many Slinkys should the firm produce?
   d. If the equilibrium price of a Slinky increases to $10, how many laborers should the firm hire, and how many Slinkys should the firm produce?

7. Suppose that you work for a marketing firm and you are in charge of deciding how many laser printers to buy for your work team of 50 people. How would the laws of specialization and diminishing returns apply to your purchases of additional laser printers? Explain.

8. Why do economists include a normal profit in the costs of production?

9. Explain how the firm's supply curve is derived from the marginal cost curve and the average variable cost curve.

10. Compare and contrast the mainstream economics view of supply decisions with the views of political and behavioral economists. In your response, explain what types of questions each approach is trying to answer.

11. Why do political economists believe that power is a key element of supply decisions? Explain and give specific examples.

L	Q	$MP_L = \Delta Q/\Delta L$	$TVC = w \times L$	$MC = \Delta TVC/\Delta Q$	$AVC = TVC/Q$
0	0				
10	1000				
20	3000				
30	5400				
40	7400				
50	9000				
60	10,200				
70	11,000				
80	11,400				
90	11,400				

FIGURE 11.8 Table for use with problem 6.

NOTES

1 Stanford News Service, "Price Tag Can Change the Way People Experience Wine, Study Shows," January 15, 2008. http://news.stanford.edu/pr/2008/pr-wine-011608. html, accessed July 26, 2021.

2 See Samuel Bowles, Richard Edwards, and Frank Roosevelt, *Understanding Capitalism*, 3rd ed. (Oxford University Press, Oxford, 2005), ch. 3.

PART IV

Market structures and corporations

Now that we have described how markets work along with the supply and demand model, the next step in understanding markets is to analyze the different market structures that we find in capitalist economies.

Chapter 12 introduces the four main types of market structures—perfect competition, monopolistic competition, oligopoly, and monopoly. Each market structure has its own dynamics and characteristics, with different kinds of competition, barriers to entry, and product differentiation. Once we can identify which market structure a particular industry fits into, that helps us to anticipate the dynamics of that industry and how firms in it will behave in response to various factors.

Chapter 13 on firm costs of production develops the mainstream microeconomic model of short-run and long-run costs. We can use the laws of specialization and diminishing returns, highlighted earlier, to derive U-shaped average cost curves in the short run and long run. The shape of long-run cost curves is driven by economies and diseconomies of scale that determine the number and size of competitors. The chapter concludes with an alternative perspective on the nature of firm costs based on the theories of political economists.

Chapter 14 develops the mainstream model of profit maximization in perfectly competitive industries. This is the perfect Smithian market structure that needs little or no regulation due to the degree of competition. The chapter lays out the assumptions behind the model, short-run profit maximization, and long-run profit maximization. The long-term model of perfect competition, where entry and exit causes firms to produce at the minimum average total cost, is discussed in relation to Adam Smith's ideas on capitalism. Counterarguments regarding the applicability of the competitive model are also considered.

Chapter 15 takes up monopoly and market power using the mainstream model of profit maximization. There are natural and nonnatural monopolies, and each of them requires a particular type of government intervention for the market to work effectively. So the chapter includes a substantial segment on the regulation of

DOI: 10.4324/9781315636924-15

monopolies of all types and a discussion of why monopolies are considered inefficient from a theoretical perspective. The role of monopoly power in political economy analysis is also discussed. The chapter includes a case study of the Google near-monopoly over search engines.

In Chapter 16, we discuss monopolistic competition, product differentiation, and the dynamics of small business competition. Most local businesses operate in monopolistically competitive markets with easy entry and exit, a large number of substitutes, and some product differentiation. This is an interesting market because it encompasses many businesses that we patronize all the time, including restaurants, gas stations, hair salons, and so on. The chapter covers the mainstream model of the monopolistically competitive firm in the short term and the long term and goes through several case studies of how such markets work in practice.

Chapter 17 focuses on oligopolies and their strategic behaviors. Oligopolies dominate global manufacturing, national retailing, and many national services. This chapter discusses the nature of oligopolies and goes through the kinked demand curve model of an oligopolistic firm. The chapter also develops a simple prisoner's dilemma game theory model to explore some of the strategic behaviors that oligopolistic firms engage in. The chapter features case studies of several industries to illustrate examples of how oligopolies function in the real world.

This section concludes with Chapter 18 on corporations and their role in society. The limited liability corporation is one of the major and most controversial forces in modern capitalism. Though some economists, such as Milton Friedman and William Baumol (author of *The Free-Market Innovation Machine*), view corporations as beneficial, other economists such as Paul Baran and Paul Sweezy (authors of *Monopoly Capital*), Veblen, and Marx see corporations as frequently destructive. This chapter contrasts the views of Austrian and mainstream economists who view corporations favorably with political economists who have an unfavorable view.

12 Different types of market structures

And how they affect market outcomes

The supply and demand model assumes that markets are extremely competitive. In actuality, some markets are competitive and others are not. Agricultural markets are extremely competitive, with thousands of small producers selling identical products. Local restaurant markets are mostly competitive, with large numbers of small restaurants competing with each other. But in the restaurant market there are differences with respect to location, quality, and branding that cause the restaurant industry to operate somewhat differently than agricultural markets.

Then we have markets that are dominated by a few huge firms. Almost all manufacturing industries as well as national service industries such as finance, banking, and insurance are dominated by a handful of large corporations. In these industries, power dynamics and strategic considerations are paramount. Finally, we have a few industries, the least competitive of all, that are monopolies, dominated entirely by one firm. This includes public utilities such as electricity, as well as some software markets. The market for search engines is almost completely dominated by Google.

Economists have identified four main types of market structures that reflect the variations described above—perfect competition, monopolistic competition, oligopoly, and monopoly. Each market faces different cost structures and different degrees and types of competition. This chapter explains the fundamental characteristics of each market structure and gives concrete examples of how they work.

Subsequently, we compare the four market structures, looking at the similarities and differences with respect to eight key characteristics: Barriers to entry, control over prices, the number of sellers, the typical size of firms, product differentiation, the existence of long-run above-normal profit, prices in the industry relative to lowest possible average total cost in long run (the degree of markup that

DOI: 10.4324/9781315636924-16

firms can impose), and long-term strategic focus. We then look at how concentrated various manufacturing and service industries are by studying the extent to which certain industries are dominated by the four largest and eight largest firms.

12.0 CHAPTER 12 LEARNING GOALS

After reading this chapter you should be able to:

- List the key characteristics of each of the four market structures— perfect competition, monopolistic competition, oligopoly, and monopoly—and describe how those key characteristics explain the dynamics of each market structure.

- Define above-normal (economic) profit, normal profit, and economic loss and explain the relevance of these terms in explaining industry behavior.

- Compare and contrast the four different market structures using the eight key market characteristics described in this chapter.

- Identify the most likely market structure for a particular industry based on its characteristics.

- Analyze the impact of competition and concentration on industries and consumers.

12.1 PERFECT COMPETITION

Economists have identified four major market structures in capitalist economic systems, ranging from the most competitive to the least competitive: (1) perfect competition, (2) monopolistic competition, (3) oligopoly, and (4) monopoly. The main characteristics of these market structures are laid out below.

The main differences between these markets exist because of varying degrees of barriers to entry. Barriers to entry are factors that make it difficult for a new firm to enter an industry or market. The major sources of barriers to entry are the existence of economies of scale that require firms to be large to be competitive, control over key resources, brand name identity, and legal restrictions (patents, copyrights, trade restrictions, and government regulations). Industries with few barriers to entry tend to be very competitive because it is easy for new firms to enter the market. The high degree of competition keeps prices low and limits the market power of any one firm. Industries with significant barriers to entry have little competition, and the huge firms that dominate such industries have immense market power.

Perfect competition is the most competitive market structure, in which large numbers of small firms produce identical products. The market is easy for new firms to enter, and firms have no control over the price they charge. Prices are determined by market supply and demand. Examples include the markets for wheat, corn, soybeans, and other agricultural products, along with some markets for local services such as babysitting and lawn mowing. These markets are so competitive that firms have no ability to increase prices. Suppliers have to charge the same price as other firms in the market because there are numerous competitors selling the exact same product—goods are perfect substitutes for each other. Any firm that charges more than the going market price charged by other firms in the industry will lose all of its sales.

More specifically, the major characteristics of a perfectly competitive market are the following:

1. **Homogenous product**: All firms sell a product that is identical to the products being sold by other suppliers. Goods are perfect substitutes for each other, so consumers will buy whatever good is cheapest. In such markets, advertising is not helpful because it raises costs but does not increase demand, because all products are identical and branding is not possible.

2. **Large number of small sellers and buyers**: This market consists of a large number of sellers and buyers in the market, all of whom are small in size. No individual seller or buyer can influence the market price of the product.

3. **Easy entry and exit**: The reason that these markets are so competitive is because anyone can enter this market. It is easy to start a firm in a perfectly competitive industry because there are no barriers to entry. It is easy to exit the market (close up operations) because the initial investment is small. The ease of entry means that if firms in this market are making above-normal profits, new firms will enter the market and drive prices down to where firms make a normal profit.

4. **Firms are price takers**: Suppliers cannot raise their prices at all because if they do, consumers will switch and buy cheaper, identical substitutes. Suppliers have no reason to lower their prices because they can sell all they want at the going market price. Thus, all firms charge the same price, and the market price is determined by the market supply and demand curves.

In perfectly competitive industries, the primary strategic, long-term focus of suppliers is on keeping costs as low as possible. Minimizing costs is the only way firms can stay in business in these most competitive of markets. Quinoa provides an excellent example of the dynamics of a perfectly competitive market.

Case study: The quinoa story

Quinoa is an ancient grain that is extremely high in protein. In 2008 it was little known outside of Bolivia and Peru, where it was a staple. It was produced there by thousands of small farmers with no branding, making quinoa a textbook example of a perfectly competitive market. In 2008 quinoa sold for $1.30 per kilogram.

Then, Oprah Winfrey, the United Nations, and others began publicizing the grain's health properties and it became trendy. Consumer tastes shifted toward quinoa, the demand skyrocketed, and the price reached $6.20 per kilogram in 2014, an increase of 377%.

But quinoa is a perfectly competitive market that is easy to enter. Other farmers around the world saw the above-normal profits being made in quinoa, so the next time farmers planted crops many of them started growing some quinoa. Quinoa was now grown in 50 countries. As a result of the entry of new quinoa growers, the supply of quinoa increased dramatically and the price fell by 40% in 2015. Prices may continue to fall further as additional growers enter the market. Eventually, any above-normal profits in the quinoa market will be competed away.

This is a classic story in a perfectly competitive market. Firms in such markets can experience a short-term boom when an increase in the demand for their product increases the market price substantially. This leads to short-term above-normal profits. But in the long term, because it is easy to enter this market (all you need is some land and some seeds and you can grow quinoa), the above-normal profits will attract new competitors, the supply of the product will increase, and the price will fall until firms earn a normal profit.

12.2 NORMAL PROFIT, ECONOMIC PROFIT, AND ECONOMIC LOSS

The quinoa story highlights the important role of profit in the entry of new firms into competitive markets. Economists use very precise definitions of different types of profit to analyze the relationship between profits and the entry and exit of firms in markets.

Economists define a normal profit as the level of profit needed for a company to remain competitive in a market. A firm earns a normal profit if it covers all of its explicit costs of production and pays a return to the firm's owners that is at least as good as they could get in other industries. In other words, to earn a normal profit, a firm must cover all of its costs of production, including the opportunity costs of the owners.

Suppose that a business owner could earn a salary of $100,000 if she closed her business and went to work for another firm. Economists consider that salary the opportunity cost of running the business: Unless the owner makes at least $100,000 in profit running her business, she should shut it down. Thus, a $100,000 profit would be a normal profit for that business owner.

Similarly, investors will want a rate of return on their investment that is at least as high as they can get elsewhere. The average rate of profit in the United States has been about 11% since 1950. This means that investors expect an 11% profit on any of their investments. If their money is tied up in a business and if that business is earning a profit of 11%, that would be considered earning a normal profit and investors would have no reason to move their money elsewhere. Interestingly, if a firm is making a 7% profit, unless they can make changes to increase that profit rate, the firm will eventually go out of business. Investors will pull their money out of the business that is only earning a 7% profit and put their money in businesses earning the normal rate of 11%. Economists consider a below-normal profit, such as 7%, to be an economic loss (see below) because investors are not getting as much return on their investment as they can elsewhere. Once all investors pull their money out of a company it will have to close. This highlights an important economic truth: Firms must earn at least a normal profit in order to stay in business.

An economic profit is an above-normal profit. A firm earning an economic profit makes a higher profit than typical firms. New firms are encouraged to enter an industry by the presence of economic profits because there are higher profits to be had in that industry than exist in other industries. For example, in the quinoa case study, when quinoa farmers started earning an economic (above-normal) profit, new farmers started entering the quinoa market, which increased the supply of quinoa. Thus, unless barriers to entry exist, economic profits in a particular market encourage new firms to enter.

An economic loss is a below-normal profit. A firm earning an economic loss makes a lower profit than typical firms. Firms will eventually exit an industry that is incurring economic losses so they can invest their money in more profitable endeavors.

Monopolistic competition is a market very similar to perfect competition, but there is one major difference: Firms in a monopolistically competitive market have a monopoly on one unique aspect of the market. This product differentiation allows some firms to charge higher prices than others, which is not possible in a perfectly competitive market.

12.3 MONOPOLISTIC COMPETITION

Monopolistic competition is another very competitive market structure with a large number of small firms due to easy entry into the market. Unlike in perfect competition, firms have a monopoly over certain unique business characteristics such as quality, brand, or location. This gives firms some control over their prices. Firms supply goods that are close but not perfect substitutes for each other. Examples include local services such as doctors, dentists, and lawyers and local retailers such as restaurants, bars, and gas stations. Businesses in all of these industries offer a similar product, but some can charge a higher price than others due to the differences in quality, brand, and location.

The major characteristics of a monopolistically competitive market are as follows:

1. **Slightly differentiated products**: Goods are close but not perfect substitutes for each other. If firms can successfully improve quality and establish brand name recognition, they can further differentiate their product from competing ones.
2. **Large number of sellers and buyers**: The large number of competitors and consumers means that no one actor has a large influence over the market. Some firms are larger than others but no firm is dominant.
3. **Easy entry and exit**: These markets are fairly easy to enter. It is relatively simple to open a restaurant or a hair salon, for example. There may be some small barriers to entry, such as startup costs or, in the case of professional services such as doctors, dentists, and lawyers, a graduate education. Nonetheless, entry into such markets is easy enough that if suppliers in a monopolistically competitive industry are earning above-normal profits, new firms will enter and compete those profits away, causing suppliers to earn normal profits in the long run.
4. **Some control over prices**: Firms in this market have a monopoly over some unique aspects of the business, including quality, location, and branding. The more successfully a supplier can differentiate their product from their substitutes, the higher the price they can charge. But the large number of substitutes limits how much one supplier can raise prices, so demand curves tend to be elastic.

In monopolistically competitive markets, the long-term focus is on keeping costs low, along with efforts to create product differentiation that would allow a firm to raise prices. As a result, we tend to see quite a bit of advertising and branding as local businesses try to draw customers away from their rivals. Convincing consumers that you are providing an especially high-quality good or service and that they will get a good deal from you are typical marketing ploys one finds in such markets. Businesses will also pay a lot more in rent to be situated in a prime location, which can increase foot traffic and visibility. Businesses also have to stay up on the latest trends in the industry to stay ahead of the competition, something we see with the rise of fast-casual restaurants in the restaurant market.

Case study: The rise of fast-casual restaurants

One of the biggest trends in the monopolistically competitive restaurant industry over the last decade has been the rise of fast-casual restaurants like Panera Bread, Jimmy John's Gourmet Sandwiches, and Chipotle Mexican Grill. Fast-casual restaurants do not offer table service, but they do offer more customizability, higher quality, and fresher and healthier options than traditional fast food restaurants. Because of higher quality, consumers spend more at fast-casual restaurants than they do at fast food restaurants, and consumers often spend almost as much at fast-casual restaurants as they do at casual full-service restaurants. The rise of fast-casual restaurants coincided with changes in consumer preferences, driven by the rise of the obesity epidemic in the United States and the increased focus of consumers on eating healthier foods from local sources.

Sales at fast-casual restaurants increased by 10%–11% per year from 2011 to 2016, much faster than growth at fast food restaurants (which experienced 3%–4% annual growth on average) and full-serve restaurants (1.5%–2% annual growth). The impact of the entry of dozens of additional competitors into the already crowded restaurant market has been interesting. Casual chains such as Applebee's and Ruby Tuesday suffered the largest decrease in demand, losing customers and being forced to close restaurants. McDonald's, the largest player in the fast food market, also suffered declines in same-store sales. Thus, the entry of fast-casual restaurants like Chipotle caused a decline in the demand for meals at Applebee's, Ruby Tuesday, and McDonald's.

Chipotle, the most rapidly growing of the fast-casual restaurants, takes a very different approach from typical fast food and casual restaurants. They spend a much higher percentage of their revenues on ingredients, which is much more similar to a high-end restaurant than to a fast food or casual restaurant, where ingredients are often processed and frozen. Many of Chipotle's ingredients are purchased fresh from local providers and hand processed by employees. They do not serve breakfast or offer a drive-through option, some of the most profitable areas for most chains. And they rarely change menu items, focusing on producing food from a small menu well. By traditional measures, Chipotle should have failed. Instead, they became the most successful of the fast-casual chains.[1]

It will be interesting to see whether the rise of fast-casual restaurants will continue or whether they have reached their capacity. This depends significantly on the whims of consumer tastes and the ability of restaurants to anticipate changes in those tastes. Meanwhile, in an attempt to reverse its decline, McDonald's has been trying to offer healthier options while at the same time adding new coffee options to compete with Starbucks.

This case study highlights the constantly shifting nature of a monopolistically competitive industry, where firms must adapt to stay ahead of the competition. Shifts in consumer preferences can create new niches such as the demand for healthier, fresher fast food. This causes new firms (Chipotle, Panera) to enter the market to take advantage of the new demand. However, as more firms enter the market, the increase in the number of substitutes takes business away from firms that were already in the market (Applebee's, McDonald's), reducing the demand for their products. Eventually, because the market is highly competitive and easy to enter, economists would expect profits to return to a normal level in the long run, where the market would stay until the next shift in market conditions disrupts it.

Monopolistic competition is one of the most common market structures we find in capitalist economic systems. Another common market structure is oligopoly, which differs from monopolistic competition in that there are significant barriers to entry, so oligopolies have much less competition.

12.4 OLIGOPOLY

An oligopoly is a market that is dominated by a few huge firms whose behavior affects each other significantly. There are large barriers to entry that keep out new competitors. In general, markets become oligopolistic when there are significant benefits to being huge. For example, in the manufacturing of cars, cell phones, steel, and other products, producing on a massive scale results in much lower costs of production. Firms can develop specialized plants utilizing very specialized equipment and labor to produce each component and additional specialized factories to assemble the components. That degree of specialization reduces costs and increases productivity significantly. Similarly, national retail chains like Walmart, Amazon, and Costco have vast networks of warehouses that allow these firms to supply goods cheaply to any corner of the country. Even more important, their huge size gives them the power to demand lower prices from their suppliers, allowing national retailers to sell goods at lower prices and thereby undercut smaller competitors. In addition, their financial resources allow huge firms in oligopolistic markets to buy out competitors and to cultivate political favors by making campaign contributions and hiring lobbyists. This allows oligopolists to continue to dominate markets, even if they are not particularly efficient. Competition to stay ahead often takes on a complex form in oligopolies (colluding, merging, advertising, lobbying), rather than the price competition we find in competitive markets.

The major characteristics of an oligopoly are listed below.

1. **Products may be differentiated or undifferentiated**: Oligopolistic industries that manufacture goods for consumers (cars, cell phones, etc.) sell differentiated products. Oligopolistic industries that manufacture materials used in the production of other goods, such as inputs like steel or aluminum, tend to produce undifferentiated products.

2. **Dominated by a few huge firms**: A handful of giant firms control most of the industry. There may be some smaller firms but the major dynamics of the market revolve around the interplay between the dominant firms.

3. **Significant barriers to entry**: In manufacturing, economies of scale are so significant that only huge firms with access to the latest technology and a global supply chain can compete. In consumer goods, brand name recognition and first mover advantages (where consumers get comfortable with a particular product, such as Facebook or the iPhone) allow certain companies to dominate. It is extremely difficult for new firms to enter such markets.

4. **Interdependence among firms**: When a handful of firms dominate an industry, the actions of one of the big players have a large and direct impact on the other firms. Firms watch each other very closely and try to match price cuts and counter advertising campaigns. This also leads to incentives for firms to collude to act like a monopoly or to merge in order to lessen competition. Most instances of collusion occur in oligopolies.

Strategic considerations in oligopolistic markets are multiple and complex. The importance of size and technology means that firms must invest substantially in research and development. The importance of brand name recognition means that there is substantial non-price competition, usually in the form of vast advertising and marketing campaigns. Collusion and mergers and acquisitions are also ways to reduce competition and enhance profits. And oligopolistic firms can secure their position in a market via hiring lobbyists and making donations to campaigns and political action committees to get reductions in taxes and regulations that inhibit their profits. An interesting example of the type of competition we see in an oligopoly is the cola wars and the efforts by Coca-Cola to preserve its market share.

Case study: Coca-Cola market dominance

One classic example of how oligopolistic companies work to dominate markets is Coca-Cola and its efforts to control shelf space and displays at grocery stores, sometimes in tacit collusion with Pepsi. Coca-Cola has a practice of paying retailers in exchange for exclusive advertising, prominent displays and signs, and a monopoly on vending machines. They even offer supermarkets special discounts and pay "slotting fees" so that their products take up more shelf space, pushing out the products of competitors or relegating them to low shelves at the end of the aisle.

Coca-Cola also appears to collude with Pepsi to alternate sale dates. Coke products are placed on sale and on featured displays one week and Pepsi the next. It is extremely unlikely that such practices are just coincidence. More likely, this is a form of tacit collusion where the two companies choose to accommodate each other rather than to engage in a price war that would hurt the profits of both companies.

What happens is a form of price leadership, where Coke establishes the pricing structure and sales dates and Pepsi matches it. Coca-Cola, with 43% of the market, is much more powerful than Pepsi, which has 27%. Coke can circulate a sheet of paper to retailers indicating the 26 weeks in the next year when it wants Coke to be featured prominently and placed on sale. That sheet somehow ends up in the hands of Pepsi. Pepsi then just happens to select the other 26 weeks of the year for its sale weeks. Evidence from North Carolina in the 1980s indicated that this sort of tacit collusion between Coke and Pepsi to alternate sale weeks was taking place, although such allegations are almost impossible to prove.[2] Interestingly, the sale prices of Coke and Pepsi also seem to be the same most of the time.

In June 2000, a jury in Texas found Coca-Cola guilty of violating Texas antitrust laws by paying retailers to exclude competitors' products, in particular the products of RC Cola. Coca-Cola used their financial clout to systematically push RC products and displays out of retailers. For example, Coca-Cola paid for 75% of display space at a convenience store chain and 100% of the space at a drug store chain. By the late 1990s, Coca-Cola was spending $900 million on these efforts. Pepsi settled out of court with RC Cola for making similar efforts to exclude RC Cola from retailers' shelves.

In the Coca-Cola example, we see how important it is to a company to maintain its dominant position. But instead of keeping ahead of competitors by innovating and keeping prices low, Coca-Cola worked to stifle competition of smaller competitors and create a stable relationship with their main competitor, Pepsi, to divide up the market. Instead of competing with prices, Coke and Pepsi competed with advertising and by buying up prime space in retailers.

The behaviors of Coca-Cola and Pepsi are typical of industries that are dominated by a small number of huge firms. Collusion and market domination are so profitable that the dominant firms will do almost anything to maintain their market position and keep out any new competition. It is only in oligopolies with more than three major competitors, such as the automobile industry with more than ten big firms, that competition provides enough check on collusive behavior and the power of dominant firms.

Colluding oligopolies, by working to control the entire market, are actually behaving much like a monopoly. Monopolies tend to be so inefficient and bad for consumers that we almost always regulate them in some way.

12.5 MONOPOLY

A monopoly is the least competitive market structure with only one firm present and no close substitutes (a unique product). Monopolies are maintained by prohibitive barriers to entry, and their control over the market gives them complete control over prices. Monopolies are generally to be avoided: Firms with monopolies can charge high prices and produce shoddy products and still make a huge profit. Consequently, there is not a single unregulated monopoly in the United States. Firms that become monopolies are usually broken up using antitrust laws or regulated if they are natural monopolies.

Most monopolies that exist today are considered to be natural monopolies. A natural monopoly is **a market where multiple firms producing a product would be less efficient than production by one firm only**. This is the case in the production of infrastructure goods such as water, sewer, and electricity. The massive investment associated with providing water, sewer, and electric lines safely to each and every house means that only one firm serving all houses could possibly be efficient. A natural monopoly will have lower costs in such industries than smaller firms. However, natural monopolies must be regulated so they do not gouge consumers. Just imagine how much you would pay for electricity if only one firm in your town sold it and if that firm's prices were unregulated!

The major characteristics of a monopolistic industry include the following:

1. **One seller**: There can be no competition for a firm to be considered a monopoly.
2. **Unique product**: There are no close substitutes for a monopoly good. The product produced by a monopolist is unique.
3. **Prohibitive barriers to entry**: There is little or no chance of another firm supplying the same product as a monopolist due to economies of scale, legal prohibitions, or other barriers to entry.
4. **Complete control over prices**: With no substitutes and no threat of new firms entering the market, a monopolist can set prices wherever they wish to make the most amount of profit possible. With no substitutes, they tend to face an extremely inelastic demand curve that allows them to raise prices without losing much in the way of sales.

Monopolies result from prohibitive barriers to entry. Public utilities (water, sewer, and electricity) are natural monopolies due to economies of scale. Drug companies get a monopoly on drugs they invent for 20 years due to patent laws designed to encourage innovation. Many states such as Pennsylvania give a single state liquor store a monopoly over liquor sales in each town or neighborhood and use the monopoly profits to fund state operations.

The key to long-term success for a monopolist is to maintain their monopoly. They can use their financial and legal resources to stymie potential competitors. This can involve buying up patents or threatening new firms with lawsuits. Because U.S. laws prohibit monopolies, monopoly firms must also lobby politicians to look the other way. Or if the firm is a regulated natural monopoly, it can lobby politicians for more favorable treatment. The Microsoft near-monopoly over personal computer operating systems in the 1990s shows us some of the dangers of monopolies and why they need to be regulated.

Case study: The Microsoft Windows monopoly

In the 1990s Microsoft developed a near-monopoly on operating systems on personal computers. At that time, more than 95% of personal computers in the world were using the Microsoft Windows operating system. (This was before Apple's resurgence as a personal computer manufacturer.) The problem was that Microsoft was using its market dominance with Windows to dominate all other software markets related to personal computers.

Here are some of the tactics Microsoft used to drive out competing products:

- In the late 1980s, Microsoft demanded that computer producers pay a fee for the Windows operating system for every computer they sold, even if that computer used a different operating system. Computer manufacturers could not afford to be shut out of the market for Windows, which was the biggest player, so they complied. Because computer manufacturing firms had to pay for Windows whether or not they installed it, they had a stronger incentive to install the Windows operating system instead of alternatives. The number of competing operating systems was reduced dramatically as a result. The Department of Justice filed an antitrust lawsuit against Microsoft and ended this practice in 1994, but the damage to the competition was already done.

- Microsoft targeted IBM, a major competitor, by charging them higher prices to install Windows on IBM computers, costing IBM almost $200 million in lost revenue, and pressuring IBM to stop selling their competing operating system. IBM sued Microsoft and received a settlement of $775 million, but IBM's operating system never recovered from this attack.

- Microsoft pressured Intel to drop development of a technology that would have allowed competing software to be installed on Windows machines. Microsoft threatened to make Windows incompatible with Intel chips if Intel continued. Intel buckled under the pressure.

- In the mid-1990s, Microsoft targeted the leading word processing software, WordPerfect, altering Windows so that WordPerfect would not work well on Windows machines and making it difficult for Windows customers to purchase WordPerfect. Within a few years Microsoft Word had become a monopoly in the word processing market. They used similar tactics to capture the spreadsheet market from Lotus 1-2-3.

- Similarly, Microsoft targeted the leading web browser of the 1990s, Netscape. Microsoft made its Internet Explorer software available for free as part of the Windows operating system so there was no need to purchase competing products. Microsoft also designed Windows so that competing browsers would not work well on Windows machines. Microsoft demanded that Apple install Internet Explorer on all Apple computers, and they threatened to stop making Office products (Microsoft Word, Excel, PowerPoint) for Apple computers if Apple didn't comply. Like other companies, Apple buckled under the pressure.

After watching Microsoft systematically use its market and financial power to drive out competition in operating systems, word processing, internet browsers, and media players, regulators in the United States and Europe finally intervened. The United States sued Microsoft for violating antitrust laws. The court found that Microsoft was a monopolist and that Microsoft had frequently abused its monopoly power and violated U.S. antitrust laws. In a settlement, Microsoft agreed to make changes to foster competition in software markets. Specifically, Microsoft would no longer be able to demand that computer manufacturers install specific software on new computers, and Microsoft was required to license their technology to rivals, so the rivals could build competing products that would run on Windows.

The European Union (E.U.) also successfully sued Microsoft. The E.U. forced Microsoft to divulge programming codes to competitors and to make a version of Windows without the Microsoft media player. In 2009 the E.U. required Microsoft to offer competing internet browsers, allowing users to select one of 12 popular browsers listed in random order. The E.U. also fined Microsoft more than $2 billion for their anti-competitive behavior.

Microsoft is still a huge player in software, dominating several markets with its Office suite and other business applications. However, the rulings in the United States and the E.U. opened space for media players such as iTunes, browsers such as Firefox and Chrome, and search engines such as Google. Without these rulings, the software market would be much less dynamic and we would not have the degree of competition we do today. However, now that Google has a near-monopoly of search engines, it may be time for regulators to target them next.

The Microsoft case shows us why we do not allow unregulated monopolies in the United States. Firms with monopoly power abuse their market dominance to reduce competition. Monopolists can also produce a shoddy product while still charging a high price. Microsoft was infamous for releasing buggy versions of Windows with numerous problems that they would fix later as issues arose. In almost any other market, a firm that regularly produced a product with major problems would lose business to competitors. However, without any significant competition, Microsoft was able to continue to release versions of Windows with major flaws and still make vast amounts of money. Fortunately, if some measure of competition is preserved by regulators, there is some check on a monopolist's behavior. The rise of Apple personal computers as an alternative to Windows machines was facilitated by the antitrust rulings that forced Microsoft to stop its anti-competitive behavior.

When monopolies do arise, one possibility is to regulate them, which is what we do in the case of public utilities like water, sewer, and electricity provision. In other cases where the monopoly is not a natural one, the best approach is to use antitrust laws to foster competition in the market to prevent abuses such as the ones we saw in the Microsoft case.

We have now covered all four of the major market structures—perfect competition, monopolistic competition, oligopoly, and monopoly. To solidify your understanding, the next section offers eight criteria that you can use to identify the similarities and differences between these market structures.

12.6 COMPARING MARKET STRUCTURES

Figure 12.1 puts all of the characteristics of market structures together into one table for comparison purposes. Many of the characteristics have to do with how competitive a market is. This is driven by how easy it is to enter a market, and that determines how much control firms have over prices, how many sellers there are in the market, whether or not firms can earn an above-normal profit in the long run, and how big a markup firms can charge over their average costs. The size of firms is determined by economies of scale—whether or not large firms have a cost advantage over small firms. Product differentiation and the strategic focus of an industry relate to the type of product being sold. Differentiated products that can be branded result in markets featuring substantial advertising. Markets for homogeneous products (wheat, steel) see firms focused on getting costs as low as possible. And the largest, most dominant firms in imperfectly competitive markets (oligopolies and monopolies) can use their financial clout to preserve their market dominance via buying out competitors or lobbying efforts. The eight key characteristics of markets are described below.

1. **Entry and exit**: First, barriers to entry are a primary determinant of how competitive an industry is. The market structure with the easiest entry and exit is perfect competition, in which firms can be very small and there is no brand name identity because everyone produces an identical product. Monopolistic competition has very few barriers to entry. It is relatively easy to open a local restaurant or salon, making such markets extremely competitive. However, there is some product differentiation in monopolistic competition, so some businesses can charge more than others. Oligopolies have significant barriers to entry, requiring huge investments in order to be competitive. And with monopolies, the barriers to entry are so high that no competition is present.

2. **Control over prices**: The control a firm has over its prices is a direct result of how many substitutes there are and how closely they resemble the firm's product. If goods are perfect substitutes for each other, as they are in perfect competition, we see a perfectly elastic (flat) demand curve. If goods are close

	Most competitive ◀────────────────────────▶ Least competitive			
Market characteristics	Perfect competition	Monopolistic competition	Oligopoly	Monopoly
1. Barriers to entry	None	Some	Significant	Complete
2. Control over prices	None Perfectly elastic demand curve	Some Relatively elastic demand curve	Significant Relatively inelastic demand curve	Complete Very inelastic demand curve
3. Number of sellers	Very many	Many	Few	One
4. Typical size of firms	Small	Small to medium	Large	Extra large (one huge firm)
5. Product differentiation	None	Some	None or some	Complete (no substitutes)
6. Long-run economic profit?	No	No	Yes (dominant firms)	Yes (unless regulated)
7. Price relative to lowest possible average total cost (ATC) in long run	Price equals minimum average total cost: $P = ATC_{min}$	$P > ATC_{min}$, but markups are small	$P > ATC_{min}$, and markups can be huge for dominant firms	$P > ATC_{min}$, and markups are extremely high unless regulated
8. Long-term strategic focus	Minimizing costs	Minimizing costs, branding, quality, location	Innovation, mergers, acquisitions, branding, quality, colluding, lobbying	Preserving monopoly, lobbying
Industries that fit each classification	Agricultural goods (corn, wheat, soybeans), wood containers, unskilled services (babysitting, lawn care), concrete, signs	Local services (doctors, lawyers, dentists), local retailers (bars, restaurants, gas stations, salons), craft goods (handmade jewelry, pottery)	Manufactured goods (cars, cell phones, breweries, chips, soft drinks), national retailers and services (warehouse clubs, department stores, cell phone service), tech firms (Amazon, Facebook)	Utilities (water, sewer, electric, gas, cable TV), Google (almost), campus bookstore (some items only)

FIGURE 12.1 Table showing the characteristics of different market structures.

but not perfect substitutes, we tend to see relatively elastic demand curves such as in monopolistic competition. With only a few main substitutes, demand curves in oligopolies are much more inelastic. And with complete control over the entire market and no close substitutes, monopolies tend to see the most inelastic demand curves.

3. **Number of sellers**: The number of sellers in a market is a direct result of how easy entry or exit is in a market. The easier it is to enter a market, the more sellers there will be. The more difficult the barriers to entry, the fewer the number of sellers a market will contain.

4. **Typical size of firms**: The size of firms is primarily related to economies of scale. If small firms can be efficient, such as when there are no significant economies of scale, we tend to find markets with lots of small firms such as in perfect competition and monopolistic competition. If firms must be huge to compete due to the existence of, for example, significant economies of scale, we find markets with very few firms—either oligopolies or monopolies.

5. **Product differentiation**: Undifferentiated products include agricultural goods such as corn, wheat, and soybeans that are sold in perfectly competitive markets and manufactured inputs such as steel and aluminum that are sold in oligopolistic markets. Firms in most consumer goods and services markets thrive on product differentiation, because this is what allows them to be more successful than their competitors. Thus, in markets with product differentiation, including monopolistically competitive local restaurant markets and oligopolistic cell phone and car markets, we see vast expenditures on advertising and other types of non-price competition to establish brand name loyalty. A monopoly product is usually unrelated to other products.

6. **Long-run economic profit**: In general, in competitive markets—perfect competition and monopolistic competition—easy entry and exit means that firms will earn a normal profit in the long run. If firms are earning an economic (above-normal) profit in the short run, in the long run new firms will enter the market, driving down prices and causing profits to fall back to a normal level. Firms in competitive markets cannot earn economic profits in the long run because the market is so easy to enter. In markets with barriers to entry, firms can earn economic profits even in the long run because new firms cannot easily enter the market. Apple made above-normal profits on its iPhones from 2007 to 2019 due to their market dominance.

7. **Price relative to lowest possible average total cost (ATC) in long run**: One of the measures of how efficient a market is has to do with whether or not prices in the market are competed down to the lowest possible level for consumers. In perfectly competitive markets, with so many firms and no product differentiation, prices end up as low as possible. Firms must produce at their lowest possible per unit cost and sell the product for the smallest possible markup—a normal profit. As we will see later, this means that firms produce at their minimum average total cost (ATC_{min}) to stay in business. But as markets become less competitive, inefficiencies get introduced. Firms in monopolistically competitive markets spend money on advertising and raise prices slightly above the minimum average total cost. Oligopolies and monopolies raise prices much more due to barriers to entry.

8. **Long-term strategic focus**: If you operate in a perfectly competitive market, you can only survive by keeping costs as low as possible. And there is no benefit to advertising and marketing because you produce a homogeneous product. In monopolistic competition, you must also keep costs low to stay competitive. But you can also spend money to create brand identity via advertising to increase the demand for your product relative to competitors. It is in oligopolies where we see the widest range of long-term strategic activities. Oligopolies can stay ahead of competitors by investing in research and development to spawn innovations or by purchasing patents or innovative firms. They can work to control more of the market via mergers and acquisitions or by (illegally) colluding with their competitors. They can develop brand

identity via sophisticated and expensive advertising campaigns. Both oligopolies and monopolies are known for using their substantial financial resources to lobby politicians for subsidies, lower taxes, protection from foreign competition, and reduced regulations.

12.7 A LOOK AT DATA ON INDUSTRY MARKET SHARES

Figure 12.2 shows the concentration ratios for various manufacturing industries. A concentration ratio measures the sales of the largest firms relative to the sales of the entire industry. The table shows the share of the market dominated by the four

Manufacturing industry	Four largest firms (%)	Eight largest firms (%)	Total number of firms	Herfindahl Index
Highly concentrated industries				
Household refrigerators, freezers	92.9	98.9	15	
Breweries	87.8	90.8	837	3561
Cigarettes (Tobacco)	87.8	93.6	91	2897
Aircraft	80.1	93.9	230	3287
Moderately concentrated industries				
Breakfast cereal	79.2	93.7	37	2333
Women's handbags and purses	75.4	82.0	111	1863
Soft drinks	68.3	74.9	254	1932
Dog and cat food	67.8	80.6	233	2019
Sufficiently competitive industries				
Automobiles	60.2	88.7	167	1178
Cookies and crackers	59.8	77.7	301	1357
Coffee and tea	57.5	70.1	417	1283
Computers (electronic)	50.9	71.6	362	846
Milk (fluid)	46.3	59.8	248	1205
Ice cream and frozen desserts	45.9	64.6	343	666
Wineries	45.3	58.0	2527	785
Footwear	45.1	65.3	198	692
Office supplies (except paper)	42.4	54.6	490	747
Bakeries (commercial)	41.2	51.1	2342	637
Guns (small arms)	33.6	53.0	316	445
Sporting and athletic goods	32.3	46.7	1571	373
Audio and video equipment	30.2	44.3	460	377
Cheese	29.9	46.9	390	374
Men's and Boys' apparel	24.9	37.0	444	254
Women's, girls', infants' apparel	21.9	30.3	1840	236
Highly competitive industries				
Wood containers and pallets	11.5	16.3	2394	55
Signs	8.5	13.3	5357	36
Bakeries (retail)	4.7	7.3	6339	12

FIGURE 12.2 Table of concentration ratios for various manufacturing industries, 2012.

largest firms and the eight largest firms. It also shows the total number of firms in the industry.

Most manufacturing firms are oligopolies due to the size necessary to compete effectively in these markets. Some manufacturing industries are highly or moderately concentrated, such as refrigerators, breweries, cigarettes, and aircraft, with a few huge firms dominating the industry. In the soft drinks industry, Coca-Cola controls 43% of the market, Pepsi controls 27%, Dr. Pepper/Snapple controls 17%, and Cott/RC has a 4% market share. In industries like these in which a few firms dominate, we tend to see a lot of collusion, along with huge expenditures on advertising and marketing (non-price competition). Heavily concentrated industries often work very poorly for consumers, with high prices and little innovation.

Sufficiently competitive industries are less of a worry to regulators because the degree of competition keeps firms innovating and working to keep prices low. Even though the automobile market is oligopolistic—firms must be huge to compete—no one firm has a dominant market share.

In 2014, market share in the automobile market was widely distributed between more than ten big players, with the largest being Toyota (11.7%), Volkswagen (11%), General Motors (10.7%), Hyundai (8.9%), Ford (6.7%), Nissan (5.7%), Fiat Chrysler (5.4%), and Honda (5%). With no dominant firm and many viable competitors, the automobile market is quite competitive even though it is an oligopoly.

As we move down the list of manufacturing companies, we find industries that are closer to monopolistic competition, with no dominant players: The concentration ratios are much lower, showing that the largest firms control very small shares of the market. There are so many companies that make men's and women's apparel and there is no dominant player, so it is usually classified as a monopolistically competitive industry. Markets like local retail bakeries verge on perfect competition due to the number of competitors and the small degree of product differentiation.

For industries with 50 firms or more, Figure 12.2 reports the Herfindahl Index. The Herfindahl Index (H) **measures the size of the largest firms relative to the industry as a whole in order to provide an indicator for the degree of competition in the industry. H is found by squaring the market shares of the largest companies in the industry (s) and then adding them together**.

$$H = \sum_{i=1}^{n} s_i^2.$$

For example, consider the desktop search engine market. As you can see in Figure 12.3, in January 2021 Google had 87.7% of the search engine market, Bing had 6.3%, Yahoo! had 3%, DuckDuckGo had 2.6%, and all other companies had a combined 0.4% of the market. If we take the percentage market share for each of

Company	Market share (%)	Herfindahl score
Google	87.7	$(87.7)^2$=7683.3
Bing	6.3	$(6.3)^2$=40.2
Yahoo!	3.0	$(3)^2$=9
DuckDuckGo	2.6	$(2.6)^2$=6.8
Other	0.4	---
Herfindahl Index for top 4 firms		7740.2

FIGURE 12.3 Table showing desktop search engine market share, 2020.

the top four companies and square it, we get a Herfindahl Index of 7740.2, making search engines one of the most concentrated industries. A complete monopoly with one firm having 100% market share would have a Herfindahl Index of 100^2 or 10,000. When Microsoft controlled 95% of the market for personal computer operating systems, they generated a Herfindahl Index of $95^2 = 9025$.

The Herfindahl Index is used by the Department of Justice and the Federal Trade Commission to determine whether a market is too heavily concentrated and, if so, what should be done about it. For example, in highly concentrated industries, mergers may be prohibited. In extreme cases where industries verge on monopolies, these government agencies may recommend splitting up the company or other actions to foster competition.

The most concentrated industries in Figure 12.2, those with the highest Herfindahl Index, are often those requiring a massive capital investment and a huge size of operations, such as airlines. However, sometimes the least competitive industries are controlled by very few firms for other reasons. There is no reason for the brewery market to lack competition. At one time there were dozens of large and small companies making beer. In recent years, however, Anheuser-Busch InBev has gradually bought up more and more beer companies, so that in 2016 it controlled 45% of the market.

Figure 12.4 displays concentration ratios for service industries. Once again we see a wide variation. Services that require national distribution centers, networks, or significant infrastructure tend to be highly concentrated and oligopolistic.

Examples of oligopolistic service industries include wireless telecommunications (cell phone service), cable TV, passenger car rental, credit card issuing, air travel, warehouse clubs, home centers (Home Depot and Lowe's), department stores, mail-order stores (Amazon), and supermarkets. On the opposite end, most local services operate in monopolistically competitive industries, including restaurants, bars, physicians, dentists, legal services, childcare, automotive repair, independent artists and performers (local musicians), insurance agents, and gas stations. Florists operate in a market very close to perfect competition in that the product is fairly homogeneous (cut flowers) and extremely easy to enter.

When studying a particular industry, you can identify which market structure best characterizes the industry by identifying a few key features. The questions to ask when attempting to classify a particular industry are the following:

	Four largest firms (%)	Eight largest firms (%)	Total number of establishments
Accommodation and food services			
Cafes (snacks, nonalcoholic beverages)	35.9	39.5	54,842
Hotels and motels	19.7	26.4	54,289
Restaurants (full-service)	7.9	10.5	231,927
Bed and breakfast inns	3.9	5.7	3004
Bars (alcoholic beverages)	2.5	3.6	41,774
Health care			
Health & medical insurance carriers	34.4	49.2	4609
Hospitals (general and surgical)	8.8	13.0	5001
Physicians' offices	5.4	7.2	220,890
Dentists' offices	2.0	3.2	133,221
Local services			
Lessors of apartment buildings	9.5	15.0	50,466
Child day care services	8.4	9.8	75,331
Legal services	2.6	4.5	186,831
Automotive repair and maintenance	2.4	3.6	157,152
Information and entertainment			
Wireless telecommunications carriers	89.1	95.2	13,458
Cable and subscription programming	58.9	83.2	772
Television broadcasting	52.0	63.0	2090
Cable TV (wired carriers)	51.3	72.9	32,688
Motion picture and video production	46.4	62.2	13,616
Book publishers	40.6	56.3	2663
Independent artists, writers, performers	2.0	3.5	22,378
Finance, insurance & national services			
Passenger car rental	90.1	92.3	9948
Credit card issuing	77.6	90.8	1095
Air travel	65.3	82.4	2231
Investment banking, securities dealing	46.7	67.8	3142
National commercial banks	45.6	62.9	53,558
Insurance agencies and brokerages	11.2	16.1	132,882
Retail trade			
Warehouse clubs and supercenters	93.6	99.9	5114
Home centers (2007)	92.7	93.0	6953
Department stores	82.7	95.8	3339
Mail-order houses (like Amazon)	40.1	19.3	6140
Supermarkets & grocery stores	31.1	44.4	66,343
Women's clothing stores	25.8	39.4	36,344
Gas stations with convenience stores	13.2	20.5	97,394
Florists	1.6	2.5	14,606

FIGURE 12.4 Table showing concentration ratios for various service industries, 2012.

1. **Are there barriers to entry (is it very difficult to start a business in this industry)?**

   If the answer is yes, then the market must be either oligopolistic or monopolistic with a few firms or one firm.

   If the answer is no, then the market must be perfectly competitive or monopolistically competitive with many firms.

2. **Is there product differentiation (do the products vary or are they identical)?**

    If the answer is yes, then the market must be either monopolistically competitive or oligopolistic.

    If the answer is no, then the market must by perfectly competitive or oligopolistic.

Using these questions, you should be able to classify any industry that you come across. That classification should then allow you to anticipate typical behaviors that one might see in such an industry.

12.8 CONCLUSION

This chapter describes the four market structures that we tend to find in industries in capitalist economies. Perfectly competitive firms sell homogeneous products in markets that are so competitive that firms have no control over prices, settling for selling all that they produce at the market price. Monopolistically competitive firms sell slightly differentiated products in competitive markets, so they have some control over prices and they can gain more control of pricing via advertising and branding. However, the high degree of competition limits how much firms can charge. Oligopolistic markets are dominated by a few large firms. In oligopolies with only two or three dominant firms, we often find collusive behavior. When oligopolies are more competitive, we tend to see a lot of innovation and efforts at cultivating product differentiation and branding. Monopolies are controlled entirely by one firm, which is deeply problematic and requires government regulation or the use of antitrust laws to make the market operate more effectively.

When economists attempt to classify industries, they look at eight key market characteristics:

1. Whether or not barriers to entry inhibit the entry of competitors
2. How much firms in the industry control prices
3. How many sellers exist in the market
4. The typical size of firms in the market
5. The degree to which products are differentiated from each other
6. Whether or not firms can earn an economic profit in the long run
7. How much firms can mark up their prices relative to average total cost
8. The long-term, strategic focus of firms.

By observing these characteristics, it is possible to identify which market structure best describes a particular industry, which then makes it possible to predict how that industry will respond in a variety of circumstances.

Now that we have described the four market structures in general terms, it is time to delve into each market structure in more detail. However, in order to do that, it is important to have a deeper grasp of the forces that drive the costs of production of firms because these are major drivers of how firms behave.

The next chapter describes models of the short-run and long-run costs of production that firms face. Subsequent chapters use those models to analyze how firms in each of the four market structures maximize profits.

QUESTIONS FOR REVIEW

1. Suppose that you are a corn farmer and the market price of corn is $5 per bushel. Explain why you should also charge $5 per bushel of corn rather than a higher or lower price.

2. If firms in an industry with easy entry and exit are earning an economic profit, what can we expect to happen in the long run to the number of firms in the industry? If firms in an industry with barriers to entry are earning an economic profit, what can we expect to happen in the long run to the number of firms in the industry? Explain and give examples.

3. Explain why a firm earning a 5% profit might end up going out of business using the concept of a normal profit.

4. Why are local hair salons considered to be a monopolistically competitive industry? If hair salons in your town were doing extremely well and earning an economic profit, what would you expect to happen to the industry in the long run?

5. Why do we tend to see the most collusion in oligopolistic industries with fewer than four main competitors?

6. How do economies of scale influence the amount of competition in an industry? Explain.

7. Would Microsoft Windows be considered a natural monopoly? Why or why not?

8. Why does the government regulate monopolies even if they are natural monopolies?

9. Which of the eight characteristics of markets laid out in Figure 12.1 is most important in determining market structure? Explain and support your answer.

10. Identify which market structure best characterizes each of the markets below. Explain your answer.
    a. Internet search engines
    b. Local banking
    c. Driveway snow shoveling
    d. Online bookstores.

11. Identify which market structure best characterizes each of the markets below. Explain your answer.
    a. T-shirts
    b. Athletic shoes (for field hockey, basketball, tennis, soccer, running, etc.)
    c. Dog walking
    d. Cable television.
12. Use the data provided in this chapter to compute a Herfindahl Index for the four largest soft drinks companies and the four largest car companies. What does this information tell us about these two industries? Explain briefly.

NOTES

1 Chipotle suffered a setback in 2015 when diners suffered from outbreaks of *Escherichia coli* and norovirus. Its sales plummeted, and it took until 2017 for Chipotle to fully recover.

2 Source: Author's personal conversations with Dr. David McFarland, Professor of Economics, University of North Carolina Chapel Hill, 1987. Dr. McFarland participated in an antitrust investigation into Coke's and Pepsi's practices.

13 Short-run and long-run costs of production

This chapter develops the mainstream economics theory of the firm involving models of firms' short-run and long-run costs and their optimizing behavior. In order to understand the dynamics of market structures, we need to know the structure of firms' short-run and long-run costs of production. As you will see below, the laws of specialization and diminishing returns, highlighted earlier, give firms U-shaped average total cost curves and upward-sloping marginal cost (supply) curves in the short run.

Once we understand what short-run costs look like for a typical firm in a competitive market, we will know what their supply curve looks like and we can predict how much the firm will produce in order to maximize profits. This will also allow us to determine whether the firm is making economic profits, normal profits, or economic losses.

Long-run costs in different market structures show us the extent of economies of scale and diseconomies of scale, and that is displayed in the long-run average total cost curve. This helps us determine the number and size of competitors in a particular industry, affecting whether or not we will see small firms, large firms, or a mix of small and large firms. We can analyze the dynamics of particular industries in the long run based on the shape of a typical firm's long-run average total cost curve, including whether or not firms will enter or exit the market.

Note that this chapter develops the mainstream microeconomic *model* of short-run and long-run costs for typical firms. As with all models, it is only as good as its predictive power, which is determined largely by the realism of its assumptions.

The chapter concludes with a section on how political economists analyze firm costs and decisions regarding how to set prices and determine what quantity to produce. According to political economists, the firm's primary goals are survival, growth, and profit maximization. Firms attempt to achieve those goals by producing quantities and setting prices based on markup pricing and the firm's strategic focus on obtaining market share or securing profits from monopoly power.

DOI: 10.4324/9781315636924-17

13.0 CHAPTER 13 LEARNING GOALS

After reading this chapter you should be able to:

■ Explain the shape of the marginal cost curve and how it relates to the marginal product of labor and the laws of specialization and diminishing returns.

■ Describe the relationship between the marginal cost curve and the average variable cost curve.

■ Derive the shape of the average total cost curve from the marginal cost, average variable cost, and average fixed cost curves.

■ Given information for a firm on total fixed cost and total variable cost at various quantities, compute marginal cost, average variable cost, average fixed cost, and average total cost. Given price information for the same firm, determine the profit-maximizing level of output.

■ Apply the concepts of economies of scale and diseconomies of scale to particular industries using the long-run average total cost curve.

■ Compare and contrast the mainstream economics theory of the firm with the political economy theory of the firm.

13.1 THE MAINSTREAM MODEL OF SHORT-RUN COSTS OF PRODUCTION

The mainstream model of short-run costs of production is derived from the short-run production function that was first described in Chapter 11 and is displayed in Figure 13.1. The short-run production function, also known as the total product of labor curve (TP_L), shows the amount of output produced by different quantities of a variable input (such as labor), holding fixed inputs such as capital constant. In other words, the TP_L curve shows how much output laborers can produce given a fixed scale of operations.

The short-run production function (TP_L) reflects two key economic laws, the law of specialization and the law of diminishing returns. At first, as more laborers are hired, the firm sees an increase in productivity due to the efficiency gains from specialization. Workers get more and more productive as specialization increases skill levels and efficiency. This occurs on the TP_L curve when the slope is increasing from 0 up to point A. The marginal product of labor (MP_L) is the increase in quantity that results from hiring another laborer. The marginal product of labor

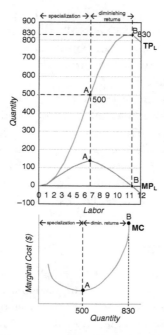

FIGURE 13.1 Marginal product and marginal cost.

increases from 0 to point A on the MP_L curve as laborers get more productive due to specialization. $MP_L = (\Delta Q/\Delta L)$, which is also the slope of the TP_L curve. (See Chapter 11 for more details.)

13.1.1 Marginal cost

Below the graph of the total product of labor and marginal product of labor curves in Figure 13.1 is a graph of the marginal cost curve. Marginal cost is the additional cost of producing another unit of output (quantity): $MC = (\Delta TVC/\Delta Q)$. Notice that as workers' marginal productivity increases, up to $Q = 500$ at point A, marginal cost decreases. Thus, the increase in the marginal productivity of labor results in a decrease in the marginal cost of production due to specialization.

Once we reach point A and a quantity of 500, the law of diminishing returns sets in. Recall that according to the law of diminishing returns, as we increase the amount of a variable input, holding fixed inputs constant, eventually, after all of the specialized jobs are filled, firms will experience diminishing marginal productivity (diminishing returns). This can be seen in the total product of labor curve when its slope starts to decrease—production is increasing at a decreasing rate—between point A and point B. We see diminishing returns in the marginal product of labor curve when MP_L starts to decrease after point A. And we see diminishing returns in the marginal cost curve when marginal cost increases after point A.

The firm reaches its short run maximum level of production given this size of operations at point B, where $Q = 830$ and $MP_L = 0$. Given its fixed inputs, it cannot produce any more output unless it can expand the size of its operations, which is only possible in the long run. If the firm hires additional laborers beyond this point, output would actually decline.

They key insight from Figure 13.1 is related to the shape of the marginal cost (MC) curve and how it determines the shape of all other firm cost curves. *The rounded check mark shape of the MC curve is due to the law of specialization, which causes the marginal cost of each additional unit to fall up to point A, and the law of diminishing returns, which causes the marginal cost of each additional unit to increase after point A.*

Now that we have an understanding of the reasons for the shape of the marginal cost curve, we need to analyze the shape of other key cost curves a typical firm uses: Average variable cost, average fixed cost, and average total cost.

13.1.2 Average variable cost

Total variable cost is the total cost of hiring all of the variable inputs, such as labor. Average variable cost (AVC) is **the variable cost per unit of output**: AVC=(TVC/Q). The shape of the AVC curve is driven directly by the shape of the marginal cost curve. The formula for marginal cost is MC=(ΔTVC/ΔQ). So MC is the *change* in total variable cost divided by the *change* in quantity—the variable cost of producing each *additional* unit—whereas AVC is the *average variable cost of all units being produced.*

We can see the relationship between MC and AVC at various quantities (Q) in a new example displayed in Figure 13.2. Both MC and AVC are undefined at a quantity of zero. At a quantity of one, $MC_{Q=1} = AVC_{Q=1} = \$9$. The additional cost of the first unit is equal to the average variable cost of all units when $Q = 1$. The second unit, $Q = 2$, only costs \$8 to produce ($MC_{Q=2} = \$8$), which lowers $AVC_{Q=2}$ to \$8.50. The third unit also costs less than the average ($MC_{Q=3} = \$7$), which pulls the average down further to $AVC_{Q=3} = \$8$. MC falls at first due to the law of specialization, as discussed earlier. And as long as MC is below AVC, AVC falls as quantity increases. When each unit costs less to produce than the average, the average cost per unit falls. At a quantity of four, MC = AVC = \$8. This is the lowest number in the AVC column. However, after this point, MC starts to increase due to the law of diminishing returns.

At a quantity of five MC is \$10, which causes AVC to increase to \$8.4. MC continues to increase faster and faster for quantities six through eight, and this continues to cause AVC to increase. As long as MC > AVC, AVC rises as more units are produced (as quantity increases). When each additional unit costs more than the average variable cost, AVC rises.

This gives us four key elements of the AVC curve:

1. AVC = MC when $Q = 1$.
2. When MC < AVC, AVC falls as quantity increases (when each additional unit costs less than the average).

3. MC = AVC when AVC is at its minimum level.
4. When MC > AVC, AVC increases as quantity increases (when each additional unit costs more than the average).

The same relationship is plotted out in the graph in Figure 13.3. MC is equal to AVC at point A when $Q = 1$. From point A to point B, MC < AVC, each additional unit costs less than the average, and that causes AVC to fall until we reach point B. At point B, the minimum point on the AVC curve, MC = AVC once again. After point B, MC > AVC, each unit costs more than the average, so AVC rises as quantity increases.

The relationship between marginal cost and average variable cost is so important that it is worth considering one additional example to drive the point home. We can use the analogy of a student's grade point average (GPA) to understand the relationship between marginal cost and average variable cost. Suppose that the *marginal* grade points are the number of grade points you get from each additional course grade you receive. The grade point *average* is the average of all of the individual (marginal) grade points. Suppose that you take one course and earn a B in that course, giving you three marginal grade points for that course.[1] Because you have only taken one course, your grade point average is (3/1)=3. After one course, your marginal grade points are equal to your grade point average. Now suppose you take a second course and get a C, which comes with two grade points. Your marginal grade points for that additional course are two. But your grade point average is now (3+2)/2=2.5. Your GPA has fallen because your marginal GPA was lower than your average. Now suppose you take a third course and get an A in

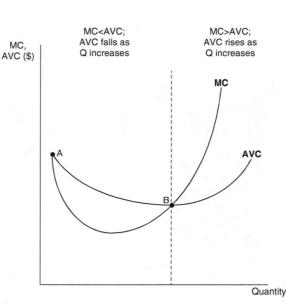

Q	MC	AVC
0	---	---
1	9	9
2	8	8.5
3	7	8
4	8	8
5	10	8.4
6	12	9
7	16	10
8	26	12

FIGURE 13.2 Table of MC
and AVC (in $).   FIGURE 13.3 Graph of MC and AVC.

that one, which comes with four grade points. Your marginal grade points on this course are four. This causes your grade point average to increase to ((3+2+4)/3)=3. When your marginal grade points are above your GPA, your GPA increases. This example illustrates the same points made above: When you only have one unit (one grade), the marginal GPA for that one course is equal to the average GPA for all of your courses. When you get an additional (marginal) grade that is lower than your average GPA, it pulls your average down. When you get an additional (marginal) grade that is higher than your average GPA, it pulls your average up.

13.1.3 Average fixed cost

Total fixed cost (TFC) is **the total cost of hiring all fixed inputs, such as capital**. In the short run, all firms must pay rent and make payments toward the cost of machinery each month. These costs are a fixed amount and cannot be increased or decreased in the short run.

Average fixed cost (AFC) is **the fixed cost per unit of output**: AFC=(TVC/ΔQ). Note that because total fixed cost is a constant amount, AFC falls as quantity increases, as you can see in the example in Figure 13.4. Total fixed cost is $48. When $Q = 1$, AFC=($48/1)=$48. When $Q = 2$, AFC=($48/1)=$24 And so on.

If we plot average fixed cost on a graph, we get a curve that looks like the one in Figure 13.5. The larger the quantity, the smaller AFC becomes. This is another important detail regarding firm costs: *The more the firm produces, the smaller its average fixed cost becomes because the firm is able to spread its fixed costs over more and more units.*

Q	TFC	AFC
0	48	---
1	48	48
2	48	24
3	48	16
4	48	12
5	48	9.60
6	48	8
7	48	6.86
8	48	6

FIGURE 13.4 Table showing AFC.

FIGURE 13.5 Graph showing that AFC always falls as Q increases.

13.1.4 Average total cost

Now it's time to put everything together to construct the average total cost curve (ATC). Total cost (TC) is **the total of all costs of production, including opportunity costs (normal profit)**: TC=TFC+TVC.

Similarly, average total cost (ATC) is **the average of all costs per unit of output**: ATC=(TC/Q)=AVC+AFC. Average total cost can be found by dividing total cost by quantity or by adding together its two components, average variable cost and average fixed cost.

Figure 13.6 begins with the MC and AVC cost curves originally depicted in Figure 13.3. The MC curve decreases at first due to the law of specialization and then increases due to the law of diminishing returns. The AVC curve starts out equal to the MC curve at a quantity of one and then it declines until it intersects the MC curve at point B, after which it increases.

To get the average total cost curve, we must add the average fixed cost curve from Figure 13.5 to the average variable cost curve: ATC = AFC + AVC. Notice in Figure 13.6 how the ATC curve starts out much higher than the AVC curve. For example, at quantity Q_1, AFC_{Q1} is quite large. But we know that as quantity increases AFC falls. At quantity Q_4 average fixed cost, AFC_{Q4}, is much smaller. The result is an average total cost curve that declines steeply at first as quantity increases

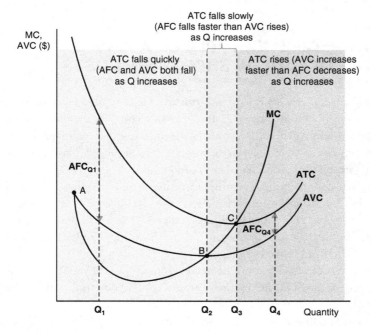

FIGURE 13.6 Marginal cost and average variable cost.

because both of its components, AVC and AFC, are declining. This happens up until quantity Q_2. After quantity Q_2, AVC starts to rise but AFC falls faster than AVC rises, so the ATC curve continues to fall, albeit more slowly, from Q_2 to Q_3. At point C, where the marginal cost curve intersects the average total cost curve, average total cost is at its minimum point.

It is important to note that marginal cost has a relationship with average total cost that is similar to its relationship with average variable cost. Marginal cost drives decreases and increases in both AVC and ATC. When MC < ATC, ATC falls as quantity increases. When each additional unit costs less than the average, the average falls. After the minimum ATC is reached at point C, MC > ATC. Each additional unit costs more than the average, which pulls the average up.

The reason that marginal cost has the same impact on both AVC and ATC is that the change in total variable cost is always equal to the change in total cost in the short run. Fixed costs do not change when quantity changes, so any change in costs from a change in quantity must be due to a change in variable costs: $\Delta TVC = \Delta TC$. This means that $MC = (\Delta TVC/\Delta Q) = (\Delta TC/\Delta Q)$.

This probably seems confusing to you at this point. In order to help you understand the relationships between all of the costs of production in the mainstream model, let's work through a detailed example using some specific numbers that display the relationships we have been discussing.

13.2 A SPECIFIC EXAMPLE OF A FIRM'S HYPOTHETICAL SHORT-RUN COSTS

Figure 13.7 contains weekly cost information for a typical lawn mowing firm. The columns in bold, quantity (Q), total variable cost (TVC), and total fixed cost (TFC), are key information that would be given to you in a typical problem involving short-run costs. All of the other information in Figure 13.7 could be computed using the formulas for all of the costs of production.

Marginal cost is found by computing the change in total variable cost and dividing by the change in quantity. From row 1 to row 2, the change in TVC is $(380 - 0) = 380$ and the change in quantity is $(10 - 0) = 10$, giving us a marginal cost of $(380/10) = \$38$. From row 2 to row 3, $MC = (\Delta TVC/\Delta Q) = ((700-380)/(20-10)) = (320/10) = 32)$. And so on.

Notice that the MC column decreases from a Q of 0 to a Q of 50 due to the law of specialization and MC increases after a Q of 50 due to the law of diminishing returns.

Average variable cost is found by dividing total variable cost by quantity: $AVC = (TVC/Q)$. The first entry is undefined due to dividing by 0. When $Q = 10$, $AVC = (380/10) = \$38$. When $Q = 20$, $AVC = (700/20) = 35$. Notice that AVC = MC at $Q = 10$ (the first unit that is produced). Then AVC falls as long as MC < AVC. At

Q	TVC	MC=$\frac{\Delta TVC}{\Delta Q}$	AVC=$\frac{TVC}{Q}$	TFC	AFC=$\frac{TFC}{Q}$	TC= TVC + TFC	ATC=$\frac{TC}{Q}$ = AVC + AFC
0	$ 0	$ ------	$ -------	$530	$ -------	$ 530	$ -------
10	380	38	38.00	530	53.00	910	91.00
20	700	32	35.00	530	26.50	1230	61.50
30	980	28	32.67	530	17.67	1510	50.33
40	1240	26	31.00	530	13.25	1770	44.25
50	1480	24	29.60	530	10.60	2010	40.20
60	1740	26	29.00	530	8.83	2270	37.83
70	2030	29	29.00	530	7.57	2560	36.57
80	2350	32	29.38	530	6.63	2880	36.00
90	2710	36	30.11	530	5.89	3240	36.00
100	3110	40	31.10	530	5.30	3640	36.40
110	3550	44	32.27	530	4.82	4080	37.09
120	4050	50	33.75	530	4.42	4580	38.17
130	4610	56	35.46	530	4.08	5140	39.54
140	5250	64	37.50	530	3.79	5780	41.29
150	5970	72	39.80	530	3.53	6500	43.33
160	6770	80	42.31	530	3.31	7300	45.63

FIGURE 13.7 Table of short-run costs for a typical lawn mowing firm (per week).

$Q = 70$, MC = AVC = 29, which is also the minimum AVC. After $Q = 70$, AVC increases because MC > AVC.

Total fixed cost is always the same: $530. This would be the weekly payment that the mowing company must make for its buildings and equipment. Average fixed cost is found by dividing TFC by Q. Notice that AFC falls as Q increases, as expected.

In Figure 13.7, total cost is found by adding total variable cost to total fixed cost. At a quantity of 0, the only costs the firm must pay are its fixed costs because it is not hiring any laborers. If the firm decides to close its doors and shut down its operations, it must still pay its total fixed cost. So this firm will lose $530 per week if it decides to shut down. This tells us something else important: The firm should stay open in the short run as long as it loses less than $530 per week and as long as it is hopeful that business will eventually improve.

Average total cost can be found in two ways: By dividing total cost by quantity or by adding together AVC and AFC. ATC falls from $Q = 10$ to $Q = 90$ when MC < ATC. ATC reaches its minimum value at $36 (at $Q = 90$) where MC = ATC. After that ATC rises as quantity increases when MC > ATC.[2]

We can also plot out all of the key information from the table in Figure 13.7 on a graph. Figure 13.8 displays a graph that contains all of the information from Figure 13.7. Most of the time in a problem you will be given either a table or a graph because they both convey the same information. The way you use the graph of MC, AVC, and ATC is as follows. For any particular quantity, you go straight up to each curve to find the amount of that particular cost at that particular quantity. For example, in Figure 13.8 if we go from a quantity of 70 up to point A and then

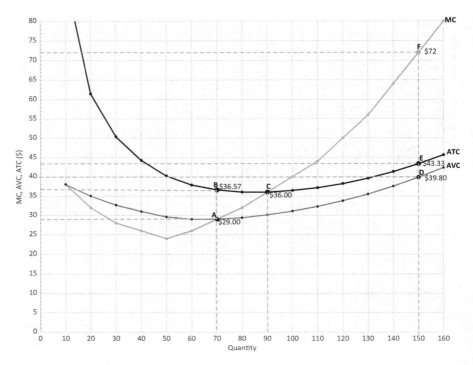

FIGURE 13.8 Marginal cost, average variable cost, and average total cost.

over to the cost axis, we see that MC = AVC = $29. Because AVC is the variable cost per unit, if we multiply AVC = 29 by Q = 70, we would get TVC = 2030. TVC at Q = 70 is equal to the area of the box that begins at the origin (0,0), goes over to Q = 70, goes up to point A, and goes over to 29.

If we continue up from a quantity of 70 to point B, we find that ATC = $36.57. And if we multiplied this by Q = 70, we would get TC of 70 × 36.57 = 2560. This is the area of the box that starts at the origin (0,0), goes over to Q = 70, goes up to point B, and then goes over to 36.57.

Even though the AFC curve is not included in the graph, we can always find AFC as the distance between AVC and ATC. Recall that ATC = AVC + AFC, so AFC = ATC − AVC. At a quantity of 70, AFC is the distance between point A and point B, which is 7.57. And if we multiply AFC by Q, we get TFC, which is the area of the box formed by point A and point B on one side and 29 and 36.57 on the other side.

The minimum ATC occurs at point C, at Q = 90 where MC = ATC = 36.

If the firm increased production to a quantity of 150, we would find the AVC at point D is 39.80, ATC at point E is 43.33, and MC at point F is 72. And we can find AFC at $Q = 150$, as the distance between point D and point E, which is 3.53. We could also find TVC, TFC, and TC by multiplying AVC, AFC, and ATC by Q. Thus, for any quantity in the graph, you can use the MC, AVC, and ATC curve to find *any* of the costs of production.

Figure 13.9 plots the total cost, total variable cost, and total fixed cost curves from the information in the table in Figure 13.7. The total cost curve has a slope that increases at a decreasing rate and then increases at an increasing rate because of the law of specialization and the law of diminishing returns. The slope of the TC and the TVC curve is the MC: $MC=(\Delta TC/\Delta Q)=(\Delta TVC/\Delta Q)$. This makes the two curves parallel to each other, and the distance between them is the firm's total fixed cost. We do not need to plot out the TFC curve because we can always find it by observing the distance between TC and TVC. Or, in mathematical terms, TC = TVC + TFC, so TFC = TC – TVC.

The graph with marginal cost and average total cost, Figure 13.8, is much more useful in determining the firm's profit-maximizing level of output and its level of profit or loss, as we will see in the next chapter, so in most cases we will use that graph rather than the graph of the TC, TVC, and TFC curves.

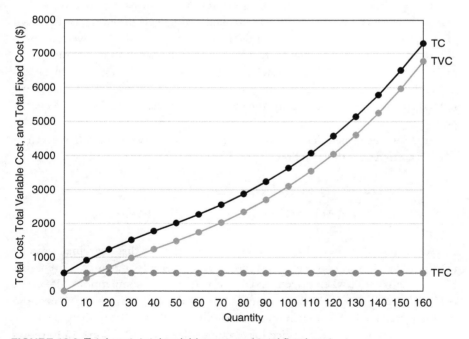

FIGURE 13.9 Total cost, total variable cost, and total fixed cost.

To complete the picture of profit maximization in the mainstream model of the firm, we need to add marginal revenue (MR) to our cost information. This is the topic of the next section.

13.3 THE MAINSTREAM MODEL OF PROFIT MAXIMIZATION

Profit maximization in the mainstream economics model of firm behavior is achieved when **firms produce every unit for which marginal revenue is greater than or equal to marginal cost**. Recall that total revenue is defined as TR=$P \times Q$. Marginal revenue (MR) is **the addition to total revenue from selling an additional unit of output**: MR=(ΔTR/ΔQ). Firms maximize profits by producing every unit for which MR≥MC.

The intuition behind this is relatively straight forward: A firm should sell any unit that makes it more in revenue than it costs the firm to supply. Recall that all costs of production include a normal profit (of about 11%) built into the costs of production. This means that a firm is still willing to sell a unit for which MR equals MC because the firm will make an 11% profit on that unit (an 11% "normal" profit is included in the costs of supplying the product).

For example, when we add marginal revenue information to the table in Figure 13.7, we can determine the profit-maximizing level of output for our lawn mowing firm. Lawn mowing is a perfectly competitive market; mowers are providing an identical service, and there is no significant product differentiation. This means that the price of lawn mowing is determined by the market supply and demand curves, and no one lawn mower can influence the price (P). As far as the individual lawn mowing company, the price they can charge is fixed at the market price.

In cases where the price the firm can charge is fixed, we find that P is equal to MR. We can derive this as follows:

$$\text{TR} = P \times Q; \text{MR} = \left(\Delta\text{TR} / \Delta Q \right) = \left(\Delta\left(PQ\right) / \Delta Q \right)$$
$$= P\left(\Delta Q / \Delta Q\right) + Q\left(\Delta P / \Delta Q\right) = P + Q\left(\Delta P / \Delta Q\right).$$

Those of you who have had calculus will recognized that marginal revenue (MR) is the derivative of total revenue with respect to quantity. Given that MR=$P+Q(\Delta P/\Delta Q)$, when price is fixed as it is in perfect competition, $\Delta P=0$ and MR=P. In other words, when the price is fixed as far as the firm is concerned, the marginal revenue they get from each unit they sell will be equal to the price.[3]

Suppose that the market price for mowing a lawn is $40. Figure 13.10 shows price (which is also equal to marginal revenue when P is constant) and total revenue information for our hypothetical lawn mowing firm, along with MC, ATC, and

Q	P=MR ($)	TR=P*Q ($)	MC ($)	AVC ($)	ATC ($)	TC ($)	Economic profit ($)=(TR−TC)
0	40	0	—	—	—	530	−530
10	40	400	38	38.00	91.00	910	−510
20	40	800	32	35.00	61.50	1230	−430
30	40	1200	28	32.67	50.33	1510	−310
40	40	1600	26	31.00	44.25	1770	−170
50	40	2000	24	29.60	40.20	2010	−10
60	40	2400	26	29.00	37.83	2270	130
70	40	2800	29	29.00	36.57	2560	240
80	40	3200	32	29.38	36.00	2880	320
90	40	3600	36	30.11	36.00	3240	360
100	40	4000	40	31.10	36.40	3640	360
110	40	4400	44	32.27	37.09	4080	320
120	40	4800	50	33.75	38.17	4580	220
130	40	5200	56	35.46	39.54	5140	60
140	40	5600	64	37.50	41.29	5780	−180
150	40	6000	72	39.80	43.33	6500	−500
160	40	6400	80	42.31	45.63	7300	−900

FIGURE 13.10 Table displaying profit maximization for a lawn mowing firm.

TC from the table in Figure 13.7. Notice that the P = MR column is fixed at $40. Total revenue is found by multiplying price and quantity, column 1 and column 2.

To determine the profit-maximizing level of output, we compare P to MC. Every unit for which $P \geq$ MC improves the financial situation of the firm, making the firm more in revenue than the firm incurs in costs. From the information in the table, we can determine that the profit-maximizing level of output for the firm is at $Q = 100$, where P = MR = MC. The firm does not want to produce less than 100 units, because it would be leaving money on the table by not producing units that are profitable. Producing more than 100 units also reduces profits. At a quantity of 110, $P = 40$ but MC = 44. The firm would lose $4 per unit for units 101 to 110 because these units cost more to supply than they make in revenue, losing the firm $40 in total.

We can also find the profit-maximizing level of output in the economic profit column. Economic profit is found by taking total revenue and subtracting total cost. If TR > TC, the firm is earning an economic profit (the economic profit column contains a positive number). If TR = TC, the firm is earning a normal profit (economic profit is 0). If TR < TC, the firm is incurring an economic loss (the economic profit column contains a negative number).

In the table, the maximum level of economic profit is $360, which occurs when $Q = 90$ and when $Q = 100$. Note that $Q = 100$ is the profit-maximizing level of output because, even though the table doesn't show it, the absolute level of profit is higher at $Q = 100$. Here it is useful to differentiate economic profit from accounting profit. Technically, Economic profit = TR − TC. We take total revenue and subtract total costs, including opportunity costs. Total costs are all of a firm's accounting costs (all of the explicit costs that we find on their balance sheets), as well as the opportunity cost of running the firm. The opportunity costs are the 11% profit plus the opportunity cost of the time owners put into running the company—the opportunity costs that a firm must cover in order to stay in business. Remember that the firm isn't truly optimizing its resources unless it makes at least a normal profit, which means covering its accounting costs *and* its opportunity costs. We could rewrite the equation for economic profit as Economic profit = Total revenue − Total accounting cost − Total opportunity cost. So why in Figure 13.10 is $Q = 100$ better than $Q = 90$ even though economic profit is the same for both quantities? Why produce the ten units for which $P = MC = \$40$? The answer is that the firm makes a normal 11% profit on those units. These profits do not show up in the economic profit column, which only measures above-normal profits. But the firm is definitely more profitable at $Q = 100$ than it is at $Q = 90$. Fortunately, if you remember the simple rule that the firm should produce every unit for which MR ≥ MC, you will always arrive at the correct profit-maximizing level of output.

We can use this rule to find out the profit-maximizing level of output (Q) for any price. For example, suppose that the price falls to \$36. In this case, the profit-maximizing level of output would be $Q = 90$, where MC is \$36. If the price increases to \$50, the profit-maximizing level of output would increase to $Q = 120$. If the price increases to \$55, the profit-maximizing level of output would still be at $Q = 120$. The firm will only increase its output to $Q = 130$ if the price goes up to at least \$56, which is the marginal cost of producing an additional unit at that quantity.

The firm should shut down if the price falls below \$29, the minimum AVC. At a price below \$29, the firm would lose all of its total fixed cost and some of its variable costs if it stayed open. If it shut down, it would be better off because it would only lose its TFC. For example, if the price fell to \$26, the best level of output for the firm if it chose to stay open would be $Q = 60$. Total revenue would be $P \times Q = \$26 \times 60 = \$1560$. Total cost at $Q = 60$ is \$2270, so the firm would lose \$1560 − \$2270 = −\$710 if it stayed open. If the firm shut down in the short run, it would produce $Q = 0$ and lose only its total fixed cost of \$530. Thus, we can qualify the profit maximization rule as follows: **In the short run, a firm should produce every unit for which MR ≥ MC as long as *P* > AVC**.

The mainstream economics model assumes that firms know all of their costs of production and that firms engage in optimizing behavior in the short run by comparing marginal revenue and marginal cost. In the long run, the mainstream economics model assumes that firms engage in similar optimizing behavior regarding what size and scale of operations to choose. This involves certain realities of particular industries based on the economies and diseconomies of scale. It is to this topic that we turn to next.

13.4 THE MAINSTREAM MODEL OF A FIRM'S LONG-RUN COSTS OF PRODUCTION

In the short run, a firm's size of operations is fixed. Our lawn mowing firm above was stuck with a fixed amount of capital (a fixed number of mowers, trimmers, trucks, and trailers to take to each mowing site), but the firm could hire more laborers in the short run if it was profitable to do so. Nonetheless, hiring more laborers while keeping the amount of capital fixed was subject to the law of diminishing returns. If the firm had only two mowers and two trimmers, there were a limited number of specialized jobs. Adding more laborers beyond the number of specialized jobs would mean marginal costs would increase as the marginal productivity of each additional laborer decreased.

In the long run, the firm's size of operations is variable. The firm can vary its capital stock: The lawn mowing firm can buy more mowers, trimmers, trucks, and trailers, if it would be profitable to do so. We can expect a firm that is maximizing its profits in a competitive market to select the optimal size of operations in the long run based on the size of the market for the product and the forces affecting economies of scale and diseconomies of scale. Economies of scale refers to **the decrease in average total cost a firm experiences as it produces a larger quantity, due to increases in productivity (increasing returns to scale) or cost advantages from being larger. The sources of economies of scale include technology (development of large, specialized plants and equipment), specialized skills (workers and managers doing highly specialized tasks), bulk purchasing, financial benefits (such as lower interest rates for larger firms), and marketing advantages (ability to target a larger audience more effectively)**. When economies of scale exist, productivity increases and costs decrease as the firm gets larger.

However, it is not always beneficial to be larger. Diseconomies of scale is **the increase in average total cost a firm experiences as it produces a larger quantity, due to management challenges. Larger firms have more difficulty with coordination of efforts, communications, bureaucratic waste, and unproductive layers of management**.

Now, let's consider how these forces would affect a lawn mowing company. If the firm were mowing 15 or fewer lawns a week, they would need only one truck, one trailer, one mower, one trimmer, and one employee. That level of capital investment (the size of operations) could work for up to two employees and 30 lawns per week. But if the firm found it profitable to mow more lawns per week, they would need more capital equipment and more employees. In addition to people who mowed and trimmed lawns, the firm might also want to purchase a computer and software and hire someone to manage billing and payroll, take orders, set up and maintain a web page, and cultivate new clients.

Each different scale of operations will have a different average total cost curve and will be optimal for producing a different level of output.

Figure 13.11 shows the average total cost curves associated with seven different sizes of firms in a particular industry. ATC_1 shows the costs associated with
the smallest firm. If the firm could only profitably sell quantity Q_1, then the firm
should choose this size of operations. Any other size of firm would have higher
costs when producing at quantity Q_1. ATC_2 is a slightly larger firm size and it can
produce quantity Q_2 for a lower cost than the other firm sizes. And so on. Notice
that ATC_4 is the optimal firm size because it has the lowest costs of production. To
compete in this industry, firms will need to operate at that size; otherwise, they
will not be able to survive.

If we connect the optimal parts of all possible short run ATC curves, we get
a long-run average total cost (LRATC) curve. The **LRATC shows the lowest cost of producing each quantity in the long run. When the LRATC
curve is declining, the firm is experiencing economies of scale. When
the LRATC curve is increasing, the firm is experiencing diseconomies of
scale.** *In the long run in perfectly competitive industries, firms must produce at the minimum
long-run average total cost to stay in businesses. Otherwise, they cannot compete.*

We see different long-run average total cost curves in different industries.
Every industry has an optimal size or range of sizes where firms can be competitive.
In the lawn mowing business, you can mow more lawns quickly and effectively
by investing in large, powerful, fast lawn mowers, along with a truck and a trailer
to haul the mowers. And you can manage the business more effectively and reach
more customers with a specialized billing and salesperson. Thus, there is a certain
minimum size of the business to be competitive, involving a certain minimum size
of investment and a minimum number of employees to do the specialized jobs.
For a lawn mowing business, the minimum optimal size involves about $40,000 to

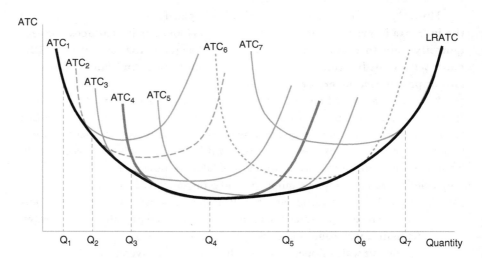

FIGURE 13.11 Deriving the long-run average total cost (LRATC) curve.

$50,000 in capital investment (for a truck, trailer, two heavy-duty lawn mowers, and two heavy-duty trimmers) and at least three workers.

However, once you reach the minimum effective size, you start to incur dis-economies of scale in the lawn mowing industry. If you want to double the size of your business, you will need twice as much equipment and twice as many employ-ees. There are no significant gains in efficiency from expanding, but you do experi-ence the problems that come with getting larger, including coordination problems and issues of bureaucratic inefficiency. In lawn mowing, there is no benefit to being larger than the minimum effective size.

But in other industries such as smartphone manufacturing, the larger the size of the firm, the lower the costs due to the technological benefits of specialization. Utilizing a separate factory for each smartphone component—the computer chips, screen, casing, camera, chips, other parts, and assembly operations—results in a significant cost savings from the development of specialized machinery and skilled laborers. The larger the smartphone manufacturer, the lower their costs.

Figure 13.12 shows different LRATC curves for three different types of indus-tries. $LRATC_1$ in graph (a) shows a firm that experiences small economies of scale (EoS) and then experiences diseconomies of scale (DoS) shortly thereafter. Firms in this type of industry must be small to be efficient and to stay competitive, produc-ing a small optimal quantity (Q^*), like the lawn mowing industry discussed earlier. $LRATC_2$ in graph (b) shows an industry in which firms can be small or large and still be competitive. There are small economies of scale, but once firms reach the minimum competitive size, they can grow larger and stay competitive (Constant Returns to Scale) until they reach the region of diseconomies of scale. For example, we see both small and large restaurants able to compete with each other. $LRATC_3$ in graph (c) of Figure 13.12 shows an industry in which the largest firms have the lowest costs. LRATC falls as firms get larger over the entire graph. This is the case in the smartphone industry and many other manufacturing industries.

In general, the mainstream model of the firm describes how firms can maxi-mize short-run profits using marginal revenue and marginal cost and how firms

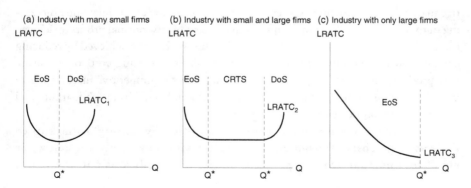

FIGURE 13.12 Long-run average total cost curves for different industries.

can select the optimal size of operations in the long run using LRATC. Empirical studies of firm behavior indicate that many firms do indeed behave in this way, forced to engage in optimizing behavior by the competitive pressures in their industry. But we also see firms engaging in other types of behavior in determining what quantity to produce and what price to charge. Political economists focus on decision making when firms operate in imperfectly competitive markets with imperfect information. This is the topic of the next section.

13.5 POLITICAL ECONOMY THEORY OF THE FIRM

As we have seen in previous chapters, political economists focus on the strategic, longer-term aspects of firm behavior. From a political economics viewpoint, prices and quantities are set by firms to achieve their primary objectives, **survival** and **growth**. Survival and growth require **profits**. Given that a firm's goals are to survive, grow, and continue to earn profits for the foreseeable future, the firm's decisions reflect short-term profit maximization and much more. In this area, as in most others, the political economy perspective is much broader than the mainstream economics perspective.

More specifically, in the mainstream economics theory of the firm, **the firm's goal is short-run and long-run profit maximization, something that the firm achieves by comparing marginal revenue and marginal cost and selecting the optimal size of operations**. In the political economy theory of the firm, **the firm's primary goals are survival, growth, and profit maximization, and those goals are achieved by determining quantities and setting prices based on markup pricing and the firm's strategic focus on surviving difficult economic conditions, gaining market share, or securing profits from monopoly power**. In political economists' studies of the behavior of actual firms, they found that firms' output and pricing decisions depend on what goals they set. If the firm's goal is to gain or preserve market share, which is crucial in competitive markets and in downturns, they try to cut prices as low as possible while increasing output. Firms may keep markups low and accept below-normal profits to achieve this goal. If the firm's goal is maximum profits, this is often best achieved by reducing competition via branding, innovation (both in terms of cutting costs or inventing new products), mergers, and acquisitions. In imperfectly competitive markets where firms have some monopoly power, firms can consistently establish high markups and earn economic profits, even in the long run.

Markup pricing is **when a firm sets its price by adding a markup to their average costs of production. That markup may be above, below, or equal to a normal profit depending on market conditions and the firm's**

strategic goals. We can define the firm's markup, m, in relationship to a normal profit, ρ:

- **If Markup (m) > Normal profit (ρ), the firm must have some monopoly power and be pursuing maximum profits by exploiting its monopoly power.**

    Monopoly power can be achieved in several ways: (1) Effective advertising and marketing that results in brand name recognition, (2) technological advances from investments in research and development that either reduce costs or result in the invention new products, (3) merging with competitors to reduce competition, or (4) acquiring competing firms or cutting-edge technology to gain a competitive advantage. Monopoly power becomes self-reinforcing, as economist Michal Kalecki argued: Economic profits from monopoly power give firms profits they can use to invest in efforts to preserve or gain additional monopoly power.

- **If $m = \rho$, the firm is operating in a competitive industry and behaving much as mainstream economic theory would predict.**

    We are most likely to see this behavior in perfectly competitive markets with no branding and so much competition that no degree of monopoly power exists.

- **If $m < \rho$, the firm is attempting to maximize market share.**

    The firm is attempting to either survive in the face of a difficult economic situation or expand its market share at the expense of competitors. In either case, the firm chooses a markup less than the going rate of profit in order to maximize its market share. This pricing strategy is often also associated with a strategic focus on cutting costs. Amazon's consistently low profit rate accompanying a relentlessly expanding market share is the quintessential example of this strategy.

For any normal rate of profit (ρ) in the economy, we can write the equation for **markup pricing** as follows: Price $= P = (1 + m - \rho)\text{ATC}$, where P is the price charged by the firm, m is the firm's markup, ρ is the normal rate of profit, and ATC is the firm's average total cost. If $m = \rho$, then $P = \text{ATC}$, just as we see in the mainstream economics model of a competitive firm in the long run. The firm earns a normal profit. If $m > \rho$, then $P > \text{ATC}$ and the firm is earning economic profits. It can use these economic profits to preserve its market dominance in the long run. If $m < \rho$, then $P < \text{ATC}$, and the firm is earning below normal profits (an economic loss). This occurs when firms are attempting to preserve market share. Sometimes firms earning an economic loss are intentionally doing so to gain market share (like Amazon) and sometimes such firms are struggling to survive due to poor economic conditions.

Research by political economists also shows that price is not directly affected by short-run demand fluctuations, and firms rarely change prices. Furthermore, firms rarely have enough information on costs to determine the marginal cost of each additional unit they produce. Instead, firms pick a strategic goal and then determine a quantity of production and pricing strategy that fits that goal. Firms tend to stick with that approach until market conditions change significantly. This is another example of **satisficing** behavior that was discussed in Chapter 11, where firms make prudent decisions using rules of thumb given limited information.

When we look at firms' pricing strategies, some interesting trends emerge. A 2012 study by Andreas Hinterhuber and Stephan Liozu, published in the *MIT Sloan Management Review*, found that firms engaged in three types of pricing strategies:

1. **Cost-based pricing** where firms use their accounting costs to determine the cost of producing each unit and then add a markup to that cost to determine what price to charge. This is similar to the mainstream model described above, although most firms determine output based on the size of operations they have found to be optimal rather than looking for where MC = MR.

2. **Competition-based pricing** where firms focus on the prices being charged by competitors to set their own prices. This is particularly common in oligopolistic industries where we see price leadership by the dominant firm and other firms following suit. Firms then engage in non-price competition, via advertising, research and development, mergers, and acquisitions.

3. **Customer-based pricing** where firms attempt to determine exactly how much consumers are willing to pay for a product. This includes anticipating price elasticity and income, as well as using marketing and other attempts to create brand name identity.

The second and third pricing strategies above occur in industries in which some degree of monopoly power exists.

The primary difference between the approach of mainstream economists and the approach of political economists has to do with how much competition you believe there is in the economy. Mainstream economists see capitalism as relentlessly competitive. Even in huge oligopolies, mainstream economists see the constant threat of innovation and entry of new firms checking the behavior of oligopolies. From the mainstream perspective, competition is the norm and most industries are similar enough to perfect competition that the model of perfect competition is useful in understanding the behavior of most firms and industries.

Political economists see monopoly power as the essential characteristic of capitalist markets. To political economists, almost all markets have some degree of monopoly power, and large firms with significant monopoly power dominate modern economic systems. From this perspective, the model of a competitive industry is much less important than studying the strategic behaviors of firms with monopoly power.

13.6 CONCLUSION

This chapter began by laying out the mainstream economics theory of the firm. Short-run costs are shaped fundamentally by the laws of specialization and diminishing returns. Once costs are established, the firm's goal is short-run profit maximization, something that the firm achieves by comparing marginal revenue and marginal cost given the size of its existing operations.

The major costs of production in the mainstream model of firm behavior are laid out in Figure 13.13. This table also includes a mathematical and verbal

Type of cost	Mathematical definition	Verbal definition	Purpose
Marginal cost (MC)	$MC = \dfrac{\Delta TVC}{\Delta Q} = \dfrac{\Delta TC}{\Delta Q}$	The increase in cost from producing another unit of a good.	MC is the firm's supply curve (above AVC). MC drives the shape of AVC, ATC. MC is shaped by laws of specialization, diminishing returns
Average variable cost (AVC)	$AVC = \dfrac{TVC}{Q}$	The variable cost per unit of output.	Below min. AVC the firm should shut down in the short run.
Average fixed cost (AFC)	$AFC = \dfrac{TFC}{Q}$	The fixed cost per unit of output.	On graphs, AFC is the distance between the ATC and the AVC curves.
Average total cost (ATC)	$ATC = \dfrac{TC}{Q}$ $ATC = AVC + AFC$	The average of *all* costs per unit of output.	ATC is used to determine if the firm is making an economic profit (P>ATC), normal profit (P=ATC), or economic loss (P<ATC).
Total variable cost (TVC)	$TVC = w * L$ (if labor is the only variable input)	The total cost of hiring variable inputs, such as labor.	TVC shows the amount of revenue a firm must make to cover its variable costs to stay open in the short run.
Total fixed cost (TFC)	Fixed amount of money that does not change in the short run.	The total cost of hiring fixed inputs, such as payments for machinery and rent.	TFC shapes a firm's economies of scale. Large fixed costs necessitate a large firm. Small fixed costs allow small firms.
Total cost (TC)	$TC = TFC + TVC$	The total of all costs of production, including opportunity costs (normal profit).	TC is used to determine if the firm is making an economic profit (TR>TC), normal profit (TR=TC) or economic loss (TR<TC).

FIGURE 13.13 Table of short-run costs of production in mainstream economics theory of the firm.

definition of each type of cost, along with a listing of the purposes for each type of cost.

In the long run in the mainstream model, firms select the optimal size of operations based on economies of scale and diseconomies of scale. Economies of scale reflect productivity and efficiency gains from being large, whereas diseconomies of scale reflect bureaucratic inefficiencies that firms experience as they grow too large. The long-run average total cost curve is used to display economies and diseconomies of scale.

In the mainstream theory of the firm, competition is assumed to be widely prevalent, so much so that firms' decisions are confined to how to minimize costs and stay competitive. Firms are assumed to have perfect knowledge of all of their costs of production, including marginal cost. The firm's primary goal is to maximize profits given the cost conditions of their industry.

In the political economy theory of the firm, the firm's primary goals are survival, growth, and profit maximization. Those goals are achieved by determining quantities and setting prices based on markup pricing and the firm's strategic focus on gaining market share or securing profits from monopoly power. Rather than engaging in optimizing behavior based on perfect information, political economists view firms as using rules of thumb based on imperfect information and strategic goals to decide how much to produce and what price to charge.

The next chapter goes into the model of perfect competition in much more detail. This model is crucial to understand because it is one of the cornerstones of mainstream economics.

QUESTIONS FOR REVIEW

1. Do you think the laws of specialization and of diminishing returns apply to a university's hiring of professors? What are professors "producing"? Will the productivity of each professor improve as they are able to specialize? Will it decline eventually as more professors are hired? Explain carefully.

2. What would it mean if a firm's marginal cost curve is always decreasing? What would it mean if a firm's marginal cost curve is always increasing? Explain carefully.

3. Why does the average total cost curve get closer and closer to the average variable cost curve as quantity (Q) increases?

4. Why does the marginal cost curve always intersect the average total cost curve at its minimum point?

5. Explain why economists include a "normal profit" as a normal cost of doing business.

6. Complete the table in Figure 13.14 and then answer the questions afterward.

Q	TFC	TVC	MC	AVC	AFC	TC	ATC
0	42	0					
1	42	10					
2	42	18					
3	42	24					
4	42	32					
5	42	42					
6	42	54					
7	42	70					
8	42	92					

FIGURE 13.14 Table for Problem 6.

    a.   Does the table display the laws of specialization and diminishing returns? Why or why not?

    b.   Using the table, explain the relationship between MC and AVC, MC and ATC, and AVC and ATC.

    c.   Using the mainstream model of profit maximization, what is the profit-maximizing level of output if the market price is fixed at $12? How much economic profit or loss would the firm make if the price is $12?

    d.   What would happen if the market price increased to $16? How much economic profit or loss would the firm make?

    e.   What would happen if the market price increased to $20? How much economic profit or loss would the firm make?

    f.   Should the firm shut down in the short run if the price falls to $6? Why or why not?

7. What would the long-run average total cost curve look like in an industry in which there were no economies of scale and no diseconomies of scale?

8. Farming is an industry that contains both very small and very large farms. Explain why this might be the case using the concepts of economies of scale and diseconomies of scale.

9. Compare and contrast the political economy theory of the firm with the mainstream economics theory of the firm. Where are they similar? What are the major differences?

10. Why do political economists argue that firms engage in *satisficing* behavior rather than *optimizing* behavior? Explain and give examples.

NOTES

1 Traditionally, grade points are allocated as follows: A = 4 grade points, B = 3 grade points, C = 2 grade points, D = 1 grade point, and F = 0 grade points.

2 In both the ATC and AVC columns, the cost curves reach their minimum points where they are equal to MC, but they also have the same value at the previous quantity. This occurs when we do not use a continuous function. If the firm could produce and sell partial units, the minimum ATC and AVC would reach their minimum values only at

the point where they intersect MC. When we do not have a continuous function, ATC and AVC will reach their minimum value one unit before where they intersect MC and then stay at that level for the unit where they are equal to MC. Nonetheless, you can always use the point where MC intersects ATC and AVC to find the minimum values of those cost curves.

3   As we will see later, in cases where the firm can affect prices, $\left(\frac{\Delta P}{\Delta Q}\right) < 0$ so $MR < P$. When a large firm increases its output, this causes P to fall.

14 Perfect competition and competitive markets

The perfect, Smithian market structure

This chapter develops the mainstream model of profit maximization in perfectly competitive industries. This perfect market structure needs little or no regulation due to the degree of competition. Recall that Adam Smith advocated laissez-faire capitalism *if* markets were truly competitive, whereas Smith was very critical of markets that were controlled by huge industries, especially when they operated with the complicity and assistance of government officials.

In theory, firms operating in perfectly competitive markets provide exactly the amount and quality of goods consumers want at the lowest possible price. If firms do not do this, their competition puts them out of the market. Firms do not bother with advertising in perfectly competitive markets—it is too costly, and it comes with no significant benefits because all products are identical and it is impossible to establish product differentiation. Instead, firms focus on providing the best product at the best price. Workers also benefit from perfectly competitive markets because dozens of small firms are bidding for their services. It seems like the perfect form of the market system. In fact, some economists are so taken with perfectly competitive market structures that they think the goal of government regulators should be to try to make all markets function like perfectly competitive ones.

But there is a dark side even to competitive markets. The same forces that require firms to produce at the lowest cost possible to stay competitive also encourage firms to ignore environmental laws and worker safety regulations. If some competitors gain a cost advantage by being unscrupulous, other firms must imitate their behavior in order to survive. Thus, even in perfectly competitive markets there is some need for regulation to prevent a race to the bottom.

DOI: 10.4324/9781315636924-18

This chapter lays out the assumptions behind the mainstream model of perfect competition. Then it works through how firms maximize profits in the short run and the long run based on this model. This model allows us to predict how firms in perfectly competitive markets will respond to changes in market prices and how perfectly competitive markets will behave in the long run. The chapter concludes by assessing the implications and the applicability of the model of perfect competition.

14.0 CHAPTER 14 LEARNING GOALS

After reading this chapter you should be able to:

■ List the assumptions and characteristics of the mainstream model of perfect competition.

■ Use a graph or table to determine the profit-maximizing level of output for a perfectly competitive firm in the short run and to determine all relevant costs, revenues, and profits at that level of output.

■ Analyze what will happen to prices and quantities for a typical firm and market in the long run using the mainstream model of perfect competition.

■ Critically analyze the implications and applicability of the mainstream model of perfect competition.

14.1 THE CHARACTERISTICS OF A PERFECTLY COMPETITIVE MARKET

As we saw in Chapter 12, the major characteristics of a perfectly competitive market are the following:

1. **Homogenous product**: Firms sell a product that is identical to all other competing products in this market. Goods are perfect substitutes for each other. Therefore, consumers will buy whatever good is cheapest. Advertising cannot be used because it raises costs, but it will not increase demand because product differentiation is not possible.

2. **Large number of small sellers and buyers**: All sellers and buyers are small relative to the size of the market, so no individual seller or buyer can influence the market price of the product.

3. **Easy entry and exit**: There are no barriers to entry or exit, so firms can enter or exit the market easily. The ease of entry means that if existing firms are making above-normal profits, new firms will enter the market and drive prices down to where firms make a normal profit in the long run. If existing firms are experiencing losses, some firms will exit the market, which drives prices up until firms earn a normal profit in the long run.

4. **Firms are price takers**: All firms charge the same price. The market price is determined by the market supply and demand curves. Individual suppliers cannot raise their prices at all because if they do, consumers will switch and buy cheaper, identical substitutes. Individual suppliers have no reason to lower their prices because they can sell all of their goods at the going market price.

In addition to the above characteristics, the model of the firm operating in perfectly competitive markets also makes the following assumptions:

1. Firms have **complete information** on all costs, resources, technologies, and prices.
2. All firms have **equal access to resources and technology**.
3. Firms make **optimal decisions** regarding how much to produce and how to produce it most efficiently. This market structure is so competitive that mainstream economists assume firms must relentlessly optimize in all decisions.
    a. Firms maximize profits in the short run by producing as long as marginal revenue is greater than or equal to marginal cost.
    b. Firms maximize profits in the long run by selecting the optimal firm size and producing as long as marginal revenue is greater than or equal to marginal cost.
4. Firms are subject to the **laws of specialization and diminishing returns** in the short run, giving them U-shaped short-run cost curves.
5. Firms are subject to **economies of scale and diseconomies of scale** in the long run, giving them u-shaped long-run cost curves.

Perfectly competitive market structures are rare, but we do see some prominent examples of markets that approach the model of perfect competition in the real world:

1. **Unprocessed agricultural products**: Unprocessed wheat, corn, soybeans, quinoa, coffee beans, and other basic agricultural products are produced and purchased by millions of small sellers and buyers in competitive markets.
2. **The market for common stocks**: Each day there are millions of buyers and sellers in the market for common, publicly traded stocks such as Amazon and Apple. (However, sometimes large, institutional investors have enough buying power that they can affect stock prices.)

3. **Homogeneous local services**: House cleaning, lawn mowing, babysitting, driveway sealing, house painting, and other local services where there is no significant product differentiation approach the model of perfect competition, although there can be very small quality differences.

4. **Used goods in plentiful supply**: New books are distributed by only one publisher, but used books are sold by thousands of small booksellers operating in various online and physical marketplaces. Most used best sellers end up selling for $0.01 (with $3.99 in shipping) on Amazon due to the level of competition.

5. **Homogeneous, easily produced local products**: Any homogeneous product that can be manufactured very simply with limited skill and easy-to-find inputs will tend toward perfect competition. Examples include simple baked goods at farmers' markets (brownies, whoopee pies), basic wood products (bird feeders, signs), and basic construction products (gravel, concrete, stone, mulch).

Based on the characteristics and assumptions above, mainstream economists developed a model of a perfectly competitive firm. This model is taken up in the next section.

14.2 THE MODEL OF THE PERFECTLY COMPETITIVE FIRM IN THE SHORT RUN

We discussed the mainstream model of the firm's short-run costs of production in the previous chapter. We will once again use that model here. We also need to incorporate the supply and demand model to show how prices are determined in perfectly competitive markets, which is where we start our development of the mainstream model of the perfectly competitive firm.

In a perfectly competitive market, the market supply curve and the market demand curve determine the market price. Individual consumers or firms have no influence on the market price—they are price takers rather than price makers. Only large movements of numerous consumers or firms can cause the market price to change. In Figure 14.1(b) the market supply and demand curves intersect to determine the equilibrium price, P_e, and the equilibrium quantity, Q_e, for the market.

Given that each firm is so small they cannot affect the market price, as far as the firm is concerned the market price is fixed and out of its control. In Figure 14.1(a) the firm's demand curve is a flat line at the market price. No matter how much the firm supplies, it will have no effect on the market price. Note also that because the market price does not change as the individual firm changes output, price is equal to marginal revenue. The revenue the firm gets for each additional unit they sell is exactly equal to the market price.

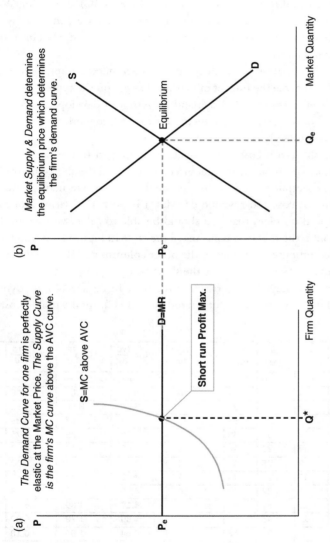

FIGURE 14.1 The firm's demand curve is the market price in perfect competition.

As discussed in the last chapter, the firm's profit-maximizing level of output is determined where marginal revenue (MR) is equal to marginal cost (MC). The firm wants to produce every unit for which MR ≥ MC because that produces the maximum possible short-run profits. Therefore, in Figure 14.1(a), the firm's profit-maximizing level of output, Q^*, occurs where MR = MC. Because marginal revenue is equal to price (P) and marginal cost (MC) above the AVC curve is the firm's supply curve, as was discussed previously, we can also say that the profit-maximizing level of output occurs where the firm's supply curve intersects the firm's demand curve.

In perfect competition, we will often include a market graph next to the firm graph so we can analyze the impact of market changes on the typical firm. You will need to use all of the supply and demand analysis you developed earlier together with the model of the perfectly competitive firm we are working through now to understand how perfectly competitive markets behave.

Using the short-run costs of production developed in the last chapter combined with information on the market price, we can find the short-run profit-maximizing level of output for a firm in a perfectly competitive market. Figure 14.2 contains short-run cost and revenue data for a hypothetical firm, Donny's Corn Farm. In a typical problem that you should be able to solve, you would be given the information in the first four columns of the table in Figure 14.2, and you would be expected to compute the values in the other columns and then to determine the profit-maximizing level of output in the short run.

There are some key characteristics of the table in Figure 14.2 that you should be aware of. First, quantity (Q), total fixed cost (TFC), total variable cost (TVC),

Q (1000s)	$P=MR$	TFC (1000s)	TVC (1000s)	TC (1000s)	$MC=\frac{\Delta TVC}{\Delta Q}$	$AVC=\frac{TVC}{Q}$	$AFC=\frac{TFC}{Q}$	$ATC=\frac{TC}{Q}$	$TR=P*Q$ (1000s)
0	$ 8	$ 17	$ 0	$ 17	$ -----	$ ------	$ ------	$ -------	$ 0
1	8	17	10	27	10	10.00	17.00	27.00	8
2	8	17	16	33	6	8.00	8.50	16.50	16
3	8	17	20	37	4	6.67	5.67	12.33	24
4	8	17	22	39	2	5.50	4.25	9.75	32
5	8	17	23	40	1	4.60	3.40	8.00	40
6	8	17	25	42	2	4.17	2.83	7.00	48
7	8	17	28	45	3	4.00	2.43	6.43	56
8	8	17	32	49	4	4.00	2.13	6.13	64
9	8	17	37	54	5	4.11	1.89	6.00	72
10	8	17	43	60	6	4.30	1.70	6.00	80
11	8	17	51	68	8	4.64	1.55	6.18	88
12	8	17	61	78	10	5.08	1.42	6.50	84
13	8	17	74	91	13	5.69	1.31	7.00	91
14	8	17	95	112	21	6.79	1.21	8.00	98
15	8	17	133	150	38	8.87	1.13	10.00	105

FIGURE 14.2 Table of cost and revenue information for Donny's Corn Farm in the short run.

total cost (TC), and total revenue (TR) are in thousands (1000s). However, per unit costs are not in 1000s. Second, the price (P) stays the same no matter how much corn Donny produces, which is a key aspect of a perfectly competitive market. In all other market structures, prices fall as firms produce more units of output. Third, the marginal cost (MC) column falls during the period of specialization and rises during the period of diminishing returns. Fourth, the average variable cost (AVC) column starts out equal to MC and then falls until it intersects MC again when $Q = 8$ and MC = AVC = \$4. Fifth, the firm's supply curve starts where $Q = 8$ and MC = \$4. The firm's supply curve is the MC curve above where MC = (minimum AVC). When finding the profit-maximizing level of output, you ignore the decreasing part of the MC column and focus on the part of the MC curve above the minimum average variable cost. This is because it is always more profitable for a firm to expand output when its costs are declining due to the law of specialization, and the firm cannot stay open unless it covers at least its minimum AVC (see the short-run shutdown condition discussed in Chapter 13).

Sixth, the average fixed cost (AFC) falls as quantity increases. Average fixed cost gets smaller and smaller as more units are produced. Seventh, the average total cost (ATC) column declines until it reaches its minimum at $Q = 10$ where MC = ATC = \$6. After that, ATC increases.

Finally, short-run profit maximization is found by comparing marginal revenue (MR = Price) and marginal cost (MC) after $Q = 8$ (the minimum AVC). Thus, the profit-maximizing level of output in the short run is where $Q = 11$ and $P = MC = \$8$. At this quantity, total revenue is \$88,000 and total cost is \$68,000, so the firm is earning an economic profit (TR − TC) of \$20,000.

This information is also plotted out in a graph in Figure 14.3. The MC, AVC, and ATC curves are plotted out from the columns in the table in Figure 14.2. (We have ignored values greater than \$13 for ATC and MC because these are not relevant to the issues we are analyzing.) The firm's demand curve is a straight line at the market price of \$8. The firm's supply curve is the MC curve above point D, where MC = AVC. To emphasize this point, we have made the MC curve solid after point D when it becomes the firm's supply curve. You can use the graph to identify all of the information contained in the table in Figure 14.2 by going through a series of steps.

- Step 1: Identify the short-run profit-maximizing level of output where MR = $P = MC$, which is point A in Figure 14.3. Dropping straight down from point A to the horizontal axis, we see that the profit-maximizing quantity in the short run is $Q^* = 11$.
- Step 2: Find the average total cost of producing the profit-maximizing quantity. This is done by going up from $Q = 11$ to the ATC curve at point B and then over to the price axis to identify that ATC at $Q = 11$ is \$6.18. *Important note: The firm is not producing at its minimum ATC here. It was more profitable for the firm to produce at a quantity with a higher ATC. The firm is willing to produce at a quantity higher than where its costs are at their lowest if it is profitable to do so.*

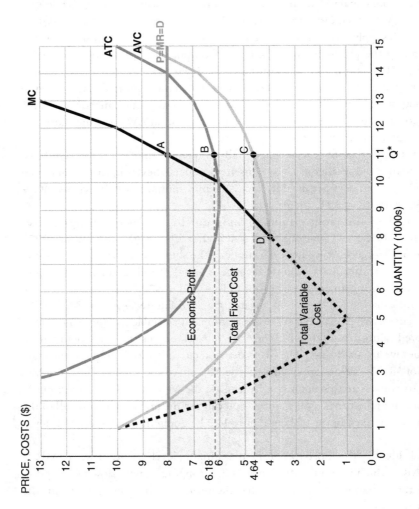

FIGURE 14.3 Graph of Donny's Corn Farm in the short run.

- Step 3: Identify any economic profit or loss by comparing price (P) and average total cost. Recall that Economic profit = TR − TC. We can rewrite this as

$$\text{Economic profit} = \text{TR} - \text{TC}$$
$$= (P \times Q) - (\text{ATC} \times Q)$$
$$= (P - \text{ATC})Q$$

$$\text{Economic profit per unit} = \frac{(\text{Economic profit})}{Q}$$
$$= \frac{(P - \text{ATC})Q}{Q}$$
$$= P - \text{ATC}$$

In Figure 14.3, economic profit per unit is $P - \text{ATC} = \$8 - \$6.18 = \$1.82$.

In Figure 14.3, economic profit per unit is the distance between point A and point B. We can find total economic profit by multiplying economic profit per unit by quantity, giving us the area of the box formed by point A, point B, $6.18 and $8.

- Step 4: Identify the average variable cost (AVC) of producing the profit-maximizing quantity by going up from $Q = 11$ to the AVC curve at point C and then over to the price axis to find AVC = $4.64. Total variable cost can then be found by multiplying AVC by quantity, giving us the area of the box going from 0 to $Q = 11$, up to point C, and then over to $4.64. *Note that the most common error in identifying AVC is the use of its minimum value, at point D, even though the firm is actually producing at a different quantity and therefore has a different AVC.*
- Step 5: Identify the average fixed cost (AFC) of producing the profit-maximizing quantity by finding the distance between ATC and AVC at $Q = 11$. On the graph in Figure 14.3, AFC is the distance between point B and point C. To get total fixed cost, we multiply AFC by Q, and that gives us the area of the box with B–C as one side and 4.64 to 6.18 on the other side.

14.2.1 The short-run shutdown condition

This firm would shut down in the short run if the price of corn fell below $4 a bushel, the minimum average variable cost. This is the lowest number in the AVC column of Figure 14.2, and it is point D in the graph in Figure 14.3 where MC = AVC. To see why, consider what would happen with a price of $3. If the price of a bushel of corn were $3, the best Donny's farm could do would be to produce at $Q = 7$ where $P = \text{MC} = \$3$. But at this quantity, total revenue would be $\$3 \times 7 = \$21$, and total costs at $Q = 7$ are $45. Donny would lose $24 by staying open. Note: TR, TC, TFC, and Q are in 1000s.

However, if Donny shut down and produced nothing ($Q = 0$), he would only lose $17, his TFC. If the price increased to $4, then Donny would be indifferent between staying open and shutting down. If $P = \$4$, then Donny would produce where $Q = 8$ and $P = MC = \$4$. His total revenue can be computed as: $TR = P \times Q = \$4 \times 8 = \$32$. His total costs at $Q = 8$ are $49. So when $P = \$4$, Donny would lose $17 if he stayed open or $17 if he shut down ($Q = 0$). When $P = AVC_{min} = \$4$, he loses the same amount of money staying open or shutting down. At any price over $4, Donny would be better off in the short run by staying open than by shutting down.

14.2.2 The firm's response to changes in price

If the market price changes, Donny would change his profit-maximizing level of output. Using the table and graph of Donny's Corn Farm above, let's consider how Donny would respond to various changes in the market price. To do this, you compare P and MC for each unit after $Q = 8$, which is where Donny's supply curve starts. Note that each time price changes the total revenue column would also change.

- If the market price increased to $9, Donny's profit-maximizing level of output is $Q = 11$. He would make more money at a price of $9 than he does when the price is $8 but not enough to make it profitable to produce the 12th unit.
- If the market price increased to $10, unit 12 would now be profitable to produce (the MC of the 12th unit is $10), so Donny would increase production to $Q = 12$. His economic profits would increase.
- If the price falls to $6, Donny's profit-maximizing level of output would be at $Q = 10$ where MC = $6. Notice that at $Q = 10$, $P = MR = \$6$, and MC = ATC = $6, so Donny would make a normal profit—his total revenue would be exactly equal to his total cost.
- If the price fell to $5, Donny's profit-maximizing level of output would be $Q = 9$ where $P = MC = \$5$. Because $P = 5$ but ATC at $Q = 9$ is $6, Donny loses $1 per unit and experiences a total economic loss of $9 when he produces nine units. However, Donny would still want to say open because he is losing less than the $17 (TFC) he would lose if he shut down.

The example above shows a perfectly competitive firm earning an economic profit when $P = \$8$ and ATC = $6.18. The other two possibilities for a firm in the short run are for it to be earning a normal profit or an economic loss.

Figure 14.4 shows a perfectly competitive firm earning a normal profit in the short run. The demand curve is just tangent to the average total cost curve, intersecting ATC at its minimum that occurs at point c. The profit-maximizing level of output, Q^*, which is shown at point a, occurs directly below point c, where MR = MC. If we were to go up from our profit-maximizing quantity to the ATC curve at point c, we would find that the ATC is equal to price, which is what happens when a firm earns a normal profit. AVC is found by going up from Q^* to the AVC

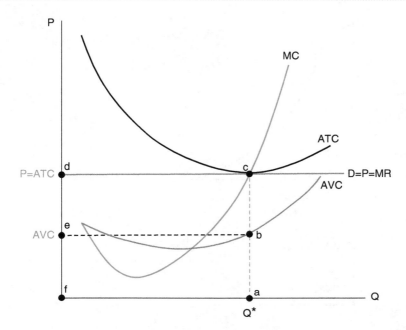

FIGURE 14.4 A perfectly competitive firm earning a normal profit.

curve at point b and then over to the price axis at point e. Average fixed cost is always the distance between ATC and AVC. At Q^*, AFC is the distance between point b and point c.

Total revenue in Figure 14.4 would be price multiplied by quantity, which is the area of the box fdca. Total cost is equal to the same box, which again signals that the firm is earning a normal profit. Total fixed cost is equal to AFC * Q, which is the box bcde. TVC is the box equal to AVC * Q, which is the box abef.

Figure 14.5 depicts a perfectly competitive firm experiencing an economic loss. The demand curve is always below ATC. The best the firm can do is to produce where the demand curve intersects the marginal cost curve at point c. This gives us the profit-maximizing (or in this case loss-minimizing) level of output of Q^* at point a. If we go up from Q^* to the ATC curve at point d, we get the firm's ATC at quantity Q^*. Note that the firm is not at its minimum ATC, which is down and to the right from point d. Average variable cost is the distance between point a and point b, and average fixed cost is the distance between point b and point d.

We can find economic profit or loss per unit by the distance between price and average total cost. In Figure 14.5 $P < $ ATC, so economic loss per unit is equal to the distance cd (or fe). Total economic loss is found by multiplying economic loss per unit by quantity, giving us the area of the box cdef in Figure 14.5. Total revenue is the area of box acfh, and TC is equal to the area of the box adeh. We can also use the graph to find that TVC = abgh, and TFC = bdeg in Figure 14.5.

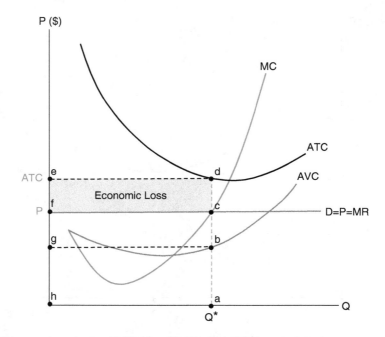

FIGURE 14.5 A perfectly competitive firm experiencing economic loss.

Even though the firm in Figure 14.5 is losing money, it should still stay open in the short run and hope things get better in the long run. Their economic loss is smaller than their loss would be if they shut down, when they would lose all of the total fixed cost. So Figure 14.5 shows a firm that is losing money but should stay open. Firms only shut down in the short run when price falls below the minimum AVC.

Figure 14.6 highlights the key points to use in analyzing graphs of perfect competition in the short run. If the demand curve goes above the minimum ATC, then the market price $P > P_2$ and the firm will earn an economic profit and produce a quantity greater than Q_2.

If the demand curve is tangent to ATC, then the market price $P = P_2$, and the firm will earn a normal profit and produce quantity Q_2. If the demand curve is always below ATC and above the minimum AVC, then the market price is between P_1 and P_2. If $P_1 < P < P_2$, then the firm will experience an economic loss but they should stay open in the short run and they will produce a quantity between Q_1 and Q_2.

If the demand curve falls below the minimum AVC, then the market price $P < P_1$. The firm should shut down in the short run, producing nothing ($Q = 0$).

Now that we have covered all of the short-run possibilities, we next turn to an analysis of perfectly competitive firms in the long run. In the short run, capital was fixed. But in the long run, all inputs are variable and the firm can adopt an entirely difference scale of operations if it is optimal to do so.

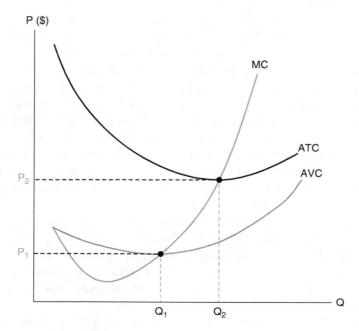

FIGURE 14.6 Possible short-run cases.

14.3 THE MAINSTREAM MODEL OF THE PERFECTLY COMPETITIVE FIRM IN THE LONG RUN

The long-run average total cost curve (LRATC) was derived in Chapter 13 from all possible short-run average total cost curves. LRATC is shaped by the forces of economies of scale and diseconomies of scale—the forces that make it more or less efficient for a firm in a particular industry to be large.

The long-run marginal cost (LRMC) curve is also shaped by economies and diseconomies of scale. Long-run marginal cost (LRMC) **is the lowest possible increase in total cost from offering one additional unit of output for sale given that all inputs are variable.** In other words, LRMC is the least cost way a firm can use any combination of its inputs to produce an additional unit of output.

14.3.1 The law of diminishing returns does not apply in the long run

The law of diminishing returns applies to increasing the amount of one input used, holding all other inputs constant. But in the long run all inputs can be varied. If a firm wants to expand in the long run, it can hire more laborers *and* it can purchase and install more machinery and expand the size of its operations. However, the law of specialization can still affect long-run marginal cost. Firms can develop specialized jobs, inputs, and machines to produce more effectively in the long run. In fact, greater specialization is one of the main sources of economies of scale.

The long-run marginal cost curve can have many different shapes depending on the characteristics of the particular industry. LRMC can decline continuously in industries with ever-increasing economies of scale that benefit from increasing specialization (e.g., smartphones where specialized factories can be developed for each component). LRMC can be flat in industries where it always takes the same amount of inputs to achieve the same proportionate increase in output. Or LRMC can look like a short-run MC curve, if there are economies of scale at first and then diseconomies of scale as firms get larger.

Perfectly competitive markets are easy to enter because there are only small economies of scale from specialization of laborers and machinery. There are also diseconomies of scale from becoming larger and more bureaucratic. So long-run average total cost and long-run marginal cost curves in perfect competition often have a U shape. This is not as likely to be true of oligopolies and monopolies, as we will see later.

Figure 14.7 shows long-run average total cost (LRATC) and long-run marginal cost (LRMC) curves for a typical perfectly competitive firm. There is no

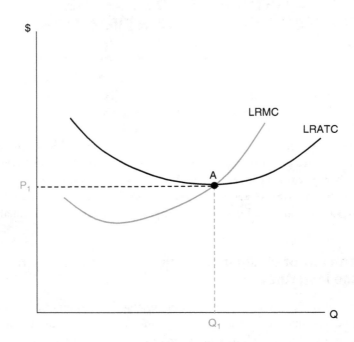

FIGURE 14.7 Possible long-run cases in perfect competition.

need for average variable cost or average fixed cost on the graph—there is no such thing as fixed cost in the long run, because every input is variable.

The major issue we are concerned with regarding long-run analysis is the entry and exit of firms in the market. In any perfectly competitive market, the ease of entry means that if firms are earning an economic profit in the short run, in the long run new firms will enter the market to take advantage of the above-normal profits. This happens in Figure 14.7 any time the price is higher than P_1, which happens whenever the demand curve is above the minimum of the LRATC curve. When firms enter the market, this causes an increase in the market supply curve and a decrease in the market price until the market returns to a normal profit.

Similarly, if firms in a perfectly competitive industry are earning economic losses, eventually, if firms keep losing money year after year, some of the firms will go out of business. This would occur at any price below P_1 in Figure 14.7, and that would happen whenever the demand curve is always below the ATC curve. When firms exit the market, this causes a decrease in the market supply curve and an increase in the market price until the market returns to a normal profit.

If the price were equal to P_1 in Figure 14.7, the firm would produce quantity Q_1, and earn a normal profit. This happens when the demand curve is just tangent to the LRATC curve at its minimum point.

Thus, *in the long run in perfectly competitive markets, firms always end up producing at their minimum long-run average total cost and earning a normal profit (point A in Figure 14.7).* As we will discuss later, this is one of the most appealing attributes of perfectly competitive markets.

Case study: A boom in the wheat market

To see how the process of long-run adjustment works, let's consider a real-world example from the perfectly competitive wheat market. In 2002 the global wheat market was in equilibrium at a price of $4 per bushel and a quantity of 20 billion bushels of wheat per year, which is point A in Figure 14.8(b). The typical wheat farmer was earning a normal profit at that price and selling 10 thousand bushels of wheat per year, which is point a in Figure 14.8(a).

From 2002 to 2012 there was a huge increase in the demand for wheat from consumers in the rapidly growing economies of China, India, Brazil, and other emerging markets. Wheat prices increased to $9 per bushel, and the equilibrium quantity of wheat produced increased to 25 billion bushels, which is shown as point B in Figure 14.8(b). This caused the demand curve for a typical wheat farmer to shift up to $9, causing them to increase production to 12.5 thousand bushels per year, which

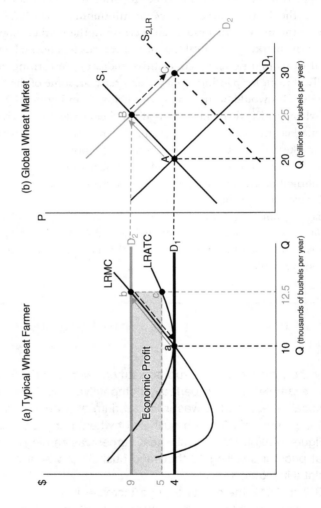

FIGURE 14.8 The global market for wheat in 2002, 2012, and 2018.

is shown at point b in Figure 14.8(a). To increase production, farmers had to use land that was less productive and rent more machinery than usual, and that increased their costs per bushel of wheat slightly. The average total cost of producing 12.5 thousand bushels of wheat was $5, which is shown at point c in Figure 14.8(a). Nonetheless, the large increase in price and small increase in ATC meant large economic profits for wheat farmers that is depicted in the graph in Figure 14.8(a).

The existence of economic profits encouraged new farmers to enter the wheat market in the long run. There was a significant increase in the market supply of wheat from 2012 to 2018 that is shown by the shift from S_1 to S_2 in Figure 14.8(b), and the movement from point B to point C. New firms kept entering the market and growing more wheat until the equilibrium price of wheat fell back to $4. Typical wheat farmers, who had earned an economic profit when the price was $9, returned to earning a normal profit at a price of $4 at point a in Figure 14.8(a). The economic profit from the boom of 2002 to 2012 was short-lived, and firms returned to earning a normal profit, as they always do in the long run in perfectly competitive markets.

Case study: A downturn in the milk market

The opposite series of events occurs if firms are earning an economic loss. In 2018, farmers producing milk were losing money at the market price of $3.20 per gallon. At that price, the typical milk farmer was producing 60 thousand gallons of milk per year, as you can see at point a in Figure 14.9(a). They also experienced average total costs of $4.20 (point b), resulting in an economic loss per unit of $1 per gallon and a total economic loss of $1 × 60,000 = $60,000. The U.S. milk market at the time was in equilibrium at a price of $3.20 per gallon and a quantity of 21 billion gallons of milk per year, point A in Figure 14.9(b).

What can we expect to happen in the long run? Eventually, the economic losses will cause some milk farmers to exit the market. This will cause a decrease in the market supply curve for milk and an increase in the market price. The exit of milk farmers will continue until the market reaches a normal profit for the typical milk producer, when the market will stabilize. As you can see in Figure 14.9(a), a typical milk farmer will earn a normal profit at a price of $4.10 per gallon and a quantity of 80

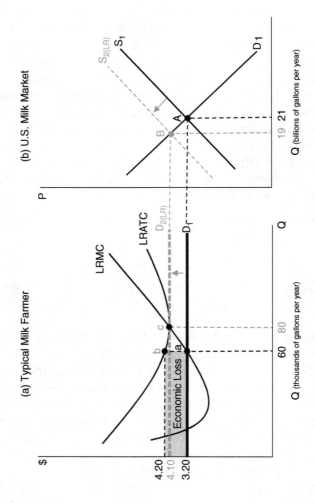

FIGURE 14.9 The U.S. market for milk in 2018.

thousand gallons per year. This can be found at point c in Figure 14.9(a) at the minimum ATC (where ATC intersects MC). Thus, we can expect firms to exit the market and the market supply to decrease until the equilibrium price of milk increases to $4.10 per gallon, the shift from S_1 to $S_{2(LR)}$ (point B in Figure 14.9(b)), at which point the firms that remained in the market will earn a normal profit producing at point c in Figure 14.9(a).

14.4 AN APPLICATION OF SUPPLY, DEMAND, AND PERFECT COMPETITION

To show how we can use the model of perfect competition together with the model of supply and demand to analyze markets, let's consider an example relevant to recent real-world events in the peanut market. In 2017 the Trump administration proposed to cut 20% of the $23 billion the United States spends annually on farm subsidies and price supports. This would involve eliminating or reducing some price supports (price floors), such as the price floor on peanuts. Let's analyze how this would affect peanut farmers.

For example, in 2017 the government-established price floor on the price of peanuts was about $360 per ton. At that price, approximately 3 million tons of peanuts were sold, about 2.5 million to the public and about 0.5 million to the government. (Recall that the government usually buys up the surplus agricultural products when it institutes a price floor.) The government spent $360 per ton for 0.5 million tons of peanuts for a total of $180 million on purchasing surplus peanuts. Economists estimate that the equilibrium price of peanuts would be $300 per ton without the price floor. Finally, peanut farmers were earning a normal profit at the price floor of $360 and producing, on average, 100 tons of peanuts per year.

It is worth mentioning that price supports on agricultural goods are considered useful in stabilizing potentially volatile food prices and in supporting other social goals. The government gives away some of the peanuts it purchases, in the form of free peanut butter for school lunch and anti-poverty programs in the United States and abroad. The government also stores some of the peanuts it purchases so that if the price of peanuts increases in the future, it can release some of their stored peanuts onto the market to reduce peanut prices back to the established price.

Now suppose that the government eliminates the price floor program and stops buying surplus peanuts as part of its cuts to farm programs. What will happen to peanut farmers and the peanut market?

Figure 14.10(b) shows a graph of the peanut market and Figure 14.10(a) depicts a typical peanut farmer based on the information provided above. The market has

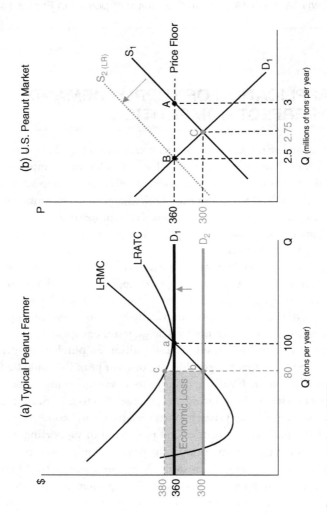

FIGURE 14.10 The U.S. peanut market in 2017.

a price floor at $360, with a total quantity of peanuts sold of 3 million tons per year (point A in Figure 14.10(b)), 2.5 million to the public (point B) and 0.5 million to the government (the distance from point A to point B). The equilibrium price is $300 per ton (point C). The typical peanut farmer depicted in Figure 14.10(a) earns a normal profit at a price of $360 per ton and a quantity of 100 tons per year, which is point a.

When the price floor program is eliminated, the price of peanuts falls to the equilibrium price of $300 per ton, point C in Figure 14.10(b). When the market price falls, the demand curve for the typical peanut farmer falls from D_1 to D_2 and the typical farmer shifts from producing 100 tons at point a to producing 80 tons at point b in Figure 14.10(a). The typical peanut farmer now earns an economic loss of about $80 per ton, the distance from point b to point c in Figure 14.10(a).

What can we expect to happen in the long run? Economic losses will cause firms to exit the market, reducing the market supply from S_1 to $S_{2(LR)}$ and causing the market equilibrium to move from point C to point B in Figure 14.10(b). This process continues until the remaining firms earn a normal profit. The peanut farmers that survive will return to earning a normal profit at point a in Figure 14.10(a), but there will be many fewer of them in the market.

This example shows how you can pair supply and demand analysis, in this case the analysis of how a price floor affects market outcomes, with the analysis of a firm operating in a perfectly competitive market. Next, we consider the implications of perfectly competitive markets for economic policy.

14.5 PERFECT COMPETITION, MARKET EFFICIENCY, AND PUBLIC POLICY

As we have seen, firms in perfectly competitive markets always end up producing at the minimum average total cost in the long run due to entry and exit as well as the lack of product differentiation that prevents any one firm from raising prices above the market price. This means that perfectly competitive markets result in economic efficiency, where **producers supply the quantity of each product that consumers demand at the lowest possible cost (minimum LRATC), no firm earns an economic profit in the long run, consumers' willingness to pay for one additional unit of the product (their marginal benefit (MB), which is reflected in the price displayed in the market demand curve) is exactly equal to the cost of producing one additional unit of the product (MB = P = MC), and producers respond quickly and effectively to any changes in consumers' tastes and preferences**. If all markets worked this way, then we would indeed be experiencing the ideal market system that Adam Smith envisioned, where small firms operating in competitive markets provide consumers with exactly what they want at the lowest possible prices and there is limited inequality because no producer can dominate the market.

The model of perfectly competitive markets underlies the supply and demand model, which is the cornerstone of mainstream economics. Many mainstream economists see competition as the essential characteristic of market economies. Even if markets sometimes depart from the competitive state, these mainstream economists see that as the exception rather than the rule. The implication is that market economies are generally efficient in allocating society's resources and that moderate amounts of government intervention can be used to correct the few cases in which market failures exist.

Political economists disagree strongly with this view of markets. Political economists see power as an essential characteristic underlying all markets. Even in markets that verge on being perfectly competitive, such as agriculture, there are major power inequities. Huge conglomerates like Monsanto control seeds and fertilizer, dictating conditions for many farmers. Large industrial farms are displacing small family farms. The government, often manipulated by wealthy lobbyists, plays a major role in shaping the agricultural sector. In recent years, this has often meant favoring industrial farming over small farms. And in less competitive markets, power relations are even more important.

One of your tasks as a student of economics is to evaluate these positions. Do you see markets as mostly competitive, needing only minor tweaks to achieve economic efficiency? Or do you see markets as mostly dominated by powerful interests, requiring major efforts by citizens and governments to reign in and correct the power imbalances? There is no right answer to these questions, and brilliant economists have come down on both sides of the issues. This is one of the crucial areas of economic debate because it shapes fundamentally one's belief in how much the government should regulate markets and how many of society's economic decisions the government should leave up to markets.

14.6 CONCLUSION

This chapter described the mainstream economics model of perfectly competitive markets. Large numbers of firms in perfectly competitive markets offer homogeneous products for sale at prices determined by market supply and demand. Prices are not influenced by individual buyers or sellers. Firms cannot earn economic profits in the long run due to the ease of entry into the market.

In order to solve problems involving tables in models of perfectly competitive markets in the short run, undertake the following steps:

1. Complete the table you are given in the problem using the formulas for the various costs and revenues.
2. Determine the profit-maximizing level of output by comparing price and marginal cost. The firm should produce every unit for which $P \geq MC$ (beginning after the minimum AVC).

3.   Compare total revenue and total cost at the profit-maximizing level of output to determine the amount of economic profit or loss.

In order to solve graphing problems involving perfectly competitive markets in the short run, you should go through a similar series of steps:

1.   Identify whether or not the firm is earning an economic profit (TR > TC, P > ATC), normal profit (TR = TC, P = ATC), or economic loss (TR < TC, P < ATC) based on comparing total revenue and total cost or price and average total cost.
2.   Put the demand curve (D) in the appropriate spot: D goes above the minimum ATC if the firm is earning an economic profit; D is tangent to the minimum ATC if the firm is earning a normal profit. D is between the minimum AVC and the minimum ATC if the firm is losing money but staying open (if the firm is losing less than its total fixed cost).
3.   Find where the demand curve intersects the marginal cost curve (after the minimum AVC) to determine the profit-maximizing level of output.
4.   Compare price and average total cost at the profit-maximizing level of output to show how much economic profit or loss the firm is experiencing.

The key to solving perfect competition problems involving the long run is determining whether or not firms will enter or exit the market. If the typical firm in a perfectly competitive market is earning an economic profit, new firms will enter the industry, increasing the market supply curve and decreasing the market price until the market reaches an equilibrium price where the typical firm earns a normal profit. If the typical firm in a perfectly competitive market is experiencing an economic loss, firms will exit the market, market supply will decrease, and market price will increase until the remaining firms earn a normal profit. Perfectly competitive markets always return to earning a normal profit in the long run thanks to easy entry and exit.

Often in problems we will assume that the firm's short-run costs are the same as its long-run costs. In competitive markets featuring small competitors, firms rarely change the size of their operations. Thus, it is safe to assume that the firm's short-run average total cost curve is very similar to its long-run average total cost curve. You will see this assumption made in some of the problems below.

Finally, we considered briefly whether or not the model of perfect competition is a reasonable description of how all markets work—competitive, efficient, and responsive to consumers and workers—or whether most markets involve significant and widespread power inequities and market failures. This is a crucial issue for you to resolve and one we will take up in some depth later in the book.

Now that we have described the functioning of the most competitive market structure, we are going to investigate its polar opposite, the least competitive market structure of monopoly. Both Adam Smith and Karl Marx railed against the evils of monopoly. But as we will see, the real world is complicated. Some monopolies are exploitative and abusive. Others serve the public interest reasonably well if they are natural monopolies that are run effectively. We will investigate monopoly as a market structure in Chapter 15.

QUESTIONS FOR REVIEW

1. Given the assumptions and characteristics of the mainstream model of perfect competition, how important and useful do you think it is for understanding the functioning of modern economies? Explain, and support your answer using examples.

2. Why is the demand curve for a perfectly competitive firm in the wheat market flat whereas the demand curve for a large firm with market power like Coca-Cola is downward sloping? Explain.

3. Why should a firm shut down in the short run if the market price falls below the firm's minimum average variable cost? Explain carefully.

4. A firm in a perfectly competitive market will earn an economic profit whenever (select the correct answer below and explain your answer):
    a. $P > AVC$.
    b. $P = ATC$.
    c. $P > ATC$.
    d. $P < ATC$.

5. Complete the table in Figure 14.11 and answer the following questions.
    a. What amount is total fixed cost in this example?
    b. What is the profit-maximizing level of output in the short run?
    c. What is the amount of economic profit or loss the firm will earn at the profit-maximizing level of output?

6. Groundworks Farm operates in the perfectly competitive market for kale.
    a. In 2010, Groundworks Farm sold 20,000 bunches of kale for a price of $2 per bunch, while incurring average total costs of $3 per bunch and average

Q	P = MR	TR	TC	ATC	MC	Economic profit
0	15		5			
1	15		15			
2	15		23			
3	15		33			
4	15		45			
5	15		60			
6	15		84			

FIGURE 14.11 Table with firm data for Problem 5.

variable costs of $1 per bunch. Show this situation a graph that includes ATC, AVC, MC, and D curves and all relevant numbers. On your graph, show each of the following as precisely as possible: (1) economic profit or loss, (2) average fixed cost (AFC), (3) average variable cost (AVC), and (4) total revenue (TR).

b.   In 2016, after kale had been labeled a "super food," the price of kale shot up to $5 per bunch. Draw a new graph of Groundworks Farm using the new market price of $5. Include ATC, AVC, MC, and D curves. Select appropriate numbers for ATC, AVC, and Q based on the numbers in part a above. Next to your graph of Groundworks Farm draw a graph of the kale market. Show what will happen to both graphs in the long run, select appropriate new numbers, and explain your answer briefly in words. Assume $LRMC = MC$, $LRATC = ATC$, and that Groundworks is a typical kale farmer.

7.   Complete the table in Figure 14.12 and answer the following questions.
   a.   What is the profit-maximizing level of output?
   b.   What is the firm's economic profit or loss at the profit-maximizing level of output?
   c.   If we assume that this firm is typical of firms in the industry and that this firm's short-run costs are the same as its long-run costs, what can we expect to happen in the long run? What price will end up being the market equilibrium price in the long run? Explain.

Q	TC	TVC	MC	AC	AVC	P	TR
0	$10,000					$20	
100	11,000					20	
200	11,800					20	
300	12,500					20	
400	13,300					20	
500	14,300					20	
600	15,500					20	
700	16,900					20	
800	18,500					20	
900	20,300					20	
1000	22,300					20	
1100	24,600					20	
1200	27,200					20	
1300	30,200					20	
1400	33,700					20	
1500	37,900					20	

FIGURE 14.12 Table with firm data for Problem 7.

Monopoly and monopoly power

Natural and nonnatural monopolies and how the government regulates them

In Chapter 14 we studied the most competitive market structure, perfect competition. Now we turn to the opposite end of the spectrum, monopoly, which is the least competitive market structure. Like perfect competition, monopoly is also a rare market structure with relatively few examples. However, one of the main reasons we do not have more monopolies is that the government has worked to preserve competition and prevent monopolies from forming by passing and enforcing antitrust laws. Most economists believe that the market system works reasonably well when it is competitive but that it works very poorly in the presence of monopoly. Therefore, unregulated monopolies are not allowed in the United States.

Monopoly is seen as one of the great evils in capitalist economic systems by most economists. Monopolies can earn economic profits indefinitely due to barriers to entry, and they have little incentive to be efficient and innovative given the lack of competition. Adam Smith railed against the power of monopolies to manipulate markets for their own benefit at the expense of consumers and workers. Karl Marx worried that the entire capitalist system was headed toward monopolies in every industry, as companies grew larger and more concentrated, swallowing up smaller competitors in the process.

However, some conservative economists worry little about monopolies because they believe that all markets, even monopolistic ones, are contestable. Economists who have complete faith in the market system believe that at some point a competitor will come along to dethrone any dominant firm. Therefore, no action needs to be taken against a monopolist—the market will solve that problem by itself. In contrast, modern political economists believe that monopolists can use their

DOI: 10.4324/9781315636924-19

power to maintain their dominance indefinitely and that the modern economy is so monopolistic that we should call it "monopoly capitalism." From this perspective, monopoly power is the source of many of the problems in modern capitalism, including inequality, corporate crime, manipulative advertising, and intense lobbying. Most mainstream economists fall somewhere in the middle, viewing monopolies as a significant problem that is sometimes, but not always, addressed by markets in the long run.

It is also important to note that there are two types of monopolies, natural and nonnatural. Natural monopolies exist where it is actually more efficient to have one firm provide a particular good or service, such as electricity, water, sewer, roads, and other public services and utilities. However, natural monopoly goods or services must be provided or regulated by the government so that consumers are not abused by the monopolistic firm. (Just imagine how much you would have to pay for water if the local, monopolistic water company were allowed to charge whatever price it wanted for water service!)

Nonnatural monopolies occur when monopolies arise in cases where it is not more efficient to have a monopoly. Nonnatural monopolies can be deeply problematic, slowing innovation and gouging consumers. Governments usually use antitrust laws to force nonnatural monopolies to be more competitive. No matter the type, monopoly firms require regulation in order to meet the needs of consumers in a fair, efficient, nonexploitative manner.

This chapter begins by working through the mainstream economics model of profit maximization in monopoly markets. We then discuss the best options for regulating natural and nonnatural monopolies and why monopolies are considered inefficient from a theoretical perspective. The chapter also contains a short case study of Google's near-monopoly over search engines in Europe. We conclude with a section on the prevalence of monopoly power in modern capitalism that has led political economists to label the current economic system as monopoly capitalism. This is contrasted with the Austrian view that almost all markets, even monopolistic ones, are contestable.

15.0 CHAPTER 15 LEARNING GOALS

After reading this chapter you should be able to:

- Explain why price (demand) is greater than marginal revenue in industries with market power and downward-sloping demand curves.

- Determine the profit-maximizing level of output for a monopolist in the short run using a table or a graph.

- Explain what a natural monopoly is and why economists prefer to have one firm in such industries.

■ Evaluate different policy options for regulating different kinds of monopolies.

■ Analyze the different views of monopolies and monopoly power by Austrian, mainstream and political economists.

15.1 MONOPOLY CHARACTERISTICS

Monopolies are industries in which there is no significant competition. The major characteristics of a monopolistic industry are the following:

1. **One seller**: There is only one firm with no competitors in a monopolistic market.
2. **Unique product**: There are no close substitutes for a monopoly good. A monopolist produces a product that is unlike other products.
3. **Prohibitive barriers to entry**: In natural monopolies no other firms can enter the market due to economies of scale. In nonnatural monopolies, the barriers to entry include ownership of a unique resource, first mover advantages, or legal prohibitions such as patents, copyrights, or legally granted franchises. With prohibitive barriers to entry, monopolies can earn an economic profit in the long run.
4. **Complete control over prices**: With no threat of competition, a monopolist can set prices wherever they wish to maximize profits. With no substitutes, their demand curve is downward sloping and tends to be extremely inelastic.

Each of these characteristics has important implications. The fact that there are no close substitutes means that a monopolist does not need to worry about competition of any kind. Monopolies do not have to keep prices low in order to compete, and they do not have to invest in innovations to keep up with competitors. They do not typically need to advertise to preserve or increase their market share.

The power that monopolies have over the market stems from barriers to entry—the forces that are keeping competitors out of the market. In the case of natural monopolies, the barrier to entry is economies of scale. The bigger the firm is, the lower their costs of production. The largest firm will have the lowest costs, driving all other firms out of business. This is true for all public utilities such as electricity, water, and sewer, as we will see below. With natural monopolies, we want to allow them to monopolize the industry because this results in the lowest possible costs of production. However, we will still need to regulate the prices that natural monopolies charge and install provisions to encourage innovation in order for them to function efficiently.

Nonnatural monopolies arise for reasons other than efficiency. Ownership or control of a key resource, such as De Beers' control over the supply of diamonds or Alcoa's control over bauxite, the main ingredient in aluminum, results in an inefficient, price-gouging monopoly. In many software markets and some technology industries, we see significant first mover advantages, where the first company to create and dominate a market stays in control and experiences a near monopoly. Amazon, eBay, PayPal, and Facebook all dominate sectors of online markets. Apple dominates tablets and smartphones. These companies were the first to dominate a particular market at a national scale. Once everyone is used to using their products, consumers are very reluctant to switch and competitors find it almost impossible to break into the market. Monopolies also exist due to patents in drug and technology markets that give companies a temporary monopoly for up to 20 years. This is designed to foster innovation so that companies have a direct incentive to invent new products. Consumers will pay a fortune in the short run for the monopoly good but will benefit in the long run. Nonnatural monopolies often need to be regulated to prevent them from abusing consumers via price gouging and poor-quality service. This usually involves using antitrust laws to prevent domination of markets and preserve a measure of competition, as we will see below.

Any form of monopoly faces a downward-sloping demand curve. The firm controls the entire market for the product it is producing, so the firm's demand curve is the market demand curve. With a downward-sloping demand curve, we get a marginal revenue curve that is downward sloping and twice as steep as the demand curve, a topic we take up in the next section.

15.2 DEMAND AND MARGINAL REVENUE CURVES FOR A MONOPOLY

Figure 15.1 contains a table with information on quantity (Q), price (P), total revenue ($TR = P \times Q$) and marginal revenue ($MR = (\Delta TR / \Delta Q)$). The P column is also the firm's demand curve ($P = D$). First notice that as the monopolist increases

Q	P=D	TR=P*Q	$MR = \frac{\Delta TR}{\Delta Q}$
0	$ 24	$ 0	$ ---
1	20	20	20
2	16	32	12
3	12	36	4
4	8	32	-4
5	4	20	-12
6	0	0	-20

FIGURE 15.1 Table showing Q, P, TR, and MR for a monopolist.

production of output, (Q), the price falls. In a monopoly, because the firm controls the entire market, the more the firm floods the market with its products, the lower the price will become. If Apple wanted to sell twice as many iPhones, it would have to lower the price significantly in order to sell that much more than it currently does.

Second, notice that the total revenue column first increases and then decreases. This is because there are two forces at work on firms that face a downward-sloping demand curve: Lowering their price brings in more money from selling additional units of output (Q), but lowering prices reduces the amount of revenue the firm gets on each unit it sells. If the firm wants to sell one unit, $Q = 1$, it charges a price of $20. The total revenue from selling the first unit is $20 ($P \times Q = \$20 \times 1 = \$20$), which is also equal to the marginal revenue of the first unit. When you only sell one unit, the revenue you get from that additional unit is the same as your total revenue.

If the monopolist wants to sell a quantity of two units, $Q = 2$, the firm has to drop its price from $20 to $16. This makes the firm an additional $P = \$16$ from selling a second unit, but the firm loses $4 on the first unit that it could have sold for $20, for a net increase in revenue of $12. Or, to put it differently, the firm faces a choice: It can sell one unit for $20 and make $20 in total revenue or it can sell two units for $16 and make $32 in total revenue. The increase in total revenue from selling the second unit, the marginal revenue, is $12.

Similarly, if the firm lowers its price to $P = \$12$ it will sell three units, $Q = 3$. The firm makes $12 when it sells a third unit, but it loses $8 by selling units one and two more cheaply, giving the firm a marginal revenue of $4.

If the monopolist lowered price even more, to $8, it would find that marginal revenue actually becomes negative; the firm loses more money from cutting prices than it gains by increasing sales. Thus, firms that experience a downward-sloping demand curve face a fundamental trade-off when they cut prices between the additional revenue from increasing sales and the decreasing revenue from cutting prices. As you can see from Figure 15.2, which plots out the demand (P) and marginal revenue curves from the table in Figure 15.1, the more the firm lowers prices, the less marginal revenue it gets for each unit. This gives us another important insight regarding monopolies: *Monopolies have a direct financial incentive to keep production low and prices high.*

Now look more closely at the relationship between the price column, which is the firm's demand curve, and the marginal revenue column in Figure 15.1, and the graph of demand and marginal revenue in Figure 15.2. When $Q = 1$, $P = \$20$ and MR $= \$20$. For each unit after that, MR $< P$. In general, the marginal revenue curve starts out touching the demand curve at the first unit and is then twice as steep as the $D = P$ curve.

Recall that in perfect competition, price was always equal to marginal revenue. Now price, which comes from the demand curve, is always greater than marginal revenue after the first unit.

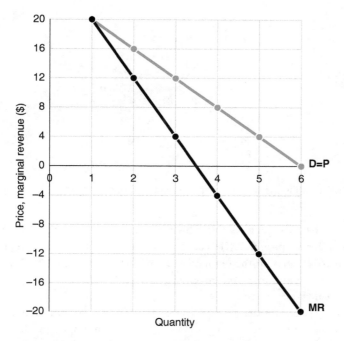

FIGURE 15.2 Demand and marginal revenue for a monopolist.

We can also look at the relationship between a demand curve and its marginal revenue curve using equations. Sometimes it is easier to see relationships between variables and curves via equations than it is with graphs.

The example above used discrete units in which the firm could not sell part of a unit. Its only choice was to sell whole units of the product. Sometimes it is possible to sell parts of units, and that gives us a continuous function.

Suppose that in point-slope form, the equation for a demand curve is $P = -4Q + 24$. The slope of the demand curve is -4 and the y-intercept is 24. This demand curve is depicted in Figure 15.3.

Because total revenue is equal to price multiplied by quantity, we can use the formula for price above and substitute that into the equation for total revenue:

$$TR = P \times Q = (-4Q + 24) \times Q = -4Q^2 + 24Q.$$

Marginal revenue is equal to $\Delta TR / \Delta Q$. For those who have had calculus, that means marginal revenue is the derivative of total revenue with respect to quantity. So we can write marginal revenue (MR) in this case as

$$MR = \frac{dTR}{dQ} = -8Q + 24.$$

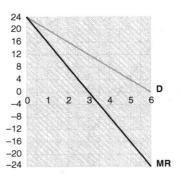

FIGURE 15.3 Continuous demand and marginal revenue functions.

The slope of the MR curve is −8, which is exactly twice as steep as the demand curve. The y-intercept of the MR curve is 24, the same as the y-intercept for the D curve. This would give us the demand and MR curves in Figure 15.2. Notice that the demand curve and marginal revenue curve still start out equal to each other, and MR is still twice as steep as D.

According to the model of optimization used in mainstream economics, a firm should produce more units as long as MR ≥ MC. In monopoly problems, we use MR and not P to determine the profit-maximizing level of output.

15.3 PROFIT MAXIMIZATION IN A MONOPOLY IN THE SHORT RUN

The table in Figure 15.4 includes information on price, total revenue, and marginal revenue from the table above and adds information on total cost (TC). From the total cost column, you can compute marginal cost (MC) and average total cost (ATC).

The profit-maximizing level of output is found by comparing marginal revenue and marginal cost for each unit. At $Q = 1$, MR = 10 and MC = 4, so the monopolist would make a significant profit on that unit. At $Q = 2$, MR = 6 and MC = 1, so that unit is also profitable to produce. At $Q = 3$, MR = 2 and MC = 2. The monopolist still wants to produce this unit because the marginal cost of $2 includes a normal profit within it. For all subsequent units MR < MC, so they are not profitable to produce.

Therefore, the profit-maximizing level of output for this monopolist is $Q = 3$. At that quantity, total revenue is $18 and total cost is $12, so the monopolist earns an economic profit of $6.

Figure 15.5 plots out a graph of the same information. You utilize a monopoly graph as follows. First, identify the profit-maximizing level of output where MR = MC. This is point **a** in Figure 15.5, and directly below point **a** is the profit-maximizing quantity, $Q^* = 3$. Now that you have the profit-maximizing quantity, go straight up from that quantity to the demand curve, to point **b**, and then go over

Q	P	TR	MR	TC	$MC=\frac{\Delta TC}{\Delta Q}$	$ATC=\frac{TC}{Q}$
0	$ 24	$ 0	$ ---	$ 12	$ ---	$ ---
1	20	20	20	18	6	18
2	16	32	12	20	2	10
3	12	36	4	24	4	8
4	8	32	-4	32	8	8
5	4	20	-12	50	18	10
6	0	0	-20	78	28	13

FIGURE 15.4 Table displaying cost and revenue information for a monopolist.

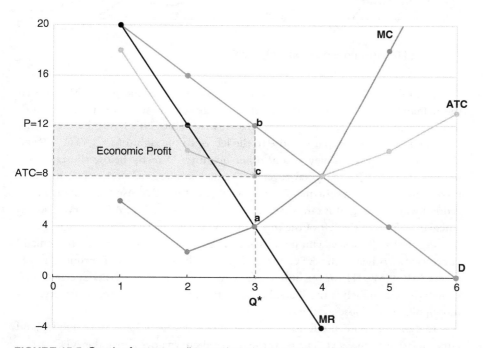

FIGURE 15.5 Graph of a monopolist earning an economic profit.

to the y ($) axis to find price, $P = 12. Also starting at $Q^* = 3$, go up to the ATC curve at point **c** to find the average total cost of producing quantity Q^*, which is $8. The difference between price and ATC is profit per unit, which is the distance between **b** and **c**. Total economic profit is profit per unit multiplied by quantity. This is the area of the shaded box in Figure 15.5 labeled economic profit.

In general, because monopolists control the entire market for their product, they will tend to earn an economic profit. However, it is possible for a monopolist to earn a normal profit or even an economic loss in an industry that is in decline. Polaroid had a monopoly on instant-developing cameras and film for many years, but as these cameras were displaced by higher quality film and digital cameras, Polaroid's profits declined.

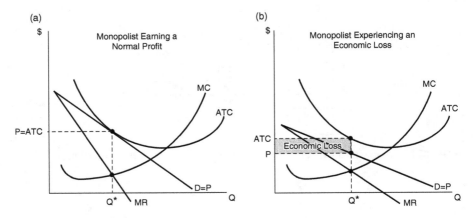

FIGURE 15.6 Other possible monopoly graphs.

Figure 15.6(a) shows a monopolist earning an economic profit. Notice that the demand curve is just tangent to the average total cost curve at quantity Q^*, so that price is equal to average total cost at that point. This has to be the profit-maximizing level of output because to the left or to the right of Q^*, ATC > P and the firm would lose money at any other quantity. Directly below the tangency point and above Q^*, marginal revenue is equal to marginal cost, a fact that also proves that Q^* is the profit-maximizing level of output. Because the demand curve is downward sloping, it is tangent to the ATC curve when the ATC curve also has a negative slope to the left of the minimum ATC.

Figure 15.6(b) shows a monopolist experiencing an economic loss. The demand curve is always below the ATC curve. The best the firm can do is produce at Q^* where MR = MC. However, at that quantity, ATC > P, so the firm experiences an economic loss, which is the shaded area on the graph. At any other quantity, this monopolist would lose even more money.

In general, you can tell how a monopolist is doing by looking at the demand curve relative to the ATC curve. If the demand curve goes above the ATC curve, the firm will earn an economic profit. If D is tangent to ATC, the firm will earn a normal profit at the tangency point. If D is always below the ATC curve, the firm will experience an economic loss. Nonetheless, the vast majority of monopolies earn economic profits, which is why we regulate them.

15.4 REGULATING NATURAL MONOPOLIES IN THE LONG RUN

In the long run, a monopolist can continue to earn economic profits indefinitely due to barriers to entry. New firms cannot enter the market. This means that monopolists will tend to charge high prices and that they have little incentive to innovate. This is objectionable to most economists because it is inefficient. The typical monopolist depicted in Figure 15.7 will earn an economic profit in the long run producing quantity Q_M, where marginal revenue is equal to long run marginal cost (LRMC), and selling at price P_M. The profit-maximizing price and quantity produced by the monopolist can be seen at point M. However, as we saw in the previous chapter, a perfectly competitive firm always produces at the minimum long-run average total cost, which is point PC in Figure 15.7. Thus, a monopolist will charge a higher price and produce a lower quantity than a perfectly competitive firm, leading to a substantial loss in consumer surplus and a substantial dead weight loss. This is extremely inefficient. And monopolists have less incentive to innovate, because they face no significant competition and no threat of new firms entering their market.

To force the firm to be more efficient and less exploitative, regulators have two choices: (1) They can use antitrust laws to split up the company and encourage more competition; or (2) they can regulate the prices that the monopolist can charge via price ceilings or government control. Encouraging competition is the better choice if the industry is not a natural monopoly. Utilizing price ceilings is the better choice if the industry is a natural monopoly.

1. **Regulating a nonnatural monopoly**: In Figure 15.8(a), the firm is a non-natural monopoly because its costs do not decline over the entire market. It

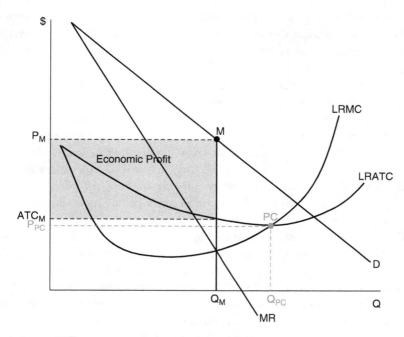

FIGURE 15.7 Monopoly vs. perfect competition.

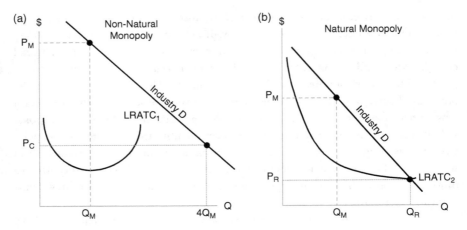

FIGURE 15.8 Long-run average total cost curves for a nonnatural monopoly and a natural monopoly.

is not more efficient for there to be one firm. This is a monopoly because the firm controls the market, not because it is more efficient to have one firm. If it is allowed to continue to control the market, the monopolist will produce a very low quantity, Q_M, and charge a very high price, P_M. But if regulators can foster competition in this market to get four different competitors of a similar size, the market could produce a quantity of $4Q_M$ and charge a price of P_C, a more competitive price. This is similar to what happened when regulators split up the Standard Oil monopoly, which controlled 91% of oil production in 1904, into 34 independent companies. Standard Oil was accused of harming consumers and other industries due to the extremely high prices it charged and the ruthless practices it used to eliminate or buy out competitors. Standard Oil's impact was so vast that it was regularly depicted as an octopus, with its tentacles controlling government and strangling industries and consumers, as depicted in Figure 15.9. This is similar to what happened when regulators forced Microsoft Windows to allow competition in media players and search engines, preventing Microsoft from dominating other markets due to its monopoly power. Nonnatural monopolies are best regulated by fostering competition. Once the market returns to being competitive, the market will function more efficiently.

2. **Regulating a natural monopoly**: Figure 15.8(b) shows a natural monopoly, whose long-run average total cost $LRATC_2$ declines over the entire market. This means that one firm can produce for the entire market more efficiently than a number of smaller firms. The monopolist can make a normal profit at quantity Q_R, producing enough to supply the entire market. If this market were split into many competitors producing much smaller quantities, the price would end up much higher because the cost, $LRATC_2$, is much higher at lower

FIGURE 15.9 Standard Oil's stranglehold on the U.S. economy.

quantities. However, just because this natural monopolist *can* produce a large quantity efficiently and sell it at a low price does not mean that it will actually do so. In fact, this natural monopoly would prefer to produce Q_M, charge price P_M, and make a large economic profit. This is why regulators would need to install a price ceiling on the price the natural monopolist could charge. If regulators imposed a price ceiling of P_R on the monopoly, then the monopoly would want to produce quantity Q_R in order to make a normal profit. This is the **regulated** price and quantity that the government can engineer with the right set of regulatory policies. To add more details regarding how natural monopolies are regulated, we will consider a hypothetical example based on a real-world case.

The table in Figure 15.10 contains monthly cost and revenue data for Comcast, which has a near-monopoly on providing internet service via cable modems in many markets in the United States. Comcast is a natural monopoly because its long-run average total cost (LRATC) column declines over the entire market. Specifically, the demand (*P*) column eventually falls below the ATC column at a quantity when ATC is still decreasing. This can also be seen in the graph of the same information in Figure 15.11. One firm can supply the entire demand for the product more cheaply than several firms. The more houses that Comcast services, the lower its costs per unit. This makes sense given the amount of infrastructure involved in providing internet service. Comcast makes a huge investment in servers and then runs wires to every house and business in a community. Interestingly, if a second company were to offer cable modem service, they would have to build

	Quantity Q (1000s)	Long run total cost, TC	Long-run marginal cost $MC=\frac{\Delta TC}{\Delta Q}$	Long-run average total cost $ATC=\frac{TC}{Q}$	Price P	Total revenue $TR=P*Q$	Marginal revenue $MR=\frac{\Delta TR}{\Delta Q}$
	0	$ 0	$	$ -----	$ 100	$ 0	$ ---
	10	840	84	84.0	95	950	95
	20	1490	65	74.5	90	1800	85
	30	2090	60	69.7	85	2550	75
	40	2660	57	66.5	80	3200	65
Q*	50	3210	55	64.2	75	3750	55
	60	3750	54	62.5	70	4200	45
	70	4280	53	61.1	65	4550	35
P=ATC	80	4800	52	60.0	60	4800	25
	90	5310	51	59.0	55	4950	15
P=MC	100	5810	50	58.1	50	5000	5
	110	6320	51	57.5	45	4950	-5

FIGURE 15.10 Table with long-run cost and revenue data for Comcast internet service.

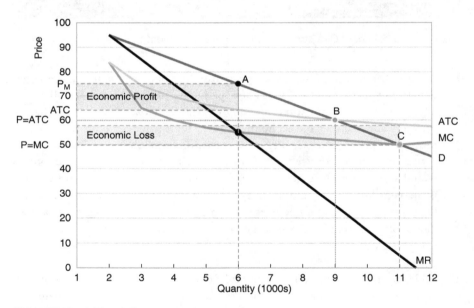

FIGURE 15.11 Regulating a natural monopoly.

the exact same infrastructure, making its cable lines available to every house and business. Having two firms competing would double the costs while keeping the number of customers being served the same! Having a second competitor would also double the cost of providing internet services.

From the table in Figure 15.10, Comcast would maximize profits by producing every unit for which MR ≥ MC. This would mean producing a quantity of $Q^* =$ 50 thousand households per month, because MR ≥ MC up to this point. Comcast would earn an economic profit of TR − TC = \$3750 − \$3210 = \$540 thousand per month.

Most municipalities grant Comcast a monopoly on cable TV and internet service because it is more efficient—a natural monopoly. But they regulate the prices that are charged to prevent consumers from being gouged. The local utilities board limits the price that Comcast can charge by setting a price ceiling. As a further benefit, because P = MR when the price is fixed by the price ceiling, and because MC is declining (this is a natural monopoly), lowering the price the monopolist can charge increases the quantity the monopolist wants to produce.

The utilities board has three different pricing regulations to choose from when it regulates a natural monopoly: (1) an ATC price ceiling (average total cost pricing), (2) a marginal cost price ceiling (MC pricing), and (3) a profits tax. Each of these strategies is used in a different circumstance. Average total cost pricing is used to give consumers a fair price, marginal cost pricing is used for goods where the government wants to encourage consumption of the product, and a profits tax is used to raise revenue and to discourage consumers from buying a product.

15.4.1 Average total cost pricing (sometimes called average cost pricing)

Under average total cost pricing, the government forces Comcast to set P = ATC. This occurs when Q = 80 and P = \$60 = ATC. Here, Comcast earns a normal profit (TR = TC) and more consumers get a cable modem at a lower price. (Note: Sometimes the curved shape of the ATC curve results in the demand curve intersecting the ATC curve twice, once at a high price and once at a low price. If this happens, regulators always choose the lower price to achieve the primary goal of lowering prices for consumers.) In this way, the government makes the natural monopoly market mimic the results of the perfectly competitive market. Average total cost pricing is the most frequently used form of natural monopoly regulation because it gets consumers a fair price, promotes economic efficiency, and does not require a subsidy from the government.

15.4.2 Marginal cost pricing

The utilities board could also use marginal cost pricing, where Comcast must set P = MC. This occurs when Q = 100 and P = \$50 = MC. Note that the price is even lower and the quantity even higher under this plan than under average total cost pricing, but Comcast now incurs an economic loss of TR − TC = \$5000 − 5810 = −\$810 thousand per month. This loss will have to be offset by a government subsidy of \$810 thousand; otherwise, Comcast would eventually go out of business. *The government would subsidize Comcast by exactly the amount of their loss, which would leave them with a normal profit.* The government should only choose marginal cost pricing if they are willing to subsidize the industry in order to encourage more consumers to purchase this product. Regulators use marginal cost pricing with vaccinations and public transportation. We want to provide these goods to as many consumers as possible because of the benefits they have for society. Vaccinations make entire communities healthier, which increases productivity. Public transportation reduces commute times for drivers and reduces pollution. These are goods that generate external benefits: They benefit the purchaser as well as other citizens. In such cases, we set the price equal to marginal cost (and below ATC) so that more people use the product, and we subsidize the company so they make a normal profit and stay in business.

15.4.3 Profits tax

Another option the utilities board can use to regulate Comcast is a profits tax. They can let Comcast charge as high a price as they want and then tax away the economic profits. This approach is designed to raise money to fund state expenditures and to discourage consumers from buying too much of the product. Casinos and state liquor stores are examples of where a state government grants a monopoly to a particular business in a particular town but the state charges that business a huge franchise fee or tax on products to capture their economic profits. Here, too, the monopolist ends up earning a normal profit, and the economic profit amount goes to the state. In the Comcast example above, this would mean the state allowing Comcast to produce $Q = 50$ and make an economic profit of $540 thousand, which would then be taken by the state. Thus, the profits tax results in the highest price and lowest quantity of any of the options.

15.4.4 State-owned enterprise

A final option the government can choose to use is to create a state-owned enterprise to provide the product. Sometimes, state-run companies are actually more efficient that the private sector. State-run health care systems in Europe cost less and have better health outcomes than the U.S. health care system, a system that relies mostly on the private sector. Municipal water and sewer companies have historically provided better services at a lower cost than private contractors. Even internet service is often provided by public enterprises in many countries rather than the private sector. In 2015, 75% of U.S. consumers lived in monopolistic markets with only one private sector company providing high-speed internet access. Meanwhile, European consumers with public internet companies paid much less for much better service (much faster download and upload speeds). In countries with effective governments, state-owned enterprises seem to be more efficient than private sector monopolies, including those monopolies that are regulated.

Interestingly, the cheapest high-speed internet service exists in London via an innovative public–private hybrid system. A public company, British Telecomm, provides high-speed fiber-optic cable to every household. (Private sector companies were unwilling to make this substantial investment.) Then, private sector companies compete with each other using the publicly provided cable to provide internet service to households. The combination of private sector competition with publicly provided infrastructure to ensure high-quality access to the internet for all households has worked spectacularly well.

In general, government officials choose the regulatory option that fits the industry. They use average total cost pricing to get a fair price for consumers. They use marginal cost pricing to encourage consumers to buy more of a product that has external benefits. They use a profits tax to discourage consumers from buying a product and to raise tax revenue to fund state programs. And they use state enterprises to provide services when the private sector cannot do so efficiently.

Figure 15.11 plots out the information in the table in Figure 15.10. If unregulated, Comcast would produce at point A and earn an economic profit at $Q = 6$. Regulators could also allow Comcast to produce at point A and then tax away their economic profits with a profits tax. Under average total cost pricing, Comcast would be forced to produce at point B and earn a normal profit. Under marginal cost pricing, it would have to produce at point C and incur an economic loss, which would have to be paid for by the government as a subsidy.

There is an added problem with the regulation of natural monopolies: Once price ceilings are installed, firms have an incentive to lie about their costs, and they have less of an incentive to produce efficiently and provide adequate service. Under average total cost pricing, firms are guaranteed a normal profit even if their costs increase. So firms could pad their costs or produce inefficiently and they would still make the same profit. Meanwhile, the guarantee of a normal profit would mean that no matter how bad their service became, they would still make the same amount of money.

To circumvent this problem, regulators often fix the price ceiling in place for long periods of time (usually five to ten years). Then if the monopolist's costs increase, the firm loses money but it cannot raise prices. If the monopolist can innovate and lower costs, it can earn an economic profit for a short period of time, after which regulators would lower the price ceiling.

15.5 THE DEBATE OVER MONOPOLIES: RIVALROUS COMPETITION VS. MONOPOLY CAPITAL

Although most economists from Adam Smith to Karl Marx view monopolies as problematic, there are some complexities in the debate over the role and behavior of monopolies. Some conservative mainstream economists and Austrian economists do not see monopolies as a problem, whereas political economists see monopoly power as one of the main problems with modern capitalism.

Conservative (laissez-faire) economists from the University of Chicago and the Austrian School of Economics are less concerned with monopoly than other economists. To them, monopoly is usually the product of superior quality and efficiency of one particular firm, rather than a result of collusion and mergers. If the monopoly firm is indeed more efficient than other firms, then using antitrust laws to split up or regulate the market could result in a decline in efficiency. From this perspective, economic concentration of an industry is assumed to be benign, unless a company actually raises its prices. These economists believe that markets are characterized by rivalrous competition, which is viewed as **a dynamic process in which entrepreneurs are constantly looking for new, profitable opportunities to satisfy consumers and no firm is safe from the entry of new competitors**. Monopolies or oligopolies will eventually be displaced by new and better competitors, so there is little need for regulators to intervene.

This view has had a major impact on antitrust policy in the United States since the 1970s. Whereas previously the U.S. government resisted mergers and fought economic concentration, in recent decades the government has done very little to prevent the increasing concentration of industries. Most mergers are allowed without government intervention.

In contrast, political economists see monopoly power as one of the great evils of modern capitalism. They see that this power is so great and so widespread that Paul Baran and Paul Sweezy dubbed the modern era "monopoly capitalism." According to 2016 World Bank data, if we ranked economic entities—countries and companies—by the total revenue they generate (gross domestic product), *69 of the 100 largest economic entities are corporations, and only 31 are countries!* Walmart is larger than Spain. The Chinese company State Grid is larger than South Korea. Royal Dutch Shell is larger than Mexico and Sweden. Exxon Mobil, Volkswagen, and Toyota are all larger than India. Apple is larger than Belgium. BP is larger than Switzerland, Norway, and Russia. Berkshire Hathaway is larger than Venezuela and Saudi Arabia. And so on.[1]

Political economists see monopoly power as an inherently destructive force. First, low prices are not necessarily a good measure of the efficiency of a particular firm. Walmart and Amazon are able to reduce prices by using their monopoly power to demand lower prices from suppliers and lower wages from employees. Their costs have declined much more than their prices, resulting in higher profits. Second, monopolists often are not innovative. Instead, they buy up good ideas that small entrepreneurs generate, allowing the monopolist to maintain its economic standing and making the monopoly appear to be innovative, when in fact it is doing nothing of the sort. Facebook's purchases of Instagram and WhatsApp and Google's purchases of Waze and Apture are simply the latest in a long line of acquisitions of dominant firms to preserve their dominance. Third, monopolies use their immense financial resources to secure tax breaks and preferential treatment from the government to ensure their dominance of markets.

Many mainstream economists fall somewhere in between. They prefer to regulate monopolies, which is seen as the least efficient market structure. But they do not see monopoly power as a widespread problem, so they do not advocate for significantly greater steps by the government to regulate industries.

Given these disparate views, it is interesting to consider whether or not Google is enough of a monopoly to merit intervention by antitrust regulators or whether they are an efficient, innovative firm that should be left alone. This is the topic of the next section.

Case study: Is the Google search engine monopoly in Europe a problem?

In the 2010s, Google controlled about 92% of the search engine market in Europe and over 97% of the search engine market in Germany. This resulted in Google grabbing 56% of digital advertising revenues in the European Union (E.U.). In the United States, Google's market share was smaller at around 66%, primarily due to the continued dominance of Windows and Microsoft's bundling and promotion of Bing with Internet Explorer. Nonetheless, Google is the dominant search engine in the U.S. market.

Google was so dominant in Europe that the European Parliament began antitrust proceedings against Google. In 2017 the E.U. fined Google $2.7 billion for abusing its market dominance to discriminate against rival comparison-shopping services. Below we describe how Google manipulates markets.

When you undertake a Google search, you will always see several "sponsored" websites that pay Google an advertising fee to list their products. As Google itself states, sponsored sites are

> products and offers that match your query. Google is compensated by these merchants. Payment is one of several factors used to rank these results. These results are based on your current search terms and may be based on your visits to other websites.

In other words, your search results are skewed toward companies that pay Google. And because of Google's dominance of searches, merchandisers have no choice but to advertise with Google in order to have a chance to sell their products.

Search results from Google Shopping are also systematically favored over options from rival shopping sites. When you search for a product, Google's shopping sites will come up more prominently than purchasing options from other websites.

Google is also accused of using its Android operating system on mobile devices to promote Google searching and shopping. Android phones utilize Google searches and Google Shopping as their default options. This is very similar to the type of bundling that Microsoft abused for so many years when it bundled its internet browser and media player software with its Windows operating system.

In addition, a 2015 study by Michael Luca from Harvard Business School and Tim Wu from Columbia Law School along with Yelp's data science team found that Google was skewing local search results in favor of Google-created content. When you search for a local business, the businesses that have paid Google or that have a relationship with Google are more likely to be listed at the top. Thus, based on Google's own statements and recent research, it is clear that Google searches are shaped to benefit Google Shopping and Google advertising. The researchers conclude that "Google appears to be strategically deploying universal search in a way that degrades the product so as to slow and exclude challengers to its dominant search paradigm."

Some laissez-faire economists argue that Google has to provide quality search results or users would switch to other search engines, so Google's market dominance isn't a problem. Also, they argue that technology firms rarely stay dominant forever. IBM dominated mainframe computers in the 1970s and 1980s but was displaced by Microsoft and personal computers. Microsoft Windows dominated personal computers in the 1990s but was displaced by Apple. Google may lose market share as people increasingly switch from laptops to mobile devices that run on non-Android platforms. It can be argued, therefore, that Google's near-monopoly is harmless.

Other economists who are more concerned with monopoly argue that there are incredibly high barriers to entry in this market. Consumers are so used to searching with Google that Google can degrade its search results selectively without fearing that users will switch. Google's purchases of other apps and companies and the extension of its dominance into Gmail and cloud computing (Google Docs) imply that Google is leveraging its market dominance in search engines to expand and dominate other software sectors. This tactic is remarkably similar to what Microsoft did when it used its monopoly of the Windows operating system to gain dominance over word processing, spreadsheets, internet browsing, media players, and other software areas. From this perspective, only a strong antitrust action to preserve competition will ensure that consumers are protected and that innovations continue in the software market.

Here, you can use your own experiences to evaluate some of these arguments. There is substantial evidence that Google's search results are driven to a certain degree by efforts to improve Google's advertising and shopping revenues. This means that Google is not providing you with the "best" search results. Has this caused you to stop using Google as much for searches? Have you investigated and experimented with other search engines, or have you continued to use Google? Do you use Google because it is the best search engine or because you are used to using it and you don't want to bother with trying another one? Or is the reality somewhere in between? Your answers to these questions would help to determine how difficult the barriers to entry are in the search engine market, which would help us predict whether they can, in fact, be displaced by a better competitor. If a better competitor is unlikely to displace Google, then this monopolistic market should be regulated to foster additional competition.

15.6 CONCLUSION

Monopolies are the least competitive market structure, where firms face no significant competition thanks to prohibitive barriers to entry. The fact that monopolies control the entire market gives them a downward-sloping demand curve and a marginal revenue curve that is twice as steep as the demand curve. Monopolists maximize profits by producing where marginal revenue is equal to marginal cost, and they usually earn an economic profit. Monopolies can continue to earn an economic profit in the long run due to barriers to entry.

It is crucial to distinguish between the two types of monopolies—natural and nonnatural—when analyzing this market structure. With natural monopolies it is actually more efficient to have one firm controlling the market, because costs per unit fall as the firm gets larger. We regulate natural monopolies with one of four polices: Average cost pricing to give consumers a fair price, marginal cost pricing to subsidize products that generate external benefits, a profits tax to raise revenue and discourage consumption of a product, or a state-owned enterprise to provide the product or service directly to consumers.

With nonnatural monopolies, it is important to use antitrust laws to preserve and foster competition. Government regulators can take dramatic steps, such as splitting a company up into smaller firms, as they did in the case of Standard Oil. The government can also prohibit mergers that lessen competition, or it can put restrictions on mergers so that the impact on competition is lessened, something they do frequently. And the government can prevent firms from using their monopoly power to disadvantage competitors, which is what regulators did in the cases of Windows and Google.

The next chapter takes up the market structure called monopolistic competition, a market structure that combines elements of monopoly and elements of perfect competition. Firms in this market structure have a monopoly on certain unique characteristics of their business, such as their location or the quality of their product, but the market has many small competitors and no one firm dominates the market. This makes it function very differently from a monopoly.

QUESTIONS FOR REVIEW

1. What are the key differences between the characteristics of a monopoly industry and the characteristics of a perfectly competitive industry? Briefly explain.
2. Explain the relationship between the demand curve and the marginal revenue curve. Why does a monopolistic firm use marginal revenue instead of price when determining the profit-maximizing level of output?
3. What will happen in the long run to a monopolist that is earning an economic profit?
4. The table in Figure 15.12 shows cost and revenue data for Citizens' Electric Co., a monopoly that sells power in the Lewisburg, Pennsylvania, area. Q is in millions of kilowatt hours per day.
   a. Complete the table.
   b. Based on the table, is Citizens' Electric a natural monopoly? Why or why not?
   c. Determine the profit-maximizing level of output. What is the firm's economic profit or loss at that level of output?
   d. What price and quantity would result if government regulators imposed average total cost pricing?

Q	TC	MC	ATC	P	TR	MR
0	90			78		
1	140			73		
2	180			68		
3	210			63		
4	232			58		
5	250			53		
6	264			48		
7	282			43		
8	304			38		
9	328			33		
10	356			28		
11	391.6			23		
12	444			18		

FIGURE 15.12 Table showing cost and revenue data for Citizens' Electric Co.

e. What price and quantity would result if government regulators imposed marginal cost pricing?

f. What would happen if government regulators installed a profits tax?

g. What is the best way to regulate this monopoly? Support your argument carefully.

5. Use Excel or another spreadsheet program to construct a graph that plots out demand, marginal revenue, average total cost, and marginal cost curves based on the table in Figure 15.12. Show the firm's profit-maximizing level of output and the price and quantity that would result from average total cost pricing, marginal cost pricing, and a profits tax.

6. The table in Figure 15.13 is cost and revenue information for a day of trash pickup and disposal by the Lewisburg Trash Company (LTC).

a. Complete the table.

b. Based on the data, if LTC wishes to maximize profits, what price should it charge and what quantity should it produce?

c. What are the maximum economic profits per day for LTC?

d. If the government decided to regulate the price of trash pickup and disposal to ensure that more businesses and consumers would have access to it, what price and quantity would result under average total cost pricing and marginal cost pricing?

e. The government is considering three options to regulate trash pickup and disposal: (1) average total cost pricing, (2) marginal cost pricing, and (3) using antitrust laws to break up LTC so that there is more competition. Compare these options and explain which option you think is best and why.

7. What incentive problems are created by guaranteeing a monopolist a normal profit? How can those incentive problems be addressed by regulators?

8. Determine which of the following monopolistic industries would be best suited for marginal cost pricing instead of average total cost pricing: Sewage, postal service, public transportation, and vaccinations. Explain your answer.

Q	TC	ATC	MC	P	TR	MR
0	$16,000			$180		
100	23,000			160		
200	29,000			140		
300	34,000			120		
400	38,000			100		
500	40,000			80		
600	41,000			60		
700	41,500			40		
800	43,500			20		
900	48,000			0		

FIGURE 15.13 Table with cost and revenue information for the Lewisburg Trash Company.

9. Do you think the government should regulate Google given its near-monopoly on search engines described above? Why or why not? Support your argument.

10. Why do you think many countries and municipalities use state-owned enterprises to supply goods and services in industries that are natural monopolies? Why might a state-owned enterprise be more efficient than a private sector monopoly?

NOTE

1 World Bank, "World's Top 100 Economies: 31 Countries; 69 Corporations," https://blogs.worldbank.org/publicsphere/world-s-top-100-economies-31-countries-69-corporations, accessed December 14, 2018.

Monopolistic competition

The market for local services and other easy-to-enter industries with unique products

The markets we studied in the previous two chapters, perfect competition and monopoly, are interesting but rare market structures. Monopolistic competition and oligopoly are the two market structures we see most frequently in modern capitalism.

Most local businesses operate in monopolistically competitive markets. Such businesses have a monopoly on one or more unique aspects of the business—their location, product cost, product quality, service quality, and/or brand. But the market is still extremely competitive, and it is not dominated by large firms. Examples of monopolistically competitive industries include local services such as doctors, dentists, lawyers, plumbers, and electricians who own their businesses. Local retailers such as restaurants, cafes, convenience stores, bars, and gas stations are also considered to be monopolistically competitive. Products and services in these markets are close but not perfect substitutes for each other.

Simple manufacturing that does not involve substantial investments in technology is also monopolistically competitive. For example, to manufacture clothing, companies only need sewing machines and workers skilled in operating them, making this an easy market to enter.

In general, this market structure is competitive largely because there are few barriers to entry. This means that if a monopolistically competitive industry is very profitable—if most firms are earning economic profits—new firms will enter in the long run and compete away the economic profits. Similarly, if most firms in the industry are experiencing economic losses, some firms will exit the market in the long run and the monopolistically competitive market structure will return to a situation where remaining firms are earning a normal profit.

Monopolistic competition has some key differences with respect to perfect competition. Perfectly competitive markets have a market supply and demand graph that determines the market price of a homogeneous product. Monopolistically competitive markets contain firms producing dozens of slightly different products. Because of those differences, each firm faces its own unique demand curve that is

DOI: 10.4324/9781315636924-20

determined by the firm's unique characteristics—brand, cost, quality, location, and service—along with the number and characteristics of substitutes.

In the long run in perfect competition, economic profits cause new firms to enter, increasing market supply and decreasing market price. The story in monopolistic competition is similar, but there are crucial differences. If new firms enter a monopolistically competitive market, existing firms will see the demand for their product **decrease and become more elastic** due to the existence of additional substitutes. If firms exit a monopolistically competitive market, remaining firms will see the demand for their product **increase and become more inelastic** due to the decrease in the number of substitutes. This type of long-run behavior is unique to monopolistic competition.

Monopolistic competition graphs and charts look and work like monopoly graphs and charts in the short run. Firms maximize profits by producing as long as MR ≥ MC. You compare price and average total cost to determine how much economic profit or loss a firm is experiencing. A key difference is that the demand and marginal revenue curves in monopolistic competition are much more elastic than those in monopolies due to the number of substitutes. And the demand and marginal revenue curves in monopolistic competition shift in the long run when firms enter or exit, whereas in monopolies there is no entry or exit in the long run. Also, firms in monopolistic competition do not need the type of regulations that monopolies need because competitive pressures force firms in monopolistic competition to innovate and to keep prices as low as possible.

This chapter covers the mainstream model of the monopolistically competitive firm in the short term and the long term. We also consider some short case studies of how such markets work and the strategic options available to firms in this type of market.

16.0 CHAPTER 16 LEARNING GOALS

After reading this chapter you should be able to:

- ◼ Use a table or graph of a monopolistically competitive firm to determine the profit-maximizing level of output and the amount of economic profit or loss the firm is experiencing in the short run.

- ◼ Determine what will happen in the long run to firms in a monopolistically competitive market.

- ◼ Analyze how institutional characteristics and barriers to entry affect monopolistically competitive markets.

- ◼ Describe and evaluate the strategic options for a monopolistically competitive firm.

16.1 THE CHARACTERISTICS OF A MONOPOLISTICALLY COMPETITIVE MARKET

Below are the major characteristics of a monopolistically competitive market:

1. **Slightly differentiated products**: Goods or services in this market are close but not perfect substitutes for each other. Differences exist based on quality, cost, branding, service, and location.
2. **Large number of sellers and buyers**: No seller or buyer has a large influence over the market.
3. **Easy entry and exit**: These markets are fairly easy to enter. Economic profits will lure new firms into the market in the long run, whereas losses will cause firms to exit. On average, suppliers earn normal profits in the long run.
4. **Some control over prices**: The unique elements of each business allow some firms to raise prices and be more successful than others. Nonetheless, the large number of substitutes makes the demand curve for every firm fairly elastic and limits how much any one firm can charge.

There are numerous examples of monopolistically competitive businesses operating in every community. We describe some of those industries below.

16.1.1 Local professional services

Doctors, lawyers, dentists, physical therapists, contractors, and plumbers who own their own businesses all operate in monopolistically competitive industries. Even though there are some barriers to entry in each of these professions, entry is still easy enough that every community has numerous professionals in each one. This means that there are limits to the amount any one professional can earn, and high salaries in one area of professional services will lure additional people to enter the market.

16.1.2 Local retailers

Restaurants, bars, cafes, convenience stores, gas stations, salons, and barbershops are examples of monopolistically competitive retail industries. There are numerous local competitors, and it is easy to enter these markets. Although there are some large players in these markets, there are also many small firms competing and the larger firms do not dominate the market.

16.1.3 Small-scale manufacturing

Manufacturing that can be done on a small or large scale and for which there are no significant barriers to entry is usually monopolistically competitive. Even though the clothing manufacturing industry has substantial amounts of branding, large companies do not dominate the market. The largest clothing manufacturing companies in 2016 were H&M (with a market share of 1.5%), Inditex (1.4%), Nike (1.2%), and Gap (1.1%). Clearly, no firm is dominant. New companies, such as Vineyard Vines, which was founded in 1998, are still able to enter the market and gain substantial market share. In addition to clothing, the manufacture of jewelry, non-athletic shoes, purses and bags, leather goods, paper, and lumber also takes place in monopolistically competitive industries.

Because firms in a monopolistically competitive market produce a unique product, their demand curve is downward sloping just like a monopoly's demand curve, and they have a marginal revenue curve that is downward sloping and twice as steep as the demand curve. However, because there are many competitors in monopolistic competition, the demand curve for each firm tends to be very elastic—recall that the major determinant of the price elasticity of demand is the number of substitutes. Even though there are many substitutes, the monopolistically competitive firm's demand curve is *not* flat, like the demand curves facing firms in perfect competition, because products are differentiated and not homogeneous. Some firms can raise their prices above those of competing firms because of quality differences, but they cannot raise their prices too much or they will lose business to competitors.

The behavior of monopolistically competitive firms is interesting in the long run. To beat out the competition and gain market share, firms focus on keeping costs down, branding and marketing, improving quality, innovating, improving service, securing a perfect location, and making other efforts to differentiate their product from those of competitors. Despite such efforts, if most firms in a monopolistically competitive market are extremely successful and earn economic profits in the short run, then new firms will enter in the long run (this market is easy to enter), the addition of new substitutes will compete away the economic profits of many existing firms, and the typical monopolistically competitive firm will earn a normal profit in the long run.

Now that you have had an overview of monopolistically competitive markets, the next section focuses on the mainstream model of profit maximization in the short run. In the short run, the model of monopolistic competition works the same way as the model of monopoly. The only difference is the elasticity of the demand curve, which tends to be downward sloping but fairly flat in monopolistic competition. Demand curves in monopolies tend to be very inelastic because there are no close substitutes.

16.2 SHORT-RUN PROFIT MAXIMIZATION IN MONOPOLISTIC COMPETITION

In the short run, firms in monopolistic competition maximize profits by producing every unit for which marginal revenue is greater than or equal to marginal cost:

Q	P (D)	TR	MR	TC	MC	ATC
0	$ 51	$ 0	$ ----	$ 92	$ ----	$ ----
1	50	50	50	132	40	132.0
2	49	98	48	164	32	82.0
3	48	144	46	190	26	63.3
4	47	188	44	214	24	53.5
5	46	230	42	240	26	48.0
6	45	270	40	270	30	45.0
7	44	308	38	308	38	44.0
8	43	344	36	358	50	44.8
9	42	378	34	424	66	47.1
10	41	410	32	510	86	51.0

FIGURE 16.1 Table displaying a firm in monopolistic competition.

$MR \geq MC$. Figure 16.1 contains hypothetical cost and revenue data for University Hair Design, a firm operating in the monopolistically competitive salon market. The information reflects the price and cost of one haircut at University Hair Design. The variables are the same as in previous tables displaying mainstream microeconomic models: Q = quantity; P = price (demand); TR = total revenue = $P \times Q$; MR = marginal revenue = $\Delta TR/\Delta Q$; TC = total cost; MC = marginal cost = $\Delta TC/\Delta Q$; and ATC = average total cost = TC/Q.

Like the small firms in perfect competition, monopolistically competitive firms have a limited number of specialized jobs, after which the law of diminishing returns applies. This explains the decline and then increase in the MC and ATC columns. In many cases in monopolistic competition small firms can be just as efficient or even more efficient than large firms by better catering to their local customers.

The firm's profit-maximizing level of output occurs at a quantity of 7, where $MR = MC = \$38$. At that quantity, TR = TC = $308, and $P = ATC = \$44$, so the firm is earning a normal profit.

Figure 16.2 plots the same information on a graph. The profit-maximizing level of output occurs at $Q = 7$ where $MR = MC$. Going up from $Q = 7$ to the ATC and demand curves, we find that $P = ATC = \$44$. There is no profit or loss box because the firm is earning a normal profit. As always, a normal profit is included in all of the costs of production.

In the short run, firms in monopolistically competitive markets maximize profits exactly like monopolies do: They produce every unit for which $MR \geq MC$. After determining the profit-maximizing level of output, you can compare price and average total cost (or total revenue and total cost) to determine whether the firm is making an economic profit, a normal profit, or an economic loss. But in the long run, monopolistically competitive markets display very different behavior than monopolies because of the possibility of new firms entering or exiting the market.

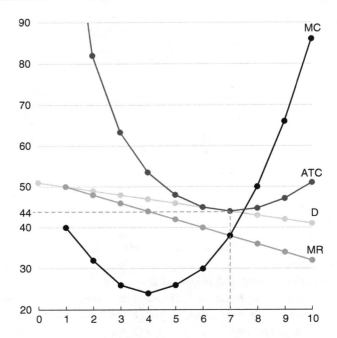

FIGURE 16.2 A monopolistically competitive firm earning a normal profit.

16.3 MONOPOLISTIC COMPETITION IN THE LONG RUN

In the long run, relatively easy entry and exit in monopolistic competition means that if the typical firm is earning economic profits, new firms will enter the market. If the typical firm is experiencing an economic loss, firms will exit the market. Eventually, the market will return to a long-run equilibrium where typical firms earn a normal profit. Now let's consider exactly how this works.

Figure 16.3(a) shows a local restaurant operating in the monopolistically competitive restaurant market earning an economic profit. Any time the demand curve, from which we obtain price, goes above the average total cost curve, the firm will earn an economic profit. The firm maximizes profits by producing quantity Q_1, where MR = MC, and selling at price P_1 (point A on the demand curve). ATC_1 is the average total cost when the firm produces at quantity Q_1. The distance between P_1 and ATC_1 is economic profit per unit, and the shaded area is total economic profit.

In the long run, because there is easy entry into this monopolistically competitive market, **more firms will enter**. This means there are **more close substitutes** competing with existing firms. As more restaurants open up nearby, the existing restaurant will see its sales decline, and it will be less able to charge high prices because consumers can go to a competitor instead of paying high prices.

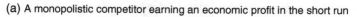

(a) A monopolistic competitor earning an economic profit in the short run

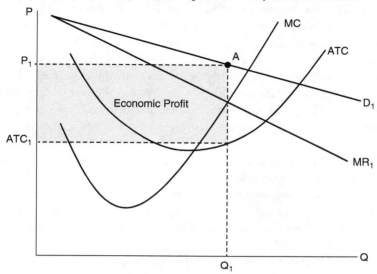

(b) Long run: Firms enter, creating more substitutes, D declines and becomes more elastic, until the firm reaches a normal profit at point B.

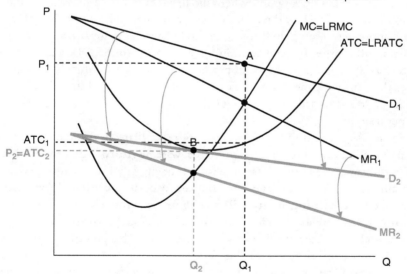

FIGURE 16.3 Economic profit and entry of firms in the long run in monopolistic competition.

The entry of new firms selling close substitutes causes the existing firm's demand curve to decrease and become more elastic (flatter). This can be seen in the new demand curve D_2 in Figure 16.3(b). The entry of new competitors continues until the typical firm in the industry earns a normal profit. This occurs at point B in Figure 16.3(b), where the new demand curve, D_2, is just tangent to the ATC curve. Notice that directly below point B, the new marginal revenue curve, MR_2, is equal to MC, identifying quantity Q_2 as the new profit-maximizing level of output. MR_2 shifts down and becomes flatter to match the changes in D_2. Because $P_2 = ATC_2$, the restaurant now earns a normal profit, and the firm is in long-run equilibrium.

Thus, the D and MR curves both shift down and to the left and become flatter with the entry of new firms producing close substitute goods. This process continues until D is tangent to ATC so the firm is earning a normal profit. The fact that $MR_2 = MC$ directly below the tangency point signals that this is the new profit-maximizing level of output. Note: We are assuming here that MC = LRMC and ATC = LRATC.

The opposite process occurs if firms in a monopolistically competitive market are losing money. Figure 16.4 depicts a firm in a monopolistically competitive industry experiencing an economic loss. The demand curve is always below the ATC curve, so there is no point where the firm could earn a normal profit or an economic profit. The best the firm can do is produce the quantity Q_1 where MR = MC at point A. Going up from Q_1 to the D curve at point B, we get the price the firm will charge, P_1. And continuing up from Q_1 to the ATC curve at point C gives us the average total cost of producing quantity Q_1, which is ATC_1. This leaves the firm with the shaded box of economic loss. The distance between P_1 and ATC_1 (the distance between point B and point C on the graph) is economic loss per unit.

In the long run, if this firm is typical of other firms in this monopolistically competitive industry, then eventually **firms will begin to exit the market as losses mount**. Firms cannot stay in business indefinitely if they are experiencing economic losses. **As firms exit the market and the number of substitutes is reduced, remaining firms will see their demand curves increase and become more inelastic.** The fewer the substitutes, the larger the increase in demand and the steeper the demand curve becomes. This process continues until the remaining firms earn a normal profit.

The demand curve in Figure 16.4(b) shifts up, becomes steeper, and eventually becomes tangent to the ATC curve at point E where $P_2 = ATC_2$ and the firm earns a normal profit. MR_2 is equal to MC at point D, directly below point E, because this is the profit-maximizing level of output. At any other quantity, $P < ATC$ and the firm would lose money.

From these examples, you can see that the typical firm in monopolistically competitive markets always earns a normal profit in the long run. If firms are earning an economic profit in the short run, in the long run firms will enter; the

(a) A monopolistic competitor earning an economic loss in the short run

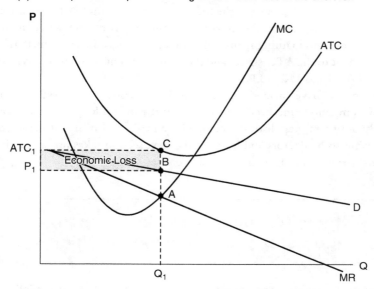

(b) Firms exit, causing D to increase and become steeper until remaining
    firms in this monopolistically competitive market earn a normal profit

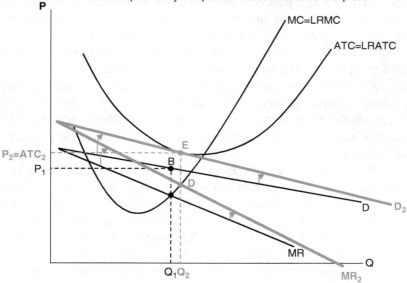

FIGURE 16.4 Economic loss and the exit of firms in the long run in monopolistic
           competition.

demand curves for existing firms will decrease and become more elastic until they are tangent to the ATC curve and the firms earn a normal profit. If firms are experiencing an economic loss in the short run, in the long run firms will exit and the demand curves for remaining firms will increase and become more inelastic until they are tangent to the ATC curve, and the firms earn a normal profit. (We assume ATC = LRATC and MC = LRMC.)

Now that we have covered the essential characteristics of how typical monopolistically competitive markets work in the short run and long run, we turn to a case study of two monopolistically competitive markets. Given that many college students want to be doctors and lawyers, the next section takes up the market for physicians' services and the market for lawyers' services.

Case study: Physicians and lawyers: An application of monopolistic competition

Physicians' services and lawyers' services are both monopolistically competitive markets. Even though there are barriers to entry that seem significant to many people—you must gain admission to a selective graduate program and undergo significant training before you can become a physician or a lawyer—dozens of people in every community are able to become physicians or lawyers. Thus, the market is quite competitive. The services are also differentiated. Physicians are differentiated by their location, quality, and the type of medicine they practice (general practice, pediatrics, gynecology, emergency medicine, palliative care, surgery, etc.). Lawyers are differentiated by their location, quality, and the type of law they practice (corporate, civil, estate, etc.).

In 2017, the median physician earned $294,000 *after* taxes and expenses. This is more than twice as much as physicians in other developed countries. Meanwhile, in 2017 the median lawyer earned $136,260. What accounts for the fact that physicians get paid so much more in the United States than in other countries and that physicians earn much more than lawyers? The answer is that the market for physicians in the United States contains much more significant barriers to entry. The schooling and training for physicians is about twice as long as the schooling and training for lawyers. But the disparity between physicians' salaries in the United States and physicians' salaries abroad has to do with the institutional characteristics of health care systems in each country and the extraordinary barriers to entry imposed by the American Medical Association (A.M.A.) in the United States.

First, in terms of institutional differences, all developed countries other than the United States have national health care systems. Most physicians in countries with national health care systems are employed by the government rather than operating private practices or working for private employers. In contrast, most physicians in the United States operate in the private sector, and that means they can charge higher prices given that the demand for medical care tends to be extremely inelastic.

Second, extraordinary barriers to entry exist in the U.S. market due to efforts by the A.M.A. to restrict the number of physicians. In a normal monopolistically competitive market we would expect extremely high salaries to lead to the entry of additional physicians into the market until physicians' salaries fell to a more reasonable level comparable with other countries. That cannot happen in the United States. The number of accredited medical schools has declined from 166 a century ago to 131 in the 2010s, despite a growing population and an increasing demand for physicians. The A.M.A., which is the body responsible for accrediting medical schools, has generally refused to license new medical schools in order to restrict the number of physicians and keep physicians' salaries high. In 2015 the United States ranked 26th out of 28 OECD (Organization for Economic Cooperation and Development) countries in medical graduates per capita due to restrictions on the number of physicians. Interestingly, because the A.M.A. does not impose similar restrictions on nursing, the United States ranks 5th out of 28 OECD countries in nursing graduates per capita. The A.M.A. restriction on the supply of physicians, coupled with a private health system that puts no limits on what a physician can charge, explains the extremely high pay of physicians in the United States.

The market for legal services used to be incredibly lucrative. The United States is one of the more litigious countries in the world, with a substantial number of lawsuits. However, a large increase in the number of lawyers in recent decades has limited lawyers' compensation. The number of law schools approved by the American Bar Association (A.B.A.) increased dramatically from 135 in 1963 to over 200 in the 2010s. The number of students enrolled in law school increased from 50,000 to over 150,000 during that same period, and the number of law school graduates per year increased from 9638 to over 44,000. The United States now has the highest number of lawyers per capita in the world! However, the number of jobs for new lawyers hovered between 27,000 and 38,000 from 2009 to 2017, meaning that there are fewer jobs than there are new lawyers. A surplus of lawyers exists and that surplus has been increasing in recent years. From 2011 to 2017, less than 90%

of law school graduates found a job utilizing their law degree. In three for-profit law schools, Arizona Summit, Charlotte, and Florida Coastal, less than 40% of law school graduates found jobs that required law degrees in 2014. This chronic surplus of lawyers has kept a lid on the salary of lawyers.

After five years of the surplus of lawyers, applications to law schools declined in the mid-2010s, and some law schools closed or reduced the number of students they accept. However, there is a structural problem in the law school market: Law schools have an incentive to keep the number of law students high so they continue to get tuition revenue, even if their students do not get jobs. Many law schools have responded to the drop in applications by lowering standards so they can continue to fill their law school classrooms and keep the law school tuition dollars rolling in. Law school graduates who attend good universities and finish in the top half of their class generally have no trouble finding jobs. But for other students, the surplus of lawyers creates a major problem.

Given the examples of the market for physicians' services compared with the market for lawyers' services, a few important trends emerge. First, market outcomes are shaped by institutional structures, including the national environment. For physicians, whether or not the health care system is public or private has a large impact on salaries. For lawyers, the litigious nature of the population and the legal code have a major impact on the market for lawyers' services. Second, market outcomes are affected significantly by the degree of barriers to entry. Substantial barriers to entry in medical schools result in higher salaries for doctors, whereas fewer barriers to entry in law schools results in lower salaries.

Markets and the institutions governing those markets also take time to adjust. The glut of lawyers was first widely discussed in 2009 during the recession that followed the financial crisis. It took about five years for the number of applicants to adjust significantly, and it is taking even longer for law schools to adjust their practices. The A.M.A. is finally discussing the possible accreditation of new medical schools given that many high-quality candidates cannot gain admission into U.S. medical schools and that the scarcity of doctors in the United States is leading hospitals and doctors' practices to hire physicians with medical degrees from other countries. Institutions often adjust slowly to major shifts in markets.

Despite the institutional variations, both the market for physicians and the market for lawyers follow the general patterns of monopolistically competitive markets to a degree. New competitors try to enter the market if it is particularly lucrative, like the market for physicians, whereas fewer people choose to enter a market that is not as likely to be as lucrative, such as law. The area in which we see the most difference in monopolistically competitive markets is the strategic focus of firms as they try to differentiate their products from their competitors, something that is studied by political economists.

16.4 STRATEGIC FOCUS: COSTS, QUALITY, LOCATION, SERVICE, AND BRANDING

Monopolistically competitive markets tend to be somewhat uneven, with some firms doing quite well while others just barely survive. A good way to think about this type of market is that even though the typical firm may be earning a normal profit, some firms are able to do better than that if they are particularly successful. However, these successes do not always last. McDonald's dominated the fast food market for many years. However, as noted earlier, the rise of fast-casual restaurants like Chipotle, Panera Bread, and Starbucks has cut into their market share. Chipotle was the most rapidly growing fast-casual restaurant until a series of health scares at their restaurants undermined their performance in the mid-2010s. Becoming one of the rare firms that is more successful than the typical firm requires luck and a strategic focus that connects with modern consumers.

In order to differentiate themselves from the other competitors, and in hopes of being one of the more successful firms in the industry, monopolistic competitors tend to focus on five strategic factors: costs, quality, location, service, and branding. We can see all of these behaviors in the clothing manufacturing industry.

16.4.1 Clothing manufacturing

In order to minimize **costs**, almost all clothing manufacturing companies use factories in developing countries where labor is inexpensive and environmental regulations are lightly enforced. China and India are the world's largest textile exporting countries and Bangladesh is the fifth largest. Some companies focus almost exclusively on low prices, which means producing clothing for the lowest cost possible.

Other firms use higher-**quality** materials and higher quality sewing subcontractors to manufacture their clothes. Some, such as True Religion, even use workers in the United States instead of less expensive workers overseas.

The **location** where the clothes are sold is also important. Inexpensive clothes need to be sold in stores where lower-income consumers shop, such as Walmart and Target. Clothing companies often offer to provide clothes to Walmart for less than they offer clothes to other retailers so Walmart will agree to sell their clothing. If you manufacture clothing for the inexpensive end of the market, getting your products into Walmart can be the key to success. Higher end clothes need to be sold in stores where higher income consumers shop, located in upscale malls and stores.

Customer **service** is also an issue, especially for high-end clothing. L.L. Bean offers a lifetime guarantee on their clothes. High-end clothing stores offer extensive customer service and often provide free alterations and other benefits. Offering free returns is another way that companies provide premier service to their customers

And **branding** is often the most important route to economic profits in the clothing industry. According to the *Wall Street Journal*, in 2011 it cost True Religion $50 to make a pair of its best-selling Super T Jeans. True Religion then sold those jeans to retailers for $152, and the retailers then sold the jeans to consumers for an average of $335. That is an extraordinary markup of 670%. Companies without brand name recognition often have to settle for a wholesale markup of 10%.

The strategic considerations change dramatically depending on the industry. Gas stations tend to make most of their profits from their convenience store and restaurant operations. Chains like Sheetz and Wawa lure consumers into their stores via inexpensive gas and then count on selling soft drinks and food to customers at high markups. To get the most customers possible into their stores, they pay a premium for locations on busy roads with lots of parking and easy access.

These examples show how complex business strategy can be in monopolistically competitive markets. The mainstream model of profit maximization described earlier can tell us about the general tendencies in these markets and whether or not we are likely to see firms entering or exiting. To understand the varied experiences of specific firms, you would need to study their particular strategies and the competitive landscape in more detail.

16.5 CONCLUSION

Monopolistically competitive market structures are some of the most common and important markets in modern capitalist economic systems. Firms in these markets sell differentiated products that are close substitutes for competing products. Easy entry and exit ensure that the typical firms earn normal profits in the long run.

In the mainstream economics model of monopolistic competition, firms maximize economic profits by producing every unit for which marginal revenue is greater than or equal to marginal cost. Once the profit-maximizing level of output is determined, the amount of economic profit or loss is determined by comparing price and average total cost or total revenue and total cost. In the long run, economic profits prompt new firms to enter, and the addition of more substitutes causes the demand curve for existing firms to decrease and become more elastic until firms earn a normal profit. Economic losses prompt firms to exit the market in the long run, and that causes the demand curve for surviving firms to increase and become more inelastic, because there are fewer substitutes. This process continues until firms earn a normal profit.

We see variations in monopolistically competitive markets due to differences in barriers to entry. And we see significant strategic differences in how monopolistically competitive firms try to differentiate their products from those of their competitors. This makes case studies of such markets interesting and complex.

The next chapter turns to the other important and common market structure we see in modern capitalism: Oligopoly. Oligopolistic markets are dominated by a few huge firms, and the strategic interplay between those huge firms is particularly complex and fascinating.

QUESTIONS FOR REVIEW

1. How does monopolistic competition differ from perfect competition? How does monopolistic competition differ from monopoly?
2. What are the major ways in which firms in a monopolistically competitive industry differentiate their products from the products of their competitors? Explain and give examples from an industry other than those that are described in this chapter.
3. The table in Figure 16.5 contains cost and revenue data for Cafe Latte, a local cafe in the monopolistically competitive cafe market. Q = quantity; P = price; TC = total cost; TR = total revenue; MR = marginal revenue; MC = marginal cost; ATC = average total cost.
    a. Complete the table and determine the profit-maximizing level of output. Compute economic profit or loss at this quantity.
    b. Now suppose that a number of new cafes enter the market. What do you expect to happen to Cafe Latte? Explain carefully.
4. In 2017, the top grossing iPhone mobile gaming apps were Pokémon Go ($2.1 billion), Candy Crush Saga ($1.6 billion), Clash Royale ($1.2 billion), and Game of War: Fire Age ($0.8 billion). There were 783,269 gaming apps available at that time, and the total annual gross revenue from iPhone mobile app gaming was estimated at over $26 billion. Revenue sources included download purchases, in-app purchases, and advertising. Would this industry be characterized as monopolistic competition? Why or why not?

Q	TC	MC	ATC	P	TR	MR
0	9			12		
1	13			10		
2	14			8		
3	16			6		
4	20			4		
5	26			2		
6	38			0		

FIGURE 16.5 Table showing cost and revenue data for Café Latte.

5. Wineries are considered to be in a monopolistically competitive industry. Suppose that the Fero Winery current sells 10,000 bottles of wine per month at a price of $15 per bottle, while incurring average total cost of $10 per bottle. Draw a graph of the Fero Winery displaying this information and show what you expect to happen in the long run. Include D, MR, ATC, and MC on your graph. Assume that the firm's short-run cost curves are the same as its long-run cost curves. Explain your answer briefly in words.

6. Suppose that Pronto Restaurant and Deli, operating in the monopolistically competitive restaurant market, currently sells meals for an average price of $12 per meal while producing a quantity of 200 meals per day and incurring average total costs of $15 per meal.

   a. Draw a graph depicting Pronto's situation, including D, MR, ATC, and MC on your graph.

   b. Show TC and any profit or loss on the graph.

   c. Assuming that Pronto is typical of other Lewisburg restaurants, what do you expect to happen in the long run?

   d. Show on the graph what you expect to happen to Pronto in the long run. Assume that the firm's short-run cost curves are the same as its long-run cost curves.

Oligopoly and strategic behavior

The nature of large firm competition and an introduction to game theory

Oligopoly is an extremely common market structure. Any industry in which firms benefit from being large due to significant economies of scale usually becomes an oligopoly. This is particularly common in large-scale **manufacturing** of all types. Companies that manufacture steel, aluminum, plastics, cars, cellular phones, breakfast cereal, soft drinks, computers, tablets, and many other inputs and products must be huge to make the massive investments in technology required to be competitive.

Oligopolies also dominate **national retail and service** markets. National distribution centers reduce costs and give firms the market power to demand lower prices from suppliers. This gives Walmart, Target, Amazon, Lowe's, Home Depot, CVS, and other huge firms significant advantages over other retailers. Wireless phone service is dominated by a handful of huge firms led by Verizon and AT&T in the United States. Pay television is dominated by AT&T (DirectTV), Comcast, Charter, and Dish Network.

Social media and other **software** markets are also oligopolistic. Facebook, Twitter, Pinterest, and Instagram dwarf their competitors. This is largely due to first mover advantages. Once consumers build a social network and get comfortable with a particular social media tool, they are usually reluctant to switch to a different one.

Oligopolies also have significant financial advantages. As huge firms, they pay the lowest interest rates and get access to the most favorable financing from banks. Oligopolies can use their vast resources to construct national and international

DOI: 10.4324/9781315636924-21

marketing campaigns that give them a far wider reach than smaller firms, which is crucial in building brand identity. They can use their financial resources to curry favor with politicians through campaign donations and by hiring an army of paid lobbyists. And the financial clout of oligopolies also allows them to buy up competing firms, purchase smaller firms with good ideas, and generally maintain their market dominance.

Oligopolies, then, are industries dominated by a few huge firms. With a small number of huge players, the actions of one huge player have a direct impact on the rest of the industry. This creates one of the most interesting characteristics of oligopolistic industries: the interdependence of firms. Oligopolistic firms have an incentive to merge or collude in order to reduce competition and increase profits. Or if they cannot collude, they need to compete relentlessly via innovation and advertising. The complex interplay of firms in oligopolistic industries makes this an extremely difficult market structure to model. Therefore, as we will see below, mainstream economists tend to focus more on strategic behavior using the kinked demand curve model of an oligopolistic firm and game theory.

This chapter begins by describing the characteristics of oligopolistic industries. Subsequently, it takes up the kinked demand curve model and the incentives oligopolists have to collude and merge. Then we develop some game-theoretic models that examine strategic behavior in oligopolistic markets. The chapter also includes some short case studies of oligopolies in wireless service, airlines, and other industries.

17.0 CHAPTER 17 LEARNING GOALS

After reading this chapter, you should be able to:

- Explain the key characteristics of oligopolistic industries and how those characteristics shape behaviors and outcomes in specific industries.

- Use the kinked demand curve model to explain why we often see sticky prices and price leadership in oligopolies and why oligopolies have an incentive to collude.

- List and describe the different types of collusion we tend to find in oligopolies.

- Use a payoff matrix to determine dominant and consistent strategies of oligopolies.

- Analyze and evaluate the behavior of specific oligopolistic industries using the economic theories and tools described in this chapter.

17.1 THE MAJOR CHARACTERISTICS OF AN OLIGOPOLISTIC INDUSTRY

Oligopolistic industries tend to have the following characteristics:

1. **Significant barriers to entry**: Firms in oligopolistic industries need to be huge in order to compete due to large economies of scale. The factors that result in significant economies of scale include the need for large-scale capital and technology, a global supply chain to minimize costs by producing where each input is cheapest, brand name recognition achieved by extensive advertising and marketing, financial advantages, political advantages, and first mover advantages. The existence of barriers to entry means that *oligopolies can earn an economic profit in the long run*.

2. **Domination of the industry by a few huge firms**: Although there may be some small firms in the industry, oligopolies are dominated by a few huge firms, ranging from duopolies with two dominant firms (Coca-Cola and Pepsi) to competitive oligopolies with four or five dominant firms (the airline industry in the United States).

3. **Finished products are differentiated; inputs may be undifferentiated**: Oligopolies in finished consumer goods markets such as cars, smartphones, and computers produce differentiated products and focus significantly on branding. Oligopolies that produce inputs for other firms such as steel, aluminum, rubber, and plastics tend to produce mostly undifferentiated products. When products are undifferentiated, the key strategic consideration is minimizing costs for a given level of quality.

4. **Interdependence among firms**: When a few firms dominate an industry, the behavior of one of the dominant firms affects all other firms in the industry. As a result, firms are constantly analyzing and attempting to predict and counter the actions of their competitors. Or, to reduce destructive competition, firms behave cooperatively.

Given these characteristics, one of the major implications is that **oligopolies are extremely diverse**. Firms in each oligopolistic industry behave very differently from firms in other industries depending on the type of industry, the magnitude of economies of scale, and the competitive landscape that exists. This makes it very difficult for economists to model and predict behavior in oligopolistic markets.

Nonetheless, we do see some patterns. In oligopolistic industries we often see the following major variations in competitive behavior:

1. **Price competition**: Firms largely ignore the interdependence that exists and maximize profits independently of the behavior of competing firms. This type of behavior occurs in the most competitive of oligopolies. In such cases, oligopolistic firms behave like firms in monopolistic competition, although the

entry of competitors is less common due to the existence of significant barriers to entry. This approach is relatively rare in oligopolies, but it does happen in heavy industries producing inputs, like steel.

2. **Strategic competition**: Firms use advertising and marketing, branding, pricing, mergers and acquisitions, research and development, lobbying, and other strategies to gain an advantage over competitors. This is the most common type of behavior in oligopolistic industries.

3. **Collusion**: Firms engage in tacit (unspoken), illegal, or legal collusion to control an industry and to act like a monopolist. This behavior is also extremely common in oligopolies.

We describe each of these types of behaviors briefly below.

17.1.1 Price competition

One of the industries in which we see a strategic focus on price competition is steel. In general, companies produce different grades of steel and whichever firm can produce a particular grade of steel for the lowest price will be the most successful. Instead of focusing on branding and the behavior of rivals, firms try to produce steel for the lowest possible price. Firms engage in some lobbying, where they try to get the government to protect their industry from foreign competition or to take actions to keep taxes and wages low. But the main focus is on production techniques, technology, and skills to keep production costs as low as possible.

17.1.2 Strategic competition

In markets with three or more competitors where there is significant interdependence, we see a lot of strategic competition. Firms will do anything they can in any area to gain a competitive advantage. Sometimes this will mean competing on price and quality. Often it means engaging in significant non-price competition via advertising or any other means possible. Consider the wireless service provider industry.

In 2017 the U.S. wireless service provider market had four huge firms, Verizon (market share of 35.7%), AT&T (33.1%), T-Mobile (16.9%), and Sprint (12.8%). This type of competitive oligopoly displays numerous types of strategic competition.

- Price: Companies regularly engage in price cutting to lure customers from competitors. From 2013 to 2018, AT&T, T-Mobile, and Sprint cut their prices below those of Verizon to try to gain market share.
- Quality: Companies invest substantial amounts to provide the largest coverage areas, fastest speeds, clearest calls, and fewest dropped calls. Verizon's lead in the market is attributed in part to their superior network quality.
- Advertising, marketing, and branding: Wireless companies spend a fortune on advertising. In 2017 firms were spending almost $200 million per month on

television advertising alone. T-Mobile and AT&T spent more than Verizon in their attempt to gain market share.

- Mergers and acquisitions: Verizon has merged with or acquired MCI, AOL, Yahoo, and numerous other companies. AT&T decided to try to acquire Time Warner in 2017 to generate more content for their mobile devices. Sprint and T-Mobile began exploring a merger in 2017, and eventually completed the merger in 2020. The Sprint brand was then discontinued.
- Investment, research, and development: Between 2010 and 2016, U.S. wireless service providers invested $200 billion. This includes efforts to expand the size and speed of networks with more investment in physical capital (wireless towers) and research and development spending to improve technology related to speed and quality.
- Lobbying: The four largest wireless service providers spent about $50 million on lobbying in 2013. In recent years they have lobbied against restrictions on automobile drivers using cell phones and against efforts by consumer advocates to ensure more competition in the wireless provider market by limiting the number of wireless frequencies one firm can own.

17.1.3 Collusion

Oligopoly is the market structure that features the largest amount of tacit, illegal, or legal collusion. In a market with a small number of dominant competitors, collusion can raise firms' profits significantly. In most oligopolistic markets we see firms adopting very similar prices and practices without discussing these strategies with each other—tacit collusion. Until recently, all wireless service providers had hefty termination fees, overage charges, and other hidden fees and charges. Airlines competing on the same route almost always charge the same fares. Almost all airlines began charging fees for checked bags in the mid-2010s. Almost all colleges raise tuition by the same amount every year. Although companies usually are not engaging in overt collusion with these practices, they are choosing not to compete with respect to prices or industry practices, which means they are engaging in tacit collusion, and they are behaving more like a monopoly than a competitive oligopoly.

Sometimes firms in an oligopoly go even further and overtly collude with each other. Most of this collusion takes the form of price fixing, where firms agree to charge a higher price than they would normally charge. Supermarkets have colluded to raise the price of milk, banks have colluded to increase the interest rate on loans, construction firms have colluded to rig the bidding process on government contracts to raise the price of construction, and airlines have colluded on extra charges. The most elaborate form of collusion is a cartel, which is **a group of sellers who work together to coordinate prices, quantities, and sales practices to reduce competition and increase profits**. The most infamous cartel is OPEC (Organization of the Petroleum Exporting Countries), a cartel of oil producing countries.

The reason that collusion is so irresistible in oligopolies is the unique nature of interdependence when a market is dominated by a few huge firms. The kinked demand curve model helps us understand the incentives faced by oligopolies, especially why they tend to adopt similar prices and practices and why they have an incentive to collude.

17.2 THE KINKED DEMAND CURVE MODEL OF AN OLIGOPOLISTIC INDUSTRY

Oligopolies that feature three or more large firms and little product differentiation, like the airline industry, display some interesting patterns:

- Prices are "sticky" and do not change as frequently as prices do in more competitive industries.
- Firms usually match each other's prices.
- Instead of competing with prices, firms use non-price competition such as advertising.
- Every so often, firms engage in a price war in which firms slash prices to gain market share.
- After price wars, these markets usually return to stability and sticky prices.

Paul Sweezy in the United States and R. L. Hall and C. J. Hitch in the United Kingdom developed the kinked demand curve model to analyze and explain these behaviors.

Figure 17.1 depicts the kinked demand curve that oligopolists with several large competitors are likely to face. The kink in the demand curve is due to the strategic dynamics of the oligopolistic industry. To understand these strategic dynamics, let's consider how the airline industry works as a classic example.

In 2018 a typical ticket for a roundtrip flight from New York to Chicago was selling for $122. All of the airlines serving this route—United, American, Delta, JetBlue, and Spirit—charged the same fare. The reason that the airlines cluster together and end up charging the same fare is because of how they expect their competitors to behave.

One of the keys to the strategic behavior of the airlines is that there is very little product differentiation. Research indicates that the vast majority of consumers will simply buy the cheapest airline ticket they can find because the airlines are almost perfect substitutes for each other. This means that no airline wants to charge higher fares than their competitors or they will lose almost all of their customers.

Suppose that United were to raise the price of a ticket on the New York to Chicago route from $122 to $130. If United charges $130 and all of the other airlines keep their prices at $122, they will lose a huge amount of business. This means that United Airlines faces an *elastic* demand curve if they raise their price and none

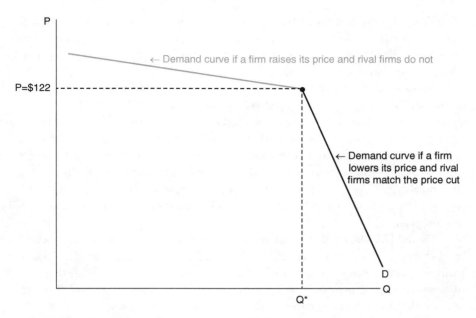

FIGURE 17.1 The kinked demand curve model of oligopoly.

of their competitors follow them in raising prices. Notice that the demand curve in Figure 17.1 is quite flat if a firm raises its price above the market price of $122. This makes United and all the other airlines extremely reluctant to raise their prices because they are afraid to end up being the most expensive option and losing most of their customers. If this happened, their total revenue would decrease when they raised their fares because quantity would fall more than price increased.

But airlines also do not want to lower prices because that will start a **price war**. If United were to lower the price of their tickets on the New York–Chicago route to $99, every other airline would almost certainly match that price cut. If the other airlines did not follow United in cutting fares, consumers would almost all want to fly United and few would purchase tickets from the other carriers. As a result, when one airline cuts its prices, all of the other airlines will also cut their prices by the same amount, engaging in a price war to be the cheapest airline. However, if all of the airlines cut their prices by the same amount, no single airline will experience a significant increase in the demand for their flights. On a typical day, only a certain number of people need to fly from New York to Chicago. Cutting the price of a ticket might cause a few more people than usual to fly, but it is unlikely to have a substantial impact on consumer demand. In other words, the demand curve for an airline ticket is *inelastic* if all of the firms reduce their prices at the same time. People tend to fly because they have a business meeting, family obligations, or a planned vacation. Very few people decide to take an additional flight just because it is inexpensive to do so.

This, of course, makes firms in the airline industry extremely reluctant to lower prices. If they lower their prices, they start a price war and their sales hardly increase at all. Total revenue would decrease because their price would fall by more than their quantity sold would increase.

So firms do not want to raise prices for fear they will lose most of their customers by being the most expensive option. And firms do not want to lower prices for fear of starting a price war. Either way, they would lose revenue by changing their prices. The rational strategy for any firm facing this dilemma would be to charge the same price as all of the other firms and then to compete in other ways. Airlines in recent years have focused on reducing costs (eliminating free meals), gaining brand name recognition (via massive advertising campaigns), and increasing customer loyalty (via frequent flier programs) instead of competing on price.

Figure 17.2 shows that firms in an industry with a kinked demand curve will charge the same price even if they have different cost structures. The kinked demand curve creates a doubly kinked marginal revenue curve. Recall that each downward-sloping demand curve comes with a marginal revenue curve that stars out touching the demand curve at the first unit and that is twice as steep. The marginal revenue curve that goes with a kinked demand curve is flat at first, to go with the flat part of the demand curve, then it drops straight down at quantity Q^* until it hits the steep MR curve that goes with the steep part of the demand curve. Notice that with a marginal cost curve of MC_1, MC_2, or anything in between, the

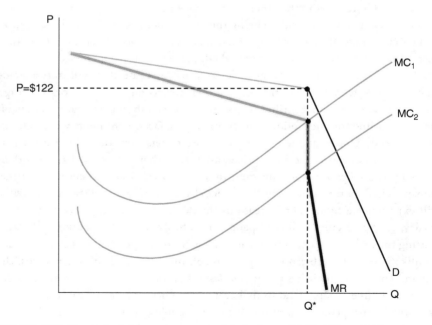

FIGURE 17.2 The kinked demand curve model of oligopoly with MR and MC.

firm will maximize profits by producing at quantity Q^* and selling at the market price of $122.

We see behavior similar to this in many industries, including beer, wireless carriers, potato chips, and soft drinks. Indeed, most oligopolies adopt similar pricing strategies when significant product differentiation does not exist.

The kinked demand curve also shows us why it is almost irresistible for companies in oligopolies to collude. The demand curve when all firms change prices together is very inelastic—the firms are acting like a monopolist with no competition. If they all raise their prices together, then they will make a lot more total revenue. But such coordination is illegal in the United States and in most other countries, so collusion must be done tacitly or illegally most of the time.

17.3 TACIT, ILLEGAL, AND FORMAL COLLUSION

Collusion between firms can take a variety of forms. Because formal collusion is illegal in most countries, most collusion is tacit or illegal.

Tacit collusion that does not violate antitrust laws is difficult to achieve. Tacit collusion occurs **when firms find a way of agreeing on prices or production quotas without actually discussing such things**. If they did engage in discussions to raise prices or reduce production, they could be prosecuted for price fixing or other actions that restrain competition and violate antitrust laws. In order to achieve stable pricing without legal violations, firms often turn to price leadership.

Price leadership is **a type of tacit collusion that occurs when one firm, the industry leader, sets the prices for the industry, and the other firms follow suit by adopting the same pricing structure**. Though this is not technically illegal, firms who do this can still get sued for violating antitrust laws because they are acting as if they are colluding even if they are not doing so formally.

We see price leadership in the airline industry repeatedly. For example, in 2008, American Airlines, the largest U.S. carrier, announced that they would start charging $15 for passengers' checked bags. Almost immediately, Delta and AirTran announced that they, too, would charge *exactly the same amount* for checked bags. By 2017 all of largest U.S. airlines settled on $25 as the charge for the first checked bag.

Interestingly, price leadership doesn't always work. Sometimes we will see one airline test the waters by announcing a fare increase. If the other airlines follow suit, the price leader will keep their fares at the higher rate. But if the other airlines do not increase their fares, the price leader will abandon the fare increase. The result is that airline fares and fees tend to move up and down together, even though the firms are not actively coordinating their pricing strategies.

Price leadership is extremely common in oligopolies. Consider the following examples:

- As the largest U.S. carmaker, General Motors announces the prices of its new model cars each year. Ford and Chrysler announce their prices a little later in the year. Usually, their prices just happen to go up by exactly the same amount as General Motors prices.
- When the United States dominated the steel industry, the largest producer, U.S. Steel, served as the price leader, announcing price increases that were followed by other steel producers.
- The largest British supermarkets, Tesco and Asda, served as price leaders on a variety of food products such as milk, coffee, and tea. Smaller supermarkets usually copied their price changes.
- The dynamite, coal, and cigarette industries in the United States have also engaged in such practices.

17.3.1 Illegal price fixing

When setting prices is done via conversations between firms to plan out price increases, this is called price fixing, and it is illegal in the United States and most other countries. Although it is hard to catch companies doing this, the number of documented cases that exist indicates that illegal price fixing is surprisingly widespread. Some famous examples from the past several decades include the following:

- In 1991, eight Ivy League universities were accused of sharing information on financial aid and tuition that involved jointly setting financial awards in order to avoid bidding against each other for students. The universities settled with the Department of Justice. (Now universities tend to follow the price leadership model, with leading colleges announcing how much their tuition will increase and other universities announcing later that they will increase tuition by the same amount.)
- In 1992, Archer Daniels Midland was caught colluding with its Japanese and Korean competitors to fix the price of lysine, an additive in animal feed.
- In 2004, De Beers, the world's largest producer of rough diamonds, pleaded guilty to the price fixing of industrial diamonds and agreed to pay a fine of $10 million.
- In 2006, 20 airlines were caught fixing the price of shipping international air cargo and were fined $3 billion.
- In 2008, LG, Chunghwa, and Sharp pled guilty and paid $585 million in criminal fines for conspiring to fix prices of liquid crystal display (LCD) panels.
- In 2012, Barclays, UBS, RBS, and other banks were caught colluding to fix the LIBOR interest rate (the interest rate that contributor banks in London offer each other for interbank deposits).
- In 2013, Apple and other online publishers were found guilty of fixing the price of e-books.

Clearly, illegal price fixing is a regular occurrence in oligopolistic markets.

17.3.2 Cartels

Cartels occur when firms engage in formal collusion by working together to coordinate prices, quantities, and sales practices. Cartels used to be fairly common in the United States before they were made illegal by the Sherman Antitrust Act of 1890. In the modern world, only a few international cartels like the OPEC oil cartel and the De Beers diamond cartel that operate outside developed country legal systems have been able to engage in formal collusive arrangements. In these cases, the cartel members meet to develop formal agreements that establish prices, quantities, and sales practices. By working together formally in this manner, the firms in the cartel end up behaving like one firm so that the market works more like monopoly than oligopoly.

The early successes and later difficulties of OPEC provide some insights into how cartels work but also why cartels are difficult to maintain. OPEC currently consists of 14 member countries that controlled 81.5% of world crude oil reserves in 2016. OPEC members also have lower costs of production than most other oil producing countries, allowing them to undercut competitors if they wish.

Historically, Saudi Arabia, with 22% of world crude oil reserves, has dominated the OPEC cartel and acted as the enforcer: When OPEC members refuse to honor OPEC agreements, Saudi Arabia can rapidly increase oil production, causing world oil prices to fall dramatically, thereby devastating other OPEC countries that rely on oil revenues. Now that Venezuela, with 25% of proven crude oil reserves, has a larger share of global reserves than Saudi Arabia, they also have significant power. However, because they do not have the accumulated wealth that Saudi Arabia has amassed, Venezuela is less able to act as an enforcer of cartel agreements.

OPEC was extremely successful in raising the price of oil in the 1970s. In 1973 oil prices quadrupled from $2.70 per barrel to $11.00 per barrel after OPEC agreed to production cuts and after OPEC placed an embargo on oil exports to the United States in retaliation for U.S. support for Israel in the Arab–Israeli War. The drop in Iran's oil production after the Iranian Revolution in 1979 caused another spike in oil prices, as they increased from $12.79 per barrel in 1978 to $35.52 in 1980.

However, these high prices didn't last. Over the next two decades more and more non-OPEC countries began producing oil because it had become so profitable. Meanwhile, with high oil and gas prices, people began to use energy more efficiently, limiting increases in demand. And OPEC countries themselves frequently "cheated" by producing more than the production quotas they had agreed to. As oil prices fell, many countries that had come to rely on oil revenues needed to increase production to make up for lost revenue, causing prices to plunge further. As a result, oil prices fell to $12.28 per barrel in 1998.

The rapid growth in China and other emerging markets in the 1990s and 2000s, along with another round of OPEC production cuts, led to an increase in oil prices to $109.45 per barrel in 2012. However, once again the dramatic increase in oil prices prompted efforts to conserve energy by consumers along with exploration into new forms of energy by producers, especially natural gas from hydraulic fracturing (fracking) and renewable energy from solar and wind power. By 2016 oil prices had fallen to $40.68 per barrel.

Some interesting lessons emerge from the OPEC cartel's experiences. First, OPEC's successes in raising prices made them a massive amount of money in the 1970s and early 1980s. However, this created incentives for consumers to use less energy and for other countries to supply more oil and alternative energy, making it harder and harder for OPEC to control oil prices. Second, it is hard to maintain collusive agreements when there are many competitors involved in the process because individual countries have an incentive to cheat on agreements. Once OPEC agrees to production cuts and prices go up, each OPEC member can make a lot of additional money by breaking the agreement and increasing production above its production quota. But if all OPEC members cheat, then the agreement falls apart and oil prices plunge. To understand the circumstances under which firms cooperate, compete, and cheat in oligopolies, economists have developed game theory.

17.4 GAME THEORY AND THE PRISONER'S DILEMMA

Game theory is **a method for modeling how economic agents such as firms, individuals, or groups interact. Each different model or game involves particular actors, who are able to choose from among two or more strategies. The strategies taken by the actors determine the outcomes of the game. The outcomes of the game, therefore, are determined by the interdependent decisions of the actors**. The strategy one actor chooses has a direct impact on the other actors and vice versa. The mutual interdependence of decisions makes game theory a useful tool in analyzing the strategies of interdependent firms in oligopolies.

17.4.1 Prisoner's dilemma

The original, classic game upon which game theory is based is called the prisoner's dilemma. It is called this because it reflects a police tactic in questioning two prisoners who have been arrested for committing two crimes. The police have evidence that the prisoners engaged in a lesser crime, but they do not have evidence for a more serious crime that occurred, so they need to get the prisoners to confess. The police separate and isolate the prisoners and offer each of them a deal: Implicate the other suspect in the serious crime and you will go free if your partner does not confess. But if the prisoner chooses not to confess and their partner does confess, the prisoner who does not confess will receive the maximum prison sentence. The police do this because, in isolation, each prisoner has a direct incentive to confess. If a prisoner thinks that his criminal partner will confess, then he must confess, too, or face the longest possible penalty. If a prisoner thinks that his fellow criminal will not confess, he will still get a shorter sentence by confessing.

This incentive structure is captured in the payoff matrix in Figure 17.3, which shows the options available to each player and the payoffs they will receive depending on each player's actions. You determine the likely outcomes of a pay-off matrix by "becoming" each of the players and trying to determine what strategy they should purse. For example, in the payoff matrix in Figure 17.3, what should Bonnie do?

Suppose Bonnie thinks that Clyde will not confess. This means Bonnie is fac-ing the choices in the first row of the payoff matrix: If Clyde chooses not to confess, then Bonnie will get 1 year in prison if she does not confess, or she will get 0 years in prison if she does confess. She has a clear incentive to confess. If Bonnie thinks Clyde will confess, then she will get 20 years in prison if she does not confess or 10 years in prison if she does confess. Once again, she will be better off if she confesses. Thus, Bonnie has a dominant strategy, which is a **situation in game theory that exists when the expected payoffs from one option are better no mat-ter what the other player does**.

Clyde also has a dominant strategy. If Clyde thinks that Bonnie will not con-fess, Clyde is looking at options in the first column of the payoff matrix. If Bonnie does not confess and Clyde does not confess, Clyde will get 1 year in prison. If Bonnie does not confess and Clyde confesses, Clyde will get 0 years in prison, which is a better option for Clyde. Similarly, if Bonnie confesses but Clyde does not, Clyde gets 20 years in prison. If Bonnie confesses and Clyde confesses, Clyde will get 10 years in prison, which is a better option for Clyde. Thus, Clyde also has a dominant strategy: He is always better off if he confesses.

Because both players have a dominant strategy, this game has a Nash equi-librium, **where each player chooses a particular strategy and no player benefits by changing strategies while the other player keeps their strategy unchanged**. In a one-time game we would expect Bonnie and Clyde to end up in the bottom right quadrant. When players are at a Nash equilibrium, they have no incentive to change their decision because they will be worse off if they change.

		Bonnie's strategies	
		Bonnie does NOT confess	**Bonnie confesses**
Clyde's strategies	Clyde does NOT confess	Bonnie: 1 year in prison Clyde: 1 year in prison	Bonnie: 0 years in prison Clyde: 20 years in prison
	Clyde confesses	Bonnie: 20 years in prison Clyde: 0 years in prison	Bonnie: 10 years in prison Clyde: 10 years in prison

FIGURE 17.3 A payoff matrix showing the prisoner's dilemma game.

Does this mean in the real world that prisoners who are caught will always confess and incriminate their partners in crime? Not at all. Often in the real world people are loyal to each other. In fact, loyalty and reciprocity are fundamental human traits that often affect the outcome of real-world interactions. Also, if Bonnie and Clyde were smart, they would have agreed on a plan ahead of time not to confess, and that would end up in both of them being better off than if they follow the dominant strategy of confessing. Thus, the strategic behavior in the prisoner's dilemma game depends on issues of trust, loyalty, reciprocity, and collusion.

There are clear parallels to the world of oligopoly. Firms are usually better off if they collude and agree on an action together, such as raising prices. But a firm will often cheat to gain an advantage over its rival firm.

Consider the rivalry between two huge firms that produce uncut diamonds, De Beers and Alrosa. Suppose that De Beers and Alrosa enter into a collusive agreement to reduce the amount of diamonds they produce and sell on global diamond markets. This will make them both a lot of money. The demand for uncut diamonds is inelastic, so small reductions in the supply of diamonds will result in large price increases, causing an increase in total revenues. However, both firms have an incentive to cheat on their agreement. They face the same incentives as the prisoners above.

In the payoff matrix in Figure 17.4, De Beers has a dominant strategy of increasing production: If De Beers thinks Alrosa will choose not to increase production, De Beers makes $5 billion by increasing production compared with only $4 billion if they do not increase production. If De Beers thinks Alrosa will chose to increase production, De Beers makes $3 billion by increasing production versus only $2 billion if they do not increase production. Either way, De Beers makes more money if they increase production. Similarly, if Alrosa expects De Beers not to increase production, they make more money by increasing production ($5 billion versus $4 billion), and if Alrosa expects De Beers to increase production, they make more money by increasing production, too ($3 billion versus $2 billion). Because both firms have a dominant strategy to increase production, this game has a Nash equilibrium outcome in which we expect firms to end up in the bottom right corner with both players choosing to increase production.

		De Beers' strategies	
		De Beers does NOT increase production	De Beers increases production
Alrosa's strategies	Alrosa does NOT increase production	De Beers earns $4 billion Alrosa earns $4 billion	De Beers earns $5 billion Alrosa earns $2 billion
	Alrosa increases production	De Beers earns $2 billion Alrosa earns $5 billion	De Beers earns $3 billion Alrosa earns $3 billion

FIGURE 17.4 A payoff matrix showing the diamond cartel game.

17.4.2 Repeated games

Note, however, that this outcome only holds if this is a one-time game. If the game is repeated multiple times—for example, if De Beers and Alrosa face the same game every year—they are much more likely to stick with their agreement and to choose not to increase production. They will make more money over the long term by continuing to collude, ending up in the top left quadrant of the game outcomes. For example, suppose that this game were repeated ten times. In a repeated game, reneging on the agreement matrix not to increase production would lead to a one-time increase in profits from increasing production when your rival does not, but after that one time, the rival would also increase production, and the firms would end up with the worst long-term outcome, having both increased production. In contrast, if the rivals stick with their agreement and choose not to increase production, they will both make a lot more money over the long term.

Consider the following payment streams for a repeated game. If De Beers and Alrosa collude by agreeing not to increase production for ten years, they will both make \$40 billion.[1] Now suppose that De Beers cheats on their agreement after one year, increasing production. They would make \$4 billion the first year when they colluded and \$5 billion the second year after they increased production. However, after De Beers cheats on the agreement, Alrosa will also increase production, so for all subsequent years both firms will make \$3 billion. This would result in De Beers making \$(4 + 5 + (8 \times 3))$ billion = \$33 billion, much less than they would make if they stayed with the collusive agreement.

Thus, with repeated games, we are much more likely to see cooperative outcomes. Indeed, such cooperative outcomes can be quite stable unless one firm thinks it can gain a long-term strategic advantage by breaking the cooperative agreement. And repeated games can be particularly stable if the largest firm is able to punish smaller firms when they cheat on agreements. For many years, Saudi Arabia was able to keep OPEC members in line by flooding the market with oil to punish any countries that defected on the OPEC agreement to reduce production.

Even in one-time games, we can get very different outcomes depending on the payoff structure. For example, consider a case in which two countries, England and Portugal, are each much better at producing one commodity than another. In Figure 17.5, England is much better at producing clothes, and its dominant strategy

		England's strategies	
		Produce wine	Produce clothes
Portugal's strategies	Produce wine	England earns \$1 billion Portugal earns \$3 billion	England earns \$8 billion Portugal earns \$8 billion
	Produce clothes	England earns \$2 billion Portugal earns \$2 billion	England earns \$3 billion Portugal earns \$1 billion

FIGURE 17.5 A payoff matrix showing the comparative advantage (invisible hand) game.

is producing clothes: England always earns more money producing clothes no matter which option they expect Portugal to choose. Similarly, Portugal is much better at producing wine, and they have a dominant strategy in producing wine. This gives us an equilibrium outcome in which England produces clothes and Portugal produces wine, which results in the highest earnings for both countries. This, in theory, is what happens when countries specialize and trade what they are best in producing.

17.4.3 A game with a dominant player

In game theory, we also get instances in which players do not have a dominant strategy but they do have a consistent strategy in which **a player in a game always behaves in a consistent fashion, either matching what the other player does or doing the opposite of what the other player does**. For example, suppose there is an industry with a dominant player, such as American Airlines, and that the other player, United Airlines, always matches whatever the dominant player does.

In Figure 17.6, American Airlines has a dominant strategy of raising fares: No matter which strategy United Airlines chooses, American Airlines earns more money by raising fares. United Airlines has a consistent strategy. If American Airlines raises fares, United Airlines also raises fares. If American does not raise fares, then United does not raise fares. Thus, this game always has a Nash equilibrium if players have perfect information about the strategies and payoffs of both players: American will always choose to raise fares, and United will always choose the same strategy as American, which will also be to raise fares in this case. This causes the game to end up in the bottom right quadrant.

17.4.3 A game with multiple Nash equilibria

Finally, there are also games in which neither player has a dominant strategy and no single equilibrium outcome is possible to discern. For example, consider the advertising Cola Wars that Coca-Cola and Pepsi have engaged in. In general, we see these two companies matching each other's strategies.

		American Airlines' strategies	
		American does NOT Raise fares	American raises fares
United airlines' strategies	United does NOT raise fares	American earns $4 billion United earns $4 billion	American earns $5 billion United earns $3 billion
	United raises fares	American earns $2 billion United earns $3 billion	American earns $12 billion United earns $10 billion

FIGURE 17.6 A payoff matrix showing the dominant player game.

		Coca-Cola's advertising strategies	
		Regular expenditures	Extreme expenditures
Pepsi's advertising strategies	Regular expenditures	Coca-Cola earns $14 billion Pepsi earns $12 billion	Coca-Cola earns $10 billion Pepsi earns $8 billion
	Extreme expenditures	Coca-Cola earns $10 billion Pepsi earns $8 billion	Coca-Cola earns $12 billion Pepsi earns $10 billion

FIGURE 17.7 A payoff matrix showing a game with no dominant strategies.

As displayed in Figure 17.7, if Coca-Cola expects Pepsi to choose regular advertising expenditures, they will make more money by also choosing regular advertising expenditures ($14 billion > $10 billion). If Coca-Cola expects Pepsi to choose extreme advertising expenditures, Coca-Cola will make more money by choosing extreme advertising expenditures ($12 billion > $10 billion). Coca-Cola has a consistent strategy, in always matching what Pepsi does. Pepsi also has a consistent strategy, choosing regular expenditures if they expect Coca-Cola to select regular expenditures and choosing extreme expenditures if they expect Coca-Cola to select extreme expenditures. Because neither company has a dominant strategy, we have no way of knowing how the outcome of this game will end up. The game has two Nash equilibria, one in the top left quadrant and one in the bottom right quadrant. We could also have a game in which there were no Nash equilibrium at all.

Along with behavioral economics, game theory is one of the most rapidly developing fields in modern, mainstream economic theory. The ability to analyze various strategic options given potential payoff structures is more useful in complex situations than the models of rational maximizing behavior used to analyze other industries. In addition, the ability to broaden games to include repeated interactions and multiple players can yield rich results.

17.5 CONCLUSION

Taking what we have discussed about oligopolies above, there are a number of important implications.

1. Oligopolies do not behave as consistently as other market structures. Therefore, we have to analyze the strategic interactions of each industry based on its unique characteristics. Sometimes we can use the kinked demand curve, sometimes we can use game theory, and other times we must turn to a detailed analysis of the competitive dynamics of a particular industry.
2. Oligopolies often result in large profits and market dominance by a few firms that can harm consumers with higher prices and less choice. Unless oligopolies are sufficiently contestable—unless there is a legitimate fear by the dominant

firms that new firms can enter and threaten their market dominance—oligopolies do not work well for consumers. Oligopolies can earn large economic profits in the long run due to their market dominance.

3. The strategic interactions of oligopolies are complex and fascinating. Oligopolies compete in a wide variety of ways, including pricing, quality, advertising and marketing, innovation, mergers and acquisitions, and lobbying. Interestingly, oligopolies can be extremely innovative by investing the economic profits they earn. However, they are only likely to invest the bulk of their profits if they are in a highly contestable market that requires them to keep ahead of the competition.

4. Oligopolies often feature sticky prices, which is captured by the kinked demand curve model. Firms are reluctant to raise prices on their own, but if they can convince other firms to raise prices with them, they can make a lot of money.

5. Oligopolies regularly collude, either tacitly, illegally, or in international cartels. By colluding, oligopolies end up behaving like a monopoly, raising prices and reducing output to increase profits.

6. Game theory can capture some of the interesting dynamics of oligopolistic markets. We can use game theory to determine how firms are likely to behave given their strategic options and potential payoffs.

Oligopolies are often considered the most important market structure. Many, if not most, of the companies we interact with on a regular basis are oligopolies, and they have an outsized influence on our economic and political systems. The behavior of huge, multinational corporations is important and highly controversial, which is why we devote the next chapter to the topic of corporations.

QUESTIONS FOR REVIEW

1. How do oligopolies differ from monopolistically competitive industries?

2. How does competition in oligopolies differ from competition in other market structures? Explain carefully.

3. Pick an oligopolistic industry that you are familiar with and that is not discussed in detail in this chapter. Explain the types of strategic competition we see in the oligopoly you picked.

4. How does the kinked demand curve model explain why prices in oligopolies tend to be sticky?

5. In December 2017, McDonald's announced a new "dollar" menu, which would contain a number of items for sale for only $1. In response, Taco Bell announced it was reducing the price of 20 items to $1. Wendy's, Burger King, and Carl's Jr. all began offering similar competing deals. How does this behavior compare with the kinked demand curve model of oligopoly? Explain carefully.

	Giant's advertising expenditures	
	Low expenditures	High expenditures
Weis's advertising expenditures — Low expenditures	Weis profits: $250,000 Giant profits: $200,000	Weis profits: $100,000 Giant profits: $180,000
High expenditures	Weis profits: $300,000 Giant profits: $100,000	Weis profits: $200,000 Giant profits: $150,000

FIGURE 17.8 A payoff matrix for use with Problem 6.

6. The payoff matrix in Figure 17.8 shows the payoffs for two supermarkets, Giant and Weis, who are considering two different strategies: Low advertising expenditures or high advertising expenditures. (a) Using the payoff matrix, what is Giant's dominant strategy (if any)? What is Weis's dominant strategy (if any)? Explain briefly. (b) In what quadrant of the payoff matrix are we likely to end up? Explain briefly.

7. The payoff matrix in Figure 17.9 shows the payoffs for two supermarkets, Giant and Weis, who are considering two different strategies: Low advertising expenditures or high advertising expenditures. (a) What is Giant's best strategy? (b) What is Weis's best strategy? (c) Does either firm have a dominant strategy or a consistent strategy? (d) Is there a Nash equilibrium where the firms will end up? Explain your answers briefly.

8. How might your answer to question 7 change if the game were a repeated game instead of a one-time game? Explain.

	Giant's advertising expenditures	
	Low ad expenditures	High ad expenditures
Weis's advertising expenditures — Low ad expenditures	Weis profits: $250,000 Giant profits: $250,000	Weis profits: $200,000 Giant profits: $300,000
High ad expenditures	Weis profits: $200,000 Giant profits: $300,000	Weis profits: $150,000 Giant profits: $250,000

FIGURE 17.9 A payoff matrix for use with Problem 7.

9. (a) Why do firms in an oligopoly have an incentive to collude? (b) What types of collusion are possible? (c) What does the OPEC case study tell us about the benefits of colluding and the difficulties in maintaining a collusive agreement?

NOTE

1 Note that technically De Beers or Alrosa could make an extra $1 billion if they cheated in the last period and increased production. However, this would destroy any chance of colluding in the future, so it is unlikely that this strategy would be adopted in the real world.

Corporations and their role in society

The good and bad sides of limited liability corporations

The limited liability corporation is one of the major and most controversial forces in modern capitalism. Whereas some economists, such as Milton Friedman and William Baumol, view corporations as primarily beneficial institutions, other economists such as John Kenneth Galbraith, Paul Baran, and Paul Sweezy see them as fundamentally destructive to people, the environment, and society. The range and strength of opinions on this topic make it fascinating to study.

In modern market-dominated capitalist economic systems, the major economic decisions of society are made by the private sector. The private sector in modern capitalism is dominated by huge, multinational corporations. This makes the corporation the dominant institution in most current economic systems. Corporations largely determine what society's priorities are; what workers' lives are like; how resources are allocated, used, and abused; and much more. As we saw earlier in this book, in some societies the government plays a significant role in regulating corporate behavior. But even in the most regulated economies, corporations play a huge role in shaping society.

There are major market failures associated with large corporations—cases where markets do not work in an efficient manner. Market failures contribute to reduced competition, inequality, production of unsafe products, mistreatment of laborers, pollution of the environment, and exploitation of scarce resources. On the other hand, corporations are also driven by the competitive process, when markets are sufficiently competitive, to be relentlessly innovative. Large corporations innovate regularly in order to stay ahead of the competition, and the innovative process often generates economic growth and products that can and do improve peoples' lives.

The chapter begins by describing the structure of the modern limited liability corporation (LLC) and its primary focus on generating short-term profits. Subsequently, the chapter takes up the dark side of corporations via a series of case studies of corporate misbehavior, reflecting the views of progressive political economists and radical political economists with an unfavorable view of LLCs.

DOI: 10.4324/9781315636924-22

The chapter then takes up the ideas of conservative economists William Baumol and Milton Friedman who view large corporations favorably, arguing that they generate innovations and economic growth. The chapter concludes by considering a middle ground between these two perspectives—that corporations are useful and productive institutions when properly regulated.

18.0 CHAPTER 18 LEARNING GOALS

After reading this chapter, you should be able to:

- Explain the role of limited liability corporations in the U.S. economy.

- Describe the principal–agent problem and moral hazard and explain how corporations use stock options to get executives to focus on short-term profits and stock prices.

- Define corporate hegemony and analyze the dark side of corporate behavior using specific examples.

- Describe and evaluate the arguments of Baumol and Friedman that large corporations are behind the best aspects of modern capitalism—innovation and growth.

- Determine the appropriate role for government in the regulation of large corporations given the arguments for and against large corporations in modern capitalism.

18.1 THE THREE TYPES OF FIRMS: SOLE PROPRIETORSHIPS, PARTNERSHIPS, AND CORPORATIONS

There are three types of firms in the United States: sole proprietorships, partnerships, and corporations. Sole proprietorships are **owned by a single person**. The owner has the legal right to all of the profits from the sole proprietorship, and they are also subject to *unlimited liability* for the firm's debts. This means that if the firm loses a lot of money, the owner is responsible for paying back all of that money to the firm's creditors. The creditors can seize the owner's house and possessions to cover losses from the sole proprietorship if they wish.

Partnerships have **two or more owners who share in the firm's profits and who are subject to** unlimited liability **for the firm's debts**. Partnerships create a vehicle to pool and share resources, so they are more able to raise money than sole proprietorships. Partnerships are particularly common in law, accounting, and medicine, and are the organizational structure chosen by many workers' cooperatives.

Limited liability corporations are **joint stock companies in which the activities and property of the firm are separated from the private property of the firm's owners, the stockholders. These are called limited liability corporations because the owners do not assume liability for the firm's debts—all they can lose is the amount they invested in the firm, limiting their liabilities** compared with sole proprietorships and partnerships. In the United States, corporations are distinct legal entities with the same rights as individuals, so a limited liability corporation is an artificial legal entity that can own property, sue others and be sued, sign contracts, donate to political campaigns, and engage in the same economic activities that individuals can.

Figure 18.1 shows that although only 17.5% of firms in the United States are corporations, they accounted for 82.2% of sales revenue in 2015. Thus, corporations dominate sole proprietorships and partnerships in terms of their economic impact. This is why corporations are an essential institution of modern capitalism.

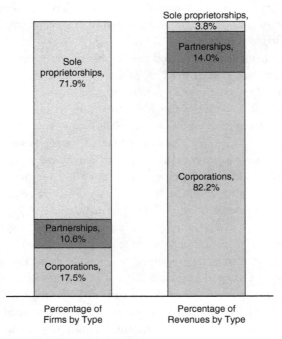

FIGURE 18.1 Types of firms by number and sales revenue, 2013.

18.2 KEY ASPECTS OF THE MODERN LIMITED LIABILITY CORPORATION

One of the key characteristics of a limited liability corporation (LLC) is the separa-tion between **ownership** and **control**. In a sole proprietorship or a partnership, owners also control the operations of the firm. However, in an LLC the owners are often stockholders who have little or no say in the day-to-day operations of the firm. The main decisions of the corporation are made by chief executive officers (CEOs) and other managers rather than owners.

This can create problems for the stockholders when the managers have differ-ent interests than the owners. Economist William Baumol observed in 1959 that the interests of managers were often to maximize sales revenue rather than profits, because the larger the corporation, the greater the prestige, salary, and prospects for promotion. Sometimes, managers would pursue increasing sales at the expense of profits. This phenomenon is known in economics as a principal–agent prob-lem, **where the agents (managers) may have different interests than the principals (owners).** The owners (principals) hire the managers (agents) to run the company to make maximum profits for the owners. However, the managers possess information and power to make decisions that do not necessarily benefit the owners, and the ramifications of those decisions may not be readily apparent to the stockholders. **When agents act in their own best interests, and when those interests are contrary to those of their principals,** economists call this moral hazard. Agents have a financial interest in behaving one way (increasing sales), even though they have a fiduciary responsibility to behave in another way (maximize profits).

The principal–agent problem and the frequent occurrences of moral hazard (managers maximizing sales instead of profits) led firms to start compensating CEOs and top-level managers with stock, stock options, and performance bonuses. In 2015, 85% of CEO compensation at Fortune 500 corporations in the United States came in the form of stock, stock options, and performance bonuses.

Employee stock options are **a type of compensation where an employer gives an employee the right to purchase a specific number of shares of stock at a fixed price over a specific period of time (in the future).** Often, the price is set at the current market price of the company's stock. Then, after a year or more with the company, the employee can purchase the company's stock at that original price, regardless of what the stock price is at that (future) time. This means that if the stock has increased in price since the employee started working, the employee can make a profit by "exercising" her stock options—purchasing the stock at the old price and selling the stock at the new price. This gives employees a direct financial incentive to take actions to increase the stock price of the company. Similarly, performance bonuses typically reward managers for earning high profits, maximizing return on investment (the rate of profit), and maximizing stock prices.

The fact that the vast majority of compensation for CEOs is directly tied to stock price gives companies a direct financial incentive to do everything in their power to increase the company's stock price. This can lead to productive outcomes, where CEOs foster conditions to generate growth and innovation. Or it can lead to destructive outcomes, where CEOs focus on padding the stock price with accounting tricks and focus too much on short-term profits without adequate consideration for the long run.

The shift to stock price–based compensation has been part of a larger shift in the global economy away from the production of goods and services toward the financial sector. Financialization refers to **the increasingly dominant role that financial motives, markets, actors, and institutions play in global economies**. We take up this phenomenon in macroeconomics. For now, the key aspect of financialization as it relates to the modern corporation is the increasing emphasis on the firm's short-term stock price to the exclusion of other goals. The best vehicle for managers to increase the firm's short-term stock price is to increase short-term profits. Thus, the primary focus of most modern U.S. corporations is on ways to increase short-term profits.

It is also worth noting that **corporations are the dominant economic institution in modern capitalist economies**. As was noted earlier, 69 of the world's largest economic entities are corporations, and only 31 are countries. These dominant corporations have massive power in deciding how society uses its scarce resources. In essence, corporations operate as the planning system for the capitalist economy, deciding whether society should emphasize the production of ever-greater amounts of consumer goods or devote resources to preserving the environment, determining whether we should use renewable energy or fossil fuels, and deciding what wages to pay workers and how much pay CEOs and stockholders should get.

In addition to controlling most of the resources in the United States, corporations shape most policy decisions and the legal environment via hired lobbyists and campaign contributions. Corporations' deep pockets allow them substantial power to sue governments and individuals when legal decisions do not go their way. In addition, corporate advertising pervades media outlets of all types, occupying almost one-third of television broadcasts, cluttering the landscape with billboards and flashing signs, placing products in movies and television shows, and generally exercising a profound influence on the culture of capitalist economies. Political economist William Dugger calls this corporate hegemony, **the cultural, legal, political, and economic power relations that make the corporation the dominant institution in modern capitalism and that give the CEOs and top managers of corporations their dominant position in capitalist society**.

So what kind of behaviors do LLCs engage in given their dominant position and their almost exclusive focus on short-term profits? The next section looks at the worst kinds of behaviors that large corporations engage in. These are the kinds of things that give corporations a bad name and seem to justify calls to reign in corporate power. But as we will see later, other economists believe that large corporations are the primary force behind the high standard of living in modern capitalist economies.

18.3 IF CORPORATIONS ARE PEOPLE, WHAT KIND OF PEOPLE ARE THEY?[1]

In 1886, the Supreme Court of the United States ruled that corporations have the same legal status as persons. The legal rights of corporations gradually have been expanded in the United States since that time to include the right to free speech and to contribute unlimited amounts to political campaigns (a product of the Supreme Court's 2010 Citizens United ruling). A key question that emerges from U.S. corporate personhood is: If corporations are people, what kind of people are they?

One of the key characteristics of a corporation is that, by its very legal structure, it is an **amoral entity**. It exists for the sole purpose of making profits, and it will do whatever is necessary to increase profits, without considering ethical issues unless those issues impinge on the bottom line. A crucial reason for this behavior is that CEOs and other corporate officers have a legal "fiduciary duty" to act in the best financial interests of stockholders. As conservative economist Milton Friedman stated in his book *Capitalism and Freedom*, "There is one and only one social responsibility of business—to use its resources and engage in activities designed to increase its profits so long as it stays within the rules of the game, which is to say, engages in open and free competition without deception or fraud." Thus, those who control corporations are obligated to do whatever they can within the law to make as much money as possible.

This can lead to behavior that some have called psychopathic. This view is common among radical political economists. In the provocative 2003 film *The Corporation*, the filmmakers argue that corporations meet the diagnostic criteria used by psychiatrists to determine whether a person is psychopathic. Those criteria are as follows:

- Callous disregard for the feelings of others
- Reckless disregard for the safety of others
- Incapacity to maintain enduring relationships
- Deceitfulness: repeated lying and conniving others for profit
- Incapacity to experience guilt
- Failure to conform to social norms with respect to lawful behaviors.

Although at first blush the claim that corporations are psychopaths seems incredible, if we consider the worst behaviors of corporations over the last few decades and the disturbing frequency with which such behaviors seem to recur, it is possible to see why so many people hold corporations in such low esteem. Below, we describe briefly some of the most horrific behaviors of large corporations in recent years.

Case study: Savar building collapse, 2013

An example of corporate abuses of subcontracting and sweatshops

For decades, U.S. and European clothing manufacturers have been moving their operations overseas to countries with extremely low wages and with few safety or environmental regulations. One of their favorite destinations in recent years has been Bangladesh, where wages for clothing workers are the lowest in the world (only $0.24 per hour until the minimum wage was raised to $0.40 per hour in 2014) and where few safety standards are enforced. Bangladesh now has more than 5000 garment factories handling orders for most of the world's top brands and retailers, and it is second in garment manufacturing output behind China.

In 2013, a building that housed several clothing factories collapsed, killing 1134 people in the worst disaster in garment industry history. It was later discovered that the building was constructed with substandard materials in violation of building codes. Even more disturbing was the fact that the owners of the factories insisted that employees return to work even after an engineer inspected the building the day before the collapse and deemed it unsafe due to cracks in the walls and clear structural deficiencies. The factories were making clothes for Walmart, Benetton, and many other large, multinational companies.

Disasters like this one, along with the torture and killing of a Bangladeshi labor activist in 2012, are a product of the subcontracting system used by large clothing manufacturers. The corporations issue specifications for the garments that they want to have manufactured and contractors around the world bid for the right to make the garments. The lowest bidder wins. But what kind of factory is likely to have the lowest bid? Given the regular occurrence of disasters and labor abuses in garment factories, it appears that the contractors who win bids are those who are the most likely to pay workers the least under the most unsafe conditions. Huge multinational clothing companies are only too eager to participate, while at the same time claiming that they are not responsible for the deaths and abuses because they themselves were not the factory owners. The factory owners in Bangladesh were charged with murder, but there were no major consequences for the clothing companies. The callous disregard for the feelings and safety of others and incapacity to experience guilt that many clothing manufacturers display is certainly consistent with the definition of a psychopath.

Case study: BP oil spill in the Gulf of Mexico, 2010

Taking chances with people's lives and the environment

The 2010 BP oil spill in the Gulf of Mexico was the worst oil spill in U.S. history. The Deepwater Horizon oil rig exploded on April 20, 2010, killing 11 people and spilling 210 million gallons of oil into the Gulf. Investigations into the causes of the spill indicated significant negligence.

- Deepwater drilling procedures were adapted from shallow water techniques, without adequate consideration of the differences between the two environments.
- Federal regulators relaxed requirements for environmental reviews, tests, and safety plans at the request of BP and encouraged but did not require key backup systems.
- BP used well casings, cement, and other equipment that violated company safety guidelines and industry best practices, despite concerns raised by BP engineers.
- Warning signs were ignored and safety tests were delayed despite the warning signs.

The human and environmental costs of the spill were devastating. In addition to the human deaths, millions of birds, turtles, dolphins, and fish died. The Gulf tourism industry was devastated for several years, costing businesses $23 billion in lost revenue. And the Gulf still has not recovered, with ongoing problems cropping up related to the environment and wildlife.

The primary culprit here was BP's relentless pursuit of lower costs. Poor quality materials plus skimping on safety measures created conditions for the explosion and meant that BP was unable to deal with the disaster once it happened. Although BP was found guilty of negligence and fined a record $18.7 billion, that amount was only about 8% of their annual revenue, and no BP official went to prison.

Case study: ExxonMobil and climate change denial, 1981–2008

Lying to people for profit

In 1981, a team of researchers at Exxon conclusively established the connection between the burning of fossil fuels, the spewing of greenhouse gases into the air (especially carbon), and climate change. Their research was supported by dozens of other studies by climate scientists. These studies have been so convincing that over 97% of climate scientists agree that climate change is occurring and that human activity is a significant cause. As anyone who studies scientific research will know, it is rare to have near-universal agreement on something as complex as climate change, which helps us to understand that the evidence for climate change is overwhelming.

Despite this evidence, Exxon, which merged with Mobil in 1999, spent millions of dollars on a public relations effort to deny the existence of climate change so that they could continue to sell as much of their oil as possible. As documented in the book (and film) *Merchants of Doubt* (2010), Exxon funded foundations who paid a small group of scientists and public relations professionals to cast doubt on the idea of climate change in order to prevent action from being taken. And their impact in the United States was dramatic. While much of the world was taking climate change seriously and enacting policies to begin reducing greenhouse gas emissions, the United States was increasing its use of fossil fuels, accompanied by increasing emissions.

ExxonMobil now states publicly that it accepts the idea that climate change is occurring, and they have stopped formally funding climate change denialism. However, ExxonMobil's reduction in public funding of denialism has coincided with a dramatic increase in untraceable "dark money" being used to fund climate change denialism.[2]

Thanks to ExxonMobil and others who have prevented progress on climate change, we are now faced with the prospect of dramatic climate events that will cost many people their lives. We are likely to see increasing droughts, food shortages, heat waves, rising sea levels, floods, and other disasters that threaten our very existence, all so that ExxonMobil could sell more barrels of oil. As is so often the case, there have been no criminal prosecutions related to these incidents.

Case study: Enron's fraudulent use of derivatives and shell companies, 1990–2002

Financial deregulation plus executive stock options are a toxic mix

One of the arguments in favor of corporations is that thanks to the profit motive, they tend to innovate in order to make money. But what kind of innovations might result from the profit motive? Enron executives Kenneth Lay and Jeffrey Skilling used the deregulated environment in financial markets in the 1990s and early 2000s (the same environment that also produced the financial crisis) to create an innovative financial model built on fraud and subterfuge.

Enron was the world's largest energy trading company, with a market value of $68 billion. But its real innovation was in shady accounting practices. Enron would start by undertaking a legitimate investment, such as building a power plant. It would then immediately claim all of the expected profit from the power plant on its books, even though it had yet to make any money on the investment, making it appear to be an incredibly profitable company. If the power plant profits ever came in below expectations, Enron would transfer the unprofitable assets to a shell company—a company that did not really exist formally, other than as a vehicle for Enron to dispose of losses—thereby hiding Enron's losses from its investors. Shell company investors were given shares of Enron common stock to compensate them for the shell company losses. Thus, Enron appeared to be incredibly profitable even while it was incurring losses, and that caused its stock price to soar.

Much of the reason for this behavior was the incentive system created by financial markets. As noted above, most CEOs and highly placed executives are paid most of their salaries in stock options. This meant that they could make more money if they could get the company's stock price to increase, and that would allow them to cash in their stock options at a higher value. In theory, paying CEOs in stock options gave them an incentive to run the company in the most profitable way possible and that would cause the stock price to go up. But stock options also gave executives an incentive to artificially prop up stock prices in order to cash in, which is what the Enron executives did. Meanwhile, the accounting auditors who were supposed to flag questionable and illegal financial transactions looked the other way in order to keep Enron's business.

As Enron's losses mounted, the executives cashed in all of their stock options and left the company bankrupt. More than 5000 employees lost their jobs and millions of investors lost their savings. Lay, Skilling, and 15 other Enron executives were found guilty of fraud. But these sordid events didn't stop an even bigger financial market manipulation from dragging down the entire global economy in the financial crisis.

Case study: Goldman Sachs, CMOs, and the financial crisis of 2007–2008

Betting against your own clients

The global financial crisis of 2007 to 2008 was a product of a number of corporate misdeeds fueled by greed and the deregulation of financial markets. To increase their profits in the early 2000s, banks started loaning money to extremely risky, sub-prime borrowers with very poor credit scores so the borrowers could purchase houses. The banks then bundled large groups of these sub-prime mortgage loans into securities called collateralized mortgage obligations (CMOs). The banks did not care about the credit-worthiness of borrowers because they immediately sold these securities (bundles of sub-prime mortgages) to investors.

As more and more sub-prime borrowers took out more and more mortgage loans, the real estate market boomed, forming a huge bubble. At the peak of the bubble in 2006 default rates on mortgages started to increase rapidly. Realizing that sub-prime loans were likely to fail, Goldman Sachs and several other big investment banks began to do something highly unethical: They sold bundles of sub-prime mortgages (CMOs) to investors, and *they used derivatives called credit default swaps to bet that the mortgages in the CMOs they sold were going to default, something that would make the CMOs worthless*. In other words, they sold investors CMO securities that they knew were going to fail, and they even made bets in financial markets that the CMOs they sold would fail. Goldman Sachs, Deutsche Bank, and Morgan Stanley all engaged in these transactions to profit at the expense of their investors.

As in so many other cases of corporate malfeasance, the legal consequences amounted to little more than a slap on the wrist. Goldman

Sachs paid a $550 million fine in 2010 to settle the fraud case brought by the Securities and Exchange Commission, an amount that was 4% of the $13.39 billion in profits Goldman Sachs made in the previous year. In 2016, Goldman Sachs agreed to an additional $5.1 billion fine for misleading investors about the quality of the CMOs they sold to investors. However, no Goldman Sachs official went to jail.

Case study: VW programs cars to cheat on emissions tests, 2009–2015

The things a company will do to become #1

Martin Winterkorn, Volkswagen's chief executive officer from 2007 to 2015, established the goal of making VW the largest car company in the world, and he embarked on an ambitious plan to achieve that goal. Much of his plan hinged on developing fuel-efficient, clean diesel cars as an alternative to hybrids. But when VW discovered that it could not develop an inexpensive technology to remove pollution without compromising the car's gas mileage and overall performance, they turned to a fraudulent approach. VW programmed 10.5 million cars so that the cars would detect when they were being tested for emissions, and during testing the cars' engines would run in a way that the cars would meet emissions standards. But when the cars were driven normally in a non-testing situation, they would spew pollutants at a rate much higher than allowed by law.

A nonprofit group, the International Council on Clean Transportation, discovered the problem when they tested numerous diesel cars in 2013. They alerted the Environmental Protection Agency (E.P.A.), which launched an investigation in 2014. As is so often the case, VW responded to the investigation aggressively, accusing regulators and testers of being incompetent. But additional testing established conclusively that VW cars had been programmed to reduce emissions when tested, while spewing large amounts of pollutants when driven normally. The E.P.A. told VW that they would no longer allow them to sell diesel cars in the United States in 2015 and accused them of violating the Clean Air Act. Particularly problematic was the fact that VW diesels spewed large amounts of nitrogen oxide in amounts up to 40 times the legal limit.

Nitrogen oxide is a pollutant that causes emphysema and bronchitis and contributes to many other respiratory diseases. The E.P.A. estimates that the additional pollution from VW diesel cars will cause as many as 34 deaths and sicken thousands of people in the United States, and other studies predict up to 200 premature deaths.

VW briefly became the largest car company in July of 2015 when they surpassed Toyota, but after the scandal became public, the company fell back. On June 27, 2016, VW agreed to pay $14.7 billion in fines (1% of the revenues VW made from 2009 to 2015) to the government and compensation to VW diesel car owners. A criminal inquiry was still underway in 2019.

Case study: General Motors' faulty ignition switches, 2005–2007

Why would anyone sell a product that they knew could kill people?

Imagine yourself as a CEO or vice president of a major corporation. An engineering report comes across your desk, noting that a part in one of your products is faulty and that the consequences of that part failing could be injury or even death for some of your customers. Would you still sell the faulty product, even knowing that it might kill people? This is what General Motors (GM) did with its faulty ignition switch.

This particularly sordid story starts in 2010, when a 29-year-old nurse named Brooke Melton died in a car crash after losing control of her car. Her parents, who knew that she was a safe driver and that her car had been behaving oddly, sued GM and hired engineering experts to try to determine the cause of the crash. They discovered that the problem was the ignition switch installed on over 22 million GM cars manufactured from 2001 to 2007. The ignition switch could turn from "On" to "Acc" just by being bumped lightly or if the car key was on a particularly heavy keychain. The shift from "On" to "Acc" could disable the power steering, anti-lock braking, and airbags and cause the car to stall.

As the investigation progressed, the full scale of GM's deceit became apparent. In 2001, GM engineers initially detected the defective part, labeling it the "switch from hell." Problems with the switch cropped up repeatedly over the next several years. In 2005, internal documents show that GM acknowledged the problem but chose not to fix it because it would be too costly. Instead, they sent a note to GM dealerships telling them to urge customers to use lighter key chains! Each year, people died as ignition switches failed and airbags failed to deploy, but GM continued to hide the problem and refused to recall cars and repair the problem.

Finally, thanks to the Melton lawsuit and government investigations that followed, GM recalled the vehicles and repaired the faulty switch— But not before at least 124 people died in crashes related to the faulty ignition switch. GM paid a $900 million fine in 2015, and other settlements with victims brought the total cost of the debacle to $2 billion. Though this put a dent in their 2015 profits of $9.7 billion, no individuals faced criminal charges for their actions.

In addition to the recent examples above, we should note that similar behaviors occurred throughout the last century. Particularly egregious examples of corporate misdeeds include the following:

- In the early 1960s, Ford would not spend three cents per car to fix transmission problems that caused the transmission to slip from park into reverse. By 1980 this had caused 400 deaths and thousands of injuries.
- In the 1970s, Ford refused to spend $11 per car to fix exploding Pinto gas tanks. Hundreds of people were killed or injured.
- In 1984, managers at a Union Carbide plant in Bhopal, India, knew of the potential for sizeable leaks of toxic chemicals but did nothing. A cyanide leak occurred, killing more than 2000 people and seriously injuring more than 30,000. Other estimates put the number of dead as high as 5000 and the number of injured as high as 40,000. Union Carbide said they were sorry and sent $1 million in disaster relief ($5 per victim).
- Dow Chemical knew that dioxins in Agent Orange and other products were extremely hazardous, but they continued to produce products containing dioxins without warning the government. As a result, there were numerous cases of cancer and birth defects in people exposed to dioxins. Dow paid $240 million in settlements, $960 per victim, to cover the damages inflicted upon people.
- In the 1970s, Firestone knew that some of its tires were prone to blowouts but chose to do nothing. When the problems were exposed, they continued to sell the tires, offering them at half price to unload them. The government fined Firestone $50,000 after there were 34 known fatalities and hundreds of injuries.

- In the 1980s, Eli Lilly marketed and sold a drug named Oraflex despite numerous deaths that had occurred in clinical trials. As deaths mounted from the drug, Eli Lilly eventually pulled the drug from the market and was fined $25,000 by the government.
- From the 1930s through the 1950s, General Motors systematically purchased and then dismantled streetcar companies serving cities. Instead of a clean, efficient train system, cities were left with clogged highways, long commutes, and terrible air pollution. GM and other co-conspirators were found guilty of conspiring to dismantle a competing form of transportation. Their fine for this misbehavior was a paltry $5000.

18.4 ARE CORPORATIONS PSYCHOPATHS?

We highlighted seven recent and seven older examples of horrific corporate behavior. In each case, corporations exhibited many of the behaviors characteristic of psychopaths, especially a callous disregard for the feelings and safety of others, deceitfulness, avoiding admitting guilt and taking responsibility for their actions, and failure to respect social and ethical norms and the law. But are these behaviors typical of powerful, profit-hungry corporations, or are they exceptions?

As we all know, many corporations behave ethically, and many invent useful and innovative products that improve our lives. Yet, every year a certain number of corporations cast ethics and morality to the side and engage in unscrupulous behavior, resulting in fraud and even deaths. There appear to be aspects of the corporate structure that encourage such behavior, including the relentless quest for maximum short-term profits, the lack of personal responsibility for any illegal actions taken by the corporation, and the power corporations have to manipulate the legal system and government regulators.

Regarding the last point, one of the elements to every story above was the inadequate efforts of government regulators. The push for deregulation by various politicians directly facilitated many of the above corporate misdeeds. And government regulators are often overmatched by corporate legal teams with almost unlimited resources, an imbalance that allows many corporations to avoid serious consequences even in cases where they have done something horribly wrong. Even when corporations have been caught red-handed in clear violation of the law, the penalties are usually little more than a slap on the wrist and are often far less than the profits from the offense in question. Corporate wealth and power appear to allow them to avoid significant checks on their behavior. Thus, instead of engaging in "open and free competition without deception or fraud," as Milton Friedman hoped that they would, it appears that some corporations use deception and fraud with near impunity in order to outdo the competition.

Ironically, such problems could be fixed easily by a regulatory system with teeth, where corporate lobbyists do not have undue influence over how corporations are regulated. And there would need to be real consequences for corporate crime. When corporations find out that their actions or products may harm people, if they refuse to take action and to inform the public and regulators of the problem, the people who make those decisions should go to prison, just as others who intentionally and knowingly harm people do.

Finally, like real people, corporations should face real consequences when they break the law. A corporation that engages in particularly egregious behavior, especially a corporation that does so repeatedly, should face sanctions that have a real impact on executives and stockholders. For cases in which a corporation causes deaths, the corporation could face the "death penalty": Having its charter revoked and its assets seized by the public. If stockholders could potentially lose all of their investment in a company that behaved illegally, they would begin checking up on companies and we would see much less illegal and unethical behavior.

Of course, all of these solutions require removing corporate money from politics. As long as corporations can buy off politicians, they can continue to act as psychopaths and face very little in the way of consequences.

Now that we have considered the dark side of corporate behavior, we need to consider other, more positive opinions of large corporations operating in a capitalist system. Although political economists tend to have a very negative opinion of corporations, most mainstream economists see corporations as benign institutions that are an essential, productive component of a capitalist economic system. We turn to those views next.

18.5 THE GOOD SIDE OF LARGE CORPORATIONS

One of the strongest arguments in favor of large corporations in capitalism comes from mainstream economist William Baumol in his book *The Free-Market Innovation Machine*. Baumol argues that the combination of capitalism and competitive oligopolies yields the most innovative and most rapidly growing economic system possible.

The existence of **private property** in capitalism is crucial in providing firms with an incentive to innovate. Firms that innovate get to keep the proceeds from their innovations due to property rights. The existence of rivalrous **competition** and the constant threat of innovation from new or existing firms yield a situation in which innovative activity "becomes mandatory, a life-and-death matter for the firm."

However, the firms most poised to be innovative are *not* firms in extremely competitive markets. Small firms in competitive markets struggle to survive, and they do not have the extra resources at their disposal to engage in the substantial investments in research and development that are required for innovation. Monopolies, of course, have no need to innovate given their control over their market and the existence of substantial barriers to entry that limit competition. Instead, it is **oligopolistic competition** that fosters the ideal market structure to generate innovation and growth.

First, oligopolies must innovate to keep ahead of their competitors, who are also doing everything in their power to supplant their rivals. Second, the focus on innovation drives firms to engage in the **routinization of innovative activities**. To keep a steady stream of innovations flowing and thereby reduce the uncertainty that comes with a competitive, constantly shifting industry, oligopolies invest vast sums of money in research and development. In the modern economy, innovation has replaced price as the prime competitive weapon. This has resulted in 70% of U.S. research and development spending now being done by private corporations rather than universities and government agencies.

Also crucial in this process is a **legal and institutional structure that rewards innovating activity**. Firms need to be encouraged to innovate with patents and licensing laws that give them a temporary monopoly on any new invention. Corporations should not be rewarded for destructive activities, such as lobbying for special treatment or inter-business lawsuits to restrict the innovations of other firms. The rule of law and enforceability of contracts are crucial to this process.

Central to Baumol's argument is also the idea that corporations generally gain more profits from licensing and disseminating their innovations than they do by keeping their innovations to themselves. This is so prevalent that Baumol notes numerous cases in which corporations even license their innovations to their direct competitors. This is because if competing firms can be more efficient at exploiting an innovation than the firm that invented it, the competing firm will pay more for the right to use that innovation than the inventing firm could earn itself. Furthermore, if the inventing firm refuses to license its innovation, competing firms will work ceaselessly to reverse engineer the innovation until they can duplicate it, a process that can happen very rapidly in the modern era. Therefore, firms have an incentive to cash in on their innovation quickly via licensing.

Baumol estimates that 20% of the benefits from an innovation go to the inventing firm, and the rest goes to society at large because the spread of innovations results in substantial **spillover benefits**. Consumers get better products at lower prices. Firms develop new products based on the new innovation. The impact of the innovation cascades through the economy.

Note, however, that overly restrictive patent laws could give firms more of an incentive to hold on to their innovations rather than licensing them, an eventuality that would reduce the benefits that society receives from innovations and slow the rate of economic growth. This makes the appropriate regulatory and legal environment a complex balancing act. Regulators must allow innovative firms enough leeway to take risks and reap the rewards from those risky investments. But regulators must also ensure that firms cannot use their dominant position to stall innovation by eliminating competition.

Baumol also agrees with Alan Greenspan, conservative mainstream econo-mist and former Chair of the Federal Reserve, that antitrust laws can actually stifle innovation by restricting oligopolies. In Greenspan's essay titled "Antitrust" he condemns the Sherman Antitrust Act of 1890 as stifling innovation and harm-ing society. He states, "No one will ever know what new products, processes, machines, and cost-saving mergers failed to come into existence, killed by the Sherman Act before they were born. No one can ever compute the price that all of us have paid for that Act which, by inducing less effective use of capital, has kept our standard of living lower than would otherwise have been possible." Greenspan summarized his view of the nature of antitrust law as "a jumble of economic irrationality and ignorance." So according to Greenspan and Baumol, firms should generally be allowed to merge because this increases efficiency and innovation.

Interestingly, mainstream economists such as Baumol and Greenspan see large corporations as a positive force in the economy *except* when corporations are involved in market failures. When corporations can make money via destruc-tive or exploitative practices, this requires government intervention. For example, when corporations have too much power over workers, corporations do not have to pay workers well or treat them fairly. When corporations can make a profit by producing unsafe products, they can also harm society. And when corporations attain so much monopoly power that they can stifle rivalrous competition, they can reduce efficiency and innovation. In theory, an effective government should be able to eliminate these market failures via effective regulation, thereby rendering large corporations relatively harmless. As we will see later, the problems with large corporations may therefore be a product of government failure from a mainstream economics perspective. Political economists, however, tend to see more fundamen-tal flaws in the limited liability corporation that cannot be corrected sufficiently with regulation.

18.6 CONCLUSION

This chapter described the most dominant economic institution of modern capital-ism—the LLC. Broadly speaking, there tend to be three perspectives on the behav-ior and role of large limited liability corporations.

Laissez-faire mainstream and Austrian economists see the corporation as a positive institution, attributing to corporations the primary responsibility for the dynamic growth and technological advances of modern capitalism. They propose that we reduce our regulations of corporations to allow them freer rein to innovate and grow. The appropriate role for government from this perspective is to ensure stable property rights, enforce contracts, resist government interference in markets, and foster oligopolistic competition.

Radical and progressive political economists view the corporation as the force that generates most of the negative outcomes of modern capitalism. As the dominant institution of modern capitalism, political economists argue that corporations put profits of stockholders ahead of all other human goals, including health and safety, decent wages and living conditions, economic stability, and the environment. Furthermore, corporations divert society's precious resources into the production of commodities that are often useless and wasteful, rather than focusing on the production of goods that directly enhance human well-being.

In the middle, we find economists who support corporate capitalism in general but who believe that corporations need to be more closely regulated to ensure that their activities are channeled into productive rather than destructive activities. These economists are the intellectual heirs to John Maynard Keynes, believing that corporate capitalism is mostly a good system but it needs appropriate regulation. From this perspective, governments need to regulate strictly corporate activities to prevent the worst abuses cited earlier, with stiff penalties for misbehavior. And governments need to preserve competition carefully in order to make sure that oligopolistic markets function in the way Baumol hoped they would.

In keeping with this theme, the next chapter focuses on market failures and government failures more explicitly. As this chapter pointed out, the limited liability corporation is the most important institution in modern capitalism, so much so that we might call the modern era "corporate capitalism." In modern mixed economies, the primary role for government is to fix the market failures created by corporate capitalism.

QUESTIONS FOR REVIEW

1. Explain the principal–agent problem and the concept of moral hazard. How are stock options designed to address this problem?
2. Using the case studies of corporate misbehavior in this chapter, identify the commonalities between the cases. Taken together, what are the major lessons regarding corporate misbehavior that emerge?
3. Critically analyze the argument that corporations are psychopaths.
4. Critically analyze Baumol's argument that large corporations are the central reason for the rapid growth and widespread wealth that is generated in modern developed capitalist economies like the United States.
5. Write an essay in which you critically analyze the arguments for and against large corporations. Given these arguments, how should the government approach regulating them? Do you think the corporate structure is fundamentally flawed, as argued by many political economists? Or do you think the corporate structure is fundamentally a useful one that is largely responsible for the high standard of living in developed countries?

6. Economist Milton Friedman argues that the only responsibility of corporations is to make profits. Do you agree with his argument? Why or why not?

7. In his book *Small Is Beautiful*, economist E. F. Schumacher argues that the problem with corporations is their bigness. When corporations become huge and impersonal, they tend to act to maximize profits without concern for people, communities, and the environment. From this perspective, only by re-embedding corporations in communities can we ensure that they serve the common interest instead of the narrower interests of stockholders. Given the information in this chapter, evaluate that perspective.

8. Do you agree with Baumol and Friedman that antitrust laws should not be used as frequently to regulate large corporations such as Google and Microsoft? Why or why not?

NOTES

1 Nghia "TN" Doan assisted with the research and writing of this material. This section was originally written for the eighth edition of *Introduction to Political Economy* by Charles Sackrey, Geoffrey Schneider, and Janet Knoedler. The author would like to thank Chris Sturr and the entire staff at Dollars and Sense for granting permission to republish this material here.

2 Douglas Fischer, "'Dark Money' Funds Climate Change Denial Effort," *Scientific American*, December 23, 2013, www.scientificamerican.com/article/dark-money-funds-climate-change-denial-effort/.

PART V

Government intervention in microeconomic markets

Part V focuses on the myriad roles that government policy plays in microeconomic markets. An economic system is a human creation, and governments set the rules of the game, determining which types of economic activities are acceptable and which types are not. Will we allow child labor to make our products, or should our government prevent such activities? How much leeway should firms have when it comes to polluting the environment? And so on. Thus, the degree and type of government intervention in microeconomic markets is a fundamental characteristic of an economic system.

As an example, consider Chapter 19, which takes up market failure and government failure. Left to their own devices, capitalist markets exhibit a number of destructive market failures. Firms sometimes produce unsafe products such as tainted meat. Workers can be exploited and markets can generate inequality and poverty. Huge firms can dominate markets and ruin the environment. Solving these problems requires carefully designed government policy. Yet, sometimes the government can create problems when it intervenes, resulting in government failure.

Chapter 20 takes up the economics of the environment and climate change. Ecological economists take a political economy approach to the study of the environment and view the economic system as situated within a natural environment. We ignore the natural environment at our peril. Environmental economists take a mainstream economics approach and focus more narrowly on the optimal level of pollution abatement using cost–benefit analysis. Both ecological and environmental economists advocate policies to reduce greenhouse gas emissions, such as a carbon tax or a cap-and-trade system. Climate change is one of the major economic issues our society is facing, so we must carefully consider the policy options for addressing climate change.

DOI: 10.4324/9781315636924-23

Chapter 21 explores the importance of public goods and services. Public goods play a crucial role in the economy, so the debate over the level of funding for public goods is an important one. National defense, infrastructure (transportation systems), public health, basic scientific research, and education are extremely important in determining the economic success of a country. Deciding on the right balance of public and private goods and how best to provide public goods are crucial decisions for any economic system.

This section begins by taking up cases in which markets and government fail.

Market failure and government failure

The primary role for government in microeconomic markets

According to the standard mainstream economics model of consumer and producer behavior, in competitive markets firms produce the goods that consumers want at the lowest possible price. If the assumptions of this model hold, unregulated markets should be efficient in providing goods and services and no government intervention is necessary.

However, economists have established eight major categories in which microeconomic markets fail to perform effectively. The market failures are as follows:

1. **Imperfect information about unsafe products**: As highlighted in Chapter 18, firms regularly produce products that are unsafe for consumers. Consumers are often unaware of those problems until it is too late.
2. **Unequal bargaining power in the labor market**: It is regularly the case in capitalist economies that many laborers have few employment options and therefore lack the ability to bargain effectively with employers for decent wages and working conditions.
3. **Monopoly power and insufficient competition**: In noncompetitive markets, monopoly power can allow firms to dominate markets, charging high prices without being particularly efficient.
4. **Negative and positive externalities**: Many markets contain spillover costs or benefits that make market outcomes inefficient. Markets tend to overproduce goods that generate negative spillovers, such as goods whose production causes pollution. Markets underproduce goods that generate positive spillovers, such as education and health care.
5. **Failure to preserve common resources and the environment**: Corporations make profits by using up resources and corporations' costs are

DOI: 10.4324/9781315636924-24

lower if they do not have to make efforts to preserve those resources. But using up precious resources and ruining the environment on which we all depend places a tremendous burden on future generations.

6. **Inadequate supply of public goods**: Unregulated markets do not provide sufficient quantities of public goods such as infrastructure (roads, bridges, train tracks, airports, and ports), and national defense, and market institutions such as laws, regulations, property rights, and contract enforcement.

7. **Increasing costs of essential services**: Essential services such as education and health care have been increasing in price so dramatically in recent years that many people cannot afford them. This presents significant economic problems to individuals and economies.

8. **Fostering of inequality and poverty**: Laissez-faire capitalist economies are associated with extremely high levels of inequality and poverty. Inequality and poverty in turn erode the health of communities.

In each of these cases of market failure, we see examples **when market outcomes are either inefficient, destructive, or counter to the public interest**. The major role for government in microeconomic markets is to correct these market failures.

Unfortunately, sometimes government efforts to correct market failures and support markets create problems of their own. Government failure occurs **when a government effort to correct market failure leads to inefficient or destructive outcomes**. Therefore, government intervention must be implemented very carefully and with substantial oversight.

This chapter discusses each type of market failure, along with some of the government policies that can be used to correct market failures. The chapter also takes up the issue of whether or not the U.S. government has been successful in correcting most market failures and the extent to which government failure has been an issue with these government efforts. The chapter concludes by describing the debate over the balance of government–market activity we should have in a capitalist market economy.

19.0 CHAPTER 19 LEARNING GOALS

After reading this chapter, you should be able to:

■ List the eight types of market failure and explain why markets are not effective in each area.

■ List the government policies that can be used to correct each type of market failure.

■ Analyze the effectiveness of U.S. efforts to deal with market failures, drawing on the examples provided in the text.

■ Identify and give examples of the major sources of government failure.

■ Critically evaluate the perspectives in the debate over how much government intervention we should have in capitalist market economies given the prevalence of market failures and government failures.

19.1 MARKET FAILURE 1: IMPERFECT INFORMATION ABOUT UNSAFE PRODUCTS

Markets can only work efficiently if all actors have complete information about the products they are buying and selling. Unfortunately, there are often cases where markets fail because buyers lack the information they need to make a good decision. This is especially true in cases of **moral hazard**, where sellers have information about negative aspects of a product but refuse to share that information with buyers so that sellers can continue to earn profits.

The existence of moral hazard is, unfortunately, all too common in capitalist markets. As we saw in Chapter 18, car companies regularly find out that some of their cars have problems that make them unsafe or unhealthy. They often hide this information from consumers in order to preserve sales, resulting in deaths and injuries. Similarly, in the food industry we regularly see meat producers selling tainted meat even after there have been cases of serious illness associated with their products. There are cases of drug companies knowing that their products generate serious and even fatal side effects, while hiding these side effects from regulators.

We also see firms attempting to hide unhealthy aspects of their products unless required to provide transparent labeling and advertising. Producers of processed food resist telling consumers the amount of sugar, salt, fat and number of calories in their products for fear of a consumer backlash. Meat producers who irradiate meat to kill harmful bacteria do not want consumers to know that the meat has been irradiated for fear of scaring off customers. Drug companies do not want to tell customers about the potential side effects of their drugs.

Unfortunately, in most cases it is impossible for consumers to have full information about all products. We cannot possibly do extensive research on every product we buy in a market system, so we will never fully know whether a product is truly safe.

As a result, countries have developed regulatory infrastructures to ensure that goods and services are safe and labeled appropriately and that consumers have the information they need to decide which products to buy. In the United States that regulatory infrastructure includes the following elements.

19.1.1 Labeling and advertising laws

Suppliers are not allowed to knowingly lie or distort facts about their goods or services. If they do, there are legal penalties, including fines. Companies producing food products are required to include labels that display health information, especially the number of calories and amount of sugar, salt, and fat. Drug companies are required to list the major side effects in any drug advertisement. The goal is to protect consumers and to provide them with more information so buyers can make more informed decisions with their purchases.

19.1.2 Lawsuits

Another check on corporate misbehavior is the legal framework that allows those who have been harmed by a product to file a lawsuit against the corporation that produces or sells it. If found guilty, firms can face fines of millions of dollars. In recent years, firms have been trying to force consumers to agree to binding arbitration, which tends to be more favorable to corporate interests and less favorable to consumers. Nonetheless, lawsuits remain a major check on corporate misdeeds.

19.1.3 Regulatory bodies

The United States has created a government agency, the Food and Drug Administration (F.D.A.), to oversee product labeling and safety. This body has the power to take dramatic steps, if necessary, against unsafe products. For example, if they find that a product is harmful to human health, they can order it pulled from shelves and prohibit it from being sold. There are similar regulatory bodies for other sectors of the economy. For example, the National Highway Transportation and Safety Administration establishes safety standards and issues recalls for cars, and the Consumer Products Safety Commission regulates products like toys and other household items.

The debates over the laws and agencies that govern product safety are intense and frequently polarized. Consumer advocates such as Public Citizen argue that consumer protections are inadequate, given the prevalence of cases in which consumers are harmed or even killed by unsafe products. Corporations counter that these laws and regulatory bodies are intrusive and extremely costly, which raises prices for consumers and slows economic growth. The fact that each year we catch a new set of corporations selling products that they know can be harmful to consumers seems to indicate that the potential benefits from concealing negative information about a product exceeds the potential costs corporations will incur from lawsuits and regulators' fines.

19.2 MARKET FAILURE 2: UNEQUAL BARGAINING POWER IN THE LABOR MARKET

In Karl Polanyi's classic book, *The Great Transformation*, he observed that market systems tend to work poorly when it comes to regulating labor markets. He labeled labor a "fictitious commodity" because labor is never produced in just the right amount that the labor market needs, the way that other inputs and commodities are produced. Thus, the labor market is rarely, if ever, in equilibrium.

The labor market fails to work properly because the consequences of disequilibrium in the labor market are devastating. A surplus of workers means unemployment, low wages, and desperation for people. A labor surplus can even lead to the devastation of entire communities if unemployment is widespread in a particular region, as has occurred due to the loss of manufacturing jobs in the rust belt cities in the United States (Detroit, Allentown, Cleveland, Flint, Gary, Youngstown, Pittsburgh, etc.). Historically, in capitalist markets there have almost always been more workers available for work than there have been jobs, especially when it comes to unskilled workers. Political economists estimate that at any given moment there are between 1.5 and 2 *billion* surplus workers in the modern global economy, a phenomenon Marx labeled as the reserve army of the unemployed.

So, what are the consequences of a chronic surplus of workers? The main problem is that workers rarely have enough bargaining power to get fair treatment in the labor market when a chronic surplus of labor exists. Firms have much more power than workers most of the time, a phenomenon that results in a market failure. Instead of workers being able to bargain for a fair wage and decent working conditions, as Adam Smith hoped they would in a rapidly growing, competitive economy, workers are often so desperate that they have to accept whatever they are offered. As a consequence of unequal bargaining power, we often see firms paying poverty-level wages and providing unsafe working conditions, especially in unskilled labor markets. To deal with this market failure, governments have developed a variety of policies and laws.

19.2.1 Legalization and support of unions

The United States and other developed countries legalized unions in order to give workers greater bargaining power in the job market. In the United States, the Wagner Act of 1935 gave all unions the legal right to organize and bargain collectively for their members. Workers bargaining individually with an employer have little or no power, and the employer does not have to respond positively to demands for higher wages or better benefits or working conditions because a single worker can be easily replaced. But a majority of workers acting together through a union have significant power. If they do not like wages, benefits, or working conditions, they can go on strike, shutting down the firm's operations. Due to the power of the strike, unions are better able to get fair deals for workers when negotiating with powerful corporations.

Note, however, that beginning with President Reagan in the 1980s, many administrations in the United States have been hostile to unions and have pushed rules and regulations that make it harder for unions to organize workers. This has contributed to a dramatic decline in the number of U.S. workers in unions. Unions represented 35% of non-farm employees in the 1950s, but the unionization rate had fallen to 11% by 2020.

19.2.2 Laws related to wages and working conditions

Since the Great Depression, the government has passed laws establishing a variety of rules and regulations of the labor market. These include the establishment of the eight-hour workday and the rule that overtime pay must be paid to hourly workers who complete over 40 hours of work in a week. The government also created worker safety laws, along with laws abolishing child labor, workers' compensation for workers injured on the job, the minimum wage, and numerous other regulations of labor markets.

19.2.3 Government agencies

In the United States, the National Labor Relations Board establishes the rules of labor negotiations and can hear appeals regarding unfair labor practices. The Department of Labor is responsible for occupational safety, wage and hour standards, unemployment insurance benefits, and reemployment services.

In general, the U.S. government provides much less support for workers than the governments of most other developed countries. U.S. workers have very low unionization rates compared with other developed countries, in part due to U.S. government hostility toward unions. As a result, as Figure 8.3 shows, U.S. manufacturing workers earn significantly less than workers in other developed countries, ranking 14th in the world and earning $10 per hour less than German workers and $28 per hour less than Norwegian workers. U.S. workers also get fewer vacation days and work more hours per week than laborers in other countries. The combination of less powerful unions, lower wages, and less leisure time indicates that U.S. workers are in a weaker position than workers in other developed countries.

19.3 MARKET FAILURE 3: MONOPOLY POWER AND INSUFFICIENT COMPETITION

When markets become too concentrated and insufficiently competitive, markets fail because firms are able to charge extremely high prices, produce poor quality goods and services, and invest little in innovation while still earning vast economic profits. Such markets work very poorly for consumers. When market power becomes too concentrated, the government can step in to regulate firms. The U.S. government has established laws and regulations that outlaw collusion, make it illegal to form a monopoly, and restrict mergers that reduce competition too much.

19.3.1 Outlawing collusion

The Sherman Antitrust Act of 1890 made it illegal for firms to collude in order to fix prices, limit output, or otherwise restrict competition. Under this statute, it is illegal to form a monopoly or a cartel to limit production, and firms cannot communicate and coordinate pricing with each other. Any overt effort to restrain competition is illegal. The government is empowered under this statute to split up huge corporations to make a market more competitive, as it did with Standard Oil.

19.3.2 Restricting mergers

The Clayton Antitrust Act of 1914 allows the government to prevent mergers between corporations that would substantially lessen competition. The Federal Trade Commission (FTC) Act of 1914 allows the government to prevent "unfair methods of competition. ... [U]nfair or deceptive acts or practices in or affecting commerce, are hereby declared unlawful." The FTC and the Antitrust Division of the Department of Justice review mergers to determine whether they will be harmful to consumers, and in certain cases they stop mergers from happening. Some of the most important cases in which the U.S. government has prevented mergers include:

- The 2018 merger of two of the largest producers of semiconductors and chips for mobile devices, Broadcom and Qualcomm.
- The 2015 merger of the two largest cable television and internet providers, Comcast and Time Warner.
- The 2011 merger of two of the largest wireless providers, AT&T and T-Mobile.
- The 2011 merger of two of the largest stock exchanges, Nasdaq and the New York Stock Exchange.
- The 2002 merger of the two largest satellite television providers, EchoStar and DirecTV.
- The 2001 merger of two of the largest airlines, US Airways and United Airlines.

Note, however, that the extent of enforcement of antitrust laws varies significantly with the particular administration in power in the government. Some administrations have adopted the approach of Milton Friedman, Alan Greenspan, and other conservative mainstream and Austrian economists. They argue that it is not a problem for large corporations to become even larger due to the efficiency gains from economies of scale and the continuous presence of rivalrous competition. Other administrations view economic concentration and monopoly power as a major problem that needs constant, vigilant attention by regulators, a view taken by liberal mainstream economists and political economists. Recent studies indicate that over 75% of U.S. industries have grown more concentrated since 2000, accompanied by increasing profits from this growing monopoly power. In general, the U.S. government seems to be allowing industries to become more concentrated, in keeping with the approach advocated by conservative economists.

19.4 MARKET FAILURE 4: NEGATIVE AND POSITIVE EXTERNALITIES

An externality **exists when markets do not effectively incorporate all costs and benefits associated with a particular good or service.** A negative externality occurs **when an economic actor (firm or individual) does something that imposes external costs—costs not included in the market transaction—on others.** A positive externality occurs **when an economic actor does something that generates external benefits—benefits not included in the market transaction—for others.**

19.4.1 Negative externalities

A negative externality occurs when a firm or individual engages in a market activity that harms others and those that are harmed are not compensated for their pain and suffering. In other words, there are "spillover costs" borne by someone other than those participating in the market transaction. There are numerous examples of goods that generate negative externalities, some of them related to the consumption of a good and others related to the production of a good. Consumption externalities include the following cases **when one person using a product imposes costs on others:**

- Smoking a cigarette generates secondhand smoke, which increases cancer rates among nonsmokers.
- Refusing to wear a motorcycle helmet increases the likelihood of a serious injury, which causes increased health care costs for others by raising the overall cost of providing medical insurance.
- Throwing large, loud parties where large amounts of alcohol are consumed in a particular residence reduces the well-being of neighbors and lowers their property values.
- Driving a car or flying in an airplane causes pollution, including carbon dioxide, which contributes to health problems and climate change, which has a negative impact on people around the globe.

Consumption externalities are usually dealt with using specific regulations regarding the use of a product. Smoking is illegal in most public places to eliminate the problems from secondhand smoke. Many states have laws mandating the use of motorcycle helmets to reduce health care costs. Communities have noise ordinances limiting how loud parties can be. And the government imposes limits on the amount of pollution that can be emitted from cars and airplanes.

Production externalities **occur when the production of a good or service imposes external costs on others.** The most significant production externality comes from goods whose production generates pollution, which in turn causes the health and well-being of others to decline as a result.

Where a negative production or consumption externality exists, a product is generating an external cost that is not incorporated into the market price. This results in a market failure because *unregulated markets tend to produce too much of a good that generates a negative externality at too low a price.* Figure 19.1 depicts a good that generates a significant negative externality: Electricity produced by burning coal and other fossil fuels.

When analyzing externalities in mainstream economics, the goal is to make sure that markets reflect *all* costs and benefits. Therefore, we will refer to the demand (D) curve as the marginal benefit (MB) curve because it shows the additional benefit that each buyer gets from consuming each unit of a product. Similarly, we will refer to the supply (S) curve as the marginal cost (MC) curve, because supply curves always reflect the additional cost of producing each unit. The efficient equilibrium in unregulated markets usually occurs where S = D, which is where MC = MB. However, when there is a negative externality, an external cost needs to be incorporated into the market before we can reach the efficient equilibrium.

In Figure 19.1, point A is the **unregulated market equilibrium**, where MB = MC. However, economists estimate that there is a marginal external cost of $20 per 1000 kilowatt hours of electricity generated by burning fossil fuels, due to the negative impact of pollution on health and the environment. Marginal external cost (MEC) is **the external cost generated by the production of each**

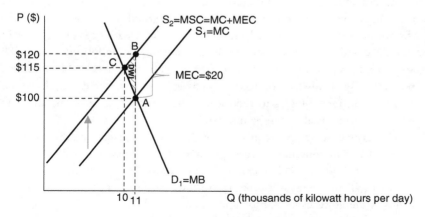

FIGURE 19.1 The effect of a negative externality on the market for electricity.

additional unit of output. If we **add the marginal external cost to the marginal cost**, we get **the true cost of producing** electricity, the marginal social cost. Note that the graph in Figure 19.1 looks like the excise tax graph we saw in Chapter 10, with the supply curve shifting up by exactly the amount of the MEC. If we use the marginal social cost curve, S_2, instead of the marginal cost curve, S_1, we get to the efficient equilibrium at point C. The efficient equilibrium results **when all costs and benefits are incorporated into the market**.

When we compare point A, the unregulated market equilibrium, with point C, the efficient equilibrium that includes all the external costs, we see that unregulated markets produce too many goods at too low a price when there is a negative externality. The unregulated market equilibrium at point A is associated with a lower price and higher quantity than the efficient equilibrium at point C. In addition, unregulated markets with a negative externality generate deadweight loss, which is the shaded area DWL on the graph. DWL is the area of the triangle made by points A, B, and C.

The government's role in the case of negative externalities is to institute a regulation or policy that moves the market from the unregulated equilibrium to the efficient equilibrium. This is called internalizing the externality because it involves **incorporating costs or benefits that are external to the market into the cost and benefit structure of the market**.

There are numerous policies that can be used to internalize a negative externality such as pollution. The goal is to establish policies that move the market to the efficient equilibrium.

1. **Assign property rights**: All externality disputes involve property rights in some way. The problem is that no one owns the water, air, or other natural resources that are being destroyed by pollution. The result is the *tragedy of the commons*: If no one owns a common resource to which everyone has access, the resource will be used until it is gone. But if you could give a community ownership of the air, then polluters would have to pay the community in order to pollute. According to economic theory, we would then arrive at a contract that would specify the optimal amount of pollution, with the polluter offering to reduce pollution or compensate the community for pollution damage. The community would only accept an offer that came with a tolerable amount of pollution. By raising the cost to the company generating the external cost, and by installing technologies to reduce pollution or by compensating the community, the externality can be internalized.

    Unfortunately, assigning property rights can be extremely difficult. Often pollution and its consequences are spread over a vast area, so it is almost impossible to identify all stakeholders, include them in the bargaining process, and get them all to agree to a binding contract. In practice, assigning property rights is therefore usually impractical due to high transactions costs—**the costs to economic actors of reaching a deal**.

2. **Corrective product tax**: To overcome high transactions costs, it is often simpler for the government to impose a direct tax on the product generating the negative externality and to use the revenue from that tax to compensate victims or to mitigate the problem in some way. This can internalize the externality, raising the cost to polluters, compensating victims, and moving the market to the efficient equilibrium.

3. **Environmental standards**: Environmental standards are the **laws, rules, and policies that require producers and consumers to behave in certain ways to protect the environment**. In the United States, all appliances must meet minimum energy efficiency standards, all gas-powered cars must have catalytic converters, all power plants must install scrubbers and other technologies to reduce emissions, firms cannot release toxic chemicals into the environment, the amount of certain pollutants a firm can release is limited, and so on. There are thousands of rules and regulations that limit environmental damage by economic actors in a variety of ways. According to firms, environmental standards can sometimes be cumbersome to comply with. And according to economists, setting legal limits on pollutants reduces the most egregious types of pollution, but it does not give firms an incentive to reduce pollution below their legal limit in the way that emissions taxes do.

4. **Emissions tax**: With an emissions tax, a government agency charges the polluter a tax based on the amount of pollution being emitted. Economists tend to prefer this option to most others because it directly taxes the substance generating the negative externality, and it gives polluters a direct financial incentive to install technologies to reduce their pollution. Via an emissions tax, polluters are forced to determine how much they are willing to pay in order to pollute. As we will see later when we study climate change in more detail, many economists think a carbon tax is the ideal way to solve the carbon emissions problem that is driving global climate change.

5. **Cap-and-trade (pollution rights and tradable emissions permits)**: A cap-and-trade pollution control system involves **the government setting a cap (a legal limit) on the amount of a certain pollutant and then allowing permits to emit that pollutant to be bought and sold**. A limited number of permits are established by the government and granted to firms. Any firm needing to pollute more than the amount their permits allow will have to pay for the right to emit the pollutant by buying additional pollution permits from other companies. Mainstream economists like the cap-and-trade system because it allows governments to determine the amount of a pollutant (the cap) and then it is up to firms to attempt to reduce pollution in the most efficient way possible. Essentially, the government creates a property right—the right to a certain amount of pollution—which can then be bought and sold!

Suppose that the government establishes a cap on emissions of a pollutant that is 10% below the amount current firms usually emit. Each firm must now either reduce their emissions by 10% or purchase emissions permits from other firms. Those firms that can easily reduce their emissions by more than 10% can make a profit by doing so and then selling off their excess pollution rights to other companies that are less able to reduce their emissions. This can lead to a very efficient reduction in pollution, and it can correct the negative externality being generated by adding the costs of generating pollution into the costs experienced by firms in the market. Cap-and-trade is being used in the United States to limit the emission of sulfur dioxide, which causes acid rain, and in Europe cap-and-trade is used to reduce greenhouse gas emissions.

6. **Voluntary programs**: Governments sometimes institute voluntary programs to encourage good behavior. Many communities offer voluntary recycling and encourage commuters not to drive every day. Most governments encourage firms to reduce their emissions and sometimes offer incentives for them to do so. Also, the threat of regulation if firms do not voluntarily reduce their emissions can spur firms to action. In general, voluntary programs have small but positive impacts, reducing emissions by up to 5% and causing small changes in behavior.

Markets for goods that generate negative externalities produce too large a quantity of the good and sell it for too low a price. Governments seek to correct these inefficiencies by internalizing the externality. Usually, this means imposing additional costs on the firm that generates the negative externality and using these revenues to correct the problem or to compensate those who experience the external cost. The United States has a mixed record when it comes to alleviation of pollution and correction of other negative externalities. We have made great strides in preventing some harmful emissions such as ozone-destroying chlorofluorocarbons and acid rain–causing sulfur dioxide. But the United States is a laggard in terms of addressing climate change, having made substantially less effort than other developed countries.

19.4.2 Positive externalities

A positive externality **occurs when an economic actor receives external benefits from a good that is purchased by someone else but does not pay for those benefits**. Essentially, the person purchasing the good gets private benefits for themselves but some external benefits spill over to others. One classic example is education. When a person receives an education, they will typically have a lifetime of better opportunities and higher pay. However, they are not the only ones who benefit from their education. Employers are able to hire a more productive worker and they are able to spend less on training, so employers reap a substantial external benefit from the educations of their workers. Society as a whole also benefits, because educated workers earn higher incomes, pay more in taxes, and contribute more to society. But in an unregulated market, there is no requirement that employers and society contribute to the educational costs of individuals to pay for the spillover benefits they receive.

Another example of a product that creates private benefits for the person who purchases the good along with public benefits for many others is the flu vaccination. Figure 19.2 shows the market for flu vaccinations. Once again we note that supply is the same as marginal cost and demand is the same as marginal benefit. The unregulated market equilibrium occurs at point A, where S = D and MC = MB. However, this is an inefficient outcome because flu vaccinations generate a marginal external benefit (MEB) of $50: Any person who gets vaccinated benefits all those around them, who are less likely to get sick. Employers benefit from healthier employees, and society as a whole benefits from a happier and healthier society and a more productive economy. Marginal external benefit is **the external benefit generated by the consumption of each additional unit of the good**. If we **add the marginal external benefit to the marginal benefit**, we get the true benefit of consuming a flu vaccination, the marginal social benefit (MSB).

To incorporate the marginal external benefit, the demand curve should shift up by exactly the amount of the MEB, giving us the marginal social benefit. This shows us the **efficient equilibrium**, which occurs at point C in Figure 19.2. Note that the efficient equilibrium at point C occurs at a higher price and higher quantity than the unregulated market equilibrium at point A, indicating that *markets should devote more resources to goods that generate a positive externality.*

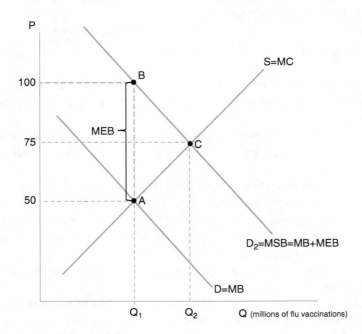

FIGURE 19.2 A positive externality (flu vaccinations).

There are two main strategies governments can choose to "internalize" a positive externality in order to move markets to the efficient equilibrium:

1. **Enact a per unit subsidy** equal to the marginal external benefit. The subsidy can be paid to either consumers or suppliers, and the cost of the subsidy should be paid by those receiving the external benefit.
2. **Government provision of the good** can also cause markets to reach the efficient equilibrium. The government directly provides flu shots at free clinics and provides free education at public schools because of the huge external benefits associated with these goods.

Either of these policies should ensure that society devotes more resources to the good and that consumers buy more of it than they would without government intervention.

Once again, the United States has a mixed record when it comes to efforts to internalize positive externalities. The United States lags behind many other developed countries in public health and public education. But the United States has the world's best (and most expensive) university system thanks to a combination of public and private universities.

19.5 MARKET FAILURE 5: FAILURE TO PRESERVE COMMON RESOURCES AND THE ENVIRONMENT

Economists identify types of goods based on the following key characteristics:

- Rivalrousness: **Whether or not the consumption or use of a good by one economic actor prevents its consumption or use by another person.**
- Excludability: **Whether or not it is possible to prevent economic actors who have not paid for a good from having access to that good.**

Private goods are rivalrous and excludable: One person or firm buys the good and they can prevent others who have not paid for that good from benefiting from it.

A good that generates a positive externality is rivalrous but nonexcludable. Purchasing a flu vaccine means that other people cannot use that same vaccine you did (making the vaccine rivalrous). But it is not possible to exclude the people around you and your employer from benefiting from your flu vaccination (nonexcludability).

Similarly, a common resource is **a particular type of good that is rivalrous in consumption—consumption by an economic actor prevents its consumption by another person—and nonexcludable—people cannot be**

stopped from consuming or using the good. A classic example is the stock of fish in a particular fishing area. When one fishing boat catches a fish, it denies other fishing boats the possibility of catching that same fish. However, no fishing boat can be prevented from fishing in an unregulated fishing area, so fishing is a nonexcludable activity.

The problem with common resources is the tragedy of the commons. **In a system in which resources are shared, economic actors (firms and individuals) that pursue self-interest will deplete or ruin the common good.** The tragedy of the commons manifests itself in different ways.

19.5.1 Depletable resources

Depletable resources **have a finite supply and cannot be replenished.** They tend to be used up in unregulated markets rather than conserved, and that can cause disruptions in the economy when they become scarce. Depletable resources include minerals, fossil fuels such as oil and natural gas, water in some aquifers, the ozone layer, and other resources that are either in finite supply or whose speed of replenishment is so slow that economists treat them as if they are finite.

Oil is one of our most important examples of a depletable resource. Scientists and economists believe that oil production will peak sometime in the very near future, after which there will be a long, steady decline in oil production. Also, we have already used up the most easily accessible oil stocks, so new supplies of oil will be increasingly expensive to obtain. This could have devastating consequences given the dependency of our economy on oil for energy and transportation. Ideally, in cases of a depletable resource we would reduce our consumption of the resource as it becomes scarce to preserve some of it for the future and to allow our economic system more time to find alternatives.

But unregulated markets do not necessarily work on the principle of safeguarding resources for the future. As a resource becomes scarce, its price increases, and this encourages additional exploration and more intensive use of the resource because of the increased profits in the industry. Markets tend to try to supply more and more depletable resources as they become scarce because the price increases that result from scarcity make it so profitable to do so. Fortunately, as the price increases, consumers start using less of the resource and they look for substitutes. Also, it becomes increasingly profitable to invest in alternatives to the scarce resource. Therefore, we can hope that by the time oil becomes scarce, we will have developed robust alternatives to fossil fuels. However, it is not clear that we can rely on this phenomenon to completely replace our dependency on oil, nor is it clear that the transition to renewable energy can be made without major shocks to the economy.

Thus, when it comes to key depletable resources, the government's job is to **encourage conservation and exploration of alternatives** so the economy is able to adjust without a major crisis. The U.S. economy experienced two major recessions in the 1970s due to oil price shocks, and we do not want to repeat those experiences. Most governments around the world are encouraging the use of alternative energies to nudge their economies away from a dependence on fossil fuels, a strategy that will cushion the disruptions the economy experiences as fossil fuels are depleted. Cultivation of alternatives also has the potential to create new profitable industries to replace the scarce resource. The United States made some efforts to reduce its dependency on fossil fuels during the Obama administration, President Trump reversed those efforts and President Biden restarted them.

19.5.2 Renewable resources

Renewable resources **can be replenished if they are not used too intensively**; however, they tend to be overused in unregulated markets so that they cannot adequately replenish themselves. Examples of renewable resources include fish, livestock, wood, water, and air.

When it comes to renewable resources, governments need to act to prevent the overuse of the resources to levels where they cannot be replenished. Fishing provides a classic example. Fishing in the North Atlantic Ocean has been suspended several times for several years at a time by the U.S. government. Overfishing depleted fish stocks to levels so low there was a danger of fish not being able to replenish themselves.

It may seem odd that fishing boats catch so many fish that they end up putting themselves out of business. But the economics of the industry make it clear why this happens. No one owns society's common resources, in this case ocean fish. Therefore, fishing firms do not have to pay for the damage they do to the common resource, and they have no direct financial incentive to limit the amount of fish they catch in an unregulated market. In addition, fishing boat owners need to make their boat payments and earn enough income to survive. As fishing stocks dwindle due to overfishing, the fishing boat owners have to stay out longer and longer to earn enough to stay in business. As all of the fishing boats go to more and more extreme efforts to catch fish, fish stocks dwindle faster and faster. The result, inevitably, is a crisis where the government must step in to stop overfishing in order to give fish stocks time to replenish themselves.

Governments approach the overuse of renewable resources by **limiting market actors' use of the resource**. In the case of fishing, the National Marine Fisheries service banned fishing in the North Atlantic until fish stocks were adequately replenished.

A new method being used in some areas is an **individual transferable quota (ITQ)**, also called a catch-share system. Under an ITQ, the regulatory body determines an overall limit for how many fish can be caught sustainably. Each fishing boat is allotted a quota that is a percentage of the overall catch limit. The fishing boat owners can even buy and sell quota allotments. In essence, the ITQ has become a property right—the right to a certain percentage of the common resource of ocean fish. Now that this resource has a price attached to it, there are limits to the amount of abuse the resource will experience. Areas using ITQs have seen a replenishment of fish stocks due to the strict limits placed on how many fish can be caught and a return to profitability for fishing boats.

There are numerous other examples of the overuse of renewable resources. The United States has had to impose restrictions on the clearcutting of timber because even though this method is cheaper and more profitable in the short run for lumber firms, clearcutting results in soil loss and renders the land inhospitable for new tree growth for many decades into the future. The government of South Africa had to impose water rationing in 2018 because a five-year drought had dramatically reduced water supplies and businesses and consumers were not conserving enough. In general, markets do not adequately protect stocks of renewable resources, so these resources have to be managed by governments in some way.

The United States tends to be reactive when it comes to preserving renewable resources. Once a crisis hits, the government steps in to fix the problem. A more active government would identify looming crises and take concrete steps before dramatic action is necessary.

19.6 MARKET FAILURE 6: INADEQUATE SUPPLY OF PUBLIC GOODS

As we saw earlier, private goods (most consumer goods) are excludable and rivalrous: When you purchase a good for yourself, you prevent others from having that good and you keep all of the benefits from that good to yourself. Common resources and goods that generate externalities are nonexcludable—the benefits (or costs) are broadly shared, but if one person purchases or takes a good or resource, others are not able to use that same good or resource.

Club goods such as streaming services (Netflix, Spotify) are excludable in that only those who pay for the service can use it, but they are nonrivalrous because one person using the service does not prevent others from also using the service (up to the limit of the network's capacity). Similarly, cinemas are excludable (you cannot get in to see the movie unless you buy a ticket) but nonrivalrous up to the cinema's capacity (many other people can also buy a ticket for the same movie until the cinema is filled).

A public good is truly unique in that public goods are both nonexcludable and nonrivalrous. Public goods are available to everyone equally, whether or not they pay. Nonexcludability means that one person using a public road does not prevent others from also using that road (the road isn't used up after one person uses it). And nonrivalrous means that people cannot be prevented from using the good, even if they do not pay for it. Someone who does not pay their taxes can still use public roads, because there is no mechanism to ensure that only those who pay taxes use public roads.

	Excludable	Nonexcludable
Rivalrous	**Private goods** Food, clothing, beer, automobiles	**Common resources, externalities** Fish stocks, oil, gas, timber
Non-rivalrous	**Club goods** Theaters, streaming services, software	**Public goods** National defense, air, roads, street lights, public parks

FIGURE 19.3 Table of the four types of goods based on excludability and rivalrousness.

Figure 19.3 lays out the four types of goods classified by excludability and rivalrousness. *Unregulated markets do not work well for resources or goods that are nonexcludable.* Unregulated markets tend to overuse common resources or overproduce goods generating negative externalities. Unregulated markets tend to under produce goods that generate positive externalities. Similarly, *unregulated markets do not produce sufficient quantities of public goods because of the free rider problem.* A free rider problem occurs **when economic actors who benefit from a resource, good, or service do not have to pay for that benefit, resulting in an undersupply**. Public goods are not sufficiently profitable to be produced by unregulated markets because some consumers will not pay for the benefits they receive.

Public radio (and television) provides a classic example of the free rider problem for public goods. Public radio depends on donations for a large percentage of its funding. It is available for free and without advertisements to anyone with a radio or internet connection, whether or not they make a donation, making it nonexcludable. One person listening to public radio does not affect the ability of anyone else to listen, making it nonrivalrous. Unfortunately, studies indicate that only about 11% of people who listen to public radio in the United States make a contribution, which means that *89% of public radio listeners are free riders*! Similar problems affect public television.

As a result, public radio and television in the United States are chronically underfunded, and they are not able to supply the level of programming that people say they want. They also have to devote long periods of time each year to regular pledge drives to try to encourage the free riders to make donations. Due to the magnitude of the free rider problem, most other countries fund public radio and television with dedicated government funds raised via taxes instead of relying on voluntary donations.

Additional examples of public goods include the following:

- **Physical infrastructure** such as roads and bridges, airports, lighthouses, and parks
- **Market infrastructure**, including the legal and regulatory framework that makes markets work

- **Public services** such as national defense, police and fire protection, the legal system, public transportation, public radio and television, and public schooling
- **The environment**, including air, water, soil, and pollution abatement
- **Public knowledge** such as scientific research
- **Public health** and disease prevention.

One of the major determinants of the quality of an economic system is the extent and condition of its public goods.

In addition to issues of quality, many public goods are subject to *congestion* if the supply of public goods is limited compared with the number of people who want to use public goods. For example, there can be too much traffic on roads and long waits at public health care clinics.

In general, **the government tries to provide the amount of public goods that citizens demand and then uses tax revenues and fees to pay for them**. Public goods cannot be provided effectively by unregulated markets due to the free rider problem, so governments either provide public goods directly through a government agency or they engage in contracts with private sector firms to provide the public goods.

For example, roads and bridges are built and maintained by either government agencies or private contractors hired by the government. Scientific knowledge is generated via public universities or subsidies to private universities. National defense is directly provided by the government, sometimes with assistance from private contractors.

So how good is the quality of U.S. public goods? According to the American Society of Civil Engineers, which studies this topic extensively, America's infrastructure earned a grade of C– in 2021. These experts see major problems in aviation, dams, drinking water, energy, hazardous waste, waterways, levees, parks, roads, schools, public transit, and wastewater. It would take $2.6 trillion to correct these problems over the next ten years but much less has been allocated. Fixing our infrastructure problems would mean a significant increase in taxes or deficit spending, which politicians seem unwilling to do.

Public goods are so crucial to the functioning of an economic system that we devote a whole chapter to public goods and services later in the book. And we devote another chapter to the economics of the environment because our survival as a species depends on its preservation.

19.7 MARKET FAILURE 7: INCREASING COSTS OF ESSENTIAL SERVICES

The uneven impact of technological change and productivity growth tends to increase the cost of essential services such as health care and education over time.

This is a market failure because unregulated markets cannot provide these essential services at a price that ensures that everyone has access to them.

The key issue with this complex market failure is the differential impact of technological change and productivity growth on the cost of manufactured goods versus the impact of such changes on the cost of services. As technology improves in manufacturing, this increases the productivity of workers and reduces the cost of manufactured goods. The quality of televisions improves every year even as the price of a high-quality television declines thanks to technological advances.

Technological advances usually have a very different impact on the service sector, however. When a new technology is invented in health care, such as robot-assisted surgery, the quality of health care improves. But the *cost* of health care increases because hospitals striving to provide the best care must invest huge amounts of money purchasing the latest technological advances. Similarly, colleges need to provide students with access to the latest technologies in order to develop the skills they need in the modern workplace. Colleges must invest vast sums of money keeping their labs and computer resources up to date. The quality of education improves as a result, but it gets increasingly expensive to educate each student.

In addition, productivity does not increase in a similar fashion in services. Providing health care still generally requires the same number of doctors and nurses even with technological improvements, so the productivity of each worker does not increase much. Similarly, college education still requires the same number of professors and support staff even with the new technologies, so the productivity of workers in education also does not change much, if at all. However, health care workers can still demand the same level of pay increases as workers in sectors with fast-growing productivity. Thus, rising salaries in manufacturing are offset by productivity increases, whereas rising salaries in services are not.

The result is that *over time the prices of key services such as health care and education, along with other services such as childcare and police protection, have increased dramatically and have taken up ever larger shares of the country's output.* As Figure 19.4 shows, from 1996 to 2016 the prices of college tuition, childcare, and health care increased by

College tuition	197%
Child care	122%
Health care	105%
Food	64%
Housing costs	61%
Average increase in prices	**55%**
New cars	2%
Clothing	-5%
Wireless service	-45%
Televisions	-96%

FIGURE 19.4 Table showing price increases of services vs. goods, 1996–2016.

far more than the average increase in prices, whereas the prices of manufactured goods stayed the same or, in some cases, fell dramatically.

Given that education, childcare, and health care are essential for the economy, **governments need to establish programs to ensure that these services are available to citizens**. Many governments, such as the social democracies of Europe, directly **provide these goods** to all citizens. The United States offers **subsidies** such as financial aid for college and tax breaks for childcare expenses and health care. The U.S. government also provides public education from kindergarten through high school and medical care to the elderly (via the Medicare program), the poor (via the Medicaid program), and veterans. However, in 2019 there were 29 million U.S. citizens who were uninsured because they were not covered by these programs and they did not have employment that came with health insurance. We will study more about health care markets in the chapter on public goods and services. The United States is the only developed country without a national health insurance system.

19.8 MARKET FAILURE 8: FOSTERING INEQUALITY AND POVERTY

After more than two centuries of capitalism, it has become clear that unregulated capitalist markets tend to foster inequality and poverty. One of the most interesting and important explanations of why this is the case comes from economist Thomas Piketty in his groundbreaking book, *Capital in the Twenty-First Century*. Piketty observes that there is a central contradiction in capitalism, which we will call the Piketty thesis: **When the rate of return going to owners of capital exceeds the rate of economic growth, inequality tends to increase because profits and other income from owning capital grow faster than wage income**. Essentially, when the economy grows very quickly and when government policies favor workers, workers' wages grow more quickly than the profits of wealthy capitalists and the economy becomes more equal. When the economy grows more slowly such that workers have less bargaining power, and when government policies favor capitalists, inequality increases. Looking at more than a century of experiences of many developed countries, Piketty finds that it is generally the case that returns to capital outstrip the rate of economic growth, so capitalism has a built-in tendency toward increasing inequality unless efforts are made to boost growth and redistribute income to workers.

We see this quite clearly from the U.S. experience since World War II. As Figure 19.5(a) shows, when the U.S. economy grew quickly and when the U.S. government pursued pro-labor and anti-poverty programs from 1950 to 1970, the share of national income going to the poorest fifth of the U.S. population dramatically increased.[1] The United States became more equal during this era. Clearly, poor people (the lowest fifth) benefited the most during this period, whereas the

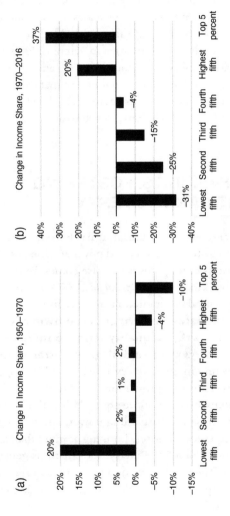

FIGURE 19.5 Changing U.S. income shares since 1950.

richest fifth, and especially the richest 5%, saw the largest decline in their share of income.

Note, however, that rich people did not experience a *decline* in income during this period. As Figure 19.6(a) shows, on average all income groups received higher incomes from 1947 to 1973.[2] The bottom 20% of the population experienced more rapid income *growth* than the top 20%.

The story is vastly different since 1970. As Figure 19.5(b) shows, from 1970 to 2016 the share of income going to the lowest fifth of the U.S. population decreased significantly, whereas the share of income going to the highest 20% and especially the top 5% dramatically increased. Even more disturbing, as Figure 19.6(b) shows, the vast proportion of increases in income since 1973 have gone to highest (richest) 20% of the population. The bottom 60% of the U.S. population has had nearly stagnant incomes during this 43-year period.

Some of the forces driving increases in inequality in recent years include the following:

- **Globalization** has resulted in declining incomes for less skilled workers in developed countries, who must now compete with unskilled workers around the world. Meanwhile, globalization has increased the demand for skilled workers.
- **Technological change** has replaced jobs for many less skilled workers while creating jobs for workers who manufacture and use advanced technology.
- **Declines in unions**, which were often due to attacks by the government, have left less skilled workers unable to demand higher wages.
- **Changes in government policy**, especially tax cuts for the rich and for corporations, coupled with cuts in welfare and assistance for the poor, have contributed to increasing inequality since 1980.

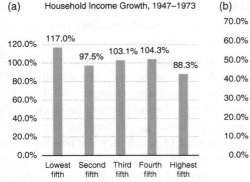

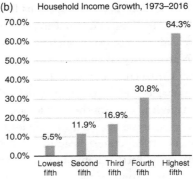

FIGURE 19.6 Household income growth since 1947.

Economists have identified five dimensions to inequality in modern capitalism that help us understand why different groups experience inequality in a variety of ways. Inequality is driven primarily by (1) social class, (2) race, (3) gender, (4) nationality, and (5) ability.

1. **Social class**: According to political economists, social class plays the dominant role in determining most people's chances in life. Due to financial capital, educational access, health access, and social capital (networks of colleagues and friends), class is the primary determinant of an individual's economic success. Parents' success is passed down to their children via superior access to education, health, and connections. Globalization, technological change, the decline in unions, and changes in government policy since 1980 have all undermined the less skilled segments of the working class and resulted in dramatic increases in inequality.

2. **Race**: Numerous economic studies indicate widespread racism in the United States. For example, with identical credentials, resumes with "white" names like Brendan are 50% more likely to get called for an interview than resumes with "black" names like Jamal. Black and Latino applicants with identical resumes and similar interview training as whites are only half as likely to get a callback or a job offer. The probability of being black, unarmed, and shot by police is about 3.5 times higher than it is for whites. And in 2015, the median hourly earnings of black men were only 73% of the median hourly earnings of white men, and Hispanic men earned only 69% of whites.

3. **Gender**: The #MeToo movement exposed the widespread existence of sexual harassment in the workplace. In addition, women face significantly unequal pay. In 2015 white women earned only 82% of what white men earned; black women earned only 65% and Hispanic women earned only 58%. Resume studies of equal candidates indicate that women are less likely to get hired than men in male-dominated fields and that women will be offered lower salaries. This highlights a major component of gender inequality: Occupational segregation. Women make up a disproportionate number of workers in low paid, female-dominated occupations like nursing, administrative assistance, reception, cleaning, and childcare. Women are also much less likely to get hired for a leadership position, such as a CEO or a law partner.

4. **Nationality**: A quick glance at the incomes of nations of the world indicates vast inequality between developed nations and underdeveloped nations. The global economy is structured so that many poor countries in Africa, Latin America, and Southeast Asia are stuck producing primary products (coffee, cocoa, minerals, etc.) or simple manufactured goods (textiles) that generate very little income. As a result, the incomes of people in those nations fall further and further behind those of developed countries.

5. **Ability**: Some of the differences in income that we see are a result of different aptitudes and abilities. This category is much less problematic than the others in

that inequality stemming from differences in ability is related to productivity. Therefore, most mainstream economists do not worry as much about inequality generated by differences in ability, except to the extent that ability is often a product of luck and therefore may not justify an excessively high return.

Inequality is considered to be a market failure due to the host of economic and social problems that it causes. Foremost among those problems is **poverty**.

To measure poverty, economists usually try to determine a minimum acceptable level of income. In the United States, the government measures poverty by establishing the cost of an "economy food plan" that constitutes the minimum expenditure on food a family needs to survive. That number is then multiplied by three because in 1961, when the poverty level was first established in the United States, families spent one-third of their incomes on food. In 2018, the poverty line for a family of four in an urban area was measured at $25,100. Families earning less than that amount are considered to be living in poverty.

Many economists believe that number is far too low. In the modern era, food costs have declined relative to the costs of housing, health care, childcare, and other crucial goods and services. Modern families usually spend only one-sixth of their income on food, which means the poverty line should probably be twice as high. As Figure 19.7 shows, in 2019, the official U.S. poverty rate was 10.5%, with 34 million people living in poverty.[3] The poverty rate among blacks was much higher at 18.8%, as was the poverty rate among Hispanics, which was 15.7%.

Figure 19.7 also shows the impact of economic growth and government policies on poverty rates. From 1962 to 1972, the war on poverty initiated by President Lyndon Johnson coupled with robust economic growth cut the poverty rate from 21% to 11.9%. Since then, the poverty rate has actually increased somewhat as

Year	All People		Black		Hispanic	
	Number	Percent	Number	Percent	Number	Percent
1962	38,625	21.0				
1972	24,460	11.9	7,710	33.3	2,414	22.8
1982	34,398	15.0	9,697	35.6	4,301	29.9
1992	38,014	14.8	10,827	33.4	7,592	29.6
2002	34,570	12.1	8,602	24.1	8,555	21.8
2012	46,496	15.0	10,911	27.2	13,616	25.6
2015	43,123	13.5	10,020	24.1	12,133	21.4
2016	40,616	12.7	9,234	22.0	11,137	19.4
2017	39,698	12.3	8,993	21.2	10,790	18.3
2018	38,146	11.8	8,884	20.8	10,526	17.6
2019	33,984	10.5	8,073	18.8	9,545	15.7

FIGURE 19.7 Table showing people below the poverty line in the United States (in thousands).

economic growth has slowed and as the government has devoted fewer resources to fighting poverty.

Poverty is associated with a number of significant economic problems, including crime, homelessness, poor health, high rates of infant mortality, obesity, family disintegration, lower productivity, depression, and lower intergenerational mobility. To address poverty and reduce the impact of these problems, **the United States has a number of anti-poverty programs**:

- **Food assistance** via the Supplemental Nutrition Assistance Program (SNAP, formerly food stamps) and the Special Supplemental Nutrition Program for Women, Infants, and Children (WIC)
- **Health care assistance** via Medicare for the elderly and Medicaid for the poor
- **Housing assistance** such as vouchers, rental assistance, or public housing
- **Tax credits** via the Earned Income Tax Credit (EITC) program
- **Welfare programs** especially Temporary Assistance for Needy Families (TANF).

These programs are almost all "means tested," which means that people must apply and prove that they qualify. TANF has work requirements along with a lifetime limit of five years. As we saw earlier, compared with other developed countries, the United States spends less on fighting poverty than other developed countries and as a result it has a much higher poverty rate.

In addition to poverty, inequality creates other problems for the economy. In particular, **inequality may reduce economic growth**. A 2014 study by International Monetary Fund economists J. Ostry, A. Berg, and C. Tsangarides found that lower inequality is "robustly correlated with faster and more durable growth," whereas higher inequality slows growth.[4] There are a number of possible reasons for this. First, rich people spend a lower percentage of income than poor people, so a redistribution of income toward the poor results in an increase in spending, which in turn stimulates business growth. Second, greater inequality reduces social cohesion and fosters instability, which can have an extremely negative impact in business investment. Third, increases in inequality necessitate greater government spending on welfare programs and greater private spending on security, which leaves less money for growth-producing public and private investment.

The United States has the most income inequality of any developed country because it does less than other countries to reduce inequality. The OECD ranks the United States 35th out of 37 countries in terms of poverty and inequality. Nonetheless, the U.S. government does take some small steps to reduce inequality. First, the United States has a modestly **progressive income tax** where rich people pay a higher percentage of their income in taxes than poor people, which is displayed in Figure 19.8. The top U.S. marginal tax rate of 37% is much lower than the top marginal tax rate we find in Sweden, which was 62% in 2018. In

Single taxable income	Marginal tax rate
$0 – $9,525	10%
$9,526 – $38,700	12%
$38,701 – $82,500	22%
$82,501 – $157,500	24%
$157,501 – $200,000	32%
$200,001 – $500,000	35%
$500,001 +	37%

FIGURE 19.8 Table of U.S. tax rates, 2018.

addition, as we will see later, the overall U.S. tax system is regressive, taxing the richest 400 families at a lower rate than everyone else, including the very poor (see Figure 29.7).

The United States has an **earned income tax credit**, which provided tax credits of up to $6318 to individuals who earned less than $20,600 and families who earned less than $53,930 in 2017.

Estate taxes also redistribute some income, although they are easy to avoid with a good tax lawyer. And **free public education** and **subsidized college education** can offer some degree of class mobility so that some of the children from lower social classes are able to move up.

The fact that the United States has the most inequality and the highest poverty rate of any developed country indicates that the U.S. government does not consider inequality and poverty to be a major market failure. This stems largely from the political ideology of supply-side economics, whose supporters in the United States are quite powerful. Supply-side advocates believe that lower taxes for the rich and for corporations will boost economic growth. In other words, designing policies to increase the revenues of suppliers should stimulate businesses to invest more and to create more jobs. Statistical evidence does not tend to support this view. Nonetheless, supply-side economics is a powerful ideology that encourages inequality. In contrast, many other economists believe that inequality is one of the major problems confronting contemporary society, so we will devote an entire chapter to the topic later in the book.

Now that we have laid out the major market failures that occur in unregulated markets, along with the government policies used to address those market failures, we also need to take up the issue of government failure. In cases where government intervention is ineffective, it may not be useful to have the government attempt to correct market failures.

19.9 GOVERNMENT FAILURE

The amount of government intervention in the United States has declined since 1980, largely due to the belief by supply-side politicians that government has become too large and intrusive and that government failure is a more significant problem than market failure. Government regulations can limit the ability of private actors to pursue maximum profits in the manner they prefer. Government bureaucracies that create and enforce polices are not always efficient. Government programs require taxes for funding, and taxes come out of funds that corporations and individuals could use in other ways. Thus, a key question for society is whether or not the benefits of government intervention to correct market failures are sufficient to offset the cost of government programs and the inefficiencies created by government failure.

According to public choice theory, put forth by economists James Buchanan and Gordon Tullock from the Austrian school of economics, government failure comes in the following varieties:

1. **Moral hazard** occurs when the pursuit of self-interest by politicians and civil servants leads them to operate for their own benefit rather than for the good of society, especially due to the role of money in politics. Example: Pennsylvania Judge Mark Ciavarella Jr. took bribes for sentencing juvenile offenders to jail time in for-profit juvenile detention centers.

2. **Short-termism** happens when politicians make decisions to look good for the next election rather than making the best long-term decisions. Example: In 2018 President Trump installed steep tariffs on steel to protect steel jobs in the short term, even though over the long term the United States will likely lose more jobs in manufacturing industries that use steel.

3. **Regulatory capture** results when industries under control of a regulatory body are able to capture the regulatory process, exerting undue influence over how laws and regulations are established and enforced. Example: A review panel of the Environmental Protection Agency with close ties to the natural gas industry ruled that fracking to extract natural gas "posed little or no threat" to drinking water despite scientific evidence to the contrary.

4. **Inefficiency** can result when government policies are badly designed, especially when they create cumbersome and inefficient bureaucratic structures and when they result in unintended consequences. Example: In the 1990s, U.S. welfare policy discouraged some people from working because they could lose more in government benefits than they gained in income if they took a job.

5. **Soft budget constraints** occur when industries expect to be continuously bailed out and therefore have no incentive to become efficient or to avoid excessive risk. Example: Many economists worry that the bailout of large banks after the financial crisis of 2008 will result in banks expecting to be bailed out whenever a crisis hits, no matter how irresponsibly they behaved. Previous bailouts have encouraged banks to continue to engage in a larger proportion of risky investments than would otherwise be the case.

Government failure can be addressed in three ways. **Laissez-faire** advocates use government failure to argue for *less government* intervention, arguing that in most cases it is not possible for the government to be as efficient as the unregulated market. **Keynesian** economists advocate *improving government* intervention to reduce government failure, arguing that where market failures are pervasive and problematic government intervention is preferable to the consequences of market failure. **Political economists** tend to see government intervention as primarily reflecting the interests of the dominant classes, and they argue for a *more extensive control of the government and the economy by democratic means.*

Eliminating or reducing government failure usually requires greater investment in salaries and resources for regulatory bodies, which in turn requires more tax revenue. Societies must therefore choose between investing more in government to better control market failures or living with the consequences of market failure and government failure.

19.10 CONCLUSION

As with so many issues, economists disagree on how to approach the issues of market failures and government failures. From a pro-corporate perspective espoused by **conservative** Austrian and mainstream **economists**, U.S. consumers and voters get exactly what they want from the U.S. economic system. If consumers cared about the environment, they would not purchase products that harmed the environment. If voters cared about public goods, they would elect politicians who made the provision of public goods a priority. Therefore, from this perspective, the poor quality of public goods in the United States and the ability of corporations to externalize costs represents the will of the people, who evidently prefer cheaper private goods to a clean environment and nice public goods. This situation indicates a widespread distrust of government intervention in the United States brought on by episodes of government failure and by a culture that prefers individual freedoms to public goods.

From a **political economy perspective**, corporations are externalizing machines. Due to their structural imperative to maximize short-term profits, corporations have an incentive to avoid paying any cost if they can. Therefore, we can expect corporations to attempt to avoid costly recalls of dangerous products, expensive worker safety measures, higher wages, environmental regulations, and any other significant cost, pushing those costs on to the rest of society. In other words, corporations have a direct financial incentive to externalize as many costs as possible. The government's job is to force corporations to internalize their external costs, making corporations responsible for their products and their impact on workers and communities. The fact that the United States has made limited progress in addressing the market failures discussed above seems to indicate that the

U.S. government is not very effective in internalizing external costs. Similarly, the fact that the U.S. infrastructure is crumbling and public goods are generally in disrepair indicates a general philosophy of supporting the private sector (via tax cuts) rather than the public sector (via greater spending on government regulatory bodies). Political economists tend to see this social imbalance as a product of the power corporations have in shaping the U.S. economic system via their financial clout and their influence over elections and legislation rather than as the will of the people.

A more middle-of-the-road **mainstream Keynesian** approach would acknowledge both perspectives. Markets clearly generate significant market failures, and the government is often successful in reducing the negative impact of market failures. The government does not always succeed in such efforts due to the existence of government failure. The goal should be to attempt to provide the optimal amount of public goods and control of external costs by weighing costs and benefits. The costs of government failure must be included in the assessment of costs and benefits to accurately determine whether the benefits of government intervention outweigh the costs.

In future chapters we will take up some of the important themes of this chapter and go into greater detail. In particular, we focus on public goods and the size and role of government, along with two of the most important economic issues of our time—increasing inequality and environmental devastation (climate change).

QUESTIONS FOR REVIEW

1. Which of the eight market failures do you think is most important? Explain your answer.
2. Construct a table in which you list each market failure, give an example of each one, and list the U.S. government programs designed to correct each market failure.
3. Which of the eight market failures is the U.S. government least effective in correcting? Why do you think the U.S. government is particularly ineffective in this area?
4. Explain the role of unions in correcting the market failure of unequal bargaining power in the labor market. Do you think the U.S. government should encourage or discourage the formation of unions? Explain your answer briefly.
5. Describe the debate over the use of antitrust laws to prevent mergers and monopolies. Why are many conservative economists untroubled by monopoly power? Why do other economists consider monopoly power to be a major market failure? Which position do you support? Why?
6. Explain what is meant by "internalizing" an externality and why governments attempt to achieve this goal when externalities are present.

7. Using a graph, explain why markets lead to inefficient outcomes when a negative externality is present. Also using the graph, explain how the government can internalize a negative externality.

8. Which market failures are created by a lack of *property rights*? Explain how cap-and-trade and "individual transferable quotas" solve the property rights problem in specific types of markets.

9. How are market failure and government failure connected with the problem of *moral hazard*? How might moral hazard be reduced or eliminated?

10. Why do unregulated markets work poorly when it comes to common resources or goods that are **nonexcludable**? Explain and give specific examples.

11. Explain why the prices of essential services such as health care and education are increasing faster than the prices of manufactured goods. How can the government deal with this market failure?

12. Analyze the issue of market failure and government failure and evaluate whether or not the United States strikes the right balance of government and markets. Should the U.S. government intervene more strongly in markets? Or do you think markets are efficient enough and government intervention inefficient enough that we should have less government intervention? Support your argument with specific examples.

NOTES

1 Source: U.S. Census Bureau, table F-2.

2 Source: U.S. Census Bureau, table H-3.

3 Source: U.S. Census Bureau, historical poverty table 2.

4 Jonathan D. Ostry, Andrew Berg, and Charalambos G. Tsangarides. "Redistribution, Inequality, and Growth," International Monetary Fund, April 2014. Note that the authors caution that extreme redistribution can have a negative impact on growth, but moderate redistribution has the opposite effect. It is also worth mentioning that other studies, relying on older and less complete data, find a negative correlation between redistribution and growth, so the issue is still somewhat contested.

The economics of the environment and climate change

A key issue of our time

This chapter discusses the economics of the environment, with a particular focus on how economic activity impacts climate change and the economic policies that could be used to address it. Economists use two major approaches to study the environment. Ecological economists study the economy as a subset of the natural environment and focus on safeguarding the health of global ecosystems. Environmental economists examine the availability and use of natural resources along with how to determine the optimal level of pollution abatement.

As we saw in Chapter 19, capitalist economies tend to use up natural resources to fuel production and profits. Once important resources become scarce and their prices increase, firms seek out substitutes. Markets are often successful in finding substitutes or designing alternatives for scarce resources, although this process takes time and it is not always easy.

Capitalist markets are usually less effective in coping with environmental damage than they are in finding alternatives for scarce resources. The environment can be seen as a public good that markets do not allocate efficiently. When markets are unregulated, pollution can rise to toxic levels and create a host of unwanted side effects. The quintessential example of this is climate change, which is fueled by the generation of greenhouse gases. In the absence of government regulation, firms and consumers have demonstrated that they will generate far more greenhouse gases than the Earth can process, resulting in a steady increase in average temperatures, rising sea levels, and increasingly extreme weather events, including stronger storms, more persistent droughts and wildfires, and more dangerous heat waves.

DOI: 10.4324/9781315636924-25

These events can have a dramatic impact on an economic system. For example, heat waves can be particularly devastating to people in regions that are unaccustomed to high heat. During the 2003 heat wave in northern Europe, temperatures reached more than 40°C (104°F), the highest in 500 years. More than 70,000 people died. Surges in wildfires in the Western United States burned millions of acres of land, devastated communities, and resulted in increasing deaths.

The long-term impacts of climate change could be much more devastating, making it increasingly difficult for the economy to support a high standard of living for people. Declining crop yields and water resources will create health crises in some regions of the world. As countries are required to invest more and more of their resources to address environmental factors, this will leave fewer investment funds for producing goods and services, thereby reducing the standard of living. If nothing is done to address climate change in the near future, scientists believe that the potential for devastating environmental crises in this century is quite high.

Fortunately, governments can institute a number of policies to put the economy on a more sustainable path. In particular, putting a price on carbon and providing incentives for people to live more sustainably could cause dramatic reductions in the production of greenhouse gases that would slow global warming.

This chapter begins by providing some background on how economists study environmental issues. Ecological economists utilize the ideas of political economists as their foundation and study the economic system as it operates within the natural environment. In contrast, environmental and natural resources economists use a mainstream economics approach, analyzing the costs and benefits of pollution abatement and studying the natural environment as a component of the economic system.

Subsequently, this chapter briefly reviews the scientific findings regarding climate change. We then use the ideas of ecological and environmental economists to analyze the economics of climate change and the economic policies we could adopt to address it. Policy options include a carbon tax, installing a cap-and-trade system, and involving the government more directly in the regulation of the economy.

20.0 CHAPTER 20 LEARNING GOALS

After reading this chapter, you should be able to:

■ Explain the approach taken by ecological and environmental economists to environmental issues.

■ List and describe the likely economic impacts of climate change.

■ Apply the principles of ecological economics and environmental economics to analyze the economics of climate change.

■ Critically analyze and evaluate various policy options to address the economic problems associated with climate change.

20.1 ECOLOGICAL ECONOMICS

Ecological economics **is the study of the interdependence between the economy and natural ecosystems, including the flow of energy and raw materials to the economy from the ecosystem's sources (mines, wells, fisheries, and land) and the return of wastes and pollutants from the economy to planetary sinks (dumps, oceans, and the atmosphere).** Sources provide us with the natural resources we need to survive and to produce goods and services. Sinks allow us to discard the waste and pollution from production, hopefully in a way that does not compromise our health or erode the future productivity of the ecosystem.

The economy tends to undervalue ecological services because many ecological services do not have a direct price associated with using them. In a path breaking study in 1997 Costanza et al. estimated that the annual value of ecological services provided by the earth was a minimum of 1.83 times the value of global gross domestic product (GDP).[1] This includes the value of land, water, natural resources, and waste disposal, much of which goes unmeasured in the economy. For example, the ability to dump waste into the ocean saves a company the cost of waste disposal, but the actual value of using the ocean as a "sink" for pollutants is not measured, nor is the potential harm to the marine environment. Assuming that the same ratio of environmental services to GDP still holds, natural ecosystems provided more than $138 trillion of value in 2016 when global GDP was $75.5 trillion. This should give you some idea of the importance of natural ecosystems to the economy!

A sustainable economic system must preserve renewable and depletable resources, and it must not overfill sinks. Renewable resources (fish stocks, forests, water, etc.) should only be depleted at a level that allows them to be replenished. Depletable resources (oil, iron ore, etc.) need to be preserved sufficiently to prevent economic disruption, via development of substitutes or conservation efforts. Planetary sinks should not be overfilled so much that the pollution harms human beings and irreparably damages resources and the ecosystem.

From the perspective of ecological economists, the inaccurate pricing of ecological services guarantees that the environment will be damaged beyond repair unless dramatic steps are taken to preserve it. Ecological economists believe strongly in the precautionary principle, which is the idea that **when an activity threatens to harm human health or the environment, precautionary measures should be taken even if some cause and effect relationships are not fully established scientifically.**[2] For example, when a new pesticide is invented, according to the precautionary principle, it should not be used until scientists have conclusively determined over a substantial period that the pesticide does not harm people or the ecosystem. This is a much more restrictive approach than is usually taken in the United States, where new pesticides are often approved without significant long-term testing.

Ecological economists are also concerned about the long-term sustainability of the economic system. They often build on the ideas of Meadows, Randers, and

Meadows, who pointed out in various editions of their pathbreaking book, *Limits to Growth*, that technology and markets are unlikely to be able to address all problems associated with resource scarcity and environmental damage because the entire system is operating unsustainably. Key resources are being depleted at a rapid rate, and planetary sinks are being filled beyond the capacity to absorb pollutants. For example, global warming is occurring because the atmosphere cannot absorb all of the carbon dioxide (CO_2) emissions that we generate.

The scale of environmental challenges facing society is immense. If society devotes its scarce resources to finding alternatives for oil, it will not have the resources necessary to develop new agricultural technologies to feed the world's rapidly growing population. If we reduce emissions dramatically to stop climate change, we will not be able to sustain our existing methods of producing goods and services, causing a reduction in our standard of living. In addition, there is often a significant delay between when an environmental crisis manifests itself and a solution can be implemented. Despite decades of discussion about addressing climate change, carbon dioxide emissions have continued to increase. From this perspective, the global economy is likely to experience **overshoot**, where a crisis results from one of three factors: (1) insufficient natural resources, (2) excessive environmental damage, or (3) inadequate investment funds to address ecological problems and still provide the other goods that society needs.

This relates to the biological concept of carrying capacity, which is **the maximum number of a species an environment can support indefinitely**. When a species exceeds its carrying capacity, its environment will start to degrade and eventually the population will experience a crisis and decline. Ecologists estimate that people are exceeding the Earth's carrying capacity by about 50%–70%, which means that, in general, our stock of resources and the quality of our environment is declining steadily. Though appropriate policies and investments in technology can reduce the impact of an environmental crisis, dramatic action will be necessary to avoid some form of crisis and collapse later this century.

Ecological economists see the economy as a subset of the natural environment, and the key to a sustainable economic system is designing economic activities that preserve natural ecosystems. This focus on preserving the natural world leads them to advocate strict regulation of the economy to prevent ecologically destructive activities. Environmental economists, on the other hand, focus more narrowly on the optimal allocation of resources and pollution abatement in specific markets.

20.2 ENVIRONMENTAL AND NATURAL RESOURCE ECONOMICS

Environmental economics **uses cost–benefit analysis to determine the efficient allocation of environmental resources, such as the optimal level of pollution.** This approach involves attempting to put a price on ecological services, as well as using government policy to require markets to incorporate the value of environmental services. In other words, environmental economists attempt to ascertain how much the environment is worth to people and then how government can implement taxes and subsidies so that markets accurately reflect the value of the environment, thereby internalizing the externality. As we saw in Chapter 19, internalizing an externality means that all environmental costs generated by a product are incorporated into the market price so that markets can produce the optimal quantity of a particular product and engage in the optimal amount of pollution abatement.

In environmental economics the socially efficient level of pollution results **when the marginal social cost of pollution abatement is equal to the marginal social benefit from abatement**. Pollution abatement refers to **any measure taken to reduce pollution and/or its impacts on people and the environment**. Environmental economists usually determine the marginal social benefit of environmental protection via surveys where they ask households to place a value on various environmental services. For example, surveys indicate that a typical U.S. household is willing to pay $257 to prevent the extinction of bald eagles and $208 to prevent the extinction of humpback whales.[3] Using these values, we can compute the marginal social benefit from preserving bald eagle habitat. Then, we can compare the marginal social benefit with the marginal cost of preserving bald eagle habitat, in terms of the foregone revenues from economic development. This would allow environmental economists to determine the optimal amount of bald eagle habitat to preserve. Similarly, environmental economists and government officials typically value a human life in the United States at $8 to $10 million based on the amounts people indicate they are willing to pay to avoid life-threatening risks. Using this method, we can put a price on an environmental practice that will result in a certain number of deaths.

For example, consider the process of hydraulic fracturing, "fracking," that is used in natural gas drilling. Water, sand, and chemicals are injected into shale rock, a process that forces out the natural gas. Wastewater from fracking returns to the surface contaminated with chemicals, buried salts, and naturally occurring radioactive material. To avoid risks to people and the environment, that wastewater should be treated before being dumped into local streams and rivers, or it should be buried deep in the ground using underground injection wells.

Environmental economists attempt to determine the optimal amount of fracking wastewater that should be treated and discharged into a local river. This helps to determine the optimal amount of pollution abatement that the fracking firm should be required to implement to reduce its wastewater pollution to the optimal level as well as what government policies can be used so that fracking firms achieve the right level of pollution abatement.

On its own, the firm only has a small interest in maintaining a clean river: The executives from the firm live far away and do not experience a negative impact from its operations. Some employees may have health issues or a decrease in well-being from the river pollution, however, so the marginal private benefit (MPB) of pollution abatement for the firm does exist, although its value tends to be low, as depicted in Figure 20.1.

The marginal cost of pollution abatement tends to increase with the amount of pollution abatement, because it gets increasingly expensive to prevent fracking wastewater from entering the river. Instead of dumping fracking fluid in streams and rivers, firms can truck fracking wastewater to a location where they can inject it deep into the ground. This is more costly than dumping the fracking wastewater in the nearest stream. In addition, some fracking wastewater still enters the groundwater and then the river via normal fracking operations. It would be prohibitively expensive to prevent *all* ground water contamination in fracking; hence the upward-sloping and increasingly steep marginal cost of abatement curve.

Without government intervention, the firm will engage in very little pollution abatement. The firm will end up at point A in Figure 20.1 where the marginal private benefit (MPB) of pollution abatement is equal to the marginal cost of pollution abatement (MC of abatement). In the early days of the fracking boom in Pennsylvania in 2008 to 2009, firms dumped minimally treated fracking wastewater into the Monongahela River, making the water unsafe to drink in local communities. Without government intervention, markets avoid paying for most of the costs of pollution abatement.

Environmental economists attempt to determine the benefits to all of society that would come from the abatement of pollution discharge. They would do this by estimating the health benefits from pollution abatement to people living along

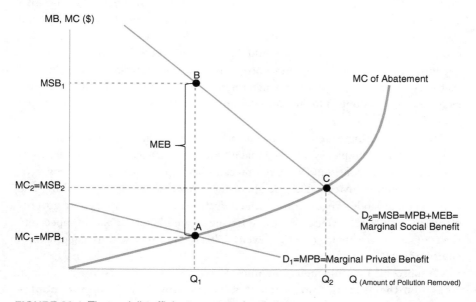

FIGURE 20.1 The socially efficient amount of pollution.

the river and drinking river water (for example, the number of lives that would be saved) and the economic value of pollution abatement in terms of improved tourism, happiness, and well-being of communities utilizing the river's environmental services. Adding up these benefits results in the marginal social benefit (MSB) curve, which is found by adding the marginal external benefit (MEB) of the river's environmental services for all people who use the river to the marginal private benefit (MPB) of the fracking firm.

The unregulated market equilibrium at point A ignores the external benefits that go to society, and an insufficient level of pollution abatement is achieved. The efficient equilibrium occurs at point C, where the marginal cost of pollution abatement is equal to the marginal social benefit.

Once the efficient equilibrium has been determined, the government can impose regulations on the firm to require them to engage in the optimal amount of pollution abatement. Possible policies include an emissions tax on the pollutant, a legal limit on the amount of the pollutant that can be emitted, and other policies that would result in the firm engaging in the optimal amount of pollution abatement.

Although ecological economists acknowledge the importance of efficiently reducing pollution, they find the approach of determining the optimal amount of pollution to be problematic in practice. It is extremely difficult to determine the health and welfare costs of pollution over the long term. We often do not know how toxic chemicals are and how they interact with other pollutants until decades later. The costs to the ecosystem are even harder to estimate. How much value should we place on a pristine river that is teeming with fish and other wildlife? Does the process of contingent valuation, where environmental economists ask people how much they are willing to pay for a particular environmental goal in a hypothetical situation, yield reliable results? Utilizing the precautionary principle, ecological economists would argue that we should not discharge fracking fluids into our water supplies until health officials determined conclusively that they are safe. This would mean suspending fracking operations until sufficient testing was done. This would, of course, be bitterly opposed by the natural gas industry.

In an interesting example of the various approaches, in 2014 New York State banned fracking completely, arguing that it was too dangerous for people and communities. This is consistent with the precautionary principle advocated by ecological economists. Meanwhile, neighboring Pennsylvania allowed fracking and imposed some modest regulations on the industry. The Pennsylvania state government required that all fracking wastewater be treated before it was dumped into rivers or that it was injected in deep wells. This is consistent with the approach of environmental economists.

A subset of environmental economics is natural resource economics, which focuses on **the pricing and efficient allocation of renewable and nonrenewable resources**. As we saw in Chapter 19, markets tend to use renewable and nonrenewable resources at unsustainable rates unless markets are carefully regulated. However, when resources become scarce, firms do have an incentive to conserve on resource use and to find alternatives. Therefore, resources prices are often prone to wide fluctuations in price over the long term.

As we saw in Chapter 9, oil prices reached a record high of $145.16 per barrel in 2008. Then a host of market-related factors caused the price to fall to $38.22 by 2015. A recession and slow growth along with efforts to conserve energy reduced demand significantly. Simultaneously, the high price of oil prompted the rapid development of alternatives on the supply side of the market via new oil exploration, new natural gas fracking technology, and the development of alternative energy sources. Thus, a combination of conservation, new technology, identification of new sources, and development of substitutes intervened to cause oil prices to fall dramatically.

In general, environmental economists are quite positive about the ability of technology and markets to save the economy from devastating shortages and environmental crises. On the other hand, ecological economists argue that dramatic policy action is needed to address the world's environmental problems because markets do not tend to anticipate major environmental crises, and the delay in responding to problems can create situations where markets overuse resources and over pollute ecosystems. The contrast between these approaches is readily apparent in the debate over how to address the economic issues associated with climate change.

20.3 THE SCIENTIFIC CONSENSUS ON CLIMATE CHANGE

Despite attempts by the fossil fuel industry to sow the seeds of doubt regarding climate change (see Chapter 18), there is an overwhelming scientific consensus on the topic. Seven different studies of scientific papers found that on average 97% of peer-reviewed scientific papers on climate change agree that climate change is happening, the planet is warming, and human activity, especially the emission of greenhouse gases, is the primary cause.[4]

The greenhouse effect works as follows: Greenhouse gases such as carbon dioxide, nitrous oxide, and methane allow solar radiation to pass into the Earth's atmosphere, but they block a significant amount of infrared heat from leaving the atmosphere. Normal amounts of greenhouse gases are crucial in warming the planet to a temperature conducive to biological life. However, human activities in the industrial age dramatically increased the production of greenhouse gases above normal levels. Burning fossil fuels releases carbon dioxide, nitrogen fertilizers in agriculture release nitrous oxide, livestock such as cows release methane, and deforestation causes trees to cease absorbing carbon dioxide and decomposing trees release carbon dioxide into the atmosphere.

The most obvious evidence of climate change is the steady increase of global temperatures in recent years and the direct correlation between temperature increases and carbon dioxide emissions, which scientists identify as the biggest contributor to global warming. Figure 20.2 plots total carbon dioxide emissions and average temperatures from 1920 to 2017.[5] The exponential increase in carbon dioxide emissions with the increasing intensity of industrialization correlates directly with a similar increase in the average temperature. The 20 warmest years since humans began measuring the Earth's temperature have all been since 1995.

Scientific predictions regarding climate change usually have been quite accurate and, if anything, tended to understate the impact increasing amounts of greenhouse gases will have on the planet. Predictions of temperature increases, sea level rise, and more extreme weather events such as heat waves, droughts, floods, and more violent storms have all proven accurate in recent years.

Countries vary widely in the quantity of greenhouse gases they emit. Oil producing countries in the Gulf states of the Middle East emit the most, with Qatar leading the world by producing more than 45 metric tons of carbon dioxide per person per year. Developed countries also produce substantial quantities of carbon dioxide per capita, as displayed in Figure 20.3.

In the developed world, the United States produces the second-highest amount of carbon dioxide per capita, after Australia, whereas European countries that have

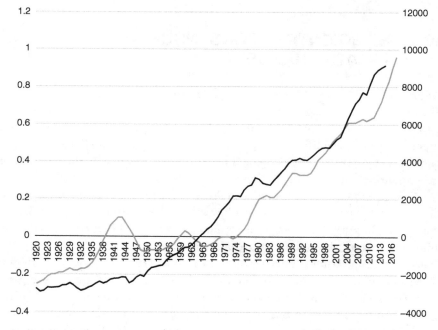

FIGURE 20.2 Total carbon dioxide emissions (black, CO_2, millions of metric tons) and global average temperatures (blue, degrees Celsius), 1920 to 2017.

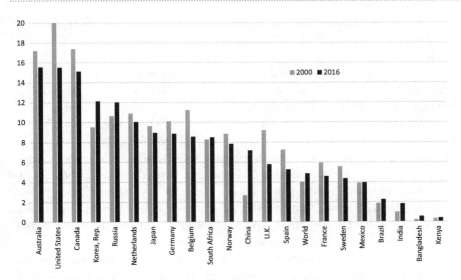

FIGURE 20.3 Carbon dioxide emissions (metric tons per capita) in 2000 and 2016. Source: World Bank, https://data.worldbank.org/indicator/EN.ATM .CO2E.PC.

more stringent environmental regulations produce much less. Notice that carbon dioxide emissions declined slightly for developed countries from 2000 to 2016, thanks to new environmental regulations, improved technologies, and the development of cleaner energy sources. However, countries that grew rapidly during this period increased their CO_2 emissions, especially China, Russia, South Korea, South Africa, Brazil, and India. Poor countries such as Bangladesh and Kenya produce a negligible amount of carbon dioxide. Overall, world emissions increased from 2000 to 2016, as the increased emissions from newly industrializing countries outstripped reductions in emissions from developed countries. Unfortunately, the continued increase in carbon dioxide emissions indicates that climate change will continue to worsen and dramatic efforts may be necessary.

The arctic regions of the Earth are warming more rapidly than other regions, contributing to melting glaciers and a steady rise in sea levels. The National Oceanic and Atmospheric Administration reports that sea levels increased by an average of 9 inches (23 centimeters) from 1880 to 2015 and that the rate of increase in sea levels is accelerating. National Aeronautics and Space Administration (NASA) and the Intergovernmental Panel on Climate Change project an additional increase in sea levels of 0.2 to 2.0 meters (0.66 to 6.6 feet) by the year 2100. Recent increases in sea levels have tended toward the upper bound of estimates, so the rise in sea levels is likely to be substantial.

Meanwhile, rising ocean temperatures and increased ocean acidification from rising carbon dioxide levels in the atmosphere are compromising marine ecosystems. Oceans absorb some carbon dioxide from the atmosphere, but this causes the ocean to become more acidic. Warmer, more acidic oceans are causing shellfish (oysters, scallops, and clams) and coral reefs to experience mass die-offs in some locations.

As some regions of the world became hotter and drier with climate change, wildfires increased in intensity and size. In Figure 20.4, data from the National Interagency Fire Center shows that the United States experienced a steady increase in acres burned by wildfires since the 1970s. California experienced one of its worst wildfire years in history in 2020, with 10.3 million acres burned.

The regions that are becoming hotter and drier are also more prone to longer and more severe droughts. Hotter temperatures increase the evaporation of water and reduce snowpack, resulting in less water availability. NASA researchers project increased droughts in the future in the U.S. southwest and central plains, as well as in many other regions of the world where warming temperatures and changing weather patterns will reduce the availability of water.

Another sobering fact is that the climate will continue to warm even if we dramatically reduce our greenhouse gas emissions right now. Once carbon dioxide is released into the atmosphere, it takes thousands of years for it to be fully reabsorbed into trees, seashells, and rocks. Therefore, our current carbon dioxide emissions will continue to warm the planet for many years to come.

Given these expected changes to the climate, some portions of the global economy are likely to experience significant impacts. Some of those impacts may be positive for the economy, but a greater proportion will have a negative impact.

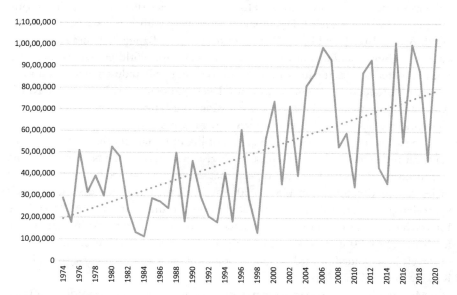

FIGURE 20.4 Millions of acres burned by wildfires in the United States, 1974–2020. Sources: https://www.nifc.gov/fireInfo/fireInfo_stats_totalFires.html, https://fas.org/sgp/crs/misc/IF10244.pdf.

20.4 THE ECONOMIC CONSEQUENCES OF CLIMATE CHANGE

So what are the economic consequences of a rapidly warming and changing climate? Climate change will have some **positive effects** on the global economy, including:

- Reduced heating costs
- Fewer deaths from exposure to the cold
- Increased agricultural production in cold climates.

Because heating costs generally exceed cooling costs in much of the world, this is a significant benefit, as is the increase in agricultural production in cold climates that now experience longer growing seasons.

Unfortunately, these positive impacts will likely be dwarfed by **negative impacts**:

- Loss of valuable, low-lying lands from rising sea levels.
- Flooding and destruction of portions of coastal cities such as New York, Miami, and Shanghai.
- Destruction of property and deaths of people, livestock, and fish from increasingly extreme weather events, including droughts, heat waves, thunderstorms, tornadoes, hurricanes, and flooding.
- Reductions in agricultural productivity in many regions from extreme weather and drought.
- Poorer health from the spread of tropical diseases.
- Loss of environmental services and resources provided by ecosystems and reductions in biodiversity and forest yields.
- Higher air-conditioning costs.

In 2018 the Organization for Economic Cooperation and Development (OECD) projected that climate change will cause a reduction of global GDP of about 2% per year by 2060, with losses increasing after that. The United Nations Environment Programme estimates that the global cost of adapting to climate change will likely be about $200 billion per year by 2030 and $390 billion by 2050. Similarly, in 2017 a group of U.S. economists and scientists from top universities estimated that damages will cost about 1.2% of GDP per year for every 1°C increase in temperature.[6] With NASA predicting a 2°C to 6°C temperature increase by 2100, that would result in an annual 2.4% to 7.2% loss in GDP. Given that GDP growth averages 1% per year in the United States, damage from climate change would put the economy in perpetual recession if the predictions are accurate.

Countries will need to engage in a large array of investments to cope with climate change, including:

- Expanding water supplies and developing water conservation efforts in drought-stricken areas.
- Developing flood management programs and building levees and seawalls in increasingly flood-prone areas.
- Resettling coastal residents and caring for refugees from flooded or drought-stricken areas.
- Adjusting crop varieties and growing techniques to cope with climate changes.
- Redesigning housing, communities, and health systems to cope with extreme heat.
- Investing in alternative energy and new technologies that conserve fossil fuels and reduce greenhouse gas emissions.

These investments will take funds away from other important human needs. Together, the negative impacts of climate change are likely to cause large-scale disruptions to human society.

Some scientists and economists believe that the consequences will be *even worse* than what was described above. A sobering report from the United Nations in 2018 estimated that we only have until 2030 to make dramatic changes in carbon emissions to avoid catastrophic consequences. Sophisticated simulations by Meadows, Randers, and Meadows in *Limits to Growth* predict that unless society takes dramatic action soon, we are likely to experience a collapse in the global economy, featuring a decline in life expectancy and the loss of numerous lives once the Earth's ecosystems are significantly compromised. If the polar ice sheets collapse more quickly than projected, sea levels could rise by up to 30 feet by the year 2100, swamping numerous coastal cities. Sudden shifts in ocean currents from climate change could cause Europe to become as cold as Alaska while other regions swelter. Warming of the arctic tundra could release large quantities of stored carbon into the atmosphere, substantially increasing carbon dioxide levels and warming global temperatures further and faster.

One of the frustrating aspects of climate change is the degree of uncertainty regarding exactly how bad things will get. We know that climate change is occurring, and we know that it will have a significant impact on the economy, but we are not certain how large the impact will be and how soon the worst impacts will be felt.

Given these looming problems, how should we address the problem of climate change? Economists offer a variety of solutions that vary based on how much faith they have in markets and technology.

20.5 MAINSTREAM, MARKET-BASED SOLUTIONS TO CLIMATE CHANGE

The one idea backed by most economists who are concerned about climate change is the need to put a price on carbon dioxide pollution. A 2015 study by Peter Howard and Derek Sylvan of the Institute for Policy Integrity at New York University found that 75% of economists who are experts in the economics of climate change advocated some form of carbon pricing or carbon tax. (Note that although it is often referred to as "carbon pricing" or a "carbon tax" in the literature, technically, this is carbon dioxide pricing and carbon dioxide taxing.[7]) The simplest way to reduce greenhouse gas emissions is with a carbon tax.

20.5.1 Carbon tax

A carbon tax is a tax on producers for every ton of carbon dioxide that the use of their product generates. This would make it less profitable to produce or use products that emit carbon dioxide, thereby encouraging the creation of technologies to reduce carbon emissions along with development of alternative, clean energy. A carbon tax would increase the price of carbon-intensive products, discouraging consumers from purchasing such products.

The conservative Climate Leadership Council, whose supporters include economists Henry Paulson, Martin Feldstein, and N. Gregory Mankiw (all of whom served in the administrations of either President Reagan or President George W. Bush), argues for the installation of a gradually increasing tax on carbon in the United States with *all* of the money from the carbon tax returned to taxpayers. They propose beginning with a $40 per ton tax on carbon, which would cost a typical four-person household $2000 per year. A $40 per ton carbon tax would increase the price of gasoline by about $0.36 per gallon. The typical household would also receive $2000 in dividend payments in the first year. Therefore, households that reduced their use of fossil fuels would receive more in dividends than they would pay in carbon taxes. This provides a direct incentive for households to use less fossil fuels.

The Climate Leadership Council also proposes a tariff on imported goods from countries that do not have a similar carbon tax so that U.S. companies do not face unfair competition. Note that conservative economists prefer an approach to addressing climate change that involves minimal government intervention where all tax revenues are returned to private individuals, keeping the size of government as small as possible.

British Colombia, Canada, tried just such an approach very successfully. They began in 2008 with a tax of $10 per ton on carbon, and they utilized the tax revenue to reduce corporate and household taxes. Subsequently, the government of British Columbia raised the carbon tax by $5 per ton per year until it reached $30 per ton in 2012. The result was quite impressive. Fossil fuel use dropped 19% relative to the rest of Canada, and the economic growth rate of British Columbia was the same as the rest of the country. The carbon tax reduced emissions without harming the economy!

Liberal mainstream economists also like the idea of a carbon tax. They usually advocate a higher carbon tax than the amount conservatives propose, and they advocate reserving some of the money generated by the carbon tax for investments in and subsidies for alternative energy development.

Liberal economists also believe in taking direct government action to address the problem of climate change more quickly and in a more dramatic fashion. For example, some have proposed banning the use of coal because it generates the largest amount of carbon relative to the amount of energy generated. Coal generates almost twice as much carbon dioxide as natural gas when generating electricity. Liberal economists argue that natural gas production also should be regulated more carefully so that methane releases from the drilling process are reduced. Even though natural gas burns cleaner than other fossil fuels, methane is a particularly harmful greenhouse gas. Using natural gas instead of oil or coal only reduces our carbon footprint if firms take great care with the drilling and delivery process.

In general, liberal economists prefer to guide the market rather than wait for the market to act. For example, the Obama administration instituted subsidies for clean energy use and for products that would reduce greenhouse emissions, such as hybrid cars. Cities such as Milwaukee with liberal governments subsidized homeowners to insulate their homes to reduce their energy use. Interestingly, such programs pay for themselves in as little as two to four years due to the substantial energy savings. Similarly, many states subsidize the installation of solar panels because they reduce energy use and pay for themselves in an average of 7.5 years. Ideally, these government policies prod the economy to reduce its carbon production more quickly than markets left to their own devices. Given the short time frame in which these projects pay for themselves, along with the fact that markets will not usually make these investments on their own, government intervention is required to make markets use energy more efficiently.

Another approach to pricing carbon is the establishment of a market for **tradable carbon permits**. This is the cap-and-trade system described in Chapter 19. Many mainstream economists prefer this approach to a carbon tax because they believe it results in a more efficient method of pollution reduction.

20.5.2 Tradable carbon permits

The government begins the process of establishing tradable carbon permits by measuring how much carbon is being emitted by each firm. Then, it sets a cap for carbon emissions below the level of existing emissions to reduce carbon pollution. The government then allocates permits to industry, with the permitted amount of carbon pollution set below each firm's past levels. (The government also could sell the permits to the highest bidder if it chose.) Faced with a limited number of permits for pollution, companies would need to reduce pollution to below their current level or purchase permits from another company that had excess carbon permits to sell. Companies would have to pay for polluting above the level of their permits, and they could profit from polluting below the number of permits they possessed by selling excess permits to other firms. This gives companies a direct financial incentive to reduce pollution. The government can reduce the cap on the number of permits each year to pressure companies to continue to reduce carbon dioxide emissions.

Mainstream economists often prefer a cap-and-trade system to an emissions tax because of the potential for efficiency gains. In theory, those firms that can reduce their emissions most easily will do so and then sell their excess pollution permits to companies less able to reduce their emissions. This could lead to a very efficient reduction in pollution, because the firms that can reduce emissions in the most cost-effective manner do so in order to profit from selling their excess pollution rights.

The European Union (E.U.) established the first international emissions trading system in 2005 that covered the greenhouse gases carbon dioxide, nitrous oxide, and perfluorocarbons. Initially, the system was ineffective. The government trusted companies to report greenhouse gas emissions prior to establishing the cap, but companies padded the numbers, which meant that permits were too plentiful and the price of permits was too low. The number of permits was adjusted in subsequent years based on actual measurements of companies' emissions, which allowed the E.U. to establish a more accurate system. In 2018, the price of a ton of carbon dioxide in the E.U. trading system was about $19, and there were modest reductions in carbon emissions as a result of the program. The E.U. experienced an 18% drop in carbon dioxide emissions between 2008 and 2014. Over the same time period, the United States, with no national cap-and-trade system, experienced an 11% drop due to new technologies that reduced carbon emissions. In appears, therefore, that the E.U. cap-and-trade system reduced emissions by about 7%.

Clearly, a cap-and-trade system can be effective, as shown by the California sulfur dioxide market described in Chapter 19. However, the E.U. experience shows that cap-and-trade programs are susceptible to lobbying and manipulation due to the permit allocation process.

Nonetheless, by 2018 more than 30 countries, including China, were using carbon trading systems, demonstrating the attractiveness of this approach. Businesses find carbon trading more attractive than a carbon tax, so cap-and-trade systems are more politically palatable in many countries.

Though carbon taxes and cap-and-trade systems have made some progress in reducing greenhouse gas emissions, progress has been limited and global emissions have continued to increase. Political economists argue that more dramatic action is necessary.

20.6 POLITICAL ECONOMY SOLUTIONS TO CLIMATE CHANGE

To ecological, progressive, and radical political economists, the problems with cap-and-trade systems are emblematic of why society should not rely on markets to solve the problem of climate change. Markets work to externalize as many costs as possible, so they will always work relentlessly to avoid paying for the environmental damage that they create. The solution to climate change, from a political economy perspective, is much more extensive, involving dramatic government intervention and less reliance on markets.

For example, in his book *Greening the Global Economy*, political economist Robert Pollin proposes the following policies:

- Make large-scale public investments in clean energy to replace fossil fuel energy.
- Install a robust carbon tax or cap-and-trade system so that fossil fuels are more expensive to use than clean energy.
- Expand public transportation systems extensively so people do not need to drive as much, especially in cities.
- Raise efficiency standards for all government buildings to reduce energy use.
- Require all government operations to utilize clean energy.
- Provide financing for private businesses and households to invest in energy efficiency, including insulation, installation of solar panels and energy efficient lighting, and other projects that pay for themselves in three to five years.

Pollin's research demonstrates that investments in energy efficiency and clean renewables will create new industries and jobs, which will more than offset job losses in fossil fuel industries. Furthermore, with retraining programs for workers in coal, oil, and other fossil fuel industries, workers need not lose out during the transition to a green economy. Thus, Pollin sees the possibility of continued economic growth as we transition to a sustainable economic system. These arguments formed the basis for the call for a "Green New Deal" by left-leaning politicians in the United States in recent years.

We see an interesting application of these ideas in Germany's approach to the environment. The German government works directly with industry to create markets and businesses that profit from higher environmental standards and that can become global leaders in various environmental sectors. With the entire world pursuing more sustainable practices, Germany worked to make its firms the leaders in sustainability.

This involved giving industry time to adapt to new environmental laws, while steadily tightening standards for pollution, waste, recycling, and energy use. The government provided funds for research and development into green technology and renewable energy projects, and the development ministry promoted German green technology solutions in global markets. As German companies developed new technologies, they were able to export those technologies to other countries. The government also required power companies to purchase green energy at preferential rates, stimulating the clean energy industry.

German recycling laws are also highly effective. Germany requires companies to be responsible for recycling all of the packaging they sell to consumers. This resulted in significant reductions in packaging and the development of materials that are easier to recycle. Car companies are responsible for recycling cars they produce at the end of their useful life, which led to cars being made of components that are easier to recycle and created an entire industry in recycling metals and other materials from old cars.

Because of these "green" policies, German companies are industry leaders in photovoltaic cells for solar panels, wind turbines, waste management, recycling, and green technology. Green technology is now one of the country's biggest industrial sectors. Green industries are growing so rapidly that they could become the largest industrial sector in Germany in the next decade.

Though Pollin argues for changes in the economic system that still largely preserve its fundamental structure, other political economists want to go even further. Ecological economist Herman Daly argues that we must end the physical growth in the use of energy and resources in order to have a sustainable economy. Society must stop spewing so many pollutants and depleting or ruining the world's resources and ecosystems. This involves a more dramatic reorientation of the economic system away from the maximum production of material goods that underlies capitalism.

Radical political economist David Harvey argues that if capitalism were to internalize all of the social and environmental costs it generates, firms would all go out of business. From this perspective, capitalism is inherently unsustainable. Fred Magdoff and John Bellamy Foster, in their book *What Every Environmentalist Needs to Know about Capitalism*, argue that market solutions will never successfully address the problems associated with climate change. They cite the following examples as evidence:

- Increased energy efficiency leads to lower costs of use, which causes people to use *more* energy than before. For example, people who purchase a fuel-efficient hybrid car tend to drive more than they did previously, offsetting the environmental benefits of greater fuel economy. Greater energy efficiency in refrigerators is offset by the increased size of refrigerators.
- New technologies that solve existing environmental problems create new problems of their own. Hydroelectric power is clean, but it causes the loss of forests and species. Wind power and hybrid cars pollute less but they use up scarce rare earth metals.
- Corporations work relentlessly to undercut efforts to impose sustainability on them. For example, when the European Union allowed firms to purchase carbon offsets elsewhere in the world as part of the cap-and-trade system, European firms paid Chinese firms to destroy their stocks of problematic greenhouse gases (HFC-23). This led Chinese firms to produce *more* HFC-23

so they could make additional revenue from E.U. companies by destroying it! This did not, of course, reduce greenhouse gas emissions.

- Capitalism has a relentless imperative to grow. Firms must invest and grow to stay ahead of competitors. They scour the world for resources and new markets to sell ever-greater quantities of products to consumers. However, this inevitably puts increasing pressure on the environment as more energy and resources are used and more pollution is generated year after year. Any slowdown in growth creates an economic crisis.
- Capitalist firms operate on an exclusively short-term basis, putting immediate profits ahead of safeguarding resources for the future. Corporations are particularly bad about exploiting common resources such as the oceans and the environment, taking advantage of such systems unless prevented from doing so and attempting to circumvent any taxes or regulations.

Magdoff and Foster argue that "Creating an entirely different system ... is a more realistic alternative than a head-in-the-sand view that refuses to recognize the incompatibility between unlimited capital accumulation and limited resources, or that denies capitalism's connection to social and ecological exploitation" (p. 134).

The views of political economists on climate change range from Pollin's proposals for a managed capitalist approach to Magdoff and Foster's proposal for a socialist approach. Such proposals are a stark contrast to the more market-based proposals of mainstream economists.

20.7 CONCLUSION

Interestingly, despite the vast differences highlighted above, there is one major area of agreement among *all* of the perspectives: Governments should implement either a carbon tax or a cap-and-trade system to establish a **price on carbon** and other greenhouse gases. Although there are a few economists who depart from this perspective, the vast majority of conservative, liberal, and radical economists agree on the need for carbon pricing.

In other areas, we see significant differences. Conservative mainstream economists want to make carbon taxes revenue neutral, with all revenues returned to businesses and households. Liberal mainstream economists want to reserve some carbon tax (or cap-and-trade) revenues for investments in clean energy, and they advocate imposing additional regulations on businesses and consumers so that the economy becomes more sustainable more quickly. However, progressive, radical, and ecological political economists question whether capitalism can ever be truly sustainable. They prefer a much greater role for government intervention in structuring the economic system to be sustainable, restricting markets to a greater degree with government regulations and investing government funds more directly in clean energy and infrastructure projects.

As is so often the case in economics, you will have to decide for yourself which approach makes the most sense to you given the significant challenges the world faces regarding climate change. Your approach will depend significantly on how much faith you have in markets and/or governments to solve the complex problems of climate change.

QUESTIONS FOR REVIEW

1. Compare and contrast ecological economics and environmental economics. Which approach do you find most compelling in addressing the issue of climate change? Explain and support your answer.
2. Critically evaluate the approach of environmental economists in determining the optimum level of pollution abatement. Do you think it is appropriate to value human life and environmental services in this way? Why or why not? How might ecological economists respond to this approach?
3. How does a carbon tax differ from a cap-and-trade system? Why do many mainstream economists prefer a cap-and-trade system? What are some of the problems that can occur with a cap-and-trade system?
4. List the various policies that economists advocate for addressing climate change.
5. Suppose that you are elected President of the United States. Design a set of economic policies to address climate change. Support the approach that you take.
6. Compare and contrast the approaches to climate change taken by the following groups:
    a. conservative mainstream economists
    b. liberal mainstream economists
    c. political economists.
7. Answer the following questions related to Figure 20.5.
    a. What price and quantity combination would an unregulated market generate? Why would economists consider this outcome inefficient? Explain carefully and make specific references to the graph in your answer.
    b. What is the socially efficient amount of pollution in this graph?
    c. How does this graph help us to understand the argument environmental economists often make that we should not strive to eliminate pollution completely?
    d. How might ecological economists respond to the environmental economic analysis displayed in this graph?

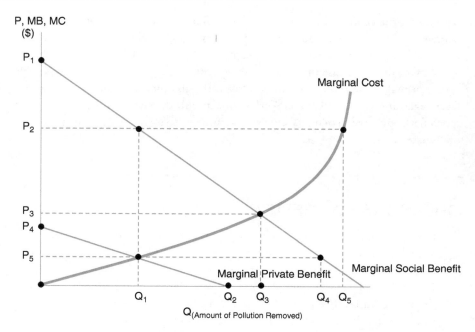

FIGURE 20.5 Determining the socially efficient amount of pollution.

8. One of the major arguments politicians make against environmental regulations is that they will reduce the number of jobs. Is this a sound argument? Why or why not? Explain using specific examples from this chapter.
9. Magdoff and Foster argue that capitalism is fundamentally incompatible with a sustainable economic system. Given what you know about capitalism and how it functions, construct an argument for or against this perspective. Use specific examples to support your answer.

NOTES

1   Robert Costanza, Ralph d'Arge, Rudolf de Groot, et al., "The Value of the World's Ecosystem Services and Natural Capital," *Nature* 387 (May 1997), pp. 253–260.

2   This definition was crafted at the Wingspread Conference on the Precautionary Principle in 1998.

3   Liz Heinzerling and Frank Ackerman, "Cost Benefit Analysis and Climate Change," *Dollars and Sense* (March/April 2003).

4   See Skeptical Science for a summary of the research on this topic at www.skeptical science.com, accessed July 10, 2018. About 12,000 scientific papers were reviewed in establishing this number.

5   Sources: Temperature data from NASA, "GISS Surface Temperature Analysis," https:// data.giss.nasa.gov/gistemp/graphs/, accessed December 8, 2018. Carbon dioxide data from T.A. Boden, G. Marland, and R.J. Andres, "Global, Regional, and National

Fossil-Fuel CO$_2$ Emissions" (Carbon Dioxide Information Analysis Center, Oak Ridge National Laboratory, U.S. Department of Energy, Oak Ridge, TN, 2017).

6 Solomon Hsiang, Robert Kopp, Amir Jina, et al., "Estimating Economic Damage from Climate Change in the United States," *Science* June 30, 2017, pp. 1362–1369. http://science.sciencemag.org/content/356/6345/1362.

7 See Peter Howard and Derek Sylvan, "Expert Consensus on the Economics of Climate Change," Institute for Policy Integrity, December 2015, http://policyintegrity.org/files/publications/ExpertConsensusReport.pdf, accessed July 13, 2018.

Public goods and services

Do we have the right balance of public and private goods and services?

One of the major economic issues confronting every economic system is the size and role of government. If citizens in the economic system wish to minimize government intervention, what legal system, regulatory framework, and public goods are necessary to keep markets operating effectively? If people prefer a state-led system, what tasks should the state be in charge of and what should be left to markets? If a country prefers a balance between markets and the state, what exactly should the balance of state and markets be?

As we saw in Chapter 8, all economic systems in the modern world are mixed economies, with some economic activities undertaken by markets and some by the state. Nonetheless, around the globe we find vast differences between market-dominated, social market, and state-dominated economic systems. Chapter 19 highlighted the importance of government intervention in correcting market failures, along with the possibility that government failure might undermine the efficacy of government intervention. This chapter focuses in more detail on one important area in which the market fails: The provision of public goods.

The quality of public goods and the ability of all citizens to access those goods are major determinants of the efficiency and equity of any economic system. Physical infrastructure, market infrastructure, public services, environmental services, and public knowledge are all crucial public goods. In addition, some "private" goods, such as education and health care, are close enough to public goods that they are usually publicly provided. These are quasi-public goods where the external benefits to society are extensive and the efficiency gains from public provision of these goods are substantial.

This chapter begins by describing the nature of public and quasi-public goods. We then examine how mainstream economists use marginal cost (supply) and marginal social benefit (society's demand) to estimate the optimal quantity of a public

DOI: 10.4324/9781315636924-26

good that the government should provide. Subsequently, we describe how governments can provide public goods directly or by using the private sector along with subsidies and regulations. Next, we take up John Kenneth Galbraith's theory of social balance and the debate over whether or not U.S. capitalism has an overabundance of private goods compared with a paucity of public goods. The chapter concludes with case studies of how governments provide two quasi-public goods, health care and education.

21.0 CHAPTER 21 LEARNING GOALS

After reading this chapter, you should be able to:

- Define and give examples of public and quasi-public goods.

- Use a graph to explain how mainstream economists attempt to determine the optimal quantity of a public good and why the private sector will not supply the optimal quantity of a public good without some form of government intervention.

- Critically analyze John Kenneth Galbraith's argument that we have a social imbalance with too many private and too few public goods.

- Describe and evaluate the different ways in which developed countries provide health care and education.

21.1 PUBLIC AND QUASI-PUBLIC GOODS

As we saw in Chapter 19, the primary role for government in microeconomic markets in a capitalist economic system is to fix market failures. One of the most important areas in which the market fails is in the provision of public goods.

21.1.1 Public goods

Recall that public goods are **nonexcludable and nonrivalrous**. With nonexcludable goods, one person using a public good does not prevent others from also using that public good. With nonrivalrous goods, people cannot be prevented from using the good, even if they do not pay for it. This results in the free rider problem, where economic actors who benefit from a public good or service will avoid paying for it unless required to do so by the government.

Public goods fall into seven major categories, each of which makes crucial contributions to the economy.

1. **Physical infrastructure** refers to transportation systems (roads, bridges, train tracks, airports, ports, public transportation), public utilities (water, sewer, gas, electric, internet, lighthouses, streetlights), public buildings (courthouses, police and fire stations, etc.), and parks. Physical infrastructure is a major contributor to economic development. Whenever a government installs new transportation infrastructure, this creates new business opportunities and increases the efficiency of existing operations. Switzerland ranked at the very top of the World Economic Forum's Global Competitiveness Index for nine straight years (2008–2017) in part due to their incredibly extensive and efficient physical infrastructure. In 2014, Switzerland led the world in manufacturing value added per capita, beating Germany by 59%, the United States by 142%, and China by 657%. If you travel around Switzerland, you will be surprised to see how many manufacturing facilities are located in small towns scattered throughout this mountainous country. Most countries have large industrial centers where factories are concentrated. The diffusion of Swiss manufacturing throughout the country can be attributed to the fact that every small town has access to one of the world's best public train systems, which is in turn linked to airports and European ports. It is extremely easy to get parts from anywhere and export products to anywhere in the world. When you combine the first-class Swiss physical infrastructure with their superb information technology infrastructure, educational system, and access to markets, you have a recipe for a very attractive business location.

2. **Market infrastructure** includes the legal and regulatory framework that makes markets work, property rights, the rules of behavior by which the private sector must abide, and government efforts to stimulate economic development, such as the fostering of systems of innovation. As we saw earlier in this book, markets can work well if the proper market infrastructure is put into place. Markets require an efficient and noncorrupt government that enforces a legal and regulatory framework that rewards firms for productive activities but penalizes them for destructive and anticompetitive practices. Laws must be clear, transparent, and fairly enforced, without too much red tape or too little protection of citizens, workers, and the environment. Markets also work more effectively if governments undertake policies to stimulate economic development. In developing countries, protecting infant industries, helping them gain market experience, and then gradually exposing them to international market competition can be very effective in developing new industries, as we saw in the United States in the 1800s and more recently in Japan, South Korea, and China. Designing a system that rewards innovation is particularly important. This can range from the U.S. innovation system, where patent laws and low taxes on the wealthy create incentives for people to start new businesses, to the Norwegian innovation system of providing a strong safety net, support, and education targeting entrepreneurs. The constant refreshing of markets with innovations keeps economic systems competitive and dynamic.

3. **Security services** consist of national and civil defense, police and fire protection, the justice system, and disaster aid. Instability is deeply destructive to economic systems. No individual or business wants to make a long-term investment if there is uncertainty about future prospects. This makes the stability provided by security services an essential ingredient in economic development. An unjust, unequal system provokes uprisings that undermine stability. Poor, desperate people who have little to live for are more likely to take extreme measures than people who have a good job and home. Therefore, economic systems need to ensure that citizens' basic needs are met via a robust safety net and efforts to foster economic development. Also, a country's justice system must be fair to all participants so that individuals and businesses have confidence in the system.

4. **Governance and public services** include government regulatory bodies (environment, education, product safety, labor, etc.) and government service providers (social security and pensions, welfare, post office, public radio and television, public health clinics, etc.). The efficiency and effectiveness of government agencies is another public good that features prominently in the health and competitiveness of an economic system. Government regulatory bodies should be prompt and responsive to constituents while also safeguarding the environment, public health, and welfare. Systems to protect against favoritism and corruption need to be put in place. Government safety nets (welfare, food, and housing assistance, etc.) need to be structured to reward productive activity and discourage fraud, while still providing those at the bottom with enough to survive. Security for the elderly and infirm is also very important. In a capitalist economic system in which people are rewarded for their productivity, those who cannot work are at a significant disadvantage and will not have sufficient income to survive unless the government establishes adequate pensions and disability support. Markets also depend on sound information so that economic actors can make good decisions. Preservation of a free press, an open and uncensored internet, and other good sources of news and information facilitates economic development and sound decision making. Many countries establish independent public broadcasting organizations, such as the British Broadcasting Corporation (BBC), so that news is presented in an unbiased manner that is not colored by the need to please advertisers. Unfortunately, government officials and news outlets that are willing to lie or distort information for their own purposes undermine confidence in news and information, which can undermine confidence in the economic system. If an investor thinks the government is likely to lie to them, they will not find government reports or forecasts reliable, fostering uncertainty and reducing the likelihood of long-term investments.

5. **Environmental services** consist of the preservation of resources (petroleum, minerals, water, air, etc.), sinks (pollution abatement via the oceans, atmosphere, ground, etc.), and ecosystems (natural plant and animal resources

necessary for the survival of life). As noted in Chapter 20, environmental services are crucial to economic systems, providing resources for production and sinks for absorbing pollution. Ecosystem preservation is a major determinant of our quality of life and our ability to survive. No one wants to live, work, or invest in a polluted, unsafe community. Furthermore, we cannot survive without the food, water, air, and other life essentials that ecosystems make possible.

6. **Public knowledge** refers to the generation and dissemination of the stock of human knowledge via libraries, scientific research, education, and shared technological innovations. The general knowledge level of a country's citizens profoundly impacts economic development. Paul Romer and other economists who developed endogenous growth theory argue that knowledge and the development of new ideas are primary sources of economic growth.[1] Therefore, a primary role for government is to foster the accumulation of knowledge and the development of new ideas. Governments do this in a number of ways. All governments provide public libraries and public education to increase the knowledge base of members of the community. Governments also fund public and university research labs to make scientific advances, which in turn creates new products and stimulates the development of entirely new industries. The very structure of economic systems can stimulate development of new knowledge and ideas. As we have seen, governments in many countries such as Japan and Sweden work with the private sector to conduct research and develop new knowledge, products, and industries. Many capitalist systems reward the creation of new ideas because new products and services can be extraordinarily profitable. But it is important for capitalist systems to be sufficiently competitive so that firms with new ideas and products can enter markets. Otherwise, firms with monopoly power can stifle innovation, limit the dissemination of knowledge, and slow development.

7. **Public health** and communicable disease prevention involve alleviating or eliminating threats to public health from diseases like measles, polio, mumps, Ebola, swine flu, malaria, and COVID-19. Some aspects of health care are a "private good" provided directly to an individual. Other elements of health care are considered a "public good," especially the prevention of communicable diseases. Everyone in the community benefits from being protected from a nasty, communicable disease. Similarly, establishing public health standards to limit the amount of toxic pollution or other hazards that people can be exposed to has broad benefits to the entire community. To address these issues, governments establish public health ministries charged with safeguarding the health of the entire community.

The line between public goods and private goods that generate external benefits is not always clear. Public goods benefit all citizens equally, whether or not they pay. Private goods with external benefits usually benefit one citizen the most, but the benefits to the entire community can be so substantial that these goods verge on public goods. To capture such cases, economists use the term quasi-public goods.

Quasi-public goods are **goods or services that have some but not all of the characteristics of public goods. Examples include the provision of health care and education to individuals, where society as a whole reaps substantial external benefits and where competition can be inefficient or wasteful**. Governments usually provide quasi-public goods as if they were public goods when the external benefits and efficiency gains from public provision are significant.

Individual health care and education are goods that generate positive externalities and that exhibit substantial economies of scale. The provision of good quality health care benefits the individual receiving the health care, but it also benefits the individual's employer (higher productivity), family (higher income), community (less communicable disease, higher standard of living), and government (higher tax revenues).

In addition to broad-based external benefits, health care is much more efficient if provided at the community level. For example, we only need one MRI machine for every 100,000 people on average according to most health experts, yet the U.S. private health care system has three times that many MRI machines. Private offices compete for patients by offering a complete range of services, such as MRIs, which leads to a lot of duplication of services. Many MRI machines in the United States sit idle, which reduces efficiency and raises costs.

Given the existence of substantial external benefits and the huge cost savings from centralization of medical services, all developed countries except the United States established a national health care system. In most countries, individual health care is treated like a public good.

Note that we are separating the health care an individual receives from public health, which works to ensure the health and safety of the entire population of a country. Even though the United States has privatized individual health care, the United States still has public health officials and the Centers for Disease Control and Prevention that work to safeguard all citizens from outbreaks of disease and other broad-based threats to public health.

Education also generates significant positive externalities and economies of scale. An individual receives the most benefit from their education, and people can be excluded from education if they do not pay, so education has many characteristics of a private good. Nonetheless, the external benefits from education are substantial: Education boosts productivity and inventions, benefiting employers, coworkers, and all of society. Educated citizens with good incomes tend to be more civically engaged, volunteering, voting, and otherwise contributing more to their communities.

And education can be delivered more efficiently on a large scale. Lecturing to 100 students is almost as effective as lecturing to one. Even education utilizing small group pedagogy can be delivered to 15 students as effectively as it can to half that many.

Therefore, as with health care, most countries treat education as a public good. All countries provide public education through high school, and many countries provide free or very low-cost education through the university level.

21.2 DETERMINING THE OPTIMAL BALANCE OF PUBLIC AND PRIVATE GOODS

Given the importance of public goods to an economic system and the fact that markets are unable to provide public goods effectively on their own, how should governments determine the optimal amount of public goods? In theory, voters express their preferences for public goods via the political process. If the political system is effective and noncorrupt, elected representatives will provide citizens with the amount of public goods that they desire.

According to mainstream economic theory, governments should attempt to estimate all of the marginal benefits received by citizens to arrive at a marginal social benefit curve. By comparing marginal social benefits with the marginal cost of providing the public good, the optimal amount of public goods can be determined.

Figure 21.1 displays a hypothetical graph of the marginal private benefits (MPB) and marginal costs (MC) associated with providing a classic public good:

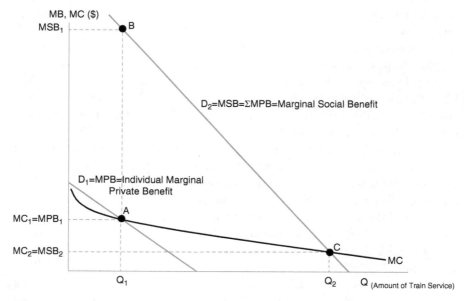

FIGURE 21.1 The optimal quantity of a public good (train service) in mainstream economics.

Train service in a city. Rail lines and trains are very expensive to build. With a high marginal cost and the marginal private benefit of only one person, the result is a very low equilibrium quantity. Point A in Figure 21.1 shows that an individual would only be willing to pay MPB_1 for quantity Q_1 of train service. Point A is the private market equilibrium. However, when we add up the benefits that *all* citizens in the city get from train service, we get demand curve D_2, the marginal social benefit (MSB) curve, which leads to the socially efficient, optimal equilibrium quantity of public goods, Q_2. According to mainstream economic theory, government officials should aim to provide quantity Q_2 of train service for the public.

Note that with public goods the marginal cost (MC) curve tends to decline over the entire market. There are huge startup costs required to build public goods like rail systems for trains and roads for cars. Once the initial investments are made, it costs very little to add another train car onto a train, so the marginal cost of increasing the quantity of train service declines steadily as quantity increases.

Of course, the process of determining the optimal quantity of a public good is not always easy in practice. It is difficult to estimate with precision the total benefits accruing to individuals from public goods. And there are significant factors that influence politicians when they make decisions regarding public goods, as we discuss below. Another problem is how best to provide public goods.

21.3 HOW BEST TO PROVIDE PUBLIC GOODS

The government can provide public goods in a variety of ways. First, the government can provide public goods directly, via a government agency. Examples in the United States include the army, public schools, and the post office. Second, the government can subsidize and regulate the private sector to provide the desired amount of the public good. The U.S. government usually contracts with private companies to provide electricity while regulating the prices that the companies can charge. Third, the government can use the public sector for some aspects of public good provision and the private sector for other aspects. The U.S. government manages the road system and determines where new roads are built, but it usually hires private contractors to build and maintain the roads. The best method of providing a public good varies with the good's particular characteristics.

The privatization of the British rail service in the 1990s provides an instructive example. The British government sold the train infrastructure (rail track, buildings, etc.) to the Railtrack Group, which then became responsible for running and maintaining track. The British government also allowed private companies to bid for the right to offer train service on those tracks, thereby creating competition in rail service.

Competition in rail service proved to be very effective. Companies bid for the right to offer train service (a franchise) on a particular line. On popular routes such as London to Manchester, three or more different companies might be granted a franchise. If a train route is a popular one with a lot of potential riders, the bidding process ensures that companies pay a premium for the franchise. If the route is not popular, a rail service provider will make a "negative" bid, which means they would require a government subsidy of a certain amount in order to operate train service on that particular train route. The company entering the bid requiring the smallest subsidy would win the contract. The government willingly provides such subsidies to ensure that every community has access to train service.

Once a rail service provider successfully wins the franchise to provide train service on a particular route, they have an incentive to get as many riders on their trains as possible. To attract passengers, train companies began running trains more frequently and offering more seats at peak times. They also improved cleanliness and food options. The result was a doubling in ridership on British trains. In this case, competition, plus a system of government subsidies, improved train service because the incentives of private firms aligned with the goals of the government.

However, privatization of the track itself proved to be a disaster. The Railtrack Group that purchased the train tracks was content to milk profits from its operations while slashing spending on maintenance. Railtrack also refused to invest in the expansion of the track to growing areas. The cuts in maintenance culminated in two major accidents, including the Hatfield rail crash that killed four people and injured 70. With mounting evidence that additional crashes would be likely, the British state was forced to retake control over track operations in 2002.

This experience tells us something important about infrastructure and the profit motive. Private sector companies tend to focus on short-term profits due to the demands from stockholders. In the infrastructure business, it is too tempting to sacrifice long-term safety and growth for short-term returns. This will increase short-term profits dramatically, but the long-term results are disastrous. In addition to poor maintenance, private sector firms often are unwilling to make long-term investments that will not be profitable for a long time. This shortsightedness makes it inappropriate for the private sector to be in charge of infrastructure most of the time.

Today, many European countries use a mixed public–private structure to provide train service, with government providing and maintaining the infrastructure and private companies competing to provide train services. However, Norway and Switzerland feature extremely efficient and entirely public train systems, demonstrating that effective train service can be provided publicly as well.

We see a similar mix of approaches in health care. Some governments provide health services and health insurance directly to the public. Some governments use private doctors, clinics, and hospitals to provide health care, but they regulate and subsidize the industry to make sure everyone has access to appropriate care. And some governments use a public–private hybrid.

Another key issue with respect to public goods is the appropriate balance between the public sector and the private sector. According to progressive political economist John Kenneth Galbraith, politicians in the United States generally provide too few public goods due to the undue influence of large corporations in the political system. Austrian economists such as Murray Rothbard disagree.

21.4 GALBRAITH AND THE THEORY OF SOCIAL BALANCE

According to mainstream economic theory, an effective political system with non-corrupt politicians should be able to provide the optimal level of public goods. But as noted in Chapter 19, the American Society of Civil Engineers gave America's infrastructure a grade of C- in 2021, identifying deficiencies in aviation, dams, drinking water, energy, hazardous waste, waterways, levees, parks, roads, schools, public transit, and wastewater. The U.S. government would need to spend more than $2 trillion over what is currently budgeted to fix these problems.

So why does the United States have an infrastructure that civil engineers believe is deficient in many areas? The answer, to Galbraith, is the overemphasis in the United States on private goods due to the dominating influence of large corporations.

Companies work to create new wants and desires via ever-increasing levels of sophisticated advertising and marketing. As legendary Apple CEO Steve Jobs said, "People don't know what they want until you show it to them." Companies need to manufacture wants for new products in order to sell them in sufficient quantities for the products to be profitable. They have to convince people who already have a house full of products to buy yet another one.

Once "early adopter" consumers start to show off their new products, other consumers will emulate them, as Veblen predicted, creating additional demand. In this way, the production of goods, coupled with sophisticated marketing, creates the demand for products. To Galbraith, **instead of consumers determining what is produced by voting with their dollars, producers determine what is desired and consumed by creating and nurturing consumer demand**.

Galbraith also observed that households became increasingly dependent on more and more commodities over time, treating new items as necessities. He called this process the **dependence effect**. We can see this phenomenon all around us in the modern world. Two decades ago in the United States, very few people owned a smartphone. Today, most people in developed countries consider smartphones a necessity. Similarly, internet service was just getting started in the 1990s and only a small proportion of the population had access. Today, most people in developed countries consider a high-speed internet connection to be essential. As Galbraith predicted, we see a relentless increase in the number of products that people see as necessities.

As people become more dependent on ever-larger quantities of commodities, Galbraith pointed out that they are not necessarily better off. Economist Richard

Easterlin corroborated Galbraith's argument with research demonstrating that despite steady increases in per capita gross domestic product (GDP) in recent decades, happiness in the United States is unchanged. From 1972 to 2008, income per capita in the United States almost doubled, whereas average happiness stayed about the same.[2] This contradicts mainstream economic theory, which predicts that consumers achieve greater satisfaction (utility) the more products they consume.

Consuming ever-increasing quantities of commodities does not seem to be making us happier, and it does come with one major negative consequence. Increasing consumption of private goods results in a decrease in the quantity and quality of our public goods. Given limited resources, if society devotes a greater share of its resources to the production of private goods, it must devote a smaller share of resources to the production of public goods.

Government infrastructure investment in the United States, which includes spending on roads, bridges, trains, mass transit, ports, airports, water, and wastewater treatment, declined steadily in recent years. The U.S. government spent about 4.5% of GDP on infrastructure investments in the 1960s, but that fell to less than 1.5% of GDP in the 2010s. Over that same time, personal consumption increased from 59% of GDP to 70% of GDP. Consumers in the United States spent more and more on private goods, at the same time that the government spent less and less on public goods.

To Galbraith, the product of such a system is a **social imbalance**, with private goods elevated over public goods even though public goods are incredibly valuable. He describes this social imbalance vividly in his famous book *The Affluent Society*:

> The family which takes its mauve and cerise, air-conditioned, power-steered, and power-braked automobile out for a tour passes through cities that are badly paved, made hideous by litter, blighted buildings, billboards and posts for wires that should long since have been put underground. They pass on into a countryside that has been rendered largely invisible by commercial art. ... They picnic on exquisitely packaged food from a portable icebox by a polluted stream and go on to spend the night at a park which is a menace to public health and morals. Just before dozing off on an air mattress, beneath a nylon tent, amid the stench of decaying refuse, they may reflect vaguely on the curious unevenness of their blessings. Is this, indeed, the American genius?

Galbraith points out in this passage how important public goods are to our enjoyment of private goods. One cannot enjoy a nice car without a good road to drive it on. A picnic of delicious food is only pleasant if the park and natural surroundings are clean and well maintained.

This is where you can use your own powers of observation to determine whether your community and country have a social imbalance. Do you see plentiful, high-quality private goods while public goods languish in disrepair? Or do you see an effective balance of private and public goods?

One of the major reasons why a country experiences a social imbalance is the powerful lobbying by corporations and business owners who benefit from increasing sales of private goods. Galbraith called this the **growth lobby** because of its ongoing efforts to pressure governments for tax cuts, deregulation, and other policies that would stimulate growth in the sales of private commodities. Typically, the growth lobby frames the public sector as an enemy of the private sector. And yet this is implicitly an argument against such crucial institutions as public schools and public education, something Galbraith pointed out in another famous quotation:

> In this discussion a certain mystique was attributed to the satisfaction of privately supplied wants. A community decision to have a new school means that the individual surrenders the necessary amount, willy-nilly, in his taxes. But if he is left with that income, he is a free man. He can decide between a better car or a television set. This was advanced with some solemnity as an argument for the TV set. The difficulty is that this argument leaves the community with no way of preferring the school. All private wants, where the individual can choose, are inherently superior to all public desires which must be paid for by taxation and with an inevitable component of compulsion. ... Finally, it was argued, with no little vigor that expanding government posed a grave threat to individual liberties. ...

As a result of the growth lobby and their relentless campaign to reduce taxes and slash government spending, public goods in the United States fell into disrepair. Similarly, the crusade against environmental regulations resulted in increasingly rapid climate change and other forms of environmental damage, while the production of private goods soared.

A related effect of this push by private interests is the undermining of careful planning. One of the important roles for government is to look ahead to ensure that our economic system remains strong for future generations. As planning shifts from the public sector to the private sector, planning changes in character. In the United States, many of the best and brightest people spend their entire careers trying to sell a few more iPhones or SUVs or whatever product upon which their job depends. Meanwhile, the great problems of society, such as solving climate change, curing cancer, or ending poverty, receive less attention and resources. Is it rational for a society to devote the largest share of its resources to the production of nonessential commodities, or do we, indeed, have a social imbalance, as Galbraith argues?

Galbraith's solution to the social imbalance he saw in U.S. capitalism was a rebalancing of political power. Galbraith advocated a system of countervailing power, **where corporations, individuals/workers, and government would have relatively equal power and no one group could dominate the others**. If corporations became too powerful, we would experience a social imbalance because private goods would dominate public goods. If government became too powerful, we could end up with a totalitarian regime that worked poorly for people. And if workers became too powerful, they might make demands that would make businesses uncompetitive, which could harm economic growth and international competitiveness. However, if all three power blocks were relatively equally balanced, as was the case in the United States in the 1950s and 1960s, we would get a system in which corporations and workers both prospered and the government provided a sufficient quantity of public goods.

There are many economists who disagree with Galbraith's analysis, especially those who prefer less government intervention. Austrian economist Murray Rothbard's views are diametrically opposed. Instead of seeing businesses as controlling and manipulating, Rothbard sees businesses working very hard to please consumers and advertising as simply providing information. Rothbard also objects to Galbraith's critique of wasteful private consumption, arguing that the luxury consumption of the rich is useful in "pioneering new ways of consumption, and thereby paving the way for later diffusion of such 'consumption innovations' to the mass of the consumers."[3] Rothbard sees government as too large and overbearing. He would prefer to see less government and more private provision of goods. Thus, Rothbard sees private producers as the source of all that is good in the U.S. economy, whereas government is an inept and inefficient force that needs to be contained and constrained.

Meanwhile, as noted above, mainstream economists usually maintain that a well-functioning democracy will tend to supply the optimal quantity of public goods. Citizens elect representatives who reflect their preferences and deliver the amount of public goods that citizens desire.

Now that we have studied how economists view the provision of public and quasi-public goods, it is worth considering in more detail how governments actually provide such goods in practice. The next section focuses on the provision of one of the most important public/quasi-public goods, health care.

21.5 HEALTH CARE AND HEALTH INSURANCE

As noted above, economists consider personal health care a quasi-public good because, even though most of the benefits from health care treatments go to an individual, society as a whole reaps substantial external benefits. The benefits from an individual's good health extend to families, employers, communities, and nations due to improved community health and productivity. Unfortunately, markets do not function effectively in providing health care or health insurance.

Health care refers to **the provision of health services and drugs by doctors, nurses, clinics, hospitals, and pharmacies**. Health care can be provided by independent practitioners operating private practices or by public hospitals and clinics. The provision of health care in unregulated markets is problematic. On the demand side, individuals rarely have enough information to know whether they need particular treatments, tests, drugs, or procedures. It is extremely difficult to be a fully informed consumer in such cases, which is why most people simply defer to their doctor. But when suppliers (doctors) are making the decisions for the consumers, problems can arise. Rather than attempting to cure people, pharmaceutical companies and doctors may have a financial incentive to keep treating people indefinitely so they can continue to collect revenue from ongoing treatments. Doctors and hospitals can increase their revenues by ordering unnecessary tests and medical procedures. There can be a conflict of interest when suppliers control the decisions of demanders (consumers).

In a competitive marketplace, doctors' offices feel the need to have the latest equipment, technology, and specialists to stay up with competitors, even if the equipment is only rarely used. But this is very costly. It is more efficient to provide health care in centralized locations due to substantial economies of scale. By treating a large number of patients, a regional hospital can offer specialized doctors and machinery at a much lower cost. Therefore, private suppliers in competitive markets do not tend to be very good at providing health care services effectively and efficiently. The same is true of health insurance.

Health insurance exists to spread the risk of costly catastrophic injury or illness to a large pool of people. Like other forms of insurance, health insurance allows households to protect themselves from an extraordinarily large expense that they might not be able to pay otherwise. Some health care treatments can cost millions of dollars and would be beyond the means of the vast majority of households. With health insurance, households make regular payments, called premiums, for which they get coverage in case they experience a large health expense. Insurance companies set premiums based on the expected average health care costs for the entire pool of people they cover. Health insurance can be sold to individuals in a competitive market or it can be provided by employers or the government.

Private health insurance companies have an incentive to insure healthy people who are unlikely to need expensive health care, and they increase profits by denying health insurance coverage to people with expensive preexisting conditions. Meanwhile, healthy, younger individuals have a disincentive to purchase health care given that they are less likely to incur substantial health care costs, whereas older people or those with chronic illnesses have a strong incentive to purchase health care. But if only sick people purchase health insurance, this defeats the purpose of insurance (spreading risk) and leads to huge increases in insurance premiums. Thus, both the supply of and demand for health care are subject to market failures.

In countries without a national health insurance system, most people get health insurance through their employer. However, this, too, creates incentive problems. Employers who provide health insurance to their employees may not want to hire individuals who might need expensive health care coverage. And employers have little or no incentive to continue to provide health care for employees after they retire. If we rely exclusively on employer-provided health insurance, retirees may end up being uninsured.

In essence, the profit motive and competition can lead to destructive behavior in the provision of both health care and health insurance. To deal with this problem, all governments intervene extensively in the market for health care. However, the degree of government intervention varies widely.

21.6 HEALTH CARE SYSTEMS

Given the extensive externalities and economies of scale in the health care market, most developed country governments opted to create a national system to provide health insurance for their citizens. Some governments provide health care directly to citizens via government clinics and hospitals, whereas other countries provide public health insurance but leave the provision of health care up to doctors operating in private practices.

The United States is the only developed country without a national health insurance system. Nonetheless, the United States does provide a substantial amount of health care, picking up most of the costs for the elderly (through Medicare), the poor (through Medicaid), and government employees (including soldiers and elected representatives). The U.S. government also provides subsidies to people in need to purchase health care in insurance marketplaces created by the Affordable Care Act (ACA). However, in 2019, 29 million U.S. citizens did not have health insurance, which is in stark contrast to the rest of the developed world where universal health insurance coverage is the norm. Figure 21.2 shows the number of Americans who are uninsured as well as those insured by their employer or the U.S. government and those who purchase their own health care.

In terms of the provision of health care, there is substantial variation between the private sector–dominated system in the United States and the public health care systems elsewhere. Figure 21.3 displays total health care expenditures as a percentage of GDP for a group of comparable developed countries. First, notice how much more of its GDP the United States devotes to health care than other developed countries. The United States devotes about 60% more of its GDP than the average of these similar countries. Second, the blend of public and private expenditure is different. About half of health care spending in the United States is undertaken by the government. This is a much smaller percentage than in other developed countries, where government provision of health care and/or health insurance is universal.

So why does the United States spend so much more on health care than other developed countries? A 2003 study by health economists Gerard Anderson, Uwe Reinhardt, Peter Hussey, and Varduhi Petrosyan from Johns Hopkins and Princeton universities found that people in the United States use about the same amount of health care as people in other wealthy countries but they pay a lot more for it.[4] The use of smaller, private sector health care providers instead of a public sector system is less cost effective.

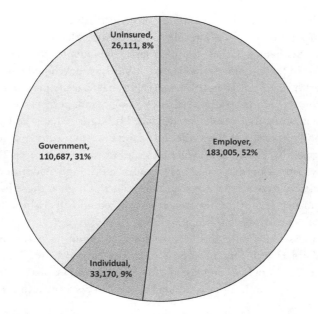

FIGURE 21.2 Health insurance coverage of Americans (in millions), 2019.

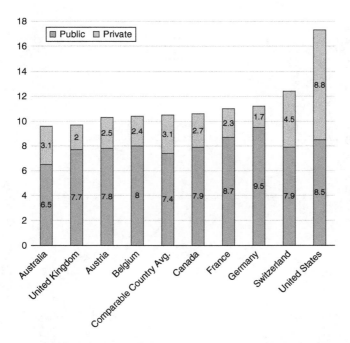

FIGURE 21.3 Total health expenditures as percentage of GDP by public and private
spending, 2016.

The high cost of U.S. health care might be justifiable if U.S. citizens experienced better health outcomes as a result. Unfortunately, that is not the reality. In a 2017 report by Schneider, Sarnak, Squires, Shah, and Doty for the Commonwealth Fund, the United States ranked dead last of 11 wealthy, developed countries in the quality of health care.[5] These health researchers analyzed the process of providing care, access to care, administrative efficiency, equity, and, perhaps most important, health care outcomes. The results are displayed in Figure 21.4. The United States does very poorly in terms of equity because so many Americans lack health insurance. Americans also pay higher deductibles and out-of-pocket costs. The lack of a centralized system means that the U.S. system has much higher administrative costs (U.S. administrative costs are more than three times as high as those in the United Kingdom) and that health information is not shared effectively between primary care physicians, specialists, and hospitals.

Other analysts also rank the U.S. health care system as extremely poor. In 2000, the World Health Organization ranked the United States 37th out of 191 countries, behind Costa Rica and just ahead of Slovenia and Cuba. Inefficiency and lack of access in the U.S. health care system cause it to perform at the level of much poorer countries.

Figure 21.5 shows OECD (Organization for Economic Cooperation and Development) data on health care indicators for eight developed countries. The United States ranks last in life expectancy, infant mortality, and obesity.

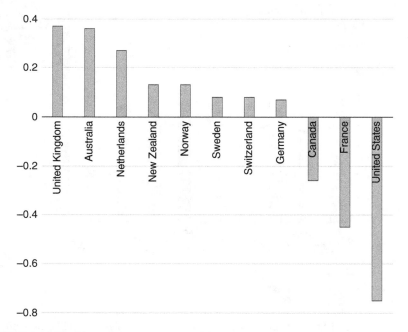

FIGURE 21.4 Health performance scores, 2017.

Country	Life expectancy	Infant mortality (deaths per 1000 live births)	Obesity (% of population)
Australia	82.8	3.1	27.9
Canada	82.0	4.7	28.1
Germany	81.0	3.2	23.6
Netherlands	81.9	3.5	20.4
Norway	82.8	2.3	23.1
Sweden	82.6	2.0	20.6
United Kingdom	81.3	3.9	26.2
United States	78.7	5.8	40.0

FIGURE 21.5 Table showing health care indicators, 2018 (or most recent year). Source: OECD.Stat.

The U.S. system does quite well in terms of providing cutting-edge care to those who are wealthy or have high-quality insurance. People around the world come to the United States for advanced medical treatments. However, the U.S. health care system does poorly by most other quality measures.

Almost all developed countries except the United States have a single-payer health care system, where **the government pays most (68%–85%) of the health care costs out of tax revenues**. Single-payer health care systems can take two different forms. In the **government provider model**, used in the United Kingdom, Sweden, and New Zealand, the government owns and runs most hospitals and clinics, the government employs some doctors, and private doctors collect most of their fees from the government. In the **national health insurance model**, doctors, clinics, and hospitals are usually private but the government provides health *insurance* to everyone, either through the government or through private insurers with payments coming from a government insurance program. Poor countries often have an **out-of-pocket model**, where there is no government health care system and only those with money receive care.

Interestingly, the United States has elements of *all* of these models. U.S. veterans receive care at government (Veterans Health Administration) hospitals and clinics, which is a variation of the government provider model. The elderly and the poor in the United States who qualify for Medicare and Medicaid receive government health insurance, but they usually see private sector doctors, which is a version of the national health insurance model. And the millions of uninsured Americans are forced to use an out-of-pocket model where they get care if they can pay for it.

One of the most dramatic changes in the U.S. health care system in recent years was the passage of the Affordable Care Act (ACA) in 2010. The ACA was fully implemented in 2014. Prior to the ACA, the number of uninsured people in the United States was increasing steadily. The combination of extraordinarily high health insurance costs, poverty, and poor-quality jobs that did not come with health benefits resulted in 47 million people, or 16% of the U.S. population (and more than 20% of working-age Americans), lacking health insurance in 2010.

The ACA was a major priority for the Obama administration. To reduce the number of uninsured, the ACA instituted four key policies. First, it prevented health insurance companies from denying coverage to someone with a preexisting medical condition. Second, it required insurance policies to allow children to be covered under their parents' health insurance policies until age 26 (adults aged 18–26 who were no longer dependents were among the least insured groups). Third, the ACA instituted subsidies to make insurance affordable to lower-income families. And fourth, the ACA required that all citizens purchase some form of medical insurance or pay a fine. The latter policy, called the "individual mandate," was important because if only sick individuals purchased health insurance, the cost of insurance would be prohibitively expensive. The only way individually purchased health care could be affordable was if it covered a large pool of people, some of whom were healthy.

The ACA also tried to control health care costs by instituting stricter oversight of health care spending and by linking health care payments to improved health outcomes rather than the number of procedures done. And the ACA created health insurance exchanges to create a marketplace for health insurance in all 50 states.

The initial results of the ACA were generally positive. The number of uninsured fell dramatically from 47 million to 28 million, and health care costs increased much more slowly. However, the individual mandate proved to be deeply unpopular politically, because healthy people resented having to purchase health insurance or pay a fine. The Trump administration and a Republican-dominated Congress eliminated the individual mandate in December of 2017. The final impact of this policy change remains to be seen, although economists predict that the removal of healthy people from the insurance pools will result in large increases in ACA premiums.

The ongoing problems with the U.S. health care system, particularly the extraordinarily high costs and the poor health outcomes, have led a number of U.S. economists and politicians to call for "Medicare for All." This would mean the creation of a national, single-payer health insurance system modeled on the existing Medicare system.

Economists and politicians, as you might expect, are divided on the best approach to providing health care and health insurance. Libertarians such as Ron Paul would prefer little or **no government** intervention in health care. Those who believe in the power of markets (e.g., *The Economist* magazine) would like the private sector to be in charge of health care and health insurance policies, but they acknowledge that the **government should make sure that all citizens have coverage** due to the market failures associated with health insurance, as is done in Switzerland. A middle-of-the-road approach, such as that taken in Sweden, involves **single-payer health insurance and the availability of government and private sector doctors, clinics, and hospitals**. Under this system, everyone can get good, government-provided health care if they wish. Or they can pay extra to receive insurance and care in the private sector. Finally, a completely national system is one where the **government provides both health insurance and health care**, which is largely the case in the United Kingdom and Cuba.

In determining life expectancy, infant mortality, and overall wellness, health care is one of the most important publicly provided goods. It is so crucial and so expensive that countries are devoting more and more of their resources to providing health care. Figure 21.6 shows the percentage of GDP a set of developed countries devoted to health care between 1992 and 2016.[6] Health care expenditures increased rapidly in all countries, as aging populations and expensive new drugs and technology increased costs. However, health care costs are highest and increasing most rapidly in the United States, whereas other developed countries with national health care systems are clustered at a lower level of spending. Nonetheless, all developed countries will need to find ways to contain health care costs as demographic and technological changes drive health care costs higher and higher.

Another quasi-public good that governments devote significant resources to is education. Education increases businesses' productivity and national income, while fostering innovation and economic growth. Public knowledge and the scientific breakthroughs that accompany education have significant spillover benefits and contribute substantially to economic development, establishing entirely new industries and improving human well-being. Thus, most countries in the world devote substantial resources to the public provision of education.

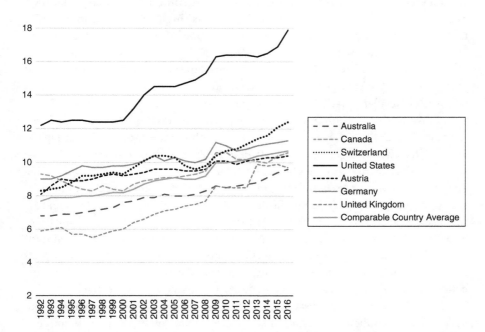

FIGURE 21.6 Health care expenditures as a percentage of GDP, 1992–2016.

21.7 EDUCATION, KNOWLEDGE, INNOVATION, AND ECONOMIC DEVELOPMENT

Education is crucial for individuals, communities, and countries for a variety of reasons. For the individual, education creates human capital—**the skills, dexterity, knowledge, habits, and creativity that improve productivity**. Human capital is directly tied to higher productivity and higher wages. Economist David Weil estimated that in developed countries only 35% of wages are paid for unskilled labor effort, whereas 65% of wages are payments for the human capital that workers acquired via education and training. There are direct correlations between education, increases in productivity, and higher incomes.

More broadly, education fosters knowledge creation, which promotes the development of new technology. Technology, in turn, complements skills and increases returns to education because workers who can understand and work with the latest technologies are particularly productive and valuable.

Education also creates numerous positive externalities. Businesses save significantly on training costs when workers are educated. Well-educated citizens tend to be healthier and wealthier, reducing crime rates and health care costs and improving tax revenues. Democratic institutions require educated citizens and leaders who can make sound decisions.

Perhaps most important from the perspective of a government considering where to devote its scarce resources, education contributes directly to economic development. The United States was an early leader in public primary education beginning in the 19th century, and it also adopted high school education earlier than other countries.[7] The high levels of education of the U.S. workforce were one of the reasons for its economic successes in the late 1900s and early 2000s. However, as we will see below, in recent years other countries caught up to and even surpassed the U.S. public education system.

It is no accident that Silicon Valley, home to the tech industry in the United States, is in close proximity to two premier universities—Stanford and the University of California Berkeley—and several other universities. Another rapidly growing tech hub, Research Triangle Park in North Carolina, is surrounded by the University of North Carolina Chapel Hill, Duke University, and North Carolina State University. Boston, with Harvard, MIT, and several other excellent universities, is a leader in biotechnology, health, and technology sectors. Technologically advanced industries tend to develop in locations with well-educated populations, leading to higher wages for everyone in the area. In one study, Enrico Moretti found that a "one percent increase in the proportion of college educated workers raises the wage of high school dropouts, high school graduates, workers with some college, and college graduates by 1.9%, 1.6%, 1.2%, and 0.4% respectively."[8]

Note that due to the substantial external benefits, private sector markets will never provide a sufficient quantity of education. As we saw in Chapter 19, unregulated markets tend to underproduce goods that generate external benefits because markets cannot charge people for the external benefits they receive. In addition, the private sector will not invest sufficiently in the pursuit of primary scientific research (basic science) of the type that is undertaken in university and government research labs utilizing public funding. Scientific breakthroughs are difficult and uncertain. Even years of effort and large investments in technology are no guarantee that a profitable breakthrough will result. This makes private companies extremely reluctant to engage in basic scientific research. But, once university and government scientists make an advance, the private sector is eager to turn those advances into new products and production techniques.

In her book *The Entrepreneurial State*, Mariana Mazzucato reports that 75% of new pharmaceutical drugs were derived from advances made in government or university research labs. Mazzucato also points out that a large number of the technologies in an iPhone were a product of government research or government funding. Government research led to the initial development of the internet, GPS technology, touchscreen displays, voice recognition, and many more aspects of the smartphone. As with many startups, Apple received initial financing from the U.S. government's small business development program. Similarly, Google's search algorithm was funded by the National Science Foundation. Thus, in addition to the provision of education, creating new knowledge by funding basic scientific research at universities and in government research labs directly stimulates the development of new industries.

Given the broad benefits of education and scientific research, most countries provide public education for all citizens or provide subsidies so all citizens can afford to purchase private education. If we look at government spending on education as a percentage of GDP (Figure 21.7), the United States falls below the level of most other high-income countries according to data from the World Bank. Public education receives the most resources in the Nordic countries and Belgium,

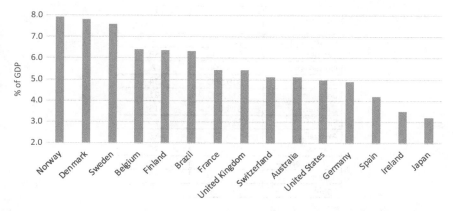

FIGURE 21.7 Government spending on education as a percentage of GDP, 2017.

followed by Brazil, France, and the United Kingdom. The governments of the United States, Germany, and Japan spend less than the others.

The United States features a lot more private spending on education than other countries. This gives U.S. education a much more unequal character than other countries. In many U.S. cities, children in wealthy, suburban school districts or in expensive, private schools get a first-rate education, whereas some public schools suffer from low levels of funding and overcrowding.

Most education analysts believe that the United States has the best university system in the world, in part because the United States spends more per student on higher education than other countries, as displayed in Figure 21.8. However, Figure 21.8 also shows many countries catching up, increasing their higher education spending much more quickly than the United States. In the United States, 62% of higher education spending comes from private sources, with the government covering the remaining 38%.

This is very different from how other countries fund higher education. Across all OECD countries, 30% of expenditures on higher education come from private sources on average, whereas 70% come from government sources. In all Nordic countries and most northern European countries, college tuition at public colleges and universities is free, paid for entirely out of government revenues.[9]

With the limited amount that the U.S. government puts toward higher education along with the high cost, most college costs in the United States are paid by students and their families. This resulted in the explosion of student debt in recent years. According to the Federal Reserve, student loan debt nearly tripled from 2006 to 2017, increasing from $500 billion to $1.466 billion. Despite the cost, college graduates earn 80% more than workers who did not graduate from college, so the investment in a college education in the United States is still beneficial to most.

In education, as with health care, we see a mix of approaches. In the United States, there are public and private schools and universities. The public pays most of

Country	Expenditure	% Change since 2005
United States	$31,600	4
Sweden	$25,300	39
Netherlands	$20,100	7
Japan	$19,500	34
Belgium	$18,900	21
Germany	$18,000	15
Finland	$17,900	19
Australia	$16,800	-13
France	$16,200	26
OECD average	$16,200	27
Ireland	$13,300	11
Spain	$13,100	6

FIGURE 21.8 Table of expenditure on higher education per student, 2016.

the costs of K–12 education, and private individuals pay most of the costs of college education. In most other developed countries, a larger proportion of the schools and universities are public, and the government covers most of the costs.

21.8 CONCLUSION

The provision of public and quasi-public goods is one of the essential roles for government and one of the key factors in determining the success of an economic system. There are seven major categories of public goods: (1) physical infrastructure, (2) market infrastructure, (3) security services, (4) governance and public services, (5) environmental services, (6) public knowledge, and (7) public health.

Quasi-public goods such as individual health care and education have some but not all of the characteristics of public goods. Even though these goods benefit individuals the most, there are broad benefits to society in ensuring that everyone has access to these goods and in providing them in the most efficient manner possible. Economies of scale usually mean that somewhat centralized public provision of quasi-public goods is more efficient than a competitive market environment with small suppliers.

The right balance of public goods and private goods is a hotly debated topic. John Kenneth Galbraith argues that the United States devotes too many resources to trivial private goods while neglecting more crucial public goods. He argues that an increase in power for workers, citizens, and the government is necessary to countervail the power of large corporations. Murray Rothbard counters that we have too much government and that we would be better off with more private goods and fewer goods provided by government.

The manner in which various countries deal with quasi-public goods like education and health care is broadly indicative of the type of economic system of that country. Market-dominated economies like the United States use less public funding for education and health care than social market economies. And the United States provides less public education and public health care services than social market economies.

Like other developed countries, the United States spends a lot of money on these goods, but it leans toward private sector spending rather than public spending. This resulted in some significant inefficiencies in the U.S. health care system. On the other hand, the U.S. higher education system, though extraordinarily expensive, delivers superb quality.

Education and human capital are directly relevant to the next topic, which we take up in Chapter 22: The labor market. Working dominates most of our lives, shaping our days and determining who we spend the most time with. Work can be a pleasant and fulfilling experience or it can be torturous.

QUESTIONS FOR REVIEW

1. List the seven categories of public goods. Which category do you think is most important for economic growth? Which category is most important for quality of life of a country's citizens? Explain briefly and support your answer.

2. How are quasi-public goods different from public goods? Explain.

3. Would vaccinations be considered a public good or a quasi-public good? Explain briefly.

4. Using a graph of the market for a public good, use mainstream economic analysis to explain carefully why markets do not tend to provide the optimal quantity of public goods.

5. Using the graph in Figure 21.9, answer the following questions:
   a. Which point represents the socially efficient equilibrium?
   b. Which point represents the private market equilibrium?
   c. What distance on the graph would represent the lost social benefits from producing at the private market equilibrium?
   d. What are some methods that can be used to move the economy to the socially efficient equilibrium?

6. Explain why privatization was effective in providing train service in Britain but not effective in providing the infrastructure for train service (the train tracks).

7. Write a short essay in which you contrast the analysis of public goods by (a) mainstream economists, (b) progressive political economist John Kenneth Galbraith, and (c) Austrian economist Murray Rothbard. Which approach do you find most convincing? Why?

8. Compare and contrast the U.S. health care system with those of other developed countries. In what ways does the U.S. system stand out?

9. Should the United States adopt a single-payer health care system? Explain and support your answer.

10. How does the U.S. education system compare with those of other developed countries? Explain briefly.

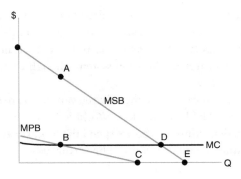

FIGURE 21.9 MC, MPB, and MSB.

11. Given the importance of education in developing human capital and fostering economic growth, how would you reform the U.S. education system? Explain and support your answer.

NOTES

1 We study other theories of economic growth in macroeconomics.

2 Rubén Hernández-Murillo and Christopher J. Martinek, "The Dismal Science Tackles Happiness Data," *Regional Economist*, January 2010, www.stlouisfed.org/publications/ regional-economist/january-2010/the-dismal-science-tackles-happiness-data, accessed December 9, 2019.

3 Murray Rothbard, "John Kenneth Galbraith and the Sin of Affluence," 2008, https:// mises.org/library/john-kenneth-galbraith-and-sin-affluence, accessed July 30, 2018.

4 Source: Bradley Sawyer and Cynthia Cox, "How Does Health Spending in the U.S. Compare to Other Countries?," Peterson-Kaiser Health System Tracker, Kaiser Family Foundation, www.healthsystemtracker.org/chart-collection/health-spending -u-s-compare-countries/#item-relative-size-wealth-u-s-spends-disproportionate- amount-health, accessed July 23, 2018.

5 See Eric Schneider, Dana Sarnak, David Squires, et al., "Mirror, Mirror 2017: International Comparison Reflects Flaws and Opportunities for Better U.S. Health Care," Commonwealth Fund, https://interactives.commonwealthfund.org/2017/july/ mirror-mirror/assets/Schneider_mirror_mirror_2017.pdf, accessed July 29, 2018.

6 See Sawyer and Cox, note 4.

7 See Claudia Goldin, "Human Capital," *Handbook of Cliometrics* (Springer-Verlag, forth- coming), http://scholar.harvard.edu/files/goldin/files/human_capital_handbook_of_c liometrics_0.pdf, accessed August 1, 2021.

8 Enrico Moretti, "Estimating the Social Return to Higher Education: Evidence from Longitudinal and Repeated Cross-sectional Data," *Journal of Econometrics* 121 (2004), pp. 175–212; p. 209.

9 Education at a Glance: OECD Indicators 2012, www.oecd.org/unitedstates/CN – United States.pdf, accessed July 24, 2018.

PART VI

Labor markets and inequality

In Part VI we take up what economists call "factor markets"—markets for the factors of production, including labor, land, and capital. Factor markets are important because in a capitalist economic system, factor markets are the primary determinants of income. Therefore, the functioning of factor markets is responsible for how much the owners of the factors of production are paid, determining the degree of inequality in society.

The most important factor market is the labor market, which governs how much workers get paid for selling their labor power to an employer (the capitalist). This is the subject of Chapter 22. Political economists focus on the conflicts that exist between laborers and capitalists as they fight over work hours, work intensity, benefits, and pay. In contrast, mainstream economists focus on how competitive labor markets work, constructing models depicting a competitive labor market in which laborers and capitalists have relatively equal bargaining power. One of the major debates in modern economics is over the minimum wage and whether or not raising the minimum wage is a good idea. Chapter 22 reviews the debate and shows that, according to the best data economists have, raising the minimum wage does not tend to increase unemployment and therefore benefits workers at the bottom of the income distribution significantly.

Chapter 23 turns to the subject of inequality in more detail. The United States is the most unequal developed country in the world, and it has been growing increasingly unequal in recent years. The fact that the United States is exceptionally unequal is largely a product of government policies, such as low taxes on the wealthy, a very unequal education system, government hostility toward labor unions, and a very small safety net to support workers who fall on hard times. Inequality also is significantly affected by class differences and the ability of the upper social classes to preserve their privileged position while denying access to others. There is also significant race and gender inequality in the United States, driven by social norms, stereotyping, unequal education, and other destructive

DOI: 10.4324/9781315636924-27

forces and policies that limit the opportunities for women and people of color. Along with the environment, increasing inequality is one of the major issues of our time.

Taken together, these chapters lay out the forces that play a huge role in shaping the opportunities we have in life. This, in turn, impacts what our lives are like, who we meet and befriend, and even who we marry.

This section begins by taking up labor markets, starting with how labor markets are evolving and how employment trends are changing.

Working for a living

The labor market and the forces that affect your working life

One of the most important aspects of economics to each and every one of us is success in the labor market. Every worker wants an interesting job that pays well and that allows them to spend time with their friends and family. But employers do not necessarily have the same interests. Employers want a worker who will give maximum effort every hour of every day, and they also prefer to pay workers as little as possible and to avoid paying for too many vacation days. These inherent conflicts between workers and employees are fundamental in driving outcomes in the labor market.

When there are very few employers bidding for the labor of a large number of workers, the market lacks competition on the demand for labor side while featuring a plethora of competition on the supply side. In such cases, employers have more power than workers in the bargaining relationship. This results in workers being exploited—that is, paid less than they are worth. Unfortunately, most markets for most workers fall into this category, with employers having undue power over workers. Nonetheless, workers with substantial education and skills usually have many options, which allows them to be more selective in what jobs they take and to demand decent pay and benefits.

Political economists study labor conditions when employers have more power than workers. Mainstream economists focus more on labor markets that are competitive and where the bargaining relationship between workers and employers is relatively equal. Thus, we get a more complete picture of labor markets by studying both perspectives.

This chapter begins with a look at how the labor market is evolving. We then take up how political economists analyze labor markets, focusing on the institutions and power structures that affect wages and working conditions. Subsequently, we study how mainstream economists analyze labor markets and the minimum wage.

DOI: 10.4324/9781315636924-28

22.0 CHAPTER 22 LEARNING GOALS

After reading this chapter, you should be able to:

■ Describe the major trends affecting employment opportunities in various industries.

■ Use the political economy model of the division of the workday to explain the conflicts between workers and employers.

■ Explain how employers are able to motivate workers using the carrot or stick approach and how these approaches tend to vary by industry.

■ Analyze the power dynamics between workers and employers and determine the major forces that seem to be driving changes in the labor market in the United States and other countries.

■ Use the mainstream economics model of the labor market to determine how various events will affect the wage rate and the number of workers employed.

■ Describe and evaluate the arguments for and against the minimum wage.

■ Use the mainstream economics model of the labor market to determine the equilibrium quantity of labor a firm should hire using marginal revenue product and marginal factor cost.

22.1 LABOR MARKET TRENDS

If you are reading this chapter, you are probably a college student working toward a degree. A key question you may be concerned with is what the labor market will be like when you graduate.

The U.S. economy moved dramatically in recent years away from manufacturing and into services. From 1990 to 2015, employment in manufacturing decreased by 30% and employment in education, health care, and business services increased by more than 80%. These structural shifts in industries sparked changes in the skills employers are looking for.

Surveys of employers indicate an increasing need for employees with **social skills**, such as:

* **Teamwork**: working closely with others in a diverse workplace
* **Cultural competency**: ability to work with and engage people from cultures around the world

- **Communications**: ability to listen, write clearly, and speak in an articulate manner
- **Influencing others**: utilizing skills relevant to sales and marketing
- **Management**: leadership, organization, ability to empower others, and capacity to be a facilitator and motivator.

Modern industries also require substantial **analytical skills**, including:

- **Problem solving and critical thinking**: finding solutions to complex, real-world problems in a shifting landscape
- **Creative thinking**: thinking outside the box and coming up with novel ideas
- **Quantitative analysis**: including a facility with statistics and math
- **Computer and technical literacy**: facility with spreadsheets, databases, and word processing software, along with coding experience
- **Ability to learn and adapt**: responding to industry, workplace, and consumer changes
- **Information literacy**: finding and processing information.

Finally, employers look for **personal skills and abilities**, including:

- **A strong work ethic**: as demonstrated by grades in difficult classes and other evidence of ability to work hard and succeed
- **Academic competence**: ability to read complex documents and understand mathematical and statistical reports
- **Multitasking**: ability to juggle multiple challenging assignments and tasks
- **Honesty and integrity**: so they can trust you with money and confidential information
- **Self-confidence**: so coworkers and clients will also have confidence in your work.

Figure 22.1 shows the industries projected to increase or contract the most in coming years.[1] Employment in health care is expected to expand the most as the population ages and as health care costs increase, which draws in additional workers, investors, and firms.

We also see a substantial projected increase in mining, education, professional and business services, leisure, and transportation and warehousing. Meanwhile, economists project declining employment in utilities, manufacturing, and the federal government. There are, of course, variations within sectors. Online retail trade is increasing with the rise of Amazon, whereas physical store retailing is in steep decline.

Notice that we can attribute the decline of numerous industries to the forces of creative destruction—shifts in technological and geopolitical forces that reshape industries. The decline in clothing manufacturing in the United States is a result of trade agreements with and lower wages in developing countries. Tobacco is

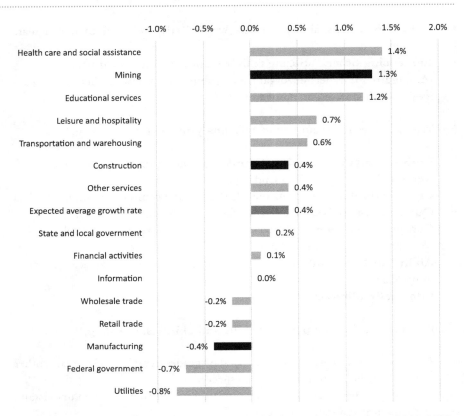

FIGURE 22.1 Projected annual rate of change (%) in industry employment, 2019–2029.

contracting due to high cigarette taxes and a public health effort to discourage smoking. The postal service is shipping less mail thanks to email and social media while facing stiff competition from UPS and Federal Express for package shipping. The decline in general government operations is a product of the current anti-government political climate, and so on.

In terms of expanding industries, it is striking the extent to which health care and social assistance dominate sectors seeing the most rapidly growing employment. We also expect to see the expansion of hiring in tech-related industries (information technology, data analysis, computer programming, social media, wireless communications) and finance. Of course, many other industries will continue to employ the same number of people as always.

One of the ways to have a successful career is to stay ahead of industry trends. Another is to make sure you have skills that are in demand so that you have many opportunities and can bargain effectively with your employer. Political economists focus their analysis of the labor market on the bargaining relationship between employers and workers because it is so fundamental in determining wages/salaries, work hours, and working conditions.

22.2 THE POLITICAL ECONOMY OF LABOR: WORKERS, EMPLOYERS, AND CONFLICT

Some workers have significant power in the labor market and can demand high wages and excellent treatment. Workers with unique skills and abilities do quite well in labor markets. But for every Giuliana Benetton, LeBron James, Oprah Winfrey, or Warren Buffett, there are millions of workers who have little power in the labor market. Political economists focus on these workers because their experiences are the most common.

As you may recall from Chapter 5, we can break the workday into the amount of time a worker pays for their wages (or salary) and benefits and the amount of time the worker is producing profits, or surplus value, for the business owner. Figure 22.2 displays this basic relationship, which is fundamental in understanding key dynamics of the labor market.

Radical political economists believe that the relationship between owners (capitalists) and workers is fundamentally an exploitative one. From this perspective, the only reason you do not get to keep all of the value you generate when you work is because you do not own the company (e.g., you do not own the means of production).

Most corporations are not owned by the person who started the company. Instead, publicly traded corporations are owned by stockholders, many of whom inherited their wealth. Why do they get to keep the profits from your work? Because they were lucky enough to be born into a rich family! To political economists, the fact that people who do not do the work are entitled to the profits generated by your labor just because they were lucky enough to be born rich is an unfair and exploitative relationship.

The amount or rate of exploitation is driven by the power imbalance between workers and employers. The less power workers have, the less they are able to demand decent wages, benefits, and working conditions. A good measure of the rate of exploitation is the **ratio of surplus value (profits) to wages** because this indicates whether or not workers are paid close to what they are worth. In a truly competitive labor market where multiple employers were bidding for the services of each laborer, we would expect workers' pay to come very close to the value of what they produce, yielding a low profit rate and a low rate of exploitation. For example, if employers made a 10% profit on what they paid a worker, we would

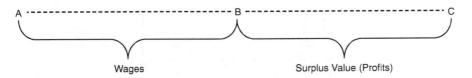

FIGURE 22.2 The division of the workday.

see a rate of exploitation of 0.10/0.90=0.11. When workers have few employment options and when they are competing with many other workers with similar skills, we expect to see a higher profit rate, a lower wage rate, and a higher rate of exploitation (Figure 22.3).

Although data on the rate of exploitation are hard to come by because companies protect this information, Neil Irwin found a useful proxy by computing the ratio of profit per worker to median worker pay.[2] Kraft Heinz foods had an exploitation ratio of 6.1, which means that earnings per worker captured by owners were 6.1 times as high as the compensation of a typical employee. Facebook was also extraordinarily profitable, with an exploitation rate of 2.6. Due to reinvestment of profits, Walmart and Amazon had an artificially low exploitation rate of 0.2, so it is important to acknowledge that profits vary with some of the particulars of each firm.

Examining how the rate of exploitation changes over time tells us much about the dynamics of the economic system. At the end of 2017, the richest 10% of the population of the United States owned 84% of the stocks and bonds. This means that the richest 10% of the population gets almost all of the profits generated by workers. They are a good proxy for the "owners" in a capitalist society. If we compare the share of national income going to workers in the form of wages and salaries to the share of income going to the top 10% (most of whom are owners), we see that there is generally an inverse relationship between wages and salaries for workers and the incomes of owners.

Figure 22.4 compares U.S. workers' share of national income to the share of income going to owners—the wealthiest 10% of the population. From 1970 to 2014, workers' share of national income declined from 52% to 42%, whereas owners' share of income increased from 34% to 47%. This highlights one of the fundamental aspects of the labor market: **There is a conflict between some of the interests of workers and some of the interests of employers**.

The primary sources of conflict between workers and employers are described below:

Company	Exploitation Ratio (profits/wages)
Kraft Heinz	6.1
McDonald's	3.2
Facebook	2.6
Wells Fargo Bank	1.4
Goldman Sachs	0.9
Alphabet (Google)	0.8
Walmart	0.2
Amazon	0.2

FIGURE 22.3 Table of exploitation ratios at U.S. companies.

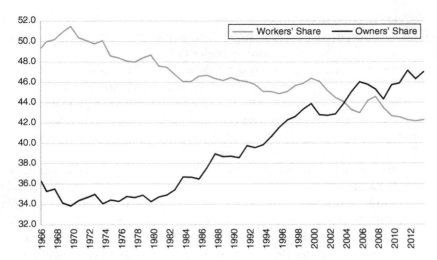

FIGURE 22.4 Workers' and owners' shares of U.S. national income, 1966–2014.

1. **Wages and salaries**: As Figure 22.4 shows, when workers' share of income rises, as it did in the 1960s, profits decrease and owners' share of income falls. When workers' share of income falls, profits rise and owners' share of income increases.

2. **Benefits**: As we saw in the material on health care, health insurance costs increased rapidly in recent years. The cost of benefits—health insurance, retirement, and other workplace perquisites (non-wage compensation)—is a substantial part of a business's costs of production. In many white-collar workplaces, benefits costs are 40% of the cost of salaries. Workers want generous benefits, whereas employers want to keep benefits costs as low as they can without compromising worker effort and health.

3. **Number of hours worked**: Workers tend to prefer fewer hours of work and lots of paid vacation time. To increase surplus value, employers want employees to work longer hours without increasing pay. We see this phenomenon in the salaried workforce in the United States. According to Wall Street Oasis, the median hours worked per week at U.S. investment banks in 2017 was 81. When you are paid a salary, your employer's incentive is to work you as many hours as you can possibly endure. Interestingly, work hours in modern investment banks are almost identical to those that workers were forced to endure during the pre-regulation period of the industrial revolution. Even workers paid by the hour are sometimes required to work mandatory overtime hours. It is often more profitable for employers to have factories operating around the clock and to have a smaller number of employees working longer hours to save on benefits costs.

4. **Intensity of work and work effort**: Employers want maximum concentration and effort at all times, whereas workers would like the ability to take

breaks, surf the internet, or social media sites, and socialize. According to the 2015 American Working Conditions Survey, two-thirds of Americans frequently work at high speeds or under tight deadlines, which is a classic indication of employers speeding up the pace of work. Only 57% of workers can take breaks when they want.[3] To coax maximum productivity out of their workforce, many employers monitor their workers, tracking internet use on their computers and installing cameras. Amazon is famous for attempting to control every aspect of how their employees find, pack, and ship products for maximum efficiency. Alternatively, employers can encourage work effort by giving employees autonomy and by offering bonuses or profit sharing.

5. **Working conditions and safety**: Workers prefer the safest environment possible, but worker safety can be expensive. More than half of U.S. workers experience hazardous conditions on the job, such as exposure to smoke, fumes, infectious materials, or extreme temperatures.[4] This is an indication of employers cutting costs while potentially compromising working conditions.

6. **Job security**: After wages and benefits, many workers cite job security as their top priority. There are few things in life more stressful than worrying about whether you will be able to keep your job and support your family. Employers prefer flexibility. They like to be able to hire workers if they need them or lay them off if they do not.

7. **Legal and political environment**: In addition to the conflicts that pervade every workplace, there are larger conflicts over the laws and policies that govern the labor market. Employers often lobby for laws that restrict unions, keep wages low, and reduce regulations on firms' behavior. Workers press for higher wages, better benefits, safety nets for workers, pro-union laws, and regulations making the workplace safer.

There are also some areas in which workers and employers have similar interests. U.S. steel workers and owners of steel companies both supported President Trump's 2018 tariffs on imported steel. Employees often benefit if their firm does well because this increases workers' prestige and offers them more opportunities. The interests of employers and employees are most aligned in firms adopting the "carrot" method of motivating employees rather than the "stick" method.

22.3 MOTIVATING LABOR: STICKS AND CARROTS

Employers tend to take one of two approaches to motivate their workers. The stick method of worker motivation refers to **efforts by employers to achieve maximum work effort via the threat of job dismissal (firing), attacking unions, and closely monitoring workers**. This approach is typical in low-wage occupations where workers are easily replaced, such as unskilled manufacturing and service sector jobs.

Some employers like this approach because they can keep wages low and spend very little on benefits and working conditions, making it very profitable. The standard way to keep employees working hard under these conditions is the stick: Prodding them to work harder with monitoring and the threat of dismissal. This conflictual approach also requires lots of managers who constantly check up on workers, creating a hierarchical structure and the accompanying bureaucratic expenses.

Amazon warehouses are known for controlling every motion of their employees under grueling conditions with low pay. Amazon monitors workers with sophisticated electronic systems to track how many boxes they pack each hour. Lunch and bathroom breaks are so short that some workers reported they had to urinate in trash cans to avoid falling behind on their quotas.[5] In 2011, when temperatures inside an Amazon warehouse in Pennsylvania exceeded 100°F, Amazon kept employees working at a grueling pace. Their only concession: They kept ambulances outside to take away workers as they collapsed from heat stroke and dehydration.[6]

The carrot method of worker motivation refers to **efforts by employers to cultivate loyalty and productivity from workers via offering job security, strong wage incentives (bonuses and profit-sharing), employee involvement in decisions, and strong unions**. In sectors where attracting and keeping skilled workers is essential, employers need to pay and treat workers well. Employers hope that the increased productivity from higher motivation will offset the increased wages and other costs associated with the carrot strategy.

Google is famous for going to great lengths to keep their skilled workers happy. Google pays high wages and good benefits, along with nontraditional perquisites such as free massages, fitness classes, gourmet meals, and snacks. Google also allows workers to bring pets to work and gives them a lot of independence and decision-making power. Workers like this autonomy and feel more invested in the company as a result.

Interestingly, we even see some carrot approaches in industries that are usually known for the stick strategy. Walmart is famous for its low wages, poor benefits, and worker monitoring. But one of their competitors in the grocery market, Wegmans, is regularly ranked as one of the best companies to work for in the United States. Like other employers utilizing the carrot approach, Wegmans empowers employees to be part of decision making and offers training and promotions from within the company to increase productivity and encourage loyalty and the development of firm-specific skills. Workers do not need to be monitored because they like their jobs and they see their loyalty to the company paying off. This saves on the cost of monitoring employees, removing a layer of bureaucracy.

Wegmans also offers flexible scheduling, which is very different from firms such as Walmart that tend to dictate when employees work. And Wegmans offers good benefits including wellness programs and discounts on food. They even provide scholarships and support for the local community, fostering loyalty and productivity.

Carrot employers can afford the costs of better pay and benefits if the increase in productivity and the decrease in monitoring costs and bureaucracy is enough to compensate. Judging by the prevalence of the stick approach in most manufacturing and service industries that employ less-skilled workers, it appears that the stick approach may be more profitable in these cases, despite how unappealing it is to workers.

Given some of the inherent conflicts between what workers want and what employers want out of the employment relationship, the balance of power between workers and employers is crucial in determining the outcomes in the seven areas of conflict described above. The next section describes the main sources of power.

22.4 POWER DYNAMICS BETWEEN EMPLOYERS AND WORKERS

The reason for the decline in workers' share of income and the increase in owners' share in Figure 22.4 has to do with the forces that drive the dynamics of the labor market. In general, political economists see wages and working conditions in labor markets as determined by the **relative power of workers and employers**. If employers have the upper hand, wages will be low and working conditions poor. If workers have the upper hand, wages will be high and working conditions better. The main factors that determine the balance of power between workers and employers are unions, political power, social attitudes, macroeconomic conditions, and the international environment.

1. **Unions and working-class solidarity**: Individual workers with few skills have very little power on their own in the workplace. If they make demands, their boss can fire them and replace them easily with a similar worker. Thus, the only way these workers can get better wages and working conditions is by joining together with other workers to demand changes—workplace solidarity. When workers act together, they can demand better pay and benefits, and if the employer does not agree to their demands, they can go on strike, temporarily shutting down the firm's operations.

   Labor unions are organizations designed to assist employees in working together to achieve their interests. A labor union is **an organization of workers formed to promote its members' interests with respect to wages, job security, benefits, and working conditions**. Labor unions engage in collective bargaining, where **the union negotiates wages and other aspects of employment with the employer**, instead of each worker negotiating separately. Workers pay a small amount every month, called "union dues," which go to support the union's activities.

After the government enacted laws during the Great Depression that legalized and supported unions, union membership increased to about 35% of the U.S. non-farm workforce in the 1950s. However, the percentage of workers in unions in the United States fell steadily from that peak as businesses and government officials attacked unions with increasing intensity. In 2020, union membership in the United States was only 11%.

2. **The balance of political power between workers and employers**: One of the major reasons for the decline in union membership in the United States was the anti-union political environment. Employers lobbied heavily to make it more difficult for unions to organize, and they generously supported politicians who agreed with their views. A recent example is the passing of so-called right to work laws in many U.S. states. Right to work laws contain provisions whereby employees who are governed by collective bargaining agreements do not have to pay union dues unless they wish to, even if the union's activities benefit them. If workers can receive the benefits of a union's bargaining efforts without paying dues, many choose to be free riders. However, as more and more workers choose to be free riders, union membership falls and unions lose the power that comes with collective bargaining. As unions weaken, this tends to put downward pressure on wages.

   In other countries where unions are more powerful, such as Sweden, Norway, and Switzerland, a workers' party or labor party advocates directly on behalf of all workers. In these countries, government policies and laws tend to be more favorable to unions. In addition, these countries provide a larger safety net, which empowers workers. If workers know that they will receive generous unemployment benefits and retraining, they do not have to take a low-paying, poor quality job. This increases the power workers have in the bargaining process, especially workers with the least skills.

3. **Social attitudes and class consciousness**: Both the degree of unionization and government policies toward workers are shaped significantly by social attitudes and the degree of class consciousness that exists in the work force. Class consciousness refers to **the awareness that people have of the existing system of social classes and their place in it**. If workers identify themselves as a member of the working class, they are more likely to form close bonds with other workers, join unions, and push for workers' rights. However, if workers identify themselves differently—for example, if people identify primarily as a member of a particular ethnic group or country—they are less likely to seek solidarity with other workers and more likely to work on behalf of a different set of values.

   U.S. employers almost always identify with other owners, pushing a set of policies that benefit owners at the expense of workers. And some U.S. workers actually identify more with owners rather than workers. Workers who hope they will strike it rich someday tend to support policies that benefit employers.

But without class consciousness and solidarity, workers do not have much power relative to employers.

Social attitudes and class consciousness are shaped considerably by the media and the education system. How unions are portrayed affects public attitudes and helps to determine whether or not unions are seen in a positive light.

4. **Market and macroeconomic conditions**: Workers have the most bargaining power when the market for their firm's product is growing rapidly, when the macroeconomic environment is strong, and when the unemployment rate is low. These three conditions create a high demand for workers. In addition, skills and education improve workers' productivity, making them more valuable and giving them more options in the labor market.

On the other hand, when the market for a firm's product is declining, when the overall economy is in a recession, and when unemployment is high, workers have little power to demand higher wages or better conditions. Also, if education is poor and workers have little access to training, they will have few skills and cannot demand better pay and benefits.

Technology can also have a big impact on wages and workers' bargaining power. The invention of robots that can replace workers will erode wages and strengthen employers. Computer technologies to monitor workers can speed up the pace of work and increase productivity, reducing the amount of time it takes for workers to pay for their wages and thereby moving point B to the left in Figure 22.2. Some technologies make workers more productive, giving workers with technological skills more power in the workplace.

5. **International environment**: Openness to trade has an uneven impact on workers' power in the workplace. If a worker is employed by a firm whose exports are growing, the increased demand for the firm's product from international consumers will increase the firm's demand for labor, putting workers in a strong position. But if a company is facing stiff competition from firms in other countries, workers are in a precarious situation. And if firms in a high-wage country can easily find workers with a similar skill set in a low-wage country, workers in the high-wage country will have little power to affect wages and working conditions.

22.4.1 The determination of wages in political economy

In general, we can expect the range of wages in a particular firm to vary based on the power dynamics we just described. The minimum wage a firm can pay is the amount workers and their families need to survive. Wages any less than this would cause workers to suffer malnutrition, ill health, and family emergencies, undermining productivity and profits. The maximum wage a firm could pay would be the entire amount of profits produced by the worker.

If labor markets are competitive and workers are powerful, workers' wages will tend toward the upper end of the range, keeping most of the profits that they

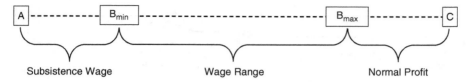

FIGURE 22.5 Wages and the division of the workday.

generate and leaving only a small amount (a normal profit) for the firm. In this case, in Figure 22.5, the wage rate part of the work day would move to the right to B_{max}, which is close to point C. Note that workers can never capture all of the value that they produce in a capitalist system because if the firm has no profits, it cannot survive. Therefore, the distance from B_{max} to C is the minimum amount of profit the firm needs to survive, which is a normal profit.

If labor markets are uncompetitive and if society's institutions support employers over workers, then wages will tend toward the lower end of the wage range. **The lowest wage rate on which a worker and their family can survive** is the subsistence wage. This is wage rate B_{min} in Figure 22.5. We often find subsistence wages in low-skill industries operating in poor countries with surplus workers. For example, in 1999, Nike announced that it was raising entry-level salaries for unskilled workers in Indonesia from $425 to $446 per year. Nike's spokesman expressed concern that the previous salary "was not meeting their basic needs."[7] Evidently $1.16 per day was not enough to live on, so Nike hoped the increase to $1.22 per day would help!

Even in the United States, some employers pay wages at or even below the subsistence level. In Ohio, one study found that 15% of Walmart workers were paid so little they qualified for food stamps, a government program designed to assist those at risk for hunger and malnourishment.[8] The workers' need for food stamps to survive at a decent level implies that Walmart was paying below subsistence wages.

Where exactly wages fall at a particular firm will depend on the power structures discussed above, including the particular characteristics of the firm, the presence or lack of a union, the skill set of employees, the market for the firm's product, the overall macroeconomic and international climate, and the political situation. Firms like wages to be as close as possible to the subsistence wage (B_{min}), and workers want wages to be as close as possible to the maximum that would still allow the firm to stay in business (B_{max}).

22.4.2 Determining work hours in political economy: Moving "C" to the right

Work hours are also a product of the power relationship between workers and firms, along with other factors such as culture and the legal system. When workers are paid a salary, such as B in Figure 22.6, their pay does not vary with the number of hours they work. They are supposed to work until the job they were hired to

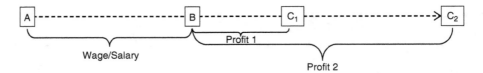

FIGURE 22.6 Wages and profits with a longer workday.

perform is done. Employers want the maximum number of work hours possible out of their salaried workforce. Increasing work hours moves point C in Figure 22.6 to the right from C_1 to C_2, which increases the rate of profit from Profit 1 to Profit 2.

Workers sometimes willingly work long hours in order to get ahead, especially in the United States with its culture emphasizing hard work and monetary achievement. But as Juliet Schor demonstrated in her book *The Overworked American*, most white-collar workers say they would prefer working fewer hours and spending more leisure time with friends and family. Most salaried workers would choose not to work so many hours if they had more bargaining power.

Manufacturing firms also like hourly workers to work long hours, so they can pay health benefits to fewer employees and so their machinery does not sit idle. What keeps U.S. manufacturing employers from demanding too many hours from workers are laws that require employers to pay overtime (at 50% higher wages) for any hours over 40 per week an employee works. Unfortunately, existing laws prevent salaried employees in the United States from receiving overtime pay when they work more than 40 hours.

Figure 22.7 shows average annual hours worked in 2019 in a variety of OECD (Organization for Economic Cooperation and Development) countries. Notice that the United States works the most hours of any developed country, averaging

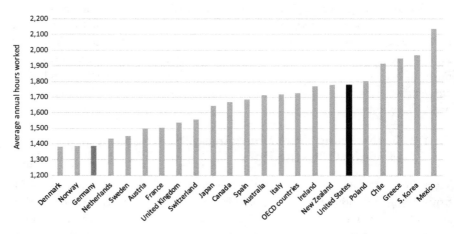

FIGURE 22.7 Average annual hours worked in 2019. Source: OECD.Stat.

1779 hours per year compared with 1386 in Germany. Americans work 28% more hours than Germans! If we consider 40 hours a normal work week, Germans are working ten fewer weeks per year (more than two months less!). German workers typically receive six weeks of vacation compared with two weeks in the United States, and they work less each week. The main reasons Germans work fewer hours but get paid more per hour than Americans include the following German institutional characteristics: A much higher unionization rate, some pro-labor political parties, high demand for German manufactured goods, and a legal system that gives workers significant input into how companies are run.

Countries in which pay is low and unions are less powerful, such as Mexico, have extremely long work hours. Mexican employees need to work very long hours to support their families, and most workers have little say in the workplace given a high unemployment rate and low levels of skills.

Mainstream economists tend to see the decrease in labor hours in most wealthy countries as an example of the labor–leisure trade-off. According to this mainstream theory, **at first as wages rise, workers want to work longer hours to take advantage of higher wages: The benefits of higher wages exceed the disutility that comes from less leisure time**. This corresponds with the change from W_1 to W_2 in Figure 22.8. **However, once a worker's income goes above their target level, increases in wages are likely to result in a worker choosing to work less and take more leisure time, while keeping their income about the same.** This corresponds with the change from W_2 to W_3 in Figure 22.8. In this region, the utility that comes from leisure is greater than the utility provided by additional income.

Political economists reject this analysis because of its problematic assumptions. For this analysis to hold, workers must be able to choose their own hours, and there can be no contracts requiring them to work a certain number of hours. Less-skilled workers are almost never in this situation. A 2017 Rand study found that more than one-third of workers have no control over work schedules and 70% of workers would like to change the number of hours they worked.[9] Clearly, most workers

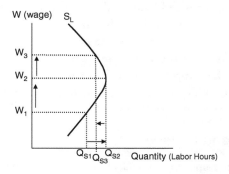

FIGURE 22.8 A backward-bending supply of labor.

are not fully able to choose how many hours they work and how much leisure time they have.

This mainstream analysis also assumes that people dislike work and like leisure, but there is no reason for this to be the case. Many people, especially those in skilled occupations, find their jobs deeply fulfilling. Human beings throughout history worked very hard at numerous tasks, for survival and because work brings with it a sense of accomplishment. This is what Thorstein Veblen referred to as the "instinct of workmanship." However, work does seem to be onerous for most workers in modern capitalism, especially those in less-skilled jobs. The 2017 Gallup poll on the American workplace found that two-thirds of Americans were "disengaged" at work. A disturbingly high number of American workers are not invested in their work. The numbers are even worse in China, where 94% of workers report being disengaged.[10]

To political economists, the active disengagement of the workforce in modern capitalism is a symptom of the hierarchical employment structure in which too many employers use sticks instead of carrots to motivate workers. From a political economy perspective, work should be meaningful and rewarding and everyone should share in the onerous tasks that no one wants to do. However, most employers who utilize unskilled labor refuse to adopt such practices. Only where labor unions and workers' political organizations are powerful do employers of unskilled workers have to address worker dissatisfaction in a significant way.

Understanding the institutional factors that undergird power structures is the key to analyzing labor markets for political economists. However, if we find a perfectly competitive labor market where workers and employers have equal bargaining power, we would see a different picture.

22.5 THE MAINSTREAM, NEOCLASSICAL MODEL OF THE COMPETITIVE LABOR MARKET

Like any market, the labor market can be depicted using supply and demand curves. But the role of firms and individuals is switched. We are used to thinking of individuals demanding consumer goods and businesses supplying those goods. In the labor market, **individuals supply the labor** and **businesses demand the labor**. The price of labor is **the wage rate. The wage rate is determined by the interaction of the supply and demand for labor and by government regulations**. In the unskilled labor market, the minimum wage can have a major impact on outcomes, as we will see below.

22.5.1 The demand for labor

The demand for labor comes from the fact that firms need workers in order to produce goods and services. Thus, the demand for labor is a derived demand in that the demand for workers' labor (and for other inputs) is derived from the demand for goods and services.

In most cases, the demand and supply of labor for one firm are extremely inelastic. Businesses need a certain number of employees to do the work to supply the goods and services that they sell. Very few (if any) businesses keep extra employees around, which means that businesses cannot lay off workers in response to higher wages without also reducing their output and lowering their total revenue. This makes the demand curve for labor very inelastic: Firms tend to keep hiring about the same number of workers, even if wages increase somewhat.

Similarly, very few workers have the option not to work. If workers do not like the wages or working conditions offered by firms, they still need to work to get income for food, lodging, and other necessities. Thus, lower wages often have little or no impact on the amount of labor individuals want to supply, making the supply curve extremely inelastic as well.

In theory, an increase in the wage rate due to an increase in the minimum wage, which is a price floor on labor, causes a very small decline in the quantity of labor demanded (a movement along the labor demand curve up and to the left). In Figure 22.9, an increase in the minimum wage from W_1 to W_2 causes a very small decline in the quantity of workers demanded, from Q_{E1} to Q_{D2}.

Note that **the number of workers hired in the labor market graph is always found on the demand curve for labor**, the curve that shows the number of workers firms want to hire at each wage rate. The supply curve of labor shows the number of laborers who want to work at each wage rate. Thus, with a minimum wage installed at W_2, more workers want to work (Q_{S2}) than firms want to hire (Q_{D2}), resulting in a surplus of workers. The surplus would be the distance between Q_{D2} and Q_{S2}.

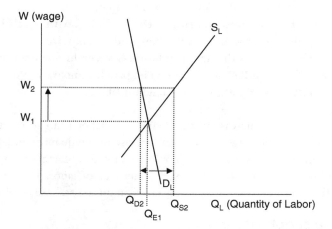

FIGURE 22.9 Increase in the wage rate causes a small decrease in Q_D and small increase in Q_S.

22.5.2 Determinants that shift the demand curve for labor

In addition to a movement along a demand curve for labor caused by a change in the minimum wage rate or a shift in the supply curve of labor, demand curves can shift to the left or to the right. The determinants of labor demand—**the factors that cause the demand curve to shift**—are listed below:

1. **Changes in the demand for the product or service that the firm produces**: The demand for labor is an indirect or *derived* demand. Firms demand labor because there is a demand for their goods and services. Thus, **changes in the demand for a product also cause changes in the demand for labor**. When the automobile market is booming, automobile manufacturers hire (demand) more laborers, shifting the demand curve for labor to the right and putting upward pressure on the wages of workers who build automobiles. When the demand for automobiles declines, the opposite occurs: The demand for automobile workers declines (shifts to the left) and there is downward pressure on their wages.

2. **Changes in the productivity of labor**: The demand for labor is affected by the productivity of labor. If laborers become more productive (due to an increase in skills, education, or technology that augments workers' skills), they increase the firm's output and lower the firm's average variable costs of production, making workers more profitable to hire. Firms usually respond to increases in labor productivity by increasing the demand for labor because of the increased revenues that accrue from the additional labor productivity. The higher demand for labor then causes upward pressure on wages.

3. **Substituting capital for labor**: When firms replace laborers with robots or other machines, this reduces the demand for labor and puts downward pressure on wages. When machines that replace labor get more expensive, firms are likely to demand more labor and use less machinery.

4. **Government taxes and subsidies that affect businesses' hiring of labor**: Payroll taxes, social security taxes paid by employers, unemployment insurance charges, and other taxes on businesses who hire workers can reduce the demand for labor. Reducing labor taxes paid by employers would cause an increase (shift to the right) in the demand for labor.

Figure 22.10 depicts an increase in the demand for labor (shift to the right) that causes an increase in the wage rate and an increase in the quantity of labor hired. The increase in the demand for labor could be caused by factors such as greater demand for the firm's products, higher productivity of labor, higher prices for machinery that replaces laborers, or lower taxes on businesses' use of labor.

22.5.3 The supply of labor

The supply of labor comes from individuals who are members of households. Under normal conditions, higher wages entice more laborers to work more hours. Thus,

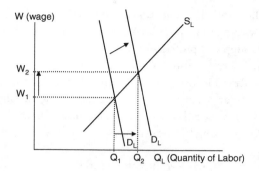

FIGURE 22.10 An increase in the demand for labor.

an increase in the wage rate prompts an increase in the quantity of labor supplied, a movement along the supply curve up and to the right. See Figure 22.9. **A movement along the supply curve of labor occurs whenever there is a change in the minimum wage or a shift in the demand curve for labor that causes a change in the wage rate.**

22.5.4 Determinants that shift the supply curve of labor

The supply curve of labor shifts when laborers decide they want to work more or less hours at a given wage rate or when other factors affecting the supply of labor change. For example, when laborers decide to work more hours to buy more goods, this increases the supply of labor and puts downward pressure on the price of labor (the wage rate). Listed below are the **major determinants that shift the supply curve of labor**:

1. **Factors making work more or less attractive**: If work becomes more attractive or more necessary, this could increase the supply of labor. Such factors could include better benefits, better treatment at work, more possibilities for advancement, and so on. Or workers might want to buy more goods and services, something that would necessitate more hours of work.
2. **Immigration**: Immigration can increase the supply of labor in a particular country or region. Outmigration can decrease the supply of labor. Stricter immigration laws, such as those proposed by the Trump administration, reduce the supply of labor for jobs that draw heavily on immigrant populations, including farmwork, slaughterhouses, meat processing, landscaping, home health care, cleaning, and construction.
3. **Government taxes and subsidies that affect workers**: Social security taxes and other charges that reduce the take-home pay of workers can reduce the supply of labor. Lower taxes on workers' labor can increase the supply of labor.
4. **Wages in substitute jobs**: Workers in a particular occupation may switch to another one if wages are better, assuming that workers can change occupations

easily. If workers switch occupations, there will be a decrease in the supply of labor in lower-paying occupations. For example, England experienced a decrease in the supply of professors when wages in other skilled service jobs for which professors were qualified increased relative to wages for professors.

5. **Barriers to entry**: Licensing requirements that make it difficult for workers to enter a particular occupation can limit the supply of labor. This can also be true for union work rules that limit the number of workers allowed to do certain jobs. Eliminating barriers to entry usually increases the supply of labor.

It is important to note that many workers have little choice in how many hours they work or in the conditions they face in the workplace, and most people have to work in order to survive. Thus, the supply curve of labor tends to be very inelastic in most cases, and workers do not always have the choices implied in the model described above.

22.6 APPLICATIONS OF THE SUPPLY AND DEMAND FOR LABOR

In 2009, the minimum wage in the United States increased from $6.55 to $7.25 an hour. That same year, businesses experienced declining sales of goods and services as the economy feel deeper into a major recession. We can show how **both** of these events affected the market for unskilled labor with the graph in Figure 22.11.

In Figure 22.11, the equilibrium in the market is at point A, at wage W_E and quantity Q_E. The initial minimum wage is set at $6.55, resulting in a quantity of labor demanded of Q_{D2} (point B) and a quantity supplied of Q_{S2} (point C). There is a small surplus of laborers (the distance between points B and C). When the minimum wage is increased to $7.25 per hour, the quantity of labor demanded falls to Q_{D3} (point D) and the quantity of labor supplied increases to Q_{S3} (point E), increasing the surplus of laborers (the distance between points D and E).

When businesses experience a decline in sales, they do not need as many workers. The demand for labor decreases, shifting from D_L to D_{L2}, moving us to point F on the graph). The demand for labor has now fallen to Q_{D4}, and the surplus of laborers has increased to the distance between point F and point E.

Note that chronic surpluses of labor result in **non-price rationing**. The existence of a large number of workers who can replace the existing workforce means that employers do not have to treat their employees very well. The quality of the job can suffer as a result. In such circumstances, employers have been known to make laborers work extra hours for no pay, reduce breaks, speed up the pace of work, reduce benefits, and treat employees poorly.

Note that Figure 22.11 probably exaggerates the impact of raising the minimum wage on employment. As we will see in the next section, most recent U.S. studies indicate that little or no job loss occurs when the minimum wage increases.

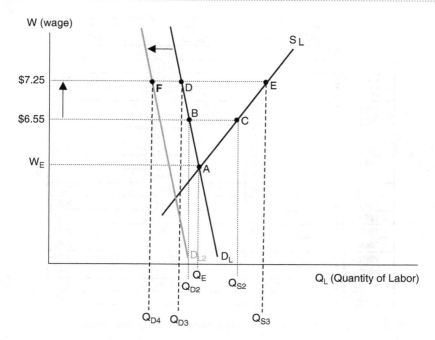

FIGURE 22.11 A higher minimum wage and a decrease in demand for labor, 2009.

22.7 THE ECONOMICS OF THE MINIMUM WAGE

The U.S. government established the minimum wage in 1938 during the Great Depression at a wage rate of $0.25 per hour. The minimum wage was created because of a recognition by economists and policymakers of a significant market failure that existed in the low-wage, unskilled labor market: In most years, there were more unskilled laborers who wanted to work than there were jobs available. When a chronic surplus of unskilled labor exists, wages will tend to be extremely low, perhaps even below the level of income people need to survive (subsistence). The minimum wage was established to give people a living wage, based on the idea that everyone who works for a living should be able to earn enough to survive. If market conditions do not result in that outcome, the government should step in to establish a minimum wage so that everyone who works for a living can afford the basic necessities of life.

As you can see from Figure 22.12, the federal government of the United States has increased the minimum wage since 1938, although not in a systematic fashion.[11] The key issue regarding the minimum wage is the standard of living of unskilled workers, so the minimum wage itself is less important than the purchasing power of the minimum wage. To determine the purchasing power of a particular wage rate, economists compute the real wage rate, and that is **the existing wage rate at**

Year	Minimum wage in current dollars	Price level (2020=1.00)	Minimum wage in 2020 dollars
1940	$ 0.30	0.05 $	5.55
1950	$ 0.75	0.09 $	8.06
1961	$ 1.15	0.12 $	9.96
1963	$ 1.25	0.12 $	10.57
1968	$ **1.60**	**0.13** $	**11.90**
1974	$ 1.60	0.19 $	8.40
1975	$ 2.10	0.21 $	10.10
1980	$ 3.10	0.32 $	9.74
1981	$ 3.35	0.35 $	9.54
1989	$ 3.35	0.48 $	6.99
1990	$ 3.80	0.50 $	7.53
1991	$ 4.25	0.53 $	8.08
1996	$ 4.75	0.61 $	7.84
1997	$ 5.15	0.62 $	8.31
2006	$ 5.15	0.78 $	6.61
2007	$ 5.85	0.80 $	7.30
2008	$ 6.55	0.83 $	7.87
2009	$ 7.25	0.83 $	8.75
2020	$ 7.25	1.00 $	7.25

FIGURE 22.12 Table showing the minimum wage in current and constant dollars.

current prices, called the nominal wage rate, divided by the price level. This gives us the wage rate in constant dollars, called the real wage rate.

$$\text{Real Wage} = \frac{\text{Nominal Wage}}{\text{Price Level}}.$$

First, consider the price level in Figure 22.12, which we compute by taking the ratio of prices in a particular year and dividing by prices in the most recent year of 2020. In 1940, the price level was $0.05. This means that, on average, something that cost $1.00 in 2020 only cost $0.05 in 1940.

Because the real wage measures how much a worker can actually purchase, the real minimum wage column in Figure 22.12 is the important one. We compute the real minimum wage column by dividing the nominal wage column by the price level column.

Notice that the real minimum wage reached its peak in 1968 at $11.90 an hour. Since that time, lawmakers raised the value of the minimum wage by less than prices increased, so minimum wage workers are earning much less now (in real terms) than before. Note in particular what happens when workers do not see an increase in the minimum wage for many years, as happened from 2009 to 2020. During this period, workers saw a decrease in the real minimum wage from $8.75 in 2009 to $7.25 in 2020. Minimum wage workers had $1.50 less per hour in purchasing power in 2020 than they did in 2009. A typical laborer who works full time for 2000 hours per year and earns a minimum wage of $7.25 per hour would have a pretax income of $14,500. That annual income is just above the poverty line for a single person but well below the poverty line for a family.

Figure 22.13 plots the real value of the minimum wage from 1940 to 2020. Each time the government increases the minimum wage, there is a spike in the real value of the minimum wage. Then, when the minimum wage stays the same and prices increase, the real minimum wage falls.

Many countries index their minimum wage to the price level so that the real minimum wage does not fall over time. However, in the United States the minimum wage is considered controversial, and conservative economists supported by the restaurant and hotel lobbies have resisted any permanent indexing of the minimum wage to the price level. A higher minimum wage imposes direct costs on businesses that hire low-wage employees, and according to these lobbyists and economists, this will lead to greater levels of unemployment for unskilled workers. They point to studies indicating that raising the minimum wage tends to increase unemployment for workers, especially teenagers.

Liberal mainstream economists and political economists, however, disagree, arguing that higher minimum wages have a host of benefits for workers and communities. Workers and their families are more able to escape poverty with a higher minimum wage. And workers spend any increases in income they get in the local community, increasing the demand for goods and services and improving the local economy. These economists also cite studies indicating that most increases in the minimum wage result in no changes at all in unemployment.

This is, in essence, a debate over the price elasticity of the demand for labor. Pro-industry economists argue that the price elasticity of the demand for labor is negative: An increase in the minimum wage will cause a decrease in the quantity of labor demanded. Pro-labor economists are arguing that the price elasticity of the demand for labor is essentially zero: An increase in the minimum wage will have no impact on the quantity of labor demanded.

So who is correct? According to a pathbreaking study by Hristos Doucouliagos and T. D. Stanley in the *British Journal of Industrial Relations*, **most studies indicate that a higher minimum wage has no impact on the unemployment rate**. The authors plot out the estimates of the labor market price elasticity in various studies and the quality of the statistical analysis involved, which we display in Figure 22.14.[12] What the authors find is that *most studies, and all of the best quality studies, show an increase in the minimum wage having no effect on employment*. If there is a negative impact on employment, it is very, very small. Some studies even indicate a positive impact of raising the minimum wage on employment.

This analysis has important implications, including the following:

1. **Employers generally minimize the number of laborers they hire**, choosing the number that will allow them to meet the needs of their customers.

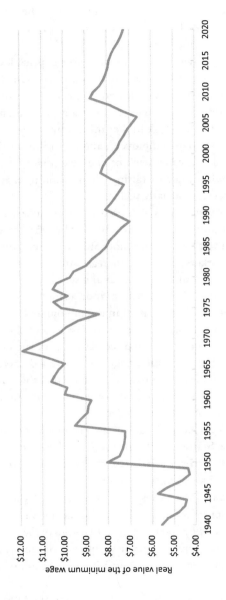

FIGURE 22.13 The real value of the minimum wage, 1940–2017.

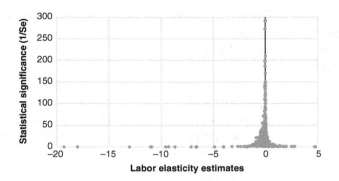

FIGURE 22.14 Labor market elasticities and the minimum wage.

Employers are not willing or able to reduce employment below existing levels given moderate increases in the minimum wage. The demand curve for labor may actually be perfectly inelastic.

2. **Higher minimum wages have a positive impact on workers' productivity.** Companies see increases in productivity after an increase in the minimum wage because workers are more satisfied with their jobs. This reduces turnover, so firms keep experienced, more productive workers longer. These increases in productivity reduce the impact of higher wages.

3. **When workers get more money from a higher minimum wage, they spend more, often at the very businesses that hire minimum wage workers.** This increase in the demand for goods and services increases the demand for workers, offsetting any negative impact of higher costs from a higher minimum wage.

In general, moderately higher minimum wages have led to no or minimal increases in unemployment and workers have gained significantly from these wage increases. Businesses who employ minimum wage labor do tend to raise prices slightly to account for higher labor costs when the minimum wage increases. Historically, those price increases have been very small—so small that consumers usually do not even notice.

Given the fact that the federal minimum wage is very low by historical standards, most states and many municipalities have enacted higher minimum wages. In 2018, 29 states had minimum wages higher than the federal minimum wage, with Washington having the highest state minimum wage at $11.50 per hour, followed by $11 per hour in California and New York.

Nationwide, workers began a "Fight for $15" campaign in 2012 to raise the minimum wage significantly across the country. This is part of the national campaign for a "living wage," in which supporters argue that any person working full time should be able to afford the basic necessities of life for their family, including food, shelter, and health care. Seattle became the largest city to agree with this goal, deciding to raise its minimum wage to $15 per hour in a series of steps. Economists are in the process of analyzing the impact of Seattle's dramatic increase in the minimum wage to see whether it has a different effect on employment than the smaller increases that had little or no impact.

As we saw above, political economists see wages determined by the balance of power between workers and employers in each business and in society. In mainstream economics, if we assume that markets are competitive and absent any market failures, then in theory workers get paid an amount exactly equal to how productive they are. We can see this via the concept of marginal revenue product.

22.8 MARGINAL REVENUE PRODUCT AND INCOME DETERMINATION IN MAINSTREAM ECONOMICS

The marginal revenue product of labor (MRP_L) is **the additional revenue the firm receives from hiring an additional laborer**. In mathematical terms, **$MRP_L = (\Delta TR / \Delta L)$**. The marginal revenue product of labor quantifies how valuable each laborer is to the firm based on how much revenue they generate. MRP_L is **also the firm's demand for labor, because MRP_L is the maximum amount a firm would be willing to pay a particular laborer**.

By multiplying by $\Delta Q / \Delta Q$ we can rewrite this equation as $MRP_L = (\Delta TR / \Delta L) = (\Delta TR / \Delta Q) \times (\Delta Q / \Delta L) = MR \times MP_L$. (Recall that marginal revenue is the change in total revenue divided by the change in quantity.) Thus, the marginal revenue product of labor depends on the firm's marginal revenue from selling products as well as the productivity of the laborer.

Figure 22.15 displays a hypothetical table showing the relationship between the number of hours a laborer works, the amount they produce (quantity, which is also call the total product of labor), marginal product of labor, MP_L (the output from each additional hour they work), and the price of output (P, which is fixed at $0.50 in this perfectly competitive output market). Given this information, we can compute the marginal revenue product of labor (MRP_L) by looking at the change in total revenue from hiring each additional unit of labor or by multiplying the MP_L column by the $MR = P$ column.

In a perfectly competitive labor market with lots of firms and workers, the wage rate will be fixed because no employer can offer less than the equilibrium wage rate and no employee will work for less than the going wage rate. In this example, the wage rate is fixed at $15, which means that the market supply curve is a flat line at a wage rate of $15 per hour. Note that even though the labor supply curve for each individual worker can be very steep, in a perfectly competitive

Labor hours L	Total product of labor $TP_L=Q$	Marginal product of labor $MP_L = \frac{\Delta Q}{\Delta L}$	Price $P=MR$	Total revenue $TR=P*Q$	Marginal revenue product of labor $MRP_L = \frac{\Delta TR}{\Delta L} = D_L$	Wage, $/hour $W = MFC = S_L$
0	0	---	$0.50	$ 0.00	$ -----	$ 15
1	10	10	$0.50	5.00	5.00	15
2	30	20	$0.50	15.00	10.00	15
3	60	30	$0.50	30.00	15.00	15
4	95	35	$0.50	47.50	17.50	15
5	135	40	$0.50	67.50	20.00	15
6	174	39	$0.50	87.00	19.50	15
7	210	36	$0.50	105.00	18.00	15
8	240	30	$0.50	120.00	15.00	15
9	262	22	$0.50	131.00	11.00	15
10	274	12	$0.50	137.00	6.00	15
11	274	0	$0.50	137.00	0.00	15

FIGURE 22.15 Table deriving the demand for labor (MRP_L), perfectly competitive output and labor market.

market with vast quantities of unskilled labor, the market supply curve for labor is flat. No matter how much the demand for labor increases, the price of labor (wage) will stay the same because there are so many workers willing to work at the going wage rate. We can define the marginal factor cost (MFC) as **the increase in cost from hiring another unit of a factor of production, such as labor**. In this case $MFC_L = \$15$.

We determine equilibrium in the labor market by comparing the demand for labor, which is the MRP_L column, with the supply of labor, which is the wage column. In economic lingo, firms want to hire each unit of labor for which the marginal revenue product of labor is greater than or equal to the marginal factor cost: $MRP_L \geq MFC_L$. In other words, firms want to hire each unit of labor that makes the firm more in revenue than it costs them. In Figure 22.15, the equilibrium occurs where $L = 8$ and $MRP_L = MFC_L = \$15$.

Figure 22.16 plots the MRP_L and MFC_L curves on a graph. Notice that the MRP_L curve increases when marginal productivity increases and decreases when marginal productivity decreases, due to the law of diminishing returns. We ignore the upward-sloping portion of the MRP_L curve because when MRP_L is increasing, the firm makes increasing amounts of revenue by hiring more units of labor. Optimization requires going past the point of maximum MRP_L. Thus, the demand for labor is **the downward-sloping portion of the marginal revenue product of labor curve**. The supply of labor is **the MFC_L curve, and it is the same as the wage rate in perfectly competitive labor markets**. Equilibrium occurs at a quantity of eight labor hours, where $MRP_L = MFC_L$.

FIGURE 22.16 Equilibrium in the labor market.

22.8.1 The marginal productivity theory of distribution

In a perfectly competitive labor market like the one depicted above, workers will tend to get paid based entirely on how productive they are ($MRP_L = W$). There are no exploitative relationships in a perfectly competitive market, so workers are paid exactly what they are worth (their marginal revenue product of labor). Economist John Bates Clark, one of the founders of the neoclassical school of economics, argued in his book *The Distribution of Wealth* that "the distribution of the income of society is controlled by a natural law, and ... this law, if it worked without friction, would give every agent of production the amount of wealth which that agent creates."[13] This, in turn, implies that people are rich because they are very productive, not because they (or their ancestors) exploited workers. This idea is vigorously disputed by political economists who argue that income is affected considerably by power relations.

Mainstream economists also study markets in which one employer has a considerable impact on the labor market and the product market. We look at these cases in the next section.

22.9 THE MAINSTREAM ECONOMICS MODEL OF LABOR IN NONCOMPETITIVE MARKETS

We can apply the mainstream economics model of the labor market to situations in which firms have monopoly power in the product market *and* the labor market. **When there is only one buyer of a product or resource** it is called a monopsony. If there is only one major employer in a small town, that firm has a huge influence on the local market. If they increase the size of their operations and hire more workers, the local wage rate will increase. If they reduce the size of their operations and lay off a lot of workers, the local wage rate will decrease. Therefore, in cases of monopsony, one firm's behavior has a large impact on wages.

Figure 22.17 depicts a hypothetical labor market in which the firm has monopoly power in the product market. Prices fall as output increases, and marginal revenue (MR) would be less than price if we computed the MR of each unit of output.

The firm has monopsony power in the labor market: Wages increase as the firm hires more workers. Notice that with monopsony power, the marginal factor cost (MFC) is greater than the wage rate. When the monopsonist hires more workers they bid up wages, which means they have to pay higher wages to new workers *and* to all existing workers to obtain all the labor they need. (An employer cannot pay newer, less experienced workers more than experienced workers without experiencing labor unrest and a decline in productivity, so when wages rise they are forced to raise the wages of all workers.)

We determine the optimal quantity of labor hours for the firm to hire in the same way as before: The firm wants to hire workers as long as $MRP_L \geq MFC_L$. In Figure 22.17, the optimal quantity of labor hours to hire is 7, where $MRP_L = MFC_L = \$14.50$. Notice that the wage rate is only $11.50 at this quantity of labor hours.

Figure 22.18 plots the key parts of this labor market on a graph. The optimal quantity of labor the firm wishes to hire is found where the MRP_L curve interests the MFC_L curve at $14.50, something that occurs when $L = 7$. At $L = 7$, we can go up to the supply of labor curve S_L to find that the wage rate is $11.50. The process is similar to that in a competitive labor market, but we find the wage rate *after* determining the optimal quantity of labor hours for the firm to hire. Note that equilibrium in a monopsonistic labor market does not occur where supply equals demand but instead at a lower quantity of labor hours.

If we contrast the mainstream approach to the labor market with the political economy approach, we see some vast differences. Political economists do not think it is possible to determine the marginal product of an individual laborer: Output is a group effort and the contribution of any one individual is extraordinarily difficult to measure. Mainstream economists maintain that firms must optimize their operations by comparing marginal revenue product and marginal factor cost or they cannot survive. Political economists study power relations between employers and workers, how these relations determine wages, and how they shift over time. Many mainstream economists tend to assume that markets are sufficiently competitive so that power relationships between employers and workers are unimportant. Interestingly, as is so often the case, both approaches capture unique aspects of the labor market due to their unique focus.

Labor hours L	Total product of labor Q	Marginal product of labor $MP_L = \frac{\Delta Q}{\Delta L}$	Price of output P	Total revenue $= P*Q$ TR	Marginal revenue product of labor $MRP_L = \frac{\Delta TR}{\Delta L}$	Wage, $/hour $=S_L$ W	Total factor Cost = TFC $W*L$	Marginal factor cost $MFC_L = \frac{\Delta TFC}{\Delta L}$
0	0	—	$ 1.00	$ 0	$ 0	$ 8.00	$ 0	$ 0
1	10	10	0.95	9.50	9.50	8.50	8.50	8.50
2	30	20	0.90	27.00	17.50	9.00	18.00	9.50
3	60	30	0.85	51.00	24.00	9.50	28.50	10.50
4	100	40	0.80	80.00	29.00	10.00	40.00	11.50
5	145	45	0.75	108.75	28.75	10.50	52.50	12.50
6	191	46	0.70	133.70	24.95	11.00	66.00	13.50
7	228	37	0.65	148.20	14.50	11.50	80.50	14.50
8	255	27	0.60	153.00	4.80	12.00	96.00	15.50
9	271	16	0.55	149.05	(3.95)	12.50	112.50	16.50
10	275	4	0.50	137.50	(11.55)	13.00	130.00	17.50

FIGURE 22.17 Table determining the optimal amount of labor to hire in a monopolistic monopsony.

FIGURE 22.18 Optimal quantity of labor hours in a monopsony.

22.10 CONCLUSION

Though many concepts in economics can be abstract and impersonal, everyone will have some significant and direct experience with the labor market. Evidence indicates that your experiences will be driven by your skills and education, along with larger forces, including technological changes, industry shifts, macroeconomic factors, the system of social classes, and the legal and political system.

Political economists use a model of the workday to understand areas in which employers and workers frequently come into conflict. They also study how employers motivate employees using the carrot or stick approach and how these approaches vary depending on skills, industry, unionization rates, and the political system. Power dynamics between workers and employers emerge as one of the major driving forces of labor market outcomes.

Mainstream economists use a different model to analyze labor markets when there are many firms and workers, so that the balance of power between employers and employees is relatively equal. In such circumstances, mainstream economists see wages determined primarily by the productivity of each worker. In the mainstream model, firms compute the optimal amount of labor to hire by comparing marginal revenue product and marginal factor cost. We can also use the mainstream model to analyze the case of monopsony, when one employer dominates the labor market so that wages increase as more workers are hired. This causes an upward-sloping supply of labor curve and a marginal factor cost of labor curve that starts out touching the supply of labor curve and then increases at a faster rate.

The mainstream model of the labor market provides a useful tool to analyze arguments for and against the minimum wage. As we saw, in general, modest increases in minimum wages tend to have little or no impact on unemployment.

However, industry groups, such as the hotel and restaurant lobbies that rely on unskilled labor, often contest this important policy result, offering their own contradictory studies. This attempt by special interests to muddy the waters is the product of a political system in the United States in which employers have substantial resources and power to sway public perceptions and public policy in their favor.

QUESTIONS FOR REVIEW

1. Given the trends described in this chapter regarding the skills employees need and the industries that are expanding and contracting, what course of study makes the most sense for you? How can you leverage your strengths into a skill set that employers would value?

2. List the major sources of conflict between workers and owners. Which of these sources of conflict do you think is most pervasive in white-collar work such as investment banking? Which sources of conflict might be most pervasive in blue-collar work in an Amazon warehouse?

3. Compare and contrast the stick approach to worker motivation with the carrot approach. How can either approach be profitable for firms operating in the same industry (e.g., Wegmans vs. Walmart)?

4. List the major sources of power in the relationship between workers and owners. Which of these do you think is most important? Why?

5. Workers in the United States are paid considerably less than workers in Germany. Using the political economy approach to the labor market, analyze why this is the case.

6. Use the political economy model of the working day to determine how each of the following events would impact wages and the rate of profit.
   a. The government increases the minimum wage.
   b. The government reduces the maximum number of work hours allowed per week from 40 to 35.
   c. New robots are invented that increase the productivity of workers.
   d. The government passes laws that make it more difficult for workers to unionize.

7. Using Figure 22.9 as your starting point, with a minimum wage of W_2 in place, analyze how each of the following events will affect the demand and supply curves for unskilled labor, the number of laborers hired by firms, and the amount of surplus labor that exists.
   a. The economy booms and the demand for goods and services significantly increases.
   b. The federal government raises the minimum wage above W_2.
   c. Immigration into the United States significantly increases.

Labor units L	Total Product of Labor Q	Price of Output P	Total Revenue TR= P*Q	Marginal Revenue Product of Labor MRP$_L = \frac{\Delta TR}{\Delta L}$	Wage W
0	0	$5.00			$1,100
1	100	$5.00			$1,100
2	300	$5.00			$1,100
3	600	$5.00			$1,100
4	950	$5.00			$1,100
5	1350	$5.00			$1,100
6	1740	$5.00			$1,100
7	2100	$5.00			$1,100
8	2400	$5.00			$1,100
9	2620	$5.00			$1,100
10	2740	$5.00			$1,100

FIGURE 22.19 Table showing output and price information for a hypothetical firm.

d. The government reduces the amount of social security taxes paid by employers who hire workers *and* reduces the amount of social security taxes withheld from workers' paychecks.
e. The government significantly cuts education spending resulting in a large decrease in the productivity of unskilled workers.
8. What are the main arguments of opponents of the minimum wage? What are the main arguments of supporters of the minimum wage? Which arguments do you find most convincing?
9. Figure 22.19 depicts hypothetical information for a firm.
   a. Is this firm a monopsony? Why or why not?
   b. Is this firm a monopoly? Why or why not?
   c. Complete the table.
   d. Determine the optimal quantity of laborers for this firm to hire.
   e. Use a spreadsheet program to plot out a graph of the demand curve for labor and the supply curve of labor. Show the optimal, equilibrium number of laborers hired on your graph.
   f. If the wage rate increases to $1200, what is the new optimal number of laborers for the firm to hire?

NOTES

1 Source: Bureau of Labor Statistics.
2 Neil Irwin, "Is Capital or Labor Winning at Your Favorite Company? Introducing the Marx Ratio," *New York Times*, May 21, 2018. Irwin calls these ratios the "Marx Ratio" in a nod to Marx's concept of the rate of exploitation.
3 Nicole Maestas, Kathleen J. Mullen, David Powell, et al., *Working Conditions in the United States: Results of the 2015 American Working Conditions Survey* (RAND Corporation,

Santa Monica, CA2017). https://www.rand.org/pubs/research_reports/RR2014.html, accessed July 17, 2018.

4 Ibid.

5 Shona Ghosh, "Peeing in Trash Cans, Constant Surveillance, and Asthma Attacks on the Job: Amazon Workers Tell Us Their Warehouse Horror Stories," *Business Insider*, April 2018. www.businessinsider.com/amazon-warehouse-workers-share-their-horror-stories-2018-4, accessed August 4, 2018.

6 Jodi Kantor and David Streitfeld, "Inside Amazon: Wrestling Big Ideas in a Bruising Workplace," *New York Times*, August 16, 2015, www.nytimes.com/2015/08/16/technology/inside-amazon-wrestling-big-ideas-in-a-bruising-workplace.html, accessed August 4, 2018.

7 CNNMoney, "Nike Raising Overseas Wages," March 23, 1999, https://money.cnn.com/1999/03/23/companies/nike/, accessed August 3, 2021.

8 Krissy Clark, "Are Walmart's Prices So Low Because Its Employees Are on Food Stamps?" *Slate*, April 2014, www.slate.com/articles/business/moneybox/2014/04/walmart_employees_on_food_stamps_their_wages_aren_t_enough_to_get_by.html, accessed August 9, 2018.

9 See note 3.

10 Sara Burrows. "85% of People Hate Their Jobs, Gallup Poll Says," Return to Now, September 22, 2017, returntonow.net/2017/09/22/85-people-hate-jobs-gallup-poll-says/, accessed July 17, 2018.

11 Source for Figure 22.12 and 22.13: Author's calculations from BLS and FRED data.

12 Source: Hristos Doucouliagos and T.D. Stanley, "Publication Selection Bias in Minimum-Wage Research? A Meta-Regression Analysis," *British Journal of Industrial Relations*, 47, No. 2 (June 2009), pp. 406–428. doi: 10.1111/j.1467-8543.2009.00723.x. © Blackwell Publishing Ltd/London School of Economics, 2009. Published by Blackwell Publishing Ltd, 9600 Garsington Road, Oxford OX4 2DQ, UK and 350 Main Street, Malden, MA 02148, USA. The author would like to thank John Wiley & Sons Ltd. and the authors for permission to publish this figure.

13 Quoted in John F. Henry, *John Bates Clark: The Making of a Neoclassical Economist* (Springer, New York, 2016), p. 71.

23 Inequality, a key modern issue

Class, race, gender, and distribution

As we have seen, radical shifts in economic systems tend to occur when the existing economic system is not working for a large number of people. As the current capitalist system in developed economies becomes more and more unequal, a major disruption becomes increasingly likely. When countries grow more unequal, it triggers unrest as people on the losing side start questioning whether their economic system is fair. This can lead to the election of politicians with more extreme views on both ends of the spectrum (liberal and conservative). And it can lead to the breakdown of civil society.

In South Africa, the world's most unequal country in 2019, the consequences of extreme inequality are readily apparent. Crime is disturbingly prevalent. Home burglaries and invasions are so common that people surround their houses with high walls topped with razor wire and broken glass. Carjacking became so bad that car companies offered to equip cars with a flamethrower system to ward off would-be car jackers. Instead of greeting people on the street, most people look away and treat anyone they do not know with suspicion and distrust.

What changes might result from the increasing inequality that is occurring across the developed world? Will it spark crime and social upheaval? Will politicians stoking populist anger such as Donald Trump in the United States and Marine Le Pen in France gain in popularity and power? Or will countries take measures to reduce inequality and stabilize their economic systems?

This chapter begins by looking at the data on income and wealth inequality in the United States and other developed countries. Subsequently, we look at explanations for increasing inequality provided by political economists. Political economists focus on factors such as social class and class power in explaining inequality. We also discuss views toward inequality coming from mainstream economists, who see inequality as driven by differences in skills, abilities, and productivity.

The chapter then turns to issues of inequality with respect to race and gender. Though some progress has been made in the United States to mitigate race and

DOI: 10.4324/9781315636924-29

gender inequality, these problems have proven to be stubbornly resistant to change. Finally, the chapter briefly describes the approaches used by feminist economists and stratification economists to analyze the inequities present in the economic system.

23.0 CHAPTER 23 LEARNING GOALS

After reading this chapter you should be able to:

■ Describe how inequality has changed in recent decades and the measures economists use to determine the degree of inequality.

■ Analyze how social class impacts inequality and people's opportunities in life.

■ List and explain additional factors that impact class inequality.

■ Describe the degree of racial and gender inequality in the United States and evaluate the effectiveness of polices to address racial and gender inequality.

■ Lay out the approach taken by feminist economists and stratification economists in their study of economic inequality.

23.1 INCOME AND WEALTH INEQUALITY IN THE UNITED STATES AND OTHER DEVELOPED COUNTRIES

Inequality has increased in all developed countries since 1980. Figure 23.1 shows that the income share of the richest 10% of the population has increased in the United States, Great Britain, France, and Europe as a whole. Notice that the increase in inequality has been particularly large in the United States, for reasons that we explore below.

Figure 23.2 provides more detail regarding the U.S. distribution of income and how it has changed since 1950. The United States grew more equal from 1950 to 1970, with the poorest 20% of the population seeing an increase in their share of national income while the richest 20% saw a decrease. However, from 1970 to 2019, inequality steadily worsened, with the bottom 80% of the population taking home a smaller share of national income while the richest 20% and the richest 5% received a much larger share.

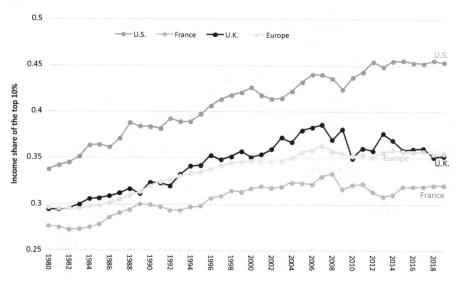

FIGURE 23.1 Income share of the top 10%, 1981–2019.

Source: World Inequality Database, https://wid.world/.

Year	Poorest 20%	Second poorest	Middle 20%	Second richest	Richest 20%	Richest 5%
1950	4.5	12	17.4	23.4	42.7	17.3
1960	4.8	12.2	17.8	24	41.3	15.9
1970	5.4	12.2	17.6	23.8	40.9	15.6
1980	5.3	11.6	17.6	24.4	41.1	14.6
1990	4.6	10.8	16.6	23.8	44.3	17.4
2000	4.3	9.8	15.4	22.7	47.7	21.1
2010	3.8	9.4	15.4	23.5	47.9	20
2019	3.9	9.2	14.8	22.5	49.5	21.9

FIGURE 23.2 Table showing changes in the U.S. distribution of income since 1950.

Source: U.S. Census Bureau, Table F-2.

Figure 23.3 shows that families in the poorest 20% of the U.S. population earn $40,000 or less per year, the middle 20% earns $69,000 to $105,038 per year, and the wealthiest 5% earn more than $304,153 per year.

The Gini coefficient measures **the degree of inequality that exists in an economy in a particular year**. To compute the Gini coefficient, economists plot out a Lorenz curve, which **shows the percentage of national income earned by each percentage of families**—the bottom 20%, 40%, 60%, 80%, and 100%. The amount that these groups actually earn is then compared to an equal distribution of income to see how unequal a society is. For example, in Figure 23.4, the Lorenz curve shows that the bottom 20% of the U.S. population has 3.9% of national income, the bottom 40% has 13.1%, the bottom 60% has 27.9%, and the

Share of population	Income range ($)		
Poorest 20%	0	-	40,000
Second poorest 20%	40,000	-	69,000
Middle 20%	69,000	-	105,038
Second richest 20%	105,038	-	164,930
Richest 20%	Above 164,930		
Top 5%	Above 304,153		

FIGURE 23.3 Table displaying family income ranges for the United States, 2019.

Source: U.S. Census Bureau, Tables F-1, F-2.

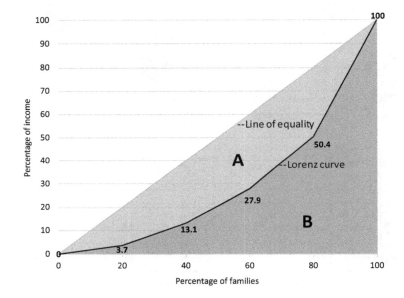

FIGURE 23.4 Lorenze curve for the United States in 2019.

Source: U.S. Census Bureau, Table F-2.

bottom 80% of the U.S. population has 50.4% of national income. An equal distribution of income would be the 45 degree line where 20% of the population has 20% of national income, 40% of the population has 40% of the income, and so on.

The Gini coefficient for the United States measures how far away the distribution of income is from equality (the difference between the line of equality and the Lorenz curve) by taking area A, the amount of inequality, and dividing it by area A plus area B, which is the area under the line of equality. In a perfectly equal society, area A would be 0, so the Gini coefficient would be 0. In a completely unequal society, the Gini coefficient would be equal to 1, because one family would have 100% of the income but every other family would have 0% of the income. Thus, **the Gini coefficient ranges from 0 to 1, with lower numbers associated with**

more equal societies and higher numbers associated with more unequal societies.

Figure 23.5 shows that the U.S. Lorenz curve has been moving further away from equality since 1970. As the Lorenz curve shifted out, the Gini coefficient for the United States increased. The Gini coefficient for the United States was 0.353 in 1970, 0.382 in 1990, and 0.390 in 2019. Thus, inequality in the United States increased by 11% from 1970 to 2019 using this measure.

Figure 23.6 shows the Gini coefficients in a variety of countries around the world. The table shows the Gini coefficient based on market income (before taxes or transfers) and the Gini coefficient based on disposable income (after taxes have been taken out and transfer payments such as welfare programs have been added in). The final column shows the amount that the government reduces inequality with its tax and transfer programs. The United States is the most unequal developed country, as you can see in this table, and its government does little to offset inequality compared to most other developed countries.

Putting these data together, after 1970 inequality increased significantly in most developed countries, especially the United States. The reason that inequality worsened much more in the United States has to do primarily with government policy.

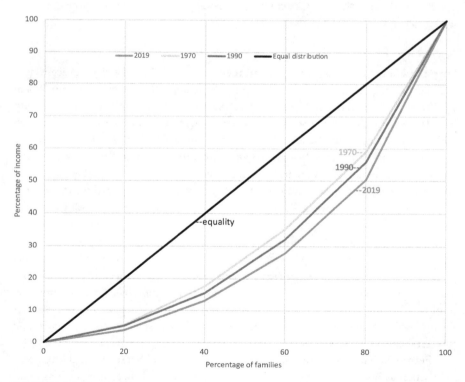

FIGURE 23.5 The U.S. Lorenz curve in 1970, 1990, and 2019.

Source: U.S. Census Bureau, Table F-2.

Country	Year	Gini based on market income	Gini based on disposable income (after taxes & transfers)	% Reduction in inequality
Iceland	2017	0.369	0.250	-32%
Belgium	2018	0.490	0.258	-47%
Norway	2018	0.429	0.262	-39%
Denmark	2017	0.446	0.264	-41%
Sweden	2018	0.428	0.275	-36%
Netherlands	2016	0.445	0.285	-36%
Germany	2017	0.500	0.289	-42%
Ireland	2017	0.535	0.295	-45%
Switzerland	2017	0.386	0.299	-23%
France	2018	0.529	0.301	-43%
Canada	2018	0.427	0.303	-29%
Australia	2018	0.454	0.325	-28%
Spain	2018	0.506	0.330	-35%
Italy	2017	0.516	0.334	-35%
Japan	2015	0.504	0.339	-33%
S. Korea	2018	0.402	0.345	-14%
United Kingdom	2018	0.513	0.366	-29%
United States	2017	0.505	0.390	-23%
Mexico	2016	0.473	0.458	-3%
South Africa	2015	0.715	0.620	-13%

FIGURE 23.6 Table showing Gini coefficients before and after taxes and transfers.
Source: OECD.Stat.

First, the United States significantly **reduced taxes on the wealthy** in recent decades. The average tax rate on the richest 0.1% of the population decreased from 55% in 1945 to about 25% in the early 2000s, and it was cut even further by President Trump in 2018. Second, the United States has a **very unequal education system**, with rich children receiving much better educations than poor children do. Third, the U.S. government has been very **hostile toward unions**, so less-skilled workers in the United States see lower wages and benefits than similar workers in other developed countries where unions are more powerful. Fourth, as we saw earlier, the United States has the **least generous safety net** of any developed country, with those who fall on hard times receiving less in benefits than the poor and destitute elsewhere.

Inequality of wealth is even more extreme than inequality in income. This is because families with high incomes can invest their extra money in additional income-generating activities, creating even more income and wealth in the future. Thus, wealth tends to pile up in families with high incomes over time. Meanwhile, poor families have little or no extra income to invest. They depend on their salaries for survival and lack access to income-generating assets such as stocks, bonds, and interest-bearing bank accounts.

Figure 23.7 shows the distribution of **net worth** of U.S. families, adding up all assets such as houses, stocks, and bonds and subtracting all liabilities such as loans

Group	Median net worth
Poorest 20%	$ 9,800
Second poorest 20%	$ 44,000
Middle 20%	$ 92,900
Second richest 20%	$ 199,100
Second richest 10%	$ 382,300
Richest 10%	$ 1,589,300

FIGURE 23.7 Table showing median net worth of families in the United States, 2019.

Asset	Bottom 50%	50%–90%	90%–99%	Wealthiest 1%
Stocks	0.6	11.1	35.6	52.7
Real estate	12.3	42.8	30.5	14.4
Total assets	5.6	30.5	36	27.9
Total debt	32.1	43.5	19.7	4.7
Total wealth	2.4	33.5	44.5	36.2

FIGURE 23.8 Table displaying the percentage of assets held by U.S. families, 2020.

and debt.[1] The poorest 20% of families have extremely very low net worth (median $9800), whereas the richest 10% have a median net worth of $1,589,300.

Figure 23.8 shows the percentage of assets held by families in various wealth groups.[2] The wealthiest 10% of U.S. families own 88.3% of stocks, whereas the bottom 90% owns only 11.7% of stocks. Most of the wealth of the bottom 90% is in their housing equity (real estate). However, the bottom 90% hold 75.6% of the country's debts.

Now that we have provided key data regarding inequality and how it has changed in recent years, it is important to examine why inequality is so persistent over time. Economists have identified five key societal factors that affect inequality: (1) social class, (2) race, (3) gender, (4) nationality, and (5) ability. Of those factors, political economists argue that the most important one in determining inequality within a particular country is the power that comes with owning and controlling society's key resources. This is another way of saying that the key driver of inequality is social class.

23.2 SOCIAL CLASS AND THE POLITICAL ECONOMY OF INEQUALITY

Research in political economics identifies social class as the primary determinant of inequality. Social class determines what opportunities we have in life, affecting the quality of schools we are able to attend, our health and self-confidence, the connections that help us to find employment, and even the people we are likely to marry.

One characteristic of a good economy that most economists support is equality of opportunity: Everyone who is willing to work hard should have the chance to succeed. Unfortunately, the rigidity of social classes is one of the major barriers to equality of opportunity.

Earlier in the book, we defined a social class as **a group of people who have a specific relationship with the production process (e.g., capitalists, workers, slaves, lords)**. In every society, those in the top social classes have more opportunities than those in the bottom. In modern capitalism, **those who own and control society's productive resources** constitute the capitalist class. People who own large businesses and vast assets, including the managers who run the businesses and the company stockholders, gain the profits and rents from business activities, making them capitalists. In a capitalist system, the capitalist class is the most powerful social group, playing a significant role in determining how a society is structured, deciding who has a job and what that job is like, and making key decisions regarding how society devotes its scarce resources.

Within the capitalist class, it is useful to distinguish between the elite group that controls the largest businesses and smaller capitalists. In his book *The Working Class Majority*, Michael Zweig identifies a group of about 57,000 people who own the largest corporations in the United States and sit on multiple corporate boards. This group, along with top political and cultural leaders, constitutes a sort of "ruling class" that has immense power along with a strong desire to preserve the status quo.

The middle class consists of middle managers who control the labor of others but are not owners of businesses, as well as small business owners who are self-employed (they work for themselves) but have very little power and control in the marketplace. Thus, the middle class is made up of **small business owners, managers, and professionals who have some control over their working lives and who often supervise others but who do not have control over a significant amount of resources or workers and who must usually answer to the ruling class**.

Finally, the working class consists of **those who must sell their labor to others in order to survive in a capitalist system**. They might own small amounts of assets, such as their home, but they have little control over the decisions in their workplace and their conditions of work.

Zweig's analysis indicates that the class composition of the United States is as follows:

- Capitalist class: 2% of the labor force
- Middle class: 35% of the labor force
- Working class: 63% of the labor force.

One of the major reasons why this is important comes from the insights of sociologist Max Weber (1864–1920), who documented the fact that *social class plays the dominant role in determining your chances in life*. First, class is the most important factor in determining income. Second, it determines one's friends and social group, shaping who we spend our time with and, usually, who we select as our partners.

Social class plays an outsized role in determining our lives largely due to what French sociologist Pierre Bourdieu (1930–2002) called personal capital. Bourdieu noted that each individual has access to a certain amount of personal capital, which is **the economic, educational, social, and cultural capital derived from a person's class position. Economic capital refers to the ownership and control of resources; educational capital refers to years of schooling and the quality of institutions attended; social capital is the network of family, friends, and associates a person can access and draw on; and cultural capital refers to the knowledge of unique cultural patterns associated with living in elite circles**. Each of these components of personal capital has a significant impact on the likelihood of success in life.

Economic capital is the most obvious reason why social class matters: Wealthy people are able to pass on resources directly to their heirs. Donald Trump, the wealthy 45th President of the United States, inherited more than $400 million from his father. A variety of economic studies indicate that about 40% of wealth is inherited, rather than created.[3] One of the biggest reasons the rich stay rich and the poor stay poor is the lingering impact of economic capital and the ability of parents to pass this on to their children.

In the modern world, access to **educational capital** is another primary determinant of one's opportunities in life. Attending elite schools opens up opportunities that are not available to others. After controlling for a host of factors such as GPA and SAT scores, Paul Attewell and Dirk Witteveen found that a decade after graduation, students from elite colleges earned 19% more than students from nonelite colleges.[4] This means that for students with relatively equal abilities, attending an elite college will help them land a higher paying job.

Social capital is the network to which a person has access, and it also presents opportunities to those who are well connected. Most employers have a demonstrated preference for hiring applicants who are "referred" to them by people they know, and studies indicate that those with connections are two to ten times more likely to be hired for a position.[5] To employers, an applicant who comes with a personal reference is much more of a sure thing, so they are much more likely to hire someone who has been vouched for. But people without connections have a much more difficult time getting an interview or a job offer.

Cultural capital is the knowledge of unique cultural attributes of elite circles, and it is also surprisingly important to one's economic success. To succeed in an interview, an applicant must fit the mold for which an employer is looking. The applicant must be dressed appropriately, speak in an articulate fashion, demonstrate knowledge of industry norms, and succeed in interviews that contain numerous cultural traps. It helps to know the right kind of wine to order and the right fork to use at a fancy restaurant, which might be part of the interview process. This cultural knowledge is readily available to those who grew up in an elite household but less accessible to others.

And cultural differences are responsible for the dissatisfaction that often accompanies success on the part of those from lower classes. As someone from a poor family becomes successful, they may lose touch with the friends and family they grew up with as their worlds no longer connect. But they may not connect well with the elites they encounter as they move up in the world. This cognitive dissonance can cause people from lower classes to be unhappy after they have achieved economic success.

Together these elements of social class serve to preserve the existing class structure. The children of the rich are likely to stay rich, bolstered by the economic, educational, social, and cultural capital they have at their disposal. The children of the poor are likely to stay poor, inhibited by their lack of access to capital despite their talents. The statistics on class mobility demonstrate that although some degree of class mobility does occur, it is limited.

Figure 23.9 displays the "Great Gatsby" curve, a term coined by economist Alan Krueger in 2012. It **shows the inverse relationship between inequality, as measured by the Gini coefficient, and intergenerational earnings mobility.**[6] As noted earlier, the Gini coefficient measures the degree of inequality in a country. Intergenerational earnings mobility **reflects the extent to which earnings of children are affected by the earnings of their parents.** Low intergenerational earnings mobility means that children's earnings are significantly impacted by the earnings of their parents, so they are unlikely to change social classes. High intergenerational earnings mobility indicates that children are only slightly affected by the incomes of their parents and that almost all children have the opportunity to thrive regardless of where they started.[7]

Unequal countries such as South Africa and Brazil have the least class mobility, whereas more equal countries such as Denmark, Norway, and Sweden have more class mobility.[8] The reasons for this inverse relationship are clear from the research on social class: Rich people have the most opportunities, whereas poor people have the least. In addition, countries such as those in Scandinavia that directly address inequality by providing free education and health care for all, paid for via progressive taxes, provide much more opportunity for those in the lower classes.

In countries with severe inequality of opportunity, it can take many generations for the effects of social class to dissipate. As Figure 23.10 shows, it takes nine generations for the typical family in South Africa to escape the circumstances they were born into and five generations in the United States. In Denmark, with their provision of education, health, training, and a safety net for all families, it takes only two generations for people to escape poverty.[9]

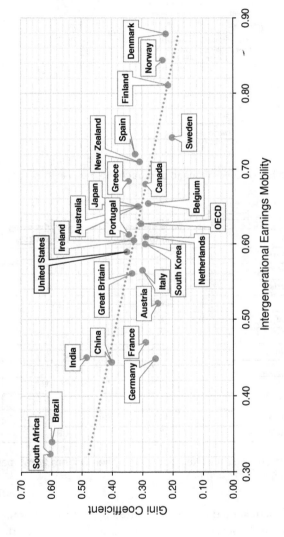

FIGURE 23.9 The Great Gatsby curve: Inequality (Gini) and intergenerational mobility, 2018.

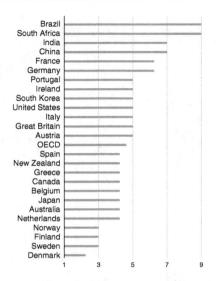

FIGURE 23.10 Number of generations to approach the mean income.

Country	Likelihood of staying in the bottom 25%	Likelihood of moving up to the top 25%
Denmark	23.5	22.0
United Kingdom	26.7	18.1
Netherlands	28.1	17.6
Spain	28.4	19.2
Greece	28.9	19.7
Austria	29.3	15.1
Belgium	29.3	16.5
Italy	30.7	18.5
Ireland	30.9	17.0
France	35.1	14.9
Germany	41.5	9.4
United States	41.8	8.5

FIGURE 23.11 Table showing the likelihood of the poor (bottom 25%) making it to the top, selected countries.

Even in very unequal countries with limited opportunities, some of the poor manage to be successful. However, we see dramatic differences in the percentage of the poor who are able to work their way to the top. As Figure 23.11 shows, a person from the poorest 25% of the population in Denmark has a 23.5% chance of staying where they are but they have a 22% chance of making it into the richest 25% of the population. At the other extreme, a U.S. citizen from the poorest 25%

has a 41.8% chance of staying poor and only an 8.5% chance of making it into the richest 25% of the population (upper middle class to wealthy).[10] Meanwhile, in the United States, nearly half of the richest 25% of the population were born in the richest 25%. Much of this stems directly from family influences. Two-thirds of managers in the United States had parents who were also managers, indicating that it is difficult for someone from outside a white-collar family to break into the ranks of management.

In 2018, a new, pathbreaking study by Nicholas Papageorge and Kevin Thom incorporating genomics and economics data found that children of low-income and high-income families have almost equal genetic endowments: It is just as likely for children of the poor to be gifted as children of the rich. However, in the United States the *least-gifted* children of the rich graduate from college at higher rates than the *most-gifted* children of the poor. The most-gifted children of the poor graduate from college at rate of just over 20%. Meanwhile, the least-gifted students from high-income families graduate from college at a rate of over 60%.[11] This is occurring in an era in which education is more important than ever before in providing opportunities for career advancement.

Thus, one of the main consequences of social class is that it has a significant impact on one's opportunities in life. In addition, social class has an important effect on health. The amount of control one has over one's job and one's life affects stress. Workers at the bottom who experience alienating work, with little control over their work life and little job security, tend to have more stress and much poorer health than people in the middle and upper classes. A 2016 study by Chetty, Stepner, and Abraham, published in the *Journal of the American Medical Association*, found that the richest 1% of men in the United States live 14.6 years longer than the poorest 1%, about ten years longer than the median man in the poorest 20%, and about five years longer than a man in the 50th percentile.[12] Similar but slightly smaller gaps were found for women. There is a direct relationship in the United States between income and expected years of life.

Clearly, class differences are quite pronounced in the modern world, and they have a dramatic effect on people's chances in life. Unfortunately, a series of changes in recent decades worsened class inequality, including globalization, the decline of unions, and skill-biased technological change.

23.3 ADDITIONAL FACTORS DRIVING CLASS INEQUALITY IN THE MODERN WORLD

When differences of class are added to modern forces of globalization, union decline, and skill-biased technological change, we have a recipe for a rapid explosion in global inequality. Below, we describe how these factors have increased inequality.

23.3.1 Globalization

Since the 1970s, the world has experienced rapid globalization. Globalization has had a very uneven impact on various groups of people. First, globalization allowed companies to locate production wherever it was cheapest. This had a dramatic impact on unskilled workers in developed countries, because corporations could easily find unskilled workers in developing countries who were willing to work for extremely low wages. A U.S. worker making $10 an hour could not compete with a worker in Myanmar making $0.08 per hour. Thus, unskilled workers in developed countries lost the most from globalization, causing their wages to stagnate or fall.

23.3.2 Decline of unions

Directly related to globalization has been the decline of labor unions in the developed world. In the 1950s when corporations could not move operations overseas, unions could safely demand higher wages without worrying that their jobs would be eliminated. With globalization, however, when unions demand higher wages, firms can simply move overseas and find cheaper labor. Globalization has steadily eroded the ability of unions to demand higher wages for their members, and that has eliminated the main benefit a worker gets from joining a union.

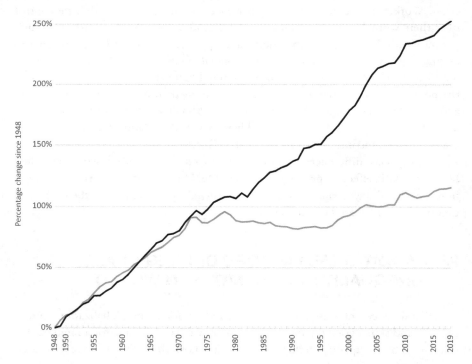

FIGURE 23.12 Percentage increases in U.S. workers' productivity and hourly compensation, 1948–2019.

23.3.3 Skill-biased technological change

In their 2008 book *The Race between Education and Technology*, economists Claudia Goldin and Lawrence Katz noted that technology was rapidly replacing unskilled workers with machines, whereas skilled workers to design and build machines were increasingly in demand. In essence, the demand for educated, skilled workers is higher than ever, but unskilled workers are less in demand because they are easily replaced by robots and other types of machinery.

The impact of these forces is depicted in Figure 23.12, which plots increases in workers' productivity and increases in their hourly wages from 1948 to 2019.[13] From 1948 to 1972, increases in workers' productivity were matched by increases in workers' wages. When workers became more productive, they were rewarded with pay increases. However, after 1972 these trends changed. Workers' wages stagnate under the influences of globalization, technological changes, and the decline in unions. From 1972 to 2000, workers' wages stayed the same, despite increases in productivity. From 2000 to 2019, workers' wages increased slightly but by much less than increases in productivity, as shown in Figure 23.12.

23.4 WHY WE SHOULD CARE ABOUT CLASS INEQUALITY AND WHAT WE CAN DO TO ADDRESS IT

There are numerous reasons why many economists are deeply concerned about inequality. Perhaps most important, recent evidence indicates that **inequality tends to reduce economic growth**. OECD researchers found that the impact of inequality on per capita gross domestic product (GDP) growth "is invariably negative and statistically significant: A 1% increase in inequality lowers GDP by 0.6% to 1.1%."[14] Meanwhile, a rise in the income share of the bottom 20% actually boosts growth. This is primarily due to the ways in which inequality limits the opportunities of the working class, reducing health, educational access, and productivity, and the fact that inequality is associated with lower levels of demand for products.[15]

23.4.1 Inequality is also associated with a host of social problems

Inequality is directly correlated with poverty in the bottom classes of society. Poverty leads to crime, substance abuse, domestic violence, malnutrition, child neglect, and more. Inequality also brings less social cohesion, and more of the population resents an economic system that is rigged on behalf of the elites. Many analysts cited such sentiments as being instrumental in the election of Donald Trump in 2016 and in the rise of right-wing, anti-immigration parties in much of Europe.

Some conservative mainstream economists are not overly concerned with inequality. For example, Martin Feldstein, the architect of supply-side, "trickle-down" economics, argues that cutting taxes on the rich will actually stimulate economic growth significantly because the rich will invest the money in productive, job-creating activities, causing the money to trickle down to workers eventually. As you will study in macroeconomics, the empirical evidence supporting this argument is quite weak. Historically, tax cuts for the wealthy have produced little or no increases in growth rates, and they have caused significant increases in government budget deficits.

Similarly, conservative mainstream economist N. Gregory Mankiw argues that the wealthy received their money due to their exceptional productivity, and if we reduce inequality we might jeopardize entrepreneurship.[16] From this perspective, a certain amount of inequality is necessary so that there are substantial rewards awaiting people willing to take risks.

Interestingly, Scandinavian countries have much higher numbers of start-up businesses per capita, a typical measure of entrepreneurship, than the United States does. Research suggests that the strong safety net in Scandinavian countries encourages people to start businesses because the risks of failure are much lower. Also, Scandinavian governments provide substantial resources and support for new businesses, and the fact that health care and other benefits are provided to all citizens removes another barrier to self-employment. In the United States, starting a business is a riskier endeavor. Thus, there is little empirical support for the idea that inequality fosters entrepreneurship.

Liberal mainstream economists and progressive political economists tend to advocate substantial policy interventions to reduce inequality, due to the likelihood that reducing inequality will foster growth and address important social problems. The countries with the greatest class mobility and least class inequality point us toward the best remedies for the inequities associated with social class divisions. Policies that would reduce class inequality include:

- Progressive income taxes that tax the rich at a higher marginal tax rate than the poor.
- Wealth taxes that tax savings and investments.
- Property taxes that tax property owners.
- Provision of high-quality education from preschool through college for all citizens.
- Provision of health care, food, shelter, and other basic necessities to all citizens.
- Minimum wage laws and other regulations that raise the wages of workers.
- Support for labor unions via a legal and regulatory framework that encourages workers to bargain collectively.
- Laws that give workers and communities input into major corporate decisions, such as whether or not a plant should be closed and moved overseas.
- A strong safety net that supports people if they fall on hard times.
- Active labor market policies that provide training and support for workers, so they have the latest skills and are matched with good jobs.

- Support for entrepreneurs and others trying to start new businesses.
- Job creation strategies, such as the triple helix approach used in Sweden where universities, employers, and the government work together to establish industrial clusters (see Chapter 8).
- Laws promoting worker cooperatives and worker ownership of companies.

The most egalitarian societies in the world, the Scandinavian countries, incorporate elements of *all* of these policies.

Market-dominated economies like the United States do much less. Indeed, it is common in the United States for the wealthiest citizens to pay *less* in taxes than the working class because investment income is taxed at a lower rate than income from work. Warren Buffet famously pointed out that U.S. tax laws allowed him to pay a lower percentage in taxes than his administrative assistant. Meanwhile, the U.S. government provides less support for the disadvantaged than all other developed countries. In addition, the U.S. educational system is extremely uneven in terms of quality and access to higher education, with the wealthy having significant advantages. So the U.S. economic system actually fosters class inequality to a significant degree.

Radical political economists want to go even further than the policies listed above. Because the root of inequality is usually social class, only in a system in which social classes do not exist would you have the elimination of inequality. Thus, radical political economists would prefer a socialist system in which workers and society collectively own and democratically control the economy's resources.

In addition to social class, race is a key influence on inequality in the United States and other countries in which the economic system historically was structured along racial lines. We noted in this chapter how social classes tend to perpetuate themselves, with the children of the rich likely to stay rich and the children of the poor likely to stay poor. Even more disturbing is the fact that minorities face even greater hurdles.

23.5 RACE AND INEQUALITY

African Americans and Hispanics in the United States tend to be heavily concentrated in lower social classes. When social class and race *both* intersect to affect a particular group of people, the results are dramatic. Not only does the working class often fare poorly under U.S. capitalism but black and Hispanic members of the working-class fare even worse. A series of powerful, recent studies demonstrate the deep-seated nature of racism in the modern United States.

- Marianne Bertrand and Sendhil Mullainathan sent thousands of resumes that were identical in terms of content to employers with publicly listed job openings. The resumes featured stereotypically African American names like

"Rasheed" and "Kareem" and stereotypically white names like "Jay" and "Brad." Applicants with resumes with stereotypically "white" names were 50% more likely to get called in for an interview. "Brad's" generic resume had a callback rate more than 500% higher than "Rasheed's."

- In another study, Devah Pager, Bruce Western, and Bart Bonikowski gave a group of black, Latino, and white applicants identical resumes and prepared them with interview training for low-wage jobs in New York City. Despite identical resumes and interview preparation, "black applicants were half as likely as equally qualified whites to receive a callback or job offer. In fact, black and Latino applicants with clean backgrounds fared no better than white applicants just released from prison."[17]

- The 2018 #livingwhileblack viral videos demonstrated the pervasiveness of overt racism in the United States. In each case, white people called the police on black people for ridiculous reasons. Rashon Nelson and Donte Robinson were handcuffed by police for sitting quietly at a table in a Philadelphia Starbucks waiting for a friend without ordering (they were planning to order after their friend arrived). Police were called on a black family trying to eat at a Subway restaurant, a black woman using a pool in the gated community in which she lived, and a black man trying to enter the apartment building in which he lived. Even black children do not escape such prejudicial attitudes: Police were called on black children for mowing part of the wrong yard, selling bottled water, and brushing a backpack against a white woman in a crowded store.

- Black people are much more likely to be subject to violence by police, as the examples of George Floyd in Minneapolis, Michael Brown in Ferguson, Eric Garner in New York, and so many others have shown. According to a 2015 study by Cody Ross, the probability of being black, unarmed, and shot by police is about 3.49 times the probability of being white, unarmed, and shot by police.[18]

- In the court system, black and Hispanic offenders face significantly greater odds of incarceration and longer sentences than white offenders convicted of the same crime.

- Studies indicate that blacks receive poorer medical care, have greater difficulty qualifying for loans and credit, pay more for cars, face discrimination in housing markets, and are less likely to get a response from political representatives.

- One-third of Latinos report discrimination when applying for jobs, negotiating salaries and promotions, and securing housing.[19]

- Latinos experienced greater racism and hostility after Donald Trump talked about Latino immigrants as "rapists," "murderers," "drug dealers," and "animals" during his campaign for President. This language shows up directly in racial incidents, such as one in which a white woman uses these exact words in a confrontation with Esteban Guzman, a Latino U.S. citizen born in southern California.[20] Unfortunately, there are many similar examples, which can be found at #livingwhilelatino.

Systematic racial discrimination has significant economic consequences. Figure 23.13 shows that median black family income as a percentage of median white family income grew from 1965 to 1975 after the Civil Rights Movement and the War on Poverty improved the situation of black families.[21] However, since 1975, black family incomes have not improved relative to white family incomes, indicating that economic progress on racial inequality has stopped. Racial wealth inequality is even more pronounced. Figure 23.14 shows that black and Hispanic households have only a fraction of the net worth of white households. Black net worth was 12.4% of white net worth in 1983 and 12.8% in 2019.[22]

To these data we add the following disturbing statistics:

- Since 2000, the black unemployment rate has been on average 4% higher than the white unemployment rate, and the Hispanic unemployment rate has averaged 2% higher.
- The poverty rate for whites in 2016 was 9%, whereas the poverty rate for blacks was 22% and the poverty rate for Hispanics was 20%.
- In 2017, the child poverty rate for blacks was 33%, for Hispanics it was 26%, and for whites it was 11%.

Year	Percentage
1955	55
1965	55
1975	61.5
1985	58
1995	60.9
2005	60
2015	61.6
2019	60.3

FIGURE 23.13 Table displaying median black family income as a percentage of median white family income.

Year	White	Hispanic	Black
1983	$98,765	9,033	12,245
1989	1,33,209	9,227	7,935
1995	1,18,594	19,303	16,863
2001	1,64,526	15,529	25,596
2007	1,95,842	24,015	19,547
2013	1,44,373	13,969	11,222
2019	1,89,000	36,050	24,100

FIGURE 23.14 Table on U.S. median household net worth by race/ethnicity, 1983–2019.

This provides substantial evidence that economic opportunities are not as prevalent for blacks and Hispanics in the United States. Unfortunately, many black and Hispanic households face all of the inequalities associated with being in a lower social class, *and* they face the added problem of racial discrimination. Black and Hispanic women also face gender discrimination, as we will see below. This highlights the concept of intersectionality, which is the **interconnectedness of various social stratifications, especially class, race, and gender along with sexual orientation, age, and disability, in creating overlapping and interdependent systems of power and discrimination**.

23.5.1 Policies to address racial inequality

Given the stubbornly intractable inequality along racial lines in the United States, it is disappointing that the government has done so little to address these issues. The U.S. government enacted laws that prevent overt discrimination in hiring on the basis of race, color, sex, religion, or ethnic origin. It is also illegal to refuse to provide service to people of different backgrounds in most cases. (Recently, the government has allowed businesses to refuse service to homosexual couples based on religious objections, which marks a major departure from this principle.)

Despite those laws, the data indicate that a substantial amount of racial discrimination still exists. The United States has not taken the most dramatic steps that would be necessary to address racial inequality, especially ensuring that all children in poor communities have access to high-quality education, health care, and other basic necessities that would allow them to succeed later in life.

One attempt to address racial and gender inequality has been affirmative action policies which many countries have adopted. Affirmative action **policies** typically **require employers who do business with the government to take "affirmative action" to increase employment of people from historically oppressed and underrepresented groups**. In the United States, affirmative action laws have a relatively small impact on hiring practices. If an employer finds two candidates who are equally qualified for a position, the employer is asked to give preference in hiring to any person from a historically underrepresented group. In practice this means that when all qualifications are equal, an employer should give the nod to the person of color or the female candidate over a white man.

Universities also attempt to diversify their student bodies via similar efforts. Universities want to attract a diverse pool of students because of the importance of diversity in the modern workplace. Each year, employers list the ability to work with people from diverse backgrounds and cultures as one of the essential characteristics they are looking for in employees. Students who graduate from a non-diverse university are not well prepared for the requirements of the modern, global workplace.

Affirmative action policies at universities are particularly important because of the vastly unequal educational opportunities in the United States. In 2017 the average score of whites on the SAT was 1118, the average score of blacks was 941, and the average score of Latinos was 987. However, research indicates that SAT scores are directly correlated with family income.[23] We saw earlier that income was not highly correlated with innate abilities. Thus, a university that admits students based on SAT scores alone would be biasing its admission standards in favor of wealthy students, who are much more likely to be white. This has led to a robust debate about what a fair admissions process would be.

To avoid the known biases of standardized test scores that favor the rich, the University of Texas simply admits the top 10% of each high school class automatically. That way, students going to low-quality public schools in poor neighborhoods can still get into a good college. Indeed, almost all universities attempt to address known biases in standardized testing by adjusting admissions criteria to give students from disadvantaged backgrounds a boost in consideration. This approach has led to numerous lawsuits by conservative activists representing a few white and Asian students, who have argued that they are being discriminated against in university admissions policies.

Despite the passing of laws and affirmative action policies, the data above indicate that the United States continues to be deeply unequal along racial lines. This has led some economists, such as William A. (Sandy) Darity, to advocate for reparations. Reparations would compensate African Americans for the trillions of dollars that were lost in wages and opportunities due to slavery and racial discrimination. Given what we know about how wealth and opportunity are passed on from one generation to the next, the best way to dramatically improve the lot of African Americans in the United States may well be to institute some sort of wealth transfer along these lines. Another problem that has proven difficult to resolve is that of gender inequality.

23.6 GENDER INEQUALITY

Though there has been much progress with respect to gender inequality in recent years, substantial inequities remain. Figure 23.15 shows the median female worker income as a percentage of median male worker income. Women earn, on average, only 82.3% of what men earn.[24]

Figure 23.16 shows one of the biggest reasons for the pay differential between men and women: Occupational segregation that occurs **when workers from a particular group, especially those of a particular gender or race, are distributed disproportionately to particular occupations.**[25] Women make up disproportionately large percentages of low-wage occupations, such as nurses, health service aids, and cashiers, but disproportionately small percentages of highly paid occupations, such as physicians, lawyers, and engineers. Note also that black workers face significant occupational segregation. There has been significant progress since 1983, with women and blacks gaining access to high-paying occupations

Year	Female/male median earnings (%)
1960	60.7
1970	59.4
1980	60.2
1990	71.6
2000	73.3
2010	76.9
2015	79.6
2019	82.3

FIGURE 23.15 Table showing median female worker income as a percentage of median male worker income.

Occupation	% Female 1983	% Female 2020	% Black 1983	% Black 2020
Engineers	5.8	16.5	2.7	6
Lawyers	15.3	37.4	2.6	6.8
Physicians	15.8	40.6	3.2	8.5
All Occupations	**43.7**	**46.8**	**9.3**	**12.1**
Elementary School Teachers	83.3	79.6	11.1	10.5
Cashiers	84.4	73.1	10.1	17.1
Health Service Aides (home)	89.2	90.3	23.5	37.4
Nurses	95.8	87.4	6.7	13.4

FIGURE 23.16 Table showing occupational segregation, 1983 and 2020.

in increasing numbers. However, there is still significant inequality with respect to occupational segregation.

The ongoing gender inequalities in the U.S. economy indicate the deeply gendered nature of the economic system. In general, when people in the United States think of a CEO or a president, they usually envision a male person in that role. When people think of a worker in a caring occupation, such as nursing or elementary school teaching, they usually have a woman in mind. Such gendered stereotypes affect the careers people choose as well as the opportunities in life that people have. Thus, culture plays a major role in establishing gender stereotypes.

The glass ceiling is a prime example of cultural attitudes toward work. In 2020 just 7.4% of CEOs of Fortune 500 companies were women,[26] and only 1.0% were black.[27] Similarly, as of 2021 there had been 46 U.S. Presidents but only one was black (Barack Obama) and the United States never had a female President. This represents an extraordinary dearth of opportunities at the top for women and minorities.

In addition, data from the U.S. Bureau of Labor Statistics show that in 2020 women earned less than men in almost every occupation. For example, female physicians earned only 82% of the salaries of male physicians, on average.[28] This indicates that occupational segregation does not tell the entire story of gender inequality.

The #MeToo movement exposed the extent to which women experience sexual harassment in the workplace. In response to the sexual assault and harassment allegations against Harvey Weinstein in October 2017, actress Alyssa Milano posted on Twitter, "If you've been sexually harassed or assaulted write 'me too' as a reply to this tweet." This was building on the original initiative begun in 2006 by Tarana Burke. The result was an outpouring as hundreds of thousands of women shared their experiences. Unfortunately, sexual harassment is disturbingly common. A 2018 survey found that 38% of women experienced some form of sexual harassment in the workplace.[29]

Women's work is also undervalued in another important way: Women tend to do much more unpaid work in the household than men do. In the United States in 2017, women spent an average of 2.19 hours per day on household activities while men spent only 1.41 hours.[30] Similar divisions are typical in the United Kingdom, Canada, and other developed countries.

The primary factor contributing to ongoing gender inequities is **culture** and the cultural beliefs that value men's work more than women's work. These beliefs stem from a history of patriarchy, **a society in which men hold power and women are largely excluded from power** structures. The following cultural factors loom particularly large:

- **Religion and "traditional" values**: Modern religions evolved from deeply patriarchal societies and feature values in which men are depicted as leaders and women are subservient. Almost all depictions of important religious figures are male.
- **Prejudice**: When members of a society are prejudiced against women, their actions will serve to discriminate against women in the economic realm.
- **Educational access**: In many societies, it is seen as more important for boys to receive education than girls. This severely limits the opportunities for women.

Cultural values and prejudices reinforce gender inequality, limiting the opportunities that women have. Due to limited opportunities, women are **crowded** into traditional, gendered occupations like nursing, administrative assistants, and cashiers, while facing barriers to more lucrative careers.

23.6.1 Policies to reduce gender inequality

As with racial inequality, the U.S. government has laws that prevent overt discrimination against women. In addition, women have been the main beneficiaries of affirmative action laws in the United States. Once affirmative action gave women access to professions that had previously been closed to them they succeeded spectacularly, and one profession after another become more equal in terms of gender representation. As Figure 23.16 shows, women made substantial inroads into high-paying professions in medicine and law in recent years.

Many countries also try to reduce gender inequality by enacting policies that make it easier for mothers to work and to return to work after having a child. In Scandinavian countries, mothers are given a full year of maternity leave and their job is waiting for them when they are ready to return to the workplace. Fathers are also encouraged to take paternity leave with similarly generous benefits. The government provides free childcare, making it easier for women to work.

In 2003 Norway grew frustrated with the slow pace of change at the very top of corporations, so they passed a law requiring that at least 40% of the seats on corporate boards of directors should be allocated to women. This caused a significant increase in the number of women in the upper echelons of businesses and had no discernible negative impact on business outcomes. Several other European countries soon followed in passing similar legislation.

Because of the unique problems associated with gender and race, groups of economists who are particularly concerned with gender and racial inequality developed robust approaches to study the relevant issues. This led to the development of two fields within economics, feminist economics and stratification economics.

23.7 ECONOMIC ANALYSIS OF INEQUALITY: FEMINIST ECONOMICS AND STRATIFICATION ECONOMICS

Economists have widely differing views about inequality. As noted above, political economists view class inequality as one of the major issues in a capitalist system. Views of mainstream economists regarding inequality are mixed, with some viewing inequality as a serious problem and others who do not find it problematic. Dissatisfaction with the lack of sophisticated analysis of gender inequality in both political economics and mainstream economics led to the formation of feminist economics.

Feminist economics is perhaps the most perceptive analysis of gender inequality. Feminist economists see gender as a key economic structure in all human societies, affecting economic outcomes in a wide variety of ways.

As we saw earlier, the mainstream economics conception of an economic actor is a man who does no housework and does not care for anyone else—economic man. This ignores gender inequalities in fundamental economic relationships. Human relationships are complicated, involving love, reciprocity, power, and mutual interdependence. Households often have similar interests, but sometimes the perspectives of household members diverge based on gendered interests. Thus, any sophisticated economic analysis must include consideration of gender issues and how gender roles affect households and household decision making.

Given the importance of gender and cultural attitudes toward gender in affecting economic outcomes, **social norms** are another key area of study. Patriarchal influences shape culture in key ways, but the manner in which patriarchy manifests itself differs in each society. This also means that power relationships are crucial in understanding the economic system and in determining the role of patriarchy in preserving power for male actors at the expense of female actors. In addition, government policies can cause changes in social norms. Providing free or subsidized childcare can encourage women to work, making them less dependent on the income of their partner. This allows women to be more independent, undermining traditional, patriarchal roles.

Like institutionalists, feminists focus on a broader definition of **social provisioning** that includes everything humans need to survive. Beyond goods and services offered for sale, feminist economists include unpaid domestic work and care as key elements of production. Feminist economists estimate that households produce or provide goods and services that add up to between 16% and 43% of the value of GDP in various countries, indicating how important household production is in the economy.[31]

The work of feminist economists has been instrumental in highlighting the unequal, gendered dynamics of power in the modern world and the often unseen and unacknowledged contributions of women to household production. Another approach highlighting oft-overlooked issues of inequality comes from stratification economics.

Stratification economics, first described in 2005 by William A. (Sandy) Darity, attempts to understand the forces behind intergroup inequality, especially racial inequality. Like feminist economics, it broadens the field of economics to include insights from sociology and psychology to understand the forces behind implicit and explicit biases. Stratification economics also emphasizes the role of power structures in supporting the relative position of those on top of existing hierarchies, such as white men in the United States, at the expense of those at the bottom.

Conservative mainstream economist Gary Becker argued in his 1957 book *The Economics of Discrimination* that discrimination was an irrational economic act that reduced profits for business owners based on their personal racial preferences. However, the analysis of stratification economists indicates that it is quite rational for most whites to discriminate against blacks, because it preserves their privileged position in the economic system. Stratification economics has identified the phenomenon of last place aversion, which is **the intense desire of a social group to preserve its relative social standing and to avoid being at the bottom of a social ranking**. In the U.S. context, this helps us understand why some poorer, less educated whites have racist attitudes toward blacks and Latinos. It also explains why empirical studies have shown little to no evidence of racial discrimination declining over time.[32]

Social prejudices also affect productivity. Perhaps the most important example of this is stereotype threat, **the adverse effect that negative beliefs about a group can have on the performance of individuals from that group**. For example, the stereotype that blacks are cognitively inferior to whites has been shown to reduce the SAT scores of black students by 13%.[33] Raising the issue of black inferiority to a black student just before a test has the impact of reducing their performance by undermining their self-confidence. The important implication is that racist stereotypes have direct bearing on productivity and therefore on one's relative success in the economy.

Stratification economics helps us understand ongoing economic inequality by analyzing how social groups are separated and stratified based on relative group status. When combined with feminist economics, we gain a more sophisticated picture of how power structures and cultural attitudes serve to preserve inequality and make it difficult to overcome.

23.8 CONCLUSION

This chapter began by describing how inequality has been increasing in developed countries in recent decades, along with the ways in which economists measure inequality, such as the Gini coefficient. The dramatic worsening of inequality, and the manner in which this change has eroded communities and faith in government and global economic systems, makes it one of the major economic issues of our time.

One of the most important drivers of inequality in capitalism is the power and control that comes with owning society's resources. This usually allows owners of capital to dictate wages for workers, unless strong unions or government intervention is present to resist the power of capitalists. The social class a person belongs to has a major influence on their life, fundamentally shaping their education, health, friendship groups, and economic opportunities.

In addition to class, race and gender play a dramatic role in shaping economic opportunities and outcomes. Racial discrimination is disturbingly common in the United States, which has the effect of limiting the wages and options for minorities. Similarly, patriarchal cultural constructs limit wages and opportunities for women. Feminist economists and stratification economists have attempted to address issues of gender and race inequality via a sophisticated analysis of the social factors that shape cultural attitudes towards race and gender.

Given the ongoing inequities faced by the working class, women, and minorities in the United States, a case can be made that we need dramatic action to break these established patterns. Some policies are refreshingly simple. The U.S. government could:

- Ensure that all citizens have access to health care, food, clothing, and shelter that guarantee everyone a healthy and productive life.
- Provide all children, including those in poor, minority communities, with high-quality education at all levels, from preschool through college.
- Institute family-friendly policies such as free childcare and year-long parental leave to make it easier for mothers to work.

There are few strong arguments against such policies, given the modest cost and the effectiveness of these policies where they have been tried.

Other policies are perhaps more controversial, such as strongly progressive income, wealth, and property taxes that would redistribute income from rich owners to those who have suffered disadvantages under our economic system—especially workers, minorities, and women. Given the power and control of wealthy capitalists, such steps are unlikely unless a mass political movement demands significant change.

QUESTIONS FOR REVIEW

1. Describe how inequality has changed in the United States and other developed countries since 1970.
2. What are the main reasons why U.S. inequality has worsened *more* than inequality in other developed countries?
3. Brazil's Gini coefficient fell from 63.3 in 1989 to 51.5 in 2014. What does this tell us about inequality in Brazil? Explain carefully.
4. List the most important factors that economists believe are contributing to inequality in the modern world.
5. Why is class correlated with inequality?
6. What is personal capital, and how does this concept help us to understand why some people are more successful than others?
7. Write an essay in which you explore the consequences of social class divisions in the modern United States. What, if anything, do you think the U.S. government should do to address social class inequality? Explain and support your answer.
8. Given the information in this chapter on racial inequality, how do you think colleges should make decisions about which students to admit?
9. Describe the degree of racial and gender inequality that exists in the modern United States. What factors explain the ongoing existence of this inequality? What could be done to reduce this type of inequality?
10. Why do feminist economists and stratification economists focus on culture as a key determinant of gender and racial inequality? Explain and give examples.

NOTES

1 Source: Federal Reserve, *Survey of Consumer Finances*, table 2, https://www.federal
   reserve.gov/publications/files/scf17.pdf, accessed January 29, 2020.

2 Source: Federalreserve.gov.

3 See, for example, Edward N. Wolff and Maury Gittleman, "Inheritances and the
   Distribution of Wealth or Whatever Happened to the Great Inheritance Boom?"
   NBER Working Paper 16840, February 2011.

4 Scott Jaschik, "College Selectivity and Income," *Insider Higher Ed*, August 22, 2016.

5 Nelson D. Schwartz, "In Hiring, a Friend in Need Is a Prospect, Indeed," *The New York
   Times*, January 27, 2013.

6 *The Great Gatsby* is a famous novel by F. Scott Fitzgerald that depicted the ostentatious
   lifestyles of the rich and famous in the United States in the 1920s and their ability to use
   connections and influence to stay on top.

7 The OECD computes intergenerational earnings mobility as 1 minus the intergenerational earnings elasticities from parent to child. This measures how income levels
   change across generations. If there is no intergenerational mobility, the intergenerational earnings elasticity is equal to 1 and the intergenerational earnings mobility is
   equal to 0. In such a case, all poor children would become poor adults and all rich
   children would become rich adults. In a highly unequal country like South Africa, the
   earnings elasticity is 0.68, which means that incomes persist across generations at a rate
   of 68%. This results in a low intergenerational earnings mobility of (1 − 0.68) = 0.32.
   A child whose parents earn $10,000 more than the average income would earn, on
   average, $6800 more than the average income. A child whose parents earn $10,000 less
   than the average income would earn, on average, $6800 less than the average income.
   Meanwhile, in a country such as Denmark, only 12% of a parent's income is passed on
   to their children, giving Denmark an intergenerational earnings mobility of 88%.

8 Source: OECD, *A Broken Social Elevator? How to Promote Social Mobility* (OECD
   Publishing, Paris, 2018), https://doi.org/10.1787/9789264301085-en.

9 Ibid.

10 Ibid.

11 See Andrew Van Dam, "It's Better to Be Born Rich Than Gifted," *Washington Post*,
   October 9, 2018, https://www.washingtonpost.com/business/2018/10/09/its-better
   -be-born-rich-than-talented/?utm_term=.c04e2a9bff45.

12 Peter Reuell, "For Life Expectancy, Money Matters," *The Harvard Gazette*, April 11,
   2016.

13 Source: Economic Policy Institute, "The Top Charts of 2016," December 22, 2016,
   https://www.epi.org/publication/the-top-charts-of-2016-13-charts-that-show-the-
   difference-between-the-economy-we-have-now-and-the-economy-we-could-have/,
   accessed August 2, 2021, and author's calculations.

14 See Orsetta Causa, Alain de Serres, and Nicolas Ruiz, "Can Growth-Enhancing
   Policies Lift All Boats? An Analysis Based on Household Disposable Incomes," OECD
   Economics Department Working Papers (OECD Publishing, Paris, 2014), http://www
   .oecd.org/economy/growth-and-inequality-close-relationship.htm, accessed October
   20, 2018.

15 In brief, rich people spend a smaller percentage of their income than poor people. When
   income is transferred to the rich from the poor, the overall level of spending declines,
   which undermines the demand for products, causing a decline in business sales and a
   decline in GDP.

16 N. Gregory Mankiw, "Defending the One Percent." *Journal of Economic Perspectives* 27, No. 3 (2013), pp. 21–34.

17 Devah Pager, Bruce Western, and Bart Bonikowski, "Discrimination in a Low-Wage Labor Market: A Field Experiment." *American Sociological Review* 74 (2009), pp. 777–799.

18 See Cody T. Ross, "A Multi-Level Bayesian Analysis of Racial Bias in Police Shootings at the County-Level in the United States, 2011–2014." *PLOS One*, November 5, 2015.

19 Joe Neel, "Poll: 1 in 3 Latinos Report Discrimination Based on Ethnicity," NPR, November 1, 2017, https://www.npr.org/documents/2017/oct/discrimination-latinos -final.pdf, accessed August 4, 2021.

20 Ashley May, "Woman Citing Trump Tells Landscapers Mexicans Are 'Rapists' and 'Animals' in Viral Video," *USA Today*, June 26, 2018.

21 Source: U.S. Census Bureau, Historical Income Tables, table F-5.

22 Source: Federal Reserve, Survey of Consumer Finances.

23 Zachary A. Goldfarb, "These Four Charts Show How the SAT Favors Rich, Educated Families," *The Washington Post*, March 5, 2014.

24 Source: U.S. Census Bureau, Historical Income Tables, P-38.

25 Source: Statistical Abstract of the United States, 2009 and Bureau of Labor Statistics.

26 See Emily Stewart, "Women Are Running for Office in Record Numbers. In Corporate America, They're Losing Ground," *Vox*, June 8, 2018, https://www.vox.com/policy -and-politics/2018/6/8/17413254/women-fortune-500-ceos-politics-blue-wave, accessed October 21, 2018.

27 Phil Wahba, "The Number of Black CEOs in the Fortune 500 Remains Very Low," *Fortune*, June 1, 2020. https://fortune.com/2020/06/01/black-ceos-fortune-500-2020 -african-american-business-leaders/, accessed August 4, 2021.

28 Source: U.S. Bureau of Labor Statistics, "Labor Force Statistics from the Current Population Survey," www.bls.gov/cps/cpsaat39.htm, accessed February 8, 2021.

29 See Susan Chira, "Numbers Hint at Why #MeToo Took Off: The Sheer Number Who Can Say Me Too," *The New York Times*, February 21, 2018.

30 See U.S. Bureau of Labor Statistics, "Economic News Release," https://www.bls.gov/ news.release/atus.t01.htm, accessed October 21, 2018.

31 Susan Himmelweit, "Feminist Economics," in *Rethinking Economics: An Introduction to Pluralist Economics*, edited by Liliann Fishcer, Joe Hasell, J. Christopher Proctor, et al. (Routledge, New York, 2017), pp. 60–75.

32 See William Darity, Darrick Hamilton, and James B. Stewart, "A Tour de Force in Understanding Intergroup Inequality: An Introduction to Stratification Economics," *Review of Black Political Economy*, June 2014.

33 See William A. Darity Jr., Darrick Hamilton, Patrick L. Mason, et al., "Stratification Economics," in *The Hidden Rules of Race*, edited by Andrea Flynn, Susan R. Holmberg, Dorian T. Warren, and Felicia J. Wong (Cambridge University Press, Cambridge, 2017), ch. 2.

PART VII

Macroeconomic issues and problems

This section provides a broad overview of the current state of macroeconomics and the key issues that macroeconomists are studying.

Chapter 24 introduces modern macroeconomics and the importance of understanding aggregate economics as a different way of thinking than microeconomics. The chapter also describes the evolution of macroeconomic policy, beginning with the Keynesian consensus of the 1950s and 1960s, the return of laissez-faire approaches from 1980 to 2007, and the switch back to Keynesian economics after the financial crisis of 2008–2010 and the coronavirus recession of 2020. Key macroeconomic topics are discussed, including the business cycle, stabilization policy, economic growth, and financial markets.

Chapter 25 discusses economic well-being. There are debates over the most important goals for an economic system and what data we should use to measure, describe, and analyze the macroeconomy. Traditionally, economists used real gross domestic product (real GDP) to measure the health of the economy. However, political economists and some mainstream economists argue that other measures, such as the OECD Better Life Index, the genuine progress indicator, and the United Nations Human Development Index are better measures of welfare due to the limitations of GDP. Some prefer to use measures of happiness.

Subsequently, in Chapter 26, we turn to the major macroeconomic market failures: unemployment and price instability. The chapter describes the different types of unemployment and the problems that occur due to unemployment. Then, the chapter discusses inflation and deflation and the problems they can cause for the macroeconomy. The chapter includes both mainstream and political economics perspectives on these topics and a case study of unemployment during the Great Recession in the United States and Europe.

We begin the section by describing the evolution of macroeconomic theory and macroeconomic trends in the modern era. The perspectives of economists on macroeconomics changed dramatically over the last century.

DOI: 10.4324/9781315636924-30

Modern macro-economics

The evolution of macroeconomic theory and the macroeconomy in the modern era

There is a crucial distinction in economics between microeconomics and macro-economics. Microeconomics is **the study of how distinct economic actors, such as consumers, workers, and firms, interact in the economic system**. In a market system, microeconomists study the interactions between buyers and sellers of goods, services, resources, and inputs. Many people have a good, intuitive grasp of how microeconomic markets work, based on their personal experiences and observations operating in markets.

Macroeconomics, however, is much harder to grasp because many of its inner workings are difficult to discern. Macroeconomics is **the study of the aggregate forces that shape national and global economies**. To aggregate means to add up all of the components. When studying the macroeconomy, economists look for trends that are affecting large numbers of consumers, producers, or investors. For example, instead of focusing on consumer demand for one particular product, macroeconomists study aggregate demand, which is **the sum of the demands for all goods and services by all economic actors, including households, businesses, banks, and government agencies**.

Macroeconomics focuses on **short-term** and **long-term** issues. A key short-term issue in macroeconomics is the **business cycle**—the patterns of booms and busts created by economic fluctuations in market capitalist economies. Short-term macroeconomic policy focuses on stabilization policies designed to avoid booms and busts, and policies to alleviate the worst problems created by the business cycle, especially policies to reduce unemployment and restore economic confidence when the economy falls into a recession. A recession is **a generalized slowdown of economic activity where reductions in production result in an increase in unemployment. A decline in production (real GDP) for six months or more** (at least two quarters) **is considered to be a recession**.

DOI: 10.4324/9781315636924-31

A key long-term macroeconomic issue is how to best generate **economic growth**. Economists try to determine what set of policies will result in the highest rate of economic growth and thereby raise the standard of living of the population. However, economic growth can have a very negative impact on the environment, and it can benefit some groups at the expense of others. Therefore, the details regarding the impact of economic growth on people and the environment are extremely important.

In studying short-term and long-term issues, macroeconomists focus on key macroeconomic goals. The most important goal of a macroeconomy is to provide for the **well-being** of the entire population. The main barriers to human well-being are the intertwined problems of unemployment and poverty, market failures that create widespread deprivation and undermine the stability of an economic system. This is why many countries established full employment as an important goal, and why all developed countries have established a safety net to support the most vulnerable in society. Well-being typically includes access to opportunities, meaningful work, leisure time, civic engagement, and the necessities of life.

Improvements in well-being usually depend to a significant degree on economic growth, another important macroeconomic goal. As far back as Adam Smith, some economists have focused on economic growth as the crucial economic topic of study. However, with the steady drumbeat of negative news about the climate and the environment, some economists such as Herman Daly now advocate zero growth and promote the macroeconomic goal of **sustainability**. Policies that promote sustainability without overly compromising economic growth are crucial in the modern era. Typically, economic growth has been accompanied by increased environmental destruction, but this does not have to be the case if appropriate environmental rules and regulations control environmental damage while also promoting the development of new industries.

Another macroeconomic goal is **stability**. Stability fosters investment and growth, whereas uncertainty undermines them. In fostering stability, governments work to avoid severe economic crises, including financial crises. This necessitates careful management of the money supply and monitoring of price levels, because deflation and inflation can both be destructive. Similarly, the financial system, and especially asset markets (such as markets for stocks, bonds, and derivatives), must be monitored and regulated because financial crises can be particularly debilitating to the macroeconomy. Governments must also work to maintain sufficient aggregate demand in crises, when declines in consumer and investor confidence cause spending to drop.

Macroeconomics is extremely complex. In 2018, the U.S. macroeconomy involved more than 329 million people, 27.9 million businesses, and 22 million government officials interacting in a $21 trillion economy. The global macroeconomy is, of course, even larger, with 7.7 billion people living in 195 countries that utilize many different approaches to economic development and produce more than \$80 trillion worth of goods and services. As a result of this complexity, it is difficult to make precise predictions about the macroeconomy, and there is much room for debate about what policies work best. Economists disagree on macroeconomic policy substantially, with a wide variety of approaches.

Broadly speaking, we can characterize four different approaches to structuring a macroeconomy. The **laissez-faire, market-dominated approach** utilizes as little government intervention as possible, even in recessions, preferring unfettered market forces. The **supply-side approach** believes in deregulating markets, while using government intervention on behalf of business. The **New Keynesian, mixed market and state approach** sees market forces as the primary driver in the economic system but recognizes the need for sound regulations, extensive stabilization policies, and a strong safety net to support those who fall upon hard times. In contrast, the **political economy, state-centered approach** sees the need for extensive government guidance of the economic system, with the state restricting or directing many market activities, guiding investment decisions, and providing significant employment via state-owned industries and services. One can also find many economists who fall in between these categories.

In addition, a country's macroeconomic approach does not always reflect the same philosophy as its microeconomic approach to regulation. The United States is considered a market-dominated economic system due to its largely deregulated markets, but its macroeconomic approach involves substantial government intervention in recessions, a mixed market and state approach. Germany is considered to be a social market economy with substantial government intervention in microeconomic markets, but its macroeconomic policy leans toward the laissez-faire approach. Sweden is more consistent, with a highly interventionist approach to both microeconomic and macroeconomic problems reflective of the political economy approach.

This chapter begins by describing the evolution of U.S. macroeconomic history from the Great Depression to present, along with the changes in macroeconomic theory that have accompanied the changes in the U.S. economic system. The chapter also briefly surveys the economic growth performance of the United States and other economic systems in the modern era.

Subsequently, the chapter discusses the modern business cycle and the different perspectives economists have regarding how the government should respond to recessions.

24.0 CHAPTER 24 LEARNING GOALS

After reading this chapter you should be able to:

■ Compare and contrast Say's law with a Keynesian understanding of macroeconomics.

- Define real GDP, unemployment, inflation, and labor force participation and explain how they illustrate an economy's macroeconomic performance.

- Describe the evolution of the U.S. macroeconomy and the global macroeconomy since the Great Depression.

- Analyze how macroeconomic theory has changed in the United States since the Great Depression in response to macroeconomic changes.

- Contrast the views of New Keynesian economists with the views of supply-side, laissez-faire, and political economists.

- Explain the characteristics of the typical modern business cycle in the United States, along with the three major perspectives of economists regarding how the government should respond to recessions.

24.1 KEYNES AND THE BIRTH OF MACROECONOMICS

We begin with a brief overview of modern macroeconomic theory, which will be developed in greater detail in subsequent chapters. As we saw earlier, classical economists such as Adam Smith and David Ricardo did not develop a workable theory to explain the regular business cycles that occur in capitalist economic systems. They focused more on the factors that caused long-term economic growth, such as technological change and the specialization of labor. The neoclassical economists such as Leon Walras and Alfred Marshall who followed Smith and Ricardo emphasized marginal analysis, developing a theory based on the assumption that individual consumers and firms optimized behavior by comparing marginal costs and marginal benefits. According to mainstream, neoclassical theory of the late 1800s and early 1900s, unregulated markets generated the optimal allocation of resources.

Specifically, according to Say's law, supply creates demand: When goods are produced and supplied, this generates an equivalent amount of income, which is then used to purchase (demand) all of the goods produced. Therefore, Say's law implies there is always enough demand to purchase all products that are produced, and overproduction or underconsumption of goods can only be a temporary phenomenon. There can be no involuntary unemployment from this perspective: All workers who desire a job can find one as long as they are willing to accept lower wages when the demand for labor falls. Capital markets efficiently allocate all savings to investment. If consumers spend less and save more, the increase in savings causes an increase in the amount of money in banks, prompting banks to lower interest rates. Lower interest rates can spur investment and offset any decrease in consumer spending. From this rosy perspective, recessions will be solved very quickly by the automatic adjustment mechanisms of the market and no government intervention is necessary.

However, the Great Depression undermined this perspective thoroughly. By 1940, the idea that that macroeconomy was self-adjusting was no longer widely accepted. The economist who most clearly and successfully explained why neoclassical theory of the time failed was John Maynard Keynes.

Keynes' research demonstrated that (1) **business investment is extremely volatile** and subject to "animal spirits." When businesses lose confidence, investment will plunge and the economy will fall into a recession. Due to the (2) **multiplier process**, once investment or consumer spending falls, this causes declines in income and businesses' sales, causing additional rounds of investment and spending cuts, multiplying the initial change many times over. Keynes also established that (3) **wages and prices are sticky** and do not fall quickly in recessions. Therefore, the economy did not experience increases in the demand for labor or goods that might accompany such price drops. Furthermore, if wages and prices do eventually fall, (4) **deflation can be ruinous for the economy**. Lower wages erode consumer demand for products, which in turn prompts businesses to reduce production and investment. Lower goods prices cause businesses to go bankrupt once the price for which they sell products falls below the cost of producing goods. The implications are that markets are inherently unstable, they do not correct themselves quickly, and they may linger in recessions indefinitely.

Keynes ushered in the era of the mixed market economy. In microeconomic markets, governments operating capitalist economic systems allowed private firms to produce most goods and services, while regulating firms to prevent the worst excesses of markets. In macroeconomic markets, governments actively engaged in stabilization policies to offset recessions and encouraged economic growth via a variety of economic policies. In the United States, growth-stimulating policies included substantial provision of infrastructure and high-quality education for workers, subsidies for research and development in key industries, and support for technology industries related to national defense. Stabilization policies included the establishment of safety nets such as unemployment insurance and welfare programs, along with increased spending, lower taxes, and lower interest rates in recessions to stimulate aggregate demand.

Meanwhile, European countries and Japan adopted an even more interventionist approach, engaging in substantial government planning to stimulate industrial development in fast-growing sectors. Many of these countries developed extensive safety nets and stabilization policies. The result in the United States, Western Europe, and Japan was rapid economic growth.

24.2 ECONOMIC GROWTH AND PAX AMERICANA, 1945–1973

Since the Great Depression, almost all economies have experienced economic growth over time, driven by technological advances and increases in labor productivity. However, the rate of economic growth in a country can vary widely from one decade to the next. Furthermore, some countries may experience robust economic growth while others stagnate. As we will see, market-dominated, social-market, and state-dominated economies experienced periods of economic growth during various time periods, with varying degrees of success.

Recall that market-dominated economies (MDEs) are economic systems in which the primary economic decisions are made by private actors (businesses, individuals) operating in markets and the government plays a secondary role. Social market economies (SMEs) are economic systems where social values take a leading role in directing the economy through the actions of a government. State-dominated economies (SDEs) are economic systems in which the government is the main economic actor in most major industries or economic decisions, owning or controlling most of the economy.

From 1945 to 1973 MDEs such as the United States and the United Kingdom and SMEs such as Sweden, Germany, and Japan saw rapid economic growth. SDEs such as the U.S.S.R. and China saw less economic growth during this period. However, as we will see below, since 1973 some SDEs such as China and Vietnam have better growth performance, as do some SMEs that feature significant government intervention, such as South Korea and Taiwan. The major causes of economic growth are thus complex, with a variety of economic systems experiencing success in different eras utilizing an assortment of approaches.

The United States emerged from World War II in a very favorable economic position. The world's other huge industrial powers, especially in Europe, were devastated by the war. The United States was the dominant economic power, producing 80% of the world's manufactured products, including cars, steel, and high-technology goods. U.S. industrial dominance allowed it to pursue a policy of tariff reductions with trading partners to promote unregulated trade flows. This benefited dominant U.S. industries significantly during this era by opening up foreign markets, and it gradually drew more and more countries into the U.S. trading orbit.

The post-World War II boom also proved to be very good for U.S. manufacturing workers, who joined unions in record numbers and experienced rapidly increasing wages. Workers used their higher wages to buy homes, cars, televisions, and other goods. When a country has a large middle class with significant spending power, the demand for products is substantial. The establishment of a basic safety net and the war on poverty under President Lyndon Johnson also supported consumer spending by those at the bottom of the income distribution. The growing consumer demand for products, coupled with Keynesian stabilization policy, provided a very profitable environment for business investment, fostering rapid economic growth.

Figure 24.1 shows how key macroeconomic variables changed since World War II in the United States. The 1950s and 1960s were the golden age of U.S. capitalism, with rapid growth in real GDP, low rates of unemployment, and low rates of inflation.

Real gross domestic product (real GDP) is **the total output of goods and services produced within an area in a given time period, corrected for changes in prices so that real GDP only measures actual changes in the amounts of goods and services produced**. Real GDP *growth* measures the percentage change in real GDP from one year to the next. Real GDP per capita is equal to **real GDP divided by the number of people in a country**. Real GDP per capita is one of the best measures of the standard of living for people in a particular country. *Growth* in real GDP per capita measures how much the standard of living of people in country increased per year, on average. The 1950s and 1960s were the decades in which the United States experienced the most rapid growth in real GDP per capita.

The unemployment rate is **the number of people actively seeking work but without a job divided by the labor force**. The labor force **is a measure of all people available for work, including all people working and all people who are unemployed and are actively seeking work**. The labor force participation rate measures **the percentage of the population working, self-employed, or unemployed divided by the number of people of working age who are eligible to work in a country**. As such, the labor force participation rate is a good measure of how many people are productively engaged in the economy, especially when combined with the unemployment rate. The unemployment rate stayed at relatively low levels and the labor force participation rate stayed high during the boom times of the 1950s and 1960s. Meanwhile, the inflation rate stayed quite low despite the booming economy.

The inflation rate is **the percentage increase in the average level of prices, such as the Consumer Price Index for urban consumers (CPI-U)**. Deflation can be destabilizing, as it was in the Great Depression, so it is to be avoided. However, high levels of inflation can also be problematic, undermining banks and those on fixed incomes. Thus, governments usually pursue price

Variable	1950s	1960s	1970s	1980s	1990s	2000s	2010s	2020
Real GDP growth	4.2	4.5	3.2	3.1	3.2	1.9	2.3	-3.4
Per capita GDP growth	2.5	3.1	2.1	2.2	2.0	1.0	1.6	-3.9
Unemployment	4.4	4.8	6.2	7.3	5.8	5.5	6.2	8.1
Labor force participation	59.3	59.2	61.8	64.8	66.7	66.2	63.3	61.7
Inflation	2.4	2.5	7.1	6.1	3.2	2.2	1.8	1.7

FIGURE 24.1 Table showing average annual rates (%) of key U.S. macroeconomic variables. Source: FRED.

stability, shooting for steady but low levels of inflation such as an inflation rate of 2% per year. The 1950s and 1960s were a wonderful time for the U.S. macro-economy, with high levels of growth and labor force participation, accompanied by low levels of unemployment and inflation. Of course, one of the problems with macroeconomic measures is that they obscure other issues. For example, the 1950s and 1960s were a sign of significant social unrest, featuring the civil rights movement, the Vietnam War protests, and the women's liberation movement, factors not captured by macroeconomic measures.

The period of Pax Americana was also very good for Western Europe, which rebuilt with assistance from the United States via the Marshall Plan. The United States gave $12 billion (an amount worth $100 billion in 2018 dollars) for reconstruction efforts. The United States also aided Japan and other Asian countries with reconstruction. This investment, along with the peace of the post-World War II era, the stability provided by Keynesian economic policy, and the increase in consumer spending from unionized workers, ushered in an era of rapid growth and prosperity for the United States, Europe, and Japan. Europe and Japan succeeded with social market economies that featured generous social welfare states, substantial investment in education and training, strong unions, and industrial policies designed to stimulate development in key sectors. Japan was particularly successful, with their real GDP per capita increasing by an astounding 9.11% per year in the 1960s.

Meanwhile, beginning in 1945, countries in Africa, Asia, and Latin America gained their independence from colonial powers, allowing them to control their own economic systems. Some were particularly successful, such as Botswana, a country that achieved rapid, sustained economic growth after it achieved independence from Great Britain. Botswana utilized newly discovered diamond deposits to invest in social welfare programs and economic development. Other countries were less successful, with the corrupting, extractive institutions of colonialism proving too tempting for new regimes to ignore. In many countries, new exploiters slipped into place following the exit of colonial exploiters. During the same period, the Soviet Union, Eastern European countries, China, and several smaller countries maintained centrally planned, state-dominated economic systems, many of which became increasingly rigid and dysfunctional over time.

Economic theory of this era was dominated by a moderate form of Keynesian economics, in which most governments undertook modest efforts to stabilize the economy. Meanwhile, a vibrant group of political economists advocated more extensive government ownership and control over markets, to better address problems such as poverty, inequality, and environmental devastation. And a growing group of Austrian and conservative mainstream economists began to challenge the Keynesian consensus. The idea that markets benefited from regulation, stabilization, and guidance was challenged with the advent of two global recessions from oil price shocks in the 1970s and the resulting stagflation, a problem that caused a major rethinking of economic theory and policy.

24.3 OPEC'S OIL SHOCKS AND THE BEGINNINGS OF NEOLIBERAL GLOBALIZATION, 1974–2000

Oil prices quadrupled in 1973 as the Organization of the Petroleum Exporting Countries (OPEC) slashed production and placed an embargo on selling oil to the United States due to U.S. support of Israel during the Arab–Israeli conflict. This exposed the Achilles heel of the U.S. economy: It was extremely dependent on imported oil to run factories and transport goods. The dramatic increase in oil prices caused businesses' costs to rise dramatically, undercutting their profitability and forcing them to lay off workers and raise prices at the same time. This generated stagflation, which occurs **when economic stagnation (declining production and worker layoffs) accompanies inflation**. As you can see in Figure 24.1, both unemployment and inflation jumped in the United States in the 1970s compared with previous decades.

Unfortunately, most mainstream Keynesian economists were confounded by how to address stagflation. Mainstream Keynesian policy of the time emphasized stimulating aggregate demand in recessions, via increased government spending, lower interest rates, or lower taxes. However, increased spending in an inflationary environment caused additional inflationary pressures. On the other hand, if policymakers targeted inflation, they could slash government spending, raise interest rates, or raise taxes, reducing spending and reducing inflationary pressures, but this would make stagnation worse, increasing unemployment. Thus, standard Keynesian economics could solve the stagnation problem or the inflation problem, but it could not solve both problems simultaneously. When oil prices doubled again at the end of the 1970s and sparked another bout of stagflation, the circumstances were ripe for a radical rethinking of economic policy.

The stagflation of the 1970s prompted a resurgence in laissez-faire ideas. Austrian and conservative mainstream economists proposed that the main problem in Western economies was too much government regulation, interference, and taxation. Three strains of conservative economics surged to the forefront of mainstream economics. Monetarists, under the guidance of Milton Friedman, suggested that government intervention was hopelessly inefficient and that economies would thrive under a minimum of regulation and intervention. New classical economists, including Robert Lucas, Jr. and Eugene Fama, argued that markets were inherently efficient due to the rational, optimizing behavior driving firms and individual actors, reaching a conclusion similar to that of monetarists that government regulation and intervention were intrusive and unnecessary.

Perhaps most important in terms of its influence on policymakers in the United States and the United Kingdom, Arthur Laffer and a group of extremely conservative economists developed the approach labeled supply-side economics. Supply-side economics refers to the belief that **the primary determinant of**

economic growth is the profitability of suppliers, including corporations and wealthy business owners. The best way to achieve profitability is therefore to eliminate regulations and to reduce taxes on corporations and the wealthy. In theory, such efforts would prompt corporations and the wealthy to invest additional funds in their businesses or to start new ones, stimulating economic growth and reversing the stagflation of the 1970s. This approach is often labeled **"trickle-down economics"** because tax cuts for the rich are supposed to lead to economic growth, which will (hopefully) create jobs and raise incomes for the poor, so tax cuts for the rich eventually trickle down to help the poor. Furthermore, Laffer argued that, in a high tax environment, cutting taxes would actually stimulate so much growth that *the tax cuts would pay for themselves.* Conservative politicians seized on this approach, which was extremely appealing because it implied that huge tax cuts for the rich would stoke economic growth but would not result in large government budget deficits.

Conservative economists also promoted the expansion of unregulated trade at the urging of certain U.S. corporations, so firms could obtain resources and labor at lower costs in other countries. In theory, this could also assist corporations by lowering their costs and restoring profitability, while opening up new markets abroad. Supply-side economists' faith in the efficiency and rapid adjustment of all markets meant they believed that workers who lost their jobs when some companies moved abroad would be quickly absorbed in growing sectors of the economy.

Another basic tenet of the supply-side approach was a reduction of the social safety net and attacks on labor unions. Supply-side economists believed that generous government benefits and labor unions undermined work efforts, productivity, and profitability.

Collectively, the package of policies was labeled neoliberalism. Neoliberalism refers to **contemporary ideas grounded in the classic, laissez-faire liberalism of Adam Smith. Market-oriented policy prescriptions include reducing trade barriers, deregulating financial markets, austerity (especially reductions in spending on the welfare state), deregulation, reduced taxation on the rich, and the privatization of government assets and functions**.

The United States and the United Kingdom entered another recession at the end of the 1970s driven by a second oil price shock generated by the Iranian Revolution of 1979, another event that disrupted oil supplies. This resulted in stagnation along with a high inflation rate that reached 14.8% in the United States. In response, Paul Volcker, the chairman of the Federal Reserve Bank of the United States (the Fed), increased interest rates to 20%, causing the economy to experience a steep decline. The Fed is the U.S. national bank, and it has the power to set interest rates, manipulate the money supply, and serve as the lender of last resort to failing banks. When the Fed increased interest rates to 20%, very few consumers were willing to buy houses and cars on credit, and very few businesses were willing to borrow to invest in new or expanded business ventures. Consumer spending and business investment spending plunged. Unemployment increased to over 10% as the economy entered a deep recession, but inflation finally began to fall. This series of events proved that *the Fed can eliminate substantial inflationary pressures but only by incurring a steep increase in unemployment*. This was a high price to pay, as millions lost jobs, devastating families and communities.

In this fraught environment, a message of tax cuts, deregulation, and unregulated trade was espoused by President Ronald Reagan in the United States and Prime Minister Margaret Thatcher in England, both of whom were elected as their countries faced a serious economic crisis. Beginning in 1979, Thatcher embarked on a radical restructuring of the U.K. economy. More than 80% of state-owned firms were privatized (sold to the private sector), including the national train system. The top tax rate on the wealthy was slashed from 83% to 40%, social programs were cut, and labor unions were attacked. The U.K. economy recovered from the recession, but inequality exploded and conditions for many workers deteriorated in the face of job and program cuts.

President Reagan undertook similar policies, cutting the tax rate on the richest individuals in the United States from 70% to 28% and working to undermine labor unions. Reagan also increased defense spending significantly as part of the cold war with the U.S.S.R., while cutting some social programs. The tax cuts and increased defense spending helped to end the deep recession of 1981–1982, along with lower interest rates and the rebounding of markets. As with Thatcher's approach, Reagan's policies affected people differently. The rich benefited significantly, but wages stayed stagnant for workers. U.S. economic growth in the 1980s was no better than in the 1970s but worse than the U.S. growth performance in the 1950s, 1960s, or 1990s. In addition, the national debt of the U.S. government quadrupled in the 1980s with the combination of increased defense spending and lower taxes. The supply-side tax cuts failed to pay for themselves.

The experience of high inflation during the 1970s made central banks such as the Fed wary of any signs of inflation. When inflation reached 6% at the end of the 1980s, the Fed once again increased interest rates dramatically, this time to 10%, to squeeze the economy and wring out inflation. High interest rates, slowing growth, and a crisis in the Middle East that led to the first Iraq war led to the recession of 1990–1991. It is important to note that both the recession of the early 1980s and the recession of 1990 were driven largely by tight monetary policy of the Fed, where they restricted the money supply to raise interest rates.

After a sluggish recovery, the rise of the internet and information technology in the late 1990s caused the U.S. economy to enter another boom. The rapid development of the internet caused companies to invest vast amounts of money in new technologies, including computing, fiber-optic cables, social media, and more. Huge numbers of start-ups grew rapidly as e-commerce and social media platforms developed for the first time.

Meanwhile, Presidents George H. W. Bush (a republican) and Bill Clinton (a democrat) continued to enact policies to deregulate markets, especially financial markets, and to reduce social programs. Bush negotiated the initial outlines of the

North American Free Trade Agreement with Canada and Mexico to dramatically reduce the tariffs between the neighboring countries, and Clinton signed the agreement into law. Clinton also signed a welfare reform bill that significantly slashed federal funding for the poorest Americans. Thus, Bush and Clinton largely continued Reagan's approach of deregulation, cuts to social programs, and the pursuit of unregulated trade. The U.S. economy in the 1980s and 1990s had been restructured so that the gains went to the richest Americans, whereas workers experienced stagnant wages.

The pursuit of unregulated trade and changes in the global economy began to devastate manufacturing communities in the United States and Western Europe in the 1970s. Manufacturing employment in the United States fell from 19 million in the 1970s to less than 13 million in the 2010s, driven by international competition, the movement of U.S. manufacturing jobs overseas, and the rise of increasingly sophisticated robotic technology that could replace workers. The U.S. Midwest suffered, including Detroit, Cleveland, Youngstown, Pittsburgh, Milwaukee, and Allentown, becoming the core of the "rust belt" of declining industrial cities. Poverty and unemployment in these communities increased. Fueled by worsening economic conditions and cuts to social programs, homelessness became a national disgrace beginning in the 1980s. The U.S. technology sector boomed with the growth of the internet and new information technologies, but manufacturing workers were unprepared for jobs in those sectors and most were unable to benefit from the tech boom. Some of these problems were tied to the rise of global competition in manufacturing.

24.4 THE RISE OF GLOBAL COMPETITORS TO THE UNITED STATES

Beginning in the 1970s, U.S. corporations faced increasing competition from international firms. By this time, Europe had recovered from World War II and European firms were globally competitive, especially in high-end manufacturing and luxury goods. Japan, South Korea, Taiwan, and Malaysia developed into industrial powerhouses, using protectionism and government support to develop from light industry (such as textiles) to heavy industry (steel, shipbuilding) to refined manufactured goods (computers, electronics, cars). Their rapid growth was facilitated by the U.S. push for less regulated trade, lower tariffs, and increasingly unregulated and open financial markets, policies that allowed financiers from all over the world to invest in emerging markets.

Figure 24.2 shows that average annual growth of real GDP per capita for a variety of regions and countries. If a country experiences rapid and sustained growth in real GDP per capita, then the economy is undergoing a tremendous economic transformation. An annual growth rate of 3% in real GDP per capita would mean that the average person is 34% better off after a decade. Japan's annual growth rate

Regions	1960s	1970s	1980s	1990s	2000s	2010s
European Union	4.21	3.07	2.04	1.94	1.29	1.37
East Asia & Pacific	6.27	2.73	3.42	2.44	3.45	3.99
Sub-Saharan Africa	1.59	1.57	-1.29	-0.77	2.47	0.87
Latin America & Caribbean	2.71	3.61	0.02	1.01	1.68	1.12
Central Europe and the Baltics				1.47	4.30	3.13
Middle East & North Africa	8.54	5.49	-3.00	2.1	2.27	1.32
South Asia (IDA & IBRD)	1.87	0.65	3.18	3.3	4.24	5.34
World	3.52	2.07	1.24	1.12	1.56	1.81
Country						
Japan	9.11	3.06	3.70	1.23	0.41	1.52
Korea, Republic of (South)	6.71	8.55	7.46	6.13	4.09	2.82
Botswana	5.41	11.77	7.48	2.72	1.56	3.30
China	1.23	5.27	8.17	8.76	9.68	7.25
Malaysia	3.55	5.55	3.11	4.53	2.69	3.93
India	1.77	0.59	3.34	3.74	4.6	5.79
Vietnam			2.23	5.59	5.62	5.15

FIGURE 24.2 Table showing average annual growth of real GDP per capita, 1961–2018.
Source: World Bank, World Development Indicators.

of 9.11% in the 1960s meant that Japanese incomes increased by 239%, more than doubling in a decade! Notice that East Asia and the Pacific, including Japan, South Korea, and Malaysia, experienced extraordinary growth in real GDP per capita in the 1960s, 1970s, and 1980s, with South Korea and Malaysia continuing to grow rapidly after that while Japan's growth slowed.

China also began to grow quickly after the death of Mao in 1978, when it began a series of dramatic reforms to move from command communism to a form of state capitalism. China began by building incentives into their central planning system, encouraging farmers and firms to increase productivity. Under Mao, farmers and firms were required to meet a production quota established by the state. They did not benefit from producing above their quota and could even end up worse off. Producing in excess of one's quota was dangerous, because the state might increase your quota the next year once you demonstrated the ability to produce a larger amount. After 1978, the Chinese state began to allow farmers and firms to sell goods they produced in excess of their state-mandated quota in newly created markets for a profit. This caused a dramatic increase in production, now that farms and firms had incentives to increase production above their government quota.

China also created special economic zones (SEZs) where firms could operate in an unregulated trade environment, sparking the development of a robust private sector. China then enticed foreign companies to these SEZs, offering them access to the vast and growing Chinese market along with low wages and government support, in exchange for a commitment from foreign firms to work with a Chinese partner and to transfer the latest technology to Chinese operations. Seeing vast potential in China, U.S. and European companies were happy to participate.

Another change in incentives came when the Chinese government began to be reward officials with bonuses and promotions when their regions experienced rapid economic growth, prompting a national focus on state-led economic development. As Figure 24.2 shows, China experienced the most rapid structural transformation in modern history, with unparalleled economic growth rates from the 1980s through the 2010s.

India followed China in becoming a rapidly growing emerging market after 1991. India was the most protected economy in the world in 1991, with an inefficient and intrusive bureaucracy. They embarked on a series of reforms to reduce tariffs, open markets, and improve government efficiency, just as the internet revolution was occurring. The combination of India's superb education system, excellent English language skills, and the new information technology revolution allowed India to become a global hub for call centers and computer services.

However, other countries were largely excluded from these shifts. Latin America and sub-Saharan Africa experienced growth in the 1960s and 1970s, but their growth in real GDP per capita was lower in the 1980s and 1990s. Most countries in these regions still depended on the export of primary products such as cocoa, coffee, copper, and other agricultural and mining products, and they were not able to move successfully into new industries. The commodity boom of the 2000s temporary sparked growth, but the 2010s saw Latin America and sub-Saharan Africa falling further behind the rest of the world as commodity prices declined.

With the opening of financial markets and the explosion of growth in Asia in the 1990s, vast sums of international money began to flow into Asia. Investors in developed countries wanted to cash in on the rapid growth that was generating huge returns in many Asian markets. Investors acted as if the good times could never end, funneling vast sums into increasingly questionable ventures. Banks loaned money to companies that were not performing well in Asian markets, and defaults began to pile up. Government support for banks and industries in many Asian countries masked growing problems. Eventually, investors realized their folly and started to pull their money out of Asian investments and markets. Panic ensued, causing bank failures and currency crashes in Thailand, Malaysia, Indonesia, South Korea, Singapore, Hong Kong, and Japan, and neighboring countries experienced smaller problems. This was the first warning sign that the deregulation of financial markets was resulting in unsustainable and destructive speculative behavior.

24.5 FINANCIALIZATION AND NEOLIBERAL GLOBALIZATION, 2000–2021

The tech boom of the 1990s prompted an internet stock bubble, called the dot-com bubble, to form late in the decade in the United States. As it became increasingly clear that the internet was the hot new business opportunity, money poured into new internet companies, and their stock prices exploded. From 1995 and 2000, the NASDAQ Composite Index of technology stocks rose 400%. Many companies saw their stock prices increase by 1000%–2000%. However, most of the companies that people were investing in were not profitable. Sparked by a recession in Japan and an increasing realization that many internet companies would never become profitable, a mass sell-off began in March of 2000. The huge loss of paper wealth caused consumers to panic, cutting spending on houses, cars, and other consumer goods. Business investment also plummeted, and the economy entered a recession. Further pessimism followed the terrorist attacks of September 11, 2001. By October of 2002, the 100 biggest companies on the NASDAQ stock index had lost 78% of their value. Numerous companies went bankrupt, and others laid off workers.

President George W. Bush, a republican and the son of President George H. W. Bush, used the recession of 2000–2001 to call for another round of tax cuts targeting investors and the wealthy. This indicated the ongoing influence of supply-side economic policy in the Republican Party. Stimulated by tax cuts, low interest rates, and the normal economic recovery process, the U.S. economy entered another period of economic growth beginning in 2003. However, the boom was to be short-lived.

As was noted above, beginning in the 1970s, the macroeconomics discipline shifted rapidly away from Keynesian economics. Supply-side economics, monetarism, and new classical economics, all strains of laissez-faire macroeconomics, gained traction. The election of conservative Presidents elevated the ideas of laissez-faire economists so that they came to influence government policy. One of the ideas used to drive policy changes was the efficient market hypothesis.

Developed by Eugene Fama, the efficient market hypothesis posited that **financial markets always incorporate all available information and function in an efficient manner, so asset prices (the prices of stocks, bonds, and derivatives) are always accurate and cannot form irrational bubbles**. Fama believed that the hypercompetitive nature of financial markets forced firms to be rational, calculating, and ruthlessly efficient.

Based on this theory, republican and democratic Presidents and Congresses systematically deregulated financial markets from the 1980s to the 2000s. What government officials and laissez-faire economists forgot were the lessons of history regarding the herd-like "animal spirits" of investors.

In the early 2000s, banks began making increasingly risky investments in derivatives. In financial markets, a derivative is **a financial security whose value is derived from an underlying asset or group of assets. Derivatives involve a contract between two or more economic actors, and the value of the derivative varies with the fluctuations in the value of the asset(s) underlying the derivative.** In many cases, a derivative is a bet between two parties, with one party betting that the value of the asset will fall and the other betting that the value of the asset will rise.

As we will see in more detail later, in the 2000s banks began issuing vast quantities of increasingly complex derivatives. For example, banks began giving large mortgages to increasingly risky "sub-prime" borrowers with bad credit ratings, including first-time homeowners and speculators lured by rapidly rising real estate prices in urban areas. Then, banks bundled millions of dollars of these risky mortgages into derivatives called collateralized mortgage obligations (CMOs), which they then sold to investors. Mortgages had historically been a very safe investment, and the derivatives were so complex that it was difficult to determine that they were risky, so investors snapped them up because of the high expected returns and their belief that mortgages would have low default rates. So much money was being made on sub-prime loans that by 2006 over 20% of all mortgages were being given to sub-prime borrowers, amounting to more than $600 billion in 2006 alone. This helped spark a large, rapid increase in the demand for homes and in home prices.

However, as one might expect, many of the high-risk, sub-prime borrowers began to default on their loans after a few years. Housing prices peaked and began to fall, causing housing speculators to default in increasing numbers. As mortgage defaults increased in number and magnitude, the derivatives on which those mortgages were based became worthless, causing the investors who purchased them to lose their investment. The crisis spun out of control, with homeowner defaults and a crash in the real estate market, followed by bankruptcies in large banks and insurance companies that had invested in housing market derivatives.

The result was the worst financial crisis since 1929. Once again, deregulated financial markets led to a speculative bubble and subsequent crash. The bank failures and the resulting crash in property values were devastating. The economy experienced the Great Recession from 2008 to 2010, which was the worst recession since the Great Depression of the 1930s.

Under President Barack Obama and a democratic Congress, a new set of financial regulations was passed to reign in banks' speculative behavior, and the government resumed Keynesian economic policy, spending large amounts to reduce the severity of the Great Recession and bail out failing banks. However, the financial crisis was so severe that economic growth remained sluggish for years after the official end of the recession. Slow growth and ongoing depressions in rust belt cities created conditions that Donald Trump was able to exploit to win the 2016 election, promising to return jobs to the United States from China, Mexico, and other countries. Trump engaged in a series of trade wars to attempt to promote U.S. exports, although these did not achieve a significant impact. Trump's other policies included traditional supply-side measures, such as huge tax cuts aimed at the very rich and corporations, and deregulation related to the environment, food, health, and safety. After a botched response to the COVID-19 pandemic of 2020, Trump was replaced by President Joe Biden, who reintroduced Keynesian stimulus policies and regulations.

Thus, the period from 2000 to 2022 found the United States lurching from supply-side tax cuts and deregulation under Bush to Keynesian-style regulation under

Obama, back to supply-side policies under Trump, and returning to Keynesian policies under Biden.

Looking back at the changes in economic policy since the Great Depression, we see Keynesian economic policy dominant until the 1970s. After that, supply-side economics became dominant in the United States and the United Kingdom, where its adherents focused on reducing businesses' costs by attacking unions, reducing regulations, and facilitating global trade, while cutting taxes for the wealthy and for businesses. Unfortunately, supply-side policies were not successful in rejuvenating economic growth in the United States. After rapid growth in the 1950s and 1960s, the United States experienced steadily declining growth in real GDP after 1970, as shown in Figure 24.3.

We will return to the debate over why economic growth in the United States slowed later in the book.

The previous several sections focused the long-term issue of economic growth, sketching out the gradual evolution of the U.S. macroeconomy and macroeconomic policy since the Great Depression. Another key issue in macroeconomics is the business cycle and what economic policies (if any) should be used to stabilize the business cycle.

24.6 MACROECONOMIC PATTERNS OF THE MODERN BUSINESS CYCLE

Economists have identified a set of macroeconomic patterns that characterize the business cycles of the mixed market economies of the world since the Great Depression. The patterns include the following key characteristics:

- The macroeconomy experiences regular business cycles, with strong growth periods followed by recessions (crises). The cycles occur approximately every 8–12 years. Economists often disagree on the causes of these regular crises and the actions that governments should take to stabilize economic systems in the face of a crisis.
- Most governments use expansionary fiscal policy (increasing government spending or decreasing taxes) and expansionary monetary policy (increasing the money supply and reducing interest rates) in recessions to stabilize the economy. This is a New Keynesian approach.
- Prices and wages tend to increase slightly during economic booms but stop increasing during recessions. However, in recent decades, increases in prices and wages have been quite limited in most developed economies even during economic booms.
- Unemployment increases dramatically in recessions and decreases during booms.

Figure 24.4 displays U.S. real GDP and potential real GDP, which is **the output of goods and services that would be produced if the economy were**

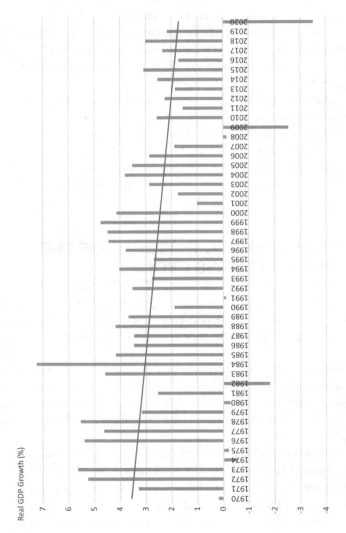

FIGURE 24.3 U.S. real GDP growth, 1970–2020.

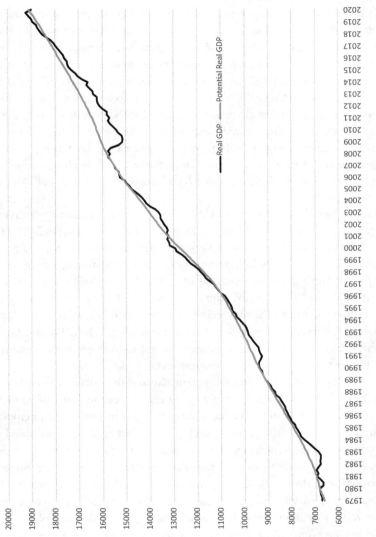

FIGURE 24.4 U.S. real GDP and potential real GDP, 1979–2019.

utilizing all of its productive resources, including all of its employable workers and all of its capital stock. To measure potential real GDP, economists estimate the general trend in real GDP, while smoothing out business cycle fluctuations. This allows economists to estimate how far above or below normal capacity the economy is at any given time. The gap between potential and real GDP can serve as a guide to macroeconomic policy.

If real GDP is below potential real GDP, the economy is operating at below capacity (a recession or a slowdown). In such cases, most economists believe that the government should undertake efforts to stimulate economic growth, including increased government spending, decreased taxes, or decreased interest rates. If real GDP is above potential real GDP, the economy is overheated, which is likely to result in inflation and/or a bubble that could lead to a crash in asset values. In an overheated economy, most economists believe that the government should attempt to slow down economic growth and reduce asset prices, which it can achieve by reducing government spending, increasing taxes, or increasing interest rates. The goal in an overheated economy is to achieve a "soft landing," gently slowing down the economy to eliminate inflationary pressures and asset bubbles to avoid a recession.

Figure 24.4 shows us that the U.S. economy grew significantly in recent decades, from a real GDP of $6742 billion in 1979 to $19,254 billion in 2019. However, it also shows that the U.S. economy regularly falls into recessions, when real GDP falls below potential real GDP, indicating that a significant number of workers are unemployed and capital resources lie idle. The United States experienced recessions in 1980 and 1982 (a double-dip recession), 1990, 2000, 2008, and 2020. After each of these recessions, the U.S. economy stayed well below its capacity, potential real GDP, for several years before finally recovering. Thus, Figure 24.4 depicts two essential characteristics of a modern, mixed market economic system: Steady growth over time, with regular recessions every 8–12 years.

Figure 24.5 shows the unemployment rate and the inflation rate in the United States from 1979 to 2020. Notice that when a recession hits, we tend to see a decrease in the rate of inflation and a sharp increase in the rate of unemployment. Unemployment then falls as the economy grows out of the recession and starts to boom, while inflation increases. The pattern repeats itself with the next recession.

A key question that emerges from these patterns is what, if anything, should the government do to address the fluctuations in the business cycle? There are four primary approaches to macroeconomic policy with respect to business cycles: Laissez-faire (noninterventionist), supply-side (trickle-down), New Keynesian (moderate intervention), and political economy (intensely interventionist, especially in recessions).

According to the **laissez–faire approach**, advocated by most monetarist, new classical, and Austrian economists, the government should not intervene significantly in the macroeconomy, even in recessions. To these economists, government intervention is too cumbersome and inept to successfully manage the economy.

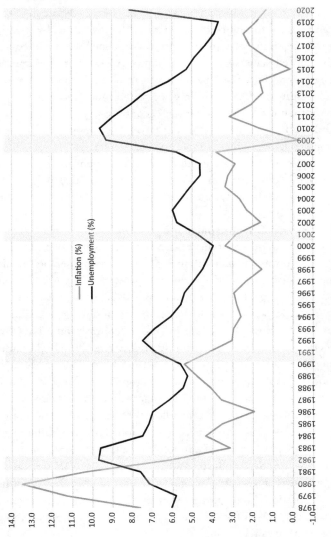

FIGURE 24.5 Unemployment rate (%) and rate of inflation (CPI-U, %), 1979–2020.

Furthermore, they oppose increased government borrowing to finance spending projects in recessions, worrying that government borrowing will displace or "crowd out" private sector investment, taking money from banks that would normally be used by the private sector.

The laissez-faire approach has had limited impact on policies in recessions in the United States. However, the European Union government and central bank subscribed to a laissez-faire approach early on in the Great Recession. They refused to take substantial steps to reduce the severity of the downturn by spending additional money and injecting new money into the financial sector. In contrast, from 2008-2010 the United States spent additional money on government projects, lowered interest rates, and purchased bad debts from banks in order to stimulate the economy. As a result, the U.S. economy recovered much more quickly from the Great Recession than the European Union's economy.

The **supply-side approach** advocates government policies to benefit suppliers in recessions to stabilize the economy. In particular, bailouts for failing businesses, low interest rates, and tax cuts for corporations and wealthy business owners are favored policies from this conservative perspective. Such policies were proposed by the George W. Bush administration in 2001 and 2008 and by the Trump administration in 2020.

The **New Keynesian approach** is advocated by most mainstream economists.[1] In recessions, these economists advocate increasing government spending and lowering taxes, both of which will increase government deficits but also stimulate economic growth. Ideally, the economic growth will spark a boom during which deficits can be repaid. New Keynesians also advocate cutting interest rates and injecting financial capital into the banking system during recessions to stimulate lending and borrowing. Meanwhile, during economic booms, New Keynesians advocate reductions in government spending, higher taxes, and higher interest rates if the economy starts to grow too quickly (e.g., if it becomes overheated and starts to form a bubble that might burst). *The U.S. government has followed a Keynesian approach in every recent recession*, working to enact stimulus programs such as lower taxes, increased spending, extended unemployment benefits, and decreased interest rates whenever the economy experienced a recession. The main difference between the New Keynesian approach and the supply-side approach is the focus of the programs. New Keynesians prefer policies and tax cuts to benefit workers and communities and to stimulate aggregate demand, whereas supply-side economists target the wealthy, corporations, and aggregate supply. The Biden administration took a New Keynesian approach in the United States in 2021 to cope with the lingering effects of the coronavirus recession.

Some economists think that the U.S. government usually does not go far enough in recessions. The **political economy approach** includes progressive and radical political economists (and a few liberal mainstream economists) who want the government to intervene more extensively. From this perspective, the capitalist economic system is inherently unstable and structured to benefit capitalists over workers. Only via active, widespread stabilization policy on behalf of workers can unemployment be minimized and growth stimulated. From this perspective, substantial government investment in infrastructure, employment, and new industrial development, such as the Green New Deal proposal to create new, environmentally friendly technologies and industries, is required to create a stable macroeconomy that benefits workers.

What we find, therefore, is that most economists agree on the necessity for Keynesian intervention in recessions, with the exception of a few far-right, laissez-faire economists. What economists usually debate is the extent of the Keynesian intervention that should take place, with conservative mainstream economists preferring the smallest possible intervention; supply-side and New Keynesian (moderate) economists preferring more interventionist actions, albeit with a different focus; and political economists preferring extensive government action on behalf of workers and the poor. We see similar divisions in the area of sustainability.

24.7 SUSTAINABILITY AND MACROECONOMICS

Sustainability refers to **the ability of an economic system to sustain itself over time by meeting its current needs without compromising its future. Sustainability has three primary dimensions, environmental, social, and financial**.

Environmental sustainability refers to the need for an economic system to preserve its environmental services, including sources and sinks, sufficiently for future generations. If an economy grows rapidly but destroys its environmental services in the process, future growth will be more difficult. The economic system will need to devote increasing amounts of investment toward correcting environmental devastation and finding alternatives to spent resources.

With climate change and an increasingly interlocked global economy, environmental sustainability has a global character. If one country reduces its carbon emissions but other countries increase theirs, then the country reducing its carbon emissions will still experience the problems associated with increasing carbon emissions globally, including global warming, ocean acidification, heat waves, and more. It is crucial in the modern world for environmental sustainability to be attacked globally rather than nationally, making global climate agreements extremely important in the current era.

A small number of far-right economists oppose efforts to reduce carbon emissions and to establish environmental regulations. Most conservative economists (laissez-faire and supply-side) believe that the government should make modest efforts to promote environmental sustainability utilizing market-based methods such as carbon taxes and subsidies for alternative energy. New Keynesian economists advocate more extensive regulations and a more elaborate system of taxes and subsidies to promote sustainability, in keeping with the mixed market-state approach. Political economists argue that capitalism is inherently unsustainable, because it promotes profit accumulation and economic growth to the exclusion of environmental preservation. From this state-centered perspective, extensive government intervention is warranted to severely constrain market activity or to promote public enterprises with a goal of sustainability.

Social sustainability refers to the importance of an economic system providing an acceptable standard of living to its entire population. Extremely unequal economic systems are prone to instability, and even revolution. Two of the market failures most commonly associated with unregulated capitalism are inequality and poverty. Therefore, most countries devote substantial resources to a safety net that protects the most vulnerable members of society to ensure that people do not become desperate. Similarly, economic systems need to be fair and to provide everyone with sufficient opportunities. Otherwise, resentment and desperation can lead to a social breakdown, with crime, homelessness, and pressures for radical change becoming more prevalent.

Laissez-faire and supply-side economists tend to believe that unregulated markets generate the most opportunities and the most robust economic growth and that most inequality is a product of poor choices of individuals. Therefore, they tend to oppose extensive safety nets, other than a modest minimum income guarantee, suggested by Friedrich Hayek to make sure that poverty and deprivation do not become too extreme. New Keynesian economists believe that a safety net is extremely important and that the government should work actively to reduce inequality and poverty. From their perspective, markets tend to be biased toward those with wealth and connections, and such imperfections need to be corrected by government policy. Political economists want to go much further, arguing that capitalist economies systematically exploit workers and leave many destitute, requiring extensive government intervention and job creation to create social stability.

Lastly, financial sustainability is important to an economic system. Financial sustainability requires an economic system to maintain manageable levels of debt in the public sector and the private sector. Growing public sector debt can become a drag on an economic system, with payments on the debt consuming an ever-increasing portion of real GDP. Growing private sector debt can make companies and individuals prone to bankruptcy, exacerbating economic crises. And debt to foreign countries can be particularly problematic if a country encounters an economic crisis.

For example, Turkey borrowed extensively from foreign banks in foreign currencies to fund construction projects under the rule of Recep Tayyip Erdoğan. Many of these were excessive and wasteful, such as the 1150-room Presidential Palace, so the economic impact was short-lived. Turkey's steadily increasing foreign debts caused the Turkish lira to lose significant value. In 2005, one U.S. dollar exchanged for 1.34 Turkish lira in international currency markets. In 2021, one U.S. dollar exchanged for 7.33 Turkish lira. By 2021 the Turkish lira was worth only 18% of what it was in 2005. This meant that money Turkey borrowed in 2005 from U.S. banks required 547% more Turkish lira to repay, placing a huge burden on the Turkish economy and contributing to the formation of a recession.

Note, however, that debt can facilitate economic growth if the money is invested wisely. If governments invest funds in growth-generating projects, such as education, infrastructure, and research and development, this sparks economic growth in the future and pays for itself over time. Governments that use their own currency to make wise investments, without incurring foreign debt, often generate better economic growth than governments that do not do so.

As with other areas, economists differ in how they approach financial sustainability. Laissez-faire conservatives tend to oppose government deficit spending, preferring to leave investment to the private sector. Supply-side conservatives do not mind government deficits for tax cuts for the wealthy, believing that this will generate enough growth to offset the tax cuts. New Keynesians tend to believe that the government is safe engaging in deficit spending in recessions and to invest in growth-generating projects, as long as the budget deficit remains a steady proportion of real GDP. They do not want the debt burden to increase over time. Political economists, on the other hand, are less concerned with government deficits and more concerned with the welfare of workers. They believe that spending money on those at the bottom stimulates aggregate demand, which stimulates economic growth. Therefore, political economists see deficit spending as one of the major sources of economic growth and prosperity. We will investigate all of these perspectives in more detail later.

24.8 CONCLUSION: THE STATE OF MODERN MACROECONOMICS

This chapter introduced the issues that are the primary focus of study for macroeconomists: economic growth, well-being, stability, and sustainability. Economists studying these issues tend to fall into four perspectives: laissez-faire, supply-side, New Keynesian, and political economy. Laissez-faire economists prefer the least possible government intervention in the macroeconomy. Supply-side economists also prefer deregulation of markets, but they are comfortable utilizing government on behalf of business and the wealthy. New Keynesian economists believe that markets usually function efficiently but that they need some government intervention when markets fail, such as in recessions. Political economists argue that markets are inherently unstable and unequal and can only function on behalf of all citizens with substantial state guidance, regulation, and direction.

Macroeconomic theory changed substantially during the last century. Prior to the Great Depression, most mainstream economists believed that capitalist economic systems were inherently efficient and would eliminate any downturn in short order, based on their belief in Say's law, an economic theory that supply creates demand. The Great Depression ushered in the ideas of John Maynard Keynes, whose research demonstrated that business investment and consumer spending are extremely volatile and cause large swings in economic output. At the same time, wages and prices are sticky and do not adjust quickly in recessions, and lower wages and prices (deflation) turns out to be very bad for the economy, undermining consumer spending and business profits. Thus, to Keynes economies tend to be unstable and prone to regular recessions, but the government can end recessions with appropriate macroeconomic policy, including increases in government spending, decreased taxes, decreased interest rates, and injecting liquidity into the banking system.

Keynesian views dominated the economics profession from the 1940s until the 1970s, the period during which the United States dominated the global economy. However, stagflation in the 1970s caused a rethinking of economic views and prompted the ascendency of laissez-faire and supply-side views. Supply-side economics became particularly powerful due to its links with conservative republican politicians beginning with Ronald Reagan. The United States and other countries such as the United Kingdom embarked on a macroeconomic approach that emphasized lowering tariffs, deregulating trade and industrial development, and cutting taxes for the wealthy and for large corporations. Meanwhile, the U.S. Federal Reserve raised interest rates dramatically in the early and late 1980s, successfully reducing inflationary pressures but causing recessions and high unemployment in the process.

Global competition to U.S. manufacturing increased substantially beginning in the 1970s, especially from Japan, followed by South Korea and the Asian tigers, and more recently by China and India. Deregulation of trade allowed U.S. corporations to move abroad, and many did so to take advantage of low wages and lax regulations. Deregulation of financial markets allowed banks and individuals to invest in increasingly risky and obtuse assets, such as derivatives, sparking a series of speculative bubbles resulting in the Asian Financial Crisis, the dot.com bubble and the sub-prime mortgage bubble. Supply-side economic policies were reversed somewhat under President Obama in the United States, they were reinstated under President Trump, and then they were reversed again under President Biden.

Throughout the recent history of the United States, its economy experienced regular recessions, usually every 8–12 years. Most economists advocate government intervention to reduce the severity of recessions, a New Keynesian approach. Some conservative economists prefer a laissez-faire approach with limited or no government intervention in recessions. In contrast, conservative, supply-side economists advocate bailouts of businesses and tax cuts in recessions, an approach that would result in large government budget deficits. Meanwhile, political economists prefer extensive government intervention to benefit workers and the poor during recessions and are comfortable with large government budget deficits from such programs.

There are similar divisions with respect to how economists view sustainability. Political economists see the need for substantial government efforts to address sustainability, New Keynesian economists want some intervention, and conservative laissez-faire and supply-side economists prefer less intervention.

Interestingly, one of the topics economists debate extensively is how we should measure the health of the macroeconomy. Since the Great Depression, most economists tended to focus on the growth of real GDP as the best measure of the health of an economic system. However, as we will see in the next chapter, real GDP does not adequately capture many aspects of well-being, so modern economists are developing a new set of measures to reflect more accurately how the macroeconomy functions in all of its multifaceted elements.

QUESTIONS FOR REVIEW

1. List the key goals economists have identified for a macroeconomic system. Which do you think is most important? Why?
2. How did Keynes demonstrate that Say's law would not hold in recessions and that the market would not self-correct?
3. Describe the evolution of post-World War II macroeconomic thinking as it relates to changes in global economies. What ideas dominated during Pax Americana? How did these ideas change with the advent of stagflation and the beginnings of neoliberal globalization? What did economists learn from the Asian financial crisis, the dot.com bubble, and the sub-prime housing bubble?
4. Define each of the following economic concepts in your own words and briefly explain why the concept is important.
   a. Real GDP.
   b. Real GDP per capita.
   c. Unemployment rate.
   d. Labor force participation rate.
   e. Inflation rate.
5. What is stagflation, and why did it prove to be difficult for mainstream Keynesian economists to cope with in the 1970s?
6. Describe the efficient market hypothesis in your own words. How did this hypothesis contribute to policies to deregulate financial markets? What were some of the results of the deregulation of financial markets?
7. What are the major patterns economists have identified in the modern business cycle?
8. Describe the different approaches to macroeconomic policy with respect to business cycles. Which approach do you find most compelling? Why?
9. Describe the different dimensions of sustainability and explain why each dimension is important.

NOTE

1 There is a debate among economists over the ideas of John Maynard Keynes. Mainstream economists who combine the ideas of Keynes with the marginal analysis of neoclassical economic theory call themselves "New Keynesians." This reflects the fact that they use some Keynesian ideas, especially stabilization policy, while using different economic methods than those Keynes used. Meanwhile, political economists, especially those from the post-Keynesian perspective, believe themselves to be the true intellectual heirs to Keynes, utilizing his ideas on macroeconomics using different models and methods. Instead of seeing investors as rational and financial markets as efficient, as implied by neoclassical models, political economists argue that investors are affected by animal spirits and financial markets are subject to wild speculative swings.

Macro-economic well-being

Measuring and describing the macroeconomy

This chapter addresses a fundamental economic question: What should the goals of an economic system be? Following immediately upon that topic, economists want to know: How can we best determine if we are successfully meeting our goals?

Establishing the goals of an economic system involves ethical considerations. For example, is a successful economic system one that maximizes the production of goods and services or one that makes sure that every person has the necessities of life and opportunities for meaningful work? Should a country maximize income, or should it pursue sustainable growth, even if that means sacrificing some income? Should citizens work long hours to maximize production, or should the government ensure that everyone has ample vacation time and a reasonable work–life balance? All of these issues come into play when an economic system establishes the goals it will pursue and the measures it will use to determine the successes or failures of that economic system.

A country's response to such ethical considerations tends to be influenced substantially by culture and values. Countries with cooperative cultures, such as the Nordic countries of Europe, tend to emphasize work–life balance as well as providing meaningful work and necessities to all citizens. Individualistic cultures such as those in the United States and the United Kingdom tend to prioritize the option of individuals to use their money as they see fit over the provision of necessities to all citizens.

In addition, there are political considerations in determining the range of feasible alternatives. Groups wielding the most political and economic power are often able to determine the goals of an economic system even when those goals diverge from the interests of the broader population. Economic systems display hegemony **when a particular group exerts undue influence within a society**. Such

DOI: 10.4324/9781315636924-32

systems are called a plutocracy if **the group that dominates the economic system is the wealthiest members of society**. Such systems contrast with well-functioning democracies where each citizen plays a role in determining the priorities of the economic system.

This chapter lays out the different goals that a variety of economists have put forward as their definition of what economic well-being looks like. We begin defining real GDP, how it is computed based on its components, and its relationship with nominal GDP and the GDP deflator. We take up some definitions of national income accounting, so you can better understand how national income (real GDP) is determined and what it shows us. We also note that although real GDP was used historically as the standard barometer of economic success, it has some substantial deficiencies as a measure of economic welfare.

Next, we discuss alternative measures that economists use to determine economic well-being. Some economists and politicians favor a focus on happiness, life satisfaction, environmental sustainability, human development, income, or a combination of all of these factors. Economists developed a variety of measures to reflect these different values, including the genuine progress indicator, the Human Development Index, and the World Happiness Index. The most comprehensive measure, the OECD Better Life Index, incorporates real GDP, environmental quality, human development, *and* life satisfaction.

25.0 CHAPTER 25 LEARNING GOALS

After reading this chapter, you should be able to:

■ Explain and demonstrate how real GDP is constructed and how it is related to nominal GDP and the price index (GDP deflator).

■ Describe the circular flow model of the economy, including the expenditure side and the income side, as well as all of the leakages and injections in the model.

■ Relate the three different ways in which GDP can be computed using the expenditure, value added, or income approach and how GDP is related to other measures of national income such as gross national product.

■ Analyze the limitations of real GDP as a measure of well-being.

■ Explain how the Better Life Index, the genuine progress indicator, and the World Happiness Index are constructed and evaluate their effectiveness relative to real GDP in measuring human economic well-being.

25.1 NOMINAL GDP, REAL GDP, AND THE GDP DEFLATOR

To understand what real GDP actually measures, we need start by discussing how real GDP is constructed. The determination of real GDP begins by first measuring nominal GDP.

Nominal GDP is **the value of all final goods and services produced in a particular place at current prices**. Nominal GDP measures the **total revenue of an entire country or region**. In mathematical terms, nominal GDP is computed by multiplying the price and the quantity sold of every *final* good or service produced in a particular time period.

Final goods are those products sold directly to consumers, whereas *intermediate* goods are the inputs that go into making final goods. The value of intermediate goods is already included in the price of final goods, so we do not include intermediate goods in GDP to avoid double counting. For example, the price of a car, a final good, already includes the value of the steel, aluminum, and other intermediate goods used as inputs in the car manufacturing process. Therefore, when computing total production in an economy, we use the prices and quantities of the cars sold but not the prices and quantities of the steel and other inputs that go into the car.

The nominal GDP of the United States in 2019 was determined by multiplying the price of every final good or service in 2019 by the quantity of that good or service sold in 2019:

$$\text{Nominal GDP}^{2019} = P_a^{19}Q_a^{19} + P_b^{19}Q_b^{19} + P_c^{19}Q_c^{19} + \ldots + P_z^{19}Q_z^{19}.$$

The price of good a in 2019 (P_a^{19}) is multiplied by the quantity of good a produced and sold in 2019 (Q_a^{19}) and so on. In 2019, nominal GDP for the United States was $21,428 billion.

Nominal GDP has limitations when it comes to measuring the productivity of an economy because it includes both prices and quantities. If prices increase by 10% but quantities stay the same, nominal GDP increases by 10% even though quantities have not changed. Thus, nominal GDP can increase when prices go up or when quantities go up.

To correct for this, economists compute real GDP, which is **the total output of final goods and services holding prices constant**. Economists pick a stable base year, such as 2012, when the economy was not experiencing a boom or a recession. To find the real GDP in 2019, economists multiply *prices* of goods and services in the base year (2012) by the *quantities* of goods and services produced in the year we are studying (2019).

$$\text{Real GDP}^{2019} = P_a^{12}Q_a^{19} + P_b^{12}Q_b^{19} + P_c^{12}Q_c^{19} + \ldots + P_z^{12}Q_z^{19}.$$

The price of good a in 2012 (P_a^{12}) is multiplied by the quantity of good a produced and sold in 2019 (Q_a^{19}) and so on. In 2019, real GDP for the United States was $19,073 billion.

Nominal GDP and real GDP use the same quantities of goods and services sold but different prices. Therefore, if we divide nominal GDP by real GDP, we get a ratio of prices:

$$\frac{\text{Nominal GDP}^{2019}}{\text{Real GDP}^{2019}} = \frac{\$21,428\,\text{b.}}{\$19,073\,\text{b.}} = 112.3(\%) = \frac{\text{Prices in 2019}}{\text{Prices in 2012}}$$

$$= \text{GDP Deflator}\left(P_{\text{GDPD}}\right).$$

The **ratio of prices in the particular year to prices in the base year** is called the GDP deflator (P_{GDPD}). The GDP deflator is the price index for all final goods in the economy. The GDP deflator for 2019 was 112.3 in percentage terms, indicating that prices in 2019 were 12.3% higher than they were in 2012 (the base year when the GDP deflator is 100).

P_{GDPD} is called a "deflator" because it can be used to deflate the value of nominal GDP to get real GDP. If we take nominal GDP and divide by the GDP deflator, we get real GDP, which is GDP without inflation.

$$\frac{\text{Nominal GDP}^{2019}}{P_{\text{GDPD}}^{2019}} = \text{Real GDP}^{2019}.$$

Figure 25.1 shows nominal GDP, real GDP, and the GDP deflator for the United States from 2000 to 2019. There are several important things to notice about this table. First, the GDP deflator increases steadily over time, which shows that the U.S. economy experiences inflation. Second, notice that nominal GDP increases more rapidly than real GDP over time. This is because in most years, both prices and quantities increase in the United States and nominal GDP goes up by the amount prices *and* quantities increase. Real GDP only goes up by the amount quantities increase, thereby concentrating on how much actual production of goods and services is increasing. Third, the GDP deflator is equal to 100% in the base year. In earlier years when prices are lower, the GDP deflator is below 100%. After the base year, the GDP deflator is above 100% because prices were higher in subsequent years. Fourth, nominal GDP is always equal to real GDP in the base year, because we are using the same prices and the same quantities for both measures.

Figure 25.2 plots U.S. nominal and real GDP on a graph so you can see these relationships clearly. Real GDP increases only when the production of goods and services increases, whereas nominal GDP increases whenever prices or the production of goods and services increase. Therefore, real GDP increases more slowly than nominal GDP.

Year	Nominal GDP	Real GDP	GDP deflator $(P_{GDPD, \%})$
2000	10252	13131	78.1
2001	10582	13262	79.8
2002	10936	13493	81.1
2003	11458	13879	82.6
2004	12214	14406	84.8
2005	13037	14913	87.4
2006	13815	15338	90.1
2007	14452	15626	92.5
2008	14713	15605	94.3
2009	14449	15209	95.0
2010	14992	15599	96.1
2011	15543	15841	98.1
2012	16197	16197	100.0
2013	16785	16495	101.8
2014	17527	16912	103.6
2015	18225	17404	104.7
2016	18715	17689	105.8
2017	19519	18108	107.8
2018	20580	18638	110.4
2019	21428	19073	112.3
2020	20933	18423	113.6

FIGURE 25.1 Table showing U.S. nominal GDP, real GDP, and the GDP deflator, 2000–2020.

Source: Federal Reserve Economic Data (FRED).

Real GDP measures national production of goods and services at constant prices and, as such, it is a good indicator of a nation's standard of living as a whole. Increases in real GDP generated by economic growth improve the standard of living of a nation. Interestingly, real GDP is equal to national income as well as national expenditure, as we can see in the circular flow model.

25.2 THE CIRCULAR FLOW MODEL OF THE MACROECONOMY

Figure 25.3 displays the circular flow model of the macroeconomy, which explains why total income for an economy is the same as total expenditure. Let's begin with the business sector. In a capitalist economic system, businesses produce goods and services, which they sell in goods markets. The sell consumer goods to households, which is classified as consumer purchases (C). Businesses sell machinery, equipment, and other capital goods to other businesses, which is called investment purchases (I). Businesses sell goods and services to the government (G), which purchases military services, buildings and building materials, and much more. Businesses also sell goods to citizens in foreign countries, which is defined as export purchases (X). And domestic businesses lose out on sales when consumers engage in import purchases (Im), buying goods from businesses located in foreign countries.

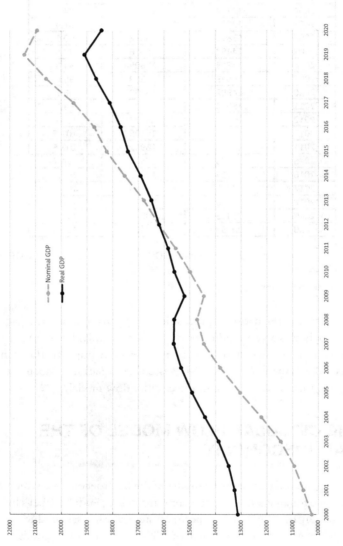

FIGURE 25.2 U.S. nominal GDP and real GDP (billions of U.S. dollars), 2000–2020.

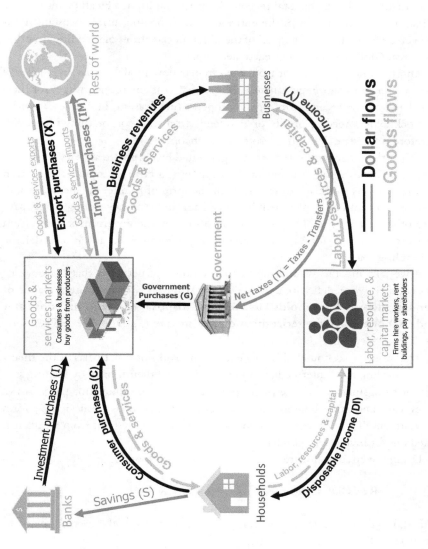

FIGURE 25.3 The circular flow model of the economy.

Adding up all purchases of goods and services in an economy, we get aggregate demand (AD). In mathematical terms,

$$AD = C + I + G + X - Im.$$

Recall that real GDP is the total revenue (all prices multiplied by all quantities) for all final goods and services in the entire economy, holding prices constant. Real GDP can be found by adding up all of the different categories of spending. In other words, real GDP is equal to aggregate demand.

Another important insight from the circular flow model is that *every dollar of income a business receives becomes income for someone*. Workers receive wages for their labor. Landowners receive rent for the property they lease to businesses. Owners and stockholders receive profits or dividends from the corporations they own. Therefore, aggregate demand is also equal to income (Y).

What, then, happens to the income generated by corporate activity? First, the government takes some of it out of the economy in taxes. A significant portion of tax revenues is paid back to taxpayers in the form of transfer payments, such as Social Security and unemployment benefits that transfer money from some taxpayers to others. Net taxes (T) is the amount of money the government keeps from taxpayers in order to fund other government programs, such as national defense and building roads.

If we take income, Y, and subtract the amount of net taxes that the government takes, T, we are left with disposable income (DI), which is **the amount of after-tax income households have at their disposal to spend on consumer goods (C) or to save for retirement or a rainy day (S)**: $DI = C + S$. Therefore, $Y = DI + T = C + S + T$.

The money that households save ends up in banks or other parts of the financial system. Financial intermediaries like banks make their money by loaning savings out to businesses for investment purchases or to consumers for purchases of homes, cars, and other household durable goods, which is also considered a form of investment. Thus, money saved goes into the banking system, from where it is loaned out for investment purchases.

Using the circular flow model, you can see the following:

$$\text{Real GDP} = \text{Income}(Y) = C + I + G + X - IM = DI + T.$$

Real GDP is equal to total income for the entire economy, and it is equal to aggregate demand for the entire economy.

If we substitute $DI = C + S$ into the above equation, we get

$$C + I + G + X - IM = C + S + T.$$

Rearranging that equation by subtracting C and adding IM to both sides, we get the important equation:

$$I + G + X = S + T + IM$$

$$\text{Injections} = \text{Leakages.}$$

Injections are purchases other than consumption that inject money into the economy. Leakages are flows of money that leak out of the economy, heading to banks, government, and other countries. When the economy is operating normally, all money that leaks out of the economy in the form of savings, taxes, and imports is injected back into the economy in the form of investment purchases, government purchases, and export purchases. As we will see later, when injections fall below leakages, the economy may be headed for a recession.

25.3 MEASURES OF NATIONAL INCOME

As noted above, national income can be measured either by total expenditures on goods and services (aggregate demand) or by total income. Figure 25.4 shows the values of consumption, investment, government spending, exports, and imports in early 2020 (before the recession hit).

Recalling that each dollar that businesses receive from expenditures becomes income for someone, we can also look at the income/cost side of U.S. nominal GDP. The costs businesses incur include compensation for employees (wages, salaries, and benefits), profits (which go to owners of corporations and small businesses), rent, interest and dividend payments, depreciation (wearing out of capital stock), production taxes, and other miscellaneous costs.[1]

Figure 25.5(a) shows how national income in the United States is divided between wages, small business owners' income (proprietors), corporate profits, income for lenders and investors in the form of interest and dividends, the amount of business income taken directly by government taxes, and depreciation (the

Personal consumption expenditures (C)	14584.9
Gross private domestic investment (I)	3626.3
Government expenditures (G)	3850.7
Exports (X)	2421.7
Imports (Im)	2947.8
Nominal gross domestic product (NGDP)	21534.9

FIGURE 25.4 Table showing U.S. nominal GDP, by component of aggregate demand, 2020.

Source: Federal Reserve Economic Data, Table 1.15.

(a) National income by type of income

Employee compensation	11,586.90
Proprietors' income	1,702.10
Rental income	797.70
Corporate profits	1,835.60
Net interest & dividends	642.70
Production & import taxes	1,612.70
Depreciation	2,220.40
Statistical discrepancy & miscellaneous	1,136.80
Gross domestic product	21,534.90

FIGURE 25.5 (a) Table showing national income by type of income.

(b) Gross value added by sector

Business	16325.9
Households and nonprofits	2743.4
General government	2465.6
Gross domestic product	21534.9

FIGURE 25.5 (b) Table showing gross value added by sector.

amount of business income lost due to the depreciation of capital stock). There is also a category for miscellaneous income and statistical discrepancies.

Last, we can also determine the income of each business by computing its value added, which is the value of what the business sells minus the value of all of the intermediate goods (inputs) it buys from other businesses. For example, in 2016, the parts in an Apple iPhone 7 cost $219.80. These intermediate goods included the display, transmitter, processor, glue, batteries, etc. The iPhone 7 sold for $649; thus, the value added was $429.20. This is the amount of money generated in the production of the iPhone. Of the value added, $5 went to compensate the workers who built the iPhone 7, leaving the remainder for Apple's profits.[2]

Thus, a business's value added is equal to the wages and profits generated by its productive activities. In addition to value added by businesses, households, nonprofits, and governments generate value added when they provide goods and services and sell them for more than the cost of intermediate goods. Figure 25.5(b) shows value added by businesses, households, nonprofits, and government.

One important insight to take away from this analysis is that *GDP can be measured in three ways*. GDP = total value added = total income = total expenditure (*AD*). All three methods give us the total economic output of the economy.

Up to this point, we have focused on GDP as the most important measure of an economy's production. We can also look at other aggregate measures to gather data on a variety of macroeconomic topics. Figure 25.6 shows other breakdowns of national income.

Domestic product and income	2019	2020*
Gross domestic product (GDP)	**21,427.69**	**21,534.91**
PLUS: Income receipts from the rest of the world	1,158.83	1,063.50
LESS: Income payments to the rest of the world	863.30	811.33
EQUALS: Gross national product (GNP)	**21,723.21**	**21,787.08**
LESS: Consumption of fixed capital	3,462.96	3,551.95
EQUALS: Net national product (NNP)	**18,260.26**	**18,235.13**
Statistical discrepancy	98.22	52.12
EQUALS: National income (NI)	**18,162.04**	**18,183.01**
LESS: Corporate profits with inventory valuation & capital consumption adjustments	2,074.64	1,835.61
Taxes on production and imports less subsides	1,420.06	1,460.85
Contributions for government social insurance, domestic	1,420.37	1,449.33
Net interest and misc. payments on assets (dividends)	644.95	642.72
Business current transfer payments (net)	170.73	175.71
Current surplus of government enterprises	-12.18	-18.57
PLUS: Personal income receipts on assets	2,992.89	3,013.94
Personal current transfer receipts	3,171.94	3,298.47
EQUALS: Personal income (PI)	**18,608.31**	**18,949.78**
LESS: Personal tax payments	2,183.16	2,214.08
EQUALS: Disposable personal income (DPI)	**16,425.15**	**16,735.70**
LESS: Personal consumption expenditures (C)	14,562.66	14,584.06
Personal interest payments by consumers	359.92	343.41
Personal transfer payments	199.76	198.44
EQUALS: Personal savings (S)	**1,302.81**	**1,609.79**

FIGURE 25.6 Table showing the relationship between gross domestic product, net national product, national income, and personal income (billions of U.S. dollars).

Source: Federal Reserve Economic Data, Tables 1.7.5 and 2.1, May 2020. Note:*2020 data is annualized from first quarter data (before the recession).

For example, gross national product (GNP) is **the total market value of goods and services produced by a country's citizens and companies during one year, and it is equal to gross domestic product plus the net income from foreign investments**. Gross *national* product includes production by U.S. corporations in the United States *and* in other countries, whereas gross *domestic* product includes production within the borders of the United States, whether or not that production is done by U.S. or foreign companies. GDP is a better indicator of a country's productive capacity, whereas GNP is a better measure of value added generated by a country's companies wherever they might be.

Net national product (NNP) is the net creation of new wealth (value added) resulting from the productive activity of the economy during the accounting period (usually one year). NNP is computed by taking GNP and subtracting the decline in the current value of the stock of fixed assets (capital) owned and used by producers as a result of physical deterioration, normal obsolescence, or normal accidental damage. By subtracting depreciation of capital that takes place during production, NNP measures the actual wealth created in a given time period.

National income (NI) measures the total monetary value of the flow of output of goods and services produced in an economy. NI is found by taking NNP and subtracting indirect business taxes and transfer payments. Indirect business taxes are primarily sales and excise taxes, customs duties on imported goods, and business property taxes. Transfer payments occur when governments redistribute income via social welfare programs such as social security, old age or disability pensions, student grants, unemployment compensation, etc. By eliminating indirect business taxes and transfer payments, we are left with the national income generated by productive market activities.

Personal income (PI) measures national income going to persons and nonprofit corporations. This includes wages and net transfer payments. To compute PI, the government begins with NI and subtracts income earned by the corporate sector (depreciation, undistributed profits), payments to the government (taxes), and adjustments such as subsidies, government and consumer interest, and any statistical discrepancy.

Disposable personal income (DPI) is the income remaining to households after the deduction of personal tax and nontax payments to the general government. After-tax income (DPI) is computed by taking PI and subtracting personal taxes, which include income and property taxes that are not deductible.

If we take DPI and subtract household interest and transfer payments, the remaining amount of money is devoted to consumption and savings. Consumption expenditures (C) are the market value of purchases of goods and services by individuals and nonprofit institutions. Savings (S) is the money that households keep in cash, bank deposits, security holdings, and private pension, health, welfare, and trust funds.

25.4 THE LIMITATIONS OF REAL GDP AS A MEASURE OF ECONOMIC WELFARE

Real GDP measures the entire country's standard of living and, as such, is a reasonable measure of economic activity and the country's total standard of living. To some economists, this makes real GDP a very good measure of the effectiveness of an economic system and a good proxy for the economic welfare of a nation. However, real GDP incorporates only measurable market-based economic activity, and it can increase for reasons that are not associated with an improvement in people's welfare. More specifically, there are four main problems that render real GDP an inaccurate measure of well-being: excluded production, inaccurate measurement of the quality of life, the inclusion of economic "bads" in real GDP calculations, and the fact that real GDP tends to be correlated with unsustainable practices.

1. Excluded production.

Real GDP only includes official market activity, neglecting unpaid household work, informal sector work, much work done for cash payments, and illegal activities.

By ignoring unpaid household work, real GDP significantly underestimates the amount of productive activity taking place in an economy. Unpaid household work includes housework, home maintenance, shopping, caring for household members (including adults and children), volunteer work in the community, and travel related to household activities. Figure 25.7 displays the typical amount of time per day devoted to paid and unpaid work by men and women from a variety of countries.[3]

The data indicate several important trends:

- Women do more unpaid work than men in *all* countries, and they do a lot more unpaid work in particular countries.
- Women spend a larger percentage of their days working on paid and unpaid work than men in almost all countries, with Denmark as one of the few exceptions.
- On average, women spend 21% more of their time on unpaid work than they do on paid work. On the other hand, men spend 145% more of their time on paid work than unpaid work.
- On average, unpaid work takes up a huge amount of time, averaging 74% of paid work. Therefore, *real GDP excludes 74% of economic activity.*

Clearly, the amount of productive household work not included in real GDP is substantial. Economists estimate that it would cost between 12% and 24% of real GDP to hire workers to do the amount of household work that is undertaken in most countries (the replacement cost of household labor). However, this number is a low estimate because the wages paid for most household work are low. If we consider the opportunity cost of workers—what they could earn in other professions if they did paid work instead of unpaid work—the increase in real GDP from including unpaid work would range from 41% to 66%.

As one example of the skewed priorities implied by real GDP, if a family places its children in day care or hires a nanny, they increase real GDP, whereas if they spend quality time with their children every day in their home but spend fewer hours in the workplace, real GDP will decline.

Furthermore, household work is only one important area of excluded production. In many countries, especially those in the developing world, much work is

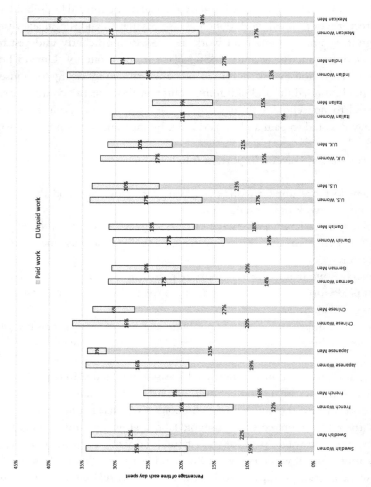

FIGURE 25.7 Percentage of time spent on paid and unpaid work, various countries, most recent year.

done in the informal sector by individuals and small businesses who engage in cash transactions and who do not report their activities to the government. Even in developed countries, many people do work for cash and do not report these payments. In 2018, the consulting firm Kearney estimated that 23% of economic activity is done "off the books."

Lastly, illegal activities are not included in real GDP. (Drug dealers do not report their income to the government!) According to the U.S. Bureau of Economic Analysis, in 2017 including illegal drugs in measures of GDP adds $111 billion, illegal prostitution adds $10 billion, illegal gambling adds $4 billion, and theft from businesses adds $109 billion. All illegal activities together add up to about 1% of U.S. real GDP.

2. **Real GDP is an inaccurate measure of human quality of life.**

Income is certainly an important determinant of quality of life. However, real GDP, in measuring national income, does not necessarily capture the experiences of most individuals, especially in a very unequal nation like the United States. Given the high poverty rate in the United States and the high rate of homelessness (554,000 people were homeless in 2017, a year during an economic boom), many people's experiences are not reflected in the high level of U.S. real GDP. Even though real GDP in the United States increased in recent decades, all or almost all of the benefit went to the richest 20% of the population, obscuring the fact that well-being is stagnant for most citizens.

In addition to income, well-being includes citizens' levels of health, happiness, security, material comfort, and leisure, categories that are not reflected by real GDP. France has a lower GDP than the United States, but French laborers work on average *19%* less than American workers. It is hard to argue that French workers are worse off than U.S. workers because they prefer more leisure time to a higher income.

3. **Real GDP includes many economic "bads."**

Real GDP increases whenever manmade or natural disasters occur. Buildings that are destroyed by hurricanes have to be rebuilt, which increases real GDP, but homeowners are no better off. The Deepwater Horizon oil spill in the Gulf of Mexico required a massive cleanup effort, increasing GDP, but people and the environment in the Gulf region suffered significantly. Having to spend increasing amounts of money on health or car insurance may safeguard against calamity, but it does not improve our well-being directly. Similarly, spending money on elaborate alarm and security systems due to high crime rates may make keep us from harm, but it is difficult to see such expenditures as an indication of increased well-being. The fact that real GDP increases whenever calamities occur or whenever households have to make defensive expenditures to ward of calamities indicates that many expenditures within real GDP do not reflect well-being.

4. **Real GDP ignores and often directly undermines sustainability.**

Real GDP usually increases when companies exploit the environment more intensively. Fracking led to a huge boom in Pennsylvania, North Dakota, and Texas as new natural gas fields were discovered, leading to substantial increases in real GDP. However, fracking processes spoiled water sources and natural beauty, and they contributed substantially to climate change. Cutting down rainforests and intensifying fishing efforts can increase real GDP in the short term, but the long-term costs can be devastating and will likely require huge corrective expenditures in the future to solve the environmental problems that are being created. In general, in our current capitalist system, exploiting the environment tends to result in increased short-term profits and real GDP, but no adjustment is made to account for the long-term environmental costs.

Thus, to most economists real GDP is at best an imperfect measure of welfare. However, measures of economic progress are crucial to determine the direction of an economy and to measure if it is functioning effectively. Therefore, the key question is how should we measure the well-being of society? In many ways, the measures we choose are a reflection of a society's priorities. The selection of real GDP as the primary criterion for economic success prioritizes market-based income growth, while ineffectively addressing household work, life satisfaction, leisure, calamities, environmental concerns, and many other important factors. A much more comprehensive measure than real GDP is the OECD Better Life Index.

25.5 THE OECD BETTER LIFE INDEX

We started off this chapter by asking some fundamental economic questions: What should the goals of an economic system be? How can we determine if we are successful in meeting those goals? Unlike real GDP, the OECD's Better Life Index was designed to answer those questions directly.

Developed in 2011 by three eminent mainstream economists, Joseph Stiglitz, Amartya Sen, and Jean-Paul Fitoussi, the Better Life Index compares well-being across OECD countries in 11 different sectors determined as essential to human well-being. These sectors are (1) housing, (2) income, (3) jobs, (4) community, (5) education, (6) environment, (7) civic engagement, (8) health, (9) life satisfaction, (10) safety, and (11) work–life balance. Each sector is measured using a set of indicators and is then ranked on a scale of 0 to 10, with 0 being the worst possible score and 10 being the best. Below, we describe briefly the determinants of the Better Life Index (BLI).

1. **Housing**: Shelter is one of our most important necessities. In addition, people desire a comfortable, safe space to raise families and spend time with friends. The Better Life Index measures housing from three vantage points: Housing

affordability, dwellings with basic facilities (access to sanitation), and rooms per person (to determine whether housing is overcrowded).

2. **Income**: Higher income levels often mean that households have greater access to high-quality education and health care and an overall better standard of living. In the Better Life Index, income is measured in terms of household net wealth (household assets such as housing equity, ownership of stocks, etc.) and net disposable (after-tax) income. These figures are adjusted for inflation and exchange rates so that they reflect purchasing power parity, making it possible to compare accurately the income and wealth of different countries. This part of the BLI is similar to GDP per capita but is broader because it includes measures of wealth.

3. **Jobs**: One of the most important characteristics of well-being is having a meaningful, fulfilling job that provides a decent standard of living. Jobs connect us to society, providing self-confidence and access to personal growth. The Better Life Index measures jobs in terms of job security, personal earnings, the long-term unemployment rate, and the employment rate.

4. **Community**: Our communities are the backbones of our personal and social lives. We rely on them for friendship, civic engagement, and help when we are in distress. In the Better life Index, community is measured through the quality of the community support network, which is determined by surveys.

5. **Education**: A good education system creates a knowledgeable, skilled labor force, as well as a more engaged, healthier, and politically conscious citizenry. Therefore, education is important for essential employment skills and for the cultivation of an informed worldview. The Better Life Index measures education on the basis of years in education, student skills, and educational attainment.

6. **Environment**: The environment directly impacts health and well-being. Green spaces let us partake in physical activities and reduce stress. The environment is a vital source of natural resources (environmental services), and a key issue is how best to preserve these resources while reaping their current benefits. Water quality and air pollution are the two indicators that serve as proxies for the quality of the environment in the Better Life Index.

7. **Civic engagement**: Regardless of ideology, a government and a political system that is responsive to and trusted by the electorate is very important to well-being. We need to be able to trust those making consequential policy decisions, which requires transparent governance. The ability of the public to engage with government and affect policy, along with the level of voter turnout, is used to measure civic engagement in the BLI.

8. **Health**: Being healthy brings so many benefits—from living a longer, more fulfilling life to spending less on health care services. Health is one of the central factors determining our success and overall quality of life. In the Better Life Index, health is measured by life expectancy as well as surveys of the levels of self-reported health by the population.

9. **Life Satisfaction**: Although this is one of the most subjective factors in the index, some people consider it the most important because it directly reflects people's general satisfaction with life. To determine this measure, people are given a survey which asks them to rate their general satisfaction with life on a scale of 0 to 10.

10. **Safety**: Feeling safe in our own community is very important. Living in areas with more crime poses a higher risk of becoming a victim of violence, increases stress, and destroys community. The Better Life Index measures safety in terms of the homicide rate and how safe individuals feel while walking alone at night.

11. **Work–life balance**: Another meaningful measure to many people is the ability to strike a balance between work and home life. Working longer hours may increase income and opportunities, but this comes at the expense of leisure, family time, and personal care. The BLI uses time devoted to leisure and personal care and the percentage of employees working very long hours (50 or more per week) as indicators for work–life balance.

Figure 25.8 shows the Better Life Index in 2019 for 27 OECD countries as well as Brazil and South Africa. Each of the 11 determinants is given equal weight in this figure.

The broadened definition of well-being in the BLI shows the strength of the Nordic model in delivering an extremely high quality of life, with Norway, Iceland, Denmark, Sweden, and Finland all in the top ten and all ahead of the United States. Nonetheless, market-dominated economies such as Australia, Canada, the United States, New Zealand, and the United Kingdom still fare well.

Figure 25.9 shows a direct comparison between the United States and Norway in each category of the Better Life Index. Norway fares particularly well with

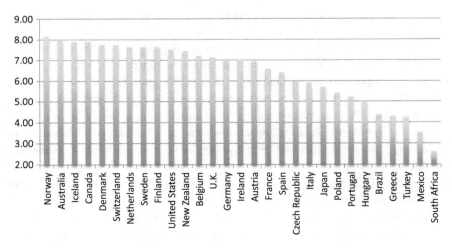

FIGURE 25.8 OECD Better Life Index, 2019.

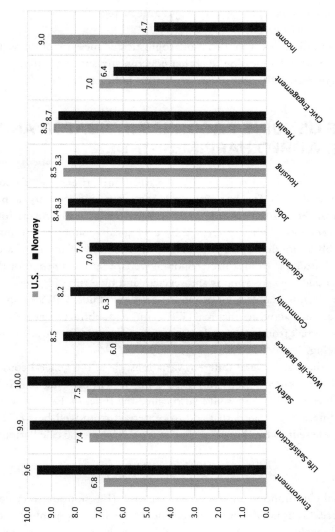

FIGURE 25.9 Better Life Index for the United States and Norway.

respect to environment, life satisfaction, safety, work–life balance, and community. The United States is particularly strong in one area: Income. Thus, the BLI indicates that high incomes in the United States, achieved via long work hours and the market-dominated system, come at the expense of other important life indicators.

One of the unique aspects of the Better Life Index is that it is an interactive tool, which lets you determine what matters most *to you* across the 11 sectors. This allows countries to make their own value judgments regarding the aspects of well-being that should prioritized.

The Better Life Index is a much more sophisticated measure of the well-being of citizens in a particular location. Another effective measure that attempts to correct the flaws in real GDP is the genuine progress indicator.

25.6 THE GENUINE PROGRESS INDICATOR AND THE WORLD HAPPINESS INDEX

The genuine progress indicator (GPI) is **a monetary measure of economic welfare that accounts for benefits and costs experienced by a particular population from investment, production, trade, and consumption of goods and services**.[4] GPI was created by ecological economists Herman Daly and John Cobb as an alternative measure of the standard of living of a country or region. GPI attempts to measure economic welfare by accounting for the benefits of market *and nonmarket* goods and services and by estimating the economic, social, and environmental costs of economic activity.[5] Thus, GPI attempts to add in positive economic activities that real GDP omits and subtract negative economic activities that detract from our well-being to come up with a more accurate measure of well-being.

Although there are several different variations, there is a general consensus of what the GPI should incorporate. In this section, we will be using the GPI developed by Cobb et al. (1995). This GPI (also called the Index of Economic Welfare) contains 27 different indicators that add to or detract from well-being. However, we can group these into five broad categories for the following calculation:

$$GPI = C_{adj} + W + G_{nd} - D - E - N.$$

C_{adj} is personal consumption adjusted for inequality. W is nonmonetary contributions to welfare. G_{nd} is nondefensive government expenditures (public goods). D is defensive and rehabilitative household expenditures, investments, and social costs. E is the costs of environmental degradation. And N is net depreciation of natural capital stocks. Each of these categories is explained more fully below.

C_{adj} = **Personal consumption, adjusted for income inequality (+).** Personal consumption captures purchases of essential goods, such as food, water, and shelter, as well as things that might not be essential but that give us some amount of happiness, like watching a movie or going to a concert. Personal consumption must be adjusted for income inequality. If per capita consumption increases but if all of the increase goes to the richest 20% of the population, as has been the case in recent decades in the United States, then per capita consumption does not accurately capture the well-being of the entire population.

W = **Nonmonetary contributions to welfare (+).** As noted above, real GDP only accounts for acts that involve the exchange of money. Real GDP excludes all unpaid work done in the home, including the time and skills it takes to raise children, cook food, and clean the house. Real GDP ignores the value of leisure time and ignores any services in the community provided by volunteers. In addition, real GDP misses external benefits from higher education and green jobs and the value contributed by infrastructure and other forms of built capital. GPI calculates and includes the value of each of these contributions to well-being.

G_{nd} = **Nondefensive government expenditures (+).** The government plays an important role in funding public goods. From public education to the maintenance of roads, a large part of government expenditure is used for the well-being of the country. The GPI does not include defensive expenditures, which are those made to offset declining levels of well-being in human, social, and environmental capital. For example, spending to clean up oil spills or toxic waste sites is crucial, but it does not lead to an improvement in human welfare. Instead, it is correcting a past problem and should not be considered genuine progress. Therefore, defensive or corrective government expenditures are not included in GPI.

D = **Defensive and rehabilitative household expenditures, investments, and social costs (−).** We all have an incentive to invest in defensive measures to minimize harm when things go wrong and to protect our future. Health insurance, car insurance, or legal services protect us from potential harm. However, these expenditures do not increase our well-being when we make them. Instead, they act as defenses when we are at risk of experiencing a decrease in well-being. Household investments in durable goods (cars, appliances) cost large amounts up front (increasing C) but provide much more limited benefits each year, so the value of future benefits is subtracted and only the current benefit is included. Other household investments that generate future benefit streams, such as home improvements and retirement savings, are discounted in a similar manner. In addition, there are significant social costs that accompany economic activity, including crime, underemployment, homelessness, time wasted commuting, and the cost of vehicle accidents. All of these items detract from well-being and are subtracted from the GPI.

E = **Costs of environmental degradation (−).** Industrialization and urbanization over the past several centuries have taken a huge toll on the environment. Climate change is but one example of the negative effects of human practices.

Many economic activities that contribute to GDP, such as the burning of fossil fuels and deforestation, create costly environment problems that will impact human society negatively in the near future but that are not accounted for. GPI includes indicators like the costs of water, land, and air pollution to calculate the impact of environmental degradation.

N = **Net depreciation of natural capital stocks (−).** Similarly, production of goods and services depletes our natural capital stocks. Many natural resources are nonrenewable, and heavy present-day consumption takes its toll on the availability of resources for future generations. Renewable resources, such as fish stocks, are often overused so much that it jeopardizes future reproduction. Therefore, GPI includes indicators like long-term nonrenewable resource depletion and long-term environmental damage. If we take the depreciation of natural capital stocks and subtract the value of services from protected natural capital from conservation efforts (a positive long-term impact), we get a measure for the net depreciation of natural capitals stocks.

Figure 25.10 tells us that U.S. real GPI per capita in 2014 was $28,459.35, which is 53.6% of real GDP per capita in the same year. The GPI tells us a number of important facts about our well-being: Almost half of our well-being comes from nonmonetary factors, demonstrating how much is missed by real GDP. And the costs of environmental damage and depreciation, coupled with defensive household expenditures that do not enhance welfare, demonstrate the extent to which well-being is mismeasured by real GDP.

Interestingly, in some countries, GPI and GDP correspond much more closely than they do in the United States.

Figure 25.11 displays the 15 OECD countries with the highest real GDP per capita and the highest real GPI per capita in 2013. Countries with strong social

Indicator	Contribution to GPI
Gross household consumption	$25,529.42
Costs of income inequality	-3,121.57
Adjusted household consumption (C_{adj})	22,407.85
Nonmonetary contributions to welfare (W)	24,122.18
Nondefensive government expenditures (G_{nd})	7,025.32
Defensive household expenditures, investments, & social costs (D)	-16,440.40
Costs of environmental degradation (E)	-3,714.65
Net depreciation of natural capital stocks (N)	-4,940.95
U.S. real GPI per capita (2014)	28,459.35
U.S. real GDP per capita (2014)	53,076.00

FIGURE 25.10 Table showing U.S. real genuine progress indicator, 2014 (in 2012 dollars).

Position	GDP per capita	GPI per capita
1	Luxembourg	Norway
2	Norway	Denmark
3	Denmark	Sweden
4	Sweden	Luxembourg
5	United States	Finland
6	Netherlands	Japan
7	Ireland	Austria
8	Austria	Netherlands
9	Japan	France
10	Finland	Belgium
11	Belgium	Ireland
12	Germany	United Kingdom
13	France	Germany
14	United Kingdom	Italy
15	Italy	United States

FIGURE 25.11 Table showing top OECD countries' GDP vs. GPI, 2013.

Source: D.F. Pais, T.L. Afonso, A.C. Marques, and J.A. Fuinhas, "Are Economic Growth and Sustainable Development Converging?" *International Journal of Energy Economics and Policy* 9, No. 4 (2019), pp. 202–213.

and environmental programs fared extremely well in both categories. For example, Norway, Denmark, and Sweden maintained a very high real GDP per capita without compromising the well-being of citizens and the environment, resulting in a similarly high real GPI per capita. The United States, however, slips from 5th in real GDP per capita to 15th in real GPI per capita, by far the largest drop of any OECD country.

In addition to the OECD Better Life Index and the genuine progress indicator, there are several other important measures of well-being. The United Nations Human Development Index focuses on three essential components of the development of human capabilities: Life expectancy at birth, years of formal education, and real GDP per capita. The Happy Planet Index looks at average life expectancy, average subjective well-being, and the ecological impact of a society.

Lastly, the United Nations World Happiness Index (WHI) incorporates real GDP per capita, healthy life expectancy at birth, social support (of relatives and friends), freedom to make life choices, generosity, and perceptions of corruption. Though the last four categories are subjective measures determined by surveys, they get at aspects of well-being that are extremely important to most people and that cannot be measured in other ways.

We can see in Figure 25.12 that the Nordic countries are at the top of the World Happiness Index, making up the first four countries and five out of the top seven. They perform particularly well on social support and freedom to make life choices. The United States does well in per capita income but poorly in healthy life expectancy, freedom to make life choices, and perceptions of corruption.

Rank	Country	Score	GDP per capita	Social support	Healthy life expectancy	Freedom for life choices	Generosity	Perceptions of corruption
1	Finland	7.77	1.34	1.59	0.99	0.60	0.15	0.39
2	Denmark	7.60	1.38	1.57	1.00	0.59	0.25	0.41
3	Norway	7.55	1.49	1.58	1.03	0.60	0.27	0.34
4	Iceland	7.49	1.38	1.62	1.03	0.59	0.35	0.12
5	Netherlands	7.49	1.40	1.52	1.00	0.56	0.32	0.30
6	Switzerland	7.48	1.45	1.53	1.05	0.57	0.26	0.34
7	Sweden	7.34	1.39	1.49	1.01	0.57	0.27	0.37
8	New Zealand	7.31	1.30	1.56	1.03	0.59	0.33	0.38
9	Canada	7.28	1.37	1.51	1.04	0.58	0.29	0.31
10	Austria	7.25	1.38	1.48	1.02	0.53	0.24	0.23
11	Australia	7.23	1.37	1.55	1.04	0.56	0.33	0.29
12	Costa Rica	7.17	1.03	1.44	0.96	0.56	0.14	0.09
13	Israel	7.14	1.28	1.46	1.03	0.37	0.26	0.08
14	Luxembourg	7.09	1.61	1.48	1.01	0.53	0.19	0.32
15	United Kingdom	7.05	1.33	1.54	1.00	0.45	0.35	0.28
16	Ireland	7.02	1.50	1.55	1.00	0.52	0.30	0.31
17	Germany	6.99	1.37	1.45	0.99	0.50	0.26	0.27
18	Belgium	6.92	1.36	1.50	0.99	0.47	0.16	0.21
19	United States	6.89	1.43	1.46	0.87	0.45	0.28	0.13
20	Czech Republic	6.85	1.27	1.49	0.92	0.46	0.05	0.04

FIGURE 25.12 Table showing World Happiness Index rankings, 2017–2019.

As the last two sections have shown, broader measures of well-being tend to favor economic systems that emphasize broad-based prosperity, significant social welfare programs, public goods, work–life balance, and sustainable economic practices. Economic systems like the United States that focus primarily on economic growth do well in terms of real GDP but fare poorly according to the Better Life Index, the genuine progress indicator, and the World Happiness Index.

25.7 CONCLUSION

This chapter began by defining and discussing the relationship between nominal GDP, real GDP, and the GDP deflator. Nominal GDP is total revenue generated by the production and sale of all final goods and services at current prices. Real GDP is equal to nominal GDP divided by the GDP deflator and represents the total revenue from sales of all final goods and services at constant prices.

We went on to discuss the circular flow model. The expenditure side of the model is composed of the components of aggregate demand: Consumption, investment, government, export, and import **purchases** of goods and services. The income side of the circular flow can be broken down into the categories of taxes and disposable income. Disposable income includes wages, rent, interest, profits, and all other sources of income generated in the production of goods and services.

The circular flow model shows that GDP is equal to aggregate demand as well as national income. National income can also be computed by measuring value added for all industries, because value added is the income generated in all productive activities. Sometimes, economists look at other measures of income, such as gross national product, to analyze different variations in how income is generated.

Determining what measure we use to determine well-being is one of the most important aspects of macroeconomics, because it determines a society's economic goals. A society focused on real GDP may well generate high levels of income, but this may not be a good indicator of how well people are doing. This is because there are four main limitations of real GDP as a measure of well-being: (1) Real GDP excludes important types of production, especially by households. (2) Real GDP is an inaccurate measure of human quality of life, ignoring key elements such as health, leisure, and the welfare of *all* citizens. (3) Real GDP includes many economic "bads" such as rebuilding from disasters or defensive expenditures. (4) Real GDP in our current capitalist economic system tends to be inversely correlated with sustainability, jeopardizing our long-term well-being.

In contrast to real GDP, the Better Life Index, the genuine progress indicator, and the World Happiness Index are constructed to generate a much more comprehensive measure of human well-being. They attempt to correct the limitations of real GDP by including excluded production, subjective measures of well-being, the costs of economic calamities, and the costs of environmental destruction. The Nordic countries fare particularly well in rankings utilizing these more comprehensive measures of well-being, whereas the United States fares poorly due to its high levels of inequality and environmental destruction and its low levels of social welfare support.

In the next chapter, we turn to two additional macroeconomic variables that are crucial to well-being: unemployment and inflation. As we will see, both of these macroeconomic market failures can be extremely harmful to a country's citizens, so government policies to limit their impact are very important.

QUESTIONS FOR REVIEW

1. In 2017, U.S. nominal GDP was $19,519 billion and U.S. real GDP (measured in 2012 dollars) was $18,108 billion. Explain the difference between these two measures of 2017 GDP and use these numbers to determine how much inflation there was from 2012 to 2017.

2. Using the circular flow model, explain why total spending (aggregate demand) tends to be equal to total income.

3. List and explain the main limitations of real GDP as a measure of well-being.

4. Do you think the Better Life Index is a better measure of economic well-being than real GDP? Why or why not? What are the strengths and weaknesses of the Better Life Index?

5. Explain how the genuine progress indicator is constructed and how it differs from real GDP and the Better Life Index.

6. How is the World Happiness Index constructed, and how does it compare to real GDP, the Better Life Index, and the genuine progress indicator?

7. Determine which indexes are most closely associated with each characteristic listed in Figure 25.13.

Characteristic	Index(es) with this characteristic (real GDP, BLI, GPI, and/or WHI)
An exclusive focus on income	
Contains no subjective measures	
Ranks countries based on a set of key indicators	
Subtracts economic "bads"	
Includes education and housing as key categories	
Includes "perceptions of corruption" as a key category	

FIGURE 25.13 Table for Problem 7.

8.   Why does the United States perform relatively well when it comes to real GDP per capita but relatively poorly when it comes to the other measures discussed in this chapter? If the United States wanted to change its performance with respect to the Better Life Index and the genuine progress indicator, what would it need to do?

9.   Write an essay in which you compare, contrast, and critically evaluate real GDP, the Better Life Index, and the genuine progress indicator. Make an argument for which measure should be used as the best barometer of a country's well-being.

10. What do you think is most important to the well-being of most people? Explain and support your position. Which measure of economic welfare would best capture well-being as you have defined it? Do you think others would agree with your determination of well-being?

NOTES

1   A good way to think about the actual profit rate is to take profits and subtract depreciation. Depreciation of capital means that machinery and equipment must be replaced, and that replacement cost comes out of profits.

2   Rakesh Sharma, "What It Costs Apple to Make an iPhone 7: $219 Parts, $5 Labor," Investopedia, Company News (2016). https://www.investopedia.com/news/what-it-costs-apple-make-iphone-7-219-parts-5-labor-aapl-snssf/. Accessed May 28, 2020.

3   Source: OECD.Stat, accessed January 17, 2020.

4   John Talberth and Michael Weisdorf, "Genuine Progress Indicator 2.0: Pilot Accounts for the US, Maryland, and City of Baltimore 2012–2014." *Ecological Economics*, 142 (December 2017), pp. 1–11. https://doi.org/10.1016/J.ECOLECON.2017.06.012.

5   Ibid.

Unemploy-ment and price instability

The major macroeconomic market failures

In the last chapter, we described various measures of economic well-being. Any discussion of macroeconomic well-being would be incomplete if it did not address the two major macroeconomic market failures: Unemployment and inflation.

Unemployment can be devastating for individuals, families, and communities. Households in which the main breadwinner loses their job have a much higher likelihood of poverty, hunger, and homelessness. Communities where large numbers of people become unemployed for a significant length of time deteriorate into poverty, crime, abandoned buildings, and outmigration of those with the means to leave. The broader macroeconomy also suffers, as unemployment results in declines in aggregate demand, reduced business sales, and, subsequently, additional rounds of layoffs due to the multiplier effect. The end result is a reduction in economic growth. The costs of unemployment can be mitigated by a generous and effective social safety net, but many countries such as the United States provide only a minimal safety net. This renders the economic impact of unemployment very high.

Price instability is the other major macroeconomic market failure. Economic systems need a degree of price stability to function effectively. Deflation is devastating, causing a rash of business failures and, as in the case of the Great Depression, contributing to an economic collapse. Rapid bouts of inflation or hyperinflation can also be destabilizing, undermining the health of the financial sector and causing the banking system to collapse. Thus, deflation or rapid inflation can both result in economic crises, demonstrating the importance of maintaining stable prices.

This chapter begins by systematically discussing the problems that occur due to unemployment and why economists consider it to be a market failure. We then describe the different types of unemployment and the potential policy solutions to solve the unemployment problem. This includes a brief discussion of some of the unemployment mitigation programs we see in economic systems around the world.

DOI: 10.4324/9781315636924-33

Subsequently, the chapter turns to how we measure inflation and deflation and how we use this measure to compute real wages and real interest rates. Next, we take up the causes of and problems created by deflation, along with the policies that can reduce its impact. We also discuss the problems created by inflation and the forces that cause inflation.

We close the chapter by discussing two important but controversial economic theories regarding the main causes of inflation. The quantity theory of money, put forth by laissez-faire economists, proposes that the major cause of inflation is increases in the money supply. The Phillips curve posits that inflation is caused by rapid economic growth and low unemployment. Adherents of these policies prefer to use austerity policies to keep inflation under control, albeit at the cost of slower growth and higher unemployment. Political economists and liberal New Keynesian economists dispute the empirical validity of these theories and argue for policies to promote economic growth and low unemployment while worrying less about inflation.

26.0 CHAPTER 26 LEARNING GOALS

After reading this chapter, you should be able to:

- Describe the costs of unemployment, how the unemployment rate is computed, and the types of unemployment.

- Evaluate the effectiveness of the unemployment rate and the labor force participation rate in reflecting the unemployment situation in a country.

- Critically analyze the possible solutions to the problems of unemployment and underemployment.

- Compute the rate of inflation, the real wage, and the real interest rate.

- Explain the causes and costs of deflation and inflation and critically evaluate potential policy solutions to these market failures.

- Compare and contrast perspectives on the quantity theory of money and the Phillips curve.

26.1 THE ECONOMIC COSTS OF UNEMPLOYMENT

Finding meaningful work is one of the most important determinants of economic well-being. People want a job that pays well enough so that they can live a good life. This includes earning enough to support their family and to provide their children with education and opportunities to succeed. People also want a job where the work that they do is important and interesting.

Unemployment, on the other hand, is devastating. In a capitalist system with no safety net, such as the laissez-faire systems in England in 1850 or the United States in 1900, unemployment means no income and brings with it the threat of poverty, homelessness, and starvation. Unemployment renders people helpless and dependent on others for their survival, something that people find deeply humiliating according to survey data. Unemployment is so devastating that having a bad job is better than having no job at all, something the famous Cambridge economist Joan Robinson alluded to when she said, "The misery of being exploited by capitalists is nothing compared to the misery of not being exploited at all."[1]

Unfortunately, unemployment is an ever-present part of a capitalist economic system. There has almost never been a time when everyone who wanted to work could find a job. The lowest unemployment rate in U.S. history was 1.2% in 1944, when the mobilization of millions of soldiers and workers for the World War II war effort employed almost everyone. Therefore, economists consider unemployment to be a market failure because it is a chronic plague in capitalist systems: Markets are not able to eliminate unemployment on their own, and unemployment imposes devastating costs on individuals, families, communities, and the macroeconomy.

First, consider the **costs of unemployment to the individual**. Unemployed individuals do not have access to the latest workplace technology and they are excluded from opportunities for training and advancement in the workplace. This results in the loss of skills and significant, long-term reductions in income for workers who experience unemployment. Similarly, numerous studies indicate that college graduates who begin work during a recession when levels of unemployment are high earn less for at least 10 to 15 years than students who graduate when economic growth is strong.[2] In addition to lost income and opportunity, unemployed individuals are more likely to experience stress, ill health, reduced life expectancy, depression, loss of motivation and self-worth, and even suicide. Unemployment also leads to social exclusion—one's social circles are often tied to employment—and the loss of various enabling freedoms, especially the freedom to have a good life free from stress and deprivation.

The costs of unemployment invariably spill over from the individual to the family. **The costs of unemployment to the family** include increased stress; the undermining of relationships and family life; increased rates of spousal abuse, child abuse, and divorce; higher rates of hunger, poverty, and homelessness; poorer health for all family members; and harm to children's development, their performance in school, and their employment futures.

Meanwhile, communities that experience high levels of unemployment are also devastated. The **costs of unemployment to the community** include increased levels of crime; a greater need for defensive expenditures on policing and security; increased poverty, hunger, and homelessness; business failures as a result of lower levels of spending; an increase in racial inequality (unemployment rates are much higher for people of color); and the loss of social cohesion.

Lastly, we need to consider how the entire economy is affected. The **macroeconomic costs of unemployment** include the loss of current output due to idled workers; the cost of government programs to support the unemployed, including unemployment insurance and welfare programs; as well as the residual costs of all of the problems to individuals, families, and communities that impact government budgets and the country as a whole. Arthur Okun attempted to estimate the relationship between unemployment and gross domestic product (GDP), coming up with Okun's law, which states that **a 1% increase in the rate of unemployment is associated with a 2% decrease in the growth of real GDP.** Thus, unemployment has huge macroeconomic costs. Spending plummets and businesses' sales decline, which leads to even more layoffs of workers, and so on. Economist Bill Mitchell estimated that, at the height of the Great Recession in the United States from September 2009 through December 2010, the United States was *losing more than $10 billion in output per day due to unemployment,* for an annual loss of more than $3 trillion![3] When this macroeconomic cost is added to the costs to individuals, families, and communities, it becomes clear how devastating a market failure unemployment can be.

26.2 THE UNEMPLOYMENT RATE AND THE TYPES OF UNEMPLOYMENT

Most people think of a person who is unemployed as someone who does not have a job but wants one. However, there are some nuances to how the official unemployment rate is calculated. In the United States, the unemployment rate is computed as follows:

$$\text{Unemployment rate} = \frac{\#\,\text{of Unemployed}}{\text{Labor force}} \times 100\%.$$

The complexities arise in the definition of the labor force, which **includes all people working or actively looking for work.** Anyone who is under 16, living in prison or another type of institution, or on active duty in the military is not included in the labor force. In recent years, about 31% of the U.S. population has fallen outside of the definition of the labor force.

However, millions of former workers have dropped out of the U.S. workforce as deindustrialization eliminated good-paying manufacturing jobs. Many searched for jobs for years but finally gave up. U.S. unemployment benefits usually run out after six months (unless extended by government mandate, which happens only in major recessions). Some former workers qualify for government disability payments due to chronic conditions from manufacturing work, such as bad backs or carpal tunnel syndrome. Others live with their family and depend on other earners for their survival. And some are in prison, after desperation from chronic unemployment caused them to resort to crime. *There are millions of people who are no longer employed but who are not counted as unemployed.*

In May 2020, the U.S. civilian labor force was 158.23 million people, the number of employed people was 137.24 million, and the number of unemployed was 20.99 million: $\dfrac{20.99}{158.23} \times 100\% = 13.3\%$. Thus, the unemployment rate in the United States in May 2020 was 13.3%.

However, the labor force was higher, 164.55 million, in February 2020. Therefore, 6.32 million people left the labor force from February to May 2020. This likely includes workers who were furloughed (temporarily laid off), discouraged workers who gave up looking for work, and more. Economists estimate that the actual unemployment rate was at least 5% higher.

Figure 26.1 shows the unemployment rate in the United States from 1950 to 2020. Notice how much higher the unemployment rate is for blacks, usually about twice as much as the unemployment rate for whites. Latinos also have higher than average unemployment rates, as do women who are the head of the household and teens. However, these official unemployment rates significantly understate the amount of unemployment due to discouraged and underemployed workers.

To understand unemployment in more detail, we need to delve into the different types of unemployment. There are *three major types of unemployment*: frictional, structural, and cyclical.

1. Frictional unemployment is **unemployment resulting from normal turnover in the labor market.**

    Workers who have decided to change jobs or occupations and college graduates looking for their first job are considered to be examples of frictional unemployment. At any given time, about 2% of the labor force is likely to fall into this category of unemployment. People in this category are fully expected to find a job in the near future, so frictional unemployment is not usually considered a major problem. Nonetheless, due to the huge costs associated with unemployment, governments try to reduce the amount and duration of frictional unemployment by offering free job search assistance and employment listings.

2. Structural unemployment is **unemployment resulting from the permanent displacement of workers due to automation, globalization, shifting demand for products, and other forces that eliminate the need for certain skills in the workplace**.

    Examples of structural unemployment include U.S. steel and textile workers who lost jobs to cheaper foreign competition from China and India, retail service workers replaced by Amazon workers selling goods online, and automobile workers replaced by sophisticated robots. Structural unemployment represents a serious problem because workers' jobs are not expected to return.

Year	All workers	By sex and age			Race/ethnicity			Married men (spouse present)	Women who maintain families
		Teens (both sexes, 16–19)	Male adults (20 & over)	Female adults (20 & over)	White	Black or African American	Hispanic or Latino ethnicity		
1950	5.3	12.2	4.7	5.1	4.9	–	–	4.6	–
1960	5.5	14.7	4.7	5.1	4.9	–	–	3.7	–
1970	4.9	15.3	3.5	4.8	4.5	8.2	–	2.6	5.4
1975	8.5	19.9	6.7	8.0	7.8	14.8	12.2	5.1	10.0
1980	7.1	17.8	5.9	6.4	6.3	14.3	10.1	4.2	9.2
1985	7.2	18.6	6.2	6.6	6.2	15.1	10.5	4.3	10.4
1990	5.6	15.5	5.0	4.9	4.8	11.4	8.2	3.4	8.2
1995	5.6	17.3	4.8	4.9	4.9	10.4	9.3	3.3	8.0
2000	4.0	13.0	4.1	3.6	3.5	7.6	5.7	2.0	5.9
2005	5.1	16.6	4.4	4.6	4.4	10.0	6.0	2.8	7.8
2010	9.6	25.9	9.8	8.0	8.7	16.0	12.5	6.7	12.3
2015	5.3	16.9	4.9	4.8	4.6	9.6	6.6	2.8	7.4
2016	4.9	15.7	4.5	4.4	4.3	8.4	5.8	2.7	6.8
2017	4.4	14.0	4.0	4.0	3.8	7.5	5.1	2.4	6.0
2018	3.9	12.9	3.6	3.5	3.5	6.5	4.7	2.0	5.4
2019	3.7	12.7	3.3	3.2	3.3	6.1	4.3	1.8	5.0
2020*	14.7	31.9	13.0	15.5	14.2	16.7	18.9	9.7	15.9

FIGURE 26.1 Table showing civilian unemployment rate, various groupings (percentage), 1950–2020.

Sources: *Economic Report of the President*, Federal Reserve Economic Data, and the U.S. Bureau of Labor Statistics. Note: *April 2020 data was used

Structurally unemployed workers will need comprehensive re-education and retraining to develop new skills to qualify for new occupations or they will be forced to accept unskilled work for low wages. The United States offers subsidized community college tuition and training programs for structurally displaced workers. Many countries in Europe, especially the Nordic countries, offer workers stipends along with comprehensive retraining and free education so they can develop a new skill set for a new, in-demand occupation. Many countries, including Sweden and Japan, also utilize industrial policies to try to create new industries to replace dying ones.

3. Cyclical unemployment is **unemployment caused by the decreased demand for labor in a recession** (due to the business cycle).

    This stems from the decrease in the demand for goods and services that occurs in recessions, which sparks repeated rounds of layoffs and large declines in the demand for labor. Cyclical unemployment can be very large and quite devastating to the entire economic system. Therefore, governments attempt to reduce cyclical unemployment via stabilization policies to stimulate aggregate demand, especially increases in government spending, reductions in taxes, and increases in the money supply. Some governments also provide subsidies or tax cuts to businesses to stimulate hiring.

To measure cyclical unemployment, mainstream economists use a concept called the natural rate of unemployment, which is **the normal rate of unemployment when the economy is not in a recession.** The natural rate of unemployment is also sometimes called **full employment.** The natural rate of unemployment is found by adding together frictional and structural unemployment. Figure 26.2 displays the U.S. unemployment rate (in black) as well as the natural rate of unemployment (in blue). The difference between the unemployment rate and the natural rate of unemployment is equal to cyclical unemployment, which are the black peaks in Figure 26.2 that occur during and after recessions. Recessions are marked by the gray sections on the figure. Note that in recessions, the unemployment rate shoots up and then it usually takes years for the unemployment rate to fall back to the natural rate.

According to mainstream economists, **the determinants of the natural rate of unemployment are (1) labor force characteristics and demographics, (2) labor market institutions, and (3) government policies**. In terms of (1) labor force characteristics and demographics, older workers with better skills tend to have a lower rate of unemployment, whereas younger, less experienced workers have higher rates of unemployment.

Determining the impact of (2) labor market institutions on the natural rate of unemployment is more complex. For example, the presence of labor unions can impact the natural rate of unemployment but sometimes in surprising ways. In some countries such as France, labor unions that can command high wages and iron-clad job security may cause employers to hire fewer employees than they

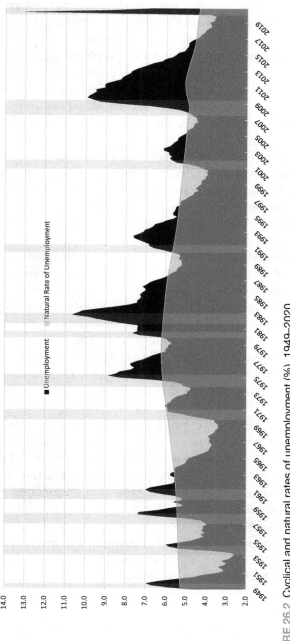

FIGURE 26.2 Cyclical and natural rates of unemployment (%), 1949–2020.

would otherwise, increasing the natural rate of unemployment. In an uncertain business environment, French employers report that they are unwilling to hire new workers because they cannot fire workers easily if the business situation changes. However, in the Nordic countries, labor unions are often more prevalent than in France, but this has not increased the natural rate of unemployment. Unions in Nordic countries are associated with higher levels of productivity, which more than offsets higher union wages. Meanwhile, the Nordic flexicurity model developed by politicians associated with labor unions ensures that unemployed workers get retrained and/or re-educated for new jobs in growing industries, reducing the structural unemployment component of the natural rate of unemployment. This is where (3) government policies become a key determinant of the natural rate of unemployment.

In general, a government unemployment system that pays workers who lose jobs but does not provide them with the skills they need for a changing workplace will tend to be ineffective, generating a higher natural rate of unemployment as well as high levels of underemployment. In contrast, an unemployment system that provides sophisticated retraining and re-education for unemployed workers coupled with policies designed to cultivate the development of new industries can work very well. We find the lowest natural rate of unemployment in countries such as Norway, the Netherlands, and Japan that utilize these policies effectively.

To political economists, the high degree of variability of the natural rate of unemployment is an indication that the concept is fundamentally flawed. From the political economy perspective, the natural rate of unemployment is the unemployment rate a country chooses to live with given its unique economic structure, and there is nothing particularly "natural" about it. From 1989 to 2019, the unemployment rate in Japan and Norway averaged about 4%, the United States averaged about 6%, France averaged 10%, and Spain had an average unemployment rate of over 16%!

Countries that want a low unemployment rate must pursue policies to achieve that goal, along with policies to limit inflation if economic activity becomes overheated. The experiences of countries who have done this successfully seem to indicate that no country needs to live with high levels of structural unemployment. Workers can be put to work doing useful tasks in the community or retrained for new occupations in growing industries.

A less important form of unemployment is seasonal unemployment, **which results from changes in the seasonal demand for labor**. Examples include farmworkers and landscapers laid off in the winter and ski instructors and snowplow operators laid off in the summer. Seasonal unemployment can be solved by setting up year-round employment systems that provide alternative jobs for workers in other seasons.

The unemployment rate is one of the most important measures of the health of the macroeconomy. Unfortunately, the unemployment rate tends to understate the degree of unemployment that actually exists.

26.3 HOW THE UNEMPLOYMENT RATE UNDERSTATES EMPLOYMENT INSECURITY

There are two major flaws with the unemployment rate that cause it to understate the level of unemployment and employment insecurity: (1) Hidden unemployment and (2) underemployment.

1. **Hidden unemployment** includes people who are unemployed and would like to work but are unable to find a job.

    They have looked for work in the last year but not in the last month. Once they quit actively looking for work, these former workers are no longer considered to be part of the labor force, and they are not counted as unemployed even though most people would consider them to be examples of unemployment. There are three categories of hidden unemployment: discouraged workers, other marginalized workers, and workers forced into retirement.

    Discouraged workers would take a job if one were available, but they have given up looking for work after repeated failures. Many structurally unemployed workers end up in this category. **Other marginalized workers** are those who would like to work but are prevented from doing so by illness, school, family responsibilities, transportation issues, or other reasons. For example, many poor people do not have access to adequate transportation or child care, which makes it very difficult to get to work even if you want to. The final category of hidden unemployment includes those in **forced retirement**. These are people who wanted to keep working but were forced to retire by their employers. Employers often use forced retirement as a cost-cutting measure during tough times.

2. **Underemployment** includes involuntary part-time workers who work fewer hours than they want to or underemployed workers confined to jobs that do not utilize their skills.

    Involuntary part-time workers are forced to work less than they want to due to labor market conditions or the actions of employers. Sometimes, only part-time jobs are available due to poor economic conditions. In addition, it is common in the United States for some employers to prevent an employee from working more than 35 hours so they do not have to pay for the employee's health care benefits. To eliminate this problem, The Netherlands passed a law requiring part-time work to come with partial benefits that were equivalent to the benefits per hour that full-time workers were getting.

    Underemployed laborers are working in a job that does not utilize the skills they developed. For example, after the collapse of investment banks in the Great Recession of 2008–2010, some people who had worked in investment banking took jobs in the fast food sector because there were no jobs available that utilized their skills and education. As automobile plants replaced skilled blue-collar workers with robots, many autoworkers turned to unskilled work in warehouses or fast food. Involuntary part-time workers and underemployed workers are employed, so they do not count in unemployment statistics. But these laborers are not working the number of hours or the type of employment that they desire.

The Bureau of Labor Statistics tracks discouraged workers, other marginalized ("marginally attached") workers, and involuntary part-time workers. On average from 1994 to 2020, the official unemployment rate averaged 5.79% and hidden unemployment and involuntary part-time employment averaged 4.64%. Thus, a more realistic measure of the unemployment rate that included hidden unemployment and involuntary part-time employment would have averaged 10.43%, *80% higher than the official unemployment rate.* In 2010 in the deepest part of the Great Recession, the official unemployment rate was 9.6%, and hidden unemployment and involuntary part-time employment totaled 7.13% of the labor force. Thus, the official unemployment rate significantly understates the level of employment insecurity (unemployment and underemployment) that is actually occurring.

Due to the prevalence of hidden unemployment, the labor force participation rate is often a much better indicator of actual employment and unemployment. The labor force participation rate measures the percentage of people of working age (ages 16–64) who are employed. A high labor force participation rate means that almost all workers who want to work are able to find a job. A low labor force participation rate indicates that many workers are unable to find work or have chosen not to work. Figure 26.3 displays labor force participation rates for selected countries in 2018. The countries to the left have the highest labor force participation rate for all persons and those to the right have the lowest.

We see the highest labor force participation rates in European social democracies such as Iceland, Switzerland, and Sweden that feature sophisticated employment creation strategies (industrial policies), active labor market policies, and generous family benefits that encourage women to work, especially generous parental leave and the provision of free childcare. In countries that are very patriarchal and/or that have poor employment creation policies and family benefits, such as Spain and the United States, we see a much lower labor force participation rate, especially for women. Countries that have chronic structural unemployment, such as South Africa, Turkey, and India, have the lowest labor force participation rates.

Notice also that the gap between male and female labor force participation is lowest in the Nordic countries that have the most generous family leave and child support policies, whereas developed countries with poor family benefits, such as the United States and the United Kingdom, have a much larger gap. The largest gender gaps in labor force participation occur in patriarchal developing countries such as Turkey and India.

A few economists argue that the unemployment rate may be overstated. In surveys, it is possible for a person to claim falsely that they are actively searching for work, or people might be working illegally off the books while reporting that they

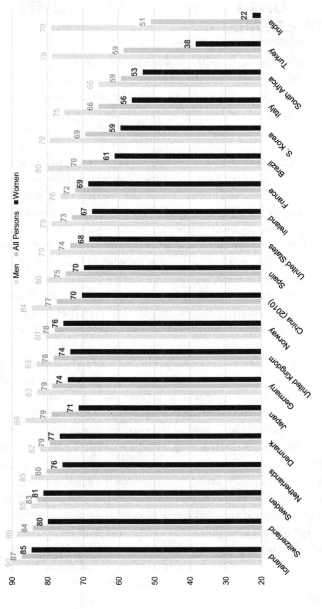

FIGURE 26.3 Labor force participation rates, select OECD countries, 2018.

are unemployed. Most economists believe these problems to be very small and are more concerned with underestimates of the unemployment rate.

26.4 SOLUTIONS TO THE UNEMPLOYMENT MARKET FAILURE

The impact of unemployment, as the major macroeconomic market failure, is so devastating to so many people that all governments enact policies to reduce unemployment. Those policies vary widely, but there are some common patterns. The most widely used policies to reduce the levels and impact of unemployment are the following:

1. **Income replacement**, via some type of unemployment insurance, minimum income guarantee, or other safety net type of program. This helps unemployed workers to afford food and shelter while they search for a new job and also serves to maintain the aggregate level of spending in the community if there are many job losses. In most countries, unemployment insurance is paid for by some combination of employed workers and employers via payroll taxes or general tax revenues. Unemployment benefits are usually time limited to discourage workers from staying unemployed for long periods.
2. **Job search assistance**, including employment listings and job counseling, is also provided by virtually all governments. Job search assistance reduces the length of time workers are unemployed and improves the efficiency of labor markets.
3. **Stabilization policies** in recessions to eliminate or reduce cyclical unemployment. In recessions, increases in government spending, tax cuts, and increases in the money supply can stimulate aggregate demand, returning many businesses to profitability and reducing unemployment. All countries use stabilization policies, although the degree of intervention varies.
4. **Retraining and reeducation** to develop new skills. This is one of the preferred methods to deal with structural unemployment. The most sophisticated of these programs are the active labor market policies in northern Europe, where unemployed workers are given a stipend and enrolled in a training and education program that is tied directly to employment at a particular business in a growing sector. These policies are often tied with industrial policies.
5. **Industrial policies** to promote regional and national economic development. An industrial policy is **a strategic initiative coordinated by the government to create favorable conditions for particular industry**. Key aspects usually include the provision of infrastructure, workforce training and education tailored to the industry, technological assistance via university and government research labs, tariff protection, various types of subsidies, and other methods to foster employment in a high-growth, high-wage industry. The

United States shies away from industrial policies, preferring to let industries develop on their own. However, northern European and newly industrialized Asian economies use industrial policies extensively and quite successfully.

6. **Private sector incentives**, such as tax cuts and hiring bonuses. Some countries, such as the United States, give employers tax credits or subsidies for creating jobs.

7. **Employer of last resort** (ELR) programs. ELR programs involve the government providing a job to anyone who wants one but does not have one at a living wage. This is also called a "job guarantee." ELR programs ensure that the economy is always at the lowest possible level of full employment and that workers always have a job if they want one. It would also mean that instead of paying unemployment benefits to people who are not working, the government would be paying people without jobs to do work that needed to be done in the community. Argentina experimented with such a program in the 2000s, and during the Great Depression, the Work Progress Administration (WPA) in the United States also took similar steps to put unemployed people to work doing useful jobs in their communities. The Nordic countries have a job guarantee for workers under age 25, who traditionally have had much higher unemployment rates. Although ELR programs are not widespread, their impacts have been quite positive where implemented.

As is usually the case, economists differ in the types of policies they advocate and the degree of government intervention they prefer. Political economists see unemployment as the most devastating macroeconomic market failure, and correspondingly they advocate dramatic actions such as ELR programs, active labor market policies, and industrial policies, in addition to the other policies listed above. Most New Keynesian U.S. economists support moderate efforts to reduce the costs of unemployment, such as unemployment insurance and stabilization policies, but not the other policies advocated by political economists. Supply-side economists prefer to alleviate unemployment via private sector incentives, especially tax cuts for businesses. Such incentives can be effective if the business climate is improving. However, business tax cuts do not tend to have much impact on employment if business confidence is low.

Laissez-faire advocates do not approve of dramatic government intervention to alleviate unemployment. Ludwig von Mises, one of the founders of Austrian economics, argued that "Unemployment in the unhampered market is always voluntary. ... [T]here is always for each type of labor a rate at which all those eager to work can get a job."[4] From this perspective, if unemployed workers would simply lower the wage that they would accept, they would find work.

The laissez-faire perspective is in direct opposition to Keynes' arguments and the data cited above, showing that there are times in which there are simply not enough jobs available for everyone who wants to work. Furthermore, when recessions are so bad and so long that wages do fall, that has eroded aggregate demand

and kept the economy in a recession. Therefore, only a small number of modern economists adopt the laissez-faire view of unemployment.

The coronavirus recession of 2020 provides an interesting case study of how different economic systems approached the economic crisis that resulted from the massive economic shutdowns required to stop the spread of the virus.[5] Only by sending most workers home and preserving social distancing were countries able to stop the spread of the virus and the accompanying deaths. But the decline in economic activity was devastating, businesses' sales dropped precipitously, and firms began to contemplate mass layoffs.

Instead of waiting for workers to lose jobs, the German government decided to pay employers a share of workers' wages. Workers were also required to share tasks, reduce their hours, and take pay cuts of about 10%. Nonetheless, almost all German workers remained employed.

Meanwhile, the United States government expanded unemployment benefits, increasing the benefit amount and the length of time that people could collect benefits. In addition to these measures, workers were given tax rebates of up to $1200, and mortgage, rent, and student loan payments were delayed for almost a year. The United States spent more per person on unemployment benefits than Germany.

The differential impact of these programs on the unemployment rate was massive. In Germany, the unemployment rate increased only slightly from 5.0% in March of 2020 to 5.8% in April of 2020. In the United States, unemployment more than tripled from 4.4% to 14.7% over the same time period. Almost all German workers kept their jobs, whereas many U.S. workers lost jobs permanently as employers went bankrupt.

The contrast between the German and U.S. approaches reflects different priorities. The German government sees maintaining employment as one of its main priorities. The U.S. government helps out unemployed workers and businesses, but it is up to the private sector to create and maintain employment.

Along with unemployment, another important macroeconomic market failure is price instability. We turn to this in the next section.

26.5 PRICE INSTABILITY: INFLATION, DEFLATION, REAL WAGES, AND REAL INTEREST RATES

The **price level** is the general level of prices of goods in a country or region compared to base year prices. The price level is measured via the construction of a **price index**, a specific measure used to compute the cost of a particular weighted combination of goods. For example, the most widely used price index is the Consumer Price Index (CPI), which is constructed by calculating the average cost over time of purchasing a basket of consumer goods, weighted by the importance of those goods in a typical consumer's budget. The CPI includes the prices of housing (the largest item in consumers' budgets), transportation, food and beverages, apparel, medical care, recreation, education, communication, and other goods and services.

$$CPI = \frac{\text{Current cost of consumer goods}}{\text{Base year cost of consumer goods}} \times 100.$$

Once we have the CPI, we can use it to compute the rate of change in prices, which tells us whether there is inflation (an increase in CPI) or deflation (a decrease in CPI) in a particular time period. Inflation is **an increase in the average level of prices in an economy**, and it is measured via the increase in a price index such as the CPI. Similarly, deflation is **a decrease in the average level of prices in an economy**. We take the CPI this year, CPI_2, subtract the CPI last year, CPI_1, and divide by the CPI last year to get the percentage change in CPI. The percentage change in the CPI is the rate of inflation if it is greater than zero or the rate of deflation if it is less than zero.

$$\text{Rate of change in prices} = \frac{CPI_2 - CPI_1}{CPI_1} \times 100\%.$$

Figure 26.4 shows the monthly rate of change in the CPI_U.[6] CPI_U is the consumer price index for urban consumers, and it is used most frequently to measure inflation.

We can see that when the economy is experiencing booms, the rate of change in prices tends to be positive (inflation). However, in deep recessions, such as 2008 and 2020, we see deflation.

The Producer Price Index (PPI) measures the average change over time in the prices of a representative basket of goods and services sold by businesses in the wholesale market to the producers of goods and services. The PPI measures the prices paid for supplies and inputs by producers.

Another important topic related to inflation is the real wage rate. Here, economists use the same terminology as they do when they refer to GDP. Nominal GDP is GDP at current prices. Similarly, the nominal wage rate is the wage rate at current prices. Real GDP is GDP at constant prices, which is found by dividing nominal GDP by the GDP deflator (a price index). The real wage rate **is equal to the nominal wage rate divided by the consumer price index** (CPI_U).

$$\text{Real wage rate} = \frac{\text{Nominal wage rate}}{CPI_U}.$$

The real wage rate is a much more accurate measure of workers' purchasing power than the nominal wage rate because it accounts for inflation. The real wage also yields another important insight: *Workers only receive a real wage increase if the increase*

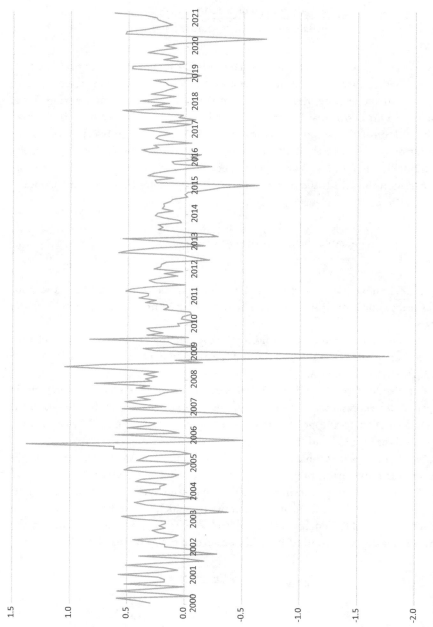

FIGURE 26.4 Monthly rate of inflation and deflation (% change in CPI$_U$, seasonally adjusted).

in nominal wages exceeds the increase in prices. If nominal wages and prices increase at the same rate, then real wages stay the same. And if nominal wages increase by less than prices increase, workers are experiencing a real wage cut. This is why many labor unions build a cost of living adjustment into their contracts, so that their nominal wages always go up at least as fast as inflation.

Figure 26.5 compares median weekly nominal wages and real wages in the United States from 1979 to 2019. Nominal wages increased dramatically over this 40-year period, from $344 per week in 1979 to $1367 per week in 2019, a 297% increase. However, wages and prices *both* increased dramatically over this time period. When we take into account increases in the price index, real wages changed very little, increasing from $322 in 1979 to $359 in 2019, an 11% increase. For 2019, if we take the nominal wage of $1367 and divide by the price index of 3.81, we get the real wage of $359. Thus, most of the increase in nominal wages over the last 40 years was a result of inflation.

Similarly, economists prefer to use the real interest rate rather than the nominal interest rate to determine how much money banks are actually making on their loans. The real interest rate is computed by taking the nominal interest rate and subtracting the rate of inflation:

$$\text{Real interest rate} = \text{Nominal interest rate} - \text{Inflation.}$$

Figure 26.6 shows the relationship between nominal interest rates, inflation rates, and real interest rates. In the 1990s, real interest rates usually fell between 3% and 4%, whereas nominal interest rates fluctuated depending on inflation. After the financial crisis, in 2008 and 2011–2012, real interest rates were negative because inflation rates exceeded nominal interest rates. When negative real interest rates occur this is very hard on banks because they end up losing money on all of their loans. This is one of the potential problems that can occur from inflation.

26.6 PRICE INSTABILITY AS A MARKET FAILURE: THE PROBLEMS CREATED BY DEFLATION AND INFLATION

Economists consider price instability to be a market failure because unregulated markets regularly generate price instability, and when price instability occurs it can have a detrimental impact on consumers, manufacturers, the financial sector, and the macroeconomy. Deflation and inflation have very different impacts. Deflation contributes directly to economic crises. Moderate levels of inflation are not problematic and economic actors can easily adjust. But higher levels of inflation, especially sudden increases and wage–price spirals, can be very problematic.

Deflation is usually a sign of an economy in distress, with prices falling due to gluts of goods. A glut of goods is usually a product of a decrease in aggregate

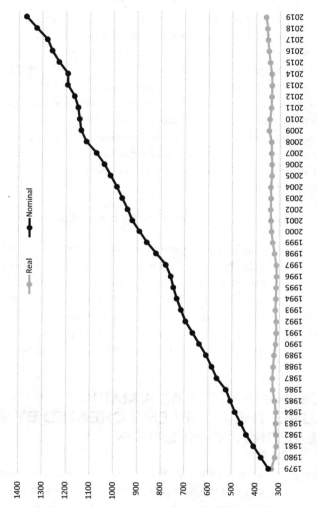

FIGURE 26.5 Median usual weekly earnings for wage and salary workers ($), 1979–2019.

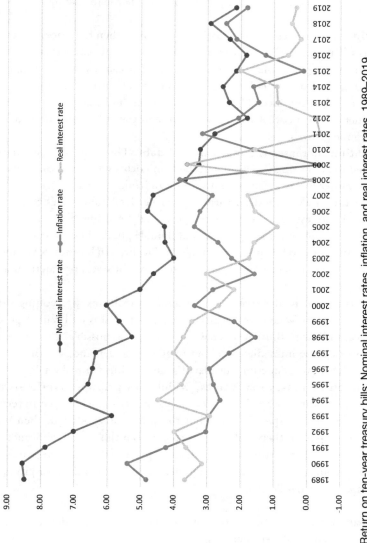

FIGURE 26.6 Return on ten-year treasury bills: Nominal interest rates, inflation, and real interest rates, 1989–2019.

demand and subsequent declines in consumer and investor confidence. The decline in aggregate demand can be caused by a stock market crash, government austerity programs, an increase in interest rates, a decrease in the money supply, an overvalued exchange rate, a political or economic crisis domestically or abroad, an increase in unemployment, and so on. Unfortunately, deflation that follows an aggregate demand shock tends to exacerbate the economic crises that caused the deflation.

The major problems created by deflation include the following:

1. **Falling output prices can bankrupt firms.** When the prices of goods that firms sell are falling but their costs remain the same (because they have already produced the goods they are trying to sell or because wages and input prices are sticky and do not fall quickly even in downturns), firms will lose money on goods they produce. These losses tend to result in layoffs and decreases in production, events that can be the first step toward a significant decline in economic growth.

2. **Deflation increases the real value of debt.** The revenues that a firm takes in tend to fall during deflation, but the firm's debts stay at the same level, making it harder to pay off loans. This, too, can bankrupt firms.

3. **Deflation makes credit more expensive.** Deflation causes real inflation-adjusted interest rates to increase, potentially causing declines in business investment and consumer purchases of durable goods (houses, cars, and appliances) that tend to be purchased on credit. Declines in business investment and consumer purchases reduce aggregate demand, business production, and real GDP.

4. **Deflation can lead consumers to delay purchases**, postponing spending until the future. When car prices are falling, consumers will wait to purchase a new car until they think prices have gone as low as possible. Therefore, falling prices can cause immediate declines in aggregate demand, which can in turn lead to business production cuts, layoffs, and declines in real GDP.

5. **Deflation increases real wages, which can prompt layoffs.** As Keynes observed, nominal wages are sticky and do not fall quickly even in recessions. If workers' wages stay the same but the prices of goods fall, then workers' purchasing power, their real wage, increases. But this makes labor more costly for firms, further cutting into profits and making layoffs increasingly likely. Layoffs reduce income and spending, decreasing the demand for products and prompting further layoffs.

Deflationary forces can also become entrenched, creating a deflationary spiral. Falling prices cause reduced spending and business failures, which prompts layoffs and more reduced spending, which causes further deflation and another bout of reduced spending and business failures, and so on.

Correcting deflation requires expansionary fiscal and monetary policies. Increased government spending and tax cuts can stimulate spending and reverse business contraction. Increasing the money supply and purchasing corporate debt can reduce interest rates and promote borrowing, which stimulates consumer spending and business investment. Governments can also prevent deflation by establishing price floors on goods and services to preserve businesses' profitability. During the Great Depression, the U.S. government placed price floors on agricultural products to prevent prices from going so low that farmers went out of business.

The opposite of deflation is **inflation**. In general, rates of inflation in the range of 0%–5% are easy for businesses and consumers to cope with and do not create significant problems. If everyone expects a 3% rate of inflation, then workers ask for a 3% raise, businesses raise prices by 3%, banks raise interest rates by 3%, and the economy adjusts to a higher price level. Modest rates of inflation can create minor problems, as we will see below. However, rapid inflation, and especially hyperinflation can create major economic problems, including a financial collapse.

The major problems created by inflation include the following:

1. **Perceptions: People are misled when looking at wages and interest rates.**

    Almost every worker can tell you a story of a boss who promised them a big raise of 2% in a year when inflation was 2.5%, meaning that the worker actually took a pay cut in real terms. "Raises" of less than the rate of inflation actually mean a decline in purchasing power, so these workers are getting a pay cut. Similarly, sometimes nominal interest rates increase, making it seem like it is more expensive to borrow but real interest rates actually decrease due to the impact of inflation. From Figure 26.6, we can see that in 2016 the nominal interest rate was 1.84% and the inflation rate was 1.26%, so the real interest rate was 0.58%. In 2017, the nominal interest rate was higher at 2.33% but the inflation rate rose to 2.13%, making the real interest rate in 2017 0.20%. Even though the nominal interest rate was higher in 2017 than it was in 2016, the real cost of borrowing money had decreased slightly from 0.58% to 0.20%. Unfortunately, homeowners often focus on nominal interest rates instead of real interest rates.

2. **Lenders lose and borrowers gain from inflation.**

    Inflation somewhat arbitrarily redistributes income from one group to another. Inflation erodes the value of assets that pay fixed (not adjusted for inflation) rates of return, including many bonds, pensions, savings accounts, and other accounts of lenders. High rates of inflation can discourage saving due to this phenomenon, which can be bad for banks and business investment. More important, substantial amounts of inflation mean that borrowers pay back money that is worth less, and lenders end up receiving money that is worth less. With inflation, it becomes easier to earn the money to pay back a loan because wages tend to increase at or above the rate or inflation. In general, the more rapid the rate of inflation, the more wages will increase, while existing loan amounts stay the same. Interestingly, most college students with student loan debt would benefit from an inflationary environment: Wages and salaries when they graduate will be higher due to inflation but their student loan amounts would have stayed the same.

3. **Inflation leads banks to raise nominal interest rates.**

    Recall that banks try to earn a real interest rate of 2%–4%, onto which they add the inflation rate to arrive at the nominal interest rate. Higher inflation leads directly to higher nominal interest rates, which can cause businesses and consumers to rethink or delay purchases that require borrowing. Thus, higher nominal interest rates can reduce business investment and consumer purchases of durable goods.

4. **Significant levels of unanticipated inflation can cause a financial crisis.**

    Banks take expected inflation into account by raising nominal interest rates, and workers take expected inflation into account by demanding wage increases. Therefore, predictable inflation is rarely a major problem. However, unexpected inflation at significant levels causes negative real interest rates to result (inflation exceeds the nominal rate of interest), which causes banks to lose money on all loans that are not indexed to inflation. High unanticipated inflation in the 1970s caused large numbers of savings and loan banks to go bankrupt due to such losses. These problems can be especially problematic if interest rate ceilings are in effect. For example, some countries limit the interest rates that banks can charge on loans to poor farmers to prevent usury. However, if the inflation rate exceeds the interest rate ceiling, banks will experience negative real interest rates, which can causes them to go bankrupt.

5. **Inflation can cause the central bank (such as the Fed in the United States) to slow down the economy.**

    In order to eliminate inflationary pressures, central banks sometimes increase interest rates significantly. In the United States, contractionary monetary policy and higher interest rates created by Fed action caused recessions in 1980 and 1990. Fears of inflation in the 2010s led the European Central Bank to maintain high interest rates (relative to those in the United States and the United Kingdom), which reduced Europe's economic growth significantly.

There are also some minor problems that inflation can cause. For example, in the United States increases in nominal wages can put you in a higher tax bracket, which will result in your paying higher taxes even though your real wages may not have changed. This may be a disincentive to earn a higher income if the tax increase is significant enough.

Though inflation is a problem, hyperinflation, which is **rapidly accelerating inflation that is out of control**, can be devastating. During episodes of hyperinflation, prices change daily. The worst modern example of hyperinflation occurred in Zimbabwe in 2007–2008, when prices increased by 98% a day. This means that prices were doubling every 24.5 hours! Zimbabwe's annual inflation rate reached 89.7 sextillion percent (89,700,000,000,000,000,000,000%) in 2009. The currency became worth so little that the government was issuing banknotes of $100 trillion, as shown in Figure 26.7.

The fact that prices change daily during hyperinflationary episodes causes people to go out and spend money as soon as they receive it, which causes prices to increase further. We also see a wage–price spiral form, where inflation causes workers to demand higher wages, which causes businesses to raise prices, which causes another round of inflation, which creates demands for more wage increases, and so on.

Eventually, hyperinflation causes people to lose faith in the currency. They buy gold and other nonmonetary assets or put their money in foreign currencies. The financial system ceases to function and people use foreign currencies or barter to make exchanges. Savings and investment collapse as a result. As we will see later, hyperinflationary episodes are usually caused by shortages of essential goods, coupled with unsustainable increases in the money supply by the government.

Given that price inflation can create some serious economic problems, it is important to recognize the causes of inflation and the policies governments can use to correct it. **Cost-push inflation** occurs when a shock to input prices, such as dramatically higher oil prices, causes businesses' costs to increase, which causes them to increase output prices. Cost-push inflation can lead to problematic spikes in inflation due to **wage–price spirals**, as higher prices lead to demands for higher wages, which causes a secondary round of price increases, and so on. This is the most important driver of inflation in the modern economy. **Demand-pull inflation** occurs when increases in the demand for goods cause prices to increase, usually due to increasing wages and input prices in a rapidly growing, overheated economy.

Both of these types of inflation are driven by increases in businesses' costs of production. This can be solved via wages and price controls that limit how much prices can increase, policies to reduce businesses' costs in other ways, or austerity policies that reduce the demand for goods and services and throw the economy into recession.

Political economists argue that inflation is a result of a conflict over the distribution of income between or within classes, such as capital and labor; landowners and peasants; between different groups of workers; or between producers in different sectors. For example, workers often benefit from low levels of unemployment and moderately higher levels of inflation because their bargaining power improves when unemployment is low. However, employers' profits are often higher when there is a higher degree of unemployment, which keeps wages low, and a lower degree of inflation, which keeps the real rate of profit high. Therefore, the pursuit of a low inflation policy by the government indicates greater support for employers than workers.

Investment banks also like austerity policies because they prefer low inflation and a strong U.S. dollar, which makes their investments more profitable. However,

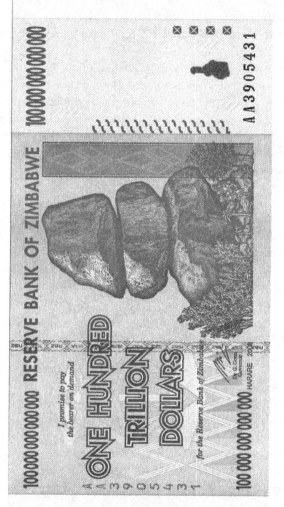

FIGURE 26.7 A one hundred trillion-dollar bank note from Zimbabwe in 2008. Source: Wikimedia Commons.

manufacturers benefit from higher demand for products, which is associated with more spending and inflation, and a weaker U.S. dollar that makes U.S. goods more competitive. So, a high growth, higher inflation, devalued currency approach tends to favor manufacturers, whereas a lower growth, lower inflation, strong currency approach tends to favor financial interests.

Mainstream economists tend to see inflation as a result of exogenous supply shocks, such as an increase in input prices, or an overheated economy that causes the cost of inputs to increase. Distributional issues associated with inflation are not a major focus of their work.

Inflation can also be driven by changes in the money supply, although there is substantial debate about this among economists. Furthermore, the austerity philosophy of conservative economists depends on an economic theory called the Phillips curve, which is also hotly debated.

26.7 ECONOMIC THEORY AND POLICY REGARDING INFLATION AND UNEMPLOYMENT

The relationship between the money supply and inflation is a contested one in economics. The money supply (abbreviated M1) **is the total amount of currency and checkable deposits in an economic system**. Some economists think that the money supply is directly tied to the rate of inflation, whereas others see the relationship as more tenuous.

As early as 1568, French economist Jean Bodin identified a relationship between the money supply and inflation. He observed that whenever there was an increase in the money supply while the quantity of goods produced remained the same, the result was inflation. This important observation was developed further in the 19th century by classical economists who developed the quantity theory of money, which posits that **the quantity of money in circulation (M1) is directly proportional to the price level of goods and services**. This theory was later reiterated by well-known laissez-faire economist Milton Friedman, who stated in 1970 that "inflation is always and everywhere a monetary phenomenon in the sense that it is and can be produced only by a more rapid increase in the quantity of money than in output."

The quantity theory of money is based on the equation of exchange:

$$\text{Money Supply} \times \text{Velocity} = \text{Price Level} \times \text{Real GDP}$$

$$M1 \times V = P \times \text{Real GDP}.$$

Velocity is **the number of times a unit of currency ($) changes hands in a year**.

P in this equation in the real GDP deflator, which is the price index for the whole economy.

The basic intuition of this model is straightforward and important. If we take the amount of money that is available and multiply by the number of times that money is spent in a year, we get total spending in the economy (nominal GDP, which is equal to P multiplied by real GDP). If an economy wants to have economic growth (an increase in Real GDP), it also must have an increase in M1. However, if M1 increases faster than real GDP, and if velocity stays constant, then the economy will experience inflation.

This equation implies a direct, proportional relationship between the money supply and the price level. To connect the money supply and inflation, Milton Friedman made three important assumptions:

1. Velocity is constant.
2. Real GDP cannot be influenced by M1 and is driven instead by productivity and technology.
3. Money can influence prices but not vice versa.

If these assumptions hold, then any increase in the money supply will lead to a similar increase in the price level.

We will study the quantity theory of money in more detail later when we take up monetary policy. For now, if we observe the relationship between the money supply (M1) and the price level (CPI), we can see that in recent years they are not closely correlated. Figure 26.8 shows that we regularly see spikes in the money supply, M1, that are not matched by corresponding increases in prices (CPI_U). These spikes in M1 are examples of the Fed engaging in "expansionary monetary policy," dramatically increasing the money supply to combat a recession (recessions occurred in 2001, 2008 and 2020 in Figure 26.8).

During the Great Recession and its aftermath from 2008 to 2012, laissez-faire economists following Milton Friedman's ideas predicted rampant inflation due to the increases in the money supply that were used to stimulate the economy to reduce the recession's severity. Instead, they recommended that money supply growth should be restricted, known as a "tight" or "contractionary" or "hawkish" monetary policy in the press. However, the inflation they predicted never materialized.

Interestingly, there was inflation of asset values when the money supply expanded. Some economists believe that there is more of a connection in the modern world between the money supply and asset values than there is between the money supply and the prices of goods and services.

The fact that increases in M1 do not seem to cause inflation in the United States in the modern era made policymakers much more willing to use expansionary monetary policy to combat recessions. With the coronavirus recession of 2020, the Fed increased the U.S. money supply by an astounding 23%, a modern record.

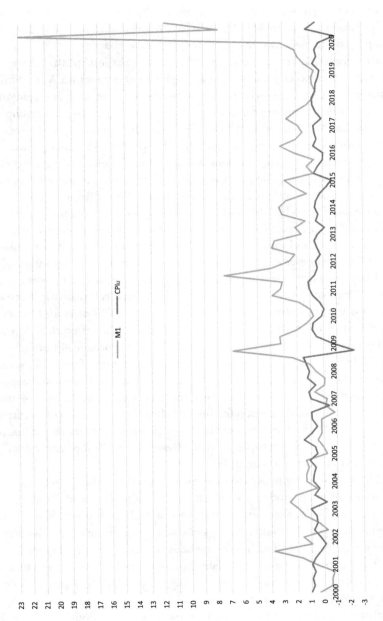

FIGURE 26.8 Percentage change in M1 and prices (CPI$_U$), 2000–2020.

At the same time, prices fell, indicating that deflation was occurring, with all of its accompanying problems. However, the increases in M1 did prop up asset values. After losing more than 33% of its value in March of 2020, the Dow Jones Industrial Average of stocks regained most of its lost ground by June of 2020 thanks largely due to the huge increase in M1. By early 2021, stock markets set new records thanks in part to the huge infusions of money from the Fed.

Another contested area of economic theory is the argument that there is an inherent trade-off between inflation and unemployment. Economist A. W. Phillips found that a stable, inverse relationship between inflation and unemployment existed in the British economy for more than a century. A similar relationship was found in the United States in the 1960s. The basic idea is that when an economy grows very quickly, unemployment tends to be very low. But rapid growth and low unemployment lead to increases in wages and input prices as the bargaining power of workers and input suppliers is improved, raising costs and causing businesses to raise prices. Strong demand for goods also allows firms to raise goods prices more easily than when demand is low. The result is low unemployment and high inflation. But in a recession, unemployment increases dramatically, reducing the demand for labor and inputs. Costs and goods prices tend to fall in recessions, reducing inflation. Therefore, in recessions we would tend to see high unemployment and low prices, whereas in booms we would see low unemployment and high prices. Thus, the Phillips curve **posits an inverse relationship between inflation and unemployment based on the impact of booms and busts on businesses' costs of production**. The Phillips curve depends on flexible wages and input prices to achieve this result, a potentially problematic assumption.

The Phillips curve has very important policy implications. If the Phillips curve relationship holds, one of the main drivers of high inflation is low unemployment. The belief that this relationship was a strong one led central banks to increase interest rates whenever unemployment rates dipped below the natural rate of unemployment. The U.S. Fed raised interest rates in the boom phase of every recent business cycle in the 1980s, 1990s, 2000s, and 2010s. However, the Phillips curve relationship is no longer as clear as it used to be.

The Phillips curve is supposed to show an inverse relationship between the percentage change in prices (inflation) and the rate of unemployment. Figure 26.9(a) shows that in the 1960s, there was a clear, inverse relationship between inflation and unemployment in the United States consistent with Phillips' ideas. However, that relationship has gotten much more tenuous in recent decades. Figure 26.9(b) plots the Phillips curve in the United States from 2000 to 2020. As we can observe, the Phillips curve became much flatter, having only a slightly negative slope, as indicated by the blue logarithmic trend line.

The flattening of the Phillips curve has important implications. The latest data indicate that an economic system can now grow quickly and have a low unemployment rate without generating significant inflation. This further implies that the austerity policies pursued in the past to reduce inflationary pressures during booms

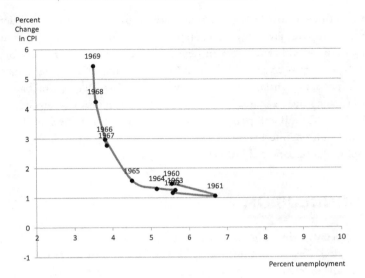

FIGURE 26.9 (a) The U.S. Phillips curve, 1960–1969.

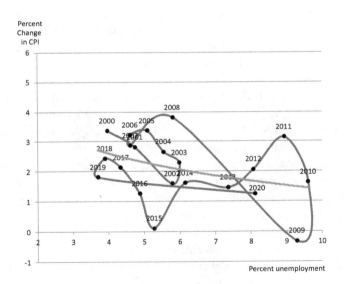

FIGURE 26.9 (b) The U.S. Phillips curve, 2000–2020.

may no longer be as necessary. Economists have theorized that in the modern, globalized economy, firms are less able to raise prices and workers are less able to demand higher wages in booms due to extensive foreign competition. This keeps input prices and wages low even when economies boom, limiting inflationary pressures. Therefore, the Phillips curve likely varies with particular aspects of markets.

We will discuss the Phillips curve and how it has changed in more detail later in the book after we have covered economic theory in more detail. For now, the key thing to note is that in modern developed economies, there may be a weak inverse relationship between inflation and unemployment. This may cause central banks to implement tight money policies in booms. However, central banks may be pressured to keep interest rates low by those who see inflation as less of a problem. Both President Trump and political economists argued that the Fed should lower interest rates in the United States during the economic boom of the late 2010s. The Fed complied, indicating a significant shift in their approach.

26.8 CONCLUSION

Unemployment is the most serious macroeconomic market failure. Its costs to people, families, communities, and the macroeconomy are devastating. Therefore, all governments enact policies to extend safety nets to workers who become unemployed, to assist the unemployed in finding jobs, and to create jobs where possible.

There are three major types of unemployment: Frictional, structural, and cyclical. The frictionally unemployed are between jobs and are expected to be rehired quickly. Structurally unemployed workers present a thornier problem because their skills are no longer in demand in the labor market. Cyclical unemployment is unemployment in excess of the natural rate of unemployment, and it occurs during and following recessions.

The natural rate of unemployment is used as a guide by mainstream economists and policymakers to indicate whether the economy is overheated (when the unemployment rate falls below the natural rate of unemployment) or in a recession (when the unemployment rate is above the natural rate of unemployment). Overheated economies can result in inflation, so policymakers often raise interest rates to slow down overheated economies to reign in inflationary pressures. Recessionary economies require expansionary fiscal and monetary policies to eliminate cyclical unemployment. Political economists argue that the concept of the natural rate of unemployment is fundamentally flawed and that it is possible to have rapid growth, low unemployment, and low inflation simultaneously with the right set of policies. They argue that the government should always pursue maximum employment to benefit workers.

The unemployment rate tends to understate the actual level of unemployment due to hidden unemployment and underemployment. Discouraged workers and part-time workers who want to work full time are important categories of unemployment and underemployment that are not included in the official unemployment rate. Therefore, economists often use the labor force participation rate instead of the unemployment rate to indicate how many people are actually working in an economy.

Policies to reduce the costs or level of unemployment include income replacement (unemployment insurance), job search assistance, stabilization policies in recessions, retraining, and re-education. Some countries, especially social market economies and state-dominated economies, use industrial policies to stimulate the development of new industries. Some of the world's most effective policies to address unemployment combine active labor market policies and industrial policies, where workers receive specific training and education to prepare for a particular job, at the same time the government creates conditions to stimulate development on an industry that will hire the workers being trained. Market-dominated economies tend to use private sector incentives instead of government-led industrial development efforts to stimulate employment creation.

A few countries have experimented with programs where the government serves as the employer of last resort, providing useful work in communities to any worker who wants a job but cannot find one. Successful examples of ELR programs included the Works Project Administration in the United States during the Great Depression and Argentina's Plan Jefes.

Price instability is another important macroeconomic market failure. Deflation can bankrupt businesses and deepen economic crises. Rapid inflation, especially hyperinflation, can destabilize the financial system and bankrupt banks. Moderate inflation, however, is straightforward for economic agents to incorporate into their expectations and causes only minor issues.

Because deflation is a major problem but low levels of inflation are not, most governments pursue economic policies designed to foster stable, moderate inflation. Both the United States and the European Union have selected 2% as their target inflation rate. If inflation falls below 2%, this may be a sign if an impending recession, so the money supply is increased and other efforts to stimulate the economy are enacted. If the inflation rate exceeds 2%, the central bank will likely increase interest rates to slow down the economy to reduce inflationary pressures and to prevent a wage-price spiral. This shows the broad adherence among policymakers to the Phillips curve idea that there is an inherent trade-off between unemployment and inflation.

Inflation is primarily driven by factors that increase businesses' costs of production. This includes higher input prices driven by supply shortages or by increased demand for inputs during expansions. According to the quantity theory of money, inflation can also be generated by increases in the money supply; however, empirical evidence indicates that this relationship in the modern world is not as clear as it once was. Also less certain in the modern era is the Phillips curve relationship between inflation and unemployment. In the United States in the 1960s there was a clear, inverse relationship between inflation and unemployment. In the

2000s and 2010s, there was a very small inverse relationship between inflation and unemployment.

The debates over the relationship between inflation and unemployment or the money supply and inflation are driven by economic theory. We turn next to economists' theories regarding how macroeconomies work in the next section to gain greater insights into these issues.

• •

QUESTIONS FOR REVIEW

1. List the major costs that result from unemployment to individuals, families, communities, and the macroeconomy.
2. (a) Define each of the three major types of unemployment in your own words and come up with at least one specific example for each type. Do not use examples from the book. (b) Explain which type of unemployment you believe to be most harmful to the economy and why.
3. Why do many economists find the unemployment rate to be problematic in terms of representing how well workers are doing? Explain carefully.
4. List the major programs that are used to reduce the levels and impact of unemployment. Which policies do you think are most effective? Why?
5. Which of the following statements about inflation are true (select one or more)? Explain each answer briefly.
   a. Inflation is worse than deflation because deflation is good for businesses.
   b. Inflation helps lenders because it leads to higher interest rates.
   c. Worries about inflation usually cause the Fed to raise interest rates.
   d. Inflation leads banks to increase nominal interest rates.
   e. Unanticipated inflation can cause a financial crisis.
   f. Inflation causes borrowers to lose and lenders to gain.
6. List the major problems created by deflation. Which of these do you think is most problematic? Why? How can deflation be solved?
7. List the major problems created by inflation. Which of these do you think is most problematic? Why? How can inflation be solved?
8. According to political economists, which groups benefit most from a low inflation, high unemployment economy, and which groups benefit from a high inflation, low unemployment economy?
9. According to the quantity theory of money and the equation of exchange, what will happen to the economy when the money supply is increased by 20% (as it was in 2020), assuming that the assumptions behind the theory hold? What are the potential problems with this approach?
10. According to the Phillips curve, if the economy experiences a rapid economic boom, what can we expect to happen? What are the potential problems with the analysis of the Phillips curve?

NOTES

1 Joan Robinson, *Economic Philosophy* (Doubleday, New York, 1965), p. 45.

2 Hannes Schwandt, "Recession Graduates: The Long-lasting Effects of an Unlucky Draw," Stanford Institute for Economic Policy Research, April 2019, https://siepr. stanford.edu/research/publications/recession-graduates-effects-unlucky#:~:text=Le aving%20school%20for%20work%20during,called%20%E2%80%9Cdeaths%20of %20despair.%E2%80%9D.

3 Bill Mitchell, "The Costs of Unemployment—Again," http://bilbo.economicoutlook. net/blog/?p=17740, accessed June 14, 2020.

4 Ludwig von Mises, *Human Action: A Treatise on Economics* (Ludwig von Mises Institute, Auburn, AL, 1998), pp. 596–597.

5 My thanks to Spandan Marasini, who conducted the research and drafted the initial text for this section.

6 Source: FRED, CPIAUCSL, https://fred.stlouisfed.org/series/CPIAUCSL.

PART VIII

Macroeconomic models

In this section, we take up the key models that economists use to analyze the macroeconomy and to determine the best policies to use to confront the major macroeconomic problems. The macroeconomy is so complex that an economist cannot possibly analyze every action of every individual or firm. In addition, microeconomic phenomena often have macroeconomic consequences that are counterintuitive. It seems rational for each individual firm to close its operations in expensive, developed countries and to reopen in cheaper, developing countries. However, as many companies moved operations overseas, wages in developed countries stagnated, growth rates slowed, and sales slowed, undermining profitability to some extent. Even though the microeconomic actions seemed rational, the macroeconomic consequences were destructive.

To analyze the macroeconomy effectively, macroeconomists rely on analysis of the broad patterns of human behavior that lead to large changes in economic outcomes. Instead of analyzing individual consumers, macroeconomists study the patterns affecting the consumption and savings habits of all consumers. Instead of analyzing the capital investment decisions of each firm, macroeconomists study the investment patterns of all firms. This requires the development of models to capture the patterns and relationships between macroeconomic variables.

Interestingly, the models of macroeconomics are not simply microeconomic models that are aggregated (added up). Sometimes, it is possible to intuit macroeconomic behavior from microeconomic models. For example, we know that when individual consumers have more money, they tend to spend more, and that holds at the macroeconomic level as well. Increases in national income will lead to increases in national consumption levels. However, there are also macroeconomic foundations for microeconomic behavior. The general macroeconomic environment, including the availability of employment, the rate of economic growth, and the value of the stock market, drives individual consumer behavior. In this sense, there are macroeconomic foundations for much microeconomic behavior. Thus,

DOI: 10.4324/9781315636924-34

macroeconomists must carefully observe what factors affect the macroeconomy writ large, to determine when microeconomic behavior results in macroeconomic outcomes and vice versa.

Chapter 27 focuses on the aggregate demand and aggregate supply (AD–AS) model, which is the cornerstone of modern New Keynesian analysis. Unlike the demand curve model of microeconomics, which focuses on individual consumers, the macroeconomic aggregate demand curve incorporates purchases by consumers, purchases of capital goods (investment) by firms, government purchases, and net purchases of goods and services from the international sector. Aggregate demand is the demand curve for all sectors of the macroeconomy. Similarly, aggregate supply is the supply curve for the whole economy, reflecting the behavior of all suppliers in all industries. Due to the complexity of the macroeconomy, there is often disagreement about the structure of macroeconomic models. Political economists dispute certain aspects of the AD–AS model, as we will see in this chapter.

Chapter 28 lays out the Keynesian aggregate expenditure–income model, sometimes called the "Keynesian cross," with a number of examples and applications. For most of the 20th century, this model was considered the cornerstone of macroeconomics. The chapter goes through how each sector (consumption, investment, government spending, and net exports) fits into the Keynesian model and how changes in the components of aggregate expenditure work with the multiplier. The chapter also includes debates over the Keynesian model.

Aggregate demand and aggregate supply

A mainstream economics model of the macroeconomy

Aggregate demand and aggregate supply is one of the most important models in mainstream macroeconomics. This chapter will lay out the basic mechanics of how that model works in the short term and the long term.

As with the supply and demand model developed earlier in the book, the aggregate demand and aggregate supply model works on a consistent set of principles. In the short run, changes in the price level cause the economy to move along the aggregate demand curve and the aggregate supply curve, whereas changes in the determinants of aggregate demand shift the aggregate demand curve and changes in the determinants of aggregate supply shift that aggregate supply curve. The aggregate demand and aggregate supply model can also be used to analyze the long-run adjustment of the economy. However, there are significant debates among economists regarding the long-term functioning of the economy, and it is important for you to understand the basic parameters of the debate.

This chapter begins by describing the short-run aggregate demand and aggregate supply (AD–AS) model. The chapter then takes up how the multiplier determines the magnitude of shifts in the aggregate demand curve. Subsequently, the chapter discusses the classical and Keynesian models of how the AD–AS model adjusts in the long run and the debate over how the government should intervene during recessions and expansions. The chapter finishes by discussing some of the problems with the AD–AS model according to political economists.

DOI: 10.4324/9781315636924-35

27.0 CHAPTER 27 LEARNING GOALS

After reading this chapter you should be able to:

■ Use an aggregate demand and aggregate supply graph to determine how a variety of factors will affect the national price index and real gross domestic product (GDP).

■ Define the marginal respending rate, list its components, and explain how the marginal respending rate and its components are related to the multiplier.

■ Compute the multiplier using the marginal respending rate.

■ Use the multiplier to determine exactly how much the aggregate demand curve will shift in response to specific changes in one of the components of aggregate demand.

■ Use the classical model and the Keynesian model to analyze how the macroeconomy will respond to a temporary downturn, a recession, and an overheated economy.

■ Critically evaluate the applicability of the classical model and the Keynesian model to the modern economy.

■ Describe and analyze the critique of the AD–AS model by political economists.

27.1 THE SHORT-RUN AGGREGATE DEMAND AND AGGREGATE SUPPLY MODEL

Figure 27.1 depicts a typical aggregate demand and aggregate supply graph for the economy. We use the price index for the whole economy, the GDP deflator, on the price axis. On the quantity axis, we use real GDP, which is the total quantity of goods and services produced in a year. Recall that, unlike nominal GDP, real GDP is corrected for changes in prices and measures the total output of goods and services.

As with regular supply and demand graphs, the aggregate demand (AD) and aggregate supply (AS) model always moves toward the equilibrium price index (P) and equilibrium real GDP. For any price above P_e in Figure 27.1, such as P_H, aggregate supply is greater than aggregate demand. At price index P_H, AS is equal to Q_2 and AD is equal to Q_3, which means that production (AS) is greater than purchases (AD). This causes businesses' inventories to increase because they are selling fewer

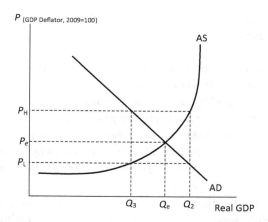

FIGURE 27.1 A typical aggregate demand and aggregate supply graph.

goods than they produced. As goods pile up in firms' warehouses, firms reduce production and lower prices, moving the economy toward equilibrium at P_e.

Similarly, for any price below equilibrium, such as P_L, aggregate demand is greater than aggregate supply. At P_L, AD is equal to Q_2 and AS is equal to Q_3. This would mean that at P_L purchases (AD) are greater than production (AS), which would cause inventories of goods decrease. As firms see goods flying out of their warehouses and their inventories of goods falling, firms would increase production and raise prices, moving the economy back toward equilibrium at P_e and Q_e. The economy always ends up at the equilibrium price level and real GDP where AD = AS.

Next, we turn to more details regarding the aggregate demand and aggregate supply curves.

Aggregate demand (AD) is **the total quantity of output (of goods and services) demanded by all sectors in the economy at various price levels. Aggregate demand is made up of five components: consumption (C), investment (I), government spending (G), exports (X), and imports (IM).**

$$AD = C + I + G + X - IM.$$

Consumption refers to consumer purchases of goods and services. Investment refers to businesses' purchases of investment goods and services, such as machinery, equipment, and construction services that expand the physical size of businesses' operations. Government spending includes all government purchases of goods and services, such as the services of soldiers and teachers, the construction of roads, and so on. Exports refers to foreign purchases of domestically produced goods and services, such as U.S. exports to Europe. Imports refers to domestic purchases of foreign-produced goods and services, such as U.S. imports from Europe. Note that imports are subtracted from aggregate demand because increased spending on imports means that *less* money is spent in the domestic economy.

Slope of aggregate demand. The aggregate demand curve slopes downward because of three effects:

1. The **real balance effect**: Higher prices mean less real wealth for consumers, causing consumers to spend less. Similarly, lower prices increase consumers' purchasing power, leading to increases in consumer spending.
2. The **real interest rate effect**: Higher prices cause real interest rates to rise because firms and individuals need to borrow more money to pay for more expensive goods. This results in decreases in spending on goods purchased with borrowed funds, including consumers' purchases of houses and cars and businesses' purchases of investment goods.
3. The **foreign trade effect**: Higher prices on U.S. goods and services makes U.S. goods less competitive, reducing exports (X) while making imports more attractive to U.S. citizens and thereby increasing imports (IM). The reduction in X and increase in IM decreases aggregate quantity demanded.

A shift in the aggregate supply curve will cause a change in the price index, which will then move the economy along the aggregate demand curve due to the three reasons listed above. It is important to note that the real balance effect, real interest rate effect, and foreign trade effect are very small according to economic research, so the real-world aggregate demand curve is much steeper than the one in Figure 27.1. In fact, as we will see later, some economists believe that the AD curve is perfectly inelastic or maybe even upward sloping. Nevertheless, to make it easier to see how the graphs work, economists tend to draw the aggregate demand curve with a flatter slope than it has in reality.

As we will see later, the aggregate demand curve *shifts* whenever there is a change in one of its components (*C, I, G, X, IM*) from something other than a change in the price level. As we will also study later, the magnitude of the shift of the aggregate demand curve depends on the initial change in spending and the multiplier.

Aggregate supply (AS) is the **total quantity of output supplied by all producers at various price levels.**

Aggregate supply is equal to the total income of the economy.

Recall that in the circular flow model, supplying goods and services generates income (GDP), which is paid to households in the form of wages, rent, interest, and profits. (Note that GDP is often abbreviated as Y in many economics texts.) The government takes a share of income in taxes (T), and the rest is left to households in the form of disposable (after-tax) income, which households use for consumption spending (C) or savings (S). Thus,

$$AS = \text{Income} = Y = GDP = C + S + T.$$

Slope of aggregate supply. The aggregate supply (AS) curve slopes upward because higher prices encourage firms to increase production, increasing real GDP. The shape of the aggregate supply curve depends on where the economy is relative to its capacity.

Full employment, also called potential real GDP (PRGDP), is the economy's normal capacity. This reflects a sustainable level of production without too much or too little unemployment. When the economy is well below its normal capacity, the aggregate supply curve is flat because real GDP can increase without increasing prices. Unemployment and excess capacity keep wages and input prices low, so firms' costs do not increase as they produce more. This corresponds with region I in Figure 27.2, where the economy is deep in a recession and well below its normal capacity (PRGDP).

As the economy nears its normal capacity, increases in real GDP cause some increases in the price level: Prices start to increase as firms increase production as laborers become relatively scarce and as firms begin to reach their productive capacity. This corresponds with region II in Figure 27.2.

Past normal capacity, the economy becomes overheated and the costs of production increase rapidly as real GDP expands. Now, firms must expand plant size to meet demand, and they must train workers for new jobs or lure skilled workers from other jobs because there are not enough skilled laborers for the new positions. Costs increase rapidly as real GDP increases when the economy is beyond is normal capacity. This corresponds with region III in Figure 27.2.

In general, a shift in the aggregate demand curve will cause a change in prices, which will cause the economy to move along the aggregate supply curve.

As we will study in more detail later, the aggregate supply curve shifts when there are changes in costs or profitability that affect most businesses. Generally, if costs increase or profitability decreases, the aggregate supply curve will shift up and to the left; if costs of production decrease or profitability increases, the aggregate supply curve will shift down and to the right.

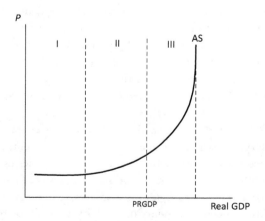

FIGURE 27.2 The slope of the aggregate supply curve.

27.2 SHIFTS IN AGGREGATE DEMAND AND AGGREGATE SUPPLY CURVES

When the aggregate demand curve shifts, this causes a change in the price index (P) and a movement along the aggregate supply curve. When the aggregate supply curve shifts, this causes a change in the price index and a movement along the aggregate demand curve. Shifts an aggregate demand and aggregate supply are a result of changes in the determinants of each curve.

27.2.1 Shifts in aggregate demand

Changes in any one of the components of aggregate demand (AD) will shift the AD curve, unless the change occurs as a result of a change in the price index. Price index changes are already built into the slope of the AD curve.

Consumption. The major factors that affect **consumption** (C) and, as a result, shift AD are changes in (1) income, (2) wealth (stocks, bonds, housing values), (3) expectations, (4) income taxes, and (5) demographic factors. The following changes would *increase* consumption and cause the aggregate demand curve to shift up and to the right:

- Higher incomes, which would give consumers more money to spend
- More wealth, which gives consumers more assets (stocks and bonds, housing equity) that they can sell to increase spending
- Positive expectations about the future, which encourage consumers to spend more than usual
- Lower income taxes, which give consumers more disposable income to spend
- More people having children and spending money on their children.

Figure 27.3 shows the impact of an increase in aggregate demand. The AD curve shifts to the right, which causes the price index to increase and real GDP to increase.

Aggregate demand would decrease if variables move in the opposite direction as those listed above. Lower incomes, reduced wealth, negative expectations, higher income taxes, and a reduction in the number of children would all result in a decrease in AD, which would in turn cause the price index and real GDP to decrease.

Investment. As noted above, investment is businesses' purchases of investment goods and services, which include machinery, equipment, construction services, and other factors that increase the physical size of businesses' operations. The major factors that affect **investment** (I) and result in a shift in aggregate demand are changes in (1) sales expectations, (2) interest rates, (3) expectations about input/output prices, (4) firms' need for production capacity, (5) technology purchases, and (6) taxes on corporate investment.

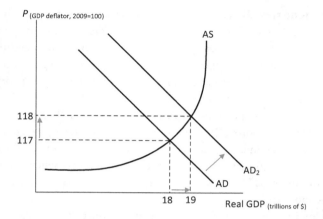

FIGURE 27.3 An increase in aggregate demand.

The following factors would increase Investment and cause an increase in aggregate demand such as the one depicted in Figure 27.3:

- Improved sales forecasts would cause firms to want to increase their productive capacity, which would mean purchasing more machinery and equipment and undertaking construction and other types of investment spending.
- Lower interest rates make it cheaper to borrow money, which makes firms more willing to borrow to finance investment spending (investments often require borrowing vast amounts of money).
- Lower expected input prices would cause firms to expect profits to increase in the future, which would spur new investment spending.
- Firms running out of production capacity when they need to produce more would necessitate investment spending to increase capacity.
- Availability of a new technology that could lower costs if implemented would prompt firms to invest in new equipment.
- Lower taxes on business investment, such as investment tax credits, would encourage businesses to make more investment purchases.

The opposites of the above (e.g., poor sales forecasts, higher interest rates, higher expected input prices, excess capacity, a lack of new technology, and higher taxes on investment) would decrease investment and aggregate demand.

Note that when businesses invest in new equipment or technology, the immediate (short-run) impact is an increase in aggregate **demand** because purchases of investment goods and services have increased. Once that new equipment or technology is implemented effectively by the firm, perhaps a few months or even a year later, the firm might see a reduction in the costs of production that might affect supply. But that is a long-term effect that is NOT reflected in short-term AD and AS analysis.

Government spending. The major factors that affect **government spending** (G) and shift AD are if Congress and the President decide to spend more or less on government programs. For example, greater government spending on infrastructure, wars, or alternative energy research would increase government spending and thereby increase aggregate demand. Lower government spending would decrease G and AD.

Net exports. Net exports are exports minus imports. The major factors that affect **net exports** (Exports (X) − Imports (IM)) and shift aggregate demand are changes in (1) U.S. income (we buy more imports when our income is higher), (2) foreign income (foreign countries buy more of our exports when their income is higher), (3) the price of U.S. goods relative to foreign goods, (4) exchange rates, and (5) taxes and tariffs.

The following factors would increase net exports $(X - IM)$ and thereby increase aggregate demand as depicted in Figure 27.3.

- Higher foreign incomes, which causes foreign countries to buy more U.S. exports
- A decrease in the prices of U.S. goods relative to foreign goods, which would cause U.S. consumers to buy fewer foreign goods (a decrease in imports) and foreign consumers to buy more U.S. goods (an increase in exports)
- Devaluing the U.S. dollar, which makes U.S. goods less expensive (promoting exports) and foreign goods more expensive (decreasing imports)
- An increase in tariffs on foreign goods, which makes foreign goods more expensive for U.S. consumers and reduces spending on imports.

The opposites of the above (e.g., lower foreign incomes, higher prices of U.S. goods, appreciation of the U.S. dollar, and a decrease in tariffs on foreign goods) would decrease net exports and aggregate demand.

Putting all of this together, the determinants of aggregate demand—the factors that cause the aggregate demand curve to shift, are listed in Figure 27.4.

Consumption	Government spending
1. Income	12. Government decisions
2. Wealth	**Net Exports**
3. Expectations	13. U.S. income
4. Income taxes	14. Foreign income
5. Demographic factors	15. Relative goods prices
Investment	16. Exchange rates
6. Sales expectations	17. Tariffs
7. Interest rates	
8. Expectations about profits	
9. Need for productive capacity	
10. Technology	
11. Taxes on investment	

FIGURE 27.4 Table showing the determinants of shifts in aggregate demand.

27.2.2 Shifts in aggregate supply

The aggregate supply curve shifts when major changes affecting costs and profitability affect most businesses in a country. Specifically, the **aggregate supply curve shifts** as a result of changes in (1) input prices (wages, oil prices, etc.), (2) the availability of productive resources (land, natural resources, labor, and capital), and (3) productivity improvements (technology implementation, worker skills, etc.). If costs increase or profitability decreases, the AS curve will shift up and to the left; if costs of production decrease or profitability increases, the AS curve will shift down and to the right.

The following factors would increase AS, shifting it down and to the right:

- Lower oil prices, which reduce energy costs and thereby reduce businesses' costs of production (all businesses use energy)
- Immigration that increases the availability of laborers, reducing costs and increasing productivity
- The invention of new computer technology that decreases businesses' costs of production and improves efficiency and productivity.

Figure 27.5 shows the effect of an increase in aggregate supply on prices and real GDP. The price index falls from 117 to 116 and real GDP increases from $18 trillion to $19 trillion.

The following factors would cause a decrease in AS (a shift up and to the left), an increase in the price index, and a decrease in real GDP: Higher oil prices, a reduction in immigration, and computer hacking, which increases businesses' costs and reduces their productivity. Figure 27.6 lists the major determinants of shifts in the aggregate supply curve.

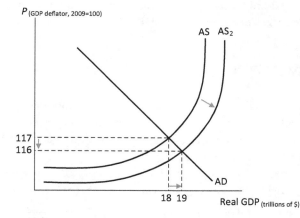

FIGURE 27.5 An increase in aggregate supply.

1.	Input prices
2.	Availability of productive resources
3.	Productivity changes

FIGURE 27.6 Table showing the determinants of shifts in aggregate supply.

In most cases, only one curve will shift (either AS or AD) and you will move along the other curve. However, there are two factors that shift both curves.

27.2.3 The factors that shift both AD and AS: Wages and exchange rates

A **change in wages** shifts both AD and AS because wages affect consumers' incomes AND businesses' costs of production. Higher wages would increase consumers' incomes, causing an increase in consumption (C) and AD. But higher wages increase costs, causing a decrease in AS. The result of an increase in AD and a decrease in AS would be no change in real GDP but a significant increase in the price index. (Try to draw a graph on your own to show this.)

A **change in exchange rates** causes a large shift in AD and a small shift in AS. Exchange rates affect foreign purchases of U.S. goods and services (X) and U.S. purchases of foreign goods and services (IM), and they also affect the cost of imported inputs, affecting AS a small amount. Imported inputs make up a small but still significant share of businesses' costs, so a change in exchange rates causes a small shift in AS.

For example, an appreciation of the U.S. dollar makes foreign goods less expensive for U.S. consumers and it makes U.S. goods more expensive for foreign consumers. This would decrease U.S. net exports and decrease AD (fewer U.S. goods would be purchased). However, the decrease in the cost of foreign inputs would reduce businesses' costs of production slightly, causing a small increase in AS. Figure 27.7 shows that an appreciation of the U.S. dollar causes a large decrease in aggregate demand and a small increase in aggregate supply, resulting in a decrease in the price index and a decrease in real GDP.

27.3 THE MULTIPLIER

One of the most important aspects of macroeconomics is how changes in the economy become amplified via the multiplier. The multiplier effect explains **how a $1 change in spending causes aggregate demand and real GDP to change by more than $1 due to a responding process.**

The responding process is driven by the marginal propensity to consume (MPC), which is **the change in consumption (ΔC) that results from a change in disposable (after-tax) income (ΔDI):** $MPC = \dfrac{\Delta C}{\Delta DI}$.

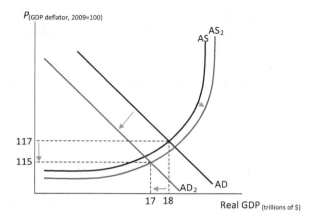

P(GDP deflator, 2009=100)

117

115

17 18

Real GDP (trillions of $)

FIGURE 27.7 The impact of an appreciation of the dollar on U.S. prices and real GDP.

If we take national income (GDP) and subtract taxes (T), we get disposable income (DI), which is the income consumers actually have at their disposal to spend. Disposable Income is either spent by consumers (C) or saved (S):

$$DI = C + S.$$

Any change in income is therefore allocated by consumers to either consumption or savings.

$$\Delta DI = \Delta C + \Delta S.$$

If we divide both sides by ΔDI, this can be rewritten as $\dfrac{\Delta DI}{\Delta DI} = 1 = \dfrac{\Delta C}{\Delta DI} + \dfrac{\Delta S}{\Delta DI}.$

Economists define the marginal propensity to save (MPS) as follows: $MPS = \dfrac{\Delta S}{\Delta DI}.$

So our equation can be rewritten as $MPC+MPS=1$. This means that any change in disposable income is divided up between the amount that consumers spend, the MPC, and the amount that consumers save, the MPS.

The responding process plays out in the following way. Suppose that the marginal propensity to consume is 0.8 $(MPC = 0.8)$, which means the MPS is 0.2. This means that consumers will spend 80% of any increase in income and save 20%. Suppose also that someone goes out and spends \$100. From the circular flow model, we know that every dollar of spending becomes someone else's income. So, what will happen to the \$100 in income that is generated by the \$100 in spending? If the marginal propensity to consume is 0.8, we know that for each \$100 in income, people will on average spend 80% of that, or \$80. Thus, from \$100 in income we would expect to see an additional \$80 in consumer spending:

$$MPC * \Delta DI = 0.8 * \$100 = \$80.$$

But this $80 in spending becomes income for another group of people, who will then spend 80% of $80, which is $64. This $64 in spending is income for yet another group of people, who will spend 80% of $64 or $51.20, which is then income for someone else.

The total change in consumption from the initial change in consumer spending of $100 is

$$\$100 + \$80 + \$64 + \$51.20 + ... = \$100\left(1 + 0.8 + 0.8^2 + 0.8^3 + ... + 0.8^n\right).$$

This is an infinite series that has a solution of the following form:

$$\text{Total change in spending} = \$100 * \frac{1}{1 - 0.8} = \$100 * 5 = \$500.$$

In this case, the **(simple) multiplier** is 5, which **is equal to** $\frac{1}{1 - MPC}$. This means that each $1 change in spending ultimately generates $5 in total spending, after the money gets spent and respent over and over.

Note that this analysis excludes the presence of taxes and imports, so this is called the "simple multiplier" because it ignores some of the more complex aspects of real-world consumer spending. To develop a fully accurate multiplier we need to build in two additional factors: Taxes and imports. Each time income is generated, the government taxes a certain percentage of that income in taxes, and that money is not able to be respent. Also, we need to factor in imports. When consumers spend money on imported goods, that money flows out of the country and is not available to be respent on domestic goods and services.

The marginal respending rate (MRR) is defined as **the additional spending that is generated from a change in income. MRR depends on the marginal propensity to consume, the net tax rate (t), and the marginal propensity to import (MPM):**

$$MRR = MPC(1 - t) - MPM.$$

The net tax rate (t) is the average amount that the government takes out of a change in income. To find the net tax rate we add up all the revenue the government takes in taxes, subtract the money the government gives back to households in the form of transfer payments (welfare payments and other income payments people get from the government), and then divide by total income. Thus, the net tax rate is the average percentage of income that the government takes in taxes. If t is the net tax rate, then $1 - t$ is the percentage of income households can actually spend—disposable income.

The marginal propensity to import (MPM) is **the increase in imports that results from an increase in disposable income.** Because this money is not available to be respent in the domestic economy, we subtract MPM from the respending rate.

What we can glean from this is that some of each $1 of income will be respent, depending on the amount consumers save, the amount the government takes in taxes, and the amount that flows overseas to pay for imports.

For example, if marginal propensity to consume (*MPC*) is 0.9, the net tax rate (*t*) is 0.2, and the marginal propensity to import (*MPM*) is 0.12, then the marginal respending rate (*MRR*) can be computed as follows:

$$MRR = MPC(1-t) - MPM = (0.9)(0.8) - (0.12) = (0.72) - (0.12) = 0.6.$$

With an MRR of 0.6, the multiplier is equal to 2.5:

$$\textbf{Multiplier} = \frac{1}{1-MRR} = \frac{1}{1-0.6} = \frac{1}{0.4} = 2.5.$$

27.4 AGGREGATE DEMAND AND THE MULTIPLIER

Because of the multiplier, an initial change in aggregate demand (AD) causes a total change in the aggregate demand curve to be larger than the initial amount. The total shift in the aggregate demand curve will be equal to the initial change multiplied by the multiplier:

$$\text{Total shift in AD} = (\Delta AD) * (\text{Multiplier}).$$

For example, suppose that consumers increase their spending by $100 billion due to an improvement in consumer confidence. With a multiplier of 2.5, a $100 initial increase in consumption will cause a total shift in aggregate demand of $250 billion:

$$(\Delta AD) * (\text{multiplier}) = (\$100\,B.)\,2.5 = \$250\,B = \text{Total shift in AD}.$$

The initial increase in consumption of $100 billion shifts the aggregate demand curve $250 billion dollars to the right. If aggregate demand equaled $14,000 billion before consumption changed, then it will now equal $14,250 (see Figure 27.8), assuming that the price level does not change.

The next question is how much real GDP will increase from this increase in aggregate demand. If the aggregate supply curve is flat between $14,000 billion and $14,250, then real GDP will increase by the same amount, as shown in Figure 27.9.

However, if any of the shift in aggregate demand occurs in the upward-sloping portion of the aggregate supply curve, then real GDP will change by *less than* the shift in aggregate demand. As Figure 27.10 shows, when the aggregate demand curve shifts by $250 billion, the increase in real GDP is only $200 billion. The

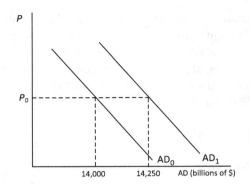

FIGURE 27.8 A shift in aggregate demand with the multiplier.

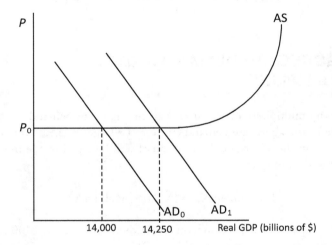

FIGURE 27.9 A shift in AD in the flat portion of aggregate supply.

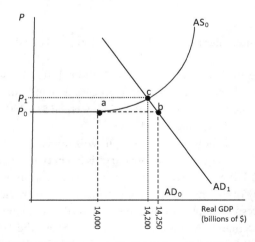

FIGURE 27.10 A shift in AD in the upward-sloping portion of AS.

increase in prices from P_0 to P_1 causes aggregate demand to decline by $50 billion (the movement along the AD curve from point B to point C as prices increase).

If the change in the aggregate demand shift occurred in a steeper portion of the aggregate supply curve, real GDP would increase by even less.

Note that the same process works in reverse. If there is a decrease in one of the components of aggregate demand, this will cause AD to shift to the left by a larger amount than the initial change due to the multiplier. Real GDP will change by less than the shift in AD (unless we are in the flat part of the AS curve), because prices will fall after the leftward shift in AD, and that will cause movement along the AD curve.

In addition to the five components that directly impact the aggregate demand curve, we need to analyze how tax increases or tax cuts affect AD via their impact on consumption. To compute the impact of tax changes, we use both the *MPC* and the *MRR*.

Suppose that the *MPC* is 0.8, the *MRR* is 0.5, and the government decides to cut taxes by $100 billion. The *MPC* tells us the percentage of disposable (after-tax) income that consumers will spend. Therefore, a $100 billion tax cut will mean that consumers have $100 billion *more* in after-tax income, and they will spend 80% of that (with an *MPC* of 0.8), for an increase in consumption of $80 billion. We would then compute the multiplier, which using the MRR of 0.5 is equal to 2, to compute the change in aggregate demand of $160 billion.

The formula to compute the change in consumption from a change in taxes is the following:

$$\Delta C = -(\Delta T * MPC).$$

Notice the minus sign in front of the parentheses in the formula for the change in consumption. When the change in taxes is negative (a tax cut), the change in consumption is positive, and vice versa.

Note that the economic impact of tax cuts is always smaller than the economic impact of directly spending government money, because consumers save a portion of tax cuts instead of spending all of it. Furthermore, consumers often become pessimistic in deep recessions, which can lead to a reduction in the marginal propensity to consume, which makes the impact of tax cuts even smaller. This is why Keynes preferred government spending to tax cuts as a way to end recessions: Government spending has a larger, more direct impact on real GDP. Tax cuts have a smaller impact, and that impact shrinks further when expectations about the future are poor.

The impact of tax cuts on AD and real GDP also depends on whose taxes are cut. The marginal propensity to consume varies with income. Rich people save more and have a lower *MPC* than poor people. For example, in recent years the marginal propensity to consume of the richest 20% of the U.S. population has been 0.88, the middle 20% has had an *MPC* of 0.94, and the *MPC* of the poorest 20%

has been 1.00. Unsurprisingly, the poorest portion of the population spends 100% of their income. This also means that *tax cuts for the poorest U.S. citizens have a 12% larger impact on aggregate demand than tax cuts for the rich.*

Now that we have described how the aggregate demand and aggregate supply model works in the short run, we next turn to long-run adjustment and the debate over whether or not the government should intervene in the business cycle.

27.5 THE CLASSICAL MODEL OF LONG-RUN ADJUSTMENT

In the long run in the classical model of aggregate demand and aggregate supply the economy tends toward a long-run equilibrium on the long-run aggregate supply (LRAS) curve. The LRAS curve is a straight line at full employment, or potential real GDP (PRGDP). Long-run aggregate supply represents **the economy at "full employment," when the economy is producing at its maximum normal capacity given existing resources and technology**. Potential real GDP (PRGDP) reflects the idea that when the economy is in a recession, production (real GDP) is below potential. When real GDP is above PRGDP, the economy is beyond its maximum safe capacity and is overheated.

In Figure 27.11, the economy is in a long-run equilibrium whenever the short-run AD and AS curves intersect on the LRAS curve directly above PRGDP.

In the short run, the economy is often in a short-run equilibrium that is above or below potential real GDP. For example, in Figure 27.12(a), the economy is in equilibrium below potential real GDP, which indicates that the economy is in a **recession**. There is a recessionary gap, which is equal to **the amount that real GDP is below potential real GDP**.

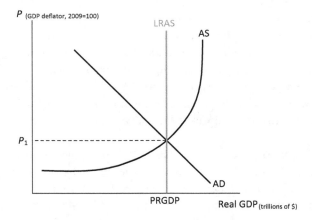

FIGURE 27.11 The long-run equilibrium at LRAS (PRGDP).

(a) A recessionary gap

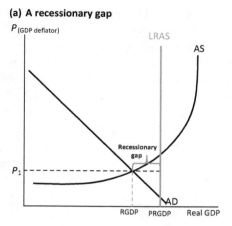

FIGURE 27.12 (a) A recessionary gap.

(b) An inflationary gap

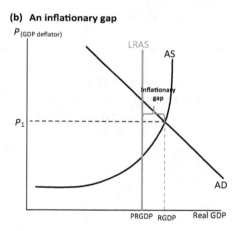

FIGURE 27.12 (b) An inflationary gap.

Figure 27.12(b) shows the economy in equilibrium above potential real GDP. This is called an **overheated economy**, and there is an inflationary gap that is equal to **the amount that real GDP is above potential real GDP**. This is called an inflationary gap because inflation usually occurs when the economy enters an overheated state.

One of the questions that economists still debate today is whether or not the economy has a tendency to return automatically to potential real GDP in the long run. The two main perspectives on this topic are the classical model and the Keynesian model.

Adherents of the classical model believe that the economy always returns to the LRAS curve at potential real GDP in the long run, and therefore the economy needs no government intervention. They are opposed by Keynesian economists who believe that the economy does not tend toward a stable equilibrium at the LRAS curve and that the government should use stabilization policy to move the economy back to potential real GDP when it strays into a recession or an overheated economy.

The classical model. According to classical economists such as J. B. Say, the economy always returns to equilibrium at potential real GDP on the long-run aggregate supply curve. Note that this perspective also has modern adherents. A small number of U.S. economists argued that the U.S. government should not intervene after the financial crisis of 2008. The European Central Bank, which is governed by modern-day adherents of the classical model, refused to intervene for many years after the financial crisis impacted Europe. The reasons for the belief that the economy is self-adjusting are outlined below with respect to three cases: Temporary downturns, recessions, and overheated economies.

Temporary downturns. Classical economists did not believe that decreases in spending would lead to recessions. Instead, they thought that a decline in consumption would only lead to a temporary downturn. If people consume less ($\downarrow C$) and save more because of worries about the economy, then the decrease in spending will cause a temporary downturn as businesses' sales decline. However, the supply of savings has increased, which means there is more money in banks, and banks want to loan that money out in order to earn profits. This leads banks to lower interest rates, which in turn increases business investment. Thus, the increase in savings by consumers is automatically counteracted by an increase in business investment. The economy stabilizes and the lower level of spending (and higher levels of saving) does not cause a recession thanks to the increase in investment (I).

Recession. In a full-fledged recession (as opposed to a temporary downturn), according to the classical model, wages and input prices tend to fall due to high levels of unemployment and slack demand. This decrease in the costs of production causes the aggregate supply curve to shift to the right, increasing real GDP until the economy reaches equilibrium at PRGDP on the LRAS curve at a lower price level. Figure 27.13(a) shows this happening.

Overheated economy. If the economy becomes overheated, according to the classical model, wages and input prices increase dramatically due to the economy operating beyond its normal capacity. Firms cannot find the skilled workers they need and they must pay higher wages to attract new workers. Inputs become more expensive due to high demand. This dramatic increase in the costs of production causes the aggregate supply curve to shift to the left until the economy reaches equilibrium back at PRGDP at a higher price level. Figure 27.13(b) shows the aggregate supply curve shifting to the left, back to LRAS. Real GDP decreases to potential real GDP.

Therefore, according to the classical model, wages and input prices always adjust to return the economy to full employment at PRGDP on the LRAS curve. Note, however, the fact that the classical model completely ignores aggregate demand and the impact of economic fluctuations on consumer and investor behavior. These are omissions taken up in the Keynesian model.

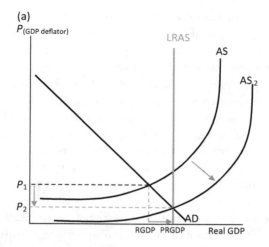

FIGURE 27.13 (a) A recessionary gap eliminated by lower wages and input prices (classical model).

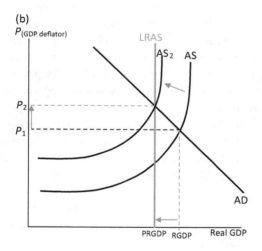

FIGURE 27.13 (b) An inflationary gap eliminated by higher wages and input prices (classical model).

27.6 THE KEYNESIAN MODEL OF LONG-RUN ADJUSTMENT

Keynes disputed the assertions by the adherents of the classical model that the economy would always adjust quickly and return to PRGDP. To Keynes, this rarely happened in the way the classical economists believed due to four concepts we first discussed in Chapter 7: The **volatility of investment, sticky wages and prices,**

macroeconomic problems created by wage and price deflation (especially their impact on aggregate demand), and the multiplier process.

Temporary downturn that is not temporary. According to the classical model, if consumers become pessimistic and spend less on consumption (C) while saving more (S), an increase in investment will offset the decline in consumption. But Keynes pointed out that this is not how investors actually behave. The primary determinant of business investment is expected sales. Only if a business expects strong sales in the future will it be willing to invest (purchase machinery and equipment and expand the size of its operations). If sales to consumers decline, this makes businesses pessimistic and they *reduce* their investment. More and more savings pile up in banks, unused because businesses do not want to borrow money to invest when the economic outlook is poor. Indeed, in every period of economic pessimism (and every downturn), money pools in banks and interest rates fall, but investors usually refuse to invest because of their pessimistic outlook for the future. Leakages out of the economy exceed injections. Thus, the temporary downturn that classical economists thought would be self-correcting can spiral into a major recession.

Recessions without end. Keynes also disputed the assertion that the economy will adjust quickly out of a recession for two main reasons. First, his research indicated that wages and input prices are sticky. They do not fall quickly, if at all, even in a recession. Firms do not like to cut wages because it erodes morale and productivity, so they lay off workers instead. Input producers often cannot cut prices because their costs have not changed and they need to sell goods for a certain price to stay in business. If there is no decrease in wages and input prices, there is no decrease in the costs of production in a recession and the increase in aggregate supply expected by the classical economists will never happen. As we saw in Chapter 7, in the worst recession in the history of the United States, the Great Depression, prices did not fall significantly for three years despite the poor economic conditions.

Second, classical economists focused only on the supply side of the economy while ignoring the demand side. This was a fatal mistake. Investment depends on expected sales more than any other factor. Once wages and input prices do fall in a major recession, this reduces the incomes of workers and the profits of input suppliers, which reduces their spending. Wage and price deflation has a devastating effect on aggregate demand: When workers and input suppliers reduce spending, the multiplier effect results in that reduction being multiplied through the economy, causing a significant decrease in aggregate demand that is much larger than the initial decrease in spending. Other businesses, seeing this reduction in consumer spending, will invest *less* due to poor expected sales. Thus, even if wages and input prices do fall in a recession, reducing costs and increasing AS, there is a corresponding decrease in AD that keeps the economy in a recession. The economy can linger in a recession for many years.

Keynes also noted that when the economy does finally pull its way out of a recession, it will be led by aggregate demand, especially consumer and investment spending, not aggregate supply. Once consumers and investors become less pessimistic and begin spending, AD will increase, which will cause firms to begin to produce (and supply) more. The government can jump-start this process by engaging in stabilization policy: Increasing spending in the recession to spur consumer and investment spending. The government can increase aggregate demand through fiscal policy, by increasing government spending or cutting taxes, or through monetary policy, by reducing interest rates to stimulate borrowing so that consumers and firms can spend more. This way the government can shorten the length and severity of recessions.

Overheated economies (booms) become busts. Keynes also disagreed with classical economists on the self-adjustment process out of an overheated economy. According to the classical model, an overheated economy causes wages and input prices to increase, which raises businesses' costs of production, causing AS to shift back to PRGDP. However, that happy story rarely ends the way that classical economists predicted. Instead, the boom sparked by an overheated economy usually turn into a full-fledged bust, causing the economy to spiral into a recession.

Keynes agreed with the classical economists that an overheated economy would cause increases in wages and input prices and that this would erode profitability for businesses. The question is what kinds of behaviors will result when profitability starts to decline in an economic boom? What we know from recent booms that have turned into busts, including the dot.com bubble of 2000 and the real estate bubble of 2007, is that when the bubble bursts the economy falls apart.

Once people realize that their financial investments in bubble assets are no longer safe, they panic and engage in a mass selloff. The prices of assets crash. There is a huge decrease in wealth as people see the value of their stocks and homes plummet. In this environment of pessimism, consumers scale back on their purchases and businesses reduce their investment spending. This decreases aggregate demand. Then, businesses that experience declining sales of goods and services lay off workers and reduce investment further, reducing incomes significantly. The decrease in incomes causes another round of declines in consumer and business investment spending, causing even larger decreases in incomes. Via the multiplier process and the volatility of investment, the economy enters a recession.

Keynes believed in avoiding an overheated economic state by reducing government spending, increasing taxes, or increasing interest rates to slow down the economy. Keeping the economy from growing too quickly can prevent booms from accelerating unsustainably and turning into busts.

Thus, according to Keynes, the economy rarely returns quickly and gently to the long-run aggregate supply curve and potential real GDP. To Keynes, careful macroeconomic policy can almost always improve on the outcomes of an unregulated macroeconomic market.

27.7 LIMITATIONS OF THE AGGREGATE DEMAND AND SUPPLY MODEL

One of the starkest areas of disagreement between mainstream economists and political economists has to do with macroeconomic modeling. Most mainstream economists see the macroeconomy as very stable, with prices adjusting to push aggregate demand and aggregate supply into equilibrium. Political economists see the macroeconomy as fundamentally unstable, and prices are largely unimportant in determining real GDP.

From the perspective of political economists, and some New Keynesian economists, the aggregate demand and aggregate supply model is fundamentally flawed. The main problems with the AD–AS framework include the slopes of the AD and AS curves, feedback effects between AD and AS, and the notion of a stable macroeconomic equilibrium.[1]

The slope of the aggregate demand curve is likely vertical or possibly upward sloping, rather than downward-sloping. The downward slope of the aggregate demand curve depends on three key effects, each of which is undermined by recent empirical research. The **real balance effect** requires that lower prices increase the real value of wealth, causing consumers to spend more and thereby increasing the aggregate quantity demanded (moving the economy along the aggregate demand curve up and to the left). However, this analysis ignores the fact that most households are net debtors—they owe more money than they have in savings. This is especially true of lower- and middle-income households. If you are a household that owes money, then a decrease in prices increases the real amount of the debt that you owe, making you poorer and causing you to spend less. Therefore, depending on the level of debt in an economy, it is quite possible for lower prices to decrease the spending by debtors as much as or more than lower prices increase the spending of those with positive wealth balances.

The **foreign trade effect** requires that lower prices make one country's products cheaper than those produced by rival countries, increasing the exports of the country with lower prices and increasing the aggregate quantity demanded. However, in both the Great Depression of the 1930s and the Great Recession of 2007–2010, the fall in prices in the United States rapidly spread to other countries as they also experienced an economic crisis. *The foreign trade effect was thus very small and short-lived because of the rapidity with which deflation spread from one country to another.*

According to the **real interest rate effect**, lower prices lead consumers and businesses to borrow less money because the prices of durable goods and investment (capital) goods have declined. In essence, loan volumes decline as people borrow smaller amounts of money now that prices are lower. However, lower prices usually occur in the presence of economic stagnation, something that is often accompanied by declines in consumer and investor purchases. Similarly, in economic booms when prices are increasing, consumers and investors are confident about the economic situation and tend to increase purchases even though prices have gone up. A more realistic aggregate demand curve that incorporated expectations would therefore be upward sloping under many circumstances.

Taking all of these factors into consideration, if the aggregate demand curve is downward sloping, then it is very, very steep. Furthermore, it might be vertical or even upward sloping depending on which effects are strongest.

Though political economists see the AD curve as very steep, **the slope of the aggregate supply curve is likely flat for almost the entire graph**. An upward slope to the aggregate supply curve depends on businesses' costs increasing as they produce more. This condition requires the existence of competitive markets where firms experience the law of diminishing returns (higher costs as they produce more) and/or where inputs are limited in supply. However, in the modern world, most firms have some market power in output markets, most experience economies of scale where it becomes less expensive to produce larger quantities, and most have multiple input sources from around the globe. This means that firms respond to changes in demand by increasing production but not necessarily by increasing prices. As long as this relationship holds true—as long as firms can increase production without experiencing higher costs—we will get a flat aggregate supply curve. The aggregate supply curve may increase in slope very slightly as the economy becomes very overheated, which is when the economy might actually see higher wages and input prices and scarcities of skilled workers. In recent decades in the United States, prices increased only during the most rapid portion of economic booms. Levels of markups are also difficult to determine. In theory, firms with monopoly power can increase prices when demand for their products increases. However, in the global era, firms have less monopoly power in output markets than they used to, even as monopsony power in input markets has increased. This, too, limits how much firms can increase prices and how much their costs increase as production increases.

Figure 27.14 shows what the AD–AS graph looks like from a political economy perspective. The AD curve is very steep, reflecting the ambiguous impact of prices on aggregate demand. The AS curve is very flat except at the very end, because prices are relatively stable as production increases until the economy becomes significantly overheated.

The concepts of potential real GDP and full employment are also fundamentally flawed from a political economy perspective. The idea of an upper limit on production is reasonable in the short run because resources are limited. However, estimating an economy's maximum production based on the concept of full employment, which assumes stable levels of frictional and structural unemployment, is problematic. As we noted in the chapter on unemployment and price instability, countries can increase production and reduce the level of structural unemployment dramatically via employer of last resort programs or via active labor market policies combined with industrial policies. Therefore, the economy's capacity, its potential real GDP, is somewhat variable.

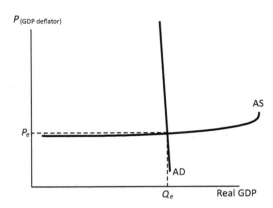

FIGURE 27.14 A political economy aggregate demand and aggregate supply graph.

In the long run, the economy's capacity is even more variable. According to mainstream economists, potential real GDP shifts out in the long run based on investments in a country's capital stock and changes in technology. To political economists, there are many more variables. For example, political economists see potential real GDP varying significantly based on whether or not governments can successfully implement industrial policies to generate economic growth and environmental policies to avoid the destruction of natural resources and environmental services upon which production depends. The notion that there is one potential real GDP that the economy returns to in the long run is therefore disputed by political economists.

Lastly, movements along aggregate demand and aggregate supply curves cannot be easily separated from shifts in these curves due to the interdependence of demand and supply factors in the macroeconomy. Here, one of Keynes' main insights looms large: In the macroeconomy, demand fluctuations tend to cause supply fluctuations. The crash of real estate prices in 2007 caused consumers and investors to reduce spending dramatically, decreasing AD. Firms responded by reducing supply dramatically as their expected sales dropped, which stimulated job losses and further decreases in aggregate demand and aggregate supply. During a boom, demand increases create business optimism, which can cause supply increases, which creates more income and sparks additional aggregate demand increases. The macroeconomy involves complex interactions that are very difficult to boil down to a simple demand and supply model.

Instead of the mainstream economics focus on stability and equilibrium, political economists believe that it is better to model the economy as an unstable, evolutionary process. Political economy analysis attempts to model the feedback loops that are an essential characteristic of the macroeconomy. From this perspective, if we focus on the shifts of the AD curve using the multiplier and ignore the effect of prices unless the economy is overheated, we would have a much more accurate model.

Despite the criticisms of political economists and some New Keynesian economists, the AD–AS model remains an important tool used by policymakers to determine how to respond to various macroeconomic situations. Therefore, it is a very important model to understand.

27.8 CONCLUSION

This chapter outlined the aggregate demand and aggregate supply model of the macroeconomy. In the basic aggregate demand and aggregate supply model, aggregate demand shifts whenever there are events that cause (a) consumers to change their spending patterns, (b) businesses to change their purchases of investment goods and services, (c) governments to change their spending patterns, and (d) international actors to shift their purchases of exports or imports. The aggregate supply curve shifts whenever businesses experience changes in profitability or the availability of productive recourses.

The multiplier helps us understand why changes to aggregate demand become magnified in the macroeconomy. Because of the respending process in macroeconomics, each dollar gets spent and respent multiple times, causing real GDP to change by more than any initial change in aggregate demand.

The chapter also laid out the debate over long run adjustment by two schools of economic thought, classical economists and Keynesian economists. Classical economists believe the economy is self-adjusting and needs little or no economic interference by government. Keynesian economists believe the economy is rarely self-adjusting and usually benefits from appropriate macroeconomic stabilization policies.

Lastly, the chapter explored some of the main criticisms of the aggregate demand and aggregate supply model. Political economists argue that AD curves are very steep, AS curves are very flat, potential real GDP is quite variable, and equilibrium if a flawed concept.

QUESTIONS FOR REVIEW

1. (a) Briefly explain why the aggregate demand curve has a negative slope in the standard AD–AS model. (b) Briefly explain the shape of the aggregate supply curve.
2. In each of the examples below, indicate what happens to aggregate demand, aggregate supply, the price level, and real GDP in the short run.
    a. The government cuts income taxes.
    b. A new, sophisticated robot is invented that dramatically reduces businesses' costs of production but that also causes millions of workers to lose their jobs.
    c. Wages of domestic workers fall due to the coronavirus pandemic.
    d. Domestic interest rates increase.

3. In 2010, the economy was at a real GDP of $12,000 billion and a price index of 101 (2009 = 100). Potential real GDP was estimated to be $13,500 billion. Due to the difficulty in gaining bipartisan agreement on the fiscal budget, the government shut down. As a result of the government shutdown, measures built into previous budgets triggered an automatic government spending cut of $200 billion. Note that the marginal respending rate (MRR) in 2010 was 0.6. Draw a graph of aggregate demand and aggregate supply displaying the U.S. economy before and after the decrease in government spending. Determine what effect these spending cuts would have on real GDP and the price index.

4. Use Figure 27.15 to answer the following questions:
   a. If the MRR = 0.6 and there is an increase in government spending of $1000 billion, then the aggregate demand curve will shift by $_____ billion. We can expect the new price index to be _____ and the new real GDP to be $_____.
   b. If the MRR = 0.8 and there is a decrease in investment of $600 billion due to a financial market crash, then the aggregate demand curve will shift by $_____ billion. We can expect the new price index to be _____ and the new real GDP to be $_____ billion.

5. If the MRR = 0.75 and the MPC = 0.9, a $1000 billion tax cut will cause a change in aggregate demand of $_____ billion. Explain and show your work.

6. Suppose real GDP falls below potential real GDP *temporarily* due to a decline in consumer spending (C), which also has the effect of increasing the pool of savings in banks.
   a. What does the classical model predict will happen to investment (purchases of capital goods) and aggregate demand in response to these events (a decrease in consumption and an increase in saving) in the short term?
   b. How does the Keynesian model differ in its predictions? Explain carefully.

7. Draw a graph showing an overheated economy. Include AD, AS, and potential real GDP on your graph.
   a. Show what will happen in the long run according to the classical model and explain your answer in words.
   b. What would Keynes like to see done in this case? Explain carefully.

8. (a) Draw a graph showing the economy in a recession. Include AD, AS, and potential real GDP on your graph. Show what will happen in the long run according to the classical model and explain your answer in words. (b) Discuss why Keynes disagrees with the assumptions of the classical model and what he would propose instead.

9. Explain the political economy critique of the aggregate demand–aggregate supply model.

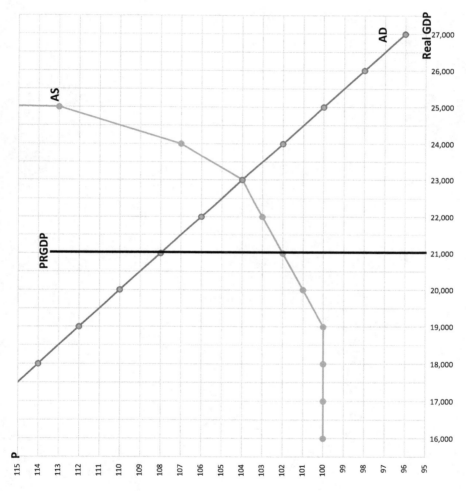

FIGURE 27.15 AD–AS graph.

NOTE

1 See Ron Baiman, *The Morality of Economics: Ghost Curve Ideology and the Value Neutral Aspect of Neoclassical Economics* (Palgrave Macmillan, London, 2016) for an excellent treatment of this topic.

28 The Keynesian aggregate expenditure model

The foundation of modern macroeconomics

In Chapter 27, we laid out the aggregate demand and aggregate supply model that is the cornerstone of modern mainstream economics. That model introduced you to a crucial aspect of macroeconomics: Sectoral analysis that details how the sectors of the macroeconomy—consisting of consumers, investors, government bodies, and foreign actors—affect aggregate demand. This chapter undertakes a more detailed sectoral analysis of the macroeconomy, based on the ideas of John Maynard Keynes as reinterpreted by Robert Samuelson and the mainstream economists who followed him.

More specifically, this chapter lays out the Keynesian aggregate expenditure model. It explains how each sector fits into Keynesian model and how changes in the components of aggregate expenditure work with the multiplier. One of the key insights from the Keynesian model is that prices often play a relatively unimportant role in determining national income. Instead, the interplay between various components of aggregate expenditure is the primary determinant.

The chapter begins by describing the consumption and savings functions, which form the basis for the aggregate expenditure model. Then, we add in each additional sector of macroeconomic spending, including investment, government spending, and net exports (exports minus imports). And we incorporate net taxes (taxes minus transfers) into the model. This gives us a comprehensive model of the macroeconomy that can help us to analyze how changes in any of the model's components will affect real gross domestic product (GDP).

DOI: 10.4324/9781315636924-36

The chapter concludes with a brief discussion regarding economic debates over the Keynesian aggregate expenditure model and the mainstream aggregate demand and supply model. Both mainstream economists and political economists utilize the aggregate expenditure model, but political economists give it much more prominence in their analysis.

28.0 CHAPTER 28 LEARNING GOALS

After reading this chapter you should be able to:

- Describe the consumption function and its relation to the savings function.

- Explain how consumption, investment, government spending, and net exports interact to determine aggregate expenditure.

- Determine the equilibrium level of national income using an aggregate expenditure chart or graph.

- Analyze how changes in the components of aggregate expenditure or in the components of the marginal respending rate affect equilibrium national income.

- Explain how the aggregate expenditure model corresponds with the aggregate demand curve in mainstream economics.

- Compare and contrast mainstream and political economy approaches to the aggregate expenditure model and aggregate demand and supply model.

28.1 THE CONSUMPTION FUNCTION AND THE SAVINGS FUNCTION

As we saw in the previous chapter, consumers' after-tax, disposable income (DI) is either consumed (C) or saved (S): $DI = C + S$. The marginal propensity to consume (MPC) is the change in consumption (ΔC) that results from a change in disposable (after-tax) income (ΔDI). In mathematical terms, $MPC = \dfrac{\Delta C}{\Delta DI}$. Similarly, the marginal propensity to save (MPS) is the change in savings from a change in disposable income, which can be expressed mathematically as $MPS = \dfrac{\Delta S}{\Delta DI}$.

In recent decades, U.S. consumers spent about 90% of their disposable income and saved about 10%. Note, however, that consumption and savings rates vary with the confidence of consumers. Figure 28.1 displays U.S. real disposable income and real consumption from 2002 to 2020. The average level of consumer spending is 90% of real disposable income; however, the amount they spend varies significantly with the economic circumstances. In 2020, U.S. consumers received a large increase in disposable income due to significant lump sum tax cuts and stimulus spending that the government enacted to offset the COVID-19 recession. Despite the increase in disposable income, consumers spent *less* as the economy shuttered from lockdowns and as people worried about their futures in the face of mass lay-offs and a stock market crash. U.S. consumers shifted from spending 89% of their disposable income on consumption goods in January of 2020 to spending only 64% in April of 2020. This is one of the reasons why tax cuts have limited effectiveness in recessions.

Due to the systematic relationship (in nonrecession years) between disposable income and its two components, consumption and savings, we can model consumption and savings functions for the U.S. economy. Figure 28.2 shows a hypothetical relationship between real disposable income (DI), consumption (C), and savings (S). (Note that in this chapter we will use only real values that have been adjusted for inflation.) The table begins with real GDP, which is national income and is abbreviated as Y. This table uses a tax rate (t) of 50%, which is the average level of taxation in many European countries, to compute real disposable (after-tax) income.

Note that whenever we talk about taxes in this chapter, we are actually talking about *net taxes*, which are taxes minus transfers. The tax rate is the percentage of income taken in by the government, not including money that is taken in and then immediately paid back out as transfer payments to the public. Transfer payments include Social Security, unemployment benefits, and other cash transfers the government pays directly to the public.

Disposable income is either consumed or saved, so at every level of disposable income, $DI = C + S$. Note that when DI = $0, consumers still need to spend money to survive, so there is still $2000 of "autonomous" consumption spending (C_a)—consumption spending that does not depend on income. With DI = $0 and C = $2000, Savings ($S$)=$DI-C$=−$2000. In other words, when consumers have no money, they have to borrow money or spend their savings in order to purchase necessities.

In the table, every time disposable income increases by $2000 billion, consumption increases by $1600. Thus, in Figure 28.2, $MPC = \dfrac{\Delta C}{\Delta DI} = \dfrac{1600}{2000} = 0.8$. Similarly, $MPS = \dfrac{\Delta S}{\Delta DI} = \dfrac{400}{2000} = 0.2$.

Figure 28.3 plots the information from Figure 28.2 to display a consumption function and a savings function. When disposable income is $0, C_a = $2000 and S = −$2000. When DI = $10,000, C = $10,000 and S = $0. Note that this is where

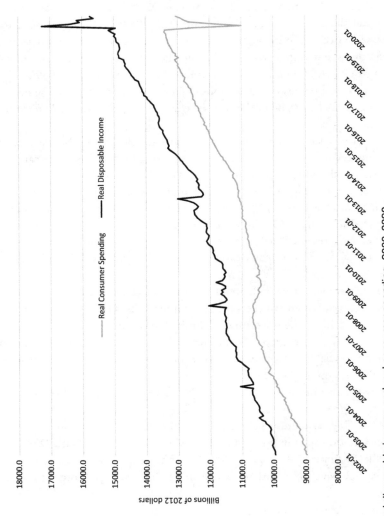

FIGURE 28.1 U.S. real disposable income and real consumer spending, 2002–2020.

Real GDP (Y)	Real disposable income (DI)	Consumption (C)	Savings (S)
0	0	2000	−2000
4000	2000	3600	−1600
8000	4000	5200	−1200
12,000	6000	6800	-800
16,000	8000	8400	−400
20,000	10,000	10,000	0
24,000	12,000	11,600	400
28,000	14,000	13,200	800
32,000	16,000	14,800	1200
36,000	18,000	16,400	1600

FIGURE 28.2 Table showing *DI*, *C*, and *S* (billions of dollars).

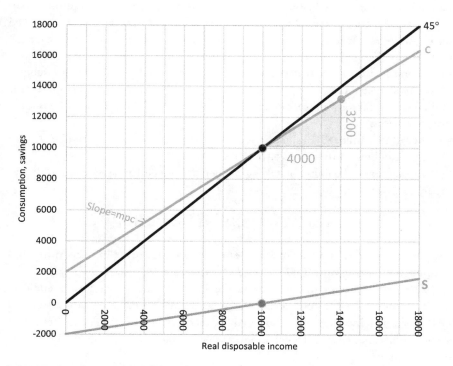

FIGURE 28.3 Consumption (*C*) and savings (*S*) functions.

the consumption function, *C*, intersects the 45° line, which indicates all points where *C* = *DI*. Also note that the slope of the consumption function is equal to $\frac{\Delta C}{\Delta DI} = 0.8$, which is the marginal propensity to consume (*MPC*). The slope of the savings function, *S*, is equal to $\frac{\Delta S}{\Delta DI} = 0.2$, which is the marginal propensity to save (*MPS*).

As mentioned previously, autonomous consumption (Ca), is **the level of consumption that does not depend on disposable income.** Even with no income, consumers must borrow money or spend their savings in order to buy food and pay rent. Induced consumption, **consumption induced by changes in income**, is found by multiplying the **MPC** by disposable income. Therefore, the equation for the consumption function in Figure 28.3 is

$$C = \text{Autonomous Consumption} + \text{Induced Consumption}$$
$$= C_a + (MPC) DI = 2000 + (0.8) * DI.$$

See the endnote for the derivation of the general form of the consumption function.[1]

Consumption can also be affected by taxes, because taxes affect disposable income, and disposable income is the main determinant of consumption. Taxes affect consumption in two different ways, depending on the type of taxes levied on consumers. Lump sum (autonomous) taxes are one-time taxes (or tax cuts) that do not change as income changes. Lump sum taxes affect autonomous consumption. The tax rate (t) is the average percentage of income that households must pay as (net) taxes. Tax rates affect the amount of disposable income that is available, and therefore the amount households can spend on induced consumption purchases.

Recall that Induced consumption$(C_i) = MPC * \text{Disposable income}(DI)$.
This can be rewritten as $C_i = MPC(Y{-}T)$.

T, total taxes, are found by taking the net tax rate percentage (t) and multiplying by income: $T = tY$.

$$\text{Substituting,} \, C_i = MPC(Y - tY) = MPC(1 - t)Y$$

Therefore, **induced consumption depends on income (Y), the marginal propensity to consume (MPC), and the tax rate (t).**

The consumption function forms the basis for the aggregate expenditure model, which plots the total level of aggregate expenditure at each level of real GDP (national income). We also need to incorporate investment, government spending, and net exports to get a more complete picture of the expenditure side of the economy.

28.2 THE COMPLETE AGGREGATE EXPENDITURE MODEL

Figure 28.4 contains a table that uses numbers that are typical for the United States to construct an aggregate expenditure model. The table begins with real GDP, which is defined as national income. Economists use **Y** to represent real GDP.

Real GDP Y	Taxes T=0.2Y	Real Disposable Income DI=Y−T	Consumption C=200+0.9DI C=200+0.72Y	Investment I I=3000	Government Spending G G=3600	Net Exports X−IM= 800−0.12Y	Aggregate Expenditure AE=C+I+G+X−IM AE=7600+0.6Y
0	0	0	200	3000	3600	800	7600
1000	200	800	920	3000	3600	680	8200
2000	400	1600	1640	3000	3600	560	8800
3000	600	2400	2360	3000	3600	440	9400
4000	800	3200	3080	3000	3600	320	10,000
5000	1000	4000	3800	3000	3600	200	10,600
6000	1200	4800	4520	3000	3600	80	11,200
7000	1400	5600	5240	3000	3600	−40	11,800
8000	1600	6400	5960	3000	3600	−160	12,400
9000	1800	7200	6680	3000	3600	−280	13,000
10,000	2000	8000	7400	3000	3600	−400	13,600
11,000	2200	8800	8120	3000	3600	−520	14,200
12,000	2400	9600	8840	3000	3600	−640	14,800
13,000	2600	10,400	9560	3000	3600	−760	15,400
14,000	2800	11,200	10,280	3000	3600	−880	16,000
15,000	3000	12,000	11,000	3000	3600	−1000	16,600
16,000	3200	12,800	11,720	3000	3600	−1120	17,200
17,000	3400	13,600	12,440	3000	3600	−1240	17,800
18,000	3600	14,400	13,160	3000	3600	−1360	18,400
19,000	**3800**	**15,200**	**13,880**	**3000**	**3600**	**−1480**	**19,000**
20,000	4000	16,000	14,600	3000	3600	−1600	19,600
21,000	4200	16,800	15,320	3000	3600	−1720	20,200
22,000	4400	17,600	16,040	3000	3600	−1840	20,800
23,000	4600	18,400	16,760	3000	3600	−1960	21,400
24,000	4800	19,200	17,480	3000	3600	−2080	22,000

FIGURE 28.4 Table of the components of aggregate expenditure at each level of real GDP (billions of dollars).

The next column of the table, taxes, is found by taking the average U.S. **tax rate** (*t*) of 20% (*t* = 0.2) and multiplying by national income, *Y*, to get **total taxes**, *T*.

$$\text{Total taxes} = (\text{tax rate}) * (\text{national income}); T = tY.$$

As before, real disposable income (*DI*) is found by subtracting total taxes (*T*) from national income (*Y*): *DI=Y−T*.

In the model depicted in Figure 28.4, the marginal propensity to consume is 0.9. Therefore, consumption (*C*) is equal to autonomous consumption (*C* when *Y* = 0, which means that C_a = $200) plus the marginal propensity to consume multiplied by disposable income: *C*=200+0.9(*DI*). Substituting *DI* = *Y* − *T*, we can rewrite the equation for consumption as *C* = 200 + 0.9(*Y* − *T*). But because T = *tY* = 0.2(*Y*), we can rewrite this further as

$$C = 200 + (0.9)(0.8)Y = 200 + (0.72)Y.$$

More generally, in aggregate expenditure models, consumption can be written as the equation

$$C = (C_a) + (MPC)(1-t)Y.$$

Investment (*I*) and government spending (*G*) are autonomous in Figure 28.4: They do not vary with national income in this particular model. Economists often assume that investment depends on factors other than current income, such as expected sales and interest rates. And government spending often depends on political factors rather than real GDP. Therefore, under some circumstances, economists find it reasonable to assume in an aggregate expenditure model that *I* and *G* are autonomous.

We can construct an aggregate expenditure model in which investment does vary with real GDP, because investment can be correlated with real GDP in some circumstances. This would mean that we would add a marginal propensity to invest, $MPI = \dfrac{\Delta I}{\Delta Y}$, to the marginal respending rate. And we could also construct a model in which government spending varies with real GDP. Governments with significant automatic stabilizers tend to increase government spending whenever income falls, resulting in a marginal propensity for government purchases that would be negative, $MPGP = \dfrac{\Delta G}{\Delta Y} < 0$. Or we might have a government that spends money whenever it gets it, resulting in a marginal propensity for government purchases that is positive, $MPGP = \dfrac{\Delta G}{\Delta Y} > 0$. This would give us a much more complex marginal respending rate of

$$MRR = MPC(1-t) - MPM + MPI + MPGP.$$

However, for simplicity, we have ignored these special cases in this chapter.

Like consumption, net exports have an autonomous component and an induced component. Exports are usually considered to be autonomous because they depend primarily on foreign incomes and preferences, not on U.S. income. Therefore, in this model exports are equal to $800 billion and they do not vary with real GDP (Y). Imports do vary with Y. The more income U.S. citizens have, the more they spend on purchases of imported goods and services. Because imports are subtracted from expenditure on U.S. goods and services, net exports decrease as U.S. income increases. Specifically, in Figure 28.4 imports increase (and net exports decrease) by an amount equal to the marginal propensity to import, $MPM = \dfrac{\Delta IM}{\Delta Y} = 0.12$, multiplied by Y. Therefore, the equation for net exports is

$$\text{Net Exports} = (X_a - IM) = 800 - (MPM)Y = 800 - (0.12)Y.$$

If we add all of the components of aggregate expenditure together, $AE = C + I + G + (X - IM)$. Using the equations for each component,

$$AE = (200 + 0.72Y) + 3000 + 3600 + (800 - 0.12Y) = 7600 + (0.6)Y.$$

In this equation, 7600 would be autonomous aggregate expenditure, AE_a.

In the previous chapter, we defined the marginal respending rate (MRR) as the amount of each dollar of income that is respent on U.S. goods and services. Mathematically, $MRR = \dfrac{\Delta AE}{\Delta Y}$. In Figure 28.4, for each change in income of 1000, there is a change in aggregate expenditure of 600, so $MRR = \dfrac{600}{1000} = 0.6$.

Also, recall that the marginal respending rate can be expressed in terms of its components:

$$MRR = MPC(1-t) - MPM = (0.9)(0.8) - (0.12) = (0.72) - (0.12) = 0.6.$$

Therefore, the equation for aggregate expenditure (AE) in its general form is

$$AE = \text{Autonomous expenditure} + \text{Induced expenditure} = AE_a + MRR(Y).$$

Equilibrium in Figure 28.4 occurs where national income (real GDP) is equal to aggregate expenditure—when $Y = AE = \$19,000$ billion. In the Keynesian aggregate expenditure model, changes in business inventories push the economy toward equilibrium where $Y = AE$.

Business inventories are **the value of unsold goods held by retailers, wholesalers, and manufacturers**. Businesses hold inventories in anticipation of future sales, and inventories tend to be particularly large in the case of goods that take a long time to manufacture.

When aggregate expenditure is greater than real GDP, purchases are greater than the total production of goods and services. In this case, $AE > Y$ and businesses are selling more goods than they are producing. Their inventories fall. The decline in inventories below their normal level is a sign to businesses that they can sell more goods and make more money. Because the goal is to maximize profits, decreases in inventories are followed by increases in production and a corresponding increase in real GDP.

When aggregate expenditure is less than real GDP, $AE < Y$, just the opposite occurs. Businesses find that their inventories increase because total spending is less than total production. As goods pile up in businesses' warehouses, they scale back on production, which decreases real GDP. Therefore, equilibrium real GDP occurs where $AE = Y$, and there is no change in business inventories because total spending is exactly equal to total production.

Using the numbers in Figure 28.4, notice that when real GDP is $17,000 billion, aggregate expenditure is $17,800 billion. This means consumers, investors, government bodies, and foreign citizens purchased $800 billion more in goods than the economy produced. Businesses then see an $800 billion decline in their inventories. This encourages businesses to increase production, which increases real GDP above $17,000 billion. This process will continue until we reach equilibrium at $Y = AE = \$19,000$ billion.

Similarly, when real GDP is $24,000 billion in Figure 28.4, aggregate expenditure is only $22,000 billion. This would result in businesses experiencing a $2000 billion increase in inventories. They would respond by reducing production, which would reduce real GDP. This process will continue until real GDP has fallen to $Y = AE = \$19,000$ billion.

We also need to recall the importance of injections and leakages in the economy. When income is equal to expenditure, leakages are also equal to injections.

$$Y = DI + T = C + S + T$$

$$AE = C + I + G + X - IM.$$

When $Y = AE$,

$$C + S + T = C + I + G + X - IM \quad \text{and}$$
$$S + T + IM = I + G + X$$

Leakages = Injections.

In Figure 28.4, when $Y = \$19,000$, $S = DI - C = 15,200 - 13,880 = 1320$. $T = 3800$. $X = 800$. Because net exports $(NE) = (X - IM)$, $IM = -NE + X = 1480 + 800 = 2280$.

Therefore, when $Y = \$19,000$, injections are equal to leakages.

$$S + T + IM = 1320 + 3800 + 2280 = 7400$$

$$I + G + X = 3000 + 3600 + 800 = 7400.$$

When $Y = \$15,000$, $S = 1000$, $T = 3000$, and $IM = 1800$, so $S+T+IM=5800$ and $I + G + X$ is still 7400 (I, G, and X are all autonomous variables in this model). Therefore, when $Y = \$15,000$, leakages are less than injections, and the extra of money injected into the circular flow of the economy causes real GDP to increase. When $Y = \$24,000$, leakages are equal to \$9400 and injections are still \$7400, meaning that more money is leaking out of the circular flow than is flowing back in. In such circumstances, we can expect real GDP to decrease.

We can also display the aggregate expenditure model using a graph. Figure 28.5 plots all of the components of aggregate expenditure. The consumption curve starts out where $Y = 0$ and autonomous consumption is 200 and proceeds at a slope of $\frac{\Delta C}{\Delta Y} = 0.72$. Adding autonomous investment of \$3000 shifts the aggregate expenditure curve up by exactly that amount, resulting in the $C + I$ curve. Adding autonomous government spending of \$3600 shifts the aggregate expenditure curve up by exactly that amount, resulting in the $C + I + G$ curve. And adding in the final component, net exports, shifts the curve up by \$800 (autonomous exports) and then reduces the slope from 0.72 to 0.60 by incorporating the marginal propensity to import (0.12 in this example) into the MRR. The aggregate expenditure curve

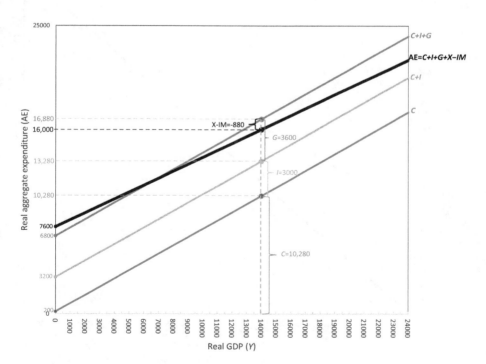

FIGURE 28.5 Construction of the aggregate expenditure curve, AE = C + I + G + X − IM.

shows **the total level of real spending, including consumption, investment, government spending, and net exports, at each level of real GDP.**

Now that we have derived the aggregate expenditure curve graphically, we can use it to find the equilibrium level of real GDP. Figure 28.6 plots aggregate expenditure at each level of income. Real GDP is displayed in the graph by the **45° line labeled Y.** The aggregate expenditure curve starts out at $Y = 0$ and $AE = AE_a$ = 7600. Then it proceeds at a slope equal to the MRR of 0.6 until $AE=Y=19{,}000$ at point **e**, which is the equilibrium level of real GDP.

The equilibrium level of real GDP can also be determined using the equation for aggregate expenditure. As we saw earlier, the equation for aggregate expenditure is $AE=AE_a+MRR(Y)$. In equilibrium, $AE = Y$. So, substituting Y for AE, we get, $Y=AE_a+MRR(Y)$. Simplifying, $Y(1-MRR)=AE_a$. Therefore, the equilibrium level of real GDP is

$$Y = \frac{AE_a}{\left(1 - MRR\right)} = AE_a * \text{Multiplier}.$$

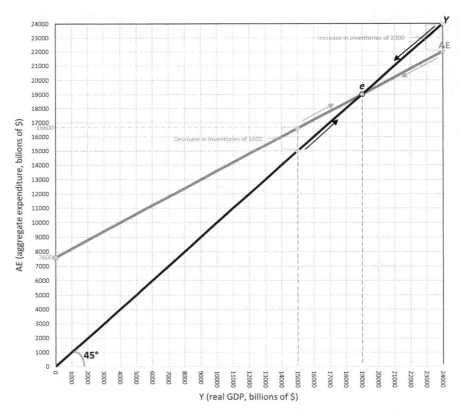

FIGURE 28.6 Keynesian equilibrium: Aggregate expenditure = Real GDP.

In Figure 28.6, $Y = 7600 * \dfrac{1}{1-0.6} = 7600 * 2.5 = \$19,000 \text{ billion}$.

Point **e** is the equilibrium level of real GDP because the economy tends to adjust until it reaches that point. To the left of point **e**, $AE > Y$, inventories are decreasing, so businesses increase production and real GDP increases as a result. To the right of point **e**, $AE < Y$, inventories are increasing, so businesses decrease production and real GDP falls.

Note that as we saw in the previous chapter, equilibrium real GDP can occur above or below potential real GDP. Once we know equilibrium real GDP and potential real GDP, we can determine whether the economy is experiencing a recessionary gap or an inflationary gap or whether the economy is at normal capacity.

We can also plot injections and leakages associated with the aggregate expenditure model. Figure 28.7 plots the injections, $I + G + X$, and the leakages, $S + T + IM$, from the table in Figure 28.4. Injections in this model are all autonomous—they do not vary with real GDP (national income)—so injections are fixed at \$7400 and the slope of the injections curve is 0. Leakages vary with income, because savings, taxes, and imports all increase as real GDP increases. This is why the leakages curve has a positive slope. In fact, the slope of the leakages curve is 0.4, which is equal to $(1-0.6)=1-MRR$.

The leakages and injections curves intersect at equilibrium when real GDP is \$19,000 billion, which corresponds to the equilibrium in Figure 28.6.

Now that we have demonstrated how the aggregate expenditure curve is constructed and how equilibrium is determined, we need to discuss the factors that cause the aggregate expenditure curve to shift.

28.3 SHIFTS IN THE AGGREGATE EXPENDITURE CURVE

As we saw above, a movement along the aggregate expenditure curve is caused by a change in real GDP (Y). When real GDP increases, consumption increases due to the marginal propensity to consume and import purchases increase because of the marginal propensity to import, moving us along the aggregate expenditure curve.

In general, shifts in the aggregate expenditure curve are caused by autonomous changes in all of the factors that shift the aggregate demand curve that we studied in the previous chapter. However, there are two major exceptions: (1) changes in national income (real GDP) cause a movement along the AE curve and a shift in the aggregate demand curve, and (2) changes in prices (the GDP deflator) in situations where prices affect macroeconomic variables cause a shift in the AE curve and a movement along the AD curve. Autonomous changes in C, I, G, X, or IM cause **parallel** shifts in AE, as we will see below.

Autonomous changes in consumption (C_a) are caused by shifts in wealth, consumers' expectations, lump sum tax changes (that do not depend on income),

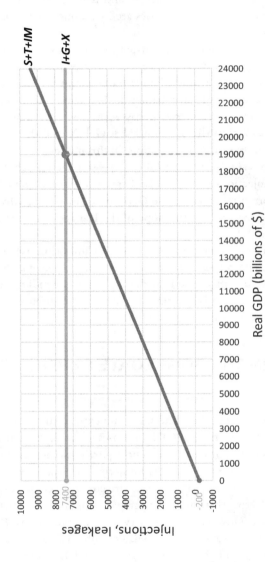

FIGURE 28.7 Injections ($I + G + X$) and leakages ($S + T + IM$).

demographic factors such as the age of the population, and prices (the GDP deflator's effect on consumer wealth). Autonomous changes in investment are driven by
changes in business sales forecasts, interest rates, expectations about profitability,
businesses' need for productive capacity, new technology opportunities, investment taxes or tax credits, and prices (the GDP deflator's effect on interest rates). All
government spending changes are considered autonomous (G_a). Lastly, autonomous
changes in net exports ($X_a - IM_a$) are caused by fluctuations in foreign income,
relative goods prices, exchange rates, tariff rates, and prices (the GDP deflator's
effect on relative goods prices).

A shift in the **slope** of the AE curve is a result of changes in the marginal respending rate and any of its components. This includes the marginal
propensity to consume, the tax rate, the marginal propensity to import, and,
possibly, the marginal propensity to invest and the marginal propensity for government purchases if these factors vary with real GDP (e.g., if these factors are
not autonomous).

Figure 28.8 lists all 22 of the factors that cause a shift in the aggregate expenditure curve.

Figure 28.9 shows how an autonomous change in aggregate expenditure affects
the AE curve and the equilibrium level of real GDP. Suppose that the economy
starts out in equilibrium at point **a** with an autonomous expenditure level of $7600
billion (the first point on AE_0), a slope of 0.6 (the MRR), and an equilibrium real
GDP of $19,000 billion. Now suppose that there is an autonomous increase in
expenditure of +$1600, which shifts the AE curve up by exactly that amount to
AE_1. This could have been caused by an autonomous increase in consumption,
investment, government spending, or net exports.

Notice that the new equilibrium, where $AE_1 = Y$, occurs at point **b** at a new
real GDP of $23,000 billion. A $1600 billion increase in autonomous aggregate
expenditure caused a $4000 billion increase in real GDP because of the multiplier.
Recall from the previous chapter that the multiplier determines how many times
each $1 of spending gets respent, which then determines the total increase in real
GDP. In this example, the multiplier is

$$\text{Multiplier} = \frac{1}{1 - MRR} = \frac{1}{1 - 0.6} = \frac{1}{0.4} = 2.5.$$

Each $1 increase in spending causes real GDP to change by $2.5, because when
people spend money it becomes someone else's income and they spend a portion of
it (equal to the MRR), which becomes someone else's income, and so on. Thus, a
$1600 billion increase in autonomous aggregate expenditure causes an increase in
real GDP of $1600 billion × 2.5 = $4000 billion.

Now suppose that, starting at point **a**, autonomous aggregate expenditure
decreases by $2000 billion. This causes a decrease in real GDP of $2000 billion*2.5=$5000 billion. Real GDP decreases from $19,000 billion to $14,000 bil-
lion, and the equilibrium point moves from point **a** to point **c**.

Determinants of shifts in *AE*
Autonomous Consumption (C_a)
1. **Wealth** (stocks, bonds, real estate values)
2. **Expectations** (consumer confidence)
3. **Income taxes** (lump sum tax changes)
4. **Demographic factors** (age structure)
5. **Prices** (effect of inflation on consumer purchases)
Autonomous Investment (I_a)
6. **Sales expectations** (business forecasts)
7. **Interest rates** (cost of financing investments)
8. **Expectations about profitability** (output, input prices)
9. **Need for productive capacity** (fully or under-utilized)
10. **Technology** (new opportunities)
11. **Taxes on investment** (or investment tax credits)
12. **Prices** (effect on borrowing costs)
Autonomous Government spending (G_a)
13. **Government decisions**
Autonomous Net Exports (X_a-IM_a)
14. **Foreign income** (directly affects exports)
15. **Relative goods prices** (foreign vs. domestic goods prices)
16. **Exchange rates** (effect on goods prices)
17. **Tariffs** (raise or lower prices of foreign or domestic goods)
18. **Prices** (inflation raises prices of domestic goods)
Changes in the slope of AE
19. Marginal Propensity to Consume (*MPC*)
20. Tax rate (*t*)
20. Marginal Propensity to Import (*MPM*)
21. Marginal Propensity to Invest (*MPI*)
22. Marginal Propensity for Government Purchases (*MPGP*)

FIGURE 28.8 Table of the determinants of shifts in the aggregate expenditure curve.

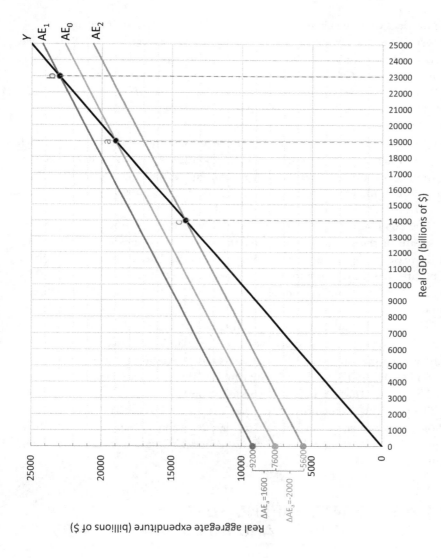

FIGURE 28.9 Shifts in the aggregate expenditure curve from autonomous changes in AE.

We can also use the equation of the aggregate expenditure curve to determine the equilibrium level of real GDP. Originally, $Y_0 = \dfrac{AE_a}{(1-MRR)} = \dfrac{7600}{(0.4)} = \$19,000\,\text{billion}$. Now that autonomous expenditure has decreased to $5600 billion, $Y_2 = \dfrac{AE_a}{(1-MRR)} = \dfrac{5600}{(0.4)} = \$14,000\,\text{billion}.$

Now let's examine changes in the slope of the AE curve in more detail.

When one of the components of the marginal respending rate (MRR) changes, the AE curve changes in slope, but autonomous expenditure does not change. Because $MRR=MPC(1-t)-MPM$, any increase in MPC, decrease in t, or decrease in MPM will increase MRR and increase the slope of the AE curve. Any decrease in MPC, increase in t, or increase in MPM will decrease MRR and reduce the slope of the AE curve.

In Figure 28.10, the original aggregate expenditure curve is AE_0, which starts out when autonomous aggregate expenditure is 8000 and has a slope of 0.6. Mathematically, $AE_0=8000+(0.6)Y$. The equilibrium level of real GDP in Figure 28.10 with aggregate expenditure curve AE_0 is $20,000 billion at point **a** where $AE_0 = Y$.

Now suppose that the marginal respending rate increases to 0.75, due to an increase in the marginal propensity to consume, a decrease in the tax rate, or a decrease in the marginal propensity to import. The aggregate expenditure curve shifts to AE_1, which starts out at 8000 and proceeds at a slope equal to 0.75: $AE_1=8000+(0.75)Y$. The new equilibrium, where $AE_1 = Y$, is at $32,000 billion at point **b**.

Or suppose that the marginal respending rate decreases to 0.5 due to a decrease in the marginal propensity to consume, an increase in the tax rate, or an increase in the marginal propensity to import. The aggregate expenditure curve would shift to AE_2, where $AE_2=8000+(0.5)Y$. Equilibrium for this aggregate expenditure curve would be where $AE_2 = Y$, at $16,000 billion at point **c**.

The aggregate expenditure curve can also be used to determine whether the economy is experiencing an inflationary or a recessionary gap and what policies might work to close the gap. Therefore, if the model is accurate, it can be extremely useful to policymakers.

28.4 AGGREGATE EXPENDITURE AND RECESSIONARY AND INFLATIONARY GAPS

A recessionary gap is the amount that equilibrium real GDP is below potential real GDP (the economy's normal capacity). An inflationary gap is the amount that equilibrium real GDP is above potential real GDP.

In Figure 28.11, potential real GDP is $20,000 billion. The economy is initially in equilibrium at point **a** where $AE_1 = Y$, so equilibrium real GDP is equal

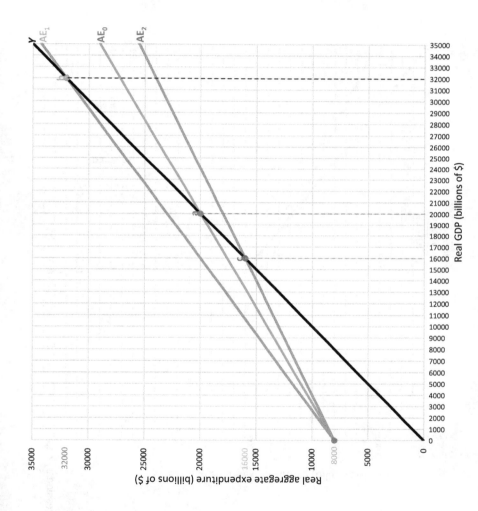

FIGURE 28.10 Shifts in the aggregate expenditure curve from a change in MRR.

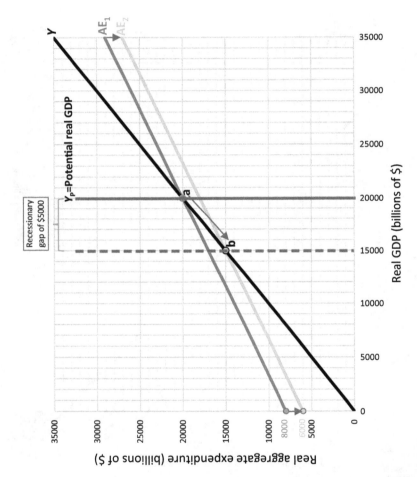

FIGURE 28.11 A recessionary gap (equilibrium real GDP < potential real GDP).

to potential real GDP (Y_p). $AE_1 = 8000 + (0.6)Y$. With an MRR of 0.6, the multiplier is equal to 2.5.

Now suppose that there is an autonomous decrease in consumption of $2000 billion, which causes the aggregate expenditure curve to shift down from AE_1 to AE_2. This causes real GDP to decrease by 2.5*2000=$5000 billion, so the new equilibrium real GDP at point **b** is $15,000 billion. Now, the economy is experiencing a recessionary gap of $5000 billion, which is the difference between equilibrium real GDP and potential real GDP.

Recall that, in a recession, economists who adhere to the classical model believe that wages and input prices will fall, reducing business costs, causing firms to produce and supply more goods and services, which increases incomes and moves the economy back to potential real GDP. In the Keynesian model, wages and input prices are sticky and do not fall quickly, if at all. Furthermore, if wages and input prices do fall, this erodes consumers' purchasing power and undermines some businesses' profitability, factors that serve to keep the economy in a recession indefinitely.

Modern policymakers adhere to the Keynesian model. Therefore, they would advocate taking steps to eliminate the recessionary gap. This would require increasing autonomous expenditure by $2000 billion to achieve a $5000 billion increase in real GDP (after the multiplier effect is incorporated). The government could increase government spending directly by $2000 billion. They could reduce interest rates and hope that consumers and investors would increase autonomous consumption and autonomous investment. Or they could give consumers a tax cut to stimulate consumption. Note, however, that the tax cut would have to be much larger than $2000 to achieve an increase in consumption of that amount because consumers save some proportion of any disposable income they receive. Recall that for tax cuts, $\Delta C = MPC(\Delta T)$. If we want to achieve a change in autonomous consumption of $2000, and if the MPC is 0.9, then we can solve for ΔT:

$$\Delta C = 2000 = 0.9(\Delta T); \Delta T = \frac{2000}{0.9} = \$2222.22.$$

It takes a $2222.22 decrease in taxes to achieve a $2000 increase in consumption when the MPC is 0.9.

Note that we are talking about a lump sum tax cut, rather than a change in the tax *rate*. A lump sum tax cut is where the government gives citizens a lump sum of money but does not change the tax rate they pay on income. For example, in 2020, the U.S. government gave most citizens a lump sum payment of $1200 to try to stimulate consumer spending in the midst of the COVID-19 recession. Unfortunately, much of that money was saved due to consumer pessimism, which caused a decline in the MPC. A change in the tax rate changes the MRR, which changes the slope of the aggregate expenditure curve. A decrease in the tax rate from 20% to 10% would have achieved a similar impact, but a tax cut of that magnitude would need to be reversed the next time the economy began to boom or it would fuel inflation. Therefore, it is much simpler to enact a straightforward, lump sum tax cut for stabilization policy than it is to make changes to tax rates.

The aggregate expenditure model can also depict the economy experiencing an inflationary gap. Figure 28.12 shows the economy initially in equilibrium at point **a** where $AE_1 = Y$, so equilibrium real GDP is equal to potential real GDP (Y_p). Now suppose that there is a huge increase in government spending of $4000 billion to fight a major war. This causes the aggregate expenditure curve to shift to AE_2, which causes equilibrium real GDP to increase to $30,000 billion, which can be seen at point **b**. There is now an inflationary gap of $10,000 billion.

To avoid inflation, the government will need to cut other areas of spending, raise interest rates to curb business investment and consumption, or increase taxes (by $11,111 billion if the MPC is 0.9) in order to shift the aggregate expenditure curve back to AE_1.

Now that we have described how the aggregate expenditure curve works, it is time to discuss the relationship between aggregate expenditure and aggregate demand and the debates economists have over which model is most useful.

28.5 THE AGGREGATE EXPENDITURE CURVE AND THE AGGREGATE DEMAND CURVE

The aggregate expenditure curve and the aggregate demand curve have identical components, but they serve different purposes. The aggregate demand curve shows the total level of spending *at each price level*. The aggregate expenditure curve shows the total level of spending *at each level of national income*. Thus, the aggregate demand model focuses on the relationship between prices and aggregate spending, whereas the aggregate expenditure model focuses on the relationship between income and aggregate spending.

In the mainstream aggregate demand model, an increase in prices causes aggregate demand spending to decline for three reasons:

1. The real balance effect: Higher prices reduce consumer wealth, causing them to spend less.
2. The real interest rate effect: Higher prices cause real interest rates to rise, which causes consumers and investors to purchase less consumption and investment goods.
3. The foreign trade effect: Higher priced domestic goods cause exports to decline and imports to increase, thereby reducing net exports.

Figure 28.13 shows the impact of higher prices on both aggregate demand (AD) and aggregate expenditure according to the mainstream model. According to the AD curve, if prices increase from P_1 to P_2, then the aggregate quantity demanded declines from Q_1 to Q_2 due to decreases in consumption, investment, and net

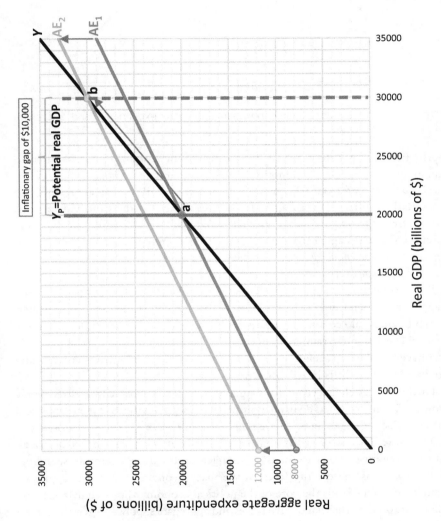

FIGURE 28.12 An inflationary gap (equilibrium real GDP > potential real GDP).

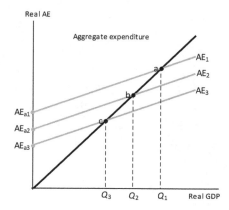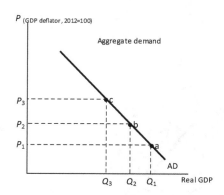

FIGURE 28.13 The correspondence between aggregate expenditure and aggregate demand.

exports. In the aggregate expenditure model, the increase in prices would cause autonomous decreases in consumption, investment, and net exports, which causes the *AE* curve to *shift* from AE_1 to AE_2, causing real GDP to decrease from Q_1 to Q_2. Similarly, if prices increase again from P_2 to P_3, aggregate quantity demanded decreases from Q_2 to Q_3 in the aggregate demand graph and the aggregate expenditure curve decreases again from AE_2 to AE_3 in the aggregate expenditure graph. Therefore, *a movement along the aggregate demand curve from an increase in prices causes a shift in the aggregate expenditure curve.*

Political economists generally believe that prices have a very minor impact on aggregate expenditure most of the time. As we saw in the previous chapter, research by political economists indicates that the real balance effect, foreign trade effect, and real interest rate effect are usually very small or even nonexistent. If prices have no effect on spending, we would have an AD curve that is vertical, and there would not be shifts in AE when prices change.

Furthermore, political economists argue that demand factors tend to drive supply responses: When consumers demand more products, suppliers increase their supply and vice versa. The aggregate supply curve is only relevant when a supply shock occurs.

Therefore, instead of utilizing a model that focuses on the impact of prices, political economists prefer to focus on the factors that drive aggregate spending, which they see as the driving force in the macroeconomy. Thus, the aggregate expenditure model forms the core of the political economy approach. Mainstream economists, on the other hand, give prices and aggregate supply a large role in their models of the macroeconomy.

28.6 CONCLUSION

This chapter laid out the Keynesian model of aggregate expenditure and income. The aggregate expenditure model begins with the consumption function.

Consumption increases as disposable income increases: Consumers spend a percentage of each increase in income on consumption purchases. That percentage is called the marginal propensity to consume. The remainder of consumers' disposable incomes is saved. Because taxes affect disposable income, they also affect consumption. Lump sum taxes affect autonomous levels of consumption, whereas tax rates (%) affect the marginal propensity to consume. As a general rule, consumption purchases are driven by income, consumers' marginal propensity to consume (or save), and the tax rate.

The aggregate expenditure model consists of consumption, investment, government spending, and net exports: $AE=C+I+G+(X-IM)$. AE contains autonomous expenditure, which involves variables that *do not* change as income changes, including autonomous consumption, autonomous investment, autonomous government spending, and autonomous exports. AE also includes induced expenditure, which involves variables that *do* vary as income changes, including induced consumption (determined via the MPC and the tax rate) and induced imports (determined by the marginal propensity to import). Thus, AE is equal to autonomous expenditure plus induced expenditure, which can be written as

$$AE = AE_a + MRR(Y).$$

The equilibrium level of aggregate expenditure can be found where real aggregate expenditure is equal to real GDP (national income): $AE=Y$. Whenever $AE>Y$, business inventories fall, causing production to increase, which causes real GDP (Y) to increase until equilibrium is reached. Whenever $AE<Y$, businesses' inventories increase and they cut production, thereby reducing real GDP (Y) until equilibrium is reached.

When $AE = Y$, injections are equal to leakages, meaning that investment plus government spending plus exports are equal to savings plus taxes plus imports. On a graph, the equilibrium level of aggregate expenditure and income is found where the AE curve intersects the Y (45°) curve.

The AE curve experiences a parallel shift whenever one of its autonomous components changes. Using the multiplier, the change in real GDP will be equal to the change in autonomous expenditure multiplied by the multiplier:

$$\Delta Y = \Delta AE_a \times \frac{1}{1-MRR}.$$

The AE curve experiences a change in slope whenever the marginal propensity to consume, tax rate, or marginal propensity to import changes, causing a change in the MRR. The equilibrium level of real GDP can be found by multiplying autonomous expenditure by the multiplier: $Y_e = AE_a^* \text{Multiplier}$. When the MRR increases the multiplier increases, which will also increase equilibrium Y. When the MRR decreases the multiplier decreases, which will decrease equilibrium Y.

Equilibrium real GDP can occur above or below potential real GDP, which means the economy can experience and inflationary gap or a recessionary gap. Policymakers can close an inflationary gap or a recessionary gap by engaging in fiscal and/or monetary policy, subjects we will study extensively in the next two chapters.

Lastly, mainstream economists tend to treat the aggregate expenditure curve as part of aggregate demand and focus on aggregate demand and supply as the key model for understanding the macroeconomy. Political economists tend to treat the aggregate expenditure curve as the key to macroeconomic understanding, and they view the aggregate demand and supply model as only useful in specialized circumstances, such as when a supply shock occurs.

In addition to debating which model is most useful, mainstream and political economists vigorously debate the extent to which fiscal policy and monetary policy should be used to stabilize the macroeconomy. It is to these subjects that we turn next.

· ·

QUESTIONS FOR REVIEW

1. Use Figure 28.14 to answer the following questions.
    a. What is the tax rate?
    b. What is autonomous consumption?
    c. What is the marginal propensity to consume?
    d. What is savings when $Y = 4000$ and $Y = 6000$?
    e. If the tax rate increased to 50%, what would consumption be when $Y = 1000$?
2. Use Figure 28.15 to answer the questions below. In this case, $t = 0.25$, $MPC = 0.8$, investment is autonomous, government spending is autonomous, exports are autonomous and equal to 200, and the MPM is 0.1.
    a. Complete the table.
    b. Determine the equilibrium level of Y and AE.
    c. What is the equation for the aggregate expenditure curve in this example?
    d. If there is an autonomous increase in investment of $500 billion, what would the new equilibrium level of Y and AE be?

Y	DI	C
0	0	600
1000	750	1200
2000	1500	1800
3000	2250	2400
4000	3000	3000
5000	3750	3600
6000	4500	4200

FIGURE 28.14 Table of Y, C, and DI for Problem 1.

Y=GDP	T	DI	C	S	I	G	X-IM	AE
0			400		600	800	200	
1000								
2000								
3000								
4000								
5000								
6000								

FIGURE 28.15 Table of AE and its components for Problem 2.

3. Use Figure 28.16 to answer the questions below.
   a. What is the equilibrium level of real GDP in Figure 28.16?
   b. What is the marginal respending rate in Figure 28.16? What is the equation for AE_1?
   c. Why is it impossible for $12,000 billion to be the equilibrium level of real GDP with aggregate expenditure curve AE_1? Explain briefly.
   d. Suppose there is a decrease in autonomous investment of $1000 billion. What will be the new equilibrium level of real GDP (Y_2)? Explain and show your work.
   e. Suppose that the marginal respending rate for aggregate expenditure curve AE_1 changes to 0.5. What will be the new equilibrium level of real GDP (Y_3)? Explain and show your work.
   f. Copy the graph in Figure 28.16. On your graph, show the new aggregate expenditure curve that results in part D when there is an autonomous decrease in investment of $1000 billion. Also show the new aggregate expenditure curve that results in part e when the marginal respending rate changes to 0.5.
4. Which of the following will cause the slope of the aggregate expenditure curve to decrease? Select one or more of the following and explain your answer briefly.
   a. A decrease in autonomous consumption expenditures.
   b. A decrease in the marginal propensity to consume.
   c. A decrease in the tax rate.
   d. A decrease in the marginal propensity to import.
5. Suppose that potential real GDP (Y_p) in Figure 28.16 is $12,000 billion and that the current aggregate expenditure curve is AE_1.
   a. How large is the inflationary or recessionary gap?
   b. How much would the government need to change government spending to move the economy from its current equilibrium on AE_1 to Y_p?
   c. Assuming that the MPC is 0.95, how much would the government need to change lump sum taxes to move the economy from its current equilibrium on AE_1 to Y_p?

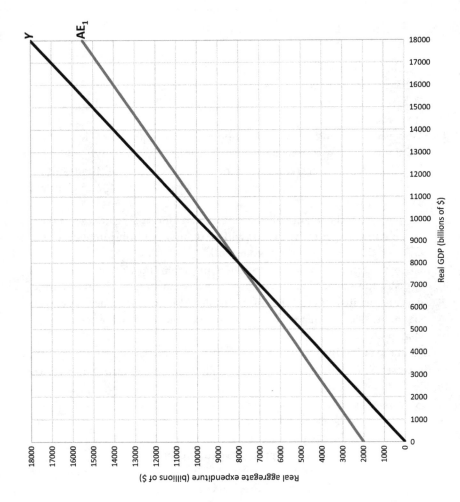

FIGURE 28.16 Graph of AE and Y for Problems 3 and 5.

6. Using Figure 28.13 (which connects AE to AD), explain what impact a decrease in prices would have on aggregate demand and aggregate expenditure according to mainstream economists. How would political economists respond to this analysis?

NOTE

1 The general form for the equation of the consumption function is the following: Consumption at any level of Y, C_Y, can be found using autonomous and induced consumption. $C_Y = C_a + (MPC)\Delta DI$.

$\Delta DI = DI_Y - DI_0$ and $DI_0 = 0$ in these models. When $Y = 0$, DI is also 0. Therefore, $\Delta DI = DI_Y$. Thus, as long as $DI_0 = 0$, $C_Y = C_a + (MPC)DI_Y$.

PART IX
Stabilization policy

Recurring economic crises are one of the features of modern capitalist economic systems. Every 8–12 years the U.S. economy enters a major crisis that requires government response to stabilize the situation. Sometimes these crises are driven by financial factors. Sometimes they are a result of austerity policies in a particularly fragile economic environment. Sometimes they are the result of shocks from factors external to the domestic economy, such as the oil price shocks of the 1970s or the COVID-19 pandemic shock of 2020. Failure to act would likely turn recessions into depressions, as we learned in the 1930s, so the government must take action to stabilize the economy when crises occur.

In Chapter 29, we study one possible method for dealing with an economic crisis: fiscal policy. Fiscal policy involves using government spending and taxation to affect the economy. One of the major debates in modern economics and politics is about how (and whether) governments should utilize fiscal policy. According to the New Keynesian approach, utilizing fiscal policy to stabilize the economy can improve on market outcomes. Critics from the right (laissez-faire economists), however, argue that the government should do less, and critics from the left (political economists) argue that the government should do much more. In addition, how the government should approach the issue of the national debt and budget deficits is an important and controversial topic. Laissez-faire economists often advocate a balanced budget, whereas political economists and supply-side economists argue that running deficits improves economic growth if the money is spent properly. The New Keynesian position falls in the middle: deficits should be run during recessions, the government should run surpluses during booms, and small deficits to fuel long-term economic growth are acceptable when the economy is at capacity. Interestingly, the fact that large deficits did not have negative consequences in the last four decades is causing economists to reconsider their objections to deficit spending.

DOI: 10.4324/9781315636924-37

Chapter 30 takes up money, banking, and the financial sector, illustrating how financial markets work in theory and practice. Every citizen needs to understand the importance of money, banking, and financial markets to a modern economy. This chapter introduces the mainstream economics view of the money market, the banking sector, and the financial sector. It also introduces students to basic financial instruments (stocks and bonds) and other important issues relevant to personal finance. The chapter also introduces the political economy model of financial markets and the role of banks in creating money. Also discussed is the rise of the Finance, Insurance, and Real Estate (FIRE) sector and the increasing financialization of modern economies.

Chapter 31 discusses monetary policy options that central banks can implement to stabilize economies. The appropriate role for monetary policy is another area where there is significant disagreement among economists. The mainstream, Keynesian view is that monetary policy should be used to stabilize the economy. In a crisis, the central bank should lower interest rates and, in the case of a liquidity trap, implement quantitative easing. This should help to avoid a potentially ruinous deflation. In a boom, monetary policy should be used to slow down the economy to prevent a bust or to engineer a soft landing. Laissez-faire economists want less intervention in money markets, whereas political economists, and especially modern monetary theory adherents, want more intervention.

Chapter 32 takes up economic crises in more detail, including the Great Depression, the financial crisis of 2007–2008, and the COVID-19 recession. One of the great problems in economics is how to avoid a financial crisis, closely followed by the problem of how to end a financial crisis once it occurs. This chapter describes mainstream views of the causes of economic crises, as well as those of laissez-faire and political economists. Particular attention is paid to the ideas of Hyman Minsky on financial fragility and modern Marxist economists studying economic crises.

Fiscal policy, debt, and deficits

Fiscal activism vs. austerity and the macroeconomic role of government

In 2019, the global economy was in fragile condition. A decade after the financial crisis of 2007–2008 and Great Recession of 2008–2009, the macroeconomy once again was unstable. Some of this was driven by a corporate debt bubble that threatened to burst. Some instability was a product of geopolitical instability, including uncertainty related to Brexit (the United Kingdom leaving the European Union, which destabilized European markets) and the U.S.–China trade war sparked by President Trump's tariffs on Chinese imports. Many economists predicted a recession in 2020 as investors signaled deep pessimism about the future.

Into this uncertain environment came the COVID-19 pandemic. Beginning in Wuhan, China in late 2019, the COVID-19 virus spread rapidly around the world, resulting in more than 224 million cases and 4.6 million deaths by September 2021. To stop the spread, most governments shut down economies and issued stay-at-home orders, and many businesses closed stores and offices. The result was a devastating global recession, which the International Monetary Fund projected would be the worst recession since the Depression. Unemployment in the United States spiked to 14.7%, and stock markets dropped initially by 30%.

It was in this environment that the U.S. government embarked on the most dramatic stimulus program in its history. Between March and June 2020, the U.S. government spent $2791 billion, 13% of U.S. gross domestic product (GDP),[1] on tax cuts, unemployment benefits, business bailouts, health care, and other emergency fiscal measures. Meanwhile, the U.S. Central Bank, the Fed, engaged in about $4000 billion of monetary stimulus, lowering interest rates to 0%, buying assets from banks and corporations, and flooding banks and asset markets with money.

The U.S. government felt comfortable engaging in its largest stimulus program ever in part because the stimulus package enacted in 2009, which was also

DOI: 10.4324/9781315636924-38

large by historical standards, was quite effective in reducing the depth of the Great Recession. In addition, the dire predictions of deficit hawks that large deficits would generate inflation and harm financial markets did not come true after the 2009 recession.

The 2020 stimulus had the immediate impact of propping up asset markets, as stocks rebounded to near their values before the pandemic hit. However, unemployment rates stayed stubbornly high, sparking debates over whether or not additional stimulus was warranted. Some economists were worried about government deficits increasing even further if new stimulus programs were enacted. Others argued that deficits were a minor problem in the face of a devastatingly deep recession. This debate over fiscal activism (stimulus) or austerity is one of the most important ones in modern macroeconomics, and it is the subject of this chapter.

The chapter begins by laying out the landscape of modern U.S. government spending and taxation policy, detailing what the U.S. government prioritizes. We compare U.S. priorities with those of other developed countries. Next, we describe automatic stabilizers and discretionary policies that governments can use to combat economic instability, especially recessions. Utilizing the aggregate demand and aggregate supply model, we show how discretionary fiscal policy affects aggregate demand and GDP, as well as how it can close recessionary or inflationary gaps.

We then turn to the debate over the role of government in the macroeconomy and the debate over fiscal activism vs. austerity regarding fiscal policy. This debate revolves in important ways around U.S. government budget deficits and whether or not deficit spending creates problems and is something to be avoided or whether deficit spending fosters prosperity and is to be embraced. Laissez-faire advocates prefer austerity, New Keynesian economists advocate deficits in recessions to stimulate aggregate demand and benefit the poor, supply-siders are fine with deficits as long as the money goes to corporate interests, and political economists advocate deficit spending if it benefits workers, families, and communities and if it fosters growth and productivity. We then take up examples of how fiscal policy was used to combat the Great Recession of 2008–2009 and the COVID-19 recession of 2020.

29.0 CHAPTER 29 LEARNING GOALS

After reading this chapter you should be able to:

■ Describe the major fiscal priorities of the U.S. government and compare and contrast those priorities with the approaches of other governments in developed countries.

■ Explain the use of automatic stabilizers and discretionary fiscal policy to stabilize the economy.

■ Use the aggregate demand–aggregate supply model to analyze the impact of changes in government spending and lump sum taxes on aggregate demand, real GDP, and prices.

■ Critically evaluate the arguments of laissez-faire, supply-side, New Keynesian and political economists on the size and role of government and the use of fiscal policy in recessions.

■ Analyze the arguments of economists regarding the appropriate size of government deficits and debt.

■ Describe and evaluate the effectiveness of the fiscal policies used in the Great Recession and the COVID-19 recession to stabilize the economy.

29.1 THE SIZE AND ROLE OF GOVERNMENT IN THE MACROECONOMY

Fiscal policy is **the use of government spending or taxation to improve economic outcomes.** Fiscal policy can be **used to address macroeconomic market failures such as recessions, unemployment, or price instability and to improve the rate of economic growth.**

The size and role of government expanded dramatically in developed countries after the Great Depression of the 1930s, marking the rise and maturation of the mixed capitalist economic system. Once governments embraced the idea that market failures could be solved, government programs in numerous areas proliferated. The major categories of government spending in the modern era are (1) public and quasi-public goods, (2) social spending, and (3) government administration.

Public and quasi-public goods include health, education, defense, policing, fire protection, infrastructure, research and development funding, basic scientific research, industrial support, and other core government functions that provide goods that markets do not supply effectively. **Social spending** includes support for children, families, the elderly, and the incapacitated, along with spending on health programs for the poor, active labor market programs to develop workers' skills, unemployment benefits, and housing subsidies. Social spending involves creating a safety net for those who cannot gain sufficient subsistence within the market system. **Social spending that involves the transfer of income from the government to individuals or businesses, such as welfare payments or direct business subsidies**, is called a transfer payment. **Government administration** involves spending on the justice system and all regulatory bodies. Performing market facilitation and regulation requires highly skilled, well-paid government officials with substantial expertise in specialized areas, along with buildings, labs, and other support structures.

The degree of spending and intervention in all three of these areas varies widely based on each country's philosophy. Market-dominated economies generally are less regulated and spend less on social programs, public goods, and government administration. Social market economies involve more regulations and administration, as well as more generous spending on social programs and public goods. State-dominated economies vary depending on the governing philosophy of the group dominating the state political infrastructure. China's Communist Party spends extensively on public goods, especially infrastructure, while providing a less generous safety net. Some areas of life in China are strictly regulated, especially labor markets, whereas environmental rules are lax. Cuba spends extensively on safety nets and public goods, and rules governing business operations are very strict.

Figure 29.1 shows the major categories of U.S. federal government spending, which amounted to $4.4 trillion in 2019. The priorities are an interesting indication of the unique aspects of the U.S. economic system. First, as with many countries, the United States provides income stabilization for those who fall on hard times. This helps individuals, families, and communities, while also supporting aggregate demand in recessions. Social Security, which is the national U.S. pension program, is the largest sources of government transfer payments, and income security, which includes unemployment insurance, welfare programs, and food assistance, also is

	Billions of $	% of budget
Social security	1,044.4	23.5%
National defense	686.0	15.4%
Medicare	651.0	14.6%
Health	584.8	13.1%
Income security	514.8	11.6%
Net interest	375.2	8.4%
Veterans benefits and services	199.8	4.5%
Education, training, employment, and social services	136.8	3.1%
Transportation	97.1	2.2%
Administration of justice	65.7	1.5%
International affairs	52.7	1.2%
Agriculture	38.3	0.9%
Natural resources and environment	37.8	0.9%
General science, space, and technology	32.4	0.7%
Community and regional development	26.9	0.6%
General government	23.4	0.5%
Energy	5.0	0.1%
Commerce and housing credit	-25.7	-0.6%
Undistributed offsetting receipts	-98.2	-2.2%
Total, federal outlays	4,448.3	100.0%

FIGURE 29.1 Table showing U.S. federal government spending, 2019.

significant. Most people do not understand the U.S. Social Security system, so it is worth taking a minute to explain why it was created and how it works.

Case study: The importance and future of the U.S. Social Security program

Without a pension, once a person can no longer work, they would have no income and would have to depend on their savings or the assistance of others. Prior to the establishment of Social Security in the United States, it was common for the elderly who had worked in low-wage jobs and who had no surviving family members to be destitute. Social Security was started as a pay-as-you-go system during the Great Depression when the elderly were the poorest segment of the U.S. population. It was decided that existing workers and employers would pay a percentage of their wages and salaries directly to retirees as a national pension system. When you work, a portion of your wages is taken out to pay Social Security benefits to a current retiree. When you retire, other workers will have money taken out of their paychecks to pay you. Your Social Security benefits are determined by your salary, with higher earning workers receiving higher payouts, although there is a cap on both Social Security taxes and Social Security benefits.

Due to the fact that future Social Security payments depend on future workers' contributions to the program, Social Security is affected by demographics. The post-World War II baby boom lasted until 1964, creating a large number of productive people. As this group retires in ever-larger numbers, and as baby boomers live longer lives, there are fewer workers to replace them because modern families have fewer children. Therefore, in the near future there will be fewer workers paying into the Social Security system while more people than ever before are drawing Social Security benefits. Beginning around 2034, the U.S. Social Security system will start running deficits. Unless the government decides to alter the structure of the program, Social Security recipients will receive reduced Social Security payments of about 79% of the level of benefits they are entitled to receive.

Some changes that would resolve the problems with Social Security include delaying the age at which people can start collecting Social Security benefits, allowing more immigrants into the United States to provide a larger workforce to support retirees, reducing Social Security benefits, or increasing Social Security taxes. None of those solutions is politically popular, so it is unclear the direction in which the government will go.

The United States is a major outlier internationally in terms of its spending on national defense. Direct national defense spending in 2019 was $686 billion, more than 15% of the federal government budget. When veterans' benefits and services are added, the total is almost $900 billion, which is 20% of the federal budget. The other big-ticket item in the federal budget is spending on health care. Medicare for the elderly and various other health programs, including Medicaid for the poor, add up to about 28% of the federal government budget. The United States spends more per capita on health care than every country in the world, despite having poor health outcomes for such a rich country.[2] Notice that the other parts of the federal budget are relatively small in comparison to spending on health, defense, and income security.

State and local governments in the United States have different priorities. Figure 29.2 shows that state and local governments are responsible for education, local infrastructure, and local services. Rather than having a national system for education and health, most of the decisions regarding these services are made at the state or local level.

Except during periods of war, the U.S. government only constituted 1.2%–3.5% of GDP from 1800 to 1930. After that, the U.S. government grew substantially with the move from a laissez-faire economy to a mixed economy with a small safety net. From 1930 to 1941, the U.S. government grew from 3.6% of GDP to 10.5% under President Roosevelt. Roosevelt's New Deal programs included substantial fiscal stimulus and the creation of programs such as Social Security and unemployment insurance. With World War II, the subsequent Cold War with the U.S.S.R., and regional conflicts in Korea, Vietnam, Iraq, and Afghanistan, the United States maintained a permanently increased military after 1941. Meanwhile, social programs, infrastructure spending, health and education services, and government regulatory agencies expanded.

Figure 29.3 shows that the U.S. government grew substantially in size and influence relative to GDP until 1976, when it reached 32% of GDP. Since 1976, the size of the U.S. government as a percentage of GDP has stayed about the same,

	Billions of $	%
State and local government spending, 2017		
Education	1010	27.6%
Public welfare (welfare, hospitals, health)	678	18.5%
Transportation (highways, airports, ports)	318	8.7%
Public safety (police, fire)	260	7.1%
Environment, parks, sewage and housing	248	6.8%
Utility expenditure (electric, water)	232	6.3%
All other (interest, administration, etc.)	913	24.9%
Total state & local spending	3660	100.0%

FIGURE 29.2 Table showing U.S. state and local government spending, 2017.

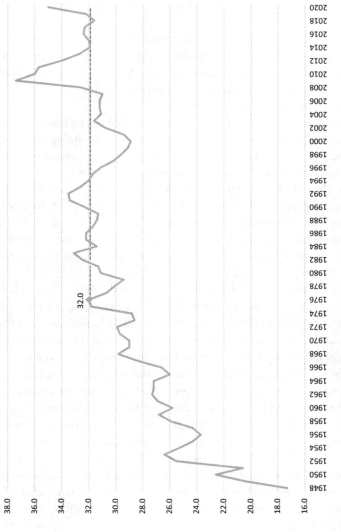

FIGURE 29.3 U.S. government spending as percentage of GDP, 1948–2020 (Q1).

increasing during recessions and decreasing with booms but averaging 31.9% of the economy.

Similarly, Figure 29.4 shows that the number of government employees in the United States increased as the mixed economy was being developed. Since the mid-1970s, however, U.S. government employment decreased as a percentage of total employment. In May of 2020, federal, state, and local government bodies in the United States employed 21.2 million people, which was 15.4% of the U.S. workforce.

Figure 29.5 compares the size of government as a percentage of GDP in the United States to other developed countries. European social democracies have much larger government sectors, primarily due to large safety nets, active labor market programs, public health care and health insurance systems, and greater spending on public goods.

Governments must also decide how to pay for their expenditures. This includes decisions on who or what to tax and how much deficit spending (and borrowing) to engage in. Figure 29.6 shows the major sources of tax revenue for the U.S. government from 1940 to 2019. Excise taxes on goods used to be a major source of income, but they are insignificant in the modern United States. Corporate taxes have also declined significantly as a source of funds, from 26.5% in 1950 to 6.6% in 2019. Much of the recent decline in corporate taxes is a result of the influence of supply-side economists on economic policy. Meanwhile, taxes on individuals— both social insurance taxes (Social Security and unemployment insurance) and individual income taxes—increased dramatically.

Another key issue is how the tax burden is shared. Most countries have a progressive tax system, in which the rich pay a larger percentage of their income in taxes than the poor. A progressive tax code reflects a philosophy that the people who have benefited from an economic system and who are more able to pay should shoulder a greater share of the tax burden and that inequality and poverty are significant market failures that need to be corrected via some measure of redistribution. The United States is a major exception here. As Emmanuel Saez and Gabriel Zucman demonstrated in their important 2019 book *The Triumph of Injustice*, the United States has a flat tax burden where the poor pay about the same percentage of their income in taxes as the rich. Figure 29.7 shows the tax rates paid by each percentile (P) of the U.S. population. The average tax rate in the United States is 28%. The poorest 10% of the population pay a 25.6% tax rate, which is, astoundingly, a higher tax rate than that paid by billionaires. The richest 400 families in the United States pay only a 23% tax rate once all of their tax dodges (such as offshore accounts and accounting tricks) and special tax rates (such as very low taxes on capital gains) are taken into account. This disparity prompted multibillionaire Warren Buffett to note the inherent unfairness of a tax code whereby he was paying a lower percentage tax rate than his hard-working secretary!

The poorest 50% of the population is hit especially hard by sales taxes and payroll taxes, which are quite regressive, meaning that the poor pay a higher percentage

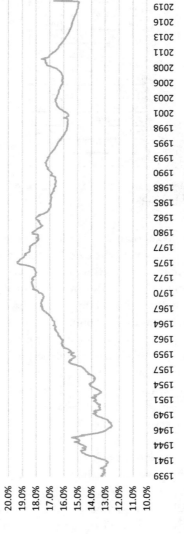

FIGURE 29.4 U.S. government employment as a percentage of total employment, 1939–2020.

France	56.13
Belgium	52.38
Denmark	51.41
Sweden	49.88
Norway	48.69
Italy	48.58
Austria	48.49
Germany	43.87
Netherlands	42.16
Spain	41.34
Canada	41.32
United Kingdom	40.84
Japan	38.74
United States	37.95
Australia	36.71
Switzerland	34.15
South Korea	32.44
India	27.29
Mexico	26.34
Ireland	25.74

FIGURE 29.5 Table of general government expenditures as a percentage of GDP, 2018. Source: OECD Stat.

of their income on these taxes than the rich. Income taxes are progressive, in that income tax rates increase as income increases, except for the top 0.01%. Here, a quirk of the U.S. tax code comes into play: Most of the super-rich get their income from capital gains—profits from buying and selling assets such as stocks, bonds, and real estate. Capital gains are taxed at a much lower rate than income, so the super-rich who have the most capital gains pay less in income taxes than the upper-middle class does. Corporate and property taxes are only slightly progressive, and the estate tax is very small, leaving the U.S. tax code flat for the most part and regressive at the top.

The U.S. tax code has changed dramatically in the last 60 years. In 1960, the super-rich paid a 56.3% tax rate, an amount 145% higher than they paid in 2018. Meanwhile, in 1960, the bottom 50% of taxpayers paid a tax rate of 21.6%, 12% lower than the 24.2% average tax rate they paid in 2018. Under the influence of supply-side economics, tax rates on corporations and the rich were lowered dramatically, tax evasion was tolerated, and tax rates on the working class were increased. Unfortunately, as we saw earlier, supply-side policies did not improve economic growth.

Putting the material in this section together, we can observe the following characteristics of U.S. fiscal policy. First, the U.S. government plays a significant role in the economy, but that role is much smaller than the role played by governments in most other developed countries. The United States spends less on public goods and safety nets, while also taxing the wealthy less than other countries. Interestingly, the United States often does more in one arena of economic policy— the utilization of discretionary fiscal policy.

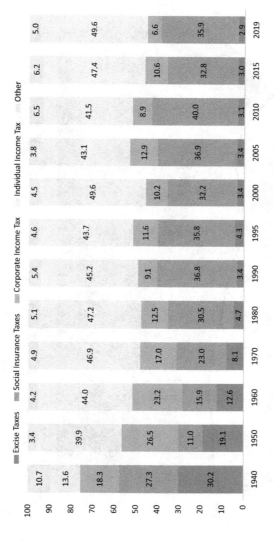

FIGURE 29.6 Sources of tax revenue as a percentage of total U.S. government revenue, 1940–2019.

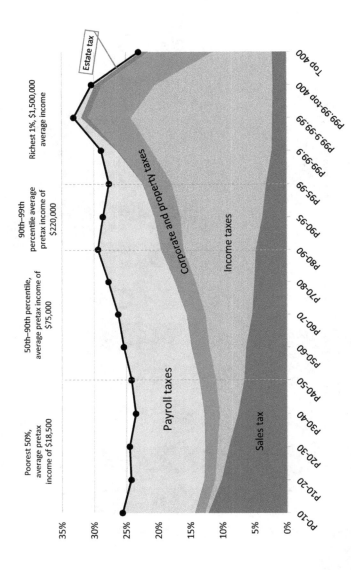

FIGURE 29.7 U.S. average tax rates by income group in 2018 (percentage of pretax income).

29.2 AUTOMATIC STABILIZERS AND DISCRETIONARY FISCAL POLICY TO CORRECT INSTABILITY

One of the major roles for fiscal policy is to stabilize the economy. The government has three fiscal policy tools at its disposal to stabilize the macroeconomy: Government spending, tax policy, and automatic stabilizers. Automatic stabilizers are **programs that automatically increase spending or reduce taxes in recessions and do the opposite when the economy is overheated**. One of the main benefits of automatic stabilizers is that they do not require political action—the programs are set up to function automatically for any citizen who falls upon hard times.

Automatic stabilizers are a key aspect of the safety net in most countries, and they include unemployment insurance, along with programs to help the poor such as welfare, food assistance, housing assistance, and government-provided health care. Whenever an economy hits a recession, governments automatically pay out increased assistance to the increasing numbers of the unemployed and the poor, increasing aggregate demand in the process. When the economy booms, spending on these programs declines. A progressive tax code also serves as an automatic stabilizer, reducing taxes when people have lower incomes in recessions and increasing taxes when incomes increase during booms.

Some governments utilize automatic stabilizers extensively because they are so effective in combating recessions quickly. Figure 29.8 shows that the Netherlands offsets 80.5% of any shocks that people experience in a recession via automatic stabilizers.[3] The United States, on the other hand, offsets only 46.1% of shocks with automatic stabilizers due to the lack of a progressive tax code and the very small U.S. safety net (featuring relatively low levels of unemployment, housing, and family benefits).

An intriguing automatic stabilizer was the Swedish policy that allowed corporations to invest tax free in recessions in the 1950s and 1960s. As a result, whenever Sweden entered a recession, there was an increase in business investment by companies that were in stable condition and that wanted to benefit from paying no corporate taxes on the money they used to invest. The tax savings was significant enough to generate additional private sector investment in Sweden at a time when private companies in other countries were cutting their investments. This example demonstrates that governments can be creative with the design of automatic stabilizers.

Even the most generous of automatic stabilizers do not replace all of the income lost in a recession. Therefore, governments need to take additional action. Discretionary fiscal policy is **fiscal policy that is "at the discretion" of government officials**, meaning that **government officials must take additional actions in order for such policy to take effect**. Expansionary fiscal

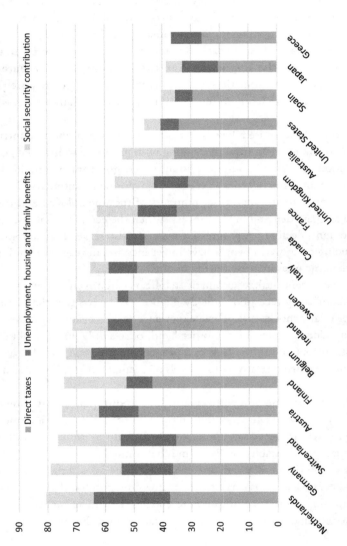

FIGURE 29.8 Automatic stabilization of shocks to household income.

policy refers to **increases in government spending or reductions in taxes that stimulate aggregate demand**. Contractionary fiscal policy, also called austerity, refers to **cuts in government spending and increases in taxes that reduce aggregate demand**.

Discretionary fiscal policy is always slower to impact the macroeconomy than automatic stabilizers. In the United States, it takes time for Congress and the President to agree on what action to take. Then, the policy takes time to be implemented and even longer to have an impact. Nonetheless, discretionary fiscal policy is considered by many economists to be the most effective tool in combating a major recession.

For example, economists estimate that infrastructure spending has the largest multiplier of any type of government spending. Spending on schools, technology, and transportation systems, including roads, bridges, trains, and airports, creates jobs directly in the construction industry, usually one of the hardest hit sectors in recessions. Such spending also makes private sector operations more efficient, reducing transit time and improving productivity. In addition, government infrastructure spending spills over into private sector investment as businesses see new opportunities. Better education, technology, and skilled workers can be a major attraction to business investment. For example, every time new train lines, roads, or airports are built, new communities and businesses spring up around the transportation hubs. Discretionary fiscal policy directly stimulates aggregate demand and can eliminate a recessionary gap.

29.3 FISCAL POLICY AND THE AGGREGATE DEMAND AND AGGREGATE SUPPLY MODEL

One of the major tasks of government is to enact the appropriate discretionary fiscal to stabilize the economy. Figure 29.9 shows the economy in a recession at point **a** with a real GDP at $18,000 billion and a price index of 101. The recessionary gap is $2000 billion—the difference between real GDP at point **a** and potential real GDP. In order to increase real GDP by $2000 billion, the government will have to enact policies that cause aggregate demand to shift by $3000 billion, from AD_1 to AD_2, and moving the economy from point **a** to point **b**. That will create inflationary pressures, causing the economy to move along the aggregate demand curve from point **b** to point **c** as inflation occurs.

The government can estimate the amount of government spending or tax cuts necessary to increase AD by $3000 billion using the multiplier. Recall that the multiplier can be computed using the marginal respending rate (MRR). Suppose that the MRR is 0.5. Using the formula for the multiplier,

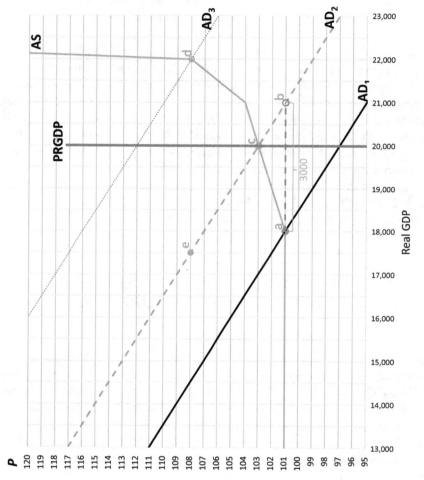

FIGURE 29.9 Fixing a recessionary gap with fiscal policy.

$$\text{Multiplier} = \frac{1}{1 - MRR} = \frac{1}{1 - 0.5} = 2.$$

Therefore, an increase in government spending of $1500 billion would cause the AD curve to shift by $1500 b. * 2 = $3000 b., moving the economy to potential real GDP. If the government spent enough money on various projects, such as building roads, bridges, schools, high-speed internet, and other infrastructure, it could eliminate the recessionary gap.

The government could also cut taxes in order to increase AD, but taxes always have a smaller impact on AD than government spending because some percentage of tax cuts is saved. In 2020 when the government sent checks for $1200 to most taxpayers to combat the COVID-19 recession, 30% of taxpayers reported that they planned to save the money instead of spending it. This information indicates that the marginal propensity to consume (MPC) in 2020 was 0.70. The MPC often drops in bad recessions because people are pessimistic about the future, causing them to save more and spend less. We can compute the change in consumption from a tax cut as follows: $\Delta C = -(\Delta T * MPC)$.[4] If we use the same multiplier of 2, then the economy needs an increase in consumption spending of $1500 to shift the AD curve by $3000 to eliminate the recessionary gap. To increase consumption by $1500, with an MPC of 0.7, we would need a tax cut of $2143 billion:

$$\Delta C = -(\Delta T * MPC); 1500 = -(\Delta T * 0.7); \frac{1500}{0.7} = -\Delta T; \Delta T = -2143.$$

A tax cut of $2143 billion causes consumers to spend 70% of that amount, given that the MPC is 0.7, which is $1500, while the remaining 30% is saved. In this example, the tax cut has to be 43% larger in absolute value than the spending increase to achieve the same impact on aggregate demand and real GDP.

The **tax multiplier** is **used to compute the impact of a lump sum change in taxes on aggregate demand.**

$$\text{Tax multiplier} = -(\text{Multiplier}) * (\text{Marginal propensity to consume})$$

$$= -\frac{MPC}{1 - MRR}.$$

In the above example, with an MPC of 0.7 and a multiplier of 2, the tax multiplier would be 1.4. A tax cut of $2143 billion would cause a change in aggregate demand of $2143 * 1.4 = $3000 billion.

Note that economists do not know the precise position of the economy at any moment, but they still attempt to estimate the position of the economy relative to potential real GDP and the amount of government intervention necessary to move the economy there. This can give us substantial insight into the appropriate amount of spending needed in a recession. Economics is an inexact social science, but it can still give us good estimates of what policies to enact and how effective they are likely to be.

Suppose that the economy is overheated and the government expects an asset bubble or an inflationary episode such as a wage-price spiral to form. In this case, the government can reduce government spending or increase taxes. Such policies, known as austerity, would cause the AD curve to decrease. As before, spending cuts would have a larger impact than tax increases. Also, if the economy was in the steep part of the AS curve, the shift in AD would have to be larger than the amount of the inflationary gap to move the economy back to potential real GDP.

For example, suppose the economy is in equilibrium at point **d** in Figure 29.7, at a real GDP of 22,000 and a price index of 108 where AD_3 intersects AS. There is an inflationary gap of $2000 billion, but the AD curve will need to shift by $4500, the horizontal distance between AD_3 and AD_2 (the distance from point **d** to point **e**), to move the economy's equilibrium from point **d** to point **c** at potential real GDP. If we use an *MRR* of 0.5 and a multiplier of 2, government spending would need to decrease by $2250 billion to shift the AD curve by $4500 billion. With an MPC of 0.7 and a tax multiplier of 1.4, a tax increase of $\dfrac{2250}{0.7} = \$3214$ billion would be needed to decrease AD by $4500 billion.

Interestingly, the government can also stimulate the economy by increasing spending and increasing taxes at the same time. If the government increases spending by $1000 billion and increases taxes by $1000 billion, aggregate demand will increase by $(1 - MPC) *$ (the change in government spending). Aggregate demand will increase by $1000 billion because of the change in government spending but decrease by $700 billion $(-MPC \times \Delta T)$ from the increase in taxes, resulting in a net initial increase in AD of $300 billion and a total increase in AD of $600 billion once the multiplier is incorporated. In this case, the balanced budget multiplier would be equal to **the multiplier minus the tax multiplier**:

$$\text{Balanced budget multiplier} = \text{Multiplier} - \text{Tax multiplier} = 2 - 1.4 = 0.6.$$

Therefore, the government can actually increase aggregate demand and real GDP by increasing government spending and increasing taxes by the same amount. The downside is that there will be a decrease in household savings as a result of the tax increase, which might impact financial markets, something we will study in the next chapter.

29.4 THE DEBATE OVER FISCAL POLICY

Now that you have a good understanding of the major areas of government spending and the major contours of fiscal policy, we next turn to debates over (1) the size and role of government in the macroeconomy and (2) the extent to which the government should use fiscal policy to stabilize the macroeconomy. There are four major perspectives on fiscal policy. Laissez-faire economists prefer a minimal role for government, and they usually oppose extensive fiscal stabilization policies. Supply-side economists prefer a small role for government regulation, though they are willing to use fiscal policy on behalf of corporate interests. New Keynesian economists see a substantial role for government regulation and stabilization policy. Political economists see the necessity for a large role for government in regulation, stabilization, and guidance of the macroeconomy.

Laissez-faire economists generally believe in a very limited role for government in the macroeconomy. They prefer few regulations and limits to the size and scope government regulatory bodies, limited spending on public and quasi-public goods, and very constrained safety nets. In fact, laissez-faire economists have argued against providing unemployment insurance or safety nets because, in their view, such programs interfere with incentives for people to work. Public goods should be provided by the private sector whenever possible.

It is worth noting that research on unemployment indicates that the vast majority of people want to work and prefer a job over accepting unemployment benefits. However, if the only option is unsatisfying work at low wages, some people might choose to collect unemployment benefits. Laissez-faire economists argue that workers should accept whatever options are available, whereas political economists argue that the state should ensure that workers have better choices.

Laissez-faire economists do not believe in undertaking significant government efforts to stabilize the economy. There are several reasons for this. First, they believe that **policy lags** render government intervention too ineffective. There is a **recognition lag**, where policymakers do not realize there is a problem until it is already too late. There is a **legislative lag** while politicians debate the best policy and negotiate with those who disagree. There is an **implementation lag**, where it can take months for the government policy to actually take effect. Implementation lags are especially problematic for fiscal policy because it takes so long for spending programs to get up and running. Then, there is a **reaction lag** where it can take additional months or even a year for policies to have their full impact on the economy. Laissez-faire economists see these lags as debilitating. New Keynesian economists acknowledge the existence of lags but believe the government can still implement effective policy given good forecasting and the fact that recessions are followed by periods of slow growth that still require expansionary fiscal policy.

Second, laissez-faire economists believe that **markets are generally self-adjusting and efficient**, so fiscal intervention is usually unnecessary. Cyclical unemployment is dismissed as a product of the unwillingness of workers to accept lower wages: In theory, according to laissez-faire theorists, if workers would accept lower wages, then they would be hired immediately by businesses, eliminating unemployment. Unemployment, from this perspective, is voluntary rather than a product of the macroeconomic environment. Like classical economists, modern laissez-faire economists see the macroeconomy as self-adjusting, returning to normal capacity without government intervention.

Third, following the ideas of Friedrich Hayek, laissez-faire advocates tend to believe that **recessions serve a useful purpose** in weeding out inefficient firms. If recessions do happen, then they are not necessarily a bad thing.

Given their criticisms of government intervention, laissez-faire advocates do not want stabilization policies to be enacted. With respect to fiscal policy, many laissez-faire advocates want to require a **balanced government budget** each year and refrain from interfering in the economy except for providing basic public goods. Each time the economy in the United States hits a recession and budget deficits increase due to declines in tax revenues and increases in spending on automatic stabilizers, some laissez-faire politician will argue that the government should balance its budget even in a recession by implementing austerity policies. However, as we will see below, austerity policies tend to devastate fragile economies.

Conservative, **supply-side** economists tend to agree with laissez-faire economists on the benefits of deregulation and reducing the size of government agencies. And they often advocate reductions in spending on social welfare programs for the poor, which also aligns with the laissez-faire approach. The differences can be found regarding policies toward tariffs, deficits, subsidies, and taxes. Laissez-faire economists prefer unregulated trade with negligible tariff rates, whereas many supply-side economists, especially those in the Trump administration, advocate protecting U.S. businesses with tariffs on foreign competitors. Laissez-faire economists prefer balanced budgets, whereas U.S. Presidents pursuing supply-side policies, including Ronald Reagan, George H.W. Bush, George W. Bush, and Donald Trump, all ran up huge budget deficits while giving generous tax cuts, tax shelters, and subsidies to the wealthy and to corporations.

During the coronavirus recession of 2020, President Trump's supply-side advisors advocated expansionary fiscal policy, including tax cuts for businesses and wealthy business owners, as well as increased government spending on infrastructure. They advocated expansionary monetary policy as well, encouraging the Fed to slash interest rates and to engage in significant quantitative easing. These policies are somewhat consistent with Keynesian economics, except that the focus of fiscal policy is on corporations and owners rather than workers and the poor.

New Keynesian economists believe that a larger degree of government intervention is necessary for the smooth operation of a capitalist economic system. The market needs oversight in many areas, including food, health, environment, and labor markets. In addition, markets require key support structures to make them work, including infrastructure; a smoothly functioning legal system; a well-educated, well-trained, and well-paid workforce; a stable banking system; support for innovation in the form of patent law and public scientific research; a national health system to prepare for pandemics; and much, much more.

Usually, the most effective way to regulate and support markets is via the creation of a government agency to oversee markets in areas where market failures exist. U.S. government administrative bodies include the offices of Management and Budget, National Intelligence, and Trade, the departments of Agriculture,

Commerce, Defense, Education, Energy, Health and Human Services, Housing and Urban Development, Interior (parks, fish, mining, land), Justice, Labor, State (diplomacy), Transportation, Treasury, Veterans Affairs, and a host of additional agencies including the Central Intelligence Agency, NASA, and the Post Office. Each of these areas was deemed important enough for Congress and the President to create an agency to regulate and support activity.

New Keynesians believe that one of the most important jobs for government is stabilization policy. The economy is fundamentally unstable and can stay in a recession indefinitely. Therefore, from this perspective the government *must* intervene to restore business and consumer confidence in recessions. This is best achieved via the stimulation of aggregate demand, rather than aggregate supply, which is an area of disagreement with supply-side economists. To New Keynesians, recessions can cause significant long-term damage without government intervention.

Workers thrown onto unemployment for several years in a deep recession will lag behind other workers in skills and experience and may never catch up to their peers who stay employed. Strong, viable businesses may go bankrupt due to temporarily terrible conditions, even though they are quite profitable under normal circumstances. General Motors, the largest U.S. automaker, declared bankruptcy in 2009 in the depths of the Great Recession. Without a government bailout they likely would have closed permanently. Instead, the government helped GM stay open. GM quickly returned to profitability after the recession, repaid the government, and earned record profits in 2015. Therefore, the government can play a significantly role in safeguarding a country's private sector base in a severe recession, preserving companies that are in trouble but that will be fine once the recession ends. Protecting profitable companies with a bright future will improve the country's economic growth performance, because those companies will grow rapidly once the economy leaves the recession.

Note, however, that the government probably should not support dying industries. Companies that are in trouble during the economic boom before a recession are likely destined for bankruptcy in the long term. Bailing such companies out during a recession would not save them. Failing companies would still need bailouts after the recession. For example, during the COVID-19 recession of 2020, J.C. Penney, Neiman Marcus, J. Crew, Pier 1, and numerous other retailers declared bankruptcy. But these companies had struggled for years as shoppers shifted from traditional retail shopping to e-commerce. Bailing out these companies would likely end up being a long-term bailout, which could end up costing the government large sums of money in perpetuity. Long-term bailouts lead to the soft budget constraint problem, where **the government continually bails out an industry that cannot become competitive in markets**. Without a limit on government bailouts—a budget constraint—companies do not need to become competitive to survive. Governments that offer companies continual bailouts can quickly find themselves in a budgetary nightmare, where they are spending large sums subsidizing companies with no future.

The United Kingdom did this in the 1970s when it bailed out steel, coal, and other declining industries. Thus, it can be important for the government to be targeted and selective with bailouts or to impose strict time limits for government support. Nonetheless, keeping companies with bright futures afloat remains a key element of effective stabilization policies.

Political economists prefer a larger degree of government intervention in all aspects of the economy. They see market failures as endemic to capitalism; therefore, markets only work with a substantial degree of government regulation and oversight. Oversight requires independently funded government agencies that have the power to regulate and even to direct markets. Most social market economies (SMEs) utilizing the political economy approach have a ministry of industry or a similar planning body that coordinates investment, conducts research into new technologies, and promotes industrial development in key growth industries. SMEs also usually have active labor market policies that train and funnel workers directly into new industries. From the political economy perspective, good governance is a source of competitive advantage that can stimulate industrial development more effectively than the private sector alone.

Similarly, political economists want the government to go much further than other approaches when it comes to stabilization policy. Given that the government has the power to end recessions via discretionary fiscal policy and stabilization policy, it should do so. The main problem in recessions is a lack of sufficient aggregate demand, as investors and consumers curtail their spending. The best way to end recessions is by spending a large amount of money, especially on infrastructure and putting people to work directly. Infrastructure spending improves the efficiency of the economy, stimulating additional rounds of investment, and it employs construction workers who are among the first to be laid off in recessions as housing starts falter and as businesses cancel construction projects. Because unemployment spikes in recessions, putting people directly to work ensures that they have an income. Instead of paying unemployment benefits to people not who are not working, the government can pay people to do productive jobs in their communities. There are plenty of things that need to be done in every community, after all.

A dramatic expansion of fiscal spending requires the government to engage in significant deficit spending, borrowing money to finance expansionary fiscal policy in recessions. Government debt and deficits is another controversial topic in economics.

29.5 THE SIZE OF GOVERNMENT DEBT AND DEFICITS

Figure 29.10 shows the annual U.S. federal budget deficit or surplus from 1970 through 2020.[5] The budget deficit or surplus is computed by taking all government spending (G) and subtracting net tax revenue (T):

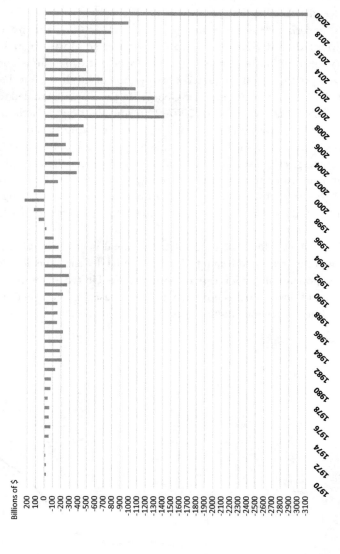

FIGURE 29.10 United States federal budget deficit or surplus, 1970–2020.

$$\text{Budget deficit} = G - T.$$

Prior to 1970, the U.S. government ran very small deficits in recessions. Budget deficits during recessions are called cyclical deficits, because they **occur as a result of recessions during the business cycle**. The government sometimes ran small surpluses when the economy was booming prior to 1970. This is a reflection of moderate Keynesian economic policy.

The U.S. government began running structural deficits, **the portion of the government deficit that exists even when the economy is at its normal capacity**, in the 1980s with the advent of supply-side economics. The boom of the 1990s and political gridlock caused a brief period of surpluses, but the return of supply-side policies in the 2000s under George W. Bush once again led to structural deficits. The Great Recession of 2007–2009 and the slow growth in subsequent years caused massive cyclical deficits, on top of existing structural deficits. Annual deficits fell from 2010 to 2016 as the economy grew under President Obama. President Trump, elected in 2016, returned to supply-side policies, and deficits increased significantly even though the economy was growing. The COVID-19 recession of 2020 was met with a massive increase in government spending (which we explain in more detail below), causing the annual budget deficit to reach record levels.

Figure 29.11 shows the total accumulated national debt of the U.S. government, which is computed by adding up all of the annual deficits. The debt seems to be increasing exponentially, so it is easy to think that the United States may soon be overwhelmed by its debts. That is not likely to be the case, however, because GDP also increased dramatically during this period.

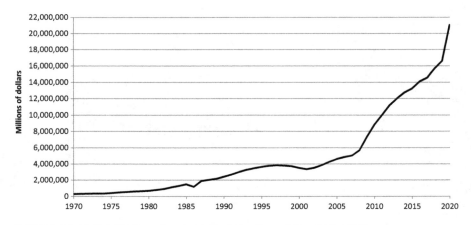

FIGURE 29.11 Total U.S. national debt held by the public, 1970–2020.

Source: Federal Reserve Economic Data (FRED).

Economists are less concerned with the total level of debt than they are the level of debt relative to GDP. This is because a high level of debt is not problematic if it is also accompanied by a high GDP.

We can explain this using the analogy of loans for home purchases. When people need a mortgage to buy a home, the bank cares much less about the buyer's total level of debt than they do the buyer's debt relative to their income. A home buyer with a high level of income will have little trouble paying off similarly high levels of debt. It is only when a buyer's debts are very high relative to income that a bank would be worried about getting paid back. Research indicates that households that exceed a debt–income ratio of more than 43% will have trouble paying back their mortgage. A higher income means a lower debt–income ratio and a higher likelihood of repayment. Similarly, a high level of debt is easy to pay back for a country with a high GDP. Total U.S. debt reached $23.2 trillion in the first quarter of 2020, but U.S. GDP was also very high at $21.5 trillion.

Figure 29.12 shows the U.S. public debt as a percentage of GDP—the debt-to-GDP ratio—from 1970 to 2020. The increase in debt as a percentage of GDP is much gentler than the increase in total debt. Nevertheless, the steady increase in the debt/GDP ratio worries some economists.

Figure 29.13 shows that though the U.S. national debt as a percentage of GDP is quite high, it is not as high as the debt–GDP ratio in Japan, Greece, and Italy, countries that experienced significant economic crises in recent years. Interestingly, the U.S. focus on military spending and tax cuts for businesses and the wealthy ends up generating much larger deficits than most social market economies that spend significant amounts on social welfare programs. Ironically, although the Nordic countries Sweden, Norway, and Denmark are considered to have some of the most

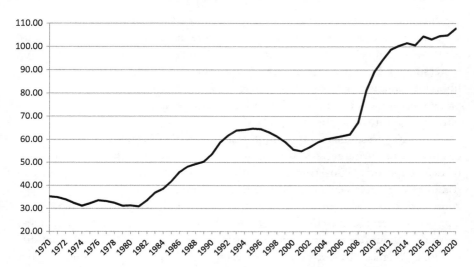

FIGURE 29.12 U.S. public debt as percentage of GDP, 1970–2020.

Source: FRED.

Japan	237.5
Greece	174.2
Italy	133.4
United States	106.7
Belgium	99.6
France	99.2
Spain	96.0
Brazil	90.4
Canada	88.0
United Kingdom	85.7
South Africa	57.8
Germany	56.9
South Korea	40.5
Switzerland	39.5
Sweden	37.2
Norway	36.8
Denmark	33.6

FIGURE 29.13 Table showing national debt as a percentage of GDP, 2020.

generous social welfare programs in the world, they also have the lowest debt ratios of developed countries.

After discussing government deficits and debt, next we need to consider the extent to which government debt is problematic. As is so often the case, economists disagree on this topic.

29.6 THE DEBATE OVER GOVERNMENT DEFICITS AND DEBT

The major opponents of deficit spending are laissez-faire economists who oppose government intervention unless there are exceptional circumstances. Laissez-faire economists generally oppose running annual budget deficits and accumulating increasing levels of government debt. They believe that deficits increase the likelihood of inflation and cause higher interest rates, which can crowd out (reduce) private sector investment and reduce economic growth. They see deficits placing a burden on future generations.

New Keynesian economists argue that any problems created by cyclical deficits that occur during recessions are minor and are more than offset by the benefits of deficit spending. Government spending, tax cuts, and interest rate cuts will stimulate aggregate demand and help to eliminate any recessionary gap, thereby contributing to economic growth. Inflation and high interest rates are almost never a problem in recessions; rather, the major recessionary problems are deflation and pessimism about future sales, both of which can be improved by expansionary fiscal policy financed by borrowing. However, New Keynesian economists are not usually in favor of structural deficits.

Supply-siders do not see deficits as a problem as long as they are created by policies that stimulate aggregate supply. Tax cuts can provide increased incentives to work, save, and invest, which should increase economic growth if the money is invested in productive new business ventures. In theory, tax cuts may pay for themselves in the long run if they stimulate enough growth.

Political economists also do not see deficits as problems, as long as deficits are generated by policies that improve the well-being of workers, stimulate aggregate demand, and enhance long-term growth prospects. Deficits that enhance productivity and create new industries are a good thing. Political economists advocate spending on education, health care, infrastructure, research and development, public transportation, technology, and a Green New Deal to create jobs in sustainable energy and other environmental areas. To political economists, unless spending results in clear signs of macroeconomic problems, such as inflation and high interest rates, a country should not worry about deficits. Deficit spending should continue until unemployment and underemployment are eliminated.

Below, we go through some specific areas of disagreement, starting with the most important area of debate—whether deficits cause the crowding out or crowding in of private sector investment.

1. Crowding out vs. crowding in of private sector investment

According to laissez-faire economists, increases in government deficits increase the demand for money, which can cause interest rates to increase. This may result in the government borrowing money that could have been used by the private sector, causing a decline in private sector investment. Because laissez-faire economists prefer private sector investment to public sector investment, this is seen in a very negative light.

New Keynesian economists note that crowding out has not been a significant problem for decades in the United States, and it is never a significant problem in recessions when private sector investment is very low. As long as the government injects sufficient liquidity (supplies of money) into the banking system, crowding out does not seem to occur in recessions. In general, the problem in recessions is too much savings and too little investment. According to the Keynesian paradox of thrift, **when consumers save more, this reduces aggregate demand, which in turn reduces GDP, which then reduces savings**. Increased saving more results in less economic activity, which decreases incomes and savings. This is especially problematic in recessions: When consumers and investors save more and spend less, savings piles up in banks. Interest rates fall, but consumers and investors do not want to borrow money due to pessimism about the future. In this environment, there is plenty of savings to go around and no crowding out of private sector investment will occur. Even in financial crises with a large number of bank failures, the central bank can increase the money supply to ensure that there is always enough money in banks for lending. Therefore, with appropriate policies, there is no reason to expect crowding out in recessions.

Furthermore, good government policy actually *crowds in* private sector investment. By improving macroeconomic conditions, government spending can encourage the private sector to invest. This is especially likely if the government spends money on infrastructure, technology development, or other programs that enhance the efficiency of the private sector, thereby providing opportunities for profitable private sector investment.

Supply-side economists are also unconcerned with deficits, in recessions or expansions, if they improve the conditions for suppliers. This usually means corporate tax cuts or decreases in taxes for the wealthy who form or invest in companies. Supply-siders hope that the tax cuts will generate sufficient economic growth in the future to offset the initial deficits the tax cuts create.

Political economists are unconcerned with deficits under most conditions, especially if the money is used to stimulate aggregate demand. Political economists agree with Keynes that stimulus money should go to the unemployed and the poor who suffer the most and who will increase their spending the most when given money. The resulting increase in aggregate demand should help to crowd in investment. Additional government investments in infrastructure, education, training, basic scientific research, technology, and other growth-generating activities will also help to stimulate growth and crowd in private sector investment.

2. **Budget deficits may contribute to trade deficits and international indebtedness**

In general, mainstream economists argue that any country consuming more than it produces must by definition run a trade deficit. Recall the leakages and injections equation from Keynes:

$$I + G + X = S + T + IM$$

$$(IM - X) = (I - S) + (G - T).$$

This equation implies that the trade deficit, the amount exports (X) are less than imports (IM), is a product of low national savings by households, businesses, and government. Trade deficits occur when savings (S) is less than investment (I) and when government spending (G) is less than net taxes (T). Figure 29.14 shows U.S. net national savings since 1950. U.S. households saved 10%–13% of their incomes from 1950 to 1984. However, after 1984 the personal savings rate averaged 7%. At the same time, government savings became significantly negative due to recurring budget deficits. The result is a net national savings rate that declined to 2% in 2019, a number that is extraordinarily low by international standards. In comparison, the net national savings rate in France is 5%, Germany is 11%, Sweden is 12%, Norway is 18%, and China is 25%.

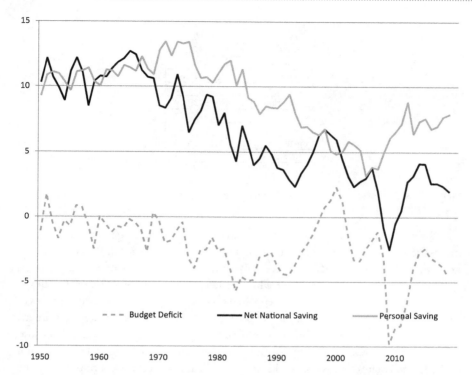

FIGURE 29.14 Net national saving, personal saving, and budget deficit as a percentage of GDP (1950–2019).

Source: FRED.

Trade deficits can be a problem, because when a country spends more than its income, it accrues debts to its trading partners in the amount of the trade deficit. If the United States produces $20 trillion worth of goods and services, it also generates $20 trillion in income in the process. However, if the United States consumes $21 trillion worth of goods when it produces $20 trillion worth of goods, then it has a trade deficit of $1 trillion. Furthermore, the United States owes domestic citizens and other countries $1 trillion for the extra goods it purchased, which it must pay for by borrowing money.

Most economists do not see the money a country owes to its own citizens as a drain on the economy, because payments to a country's own citizens increases the home country's income and stimulates its economy. However, the external debt—the money a country owes to foreign countries—is usually seen as a drain on the economy, because those payments flow out of the country. In the mid-1980s, 11.5% of U.S. government debt was held by foreign governments, corporations, and citizens. By 2019, 39% of U.S. government debt was held by foreign countries. Figure 29.15 shows the countries that hold the largest amounts of U.S. government treasury debt. The United States has a large trade deficit with most of these countries.

Japan	$1119.52
China	$1107.54
United Kingdom	$325.03
Brazil	$304.03
Ireland	$273.64
Luxembourg	$239.57
Switzerland	$230.14
Cayman Islands	$222.23
Hong Kong	$214.42
Belgium	$198.25
Taiwan	$178.89
Saudi Arabia	$176.72

FIGURE 29.15 Table showing U.S. Treasury debt held in 2019 (billions of dollars).

When the U.S. government makes payments to foreign countries, those payments are a leakage from the U.S. economy that can reduce U.S. GDP if the money is not returned to the United States. We will study the issue of trade deficits and foreign exchange flows in more detail later when we take up international financial issues.

Laissez-faire economists see unregulated trade as a great benefit to consumers everywhere. Trade deficits indicate a larger benefit accruing to home country consumers, who get lots of inexpensive foreign goods and a higher standard of living. They also believe that trade deficits will be naturally corrected by an exchange rate devaluation as the United States floods the world with dollars, although this has not proven to be the case. Prior to President Trump, most supply-side politicians in the United States adhered to the laissez-faire position. Trump saw trade deficits as a threat to the United States and imposed tariffs on China and other trading partners to reduce trade deficits.

Political economists from the modern monetary theory (MMT) perspective also see little problem with trade deficits. Bill Mitchell argues that when a foreign country runs a trade surplus, it is depriving its citizens of the use of their own resources, goods, and services, selling these items to the country with the trade deficit in exchange for assets. The trade surplus country has a lower standard of living, and the trade deficit country a higher one as a result.

Other political economists, however, argue that trade deficits undermine jobs and wages in countries that run trade deficits, making workers worse off. Similarly, John Maynard Keynes believed in the regulation of international trade to reduce or eliminate trade imbalances, which he saw as destabilizing. However, many New Keynesian economists view unregulated trade more favorably, agreeing largely with laissez-faire economists that trade deficits are a minor problem and that they will eventually correct themselves. As you can see, economists' perspectives regarding budget deficits and trade deficits do not fall neatly into clear patterns.

3. **Budget deficits can be inflationary**

Laissez-faire economists argue that increases in spending, and the increases in the money supply that tend to accompany expansionary fiscal policy, will inevitably lead to inflation. However, empirical evidence indicates otherwise, according to other economists. Vast increases in government spending and the money supply did not generate significant inflation in any recessionary period in the United States, so most economists discount this argument.

4. **Large deficits, especially during booms, can cause the government to lose the ability to use expansionary fiscal policy when needed and represent a burden on the macroeconomy**

Due to worries about budget deficits becoming a drain on the economy, politicians are often unwilling to back additional spending when deficits are high. In the depths of the financial crisis and Great Recession of 2007–2009, conservative U.S. Congressional representatives refused to engage in additional expansionary fiscal policy due to worries about budget deficits, which had increased to record levels. However, New Keynesian and political economists argued that additional spending would shorten the length of the recession and improve the strength of the recovery.

This leads us to the central question: Are large budget deficits and a growing national debt a bad thing? To laissez-faire economists, the answer is invariably yes: Deficits reduce private sector growth and mortgage a country's economic future. Many New Keynesian economists agree, arguing that deficits in recessions are fine but they should be offset by surpluses during expansions to balance the budget over the course of the business cycle. However, political economists disagree, arguing that deficits are central to economic growth.

20.6.1 Is the deficit a myth?

One of the most interesting and important arguments in favor of deficit spending was made by Stephanie Kelton, a leading MMT economist, in her 2020 book *The Deficit Myth*.[6] Most economists argue that the total amount of government spending is limited by the amount of tax revenues. Modern monetary theory instead asserts that a sovereign country that conducts transactions in its own currency backed by the state (fiat currency) can run up unlimited deficits as long as it has sufficient resources (labor, capital, and natural resources). Therefore, **there is no limit to federal spending. The government can create money out of thin air by printing it or transferring it to banks or people with a single keystroke.** The federal government can never run out of money, and the only thing stopping it from spending is political support and the upper limit of resource capacity. There should never be crowding out, because as soon as money is in short supply, the government can simply print/create more of it. The government controls the rate of interest and can set it wherever it wishes.

The philosophy Kelton is articulating here is called functional finance based on the ideas of Abba Lerner, which proposes that **governments should decide how much to spend and tax based on the impact of these policies** on prosperity for all, not based on how large the deficit is. **Deficits are largely unimportant in sovereign nations that control their own currency**.

According to MMT, **inflation, not a budget deficit, is the sign of government overspending**. If an economy is operating close to full employment and there is no more capacity for output, then additional spending could cause inflationary pressures. But, unless a country is actively experiencing inflation, it can safely continue to increase government spending and promote greater prosperity.

In addition, when a government pays out more money than it receives, the nongovernment sector experiences a surplus. **Government deficits directly enrich the private sector.** On the other hand, government surpluses take money out of the private sector, reducing economic activity.

Critics of MMT argue that it is never clear where the limits to economic capacity are, nor can we assume that government spending will necessarily be useful and productive. If government money is funneled into financial markets, it could create destructive bubbles. Too much circulation of a currency might also cause people and corporations to be less willing to accept it, which could undermine the goals of expansionary fiscal policy and cause a currency crisis. Despite these criticisms, the argument that the government should spend money on useful programs until problems materialize remains compelling to many political economists. Interestingly, although most economists do not accept the MMT approach, there has been a remarkable movement toward acceptance of large government deficits in recent years, indicating the increasing influence of the MMT approach. We see this in the fiscal policy approaches to the Great Recession and the COVID-19 recession.

29.7 FISCAL POLICY IN ACTION: FIGHTING THE GREAT RECESSION AND THE COVID-19 RECESSION

After the financial crisis of 2007, the U.S. economy plunged into the Great Recession of 2008–2009. Economists estimated that aggregate demand fell by $1200 billion as the stock market plunged and consumers and investors curtailed their spending. Though some laissez-faire economists opposed enacting expansionary fiscal policy, the vast majority of economists advocated a very large fiscal stimulus due to the severity of the recession.

In response to the recession, one of the first acts of the Obama administration was to pass the American Recovery and Reinvestment Act (ARRA) of February 2009. ARRA included $288 billion in tax cuts for households and businesses, especially for the poor; $224 billion for extended unemployment benefits, education, training, and health care; $105 billion for infrastructure spending; and $175 billion on other types of job-creating spending. At the time, this was the largest fiscal stimulus ever passed by the U.S. government.

Although it is hard to be precise, the Congressional Budget Office[7] estimated that the ARRA had the following impact:

- Increased real GDP by 1.7%–9.2%
- Reduced unemployment by 1.1%–4.8%
- Increased full-time employment-years by 2.1 million–11.6 million.

If we take the average of the low and high estimates for the economic impact, which is a reasonable approach, the ARRA has a very positive impact on the U.S. economy, increasing real GDP by about 5.5% and reducing unemployment by about 3%. However, the economic recovery after the Great Recession was sluggish, which seems to indicate that the stimulus was not large enough to eliminate the recessionary gap. Nevertheless, the U.S. stimulus was much more effective in restarting economic growth than the austerity policies pursued in the European Union (E.U.).

The Great Recession provided a dramatic contrast between the Keynesian expansionary fiscal policies implemented in the United States and the laissez-faire austerity policies implemented in the euro area of the E.U. The U.S. Great Recession was deep and lasted about a year and a half. As noted above, expansionary fiscal policy improved economic growth and the U.S. economy grew steadily but slowly after 2009. The euro area of the E.U. also experienced a deep recession in 2008–2009, recovered briefly, and then entered a second recession beginning in 2011 that lasted an additional two years.

The reason for the double-dip recession in the E.U. stemmed largely from the austerity policies its policymakers adopted. After a small initial stimulus in 2009, E.U. policymakers insisted that countries that were hard hit by the financial crisis, including Greece and Spain, slash government spending and raise taxes to reduce their budget deficits. Laissez-faire economists recommending this policy hoped that reductions in government deficits would improve business confidence, reduce crowding out, and stimulate business investment. However, just the opposite occurred. Decreases in government spending and higher taxes in fragile E.U. economies caused consumer spending and business investment to plummet. Unemployment in Greece and Spain reached 29% and 27%, respectively.

From 2008 to 2015, the U.S. economy grew by an annual average of 1.36%, while the euro area of the E.U. experienced an average annual growth rate of only 0.26%. The euro area was almost completely stagnant for seven years thanks to their policy choices. To New Keynesian economist Paul Krugman, laissez-faire economists who thought austerity would improve business confidence and investment in recessions were engaging in magical thinking, believing in the "Confidence Fairy." Unfortunately, like the tooth fairy, the Confidence Fairy proved to be a myth.[8]

The contrasting experiences of the United States and the E.U. in the Great Recession helped to convince most economists and policymakers that fiscal and monetary stimulus policies were crucial in addressing a major recession. Both the United States and the E.U. took more dramatic steps in the next recession.

When the economy plunged into the even deeper COVID-19 recession in 2020, President Trump and the U.S. Congress were willing to enact a much larger stimulus. In late March of 2020, the U.S. government passed the $2 trillion Coronavirus Aid, Relief, and Economic Security (CARES) Act. Reflecting the supply-side focus of the Trump administration, the biggest benefits went to large corporations, followed by small businesses, as shown in Figure 29.16. Households were given cash directly, as were the unemployed, but little direct government spending or job creation took place.

The result of the fiscal stimulus plus a huge monetary stimulus from the Fed was a dramatic resurgence of the stock market. The Standard and Poor's 500 index of the 500 largest U.S. companies had dropped from 3386.15 on February 19, 2020, to 2237.40 on March 23. After the stimulus, the stock market rebounded to almost the same level, reaching 3215.60 on July 16. In previous recessions, it usually took stock markets years to rebound.

However, the stimulus had a much smaller impact on unemployment at first. The unemployment rate increased from 3.5% in February 2020 to 14.7% in April at the start of the recession. By June of 2020, the unemployment rate dropped thanks to the stimulus but only to 11.1%.

Figure 29.17 shows that the United States initially allocated more money as a percentage of GDP than other developed countries on spending and tax cuts but less in total stimulus than some countries. Germany and Denmark spent most of their stimulus funds on keeping workers employed.

Fiscal policy remains somewhat controversial, although it appears that a modern consensus in favor of expansionary fiscal policy has re-emerged in the wake of the Great Recession. It will be interesting to see whether this consensus continues.

Subsidies and tax cuts for large corporations	$500
Small business loans and grants	$377
State & local government funding for COVID-19 response, other programs	$340
Cash payments to households	$300
Extra unemployment payments	$260
Public health spending on hospitals, other areas	$154
Student loan & other loan forgiveness	$44
Safety net support (food)	$26
National security spending	$17

FIGURE 29.16 Table showing CARES Act of 2020 major spending categories (in billions of dollars).

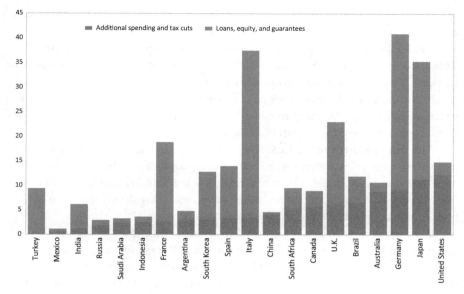

FIGURE 29.17 Fiscal (gray) and monetary (blue) response to the COVID-19 recession as a percentage of GDP.

29.8 CONCLUSION

The role of government in the United States increased steadily from the Great Depression until the 1970s, after which it stabilized at an average of 31.9% of the economy. The major areas of government spending are the purchase of public and quasi-public goods, social spending, and government administration. The U.S. government plays a significant role in the economy, but it spends less on public goods and safety nets than most other developed countries. The United States also taxes the wealthy much less than other countries and has a relatively flat tax structure instead of a progressive one. Other developed countries have progressive tax structures where the rich pay a larger percentage of their income in taxes than the poor.

Governments can use automatic stabilizers and discretionary fiscal policy to stabilize economies. In recessions, increases in government spending and decreases in taxes increase aggregate demand, and if they are large enough, they can eliminate any recessionary gap and return the economy to potential real GDP. In an overheated economy, the government can decrease spending or increase taxes to eliminate any inflationary gap.

Economists often disagree on the utilization of fiscal policy. Laissez-faire economists generally oppose the use of fiscal policy in recessions, arguing that markets quickly correct themselves and that crowding out, policy lags, and other problems render fiscal policy ineffective. They often advocate austerity and oppose increasing government deficits. New Keynesian economists strongly advocate the use of fiscal policy in recessions, seeing it as the best way to stabilize the economy and arguing that government spending tends to crowd in private sector investment. They are comfortable with deficit spending in recessions. Supply-side economists advocate the use of tax cuts for corporations and the wealthy to stimulate aggregate supply and are not concerned with deficit spending. Political economists advocate strategic government spending to benefit workers and to generate growth. Deficit spending in service of these goals is encouraged.

The steady growth of the U.S. federal debt and growing budget deficits even in non-recession years indicate an increasing acceptance of debt by U.S. politicians. Most economists are troubled by the increasing debt levels, but political economists from the modern monetary theory perspective argue that deficit spending is not problematic as long as the economy is below full capacity.

Expansionary fiscal policy was used to combat the Great Recession of 2008 and the COVID-19 recession of 2020. In the Great Recession, expansionary fiscal policy in the United States proved to be much more effective than austerity policy in the euro area in stabilizing the macroeconomy. The E.U., United States, and other developed countries engaged in record fiscal stimulus in 2020, causing an explosion in national debts. Time will tell whether these stimulus policies were effective or whether the debts proved to be debilitating.

QUESTIONS FOR REVIEW

1. Describe the priorities that emerge from role and size of the U.S. government. What does the United States prioritize? How do U.S. priorities differ from those in other developed countries?
2. Explain the difference between automatic stabilizers and discretionary fiscal policy. Give examples in your answer.
3. Use Figure 29.18 to answer the following questions. Suppose the economy is currently in equilibrium where AD₁ intersects AS.
   a. What is the amount of the recessionary or inflationary gap?
   b. If the marginal respending rate (MRR) is 0.6, how much will the government need to change spending to move the economy to a new equilibrium at potential real GDP?
   c. If the marginal propensity to consume is 0.8, how large a lump sum tax change would be needed to move the economy to a new equilibrium at potential real GDP?
4. Use Figure 29.18 to answer the following questions. Suppose the economy is currently in equilibrium where AD₂ intersects AS.
   a. What is the amount of the recessionary or inflationary gap?

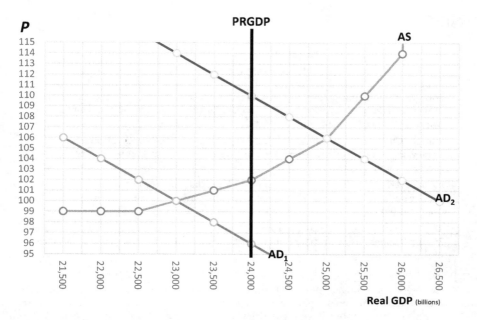

FIGURE 29.18 Aggregate demand and supply problem.

    b.   If the marginal respending rate is 0.8, how much will the government need to change spending to move the economy to a new equilibrium at potential real GDP?

    c.   If the marginal propensity to consume is 0.95, how large a lump sum tax change would be needed to move the economy to a new equilibrium at potential real GDP?

5.   Compare and contrast the different perspectives of economists on fiscal policy. Which perspective do you find most convincing? Why?

6.   Describe what has happened to U.S. budget deficits and the national debt of the federal government over the last 50 years.

7.   Critically evaluate the different perspectives of economists on government budget deficits and debt. What are the main areas of disagreement? How do you think the government should approach the issue of deficit spending? Explain and support your answer.

8.   Explain Stephanie Kelton's argument that the government should not worry about large government budget deficits except under certain conditions. What are some criticisms of this approach?

9.   Describe the fiscal policies used to stabilize the economies of the United States and the euro area during the Great Recession of 2008. Were the policies effective? Why or why not? How did developed countries change their policies to combat the COVID-19 recession of 2020?

NOTES

1 2019 U.S. GDP was used for this calculation.

2 See Geoffrey Schneider, *Microeconomic Principles and Problems* (Routledge, London, 2019), ch. 21 for more details. Most health economists attribute high U.S. costs and poor health outcomes to the emphasis on private sector health care and the inefficiencies in private health care markets. The U.S. pays far more for prescription drugs and basic medical services than any other country.

3 Source: OECD, *OECD Economic Outlook*, Volume 2019, No. 2, https://www.oecd-i library.org/sites/f21b05be-en/index.html?itemId=/content/component/f21b05be-en, accessed August 6, 2021.

4 Note that for simplicity we are assuming here that the tax change is a "lump sum" change and does not vary with income, and we are assuming the marginal propensity to import is 0 when it comes to the impact of lump sum tax cuts.

5 The 2020 deficit figure was estimated by the Congressional Budget Office in June of 2020. Changes in government policies or tax collection after this date are not reflected in this estimate.

6 My thanks to Spandan Marasini, who wrote the initial draft of this section.

7 Congressional Budget Office, "Estimated Impact of the American Recovery and Reinvestment Act on Employment and Economic Output in 2014," February 2015, https://www.cbo.gov/sites/default/files/114th-congress-2015-2016/reports/49958-ARRA.pdf, accessed August 6, 2021.

8 Paul Krugman, "Myths of Austerity," *New York Times*, July 1, 2010. https://www.ny times.com/2010/07/02/opinion/02krugman.html?ref=paulkrugman, accessed August 6, 2021.

30 Money, banking, and the financial sector

How money markets make the world go around

In modern capitalist economies, money seems to be the most important priority. Many individuals and businesses spend their entire existence trying to accumulate as much money as possible. Ironically, money has no intrinsic value: It is only worth the paper it is printed on or the electronic credit in your account. But money is important because people believe in its enduring value and they are willing to part with goods, services, labor, property, and assets in exchange for money.

Money started out as a simple social construct—as a registry of debts or as a commodity such as a unit of wheat to keep track of who owed what to whom. However, the modern monetary system is much more complicated. Money is now mostly a system of electronic debits and credits, and printed money is becoming less and less important. Banks and financial markets that control much of a country's money loom ever larger in importance, so much so that they often influence economic policy to be more favorable to money markets than to workers and manufacturers. Thus, money is about claims on resources, but it is also about economic and political power.

This chapter takes up money, banking, and the financial sector, illustrating how money markets and financial markets work in theory and practice. Given their importance, every citizen needs to understand the role of money, banking, and financial markets in modern economies.

This chapter begins by discussing the history of money and its role in the modern world. Next, we take up the banking sector and how banks create money. Subsequently, we introduce the mainstream economics and political economy models of the money market. Next, we take up financial markets, including stocks,

DOI: 10.4324/9781315636924-39

bonds, and real estate. Financialization, a term used to describe the rise and increasing dominance of the Finance, Insurance, and Real Estate (FIRE) sector, is then discussed.

30.0 CHAPTER 30 LEARNING GOALS

After reading this chapter, you should be able to:

■ Describe the history of money and the role it has played in various economies.

■ Differentiate between commodity money and fiat money and explain why economists believe that fiat money is better for economic stability.

■ Explain how banks work and how they can create money via the money (deposit) multiplier.

■ Use the mainstream and political economy models of the money market to determine how changes in key variables will affect the money supply and the interest rate.

■ Compare and contrast the mainstream economics and political economy models of the money market and explain the debate over whether money is exogenously or endogenously determined.

■ Describe the role that financial markets, especially stock markets, play in the economy.

■ Critically analyze the concept of financialization and whether or not financialization presents a significant problem in modern economies.

30.1 DEFINING MONEY—IT'S NOT WHAT YOU THINK

To many people, money is the central focus of their existence due to its importance in modern capitalism. Having money means you can buy the necessities of life. If you successfully accumulate money, you are an important person with power and influence. It often seems that money is the central driver of the modern world—that "money makes the world go around."

This is ironic given that some economists do not see money as particularly important. Many laissez-faire economists argue that money has no significant impact on the "real" economy, affecting only prices. In economic terminology, laissez-faire economists argue that money is "neutral," having no positive or negative impact on the real economy. Other economists disagree, arguing that money has a very important impact on real economic variables. And, as we will see, a poorly managed monetary system is a recipe for disaster.

In the modern economy, money is **a unit of account, which may also be a physical item such as a printed piece of paper, that is accepted as payment for taxes, debts, and goods and services. Money can also be issued as credit (loaned out).** Historically, money has taken on two main forms, as **an account of debits and credits in a ledger and as a medium of exchange for trading**.

Anthropological research has established that most exchanges in ancient human societies were gifts, with an understanding that at some point there was likely to be a reciprocal gift. You would share what you had with other community members, with the understanding that you would be "paid back" in the future when you needed something. Ancient societies featured strong bonds of community, including reciprocity and redistribution, because larger, more united groups had a greater likelihood of success in the challenging environment facing hunter-gatherer societies. The fact that exchanges took the form of gifts (redistribution) and reciprocity meant that money was unnecessary, so it did not exist in the modern sense.

According to anthropologist David Graeber, the earliest form of money probably happened when, "I owe you one," became "I owe you one unit of something."[1] There is evidence that units of wheat were the first units of account—in essence the first form of money. In ancient Babylonia, the mina was the unit of account, and it was equal to 10,800 grains of wheat.[2] Thus, the earliest forms of economic exchange seem to have taken the form of loans and an early form of debt bondage. Debts were kept track of on "tally sticks," such as the one displayed in Figure 30.1.[3] Eventually, debts denoted on tally sticks were replaced with loans of money, along with the idea of interest payments or some other form of return on loans.

The development of commodity money, where **gold, silver, or other precious commodities are used as the primary unit of account**, accompanied the rise of private property and the development of a government (state) that needed to engage in taxation to support itself. Figure 30.1 shows ancient Chinese metal coins, carved with official characters to make them harder to duplicate and counterfeit.

Many different commodities have served as money in human societies. Livestock, grains, salt, peppercorns, cocoa beans, tea, precious metals, rare Cowrie shells, decorated belts, large carved stones, and beaver pelts have all served as commodity money in particular times and places. Even in the modern world we occasionally see commodities serving as money. In prisons, cigarettes sometimes serve as a form of currency. In Russia in the late 1990s when the Russian ruble lost all of its value, people started to use cases of vodka as currency. In the isolated regions of Colombia where cocaine is produced, coca paste is often accepted as payment.

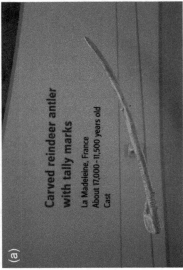

FIGURE 30.1 An ancient French tally stick (left) and ancient Chinese coins (right).

In general, commodity monies have two important things in common: They are scarce, but they are not impossibly rare. If leaves on trees were money, then everyone would have vast amounts and the money would not be able to maintain its value. If money was something impossibly rare, there would not be enough of it to facilitate debt payments and exchange.

Commodity money is useful because it makes exchanges much more efficient. Without money, exchanges have to be done via barter, with both people trying to trade something they have for something they want. Barter, however, is very inefficient: If either party does not want what the other person is trading, then no exchange will take place. That is, there has to be a "coincidence of wants" in order for barter to take place. Barter is also made difficult by the lack of common prices. For barter to work, there has to be a common understanding of the worth of each commodity in terms of all other commodities.

Money simplifies this process immensely. Each person can sell what they have for money to a person who wants it. Then they can use that money to buy what they want. In addition, the prices of all items can be expressed in terms of money, so it is easy to establish relative prices for all goods and services. Money facilitates commerce by serving as a medium of exchange.

In theory, commodity money has intrinsic value, in that the commodity being used as money—often gold or silver—is useful and pretty. Human beings have long valued shiny things like gold, silver, and diamonds. However, commodity money's primary source of value is that the state requires its citizens to use it and because people have to pay taxes and debts in commodity money. This is why the move from commodity money to fiat money occurred without significant problems.

Fiat money is **money that is established as legal tender by government fiat**, which is an official government decree. In the modern world, fiat money is **paper money or electronic accounts that have value because the state declares that they do and because people need the fiat money to pay their taxes and debts and to engage in economic activities in a particular society**.

Fiat (paper) money originated in China in the 11th century. Initially, the paper money could be exchanged for a certain amount of silk, silver, or gold, linking the paper money to a commodity. By the 13th century, the link between paper money and commodities had been severed. Unfortunately, excessive spending by the Chinese government in the face of commodity shortages resulted in hyperinflation and an economic collapse. This episode highlights the fact that *one of the main roles for government in a fiat money system is preserve the value of its currency and to avoid price instability*. Fiat money only has value as long as people believe it does. Fiat money must be useful for paying taxes and debts and for purchasing goods and services or it loses its value.

Officially, the U.S. dollar was on the "gold standard" for much of its history. A government whose currency is on the gold standard promises that each unit of currency (such as one dollar) can be exchanged for a certain amount of gold. The gold standard was important early in U.S. history in giving people confidence in the value of the dollar. Currencies only work to facilitate exchange, including government purchases, if they are widely accepted.

The United States partially abandoned the gold standard in 1933 when financial panics during the Great Depression caused people to withdraw their money from banks and to hoard gold. President Roosevelt and Congress stopped allowing dollars to be exchanged for gold so they could shore up the nation's money supply. Nonetheless, the United States officially maintained an exchange rate of one ounce of gold equal to $35 until 1971, when President Nixon completely abandoned the gold standard to stop foreign countries with large dollar holdings from buying up U.S. gold reserves. Since then, the U.S. dollar has been exclusively a fiat currency. Other countries quickly followed and the gold standard became a relic of history.

The abandonment of commodity money and the gold standard relate to the fundamental problem with commodity money: Fluctuations in the value of gold (or whatever commodity is being used as the basis for money) cause instability in the macroeconomy, with severe fluctuations in prices and output. The equation of exchange illustrates how this can play out.

According to the equation of exchange:

$$\text{Money supply}\,(M1) \times \text{Velocity}\,(V) = \text{Price level}\,(P) \times \text{Real GDP}\,(Y).$$

Recall that velocity is the number of times a dollar changes hands in a year.

Now consider what it would mean for an economy utilizing a commodity like gold as its currency. A fixed money supply implies that there can be no growth in real GDP. Thus, economic growth is at the mercy of supplies of gold. The only choice a country would have if it wanted to stimulate growth would be to put less gold into each coin (called "debasing" the currency), thereby increasing M1 enough to facilitate economic growth.

Another way to think about this is as follows: If more goods are produced (higher real GDP), the only way consumers can purchase more goods is if they have more money. If more goods are produced but the amount of money available to consumers stays the same, then some goods will not be purchased, potentially causing a glut, deflation, and a serious downturn. Therefore, having too little money presents a major constraint on macroeconomic growth.

Having too much money can also be problematic. When the United States used gold coins as money, every time there was a large influx of gold, if there was not a similar increase in the production of goods, the economy would experience significantly higher prices. Using the equation of exchange above, if M1 increases substantially, and if velocity and real GDP are stable, then the result will be an increase in P equal to the increase in M1.

When the United States used the gold standard, it experienced dramatic bouts of inflation and deflation, more regular economic crises, and lower levels of economic growth. Meanwhile, with fiat money the central bank is able to increase the money supply when needed to facilitate growth and prevent deflation, and it can decrease the money supply to reduce inflationary pressures when needed. Thus, fiat money improved economic stability and performance markedly. As one example, during the financial crisis of 2007–2008, a time of huge upheaval and deflationary pressures, the U.S. Central Bank (the Fed) was able to dramatically increase the money supply to offset the crisis. Though the huge increase in the money supply scared many politicians and commentators, who predicted rampant inflation, that did not occur. Instead, deflationary pressures subsided and real GDP growth was restored, stabilizing the economy. Economic research shows that there was *23 times* less variance in prices during the financial crisis with fiat money and activist Fed policy than there was under the gold standard from 1919 to 1933.[4] Thus, fiat money plus sound macroeconomic policy fosters stability and growth much better than the gold standard did. As we will see in the next chapter, managing the money supply in a manner that fosters economic growth while maintaining price stability is the major job of central bank officials.

Interestingly, in the modern economy, very few people handle paper money. Money is mostly a unit of account, transferred electronically between employers and employees, consumers and businesses, business and the government, and so on. This is why in the modern economy money is defined as a "unit of account" that facilitates transactions of all types.

30.2 THE USES AND MEASUREMENT OF MONEY

In all economic systems, money is a crucial tool of the government. Money is issued by the government to purchase what it needs to function. Taxes are levied by the government to create a demand for money so that its citizens must use the currency to pay taxes. Once accepted as a medium of exchange, money becomes the primary unit for economic transactions.

The main purposes of money are as follows:

1. Money is a **unit of account**, which is used to express the value of items and the amount of debts.
2. Money is a **medium of exchange**, which is used in transactions. Money eliminates the need for barter and thereby increases the efficiency of the economy.
3. Money is a **store of value**. It is a financial asset that, if saved, can be used in the future to make purchases. Money can also be loaned out so others can make purchases for a fee (an interest payment). Also, money is extremely "liquid," in that it can easily be used to buy goods or to purchase financial assets.

Note that money can only serve as a unit of account for debts and as a store of value if its value will be relatively stable over time. If people expect a currency to be worthless in the future, they will not hold it as an asset, nor will they be willing to loan money to someone with the expectation of future payments.

In general, money must have a stable supply and be difficult to counterfeit. If money will be used for physical spending in a store or a market, it must also be easy to carry and durable.

Interestingly, so-called cryptocurrencies like Bitcoin have some but not all of the characteristics of fiat money. Cryptocurrencies can be created (mined) in limited amounts via powerful computers. They have deep, complex encryption that prevents simple duplication. Therefore, Bitcoin is supplied by market participants, although the supply is limited to preserve the value of a Bitcoin. Enough people accept Bitcoin that it can serve as a medium of exchange and as a unit of account for short-term transactions. Where Bitcoin encounters problems is with respect to stability of value over time.

National currencies always have value as long as the governments issuing them have the ability to tax. You will always need to have some of the government-issued currency to pay your taxes. The value of Bitcoin, however, would fall to nothing as soon as people lost faith in it. Bitcoin is not a government currency and no one can make you use it. Thus, the value of a Bitcoin depends entirely on the faith of those who hold it. The dramatic fluctuations in the price of a Bitcoin demonstrate the fundamental instability of a nongovernmental form of money.

The first Bitcoin exchange was created in 2010. In its first year, the value of a Bitcoin increased by 900% in five days. Later in the year, it fell by 94%. Even after becoming more established, the value fluctuated dramatically. In the mid-2010s, the value of a Bitcoin sometimes changed by as much as 30% in one day and 500% in three weeks. National currencies are much more stable as long as they are well managed.

Some people continue to use Bitcoin because it bypasses government and no record is kept of Bitcoin transactions, making it very good for illegal transactions. Bitcoin's success prompted numerous imitators, and many Wall Street banks started to become involved in the cryptocurrency market. Nevertheless, cryptocurrencies like Bitcoin remain a relatively small part of financial markets as of 2021.

In modern economic systems, we use different measures of the amount of money in the economy based on different definitions of liquidity. Liquidity in financial economics refers to **the ease with which an asset can be converted into cash**. Therefore, cash money is the most liquid asset because it is already cash. Economists also consider checking accounts, traveler's checks, demand deposits, and other types of accounts that consumers can spend immediately as the same as cash.

The money supply, M1, also called the money stock, is equal to **cash held by the public and near-cash accounts** (checkable deposits). These liquid assets are spent the most frequently.

M2 is equal to M1 plus short-term accounts that can be easily converted into cash, usually with one simple step. M2 includes savings accounts, money market accounts, mutual funds, and other fairly liquid assets that can be converted into cash by making a transfer in an online account or going to the bank.

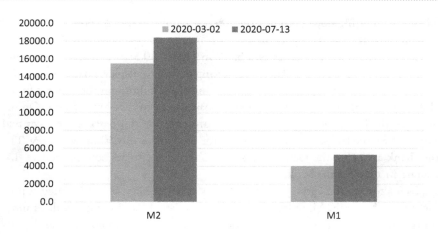

FIGURE 30.2 M1 and M2 (billions of dollars).

M3 is equal to M2 plus large certificates of deposit and savings accounts as well as business savings. Because banks only keep a small amount of cash as reserves, large withdrawals from M3 will often take several days, which means that large deposits are the least liquid form of money in banks.

The amount of money in the economy—M1 and M2—is a crucial variable in determining how much money will be spent by consumers. Therefore, it is tracked very carefully by economists. One of the major jobs of the central bank is to manage M1 and M2 such that there is enough money for purchases and for economic growth but not too much money so that inflation is generated.

Figure 30.2 shows the amount of money (M1 and M2) in the U.S. economy on March 2 and July 13 of 2020. The Fed increased the money supply dramatically during this period to combat the COVID-19 recession, something we will take up later in more detail.

Though the government establishes a country's currency, banks have a tremendous influence over the total amount of money in an economy. Banks perform a useful service in a capitalist economy, but they can also contribute to instability if not properly regulated.

30.3 BANKS, THE BANKING SYSTEM, AND THE MONEY MULTIPLIER

Banks make profits by loaning out money to people, businesses, and institutions and charging those borrowers interest on their loans. The money that banks loan out comes from bank owners as well as depositors. Thus, banks are called **financial intermediaries** because they match savers with borrowers: They take in deposits from savers and they use those deposits to make loans to borrowers. Bank profits depend on the difference between the interest banks receive from borrowers and the interest banks pay to depositors.

We can see these two sides of a bank in Figure 30.3(a), which shows a bank T-account. A T-account is a classic accounting device to display a balance sheet for an organization with the assets on one side and the liabilities on the other. On the liability side, banks owe money to their depositors and to the bank owners. On the asset side, the bank keeps reserves, which are **cash or deposits at the central bank** that can be transferred to any depositor who needs to withdraw money. The other bank assets are the loans, stocks, bonds, other securities, and properties that generate income for the bank.

To make the most money possible, banks prefer to keep as little money as possible on hand as cash. More loans or purchases of stocks and bonds result in more profits. Therefore, banks only keep enough money on hand to cover what depositors need or a larger amount if required by law.

The banking required reserve ratio (RRR) is **the percentage of deposits that banks are required by law to hold as reserves**. In order to qualify for federal banking insurance in the United States, banks must agree to abide by the RRR.

Historically in the United States, the required reserve ratio on checking accounts has been 10%, whereas the RRR for savings accounts and other deposits is much lower because these accounts are used less frequently for spending. In Figure 30.3(b), if a bank customer deposits $100,000 in their checking account, the bank's liabilities have increase by $100,000. With an RRR of 10%, the bank will keep $10,000 of the checking account deposit in reserves, as required by law, and loan the rest out ($90,000) to increase their profits.

(a) A Bank T-Account

Assets	Liabilities
Reserves	Checkable deposits
Loans	Savings and time deposits
Stocks, bonds, securities	Owner equity
Property	

FIGURE 30.3 (a) A bank T-account.

(b) A Bank T-Account
after a deposit of $100,000

Assets	Liabilities
Reserves $10,000	Deposits $100,000
Loans $90,000	

FIGURE 30.3 (b) The effect of a deposit on reserves.

The fact that banks do not keep most of their deposits in cash means that there can be a "run on the bank" if a large number of depositors try to withdraw a lot of money at the same time. This situation is depicted memorably in the classic Christmas film *It's a Wonderful Life*, when panicked depositors come into their community bank to withdraw money at the same time. The protagonist, George Bailey, responds,

> You're thinking of this place all wrong. As if I had the money back in a safe. The money's not here. Your money's in Joe's house ... right next to yours. And in the Kennedy house, and Mrs. Macklin's house, and a hundred others. Why, you're lending them the money to build, and then, they're going to pay it back to you as best they can.

Bank runs tend to occur when people lose faith in a bank or the banking system. During the Great Depression, banks failed one after another as people lost confidence in banks. Even healthy banks experienced bank runs. This is why the government established the Federal Deposit Insurance Corporation, the Federal Savings and Loan Insurance Corporation, and other banking insurance programs. The government guarantees that it will replace the money in your accounts if the bank loses it. This way, depositors can always have faith that their money will be safe, even if the bank fails.

Meanwhile, the government regularly inspects the books of federally insured banks to make sure they are not engaging in overly risky behavior. This helps to assure the stability of the financial system. As we will see later, deregulation of banking in the 1980s and 1990s set the stage for two speculative bubbles and the financial crisis of 2007–2008.

Banks also have a dramatic impact on the economy because of how they create money. Deposit creation occurs as banks take in and loan out money. The money multiplier, also called the deposit multiplier, is **the amount of money that banks create with each dollar of reserves**. The money multiplier works much like the spending multiplier we studied earlier.

If we start with an initial $100,000 deposit and a required reserve ratio (RRR) of 10%, as we saw above, the bank will loan out $90,000 and keep $10,000 in required reserves. As long as economic conditions are favorable, banks tend to loan out all of their excess reserves because this is how they make money.

Now suppose that $90,000 is loaned to a home buyer, who writes a check to the homeowner for that amount. The homeowner deposits the check in the checking account at their bank, giving that bank $90,000 in reserves. This bank will keep $9,000 in required reserves and loan out the $81,000 in excess reserves. That $81,000 loan gets spent on something else, perhaps a sports car, which is deposited in the car dealership's bank. The car dealership's bank now has $81,000 in reserves. It will keep $8100 in required reserves and make $72,900 in new loans. And so on.

The total amount of deposits created is equal to $100,000 + 90,000 + 81,000 + 72,900 + ...

This can be rewritten as $100,000*(1+0.9+0.9^2+0.9^3+...)$. This infinite series has a solution in the following form:

$$\Delta \text{Deposits} = \Delta M1 = (\$100,000) * \frac{1}{(1-0.9)} = (\$100,000) * \frac{1}{0.1}$$

$$= \$100,000 * 10 = 1,000,000.$$

In this case, the money multiplier is 10. Each $1 increase in deposits ends up creating $10 in total deposits, because the same money is lent and relent multiple times by multiple banks.

From this equation, we can also see that the equation for the money multiplier is

$$\text{Money multiplier} = \frac{1}{\text{Required reserve ratio}(\text{RRR})}.$$

The money multiplier will be smaller if banks hold excess reserves or if people hold cash instead of depositing money. Holding excess reserves means that a bank is not lending out money that it is legally allowed to lend and is therefore willingly sacrificing profits. Banks only hold excess reserves if the likelihood of default is so high that it is better to hold cash and give up on earning interest than it is to make a risky loan.

The money multiplier will be larger if banks can easily borrow reserves to loan out money whenever they see a good opportunity. Some classes of assets have no required reserve amount, making the money multiplier effectively infinite for such assets. Due to the dramatic effect of banks on the money supply, they can be a significant source of instability.

Like any business, banks exist to make the maximum amount of money possible. They do this by paying depositors as little interest as possible on their deposits. And they try to charge borrowers as much interest as possible on loans while minimizing the risk of default. Higher risk loans will come with higher interest rates, as well as a higher risk of default. If the banking market is sufficiently competitive, depositors and borrowers will get fair interest rates, but if banks have monopoly power, banks are able to extract monopoly profits.

To reduce the risk of making loans, banks demand collateral from borrowers. Collateral is **something pledged by a borrower to provide security for repayment of a loan. Collateral is forfeited to the bank if the borrower defaults on the loan.** For most bank loans, the bank is entitled to keep the home or business if the homeowner or business owner defaults on their loan. The bank can then sell the home or business to recoup their losses.

Banks have a financial incentive to loan out as much money as possible, but the more banks loan out, the riskier their financial situation is. This is because banks are loaning money to increasingly risky borrowers as they expand their lending. In addition, bank loan defaults tend to come in clumps when economic conditions deteriorate. If large numbers of borrowers default at the same time, banks can end up without enough cash to meet the needs of depositors, who want to write checks to pay bills and get cash when they need it. This is why **one of the main roles of the central bank is as a lender of last resort**, to lend money to banks when they run short of cash.

Once banks have substantial losses greater than or equal to the ownership stake of the bank owners, banks have an incentive to undertake risky loans to try to recoup their losses. Often, bank owners' stake in the bank is as little as 3%, and the rest of the money belongs to depositors. If bank losses exceed 3% and bank owners have lost all of their own investment, they are gambling entirely with other people's money, so they have less incentive to be prudent with their loans. In many instances, we find that failing banks make increasingly risky loans to try to recoup losses. This is another reason why government regulation of banking is so important.

There are many different types of banks in the modern world. **Retail** banks, **savings and loan** banks, and **credit unions** take in deposits and make loans to individuals and small businesses. **Commercial** banks deal primarily with businesses. **Private** banks offer traditional banking services as well as financial investment services and trust and estate planning for wealthy individuals. **Investment** banks handle large corporate investments, including underwriting and issuing securities (stocks and bonds); supporting mergers and acquisitions; creating, selling, and insuring derivatives; and investing directly in all types of domestic and international asset markets. The **central** bank oversees the banking system and manipulates the money supply and interest rates via monetary policies.

Banks are regulated carefully due to their substantial impact on the economy. In the United States the Glass–Steagall Act of 1933 separated the banking sector into traditional banking, where banks take in deposits and make loans to families and businesses, and investment banking, where banks make riskier, more speculative investments. The idea was to insulate insured, safe banks from high-risk banks that were not insured by the government. However, beginning in the 1980s banking regulations were relaxed and investment banks were allowed to merge with retail banks and savings and loans. Unfortunately, this corresponded with more regular banking crises, as we will see later.

One of the most important aspects of money is its relationship to interest rates. Interest rates are a major determinant of the amount of business investment and consumer spending that occur. The amount of items purchased using borrowed money is so vast that credit markets loom large in macroeconomic analysis. To understand the relationship between money and interest rates, economists developed various models of the money market.

30.4 THE MAINSTREAM ECONOMICS MODEL OF THE MONEY MARKET

The mainstream model of the money market depicted in Figure 30.4 shows a supply and demand curve for money (M1). M1 includes cash and checkable deposits and it is the money that households and businesses use to make most of their purchases. The first important thing to note about this graph is that the price of money—the price of holding cash—is the interest rate. If you keep your money as cash instead of depositing it in an interest-bearing account in a bank or buying a bond, you are losing the return that you could make on your money, which is the going rate of interest. In essence, the interest rate is the opportunity cost of holding cash.

People demand money—that is, they desire to hold cash—for three reasons, which are listed below.

1. **Transactions demand.** The transactions demand for money is **the amount of cash or checkable deposits that individuals need to keep available to make purchases (transactions).** If interest rates are high, people will keep as little cash as possible and instead put their money into bonds or interest-bearing money market accounts. If interest rates are low, they will keep more of their money in cash or checkable deposits for convenience.
2. **Precautionary demand.** The precautionary demand for money is **the amount of cash or checkable deposits that people keep as a contingency to meet unexpected expenses.** When people are worried about keeping their job, they often keep a larger amount of cash on hand. However, higher interest rates encourage people to hold less cash and to place more money into interest-bearing accounts and securities.
3. **Speculative demand.** The speculative demand for money reflects **the amount of cash or checkable deposits that people want to hold as a**

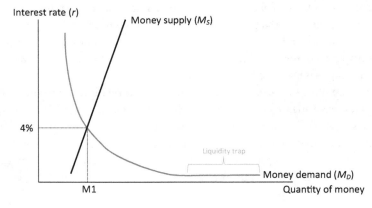

FIGURE 30.4 The mainstream model of the money market.

safe asset to maximize returns on all of their assets. Investors nearly always hold a certain amount of their portfolio as cash because it is safe and because having cash allows them to take advantage very quickly of any opportunities that arise.

In general, the money demand curve is downward sloping because people want to hold less cash and more interest-bearing securities and accounts when interest rates are high. When interest rates are low, there is very little return on interest-bearing assets, so people tend to hold more cash. Thus, an increase in the interest rate causes a decrease in the quantity of money demanded and a decrease in the interest rate causes an increase in the quantity of money demanded.

Notice that the money demand curve becomes flat when interest rates approach 0%. The flat part of the demand curve for money is called a liquidity trap, which **occurs when people believe that interest rates can fall no further and can only increase**. When a liquidity trap occurs, no matter how much the central bank increases the money supply, interest rates will stay the same and **people will hold all new money as cash because they believe interest rates will increase in the near future**. No one will buy a government bond at a low interest rate and lock themselves into a low rate of return if they expect the interest rate to increase very soon. The existence of a liquidity trap indicates that there are limits to how effective monetary policy that increases the money supply can be in stimulating the economy.

The **determinants of the demand for money**, the factors that *shift* the money demand curve, are the following:

1. **Income** (real GDP): Higher incomes result in people spending more money, which increases the demand for money in order to engage in more transactions.
2. **Price level**: The higher the price level, the more money (cash) people need to buy goods and services, increasing the demand for money.
3. **Expectations**: When investors expect the price of stocks to crash, they will sell their stocks and hold their assets as cash until the crash occurs or their expectations change. This increases the demand for money.
4. **Preferences**: If people are risk averse, they tend to hold more money as cash and to place less money in riskier assets like stocks. If they have a high level of risk tolerance, they will hold less cash and invest more of their money in riskier assets. If people prefer to use credit cards for purchases, they have a lower demand for cash.
5. **Asset transfer costs**: Moving money out of stocks, bonds, and some money market accounts comes with a fee, and sometimes those fees can be significant. If fees are low, investors can keep their money in stocks or bonds and sell those assets whenever they need cash. If fees are high, investors will tend to keep more money in cash to avoid the costs associated with transactions.

6. **Changes in regulations**: The government can affect the amount of money
    that people want to hold as cash via regulations. For example, in 1980 the
    U.S. government allowed banks to start paying interest on checking accounts,
    which made it more attractive to keep money in checkable deposit accounts,
    increasing the demand for money.

Suppose there is an economic boom that dramatically increases incomes. We would
expect a significant increase in money demand because people need more cash to
make more purchases. This would cause the money demand curve to increase (shift
up and to the right), causing interest rates to increase, as depicted in Figure 30.5(a).

In mainstream economics, the money supply is determined by the amount
of money the central bank prints and distributes electronically and by the money
multiplier. The money supply curve is straight up and down (vertical) under some
conditions. This model assumes that banks loan out all excess reserves and that
banks cannot borrow reserves when they want them. The money supply curve
would be upward sloping if banks hold excess reserves when interest rates are low
and no good loan opportunities are available, whereas banks increase lending as
interest rates rise and loans become more profitable.

Shifts in the money supply curve (the *determinants* of money supply) occur due
to changes in the behavior of the central bank. The money supply curve would
increase (shift to the right), as it does in Figure 30.5(b), if the central bank decides
to increase the money supply by printing money, purchasing bonds or other assets,
or crediting banks' accounts. The money supply curve would decrease if the central
bank decided to take in money from banks by selling government bonds or if it
printed less money than usual.

As we will see in the next section, political economists have a very different
model of the money market.[5] Political economists argue that banks rely intensively

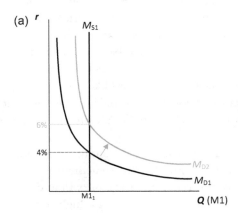

FIGURE 30.5 (a) An increase in money demand.

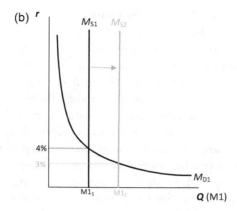

FIGURE 30.5 (b) An increase in money supply.

on borrowing reserves to create new loan opportunities, which means that the money market is driven in a fundamental way by private bank money creation.

30.5 POLITICAL ECONOMISTS ON ENDOGENOUS MONEY

In mainstream economics, it is typically assumed that banks do not hold excess reserves, and the money supply is typically depicted as a vertical line that is controlled entirely by the central bank (the Fed in the United States). The money supply from this view is *exogenous*, determined (externally) by the Fed and unaffected by the internal dynamics of banks and the economic system. The Fed changes the interest rate by increasing or decreasing the money supply (M1) in a very controlled fashion by changing the quantity of banks' excess reserves, precisely determining the amount of money in the economy. If the Fed wants banks to loan out more money, they purchase bonds and other securities from the public, the public gets more money in their bank accounts, banks have excess reserves, and banks reduce interest rates to encourage more people to borrow these excess reserves. Banks then loan out those excess reserves to increase profits.

An open market sale would do the opposite. If the Fed undertakes an open market sale in the mainstream model of the money market, it sells bonds to the public, taking money out of the banking system in exchange for government bonds and increasing the interest rate. *In this model, the central bank determines the money supply and money demand curve determines the rate of interest.*

Research by political economists shows that, in general, the money supply is *not* controlled with precision by the central bank. Instead, they see an endogenous money supply, which means that **the money supply is determined by economic variables *within* the economic system, especially real GDP,** expected business sales, business investment, consumer confidence, and consumer spending. What we see is that banks and the Fed generally respond to increases in the demand for money from borrowers by supplying more money.

For example, banks extend large amounts of credit to numerous businesses, and especially to the largest corporations. These lines of credit are negotiated ahead of time, so that any time a corporation needs money, for whatever purpose, it can access funds. This is similar to a consumer who has a credit card with a prearranged credit limit that allows them to *borrow funds at any time* to finance purchases.

Most important, **large loans from banks to corporations take place whether or not the bank has excess reserves**. If a corporation needs to borrow money, it writes a check (or debits its account), and the bank automatically extends the corporation a new loan to cover that check. If the bank does not have enough excess reserves to cover the new loan, as is often the case, they simply borrow the money from other banks (or other financial institutions), paying the federal funds rate of interest, which is the interest rate banks charge each other for lending reserves. If enough banks do this simultaneously, the federal funds rate may rise. However, the Fed, which usually seeks to maintain the federal funds rate at a targeted level, will then increase the supply of money to keep the federal funds rate at its target. Thus—and this is the key insight—**the money supply tends to increase whenever borrowers, as a group, demand more money to finance their purchases of investment and consumer goods**. *Banks create the money that borrowers need by crediting borrowers' accounts and borrowing any necessary reserves.* In this analysis of the money market, **the central bank sets the interest rate and the demand for money determines the amount of money supplied**, as depicted in Figure 30.6.

Banks do this because it is how they make money. Why turn down a borrower with good credit who wants to borrow more money when all the bank needs to

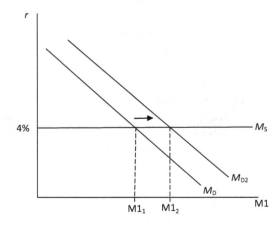

FIGURE 30.6 The political economy model of an increase in the money supply.

do is borrow a portion of the loan to cover the reserve requirements? If real GDP is expanding and there are good investment opportunities, banks will gladly create money to loan to creditworthy borrowers.

Banks also become creative in circumventing reserve requirements when it is profitable to do so. If the Fed is trying to slow down the economy by tightening credit and raising interest rates, banks can create new financial instruments that are not subject to the same level of regulation and thereby create additional funds for lending. During the housing bubble of 2006–2008, banks created new mortgage instruments, called collateralized mortgage obligations (CMOs), where they loaned money to sub-prime (bad credit) borrowers who wanted to buy homes. Banks then bundled those mortgages into large packages of loans and sold those loan packages as CMOs to banks, investors, and insurance companies, leaving CMO-creating banks with large sums of newly created money. CMOs were not subject to reserve requirements, so the amount of loans banks could create was *virtually unlimited*.

Note that the central bank still has considerable power even in the political economy model. The central bank can regulate the demand for credit by raising interest rates to slow down the economy or by lowering interest rates to stimulate it. These efforts are of necessity imprecise because, as we have seen, business investment is erratic and driven by expectations of future sales and profits. If businesses expect bad days ahead, decreases in interest rates usually have a negligible impact on investment. If the economy is booming and opportunities abound, slightly higher interest rates are unlikely to deter investors.

The political economy model of the money market also implies that the equation of exchange is wrong about several things. First, M1 is not determined by the Fed; it is determined by banks' lending opportunities. Second, inflation usually stems from rapid increases in real GDP, not increases in M1.

Another important implication is that banks are pro-cyclical accelerators. They loan out ever-increasing amounts of money when the economy is booming, dramatically expanding the money supply in response to increased borrowing requests. But, when the bottom falls out, banks curtail lending, so banks exacerbate busts by ceasing money creation. The fact that the banking system inherently destabilizes the economic system, fueling both booms and busts, is why political economists generally favor increased regulation of banks. This is very different from the view of financial markets promoted by laissez-faire economists, in which banks and financial markets are seen as so efficient and competitive that no regulations are necessary.

30.5.1 A hybrid model of the money market

If we take the insight from the mainstream model that the Fed can manipulate the money supply to some degree and add to that the political economy insight that the supply of money is endogenous but that increases in the demand for money can result in increases in interest rates, we get the graph in Figure 30.7. The Fed sets

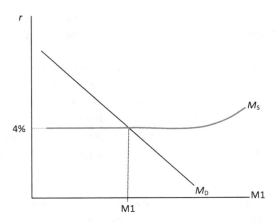

FIGURE 30.7 A hybrid model of the money market.

the interest rate based on their goals for the economy (stimulus, contraction, or stability). The money demand curve shifts based on business and consumer demand for funds, which is driven by expectations and the macroeconomic environment. Large shifts in the demand for money can cause interest rate changes. The Fed can shift the money supply, but it is not clear how large an impact that will have on business investment or consumer purchases unless they take dramatic action.

Now that we have explored the banking sector and the money market, the other key component of the financial sector is asset markets. The markets for stocks, bonds, and real estate are one of the most important components of the economy, and yet they are largely disconnected from the well-being of many workers and families.

30.6 ASSET MARKETS: STOCKS, BONDS, AND REAL ESTATE

There are six main types of assets: **cash** or checkable deposits, **stocks** (equities), **bonds** (fixed income assets), **derivatives**, **insurance**, and **real estate**. Stocks, bonds, derivatives, and other financial instruments bought and sold by financial investors are called *securities*. Purchasing securities or real estate involves a higher risk than keeping your money in cash, but returns tend to be higher on average the more risk you are willing to take, except when securities markets crash, of course. Thus, securities markets feature high-risk, high-reward options.

Securities markets are regulated by the Securities and Exchange Commission. There are extensive rules prohibiting insider trading (buying or selling stocks because you have special knowledge about a transaction or company that is not available to the public) and limiting other types of harmful behavior.

It is very important to distinguish financial investment in securities, sometimes called financial capital, from investment purchases, which are business purchases of machinery, equipment, and other capital goods. Financial capital is invested in financial markets, where it has an indirect impact on aggregate demand by impacting consumer and investor behavior. Business investment purchases are a direct and important component of aggregate demand. For most economic analysis, investment purchases are much more important than financial investment.

Stocks are **an ownership share in a company, which entitles the owner to a share of the company's earnings. Earnings are realized either through a higher stock price as a company becomes more profitable or by dividend payments to stockholders**. Stock shares for a company come into being during an initial public offering (IPO), where a company offers the opportunity for investors to buy shares of the company. IPOs serve the purpose of cashing out the founders of the company and/or raising new funds so the company can expand. After the IPO, investors buy or sell shares of previously issued stocks.

The prices of previously issued stocks tend to reflect financial investors' expectations regarding future profitability. For example, for many years Tesla and Amazon featured soaring stock prices even though they were not yet profitable, because investors had faith in their business models. Stock prices tend to fluctuate dramatically but typically have a higher average rate of return than bonds.

Corporate **bonds** are loans from the person who buys the bond to the corporation that issues the bond. Bonds pay a fixed rate of return (similar to a rate of interest) on the date that the bond matures. Bonds come with various levels of risk and various maturity dates. If an investor does not want to hold a bond until it matures, they can sell it before the maturity date.

The price of a previously issued bond is inversely related to interest rates. For example, if a corporate bond is issued guaranteeing a 5% return but interest rates fall to 3%, the corporate bond will increase in value because it is paying a higher return than other types of interest-bearing financial instruments.

Bond values are much more stable than stock prices and they come with a guaranteed return. Therefore, on average, bonds are lower risk and they pay a lower rate of return than stocks.

A derivative is **a contract between two or more economic actors where the value of the derivative is based on particular financial assets and the conditions under which those assets are exchanged**. A futures contract for wheat is a form of derivative where one party would agree to sell a certain amount of wheat to another party on a certain date in the future for a certain price. Derivatives are essentially bets and hedges.

For example, suppose the current price of a bushel of wheat is $5 per bushel but you think the price of wheat will fall to $4 per bushel in the future because there will be a bumper crop this year. To make money, you can create a derivative contract to sell 1 million bushels of wheat in the future at $5 per bushel when the next crop comes in. If you are correct and the price of wheat has fallen to $4 per bushel by the time your contract comes due, you can buy 1 million bushels of wheat for $4 per bushel in wheat markets and sell wheat to the business who agreed to pay $5 per bushel via the futures contract, thereby making $1 million. Note, however, that if you were wrong and if the price of wheat increased to $6 per bushel, you would lose $1 million. Meanwhile, the person willing to buy wheat in the future at $5 per bushel might want to enter into this contract as a hedge against risk. For example, the King Arthur Baking Company needs wheat to make its flour. Not knowing what the price of wheat will be in the future presents a large risk for their business. But, if they lock in the price of wheat at $5 per bushel, then no matter what happens to the wheat market, they know they will get the wheat they need at a price that is acceptable to them.

Derivatives are the riskiest form of financial assets. They involve making bets on futures markets that are inherently uncertain and variable.

Insurance involves **the purchase of a hedge against risk or an untimely event, where the insurer collects premium payments and provides compensation for a specified loss**. Therefore, insurance is also a financial bet. When a company sells you life insurance, they are making a bet that the premiums you pay for insurance coverage and the returns that the insurance company receives on those premiums will be greater than the payout from the insurance company when you die. Insurance companies invest heavily in stocks, bonds, and derivatives to achieve the highest return possible, so they can fall victim to the booms and busts of asset markets.

Real estate investments involve **the purchase, rental, and sale of all types of property, including land and buildings**. Real estate markets can be stable for years, but they also sometimes fluctuate wildly with interest rates and recessions. They are like any other asset in that they have an underlying value, a rate of return, and their value can fluctuate dramatically depending on market conditions.

Stocks are the most visible and important securities, so it is worth spending a little time discussing how stock markets work and what drives them. First, stocks fluctuate dramatically on a daily basis. Every day in stock markets, huge amounts of money change hands as financial investors make bets on whether or not stocks are going to go up in the short run or in the long run. Many short-run fluctuations are driven by program trading, where computer programs analyze market trends and make trades buying or selling stocks based on those trends. Value investors like Warren Buffett focus instead on the long term, investing in companies that have the best prospects for future growth.

Stocks are very hard to predict because they do not follow a systematic model. Economic analysis indicates that stock prices follow a **random walk**, such that it is virtually impossible to predict their movements. Nonetheless, there are certain metrics that can give us a general idea of whether stocks or priced correctly.

One of the best ways to determine whether stock prices are overvalued or undervalued is to look at the price-earnings (P/E) ratio, which compares a company's stock price (P) to the company's earnings (profits) per share (E):

$$\frac{P}{E} = \frac{\text{Share price}}{\text{Earnings per share}}.$$

In general, a stock with a higher P/E ratio than other stocks is expensive—it has a relatively high price and a relatively low level of profits. A low P/E ratio indicates a relatively inexpensive stock that may be a good buy. If a stock's price is $100 a share and its earnings per share are $5, its P/E ratio is 20, and it would take 20 years for an investor to get a return that was equal in value to their stock purchase.

However, there are additional complexities that go into evaluating a P/E ratio. A company that is growing rapidly may have a high P/E ratio based on investors' expectations of future profits rather than the current level of earnings. For example, in 2020 Amazon's P/E ratio was 144, when the average P/E ratio for most companies was around 20. But this does not necessarily mean that Amazon's stock was overvalued. In 2020 Amazon's sales were exploding during the COVID-19 pandemic and investors expected large future profits as Amazon's dominance of retail sales increased. Due to the limitations of P/E as a measure of the value of stocks, investors also look at dividend yields, price-to-book value ratios, and price-to-sales ratios to get a comprehensive picture of how a firm's stock is doing.

Economist Robert Shiller, who successfully predicted the internet stock crash of 2000 and the housing crash of 2007, constructed a variation of the P/E ratio called the cyclically adjusted price-to-earnings (CAPE) ratio to determine whether an asset market is overvalued, undervalued, or accurately valued. Because earnings fluctuate widely with the business cycle, CAPE takes the average of ten years of earnings (E10) and adjusts them for inflation. Current stock prices divided by average real earnings over the last decade gives us an indication of whether stocks are generally overvalued or undervalued compared to historical averages.

Figure 30.8 shows the Shiller CAPE from 1881 to 2020 for the S&P 500, which is a stock market index measuring the value of 500 large, important, and representative publicly traded U.S. companies.[6] Historically, whenever the CAPE index gets over 20 it has been as sign that returns over the next 20 years will decline. CAPEs over 30 usually are followed by steep drops.

Stock markets tend to reflect the profitability and growth prospects of publicly traded companies—those companies that have issued stock for sale to the general public and whose stocks are publicly traded on stock markets. Generally speaking, stock markets are not a good reflection of the performance of the economy as a whole. When workers are less powerful and wages are low, this can support corporate profitability and lead to high stock prices. From March 20 to July 20, 2020, in the midst of the COVID-19 pandemic of 2020, the S&P 500 stock market index increased by 46.4% while unemployment stayed stubbornly high at over 11%. Conditions for workers and communities were miserable. But the Fed injected trillions of dollars into financial markets and interest rates were at historic lows, so

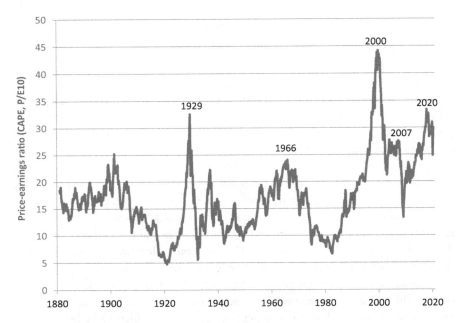

FIGURE 30.8 Shiller CAPE price–E10 ratio, 1881–2020.

money poured into stock markets and stock prices rose dramatically even as the rest of the country was suffering.

The fact that the interests of financial markets—Wall Street—are often diametrically opposed to the interests of workers and communities—Main Street—is particularly troubling given the extent to which financial markets have become an increasingly dominant force in global economies. This phenomenon has been labeled "financialization" by political economist Gerald Epstein.[7]

30.7 FINANCIALIZATION

Financialization refers to **the increasingly dominant role of financial motives, financial markets, financial actors, and financial institutions in the operation of the domestic and international economies**. The financial sector includes Financial, Insurance, and Real Estate (FIRE) markets. FIRE grew significantly in value, profits, and political power over the last five decades.

The process of financialization of the global economy began in the 1970s. Manufacturing in developed countries stagnated during this decade, so investors' money flowed increasingly into the profitable FIRE sector. The rise of FIRE was further driven by the neoliberal (laissez-faire plus supply-side) economic philosophy that swept the globe beginning with Margaret Thatcher in England in 1979 and Ronald Reagan in the United States in 1980. Neoliberal policymakers attacked unions while pushing for deregulation of financial markets, laissez-faire trade policies, tax cuts for the wealthy and for corporations, and reductions in the size of the state (austerity).

From 1969 to 2019, the FIRE sector increased in size from 14% of U.S. GDP to 21%. Over the same period, the share of corporate profits belonging to the FIRE sector increased almost twofold to 26.4%, indicating that the FIRE sector receives a disproportionately larger share of profits.

Significant income and capital gains tax cuts incentivized the nation's top earners to invest in securities, flooding financial markets with money. Maximizing shareholder value became the mantra of corporations, resulting in waves of mergers and corporate takeovers, accompanied by layoffs for workers. Financial innovations, such as the creation of complex derivatives and other forms of securitization, offered new opportunities for speculative investments. As FIRE profits surged, workers' wages stagnated and the number of jobs in manufacturing industries continued to decline.

The FIRE sector's increased size and power gave them the ability to get politicians to adopt increasingly favorable policies toward the FIRE sector. Policies liberalizing international financial flows and facilitating the use of tax havens allowed investors to move their money anywhere in the world where returns were the highest and taxes the lowest. In the United States, burgeoning trade deficits and manufacturing job losses were largely ignored in favor of policies to encourage a strong dollar and an emphasis on unregulated trade and financial flows. These policies undermined manufacturing but were extremely profitable for the FIRE sector.

The speculative core of the FIRE sector, however, led to increasingly common financial crises. These included the Savings and Loan Crisis and Latin American Debt Crisis of the 1980s, the Asian Financial Crisis of the late 1990s, the internet stock crash of 2000, and the real estate bubble and financial crisis of 2007–2008. Demonstrating the power of the FIRE sector, U.S. investment banks were bailed out during the financial crisis to the tune of more than $700 billion, while many workers lost their homes and ended up destitute and desperate. The U.S. government's willingness to bail out Wall Street while it let Main Street suffer sparked the Occupy Wall Street movement and led to an increasing number of young people rejecting the U.S. economic model.

The coronavirus pandemic exposed additional weaknesses of the neoliberal model and its emphasis on the FIRE sector. The underfunding of public health systems left many countries unable to cope with the pandemic. In the United States, however, Wall Street continued to receive the bulk of bailouts, while workers, communities, hospitals, and public health systems continued to struggle. Thus, in 2020 the FIRE sector seemed to be as dominant as ever in the United States.

Political economists are very critical of financialization, arguing that it has reshaped the world in favor of financial corporations and against workers. Political economists advocate policies to reign in the FIRE sector, taxing financial transactions and the wealthy, re-imposing capital controls to limit global speculative behavior and tax havens, and enacting policies that benefit workers and communities and protect them from the destabilizing tendencies of the FIRE sector.

Laissez-faire and supply-side economists, who were the architects of the neoliberal policies that fostered the rise of the FIRE sector, continue to see financial markets as dynamic and essential to modern capitalism and deregulation as a benefit to economic growth. The growth of the FIRE sector is, from this perspective, a natural result of markets pursuing efficiency and the maximum possible economic growth.

New Keynesian economists strive for a middle path, with increased regulation of the FIRE sector that will preserve its essential characteristics while reigning in its excesses. After the financial crisis, New Keynesian economists advocated significant regulations on banking and derivatives markets, while proposing that the core of the FIRE sector be left unchanged. We will explore these debates further in the next two chapters.

30.8 CONCLUSION

Money, banking, and financial markets are very important in modern economic systems. How they work is often unclear to most people, so this chapter attempted to describe the essential features of money, banking, and financial markets.

Money is a unit of account that forms a crucial component of modern economic systems. Money is created by governments so they can provision themselves. Money gives governments the ability to tax their citizens in their own currency and to spend money on the goods and services the government needs in order to function. A nation that has a sovereign currency controls the supply of its own money.

Modern economies use fiat money, rather than commodity money or the gold standard, so that the government has greater control over the money supply. This allows the government to increase the supply of money to foster economic growth or in the case of a banking crisis.

Banks make money by making loans to borrowers and charging interest on those loans. The money for bank loans comes from depositors or from borrowed reserves. Banks create money via the money multiplier, whereby the same deposit is loaned out again and again by one bank after another, albeit in ever-decreasing amounts.

Mainstream economists use a model of the money market to try to anticipate the factors that will cause interest rates to rise or fall. In the mainstream New Keynesian model, the money supply curve is vertical and determined by the central bank, so the money supply is viewed as exogenous—determined by factors external to the economy (the central bank decision-making process). The money demand curve is downward sloping and becomes flat as it nears 0% interest to reflect a liquidity trap. A liquidity trap occurs when interest rates cannot fall further and investors prefer to hold cash rather than to invest in low-return bonds or risky stocks. In a liquidity trap situation, monetary stimulus is usually ineffective.

In the political economy model of the money market, the money supply curve is flat, with interest rates set by the central bank. The money demand curve is steep. The quantity of money in the economy is determined by the demand curve for money, because banks can always borrow reserves if people want to borrow and spend more money than usual. This makes the money supply endogenous—determined by the level of economic activity and the demand for loanable funds.

In addition to banks, securities markets for stocks, bonds, and derivatives and real estate markets play an important role in the economic system. The Finance, Insurance, and Real Estate (FIRE) sector comes with higher levels of risk but pays a higher level of return in exchange for that risk. Stock markets form regular bubbles that burst, often dragging the rest of the economy into a recession when that happens. The Shiller CAPE index in one good measure of when a stock market is in a bubble situation.

The FIRE sector became increasingly dominant over the last 50 years with the advent of neoliberal policies—a process called financialization. Political economists see financialization as problematic because it involves society's resources being increasingly captured by the wealthy individuals and corporations who control the FIRE sector. Laissez-faire and supply-side economists prefer the deregulatory, low-tax environment that gave rise to financialization. New Keynesian economists prefer more regulation of the FIRE sector than laissez-faire economists but less than the amount advocated by political economists. The next two chapters explore financial regulation and financial crises in more detail.

QUESTIONS FOR REVIEW

1. Explain why the gold standard and commodity money fell out of fashion and why modern economists prefer fiat money.
2. Why will a government-issued form of money always be safer to hold than a cryptocurrency such as Bitcoin?
3. How is the money multiplier related to the required reserve ratio? Explain briefly. What factors would cause the money multiplier to be larger? What factors would cause the money multiplier to be smaller?
4. Explain why banks rarely hold excess reserves. What might prompt a bank to hold excess reserves?
5. Why do economists consider the interest rate to be the opportunity cost of holding your money as cash?
6. Explain the slope of the money demand curve in the mainstream model of the money market. Why is it downward sloping? Why does it get flatter as interest rates approach 0%?

7. How would each of the following factors affect the money market according to mainstream economists?
   a. A major recession causes real GDP to fall significantly.
   b. Inflation occurs due to an increase in oil and other energy prices.
   c. Investors expect a major economic boom.
   d. The central bank decreases the amount of money in circulation.
8. What are the main differences between the mainstream model of the money market and the political economy model of the money market? Why does it matter if the money supply is exogenous or endogenous?
9. According to the political economy theory of endogenous money, which of the following are true (select one or more options)?
   a. The Fed determines the money supply.
   b. The Fed sets the rate of interest.
   c. Money demand determines the rate of interest.
   d. Banks create money by making new loans and later finding the reserves they need.
   e. Banks can only create money out of excess reserves.
   f. The money supply is determined by the demand for money from businesses and households.
   g. The money supply is determined by the Fed.
   h. Banks need to be carefully regulated.
   i. Financial markets are so efficient that banks do not need to be regulated.
10. In your own words, define the term "financialization." Why do political economists see financialization as a problem? Why do laissez-faire and supply-side economists disagree?

NOTES

1 David Graeber, *Debt: The First 5000 Years* (Melville House, Brooklyn, NY), 2011.

2 L. Randall Wray, "Introduction to an Alternative History of Money." Levy Economics Institute of Bard College, Working Paper No. 717, May 2012. http://www.levyinstitute.org/publications/introduction-to-an-alternative-history-of-money, accessed August 6, 2021.

3 Source: Wikimedia commons, public domain files. See: https://commons.wikimedia.org/wiki/File:Carved_reindeer_antler_with_tally_marks_(4697848661).jpg   and https://commons.wikimedia.org/wiki/File:Chinese_cash_coins_b.jpg.

4 See Matthew Obrien, "Why the Gold Standard Is the World's Worst Economic Idea, in 2 Charts," *The Atlantic*, August 26, 2012.

5 Section 30.5 draws heavily on James K. Galbraith and William Darity Jr., *Macroeconomics* (VSSD, Delft, The Netherlands, 2005), as well as various works by L. Randall Wray.

6 Source: Robert Shiller, "Online Data Robert Shiller," http://www.econ.yale.edu/~shiller/data.htm, accessed January 31, 2021. The S&P 500 is considered to be a very good indicator of the stock values of the largest corporations in the U.S.

7 Spandan Marasini did some of the research and writing for section 30.7.

Monetary policy

The role of central banks in stabilizing economies and regulating financial markets

When the economy falls apart, the first place people turn is to central banks, institutions that can use monetary policy quickly to try to stabilize the economy. Central bankers are the first responders in an economic crisis, able to take dramatic action as soon as an economy experiences a crisis. However, as we will see, the ability of central banks to stabilize an economy in a major crisis is limited, so monetary policy often must be combined with fiscal policy.

The appropriate role for monetary policy is an area of significant debate and disagreement among economists. The mainstream New Keynesian view is that the central bank can and should use monetary policy to stabilize the economy. In a recession, the central bank should increase the money supply, lower interest rates, and, in the case of a liquidity trap, implement quantitative easing. This should help to avoid a potentially ruinous deflation and to jump-start economic growth. In an overheated economy, monetary policy should be used to slow down the economy to prevent a bust and to engineer a soft landing.

Laissez-faire economists want less government intervention in money markets. They see central bank intervention as destructive, especially given policy lags, and prefer to have the establishment of a monetary rule whereby the government allows the money supply to grow at a fixed rate each year.

Political economists, and especially modern monetary theory (MMT) adherents, want more central bank intervention and regulation. They argue that the central bank should increase the money supply until there are clear, definite signs of inflation. They are much more concerned with unemployment than inflation, so they encourage the use of monetary stimulus to foster growth and reduce unemployment until the economy reaches its maximum capacity.

Supply-side economists see low interest rates as a policy with clear benefits for suppliers. In recent years they agreed with political economists that substantial

DOI: 10.4324/9781315636924-40

monetary stimulus was warranted to encourage economic growth even when the economy was booming.

The regulatory landscape in an economy is also important. Some economies, like the United States and the United Kingdom, feature freewheeling financial markets with few restrictions in which investment banks and other financial entities are free to create new financial instruments and engage in risky speculation. Other economies, such as China, feature a very constrained financial system featuring significant state control. As is usually the case, social democracies fall in between the market-dominated approach and the state-dominated approach, offering financial markets that are more contained than those in the United States but much freer than those in China.

This chapter begins by describing how the regulation of the banking sector and financial markets has evolved in the United States. Next, the chapter lays out the five policy tools that the Fed can use to change the money supply and interest rates. Fed policy changes have an impact on aggregate demand, aggregate supply, and real gross domestic product (GDP), although as we will see, the impact of contractionary monetary policy is much greater than the impact of expansionary monetary policy. The chapter concludes by taking up two controversial areas of monetary policy: The debate over the nonaccelerating inflation rate of unemployment theory and the debate over the connection between expansion of the money supply and inflation.

31.0 CHAPTER 31 LEARNING GOALS

After reading this chapter, you should be able to:

- Describe the regulatory landscape of U.S. banking and financial markets.

- List, explain, and analyze the impact of the U.S. Federal Reserve Bank policy tools.

- Use graphs of the money market and aggregate demand and aggregate supply to analyze the impact of different monetary policies.

- Explain the theory and debate over the nonaccelerating inflation rate of unemployment.

- Summarize and critically evaluate the views of laissez-faire, New Keynesian, supply-side, and political economists on expansionary monetary policy and its relationship with inflation.

31.1 THE REGULATORY LANDSCAPE OF U.S. FINANCIAL MARKETS

The central bank of a country is one of the most important economic institutions. It is often said that, after the head of state, the head of the central bank is the next most important government official in terms of their impact on the economy.

The U.S. banking system evolved in fits and starts after independence from England in 1776. There were several attempts at creating a central bank, but these ended in failure, often because the central bank was undermined by state banks. From 1837 to 1863, bank charters were easy to obtain and many private banks were created, issuing their own currency (banknotes) backed by gold and silver. Reserve requirements and interest rates for state banks were set by state governments. However, regular banking panics led to the National Banking Acts of 1863 and 1864, which established a national currency backed by gold and authorized a newly created Department of the Treasury to regulate nationally chartered banks.

Throughout the 1800s, the gold standard continued to cause destabilizing fluctuations in the economy, slowing growth when too little gold was available but fueling inflation when new discoveries of deposits or new technologies to improve extraction increased the supply of gold. During the late 1800s and early 1900s, the banking industry consolidated under the influence of a few huge investment banks, led by J.P. Morgan and Company. These banks controlled a majority of the nation's wealth, and they were able to use their power to gain control over the major industries of the era, leading to even more consolidation of wealth.

Outraged by the dominance and exploitation of a handful of wealthy bank owners and industrialists, the regular banking panics, and the open corruption of politicians of the era, members of the Progressive Movement organized in resistance and demanded substantive change. The Federal Reserve Act of 1913 established a new national central bank that would manage the currency and that could serve as the lender of last resort during a banking liquidity crisis. The first U.S. dollar was printed in 1914. The Federal Reserve Act also established the Federal Reserve banking system to regulate banks in each region of the United States.

Political pressure also resulted in the ratification of the 16th Amendment to the U.S. Constitution in 1913 allowing the income tax. This was important in creating demand for dollars. All citizens now needed U.S. dollars to pay their taxes, so the dollar replaced banknotes and gold as the standard currency. The passage of the Clayton Antitrust Act of 1914 reduced the power of heavily concentrated industries, fostering competition in banking, steel, and other key industries.

The Federal Reserve system was refined significantly during the Great Depression, allowing the Fed to engage in emergency support of banking and establishing the deposit insurance system to restore depositors' faith in banks. To reduce the negative impact of speculative behavior on the banking system, the

Glass–Steagall Act separated commercial (safe) banking from investment (risky) banking. Commercial banking was insured by the government, whereas investment banking was not.

After World War II, the Bretton Woods system of international monetary management was established. The system included the creation of the International Monetary Fund (IMF) and the World Bank to promote stability in countries that face a crisis but do not have the resources to cope with the crises themselves. Bretton Woods also established a foreign exchange convertibility system whereby all currencies would be convertible into U.S. dollars, and the dollar became the world's reserve currency. As we will see later, serving as the world's reserve currency has meant that people, firms, and governments around the world like to hold dollars, which has increased the value of the dollar in foreign exchange markets above levels where it would normally trade. This is one of the factors contributing to chronic U.S. trade deficits.

With the advent of neoliberal economic philosophy and policy in the United States beginning around 1980 under President Reagan, the banking sector in the United States was deregulated to a significant degree. Instead of being restricted to small business loans and home mortgages, savings and loan banks were allowed to merge with commercial banks and to make loans for speculative purposes. To increase their profits, savings and loans engaged in real estate speculation and loaned money to governments in developing countries that paid high interest rates. However, many real estate investments collapsed, and several large Latin American governments were unable to make their debt payments. Following the first wave of banking deregulation in the United States, more than 23% of savings and loan banks failed, and they had to be bailed out by the government to prevent a wider shock to the economy.

In 1999 the Glass–Steagall Act was repealed and investment banks were allowed to gain control over commercial banks and savings and loans. A huge wave of mergers and acquisitions ensued, as Wall Street firms snapped up smaller banks to expand their opportunities. This set the stage for the massive real estate and derivative speculation of the 2000s, which culminated in the financial crisis of 2007–2008 and that required another government bailout. We will study the financial crisis in more detail in the next chapter.

A modicum of regulation was reinstated with the Dodd–Frank Wall Street Reform and Consumer Protection Act of 2010. Dodd–Frank increased Fed oversight of banks and required large banks to demonstrate that they were behaving responsibly and not in a manner that was likely to require future bailouts. However, much of Dodd–Frank was repealed under the Trump administration's return to neoliberal policies, which left the U.S. banking system in a relatively deregulated state as of 2020. It will be interesting to see whether the latest round of deregulation follows the same pattern and contributes to another bout of speculation, bank failures, and bailouts. The main overseer of the banking system in the United States is the Fed.

The Federal Reserve Bank or "Fed" is the central bank of the United States. It is an independent institution that does not have to answer directly to politicians. The chair of the Fed and the members of the Federal Reserve Bank Board of Governors are nominated by the President and approved by the Senate. Once approved, the Fed can act with complete autonomy, although it may sometimes react to pressure from government officials or businesses. This structure is designed to give the Fed the ability to resist political pressure and to act as it sees fit with respect to monetary policy.

Central bank independence can prevent bad economic policies from being enacted for political ends. For example, politicians who are in power prefer to have the central bank keep interest rates low in order to stimulate growth and fuel their re-election prospects. President Trump frequently called on the Fed to lower interest rates when the economy was booming in 2018 and 2019. The Fed, however, was worried about inflationary pressures at the time and resisted Trump's calls for lower interest rates.

Central banks in most developed countries are independent from political influence, including the European Central Bank, the Bank of England, and the Bank of Japan. In these countries, it is not uncommon for central banks to undertake actions that politicians dislike. However, in other countries, including China, Russia, and a host of developing countries, the central bank is controlled directly or indirectly by government officials. In these countries, central bank actions are an extension of the state's goals and priorities and the political interests of those in power.

In the modern era, central banks are tasked with crucial but potentially conflicting macroeconomic goals: Minimizing unemployment and promoting economic growth while preserving price stability. Federal Law established the **U.S. Fed's goals** as **maximum employment, stable prices, and moderate long-term interest rates**. The European Central Bank, on the other hand, is only tasked with maintaining stable prices. The issue of the appropriate focus of the central bank in terms of employment and inflation is complex and controversial, as we will see later.

Next, we turn to the tools the Fed has at its disposal to affect the economy. Understanding *how* the central bank does its work will help you anticipate how changes in central bank policy will affect interest rates, financial markets, and you!

31.2 THE FED'S FIVE POLICY TOOLS

The U.S. Fed has five policy tools that it can use to affect interest rates. (Other central banks have a similar toolbox.) These policy tools are open market operations, changes to the discount rate, changes to the federal funds rate, changing the required reserve ratio or the interest rates on banks' excess reserves, and quantitative easing or tightening. We explain each of these tools below.

Open market operations, the first Fed policy tool, involve **the purchase or sale of government securities (bonds)**.

An open market purchase is a **central bank (Fed) purchase of government bonds from the public**. The Fed offers to buy bonds for slightly above market value, which makes individuals want to sell more bonds than they usually would. When individuals accept the Fed's offer, the Fed takes in people's bonds and credits their accounts with cash. Thus, **the impact of an open market purchase is to increase the amount of money people have in their bank accounts**. As people's accounts increase in size, banks experience an increase in excess reserves that they can lend out. Therefore, the money supply increases by the amount of the Fed purchases of bonds multiplied by the money multiplier. According to the mainstream economics model of the money market, an increase in the money supply causes interest rates to fall, and this will lead to increases in business investment purchases and consumer durable purchases, increasing aggregate demand and stimulating the economy.

An open market sale does the opposite. An open market sale is **a central bank (Fed) sale of government bonds to the public**. The Fed offers buyers an attractive rate of return, usually slightly above the going rate of return, to encourage people to buy bonds. Once the sale is accepted, the Fed gives the public bonds but takes money from the accounts of the public as payment for the bonds. This leaves the public with more bonds but less cash. **The impact of an open market sale is therefore to decrease the amount of money people have in their bank accounts.** This decreases banks' reserves, decreasing the money supply, causing interest rates to increase, and spurring reductions in business investment and consumer durable purchases. The reduction in investment and consumer spending would, in turn, decrease aggregate demand and slow the economy.

The discount rate, the second Fed policy tool (also called the primary credit rate) is **the rate of interest the Fed charges banks to borrow reserves**. Recall that the Fed is the lender of last resort. Banks who want to lend out more money can always borrow reserves from the Fed, but they have to pay the Fed interest on what they borrow. If the Fed wants to increase the money supply, it can lower the discount rate. This means banks can borrow reserves more cheaply, which means that it is more profitable for banks to make loans. To decrease the money supply, the Fed can raise the discount rate. This discourages bank lending by making it more expensive for banks to obtain the reserves they need to make loans.

The federal funds rate is the third Fed policy tool and **is the rate of interest banks charge each other on extremely short-term loans (often overnight), and it is controlled indirectly by the Fed**. Though the Fed does not set this interest rate, the Fed manipulates it via open market operations. By increasing the amount of money in banks via open market purchases, the Fed can drive down the federal funds rate. Open market sales will reduce the amount of money in banks and increase the federal funds rate. The federal funds rate is very important because it is a key determinant of whether or not it is profitable for banks to borrow to create new loans.

Figure 31.1 shows the effective federal funds rate and the discount rate from 2004 to 2020. The Fed sets a target interest rate range for the federal funds rate and then it engages in open market purchases or sales of bonds until it achieves the "effective" federal funds rate within the range it is targeting. The Fed sets the discount rate about 1% higher than the federal funds rate. The prime interest rate is **the rate of interest private banks charge their best customers—the biggest corporations with the most collateral and the most secure financial situation**. The prime rate of interest clearly moves with the federal funds rate, averaging 3.09% higher since 2004. Thus, it is clear that *the Fed is the primary force determining interest rates in the U.S. economy.*

Figure 31.1 shows the Fed engaging in contractionary monetary policy from 2004 to 2006 and from 2016 to 2019, when it raised the federal funds rate and the discount rate when the economy was overheated to slow down the economy. From 2007 to 2009 and in 2020, the Fed lowered the federal funds rate and the discount rate significantly to stimulate the economy in the face of serious recessions.

The fourth Fed policy tool, changing the required reserve ratio, also has a dramatic influence on the money supply and interest rates. Decreasing the required reserve ratio allows banks to loan out more of their reserves and increases the size of the money multiplier. To stimulate borrowing in the COVID-19 recession of 2020, the Fed lowered the reserve requirement to 0%, allowing banks to loan out a lot more money if they wanted to. Increasing the required reserve ratio reduces the amount banks can loan out and reduces the size of the money multiplier, decreasing the money supply.

The Fed can also manipulate banks' reserves by **changing the interest rate the Fed pays to banks who hold excess reserves**. If the Fed wants banks to hold fewer excess reserves, it can reduce the interest rate it pays. If the Fed wants banks to hold more excess reserves, it can increase the interest rate it pays on banks' excess reserves.

The Fed's fifth policy tool is a relatively new one, quantitative easing or tightening. Quantitative easing (QE) occurs **when the Fed purchases bonds or other assets from banks and businesses**. QE was used for the first time in the U.S. after the financial crisis of 2007–2008. The Fed makes these purchases with new money that is injected into the banking system at a time when banks would normally be saddled with bad loans that would require banks to scale back on lending and devote resources to covering losses. New money then swells the size of the bank reserves in the economy equal to the quantity of assets purchased. Banks take the new money and buy assets to replace the ones they sold to the central bank. This leads to an increase in stock prices and lowered interest rates, which in turn may help to boost businesses' investment purchases. Buying "toxic" assets can be extremely helpful to troubled banks given that banks could not sell such assets on the open market because there is no demand for them.

Figure 31.2 shows that the Fed began to conduct significant quantitative easing in late 2008, buying more than $1 trillion in assets. As the financial crisis deepened,

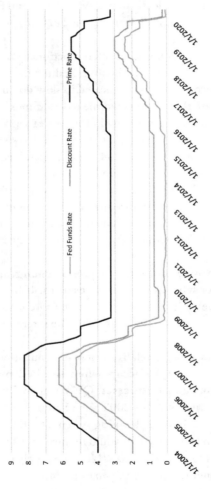

FIGURE 31.1 Effective federal funds rate and primary credit (discount) rate (%), 2004–2020.

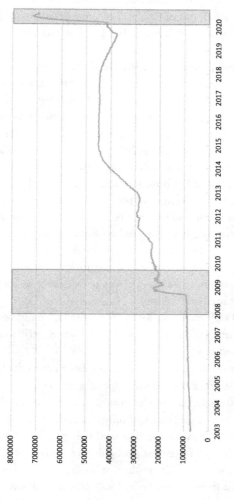

FIGURE 31.2 Total assets held by the Fed (in millions of dollars), 2003–2020.

the Fed continued with its QE asset purchases, until it accumulated $4.5 trillion by 2014.

The opposite of quantitative easing is quantitative tightening, which occurs **when the Fed sells bonds and assets from its portfolio back to investors**. Figure 31.2 shows that the Fed began selling some of the assets it had accumulated, also called "unwinding," in 2018.

Statistical evidence from the Fed indicates that the QE asset purchases after the financial crisis probably reduced the U.S. unemployment rate by 1.5% and increased real GDP by 3%. Bank of England economists estimate that the first €200 billion QE purchases caused a 3% cut in the interest rate and raised Britain's real GDP by 2%.

There are also some potential dangers from QE. Pushing interest rates to 0% could make it hard to rein in inflation in the future. Low interest rates could prompt the government to borrow too much and investors to take on risky investments. However, economists worry more about deflation and low levels of investment than inflation and excessive borrowing in an economic crisis.

Furthermore, *QE is the only major policy option that the Fed can use if the economy is in a liquidity trap*. Recall that in a liquidity trap, interest rates have fallen to near 0% and investors hold cash instead of buying bonds or putting their money in interest-bearing accounts because the return is too low to justify tying your money up. Additional increases in the money supply have no effect on the economy: Interest rates cannot drop further and investors and consumers are too pessimistic to spend money. With increases in the money supply ineffective, the only expansionary monetary policy option that can work is quantitative easing. Fed purchases of assets, especially toxic ones, cause asset prices to increase, restoring confidence in asset markets and the broader economy.

When the COVID-19 recession hit in 2020, the Fed embarked on a significant monetary stimulus using QE, purchasing more than $3 trillion from banks and other financial intermediaries.

Many of the QE purchases amount to bailouts of banks for bad decisions they made. As we will see later, banks made a lot of very bad, very risky investments in the sub-prime housing market in the 2000s, which sparked the financial crisis. Despite the fact that banks exercised bad judgment, the Fed felt compelled to bail out the banking sector to prevent the financial collapse from spiraling into a full-on depression. Though this move was probably necessary from a macroeconomic standpoint, it did not sit well with workers who lost jobs in the Great Recession but who did not benefit from a massive bailout. When bank executives went ahead and awarded themselves huge bonuses in the midst of the Fed bailout, it sparked an outcry that culminated in the Occupy Wall Street movement in 2011.

Next, we go into how Fed policy works in theory using the mainstream model of the money market and the aggregate demand and aggregate supply model developed earlier. However, as we will discuss later, the reality is often different from the theory when it comes to monetary policy.

31.3 USING MODELS TO ANALYZE HOW MONETARY POLICY AFFECTS THE ECONOMY

Figures 31.3(a) and 31.3(b) depict the mainstream model of the money market and the aggregate demand and aggregate supply model, respectively. Point **a** in Figure 31.3(b) shows the economy deep in a recession, with a $3 trillion recessionary gap. To eliminate the recession, the Fed needs to enact policies that will cause the aggregate demand curve to shift from AD_1 to AD_2, which is a $4 trillion difference measuring horizontally along the price line. If the marginal respending rate is 0.5, which would make the multiplier equal to $\frac{1}{1-0.5} = 2$, the Fed needs to enact policies that will cause an initial increase in aggregate demand of $2 trillion, which will cause a total change in aggregate demand of $4 trillion after the multiplier effect plays out.

The Fed's uses its key policy tools to control the money supply and interest rates. To increase the money supply and reduce interest rates, the Fed can conduct an open market purchase of bonds, reduce the discount rate and the target federal funds rate, reduce reserve requirements, and engage in quantitative easing. If the Fed does enough of this, it can lower interest rates significantly. In Figure 31.3(a), the Fed increases the money supply from M_{S1} to M_{S2}, which causes interest rates to decrease from 3% to 1%.

This significant decrease in interest rates will cause businesses to increase their investment purchases and consumers to increase their durable goods purchases, increasing aggregate demand. Lowering interest rates significantly also makes it more profitable for financial investors to put their money into the stock market,

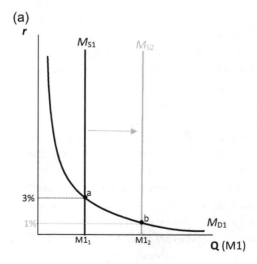

(a)

FIGURE 31.3 (a) An increase in money supply.

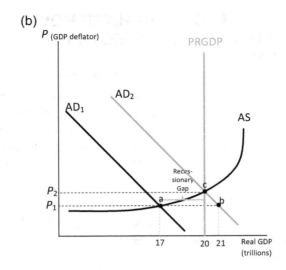

(b)

FIGURE 31.3 (b) The goal of expansionary monetary policy.

because the return on money market accounts and bonds is so low. Therefore, the decrease in interest rates would also improve stock market values. If the Fed undertakes enough monetary stimulus, it might be able to increase aggregate demand by the amount that is needed.

Unfortunately, the real world does not always respond in the hoped-for manner. Monetary policy tends to have limited effectiveness in recessions. Since the Great Depression, economists have known that monetary policy can easily pull back the economy via contractionary monetary policy, but using monetary policy to cause the economy to expand in a recession is like **"pushing on a string."**

There are a number of reasons why expansionary monetary policy is often ineffective in recessions. First, liquidity traps occur when the Fed lowers interest rates to near 0%. After that point, further increases in the money supply have no effect on interest rates or aggregate demand. Second, consumer confidence plummets in recessions due to layoffs and wage freezes. Consumer spending declines and consumer saving increases. Increasing the money supply in such an environment does not tend to encourage additional consumer spending. Third, business confidence also declines in recessions, which reduces business investment purchases. Few businesses want to expand the size of their operations when sales are falling, even if interest rates are low. Thus, *there is often very little change in aggregate demand from expansionary monetary policies in deep recessions.*

This is why truly effective stabilization policy in recessions involves a combination of expansionary fiscal policy *and* expansionary monetary policy. If the Fed makes sure interest rates are as low as possible, and if the government increases spending on infrastructure and other items that stimulate job growth and business expansion, then consumers and businesses may start to spend again. This is known as "priming the pump."

Monetary policy is effective at slowing the economy. If the central bank raises interest rates high enough, it will strangle business investment purchases and consumer durable goods purchases, decreasing aggregate demand. The Fed played a significant role in the recessions of 1982, 1990, 2000, and 2007 by engaging in contractionary monetary policy, raising interest rates, and decreasing the money supply. The Fed always hopes to effect a "soft landing," where aggregate demand decreases slightly and returns to potential real GDP, where the economy settles. However, once an economy experiences a decline in aggregate demand, the layoffs and financial market declines that follow tend to undermine consumer and investor confidence. This sparks additional rounds of decreased spending and sends the economy into a recession.

We now know the different types of policies the Fed can use to affect the money supply, interest rates, aggregate demand, and real GDP. However, choosing which policy to apply and how large the stimulus or contraction should be is a complicated decision that is driven by the theoretical framework being used by policymakers. As is so often the case, economists do not agree on the best theoretical approach to monetary policy.

31.4 THE DEBATE OVER THE NAIRU THEORY

In Chapter 27 we discussed the concept of the natural rate of unemployment. This idea was related to the Phillips curve, which posited an inverse relationship between inflation and unemployment. In the United States in the 1960s, there seemed to be a clear, inverse relationship.

Drawing on this information, Milton Friedman and a group of laissez-fare economists developed the nonaccelerating inflation rate of unemployment (NAIRU) theory. According to the NAIRU theory, **when the unemployment rate falls below the natural rate of unemployment** (the normal rate of unemployment when the economy is not in a recession), **inflation is expected to increase and perhaps to accelerate** (increase at an increasing rate). Once inflation got started, the theory was that it would accelerate because of a wage–price spiral and changing inflationary expectations. When inflation occurred, workers would demand higher wages to maintain their purchasing power and businesses would raise prices because they expected costs to increase. This would cause another round of inflation and another round of wage demands and price increases. In essence, the rate of unemployment that prevents inflation, the NAIRU, is the natural rate of unemployment. Similarly, **when the unemployment rate goes above the natural rate of unemployment, inflation is expected to fall**.

Economists estimate that the natural rate of unemployment ranged between 4.5% and 6% in the United States in recent decades. The NAIRU theory was used by laissez-faire economists to argue against the utilization of government spending to stimulate the economy, arguing that it would eventually result in inflation.

Furthermore, whenever the unemployment rate dropped below 6%, economists subscribing to the NAIRU theory would argue in favor of contractionary monetary policy to eliminate inflationary pressures.

However, in the last three decades, there is no clear relationship between inflation and unemployment in the United States. During the 1990s, 2000s, and 2010s, booms resulted in unemployment rates significantly below the natural rate of unemployment, yet there was no significant increase in inflation during these episodes. Thus, most New Keynesian economists are skeptical that the government must adhere strictly to the natural rate of unemployment idea.

Nonetheless, most New Keynesian economists believe there is some level of unemployment that would trigger inflation, so the underlying core idea of the NAIRU theory is still widely believed. As Paul Krugman argued,

> A market economy ... requires that a certain number of people who want to work be unable to find jobs so that their example will discipline the wage demands of those who are already employed. Even liberal economists like myself grudgingly accept the conclusion that a responsible Fed must sometimes raise interest rates in order to limit the number of jobs and maintain a suitably high rate of unemployment.[1]

The debate is over how low the level of unemployment would need to drop before generating inflation. In 2019 the U.S. unemployment rate dropped to 3.5% without significant inflation. The natural rate of unemployment may have fallen dramatically as globalization and the decline of unions undermined the ability of workers to demand higher wages and the ability of firms to raise prices.

The idea that we need to maintain a high rate of unemployment to contain prices is unacceptable to political economists. The NAIRU theory has been deeply destructive as well as inaccurate according to this perspective. As Stephanie Kelton wrote,

> This underlying faith in the idea that there's some inescapable constraint on the economy's employment potential ... caused the Fed to systematically underestimate the extent to which the unemployment rate could safely fall. This misreading drove the Fed to raise interest rates in the hope of choking off a further drop in unemployment, essentially aiming to deny millions of underemployed and unemployed people access to jobs on the belief that the NAIRU limit had already been reached.[2]

Many countries have reduced the unemployment rate to below 2% without facing inflationary pressures. Wage and price controls can be used to limit inflation to get the unemployment rate even lower without generating inflationary pressures. Thus, there is no reason that a government cannot pursue true full employment, where everyone who wants to work has a job.

From the political economy perspective, the government should continue to create jobs, spend money, and increase the money supply until inflation actually occurs, rather than decreasing the money supply just because we think that inflation might happen. Thus, instead of the current practice of maintaining a relatively high rate of unemployment to keep inflation low, *political economists want to reduce unemployment until there are concrete signs of inflation*. Political economists see the NAIRU theory as beneficial to employers because it maintains a level of unemployment that keeps wages low and profits high, but this comes at a direct cost to workers.

Most central banks follow the NAIRU/New Keynesian approach, raising interest rates if the unemployment rate drops significantly below the natural rate of unemployment. When the unemployment rate in the United States dropped below 5% in 2015, the Fed began nudging up interest rates, and it increased them steadily for the next four years as the unemployment rate fell further. Subsequently, the Fed lowered interest rates as fragile conditions emerged in 2019, and the Fed decreased interest rates to 0% when the COVID-19 recession hit in 2020.

Another related area of debate is regarding the relationship between monetary policy and inflation. Here again, the theoretical background adopted by the Fed chair will drive their selection of policies.

31.5 THE DEBATE OVER EXPANSIONARY MONETARY POLICY AND INFLATION: HAWKS, DOVES, AND OWLS

There are three major perspectives on how the Fed should manage the money supply to deal with recessions. Economists from the **laissez-faire** perspective do not want to Fed to engage in activist management of the money supply. They tend to be aggressive "**hawks**" on inflation, opposing dramatic efforts to stimulate the economy in recessions due to worries about inflation and advocating austerity to control inflationary pressures. "**Doves**" are **New Keynesian** economists and many **supply-side** economists who support extensive monetary stimulus policies in recessions, including quantitative easing. However, there are limits to how far doves want to go with monetary stimulus. Lastly, **political economists**, especially modern monetary theory economists, want even more extensive stimulus policies. They advocate increasing monetary stimulus significantly while carefully monitoring the economy for signs of inflation, which involves a more detailed and complex macroeconomic management approach. Here, you might think of an "**owl**," keenly observing the situation and adjusting if it sees signs of trouble. We go into each group in more detail below.

Inflation hawks are opposed to significant monetary stimulus in recessions due to worries about inflation. The hawk moniker is intended to signify a very aggressive stance with respect to fighting inflation. The group most against central bank monetary stimulus is the strand of laissez-faire economics called monetarism, founded by Milton Friedman. As with other laissez-faire strands, monetarists believe in the efficiency and self-adjusting properties of unregulated markets and oppose government intervention utilizing monetary policy. Therefore, laissez-faire advocates do not want stabilization policies to be enacted by the central bank.

In addition to subscribing to the NAIRU theory (see above), Friedman opposed expansionary fiscal policy in recessions because he thought private sector investment would be crowded out. (See the debate on this topic in the chapter on fiscal policy.) He also opposed expansionary monetary policy in recessions because of **policy lags**. To Friedman, the central bank takes time to realize there is a recession and then it must meet to decide on a policy. Once the central bank implements a policy, it takes the policy time to affect the economy. Friedman's research showed that it could take up to 18 months for monetary policy to affect the economy. By then, the recession might already be over.

Instead, in the realm of monetary policy Milton Friedman argued for a **monetary rule**, whereby the Fed would set money supply growth just above the expected rate of growth in real GDP. If real GDP was expected to grow by 2%, the money supply would be allowed to grow by 3%. This would allow enough increase in the money supply for economic growth to occur but not enough to generate significant inflation. Recall the equation of exchange:

$$\text{M1} \times \text{Velocity} = P \times \text{Real GDP}.$$

The second component of Friedman's analysis was the quantity theory of money: **If we assume that velocity is constant, that real GDP cannot be influenced by M1, and that money can influence prices but not vice versa, then** Friedman's famous dictum that **inflation is always caused by too much money** will hold.

For example, if velocity is fixed, a 3% increase in M1 with a 2% rate of growth in real GDP would keep inflation to 1%. However, if they Fed engages in significant monetary stimulus, allowing the money supply to grow by 10%, then with 2% real GDP growth this action would generate 8% inflation.

The monetary rule Friedman proposed would prevent the Fed from actively intervening to stabilize the economy. With this approach, the Fed would be more concerned with fighting inflation—a hawkish approach—than with reducing the unemployment that accompanied a recession.

History has not been kind to the laissez-faire, hawkish approach to monetary policy. As we saw in Chapter 27, there is no systematic correlation between the money supply (M1) and inflation as predicted by the quantity theory of money. As we saw in Chapter 29, austerity policies in Europe, which included less monetary stimulus than in the United States, slowed economic growth in the E.U. relative to the United States. Thus, central bankers in most countries, even those with conservative political leanings, have dismissed the most strident views of inflation hawks. Instead of targeting the money supply, as Friedman advocated, *central banks now target the interest rate* and worry about maintaining enough growth in recessions.

Most mainstream economists from the **New Keynesian** perspective qualify as inflation **doves**, in that they are comfortable with substantial monetary stimulus in recessions. They are more concerned with generating employment and avoiding deflation than they are with inflation when the economy enters a downturn.

New Keynesians point out that M1 is only one influence on nominal GDP and other factors are far more important. Factors influencing business investment and consumer confidence are particularly crucial in a recession. Increasing the money supply, lowering interest rates to 0%, and purchasing toxic assets can all play a role in propping up financial markets and improving business and consumer confidence. Therefore, the monetarist assumption that M1 cannot affect real GDP is incorrect.

Furthermore, the crowding out of private investment from government borrowing is a non-problem in recessions when firms are not investing anyway. Instead, government borrowing and investment can crowd in private sector investment.

The assumption that velocity, V, is constant is also inaccurate. As Figure 31.4 shows, the velocity of money changes significantly with the business cycle. The velocity of M1 fell in every recession (2000–2001, 2007–2009, 2020), and in the worst recessions, it fell sharply. From January 1 to April 1 of 2020, velocity fell by 27%! This means that the Fed must increase M1 significantly just to offset declines in velocity, and the Fed needed to increase M1 by more than 27% for it to have any expansionary impact. In such a situation, a monetary rule would have been a disaster, resulting in massive declines in prices and real GDP.

Figure 31.4 also shows that the velocity of money increased during the boom from 2004 to 2007. This is one of the reasons the Fed felt the need to increase

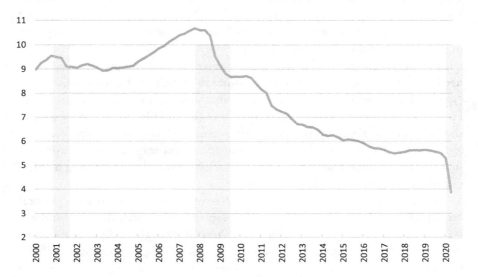

FIGURE 31.4 Velocity of money in the United States, 2000–2020.

interest rates during this period to reduce inflationary pressures. New Keynesians worry about economic growth and increases in M1 or velocity generating inflation during expansions, so they often advocate contractionary monetary policy at such times.

Most modern central bankers subscribe to the new Keynesian approach. In recessions, they are dovish on inflation, willing to increase M1 to reduce unemployment and not worrying about inflationary pressures. In a boom, New Keynesians believe that the money supply should be reduced and interest rates should be increased to reduce inflationary pressures. Thus, *the core new Keynesian approach is that effective monetary policy can and should be used to stabilize an economic system.*

Political economists want to go much further than New Keynesians in stimulating the economy. They are more dovish than the New Keynesian doves, in that they view unemployment as the most important macroeconomic problem and inflation as a relatively minor and quite controllable problem. Political economists note that capitalist economies almost always operate with insufficient aggregate demand, which means that there is almost always too much unemployment. Only once in the last century—during World War II—was there true full employment in the United States such that everyone who wanted to work was able to find a job. In all other periods, there has been room for more monetary and fiscal stimulus.

Rather than relying on the NAIRU theory and the quantity theory of money, many political economists advocate an approach originated by Abba Lerner called functional finance. With the functional finance approach, **central banks and governments make decisions based on achieving explicit macroeconomic goals, including stabilizing the business cycle, achieving true full employment, fostering economic growth, and maintaining price stability**. From this perspective, the government should engage in deficit spending, fund job creation, and increase the money supply to foster growth and unemployment until there is actual evidence of inflation.

Note that to achieve full employment without inflation, the government would need to monitor the macroeconomy carefully to make sure it does not exceed its "speed limit," which is the where the economy grows so quickly that inflation accelerates. Resource and labor markets need to be carefully monitored for signs of shortages that might result in inflationary pressures. Thus, the political economy approach involves a greater level of government intervention and macroeconomic monitoring, with the goal of stimulating aggregate demand and achieving true full employment that is well below the NAIRU.

President Trump and his supply-side economic advisors sided with political economists in advocating significant monetary stimulus when the economy was booming in 2018–2019. They agreed with New Keynesians and political economists that monetary stimulus was necessary in the COVID-19 recession of 2020. Cutting businesses' borrowing costs is consistent with the supply-side focus on reducing businesses' costs and stimulating financial markets to improve the business investment climate. The Fed continued engaging in monetary stimulus in 2021 under President Biden.

With regard to monetary policy, we see some predictable positioning, with laissez-faire economists advocating no government intervention, New Keynesian economists preferring some government intervention, and political economists arguing for extensive government intervention. Interestingly, supply-siders, who often side with laissez-faire economists, differ in the realm of monetary policy, where they side more with political economists due to their desire to stimulate financial markets.

31.6 CONCLUSION

This chapter began by describing how the U.S. government regulated banks and financial markets during its history. The banking sector was constantly shifting and quite unsteady for the first 160 years. The establishment of a central bank and national currency during the Civil War did not end that instability. The gold standard, regular banking panics, and the massive consolidation of banking in the hands of the robber barons exacerbated the problems with the unstable and unequal financial system. Banking regulation began in the early 1900s and increased dramatically during the Great Depression, after which the system became more stable. However, the deregulation of banking beginning in the 1980s set the stage for another round of financial market instability for the next four decades.

In the modern United States, the Fed has five central bank policy tools it can use to stabilize the economy: Open market operations, the federal funds rate, the discount rate, reserve requirements, and quantitative easing or tightening. The Fed can decrease the money supply and increase interest rates in booms to slow the economy as it tries to engineer a soft landing. The Fed can increase the money supply and decrease interest rates in recessions to stimulate aggregate demand. However, Fed policy is much more effective in slowing the economy than stimulating it.

Fed policy choices can be controversial. Laissez-faire economists subscribe to the nonaccelerating inflation rate of unemployment (NAIRU) theory, arguing that low unemployment will cause accelerating inflation so the Fed should maintain tight monetary policy. New Keynesian economists worry more about unemployment than inflation, so they advocate somewhat more expansionary monetary policy. Political economists see unemployment as the most important macroeconomic problem, so they advocate significant monetary expansion until virtually all unemployment is eliminated.

There are similar disagreements regarding the relationship between the money supply and inflation. Laissez-faire economists argue that the Fed should not increase the money supply in recessions because it will cause inflation without improving growth. New Keynesian economists disagree with this argument, given that deflation is the big risk, not inflation, in recessions, and that increases in the money supply can, if paired with expansionary fiscal policy, stimulate aggregate demand. Political economists advocate even more dramatic monetary policy expansion until signs of inflation actually emerge.

Central bankers have more economic power and influence than most heads of state. That is why these debates over monetary policy are so crucial. The decisions on monetary policy loom particularly large during economic crises, as we will see in the next chapter.

QUESTIONS FOR REVIEW

1. How has the regulation of banks and financial markets changed over the course of U.S. history?
2. List the Fed's monetary policy tools. Explain how the Fed could use each policy tool to reduce the money supply and increase interest rates.
3. What happens to banks, the money supply, and interest rates if the Fed engages in an open market purchase?
4. What is quantitative easing, and how can it help to stimulate the economy?
5. Figure 31.5 shows the economy in an overheated state at point **a**.
   a. How large is the inflationary gap?
   b. What policies can the Fed use to cause a decrease in aggregate demand? Explain.
   c. If the marginal respending rate is 0.8, how large a decrease in investment and consumption would it take to move the economy back to PRGDP?
6. In your own words, define the NAIRU theory. Explain the different perspectives on NAIRU.

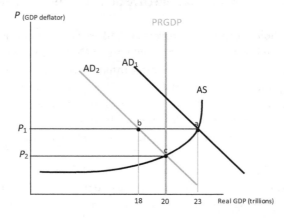

FIGURE 31.5 An inflationary gap at point **a**.

7. Explain the perspectives of hawks, doves, and owls on expansionary monetary policy and its relationship to inflation. Which perspective do you find most compelling? Why?

8. You have just been appointed the new chair of the Federal Reserve Bank. The President wants your immediate input on (a) how best to regulate banks and financial markets and (b) the best monetary policy to use given the current state of the economy. Write an essay in which you take up these key issues. Refer to specific macroeconomic schools of thought in your essay and the ideas you find most compelling in understanding banking and monetary policy.

NOTES

1 Paul Krugman, "The Way We Live Now," *New York Times*, May 23, 1999, section 6, p. 24.

2 Stephanie Kelton, *The Deficit Myth: Modern Monetary Theory and the Birth of the People's Economy* (Public Affairs, New York, 2020).

Crises, financial and otherwise

On the causes and consequences of economic crises and how they can be averted

What causes an economic crisis? To some economists, recessions are one of the great mysteries in economics, caused by unpredictable shocks that are external to the system. From this perspective, crises are virtually impossible to predict.

Other economists have made their living predicting crises. Keynes was certainly very good at it, as was Hyman Minsky. Their insights give us ideas for what the underlying causes of crises might be.

Keynes focused on investment volatility as the driving force behind recessions. Political economists extend this analysis to include all factors that can cause a profit squeeze toward the end of a boom. After the oil shocks of the 1970s, economists added supply shocks to the list of factors that could cause recessions. Minsky and political economists analyzed the role that asset bubbles could play in driving the business cycle. Meanwhile, laissez-faire economists focused on monetary and productivity shocks, misperceptions, and government errors as factors likely to create recessions. Taken together, these approaches provide insights into the factors that might lead to the next recession. We can also learn a lot from analyzing history.

The dot-com recession of 2000–2001 and the Great Recession of 2007–2009 were both driven by asset bubbles in which speculators invested in risky assets that eventually crashed, dragging the rest of the economy with them. Indeed, asset bubbles have increased in importance as a driver of crises in recent decades as financial markets have been deregulated. The COVID-19 recession of 2020, on the other hand, was caused by a pandemic that forced economies to shut down to contain the virus, simultaneously eroding supply and demand.

The degree of fiscal and monetary stimulus enacted by governments has increased dramatically in each of the last three recessions, helping to alleviate the worst problems created by the recessions but failing to lift the economies into full recovery quickly. Thus, macroeconomic management of the business cycle remains a complex and inexact science about which there is much disagreement.

DOI: 10.4324/9781315636924-41

We begin the chapter by reviewing the classic analysis of recessions pioneered by John Maynard Keynes.

32.0 CHAPTER 32 LEARNING GOALS

After reading this chapter, you should be able to:

■ List and explain the different factors economists have identified that can result in a recession.

■ Compare and contrast the different explanations of the business cycle put forth by Keynesian, political, and laissez-faire economists.

■ Identify and describe the characteristics of the last three U.S. recessions.

■ Critically evaluate the ideas of economists regarding recessions and their applicability to the last three U.S. recessions.

Economists have put forth a variety of explanations regarding the causes of recessions. We go through the most important ones below. The major factors that have caused recessions include (1) investment volatility, (2) a profits squeeze, (3) supply shocks, and (4) asset bubbles. As we go through these different factors, we will also outline the different economic perspectives on the causes of crises. We begin with Keynes, who significantly advanced our understanding of the business cycle through his studies of investment volatility.

32.1 CYCLICAL INVESTMENT VOLATILITY (KEYNES)

Some of the best analysis of the causes of recessions comes from John Maynard Keynes and the modern economists who center their analysis on Keynesian ideas. This includes New Keynesians as well as political economists who focus on the role of aggregate demand and the volatility of business investment purchases as a major driver of many recessions.

In Keynesian analysis, there is a natural cycle of business investment given the uncertainty of profitability. According to Keynes, businesses' investment purchases, in which they buy capital goods in order to expand the size of their operations, is the most volatile component of gross domestic product (GDP) and is the component most likely to drive changes in the business cycle. As political economist John Harvey observed, in every U.S. business cycle since 1950 save one, [businesses'] physical investment [purchases] rapidly decelerated at the end of the expansion and then collapsed to bring on recession (the exception being the 1960s, when the data are affected by the fact that government spending on the Vietnam War and the War on Poverty propped up the economy longer than the market would have done by itself). On average, construction of new capacity rose at nearly 16% (adjusted for inflation) in every year of expansions but the last, when it dropped to 6.6%. Over the recessions, it "grew" at −13.5% per year. There is no other economic variable that is more tightly associated with the business cycle than this, nor is there one whose variability is more dramatic.[1]

Thus, we see a dramatic decline in the rate of business investment purchases just before a recession, and then a crash after the recession begins. Real GDP growth parallels changes in business investment purchases, declining from 5.6% to 3.5% after the initial decline in investment and dropping to −1.2% during recessions.

The Keynesian recession story starts in the ashes of a recession. After several years of slow growth and declining investment, opportunities begin to emerge. New technologies, new products, and new markets offer promising potential profits, encouraging businesses to expand and sparking an increase in business investment purchases of capital goods. This creates jobs and income, which spurs an increase in consumer spending, which creates additional opportunities for profitable investment. The boom boosts consumer and investor confidence, which causes additional rounds of spending on consumer durables and business capital goods.

After several years of expansion, however, consumers have all of the durable goods they need and the most promising investment opportunities are gone. Now all that is left are riskier investments. Profit rates inevitably decline in the late stages of the business cycle from these forces. The decline in investment that usually accompanies the decline in profit rates sows the seeds of the recession. Demand for construction workers, materials, and numerous other sectors declines as businesses stop expanding, and this reduces income and employment. Now households do not have enough income to buy everything that is produced, and gluts of goods start to emerge.

As the economy becomes fragile late in the expansion, all it takes is a nudge to push the economy into a recession. The precipitating event could be a steep increase in interest rates by the Fed, a plunge in the stock market as investors lose confidence, or many other factors. Whatever sparks the crash, once business and consumer confidence is undermined, there will be dramatic declines in business investment and consumer durable purchases, pushing the economy into a recession. After a period of declining growth and then slow growth, which can be minimized with enough government stimulus, the cycle begins anew.

Note that declines in investment can be caused by numerous factors. They can be driven by the normal dynamics of the business cycle, as described above. Investment may also decline due to rapid and large increases to interest rates, such as those that occurred in the United States in 1980 and 1990. This would be characterized as an aggregate demand shock—**a decrease in aggregate demand from something other than the normal, cyclical investment patterns**. Indeed, according to political economists, any factors that reduce profit rates in most businesses will cause a decline in business investment purchases and nudge the economy toward a recession.

32.2 PROFIT SQUEEZE (POLITICAL ECONOMISTS)

A similar theory to the Keynesian approach is the political economy approach grounded in Marxian and post-Keynesian ideas that focus on the **profit rate** as the major driver of the business cycle. The profit rate is equal to **the total amount of profit accrued by a firm divided by the total capital invested by the firm**:

$$\text{Profit rate} = \frac{\text{Total profits}}{\text{Total}\left(\text{physical}\right)\text{capital investment}}.$$

As noted above, early in the business cycle, firms' investment purchases of capital goods tend to be very profitable. They are investing in productive new technologies and expanding into profitable new areas. This profitability draws in even more new investment as businesses see opportunities expanding. Also, the profits that are generated as the boom gets started become available to be invested, providing a further stimulus to investment.

Eventually, however, the profit rate starts to decline later in the business cycle, and that stifles investment. A declining profit rate makes firms more reluctant to make investment purchases, and it gives firms less money with which to make those purchases. So far, the story is similar to the Keynesian one. What political economists add are some additional reasons why the profit rate may decline.

The profit rate can decline due to a number of factors. One reason is (1) **underconsumption**. If businesses have expanded their capacity significantly but if consumers scale back on their goods purchases, as they tend to do in booms after they have purchased all of the durable goods they need, the profit rate falls.

A second reason the rate of profit can decline during a boom is a (2) **wage squeeze**. As the economy grows and unemployment falls, workers are able to demand higher wages. This increases businesses' costs and reduces their profit rate.

The third reason is the (3) **increasing difficulty in squeezing profit out of a business with ever-larger amounts capital**.[2] As the business cycle progresses, the capital investments tend to become less and less productive as increasingly marginal projects get funded. Once capital investment purchases boost productivity by a smaller amount than they increase costs, there will be a decline in the profit rate.

Empirical work by Tom Weisskopf indicates that the most important reason for the decline in the profit rate in business cycles prior to 1970 was the wage squeeze. When unions were powerful and the U.S. economy was a manufacturing powerhouse, workers received significant real wage increases during booms, which undermined profit rates and fostered conditions for a recession. However, as the decline of unions, globalization, and neoliberal government policies reduced the power of workers to demand wage increases, the factors driving the decline in the profit rate at the end of the business cycle changed.

Instead of wage increases undermining profits, Erdogan Bakir shows that other factors became more important in undermining businesses' profit rates late in U.S. business cycles after 1970.[3] The major factors undermining profits were (4) higher domestic prices and the deterioration in U.S. terms of trade, (5) declining productivity from increasing bureaucratization of businesses, and (6) financialization.

In the global, neoliberal era, the output prices U.S. corporations can charge are kept low by global competition, while the costs of food, rent, health care, and other goods purchased by U.S. workers keep increasing. Even though real wages are stagnant, the cost of workers relative to the price of output is increasing, undermining the profit rate. In essence, U.S. businesses are experiencing higher costs (higher nominal wages) toward the end of boom periods, but the higher costs are due to increases in health care, food, and housing prices, not from higher wages.

In addition, U.S. corporations expanded the size of management relative to the number of productive workers since the 1970s. U.S. firms are now significantly more bureaucratic on average than overseas firms, and this costly bureaucratic structure increases businesses' costs of production and reduces productivity and profits. Lastly, the additional interest and dividend payments that firms have to make as the financial sector has increased its dominance also erodes the profit rate.

Figure 32.1 shows how useful the profit rate analysis of political economists can be. Bakir's work demonstrates that late in every economic expansion and immediately prior to every recession, there is a sharp drop in the profit rate. This analysis can be used to predict when recessions occur as long as future business cycles follow similar patterns.

Figure 32.1 also shows a steady decline in businesses' capital investment purchases since the 1970s, which is a significant factor driving slower growth of real GDP in the United States in recent decades.

So far, we have focused on demand factors, and especially business investment purchases, as the major driver of crises. However, supply factors can also play a role.

32.3 SUPPLY SHOCKS

Supply shock recessions are caused by factors that cause aggregate supply to decrease. The most important modern examples of supply shocks are the recession of 1973–1975 and the double-dip recession of 1980–1982, both of which were

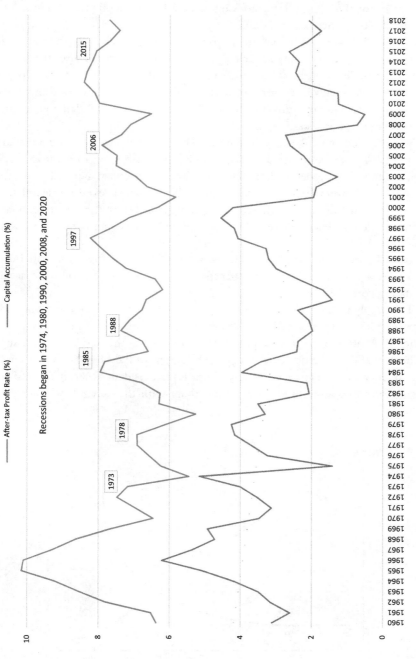

FIGURE 32.1 Profit rate and capital accumulation, 1960–2018.

driven by significantly higher oil prices. The price of oil quadrupled in 1973, raising costs for all businesses, and particularly those that used a lot of energy. This
was accompanied by a significant stock market crash, as high oil prices undermined
profitability for numerous businesses.

Figure 32.2 shows the economic impact of a supply shock using the aggregate
demand and aggregate supply model. The increase in oil prices causes the profitability of virtually all non-oil businesses to decline. Businesses have to raise prices
and cut costs to survive, resulting in mass layoffs. The result is one of the worst
macroeconomic outcomes possible: Stagflation, which is the simultaneous occurrence of stagnation (a recession) and inflation.

Whereas demand shocks can be corrected by expansionary fiscal and monetary
policy to stimulate aggregate demand, supply shocks are more difficult to solve.
Increases in aggregate demand can eliminate the recessionary gap and move the
economy back to potential real GDP (PRGDP). However, even more inflation
may result from this expansion. Reducing aggregate demand via contractionary
policies would eliminate inflation, but it would push the economy deeper into the
recession.

In 1979, Fed Chair Paul Volcker raised interest rates to 20% to eliminate inflationary pressures. His efforts were successful in eliminating inflation but at the
devastating cost of a major recession.

The supply shocks of the 1970s spurred economists to analyze the supply side
of the economy in more detail and prompted the development of supply-side economics as an attempt to solve supply shocks. In theory, the best cure for a supply shock that caused a decrease in aggregate supply would be policies that could
cause an increase in aggregate supply. Therefore, President Reagan focused on
tax cuts for corporations and the wealthy, along with the deregulation of trade,

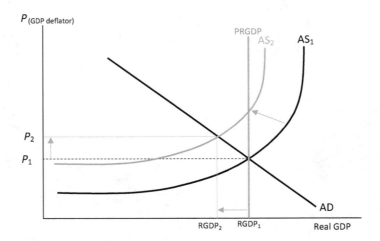

FIGURE 32.2 Stagflation from a supply shock.

the environment, labor markets, and other aspects of the economy. Unfortunately, Reagan's supply-side policies did not stimulate business investment enough to generate a significant improvement in economic growth. Stimulating the supply side of the economy remains a difficult goal to achieve. We will return to this topic in the chapter on economic growth later in the book.

Whereas supply shocks dominated economic conversations in the 1970s and 1980s, asset price bubbles were a major issue in the 1990s and 2000s. Some of the most perceptive observations on asset bubbles come from political economist Hyman Minsky.

32.4 ASSET BUBBLES AND MINSKY'S FINANCIAL INSTABILITY HYPOTHESIS[4]

Perhaps no factor looms so large in recent recessions as the ability of asset bubbles to drag the economy into a recession when they burst. Asset bubbles occur when financial markets make huge bets on assets that prove, in retrospect, to be overvalued. Such behavior prompted John Maynard Keynes to remark, "When the capital development of a country becomes a by-product of the activities of a casino, the job is likely to be ill-done."

In modern capitalism, finance has become a major force affecting the entire global economy. Thus, any analysis that ignores the role of finance is bound to be fundamentally flawed. In mainstream economics, it is typical to ignore the financial sector, assuming that it simply links borrowers with lenders without impacting the rest of the economy. Mainstream economists typically assume that markets are stable, assets are always priced correctly (the efficient market hypothesis), investors rationally balance risks and rewards (the capital asset pricing model), and any deviations from this situation are small or temporary. That approach is difficult to support given the recent financial crisis and the increasing occurrence of asset bubbles.

One of the most useful analyses of the role of finance in modern capitalism comes from Hyman Minsky in the form of his **financial instability hypothesis**. Building on the foundation of the Keynesian business cycle, Minsky adds the role of psychology in financial investments to help us understand why financial markets are prone to recurring crises and why stability breeds excess, which is, in turn, destabilizing.

One of Minsky's major insights is that in financial markets "stability is destabilizing."[5] Rather than tending toward a stable equilibrium, stability breeds excessive risk taking. As investors gain confidence that the good times will never end, as they did in the booms of the 1990s and early 2000s, they engage in increasingly risky investments. The spectacular booms in asset markets are followed by equally spectacular busts. In the modern economy, *the financial sector tends to* exacerbate *the trends in the goods and services sector*, amplifying the business cycle. To understand exactly how this takes place, we need to understand the **Minsky cycle**.

32.4.1 The Minsky cycle

As Keynes noted, in the typical business cycle, after one to two years in a recession followed by another two to three years of slow growth, new business opportunities start to arise. Firms identify new products that could be sold, new markets they can exploit, new technologies that can reduce costs, and so on. Meanwhile, consumer confidence starts to improve along with job growth. Thus, after several years in which very little investment takes place, firms begin to invest again, expanding purchases of plants and equipment and increasing their productive capacity. This causes incomes to increase and unemployment to fall, starting the economic expansion.

What Minsky adds to this story is the role of financial institutions in the boom. The increase in business investment must be financed somehow. In order to finance billions of dollars in new investments, firms borrow from banks.

32.4.1.1 Phase 1: Stable finance (the "hedge finance" phase)

The investments early in a boom are usually fairly safe. Businesses invest in sound opportunities with a high expected return. They are confident that the increases in revenues from their investments can easily pay off the interest and the principal that they borrowed from banks.

Minsky calls this safest stage of the cycle "hedge finance." Investments are "hedged" in that they are very safe and unlikely to experience financial losses. (This has nothing to do with hedge funds, which are often very risky.) Expected revenues from investments exceed payments on interest and the principal, so the risk of default is very low. Both businesses and banks are in a stable situation. But, as noted above, stability breeds instability. Success leads to excess, which leads to a crash.

32.4.1.2 Phase 2: Risky finance (the "speculative finance" phase)

As the boom gathers speed, business confidence improves, and this has a major consequence: Firms are now willing to take on much more risk. Once all of the best investment opportunities are taken, firms must increasingly look for higher risk investments. High levels of confidence encourage businesses to borrow even more money to finance these higher risk investments. In the process, they take on even more debt, committing larger and larger portions of their expected revenues to debt service.

This phase of the Minsky cycle is termed the "speculative" phase. As businesses borrow more and more money for riskier and riskier investments, the expected revenue from the investments will reach a point where it covers the interest payments but not the principal. Thus, the only way businesses can pay off their debt is if the investment ends up being unexpectedly successful and revenues increase. But, until they experience a revenue increase, businesses will have to keep refinancing their loans whenever they come due. They will make the interest payments on the loan, but they will not pay any principal. This phase of the cycle is called "speculative finance" because businesses are speculating that their investments will eventually result in an increase in revenues sufficient to pay off their debts.

Meanwhile, banks, assuming that the boom will continue and that businesses will have no problem paying off their debts, are quite comfortable making riskier loans that require less collateral. Collateral is security that is provided for repayment of a loan, which is forfeited in the event of a default. For example, a business financing an expansion of their operations would have to put up as collateral their existing business assets in order to secure bank financing. That way, if the investment fails and the firm cannot pay the bank, the bank can seize the assets of the business as compensation. Normally, a bank would not loan to a business without significant collateral, but when confidence is high, banks tend to relax their rules regarding collateral. And normally banks would require borrowers to pay off the interest and some of the principal of the loan. This, too, is relaxed when confidence is high.

Banks, flush with cash because of the boom (savings and business profits are pouring into bank accounts), also start to create new financial products and to work to circumvent rules and regulations in order to take advantage of new opportunities. Hence, we get bank speculation to go along with the business speculation already underway.

Meanwhile, as the economy booms the government tends to take in larger amounts of tax revenues and reduces spending on unemployment and social programs (austerity). This happens at the same time that the central bank (Federal Reserve) raises interest rates. Austerity and higher interest rates combine to slow the economy somewhat and increase the risk of default on speculative investments. The good times also prompt calls for deregulation because all is well in financial markets. When financial markets have seemingly exhausted the less risky investments, they clamor for deregulation to be able to invent new financial instruments, as savings and loan banks did in the 1980s (leading to the savings and loan crisis of the late 1980s) or as investment banks did in the late 1990s and early 2000s (leading to the financial crisis of 2007–2009). This combination of deregulation, fiscal and monetary tightening, and riskier investment opportunities moves the economy from a stable structure to a fragile financial situation.

32.4.1.3 Phase 3: The Ponzi finance phase and the crash

As the bubble reaches a fever pitch and confidence improves even more, businesses increase investment further in the riskiest ventures and take on debt they cannot afford, relying on the hope that the investments will be more successful than they appear. Businesses take on so much debt that they cannot make the principal or the interest payments, which means that they must borrow more and more money just to make the interest payments on their debts. Their debts continue to mount until the hoped-for increase in revenue from the investment happens.

This is called the "Ponzi" phase of the cycle because businesses are borrowing money that they cannot pay back given existing conditions. Their only hope of paying back their loans is if their investments generate substantial new revenues.

This is very similar to a Ponzi scheme, such as that perpetrated by Bernie Madoff, where an unscrupulous investment manager takes in money from investors but, rather than investing it, squanders it. His only hope of paying off the original investors is if new investors also entrust him with their money, at which point the Ponzi scheme operator uses the money from the new investors to pay dividends to the original investors. The Ponzi scheme can only continue as long as new investors continue to give new money to the Ponzi investment manager so he can continue to pay off his other investors. Once new investments dry up, the whole Ponzi scheme will collapse.

Similarly, in the Ponzi phase of the business cycle, businesses are borrowing money that they cannot possibly pay back unless their risky investment is actually successful in generating new revenues. While they wait for the hoped-for increase in revenues, they must continue to receive financing from banks to cover their principal and interest payments. There is an inherent instability in such a situation.

Businesses in this phase of the cycle will not default as long as banks continue to loan them increasing amounts of money. However, once the economy becomes this fragile, numerous factors can derail the boom. Multiple defaults can occur if (1) revenue flows from investments turn out to be lower than expected, (2) interest rates increase,[6] (3) banks get scared and curtail lending, or (4) a prominent firm or bank defaults on payments and scares investors or lenders.

Once businesses, investors, or banks are spooked, we have reached the "**Minsky moment**," and the financial bubble collapses rapidly. As everyone tries to unload risky assets, their prices plummet, and bankruptcies and defaults ensue. The risky investments collapse. Firms lay off workers and income and employment fall, reducing consumer spending and making the situation even more dire. The economy spirals into recession and only a significant injection of money into financial markets by the central bank (such as the Fed) and a large increase in government spending can stop the crash.

32.4.2 The super-Minsky cycle

There is also a trend in financial markets where the likelihood of a severe financial crash increases over a period of several decades. If the regular recessions and crashes are mild, there will be increasing calls for deregulation over time. For example, financial markets were deregulated substantially in the 1990s and early 2000s after two decades of relatively stable growth. The more financial markets are deregulated, the riskier the behavior can be. This will tend to increase the severity of the crash as deregulation proceeds, resulting in a major crash such as the Great Depression of the 1930s or the Great Recession of 2007–2009. Of course, in the wake of a major crash, calls for new regulations emerge and safeguards are put back into place. This stabilizes the system and reduces the severity of the next several recessions. That is, until the lessons have been forgotten and renewed calls for deregulation are heeded, setting up the next major crash.

As numerous publications and economists from both mainstream and political economy perspectives have noted, Minsky's financial instability hypothesis is very important in understanding the modern business cycle. Minsky left us with a number of key ideas that we can use to anticipate and possibly to avoid future crises:

- Stability is destabilizing: Stability encourages excessive risk-taking, which leads to fragility and crisis.
- Over the long term (several decades), stability is destabilizing partly because it encourages deregulation of financial markets, which encourages a larger speculative boom and much deeper bust.
- Over the typical ten-year business cycle, stability is destabilizing because of the manner in which improvements in confidence encourage businesses and banks to engage in increasingly risky behavior.
- In the first "stable" or "hedge" phase of the business cycle, firms make sound investments and banks make sound loans that should be successful and that have a low probability of default.
- In the second "risky" or "speculative" phase, as the economy grows and confidence improves, firms take on more debt and make increasingly risky investments while banks create new, riskier financial securities. The probability of defaults increases.
- In the third "Ponzi" phase, rapid growth and appreciating asset values cause the boom to reach a fever pitch as firms and banks make even riskier investments and the probability of defaults becomes very high.
- At some point, when it becomes clear that the risky investments will not generate the necessary returns, the economy reaches a "Minsky moment," panic selling ensues, and the market crashes. The financial market crash causes reduced investment and consumer spending, unemployment increases, and the economy falls into a recession.

If we take Minsky's analysis to heart, then financial markets, and markets in general, must always be regulated to prevent Ponzi-like behaviors. Only then can we avoid the worst excesses of financial markets and the deep recessions that follow a financial market collapse.

Political economists and New Keynesian economists study crises and how they work. Most laissez-faire economists tend to assume that recessions will be short-lived and focus instead on long-term characteristics of macroeconomic markets.

Nonetheless, laissez-faire economists developed some ideas on what might cause a recession, which are taken up in the next section.

32.5 LAISSEZ-FAIRE ECONOMISTS' THEORIES OF THE BUSINESS CYCLE

Building on Milton Friedman's research, monetarist theories of the business cycle **credit monetary factors with driving fluctuations in real GDP**. Some of Friedman's most important research showed that one of the major causes of the Great Depression was the huge decrease in the money supply that occurred as one bank after another failed. Using Friedman's quantity theory of money, M1 $*$ V $=$ P $*$ Real GDP, a large decrease in M1 can cause deflation (a decrease in P) and a large decrease in real GDP.

In the modern era, most central banks have learned this key lesson: The central bank must act as the lender of last resort and must ensure that banks and financial markets have sufficient liquidity in a crisis. This is why the Fed injected trillions of dollars into the economy in 2008 and in 2020. Friedman thought that monetary stimulus might be enough to stop a recession, so he did not advocate additional fiscal stimulus. However, as we saw in the chapter on fiscal policy, countries that combined monetary and fiscal stimulus fared much better in response to the Great Recession than those that did not use both.

Laissez-faire economists also developed real business cycle theory, which **attributes recessions to productivity shocks caused by changes in technology and the legal and regulatory environment**. A major innovation in one sector, such as the development of the internet, can cause huge disruptions in other sectors, such as retail shopping. Also, a major shift in government, such as the switch in Russia from communism to capitalism, can undermine existing productive institutions and cause a crisis. Though it is certainly true that productivity shocks can cause recessions, this does not explain the regularity with which recessions occur.

Laissez-faire economists are also less concerned with recessions than other economists because of their belief in the flexibility of markets. For example, laissez-faire economists often argue that recessions are a result of workers demanding wages that are too high. From this perspective, if workers would reduce their reservation wage—the lowest wage rate that they will accept—in recessions, they would all find work. This market misunderstanding theory **attributes the cause of a recession to misperceptions by workers or other economic actors**.

The political business cycle theory argues that **business cycles can result from policies of politicians to improve their re-election chances**. There are definite indications that political behavior can contribute to business cycles. Republican Senate Majority Leader Mitch McConnell stymied efforts by the democratic Obama administration to engage in fiscal stimulus after the Great

Recession, but he supported large stimulus packages under republican President Trump. Thus, it is always important to include political considerations in economic analysis of the business cycle given the importance of political decisions on fiscal policy.

Laissez-faire economists often highlight the political business cycle because it reinforces their belief that government intervention is usually self-serving and inefficient. This contrasts with the other theoretical approaches that emphasize the need for effective government intervention to fix recessions and, possibly, to alter economic conditions such that recessions are less likely.

Now that we have studied economists' theories regarding the factors that drive the business cycle, we turn to case studies of recent recessions. This will help you understand the unique dynamics that drive each business cycle, as well as the patterns that emerge.

32.6 THE RECESSION OF 2001: INTERNET/TECH OVERINVESTMENT AND STOCK BUBBLE

After the 1990 recession, the U.S. economy began to grow rapidly. Much of this growth was driven by the so-called new economy, which included businesses in the information technology sector such as fiber-optic cables, personal and business computers, and the development of the internet. Computer ownership in the United States more than doubled during this decade as computers changed from a luxury to a necessity. Internet use exploded. As investors began to see the internet as the next big thing, investment in the tech sector also exploded.

Herd behavior is **the tendency of human beings to emulate the behavior of others**. Emulation, where people copy others with the goal of doing as well as they are, is a pattern found in much human behavior. Veblen identified pecuniary emulation, where people imitate the tastes and fashions of the classes above them and strive to fit in, as one of the major forces shaping human behavior. Similarly, in financial markets investors emulate others to make sure they are not missing out on the next big thing. FOMO, fear of missing out, is a major driver in financial markets. Once a handful of big investors decided that the internet was the next big thing, huge numbers of investors followed suit, to the point of incredible irrationality.

A few new internet companies showed incredible promise, such as Netscape and the other first internet browsers. They were quickly followed by dozens of "dot-com" companies, so-named because of the .com end on their website address. The dot-coms ended up with huge stock valuations, even though most of them had never made a profit and some of them had never even sold a product!

Tech stocks at the time were concentrated in the NASDAQ Composite Stock Index because they were too small and new to be listed on the larger stock indexes. Figure 32.3 shows that from 1995 to 2000, the NASDAQ Composite Index

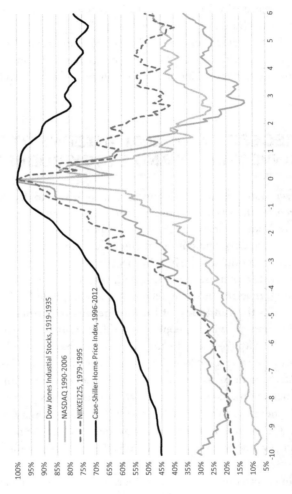

FIGURE 32.3 Asset bubbles (% of peak value).

increased 400%, reaching a price-to-earnings ratio of 200, which is more than ten times the price-to-earnings ratio that is considered to be dangerously high.

This situation is what economists call an asset bubble, which occurs **when a particular asset, such as stocks or property, increases in price rapidly and irrationally in a relatively short period of time** (less than ten years). An asset value is irrational when its price is wildly out of line with traditional asset valuation measures, such as the price-to-earnings ratio for stocks.

In 2000, a series of events undermined confidence in the tech sector. The Fed increased interest rates, which raised the costs of borrowing. Japan entered a recession, spooking investors that a global recession was coming. U.S. Judge T. P. Jackson ruled that Microsoft was engaged in monopolistic practices and should be broken up (a ruling later softened on appeal), which reduced confidence in the tech sector's big players. And investors and business publications began questioning the value of tech stocks.

As a result, the tech bubble burst. Over the next two years, tech stocks lost 75% of their value. As you can see in Figure 32.3, compared with other asset bubbles, the NASDAQ bubble had the steepest increase and steepest initial crash in modern history. This crash was more extreme than the stock market bubble and crash that preceded the Great Depression and the crash of the Japanese Nikkei stock index in 1989.

One might think that after one asset bubble, investors would not be so quick to jump into another one. Unfortunately, the dot-com bubble was followed by an even more devastating crash, this time in the housing market in 2007.

32.7 THE GREAT RECESSION OF 2007–2009: THE SUB-PRIME MORTGAGE BUBBLE

The story of the financial crisis and Great Recession begins in the ashes of the dot-com crash. With the recession of 2001, the Fed lowered interest rates significantly to 1% and kept interest rates there through 2004. This provided lots of inexpensive money for banks to loan out.

Meanwhile, housing prices were increasing rapidly, as shown in Figure 32.3 with the Case–Shiller Home Price Index. Cheap money and booming home prices meant that a lot of money could be earned in real estate speculation, so investors began to move money into real estate markets, pushing up home prices even faster. Meanwhile, homeowners saw booming house prices as evidence of newfound wealth, so many households borrowed heavily against their increased home values to buy goods. Unfortunately, the increase in household debt also meant a greater risk of default, as we will see later.

Banks, flush with cash and able to obtain more cash for almost no cost, began to look for new people to whom they could loan money. Once all of the credit-worthy borrowers had taken out mortgages to purchase homes, banks and mortgage companies turned to high-risk borrowers: Real estate speculators and sub-prime borrowers. To entice borrowers, banks set up high-risk loans with a low, two-year "teaser" rate around 4%, often with no down payment but with interest rates set to balloon to as much as 27% after two years.

Real estate speculators saw the rapidly rising housing prices as an opportunity to make a lot of money fast. They borrowed huge amounts of money from banks and bought houses in areas where home prices were increasing rapidly. The speculators assumed that home values would continue to rise, which would allow them to flip the house (resell it) within two years, before the high interest rates on their loans kicked in. The percentage of houses sold to speculators increased from 20% in 2000 to 35% in 2007.

Sub-prime borrowers are **people who are likely to have difficulty making loan payments on time and have a high risk of default**. Normally banks would be reluctant to loan money to sub-prime borrowers due to the high likelihood of default. However, two factors reduced their concerns. First, the historically steady increase in home prices, along with the recent boom in real estate markets, provided them with a false sense of security that home loans were not very risky. Historically, home loans have much lower rates of default than other loans, and with increasing house prices, banks could recoup their mortgage losses by foreclosing on and selling any homes where borrowers stopped paying.

With financial markets awash with cash and interest rates low, retirement funds and other institutional investors were looking for higher returns wherever they could find them. To satisfy this demand, banks began engaging in the process of **securitization** of mortgages, bundling mortgages together and selling them as particular kinds of derivatives called a collateralized mortgage obligations (CMOs) and collateralized debt obligations (CDOs).

A collateralized mortgage obligation, also called a mortgage-backed security, is **a derivative consisting of a bundle of many home mortgages, which is sold to investors who expect to get a return on their CMO purchase but who also assume the risk of default associated with the mortgages**. In essence, a CMO is a financial security that investors can purchase whose underlying value is derived from the expected mortgage interest and principal payments, subject to the risk of default. Individual CMOs packaged loans valued at over $100 million, and investors could buy into many different levels of each CMO. The highest level, or "tranche," had a lower expected return but the least default risk, and the lowest tranche had the highest expected return and the highest default risk. Most CMOs contained four or five different tranches, and they were sold primarily to institutional investors such as insurance companies and banks.

Figure 32.4 shows the explosion of CMOs from 2002 to 2007, where they went from $0 per year to $126 trillion! Sub-prime loans increased from 8% of mortgages in 2004 to 20% in 2006, and the ratio was much higher in places where home prices were rising fastest, which is also where real estate speculation was at its highest.

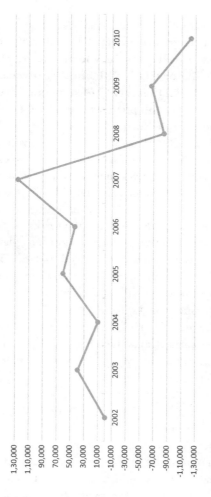

FIGURE 32.4 Flow of private CMOs (millions of dollars), 2002–2010.

A collateralized debt obligation is **a derivative consisting of a bundle of various forms of debt instruments, such as mortgages, auto loans, student loans, credit card debt, and so on**. In the 2000s, CDOs often contained several CMOs along with other kinds of debt, making them extremely complex bundles of bundles of loans that were hard for investors to assess accurately. CMOs and CDOs are similar, because they are both **a security that is backed by a pool of debt**, so they are often lumped together under the label of collateralized loan obligations (CLOs).

Because they knew that CLOs could be risky, investment banks used another type of derivative called a credit default swap (CDS) to reduce their risk exposure. A credit default swap is **a derivative in which one investor pays to swap their credit risk on a CMO or CDO with another investor. The purchaser of a CDS pays a fee to the CDS issuer. In exchange, if the CMO or CDO defaults, the CDS issuer pays the purchaser of the CDS**.

CDSs were at the heart of the financial crisis. An investor could buy a risky CMO, but if they bought a CDS as insurance, they were taking on no significant risk themselves. This meant they had no financial incentive to care about how risky the CMO might be. Meanwhile, CDS issuers were happy to issue CDSs because they thought the risk of default on mortgages would continue to be low, as it had been historically. And most CLOs were given the highest possible ratings by the agencies that were supposed to accurately assess their risks.

Here is where another incentive problem comes into play. Ratings agencies in the United States are private firms that are paid by large investment banks to rate securities in an objective fashion. Ratings can range from "D" to "AAA." However, ratings agencies make the bulk of their money by rating the most complex derivatives, and investment banks issuing the derivatives like to pick the ratings agency that issues the most favorable ratings. Therefore, ratings agencies have a direct financial incentive to give investment banks higher ratings on their derivatives than is warranted. Leading up to the financial crisis, this is exactly what happened. Ratings agencies like Moody's, Standard & Poor's, and Fitch gave subprime CMOs and CDOs AAA ratings, even though there was an extremely high likelihood of default. From 2004 to 2006, CMOs and CDOs looked like a sure thing to investors: They paid high interest rates and they came with the highest possible rating, which seemed to indicate that they were secure.

Now we can add another layer to the story, excessive leveraging, which is a problem in most financial crises. Leveraging refers to **the use of debt to purchase an asset, with the hope that the profit from the asset purchase will exceed the borrowing cost**. Buying an asset with borrowed money is doubly risky. There is a risk to the asset purchaser that the asset may not pay off and there is a risk to the bank loaning money because if the asset purchase does not pay off, the purchaser may default on the loan used to make the purchase.

Derivatives were not regulated by the Fed prior to 2010, and they had no reserve requirement. When a bank makes a "bet" by purchasing a CMO—betting that they will get a good return on their purchase—the CMO is an asset. Then the bank can go to another lender and say, we need to borrow money for another investment; here is a CMO as collateral in case we default on the loan. Then they can use the money they borrow to buy another CMO, which is now another asset in their portfolio, which they can borrow against to buy another CMO. Banks were making bets, funded by other bets, funded by still more bets. The analogy is a house of cards, because the bank has accumulated a mountain of debt, but it has very little equity, and if it loses its equity, the bank will default on its loans.

The assets-to-equity ratio is a measure of how many assets a bank has relative to the amount of equity the owners have in the bank. In 2003, the huge investment banks Morgan Stanley, Lehman Brothers, Bear Stearns, Merrill Lynch, and Goldman Sachs had an asset-to-equity ratio of about 19 to 1. By 2007 the ratio had increased to over 32 to 1.

As if investment in high-risk CLOs was not enough, banks started engaging in highly unethical CDS speculation. As we saw above, CDSs started out as insurance in case your CLO defaulted. Now, however, Wall Street firms started purchasing CDS policies on CLOs that they did not own themselves. Goldman Sachs, Deutsche Bank, Morgan Stanley, and other big investment banks sold sub-prime mortgages packaged as CLOs to investors, and they purchased credit default swaps sold by a third party, often AIG insurance, to bet that the CLOs they sold were going to default. In essence, *in a classic example of moral hazard, investment banks sold CLOs they knew were likely to fail and then used CDSs to place bets that the CLOs would fail.*

Eventually, the house of cards started to collapse. U.S. home prices began to decline steeply in 2006 as the Fed increased interest rates to more than 5%, which undermined new home sales, and as the two-year "teaser" rates on sub-prime loans started to increase. Overbuilding also contributed. By 2008, home prices had fallen by more than 20%.

Mortgage default rates increased dramatically, as did foreclosure rates. Many speculators and homeowners simply walked away from their mortgages, because they owed more money on their house than it was now worth. The sub-prime market collapsed, so the trillions of dollars in CLOs based on those sub-prime mortgages lost almost all of their value. Investment banks that invested heavily in CLOs—and this was most of the big banks—began to collapse. Companies that sold credit default swaps taking the default risk from the CLOs were liable for huge payouts, and they also collapsed. Banks were so intertwined that when one failed, the other banks who had investments in the failing bank also were at risk of failure.

Banks were now so short of liquidity due to their huge losses that many stopped loaning out money. Lehman Brothers went bankrupt, and Merrill Lynch was on the verge of failure until it was purchased by Bank of America. Goldman Sachs and Morgan Stanley were forced to get emergency loans from the Fed. Ninety banks failed from late 2007 to mid-2009.

Consumers, seeing the value of their home decline dramatically, cut back on consumption spending. The rest of the economy followed the housing and banking sectors into the crash. Stock prices decreased by 40% in 2008. The result was the worst recession since the Great Depression.

Putting all of this together, we can list the following factors as crucial drivers in the financial crisis:

- Deregulation of the banking sector that allowed federally insured banks to combine risky investment banking (derivatives) with mortgage banking
- An abundance of cheap money searching for a higher return
- Moral hazard, herding, and a lack of ethics, as mortgage companies increasingly pursued sub-prime and real estate speculation loans, only to convert these loans to CMOs and CDOs, which they sold at inflated values
- The rise of housing speculation and sub-prime lending driving a bubble in the housing market
- Improper standards and incentives in the ratings industry, which benefited financially from giving high ratings to unsafe derivatives
- Moral hazard, herding, and a lack of ethics driving investment banks to sell high-risk CLOs and then bet against them
- Overleveraging of investment banks as they made bets on top of bets in risky markets.

The crisis was so dire that the government responded quickly and dramatically with a massive bailout of financial markets. The Fed pushed interest rates to near 0% and injected liquidity into the banking system, loaning trillions of dollars to banks that needed funds. They bailed out huge banks and insurers that were considered too big to fail. They purchased $700 billion in stock and toxic assets from troubled banks as part of the Troubled Asset Relief Program (TARP) of 2008. The government bailed out failing companies including General Motors and Chrysler, whose car sales had dried up. In one of the most controversial steps, the Fed engaged in quantitative easing over and beyond TARP, buying securities of all types in financial markets to prop up asset values and to stabilize the financial sector.

In terms of fiscal policy, the Obama administration spent more than $800 billion on the American Recovery and Reinvestment Act (ARRA), which was passed in February of 2009. This included a mix of tax cuts, extended unemployment benefits, and about $300 billion in direct spending on infrastructure and other job-creating activities. At the time, New Keynesian economists noted that this would not be enough to end a recession as deep as this one, and they were correct. The economy struggled with slow growth until 2015, when U.S. real GDP growth per capita finally exceeded 2%.

To address the problems with the banking system, the U.S. government passed the Dodd–Frank Wall Street Reform and Consumer Protection Act of 2010. This act imposed stricter regulation on banking and extended basic banking regulations to other parts of the financial sector, including derivatives markets. The Act empowered government regulators to identify threats to financial stability, such as when banks become too big and too dominant. And it established the Consumer Financial Protection Bureau to protect investors from fraudulent behavior in asset markets. To address the manipulations of Goldman-Sachs and other investment banks, the Dodd–Frank Act instituted a basic regulation: Financial advisors must act in the client's interest and cannot recommend assets to clients that are known to be likely to fail without full disclosure of information. Writing in 2017, Federal Reserve Chair Janet Yellen observed that Dodd–Frank "substantially boosted resilience without unduly limiting credit availability or economic growth."

However, parts of Dodd–Frank caused investment banks much angst, especially the rule that they had to act in their client's interests, which they saw as too difficult to interpret and apply. This and other parts of Dodd–Frank were repealed by the Trump administration as part of its move to deregulate industries.

The dramatic fiscal and monetary stimulus enacted by the U.S. government was successful in forestalling another depression, and the new regulations stabilized the financial sector, but these efforts were not enough to stimulate a return to robust economic growth for several years. Interestingly, the large deficits the government ran from 2008 through 2019, ranging from $440 billion to $1410 billion, did not result in high interest rates or inflation. This gave government officials more confidence in running large deficits when the COVID-19 recession hit in 2020.

32.8 THE INVERTED YIELD CURVE AND THE COVID-19 RECESSION OF 2020

In addition to signs of a bubble, one of the other signs of an impending recession is an inverted yield curve. The yield curve is **the difference between interest rates on short-term bonds and interest rates on long-term bonds**. In general, long-term bonds pay a higher interest rate because you are tying your money up for a longer period of time and your money is subject to more inflation risk. If you purchase a ten-year bond paying 2% interest, and if the inflation rate surges to 5% before your bond matures, you will lose a lot of money in real terms. As a result, bond buyers usually need to be paid a premium to put their money into long-term bonds.

However, every so often the yield curve *inverts*, such that interest rates on short-term bonds are higher than interest rates on long-term bonds. The factors behind an inverted yield curve include the following: (1) Investors expect slow growth and low inflation, so they are willing to buy a bond promising a steady but low long-term return or (2) investors expect the Fed to keep cutting short-term interest rates to stimulate the economy, so they wait to purchase short-term bonds and the return on short-term bonds falls as a result.

In essence, an inverted yield curve is a sign that large numbers of investors expect a recession and, as we have studied, when businesses expect a recession, this tends to cause behaviors that cause a recession. Furthermore, *every recession in the United States since 1955 was preceded by an inverted yield curve*. As Figure 32.5 shows, the United States experienced an inverted yield curve, with interest rates on ten-year treasury bonds lower than interest rates on two-year treasury bonds, just before the advent of the recessions of 1990, 2000, and 2007. Interestingly, the yield curve also inverted briefly in 2019, leading many economists to predict a recession in 2020 even before the COVID-19 pandemic hit. The economy was clearly in a fragile state when the pandemic forced economies into lockdowns and caused a massive, sharp recession.

In the second quarter of 2020, the U.S. economy shrank by 9.5% (an annual rate of 32.9%) and the eurozone economy shrank by 12.1%, the steepest declines since the creation of modern economic statistics in the 1950s. This was a product first and foremost of the shutdown to control the pandemic, as governments forced businesses to close and workers to stay home to contain the novel coronavirus that causes the deadly COVID-19 disease.

The shutdown also led to declines in consumer spending, especially on travel, entertainment, and restaurant purchases, and declines in business investment as expected sales plummeted. There were also disruptions in supply chains, as manufacturers had trouble getting parts from places hard hit by the virus and as global trade slowed.

The United States, the E.U. and most other developed countries engaged in massive fiscal and monetary stimulus to combat the recession (see the chapters on fiscal and monetary policy for details). In the United States, tax cuts, bailouts, and quantitative easing were extremely effective in returning the stock market to its previous levels. The stock market dropped more than 30% from February 20 to March 23, 2020, but it recovered all the ground it lost by August 19, 2020, thanks to the trillions of dollars injected into financial markets.

However, unemployment rates remained extremely high. More important, the fractured U.S. public health system and the ineffective response of the Trump administration meant that the rate of infections soared in the United States well after most other developed countries contained it. As U.S. colleges attempted to reopen in the fall of 2020, one college after another had to close their campuses and move to remote instruction due to virus outbreaks. Meanwhile, European universities, where the virus was more contained, were able to stay open thanks to extensive testing, quarantine, and contact-tracing infrastructure managed by the national government.

As of August 2021, it appeared that the largest stimulus in U.S. history was successful in quickening the end of the COVID-19 recession. The unemployment rate dropped from 15% in April 2020 to 5.4% in July 2021. However, additional waves of infections continued to threaten the still-fragile recovery.

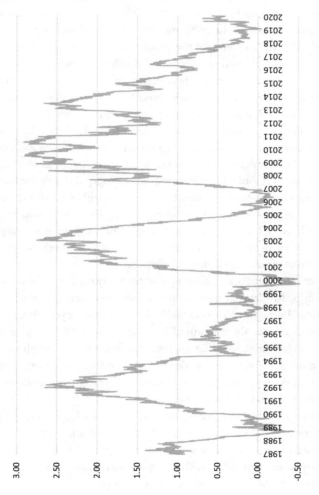

FIGURE 32.5 Ten-year minus two-year treasury spread, 1987–2020.

32.9 CONCLUSION

Recessions are difficult to predict with precision, but patterns do emerge that help us anticipate when recessions are likely to occur. John Maynard Keynes focused on the cyclical patterns in business investment purchases. After a recession and a period of slow economic growth, new technologies, products, and markets emerge that offer the promise of above-normal profits, enticing businesses to expand into new areas. The increase in business investment purchases creates jobs and raises incomes, sparking expansions in consumer spending and starting a boom. After several years of a booming economy, the promising investment opportunities have all been taken and consumers have purchased the houses and cars that they need, so a decline in investment and consumption tends to occur. The economy becomes fragile and is nudged into a recessionary spiral by an event that causes businesses and consumers to lose confidence and dramatically curtail spending.

Political economists broaden Keynesian analysis to include additional factors that can cause the profit rate to fall during a boom. Underconsumption can lead to a glut of goods and declining profits. A wage squeeze can occur as workers demand higher wages during a boom. It can become increasingly difficult for businesses to squeeze profit out of ever-larger amounts of capital. Higher domestic prices cause higher nominal wages, a factor that undermines profits. Declining productivity from increasing bureaucratization can raise costs and lower productivity. And the increasing dominance of the financial sector can extract revenues out of other sectors, reducing profit rates of nonfinancial corporations.

Laissez-faire economists attribute recessions to exogenous shocks or market misunderstandings. Monetarist theories of the business cycle credit monetary factors with driving fluctuations in real GDP. Real business cycle theory attributes recessions to productivity shocks caused by changes in technology and the legal and regulatory environment. Market misunderstanding theory attributes the cause of a recession to misperceptions by workers or other economic actors. And political business cycle theory notes that business cycles can result from policies of politicians to improve their re-election chances.

When we examine the last three recessions, we see the importance of asset bubbles in driving the boom–bust cycle. In the 1990s, tech stocks increased in value by 400%, even though tech companies where not very profitable. In the 2000s, home prices increased by more than 100% and sub-prime mortgages increased dramatically, even though many of the people buying homes had poor credit and were unlikely to be able to pay off their mortgages. In both cases, the asset markets crashed once investors realized their folly. When asset markets crashed, this spooked investors and consumers, caused bank failures, and resulted in a full-fledged recession.

In addition to the home price bubble, the financial crisis of 2007–2008 was driven by the creation of opaque derivatives called collateralized loan obligations that disguised the amount of risk they contained, especially when they were given AAA ratings by self-interested ratings agencies. Frustration with financial shenanigans led to the passage of the Dodd–Frank Act in 2010, which imposed stricter financial market regulations to prevent such events from reoccurring. However, much of Dodd–Frank was repealed during the Trump administration's push to deregulate markets.

The COVID-19 recession marked a different type of downturn, driven by a public health crisis and the necessity to close businesses and to require people to work from home to contain the pandemic. Record-breaking stimulus efforts caused financial markets to rebound, but unemployment proved much more difficult to address as numerous businesses shuttered in the difficult conditions. Countries with robust public health systems fared much better than those without, demonstrating the importance of systematic health care in protecting a country's citizens and economy in a globalized world where viruses spread rapidly.

Interestingly, the forces driving recessions seem to be shifting in the modern United States. Asset bubbles, trade flows and relative prices, and global disease transmission now loom large. The clear policy response to minimize these destructive forces would be greater regulation of financial markets, stabilization of trade flows and wages for workers, and investment in public health systems. However, vested interests make such public policy decisions difficult.

QUESTIONS FOR REVIEW

1. Explain the Keynesian idea that the patterns in business investment purchases drive the business cycle.
2. According to political economists, what are the major factors that can reduce the profit rate and lead to a recession? Explain each one briefly.
3. Using Figure 32.2, explain why a supply shock presents a difficult conundrum for policymakers, forcing them to choose between fighting inflation and fighting unemployment. How are supply-side policies designed to resolve this conundrum?
4. Explain the key ideas in Minsky's financial instability hypothesis in your own words. In your answer, describe each phase of the business cycle carefully.
5. Describe the different laissez-faire theories of the business cycle. What are the main differences between laissez-faire approaches to recessions and those of new Keynesian and political economists?
6. What is an asset bubble? How does this concept help us understand the recessions of 2000–2001 and 2007–2009?
7. What is a CLO (collateralized loan obligation)? What is a CDS (credit default swap)? Explain briefly in your own words. How did these derivatives feature in the financial crisis of 2007–2008?
8. What are the essential features of the financial crisis of 2007–2008? Who was primarily to blame? How did economic theory promoting deregulation

contribute to the financial crisis? Given the major causes of the financial crisis, how do you think the government should approach regulating financial markets in the modern era?

9. What is an inverted yield curve? Why do many economists see this as a precursor to a recession?

NOTES

1 John T. Harvey, "Why Do Recessions Happen? A Practical Guide to the Business Cycle," *Forbes*, April 18, 2011, https://www.forbes.com/sites/johntharvey/2011/04/18/why-do-recessions-happen-a-practical-guide-to-the-business-cycle/#762aa0407100.

2 Marx used the term the "organic composition of capital" to refer to the ratio of labor expenditure to capital investment purchases. As businesses invest more and more in capital, they will experience a decline in the profit rate if the productivity increases from the new capital are not greater than the increase in costs from the capital purchase.

3 Erdogan Bakir, "Capital Accumulation, Profitability, and Crisis: Neoliberalism in the United States," *Review of Radical Political Economics*, Vol. 47, No. 3, 2015, pp. 389–411.

4 The author would like to thank Janet Knoedler and Erdogan Bakir for their feedback on this section. Any errors are, of course, my own.

5 L. Randall Wray, *Why Minsky Matters* (Princeton University Press, Princeton, NJ, 2016), p. 15.

6 Higher interest rates mean that firms have to borrow even more money to keep financing their risky investments and the return from the investments has to been even higher in order to stave off losses.

PART X

Growth and global interconnectedness

The modern global economy features a wide variety of economic systems, some of which are growing quickly and some of which are growing slowly or not at all. China and South Korea, two of the economies that grew most rapidly in recent decades, used a state-led approach to innovation and growth, with the government directing resources into strategically important areas. Other rapidly growing economies, such as India and Ireland, used a more market-based approach. However, state-led and market-focused economies elsewhere are not experiencing the same level of economic growth as these successful economies.

Chapter 33 explores theories and polices related to the sources of economic growth. Economic growth is one of the most complex and least understood topics in economics. If there were a simple formula for economies to implement in order to achieve rapid economic growth and the prosperity that accompanies it, all countries would adhere to this formula. In actuality, there are many different methods for achieving rapid economic growth. Some successful approaches to growth are largely state directed, whereas others take a more laissez-faire, market-oriented approach. This chapter lays out the approaches to economic growth taken by economists from the New Keynesian, laissez-faire, and political economy perspectives. The chapter then discusses the growth approaches and experiences of real-world economies in the modern era and whether or not economic growth can be achieved in a sustainable way to preserve the environment.

Chapter 34 takes up another set of issues related to economic growth—international trade and protectionism. Laissez-faire economists advocate unregulated (free) trade based on the theory of comparative advantage, which posits that unregulated trade increases productivity and efficiency, and results in a higher standard of living (and rate of growth) for people in countries that pursue unregulated trade. New Keynesian economists prefer trade with modest regulation. Political economists believe that trade should be managed carefully and that key industries should be protected in order to stimulate domestic economic development. The debate

DOI: 10.4324/9781315636924-42

over whether or not to pursue unregulated or regulated trade is an ongoing and important one in economics, underlying debates over trade agreements and economic integration (such as the European Union). Trade also has a major impact on macroeconomic flows of money and resources. In addition, trade can be a major driver of economic growth for globally competitive, export-oriented economies, or it can result in deindustrialization and stagnation.

Chapter 35 on international finance and financial flows begins with economic theories regarding the market for foreign exchange. We examine how the supply and demand for foreign exchange affect exchange rates. Exchange rates in turn affect the prices of domestic and foreign goods, so exchange rates play an important role in determining which industries are successful in a particular country. Countries can choose fixed or flexible exchange rate systems, which can cause very different outcomes. Next, we turn to a discussion of the balance of payments, trade deficits, and trade surpluses. Trade deficits are an important and controversial topic in U.S. economics and politics. Financial flows, which are a product of trade flows and other factors, can be managed by the government or allowed to flow freely. This is related to the issue of exchange rate instability, a significant problem of developing countries that can result in currency crises. The chapter concludes with a discussion of fiscal and monetary policy in an open economy.

33 The sources of economic growth

Economic growth is one of the most important goals for an economic system. Governments across the world prioritize economic growth because if it occurs, the standard of living of a country's population improves. In general, people with a higher material standard of living are happier and healthier.

Despite the prioritization of growth, it can be quite difficult to achieve sustained economic growth over a long period of time. The drivers of economic growth are complex and not well understood. As evidence of this, despite the fact that almost all countries pursue strategies to stimulate economic growth, the growth rates of countries vary widely. In the last two decades, China, India, and Vietnam experienced per capita gross domestic product (GDP) growth rates of more than 5% per year, whereas Japan, the E.U., and the United States experienced annual per capita GDP growth of about 1%. If there were a clear set of policies to stimulate rapid economic growth, then all countries would be able to achieve it simply by adopting those policies, but clearly that is not the case.

The reality is that there are many different ways to achieve sustained economic growth, from the state-directed approach of China and South Korea to the more laissez-faire approach of India and Ireland. Furthermore, governments that try to emulate the policies of countries that are growing rapidly are often unsuccessful despite adopting similar approaches.

There are also complexities surrounding the relationship between growth and sustainability. Historically, economic growth has been associated with environmental destruction. However, with the potentially devastating consequences of climate change, a key question emerges: How can economies continue to grow while also preserving the environment? Some countries, such as Germany, are incorporating sustainability into their approach to economic growth with great success. Growth in Germany has been accompanied by improvements in their environmental record in recent decades. Other countries, such as China, have adopted a

DOI: 10.4324/9781315636924-43

very resource-intensive approach to generating growth, which means that Chinese growth has come at the expense of the environment.

The complexities of economic growth are reflected in the wide varieties of views on the topic seen in the economics profession. This chapter features both mainstream and alternative views regarding the major forces that drive economic growth. Mainstream New Keynesian theories tend to stress the growth of factors of production (capital and labor), technological progress, and certain key institutions (property rights, rule of law, stability). Supply-side economists focus on private sector incentives, preferring to minimize government intervention and maximize private sector flexibility. Political economists highlight the role of a wider range of institutions on growth, especially the role of government as a facilitator and engine of growth, the importance of aggregate demand and the profit rate, and the need for labor market arrangements that foster equality, productivity, and innovation.

The chapter begins by discussing the importance of economic growth in determining the standard of living of people within an economic system, along with some of the variations in growth experiences around the world. We then turn to the mainstream New Keynesian model of economic growth, which focuses on the role of capital goods, improvements in technology, and human capital as key drivers of growth. Utilizing these ideas, mainstream economists advocate policies to increase savings and investment, stimulate innovation, and improve education and training. In contrast, supply-side (laissez-faire) economists take a different approach to growth, arguing that deregulation along with tax cuts for the wealthy, corporations, and workers will be most effective in stimulating growth. Next, we turn to the ideas of political economists, who see the effectiveness of the state as the main driver of growth along with the overall macroeconomic environment.

The chapter concludes by discussing growth and sustainability, as economists try to determine how modern economic systems can continue to grow without creating excessive environmental devastation. Effective policies that stimulate the development of green technologies and industries while phasing out dirty ones could allow modern economies to grow sustainably. Establishing such a system is one of the major issues of our time.

33.0 CHAPTER 33 LEARNING GOALS

After reading this chapter you should be able to:

■ Explain how exponential growth affects the standard of living of various countries.

■ Describe, compare, and evaluate the New Keynesian, supply-side, and political economy models of economic growth and the policies each group advocates to stimulate growth.

■ Discuss the various perspectives on growth and sustainability and determine what you think would be the best approach to resolve the seeming contradictions between growth and environmental preservation.

We begin by taking up the importance of economic growth in determining a nation's standard of living, along with some of growth experiences of countries around the globe.

33.1 THE IMPORTANCE OF ECONOMIC GROWTH

To classical economists such as Adam Smith and Karl Marx, economic growth and the distribution of income were the most important topics of study. Economic growth determined a country's standard of living, which was seen as the major determinant of well-being. And the distribution of income determined whether or not most of the population was benefiting from economic growth. Growth still occupies an important place in modern economics and remains the top economic priority for most countries.

Growth is an exponential process, which means that its impact grows larger and larger with time. In a typical year in the United States, real per capita GDP grows by about 2%, so output is 102% as large as output the previous year. This is a result of an increase in the number of businesses, productivity from business investment in additional capital goods, better technology that increases productivity even further, an increase in the quantity of laborers, and better skills and knowledge that increase labor productivity. Next year, even more businesses will form, more capital goods will be purchased, new technologies will be invented, and new skills and knowledge will be created, increasing real per capita GDP by another 2%. In essence, *machines, factories, and businesses can create additional machines, factories, and businesses.* Now real per capita GDP is 2% higher than 102%, or 104.04% of the amount two years ago. The following year real per capita GDP will be 106.12% of the original level. Then 108.24%. Then 110.4%. And so on. Notice that because growth builds on growth exponentially, real GDP per capita goes up slightly faster than the 2% rate of growth.

Due to the fact that growth is an exponential process, over time small differences in growth lead to large differences in a country's standard of living, as measured by per capita GDP. A simple way to observe these differences is with the rule of 70, **a mathematical formula that estimates how many years it takes for a variable growing at an exponential rate to double**.

$$\text{Number of years for a variable to double}(t) = \frac{70}{\text{Annual \% growth rate of the variable}(g)}.$$

To give an example of the impact of different rates of economic growth, from 1960 to 2018, the average annual rate of growth in U.S. per capita GDP was 2%: $t = \dfrac{70}{2} = 35$. This meant that U.S. income doubled every 35 years. However, since 2000, annual growth in U.S. per capita GDP has been closer to 1%, which means that it will take 70 years for our income to double if this lower growth rate persists. From 1980 to 2018, China experienced an annual rate of growth in per capita GDP of 8.5%, which meant that incomes in China doubled every 8.2 years ($t = \dfrac{70}{8.5} = 8.2$)! As a result, a Chinese worker earning $1000 in 1980 would see their income double five times in 41 years to reach $32,000 in 2021.

We can solve for the increase in the worker's income as follows. The worker's income starts at $1000, doubles once to $2000, doubles a second time to $4000, doubles a third time to $8000, doubles a fourth time to $16,000, and doubles a fifth time to $32,000. Mathematically, we can use the following formula:

$$\text{New income} = \left(\text{Original income}\right) * 2^{\left(\text{Number of doublings}\right)}$$

In this example, the new income is $1000*2^5=$32,000. Thus, the rate of growth determines how quickly incomes increase.

Rapid economic growth has transformed poor countries into rich countries. Poor economic growth has constrained citizens in other countries to poverty for the long term. Figure 33.1 shows the large countries that have grown the most quickly in recent decades, with China, South Korea, Vietnam, and India leading the way. Most developed countries are clustered in the middle, close to the world average, with Ireland and Norway above average and Italy and Switzerland below average. Toward the bottom is Nigeria with growth averaging only 0.54%, Iran experiencing no growth, and Saudi Arabia experiencing negative growth with the decline in oil prices, its major export, in recent years.

According to the convergence hypothesis put forth by Clark Kerr and some other mainstream economists, **the productivity growth rates (and growth in per capita real GDP) of poor countries should tend to be higher than for rich countries, because poor countries can imitate and learn from the experiences of rich countries. If this occurs, then all economies should eventually converge to the same level of per capita income**. However, Figure 33.1 shows us a much more uneven pattern. China, South Korea, Vietnam, and other countries with the most rapid economic growth rates are converging with rich countries. However, Brazil, Kenya, Mexico, and Nigeria, among others, are actually falling further and further behind. Thus, one of the major trends in recent decades has been the amazing success of some developing countries, while most developing countries are still mired in poverty. Below we explore some of the reasons for these widely disparate growth experiences and the theories economists developed to explain economic growth patterns.

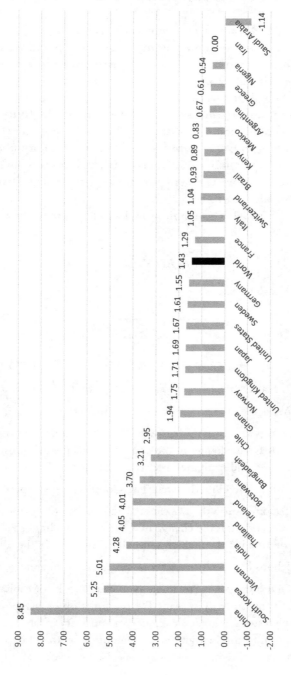

FIGURE 33.1 Average annual growth of real GDP per capita (%), 1980–2019.

33.2 THE MAINSTREAM, NEW KEYNESIAN APPROACH TO ECONOMIC GROWTH

To mainstream New Keynesian economists, economic growth is **the long-term, sustained increase in the economy's capacity (potential real GDP). Sustained economic growth from the mainstream perspective is driven by improvements in labor productivity**—when each laborer can produce a greater quantity of goods and services.

The **three sources of improvements in labor productivity**, which are the primary drivers of economic growth from this perspective, are (1) **increases in physical capital goods**, (2) **improvements in technology** (the quality of capital goods), and (3) **the quality of laborers** (often referred to as human capital). Mainstream economists estimate that improvements in technology have the greatest impact on economic growth.

The mainstream model of economic growth can be expressed by the following equations:

$$Y = \text{AF}(K, L) \tag{1}$$

$$\frac{\Delta Y}{Y} = \frac{\Delta A}{A} + \alpha_K \frac{\Delta K}{K} + \alpha_L \frac{\Delta L}{L}. \tag{2}$$

In these equations, Y is real GDP and ΔY is the change in real GDP, so $\frac{\Delta Y}{Y}$ is the growth rate in real GDP. A is total factor productivity, which is a measure of technology, and ΔA is the change in total factor productivity, so $\frac{\Delta A}{A}$ is the contribution of technology to economic growth. K is the country's existing physical capital stock, and ΔK is the change in the country's capital stock (business investment purchases of plants and equipment). α_K is capital's share of total income, which is usually 30% (0.30) in the United States. Therefore, $\alpha_K \frac{\Delta K}{K}$ represents capital's contribution to economic growth. L is the size and quality (human capital) of the country's labor force, and ΔL is the change in the size and quality of the labor force. α_L is labor's share of total income, which is usually 70% (0.70) in the United States. Thus, $\alpha_L \frac{\Delta L}{L}$ is labor's contribution to economic growth. Therefore, equation (1) tells us that real GDP depends on technology and the stocks of capital and labor. Equation (2) tells us that growth in real GDP is a function of changes in (a) technology, (b) the capital stock, and (c) the quality and quantity of labor. These factors and their contribution to productivity and economic growth are explored below, starting with what happens when there is an increase in the capital stock.

33.2.1 Increase in the capital stock

Mainstream economists use a production function (the total product of labor) to show the relationship between labor and output. Figure 33.2 shows the total product of labor curve for two different levels of capital goods, a smaller level K_1 and a larger level K_2. With a given amount of labor, L_1, the amount of output varies directly with the amount and quality of capital goods. With a smaller amount of capital, K_1, the economy produces an output (real GDP) of Y_1. When economic actors invest in additional capital goods, such that $K_2 > K_1$, output increases from Y_1 to Y_2. There is a direct, positive relationship between the amount of capital goods and the productivity of laborers. If workers have more capital or better capital to work with, they are more productive during each hour they work and therefore output will increase for each amount of labor hours. Or, to be more precise, *for a given level of technology and number of labor hours, labor productivity tends to increase as the capital stock increases.* As a classic example, a lumberjack with a chainsaw can cut down eight times as many trees in the same amount of time as a lumberjack with an axe—an 800% increase in productivity per labor hour.

An increase in the quantity of labor hours from L_1 to L_2 (holding capital constant), perhaps from an increase in immigration or an increase in the working-age population, would move the economy along the production function, causing real GDP to increase from Y_1 to Y_3. Note that productivity per labor hour does not increase but total production of goods and services does increase because there are more laborers performing more work. This analysis assumes that there are additional jobs for the new laborers to do.

33.2.2 Improvements in technology

Mainstream economists estimate that as much as 60%–80% of economic growth is a result of technological change. The impact of an improvement in technology is

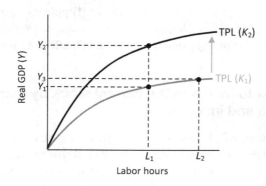

FIGURE 33.2 Change in a country's production function from an increase in capital.

similar to the impact of an increase in the capital stock: *With better technology, workers can produce more output per hour of labor.* This would shift the production function in Figure 33.2 up in the same way that an increase in the capital stock would.

33.2.3 Improvements in the quality of labor (human capital)

One of the key drivers of productivity is the level of education and training of laborers. This is sometimes called "human capital" to capture the idea that the value of human labor increases with the amount of education and training they receive. Economists estimate that improvements in human capital are more important than increases in physical capital in increasing growth. German manufacturing firms, which produce many of the highest value manufactured goods in the world (everything from BMW, Mercedes, Audi, and VW cars to Kuka industrial robots to Sennheiser and Bosch electronics), invest between $25,000 and $200,000 in training for each worker in addition to the education and training provided by the government. They see this training as essential in the production of the highest quality goods. An improvement in human capital would also shift the production function in Figure 33.2 up in the same manner as an increase in the capital stock or an improvement in technology. After an increase in human capital, production of goods and services would be higher for each labor hour worked.

33.3 NEW KEYNESIAN POLICIES TO STIMULATE ECONOMIC GROWTH

Given the mainstream New Keynesian view that economic growth is driven by improvements in labor productivity, and increases in labor productivity are driven by improvements in the capital stock, technology, or human capital, New Keynesian policies to encourage economic growth focus on these three areas. The most important policies from this perspective are (1) policies to stimulate savings and investment, including a stable political system with secure property rights; (2) policies to stimulate technology development; and (3) efforts to improve education and training.

33.3.1 Policies to increase the capital stock by stimulating savings and investment

Investment purchases of physical capital result in a larger capital stock, which increases productivity and economic growth. Recall that physical capital includes **plants** (factories, office buildings, other physical structures) and **equipment** (computers, software, robots, internet infrastructure, and so on). Policies that stimulate investment in plants and equipment tend to increase economic growth. However, sparking increases in investment purchases of physical capital goods is extremely difficult given its unpredictability. As John Maynard Keynes pointed out, investment is extremely risky and uncertain, so it requires just the right conditions.

We can utilize the major determinants of investment from previous chapters to come up with policies that might stimulate additional amounts of business investment purchases. First, the largest determinant of business investment is expectations of future sales. Therefore, **policies that lead to sustained growth in the demand** for businesses' products will stimulate investment, because businesses will have confidence that their investment will see a return. Possible policy options include **stabilization policies** in recessions to stimulate growth and **policies to increase wages and incomes**, especially of workers who spend most of their incomes. In the United States in the 1950s and 1960s, government support of unions and U.S. manufacturing dominance created a virtuous circle, where higher wages sparked an increase in consumer purchases that caused businesses to increase investment in the size of their operations, which then caused additional job creation and even higher wages.

More controversially, a country might **protect domestic markets** from foreign competition to give domestic companies a larger market share. However, such policies may not be successful if trading partners respond with similar protective efforts, as is often the case.

Policies to **reduce real interest rates** can also lead to increases in investment purchases if the macroeconomic conditions are right. If businesses have good investment opportunities and if interest rates are low, then the conditions for an increase in investment are good. But as we know from decades of research, when economic prospects are poor, lowering interest rates tends to have little or no impact on investment purchases.

Investment tax credits or other **tax policies that increase the profitability of investing** may increase investment. These can include investment tax credits, subsidies for key inputs such as imported technology to reduce the costs of investing, and subsidized loans. Some economists advocate policies to increase savings so banks have more money to loan out. However, as we know from Keynes, more savings means less consumption spending, which can erode aggregate demand and the investment climate. Thus, economists tend to disagree on whether or not prioritizing savings is a good idea.

Many economists also advocate **making an economy open to foreign direct investment (FDI)** in order to stimulate investment purchases in the domestic economy. In theory, foreign direct investment, which is purchases of domestic companies and capital goods by foreign companies and investors, can increase a country's capital stock directly. Even though FDI capital is controlled by foreign owners, it will increase productivity and jobs in the domestic economy. New Keynesian economists tend to encourage developing economies with low savings rates to try to attract foreign direct investment as a means to improve economic growth. For example, a study by Bellak et al. indicated that lowering taxes, improving labor productivity, providing infrastructure, increasing research and development funding, and lowering labor costs tend to increase foreign direct investment.[1] China is credited with attracting substantial FDI via all of these policies. Note, however, that China insisted that all foreign investors have a local partner and utilize the latest technology, which guaranteed that Chinese firms would gain the latest technical knowledge and experience in order to become globally competitive. Other countries that do not have China's clout are often at the mercy of foreign investors, which can lead to a "sweatshop model" of foreign direct investment based on low wages and exploitative working conditions. The sweatshop model is not generally associated with significant, long-term growth because it does not stimulate domestic aggregate demand, local knowledge, or local technology in a significant way, and the country owning the sweatshops reaps the lion's share of the benefits.

Another crucial variable is the **stability of the political climate**. Investment is highly risky, so it thrives in an environment that fosters stability. Political stability is very important. Countries where regular coup attempts happen or where elections are frequently disputed experience instability, which tends to reduce investment. Countries that have a stable government with a cohesive set of laws and rules that are applied systematically and fairly provide a stable basis for firms to invest. New Keynesian economists also emphasize the role of stable **property rights** in fostering investment. Businesses that are secure that they will be able to reap the benefits from their investments, and not have them stolen, will tend to invest more. Corrupt governments where insiders regularly seize private businesses, such as Russia in the 2000s, have the effect of stifling investment.

33.3.2 Policies to stimulate technological innovation

Improvements in technology allow firms to get more output from the same amount of labor or to keep output the same while employing fewer laborers. Either way, technological development can improve the profit rate for businesses. However, technological development is uncertain. A firm can invest huge sums on new technology only to have it flounder. For example, the Google+ social media platform intended as an alternative to Facebook or Samsung's fragile Galaxy Fold folding smartphone both involved substantial investments in new technologies that did not pay off. Or a new technology can lead to huge profits if successful—for example, Google's internet search engine and Apple's iPhone.

One of the major roles for governments is to structure a nation's economy in such a way that technological development is encouraged. Given that New Keynesian economists credit technology with the primary role in driving economic growth, innovation policy should be one of the most important priorities for a government striving to stimulate growth.

One of the most direct and effective ways to promote innovation is to increase funding for research and development (R&D), which involves **activities designed to result in scientific breakthroughs, design and introduce new**

products, or improve existing products or manufacturing processes. Government funding for scientific research at universities and government research labs, often called "basic" science, can lead to transformational breakthroughs. For example, the internet was created by university researchers with funding from the U.S. military. In general, due to the uncertainty and long timeframe involved in scientific breakthroughs, corporations rarely devote significant amounts to such endeavors. This is why government funding is so crucial and why governments are the primary source of funding for the basic scientific research that results in major innovations.

However, the private sector is good at using scientific breakthroughs to design and introduce new products or new manufacturing techniques. Corporations turned the internet, originally designed for sharing information between researchers, into a vehicle for ecommerce, social media, coordinating supply chains, and much more. The government can encourage private sector spending on research and development by offering tax breaks to reduce the cost of spending on private sector R&D. But there is no substitute for government funding for scientific research at universities and government research centers, which generates regular scientific breakthroughs that spill over into the private sector, creating new products, industries, and jobs in the process. As another example, *every* new drug developed and approved in the United States from 2010 to 2016 was based at least in part on research from the National Institutes of Health. This research involved more than $100 billion in funding, more than 90% of which was considered "basic" scientific research.[2]

Due to the importance of R&D and a skilled workforce, **increasing access to higher education and improving its quality**, especially in technology-related fields in science, technology, and engineering, can be a good way to foster technological innovation. One of the reasons the United States is the leader in many tech industries is its impressive university system, generally seen as the best in the world.

Given the importance of innovation for economic growth, researchers have tried to identify the best ways to stimulate innovation. Authors of the Global Innovation Index, constructed by researchers at Cornell University, INSEAD (Institut Européen d'Administration des Affaires), and the United Nations, determined that the following elements have a direct impact on innovation: Political stability, government effectiveness, regulatory quality, rule of law, ease of starting or closing a business, education, research and development, information and communication technologies, infrastructure, ecological sustainability, market sophistication, number of knowledge workers, innovation linkages (between universities, governments, and businesses), knowledge absorption and creation, and creative outputs.[3] Based on these measures, the top ten countries in the Global Innovation Index rankings for 2020 are displayed in Figure 33.3.

Switzerland leads the way (as it has for the last ten years) with an economic system that features extremely skilled, well-trained, and knowledgeable workers; high research and development expenditures; advanced universities that collaborate

Rank	Economy	Score
1	Switzerland	66.1
2	Sweden	62.5
3	United States	60.6
4	United Kingdom	59.8
5	Netherlands	58.8
6	Denmark	57.5
7	Finland	57.0
8	Singapore	56.6
9	Germany	56.5
10	South Korea	56.1

FIGURE 33.3 Table showing the Global Innovation Index, 2020.

effectively with industries; science and technology clusters; efficient, noncorrupt government; strong sustainability; and an infrastructure that may be the world's most efficient. Sweden, ranked second for many years, features a similar set of characteristics, along with some of the most sophisticated government–university–industry partnerships in existence, as we discuss below. Interestingly, the United States, ranking third, has some similarities, especially its top-quality universities, science and technology clusters, and innovative private sector. The United States has some unique strengths, such as its entrepreneurial climate, creative sector, and incentives for revolutionary innovation, but it also has some notable weaknesses, including uneven government quality and poor performance with respect to sustainability.

It often surprises people that an emphasis on sustainability is a contributor to innovation. However, the world is increasingly demanding sustainable products. Those companies that can produce sustainably have a huge advantage in the modern marketplace, making sustainability a key ingredient in successful innovation.

People often do not expect a vibrant creative sector, including art, literature, music, cinema, and theater, to be an essential contributor to innovation. Creative thinking is where new ideas come from, which directly fosters innovation, so countries featuring strong creativity tend to be very innovative. This is why U.S. employers regularly rank creativity as one of the top abilities they are looking for in job applicants.

Interestingly, only one of the countries atop the Global Innovation Index, South Korea at #10, ranks in the top ten for per capita economic growth (shown in Figure 33.1). Thus, there is much more to economic growth than fostering innovation, as we will discuss below.

33.3.3 Policies to improve education quality and access, training, and skills

In addition to its contributions to innovation, human capital is crucial to economic growth in other ways. More educated and better trained workers are more productive and earn higher incomes, which stimulates aggregate demand at the same time it improves the functioning of firms. Economists estimate that education is more important than investment in stimulating economic growth.

Figure 33.4 shows educational spending as a percentage of GDP in various OECD countries. Norway spends the most, at 6.6% of GDP, and Ireland spends the least, at 3.4% of GDP. Notice that the Anglo-Saxon economies—the United Kingdom and its former colonies such as the United States, Ireland, and Australia—spend less on public education and more on private education than other countries.

The Nordic countries, whose educational systems are rated the most effective in terms of student learning and overall access, feature high levels of public spending and very little private spending. This is largely because they have decided that quality education is a human right and that the economy benefits from everyone receiving a first-rate education. Even poor children in these economic systems get a quality education and a (free) college education.

The United States usually ranks below the OECD average in math, science, and reading skills, primarily due to the extreme inequality of the U.S. educational system. In the United States, where property taxes tend to determine how much money each school district has, rich towns have excellent schools, whereas poor towns have poor schools.

Education in only one component of human capital. Training and skill development are another key component. Note that although Germany spends a below-average amount on education, they spend an above-average amount on training and skills, which is a major reason their manufacturing firms are so productive and their manufactured goods of such high quality. U.S. spending on worker training is among the lowest of developed countries, whereas the social market economies of Europe spend the most.

Now that we have examined the mainstream approach to economic growth, we need to consider other perspectives. First, we discuss the laissez-faire, supply-side approach to economic growth. Then, we take up the political economy approach.

33.4 THE SUPPLY-SIDE (LAISSEZ-FAIRE) APPROACH TO ECONOMIC GROWTH

As we saw earlier, supply-side economists prefer a laissez-faire approach to the economy. Government interventions from this perspective are confined primarily to assisting corporations (suppliers) and the wealthy (investors), so that they create jobs and wealth that trickle down to average people.

More specifically, supply-side economists have the following theories regarding growth:

1.   Economic growth is determined primarily by aggregate supply rather than aggregate demand (supply creates demand according to supply-side theories), so the conditions impacting firms are paramount.

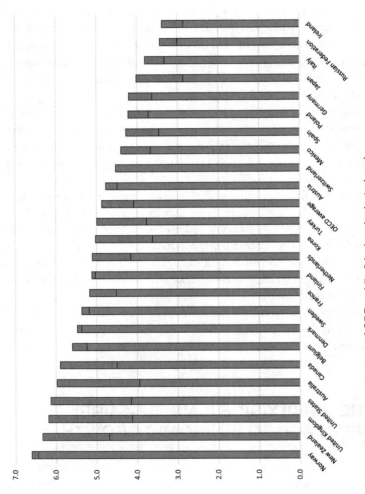

FIGURE 33.4 Educational spending as a percentage of GDP, public (blue) and private (gray).

2. As with mainstream economists, supply-siders believe that the major drivers of growth are increases in investment purchases (capital), technological change, and increases in the number and productivity of laborers. However, they believe that different factors drive changes in these variables.

3. Incentives for saving and investment are the primary determinants of economic growth. The major factors affecting saving and investment are policies that determine their after-tax returns. According to the supply-side approach, tax cuts for the wealthy, reductions in capital gains taxes, and tax cuts for businesses are the preferred policies to increase saving and investment and thereby stimulate growth.

4. Labor supply can be increased via tax policy as well by reducing the marginal tax rates that workers pay. In theory, this gives workers an incentive to work more, increasing labor supply, and promoting productivity and growth.

5. Deregulation of businesses can facilitate investment and growth and should be pursued vigorously.

President Trump used these ideas to argue that his 2017 tax cuts for U.S. corporations and the wealthy would provide "rocket fuel" for the economy, generating jobs and growth in the process. However, a comprehensive 2020 study by David Hope and Julian Limberg of Kings College London examined 18 advanced countries over 50 years and found that major tax cuts for the rich increase inequality but have no significant effect on economic growth or unemployment.[4] Their research compared countries that passed laws for major tax cuts in a given year with those that did not. The impact of tax cuts over the next five years included permanent increases in inequality but no increase in growth or employment relative to countries that did not implement tax cuts for the rich.

There is some evidence that tax cuts for laborers can increase labor supply slightly, especially for adults who are the second earner in a family. However, the impacts on labor supply are very small, and there is no measurable increase in economic growth as a result.

Though the latest economic research has not been kind to supply-side theories, these ideas continue to be important in the United States and some countries where conservative politicians still subscribe to these views. In other countries such as the social democracies of Europe, political economy theories have held much more influence. We turn to these ideas next.

33.5 THE POLITICAL ECONOMY APPROACH TO ECONOMIC GROWTH

Political economists agree with much of the mainstream Keynesian approach to economic growth, but they have a few disagreements. In particular, they argue that a much broader set of factors determine the rate of economic growth and that the government is the most important determinant of the growth rate, followed by aggregate demand.

First, political economists see the **government, its quality, and the economic system it establishes with its policies** as the most important factors in determining the level of innovation and growth. In Mariana Mazzucato's book *The Entrepreneurial State*, she points out that governments do much more than support basic scientific research. In addition to basic science, governments fund areas along the entire innovation chain, including applied research, early stage financing for high-risk endeavors, infrastructure support, education and training support, and much more. As one example from the United States, Apple received money from the Small Business Investment Corporation and then developed the smartphone based on technologies that were almost all developed through government funding and projects, including the internet, GPS, touchscreens, and voice activation.

Some governments partner directly with the private sector in collaborative projects designed to stimulate innovation and job creation. Perhaps the most sophisticated example of this is the triple helix approach to innovation utilized by Sweden and the other Nordic countries, in which **government, universities, and industry interact as partners to generate ideas, invent and spread technologies, and develop industries and communities**. Governments establish the partnerships, fund the research, and build the infrastructure for the developing industry. Universities conduct the scientific research that leads to breakthroughs and train workers and managers in the best techniques for the new product or industry. And the private sector designs and introduces new products and processes based on the scientific breakthroughs, utilizing the infrastructure, training, and new ideas. This approach is credited with stimulating the biotechnology industry and the information and communications technology industry in Sweden, now among the leaders in these sectors in the E.U. Twenty percent of new private sector products in Sweden can be tied directly to research partnerships with universities, and the impact of the triple helix model is felt more broadly in the development of technology clusters featuring universities, multiple firms, workers, and government support tailored to a particular industry.

Interestingly, countries that have grown the most rapidly over the last 50 years have all used what economists call a developmental state, where **the government undertakes macroeconomic planning and policies to stimulate industrial development in strategic sectors**. Japan, China, and South Korea have been particularly effective with this approach. China has some unique advantages as the world's largest country with a vast potential market, which made it easier for China to attract foreign investment and technology under favorable conditions. Therefore, South Korea's economic performance as the country with the second-most rapid growth of per capita GDP may be more impressive.

The South Korean developmental state featured the following key characteristics:

- **Land reform.** South Korea seized vast estates from absentee Japanese land-owners and redistributed the land to independent, family proprietors, firmly establishing property rights, incentives for productivity, and a strong agricultural base from which to grow.

- **Industrial policy and planning.** The South Korean government identified industries in which the country could succeed, spent money on R&D to identify the best technologies for those industries, subsidized local conglomerates to enter those industries, and invested massively in infrastructure (postal service, telecom, rails, air, and ports), education, and training to give those industries a competitive advantage.

- **Protectionism and monitorable performance standards.** Using the infant industry approach, South Korea protected the new industries from foreign competition with tariffs until they could be internationally competitive. The government also subsidized key inputs to keep their costs low. However, firms receiving protection were required to increase domestic investment and employment, R&D spending, and exports. The strong export orientation forced firms to become internationally competitive quickly or be faced with the withdrawal of government support. Once firms were competitive, subsidies could be reduced or eliminated, and funding could shift to new areas.

- **Sequential industrialization.** South Korea began by producing simple manufactured goods that fit with their existing skills and resources, including grain production, energy, and textiles. As their manufacturing experience, skills, and technology improved, they shifted to steel, electronics, and machinery and then to cars and shipbuilding. More recently, they dramatically increased R&D spending, developed an advanced technology sector, and increased efforts to spur creative thinking and creative industries to fuel new ideas and innovations.

The results were impressive. In 1960 South Korea was one of the poorest countries in the world. By 2020, South Korea was a wealthy country, with a higher GDP per capita the most E.U. countries. South Korea's per capita rate of economic growth has averaged 5.25% for the last four decades, and its products are admired around the world, including Hyundai and Kia cars, Samsung and LG phones, TVs and appliances, and K-Pop.

Thus, from a political economy perspective, the effectiveness of government, including planning and execution of economic development programs, is paramount in driving economic growth. The impact of government on innovation and growth is based on far more than support for basic science and the establishment of stable property rights.

Second, political economists stress the **importance of aggregate demand** to investment and growth. Without the expectation of future sales and profits, businesses will not invest in new capital or spend on R&D to develop new technology. Future sales depend on having sufficient aggregate demand. Aggregate demand depends most importantly on the income and willingness to spend of the population as a whole. This is one of the reasons why infant industry protection can stimulate investment and growth—it ensures that a new industry will have a protected market with sufficient demand for its products. The key is to make sure the protection eventually is removed or reduced, as South Korea did, so that firms become internationally competitive rather than serving as a perpetual drain on the economy.

From the political economy perspective, economic growth can be driven by higher wages, in direct contradiction to the supply-side argument. Higher wages increase aggregate demand, causing businesses to increase production. Businesses produce at a higher rate of capacity when demand is high and may even start to run out of excess capacity if the surge in demand is large enough. The combination of **higher profits** from increased sales and running out of production capacity (**higher capacity utilization**) stimulates new investment and growth. This helps us to understand why the most rapid and sustained period of economic growth in the United States in the last century was during the 1950s and 1960s, when U.S. real wages also increased rapidly.

Correspondingly, one of the reasons for the slowing of growth in the United States and in other developed countries in recent decades is the significant increase in **inequality** and its impact on aggregate demand. Because rich people spend a smaller percentage of their income than the middle class and the poor, the redistribution of income from the poorest 80% to the richest 1% results in a decline in aggregate demand, which undermines expected sales and profits for most businesses.

Some economies try to circumvent insufficient domestic demand by orienting their economies toward exports. This is true of Germany, China, South Korea, and Japan, all of whom established policies to promote exports. Export-oriented policies include low-cost government loans, subsidies, protection from foreign competition as new industries are being established (infant industry protection), and policies to keep labor costs low.

The degree of inequality is also important in determining if the benefits of economic growth are broadly shared. Economic growth that is only experienced by the richest portion of a country's population, as has been the case in the United States in recent decades, does not improve the lives of most of the population. This defeats the primary purpose of economic growth, which is to improve the lives of a country's residents.

The third major determinant of investment and growth from a political economy perspective is the **profit rate**. Businesses cannot invest unless they have a sufficient rate of profit over and above their costs of production. But they also need a reason to invest their profits, instead of just sitting on them. In 2019, Apple kept more than $200 billion in cash because they did not have good opportunities for investment that would have a good expected return. Apple also did not face stiff enough competition that they felt compelled to put that money toward R&D. Thus, investment requires a sufficient profit rate along with enough competition, demand, and stability to encourage firms to invest. To the extent the state can establish a stable or increasing level of aggregate demand, sufficiently competitive markets, and a macroeconomic environment in which corporations can earn adequate profits, a country can expect a high level of investment.

This highlights the extent to which **incentives for firms** to invest are a key determinant of the rate of investment. After the supply-side Trump tax cuts in 2017, most firms used their windfall for stock buybacks, which increased the value of their stock but had no impact on the amount of investment in capital goods. As noted above, there was no uptick in economic growth as a result of the tax cuts. On the other hand, South Korea's insistence that corporations use tax breaks or subsidies for investment in R&D activities meant that government funds were channeled directly into productive corporate activities.

Another interesting focus in political-economic analysis is on **the use of society's surplus** and whether or not the surplus is invested productively in capital goods or spent wastefully on consumer goods. Under feudalism, most of the surplus generated by society was spent on churches, castles, riches for nobles, and other consumption goods rather than on capital goods that could have increased productivity and growth. The result was a stagnant society.

We still see this distinction today. In many dictatorships, government officials use the country's surplus to fund luxurious living for themselves rather than investing in new productive capacity or human capital. Turkey's President Recep Tayyip Erdogan built himself a presidential palace with 1150 rooms and opulent furnishings at a cost of more than $1 billion. Imagine how many productive businesses could have been funded and how many educations paid for had that money been spent on productive activities.

In contrast, economic systems that promote investment in physical and human capital tend to experience more rapid economic growth. The governments of China and South Korea channel society's surplus funds directly to investments that will enhance economic growth. In the United States, tax cuts for corporations and the wealthy in 2017 did not stimulate investment largely because there was no requirement that the funds be used in a particular way.

Another key factor in political economy is the importance of incentives in the workplace to give workers reasons to be productive. Worker productivity is directly tied to the intensity with which workers apply themselves during work, which is driven by **labor market incentives**. In coercive, exploitative systems— the "stick approach"—workers are more likely to have a hostile attitude toward their employer and to shirk work whenever possible. In more cooperative systems where workers are involved in decision making and rewarded for their productivity—the "carrot approach"—workers tend to enjoy their work and to enthusiastically embrace efforts to increase productivity.

Germany, Japan, and South Korea are famous for their labor productivity, which is tied to worker involvement in key decisions about how work is done, incentives for workers to come up with ideas to improve the efficiency of their work, and relatively cooperative labor–management relations that foster shared interests and identity. Unions often play a positive role in establishing these types of employment relations in particular industries. Germany led the world in labor productivity in 2017 due to their combination of worker incentives and training, along with their cutting-edge technology.

Related factors that affect worker productivity include health care, childcare, and other forms of family support. Better medical coverage makes workers healthier and more productive. Free or subsidized childcare makes it easier for people to work and makes it less likely that they will need to miss work. Generous family leave programs encourage parents, and especially women, to stay in the workforce after they start a family, increasing the country's labor force participation rate and its productivity over the long time.

Taken together, the political economy approach to growth focuses much more on the role of the state and the overall environment affecting innovation and investment. Furthermore, political economists emphasize the importance of aggregate demand and the profit rate in determining investment and growth. As a result, political economists support much more extensive government intervention to increase the rate of growth, whereas laissez-faire, supply-side economists support less government intervention and New Keynesian economists pursue a middle path. Another area in which political economists see the need for extensive government intervention surrounds the topic of growth and sustainability.

33.6 GROWTH AND SUSTAINABILITY

Increasing alarm at environmental devastation and climate change in recent decades has resulted in a new emphasis on sustainable growth in the modern world. As we know, without adjustments in how we structure our economic systems, it is likely that we will not be able to continue to experience the same amount of economic growth that we have in the past.

Until very recently, economists tended to emphasize economic growth above all other economic goals. One of the reasons environmental issues were ignored was due to an idea called the environmental Kuznets curve, which theorized that **as countries grow and became wealthier, they can afford to pay more attention to the environment, developing technologies, regulations, and clean production methods that reduce their environmental impact**. According to this theory, **environmental destruction should increase during the first step of industrialization, then level off, and then decline as a country's standard of living increases**.

Figure 33.5 shows an environmental Kuznets curve for the United States, plotting tons of carbon dioxide emissions per capita against real GDP per capita. We can see the inverted U shape that the environmental Kuznets theory predicts, but the drop in CO_2 emissions has not been dramatic considering how wealthy the

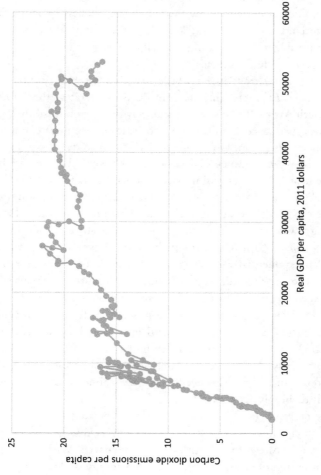

FIGURE 33.5 The U.S. environmental Kuznets curve for CO_2, 1800–2016.

United States has become. If other countries follow the same pattern, then we will not get rich enough fast enough to stave off disastrous climate change.

Figure 33.6 plots carbon dioxide emissions in tons per capita and real GDP per capita for every country in the world in 2019. Instead of an inverted U shape we see a general upward trend, indicating that as countries get wealthier, they emit more CO_2. It appears that the environmental Kuznets curve does not accurately explain the connection between growth and environmental destruction.

Instead, we see the influence of sustainability policies on a country's environmental impact. Countries well below the trend line, such as Norway, Singapore, Sweden, Switzerland, and Costa Rica, actively purse sustainability via government policies. They are able to achieve a much smaller impact on the environment at the same income level as other countries.

Countries above the trend line pay little attention to the environmental impact of their economies. Examples include Kuwait, Saudi Arabia, the United States, Russia, and South Africa. These countries all rely heavily on fossil fuels, including the dirtiest ones such as coal and oil, and do little to promote renewable energy use and carbon sequestration. Given that global efforts to date have not been very effective in reducing environmental destruction, there could be devastating consequences in the near future that will impact economic growth.

Climate change and other forms of environmental degradation are eroding the productive capacity of numerous industries. Therefore, countries that prioritize unsustainable growth now will pay the price of devastating economic declines in the future. In *Limits to Growth*, systems analysts Meadows, Randers, and Meadows observe that "an exponentially growing economy depletes resources, emits wastes, and diverts land from the production of renewable resources."[5] Eventually, sometime later this century, the exhaustion of nonrenewable resources like oil and the reductions in food and renewable resource production from ocean acidification, climate change, soil loss, and pollution will lead to reductions in productivity, declines in real GDP per capita, decreases in human well-being, and possibly even mass starvation. Only immediate and dramatic efforts to establish a sustainable economic system can prevent this eventuality according to their forecasts, which have proven disturbingly accurate so far.

Given the fact that growth to date has been associated with greater environmental destruction, some economists, such as Nicholas Georgescu-Roegen and E. F. Schumacher, advocate zero growth or even **degrowth**. Without people reducing their consumption of products, resources, and energy, and without a reframing of society's orientation away from unlimited economic growth, these economists see little hope for the planet. Schumacher, in his famous book *Small Is Beautiful*, argues that material wealth is hollow and unfulfilling, and we can actually achieve greater happiness and well-being by focusing on meaningful work, deep human relationships, and living in harmony with nature, while reducing our consumption of material goods and our ecological footprint.

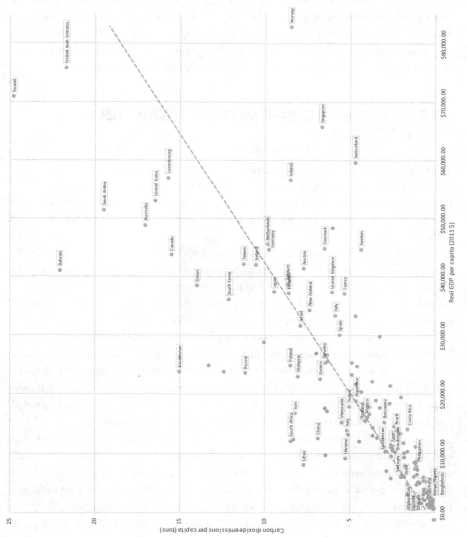

FIGURE 33.6 Real GDP per capita and CO₂ emissions per capita, 2019.

As an alternative to degrowth, most political economists push for **sustainable growth**. As noted earlier, evidence indicates that most environmental regulations do not reduce economic growth, and if done effectively, environmental policy can actually increase growth. In order to increase economic growth, environmental regulations need to be structured to promote investment in new technologies, which can then lead to lower costs and the development of new products. Germany's investments in green technology and Costa Rica's investments in eco-tourism and geo-thermal energy have fueled economic growth. This is the reason why many political economists believe that governments should enact targeted policies that improve sustainability and promote growth at the same time.

33.7 POLICIES TO PROMOTE SUSTAINABLE GROWTH

Most people desire a higher standard of living, but we also need to preserve our environment if we want to be able to maintain our standard of living in the future. Therefore, a key question for modern economic systems is to identify the best policies to generate sustainable growth. Some of the best ideas are described below.

Incentivize pollution reductions via taxes or tradable emissions permits. One of the best ways to move away from pollution-generating activities is to tax them or make them costly. The vast majority of economists support a carbon tax to impose a cost on any activity that generates carbon dioxide, which is the main driver of global climate change. Or governments can establish markets for pollution rights via tradable emissions permits, which similarly incentivize economic actors to pollute less. (See the chapter on the economics of the environment and climate change for more details.) Also, governments should reduce subsidies for environmentally destructive activities, such as U.S. subsidies for oil exploration. So far, countries that have implemented these programs have not experienced declines in economic growth and have experienced some of the largest reductions in pollution.

Similarly, industrial agriculture contributes significantly to climate change and should be discouraged, whereas regenerative grazing and sustainable agriculture, which sequester carbon and generate healthier food, should be subsidized. Suburbanization and production that results in deforestation must be curtailed, and tree planting and measures to preserve valuable natural areas such as the Amazon rain forest must be established. Fossil fuel-based cars and airplanes need to be phased out and replaced with public transportation and electric vehicles that utilize sustainably generated electricity. Recycling and composting can be required to disincentivize and reduce waste.

Incentivize or directly engage in investment in sustainable practices and alternatives. The key to sustainable growth is the development of new technologies that reduce pollution and resource use while improving productivity. Governments can conduct extensive research and development on such initiatives and subsidize research at universities and business research labs. Governments can also establish industrial clusters with the appropriate infrastructure, education, and private sector partners to develop new processes and products utilizing the green technologies they develop.

The right set of policies could lead to a complete reorientation of an economic system from unsustainable growth to sustainable growth. Indeed, this is the whole premise of the "Green New Deal" proposed in various countries, which seeks to create jobs in new, sustainable industries at a faster rate than jobs in dirty industries are destroyed. Unfortunately, even though evidence indicates that these policies are likely to work, they are opposed vigorously by the vested interests who would be harmed by this change toward environmental preservation. Fossil fuel producers, dirty industries, and producers of goods that harm ecological sustainability all oppose the Green New Deal, and their political clout makes such changes difficult to implement. It will be interesting to see whether the groundswell of support for sustainable practices is strong enough to overcome the inertia created by the opposition of unsustainable industries toward sustainable growth.

33.8 CONCLUSION

We began this chapter by discussing how economic growth is a major determinant of the standard of living of people within a country. Some countries such as China, South Korea, and Vietnam are growing quickly using a state-led approach. Other countries, including India and Ireland, have been successful in recent decades with a more market-oriented approach. Using the rule of 70, we can determine that these rapidly growing countries are seeing a doubling in their GDP per capita every 8 to 17 years. But other countries utilizing state-led approaches (such as Brazil) and market-led approaches (such as Mexico and Kenya) have been much less successful. Therefore, a country's broad approach to generating growth is not enough to explain divergences in growth rates.

To attempt to explain growth patterns, the New Keynesian model of economic growth focuses on the role of capital goods, improvements in technology, and human capital. New Keynesian economists advocate policies to increase savings and investment, stimulate private sector innovation, and improve education and training to stimulate growth.

Supply-side economists believe that public sector intervention reduces growth and prefer deregulation of the economic system as well as tax cuts for the wealthy and corporations—a trickle-down approach. In contrast, political economists argue that the effectiveness of the state is the main contributor to economic growth. In addition, political economists view the overall macroeconomic environment, and especially the maintenance of adequate aggregate demand to spur investment, as crucial.

Lastly, we discussed how economic systems need to adjust their approach to engineer more environmentally sustainable growth. Countries need to implement policies that encourage R&D activities and investment in green technologies and sustainable industries to replace dirty ones. This could result in growth that is not as environmentally destructive as has historically been the case. With the looming problems associated with climate change and other environmental choke points, creating economies that feature sustainable growth is an urgent priority.

QUESTIONS FOR REVIEW

1. Vietnam's real GDP per capita has been growing by 5% per year, whereas Switzerland's has been growing at 1% per year. Using the *rule of 70* and assuming that these growth rates stay the same, if Vietnam's real GDP per capita is currently $3000 and Switzerland's real GDP per capita is $90,000, what will each country's real GDP per capita be in 70 years? What will each country's real GDP per capita be 140 years?

2. Explain the convergence hypothesis in your own words. Does evidence indicate that the convergence hypothesis accurately explains growth patterns?

3. Using the graph in Figure 33.7, show what will happen to the U.S. economy if (a) there is a major breakthrough in robotics that improves productivity and (b) the number of workers in the United States declines significantly due to immigration restrictions.

4. According to the New Keynesian approach, what are the major factors that contribute to economic growth? What policies do New Keynesian economists advocate in order to stimulate growth? Which of these policies do you find most compelling? Why?

5. What are the key elements of the supply-side approach to economic growth?

6. What are the key elements of the political economy approach to economic growth?

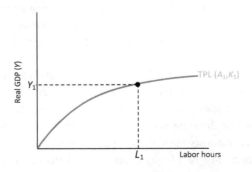

FIGURE 33.7 Production function for the United States.

7. Compare and contrast the approaches to innovation and growth taken by (a) New Keynesian economists, (b) supply-side economists, and (c) political economists. Which approach do you find most compelling? Explain and support your answer.

8. Explain the environmental Kuznets curve. Does the evidence support this theory? Why or why not?

9. Suppose that you are appointed the chair of the U.S. president's council of economic advisors and you are asked to suggest a set of policies to promote economic growth while preserving sustainability. What policies would you prioritize and why?

NOTES

1 C. Bellak, M. Leibrecht, and R. Stehrer, "Policies to Attract Foreign Direct Investment: An Industry-Level Analysis," OECD Global Forum on International Investment VII, 2008, https://www.oecd.org/investment/globalforum/40301081.pdf.

2 See E.G. Cleary, J.M. Beierlein, N.S. Khanuja, et al., "Contribution of NIH Funding to New Drug Approvals 2010–2016," *Proceedings of the National Academy of Sciences (PNAS)*, 155, No. 10, pp. 2329–2334, 2018. https://www.pnas.org/content/115/10/2329.

3 See Global Innovation Index, "Global Innovation Index 2020," https://www.global innovationindex.org/, accessed August 7, 2021.

4 See David Hope and Julian Limberg, "Footing the COVID-19 Bill: The Economic Case for Tax Hike on Wealth," *The Conversation*, https://theconversation.com/footing -the-covid-19-bill-economic-case-for-tax-hike-on-wealthy-151945, accessed August 7, 2021.

5 Donella Meadows, Jorgen Randers, and Dennis Meadows, *Limits to Growth: The 30-Year Update* (Chelsea Green Publishing, White River Junction, VT, 2012), p. 147.

International trade and integration

How unregulated trade, protectionism, and trade agreements affect economies

The global integration of economic systems completely restructured modern economies over the last 50 years. Economies went from being relatively isolated in the first half of the 20th century to extremely integrated by the 2020s. The impact of global integration was complex, with some people and some countries benefiting significantly while others lost ground.

Globalization, and the international trade that drives it, dramatically reshaped many countries and communities. Developed countries saw their manufacturing industries and blue-collar wages decline, while their tech and service sectors boomed. Global manufacturing shifted to China, South Korea, India, Taiwan, and other newly industrialized economies, although some developed countries like Germany and Japan were able to maintain their high-end manufacturing. Some developing countries caught up with the wealthy nations of the world, and others fell further behind and became increasingly marginalized.

During the globalization era, the United States pursued unregulated ("free") trade policies for the most part. This approach changed somewhat under the Trump administration. By the middle of 2021 it appeared to be the case that President Biden would maintain elements of Trump's protectionism, especially policies that seemed to be helping workers keep jobs in previously declining industries.

Most other developed countries opened up their markets to trade and foreign investment somewhat but continued to pursue neo-mercantilist trade policies intended to give advantages to key domestic industries. Europe became much more integrated internally with the creation of the European Union, at the same time that they maintained protections against countries elsewhere. The United States integrated to a lesser degree with the Mexican and Canadian economies under the North American Free Trade Agreement. As a result, by the 2020s the global trading system was a hodgepodge of trading blocs and trade agreements with a wide variety of provisions.

DOI: 10.4324/9781315636924-44

At its heart, the debate over trade policy and globalization is a debate about economic theory. The arguments for unregulated trade are based on the theory of comparative advantage, developed two centuries ago by economist David Ricardo. According to this theory, trade makes everyone better off, increasing global efficiency and raising average standards of living. One of the key questions confronting modern policymakers is whether or not this theory still applies. Most mainstream New Keynesian economists believe that it does. For example, Gregory Mankiw states, "*Economists* view the United States as an ongoing experiment that confirms the benefits of free trade."[1] However, Mankiw glosses over the many problems that trade has created in communities in the United States, as evidenced by the widespread opposition to free trade policies in large swaths of the country.

Unlike mainstream economists, political economists find unregulated trade to be problematic on many levels. Whereas Mankiw and most mainstream economists prefer unregulated ("free") trade, some liberal mainstream economists and most political economists believe that protecting specific industries with tariffs can be useful in fostering economic growth, especially in the case of new, "infant" industries. Tariffs and other forms of protection can have a dramatic effect on the fortunes of particular industries. A sound set of policies to manage trade can lead to more robust economic development and better outcomes for most people according to the political economy view.

This chapter begins by discussing why countries trade. We then outline the theory of comparative advantage, which underlies the reasoning for mainstream economists' support of unregulated trade. We go on to discuss the limitations of this theory as it applies to the modern world. Subsequently, the chapter takes up issues of protectionism and tariff and non-tariff barriers that countries use to protect particular industries. The chapter then turns to current trade patterns, political economy approaches to trade, and economic integration via international trade agreements such as the North American Free Trade Agreement (NAFTA) and the European Union (E.U.).

34.0 CHAPTER 34 LEARNING GOALS

After reading this chapter, you should be able to:

- Explain the theory of comparative advantage in words and using a graph.

- Use production possibilities curves to determine comparative advantage and to construct consumption possibilities curves.

- List and analyze the assumptions behind the comparative advantage model.

- ■ Explain the arguments for and against protectionism.

- ■ Describe U.S. trade patterns and analyze political economy theories that attempt to explain these trade patterns.

- ■ Evaluate the costs and benefits of economic integration via trade agreements versus a managed trade approach.

We begin with the cornerstone belief of economists who advocate unregulated trade, the theory of comparative advantage.

34.1 TRADE AND THE THEORY OF COMPARATIVE ADVANTAGE

Human beings have traded goods and services for thousands of years. There is sometimes a social goal in such exchanges. Trading goods with another community or country can build ties and relationships, which can reduce the likelihood of conflict.

But the primary reason for trade is for people in one geographical location (the importer) to obtain goods that are unavailable to them from another geographical area that has the desired goods (the exporter). For trade to occur it must be mutually beneficial: Both parties must be willing to make the exchange. Thus, in theory, trade makes both parties better off. The exporter benefits financially from selling more goods and the importer benefits from obtaining goods that they could not have obtained without trade.

Economists often go even further in extolling the virtues of unregulated trade. If every country specializes in the production of the goods that it can produce best (highest quality for the lowest cost) and then exports those products to the rest of the world, while importing the products that it is least effective at producing, the entire world will see a higher standard of living. In theory, with unregulated trade, goods will be produced and exported from locations where it is most efficient to do so. However, as we will see later, this rosy depiction of unregulated trade does not capture many of the modern realities.

Economists developed the theory of comparative advantage to explain the benefits of specialization and trade in more detail. The basic principle of the theory of comparative advantage is that **a country should produce and specialize in those goods that it can produce for a lower opportunity cost than its trading partners**. In other words, a country should produce what it is *relatively* best at producing.

For example, suppose that the United States can produce both computers and textiles more efficiently than Mexico. But, due to a lack of technology and skilled labor, computers have a much higher *opportunity cost* in Mexico. This means that Mexico would have to give up the production of a huge proportion of its other goods in order to be able to produce small amounts of computers.

Meanwhile, textiles have a very low opportunity cost in Mexico. Despite the fact that textile production is less efficient in Mexico than it is in the United States, the plentiful supply of inexpensive labor means that Mexico can produce textiles for a very low opportunity cost. Increasing the production of textiles will result in very little loss in the production of other goods.

In the United States, producing textiles has a very high opportunity cost—it takes away resources that could be used in the production of other high-value goods, such as computers. So it is **relatively** cheaper to produce textiles in terms of computers in Mexico. In other words, the resources used to produce textiles in Mexico are more abundant and relatively less expensive than in the United States.

In theory, the United States benefits from trade with Mexico because by **specializing** in the production of computers and exporting them to Mexico in exchange for textiles, the United States can gain more computers and textiles than it could possibly produce by itself. Mexican consumers are willing to give up a lot of textiles for each computer because they are so expensive (they have a high opportunity cost) in Mexico before trade occurs.

34.1.1 A graphical illustration of comparative advantage

To illustrate the theory of comparative advantage, economists use production possibilities curves and consumption possibilities curves. Recall that a production possibilities curve (PPC) **shows all combinations of two goods that a country can produce given its existing resources and technology**. For simplicity, we will assume that resources are not specialized, so opportunity costs stay constant along the production possibilities curve, making the PPC a straight line.

Suppose that, using a certain amount of resources, the United States can produce either 10 units (tons) of textiles or 40 units (thousands) of computers. Meanwhile, with the **same** amount of resources, Mexico can produce either 5 tons of textiles or 10 units of computers (in thousands). These production possibilities curves are illustrated in Figure 34.1.

In this example, the United States has an absolute advantage in both goods, meaning that **the United States can produce more of both goods with the same amount of resources than Mexico**. But the United States does not have a **comparative advantage** in the production of both goods.

If we use T for textiles (in tons) and C for computers (in thousands), then in the United States, $10T = 40C$. U.S. resources can produce either $10T$ or $40C$, so these amounts are equal in terms of the amount of resources they require. Dividing both sides by 10, we get $1T = 4C$. This means that the opportunity cost of one unit of textiles ($1T$) is equal to 4 units of computers ($4C$). Each time the United States produces 1 unit of textiles, it is using resources that instead could have produced 4 units

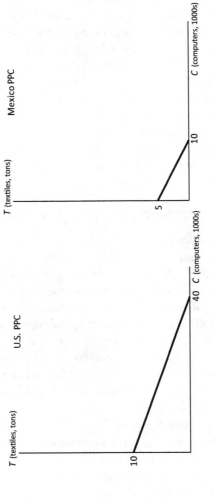

FIGURE 34.1 Production possibilities curves for the United States and Mexico.

of computers. Similarly, if we take our original equation of $10T = 40C$ and divide both sides by 40, we get $1C = \frac{1}{4}T$. Each time one unit of computers is produced, the United States is sacrificing the production of one-quarter of a unit of textiles.

In Mexico, using the PPC in Figure 34.1 we can see that $5T = 10C$. Mexico can produce either 5 units of textiles or 10 units of computers with its existing resources. Dividing both sides of the equation by 5, we can rewrite that equation as $1T = 2C$. Therefore, in Mexico the opportunity cost of producing one unit of textiles is 2 units of computers. Similarly, $1C = \frac{1}{2}T$ in Mexico.

Putting these results together, each unit of textiles "costs" 2 computers in Mexico ($1T = 2C$), and in the United States each unit of textiles "costs" 4 computers ($1T = 4C$). Mexico has a **comparative advantage** in the production of textiles, because *Mexico can produce textiles for a lower opportunity cost.*

But in Mexico, $1C = \frac{1}{2}T$, whereas in the United States, $1C = \frac{1}{4}T$. Thus, the United States has a comparative advantage in computer production because the United States can produce computers for a lower opportunity cost:

$$\left(\frac{1}{4}T_{(US)}\right) < \left(\frac{1}{2}T_{(Mex)}\right).$$

According to mainstream economists, in order to increase efficiency, the United States should specialize in what it produces most efficiently (computers) and trade them to Mexico for what they produce most efficiently (textiles).

When countries trade, the opportunity costs in each country adjust and end up in between the original opportunity costs that existed in each country before trade occurred. Before trade, computers would have been very expensive in Mexico and textiles would have been very expensive in the United States due to opportunity costs. After trade, computers will become cheaper in Mexico thanks to U.S. computer exports and textiles will become cheaper in the United States thanks to Mexican textile exports. For example, suppose that after trading, the opportunity costs in the United States and Mexico settled on a ratio of $1T = 3C$, in between the opportunity costs in each country that existed before trade. This is known as the international terms of trade, which is **the opportunity cost at which goods will trade internationally**.

At the international terms of trade of $1T = 3C$, both Mexico and the United States can be better off by specializing in the good in which they have a comparative advantage and trading for the other good. (Note: In comparative advantage problems, you will usually be given the international terms of trade.) Now, both countries can exchange $1T$ for $3C$. Note also that both countries can exchange $1C$ for $\frac{1}{3}T$ given the international terms of trade $\left(1C = \frac{1}{3}T\right)$.

The gains from trade are illustrated in the graph in Figure 34.2 showing production possibilities curves and the **consumption possibilities curves** that result after trade. A consumption possibilities curve (CPC) **shows all combinations of two goods that can be consumed by a country after specialization and trade. The CPC is constructed by starting at the point where the country specializes entirely in the good in which they have a comparative advantage. The other endpoint of the CPC is found by determining how much of the other good the country could get if it traded *all* of the specialized goods it produces to the other country at the international terms of trade**.

In Figure 34.2, the U.S. PPC runs from $10T$ to $40C$. But with trade, the United States should specialize and produce only computers, $40C$. If the United States decides to export all $40C$, then using the international terms of trade of $1C = \frac{1}{3}T$, the United States will get in exchange $40C = 40 * \frac{1}{3}T = 13.3T$. (You multiply both sides of the international terms of trade by the number of units of computers the United States can produce.) Thus, the U.S. consumption possibilities curve is the straight line between $40C$ and $13.3T$ in Figure 34.2.

If the United States were originally consuming at point A on its PPC, it can now consume **more of both goods** after trade at point B on its CPC.

Mexico's CPC starts at $5T$ and extends to $15C$, because $1T = 3C$ at the international terms of trade, which means that $5T = 15C$. Mexico can also consume more of both goods than it did before (unless it only desired to consume textiles).

Both countries can now consume more of both goods along their consumption possibilities curves by specializing in the production of the good in which they have a comparative advantage and trading this good to their trading partner. Specialization and trade increase efficiency and trade makes both countries better off.

According to the theory of comparative advantage, unregulated trade will result in maximum global productivity and increased standards of living. Each country specializes in what it is relatively best at producing, which increases productivity and makes people in all trading countries better off. As one concrete example, economists Robert Lawrence and Lawrence Edwards estimated that trade with China increased the standard of living of U.S. citizens by $250 a year in 2008. However, as we will see below, political economists find that this analysis misses key aspects of modern trade.

34.2 PROBLEMS WITH THE THEORY OF COMPARATIVE ADVANTAGE

The first problem with the theory of comparative advantage is that unregulated trade tends to benefit countries that have an advantage in lucrative industries more

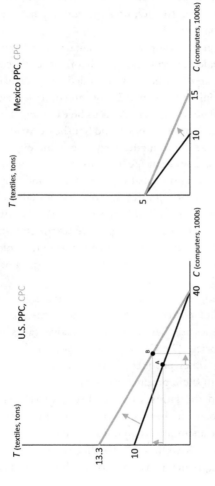

FIGURE 34.2 Consumption possibilities curves for the United States and Mexico.

than countries that do not. David Ricardo promoted unregulated trade in England in the 1800s when such policies were clearly advantageous to England. England was the first country in the world to industrialize, so they had an advantage over other countries in most manufactured goods. Unregulated trade allowed their industries to dominate potential competitors, helping them to maintain their status as the leading industrial power.

This is why other countries such as the United States and continental Europe protected their industries to give their companies time and space to develop and to become globally competitive. To date, no large country has successfully developed its economy via unregulated trade.

In addition, the theory of comparative advantage is often wrong when it comes to explaining global trade patterns. For much of the 20th century, countries in Africa, South America, and Southeast Asia tended to specialize in producing raw materials, whereas the United States and European countries tended to specialize in producing manufactured goods, which seems to be explained by the theory of comparative advantage. Africa, South America, and Southeast Asia have abundant natural resources, so they specialize in producing these goods and export them to developed countries. The United States and Europe have advanced technology and skilled labor, so they specialize in exporting financial services and manufactured goods.

However, this trade pattern ignores the role of colonialism in destroying manufacturing in developing countries and supporting manufacturing in Europe. For example, England destroyed India's cutting-edge textile industry and forced India to grow cotton for British textile manufacturers during the colonial era. England's industrial dominance was a product of imperial strategy, not a result of greater efficiency.

Furthermore, developed countries like the United States and those in Europe import *and* export manufactured goods from each other, as we will see below. These countries simultaneously have comparative advantages and disadvantages in the same product categories. The United States *imports and exports* cars, computers, smartphones, and many other products. It is not at all clear which country has a comparative advantage in these product categories.

The reasons behind the failures of the theory of comparative advantage to explain modern trade patterns has to do with the unrealistic assumptions upon which it is based. If these assumptions do not hold, then there is no reason to expect trade to improve everyone's welfare as the theory predicts. Political economists offer the following critique of the assumptions behind the theory of comparative advantage.

34.2.1 Assumption 1: Factors of production (labor and capital) are mobile internally but not externally

In Ricardo's era, it was uncommon for firms to move their operations outside of their home country. But in the modern world, multinational corporations can move their factories almost anywhere in the world. Companies move operations to where labor is cheaper or environmental regulations are lighter, which leads to lower costs and more profits.

As a result, it has become less meaningful to talk about a *country* having a comparative advantage—the real source of advantage may be the resources, technology, and skills controlled by a particular *company*. Political economists argue that **comparative advantage of countries has been replaced by the competitive advantage of companies**. As a result, the flow of capital around the globe in search of lower costs can lead to changes in a country's comparative advantages. The United States once had a significant comparative advantage in automobiles. Now, a significant amount of U.S. car manufacturing is done in Mexico. The Apple iPhone is a U.S.-designed product, but it is assembled in China from parts made all over the globe.

Apple's supply chain used parts sourced all over the globe to make the iPhone 6, as identified in the list below:

- Accelerometer: Bosch in Germany, InvenSense in the United States
- Audio chipsets and codec: Cirrus Logic in the United States (outsourced for manufacturing)
- Baseband processor: Qualcomm in the United States (outsourced for manufacturing)
- Batteries: Samsung in South Korea, Huizhou Desay Battery in China
- Cameras: Sony in Japan; OmniVision in the United States produces the front-facing FaceTime camera chip but subcontracts to TSMC in Taiwan for manufacturing
- Chipsets and processors: Samsung in South Korea and TSMC in Taiwan, alongside partner GlobalFoundries in the United States
- Controller chips: PMC Sierra and Broadcom Corp in the United States (outsourced for manufacturing)
- Display: Japan Display and Sharp in Japan, LG Display in South Korea
- DRAM: TSMC in Taiwan, SK Hynix in South Korea
- eCompass: Alps Electric in Japan
- Fingerprint sensor authentication: AuthenTec makes it in China but outsources it to Taiwan for manufacturing
- Flash memory: Toshiba in Japan and Samsung in South Korea
- Gyroscope: STMicroelectronics in France and Italy
- Inductor coils (audio): TDK in Japan
- Main chassis assembly: Foxconn and Pegatron in China
- Mixed-signal chips (such as NFC): NXP in the Netherlands
- Plastic constructions (for the iPhone 5c): Hi-P and Green Point in Singapore
- Radio-frequency modules: Win Semiconductors (module manufacturers Avago and RF Micro Devices) in Taiwan, Avago Technologies and TriQuint

Semiconductor in the United States, Qualcomm in the United States for LTE connectivity

- Screen and glass (for the display): Corning (Gorilla Glass) in the United States; GT Advanced Technologies produces the sapphire crystals in the screens
- Semiconductors: Texas Instruments, Fairchild, and Maxim Integrated in the United States
- Touch ID sensor: TSMC and Xintec in Taiwan
- Touchscreen controller: Broadcom in the United States (outsourced for manufacturing)
- Transmitter and amplification modules: Skyworks and Qorvo in the United States (outsourced for manufacturing)

The software and design for the iPhone is developed in the United States but the assembly and most parts production take place in China at Foxconn and other large Chinese firms. Apple may move some assembly to India in the near future due to cost savings available there.[2] Thus, even though the iPhone was invented in the United States and Apple is a U.S. company, it is hard to say that the United States has a comparative advantage in smartphones. That advantage lies with Apple and its supply chain located all over the globe, and especially in China.

34.2.2 Assumption 2: Technology is fixed and does not change over time

The theory of comparative advantage is static and assumes that a country will maintain a comparative advantage in the same types of products over time. However, technological changes can alter export patterns. As technology is assimilated and disseminated, other countries may end up exporting goods that were originally invented and exported by a different country, so the pattern of comparative advantage can change dramatically. For example, the United States invented the television, but it produces very few televisions today. Production has moved to other locations, such as Taiwan, South Korea, and China, where costs are lower and technology is better.

Countries can use technological assimilation and development to capture industries. For example, when South Korea was starting to produce cars, they protected their market against imported cars using tariffs until their car companies were globally competitive. By imitating and improving technology, they were able to become efficient. Only then did South Korea lower trade barriers and begin engaging in less regulated trade. As we saw in the previous chapter, this is known as **infant industry protection**, where a country protects firms when they are starting out so that they can gain a foothold in an established industry. Today, South Korean car companies Hyundai and Kia are internationally competitive and have a steadily increasing share of the global automobile market.

There are also spillover benefits from creating clusters of industries, such as Silicon Valley in California, Research Triangle Park in North Carolina, and the special economic zone in Shenzhen, China. Creating industrial clusters spurs innovation and technological development, and it can create jobs in high-wage sectors of the economy. Governments can play a role in stimulating industrial clusters through infrastructure, education, and subsidies, which can have a large payoff if a cluster becomes a dynamic source of innovation and growth. Technological development thus becomes a key reason why comparative advantage can shift. And technological development can be manipulated via government policies to protect infant industries, attract foreign investment, and promote innovation.

34.2.3 Assumption 3: Productive resources are fully employed and move quickly and easily between industries

The theory of comparative advantage assumes that resources—labor and capital—will flow quickly and easily from the sector *without* a comparative disadvantage into the sector *with* the comparative advantage. Resources should flow out of dying industries and into growing industries. The real world seldom works this way, unfortunately. The United States used to have a comparative advantage in manufacturing steel. In recent years, it lost the comparative advantage in steel but gained a comparative advantage in software and technology. However, the U.S. rust belt still features decrepit steel plants in run-down towns and cities such as Detroit, Youngstown, and Allentown. Workers and resources in these locations were not able to find new jobs and purposes in new industries. Instead, these regions feature chronically underemployed workers and unused resources. Former steel workers do not have the skills required by the new industries, nor can they afford the kind of retraining they would need to be successful in a new industry.

In addition, the theory of comparative advantage assumes that all countries are producing at full capacity—that is, they are on their production possibilities curve. However, as noted in earlier chapters, economies are rarely at full employment. This means that countries need to expand the production of goods to reach full capacity, which implies that countries can reduce unemployment by producing more goods domestically rather than importing goods from other countries.

Furthermore, as Keynes demonstrated, demand creates supply; therefore, employment and income are driven first and foremost by demand factors (the autonomous level of spending). Unregulated trade has the impact of reducing employment and income in less competitive countries as demand for their products declines and increasing incomes in more competitive countries as demand for their products increases.

To political economists, this is a strong argument in favor of protectionism. Indeed, the need to create or preserve jobs has been used to justify protectionism in the United States from Alexander Hamilton in 1790 to Donald Trump in 2020. This is why most countries today pursue neo-mercantilist policies in which they subsidize exports and put up barriers to imports, including tariff and non-tariff barriers.

34.2.4 Assumption 4: Trade benefits everyone

Economists who believe in the theory of comparative advantage argue that the benefits from trade are widespread, increasing the standard of living of citizens. However, this ignores the fact that the distribution of the benefits from trade is extremely uneven. The workers and owners of firms in exporting industries see a higher demand for their products, increasing incomes and benefiting the communities in which they are located. Workers and owners of firms in industries losing out to imports end up with lower incomes and their communities fall on hard times.

Furthermore, trade has increased the incomes of skilled workers and business executives, while reducing the incomes of blue-collar workers in developed countries. Because most people are blue-collar workers, trade has reduced wages for most workers in developed countries. Thus, trade has contributed directly to inequality.

34.2.5 Assumption 5: Trade is free and fair

As trade disputes show, trade is often unfair. Chinese firms have been accused of stealing the technology and intellectual property of U.S. firms, undermining the U.S. comparative advantages in key tech sectors. In Japan, collaborative business arrangements make it extremely difficult for foreign firms to compete in some sectors, such as the car market, which has the effect of reducing imports. In addition, countries should not be able to gain an advantage in trade by repressing laborers or ignoring environmental problems. If countries can gain an advantage via a race to the bottom by paying lower wages and reducing environmental regulations, this undermines the notion that trade makes all people better off and that trade is fair.

34.2.6 Assumption 6: Interdependence created by trade is not a problem

With specialization and trade, countries produce a smaller range of products. However, less developed countries (LDCs) that specialize in primary products such as coffee or cocoa are vulnerable to price fluctuations and can experience a deterioration in their terms of trade over time (the prices of their exports fall while their imports increase in price). Countries actually need diversified exports to provide a stable export sector to generate funds to pay for imported goods. Specializing in a narrow range of goods can foster instability. Countries may also wish to protect key sectors for national defense reasons, so they do not have to depend on key imported goods in the event of a major conflict.

One of the implications of the interdependence issue is that all industries are not equal. Some industries, especially those that come with high-wage jobs and linkages to many other industries, are better for economic growth than others. A country may want to protect high-linkage, high-wage industries to preserve good quality jobs and maintain export diversification.

34.2.7 Assumption 7: Exchange rates will adjust to equalize trade flows so that exports will equal imports

In theory, a country that runs chronic trade deficits will experience an outflow of currency, causing its currency to depreciate. The depreciation of the currency, in turn, causes exports to become more competitive and imports to become more expensive, which should eliminate any trade deficit. (Trade surpluses should be eliminated by an identical process in reverse.) However, in reality many countries run chronic trade deficits or trade surpluses. This topic is taken up in more detail in the chapter covering international financial flows. For current purposes, the important issue is that countries are affected differently by trade flows. Countries like the United States that run chronic trade deficits benefit from inexpensive imported goods, but they lose industries and jobs to foreign countries. Countries like China and Germany that run chronic trade surpluses experience more job growth, but their consumers receive fewer benefits from trade.

In conclusion, we see that trade provides broad, general benefits in the form of lower prices and better quality goods. It does seem to be the case that trade has increased the standard of living of people *on average*.

However, it is not the case that trade benefits everyone. There are clear winners and losers from trade. If a country worked to make sure that those harmed by trade received some of the benefits it might be possible to argue that trade would indeed make everyone better off. But without substantial trade adjustment assistance, many workers, firms, and communities have strong reasons to oppose unregulated trade. The differential impact of trade is one of the reasons many countries turn to protectionism.

34.3 PROTECTIONISM: USING TARIFF AND NON-TARIFF BARRIERS TO PROTECT INDUSTRIES

The main policies a country can use to protect specific industries are tariffs and quotas. A tariff is **a tax on imported goods**. An import quota is **a limit on the quantity of a good that can be imported**. Other policies a country can use to protect industries include subsidies and laws or regulations that prevent or impede trade.

There are a number of reasons why a country may want to protect some of its industries:

1. **Infant industry protection.** As noted above, one of the strongest reasons to protect an industry is to foster economic development. New industries usually need protection until they gain the size and experience necessary to compete at the international level.

2. **Strategic industry protection.** Certain industries may be deemed so essential to a country's interests that they cannot be entrusted to production in foreign locations. Typically, industries associated with national defense fall within this category. The United States has protected its steel, electronics, and metalworking industries for national defense reasons. Similarly, certain industries are essential for clusters of economic development. The U.S. technology industry is centered in Silicon Valley outside of San Francisco, where Google, Apple, Xerox, Intel, IBM, Adobe, and many other companies are clustered. There are substantial spillover benefits to industrial clusters: Inventions in one company are picked up and utilized by another company and vice versa. For this reason, the U.S. government protected Intel from foreign competition during a period in which foreign microchips were threatening its business. This allowed for continuing, fruitful collaborations between Intel and other U.S.-based computer companies such as Apple and Dell. Some countries also choose to protect industries that employ large numbers of people.

3. **Strategic trade policy.** When other countries are engaging in unfair trade practices, tariffs are one of the best options a country can use to force foreign countries to change their trade practices. For example, in 2018 the Trump administration argued that China was pursuing unfair trade practices by stealing U.S. intellectual property, requiring U.S. firms to invest in China in order to sell goods there, and unfairly subsidizing the manufacturing of steel, aluminum, and other products. President Trump imposed tariffs on Chinese goods to try to force them to reduce their trade barriers and buy more U.S. goods. Similarly, tariffs can be used to reduce imports by countries that face chronic trade deficits (when exports exceed imports).

4. **Raise revenue.** In many developing countries with large informal economies, it is difficult to raise tax revenues. Incomes are low and many transactions occur in cash, which makes them untraceable and difficult to tax. But imported goods are tracked carefully and come through specific international shipping outlets, such as ports or airports. This makes taxes on imported goods one of the easiest ways for governments to raise revenue.

Note that protectionism may not help a particular industry if the foreign country retaliates. As soon as President Trump imposed tariffs on Chinese goods in 2018, the Chinese government imposed tariffs on U.S. goods in response. Thus, protecting particular industries may only be effective for a country if no retaliation occurs.

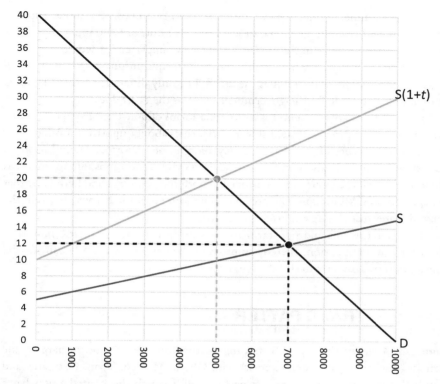

FIGURE 34.3 The effect of a 100% tariff.

Tariffs have the effect of increasing the price and reducing the quantity of an imported good purchased in the country that imposes the tariff. Figure 34.3 shows the impact of a 100% tariff on a foreign good. The market is initially in equilibrium at a price of $12 and a quantity of 7000. Then, the government imposes a 100% tariff on the product, which has the effect of doubling the price at which each quantity can be sold. If the firm exporting the product sells it for $5, the government adds a tariff of 1.00 * 5 = $5, so the new price with the 100% tariff is $10. If the firm's product sells for $10, the tariff is $10 and the new price with the tariff becomes $20. The new supply curve S(1 + tariff) = 2S is twice as steep as the original supply curve S. The new equilibrium that results is at a price of $20 and a quantity of 5000. The tariff has the effect of increasing the equilibrium price and reducing the equilibrium quantity sold.

This is very bad for the foreign seller of the product. Not only do they sell a smaller quantity, but they make a lot less money than they used to. They supply 5000 units of their product at a price of $10 and then the government adds another $10 to that in the form of the 100% tariff, making the price to consumers $20. In the tariff graph, the original supply curve reflects the money going to the seller, and the new supply curve adds in the cost of the tariff. The government would take $10 * 5000 = $50,000 in tariff revenue.

The government could achieve a similar result by imposing a quota. Suppose the government instituted a quota, or a maximum limit, of 5000 units on exports of the product depicted in Figure 34.3. The new supply curve would become a vertical line at $Q = 5000$, which would result in an equilibrium at $Q = 5000$ and $P = \$20$, achieving the same result as the tariff. The only difference is that the quota does not raise revenue for the government whereas the tariff does.

Occasionally, governments resort to other forms of non-tariff barriers in trade. For example, countries can establish very strict rules about importing goods or they can restrict the types of products that they allow to be imported. Many European countries ban genetically modified organism (GMO) food crops due to concerns about health and the environment associated with the pesticides and herbicides that are sprayed on GMO crops. The prevents genetically modified crops grown in the United States from being exported to Europe.

In general, tariffs and non-tariff barriers protect specific domestic industries from foreign competition, thereby improving their profitability. We can see the impact of tariffs directly in the changes of trade patterns.

34.4 U.S. TRADE PATTERNS

Figure 34.4 shows the top U.S. trading partners in 2017. Note the large trade deficits (imports greater than exports) with China, Mexico, Japan, Germany, and South Korea. The only top trading partners with which the United States has a trade surplus are the United Kingdom and Brazil. As we will see in the next chapter, mainstream economists link U.S. trade deficits to the low U.S. savings rate and an extremely strong currency.

China dropped from our top trading partner in 2017 to third place in 2019. This happened after a major trade dispute between the United States and China, in which both countries imposed significant, wide-reaching tariffs on the other. As a result, U.S. imports from China declined by $53 billion and U.S. exports to China declined by $24 billion in 2019.

According to the theory of comparative advantage, the United States should specialize in the goods in which it has a comparative advantage and import the goods in which it does not. It is instructive to look at the categories of products that form the largest U.S. exports and imports. Figure 34.5 shows the top ten categories of exports and imports for the United States in 2019. Interestingly, for the most part the United States both exports and imports the same product categories. The United States exports and imports computers, oil, vehicles, electrical machinery and equipment, medical equipment, plastics, precious metals, pharmaceuticals, and organic chemicals. In these goods categories, no clear pattern of comparative advantage emerges.

The only seemingly clear areas of comparative advantage are in the categories of aircraft and spacecraft, which U.S. industry dominates, and furniture, which

Rank	Country	Exports 2017	Imports 2017	Exports 2019	Imports 2019	Total trade 2019	% of total trade, 2019
1	Mexico	243.0	314.0	256.4	358.1	614.5	14.80%
2	Canada	282.4	300.0	292.7	319.7	612.4	14.80%
3	China	130.4	505.6	106.6	452.2	558.9	13.50%
4	Japan	67.7	136.5	74.7	143.6	218.3	5.30%
5	Germany	53.5	117.7	60.3	127.5	187.8	4.50%
6	South Korea	48.3	71.2	56.9	77.5	134.4	3.20%
7	United Kingdom	56.3	53.1	69.2	63.2	132.3	3.20%
8	France	33.6	48.9	37.8	57.4	95.2	2.30%
9	India	25.7	48.6	34.4	57.7	92.1	2.20%
10	Taiwan	25.8	42.5	31.2	54.3	85.5	2.10%
11	Netherlands	42.2	17.7	51.2	29.8	81.0	2.00%
12	Italy	18.3	50.0	23.8	57.2	80.9	2.00%
13	Vietnam	8.1	46.5	10.9	66.7	77.6	1.90%
14	Brazil	37.1	29.4	43.1	30.9	73.9	1.80%
15	Ireland	10.7	48.8	9.0	61.8	70.8	1.70%

FIGURE 34.4 Table showing top U.S. trading partners, 2017 and 2019.

Source: U.S. Census Bureau, "Foreign Trade," www.census.gov/foreign-trade, accessed February 2, 2021.

U.S. top exports (and import rank)	Volume (billions)	% of exports	U.S. top imports	Volume (billions)	% of imports
1. Machinery including computers (1)	$206	12.5%	1. Machinery including computers	$379	14.8%
2. Mineral fuels including oil (4)	$200	12.1%	2. Electrical machinery, equipment	$352	13.7%
3. Electrical machinery, equipment (2)	$173	10.5%	3. Vehicles	$310	12.1%
4. Aircraft, spacecraft	$136	8.3%	4. Mineral fuels including oil	$210	8.2%
5. Vehicles (3)	$133	8.1%	5. Pharmaceuticals	$128	5.0%
6. Optical, technical, medical apparatus (6)	$91	5.5%	6. Optical, technical, medical apparatus	$97	3.8%
7. Plastics, plastic articles (8)	$65	3.9%	7. Furniture, bedding, lighting, signs, prefab bldgs.	$67	2.6%
8. Gems, precious metals (9)	$60	3.6%	8. Plastics, plastic articles	$61	2.4%
9. Pharmaceuticals (5)	$54	3.3%	9. Gems, precious metals	$58	2.3%
10. Organic chemicals (10)	$39	2.4%	10. Organic chemicals	$55	2.1%

FIGURE 34.5 Table showing largest export and import products for the United States, 2019.

our trading partners dominate. Thus, in the modern era it is misleading to assume that a country has a comparative advantage in an entire product category. Instead, we see competitive companies in the United States and competitive companies in other countries within the same product category. For example, the United States exports cars made by Ford, Chevrolet, Chrysler, and Tesla, and it imports cars made by Toyota, Honda, Hyundai, Mercedes, VW, BMW, and some others.

The patterns that emerge from the trading data on the United States and other developed countries indicate that countries tend to trade the most with other countries that (1) are geographically close, (2) have similar tastes and preferences, (3) have similar resource endowments and technologies, and (4) are open to trade. In essence, developed countries tend to trade the most with other developed countries that are similar to them.

Countries do get some goods from countries with different resource endowments, as predicted by the theory of comparative advantage. The United States imports clothing, which requires labor-intensive production, from Bangladesh, China, India, and other countries where labor is cheap and plentiful. The United States imports cocoa, coffee, and tropical fruits from countries with climates that can easily produce such goods. The United States exports high-technology goods and airplanes because of its technological edge in those products. However, the goods that the United States either exports or imports make up a small portion of U.S. trade.

So, if resource endowments that determine comparative advantage are not the major influence over what goods and services a country exports, what is? Political economists focus on absolute advantage, comparative institutional advantage, and other factors to explain international competitiveness.

34.5 POLITICAL ECONOMY VIEWS ON TRADE AND COMPETITIVENESS

The theory of comparative advantage argues that specialization and trade derive from a country's abundant resources. If a country has lots of good agricultural land, it will specialize in agricultural products. If a country has abundant skilled labor and advanced technology, it will specialize in tech goods. However, as noted above, trade patterns do not support the theory of comparative advantage much of the time because countries both import and export the same categories of goods. Given the problematic assumptions behind the theory of comparative advantage and the observed trade patterns in the modern world, political economists developed a different set of principles regarding trade.

Political economists argue that firms, not countries, are the appropriate level of analysis for trade flows. And firms in competitive markets must produce goods for a lower costs than their competitors if there are no significant quality differences. This means that (1) **to political economists, absolute advantage is usually**

more important than comparative advantage in determining trade flows. International trade occurs between firms, not countries, and firms operating in competitive global markets must have the lowest prices, and therefore the lowest costs, to be successful.

The need for firms to have the lowest costs possible also helps us to understand globalization and the shift of global manufacturing to low-cost locations. When Apple began to worry about how much more the iPhone cost than the smartphones made by Samsung, they started to outsource more of their production to China. This is why it does not matter that U.S. engineers designed and created the iPhone and that production was initially based primarily in the United States. To political economists, the United States does not have a comparative advantage in smartphones. Apple has an absolute advantage in smartphones.

Political economists also note the extent to which (2) **unregulated trade policies tend to undermine workers**. Although the theory of comparative advantage implies that workers will be better off with trade, experiencing a higher standard of living and shifting out of declining sectors into growing ones, the reality has been much different. During the neoliberal era of deregulated trade and globalization, U.S. labor's share of national income declined from 65% in 1970 to 60% in 2019. Similar declines occurred in other developed countries. Even in developing countries, the threat that employers can move wherever labor is cheapest is used as a way to keep wages low and workers compliant. With the steady erosion in workers' well-being during the era of "free" trade, the theory of comparative advantage appears to be more of an ideological argument in favor of multinational firms and against the majority of workers than an accurate descriptor of real-world trade patterns.

Therefore, political economics advocate policies to prevent trade from becoming a race to the bottom, where firms seek out the most vulnerable workers and the most lax environmental standards to reduce their costs and gain a competitive advantage. **Corrective tariffs** can be applied to countries or regions that exploit laborers or that do not adhere to the same environmental standards. This evens the playing field and ensures that domestic companies do not have to face unfair competition.

Political economists also argue that (3) **unregulated trade can undermine effective aggregate demand**, reducing employment and incomes. Political-economic research indicates that demand factors are usually more important than supply factors in driving production, employment, and growth. To the extent that unregulated trade undermines aggregate demand by driving down wages and bankrupting uncompetitive businesses, it will have a detrimental impact. After their pursuit of unregulated trade policies, the United States and the United Kingdom developed rust belts featuring empty, rusting factories, and impoverished cities, but new industries did not develop to replace the dying ones in these locations. To political economists, **managed trade policies** to stimulate exports and limit trade deficits are better for the majority of workers than unregulated trade, which tends to benefit multinational corporations.

Political economists also argue that trade patterns between countries can be exploitative. Throughout most of the last century, less developed countries were constrained to producing primary products such as agricultural goods and minerals. Unfortunately, the real prices of primary products have fallen in recent years, indicating that primary product exporters are getting less money for their products than they used to. The primary reason for this is the difference in income elasticity between manufactured goods and high-end services on the one side and primary products on the other. As economies get richer, their expenditure on high-end goods and services increases relative to their expenditure on primary products. Over time, this means the demand for high-end manufactured goods and services outstrips the demand for primary products and the relative prices of manufactured goods will increase relative to the prices of primary products.

This highlights the extent to which (4) trade patterns result in unequal exchange, where **resources are systematically transferred by global trade flows from developing countries that produce primary products to developed countries**. When we consider the fact that the former colonial powers, especially England, Spain, Portugal, the Netherlands, and Belgium, systematically dismantled manufacturing in their colonies and set up the colonies to supply them with primary products, the persistence of the resulting trade patterns is deeply troubling. Only a small number of former colonies have been able to escape the trap of primary product specialization to engineer the structural transformation of the economy toward higher value manufactured goods.

Nevertheless, the fact that some countries have been able to transform their economies via a developmental state, as discussed in the chapter on economic growth, indicates that (5) *the right set of policies can be beneficial in creating the appropriate environment for manufacturing*. This is the essential insight behind the theory of comparative institutional advantage as developed by political economists.

The theory of comparative institutional advantage posits that **trade patterns are driven by particular combinations of institutions (government policies and support, infrastructure, labor skills and training, education systems, communities, industrial clusters, and innovation systems) that create advantages for specific types of production in particular places, attracting economic actors to locate production in certain geographical locations**. One of the most important implications of the theory of comparative institutional advantage is that governments can guide and shape trade patterns by altering local institutions and incentives. This was the strategy pursued by the developmental states and triple helix models we studied in the previous chapter.

According to the theory of comparative institutional advantage, trade and industrial development are driven largely by state policies. Economic growth and development are stimulated by fostering the best possible institutional environment for growing industries. This includes the provision of infrastructure, efforts to develop technology via R&D spending or foreign direct investment (with local partners), education and training, protectionism or other measures to ensure a sufficient demand for products, provision of subsidized financing, and more. China, South Korea, and Japan have been particularly adept with this approach.

Interestingly, supply-side economists also emphasize the institutional environment facing businesses, although they advocate a very different set of policies. Supply-side economists focus primarily on business profits, arguing that the government should work to give domestic companies advantages and disadvantage foreign competition, usually via tariffs. This was the approach taken during the Trump administration in the United States from 2017 to 2020. However, without the other types of support noted above, this approach had limited impact in rejuvenating U.S. manufacturing.

Despite these criticisms of unregulated trade and the theory of comparative advantage, in recent decades countries moved increasingly toward free trade. Most of these changes occurred as a result of international trade agreements to reduce tariffs. These efforts to integrate global economies have caused major changes in the world and a recent backlash against globalization.

34.6 GLOBAL INTEGRATION AND RESISTANCE TO GLOBALIZATION

During the Great Depression and World War II, global trade collapsed and countries retreated from international entanglements. With the end of World War II, the United States emerged as the globally dominant power and began pushing unregulated trade and a greater degree of international cooperation. Partly this effort was to bring countries together to avoid future conflicts, and partly it was intended to open up new markets to dominant U.S. manufacturers.

The effort at global economic integration began with the General Agreement on Tariffs and Trade (GATT) of 1947, which reduced tariffs and promoted trade among countries signing the agreement. At the same time, the World Bank and the International Monetary Fund were established to assist struggling economies and to promote market-based development in the developing world, in part as a counter to the Soviet Union's influence. GATT was followed by the creation of the World Trade Organization (WTO) in 1995 to further reduce tariffs and facilitate trade between nations. The creation of the WTO, along with the fall of the Soviet Union in 1990, ushered in the era of neoliberalism in which the entire world became enmeshed in a global system of international trade that was less regulated and less protectionist than in any previous era. The neoliberal era was very good for some regions, countries, and individuals and very bad for others.

GATT and the WTO established rules for countries who joined their organizations with respect to tariffs, intellectual property, regulation of foreign corporations, and other aspects of international exchange. Multinational corporations played a key role in shaping WTO policies, which resulted in rules that are very favorable to corporations and less favorable to workers and other interests. The result has been very good for multinational corporations, who can now move easily to most countries who are WTO members and be confident that there will be little interference with their operations. Few countries felt like they could stay out of the WTO because the world's largest consumer markets, especially the United States and the E.U., would not be as accessible otherwise.

However, the WTO is deeply controversial, in part due to the way in which they have impeded the ability of countries to institute modest regulations that affect foreign companies. Companies with a complaint against any regulation or trade policy of a country can lodge a complaint with the WTO. In its findings, the WTO tends to be more sympathetic to companies than to regulators. For example, Japan passed a law prohibiting the importation of apples sprayed with toxic pesticides and Europe tried to ban hormone-treated beef due to the potentially negative impact on health. In both cases, the WTO ruled that these laws were unfair restrictions of international trade and countries were not allowed to impose these restrictions that were intended to protect the health of their populations.

At the same time that the WTO was expanding, countries were forming trading blocs in which they eliminated tariffs with particular trading partners, usually those in close geographic proximity. According to the World Bank, average global tariff rates fell steadily from around 10% in 1990 to about 2% in 2015, thanks largely to the WTO and to trade agreements that eliminated tariffs among trading bloc members. By the 2010s, international trade was less regulated than it has ever been.

There are four major types of trading bloc agreements:

1. A **free trade area** reduces or eliminates tariffs between member countries. The result of a free trade area is increased trade with group members but reduced trade with the rest of the world.
2. A **customs union** creates common external tariffs (customs) on nonmember countries, while reducing or eliminating tariffs between member countries. Countries in a customs union behave like a single country with respect to trade.
3. **Common markets** go even further, allowing capital and labor mobility between countries in the bloc, along with lower (or no) internal tariffs and common external tariffs. Workers and firms can move freely within member countries.
4. An **economic union** involves central economic coordination and a common currency, along with capital and labor mobility, low or no internal tariffs, and common external tariffs. An economic union functions like a single-country economy in most respects.

34.6.1 The European Union

The European Economic Community was created in 1957 to open up European economies to each other and to bring about a degree of economic integration between member states. This was followed by the European Union, which began as a common market and in 1999 became an economic union with the adoption of a common European currency, the euro. By this point, European economies were closely integrated.

Tariffs between E.U. countries were completely eliminated, and the E.U. maintained common tariffs on goods from other countries. Companies could move any part of their operations to other E.U. countries and workers could move freely between countries to find work. In these respects the E.U. economy operates like that of a single country, although individual member states still retain much autonomy in other arenas. The E.U. government is therefore more of a body to regulate competing interests than a central government.

Most economic studies indicate that joining the E.U. had substantial benefits for almost all member states (except for Greece, as we will see later). The share of trade between member countries increased substantially, and it decreased with the rest of the world. Companies were able to become more competitive, and workers could seek out new opportunities. Meanwhile, generous safety nets and social programs ensured that no one was excessively disadvantaged by changes caused by the economic integration. Campos et al. found that joining the E.U. increased a country's per capita economic growth by about 0.67% per year for most countries and by more than double that for Ireland and a few other countries.[3]

Some interesting collaborations between countries resulted in the formation of new industries and research institutes that would not have been possible without economic integration. For example, Airbus, a European multinational aerospace corporation with significant operations in France, Germany, Spain, and the United Kingdom, was founded in 1970 and became the world's largest airplane manufacturer in 2019. The European Organization for Nuclear Research built the Large Hadron Collider, the world's largest machine, to conduct research and develop scientific breakthroughs.

However, the organization of the E.U. had some significant flaws. It was ill-equipped to deal with economic crises, especially the financial crisis of 2008–2010. One of the main problems was that the E.U. had no mechanism to deal with member states experiencing a major economic shock related to trade deficits.

As one of the least developed countries in the E.U., Greece regularly ran trade deficits with countries like Germany because it imported expensive German manufactured goods like cars and electronics and exported lower value goods like tourist services. When Greece was an independent country, it could devalue its currency, the drachma, to increase the prices of imported goods and decrease the prices of its exports, improving the competitiveness of its export products and reducing its trade deficits. This would stem the outflow of money and stabilize the economy.

After Greece joined the E.U. and adopted the euro, it could no longer devalue its currency to stay competitive. Greece's outflows of money accelerated, and by the time of the financial crisis of 2008 Greece could no longer pay its debts. However, instead of bailing out a struggling member state, like the U.S. government does when one of its 50 states falls on hard times, the E.U. insisted on austerity policies (higher taxes and cuts to government spending) to reduce Greece's debts. As is always the case, austerity reduced Greece's gross domestic product (GDP) and increased unemployment, making the situation even worse. Thanks to these short-sighted policies, Greece entered a depression that lasted from 2008 to 2016, and even in 2019 after growth had returned, the unemployment rate remained above 17%. The E.U. had no mechanism to deal with a macroeconomic crisis of one of its member states, demonstrating that a currency union without macroeconomic policy coordination and stabilization was a poor structure.

The E.U. also failed to anticipate the impact of adding impoverished Eastern European countries to the bloc and the hostility that immigrant workers would face as they moved to different countries within the E.U. In 2004 the E.U. added eight Eastern European countries from the former Soviet Union bloc, including Poland, Hungary, and Czechia (Czech Republic). In 2007 Bulgaria and Romania were added. These were poor countries relative to the rest of Europe, and their economies were still struggling after the conversion from centralized state communism to capitalism. Once they joined the E.U. and people were able to move freely, workers left Eastern Europe in droves seeking better jobs and pay in other countries, especially England, which was growing more quickly than the rest of the E.U. at the time.

The share of foreign-born residents soared in England to 13.4% of the population. Eastern Europeans filled low-wage service jobs and put a strain on public services. British workers saw this as a major threat to their well-being and started backing initiatives to get the United Kingdom to leave the E.U.—**Brexit**. However, British banks and manufacturers, who depended on selling to E.U. markets, opposed Brexit, fearing the loss of a huge portion of their business. After a bitter and divisive campaign filled with disinformation, the United Kingdom voted narrowly to leave the E.U. Brexit took place on January 31, 2020, marking the first departure from the E.U. Only time will tell whether the E.U. fractures further in the face of ongoing challenges.

34.6.2 The North American Free Trade Agreement

As Europe became increasingly integrated, the United States felt the need to expand its access to nearby markets and resources, which it achieved with the North American Free Trade Agreement and the subsequent revision labeled the United States–Mexico–Canada Agreement (USMCA). NAFTA took effect in 1994, immediately eliminating tariffs on more than half of industrial products. By 2009, tariffs on all industrial and agricultural products traded between the three countries were completely eliminated. The goal was to create a North American supply chain, adding cheap Mexican labor and Canadian natural resources and skilled labor to U.S. manufacturing prowess. It was also hoped that the agreement would make U.S. and Canadian companies more competitive, boost Mexico's GDP, and reduce the number of Mexican migrants as a result.

Trade between the three countries increased sharply after NAFTA was implemented, increasing from $290 billion in 1993 to $1100 billion in 2016, an increase of 279%. The U.S. stock of foreign direct investment in Mexico increased from $15 billion to $100 billion during the same time frame. Economists estimate that NAFTA had no significant impact on U.S. GDP, leaving it essentially unchanged from its normal growth trajectory. There were some benefits for North American consumers as the prices of some products dropped.

However, the impact on many workers was quite negative. Economist Robert Scott estimates that 683,000 U.S. jobs were lost from 1993 to 2010.[4] U.S. manufacturers did move to Mexico as predicted, but wages in Mexico stayed very low. According to Luis Villanueva, the Mexican "sectors that produce for the export market are sectors that pay among the lowest wages within the manufacturing sector."[5] The Mexican maquiladoras—factories along the U.S. border producing for export—are infamous for low wages, unsafe working conditions, and lax environmental standards. Meanwhile, almost 2 million Mexican corn farmers were put out of work when they could not compete with heavily subsidized U.S. corn, leading to an explosion of Mexican immigration to the United States. This was, of course, the opposite of what NAFTA architects hoped to achieve.

The USMCA agreement tweaked NAFTA slightly, establishing new rules of origin that required 75% of automobiles to originate in member countries to qualify for no tariffs (an increase from 62.5%) and rules requiring 40% of each vehicle to come from factories paying at least $16 per hour (e.g., U.S. and Canadian factories). In most other regards, the trade agreement was largely unchanged.

The NAFTA/USMCA experience illustrates some of the classic lessons of unregulated trade. Consumers tend to benefit somewhat, paying lower prices for goods. Producers and workers in competitive industries benefit, seeing higher demand for their products, more jobs, and higher profits. Producers and workers in uncompetitive industries experience significant harm, as businesses close, jobs are eliminated, and communities that depend on the income from these jobs experience economic decline. Workers tend to lose bargaining power and many experience lower wages as they are forced to compete with low-wage workers from other countries.

As another indication of the problems that trade agreements can create for workers, U.S. job losses were even higher after China joined the WTO and qualified for lower tariffs. Daron Acemoglu et al. (2016) estimated that import competition from China eliminated more than 2 million U.S. jobs from 1999 to 2011.[6]

As we can see from the information above, after World War II most countries in the world reduced tariffs, increased trade, and formed a series of trading blocs that reduced protectionism and increased the economic integration of particular regions of the world. Between WTO rulings hostile to labor, health, and the environment and the steady erosion of jobs and wages in developed countries as manufacturing moved to China, India, South Korea, Mexico, and other less expensive locations, globalization led to increasing dissatisfaction with unregulated trade.

34.6.3 Resistance to neoliberal globalization

Throughout the period during which trade was liberalized (deregulated) and economies were increasingly opened to international competition, there was resistance from workers and communities threatened by globalization. Each time the WTO meets there are mass protests by labor unions and activists who see unregulated trade as a fundamental threat to people, communities, and the global environment. Donald Trump was elected in the United States in 2016 in part due to his pledge to renegotiate NAFTA and prevent U.S. jobs from moving to China. During his presidency, Trump began many trade wars with other countries, raising tariffs to try to increase U.S. jobs. His efforts were often canceled out, however, by retaliatory foreign tariffs on U.S. goods. Boris Johnson was elected U.K. prime minister on his Brexit platform to end the United Kingdom's participation in the E.U., which he successfully delivered.

Interestingly, even though tariffs were reduced in recent decades, most countries still utilize some form of strategic trade policy to protect and promote key domestic industries. In cases where the use of tariffs is limited by trade agreements, countries use subsidies and non-tariff barriers to protect and assist industries. These countries are adopting more of a managed trade approach drawing on the ideas of political economists instead of the laissez-faire approach promoted by the WTO and the theory of comparative advantage.

To a large degree, modern economists appear to be repeating the debates of the great economists of earlier eras. Adam Smith and David Ricardo argued in favor of unregulated trade to improve people's standard of living, whereas Karl Marx maintained that international trade fosters a race to the bottom that results in labor exploitation and environmental devastation. Keynes, of course, falls somewhere in the middle, arguing in favor of trade as long as it is regulated carefully to ensure that everyone benefits.

34.7 CONCLUSION

Most mainstream New Keynesian economists are staunch believers in unregulated trade. This belief is grounded in the theory of comparative advantage, which posits that if all countries engage in unregulated trade, they will end up specializing in goods that they are relatively best at producing. If every country specializes in this manner, global productivity will improve and everyone will experience a higher standard of living. Countries specialize in those goods that reflect their endowments of resources (land, labor, capital, and natural resources). Some government policies may be necessary to assist those harmed by trade but, in general, unregulated trade is viewed as the best policy.

However, the United States does not tend to trade the most with countries that have different resource endowments. Instead, the largest trading partners of the United States are nearby, open to trade, have similar tastes and preferences, and have similar resource endowments and technologies. This has important implications for trade theory and policy.

Political economists are skeptical of the theory of comparative advantage. Instead, they focus on the winners and losers from unregulated trade, noting that workers and manufacturing communities in developed countries have paid a steep price for globalization. Global multinational corporations have been the main beneficiaries, because they are able to scour the globe to find new markets and the lowest possible costs of production. Political economists prefer to manage trade to protect key industries and to ensure that workers and communities are shielded from the destructive side of global trade. They also argue that comparative advantage in key industries can be gained via the right set of policies.

Trade policy and economic integration can be deeply controversial. The United States pursued unregulated trade beginning in the 1970s and later through the vehicles of NAFTA and the WTO, believing that these policies and trade agreements were broadly beneficial. But the election of Donald Trump in 2016 ushered in a new era of protectionism that indicated a shift in approach. Similarly, the E.U. pursued economic integration and less regulated trade until very recently, when its stability was shattered by the financial crisis and the collapse of the Greek economy. Subsequently, the mass movement of Eastern Europeans to the United Kingdom spawned Brexit and further E.U. disintegration. It will be interesting to see whether the pro-trade arguments of mainstream economists hold sway or whether the United States and the E.U. continue to move toward a more protectionist stance in the future.

The debate over trade policy reflects the deep divisions between mainstream economists and political economists. Laissez-faire economists for the most part put their faith in markets and the ability of private actors to innovate and yield outcomes that tend to benefit society. Unregulated trade is the ultimate expression of a market-oriented philosophy in that corporations determine what goods are produced, how they are made, and *where* they are made. New Keynesian economists generally prefer unregulated trade, but there must be adequate trade adjustment assistance, retraining, reeducation, community redevelopment, and other measures to insure that trade benefits everyone.

Political economists distrust markets to make those decisions without government oversight, worrying about ethical lapses (worker and environmental exploitation) by corporations as well as the destruction of communities as industries move abroad. Political economists advocate the use of industrial policies such as the triple helix to construct a comparative institutional advantage in key industries to create jobs and increase incomes in the domestic economy.

As always, it is left to the reader to determine which perspective you find most compelling.

QUESTIONS FOR REVIEW

1. (a) Explain the theory of comparative advantage and why most mainstream economists believe that unregulated trade increases the welfare of citizens on average. (b) List and briefly explain the main problems with the theory of comparative advantage.

2. Protectionism has long been utilized as a tool for economic development.
    a. What are the major policies used in protectionism?
    b. What are the main arguments for protectionism?
    c. What are the main costs generated by protectionism?

3. The theory of comparative advantage demonstrates that, in theory, *all* countries can benefit through specialization and trade.
    a. The graphs in Figure 34.6 show production possibilities curves for the United States and Kuwait, using an identical amount of resources for one month. Copy the graphs onto a sheet of paper. Determine which country has a comparative advantage in oil and which in rocket launchers using the PPCs. Show your work.
    b. Draw consumption possibilities curves on your graphs. Assume that the international terms of trade are one rocket launcher for two units of oil $(1RL = 2O)$.

4. The graphs in Figure 34.7 show production possibilities curves for the United States and Japan, using an identical amount of resources for one day. Determine which country has a comparative advantage in beef and which in automobiles using the PPCs. Show your work. Copy the graphs onto a sheet of paper. Draw consumption possibilities curves on your graphs. Assume that the international terms of trade are 1 automobile for 3 units of beef $(1A = 3B)$.

5. In 2018, the Trump administration imposed 25% tariffs on imports of steel into the United States. Using a graph, show how that tariff would affect the equilibrium price and quantity of imported steel. Assume that the initial price of steel is $2000 per ton. What impact would these tariffs have on U.S. steel

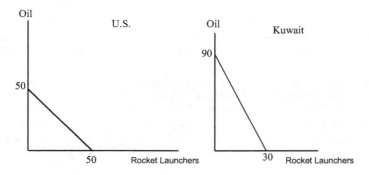

FIGURE 34.6 PPCs for the United States and Kuwait.

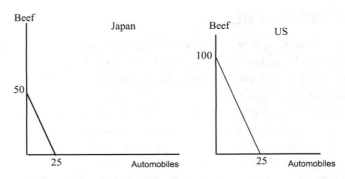

FIGURE 34.7 PPCs for Japan and the United States.

makers? What impact would the steel tariffs have on U.S. car companies that use a lot of steel to manufacture cars?

6. Describe U.S. trade patterns. Compare these trade patterns with the predictions of the theory of comparative advantage and political economy trade theories regarding the products that countries should specialize in producing and export. Which ideas do you find most accurately capture the realities of U.S. trade patterns? Explain and support your answer.

7. Describe the experiences of the E.U. and the United States with economic integration via trade agreements. What are the benefits of economic integration? What are the costs? Do you think the United States should continue to pursue the economic integration of North America? Why or why not?

8. Write an essay in which you assess the strongest arguments in favor of unregulated trade and the strongest arguments in favor of protectionism. Determine what approach you think your country should utilize when it comes to trade and exchange rates and support your arguments with examples from the text and from other sources.

NOTES

1 Gregory Mankiw, *Principles of Economics* (Cengage, Boston, 2015), p. 188.

2 See Christopher Minasians, "Where Are Apple Products Made?" September 18, 2017, https://www.macworld.co.uk/feature/apple/where-are-apple-products-made-3633 832/, accessed April 1, 2018.

3 Nauro Campos, Fabrizio Coricelli, and Luigi Moretti, "The Eye, the Needle and the Camel: Rich Countries Can Benefit from EU Membership (VOX, CEPR Policy Portal, 2016), https://voxeu.org/article/how-rich-nations-benefit-eu-membership.

4 See Robert Scott's work for the Economic Policy Institute, summarized at https://www.epi.org/blog/and-if-you-believe-this-ive-got-a-great-deal-to-sell-you-the-econ omic-impacts-of-the-revised-nafta-usmca-agreement/, accessed January 24, 2021.

5 Luis Villanueva, "Are Manufacturing Workers Benefiting from Trade? The Case of Mexico's Manufacturing Sector," *International Journal of Development Issues* 16, No. 1 (2017), pp. 25–42.

6 Daron Acemoglu, David Autor, David Dorn, et al., "Import Competition and the Great U.S. Employment Sag of the 2000s," *Journal of Labor Economics* 34, No. 1 (2016).

International finance and open economy macroeconomics

Exchange rates, financial flows, and the balance of payments

International finance is a complex and important topic. Exchange rates can fluctuate widely, causing large swings in the prices of imports and exports. Billions of dollars can be made or lost very quickly in foreign exchange markets. International flows of money can fuel economic growth or cause an economic system to crash. This instability sometimes prompts governments to attempt to fix exchange rates in place and to regulate financial flows, although problems can result from such efforts.

This chapter beings with the market for foreign exchange and how the supply and demand for foreign currency affect exchange rates. Exchange rates in turn affect the prices of domestic and foreign goods, so exchange rates play an important role in determining which industries are successful in a particular country. In general, the exchange rate for a particular currency is determined by the supply and demand for that currency. Exchange rates change when people shift the amount of foreign goods or investments that they want, which in turn affects the relative prices of goods and assets. By affecting the relative prices of goods in different countries, exchange rates are an important factor in determining the demand for domestic and foreign goods, which can have a large influence on the success or failure of particular industries.

Next, we turn to the balance of payments and how international flows of money impact the economy. Inflows of money into an economy result from selling

DOI: 10.4324/9781315636924-45

exports to other countries or from foreign investment in domestic assets. Outflows of money occur due to buying imports or from corporations and individuals investing in overseas assets. Being an accounting identity, the inflows and outflows of money in the balance of payments must be equal. However, analysis of the balance of payments also makes it clear that when countries experience a trade deficit (imports greater than exports), they also end up with a financial account surplus (inflows of foreign capital greater than outflows of domestic capital). Trade deficits therefore result in greater foreign ownership of domestic assets. Most laissez-faire and New Keynesian economists see no significant problem with trade deficits, whereas political economists argue that trade deficits are likely to eliminate jobs and reduce growth.

Some countries allow market forces to dictate exchange rates, whereas other countries adjust currency flows to achieve a fixed exchange rate in order to try to achieve greater stability. Similarly, some countries allow international financial capital to flow in and out freely, whereas other countries strictly limit international financial flows. The variation in approach depends on a country's tolerance for the instability that can come from rapid swings in exchange rates and international investment flows and the country's willingness to utilize government intervention to achieve greater stability.

35.0 CHAPTER 35 LEARNING GOALS

After reading this chapter, you should be able to:

■ Use a supply and demand graph of the foreign exchange market to analyze how particular events will affect exchange rates, exports, and imports.

■ Describe the components of the balance of payments and explain how trade deficits and surpluses relate to financial account surpluses and deficits.

■ Critically evaluate the arguments for and against trade deficits.

■ Compare and contrast the different types of exchange rate regimes.

■ Assess the arguments for and against regulating the flows of international capital.

We begin with the mainstream economic model of the market for foreign exchange.

35.1 EXCHANGE RATES AND THE FOREIGN EXCHANGE MARKET

An exchange rate refers to **the amount of one currency that exchanges for another** in a foreign exchange market. For example, in 2008, one U.S. dollar ($) exchanged for half of a British pound (£): $1 = £0.5. This also meant that one British pound was equal to two U.S. dollars: £1 = $2.

Then, from 2009 to 2021, the dollar appreciated—increased in value—relative to the pound. In 2021, one U.S. dollar exchanged for 0.75 pounds ($1 = £0.75). If we divide both sides by 0.75, we find that $£1 = \$\dfrac{1}{0.75} = \$1.33$. Therefore, the British pound depreciated—decreased in value—relative to the U.S. dollar.

A currency appreciates **when the currency's value increases relative to a foreign currency**. A currency depreciates **when its value decreases relative to a foreign currency**. Because exchange rates measure the value of one currency in terms of another currency, *whenever the domestic (home country) currency appreciates against a foreign currency, the foreign currency depreciates against the domestic currency and vice versa.*

In the mainstream economics model of the foreign exchange market, the value of a country's currency—the exchange rate of one currency with respect to another—is determined by the forces of supply and demand in the **foreign exchange market**. The foreign exchange market is where all buyers and sellers of a currency interact. Actors in foreign exchange markets include central banks, private banks, companies, investment firms, brokers, investors, and individuals.

In a foreign exchange market, the price of a currency is the exchange rate, which is the amount of a foreign currency that one unit of the domestic currency can purchase. On the quantity axis, the equilibrium quantity is the total amount of domestic currency exchanged for the foreign currency. The supply of the domestic currency comes from domestic country banks, businesses, investors, and consumers who want to exchange domestic country currency for foreign currency, usually so they can purchase foreign country goods or invest in foreign country assets. Basically, anyone who wants foreign goods or assets must supply their domestic currency in exchange for foreign currency at some point to buy the foreign goods or assets. The demand for domestic currency in a foreign exchange market comes from foreign country banks, businesses, investors, and individuals who want domestic country goods or assets. The exchange rate determines the prices of domestic country goods and assets relative to the prices of foreign goods and assets.

Figure 35.1(a) shows a graph of the foreign exchange market for U.S. dollars relative to the British (U.K.) pound. The price of the dollar is the amount of foreign currency one dollar will buy—in this case, 0.5 pounds (£). The **supply curve** reflects U.S. citizens, banks, and businesses who are exchanging dollars for pounds. They are supplying (selling) U.S. dollars and demanding (purchasing)

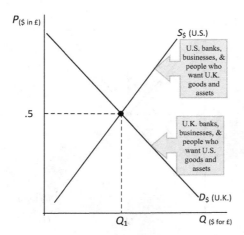

FIGURE 35.1 (a) The foreign exchange market for U.S. dollars.

British pounds, because they want something British and you can only buy British items with British pounds. Typically, the supply curve of dollars is U.S. actors who want to buy British goods, travel in the United Kingdom, or buy British stocks and bonds.

The **demand curve** in the foreign exchange market for the dollar consists of U.K. citizens, banks, and businesses that are exchanging pounds for dollars. They are demanding dollars, which they purchase by supplying pounds. U.K. actors want U.S. dollars because they need dollars in order to buy U.S. goods, stocks, or bonds or to travel in the United States.

The demand curve for a currency slopes downward because as a currency increases in value (appreciates), home country goods and assets get more expensive and foreign citizens reduce their quantity demanded. The supply curve slopes upward because as a currency appreciates in value, foreign goods and assets get cheaper, so home country citizens supply more home currency to obtain more foreign currency, which they use to buy more foreign goods and assets.

As with all supply and demand graphs, a change in the exchange rate (the price of the dollar) causes a movement along the supply and demand curves. Shifts in supply and demand curves are caused by changes in the fundamental determinants of the location of the curves. (Recall the supply and demand model in earlier chapters.)

Figure 35.1(b) shows what happened to the foreign exchange market for U.S. dollars from 2007 to 2021. After the financial crisis hit in 2008, investors flocked to U.S. treasury bonds, which are often considered the world's safest asset. Also, the U.S. economy recovered more quickly than the U.K. economy from the financial crisis, making it a more attractive investment location. And in 2016 when the United Kingdom decided to exit from the European Union (Brexit), investors feared that the British economy would face some major economic problems. For all of these reasons,

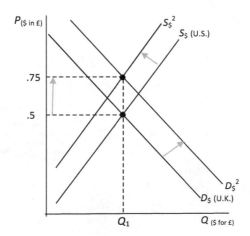

FIGURE 35.1 (b) U.S. assets become more attractive.

U.S. investors decided to reduce their purchases of U.K. stocks and bonds from 2007 to 2021, reducing the supply of dollars (they did not need as many British pounds as usual because they were not investing as much in the U.K. economy). The supply of U.S. dollars decreases from $S_\$$ to $S_\$^2$. Meanwhile, U.K. investors purchased more U.S. stocks and bonds than usual because the United States was a safer place to invest, increasing the demand for dollars. The demand for dollars increased from $D_\$$ to $D_\$^2$. The result was a significant appreciation of the U.S. dollar, which was matched by an equally severe depreciation of the British pound.

As a general rule, whenever the domestic country (in this case the United States) changes its behavior, the supply curve of the domestic currency shifts. Whenever the foreign country (in this case the United Kingdom) changes its behavior, the demand curve for the domestic currency shifts. Notice that foreign exchange markets often feature double shifts with both supply and demand curves shifting in opposite directions, because events often affect consumers or investors in both countries.

In the modern economy, international financial flows are so large, exceeding $1 trillion per day, that they have a major impact on currency values. In most cases, when an economy's expected economic performance is strong, there is a strong demand for that country's currency as investors seek out that country's assets. Therefore, *currencies tend to appreciate in countries with strong expected growth.*

35.2 THE DETERMINANTS OF SHIFTS IN SUPPLY AND DEMAND IN FOREIGN EXCHANGE MARKETS

The same rules that apply to regular supply and demand models apply to foreign exchange markets. A change in the price (exchange rate) causes a movement along the supply and demand curves. A change in one of the determinants of demand shifts the demand curve. A change in one of the determinants of supply shifts the supply curve.

35.2.1 Determinants of demand

The location of the demand curve in the mainstream foreign exchange market model is determined by the following factors:

1. **Government demand for its own currency.** Governments can purchase their own currency using gold or reserves of foreign currencies that they keep on hand.
2. **Changes in foreign incomes.** If foreign incomes increase, they will want more domestic country exports, which will cause them to increase their demand for domestic country currency.
3. **Changes in foreign tastes and preferences for domestic goods and investments.** If citizens' tastes in the foreign country change so that they want more domestic country products, their demand for domestic currency increases.
4. **Changes in relative interest rates.** If interest rates increase in the domestic country relative to the foreign country, foreign investors who seek out high interest rates (the highest return) for their money will demand more domestic country currency so they can buy more domestic interest-bearing bonds.
5. **Changes in relative prices of goods.** If goods prices decrease in the domestic country relative to the foreign country, consumers in the foreign country will want more domestic country goods, increasing the demand for domestic currency.

Decreases in the demand for a nation's currency would be a result of decreased government purchases of the nation's own currency, decreases in foreign incomes, foreign tastes changing so they demand less domestic country goods, a decrease in relative interest rates, and an increase in domestic country goods prices.

Most of the factors affecting the demand curve for a currency are a product of changes in foreign country behavior. In general, any factor that causes foreign citizens to want more goods or assets (stocks or interest-bearing bonds) from the domestic country will cause an increase in the demand for the domestic country's currency, shifting the demand curve up and to the right. Any factor causing foreign citizens to want less of the domestic country's goods or assets would cause a decrease in the demand curve.

35.2.2 Determinants of supply

The location of the supply curve in the mainstream foreign exchange market model is determined by the following factors:

1. **Changes in the government's supply of its own currency.** Governments can supply more of their own currency, using it to purchase foreign currencies.

2. **Changes in domestic country incomes.** When home country consumers have more money, they will buy more goods, and some of those goods will come from foreign countries. To buy more foreign goods, they must increase the supply of home country currency in exchange for foreign currency.

3. **Changes in home country tastes and preferences for foreign country goods and investments.** If home country consumers prefer more foreign country goods than they used to, more home country currency will be supplied to purchase more foreign goods.

4. **Changes in relative interest rates.** If interest rates decrease in the home country relative to the foreign country, home country investors who seek out high interest rates for their money will invest *more* money abroad, buying more foreign interest-bearing bonds and increasing their supply of home country currency.

5. **Changes in relative prices of goods.** If goods prices increase in the home country relative to the foreign country, consumers in the home country will want more foreign country goods, increasing the supply of home country currency.

A decrease in the supply of a currency would result from a decrease in government supply of its own currency, a decrease in home country incomes, reduced home country preferences for foreign goods or investments, higher relative home country interest rates, and lower relative home country prices.

Notice that changes in relative interest rates and changes in relative prices appear in *both* the demand and the supply list of determinants in exchange markets. These factors cause **double shifts**.

Now let's consider some examples. And to get you used to applying this model to any country, we will use Japan and the euro area as the two sides of the foreign exchange market. In the foreign exchange market for the Japanese yen, Japanese banks, consumers, and investors are the ones supplying yen in exchange for euros. Japan is the domestic (home) economy. The amount of yen Japanese actors supply depends on how many European goods and assets they want. Meanwhile, the demand for yen comes from European banks, consumers, and investors who want Japanese goods and assets. The amount of yen they demand (which is also the amount of euros they supply) depends on how many Japanese goods and assets Europeans want.

Figure 35.2(a) shows what happens to the foreign exchange market for Japanese yen (¥) when incomes in the euro area (€) increase. When European consumers have more income, they buy more products, and some of the products they buy will be Japanese. When the demand for Japanese exported goods increases, European importers must pay for those goods in Japanese yen, so the demand for yen increases, shifting up and to the right and moving the equilibrium from point

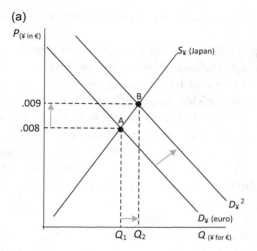

FIGURE 35.2 (a) Increase in incomes in Europe.

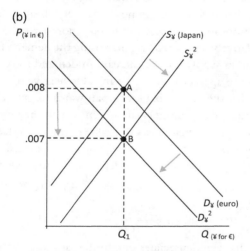

FIGURE 35.2 (b) Interest rates in the euro area increase.

A to point B. The result is an appreciation of the yen, whose exchange rate value increases from €0.008 to €0.009. The quantity of yen exchanged for euros increases from Q_1 to Q_2.

In Figure 35.2(b), we see what happens to the exchange rate value of the Japanese yen when interest rates in the euro area increase. A very important thing to understand in foreign exchange markets is that *international money tends to flow wherever interest rates are higher.* At any given time, there are a lot of international investors looking to put their money in bonds that pay a high interest rate. So, any country that has higher interest rates relative to other countries will see an inflow of foreign money.

In this example, interest rates in the euro area increase. This causes a double shift in the foreign exchange market. Japanese investors want to move some of their money to Europe to take advantage of the higher interest rates there, so there is an **increase in the supply of yen**. Japanese investors exchange yen for euros so they can buy European bonds and other interest-bearing securities. Meanwhile, European investors who usually invest some of their money in Japanese bonds decide to invest less than usual in Japan, preferring to invest their money in European bonds that come with newly higher interest rates. Therefore, the **demand for Japanese yen decreases** as euro-area investors exchange fewer euros for yen. This increase in supply and decrease in demand for yen causes the value of the yen to depreciate from €0.008 to €0.007.

Now let's go through some additional examples to make sure you understand how foreign exchange markets work.

Suppose that the prices of Japanese goods decline relative to the prices of European goods. What would happen to the foreign exchange market for the Japanese yen? Japanese consumers who usually buy European goods would buy less than usual, because Japanese goods are now relatively cheaper. The supply of yen would decrease. European consumers would buy more Japanese goods than usual because they are relatively less expensive, increasing the demand for yen. The result would be a decrease in supply and an increase in demand for yen, both of which would cause the yen to appreciate (increase in value relative to the euro).

Now suppose that the central bank of Japan wants to give a boost to Japanese exports. To do so, they supply more Japanese yen, which they use to buy up euros. This increase in the supply of yen causes the value of the yen to fall. The yen depreciates relative to the euro. How does this help Japanese exports?

Suppose that a Toyota Prius, made in Japan, normally sells for ¥2,500,000. If the exchange rate is 1¥ = 0.008€, then $1€ = \dfrac{1}{0.008}¥ = 125¥$. That means a Prius selling for ¥2,500,000 will sell for $€\dfrac{2,500,000}{125} = €20,000.$[1]

Now suppose that yen depreciates due to the Japanese central bank's actions, falling to 1¥ = €0.00666. This means that $1€ = \dfrac{1}{0.00666}¥ = 150¥$. The Prius, which still sells for ¥2,500,000 in Japan, now costs $€\dfrac{2500000}{150} = €16,667.$ The Japanese central bank action reduced the price of the Prius, and of all Japanese export goods, significantly, which will help Japanese exporters sell more goods in Europe. Exchange rates can have a major impact on a country's imports and exports as well as their financial markets.

Political economists view exchange rate markets as extremely speculative in nature. The vast majority of currency market trades involve speculation rather than exchanges related to international trade or investment. This makes exchange markets subject to extreme fluctuations and speculative bubbles that can be destabilizing (and that are hard to model). Hence, as we will see later, many political economists advocate the regulation of exchange markets to improve stability.

35.3 EXCHANGE RATES, TRADE, AND MARKETS FOR GOODS AND SERVICES

Exchange rates directly affect the prices of imports and exports as well as the value of assets. Therefore, exchange rates impact goods markets and financial markets significantly, and they affect aggregate demand and aggregate supply.

The following are the key principles regarding how exchange rates affect other markets:

- Depreciation of a home country's currency makes foreign goods more expensive for home country consumers (reducing imports) and makes home country goods cheaper for foreign consumers (increasing exports). When a currency depreciates, each unit of that currency buys fewer foreign goods than it used to, making them more expensive. The decreases in imports and increases in exports increase aggregate demand. Imported inputs become more expensive, however, so aggregate supply decreases slightly, with the degree of the shift depending on the percentage of a country's inputs that are imported.
- Depreciation of a home country's currency makes its money worth less relative to foreign money, which reduces the value of home country assets. This can hurt home country financial institutions, especially banks.
- Appreciation of a home country's currency makes its goods more expensive relative to the prices of foreign products, reducing exports and increasing imports. This has the effect of decreasing aggregate demand. Aggregate supply increases slightly with a currency appreciation because foreign inputs become less expensive.
- Appreciation of a home country's currency makes its money worth more relative to foreign currencies, which increases the value of home country assets.

Because of the impact on exports, currency devaluation has been a frequent tool used by countries to promote export industries. The 2015 World Economic Outlook published by the International Monetary Fund found that a 10% devaluation of a nation's currency can boost exports by an average of 1.5% of gross domestic product (GDP).[2] Thus, currency devaluation can provide a significant boost to economic growth.

There are some potential problems with devaluing a nation's currency to promote growth, however. First, devaluation tends to increase prices and harm consumers. Devaluation makes all foreign goods prices higher, because the home country currency buys less than it used to. Imported inputs get more expensive, raising the costs of production. The increase in the prices of imported goods also allows domestic firms to raise their prices. And devaluation reduces the value of a country's financial assets. Assets in foreign countries become relatively more expensive. Thus, devaluing a currency has some substantial benefits, along with some costs.

China has regularly been accused of maintaining an artificially low exchange rate in order to promote exports. After the financial crisis hit in 2009, numerous countries engaged in competitive devaluations of their currencies to try to promote exports. Of course, if countries simultaneously attempt to devalue their currencies, there will be no impact on exchange rates or exports. For example, if the Japanese government supplies more yen to buy euros but the European government supplies more euros to buy yen, their actions cancel each other out. However, countries that did not devalue their currency in 2009 saw reduced exports to countries that did devalue their currency.

The impact of exchange rates on trade and financial flows is one of the major factors driving changes in a country's balance of payments. It is to this topic that we turn next.

35.4 INTERNATIONAL FINANCE AND THE BALANCE OF PAYMENTS

International finance involves the flows of goods and services, income, assets, and other forms of financial capital between countries. These flows can have a large influence on economic outcomes, so it is important to understand how they work.

The balance of payments measures **all of the transactions in which the currency of one nation is exchanged for the currency of another nation during a particular period of time** (usually one year). Mostly, currency exchanges occur because of trade (exports or imports) or because of purchases of another country's assets (financial investments). The balance of payments is an accounting identity tracking these flows, and all of the inflows of money, the credits, must balance all of the outflows of money, the debits (Figure 35.3).

Within the balance of payments, the major issues economists focus on are the following:

- The current account deficit or surplus, which is driven primarily by any trade deficit (the amount imports exceed exports) or trade surplus (the amount exports exceed imports)
- The financial account surplus (the amount foreign purchases of home country assets exceed home country purchases of foreign country assets) or deficit.
- Because credits (inflows) always balance debits (outflows), **any current account deficit is always matched by a financial account surplus, and any current account surplus is always matched by a financial account deficit.**

Home Country Balance of Payments **Credits**	Home Country Balance of Payments **Debits**
Any inflow of money from a foreign country	*Any outflow of money to a foreign country*
Current Account	Current Account
Incoming money from **exports** of home country goods & services	Outgoing money to pay for **imports** of foreign country goods & services
Investment and salary income earned by home country citizens in foreign countries	**Investment and salary income** earned by foreign country citizens in the home country
Foreign aid (unilateral transfers) given from foreign countries to the home country	**Foreign aid** (unilateral transfers) given from the home country to foreign countries
Financial Account	Financial Account
Foreign purchases of home country assets (stocks, bonds, property, and other assets)	**Home country purchases of foreign country assets** (stocks, bonds, property, etc.)
Money from the **sale of foreign assets** (stocks, bonds, property, and other foreign assets) by the home country	Money from the **sale of home country assets** (stocks, bonds, property and other assets) by the foreign country
Incoming transfers of assets (migrants' remittances, fund and asset transfers)	**Outgoing transfers** of assets (migrants' remittances, fund and asset transfers)
Capital Account: debt forgiveness, and other capital and nonfinancial transfers to foreign citizens	**Capital Account:** debt forgiveness, and other capital and nonfinancial transfers to home country citizens

FIGURE 35.3 Table showing the two sides of the balance of payments.

35.4.1 Trade deficits and the current account

Figure 35.4 displays the U.S. current account for 2017 and 2018. Notice in particular that in 2018 U.S. exports of goods were $1672 billion, and U.S. imports of goods were $2563 billion, which means that in 2018, the United States experienced a trade deficit in goods of $891 billion. This was offset somewhat by a trade surplus in services. This left the United States with a current account deficit of $479 billion in 2018. That money flowed out of the United States to foreign countries.

Figure 35.5 shows the countries with which the United States experienced its largest trade deficits in 2019. The trade deficits with China are particularly large, followed by those with Mexico, Japan, Germany, Vietnam, and Ireland.

Figure 35.6 shows the U.S. financial account and capital account in 2017 and 2018. The financial account includes all financial flows into and out of a country. The U.S. financial outflow is primarily the purchase of capital assets outside the United States by the U.S. government, institutions, citizens, or businesses. Meanwhile, the U.S. financial inflow is the purchase of U.S. capital assets by foreign governments, institutions, citizens, or businesses. The difference is the statistical discrepancy, which has to do with the amounts of money that vanish each year, held as cash for a variety of reasons (some of them illegal!).

Notice that the financial account surplus is very close to the amount of current account deficit. This has an important implication: *A nation with a trade deficit is also experiencing foreign purchases of domestic assets.* A nation with a trade surplus is acquiring foreign assets. The capital account includes various other transfers of assets and is so small for the United States that it has a negligible impact on the balance of payments.

When we compare the current account deficit for the United States with the financial and capital account surpluses, we see the mirror image graph depicted in Figure 35.7. The larger the current account deficit, the larger the financial account surplus.

Normally, mainstream economists expect exchange rates to adjust when a nation has a large trade deficit. Trade deficits cause a large outflow of a country's currency. By flooding the international market with its currency, a country causes its currency to depreciate. The depreciation in currency causes home country goods to become cheaper, which boosts exports and reduces imports, thereby eliminating the trade deficit. Trade surpluses would have the opposite effect. Thus, according to mainstream economic theory, trade deficits and surpluses should automatically be eliminated by adjustments in exchange rates.

However, political economists point out that in the modern era, chronic trade deficits and surpluses are the norm for many countries. Furthermore, these

	2017	2018
Exports of goods and services and income receipts (credits)	3,433,239	3,701,694
Exports of goods and services	2,351,072	2,500,756
Goods	1,553,383	1,672,331
Services	797,690	828,425
Primary income receipts (investment income, compensation)	928,118	1,060,362
Secondary income (current transfer) receipts	154,049	140,576
Imports of goods and services and income payments (debits)	3,882,380	4,190,166
Imports of goods and services	2,903,349	3,122,862
Goods	2,360,878	2,563,651
Services	542,471	559,211
Primary income payments (investment income, compensation)	706,386	816,066
Secondary income (current transfer) payments	272,645	251,237
Capital transfer receipts and other credits	24,788	9,418
Capital transfer payments and other debits	42	10
Current account deficit	-424,395	-479,064

FIGURE 35.4 Table of U.S. current account (millions of dollars).

Country	Exports	Imports	Trade deficit
China	106.6	452.2	345.6
Mexico	256.4	358.1	101.7
Japan	74.7	143.6	68.9
Germany	60.3	127.5	67.2
Vietnam	10.9	66.7	55.8
Ireland	9.0	61.8	52.8
Italy	23.8	57.2	33.4
Canada	292.7	319.7	27.0
India	34.4	57.7	23.3
Taiwan	31.2	54.3	23.1
South Korea	56.9	77.5	20.6
France	37.8	57.4	19.6

FIGURE 35.5 Table showing largest U.S. trade deficits, 2019.

	2017	2018
Net U.S. acquisition of financial assets excluding financial derivatives	1,182,749	301,618
Net U.S. incurrence of liabilities excluding financial derivatives	1,537,683	800,913
Financial derivatives other than reserves, net transactions	23,074	−20,261
Financial account surplus	**331,860**	**519,556**
Statistical discrepancy	**92,536**	**−40,492**
Current account deficit	**−424,395**	**−479,064**

FIGURE 35.6 Table showing U.S. financial account (millions of dollars).

imbalances can lead to some significant problems, even though there are benefits to consumers from the "extra" imports.

The root cause of trade deficits can be determined by analyzing the key GDP accounting identities behind the balance of payments that were described earlier in the book.

$$GDP = C + S + T = C + I + G + X - IM$$

$$S + T + IM = I + G + X$$

$$(S - I) + (T - G) = (X - IM).$$

Therefore, trade deficits $(X - IM)$ are a product of the amount that savings is less than investment $(S < I)$ and the amount that taxes are less than government spending $(T < G$; budget deficits).

35.5 THE CAUSES OF U.S. TRADE DEFICITS

There are three major causes of U.S. trade deficits that economists from various perspectives have identified: (1) Low U.S. national savings, (2) high savings rates

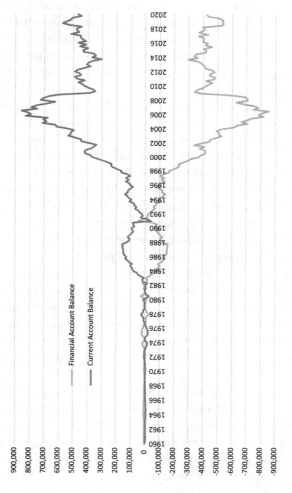

FIGURE 35.7 U.S. financial account and current account (millions of dollars), 1960–2020.

in several countries that are important U.S. trading partners, and (3) high demand for U.S. assets.

1. **Low U.S. national savings.** The U.S. government runs chronic budget deficits and U.S. consumers save very little compared with consumers in the rest of the world. Mainstream economists therefore identify *low U.S. national savings as the major source of the U.S. trade deficit.* Any country that consumes more than it produces is by definition consuming more than its income, so it *must* run a trade deficit. The extra goods being consumed must be produced by a foreign country. Therefore, if the United States wants to eliminate the trade deficit, it would need to save more and consume less and the government would need to balance its budget. This would be quite painful, involving major decreases to aggregate demand and possibly a recession.

    Whereas mainstream economists focus on low national savings as the primary culprit, political economists focus on a different set of issues. Political economists argue that the major source of U.S. trade deficits is the surge of foreign investments in U.S. assets, which takes the form of foreign purchases of U.S. stocks, bonds, property, companies, and other assets. This is a product of high foreign savings, the status of the U.S. dollar as the world's reserve currency that central banks and investors prefer to hold, and active efforts by foreign central banks and foreign investors to purchase U.S. assets. High demand for U.S. assets increases the demand for the dollar, causing the dollar to appreciate and U.S. exports to increase in price.

2. **High foreign savings.** Many trading partners of the United States have extremely high rates of savings and low levels of consumption. As a result, these high-savings countries end up producing more goods than they purchase, resulting in a trade surplus in their country. This is especially true of Japan, South Korea, China, and Germany. Figure 35.8 shows that the savings rates in these countries, especially China, are much higher than the savings rate in the United States.[3]

    Sometimes high savings rates can be attributed to culture: Citizens of some countries have always had high rates of savings. However, high savings rates and low levels of consumption are also a product of specific economic policies. For example, (a) some countries actively suppress wages. In China and Germany, the state actively pursues low wage policies. This limits the amount of goods their consumers purchase, leading to low levels of consumption and high savings rates. Another factor is (b) the subsidization of exports, something that China, Japan, South Korea, and Germany all engage in. Subsidizing exports takes domestic money that could have been spent on consumption and uses it instead for production. In addition, (c) high domestic taxes on the consumption of goods and services, such as Germany's 19% value-added tax, reduce domestic consumption. Trading partners that systematically suppress

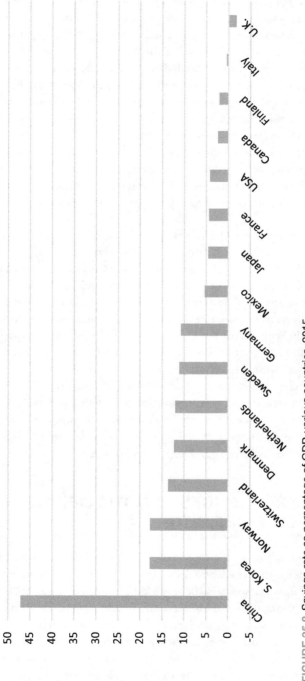

FIGURE 35.8 Savings rate as percentage of GDP, various countries, 2015.

consumer demand while subsidizing production tend to run trade surpluses, which generate large inflows of foreign (U.S.) currency into their countries.

3. **High demand for U.S. assets and currency.** Financial markets in the United States are viewed as a uniquely profitable investment environment, with little regulation and generous government bailouts if things get bad. U.S. government bonds are viewed as one of the world's safest assets. As a result, investors all over the world have a high demand for U.S. assets.

Similarly, the U.S. dollar was set up after World War II as the world's reserve currency in order to make international transactions easier. The dollar continues to serve this role, with more than 90% of foreign exchange transactions involving the dollar and more than 60% of international reserves held in dollars. In essence, the dollar is used around the world in transactions that have little or nothing to do with the U.S. economy. Consequently, there is generally more demand for the dollar than for other currencies, which causes the dollar to appreciate in value above its normal level, contributing to trade deficits.

Outsized financial flows into the United States are exacerbated when the countries that run trade surpluses with the United States take the dollars they earned on exports and invest those sums in U.S. asset markets. This provides an additional factor that keeps the U.S. dollar overvalued, while providing an outlet for the surplus of funds generated in trade surplus countries. The high demand for U.S. assets, coming from foreign savings, foreign asset demand, and foreign trade surplus revenues, increases the demand for the U.S. dollar, causing the dollar to appreciate in value and making U.S. goods more expensive, thereby reducing exports and contributing directly to the trade deficit.

Note that, regardless of the primary reason for trade deficit (low U.S. national savings, high savings in trading partner economies, or high demand for U.S. assets), the consequences are the same: *A country with chronic trade deficits will experience increasing levels of foreign ownership of domestic assets as long as these relationships persist.* Some economists see this as a major problem, whereas others do not.

35.6 THE CONSEQUENCES AND THE DEBATE OVER TRADE DEFICITS

There are a number of different perspectives on trade deficits. Most political economists find trade deficits problematic because they can reduce employment in the United States, hurting U.S. workers. Supply-side economists argue that foreign countries unfairly advantage their own firms and disadvantage U.S. firms, which is bad for U.S. industrial development. Laissez-faire economists believe that trade deficits are primarily a product of too much government spending, which they would like to rein in via austerity policies. Most mainstream New Keynesian economists, however, see trade deficits as a relatively harmless phenomenon that enhances the U.S. standard of living without significant costs. These perspectives are described in more detail below.

Critics of U.S. trade deficits include U.S. labor leaders, political economists, and liberal mainstream economists who argue that *foreign countries are hurting U.S. employment* via their manipulative trade practices. Note that this problem occurs under very specific circumstances.

By engineering their economies to increase production while holding consumption levels steady, trade surplus countries can increase their own employment levels at the expense of employment in countries running trade deficits. Production in trade surplus countries outstrips domestic consumption, and the excess supply is sold to foreign country consumers. At the same time, when the United States exports less than it imports, aggregate demand is lower than it would have been otherwise (recall that aggregate demand includes net exports, $X - IM$).

If the inflow of foreign money from the trade deficit stimulates new investment, then aggregate demand (and U.S. income and employment) will be maintained and the trade deficit will not harm U.S. employment. However, in recent years in the United States, there has been an overabundance of money in financial markets, which means that *the addition of foreign funds is not being invested productively*. Therefore, *any country with excess liquidity in financial markets that exports less than it imports will see lower levels of aggregate demand, lower GDP, and fewer jobs*. Unfortunately, this has been the U.S. experience in recent years, meaning that *the United States is directly experiencing economic costs (lower employment and GDP) from the trade deficit*.[4] From the perspective of political economists and some liberal mainstream economists, U.S. workers should be protected from subsidized foreign competition to prevent these negative outcomes.

It is worth pointing out that although the trade deficit may be costing U.S. workers jobs, it is very good for U.S. financial markets. The flood of international money keeps interest rates low, and the flood of foreign purchases of U.S. assets increases the value of the U.S. stock market and other U.S. assets. Some investors, like Warren Buffet, worry that the United States will be "colonized by purchase" of assets by foreign countries, steadily losing control of its assets.[5] Other investors argue that the infusion of foreign investment provides liquidity and opportunities that lead to job and income creation.

President Trump, and the supply-side economists who supported him, made U.S. trade deficits a major political issue. Trump engaged in trade wars with China and numerous other countries, imposing tariffs on their goods and threatening to keep those tariffs in place until the trade surplus countries started purchasing more U.S. exports. These countries then retaliated by imposing tariffs on U.S. goods. Trump succeeded in reducing the U.S. trade deficit slightly but at a huge cost to numerous U.S. businesses that experienced higher costs from tariffs on inputs and declining export sales.

Laissez-faire advocates like Martin Feldstein argue that the U.S. trade deficit is primarily a result of too much government spending. Laissez-faire economists would like to resolve the issue by dramatically reducing the amount of government spending.

However, the majority of mainstream New Keynesian economists see the trade deficit as mostly harmless. First and foremost, U.S. trade deficits indicate that U.S. consumers have a higher standard of living, consuming more goods than they could afford without having access to surplus goods from trading partners. In addition, foreign investment increases U.S. asset values and allows the United States to maintain a high level of domestic investment. The increased payments to foreign owners have not, as yet, proved to be a problem. This led conservative mainstream economist Gregory Mankiw to argue, "Whether a trade deficit represents a problem depends on whether our spending is prudent or profligate."[6] As long as businesses are investing money wisely and consumers are not spending beyond their means, trade deficits are not a problem from this perspective. According to the standard mainstream economic models, rational, well-informed consumer and investor behavior ensures that trade deficits are not problematic.

In contrast, most political economists dispute that injections of foreign capital are being invested productively given low levels of business investment (in capital goods) in the United States in recent decades. Furthermore, consumer debt levels are extremely high, calling into question the rationality of the spending behavior of the modern U.S. consumer. And, as noted above, political economic research notes the negative impact of trade deficits on U.S. aggregate demand and employment.

We have focused on the U.S. experience in this section. Other countries, however, experience balance of payments issues very differently. Developing countries cannot run persistent current account deficits like those of the United States because international investors usually are not willing to purchase large quantities of developing country assets. Running current account deficits can cause a developing country to experience rapid currency depreciation, inflation, and unemployment. In this sense, developing countries are often balance of payments constrained, in that they are forced to balance international inflows and outflows.

Given that trade deficits or surpluses depend in part on exchange rates, countries can affect their trade balance by manipulating their exchange rate. Alternatively, they can allow market forces to determine their exchange rate. The decision to manage a country's exchange rate or let it "float" is discussed in the next section.

35.7 FIXED VS. FLOATING EXCHANGE RATE REGIMES

One of the major issues that each government must decide when it comes to international finance is whether or not it will allow its currency to float freely based on the forces of supply and demand or whether it wants to try to maintain a fixed exchange rate to build more stability into the economic system. Each option comes with its benefits and potential problems.

In general, there are three major types of exchange rate regimes, freely floating, managed float, or fixed. A floating exchange rate regime is when **the government does not regulate the exchange rate, allowing its country's currency to fluctuate with market forces**. This can lead to widespread fluctuations in a nation's currency. Figure 35.9 shows the fluctuations in the price of one euro in U.S. dollars from 2016 to 2021. These are two relatively stable currencies, but it is common for the exchange rate to fluctuate by 15%–20% in a single year. For businesses that depend on importing and exporting, this introduces a significant amount of variability into their operations.

Countries sometimes turn to fixed exchange rates to facilitate exchange with particular trading partners, such as countries within the euro region, or to stabilize an economic system and give confidence to investors that their money will retain its value. Foreign exchange risk is one of the biggest hurdles facing an international investor or trader. If you invest in a country and its currency crashes, your money will lose a large share of its value. For example, if you invested in Venezuela's major industry, oil and gas, at the beginning of 2020, by the end of 2020 your investment would have lost 70% of its value due to the dramatic depreciation of Venezuela's currency. Investors can purchase futures contracts that allow them to lock in a particular exchange rate, but such contracts can be expensive, especially when a country is unstable.

A fixed exchange rate regime exists **when the government of a country pegs (fixes) the value of its currency relative to another currency**. Given the constant fluctuations in the supply and demand for a country's currency, a fixed exchange rate can only be maintained through vigilant efforts by a country's central bank. In reality, fixed exchange rates fluctuate slightly around the official rate.

There are numerous examples of fixed exchange rates. Before European Union members adopted the euro, they pegged their currencies to the German deutsche mark to make the currency conversion possible. Rather than adopt the euro, Denmark pegs its currency to the euro so that it can trade easily with other E.U. countries. And Denmark can adjust its currency if it experiences a crisis, something that Greece was unable to do once it adopted the euro as its currency.

Small countries also sometimes peg their currencies to an established one to reduce fluctuations and stabilize the economy. Panama and Cuba peg their currencies to the U.S. dollar.

Governments have three main tools they can use to alter the supply or the demand for their currency in order to maintain its value: (1) Purchase or sell its own currency, (2) restrict access to international exchange, or (3) change interest rates.

Suppose that Japan wants to peg its currency to the euro at €1 = ¥100 (¥1 = €0.010) to facilitate trade with Europe, thereby making exporters and importers in Japan and Europe secure in the knowledge that investments and exchanges will garner a reliable return. The government of Japan will need to manipulate the demand or supply of their currency to keep the exchange rate with the euro steady.

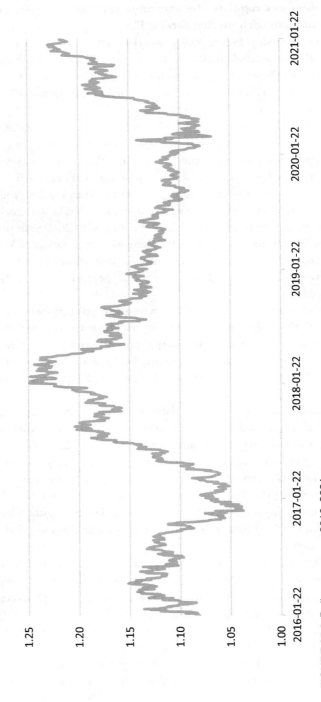

FIGURE 35.9 Dollars per euro, 2016–2021.

(a)

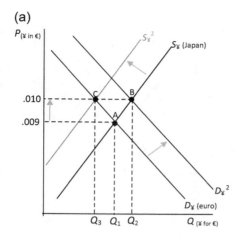

FIGURE 35.10 (a) Actions to increase the value of the yen.

Figure 35.10(a) shows the yen originally in equilibrium at point A at an exchange rate of ¥1 = €0.009, below the target the government set. The government has three choices to increase the value of the yen, all of which involve decreasing the supply and/or increasing the demand for yen.

1. The government can increase the demand for yen by **buying its own currency** (yen) utilizing gold or foreign exchange reserves it has accumulated. This will increase the demand for yen from $D_¥$ to $D_¥^2$, moving the market to a new equilibrium at point B and increasing the value of the yen back to its target of ¥1 = €0.010. In order to buy more of its own currency, governments must accumulate gold or the currencies of their trading partners. This action is only possible until the government runs out of its precious metal and foreign exchange reserves.

2. The government can reduce the supply of yen by instituting **foreign exchange controls** such as instituting a licensing system that strictly limits the amount of foreign exchange that individuals and firms can purchase. The result is that fewer domestic entities are able to supply their currency in exchange for a foreign currency, reducing the supply of yen. The shifts the supply curve of yen in Figure 35.10(a) from $S_¥$ to $S_¥^2$, causing the value of the yen to increase back to its target of €0.010. Many developing countries install limits on purchases of foreign currencies to keep financial capital from leaving the country.

3. The government can **increase interest rates** to draw money into the country. As shown in Figure 35.10(b), higher interest rates in Japan will decrease the supply of yen from $S_¥$ to $S_¥^3$ as Japanese investors keep more of their money in Japanese interest-bearing securities. Meanwhile, the demand for yen will increase from $D_¥$ to $D_¥^3$ as foreign investors also seek out Japanese interest-bearing securities. The result is an appreciation of the yen from €0.009 to

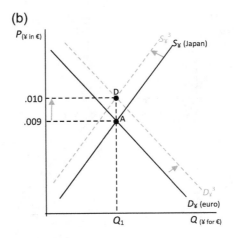

FIGURE 35.10 (b) Increase in interest rates in Japan.

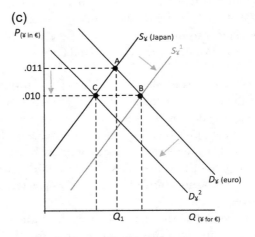

FIGURE 35.10 (c) Actions to decrease the value of the yen.

€0.010. Note that though higher interest rates do help to raise the value of a country's currency, there will be some negative consequences due to the impact of higher interest rates on domestic consumption and investment.

Maintaining a strong currency makes it easier for a country to accumulate foreign assets and purchase foreign goods, although it makes a country's exports more expensive.

If a country's currency is above its target exchange rate, the government will have to take actions that would reduce demand and/or increase supply of its currency. Figure 35.10(c) shows Japan in equilibrium at point A with an overvalued currency of ¥1 = €0.011. The government has three choices to cause the yen to depreciate:

1. The government can **increase the supply of its own currency** (yen) and use it to buy the foreign currency (euros). This increases the supply of yen from $S_¥$ to $S_¥{}^1$, causing the value of the yen to depreciate to the target of ¥1 = €0.010 at point B. Because governments can create unlimited amounts of their own currency, there are no limits on the amount of this a government can undertake. However, too much supply of a currency could cause its value to drop too much, which would lead to inflationary pressures and eventually could result in people refusing to accept a currency. Therefore, governments use this option judiciously.

2. The government can **impose foreign exchange controls on the amount of domestic currency that foreign investors can purchase**. This reduces the demand for the domestic currency (yen), shifting the demand curve from $D_¥$ to $D_¥{}^2$ and causing the value of the yen to depreciate from 0.11 to 0.10 euros at point C. Countries that want to limit foreign control over domestic markets often impose this type of foreign exchange control.

3. The government can **decrease interest rates**, which will cause domestic investors to supply more yen in order to purchase more euro-denominated bonds that pay higher interest rates. The supply of yen shifts from $S_¥$ to $S_¥{}^3$ in Figure 35.10(d). Similarly, European investors will decrease their demand for yen, as they buy fewer Japanese bonds than normal due to lower interest rates in Japan. The demand for yen shifts from $D_¥$ to $D_¥{}^3$. The new equilibrium at point D in Figure 35.10(d) has returned the yen to its pegged rate of 0.010 euros.

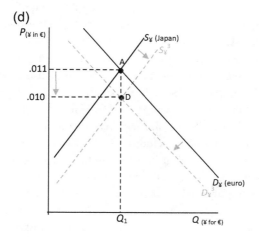

(d)

FIGURE 35.10 (d) Decrease in interest rates in Japan.

Many countries maintain their currencies at an artificially low exchange rate to promote exports. However, this hurts consumers by increasing the prices of imported goods and it hurts investors by reducing the value of domestic currency.

Countries who find the fluctuations in floating exchange rate regimes too destabilizing but see the fixing of exchange rates as overly restrictive can opt for a middle ground. A managed float exchange rate regime is **when the government establishes a target zone for its currency and intervenes whenever its currency leaves the target zone**. Thus, a currency would be allowed to appreciate or depreciate somewhat but the government would step in to intervene if the changes in the currency's value were too dramatic.

According to the International Monetary Fund, in 2013, 82 countries used a managed float exchange rate regime, 25 countries used a fixed regime, and 65 countries used a floating regime. So most countries manage their currencies in some manner, although many of the world's largest economies, including the United States and the E.U., allow their exchange rates to float.

Laissez-faire and New Keynesian economists tend to prefer floating exchange rates due to their faith in markets. Political economists often prefer managed float or fixed exchange rate systems due to their emphasis on stability, although there are some notable dissenters who think that floating exchange rates allow for more expansionary fiscal policies.

One of the main sources of instability in many economies, especially smaller ones, is the impact of large flows of international capital. Therefore, another issue for governments is whether or not to manage flows of financial capital.

35.8 UNREGULATED VS. MANAGED FINANCIAL CAPITAL FLOWS

In the modern world, international "hot" money flows rapidly around the globe seeking the highest return and the next big thing. A small economy can find itself devastated by withdrawals of financial capital or buoyed by inflows. And international financial flows can switch directions very quickly depending on the whims of investors. This makes the management of international financial flows a major issue for most countries, and especially for small ones. The Asian financial crisis of 1997 shows the difficulties that can result from large swings in financial flows.

In the 1980s and early 1990s, international investors poured money into rapidly growing Asian economies, including South Korea, Thailand, Hong Kong, Malaysia, and the Philippines. High interest rates and rapid growth in these countries attracted a spike in international investment, which in turn caused a huge increase in asset prices, especially stocks and real estate prices. These Asian countries borrowed extensively from Western investors to finance economic expansion. So much money was available that companies began to invest in very risky endeavors. At the same time, many of these countries were running current account deficits, driven at least in part by their financial account surpluses, and they were trying to maintain a fixed exchange rate.

By the mid-1990s, economic growth picked up in the United States and Europe driven by the tech boom. As these developed countries grew, their central banks increased interest rates to rein in inflation. The combination of rapid growth and high interest rates in the United States and Europe drew international financial investors back to developed countries, and they began pulling their money out of their Asian investments. Meanwhile, Chinese competition began to displace other competitors in Asia.

Investors pulled money out of their non-Chinese Asian investments en masse, causing real estate prices and stock prices to crash. As investors sold Asian currencies, the currencies also began to depreciate rapidly, forcing governments trying to maintain fixed currencies to raise domestic interest rates and buy up their own currency using their foreign exchange reserves. But the governments ran out of foreign exchange reserves quickly given the volume of money being withdrawn from their countries, and the high interest rates they established were devastating to their domestic economies. Countries were forced to abandon their fixed exchange rates and allow their currencies to float, at which point currency values plummeted. After the devaluation, companies that borrowed extensively from Western banks could not meet their payment obligations. The Thai baht devalued from 25 baht per dollar to almost 50 baht per dollar, losing half its value. This meant that the amount of payments of Thai debts to U.S. banks doubled within a few months.

One after another, Asian economies crashed. The IMF and the World Bank had to step in to bail out the countries to prevent an even worse disaster.

The Asian financial crisis had disturbing similarities to the Latin American debt crisis of the 1980s and the Mexican peso crisis of 1994–1995. In each case, international "hot" money flooded into smaller, developing economies to take advantage of good returns, leading to a speculative asset bubble and unsustainable borrowing. Then, when the international money was withdrawn, the result was devastating crashes and significant suffering. The frequency of these speculative bubbles has led to calls in many countries for regulation of international financial flows.

International capital controls are **rules or laws that restrict the movement of inflows and/or outflows of financial capital**. There are two main types of international capital controls, (1) direct controls where the government imposes limits on capital flows and (2) taxes or other incentives that increase the cost of shifting capital internationally. Many developing countries restrict outflows of international investment to prevent the types of panics that sparked the Asian financial crisis. International capital controls are extremely useful to countries attempting to maintain a fixed exchange rate system, because it prevents destabilizing outflows of currency. And capital controls can be helpful to countries trying to promote economic development because they prevent foreign investors from flooding in and driving up exchange rates and asset values.

Laissez-faire economists argue that restricting international financial flows introduces distortions into markets that will lead to inefficiencies in the allocation of capital, pushing it into less productive uses. New Keynesian economists prefer a middle ground, imposing capital controls in emergency situations but allowing market forces to work most of the time.

35.9 CONCLUSION

This chapter began by examining how markets for foreign exchange work. Currencies tend to appreciate in value when a country offers higher rates of return or when a country's assets are viewed as a good investment due to strong economic prospects. Currencies also tend to appreciate when a country's inflation is low, because global consumers snap up low-priced goods. Currencies tend to depreciate when a country's rates of return are low or when a country's goods prices are relatively high.

Some countries actively maintain a depreciated currency in order to promote exports. There is some evidence that this policy can stimulate economic growth by boosting exports. However, this aggressive posture can spark trade wars, such as the one between the United States and China in 2018. Trade wars can end up hurting both countries as exports plummet and goods prices increase.

The balance of payments catalogs all international flows of money. It yields one very important insight: Current account deficits are matched by financial account surpluses. Normally, according to mainstream economic theory, exchange rate fluctuations would tend to eliminate any trade deficits or surpluses. However, in the modern world, we see the perpetuation of trade deficits in some countries like the United States and the perpetuation of trade surpluses from some countries such as China, Germany, Japan, and South Korea. Political economists attribute these chronic imbalances to the importance of asset flows and their role in altering currency values.

U.S. trade deficits are a hotly debated topic among economists. Trade deficits tend to hurt U.S. workers and businesses who lose out to foreign competition, but they benefit U.S. consumers who get cheap foreign goods and U.S. investors who experience higher asset values. Foreign consumers in trade surplus countries are harmed in the process, because they are not able to purchase as many consumer goods as they would otherwise. Foreign workers and firms benefit from the expanded levels of production they experience with trade surpluses.

Most political economists and supply-side economists tend to oppose trade deficits due to their negative impact on U.S. workers and firms. Laissez-faire economists oppose trade deficits because they are emblematic of too much government spending. On the other hand, most mainstream New Keynesian economists believe that trade deficits are a boon for consumers and do not have significant economic costs because foreign investment is, in theory, used productively for job-creating activities.

The chapter also took up fixed, flexible, and managed exchange rate regimes. Fixed exchange rates promote stability but can be hard to maintain in the face of international financial flows. Flexible exchange rates require no government intervention, but they can be very unstable. Most countries use a managed float regime to give exchange rates a degree of stability without being overly restrictive.

Lastly, international financial flows can be destabilizing to an economy, as was the case with the Asian financial crisis of 1997. International "hot" money can flood into a booming small economy, causing an asset price bubble and an exchange rate appreciation. Both of these events can destabilize a developing economy and result in a subsequent crash. As a result, some countries use capital controls to limit the degree of fluctuation in international financial flows.

QUESTIONS FOR REVIEW

1. For each question below, draw a graph of the foreign exchange market for U.S. dollars in British pounds, and show how each of the following events will affect the price of the dollar and the quantity of dollars exchanged for British pounds. Explain your answer briefly.
    a. Incomes in the United Kingdom decrease.
    b. Interest rates in the United States decrease.
    c. The prices of U.S. goods decrease.
2. Suppose that U.S. interest rates rise relative to those in Europe. What effect will this have on the value of the U.S. dollar relative to the euro?
3. Suppose that the European Central Bank decides to sell euros in order to buy dollars. What effect will this have on the value of the euro relative to the U.S. dollar? Explain using a graph of the foreign exchange market for euros.
4. Describe the relationship between current account deficits and financial account surpluses.
5. Under what circumstances will a trade deficit lead to reductions in employment? Explain carefully.
6. Who benefits the most from a trade deficit? Who is harmed the most by a trade deficit?
7. Describe the major perspectives on why trade deficits are problematic. Also explain why many economists do not consider trade deficits to be a problem.
8. Suppose that the U.S. dollar is pegged to the euro at a rate of 1\$ = 1€. Suppose also that the value of the dollar falls to 1\$ = 0.8€. What policies can the U.S. government implement to return the value of the dollar to its pegged (fixed) rate of 1\$ = 1€?
9. Explain the causes of the Asian financial crisis. How might capital controls prevent such a crisis from happening in the future?

NOTES

1 We are assuming there are no tariffs or transportation costs in this example.

2 See International Monetary Fund, "Adjusting to Lower Commodity Prices," *World Economic Outlook*, September 2015. https://www.imf.org/en/Publications/WEO/Issues /2016/12/31/Adjusting-to-Lower-Commodity-Prices, accessed February 2, 2021.

3 Source: OECD stat.

4 Paul Krugman, "Trade Deficits: These Times Are Different," *New York Times*, March 28, 2016.

5 Warren E. Buffett, "America's Growing Trade Deficit Is Selling the Nation Out from under Us." *Fortune*, November 10 (2003), p. 106.

6 Gregory Mankiw, "Surprising Truths about Trade Deficits," *New York Times*, October 5, 2018, https://www.nytimes.com/2018/10/05/business/surprising-truths-about-trade-deficits.html.

Glossary of key terms and concepts

Absolute advantage: when a country can produce more of a good with the same amount of resources as another country.

Affirmative action: policies that require employers who do business with the government to take "affirmative action" to increase employment of people from historically oppressed and underrepresented groups.

Aggregate demand (AD): the sum of the demands for all goods and services by all economic actors, including households, businesses, banks, and government agencies, at various price levels. $AD = C + I + G + X - Im$.

Aggregate expenditure curve: the total level of real spending, including consumption, investment, government spending, and net exports, at each level of real GDP.

Aggregate supply (AS): the total quantity of output supplied by all producers at various price levels. $AS = \text{Income} = GDP = C + S + T$.

Anchoring: when people rely too heavily on the first piece of information shared with them when making a decision.

Appreciation: when a currency's value increases relative to a foreign currency.

Asset bubble: when a particular asset, such as stocks or property, increases in price rapidly and irrationally in a relatively short period of time.

Austerity: a government policy to reduce or eliminate social programs like food stamps, unemployment insurance, and education, in order to balance the government budget.

Automatic stabilizers: programs that automatically increase spending or reduce taxes in recessions and do the opposite when the economy is overheated.

Autonomous consumption (Ca): the level of consumption that does not depend on disposable income.

Average fixed cost (AFC): the fixed cost per unit of output. $AFC = TFC/Q$.

Average total cost (ATC): the average of all costs per unit of output. $ATC = TC/Q = AVC + AFC$.

Average variable cost (AVC): the variable cost per unit of output. AVC is equal to total variable cost divided by quantity (TVC/Q).

Balance of payments: all of the transactions in which the currency of one nation is exchanged for the currency of another nation during a particular period of time.

Balanced budget multiplier: the multiplier when government spending increases by the same amount that taxes decrease. It is equal to the multiplier minus the tax multiplier.

Bandwagon effect: the more people who have a good, the more other people also want it.

Barriers to entry: factors that make it difficult for a new firm to enter an industry or market. The major sources of barriers to entry are economies of scale (efficiencies from being large), control over key resources, brand name identity, and legal restrictions (patents, copyrights, trade restrictions, and government regulations).

Business cycle: the pattern of booms and busts created by economic fluctuations in market capitalist economies.

Business inventories: the value of unsold goods held by retailers, wholesalers, and manufacturers.

Capital goods: the machinery, equipment, buildings, and productive resources (other than labor) used to produce goods and services.

Capitalism: an economic system in which the capital goods and other productive resources (land, natural resources) are privately owned and are bought and sold in markets based on the pursuit of profits.

Capitalist class: those who own and control society's productive resources in a capitalist system.

Carrot method of worker motivation: efforts by employers to cultivate loyalty and productivity from workers via offering job security, strong wage incentives (bonuses and profit-sharing), employee involvement in decisions, and strong unions.

Carrying capacity: the maximum number of a species an environment can support indefinitely.

Cartel: a group of sellers who work together to coordinate prices, quantities, and sales practices to reduce competition and increase profits.

Ceteris paribus assumption: all other relevant factors do not change.

Choice: when consumers, producers, and governments select from among the limited options that are available to them due to scarcity.

Class: a group of people that has a specific relationship with the production process (e.g., capitalists, workers, slaves, lords).

Class consciousness: the awareness that people have of the existing system of social classes and their place in it.

Collateral: something pledged by a borrower to provide security for repayment of a loan. Collateral is forfeited to the bank if the borrower defaults on the loan.

Collateralized debt obligation (CDO):   a derivative consisting of a bundle of various forms of debt instruments, such as mortgages, auto loans, student loans, credit card debt, and so on.

Collateralized loan obligations (CLOs):   a security that is backed by a pool of debt.

Collateralized mortgage obligation (CMO) (mortgage-backed security)**:**   a derivative consisting of a bundle of many home mortgages, which is sold to investors who expect to get a return on their CMO purchase but who also assume the risk of default associated with the mortgages.

Collective bargaining: when workers bargain as a group (union) with employers instead of each worker bargaining separately with an employer.

Commodity money: when gold, silver, or other precious commodities are used as the primary unit of account. Example: the gold standard.

Common resource: a particular type of good that is rivalrous in consumption—consumption by an economic actor prevents its consumption by another person—and nonexcludable—people cannot be stopped from consuming or using the good.

Communism: an economic system in which the government controls society's productive resources and makes the major economic decisions. Each person works according to their abilities and is paid according to their needs.

Comparative advantage (theory of): a country should produce and specialize in those goods that it can produce for a lower opportunity cost than its trading partners.

Comparative institutional advantage (theory of): trade patterns are driven by particular combinations of institutions (government policies and support, infrastructure, labor skills and training, education systems, communities, industrial clusters, and innovation systems) that create advantages for specific types of production in particular places, attracting economic actors to locate production in certain geographical locations.

Complementary good: a product that consumers tend to purchase along with another good; when the price of one good increases and consumers buy less of it, there will also be a decrease in the demand for any complementary goods.

Consistent strategy: when a player in a game always behaves in a consistent fashion, either matching what the other player does or doing the opposite of what the other player does.

Conspicuous consumption: the practice of consumers purchasing and using goods for the purposes of displaying their status and importance to others.

Consumer goods: goods that are purchased and used by consumers but that do not contribute to future productivity.

Consumer surplus: the difference between the amount consumers value a good and are willing to pay for it and the price of that good. On a graph, consumer surplus is the area below the demand curve and above the equilibrium price.

Consumption possibilities curve (CPC): shows all combinations of two goods that can be consumed by a country after specialization and trade. The CPC is constructed by starting at the point where the country specializes entirely in the good in which they have a comparative advantage. The other end point of the CPC is found by figuring out how much of the other good the country could get if it traded all of the specialized goods it produces to the other country at the international terms of trade.

Contractionary fiscal policy (austerity): cuts in government spending and increases in taxes that reduce aggregate demand.

Convergence hypothesis: the productivity growth rates of poor countries should tend to be higher than those for rich countries, because poor countries can imitate the experiences of rich countries. All economies should eventually converge to the same level of per capita income.

Corporate hegemony: the cultural, legal, political, and economic power relations that make the corporation the dominant institution in modern capitalism and that give the CEOs and top managers of corporations their dominant position in capitalist society.

Countervailing power: a configuration in which corporations, individuals, and government would have relatively equal power and no one group could dominate the others.

Creative destruction: the process by which businesses are forced to invent constantly to stay one step ahead of the competition and where creative, new industries inevitably destroy and replace older ones.

Credit default swap: a derivative in which one investor pays to swap their credit risk on a CMO or CDO with another investor. The purchaser of a CDS pays a fee to the CDS issuer. In exchange, if the CMO or CDO defaults, the CDS issuer pays the purchaser of the CDS.

Cross-price elasticity of demand: the responsiveness of the quantity of one good demanded to the price of a different good.

Cyclical deficits: government budget deficits that occur as a result of recessions during the business cycle.

Cyclical unemployment: unemployment caused by the decreased demand for labor in a recession.

Deadweight loss: the decrease in consumer and producer surplus that results from a market regulation, such as an excise tax, subsidy, price floor, or price ceiling.

Deflation: a decrease in the average level of prices in an economy.

Demand curve: a curve that shows the quantity of a good buyers would like to purchase at each price within a particular period of time.

Demand for labor: in mainstream economics, the downward-sloping portion of the marginal revenue product of labor curve.

Demand shock: a decrease in aggregate demand from something other than the normal, cyclical investment patterns.

Democratic socialism: an economic system where the most important resources of society are controlled democratically by all citizens, including workers, who usually have little say in how market capitalist economies are run.

Depletable resources: resources that have a finite supply and cannot be replenished.

Depreciation: when a currency's value decreases relative to a foreign currency.

Derivative: a financial security whose value is derived from an underlying asset or group of assets. Derivatives involve a contract between two or more economic actors, and the value of the derivative varies with the fluctuations in the value of the asset(s) underlying the derivative.

Derived demand: the demand for workers' labor (and for other inputs) is derived from the demand for goods and services.

Determinants of demand: the six factors that determine the location of the demand curve and whether or not it shifts to the left or to the right. The determinants of demand are (1) disposable income and wealth, (2) tastes and preferences, (3) the prices of substitute and complementary goods, (4) the number and size of buyers, (5) buyers' expectations about the future, and (6) the availability and cost of consumer credit.

Determinants of supply: the five factors that determine the location of the supply curve and whether or not it shifts to the left or to the right. The determinants of supply are (1) the cost, productivity, and availability of inputs; (2) the technology available to make the product; (3) sellers' expectations about the future; (4) changes in the profitability of other markets the seller can supply; and (5) the number and size of sellers.

Developmental state: the government undertakes macroeconomic planning and policies to stimulate industrial development in strategic sectors.

Dialectics: a method of analysis focusing on contradictions and the struggle of opposing forces.

Diminishing returns (law of):   as more units of a variable input (such as labor) are added to a fixed amount of other inputs (such as capital), the marginal productivity of the variable input will eventually decrease (after all specialized tasks are filled).

Discount rate (primary credit rate):   the rate of interest the Fed charges banks to borrow reserves.

Discretionary fiscal policy: fiscal policy that is "at the discretion" of government officials. Government officials must take additional actions in order for such policy to take effect.

Diseconomies of scale: the increase in average total cost a firm experiences as it produces a larger quantity, due to management challenges. Larger firms have more difficulty with coordination of efforts, communications, bureaucratic waste, and unproductive layers of management.

Disposable income (DI): the income people have to spend after the government has taken out taxes (after tax income). $DI = C + S$.

Dominant strategy: a situation in game theory that exists when the expected payoffs from one option are better no matter what the other player does.

Double movement: Polanyi's term for the push for the development of markets by businesses (first mercantilists and then capitalists), which was met by a counter movement by workers and communities to regulate markets.

Ecological economics: the study of the interdependence between the economy and natural ecosystems, including the flow of energy and raw materials to the economy from the ecosystem's sources (mines, wells, fisheries, and land) and the return of wastes and pollutants from the economy to planetary sinks (dumps, oceans, and the atmosphere).

Economic efficiency: producers supply the quantity of each product that consumers demand at the lowest possible cost (minimum LRATC), no firm earns an economic profit in the long run, consumers' willingness to pay for one additional unit of the product is exactly equal to the cost of producing one additional unit of the product ($MB = P = MC$), and producers respond quickly and effectively to any changes in consumers' tastes and preferences.

Economic growth: the long-term, sustained increase in the economy's capacity (potential real GDP), driven by improvements in labor productivity.

Economic model: a theoretical, simplified construct designed to focus on a key set of economic relationships.

Economies of scale: the decrease in average total cost a firm experiences as it produces a larger quantity, due to increases in productivity (increasing returns to scale) or cost advantages from being larger. The sources of economies of scale include technology, specialized skills, bulk purchasing, financial benefits, and marketing advantages.

Efficiency (productive)**:** in mainstream economics, a situation in which all resources are employed as productively as possible.

Efficient equilibrium: when all costs and benefits (internal and external) are incorporated into the market.

Efficient market hypothesis: financial markets always incorporate all available information and function in an efficient manner, so asset prices (the prices of stocks, bonds, and derivatives) are always accurate and cannot form irrational bubbles.

Employee stock options: a type of compensation where an employer gives an employee the right to purchase a specific number of shares of stock at a fixed price over a specific period of time (in the future).

Endogenous money supply: the money supply is determined by economic variables within the economic system, especially real GDP, expected business sales, business investment, consumer confidence, and consumer spending.

Environmental economics: the use of cost–benefit analysis to determine the efficient allocation of environmental resources, such as the optimal level of pollution.

Environmental Kuznets curve: a theory that as countries grow and became wealthier, they can afford to pay more attention to the environment, developing technologies, regulations, and clean production methods that reduce their environmental impact. Environmental destruction should increase during the first step of industrialization, then level off, and then decline as a country's standard of living increases.

Equation of exchange: Money supply (M1) $\times$ Velocity (V) = Price level (P) $\times$ Real GDP (Q).

Exchange rate: amount of one currency that exchanges for another.

Excise tax: a per unit tax paid by sellers to the government.

Excludability: whether or not it is possible to prevent economic actors who have not paid for a good from having access to that good.

Expansionary fiscal policy: increases in government spending or reductions in taxes that stimulate aggregate demand.

Externality: when markets do not effectively incorporate all costs and benefits associated with a particular good or service.

Federal funds rate: the rate of interest banks charge each other on extremely short-term loans (often overnight), which is controlled indirectly by the Fed.

Fiat money: money that is established as legal tender by government fiat (an official government decree); paper money or electronic accounts that have value because the state declares that they do and because people need the fiat money to pay their taxes and debts and to engage in economic activities in a particular society.

Financialization: the increasingly dominant role that financial motives, markets, actors, and institutions play in global economies.

Fiscal policy: the use of government spending or taxation to improve economic outcomes. Fiscal policy can be used to address macroeconomic market failures such as recessions, unemployment, or price instability and to improve the rate of economic growth.

Fixed exchange rate regime: when the government of a country pegs (fixes) the value of its currency relative to another currency.

Floating exchange rate regime: when a government does not regulate the exchange rate, allowing its country's currency to fluctuate with market forces.

Free rider problem: when economic actors who benefit from a resource, good, or service do not have to pay for that benefit, resulting in an undersupply.

Frictional unemployment: unemployment resulting from normal turnover in the labor market.

Functional finance: governments should decide how much to spend and tax based on the impact of these policies on prosperity for all, not based on how large the deficit is. Deficits are largely unimportant in sovereign nations that control their own currency.

Game theory: a method for modeling how economic agents such as firms, individuals, or groups interact. Each different model or game involves particular actors, who are able to choose from among two or more strategies. The strategies taken by the actors determine the outcomes of the game. The outcomes of the game, therefore, are determined by the interdependent decisions of the actors.

GDP deflator: the ratio of prices in the particular year to prices in the base year.

Genuine progress indicator (GPI): a monetary measure of economic welfare that accounts for benefits and costs experienced by a particular population from investment, production, trade, and consumption of goods and services.

Gini coefficient: a measure of the degree of inequality that exists in an economy in a particular year. The Gini coefficient ranges from 0 to 1, with lower numbers associated with more equal societies and higher numbers associated with more unequal societies.

Government: provides the institutions that develop and implement policies for the state.

Government failure: when a government effort to correct market failure leads to inefficient or destructive outcomes.

Great Gatsby curve: a curve that shows the inverse relationship between inequality, as measured by the Gini coefficient, and intergenerational earnings mobility.

Gross national product (GNP): the total market value of goods and services produced by a country's citizens and companies during one year, which is equal to gross domestic product plus the net income from foreign investments.

Herd behavior: the tendency of human beings to emulate the behavior of others.

Herfindahl Index (*H*): an index that measures the size of the largest firms relative to the industry as a whole in order to provide an indicator for the degree of competition in the industry. *H* is found by squaring the market shares of the largest companies in the industry and then adding them together.

Hegemony: when a particular group exerts undue influence within a society.

Historical materialism: Marx's approach to the study of economics, focusing on the class conflicts and technological changes that provoke changes in the material conditions of society over time.

Human capital: the skills, dexterity, knowledge, habits, and creativity that improve productivity.

Hyperinflation: rapidly accelerating inflation that is out of control.

Imperialism: when one country gains control of another country or territory.

Import quota: a limit on the quantity of a good that can be imported.

Income elasticity of demand (e_{GDP}): the responsiveness of the quantity demanded to changes in income (GDP).

Induced consumption: consumption induced by changes in income, found by multiplying the MPC by disposable income.

Industrial policy: a strategic initiative coordinated by the government to create favorable conditions for particular industry.

Infant industry promotion strategy: a country protects and subsidizes a new industry until it can be globally competitive.

Inferior goods: goods that consumers want to buy less of as their income or wealth increases or more of as their income or wealth decreases.

Inflation rate: the percentage increase in the average level of prices, such as the Consumer Price Index for urban consumers.

Inflationary gap: the amount that real GDP is above potential real GDP.

Inputs: the factors of production—labor, capital, land, and natural resources—used to produce goods and services.

Institutional economics: the study of the institutions that shape an economy, how the economy and those institutions evolve, and how human beings are shaped by culture and institutions and seek status and power within those structures.

Institutions: the organizations, social structures, rules, and habits that structure human interactions and the economy.

Insurance: the purchase of a hedge against risk or an untimely event, where the insurer collects premium payments and provides compensation for a specified loss.

Intergenerational earnings mobility: the extent to which earnings of children are affected by the earnings of their parents. Low intergenerational earnings mobility means that children's earnings are significantly impacted by the earnings of their parents.

Internalizing an externality: incorporating costs or benefits that are external to the market into the cost and benefit structure of the market.

International capital controls: rules or laws that restrict the movement of inflows and/or outflows of financial capital.

International terms of trade: the opportunity cost at which goods will trade internationally.

Intersectionality: the interconnectedness of various social stratifications, especially class, race, and gender, along with sexual orientation, age, and disability, in creating overlapping and interdependent systems of power and discrimination.

Labor force: a measure of all people available for work, including all people working and all people who are unemployed and are actively seeking work.

Labor force participation rate: the percentage of the population working, self-employed, or unemployed divided by the number of people of working age who are eligible to work in a country.

Labor-leisure trade-off: according to this mainstream theory, at first as wages rise, workers want to work longer hours to take advantage of higher wages: the benefits of higher wages exceed the disutility that comes from less leisure time. Once a worker's income goes above their target level, increases in wages are likely to result in a worker choosing to work less and take more leisure time, while keeping their income about the same.

Labor union: an organization of workers formed to promote its members' interests with respect to wages, job security, benefits, and working conditions.

Law of demand: other things being equal, the quantity of a good demanded is inversely related to its price. When price increases, quantity demanded decreases. When price decreases, quantity demanded increases.

Law of diminishing marginal utility: as a person consumes more and more of one product, while holding consumption of other products constant, that person experiences a decline in the additional (marginal) utility from each additional unit of that product consumed.

Law of increasing opportunity cost: if resources are specialized and if all resources are being used efficiently, then as more and more of one good is produced, the opportunity cost of producing each additional unit of that good will increase.

Law of supply: other things being equal, the quantity of a good supplied is directly related to its price. When price increases, quantity supplied increases. When price decreases, quantity supplied decreases.

Leveraging: the use of debt to purchase an asset, with the hope that the profit from the asset purchase will exceed the borrowing cost.

Limited liability corporations: joint stock companies in which the activities and property of the firm are separated from the private property of the firm's owners, the stockholders. Owners do not assume liability for the firm's debts—all they can lose is the amount they invested in the firm, limiting their liabilities.

Liquidity: in financial economics, the ease with which an asset can be converted into cash.

Liquidity trap: when people believe that interest rates can fall no further and can only increase, so people hold all new money as cash because they believe interest rates will increase soon.

Long run: the period of time in which all inputs are variable and can be adjusted. Suppliers can build entirely new plants, install new technology and equipment, and increase their productive capacity in the long run.

Long-run aggregate supply: the economy at "full employment," when the economy is producing at its maximum normal capacity given existing resources and technology.

Long-run average total cost curve (LRATC):   a curve showing the lowest cost of producing each quantity in the long run. When the LRATC curve is declining, the firm is experiencing economies of scale. When the LRATC curve is increasing, the firm is experiencing diseconomies of scale.

Long-run marginal cost (LRMC):   the lowest possible increase in total cost from offering one additional unit of output for sale given that all inputs are variable.

Lorenz curve: a curve showing the percentage of national income earned by each percentage of families.

Macroeconomic problems created by wage and price deflation: Declines in wages undermine aggregate demand and declines in prices undermine business profitability, both of which harm the economy in particular ways.

Macroeconomics: the study of the aggregate forces that shape national and global economies.

Mainstream economics (ME):   the study of how society manages its scarce resources to satisfy individuals' unlimited wants.

Managed float exchange rate regime: when the government establishes a target zone for its currency and intervenes whenever its currency leaves the target zone.

Marginal cost (MC):   the increase in cost from producing another unit of a good. $MC = (\Delta TVC/\Delta Q)$.

Marginal external benefit: the external benefit generated by the consumption of each additional unit of the good.

Marginal external cost (MEC):   the external cost generated by the production of each additional unit of output.

Marginal factor cost (MFC):   the increase in cost from hiring another unit of a factor of production, such as labor.

Marginal product of labor (MPL):   the additional output that results from hiring an additional unit of a variable input (labor). MPL is equal to the change in quantity divided by the change in labor $(\Delta Q/\Delta L)$.

Marginal productivity theory of distribution: the neoclassical theory that people are paid exactly what they are worth based on their marginal productivity under a competitive, capitalist economic system. This theory assumes that there are no power imbalances and so no exploitative relationships exist.

Marginal propensity to consume (MPC):   the change in consumption (ΔC) that results from a change in disposable (after tax) income (ΔDI). $MPC = \Delta C/\Delta DI$.

Marginal propensity to import (MPM):   the increase in imports that results from an increase in disposable income.

Marginal respending rate (MRR):   the additional spending that is generated from a change in income. MRR depends on the marginal propensity to consume, the net tax rate (t), and the marginal propensity to import (MPM): $MRR = MPC(1 - t) - MPM$.

Marginal revenue (MR):   the addition to total revenue from selling an additional unit of output. $MR = \Delta TR/\Delta Q$.

Marginal revenue product of labor (MRP$_L$):   the additional revenue the firm receives from hiring an additional laborer. MRP$_L$ is the firm's demand for labor, because MRP$_L$ is the maximum amount a firm would be willing to pay a particular laborer.

Marginal social benefit (MSB):   the true cost of a product that generates a marginal external cost. Marginal social benefit is computed by adding the marginal external benefit to the marginal benefit.

Marginal social cost: the true cost of a product, which generates a marginal external cost. Marginal social cost is equal to marginal cost plus marginal external cost: MSC = MC + MEC.

Market: an institution that organizes and facilitates transactions between buyers and sellers.

Market-dominated economies (MDEs):   economic systems in which the primary economic decisions are made by private actors (businesses, individuals) in the market. Governments and social values play a secondary role.

Market failure: when market outcomes are either inefficient, destructive, or counter to the public interest.

Market misunderstanding theory: the cause of a recession is misperceptions by workers or other economic actors.

Market-supporting institutions: the set of institutions that must exist in order for markets to function effectively; these include property rights, laws to facilitate the aggregation of capital, trust, contract laws, competition, a lack of coercion, and physical, market, and financial infrastructure to lower transactions costs.

Markets always clear: the neoclassical theory that supply always equals demand in all markets, so the invisible hand of the market always allocates resources efficiently.

Markup pricing: when a firm sets price by adding a markup to their average total (accounting) costs of production. That markup may be above, below, or equal to a normal profit depending on market conditions and the firm's strategic goals.

Microeconomics: the study of distinct economic actors, such as consumers, workers, and firms, and how they interact in the economic system.

Middle class: small business owners, managers, and professionals who have some control over their working lives and who often supervise others but who do not have control over a significant amount of resources or workers and who must usually answer to the ruling class.

Mixed market capitalism: an economic system in which private sector firms and individuals produce goods and services for markets for profits and a public sector established by the government regulates those markets and provides public goods such as schools, roads, airports, health care, and other goods and services that are usually provided inadequately by private markets.

Monetarist theories of the business cycle: monetary factors with driving fluctuations in real GDP.

Money: a unit of account, which may also be a physical item such as a printed piece of paper, that is accepted as payment for taxes, debts, and goods and services. Money can be issued as credit (loaned out). Money takes two main forms: as an account of debits and credits in a ledger, and as a medium of exchange for trading.

Money (deposit) multiplier: the amount of money that banks create with each dollar of reserves. Money multiplier = 1/(required reserve ratio (RRR)).

Money supply (M1) (money stock):   cash held by the public and near-cash accounts (checkable deposits).

Monopolistic competition: a very competitive market structure with a large number of small firms due to easy entry, and firms have a monopoly over certain unique business characteristics such as quality, brand, or location. This gives firms some control over their prices. Firms supply goods that are close but not perfect substitutes for each other.

Monopoly: the least competitive market structure with only one firm present and no close substitutes (a unique product). Monopolies are maintained by prohibitive barriers to entry, and their control over the market gives them complete control over prices.

Monopoly power: the ability of large firms to control prices.

Monopsony: when there is only one buyer of a product or resource.

Moral hazard: In a principal–agent problem, when agents act in their own best interests and when those interests are contrary to the interests of their principals.

Multiplier: a respending process whereby a dollar in spending becomes income for someone else, which they then spend, which becomes additional income, and so on, so that a dollar of spending is respent multiple times. Multiplier = $1/(1 - \text{MRR})$.

Nash equilibrium: in game theory, when each player chooses a particular strategy and no player benefits by changing strategies while the other player keeps their strategy unchanged.

Natural monopoly: a market where multiple firms producing a product is less efficient than production by one firm.

Natural rate of unemployment: the normal rate of unemployment when the economy is not in a recession (full employment).

Natural resource economics: a subset of economics that focuses on the pricing and efficient allocation of renewable and nonrenewable resources.

Necessary product: the resources necessary for a community's survival, including food, shelter, and the replacement of tools and materials used up in production.

Negative externality: when an economic actor (firm or individual) does something that imposes external costs—not included in the market transaction—on others.

Neoclassical economics: the study of how rational actors in competitive markets determine incomes and the prices and quantities of goods and services through the interaction of supply and demand.

Neoliberalism: contemporary ideas grounded in the classic, laissez-faire liberalism of Adam Smith. Market-oriented policy prescriptions include reducing trade barriers, deregulating financial markets, austerity (especially reductions in spending on the welfare state), deregulation, reduced taxation on the rich, and the privatization of government assets and functions.

Nominal GDP: the value of all final goods and services produced in a particular place at current prices (the total revenue of a country or region).

Nonaccelerating inflation rate of unemployment (NAIRU) theory: when the unemployment rate falls below the natural rate of unemployment, inflation is expected to increase and perhaps to accelerate.

Non-price rationing: the development of methods of rationing goods and services other than by price, such as queues and black markets.

Normal goods: goods that consumers want to buy more of when their income or wealth increases and that they want to buy less of when their income or wealth decreases.

Occupational segregation: when workers from a particular group, especially those of a particular gender or race, are distributed disproportionately to particular occupations.

Okun's law: a 1% increase in the rate of unemployment is associated with a 2% decrease in the growth of real GDP.

Oligopoly: a market that is dominated by a few huge firms whose behavior affects each other significantly. There are difficult barriers to entry that keep out new competitors.

Opportunity cost: what is given up when a choice is made to allocate resources in a particular way.

Paradox of thrift: when consumers save more, this reduces aggregate demand, which in turn reduces GDP, which then reduces savings.

Patriarchy: a society in when men hold power and women are largely excluded from power.

Pecuniary emulation: when people from the lower classes imitate the culture, habits, and spending of the upper classes to achieve status for themselves.

Perfect competition: the most competitive market structure, in which large numbers of small firms produce identical products. The market is easy for new firms to enter, and firms have no control over the price they charge. Prices are determined by market supply and demand.

Personal capital: the economic, educational, social, and cultural capital derived from a person's class position. Economic capital refers to the ownership and control of resources; educational capital refers to years of schooling and the quality of institutions attended; social capital is the network of family, friends, and associates a person can access and draw on; and cultural capital refers to the knowledge of unique cultural patterns associated with living in elite circles.

Per unit subsidy: the government pays suppliers a fixed amount for each unit they sell.

Phillips curve: a theory positing an inverse relationship between inflation and unemployment based on the impact of booms and busts on businesses' costs of production.

Piketty thesis: when the rate of return going to owners of capital exceeds the rate of economic growth, inequality tends to increase because profits and other income from owning capital grow faster than wage income.

Pluralist economics: a social science whose practitioners, from a variety of distinct schools of thought, study economies, how they grow and change, and the how they produce and distribute the goods societies need and want.

Plutocracy: a situation in which the group that dominates the economic system is made up of the wealthiest members of society.

Political business cycle theory: business cycles can result from policies of politicians to improve their reelection chances.

Pollution abatement: any measure taken to reduce pollution and/or its impacts on people and the environment.

Positive externality: when an economic actor does something that generates external benefits—benefits not included in the market transaction—for others.

Potential real GDP: the output of goods and services that would be produced if the economy were utilizing all of its productive resources, including all of its employable workers and all of its capital stock.

Precautionary demand for money: the amount of cash or checkable deposits that people keep as a contingency to meet unexpected expenses.

Precautionary principle: when an activity raises threats of harm to human health or the environment, precautionary measures should be taken even if some cause-and-effect relationships are not fully established scientifically.

Price ceiling: a legally set maximum price. Suppliers cannot raise their price above the price ceiling. A price ceiling must be set *below* the equilibrium price to be effective.

Price elasticity of demand: the responsiveness of quantity demanded to changes in price. In mathematical terms, the price elasticity of demand, ED, is equal to the percentage change in the quantity demanded divided by the percentage change in price.

Price elasticity of supply: the responsiveness of quantity supplied to changes in price; equal to the percentage change in the quantity supplied divided by the percentage change in price.

Price floor: a legally set minimum price. Sellers cannot lower their price below the price floor. A price floor is set above the equilibrium price in order to support sellers of a particular good.

Price leadership: a type of tacit collusion that occurs when one firm, the industry leader, sets the prices for the industry and the other firms follow suit by adopting the same pricing structure.

Prime interest rate: the rate of interest private banks charge their best customers—the biggest corporations with the most collateral and the most secure financial situation.

Principal-agent problem: when the agents (managers) may have different interests than the principals (owners).

Producer surplus: the difference between the amount for which sellers are willing to sell each unit of a good and the price at which they actually sell the good. On a graph, producer surplus is the area above the supply curve and below the equilibrium price.

Production possibilities curve (PPC): a model that shows all combinations of two goods that can be produced, holding the amount of resources and the level of technology fixed.

Profit maximization (mainstream economics): firms produce every unit for which marginal revenue is greater than or equal to marginal cost.

Profit rate: the total amount of profit accrued by a firm divided by the total capital invested by the firm.

Progressive political economics (PPE): the study of social provisioning—the economic processes that provide the goods and services required by society to meet the needs of its members.

Property rights: when a productive resource such as land or a slave belongs to a particular person or group instead of to society as a whole.

Public good: a good that is nonexcludable and nonrivalrous. Public goods are available to everyone equally, whether or not they pay.

Quantitative easing (QE): when the Fed purchases bonds or other assets from banks and businesses.

Quantitative tightening: when the Fed sells bonds and assets from its portfolio back to investors.

Quantity demanded: the amount of a good or service that buyers are willing to purchase at each price in a particular time period.

Quantity supplied: the amount of a good or service that sellers are willing to offer for sale at each price in a particular time period.

Quantity theory of money: a theory that the quantity of money in circulation (M1) is directly proportional to the price level of goods and services. $MV = PQ$. Assumes velocity is constant and real GDP cannot be influenced by the money supply.

Quasi-public goods: goods or services that have some but not all of the characteristics of public goods. Examples include the provision of health care and education to individuals, where society as a whole reaps substantial external benefits and where competition is inefficient or wasteful.

Radical political economics (RPE): the study of power relations in society, especially conflicts over the allocation of a society's resources by various social classes and how those conflicts cause society to evolve.

Rate of exploitation: the ratio of surplus value (profits) to wages.

Real business cycle theory: recessions are due to productivity shocks caused by changes in technology and the legal and regulatory environment.

Real estate investments: the purchase, rental, and sale of all types of property, including land and buildings.

Real gross domestic product (real GDP): the total output of goods and services produced within an area in a given time period, corrected for changes in prices so that real GDP only measures actual changes in the amounts of goods and services produced.

Real gross domestic product per capita: real GDP and divided by the number of people in a country.

Real wage rate: the existing wage rate at current prices, called the nominal wage rate, divided by the price level. This gives us the wage rate in constant dollars, called the real wage rate.

Recession: a generalized slowdown of economic activity where reductions in production result in an increase in unemployment. A decline in production (real GDP) for six months or more (at least two quarters) is considered to be a recession.

Recessionary gap: the amount that real GDP is below potential real GDP.

Renewable resources: resources that can be replenished if they are not used too intensively.

Required reserve ratio (RRR): the percentage of deposits that banks are required by law to hold as reserves.

Research and development (R&D): activities designed to result in scientific breakthroughs, design and introduce new products, or improve existing products or manufacturing processes.

Reserves (bank)**:** cash or deposits at the central bank.

Rivalrous competition: a dynamic process in which entrepreneurs are constantly looking for new, profitable opportunities to satisfy consumers and no firm is safe from the entry of new competitors.

Rivalrousness: whether or not the consumption or use of a good by one economic actor prevents its consumption or use by another person.

Rule of 70: a formula that estimates how many years it takes for a variable growing at an exponential rate to double. The number of years for a variable to double = 70/(annual % growth rate of the variable).

Satisficing: making prudent decisions using rules of thumb given limited information.

Say's law: supply creates its own demand, and savings is always equal to investment.

Scarcity: when a society's seemingly unlimited desire for goods and services exceeds the resources available to produce and provide those goods and services.

Seasonal unemployment: unemployment that results from changes in the seasonal demand for labor.

Short run: the period of time in which the supplier cannot adjust the size of operations (their capacity). The supplier's capital stock (buildings, machinery, and equipment) is fixed. Suppliers are only able to adjust their variable inputs in the short run, especially the amount of labor they hire.

Short-run production function: a function that shows the relationship between the quantities of variable inputs (such as labor) and the amount of output produced, holding fixed inputs (such as capital) constant.

Single-payer health care system: a system where the government pays most health care costs for its citizens out of tax revenues. Care and insurance can be provided directly by the government or guaranteed by the government but provided by the private sector.

Snob effect: price is assumed to represent quality.

Social market economies (SMEs):   economic systems in which social values take a leading role in directing the economy, usually through the actions of a government that manages the economy in accordance with social values.

Socialist economic system: an economic system in which the means of production and distribution are either owned or regulated by society.

Socially efficient level of pollution: when the marginal social cost of pollution abatement is equal to the marginal social benefit from abatement.

Soft budget constraint problem: when a government continually bails out an industry that cannot become competitive in markets.

Specialization (law of):   when laborers specialize in a specific task, their productivity increases because (a) their skill and dexterity in completing that task improves, (b) they spend less time switching between jobs, and (c) specialized machinery and equipment can be developed to increase productivity related to the specialized task.

Specialization of labor: particular tasks are performed by specific individuals, rather than everyone performing all tasks.

Specialization of resources: when some resources cannot be easily adapted from one use to another.

Speculative demand for money: the amount of cash or checkable deposits that people want to hold as a safe asset to maximize returns on all of their assets.

Stabilization policy: increasing government spending, reducing taxes, and reducing interest rates in recessions, while doing the opposite when the economy is growing too quickly.

Stagflation: when stagnation (declining production and worker layoffs) and inflation occur at the same time.

State-dominated economies (SDEs):   economic systems in which the government is the main economic actor in most major industries or economic decisions, owning or controlling most of the economy.

Status-seeking: the human propensity to try to achieve the highest social status possible, as defined by the particular culture of the community.

Stick method of worker motivation: efforts by employers to achieve maximum work effort via the threat of job dismissal (firing), attacking unions, and closely monitoring workers.

Sticky wages and prices: in a recession, wages and prices do not fall fast enough to encourage businesses to hire more workers and consumers to buy more goods.

Stocks: an ownership share in a company, which entitles the owner to a share of the company's earnings. Earnings are realized either through a higher stock price as a company becomes more profitable or by dividend payments to stockholders.

Structural deficits: the portion of the government deficit that exists even when the economy is at its normal capacity.

Structural unemployment: unemployment resulting from the permanent displacement of workers due to automation, globalization, shifting demand for products, and other forces that eliminate the need for certain skills in the workplace.

Sub-prime borrowers: people who are likely to have difficulty making loan payments on time and have a high risk of default.

Subsistence wage: the lowest wage rate on which a worker and their family can survive.

Substitute good: a product that consumers are willing to purchase instead of another good; when the price of one good increases, many consumers will switch to buying the substitute good, increasing the demand for the substitute.

Superior goods: normal goods whose income elasticity is greater than 1: $e_{GDP} > 1$.

Supply curve: a curve that shows the quantity of a good sellers will offer for sale at each price within a particular period of time.

Supply curve for a firm: the marginal cost curve above where MC intersects AVC.

Supply of labor: in mainstream economics, the amount of labor supplied at each wage rate. In perfectly competitive markets, the supply of labor is the marginal factor cost curve, which is the same as the wage rate.

Supply-side economics: the belief that the primary determinant of economic growth is the profitability of suppliers, including corporations and wealthy business owners. The best way to achieve profitability is therefore to eliminate regulations and to reduce taxes on corporations and the wealthy.

Surplus product: the amount that is produced over and above what is needed for the community's survival (the necessary product).

Surplus value: the amount of value produced by workers over and above the cost of their wages (including benefits).

Sustainability: the ability of an economic system to sustain itself over time by meeting its current needs without compromising its future. Sustainability has three primary dimensions: environmental, social, and financial.

Tacit collusion: when firms find a way of agreeing on prices or production quotas without discussing such things.

Tariff: a tax on imported goods.

Tax multiplier: a measure used to compute the impact of a lump sum change in taxes on aggregate demand. Tax multiplier = MPC/(1 − MRR).

Technology: the tools, skills, and scientific knowledge that society develops in the use of resources to produce goods and services.

Theory of demand: in mainstream economics, consumers' willingness to pay for a product (demand) depends on the benefit (marginal utility) they expect to get from consuming the product, the price of the product, disposable income and wealth, tastes and preferences, the prices of substitute and complementary goods, the number and size of buyers, expectations about the future, and the availability and cost of consumer credit.

Theory of supply: in mainstream economics, a seller's willingness to offer a product for sale (supply) in a perfectly competitive market depends on the price they expect to get from selling the product, the cost, productivity and availability of inputs, the technology available to make the product, sellers' expectations about the future, changes in the profitability of other markets the seller can supply, and the number and size of suppliers.

Theory of the firm, mainstream economics: the firm's goal is short-run and long-run profit maximization, which the firm achieves by comparing marginal revenue and marginal cost and selecting the optimal size of operations.

Theory of the firm, political economy: the firm's primary goals are survival, growth, and profit maximization, and those goals are achieved by determining quantities and setting prices based on markup pricing and the firm's strategic focus on gaining market share or securing profits from monopoly power.

Total cost (TC): the total of all costs of production, including opportunity costs (normal profit). TC = TFC + TVC.

Total fixed cost (TFC): the total cost of hiring all fixed inputs, such as capital.

Total revenue (TR): Price multiplied by quantity sold. TR = $(P \star Q)$.

Total variable cost (TVC): the total cost of hiring variable inputs, such as labor. TVC = $W \star L$.

Traditional economy: an economy in which resources are allocated based on communal patterns of reciprocity and redistribution, and in which tasks are allocated and knowledge and skills are preserved through established social relationships.

Tragedy of the commons: in a system in which resources are shared, firms and individuals that act in a self-interested fashion will deplete or ruin the common good.

Transaction: an agreement between economic agents—buyers and sellers—to exchange goods, services, or assets.

Transactions costs: the costs incurred when engaging in a transaction, including transportation costs, information costs that are incurred when actors identify and evaluate different opportunities, and bargaining, monitoring, and enforcement costs.

Transactions demand for money: the amount of cash or checkable deposits that individuals need to keep available to make purchases (transactions).

Transfer payment: social spending that involves the transfer of income from the government to individuals or businesses, such as welfare payments or direct business subsidies.

Triple helix approach to innovation: government, universities, and industry interact as partners to generate ideas, invent and spread technologies, and develop industries and communities.

Unemployment rate: the number of people actively seeking work but without a job divided by the labor force.

Unequal exchange: when resources are systematically transferred by global trade flows from developing countries that produce primary products to developed countries.

Unregulated market capitalism (laissez-faire): an economic system in which the main productive resources of society—the labor, land, machinery, equipment, and natural resources—are owned by private individuals, who use those resources to produce goods and services that are bought and sold in markets for profits.

Utility: the amount of satisfaction a person gains from consuming a product.

Veblen good: the quantity of the good demanded increases as the price increases because the scarcity and exclusivity associated with the good increase the display value and honorific character of the good.

Velocity: the number of times a unit of currency ($) changes hands in a year.

Vested interests: the group dominating society, whose goal is usually to preserve the status quo that they benefit from.

Volatility of investment: the Keynesian theory that business purchases of capital goods (investment) depend primarily on expected future profits, which is driven largely by expected sales, and expectations can vary dramatically.

Wealth: the value of the assets held by individuals and households.

Working class: those who must sell their labor to others in order to survive in a capitalist system.

Yield curve: the difference between interest rates on short-term bonds and interest rates on long-term bonds.

Index

Locators in **bold** refer to tables and those in *italics* to figures.

aggregate expenditure 704–708;
aggregate expenditure curve 708–710;
complete aggregate expenditure model
692–699; consumption function
688–692; inflationary gap 704–708,
709; recessionary gap 704–708, *706*;
savings function 688–692; shifts in the
aggregate expenditure curve 699–704
knowledge as public good 476, 492–495
Krueger, Alan 13–14, 544

labeling laws 422
labor force: definition 625; size of 625–626;
see also employment
labor force participation rate 573, 632, *633*
labor-leisure trade-off 515
labor market 501; the 1800s and worker
conditions 88–90; employer-worker
power dynamics 510–516; exploitation
93–97; as factor market 499; income
determination 526–528; industrial
revolution 82–83; legislation 424;
minimum wage - economic effects
13–14, *521*, 521–526; motivation
508–510; neoclassical economics
516–520; New Deal 139;
noncompetitive markets 528–529,
530, *531*; operation of 177; political
economy 505–508; supply and demand
520; Swedish policy 161–162; trade
865; trends 502–504, *504*; unequal
bargaining power 423–424
labor market incentives 853
labor productivity 840–841, 842, 853–854
labor quality *see* human capital
labor, specialization of 49–50, 60
labor unions: class inequality 548;
employer-worker power dynamics
510–511; Great Depression 101–102;
legalization and support of 423–424
Laffer, Arthur 575–576
laissez-faire economics: business cycles
586–588, 818–819; corporations 414;
economic growth 847–849; fall of
122–123; financialization 782; fiscal
policy 737–738, 748; free trade 81–82,
863, 890; government failure 447;
macroeconomics 569, 581; monetary
policy 785, 799–800; money 758–759;
monopolies 353–354; nonaccelerating
inflation rate of unemployment

(NAIRU) theory 797–798; poor laws
77–79; Say's law 79–81; as school of
thought 17; size of government *18*;
Smith, Adam 72–73; sustainability as
macroeconomic goal 590, 591; trade
deficits 912–914; unemployment 624,
635–636
land ownership: Catholic Church 58;
industrial revolution 70–71
last place aversion 559
Latin America: debt crisis 788, 921;
economic growth 580; imperialism 110;
independence 574
law of demand 10, 189–190, 242
law of diminishing marginal utility 189
law of diminishing returns 248–249; long
run 325–326; short-run 290, 291–292
law of increasing opportunity cost 29–31
law of specialization 248, 249, 290
law of supply 197
lawsuits 422
lawyers' services 370–372
legal system: corporations 402; making
markets work 180–182; United States
157; *see also* regulations
legislative lag 737
lender of last resort 769
Lerner, Abba 749–750, 802
leveraging 824
liberal (progressive political economy) *see*
progressive political economics (PPE)
life satisfaction 612; *see also* macroeconomic
well-being
lifetime employment 165
Lilly, Eli 411
limited liability corporation 105, 397,
399–402
limits to growth 452–453, 462, 856
liquidity 764
liquidity trap 771
living wage 525–526
local professional services 363, 370–372
local retailers 363
location, monopolistic competition 373
long run: aggregate demand and aggregate
supply (AD-AS) model 682; Keynesian
model of adjustment 677–679;
macroeconomics 567; market structures
281; monopolistic competition
366–373; perfect competition 325–
331; production costs 289, 303–306;

CPSIA information can be obtained
at www.ICGtesting.com
Printed in the USA
LVHW020857120822
725644LV00002B/21